Substance Abuse:
Therapist Jean Obert
"Being addicted to heroin is one of the most difficult things to kick."

Substance Abuse:
Therapist Louise Roberts
"You try to make sense out of an addiction that doesn't make sense."

Anorexia Nervosa—Binge-Eating/ Purging Type:
The Case of Jessica
"The diet started being my only way of getting control."

Bulimia:
The Case of Ann
"I was just afraid to go home and be around food."

Anorexia Nervosa:
The Case of Tamora
"If someone had told me how ugly I looked, being that thin, I wouldn't have done it. I mean, it was...part beauty and...part power."

Attention-Deficit/Hyperactivity Disorder (ADHD):
The Case of Jimmy
"Sometimes I just drift off."

Eating Disorders:
Nutritionist Alise Thresh
"Some people are normal eaters...some people are concerned about their eating...and to an extreme, there is an eating disorder."

Gender Identity Disorder:
The Case of Denise
"My earliest memories, back when I was about 4 years old...I remember cross-dressing back then, all the way until really around my puberty."

Childhood Sexual Abuse:
The Case of Karen
"He started when I was six years old...He would always get one bed in motel rooms because he said he needed to save money."

Schizophrenia:
The Case of Larry
"I have all kinds of voices."

Autism:
Dr. Kathy Pratt

Attention-Deficit/Hyperactivity Disorder (ADHD):
Dr. Raun Melmed

Schizophrenia:
The Case of Georgiana
"Then it got out of hand, where I couldn't control coming and going, back and forth, and in my body, out of my body, it was no longer under my control."

Schizoaffective Disorder:
The Case of Josh
"I looked out the window and saw this guy with a machete chasing one of the psychiatrists."

Antisocial Personality Disorder:
The Case of Paul
"I went to prison for kicking down my wife's door."

Borderline Personality Disorder:
The Case of Liz
"I have problems with anger management."

Autism:
The Case of Xavier
"He'll watch a DVD, same scene over and over and over again."

Alzheimer's Disease:
The Case of Wilburn "John"
"You kinda have hope whenever you have cancer...but then, [with] Alzheimer's...you die, just a little each day."

Abnormal Psychology
in a Changing World

SEVENTH EDITION

JEFFREY S. NEVID
St. John's University

SPENCER A. RATHUS
New York University

BEVERLY A. GREENE
St. John's University

PEARSON

Prentice
Hall

Upper Saddle River, New Jersey 07458

Library of Congress Cataloging-in-Publication Data

Nevid, Jeffrey S.
  Abnormal psychology in a changing world/Jeffrey S. Nevid, Spencer A. Rathus,
Beverly Greene.—7th ed.
        p. cm.
  Includes bibliographical references and index.
  ISBN 0-13-512897-8
  1. Psychology, Pathological—Textbooks.   I. Rathus, Spencer A. II. Greene, Beverly.
III. Title.
  RC454.N468 2008
  616.89—dc22

2007039553

Editorial Director: *Leah Jewell*

Executive Editor: *Jeff Marshall*

Associate Editor, Editorial: *LeeAnn Doherty*

Editorial Assistant: *Aaron Talwar*

Director of Marketing: *Brandy Dawson*

Senior Marketing Manager: *Jeanette Koskinas*

Marketing Assistant: *Laura Kennedy*

Senior Pegasus Program Manager: *Brian Hyland*

Pegasus Program Manager: *Richard Virginia*

Senior Managing Editor: *Ann Marie McCarthy*

Associate Managing Editor: *Maureen Richardson*

Production Liaison: *Maureen Richardson*

Senior Operations Supervisor: *Sherry Lewis*

Director, Image Resource Center: *Melinda Patelli*

Manager, Rights & Permissions: *Zina Arabia*

Interior Image Specialist: *Beth Brenzel*

Cover Image Specialist: *Karen Sanatar*

Image Permission Coordinator: *Debbie Latronica*

Photo Researcher: *Teri Stratford*

Senior Art Director: *Nancy Wells*

Art Director: *Anne Bonanno Nieglos*

Interior Design: *Jill Lehan*

Concept Map Design: *Ximena Tamvakopolous*

Cover Design: *Jill Lehan*

Cover Illustration/Photo: *Katrina Wittkakamp/Taxi-Getty Images*

Composition/Full-Service Project Management: *Prepare Inc.*

Printer/Binder: *Courier Companies, Inc.*

Cover Printer: *Phoenix Color Corp.*

*Credits and acknowledgments borrowed from other sources and reproduced, with permission, in this textbook
appear on appropriate page within text (or on page 608).*

Pearson Education, Ltd. London
Pearson Education Australia PTY, Limited
Pearson Education Singapore, Pte., Ltd.
Pearson Education North Asia Ltd.
Pearson Education, Canada, Ltd.
Pearson Educación de Mexico, S.A. de C.V.
Pearson Education—Japan
Pearson Education Malaysia, Pte., Ltd.
Pearson Education, Upper Saddle River, New Jersey

10 9 8 7 6 5 4 3 2 1

ISBN-10:   0-13-512897-8
ISBN-13: 978-0-13-512897-8

1 Introduction and Methods of Research 2

2 Contemporary Perspectives on Abnormal Behavior 36

3 Classification and Assessment of Abnormal Behavior 68

4 Methods of Treatment 102

5 Stress, Psychological Factors, and Health 140

6 Anxiety Disorders 170

7 Dissociative and Somatoform Disorders 210

8 Mood Disorders and Suicide 246

9 Substance Abuse and Dependence 290

10 Eating Disorders and Sleep Disorders 330

11 Disorders Involving Gender and Sexuality 358

12 Schizophrenia and Other Psychotic Disorders 396

13 Personality Disorders and Impulse Control Disorders 434

14 Abnormal Behavior in Childhood and Adolescence 474

15 Cognitive Disorders and Disorders Related to Aging 514

16 Abnormal Psychology and the Law 542

Preface xi
About the Authors 1

CHAPTER 1

Introduction and Methods of Research   2

How Do We Define Abnormal Behavior? 6
Criteria for Determining Abnormality 6
Cultural Bases of Abnormal Behavior 9

Historical Perspectives on Abnormal Behavior 10
The Demonological Model 10
Origins of the Medical Model: In "Ill Humor" 11
Medieval Times 11
Witchcraft 12
Asylums 13
The Reform Movement and Moral Therapy 13
A Step Backward 14
The Community Mental Health Movement: The Exodus
   from State Hospitals 15
Contemporary Perspectives on Abnormal Behavior 15

 CONTROVERSIES IN ABNORMAL PSYCHOLOGY
   What Is Abnormal Behavior? 18

Research Methods in Abnormal Psychology 19
Description, Explanation, Prediction, and Control:
   The Objectives of Science 19
The Scientific Method 21
Ethics in Research 21
Naturalistic Observation 22
The Correlational Method 22
The Experimental Method 23
Epidemiological Studies 26
Kinship Studies 27
Case Studies 29

 A CLOSER LOOK
   Thinking Critically About Abnormal Psychology 31

 CONTROVERSIES IN ABNORMAL PSYCHOLOGY
   **Psychoquackery: Discredited Psychological Treatments
      in Mental Health 32**

Summing Up 33

CHAPTER 2

Contemporary Perspectives on Abnormal Behavior   36

The Biological Perspective 38
The Nervous System 38
Evaluating Biological Perspectives on Abnormal Behavior 43

 CONTROVERSIES IN ABNORMAL PSYCHOLOGY
   Is It All in the Genes? 44

The Psychological Perspective 45
Psychodynamic Models 45
Learning Models 52
Humanistic Models 56
Cognitive Models 58

The Sociocultural Perspective 60
Ethnicity and Mental Health 60
Evaluating the Sociocultural Perspective 63

The Biopsychosocial Perspective 63
The Diathesis–Stress Model 64
Evaluating the Biopsychosocial Perspective 65
The Case of Jessica—A Final Word 66

Summing Up 66

CHAPTER 3

Classification and Assessment of Abnormal Behavior   68

How are Abnormal Behavior Patterns Classified? 70
The *DSM* and Models of Abnormal Behavior 70

Standards of Assessment 77
Reliability 77

 CONTROVERSIES IN ABNORMAL PSYCHOLOGY
   The Bible of Psychiatry 78
Validity 79

Methods of Assessment 80
The Clinical Interview 80

Computerized Interviews 81
Psychological Tests 82
Neuropsychological Assessment 90
Behavioral Assessment 92
Cognitive Assessment 95
Physiological Measurement 96

**Sociocultural and Ethnic Factors
in Assessment 99**

Summing Up 100

CHAPTER 4

Methods of Treatment   102

Types of Helping Professionals 104

Psychotherapy 104

 A CLOSER LOOK
How Do I Find Help? 106
Psychodynamic Therapy 107
Behavior Therapy 110
Humanistic Therapy 111
Cognitive Therapy 113
Cognitive-Behavioral Therapy 116
Eclectic Therapy 117
Group, Family, and Couple Therapy 118

 CONTROVERSIES IN ABNORMAL PSYCHOLOGY
Online Therapy: A New Therapeutic Tool, or Pandora's Box? 119
Evaluating Methods of Psychotherapy 119

 CONTROVERSIES IN ABNORMAL PSYCHOLOGY
The Controversy Over Evidence-Based Practice: Repairing the Rift 121

Multicultural Issues in Psychotherapy 123

Biomedical Therapies 126
Drug Therapy 126
Electroconvulsive Therapy 128
Psychosurgery 130
Evaluation of Biological Approaches 130

Hospitalization and Community-Based Care 131
Roles for Hospitalization 131
The Community Mental Health Center 131
Ethnic Group Differences in Use of Mental Health Services 133
Racial Stereotyping and the Mental Health System 135
Evaluation of Deinstitutionalization 136

Summing Up 137

CHAPTER 5

Stress, Psychological Factors, and Health   140

Adjustment Disorders 142

Stress and Illness 144
Stress and the Endocrine System 144
Stress and the Immune System 145
Terrorism-Related Trauma 146
The General Adaptation Syndrome 147

 A CLOSER LOOK
Warning Signs of Trauma-Related Stress 148
Stress and Life Changes 149

 QUESTIONNAIRE
Going Through Changes 150
Acculturative Stress: Making It in America 150

 CONTROVERSIES IN ABNORMAL PSYCHOLOGY
Coming to America: The Case of Latinos 153

Psychological Factors That Moderate Stress 153

Psychological Factors and Physical Disorders 156

 QUESTIONNAIRE
The Life Orientation Test 157

 A CLOSER LOOK
Psychological Methods for Lowering Arousal 157
Headaches 159
Cardiovascular Disease 160

 A CLOSER LOOK
Dying of a Broken Heart 162
Asthma 163
Cancer 164
Acquired Immunodeficiency Syndrome (AIDS) 165

Summing Up 168

CHAPTER 6

Anxiety Disorders   170

Overview of Anxiety Disorders 171

Panic Disorder 172
Theoretical Perspectives 175
Treatment Approaches 177

 A CLOSER LOOK
Coping with a Panic Attack 179

Phobic Disorders 179

Types of Phobic Disorders 180
Theoretical Perspectives 184
Treatment Approaches 189

Obsessive–Compulsive Disorder 194
Theoretical Perspectives 195
Treatment Approaches 198

Generalized Anxiety Disorder 198

Theoretical Perspectives 199
Treatment Approaches 200

**Acute Stress Disorder and Posttraumatic
Stress Disorder 200**
Features of Traumatic Stress Disorders 203
Theoretical Perspectives 204
Treatment Approaches 204

Ethnic Differences in Anxiety Disorders 204

 **CONTROVERSIES IN ABNORMAL PSYCHOLOGY
EMDR: Fad or Find? 205**

 TYING IT TOGETHER 206

Summing Up 206

CHAPTER 7

Dissociative and Somatoform Disorders   210

Dissociative Disorders 212
Dissociative Identity Disorder 212
Dissociative Amnesia 217

 **CONTROVERSIES IN ABNORMAL PSYCHOLOGY
Are Recovered Memories Credible? 219**
Dissociative Fugue 219
Depersonalization Disorder 221

 **QUESTIONNAIRE
The Dissociative Experiences Scale 223**
Culture-Bound Dissociative Syndromes 223
Theoretical Perspectives 223
Treatment of Dissociative Disorders 225

 TYING IT TOGETHER 226

Somatoform Disorders 227

 **A CLOSER LOOK
Münchausen Syndrome 230**
Conversion Disorder 231
Hypochondriasis 232
Body Dysmorphic Disorder 233
Pain Disorder 234
Somatization Disorder 235
Koro and Dhat Syndromes: Far Eastern Somatoform
    Disorders? 236
Theoretical Perspectives 237
Treatment of Somatoform Disorders 240

Summing Up 241

CHAPTER 8

Mood Disorders and Suicide   246

Types of Mood Disorders 248
Major Depressive Disorder 249

 **CONTROVERSIES IN ABNORMAL PSYCHOLOGY
Why Are More Women Depressed? 253**

 **QUESTIONNAIRE
Are You Depressed? 254**
Dysthymic Disorder 254
Bipolar Disorder 256
Cyclothymic Disorder 258

Causal Factors in Depressive Disorders 259
Stress and Depression 259
Psychodynamic Theories 260
Humanistic Theories 261
Learning Theories 261
Cognitive Theories 263
Learned Helplessness (Attributional) Theory 266
Biological Factors 268

 **A CLOSER LOOK
Something Fishy About This 269**

Causal Factors in Bipolar Disorders 269

Treatment of Mood Disorders 270
Treating Depression 270
Biological Approaches 273
Treating Bipolar Disorder 276

 TYING IT TOGETHER 277

 **A CLOSER LOOK
Magnetic Stimulation Therapy
    for Depression 278**

Suicide 278
Who Commits Suicide? 279
Why Do People Commit Suicide? 281
Theoretical Perspectives on Suicide 281
Predicting Suicide 284

 **A CLOSER LOOK
Suicide Prevention 285**

Summing Up 285

CHAPTER 9

Substance Abuse and Dependence   290

Classification of Substance-Related Disorders 291
Substance Abuse and Dependence 292
Addiction and Other Forms of Compulsive Behavior 294
Racial and Ethnic Differences in Substance Use Disorders 295
Pathways to Drug Dependence 295

Drugs of Abuse 296
Depressants 296

 QUESTIONNAIRE
Are You Hooked? 298

 A CLOSER LOOK
Binge Drinking, a Dangerous College Pastime 301
Stimulants 305
Hallucinogens 308

Theoretical Perspectives 310
Biological Perspectives 310
Learning Perspectives 312

Cognitive Perspectives 315
Psychodynamic Perspectives 315
Sociocultural Perspectives 316

Treatment of Substance Abuse and Dependence 316
Biological Approaches 317
Culturally Sensitive Treatment of Alcoholism 319
Nonprofessional Support Groups 319
Residential Approaches 320
Psychodynamic Approaches 320
Behavioral Approaches 320
Relapse-Prevention Training 322

 CONTROVERSIES IN ABNORMAL PSYCHOLOGY
In the Eye of the Storm: The Controlled Drinking Controversy 323

 TYING IT TOGETHER   325

Summing Up 325

CHAPTER 10

Eating Disorders and Sleep Disorders   330

Eating Disorders 332
Anorexia Nervosa 333
Bulimia Nervosa 334
Causes of Anorexia and Bulimia 336

 CONTROVERSIES IN ABNORMAL PSYCHOLOGY
Should Barbie Be Banned? 339

 QUESTIONNAIRE
The Fear of Fat Scale 341
Treatment of Eating Disorders 341
Binge-Eating Disorder 342

 TYING IT TOGETHER   343

 A CLOSER LOOK
Obesity: A National Epidemic 343

Sleep Disorders 345
Dyssomnias 346
Parasomnias 349
Treatment of Sleep Disorders 351

 A CLOSER LOOK
To Sleep, Perchance to Dream 354

Summing Up 354

CHAPTER 11

Disorders Involving Gender and Sexuality   358

Gender Identity Disorder 360
Theoretical Perspectives 363

 A CLOSER LOOK
Homophobia: Social Prejudice or Personal
    Psychopathology? 364

Sexual Dysfunctions 365
Types of Sexual Dysfunctions 366
Theoretical Perspectives 367
Treatment of Sexual Dysfunctions 372

Paraphilias 376
Types of Paraphilias 376

Theoretical Perspectives 383

 CONTROVERSIES IN ABNORMAL PSYCHOLOGY
"Cybersex Addiction"—A New Psychological Disorder? 384
Treatment of Paraphilias 385

Rape 387
Types of Rape 389
Theoretical Perspectives 390

 QUESTIONNAIRE
Cultural Myths That Create a Climate That
    Supports Rape 391

Summing Up 391

CHAPTER 12

Schizophrenia and Other Psychotic Disorders   396

Schizophrenia 397
Course of Development 398
Prevalence 400
Diagnostic Features 401
Perceptual Disturbances 405
Subtypes of Schizophrenia 408
Theoretical Perspectives 410

 CONTROVERSIES IN ABNORMAL PSYCHOLOGY
Is Mental Illness a Myth? 417

 TYING IT TOGETHER
The Diathesis–Stress Model 420

Treatment Approaches 422

Other Forms of Psychosis 426
Brief Psychotic Disorder 426
Schizophreniform Disorder 426
Delusional Disorder 426

 A CLOSER LOOK
The Love Delusion 427
Schizoaffective Disorder 428

Summing Up 429

CHAPTER 13

Personality Disorders and Impulse Control Disorders   434

Types of Personality Disorders 435
Personality Disorders Characterized by Odd or Eccentric Behavior 437
Personality Disorders Characterized by Dramatic, Emotional,
   or Erratic Behavior 440

 A CLOSER LOOK
**"In Cold Blood:" Peering into the Minds of Psychopathic
   Murderers 443**
Personality Disorders Characterized by Anxious or Fearful Behavior 449
Problems with the Classification of Personality Disorders 452

Theoretical Perspectives 454
Psychodynamic Perspectives 454
Learning Perspectives 456
Family Perspectives 458
Biological Perspectives 459

 CONTROVERSIES IN ABNORMAL PSYCHOLOGY
Bad Genes, Bad Behavior? 460

Sociocultural Perspectives 461

 QUESTIONNAIRE 462
The Sensation-Seeking Scale 462

 TYING IT TOGETHER 463

Treatment of Personality Disorders 463
Psychodynamic Approaches 463
Behavioral Approaches 464
Biological Approaches 464

Impulse Control Disorders 465
Pathological Gambling 465
Kleptomania 467

 CONTROVERSIES IN ABNORMAL PSYCHOLOGY
Losing $10 Million: A Case of Pathological Gambling? 468

Summing Up 469

CHAPTER 14

Abnormal Behavior in Childhood and Adolescence   474

**Normal and Abnormal Behavior in Childhood
and Adolescence 475**
Cultural Beliefs About What Is Normal and Abnormal 476
Prevalence of Mental Health Problems in Children and Adolescents 476
Risk Factors for Childhood Disorders 477

Pervasive Developmental Disorders 478
Autism 480

Mental Retardation 485
Causes of Mental Retardation 485
Intervention 488

Learning Disorders 489
Types of Learning Disorders 490
Understanding and Treating Learning Disorders 490

A CLOSER LOOK
The Savant Syndrome 491

Communication Disorders 492

**Attention-Deficit and Disruptive Behavior
Disorders 493**
Attention-Deficit Hyperactivity Disorder 493
Conduct Disorder 496
Oppositional Defiant Disorder 497

Childhood Anxiety and Depression 499
Separation Anxiety Disorder 499
Understanding and Treating Childhood Anxiety Disorders 501
Childhood Depression 502
Understanding and Treating Childhood Depression 502

CONTROVERSIES IN ABNORMAL PSYCHOLOGY
Are We Overmedicating Our Kids? 504

Suicide in Children and Adolescents 505

Elimination Disorders 506

Enuresis 507

Encopresis 508

Summing Up 509

CHAPTER 15

Cognitive Disorders and Disorders Related to Aging   514

Cognitive Disorders 515

Dementia 517

Delirium 518

Amnestic Disorders 520

Psychological Disorders Related to Aging 522

Anxiety Disorders and Aging 523

Depression and Aging 523

Sleep Problems and Aging 525

Dementia of the Alzheimer's Type 525

Vascular Dementia 531

 QUESTIONNAIRE
Examining Your Attitudes Toward Aging 532

Dementias Due to General Medical Conditions 532

Dementia Due to Pick's Disease 532

Dementia Due to Parkinson's Disease 532

Dementia Due to Huntington's Disease 534

Dementia Due to HIV Disease 534

Dementia Due to Creutzfeldt-Jakob Disease 535

Dementia Due to Head Trauma 535

Neurosyphilis 535

 CONTROVERSIES IN ABNORMAL PSYCHOLOGY
The Danger Lurking Within: Would You Want to Know? 536

Summing Up 537

CHAPTER 16

Abnormal Psychology and the Law   542

Psychiatric Commitment and Patients' Rights 544

Predicting Dangerousness 545

 CONTROVERSIES IN ABNORMAL PSYCHOLOGY
**What Should We Do About the "Wild Man of West
     96th Street"? 547**

Patients' Rights 550

 A CLOSER LOOK
The Duty to Warn 552

The Insanity Defense 555

Legal Bases of the Insanity Defense 556

Determining the Length of Criminal Commitment 557

Perspectives on the Insanity Defense 558

Competency to Stand Trial 559

Summing Up 560

Glossary 562

References 568

Photo Credits 608

Author Index 609

Subject Index 622

Welcome to the new edition of *Abnormal Psychology in a Changing World*. Research developments continue to sharpen our understanding of abnormal behavior and we endeavor to bring these advances to students in a way that both stimulates interest and makes complex material understandable. We also recognize that there is a basic human dimension to the study of abnormal psychology. Our approach is to help students enter the world of people suffering from the range of disorders we encounter in the text. We seek to accomplish this challenging goal by including many illustrative case examples drawn from our own case experiences and those of other practitioners, as well as through a supplementary video casebook, of interviews with real people diagnosed with different disorders, and by a pedagogical feature that takes this approach an important step further: the "I" feature.

PUTTING A HUMAN FACE ON THE STUDY OF ABNORMAL PSYCHOLOGY

The unique **"I"** feature in the text takes students directly into the world of people affected by psychological disorders. This feature consists of first-person narratives and allows students to learn from people struggling with many types of psychological disorders as they tell their stories in their own words.

"My Dark Place"

There are times in my life when I go to a dark place. I find it hard to run or hide from this symptom that feels like it controls my life. It's called self-mutilation or cutting. It's part of my . . . diagnosis called borderline personality disorder (BPD). Cutting is when you feel an urge to cut different places on your body. In my case, it's my arms and legs. I remember being depressed at a very young age. At age eight-years-old, I cut myself for the first time. I was very alone in my pain and no one noticed my scar. But, even at that very young age, after I cut, I felt a sense of relief. For a while I was able to block out everything and just feel free. Even today, I still feel a need to comfort myself. Now that I'm older I must find other outlets for my pain. It's something that's going to take a lot of work and therapy.

Source: New York City Voices. *Reprinted with permission*

By having students enter the world of people facing the many challenges posed by psychological disorders, the text breaks down barriers between "us" and "them" and helps students see that mental health problems are a concern to us all.

The human side of the study of abnormal psychology is further emphasized through integrated case examples and video case interviews. This edition expands upon the "I" feature by including several more first-person narratives:

- **"Just Checking"** (Obsessive–Compulsive Disorder; Chapter 6)
- **"Walking on Eggshells"** (Borderline Personality Disorder; Chapter 13)

- **"Rubbing Salt into a Wound"** (Narcissistic Personality Disorder; Chapter 13)
- **"Living in the Labyrinth"** (Alzheimer's Disease; Chapter 13).

The other "I" features that students will encounter in the text are listed here:

- **"Cowering Under the Covers"** (Bipolar Disorder; Chapter 1)
- **"Thomas Hears Voices"** (Schizophrenia; Chapter 1)
- **"Pretty Grisly Stuff"** (Claustrophobia; Chapter 1)
- **"Jessica's Little Secret"** (Bulimia; Chapter 2)
- **"Jerry Has a Panic Attack on the Interstate"** (Panic Disorder; Chapter 3)
- **"Susanna—'A Girl, Interrupted'"** (Suicide attempt; Chapter 4)
- **"Go! Go! It's Coming Down!"** (Traumatic stress; Chapter 5)
- **"I Felt Like I Was Going to Die Right Then and There"** (Panic attack; Chapter 6)
- **"We Share a Single Body"** (Dissociative Identity Disorder; Chapter 7)
- **"Sickened"** (Münchausen Syndrome; Chapter 7)
- **"Darkness Visible"** (Major depression; Chapter 8)
- **"An Unquiet Mind"** (Bipolar Disorder; Chapter 8)
- **"Electroboy"** (Manic Episode; Chapter 8)
- **"Leading a Normal Life"** (Bipolar Disorder; Chapter 8)
- **"Nothing and Nobody Comes Before My Coke"** (Substance Dependence; Chapter 9)
- **"Taking Away the Hurt I Feel"** (Substance Dependence; Chapter 9)
- **"Surely They Can't Mean Beer!"** (Alcohol Dependence; Chapter 9)
- **"What's Up with That?"** (Bulimia; Chapter 10)
- **"He's Only Sleepwalking"** (Sleepwalking Disorder; Chapter 10)
- **"I Know Something None of You Will Ever Know"** and **"Everybody Is Born Unique, but Most of Us Die Copies"** (Gender Identity Disorder; Chapter 11)
- **"Paralyzed with Anxiety"** (Male Erectile Disorder; Chapter 11)
- **"I Never Thought It Would Happen to Me"** and **"Why Did She Put Up Such a Big Struggle?"** (Date Rape; Chapter 11)
- **"I Hear Something You Can't Hear"** (Schizophrenia; Chapter 12)
- **"I and I, Dancing Fool, Challenge You the World to a Duel"** (Schizophrenia; Chapter 12)
- **"The Poverties"** (Schizophrenia; Chapter 12)
- **"The Voices Grow Softer"** (Schizophrenia; Chapter 12)

- **"My Dark Place"** (Borderline Personality Disorder; Chapter 13)
- **"A World of My Own Creation"** (Autistic Disorder; Chapter 14)
- **"I Didn't Know What They (People) Were For"** (Autistic Disorder; Chapter 14)
- **"Now Is the Last Best Time"** (Alzheimer's Disease; Chapter 15)
- **"A Daughter's Dilemma"** (Alzheimer's Disease; Chapter 15)
- **"Please Look into Your Heart"** (John Hinckley's diary; Chapter 16)

Fostering Critical Thinking: Controversies in Abnormal Psychology

The field of abnormal psychology is not a "done deal." Many students begin the course with an expectation that our knowledge of the disorders we cover is complete and incontrovertible. They soon learn that while we have learned much about the underpinnings of these disorders, much remains to be learned. They also learn that there are many current controversies in the field. By spotlighting these controversies, we encourage students to think critically about these important issues and examine different points of view.

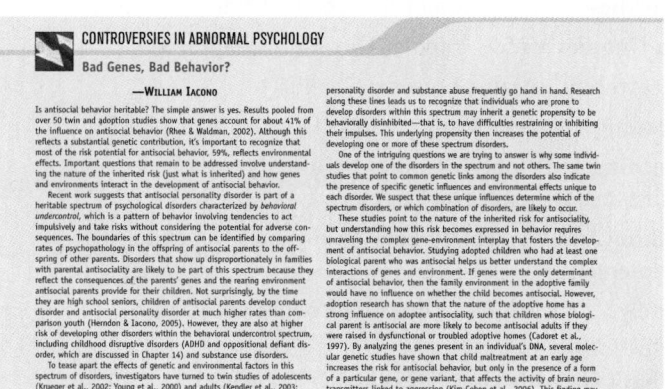

We are extremely grateful to our colleagues from other universities who have contributed to this edition by writing about particular controversies in abnormal psychology. The contributors include a number of the major researchers in the field today:

- **John Norcross** and **Gerald Koocher** on discredited treatments: "Psychoquackery and Discredited Psychological Treatments in Mental Health"
- **Thomas Widiger** on the *DSM*: "The Bible of Psychiatry"
- **William Sanderson** on EBP: "The Controversy Over Evidence-Based Practice: Repairing the Rift"
- **Charles Negy** on acculturation and mental health: "Coming to America: The Case of Latinos"
- **Mark and Linda Sobell** on the controlled drinking controversy: "In the Eye of the Storm: The Controlled Drinking Controversy"
- **William Iacono** on genetic bases of antisocial behavior: "Bad Genes, Bad Behavior?"

- **Wendy Slutske** on pathological gambling: "Losing $10 Million: A Case of Pathological Gambling?"

We also address these other controversial issues in the field today:

- Online Therapy: A New Therapeutic Tool or Pandora's Box?
- Is It All in the Genes?
- EMDR: Fad or Find?
- Are Recovered Memories Credible?
- Why Are More Women Depressed?
- Should Barbie Be Banned?
- "Cybersex Addiction"—A New Psychological Disorder?
- Is Mental Illness a Myth?
- Are We Overmedicating Our Kids?
- The Danger Lurking Within: Would You Want to Know? (Genetic testing)
- What Should We Do About the "Wild Man of West 96th Street"?

Introducing a New Visual Learning Tool: Concept Maps in Abnormal Psychology

The *Tying It Together* feature helps students integrate diverse theoretical viewpoints to better understand the complex causal pathways leading to abnormal behavior patterns. In this edition, we introduce a new visual learning tool to complement the text description of theoretical perspectives: *Concept Maps in Abnormal Psychology.* These unique diagrams are crafted to help students "see at a glance" the linkages between specific disorders, underlying causal factors, and treatment approaches.

Keeping Pace with an Ever-Changing Field

The text integrates the latest research findings and scientific developments in the field that inform our understanding of abnormal psychology. The content is comprehensive and up-to-date and is presented in a way that makes complex material engaging and accessible.

Expanded Focus on Neuroscience

Research findings on brain-behavior relationships greatly expand our understanding of abnormal behavior patterns. In this edition, we expand our coverage of neuroscience research by including such cutting edge developments as the hunt for endophenotypes in schizophrenia, the use of magnetic stimulation therapy for depression, the role of neurotransmitters in explaining drug abuse and dependence, and developments in the search for genetic factors in a wide range of psychological disorders.

Expanded Topics

This text expands upon previous editions by including a major new section on impulse control disorders, with an emphasis on pathological gambling and kleptomania. We welcome the contribution of Professor Wendy Slutske, a leading authority on pathological gambling.

THE FULLY INTEGRATED TEXTBOOK

Integrating Diversity Throughout the Text

We examine abnormal behavior patterns in relation to such factors of diversity as ethnicity, culture, gender, sexual orientation, and socioeconomic status. We believe students need to understand how issues of diversity affect the conceptualization of abnormal behavior as well as the diagnosis and treatment of psychological disorders. We also believe that coverage of diversity should be integrated directly in the text, not separated off in boxed features.

Integrating Theoretical Perspectives

Students often feel as though one theoretical perspective must ultimately be right and all the others wrong. We examine the many different theoretical perspectives that inform contemporary understanding of abnormal psychology. As mentioned, we also help students integrate these diverse viewpoints in the *Tying it Together* features within the text. We also explore potential causal pathways involving interactions of psychological, sociocultural, and biological factors. We hope to impress upon students the importance of taking a broader view of the complex problems we address by considering influences of multiple factors and their interactions.

TYING IT TOGETHER

Throughout the text we've endorsed the value of a multifactorial model of abnormal behavior, the view that psychological disorders result from a complex web of psychological, sociocultural, and biological factors. Our understanding of personality disorders is no exception. A history of childhood abuse, neglectful or punitive parents, and learning experiences that breed fear of social interactions rather than self-confidence may underlie the development of personality disorders. Social-cognitive factors, such as the effects of modeling aggressive behavior and cognitive biases that predispose people to misconstrue other people's behavior as threatening, also influence the development of maladaptive ways of relating to others that become identified with personality disorders. Evidence also suggests a genetic contribution to several types of personality disorders, including antisocial, schizotypal, and borderline types. Other biological factors implicated in antisocial personality disorder include a lack of emotional responsiveness to threatening cues, excessive need for stimulation, and underlying brain abnormalities. Sociocultural factors, such as social stressors associated with poverty and living in a disintegrating, crime-ridden neighborhood, are linked to a greater likelihood of child abuse and neglect, which in turn sets the stage for lingering resentments and lack of empathy for others that typify the antisocial personality.

How are these factors linked together? Typically, we find common themes in the development of specific personality disorders, such as harsh or punitive parenting in the case of antisocial personality. However, we need to allow for different combinations of factors and causal pathways to come into play. For example, some people with antisocial personality disorder were raised in economically deprived conditions and lacked consistent parenting. Others were raised in middle-class families but experienced neglectful or harsh parenting. Clinicians need to evaluate how each person's developmental history may have shaped his or her way of relating to others.

The *Concept Map for Abnormal Psychology* at the end of the chapter lists the *DSM* clusters of personality disorders, the major theoretical perspectives discussed in this chapter, and several key treatment approaches. The concept map also illustrates a potential causal pathway leading to the development of antisocial personality disorder.

Integrating Video Case Examples

Video case examples provide students with opportunities to see and hear individuals who are diagnosed with different types of psychological disorders. Students can read about the clinical features of specific disorders and with a few clicks of a computer mouse, see a video case example that illustrates the concepts discussed in the text. The video case examples are highlighted in the margins of the text with an icon and can be accessed through MyPsychLab or by purchasing the supplementary CD-ROM through prenhall.com.

The video case examples supplement the many case examples we include in the text itself. Putting a human face on the subject matter helps make complex material more accessible.

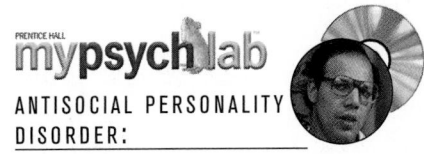

The Case of Paul
"I went to prison for kicking down my wife's door."

Many of these case examples are drawn from our own clinical files and those of leading mental health professionals.

Integrating Text and Companion Web Site

Web content related to the text helps students reinforce and expand their learning. By visiting the companion Web site, students can take quizzes that help them review what they've learned and find related resources on the Web.

Integrating Key Terms

We include a running glossary within the chapters so students will not need to thumb to the back of the book to find definitions of key terms. Key terms are boldfaced in the text and defined in both the glossary in the back of the book and in the margins of the text where the terms appear.

MAINTAINING OUR FOCUS

Abnormal Psychology in a Changing World is a complete learning and teaching package that brings into focus four major objectives: (1) integrating an interactionist or biopsychosocial model of abnormal behavior; (2) underscoring the importance of issues of diversity to the understanding and treatment of psychological disorders; (3) maintaining currency; and (4) adopting a student-centric pedagogy.

Focus on the Interactionist Approach

We approach our writing with the belief that a better understanding of abnormal psychology is gained by adopting a biopsychosocial orientation that takes into account the roles of psychological, biological, and sociocultural factors and their interactions in the development of abnormal behavior patterns. We emphasize the value of taking an interactionist approach as a running theme throughout the text. We feature a prominent interactionist model, the diathesis–stress model, to help students better understand the factors contributing to different forms of abnormal behavior.

Focus on Exploring Key Issues in Our Changing World

The *A Closer Look* boxed features provide opportunities for further exploration of selected topics that reflect contemporary issues and concerns. Several *A Closer Look* features provide information and resources that enable students to apply information in the text to their own lives. Examples include:

- Thinking Critically About Abnormal Psychology (Chapter 1)
- How Do I Find Help? (Chapter 4)
- Warning Signs of Trauma-Related Stress (Chapter 5)
- Psychological Methods for Lowering Arousal (Chapter 5)
- Coping with a Panic Attack (Chapter 6)
- Suicide Prevention (Chapter 8)
- To Sleep, Perchance to Dream (Chapter 10)

Other *A Closer Look* features focus on intriguing research findings or emerging developments in the field:

- Something Fishy About This (Chapter 8)
- Magnetic Stimulation Therapy for Depression (Chapter 8)
- "In Cold Blood": Peering into the Minds of Psychopathic Murderers (Chapter 13)

Still others focus on specific topical issues, providing opportunities for more in-depth exploration of these topics:

- Dying of a Broken Heart (Chapter 5)
- Homophobia: Social Prejudice or Personal Psychopathology? (Chapter 11)
- Münchausen Syndrome (Chapter 7)
- Binge Drinking, a Dangerous College Pastime (Chapter 9)
- The Savant Syndrome (Chapter 14)
- The Love Delusion (Chapter 12)

Focus on Student-Centric Pedagogy

We continually examine our pedagogical approach to find even better ways of helping students succeed in this course. We believe that to foster deeper understanding, we must first engage student interest through such pedagogical aids as *Truth or Fiction* chapter openers and *self-scoring questionnaires* that encourage active learning through self-examination. We also believe that effective learning occurs through repeated practice and review of textbook material.

"Truth or Fiction" Chapter Openers

Each chapter begins with a set of *Truth or Fiction* questions to whet the student's appetite for the subject matter within the

chapter. Some items challenge preconceived ideas and common folklore and debunk myths and misconceptions, whereas others highlight new research developments in the field. Instructors and students have repeatedly reported to us that they find this feature stimulating and challenging. Examples of *Truth or Fiction* entries include:

- Despite changing attitudes in society toward homosexuality, the psychiatric profession still continues to classify homosexuality as a mental disorder.
- Recent research shows that most psychological disorders are caused by defective genes.
- Depressant drugs are drugs that cause depression.
- Although it is not an exact science, the measurement of the bumps on a person's head can be used to determine the person's personality traits.
- Writing about traumatic experiences may be good for your health.
- Exposure to combat is the most common trauma linked to posttraumatic stress disorder (PTSD).
- The term split personality refers to schizophrenia.
- Placing a powerful electromagnet on the scalp can help relieve depression.
- Obesity is one of the most common psychological disorders in the United States.
- Coca-Cola originally contained cocaine.
- Drugs used to treat depression may also help curb binge eating in people with bulimia.
- Some people literally gasp for breath hundreds of times during sleep without realizing it.
- If you have two parents with schizophrenia, it's nearly certain that you will develop schizophrenia yourself.
- A form of dementia is linked to mad-cow disease.
- An attempt to assassinate the president of the United States was seen by millions of television viewers, but the would-be assassin was found not guilty by a court of law.

The *Truth or Fiction* questions are revisited and answered in the sections of the chapter where the topics are discussed. Students are thus given feedback concerning the accuracy of their preconceptions in the light of the material being addressed.

Self-scoring questionnaires involve students in the discussion at hand and permit them to evaluate their own attitudes and behavior patterns. In some cases, students may become more aware of troubling concerns, such as states of depression or

TRUTH or FICTION

Personality disorders can be successfully treated with psychiatric drugs.

☑ **FALSE.** Drugs can be used to relieve anxiety or depression associated with some personality disorders, but they do not change the underlying maladaptive and inflexible patterns of behavior that typify these disorders.

problems with drug or alcohol use, which they may want to bring to the attention of a helping professional. We have carefully screened the questionnaires to ensure they will provide students with useful information to reflect upon as well as serve as a springboard for class discussion. *Questionnaires* in this edition include:

- The Life Orientation Test (Optimism Scale) (Chapter 5)
- The Dissociative Experiences Scale (Chapter 7)
- Are You Depressed? (Chapter 8)
- The Fear of Fat Scale (Chapter 10)
- Examining Your Attitudes Toward Aging (Chapter 15)

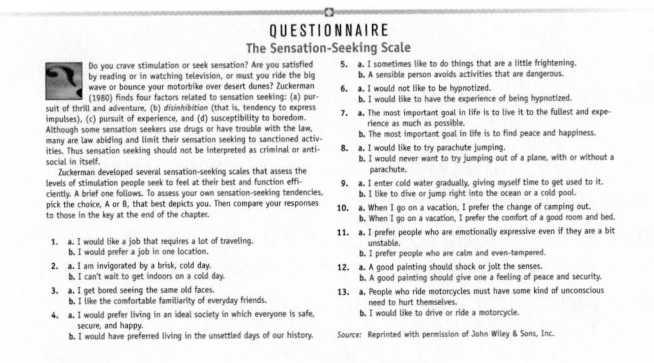

Overview Charts

Overview charts provide summaries of various disorders. We are gratified by the many comments from students and professors regarding the value of these study charts.

"Summing Up" Chapter Summaries

The *Summing Up* chapter summaries are organized in a question-and-answer format, rather than a traditional narrative summary. We believe that students learn better when material is framed in terms of questions to answer rather than simply as narrative text.

SUMMING UP

Types of Personality Disorders
What are personality disorders? Personality disorders are maladaptive or rigid behavior patterns or personality traits associated with states of personal distress that impair the person's ability to function in social or occupational roles. People with personality disorders do not generally recognize a need to change themselves. *What are the classes of personality disorders within the DSM system?* The DSM classifies personality disorders on Axis II and categorizes them according to the following clusters of characteristics: odd or eccentric behavior; dramatic, emotional, or erratic behavior; or anxious or fearful behavior.

What are the features of personality disorders characterized by odd or eccentric behavior? People with paranoid personality disorder are unduly suspicious and mistrustful of others, to the point that their relationships suffer. But they do not hold the more flagrant paranoid delusions typical of schizophrenia. Schizoid personality disorder describes people who have little if any interest in social relationships, show a restricted range of emotional expression,

ANCILLARIES

No matter how comprehensive a textbook is, today's instructors and students require a complete teaching package to advance teaching and comprehension. *Abnormal Psychology in a Changing World* is accompanied by the following ancillaries:

Current Directions in Abnormal Psychology

Prentice Hall is pleased to announce the availability of the reader, *Current Directions in Abnormal Psychology*, which is a collection of scientific articles taken from the Association for Psychological Science (APS) journal, *Current Directions in Psychological Science*. The *Current Directions in Abnormal Psychology* reader can be packaged with this text upon request.

Current Directions in Psychological Science was created as a means by which scientists could quickly and easily learn about new and significant research developments outside their major field of study. The journal's concise reviews span all of scientific psychology, and because of the journal's accessibility to audiences outside specialty areas, it is a natural fit for use in college courses. These readers offer a rich resource that connects students and scholars directly to leading scientists working in psychology today.

The Association for Psychological Science is the only association dedicated solely to advancing psychology as a science-based discipline. APS members include the field's most respected researchers and educators representing the full range of topics within psychological science. The society is widely recognized as a leading voice for the science of psychology in Washington, and is focused on increasing public understanding and use of the knowledge generated by psychological research.

Print Supplements for Instructors

Instructor's Resource Manual

The Instructor's Resource Manual includes *Lecture and Discussion* suggestions, *Student Activities, Classroom Demonstration* ideas, and suggestions on how to integrate the *Abnormal Psychology* CD-ROM into your course. The *Instructor's Resource Manual* also includes notes and suggestions on how to integrate the new *Speaking Out* video segments into your course.

Test Item File

The comprehensive test bank has been updated to include new questions on revised text material. It contains over 4,000 multiple choice, true/false, short answer, and essay questions.

PH Color Transparencies for *Abnormal Psychology Series II*

This set of full-color transparencies includes illustrations, figures, and graphs from the text, as well as images from a variety of other sources. It has been designed with lecture hall visibility and convenience in mind.

Media and Online Resources for Instructors

MyPsychLab

This new course management platform promises to revolutionize the way in which instructors teach and students learn. Developed by an elite team of Prentice Hall publishing and technology experts, the MyPsychLab platform is inspired by the higher education "outcomes assessment" revolution of the new millennium. This robust course management platform enables instructors to assign tests, quizzes, and projects online, and view the results of those assignments as a class aggregate, or as focused on a student-by-student, text section-by-text section basis. Based upon these assignment results, instructors are presented with a detailed teaching plan to bolster student comprehension of any topic areas not well understood, and to supplement all other chapter sections. A series of self-diagnostic tests serve as the foundation of this exciting new platform, which also includes and integrates assignments, remediation content, and study activities that feed results into the platform's gradebook. The diversified collection of study content and activities encompasses *Live!Psych* animations, Patient Interview videos, the APS reader *Current Directions in Abnormal Psychology*, author-recommended Web sites, and more. All supplementary resources will be housed on the MyPsychLab platform, and Blackboard cartridges and WebCT ePacks will also be available.

Speaking Out: Interviews with People who Struggle with Psychological Disorders

This set of video segments allows students to see firsthand accounts of patients with various disorders. The interviews were conducted by licensed clinicians and range in length from 8 to 25 minutes. Disorders include major depressive disorder, obsessive–compulsive disorder, anorexia nervosa, PTSD, alcoholism, schizophrenia, autism, ADHD, bipolar disorder, social phobia, hypochondriasis, borderline personality disorder, and adjustment to physical illness. These video segments are available on VHS cassettes, DVD, CD-ROM, or through MyPsychLab. The *Instructor's Resource Guide* provides background notes and suggested discussion questions.

Instructor's Resource Center on CD-ROM

This valuable, time-saving supplement provides you with an electronic version of a variety of teaching resources all on one disk so that you may customize your lecture notes and media presentations.

The CD-ROM includes PowerPoint Lecture and CRS slides, and electronic versions of text artwork, overhead transparencies, Instructor's Resource Manual, and the Test Item File.

TestGen Assessment Software

Available on one dual-platform CD-ROM, this test generating software provides instructors *Best in Class* features in an easy to use program. Create tests using the TestGen Wizard and easily select questions with drag-and-drop or point-and-click functionality. Add or modify test questions using the built-in Question Editor and print tests in a variety of formats. Full technical support is available for instructors using the TestGen software.

PowerPoint Lecture Slides with Classroom Response System Questions

These slides are not only intended to be the basis for class lectures, but also for class discussions. The incorporation of the CRS questions into each chapter slideshow facilitates the use of "clickers"—small hardware devices similar to remote controls, which process student responses to questions, and interpret and display results in real time. CRS questions are a great means to engage students in learning and precipitate contemplation of text concepts. The slides concisely reinforce the content, and feature prominent figures and tables, from the text. The PowerPoint Lecture Slides with Classroom Response System Questions will be available for download via the Prentice Hall eCatalog or the MyPsychLab platform.

Student Supplements

MyPsychLab

With this exciting new tool students are able to self-assess using embedded diagnostic tests and instantly view results along with a customized study plan. The customized study plan will focus on the student's strengths and weaknesses, based upon the results of the diagnostic testing, and present a list of activities and resources for review and remediation, organized by chapter and section. Students can also access the *Speaking Out* Patient Interview videos called out in the margin of the text. Some study resources intended for use with portable electronic devices are made available exclusively through the MyPsychLab, such as key terms, flashcards, and video clips optimized for use with portable electronic devices. Students will be able to quickly and clearly analyze their own comprehension level of the course material, and study more efficiently, leading to exceptional exam results!

Speaking Out: Interviews with People who Struggle with Psychological Disorders

Available on MyPsychLab or by purchasing the supplementary CD-ROM through prenhall.com, these video clips show skilled clinicians interviewing real patients who have been diagnosed with various disorders. The videos cover disorders such as panic disorder, schizophrenia, anorexia nervosa, bipolar disorder, PTSD, major depression, autism, ADHD, borderline personality disorder, hypochondriasis, alcoholism, and others. Icons in the text margins indicate when students should go to the video interviews.

Companion Web Site
(www.prenhall.com/nevid)

All of the resources on the Companion Web site have been carefully created and selected to reinforce students' understanding of the concepts in the text. Students can take online quizzes and receive immediate scoring and feedback, use interactive flashcards to review key terms, and link to related Web sites for more information on each chapter's topics.

Research Navigator

Research Navigator is an online resource that features three exclusive databases full of source material, including:

- EBSCO's *ContentSelect Academic Journal Database*, organized by subject. Each subject contains 50 to 100 of the leading academic journals by keyword, topic, or multiple topics. Articles include abstract and citation information and can be cut, pasted, e-mailed, or saved for later use.

- *The New York Times Search-by-Subject One Year Archive*, organized by subject and searchable by keyword or multiple keywords. Instructors and students can view the full text of the article.

- *Link Library*, organized by subject, offers editorially selected best of the Web sites. Link Libraries are continually scanned and kept up to date, providing the most relevant and accurate links for research assignments. To see how this resource works, take a tour at www.researchnavigator.com, or ask your local Prentice Hall representative for more details. Access to the Research Navigator is a component of MyPsychLab.

Study Guide

The student Study Guide includes numerous review and study questions, and other learning aids to help reinforce students' understanding of the concepts covered in the text. The Study Guide is available for packaging with this text.

ACKNOWLEDGMENTS

With each new edition, we try to capture a moving target, as the literature base that informs our understanding continues to expand. We are deeply indebted to the thousands of talented scholars and investigators whose work has enriched our understanding of abnormal psychology. Thanks to our colleagues who reviewed our manuscript through earlier editions and continue to help us refine and strengthen our presentation of this material:

Reviewers of the Seventh Edition

Joshua Broman-Fulks, *Appalachian State University*

Ann Butzin, *Owens State Community College*

Dennis Cash, *Trident Technical College*

Michael Connor, *California State University*

Charles Cummings, *Asheville-Buncombe Technical Community College*

Nora Lynn Gussman, *School Forsyth Technical Community College*

Marc Henley, *Delaware County Community College*

Jennifer Hicks, *Southeastern Oklahoma State University*

Kristine Jacquin, *Mississippi State University*

Jennifer Langhinrichsen-Rohling, *University of South Alabama*

Don Lucas, *Northwest Vista College*

Mindy Mechanic, *California State University, Fullerton*

Gary Noll, *University of Illinois at Chicago*

Jackie Robinson, *Florida A&M University*

Sandra Sego, *American International College*

Nancy Simpson, *Trident Technical College*

Charles Spirrison, *Mississippi State University*

Tamara Sullivan, *SUNY-Brockport*

Deborah Thomas, *Washington State Community College*

Naomi Wagner, *San Jose State University*

Thomas Weatherly, *Georgia Perimeter College*

Reviewers of the Previous Edition

Sally Bing, *University of Maryland Eastern Shore*

Christiane Brems, *University of Alaska Anchorage*

Barbara L. Brown, *Georgia Perimeter College*

Lorry Cology, *Owens Community College*

Nancy T. Dassoff, *University of Illinois—Chicago*

David Dooley, *University of California at Irvine*

Heinz Fischer, *Long Beach City College*

John H. Forthman, *Vermillin Community College*

Pam Gibson, *James Madison University*

Karla J. Gingerich, *Colorado State University*

Bernard Gorman, *Nassau Community College*

Gary Greenberg, *Connecticut College*

John K. Hall, *University of Pittsburgh*

Bob Hill, *Appalachian State University*

Robert Kapche, *California State University at Los Angeles*

Stuart Keeley, *Bowling Green State University*

Cynthia Diane Kreutzer, *Georgia Perimeter College*

J. Langhinrichsen-Rohling, *University of Nebraska—Lincoln*

Tom Marsh, *Pitt Community College*

Shay McCordick, *San Diego State University*

Linda L. Morrison, *University of New England*

Martin M. Oper, *Erie Community College*

Joseph J. Palladino, *University of Southern Indiana*

Carol Pandey, *L. A. Pierce College*

Ramona Parish, *Guilford Technical Community College*

Esther D. Rosenblum, *University of Vermont*

Harold Siegel, *Nassau Community College*

Ari Solomon, *Williams College*

Robert Sommer, *University of California—Davis*

Linda Sonna, *University of New Mexico, Taos*

Stephanie Stein, *Central Washington University*

Joanne Hoven Stohs, *California State University—Fullerton*

Larry Stout, *Nicholls State University*

Theresa Wadkins, *University of Nebraska—Kearny*

Max Zwanziger, *Central Washington University*

We also wish to recognize the exemplary contributions of the publishing professionals at Prentice Hall who helped guide the development of this edition, especially Jeff Marshall, Executive Editor, whose vision and insights helped us create the pedagogical platform and unique learning aids incorporated in this text; LeeAnn Doherty, Associate Editor, for keeping us on track and on time and managing the many editorial features that comprise this work; and Maureen Richardson, Associate Managing Editor for Production, for overseeing production and managing to bring everything together in a finished work.

Finally, we especially wish to thank the two people without whose inspiration and support this effort never would have materialized or been completed, Judith Wolf-Nevid and Lois Fichner-Rathus.

J.S.N
New York, New York

S.A.R.
Short Hills, New Jersey
SRathus@aol.com

B.A.G
Brooklyn, New York

Jeffrey S. Nevid is Professor of Psychology at St. John's University in New York, where he directs the Doctoral Program in Clinical Psychology, teaches at both the undergraduate and graduate levels, and supervises doctoral students in clinical practicum work. He received his Ph.D. in Clinical Psychology from the State University of New York at Albany and was a staff psychologist at Samaritan Hospital in Troy, New York. He later completed a National Institute of Mental Health Post-Doctoral Fellowship in Mental Health Evaluation Research at Northwestern University. He holds a Diplomate in Clinical Psychology from the American Board of Professional Psychology, is a Fellow of the Academy of Clinical Psychology, and has served on the editorial boards of several journals and as Associate Editor of the *Journal of Consulting and Clinical Psychology*. His publications have appeared in such journals as *Journal of Consulting and Clinical Psychology, Health Psychology, Journal of Occupational Medicine, Behavior Therapy, American Journal of Community Psychology, Professional Psychology: Research and Practice, Journal of Clinical Psychology, Journal of Nervous and Mental Disease, Teaching of Psychology, American Journal of Health Promotion,* and *Psychology and Psychotherapy.* Dr. Nevid is also author of the book *Choices: Sex in the Age of STDs* and the introductory psychology text, *Psychology: Concepts and Applications,* as well as several other college texts in the fields of psychology and health that he coauthored with Spencer A. Rathus. Dr. Nevid has also been involved in conducting a program of pedagogical research focusing on helping students become more effective learners.

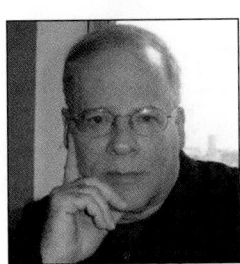

Spencer A. Rathus received his Ph.D. from the University at Albany. He is on the faculty at the New York University School of Continuing and Professional Studies. His areas of interest include psychological assessment, cognitive behavior therapy, and deviant behavior. He is the originator of the Rathus Assertiveness Schedule, which has become a Citation Classic. He has authored several books, including *Psychology in the New Millennium, Essentials of Psychology,* and *The World of Children.* He coauthored *Making the Most of College* with Lois Fichner-Rathus; *AIDS: What Every Student Needs to Know* with Susan Boughn; *Behavior Therapy, Psychology and the Challenges of Life, Your Health* and *Health in the New Millennium* with Jeffrey S. Nevid; and *Human Sexuality in a World of Diversity* with

Jeffrey S. Nevid and Lois Fichner-Rathus. His professional activities include service on the American Psychological Association Task Force on Diversity Issues at the Precollege and Undergraduate Levels of Education in Psychology, and on the Advisory Panel, American Psychological Association, Board of Educational Affairs (BEA) Task Force on Undergraduate Psychology Major Competencies.

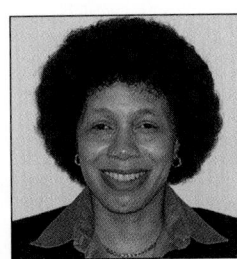

Beverly A. Greene is Professor of Psychology at St. John's University and is a Fellow of seven divisions of the American Psychological Association, as well as a Fellow of the American Orthopsychiatric Association and the Academy of Clinical Psychology. She holds a Diplomate in Clinical Psychology and serves on the editorial boards of numerous scholarly journals. She received her Ph.D. in Clinical Psychology from Adelphi University and worked in public mental health for over a decade. She was founding coeditor of the APA Society for the Study of Lesbian, Gay, and Bisexual Issues series, *Psychological Perspectives on Lesbian, Gay and Bisexual Issues.* She is also coauthor of the recent book, *What Therapists Don't Talk About and Why: Understanding Taboos That Hurt Ourselves and Our Clients,* and has more than 80 professional publications that are the subject of nine national awards. Dr. Greene was recipient of the APA 2003 Committee on Women in Psychology Distinguished Leadership Award, 1996 Outstanding Achievement Award from the APA Committee on Lesbian, Gay, and Bisexual Concerns, the 2004 Distinguished Career Contributions to Ethnic Minority Research Award from the APA Society for the Study of Ethnic Minority Issues, the 2000 Heritage Award from the APA Society for the Psychology of Women, the 2004 Award for Distinguished Senior Career Contributions to Ethnic Minority Research (APA Division 45), and the 2005 Stanley Sue Award for Distinguished Professional Contributions to Diversity in Clinical Psychology (APA Division 12). Her coedited book, *Psychotherapy with African American Women: Innovations in Psychodynamic Perspectives and Practice,* was also honored with the Association for Women in Psychology's 2001 Distinguished Publication Award. In 2006 she was the recipient of the Janet Helms Award for Scholarship and Mentoring from the Teacher's College, Columbia University Cross Cultural Roundtable, and of the 2006 Florence Halpern Award for Distinguished Professional Contributions to Clinical Psychology (Div. 12 APA). She is an elected representative to the APA Council and member at large of the Women's and Public Interest Caucuses of the Council.

Introduction and Methods of Research

CHAPTER OUTLINE

HOW DO WE DEFINE ABNORMAL BEHAVIOR? 6–10

Criteria for Determining Abnormality
Cultural Bases of Abnormal Behavior

HISTORICAL PERSPECTIVES ON ABNORMAL BEHAVIOR 10–19

The Demonological Model
Origins of the Medical Model:
  In "Ill Humor"
Medieval Times
Witchcraft

Asylums
The Reform Movement and Moral Therapy
A Step Backward
The Community Mental Health Movement:
  The Exodus from State Hospitals
Contemporary Perspectives
  on Abnormal Behavior

RESEARCH METHODS IN ABNORMAL PSYCHOLOGY 19–33

Description, Explanation, Prediction,
  and Control: The Objectives of Science

The Scientific Method
Ethics in Research
Naturalistic Observation
The Correlational Method
The Experimental Method
Epidemiological Studies
Kinship Studies
Case Studies

SUMMING UP 33–34

"I" "Pretty Grisly Stuff"

I never thought I'd ever see a psychologist or someone like that, you know. I'm a police photographer and I've shot some pretty grisly stuff, corpses and all. Crime scenes are not like what you see on TV. They're more grisly. I guess you kind of get used to it. It never bothered me, just maybe at first. Before I did this job, I worked on a TV news chopper. We would take shots of fires and rescues, you know. Now I get uptight sitting in the back seat of car or riding an elevator. I'll avoid taking an elevator unless I really have no other choice. Forget flying anymore. It's not just helicopters. I just won't go in a plane, any kind of plane.

I guess I was younger then and more daring when I was younger. Sometimes I would hang out of the helicopter to shoot pictures with no fear at all. Now, just thinking about flying makes my heart race. It's not that I'm afraid the plane will crash. That's the funny thing. Not ha-ha funny, but peculiar, you know. I just start trembling when I think of them closing that door, trapping us inside. I can't tell you why.

—Phil, 42, a police photographer

Source: From the Author's Files

"I" Cowering Under the Covers

When I start going into a high, I no longer feel like an ordinary housewife. Instead I feel organized and accomplished and I begin to feel I am my most creative self. I can write poetry easily. I can compose melodies without effort. I can paint. My mind feels facile and absorbs everything. I have countless ideas about improving the conditions of mentally retarded children, of how a hospital for these children should be run, what they should have around them to keep them happy and calm and unafraid. I see myself as being able to accomplish a great deal for the good of people. I have countless ideas about how the environment problem could inspire a crusade for the health and betterment of everyone. I feel able to accomplish a great deal for the good of my family and others. I feel pleasure, a sense of euphoria or elation. I want it to last forever. I don't seem to need much sleep. I've lost weight and feel healthy and I like myself. I've just bought six new dresses, in fact, and they look quite good on me. I feel sexy and men stare at me. Maybe I'll have an affair, or perhaps several. I feel capable of speaking and doing good in politics. I would like to help people with problems similar to mine so they won't feel hopeless.

It's wonderful when you feel like this. . . . The feeling of exhilaration—the high mood—makes me feel light and full of the joy of living. However, when I go beyond this stage, I become manic, and the creativeness becomes so magnified I begin to see things in my mind that aren't real. For instance, one night I created an entire movie, complete with cast, that I still think would be terrific. I saw the people as clearly as if watching them in real life. I also experienced complete terror, as if it were actually happening, when I knew that an assassination scene was about to take place. I cowered under the covers and became a complete shaking wreck. . . . My screams awakened my husband, who tried to reassure me that we were in our bedroom and everything was the same. There was nothing to be afraid of. Nevertheless, I was admitted to the hospital the next day.

—A firsthand account of a 45-year-old woman with bipolar disorder

Source: Fieve, 1975, pp. 27–28

TRUTH or FICTION

T☐ F☐ Psychological disorders affect relatively few Americans. (p. 4)

T☐ F☐ Behavior deemed abnormal in one society may be perceived as normal in another. (p. 10)

T☐ F☐ A night's entertainment in London a few hundred years ago might have included gaping at the inmates at the local asylum. (p. 13)

T☐ F☐ Despite changing attitudes in society toward homosexuality, the psychiatric profession still continues to classify homosexuality as a mental disorder. (p. 18)

T☐ F☐ Recent evidence shows there are literally millions of genes in the nucleus of every cell in the body. (p. 27)

T☐ F☐ Fraternal twins share the same genetic inheritance as do pairs of other siblings who are not twins. (p. 28)

T☐ F☐ Case studies have been conducted on dead people. (p. 29)

"I"
Thomas Hears Voices

I've been diagnosed as having paranoid schizophrenia. I also suffer from clinical depression. Before I found the correct medications, I was sleeping on the floor, afraid to sleep in my own bed. I was hearing voices that, lately, had turned from being sometimes helpful to being terrorizing. The depression had been responsible for my being irritable and full of dread, especially in the mornings, becoming angry over frustrations at work, and seemingly internalizing other people's problems. . . .

The voices, human sounding, and sounding from a short distance outside my apartment, were slowly turning nearly all bad. I could hear them jeering me, plotting against me, singing songs sometimes that would only make sense later in the day when I would do something wrong at work or at home. I began sleeping on the floor of my living room because I was afraid a presence in the bedroom was torturing good forces around me. If I slept in the bedroom, the nightly torture would cause me to make mistakes during the day. A voice, calling himself Fatty Acid, stopped me from drinking soda. Another voice allowed me only one piece of bread with my meals.

—Thomas, a young man diagnosed with schizophrenia and major depression

Source: Campbell, 2000, reprinted with permission of the National Institute of Mental Health

---

psychological disorder Abnormal behavior pattern that involves a disturbance of psychological functioning or behavior.

abnormal psychology The branch of psychology that deals with the description, causes, and treatment of abnormal behavior patterns.

T R U T H or F I C T I O N

Psychological disorders affect relatively few Americans.

☑ **FALSE.** In one way or another, psychological disorders affect all of us.

THESE THREE PEOPLE—LIKE MANY OF THE PEOPLE YOU WILL MEET IN THIS TEXT—STRUGGLE with problems that mental health professionals classify as psychological or mental disorders. A **psychological disorder** is a pattern of abnormal behavior that is associated with states of emotional distress, such as anxiety or depression, or with impaired behavior or ability to function, such as difficulty holding a job or even distinguishing reality from fantasy. **Abnormal psychology** is the branch of psychology that studies abnormal behavior and ways of helping people who are affected by psychological disorders.

The problem of abnormal behavior might seem the concern of only a few of us. After all, relatively few people are ever admitted to a psychiatric hospital. Most people never seek the help of a mental health professional, such as a psychologist or psychiatrist. Fewer still ever plead not guilty to crimes on grounds of insanity. Most of us probably have at least one relative we consider "eccentric," but how many of us have relatives we consider "crazy"? And yet, the truth is that abnormal behavior affects all of us in one way or another. If we limit ourselves to diagnosable mental disorders, nearly one in two of us (46%) are directly affected at some point in our lives (Kessler et al., 2005a; see Figure 1.1). More than one in four adult Americans (26%) experience a diagnosable psychological disorder in any given year (Kessler et al., 2005b; WHO, 2004). If we also include the mental health problems of our family members, friends, and coworkers and take into account those who foot the bill for treatment in the form of taxes and health insurance premiums and lost productivity due to sick days, disability leaves, and impaired job performance inflating product costs, then clearly all of us are affected to one degree or another.

The study of abnormal psychology is illuminated not only by the extensive research on the causes and treatments of psychological disorders reported in scientific journals, but also by the personal stories of people affected by these problems. In this text, we will learn from these people as they tell their stories in their own words. Through first-person narratives, case examples, and video interviews, we enter the world of people struggling with various types of psychological disorders that affect their moods, thinking, and behavior. Some of these stories may remind you of the experiences of people close to you, or perhaps even yourself. We invite you to explore with us the nature and origins of these disorders and ways of helping people who face the many challenges they pose.

Let us pause for a moment to raise an important distinction. Although the terms *psychological disorder* and *mental disorder* are often used interchangeably, we prefer using the term *psychological disorder*. The major reason is that the term *psychological disorder* puts the study of abnormal behavior squarely within the purview of the field of

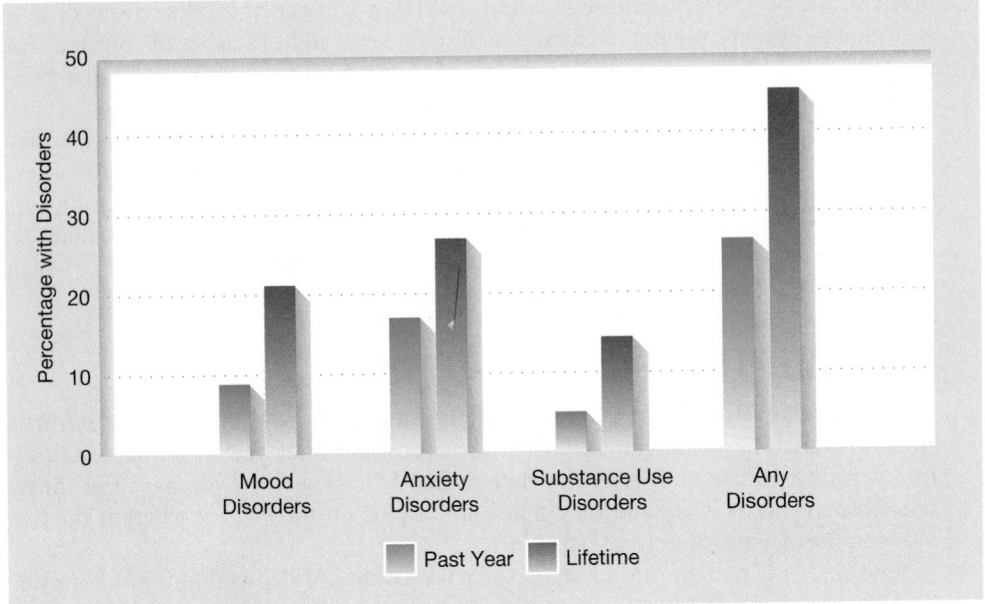

FIGURE 1.1 Lifetime and past-year prevalences of psychological disorders.
This graph is based on a nationally representative sample of 9,282 English-speaking U.S. residents aged 18 and older. Here we see percentages of individuals with diagnosable psychological disorders either during the past year or at some point in their lives for several major diagnostic categories. The mood disorders category includes major depressive episode, manic episode, and dysthymia (discussed in Chapter 8). Anxiety disorders include panic disorder, agoraphobia without panic disorder, social phobia, specific phobia, and generalized anxiety disorder (discussed in Chapter 6). Substance use disorders include abuse or dependence disorders involving alcohol or other drugs (discussed in Chapter 9).
Source: Kessler et al., 2005a; Kessler et al., 2005b.

psychology. Moreover, the term *mental disorder* (also called *mental illness*) is derived from the **medical model** perspective that holds abnormal behavior patterns to be symptoms of underlying illness. Although the medical model is a major contemporary model for understanding abnormal behavior, we believe we need to take a broader view of abnormal behavior by incorporating psychological and sociocultural perspectives as well.

Recently, the U.S. Surgeon General issued a report on the nation's mental health. Here are some key conclusions from the report (Satcher, 2000; USDHHS, 1999b):

- Mental health reflects the complex interaction of brain functioning and environmental influences.
- Effective treatments exist for most mental disorders, including psychological interventions such as psychotherapy and counseling and psychopharmacologic or drug therapies. Treatment is often more effective when psychological and pharmacological treatments are combined.
- Progress in developing effective prevention programs in the mental health field has been slow because we do not know the causes of mental disorders or ways of altering known influences, such as genetic predispositions. Nonetheless, some effective prevention programs have been developed.
- Although 15% of American adults receive some form of help for mental health problems each year, many who need help do not receive it.
- Mental health problems are best understood when we take a broader view and consider the social and cultural contexts in which they occur.
- Mental health services need to be designed and delivered in a manner that takes into account the viewpoints and needs of racial and ethnic minorities.

The Surgeon General's report forms a backdrop for our study of abnormal psychology. As we shall see throughout the text, we believe that understandings of abnormal

medical model A biological perspective in which abnormal behavior is viewed as symptomatic of underlying illness.

behavior are best revealed through a lens that takes into account interactions of biological and environmental factors. We also believe that social and cultural (or *sociocultural*) factors need to be considered in the attempt to both understand abnormal behavior and develop effective treatment services.

In this chapter we first address the difficulties of defining abnormal behavior. We see that throughout history, abnormal behavior has been viewed from different perspectives. We chronicle the development of concepts of abnormal behavior and its treatment. We see that in the past, treatment usually referred to what was done *to*, rather than *for*, people with abnormal behavior. We then describe the ways in which psychologists and other scholars study abnormal behavior today.

HOW DO WE DEFINE ABNORMAL BEHAVIOR?

We all become anxious or depressed from time to time, but is this abnormal? Becoming anxious in anticipation of an important job interview or a final examination is perfectly normal. It is appropriate to feel depressed when you have lost someone close to you or when you have failed at a test or on the job. So, where is the line between normal and abnormal behavior?

One answer is that emotional states such as anxiety and depression may be considered abnormal when they are not appropriate to the situation. It is normal to feel down when you fail a test, but not when your grades are good or excellent. It is normal to feel anxious before a college admissions interview, but not to panic before entering a department store or boarding a crowded elevator.

Abnormality may also be suggested by the magnitude of the problem. Although some anxiety is normal enough before a job interview, feeling that your heart might leap from your chest—and consequently canceling the interview—is not. Nor is it normal to feel so anxious in this situation that your clothing becomes soaked with perspiration.

Criteria for Determining Abnormality

Mental health professionals apply various criteria in making judgments about whether behavior is abnormal. The most commonly used criteria include the following:

1. *Unusualness.* Behavior that is unusual is often considered abnormal. Only a few of us report seeing or hearing things that are not really there; "seeing things" and "hear-

Is this abnormal? One of the criteria used to determine whether or not behavior is abnormal is whether it deviates from acceptable standards of conduct or social norms. The behavior and attire of these men is abnormal in a classroom or workplace, but not at a football game.

ing things" are almost always considered abnormal in our culture, except, perhaps, in the case of certain types of religious experiences (USDHHS, 1999a). Moreover, "hearing voices" and other forms of hallucinations under some circumstances are not considered unusual in some preliterate societies.

Becoming overcome with feelings of panic when entering a department store or when standing in a crowded elevator is uncommon and considered abnormal in our culture. Uncommon behavior is not in itself abnormal. Only one person can hold the record for swimming the fastest 100 meters. The record-holding athlete differs from the rest of us but, again, is not considered abnormal. Thus rarity or statistical deviance is not a sufficient basis for labeling behavior abnormal; nevertheless, it is one yardstick often used to judge abnormality.

2. *Social deviance.* All societies have norms (standards) that define the kinds of behaviors acceptable in given contexts. Behavior deemed normal in one culture may be viewed as abnormal in another. For example, people in our culture who assume that all male strangers are devious are usually regarded as unduly suspicious or distrustful. But such suspicions were justified among the Mundugumor, a tribe of cannibals studied by anthropologist Margaret Mead (1935). Within that culture, male strangers *were* typically malevolent toward others, and it was normal to feel distrustful of them. Norms, which arise from the practices and beliefs of specific cultures, are relative standards, not universal truths.

Thus, clinicians need to weigh cultural differences when determining what is normal and abnormal. Moreover, what strikes one generation as abnormal may be considered normal by the next. For example, until the mid-1970s homosexuality was classified as a mental disorder by the psychiatric profession (see the *Controversies in Abnormal Psychology* feature on page 18). Today, however, the psychiatric profession no longer considers homosexuality a mental disorder, and many people argue that contemporary societal norms should include homosexuality as a normal variation in behavior.

Another result of basing normality on compliance with social norms is the tendency to label nonconformists as mentally disturbed. We may come to brand behavior that we do not approve as "sick" rather than accept that the behavior may be normal, even though it offends or puzzles us.

3. *Faulty perceptions or interpretations of reality.* Normally, our sensory systems and cognitive processes permit us to form accurate mental representations of the environment. Seeing things and hearing voices that are not present are considered hallucinations, which in our culture are generally taken as signs of an underlying mental disorder. Similarly, holding unfounded ideas or *delusions,* such as *ideas of persecution* that the CIA or the Mafia are out to get you, may be regarded as signs of mental disturbance—unless, of course, they *are.* (As former Secretary of State Henry Kissinger is said to have remarked, "Even paranoid people have enemies.")

It is normal in the United States to say that one "talks" to God through prayer. If, however, a person insists to have literally seen God or heard the voice of God—as opposed to, say, being divinely inspired—we may come to regard her or him as mentally disturbed.

4. *Significant personal distress.* States of personal distress caused by troublesome emotions, such as anxiety, fear, or depression, may be abnormal. As we noted earlier, however, anxiety and depression are sometimes appropriate responses to the situation. Real threats and losses do occur in life, and *lack* of an emotional response to them would be regarded as abnormal. Appropriate feelings of distress are not considered abnormal unless they persist long after the source of anguish has been removed (after most people would have adjusted) or if they are so intense that they impair the individual's ability to function.

5. *Maladaptive or self-defeating behavior.* Behavior that leads to unhappiness rather than self-fulfillment can be regarded as abnormal. Behavior that limits our ability

When is anxiety abnormal? Negative emotions such as anxiety are considered abnormal when they are judged to be excessive or inappropriate to the situation. Anxiety is generally regarded as normal when it is experienced during a job interview (top), so long as it is not so severe that it prevents the interviewee from performing adequately. Anxiety is deemed to be abnormal if it is experienced whenever one boards an elevator (bottom).

to function in expected roles, or to adapt to our environments, may also be considered abnormal. According to these criteria, heavy alcohol consumption that impairs health or social and occupational functioning may be viewed as abnormal. Agoraphobic behavior, characterized by intense fear of venturing into public places, may be considered abnormal in that it is both uncommon and maladaptive because it impairs the individual's ability to fulfill work and family responsibilities.

6. *Dangerousness.* Behavior that is dangerous to oneself or other people may be considered abnormal. Here, too, the social context is crucial. In wartime, people who sacrifice themselves or charge the enemy with little apparent concern for their own safety may be characterized as courageous, heroic, and patriotic. But people who threaten or attempt suicide because of the pressures of civilian life are usually considered abnormal.

Football and hockey players who occasionally get into fistfights or altercations with opposing players may be normal enough. Given the nature of the sports, unaggressive football and hockey players would not last long in college or professional ranks. But individuals involved in frequent altercations may be regarded as abnormal. Physically aggressive behavior is most often maladaptive in modern life. Moreover, physical aggression is ineffective as a way of resolving conflicts—although it is by no means uncommon.

Abnormal behavior thus has multiple definitions. Depending on the case, some criteria may be weighted more heavily than others. But in most cases, a combination of these criteria is used to define abnormality.

Let's now return to the three cases we introduced at the beginning of the chapter. Consider the criteria we can apply in determining that the behaviors reported in these case vignettes are abnormal. For one thing, the abnormal behavior patterns in these three cases are unusual in the statistical sense. Most people do not encounter these kinds of problems, although we should add that these problems are far from rare. The problem behaviors also meet other criteria of abnormality, as we shall see.

Phil suffered from *claustrophobia,* an excessive fear of enclosed spaces. (This is an example of an anxiety disorder and is discussed more fully in Chapter 6.) His behavior was unusual (relatively few people are so fearful of confinement that they avoid flying in airplanes or riding on elevators) and was associated with significant personal distress. His fear also impaired his ability to carry out his occupational and family responsiblities. But he was not hampered by faulty perceptions of reality. He recognized that his fears exceeded a realistic appraisal of danger in these situations.

What criteria of abnormality applies in the case of the woman who cowered under the blankets? She was diagnosed with *bipolar disorder* (formerly, manic-depression), a type of mood disorder in which a person experiences extreme mood swings from the heights of elation and seemingly boundless energy to the depths of depression and despair. (The vignette described the manic phase of the disorder.) Bipolar disorder, which is discussed in Chapter 8, is associated with extreme personal distress and difficulty functioning effectively in normal life. It is also linked to self-defeating and dangerous behavior, such as reckless driving or exorbitant spending during manic phases and suicide during depressive phases. In some cases, like the one presented here, people in manic phases sometimes have faulty perceptions or interpretations of reality, such as hallucinations and delusions.

Thomas, whose story was featured in the third vignette, suffered from both schizophrenia and depression. It is not unusual for people to have more than one disorder at a time. In the parlance of the psychiatric profession, these clients present with *comorbid* (co-occurring) diagnoses. Comorbidity complicates treatment because clinicians need to design a treatment approach that focuses on treating two or more disorders. Schizophrenia meets a number of criteria of abnormality in addition to statistical infrequency (it affects about 1% of the general population). The clinical features of schizophrenia include socially deviant or bizarre behavior, disturbed perceptions or interpretations of reality (delusions and hallucinations), maladaptive behavior (difficulty meeting responsibilities of daily life), and personal distress. (See Chapter 12 for more detail on schizophrenia.) Thomas, for example, was plagued by auditory hallucinations (terrorizing voices), which were certainly a source of significant distress. His thinking was also delusional, because he believed that "a presence" in his bedroom was "torturing good forces" surrounding him and causing him to make mistakes during the day. In Thomas's case, schizophrenia was complicated by depression that involved feelings of personal distress (irritability and feelings of dread). Depression is also associated with dampened or downcast mood, maladaptive behavior (difficulty getting to work or school or even getting out of bed in the morning), and potential dangerousness (possible suicidal behavior).

It is one thing to recognize and label behavior as abnormal; it is another to understand and explain it. Philosophers, physicians, natural scientists, and psychologists have used various approaches, or *models,* in the effort to explain abnormal behavior. Some approaches have been based on superstition; others have invoked religious explanations. Some current views are predominantly biological; others are psychological. In considering various historical and contemporary approaches to understanding abnormal behavior, let's first look further at the importance of cultural beliefs in determining which behavior patterns are deemed abnormal.

Cultural Bases of Abnormal Behavior

As noted, behavior that is normal in one culture may be deemed abnormal in another. Australian aborigines believe they can communicate with the spirits of their ancestors and that people, especially close relatives, share their dreams. These beliefs are considered normal within Aboriginal culture. But were such beliefs to be expressed in our culture, they would likely be deemed delusions, which professionals regard as a common feature of schizophrenia. Thus, the standards we use in making judgments of abnormal behavior must take into account cultural norms.

Kleinman (1987) offers an example of "hearing voices" among Native Americans to underscore the ways in which judgments about abnormality are embedded within a cultural context:

> Ten psychiatrists trained in the same assessment technique and diagnostic criteria who are asked to examine 100 American Indians shortly after the latter have experienced the death of a spouse, a parent or a child may determine with close to 100% consistency that those individuals report hearing, in the first month of grieving, the voice of the dead person calling to them as the spirit ascends to the afterworld. [Although such judgments may be consistent across observers] the determination of whether such reports are a sign of an abnormal mental state is an interpretation based on knowledge of this group's behavioural norms and range of normal experiences of bereavement. (p. 453)

To these Native Americans, bereaved people who report hearing the spirits of the deceased calling to them as they ascend to the afterlife are normal. Behavior that is normative within the cultural setting in which it occurs should not be considered abnormal.

Concepts of health and illness have different meanings in different cultures. Traditional Native American cultures distinguish between illnesses that are believed to arise from influences outside the culture, called "White man's sicknesses," such as alcoholism and drug addiction, from those that emanate from a lack of harmony with traditional tribal life and thought, which are called "Indian sicknesses" (Trimble, 1991). Traditional healers, shamans, and medicine men and women are called on to treat "Indian sickness." When the problem is thought to have its cause outside the community, help is sought from "White man's medicine."

Abnormal behavior patterns take different forms in different cultures (USDHHS, 1999a). Westerners experience anxiety, for example,

A traditional Native American healer. Many traditional Native Americans distinguish between illnesses believed to arise from influences external to their own culture ("white man's sicknesses") and those that emanate from a lack of harmony with traditional tribal life and thought ("Indian sicknesses"). Traditional healers such as the one shown here may be called on to treat "Indian sickness," whereas "white man's medicine" may be sought to help people deal with problems whose causes are seen as lying outside the community, such as alcoholism and drug addiction.

in the form of worrying about paying the mortgage, losing a job, and so on. Yet "in a number of African cultures, anxiety is expressed as fears of failure in procreation, in dreams and complaints about witchcraft" (Kleinman, 1987). Australian aborigines can develop intense fears of sorcery, accompanied by the belief that one is in mortal danger from evil spirits (D. J. Spencer, 1983). Trancelike states in which young aboriginal women are mute, immobile, and unresponsive are also quite common. If these women do not recover from the trance within hours or, at most, a few days, they may be brought to a sacred site for healing.

The very words that we use to describe psychological disorders—words such as *depression* or *mental health*—have different meanings in other cultures or no equivalent meaning at all. This doesn't mean that depression doesn't exist in other cultures. Rather, it suggests we need to learn how people in different cultures experience emotional distress, including states of depression and anxiety, rather than imposing our perspectives on their experiences. Among people in China and other countries in the Far East, depression is often expressed through the development of physical symptoms, such as headaches, fatigue, or weakness, rather than by the feelings of guilt or sadness that are more common in the West (American Psychiatric Association, 2000; Draguns & Tanaka-Matsumi, 2003; Parker, Gladstone, & Chee, 2001).

These differences demonstrate how important it is that we determine whether our concepts of abnormal behavior are valid before we apply them to other cultures (Dana, 2000). Research efforts along these lines have shown that the abnormal behavior pattern associated with our concept of schizophrenia exists in countries as far flung as Colombia, India, China, Denmark, Nigeria, and the former Soviet Union, among others (Jablensky et al., 1992). Furthermore, rates of schizophrenia appear similar among the countries studied. However, differences have been observed in some of the features of schizophrenia across cultures (Thakker & Ward, 1998).

Views about abnormal behavior vary from society to society. In our culture, models based on medical disease and psychological factors are prominent in explaining abnormal behavior. But in traditional native cultures, models of abnormal behavior often invoke supernatural causes, such as possession by demons or the devil (Lefley, 1990). In Filipino folk society, for example, psychological problems are often attributed to the influence of "spirits" or the possession of a "weak soul" (Edman & Johnson, 1999).

HISTORICAL PERSPECTIVES ON ABNORMAL BEHAVIOR

Throughout the history of Western culture, concepts of abnormal behavior have been shaped, to some degree, by the prevailing worldview of the time. For hundreds of years, beliefs in supernatural forces, demons, and evil spirits held sway. (And, as we've just seen, these beliefs still hold true in some societies.) Abnormal behavior was often taken as a sign of possession. In modern times, the predominant—but by no means universal—worldview has shifted toward beliefs in science and reason. In our culture, abnormal behavior has come to be viewed as the product of physical and psychosocial factors, not demonic possession.

The Demonological Model

Why would anyone need a hole in the head? Archaeologists have unearthed human skeletons from the Stone Age with egg-sized cavities in the skull. One interpretation of these holes is that our prehistoric ancestors believed abnormal behavior was caused by the inhabitation of evil spirits. These holes might be the result of **trephination**—the drilling of the skull to provide an outlet for those irascible spirits. Fresh bone growth indicates that some people did survive this "medical procedure."

Just the threat of *trephining* may have persuaded some people to comply with tribal norms. Because no written accounts of the purposes of trephination exist, other explanations are possible. For instance, perhaps trephination was simply a form of surgery to remove shattered pieces of bone or blood clots that resulted from head injuries (Maher & Maher, 1985).

trephination A harsh, prehistoric practice of cutting a hole in a person's skull, possibly in an attempt to release demons.

The notion of supernatural causes of abnormal behavior, or demonology, was prominent in Western society until the Age of Enlightenment. The ancients explained nature in terms of the actions of the gods: The Babylonians believed the movements of the stars and the planets expressed the adventures and conflicts of the gods. The Greeks believed the gods toyed with humans, unleashed havoc on disrespectful or arrogant humans, and clouded their minds with madness.

In ancient Greece, people who behaved abnormally were sent to temples dedicated to Aesculapius, the god of healing. The Greeks believed that Aesculapius would visit the afflicted while they slept in the temple and offer them restorative advice through dreams. Rest, a nutritious diet, and exercise were also part of the treatment. Incurables were driven from the temple by stoning.

Origins of the Medical Model: In "Ill Humor"

Not all ancient Greeks believed in the demonological model. The seeds of naturalistic explanations of abnormal behavior were sown by Hippocrates and developed by other physicians in the ancient world, especially Galen.

Hippocrates (ca. 460–377 B.C.E.), the celebrated physician of the Golden Age of Greece, challenged the prevailing beliefs of his time by arguing that illnesses of the body and mind were the result of natural causes, not possession by supernatural spirits. He believed the health of the body and mind depended on the balance of **humors,** or vital fluids, in the body: phlegm, black bile, blood, and yellow bile. An imbalance of humors, he thought, accounted for abnormal behavior. A lethargic or sluggish person was believed to have an excess of phlegm, from which we derive the word *phlegmatic.* An overabundance of black bile was believed to cause depression, or *melancholia.* An excess of blood created a *sanguine* disposition: cheerful, confident, and optimistic. An excess of yellow bile made people "bilious" and *choleric*—quick-tempered, that is.

Though we no longer subscribe to Hippocrates's theory of bodily humors, his theory is important because of its break from demonology. It foreshadowed the modern medical model, the view that abnormal behavior results from underlying biological processes. Hippocrates made other contributions to modern thought and, indeed, to modern medical practice. He classified abnormal behavior patterns, using three main categories that still find equivalents today: *melancholia* to characterize excessive depression, *mania* to refer to exceptional excitement, and *phrenitis* (from the Greek "inflammation of the brain") to characterize the bizarre behavior that might today typify schizophrenia. To this day, medical schools honor Hippocrates by having students swear an oath of medical ethics that he originated, the Hippocratic oath.

Galen (ca. 130–200 C.E.), a Greek physician who attended Roman emperor–philosopher Marcus Aurelius, adopted and expanded on the teachings of Hippocrates. Among Galen's contributions was the discovery that arteries carry blood, not air, as had been formerly believed.

Medieval Times

The Middle Ages, or medieval times, cover the millennium of European history from about 476 C.E. through 1450 C.E. After the passing of Galen, belief in supernatural causes, especially the doctrine of possession, increased in influence and eventually dominated medieval thought. This doctrine held that abnormal behaviors were a sign of possession by evil spirits or the devil. This belief was part of the teachings of the Roman Catholic Church, the central institution in Western Europe after the decline of the Roman Empire. Although belief in possession preceded the Church and is found in ancient Egyptian and Greek writings, the Church revitalized it. The Church's treatment of choice for possession was exorcism. Exorcists were employed to persuade evil

Trephination. Trephination refers to a procedure by which a hole is chipped into a person's skull. Some investigators speculate that the practice represented an ancient form of surgery. Perhaps trephination was intended to release the demons responsible for abnormal behavior.
Image #283253. Photo by: Bierwert. American Museum of Natural History Library.

humors According to the ancient Hippocratic belief system, the vital bodily fluids (phlegm, black bile, blood, yellow bile).

Exorcism. This medieval woodcut illustrates the practice of exorcism, which was used to expel the evil spirits that were believed to have possessed people.

The water-float test. This so-called test was one way in which medieval authorities sought to detect possession and witchcraft. Managing to float above the water line was deemed a sign of impurity. In the lower right-hand corner, you can see the bound hands and feet of one poor unfortunate who failed to remain afloat, but whose drowning would have cleared away any suspicions of possession.

spirits that the bodies of the "possessed" were no longer habitable. Methods of persuasion included prayer, incantations, waving a cross at the victim, beating and flogging, even starving the victim. If the victim continued to display unseemly behavior, there were yet more persuasive remedies, such as the rack, a device of torture. No doubt, recipients of these "remedies" fondly wished the devil would vacate the premises immediately.

The Renaissance—a great revival of classical learning, art, and literature—began in Italy in the 1400s and spread throughout Europe. Ironically, although the Renaissance is considered the transition from the medieval to the modern world, the fear of witches also reached its height during this period.

Witchcraft

The late 15th through the late 17th centuries were especially bad times to annoy your neighbors. These were times of massive persecutions, particularly of women, who were accused of witchcraft. Church officials believed that witches made pacts with the devil, practiced satanic rituals, ate babies, and poisoned crops. In 1484, Pope Innocent VIII decreed that witches be executed. Two Dominican priests compiled a notorious manual for witch-hunting, called the *Malleus Maleficarum* (The Witches' Hammer), to help inquisitors identify suspected witches. Many thousands were accused of witchcraft and put to death in the next two centuries.

Witch-hunting required innovative "diagnostic" tests. In the case of the water-float test, suspects were dunked in a pool to certify they were not possessed by the devil. The test was based on the principle that pure metals settle to the bottom during smelting, whereas impurities bob up to the surface. Suspects who sank and drowned were ruled pure. Suspects who kept their heads above water were judged to be in league with the devil. As the saying went, you were "Damned if you do and damned if you don't."

Modern scholars once believed these so-called witches were actually people with psychological disorders who were persecuted because of their abnormal behavior. Many suspected witches did confess to bizarre behaviors, such as flying or engaging in sexual intercourse with the devil, which suggests the types of disturbed behavior associated with modern conceptions of schizophrenia. Yet these confessions must be discounted because they were extracted under torture by inquisitors who were bent on finding evidence to support accusations of witchcraft (Spanos, 1978). We know today that the threat of torture and other forms of intimidation are sufficient to extract false confessions. Although some of those who were persecuted as witches probably did show abnormal behavior patterns, most did not (Schoenman, 1984). Rather, accusations of witchcraft appeared to be a convenient means of disposing of social nuisances and political rivals, of seizing property, and of suppressing heresy (Spanos, 1978). In English villages, many of the accused were poor, unmarried elderly women who were forced to beg their neighbors for food. If misfortune befell the people who declined to give help, the beggar might be accused of having cast a curse on the household. If the woman was generally unpopular, the accusation of witchcraft was likely to follow.

Demons were believed to play roles in both abnormal behavior and witchcraft. However, although some victims of demonic possession were perceived to be afflicted as retribution for their own wrongdoing, others were considered to be innocent victims—possessed by demons through no fault of their own. Witches, on the other hand, were believed to have renounced God and voluntarily entered into a pact with the devil. Witches were generally seen as more deserving of torture and execution (Spanos, 1978).

Historical trends do not follow straight lines. Although the demonological model held sway during the Middle Ages and much of the Renaissance, it did not completely supplant belief in naturalistic causes. In medieval England, for example, demonic possession was only rarely invoked in cases in which a person was held to be insane by legal authorities (Neugebauer, 1979). Most explanations for unusual behavior involved natural causes, such as physical illness or trauma to the brain. In England, in fact, some disturbed people were kept in hospitals until they were restored to sanity (Allderidge, 1979). The Renaissance Belgian physician Johann Weyer (1515–1588) also took up the cause of Hippocrates and Galen by arguing that abnormal behavior and thought patterns were caused by physical problems.

"Bedlam." The bizarre antics of the patients at St. Mary's of Bethelem Hospital in London in the 18th century were a source of entertainment for the well-heeled gentry of the town, such as the two well-dressed women in the middle of the painting.

Asylums

By the late 15th and early 16th centuries, asylums, or madhouses, began to crop up throughout Europe. Many were former leprosariums, which were no longer needed because of the decline in leprosy after the late Middle Ages. Asylums often gave refuge to beggars as well as the mentally disturbed, and conditions were appalling. Residents were chained to their beds and left to lie in their own waste or to wander about unassisted. Some asylums became public spectacles. In one asylum in London, St. Mary's of Bethlehem Hospital—from which the word *bedlam* is derived—the public could buy tickets to observe the antics of the inmates, much as we would pay to see a circus sideshow or animals at the zoo.

The Reform Movement and Moral Therapy

The modern era of treatment begins with the efforts of the Frenchmen Jean-Baptiste Pussin and Philippe Pinel in the late 18th and early 19th centuries. They argued that people who behave abnormally suffer from diseases and should be treated humanely. This view was not popular at the time; mentally disturbed people were regarded as threats to society, not as sick people in need of treatment.

From 1784 to 1802, Pussin, a layman, was placed in charge of a ward for people considered "incurably insane" at La Bicêtre, a large mental hospital in Paris. Although Pinel is often credited with freeing the inmates of La Bicêtre from their chains, Pussin was actually the first official to unchain a group of the "incurably insane." These unfortunates had been considered too dangerous and unpredictable to be left unchained. But Pussin believed that if they were treated with kindness, there would be no need for chains. As he predicted, most of the shut-ins were manageable and calm after their chains were removed. They could walk the hospital grounds and take in fresh air. Pussin also forbade the staff from treating the residents harshly, and he fired employees who ignored his directives.

The unchaining of inmates at La Bicêtre by 18th-century French reformer Philippe Pinel. Continuing the work of Jean-Baptiste Pussin, Pinel stopped harsh practices, such as bleeding and purging, and moved inmates from darkened dungeons to sunny, airy rooms. Pinel also took the time to converse with inmates, in the belief that understanding and concern would help restore them to normal functioning.

Pinel (1745–1826) became medical director for the incurables' ward at La Bicêtre in 1793 and continued the humane treatment Pussin had begun. He stopped harsh practices, such as bleeding and purging, and moved patients from darkened dungeons to well-ventilated, sunny rooms. Pinel also spent hours talking to inmates, in the belief that showing understanding and concern would help restore them to normal functioning.

The philosophy of treatment that emerged from these efforts was labeled *moral therapy*. It was based on the belief that providing humane treatment in a relaxed and decent environment could restore functioning. Similar reforms were instituted at about this time in England by William Tuke and later in the United States by Dorothea Dix. Another influential figure was the American physician Benjamin Rush (1745–1813)—also a signatory to the Declaration of Independence and an early leader of the antislavery movement (Farr, 1994). Rush, considered the father of American psychiatry, penned the first American textbook on psychiatry in 1812: *Medical Inquiries and Observations Upon the Diseases of the Mind.* He believed that madness is caused by engorgement of the blood vessels of the brain. To relieve pressure, he recommended bloodletting, purging, and ice-cold baths. But he did advance humane treatment by encouraging the staff of his Philadelphia Hospital to treat patients with kindness, respect, and understanding. He also favored the therapeutic use of occupational therapy, music, and travel (Farr, 1994). His hospital became the first in the United States to admit patients for psychological disorders.

Dorothea Dix (1802–1887), a Boston schoolteacher, traveled about the country decrying the deplorable conditions in the jails and almshouses where mentally disturbed people were placed. As a result of her efforts, 32 mental hospitals devoted to treating people with psychological disorders were established throughout the United States.

A Step Backward

In the latter half of the 19th century, the belief that abnormal behaviors could be successfully treated or cured by moral therapy fell into disfavor (USDHHS, 1999a). A period of apathy ensued in which patterns of abnormal behavior were deemed incurable (Grob, 1994). Mental institutions in the United States grew in size but provided little more than custodial care. Conditions deteriorated. Mental hospitals became frightening places. It was not uncommon to find residents "wallowing in their own excrements," in the words of a New York State official of the time (Grob, 1983). Straitjackets, handcuffs, cribs, straps, and other devices were used to restrain excitable or violent patients.

Deplorable hospital conditions remained commonplace through the middle of the 20th century. By the mid-1950s, the population in mental hospitals had risen to half a million patients. Although some state hospitals provided decent and humane care, many were described as little more than human snakepits. Residents were crowded into wards that lacked even rudimentary sanitation. Mental patients in back wards were essentially *warehoused;* that is, they were left to live out their lives with little hope or expectation of recovery or return to the community. Many received little professional care and were abused by poorly trained and supervised staffs. Finally, these appalling conditions led to calls for reforms of the mental health system.

The Community Mental Health Movement: The Exodus from State Hospitals

In response to the growing call for reform, Congress in 1963 established a nationwide system of community mental health centers (CMHCs) that was intended to offer an alternative to long-term custodial care in bleak institutions. CMHCs were charged with providing continuing support and care to former hospital residents who were released from state mental hospitals under a policy of deinstitutionalization. Another factor that laid the groundwork for the mass exodus from mental hospitals was the development of a new class of drugs—the *phenothiazines*. This group of antipsychotic drugs, which helped quell the most flagrant behavior patterns associated with schizophrenia, was introduced in the 1950s. *Phenothiazines* reduced the need for indefinite hospital stays and permitted many people with schizophrenia to be discharged to halfway houses, group homes, and independent living. The mental hospital population across the United States plummeted from 559,000 in 1955 to fewer than 100,000 by the 1990s (Grob, 2001). Some mental hospitals were closed entirely.

The community mental health movement and the policy of deinstitutionalization were developed with the hope that mental patients could return to their communities and assume more independent and fulfilling lives. However, the exodus from state hospitals left tens of thousands of marginally functioning people in communities that lacked adequate housing and other forms of support. Even today, many of the homeless we see wandering city streets and sleeping in bus terminals and train stations are discharged mental patients. (In Chapter 4, we take a closer look at the policy of deinstitutionalization and the problems faced by the psychiatric homeless population.)

Contemporary Perspectives on Abnormal Behavior

Beliefs in possession or demonology persisted until the 18th century, when society began to turn toward reason and science to explain natural phenomena and human behavior. The nascent sciences of biology, chemistry, physics, and astronomy promised knowledge derived from scientific methods of observation and experimentation. Scientific observation in turn uncovered the microbial causes of some kinds of diseases and gave rise to preventive measures. Scientific models of abnormal behavior also began to emerge, including models representing biological, psychological, sociocultural, and biopsychosocial perspectives. We briefly discuss each of these models here, particularly in terms of their historical background, which will lead to a fuller discussion in Chapter 2.

The Biological Perspective Against the backdrop of advances in medical science, the German physician Wilhelm Griesinger (1817–1868) argued that abnormal behavior was rooted in diseases of the brain. Griesinger's views influenced another German physician, Emil Kraepelin (1856–1926), who wrote an influential textbook on psychiatry in 1883 in which he likened mental disorders to physical diseases. Griesinger and Kraepelin paved the way for the modern medical model, which attempts to explain abnormal behavior on the basis of underlying biological defects or abnormalities, not evil spirits. According to the medical model, people behaving abnormally suffer from mental illnesses or disorders that can be classified, like physical illnesses, according to their distinctive causes and symptoms. Adopters of the medical model don't necessarily believe that every mental disorder is a product of defective biology, but they maintain that it is useful to classify patterns of abnormal behavior as disorders that can be identified on the basis of their distinctive features or symptoms.

Kraepelin specified two main groups of mental disorders or diseases: **dementia praecox** (from roots meaning "precocious [premature] insanity"), which we now call schizophrenia, and manic–depressive psychosis, which is now labeled *bipolar disorder*. Kraepelin believed that dementia praecox was caused by a biochemical imbalance and

dementia praecox The term given by Kraepelin to the disorder now called schizophrenia.

manic–depressive psychosis by an abnormality in body metabolism. His major contribution was the development of a classification system that forms the cornerstone of current diagnostic systems.

The medical model gained support in the late 19th century with the discovery that an advanced stage of *syphilis*—in which the bacterium that causes the disease directly invades the brain itself—led to a form of disturbed behavior called **general paresis** (from the Greek *parienai*, meaning "to relax"). General paresis is associated with physical symptoms and psychological impairment, including personality and mood changes, and with progressive deterioration of memory functioning and judgment. With the advent of antibiotics for treating syphilis, general paresis has become extremely uncommon.

General paresis is of interest to us mostly for historical reasons. With the discovery of the connection between general paresis and syphilis, scientists became optimistic that other biological causes would soon be discovered for many other types of disturbed behavior. The later discovery of Alzheimer's disease (discussed in Chapter 15), a brain disease that is the major cause of dementia, lent further support to the medical model. Yet we realize today that the great majority of psychological disorders involve a complex web of factors we are still struggling to understand.

Much of the terminology used in abnormal psychology has been "medicalized." Because of the medical model, we commonly speak of people whose behavior is abnormal as being mentally ill. Because of the medical model we commonly refer to the symptoms of abnormal behavior, rather than the features or characteristics of abnormal behavior. Other terminological offspring of the medical model include *mental health, syndrome, diagnosis, patient, mental patient, mental hospital, prognosis, treatment, therapy, cure, relapse,* and *remission*.

The medical model is a major advance over demonology. It inspired the idea that abnormal behavior should be treated by learned professionals, not punished. Compassion supplanted hatred, fear, and persecution. But the medical model has also led to controversy over the extent to which certain behavior patterns should be considered forms of mental illness. We address this issue in *Controversies in Abnormal Psychology* on page 18.

general paresis A degenerative brain disease occurring when the bacterium that causes syphilis directly invades brain tissue.

Charcot's teaching clinic. Parisian neurologist Jean-Martin Charcot presents a woman patient who exhibits the highly dramatic behavior associated with hysteria, such as falling faint at a moment's notice. Charcot was an important influence on the young Sigmund Freud.

The Psychological Perspective Even as the medical model was gaining influence in the 19th century, some scientists argued that organic factors alone could not explain the many forms of abnormal behavior. In Paris, a respected neurologist, Jean-Martin Charcot (1825–1893), experimented with the use of hypnosis in treating *hysteria*, a condition characterized by paralysis or numbness that cannot be explained by any underlying physical cause. [Interestingly, cases of hysteria were common in the Victorian period, but are rare today (Spitzer et al., 1989).] The thinking at the time was that people with hysteria must have an affliction of the nervous system, which caused their symptoms. Yet Charcot and his associates demonstrated that these symptoms could be removed in hysterical patients or, conversely, induced in normal patients, by means of hypnotic suggestion.

Among those who attended Charcot's demonstrations was a young Austrian physician named Sigmund Freud (1856–1939). Freud reasoned that if hysterical symptoms could be made to disappear or appear through hypnosis—the mere "suggestion of ideas"—they must be psychological, not biological,

Sigmund Freud and Bertha Pappenheim (Anna O.). Freud is shown here at around age 30. Pappenheim (1859–1936) is known more widely in the psychological literature as "Anna O." Freud believed that her hysterical symptoms represented the transformation of blocked-up emotions into physical complaints.

in origin (E. Jones, 1953). He concluded that whatever psychological factors give rise to hysteria, they must lie outside the range of conscious awareness. This insight underlies the first psychological perspective on abnormal behavior—the **psychodynamic model.** "I received the proudest impression," Freud wrote of his experience with Charcot, "of the possibility that there could be powerful mental processes which nevertheless remained hidden from the consciousness of men" (as cited in Sulloway, 1983, p. 32).

Freud was also influenced by the Viennese physician Joseph Breuer (1842–1925), 14 years his senior. Breuer too had used hypnosis to treat a 21-year-old woman, Anna O., with hysterical complaints for which there was no apparent medical basis, such as paralysis in her limbs, numbness, and disturbances of vision and hearing (E. Jones, 1953). A "paralyzed" muscle in her neck prevented her from turning her head. Immobilization of the fingers of her left hand made it all but impossible for her to feed herself. Breuer believed there was a strong psychological component to her symptoms. He encouraged her to talk about her symptoms, sometimes under hypnosis. Recalling and talking about events connected with the appearance of the symptoms—especially events that evoked feelings of fear, anxiety, or guilt—provided symptom relief, at least for a time. Anna referred to the treatment as the "talking cure" or, when joking, as "chimney sweeping."

The hysterical symptoms were taken to represent the transformation of these blocked-up emotions, forgotten but not lost, into physical complaints. In Anna's case, the symptoms disappeared once the emotions were brought to the surface and "discharged." Breuer labeled the therapeutic effect *catharsis,* or emotional discharge of feelings (from the Greek word *kathairein,* meaning to clean or to purify).

Freud's theoretical model was the first major psychological model of abnormal behavior. As we'll see in Chapter 2, other psychological perspectives on abnormal behavior soon followed based on behavioral, humanistic, and cognitive models. Each of these perspectives, as well as the contemporary medical model, spawned particular forms of therapy to treat psychological disorders.

psychodynamic model The theoretical model of Freud and his followers, in which abnormal behavior is viewed as the product of clashing forces within the personality.

CONTROVERSIES IN ABNORMAL PSYCHOLOGY

What Is Abnormal Behavior?

The question of where to draw the line between "normal" and "abnormal" behavior continues to be a subject of debate within the mental health field and the broader society. Unlike medical illness, a psychological or mental disorder cannot be identified by a spot on an X-ray or from a blood sample. Classifying these disorders involves clinical judgments, not findings of fact; and as we have noted, these judgments can change over time and can vary from culture to culture. For example, medical professionals once considered masturbation a form of mental illness. Although some people today may object to masturbation on moral grounds, professionals no longer regard it as a mental disturbance.

Consider other behaviors that may blur the boundaries between normal and abnormal: Is body-piercing abnormal, or is it simply a fashion statement? (How much piercing do you consider "normal?") Might excessive shopping behavior or overuse of the Internet be forms of mental illness? Is bullying a symptom of an underlying disorder, or is it just "bad behavior?" Mental health professionals base their judgments on the kinds of criteria we outlined in this text. But even in professional circles, debate continues about whether some forms of behavior should be classified as forms of abnormal behavior or mental disorders.

One of the longest of these debates concerns homosexuality. Until 1973, the American Psychiatric Association classified homosexuality as a mental disorder. In that year, however, the organization voted to drop homosexuality from its listing of classified mental disorders in its diagnostic manual, the *Diagnostic and Statistical Manual of Mental Disorders,* or *DSM* (discussed in Chapter 3). The *DSM* retained, however, a diagnostic classification that could be applied to individuals who are distressed or confused about their sexual orientation.

The decision to declassify homosexuality as a mental disorder was not unanimous among the nation's psychiatrists. Many argued that the decision was motivated more by political reasons than by good science. Some objected to basing such a decision on a vote. After all, would it be reasonable to drop cancer as a recognized medical illness based on a vote? Shouldn't scientific criteria determine these kinds of judgments, rather than a popular vote?

What do you think? Is homosexuality a variation in the normal spectrum of sexual orientation, or is it a form of abnormal behavior? What is the basis of your judgment? What criteria did you apply in forming a judgment? What evidence do you have to support your beliefs?

Is homosexuality a mental disorder? Do you consider homosexuality abnormal? Until 1973, homosexuality was classified as a mental disorder by the American Psychiatric Association. What criteria should be used to form judgments about determining whether particular patterns of behavior comprise a mental or psychological disorder?

T R U T H or F I C T I O N

Despite changing attitudes in society toward homosexuality, the psychiatric profession still continues to classify homosexuality as a mental disorder.

☑ **FALSE.** The psychiatric profession dropped homosexuality from its listing of mental disorders in 1973.

Within the *DSM* system, mental disorders are recognized on the basis of behavior patterns associated with either emotional distress and/or significant impairment in psychological functioning. Researchers have found that people with a gay male or lesbian sexual orientation tend to have a greater frequency of suicide and of states of emotional distress, especially anxiety and depression, than people with a heterosexual orientation (Bagley & D'Augelli, 2000; Cochran, Sullivan, & Mays, 2003; Skegg et al., 2003).

Even if gay males and lesbians are more prone to develop psychological problems, it doesn't necessarily follow that these problems are the result of their sexual orientation. Gay adolescents in our society come to terms with their sexuality against a backdrop of deep-seated prejudices and resentment toward gays. The process of achieving a sense of self-acceptance against this backdrop of societal intolerance can be so difficult that many gay adolescents seriously consider or attempt suicide (Bagley & D'Augelli, 2000; Simonsen et al., 2000). As adults, gay men and lesbians often continue to bear the brunt of prejudice and negative attitudes toward them, including negative reactions from family members that often follow the disclosure of their sexual orientation. The social stress associated with stigma, prejudice, and discrimination that gay people encounter may directly cause mental health problems (Meyer, 2003).

Understood in this context, it is little wonder that many gay males and lesbians develop psychological problems. As a leading authority in the field, psychologist J. Michael Bailey (1999) wrote, "Surely, it must be difficult for young people to come to grips with their homosexuality in a world where homosexual people are often scorned, mocked, mourned, and feared."

Should we then accept the claim that societal intolerance is the root cause of psychological problems in people with a homosexual orientation? As critical thinkers, we should recognize that other factors may be involved. We need more evidence before we can arrive at any judgments concerning why gay males and lesbians are more prone to psychological problems, especially suicide.

One of these other factors may be lifestyle choice. A classic study of gay couples showed that those living in committed, close relationships were as well adjusted as married heterosexual couples (Bell & Weinberg, 1978). Differences in psychological adjustment or mental health may be more of a reflection of lifestyle factors than sexual orientation.

Imagine a society in which homosexuality was the norm and heterosexual people were shunned, scorned, or ridiculed. Would we find that heterosexual people are more likely to have psychological problems? Would this evidence lead us to assume that heterosexuality is a mental disorder? What do you think?

Critical Thinking

- How do you decide when any behavior, such as social drinking or even shopping or Internet use, crosses the line from "normal" to "abnormal"?
- Is there a set of criteria you use in all cases? How does your criteria differ from the criteria specified in the text?
- Do you believe that homosexuality is abnormal? Why or why not?

The Sociocultural Perspective Mustn't we also consider the broader social context in which behavior occurs to understand the roots of abnormal behavior? Sociocultural theorists believe the causes of abnormal behavior may be found in the failures of society rather than in the person. Accordingly, psychological problems may be rooted in the ills of society, such as unemployment, poverty, family breakdown, injustice, ignorance, and the lack of opportunity. Sociocultural factors also focus on relationships between mental health and social factors such as gender, social class, ethnicity, and lifestyle.

Sociocultural theorists also observe that once a person is called "mentally ill," the label is hard to remove. It also distorts other people's responses to the "patient." Mental patients are stigmatized and marginalized. Job opportunities may disappear, friendships may dissolve, and the "patient" may feel increasingly alienated from society. Sociocultural theorists focus our attention on the social consequences of becoming labeled as a "mental patient." They argue that we need to provide access to meaningful societal roles, as workers, students, and colleagues to people with long-term mental health problems, rather than shunt them aside.

The Biopsychosocial Perspective Aren't patterns of abnormal behavior too complex to be understood from any one model or perspective? Many mental health professionals endorse the view that abnormal behavior is best understood by taking into account multiple causes representing the biological, psychological, and sociocultural domains (Levine & Schmelkin, 2006). The **biopsychosocial model,** or interactionist model, informs this text's approach toward understanding the origins of abnormal behavior. We believe it's essential to consider the interplay of biological, psychological, and sociocultural factors in the development of psychological disorders. Although our understanding of these factors may be incomplete, we must consider all possible pathways and account for multiple factors, influences, and interactions.

Perspectives on psychological disorders provide a framework not only for explanation but also for treatment (see Chapter 4). The perspectives we use also lead to the predictions, or *hypotheses,* that guide our research or inquiries into the causes and treatments of abnormal behavior. The medical model, for example, fosters inquiry into genetic and biochemical treatment methods. In the next section, we consider the ways in which psychologists and other mental health professionals study abnormal behavior.

biopsychosocial model An integrative model for explaining abnormal in terms of the interactions of biological, psychological, and sociocultural factors.

RESEARCH METHODS IN ABNORMAL PSYCHOLOGY

Abnormal psychology is a branch of the scientific discipline of psychology. Research in the field is based on the application of the **scientific method.** Before we explore the basic steps in the scientific method, let us consider the four overarching objective of science: description, explanation, prediction, and control.

scientific method A systematic method of conducting scientific research in which theories or assumptions are examined in the light of evidence.

Description, Explanation, Prediction, and Control: The Objectives of Science

To understand abnormal behavior, we must first learn to describe it. Description allows us to recognize abnormal behavior and provides the basis for explaining it. Descriptions should be clear, unbiased, and based on careful observation. Let us pose a vignette that challenges you put yourself in the position of graduate student in psychology who is asked to describe the behavior of a laboratory rat the professor places on the desk in front of you:

Imagine you are a brand-new graduate student in psychology and are sitting in your research methods class on the first day of the term. The professor, a distinguished woman of about 50, enters the class. She is carrying a small wire-mesh cage containing a white rat. The professor removes the rat from the cage and places it on the desk. She asks the class to observe its behavior. As a serious student, you attend closely. The animal moves to the edge of the desk, pauses, peers over the edge, and seems to jiggle its whiskers at the floor below.

It maneuvers along the edge of the desk, tracking the perimeter. Now and then the rat pauses and vibrates its whiskers downward in the direction of the floor.

The professor picks up the rat and returns it to the cage. She asks the class to describe the animal's behavior.

A student responds, "The rat seems to be looking for a way to escape."

Another student says, "It is reconnoitering its environment, examining it." "Reconnoitering?" you think. That student has seen too many war movies.

The professor writes each response on the blackboard. Another student raises her hand. "The rat is making a visual search of the environment," she says. "Maybe it's looking for food."

The professor prompts other students for their descriptions.

"It's looking around," says one.

"Trying to escape," says another.

Your turn arrives. Trying to be scientific, you say, "We can't say what its motivation might be. All we know is that it's scanning its environment."

"How so?" the professor asks.

"Visually," you reply, confidently.

The professor writes the response and then turns to the class, shaking her head. "Each of you observed the rat," she said, "but none of you described its behavior. Instead, you made inferences that the rat was 'looking for a way down' or 'scanning its environment' or 'looking for food,' and the like. These are not unreasonable inferences, but they are inferences, not descriptions. They also happen to be wrong. You see, the rat is blind. It's been blind since birth. It couldn't possibly be looking around, at least not in a visual sense."

The vignette about the blind rat illustrates that our descriptions of behavior may be influenced by our expectations. Our expectations reflect our preconceptions or models of behavior, and they may incline us to perceive events—such as the rat's movements and other people's behavior—in certain ways. Describing the rat in the classroom as "scanning" and "looking" for something is an inference, or conclusion, we draw from our observations based on our model of how animals explore their environments. In contrast, description would involve a precise accounting of the animal's movements around the desk, measuring how far in each direction it moves, how long it pauses, how it bobs its head from side to side, and so on.

Nevertheless, inference is important in science. Inference allows us to jump from the particular to the general—to suggest laws and principles of behavior that can be woven into a model or **theory** of behavior. Without a way of organizing our descriptions of phenomena in terms of models and theories, we would be left with a buzzing confusion of unconnected observations.

Theories help scientists explain puzzling data and predict future data. Prediction entails the discovery of factors that anticipate the occurrence of events. Geology, for example, seeks clues in the forces affecting the earth that can forecast natural events such as earthquakes and volcanic eruptions. Scientists who study abnormal behavior seek clues in overt behavior, biological processes, family interactions, and so forth, to predict the development of abnormal behaviors as well as factors that might predict response to various treatments. It is not sufficient for theoretical models to help us explain or make sense of events or behaviors that have already occurred. Useful theories must allow us to predict the occurrence of particular behaviors.

The idea of controlling human behavior—especially the behavior of people with serious problems—is controversial. The history of societal response to abnormal behaviors, including abuses such as exorcism and cruel forms of physical restraint, render the idea particularly distressing. Within science, however, the word *control* does not imply that people are coerced into doing the bidding of others, like puppets dangling on strings. Psychologists, for example, are committed to the dignity of the individual, and the concept of human dignity requires that people be free to make decisions and exercise choices. Within this context, *controlling behavior* means using scientific knowledge to help people shape their own goals and more efficiently use their resources to accomplish them. Today, in the United States, even when helping

theory A formulation of the relationships underlying observed events.

professionals restrain people who are violently disturbed, their goal is to assist them to overcome their agitation and regain the ability to exercise meaningful choices in their lives. Ethical standards prohibit the use of injurious techniques in research or practice.

Psychologists and other scientists use the *scientific method* to advance the description, explanation, prediction, and control of abnormal behavior.

The Scientific Method

The scientific method tests assumptions and theories about the world through gathering objective evidence. Gathering evidence that is objective requires thoughtful observational and experimental methods. Here let us focus on the basic steps involved in using the scientific method in experimentation.

1. *Formulating a research question.* Scientists derive research questions from previous observations and current theories. For instance, based on their clinical observations and theoretical understanding of the underlying mechanisms in depression, psychologists may formulate questions about whether certain experimental drugs or particular types of psychotherapy help people overcome depression.

2. *Framing the research question in the form of a hypothesis.* A **hypothesis** is a prediction tested in an experiment. For example, scientists might hypothesize that people who are clinically depressed will show greater improvement on measures of depression if they are given an experimental drug than if they receive an inert placebo (a "sugar pill").

3. *Testing the hypothesis.* Scientists test hypotheses through experiments in which variables are controlled and the differences observed. For instance, they can test the hypothesis about the experimental drug by giving the drug to one group of people with depression and giving another group the placebo. They can then test to see if the people who received the active drug showed greater improvement over a period of time than those who received the placebo.

4. *Drawing conclusions about the hypothesis.* In the final step, scientists draw conclusions from their findings about the accuracy of their hypotheses. Psychologists use statistical methods to determine the likelihood that differences between groups are significant, as opposed to chance fluctuations. Psychologists can be reasonably confident that group differences are significant—that is, not due to chance—when the probability that chance alone can explain the difference is less than 5%. When well-designed research findings fail to bear out hypotheses, scientists rethink the theories from which the hypotheses are derived. Research findings often lead to modifications in theory, new hypotheses, and in turn, subsequent research.

Let us consider the major research methods used by psychologists and others in studying abnormal behavior. Before we do so, let us consider some of the principles that guide ethical conduct in research.

Ethics in Research

Ethical principles are designed to promote the dignity of the individual, protect human welfare, and preserve scientific integrity (APA, 2002). Psychologists are prohibited by the ethical standards of their profession from using methods that cause psychological or physical harm to subjects or clients. Psychologists also must follow ethical guidelines that protect animal subjects in research.

Institutions such as universities and hospitals have review committees, called *institutional review boards* (IRBs), that review proposed research studies in the light of ethical guidelines. Investigators must receive IRB approval before they are permitted to begin their studies. Two of the major principles on which ethical guidelines are based are (a) *informed consent* and (b) *confidentiality*.

The principle of **informed consent** requires that people be free to choose whether they want to participate in research studies. They must be given sufficient information in advance about the study's purposes and methods, and its risks and benefits, in order

hypothesis An assumption that is tested through experimentation.

informed consent The principle that subjects should receive enough information about an experiment beforehand to decide freely whether to participate.

to make an informed decision about their participation. Subjects must also be free to withdraw from a study at any time without penalty. In some cases, researchers may withhold certain information until all the data are collected. For instance, subjects in placebo control studies of experimental drugs are told that they may receive an inert placebo rather than the active drug. In studies in which information was withheld or deception was used, subjects must be debriefed afterward. That is, they must receive an explanation of the true methods and purposes of the study and why it was necessary to keep them in the dark. After the study is concluded, participants who received the placebo would be given the option of receiving the active treatment, if warranted.

Subjects also have a right to expect that their identities will not be revealed. Investigators are required to protect their **confidentiality** by keeping the records of their participation secure and by not disclosing their identities to others.

We now turn to discussion of the research methods used to investigate abnormal behavior.

Naturalistic Observation

In **naturalistic observation,** the investigator observes behavior in the field, where it happens. Anthropologists have observed behavior patterns in preliterate societies to study human diversity. Sociologists have followed the activities of adolescent gangs in inner cities. Psychologists have spent weeks observing the behavior of homeless people in train stations and bus terminals. They have even observed the eating habits of slender and overweight people in fast-food restaurants, searching for clues to obesity.

Scientists try to ensure that their naturalistic observations are unobtrusive, so as to minimize interference with the behavior they observe. Nevertheless, the presence of the observer may distort the behavior that is observed, and this must be taken into consideration.

Naturalistic observation provides information on how subjects behave, but it does not reveal why they do so. It may reveal, for example, that men who frequent bars and drink often get into fights. But such observations do not show that alcohol *causes* aggression. As we shall see, questions of cause and effect are best approached by means of controlled experiments.

The Correlational Method

One of the primary methods used to study abnormal behavior is the **correlational method,** which involves the use of statistical methods to examine relationships between two or more factors that can vary, which are called *variables*. For example, in Chapter 8 we will see that there is a statistical relationship, or *correlation*, between the variables of negative thinking and depressive symptoms. The statistical measure used to express the association or correlation between two variables is called the **correlation coefficient,** which can vary along a continuum ranging from −1.00 to +1.00. When higher values in one variable (negative thinking) are associated with higher values in the other variable (depressive symptoms), there is a *positive correlation* between the variables. If higher levels of one variable are associated with lower values of another variable, there is a *negative correlation* between the variables. Positive correlations carry positive signs; negative correlations carry negative signs. The higher the correlation coefficient—meaning the closer it is to either −1.00 or +1.00—the stronger the relationship is between the variables.

The correlational method does not involve manipulation of the variables of interest. In the previous example, the experimenter does not manipulate people's depressive symptoms or negative thoughts. Rather, the investigator uses statistical techniques to determine whether these variables tend to be associated with each other. Because the experimenter does not directly manipulate the variables, a correlation between two variables does not prove that they are causally related to each other. It may be the case

confidentiality Protection of the identity of participants by keeping records secure and not disclosing their identities.

naturalistic observation A form of research in which behavior is observed and measured in its natural environment.

correlational method A scientific method of study that examines the relationships between factors or variables expressed in statistical terms.

correlation coefficient A statistical measure of the strength of the relationship between two variables expressed along a continuum that varies between −1.00 and +1.00.

that two variables are correlated but have no causal connection. For example, children's foot size is correlated with their vocabulary, but growth in foot size does not cause the growth of vocabulary. Depressive symptoms and negative thoughts are correlated, as we shall see in Chapter 8. Though negative thinking may be a causative factor in depression, it is also possible that the direction of causality works the other way—that depression gives rise to negative thinking. Or perhaps the direction of causality works both ways, with negative thinking contributing to depression and depression in turn influencing negative thinking. Then again, depression and negative thinking may both reflect a common causative factor, such as stress, and not be causally related to each other at all. In sum, we cannot tell from a correlation alone whether or not variables are causally linked. To address questions of cause and effect, we need to use experimental methods in which the experimenter manipulates one or more variables of interest and observes their effects on other variables or outcomes under controlled conditions.

Although the correlational method cannot determine cause-and-effect relationships, it does serve the scientific objective of prediction. When two variables are correlated, we can use one to predict the other. Knowledge of correlations among alcoholism, family history, and attitudes toward drinking helps us predict which adolescents are at great risk of developing problems with alcohol, although causal connections are complex and somewhat nebulous. Knowing which factors predict future problems helps direct preventive efforts toward high-risk groups.

The Longitudinal Study   The **longitudinal study** is a type of correlational study in which individuals are periodically tested or evaluated over lengthy periods of time, perhaps for decades. By studying people over time, researchers seek to identify factors or events in people's lives that predict the later development of abnormal behavior patterns, such as depression or schizophrenia. Prediction is based on the *correlation* between events or factors that are separated in time. However, this type of research is time consuming and costly. It requires a commitment that may literally outlive the original investigators. Therefore, long-term longitudinal studies are relatively uncommon. In Chapter 12 we examine one of the best-known longitudinal studies, the Danish high-risk study that has tracked, since 1962, a group of children whose mothers had schizophrenia and who were themselves at increased risk of developing the disorder (Mednick, Parnas, & Schulsinger, 1987; Parnas et al., 1993).

The Experimental Method

The **experimental method** allows scientists to demonstrate causal relationships by manipulating the causal factor and measuring its effects under controlled conditions that minimize the risk of other factors explaining the results.

The term *experiment* can cause some confusion. Broadly speaking, an experiment is a trial or test of a hypothesis. From this vantage point, any method that seeks to test a hypothesis could be considered experimental—including naturalistic observation and correlational studies. But investigators usually limit the use of the term *experimental method* to refer to studies in which researchers seek to uncover cause-and-effect relationships by directly manipulating possible causal factors.

The factors or variables hypothesized to play a causal role are manipulated or controlled by the investigator in experimental research. These are called the **independent variables.** The observed effects are labeled **dependent variables** because changes in them are believed to depend on the independent or manipulated variable. Dependent variables are observed and measured, not manipulated, by the experimenter. Examples of independent and dependent variables of interest to investigators of abnormal behavior are shown in Table 1.1.

In an experiment, subjects are exposed to an *independent variable,* for example, the type of beverage (alcoholic vs. nonalcoholic) they consume in a laboratory setting. They are then observed or examined to determine whether the independent variable makes a difference in their behavior, or more precisely, whether the independent variable affects

Naturalistic observation. Psychologists take their research into the streets when they conduct naturalistic observation studies—and into the homes, restaurants, schools, and other settings where behavior can be directly observed. For example, psychologists have unobtrusively positioned themselves in school playgrounds to observe how aggressive or socially anxious children interact with peers.

longitudinal study A research study in which subjects are followed over time.

experimental method A scientific method that aims to discover cause-and-effect relationships by manipulating independent variables and observing the effects on the dependent variables.

independent variables Factors that are manipulated in experiments.

dependent variables Outcomes of an experiment believed to be dependent on the effects of an independent variable.

TABLE 1.1

Examples of Independent and Dependent Variables in Experimental Research

Independent Variables	Dependent Variables
Type of treatment: for example, different types of drug treatments or psychological treatments	Behavioral variables: for example, measures of adjustment, activity levels, eating behavior, smoking behavior
Treatment factors: for example, brief vs. long-term treatment, inpatient vs. outpatient treatment	Physiological variables: for example, measures of physiological responses such as heart rate, blood pressure, and brain wave activity
Experimental manipulations: for example, types of beverage consumed (alcoholic vs. nonalcoholic)	Self-report variables: for example, measures of anxiety, mood, or marital or life satisfaction

the dependent variable—for example, whether they behave more aggressively if they consume alcohol. Studies need to have a sufficient number of participants (subjects) to be able to detect statistically meaningful differences between experimental groups.

Experimental and Control Groups Well-controlled experiments randomly assign subjects to experimental and control groups. The **experimental group** is given the experimental treatment, whereas the **control group** is not. Care is taken to hold other conditions constant for each group. By using **random assignment** and holding other conditions constant, experimenters can be reasonably confident that the experimental treatment, and not uncontrolled factors, such as room temperature or differences between the types of subjects in the experimental and control groups, brought about the differences in outcome between the experimental and control groups.

Why should experimenters assign subjects to experimental and control groups at random? Consider a study intended to investigate the effects of alcohol on behavior. Let's suppose we allowed subjects themselves to decide whether or not they wanted to be in an experimental group that drank alcohol or a control group that drank a non-alcoholic beverage. If this were the case, differences between the groups might be due to an underlying **selection factor** rather than the experimental manipulation.

For example, subjects who *chose* the alcoholic beverage might differ in their personalities from those who chose the control beverage. They might be more willing to explore or to take risks, for example. Therefore, we would not know whether the independent variable (type of beverage) or a selection factor (difference in the kinds of subjects making up the groups) was ultimately responsible for observed differences in behavior. Random assignment controls for selection factors by ensuring that subject characteristics are randomly distributed across groups. Thus it is reasonable to assume that differences between groups result from the treatments they receive rather than from differences between the subjects making up the groups. Still, it is possible that apparent treatment effects stem from subjects' expectancies about the treatments they receive rather than from the active components in the treatments themselves. In other words, knowing you are being given an alcoholic beverage to drink might affect your behavior, quite apart from the alcoholic content of the beverage itself.

Controlling for Subject Expectancies To control for subject expectancies, experimenters rely on procedures that render subjects **blind,** or uninformed about the treatments they are receiving. For example, participants in a study designed to test an investigational medication for depression would be kept uninformed about whether they are receiving the actual drug or a **placebo,** an inert drug that physically resembles the active drug. We use placebos to control for the possibility that positive treatment outcomes result from hopeful expectancies people hold, rather than the chemical properties of the drug or specific features of the treatment (Dar, Stronguin, & Etter, 2005).

experimental group In an experiment, a group that receives the experimental treatment.

control group In an experiment, a group that does not receive the experimental treatment.

random assignment A method of assigning research subjects at random to experimental or control groups to balance these groups on the characteristics of people that comprise them.

selection factor A type of bias in which differences between experimental and control groups result from differences in the types of participants in the group, not from the independent variable.

blind A state of being unaware of whether one has received an experimental treatment.

placebo An inert medication or bogus treatment that is intended to control for expectancy effects.

In a *single-blind placebo-control study*, subjects are randomly assigned to treatment conditions in which they receive either an active drug (experimental condition) or an inert placebo (placebo-control condition), but are kept blind, or uninformed, about which drug they receive. It is also helpful to keep the researchers blind as to which substances the subjects receive, so as to prevent the researchers' own expectations from affecting the results. So in the case of a *double-blind placebo design*, neither the researcher nor the subject is told whether an active drug or a placebo is administered. Double-blind studies are used to control for both subject and experimenter expectancies. But a major limitation of single-blind and double-blind studies is that subjects and experimenters can sometimes "see through" the blind (Mooney, White, & Hatsukami, 2004). Telltale side effects or obvious drug effects can break the blind, making it seem more like a Venetian blind with the slats slightly open. Still, the double-blind placebo control is among the strongest and most popular experimental designs, especially in drug treatment research (Leber, 2000).

Although placebos are routinely used in clinical research, evidence indicates that the effects of placebos are generally weak (Bailar, 2001; Hrobjartsson & Gotzsche, 2001). Placebo effects are generally strongest in pain studies, presumably because pain is a subjective experience that may be influenced more by the power of suggestion than other physiological factors that rely on objective measures, such as blood pressure.

Placebo-control groups are also used in psychotherapy research to control for subject expectancies. Assume you were to study the effects of therapy method A on mood. You could randomly assign research participants to either an experimental group in which they receive the new therapy or to a (no-treatment) waiting-list control group. But in that case, the experimental group might show greater improvement because participation in treatment engendered hopeful expectations, not because of the particular therapy method used. Although a "waiting-list" control group might control for positive effects due simply to the passage of time, it would not account for placebo effects, such as the benefits of therapy resulting from instilling a sense of hope and expectations of success.

To control for placebo effects, we might use an *attention-placebo* control group in which participants are exposed to a believable or credible treatment that contains the nonspecific factors that all therapies share—such as the attention and emotional support of a therapist—but not the specific therapeutic ingredients represented in the active treatment. Attention-placebo treatments commonly substitute general discussions of participants' problems for the specific ingredients of therapy contained in the experimental treatment. Unfortunately, although we may keep attention-placebo subjects blind as to whether they are receiving the experimental treatment, their therapists are generally aware of which treatment is being administered. Therefore, the attention-placebo method may not control for therapists' expectations.

Experimental Validity Experimental studies are judged on whether they are valid, or sound. There are many aspects of validity, including *internal validity, external validity,* and *construct validity*. We will see in Chapter 3 that the term *validity* is also applied in the context of tests and measures to refer to the degree to which these instruments measure what they purport to measure.

Experiments have **internal validity** when the observed changes in the dependent variable(s) can be causally related to the independent or treatment variable. Assume a group of depressed subjects is treated with a new antidepressant medication (the independent variable), and changes in their mood and behavior (the dependent variables) are tracked over time. After several weeks of treatment, the researcher finds most subjects have improved and claims the new drug is an effective treatment for depression. Not so fast! How does the experimenter know that the independent variable and not some other factor was causally responsible for the improvement? Perhaps the subjects improved naturally as time passed, or perhaps they were exposed to other events responsible for their improvement. Experiments lack internal validity to the extent

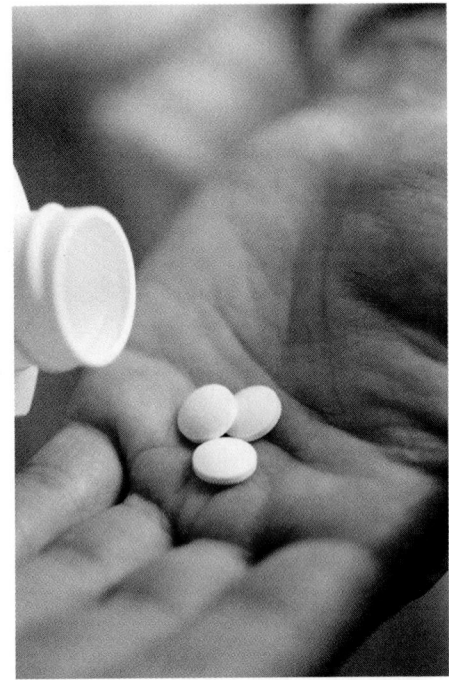

The real thing or a placebo? Placebos are inert pills that physically resemble active drugs. What are the two major types of placebo-control studies? What are they intended to control? What is the major limitation of these designs?

internal validity The degree to which manipulation of the independent variables can be causally related to changes in the dependent variables.

they fail to control for other factors (called *confounds,* or threats to validity) that might pose rival hypotheses for the results.

Experimenters *randomly assign* subjects to treatment and control groups to help control for such rival hypotheses. Random assignment helps ensure that subjects' attributes—intelligence, motivation, age, race, and so on—are randomly distributed across the groups and are not likely to favor one group over the other. Through the random assignment to groups, researchers can be reasonably confident that significant differences between the treatment and control groups reflect the effects of independent (treatment) variables and not confounding selection factors. Studies need to include large enough samples of subjects to be able to randomize sufficient numbers of participants to experimental conditions and to be able to discern significant statistical differences between groups.

External validity refers to the generalizability of results of an experimental study to other subjects, settings, and times. In most cases, researchers are interested in generalizing the results of a specific study (for example, effects of a new antidepressant medication on a sample of people who are depressed) to a larger population (people in general who are depressed). The external validity of a study is strengthened to the degree that the *sample* is representative of the target population. In studying the problems of the urban homeless, it is essential to recruit a representative sample of the homeless population, for example, rather than focusing on a few homeless people who happen to be available. One way of obtaining a representative sample is by means of random sampling. In a *random sample,* every member of the target population has an equal chance of being selected.

Researchers may seek to extend the results of a particular study by means of replication, which refers to the process of repeating the experiment in other settings, with samples drawn from other populations, or at other times. A treatment for hyperactivity may be helpful with economically deprived children in an inner-city classroom but not with children in affluent suburbs or rural areas. The external validity of the treatment may be limited if its effects do not generalize to other samples or settings. That does not mean the treatment is less effective, but rather that its range of effectiveness may be limited to certain populations or situations.

Construct validity is a conceptually higher level of validity. It is the degree to which treatment effects can be accounted for by the theoretical mechanisms or constructs represented in the independent variables. A drug, for example, may have predictable effects but not for the theoretical reasons claimed by the researchers.

Consider a hypothetical experimental study of a new antidepressant medication. The research may have internal validity in the form of solid controls and external validity in the form of generalizability across samples of seriously depressed people. However, it may lack construct validity if the drug does not work for the reasons proposed by the researchers. Perhaps the researchers assumed that the drug would work by raising the levels of certain chemicals in the nervous system, whereas the drug actually works by increasing the sensitivity of receptors for those chemicals. "So what?" we may ask. After all, the drug still works. True enough—in terms of immediate clinical applications. However, a better understanding of why the drug works can advance theoretical knowledge of depression and give rise to the development of yet more effective treatments.

We can never be certain about the construct validity of research. Scientists recognize that their current theories about why their results occurred may eventually be toppled by other theories that better account for the findings.

Epidemiological Studies

Epidemiological studies examine the rates of occurrence of abnormal behavior in various settings or population groups. One type of epidemiological study is the **survey method,** which relies on interviews or questionnaires. Surveys are used to ascertain the rates of occurrence of various disorders in the population as a whole and in various subgroups classified according to such factors as race, ethnicity, gender, or social class. Rates of occurrence of a given disorder are expressed in terms of

external validity The degree to which experimental results can be generalized to other settings and conditions.

construct validity The degree to which treatment effects can be accounted for by the theoretical mechanisms (constructs) represented in the independent variables.

epidemiological studies Research studies that track rates of occurrence of particular disorders among different population groups.

survey method A research method in which large samples of people are questioned by means of a survey instrument.

incidence, the number of new cases occurring during a specific period of time, and **prevalence,** the overall number of cases of a disorder existing in the population during a given period of time. Prevalence rates, then, include both new and continuing cases.

Epidemiological studies may point to potential causal factors in medical illnesses and psychological disorders, even though they lack the power of experiments. By finding that illnesses or disorders "cluster" in certain groups or locations, researchers can identify distinguishing characteristics that place these groups or regions at higher risk. Yet such epidemiological studies cannot control for selection factors—that is, they cannot rule out the possibility that other unrecognized factors might play a causal role in putting a certain group at greater risk. Therefore they must be considered suggestive of possible causal influences that must be tested further in experimental studies.

Samples and Populations In the best of possible worlds, we would conduct surveys in which every member of the population of interest would participate. In that way, we could be sure the survey results accurately represent the population we want to study. In reality, unless the population of interest is rather narrowly defined (say, for example, designating the population of interest as the students living on your dormitory floor), surveying every member of a given population is extremely difficult, if not impossible. Even census takers can't count every head in the general population. Consequently, most surveys are based on a sample, or subset, of the population. Researchers must take steps when constructing a sample to ensure that it *represents* the target population. For example, a researcher who sets out to study smoking rates in a local community by interviewing people drinking coffee in late-night cafés will probably overestimate its true prevalence.

One method of obtaining a representative sample is random sampling. A **random sample** is drawn in such a way that each member of the population of interest has an equal probability of selection. Epidemiologists sometimes construct random samples by surveying at random a given number of households within a target community. By repeating this process in a random sample of U.S. communities, the overall sample can approximate the general U.S. population, based on even a tiny percentage of the overall population.

Random sampling is often confused with random assignment. *Random sampling* refers to the process of randomly choosing individuals within a target population to participate in a survey or research study. By contrast, *random assignment* refers to the process by which members of a research sample are assigned at random to different experimental conditions or treatments.

Kinship Studies

Kinship studies attempt to disentangle the roles of heredity and environment in determining behavior. Heredity plays a critical role in determining a wide range of traits. The structures we inherit make our behavior possible (humans can walk and run) and at the same time place limits on us (humans cannot fly without artificial equipment). Heredity plays a role in determining not only our physical characteristics (hair color, eye color, height, and the like) but also many of our psychological characteristics. The science of heredity is called *genetics.*

Genes are the basic building blocks of heredity. They regulate the development of traits. *Chromosomes,* rod-shaped structures that house our genes, are found in the nuclei of the body's cells. A normal human cell contains 46 chromosomes, organized into 23 pairs. Chromosomes consist of large complex molecules of deoxyribonucleic acid (DNA). Genes occupy various segments along the length of chromosomes. Scientists believe there are about 20,000 to 25,000 genes in the nucleus of a human body cell (Lupski, 2007; Volkow, 2006).

The set of traits specified by our genetic code is referred to as our **genotype.** Our appearance and behavior are not determined by our genotype alone. We are also influenced by environmental factors such as nutrition, learning, exercise, accidents and illnesses, and culture. The constellation of observable or expressed traits is called a **phenotype.** Our phenotype represents the interaction of genetic and environmental

incidence The number of new cases of a disorder that occurs within a specific period of time.

prevalence The overall number of cases of a disorder in a population within a specific period of time.

random sample A sample that is drawn in such a way that every member of a population has an equal chance of being included.

T R U T H (or) F I C T I O N

Recent evidence shows there are literally millions of genes in the nucleus of every cell in the body.

☑ **FALSE.** Although no one yet knows the precise number, scientists believe there are about 20,000 to 25,000 genes in the nucleus of each body cell, but certainly not millions.

genotype The set of traits specified by an individual's genetic code.

phenotype An individual's actual or expressed traits.

influences. People who possess genotypes for particular psychological disorders are said to have a *genetic predisposition* that makes them more likely to develop the disorder in response to stress or other factors, such as physical or psychological trauma.

The more closely people are related, the more genes they have in common. Children receive half their genes from each parent. Thus there is a 50% overlap in genetic heritage between each parent and his or her offspring. Siblings (brothers and sisters) similarly share half their genes in common.

To determine whether abnormal behavior runs in a family, as we would expect if genetics plays a role, researchers locate a person with the disorder and then study how the disorder is distributed among the person's family members. The case first diagnosed is referred to as the index case, or **proband.** If the distribution of the disorder among family members of the proband approximates their degree of kinship, there may be a genetic involvement in the disorder. However, the closer their kinship, the more likely people also are to share environmental backgrounds. For this reason, twin and adoptee studies are of particular value.

Twin Studies   Sometimes a fertilized egg cell (or *zygote*) divides into two cells that separate, so each develops into a separate person. In such cases, there is a 100% overlap in genetic makeup, and the offspring are known as identical twins, or monozygotic (MZ) twins. Sometimes a woman releases two egg cells, or ova, in the same month, and they are both fertilized. In such cases, the *zygotes* develop into fraternal twins, or dizygotic (DZ) twins. DZ twins overlap 50% in their genetic heritage, just as other siblings do.

Identical, or MZ, twins are important in the study of the relative influences of heredity and environment because differences between MZ twins are the result of environmental rather than genetic influences. In twin studies, researchers identify individuals with a specific disorder who are members of MZ or DZ twin pairs and then study the other twins in the pairs. A role for genetic factors is suggested when MZ twins (who have 100% genetic overlap) are more likely than DZ twins (who have 50% genetic overlap) to share a disorder in common. The term *concordance rate* refers to the percentage of cases in which both twins have the same trait or disorder. As we shall see, investigators find higher concordance rates for MZ twins than DZ twins for some forms of abnormal behavior, such as schizophrenia and major depression.

proband   The case first diagnosed of a given disorder.

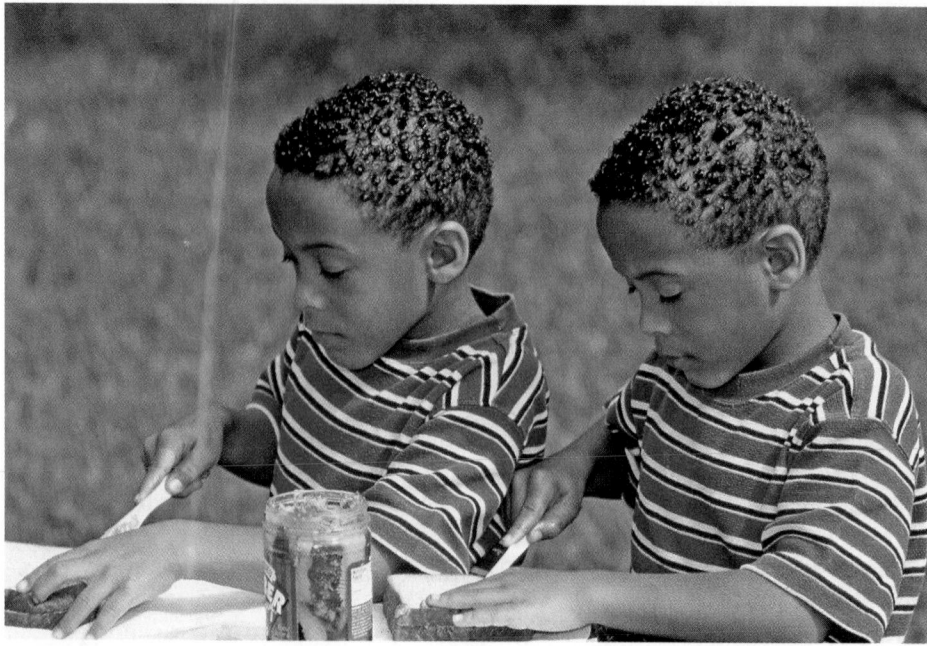

Twin studies. Identical twins have 100% of their genes in common, as compared to 50% overlap among fraternal twins or any two other siblings. Establishing that identical twins are more likely to share a given disorder than are fraternal twins provides strong evidence for a genetic contribution to the disorder.

Even among MZ twins, though, environmental influences cannot be ruled out. Parents and teachers, for example, often encourage MZ twins to behave in similar ways. Put in another way: If one twin does X, everyone expects the other to do X also. Expectations have a way of influencing behavior and making for self-fulfilling prophecies. We should also note that twins might not be typical of the general population, so we need to be cautious when generalizing the results of twin studies to the larger population.

Adoptee Studies **Adoptee studies** provide powerful arguments for or against a role for genetic factors in the appearance of psychological traits and disorders. Assume that children are reared by adoptive parents from a very early age—perhaps from birth. The children share environmental backgrounds with their adoptive parents but not their genetic heritages. Then assume we compare the traits and behavior patterns of these children to those of their biological parents and their adoptive parents. If the children show a greater similarity to their biological parents than their adoptive parents on certain traits or disorders, we have strong evidence for genetic factors in these traits and disorders.

The study of monozygotic twins reared apart can provide even more dramatic testimony to the relative roles of genetics and environment in shaping abnormal behavior. However, this situation is so uncommon that few examples exist in the literature. Although adoptee studies may represent the strongest source of evidence for genetic factors in explaining abnormal behavior patterns, we should recognize that adoptees, like twins, may not be typical of the general population. In later chapters we explore the role that adoptee and other kinship studies play in ferreting out genetic and environmental influences in many psychological disorders.

Case Studies

Case studies have been important influences in the development of theories and treatment of abnormal behavior. Freud developed his theoretical model primarily on the basis of case studies, such as that of Anna O. Therapists representing other theoretical viewpoints have also reported cases studies.

Types of Case Studies **Case studies** are intensive studies of individuals. Some case studies are based on historical material, involving subjects who have been dead for hundreds of years. Freud, for example, conducted a case study of the Renaissance artist and inventor Leonardo da Vinci. More commonly, case studies reflect an in-depth analysis of an individual's course of treatment. They typically include detailed histories of the subject's background and response to treatment. The therapist attempts to glean information from a particular client's experience in therapy that may be of help to other therapists treating similar clients.

Despite the richness of material that case studies can provide, they are much less rigorous as research designs than experiments. Distortions or gaps in memory are bound to occur when people discuss historical events, especially those of their childhoods. Some people may intentionally color events to make a favorable impression on the interviewer; others aim to shock the interviewer with exaggerated or fabricated recollections. Interviewers themselves may unintentionally guide subjects into reporting histories that mirror their theoretical preconceptions.

Single-Case Experimental Designs The lack of control available in the traditional case-study method led researchers to develop more sophisticated methods, called **single-case experimental designs** (sometimes called *single-participant research designs*), in which subjects serve as the own controls (Morgan & Morgan, 2001). One of the most common forms of the single-case experimental design is the A-B-A-B, or **reversal design** (see Figure 1.2). This method involves repeated measurement of behavior across four successive phases:

1. A baseline phase (A). This phase occurs prior to treatment and allows the experimenter to establish a baseline rate for the behavior before treatment begins.
2. A treatment phase (B). Now the target behaviors are measured as the client undergoes treatment.

adoptee studies Studies that compare the traits and behavior patterns of adopted children to those of their biological parents and their adoptive parents.

case study A carefully drawn biography based on clinical interviews, observations, and psychological tests.

TRUTH or FICTION

Case studies have been conducted on dead people.

☑ **TRUE.** Case studies have been conducted on people who have been dead for hundreds of years. An example is Freud's study of Leonardo da Vinci. Such studies rely on historical records rather than interviews.

single-case experimental design A type of case study in which the subject is used as his or her own control.

reversal design An experimental design that consists of repeated measurement of a subject's behavior through a sequence of alternating baseline and treatment phases.

FIGURE 1.2 Diagram of an A-B-A-B reversal design.

3. A second baseline phase (A, again). Treatment is now temporarily withdrawn or suspended. This is the reversal in the reversal design, and it is expected that the positive effects of treatment should now be reversed because the treatment has been withdrawn.
4. A second treatment phase (B, again). Treatment is reinstated, and the target behaviors are assessed yet again.

The investigator looks for evidence that change in the observed behavior occurs coincident with treatment. If the behavior improves whenever treatment is introduced (during the first and second treatment phases) but returns (or is reversed) to baseline levels during the reversal phase, the experimenter can be reasonably confident the treatment had the intended effect.

A reversal design is illustrated by a case in which Azrin and Peterson (1989) used a controlled blinking treatment to eliminate a severe eye tic—a form of squinting the eyes shut tightly for a fraction of a second—in a 9-year-old girl. The tic occurred about 20 times a minute when the girl was at home. In the clinic, the rate of eye tics or squinting was measured for 5 minutes during a baseline period (A). Then the girl was prompted to blink her eyes softly every 5 seconds (B). The experimenters reasoned that voluntary "soft" blinking would activate motor (muscle) responses incompatible with those producing the tic, thereby suppressing the tic. As you can see in Figure 1.3, the tic

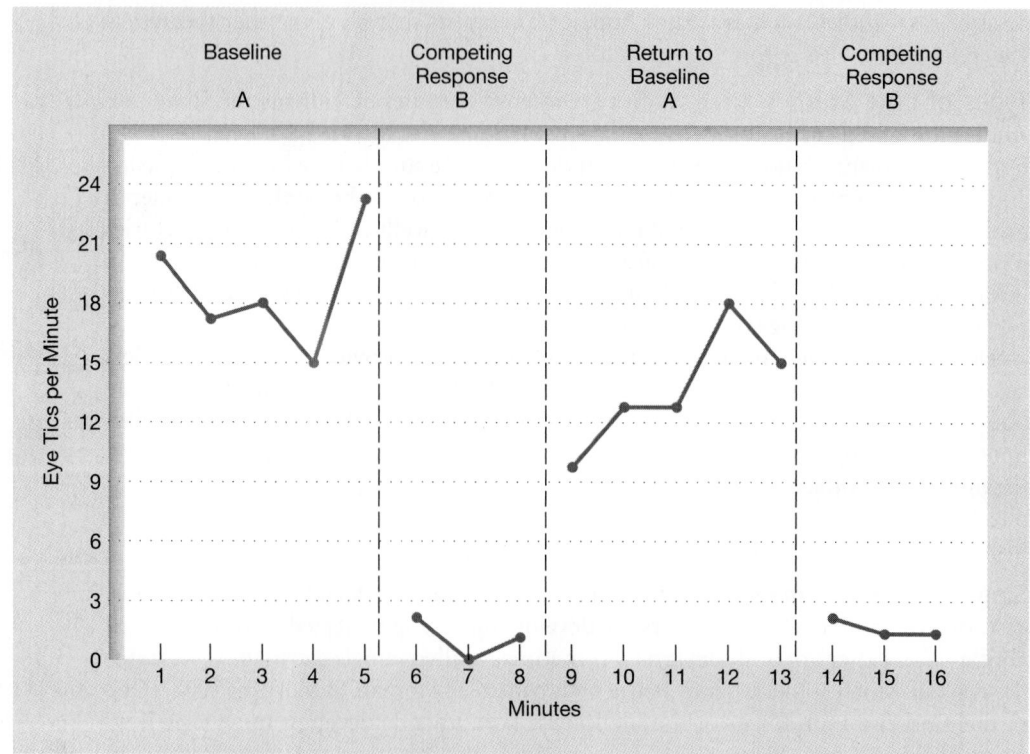

FIGURE 1.3 Use of an A-B-A-B reversal design in the Azrin and Peterson study.
Notice how the target response, eye tics per minute, decreased when the competing response was introduced in the first "B" phase. The rate then increased to near baseline levels when the competing response was withdrawn during the second "A" phase. It decreased again when the competing response was reinstated in the second "B" phase.

was virtually eliminated in but a few minutes of practicing the incompatible, or competing, response ("soft" blinking) but returned to near baseline levels during the reversal phase (A), when the competing response was withdrawn. The positive effects were quickly reinstated during the second treatment period (B). The child was also taught to practice the blinking response at home during scheduled 3-minute practice periods and whenever the tic occurred or she felt an urge to squint. The tic was eliminated during the first 6 weeks of the treatment program and remained absent at a follow-up evaluation 2 years later.

A CLOSER LOOK

Thinking Critically About Abnormal Psychology

We are exposed to a flood of information about mental health streaming through the popular media—television, radio, and print media, including books, magazines, and newspapers, and increasingly, the Internet. We may hear a news report touting a new drug as a "breakthrough" in the treatment of anxiety, depression, or obesity, only to later learn that the so-called breakthrough doesn't live up to expectations or carries serious side effects. Some reports in the media are accurate and reliable, whereas others are misleading, biased, or contain half-truths, exaggerated claims, or unsupported conclusions.

Some therapies offered to the general public are nothing but pure shams. In the nearby *Controversies in Abnormal Psychology* feature, two leading clinical psychologists, John Norcross and Gerald Koocher, take a critical look at the problem of *psychoquackery*.

To sort through the welter of confusion, we need to ready ourselves with the skills of critical thinking, to adopt a questioning attitude toward the information we hear and read. Critical thinkers weigh evidence to see if claims stand up to scrutiny. Becoming a critical thinker means never taking claims at face value. It means looking at both sides of the argument. Most of us take certain "truths" for granted. Critical thinkers, however, evaluate assertions and claims for themselves.

We encourage you to apply critical-thinking skills as you study this book. Adopt a skeptical attitude toward information you receive. Carefully examine the definitions of terms. Evaluate the logical bases of arguments. Evaluate claims in the light of available evidence. Here are some key features of critical thinking:

1. *Maintain a skeptical attitude.* Don't take anything at face value, not even claims made by respected scientists or textbook authors. Consider the evidence yourself. Seek additional information. Investigate the credibility of your sources.
2. *Consider the definitions of terms.* Statements may be true or false depending on how the terms they use are defined. Consider the statement, "Stress is bad for you." If we define *stress* in terms of hassles and work or family pressures that stretch to the max our ability to cope, then there is substance to the statement. However, if we define stress (see Chapter 5) as conditions that require us to adjust, which may include such positive life events as a new marriage or the birth of a child, then certain types of stress can be positive, even if they are stressful. Perhaps, as we'll see, we all need some amount of stress to be energized and alert.
3. *Weigh the assumptions or premises on which arguments are based.* Consider a case in which we are comparing differences in the rates of psychological disorders across racial or ethnic groups in our society. Assuming we find differences, should we conclude that ethnicity or racial identity accounts for these differences? This conclusion might be valid if

we can assume that all other factors that distinguish one racial or ethnic group from another are held constant. However, ethnic or racial minorities in the United States and Canada are disproportionately represented among the poor, and the poor are more apt to develop more severe psychological disorders. Thus, differences we find among racial or ethnic groups may be a function of poverty, not race or ethnicity. These differences may also be due to stereotyping of minorities by clinicians in making diagnostic judgments, rather than to true differences in underlying rates of the disorder.

4. *Bear in mind that correlation is not causation.* Consider the relationship between depression and stress. Evidence shows a positive correlation between these variables, which means depressed people tend to encounter high levels of stress (e.g., Drieling, Calker, & Hecht, 2006; Kendler et al., 2004; Monroe et al., 2001). But does stress cause depression? Perhaps it does. Or perhaps depression leads to greater stress. After all, depressive symptoms are stressful in themselves and may lead to additional stress as the person finds it increasingly difficult to meet life responsibilities, such as keeping up with work at school or on the job. Perhaps the two variables are not causally linked at all but are linked through a third variable, such as an underlying genetic factor. Is it possible that people inherit clusters of genes that make them more prone to both depression and stress?
5. *Consider the kinds of evidence on which conclusions are based.* Some conclusions, even seemingly "scientific" conclusions, are based on anecdotes and personal endorsements, not sound research. There is much controversy today about so-called recovered memories that are said to suddenly resurface in adulthood, usually during psychotherapy or hypnosis, and usually involving incidents of sexual abuse committed during childhood by the person's parents or family members. Are recovered memories accurate? (See Chapter 7.)
6. *Do not oversimplify.* Consider the statement "Alcoholism is inherited." In Chapter 9, we review evidence suggesting that genetic factors may create a predisposition to alcoholism, at least in males. But the origins of alcoholism, as well as of schizophrenia, depression, and physical health problems such as cancer and heart disease, are complex and reflect the interplay of biological and environmental factors. For instance, people may inherit a predisposition to develop a particular disorder but may be able to avoid developing it if they live in a healthy environment or learn to manage stress effectively.
7. *Do not overgeneralize.* In Chapter 7, we consider evidence showing that a history of severe abuse in childhood figures prominently in the great majority of cases of people who later develop multiple personalities. Does this mean that most abused children go on to develop multiple personalities? Actually, very few do.

No matter how well controlled the design, or how impressive the results, single-case designs suffer from weak external validity because they cannot show whether a treatment effective for one person is effective for others. Replication with other individuals can help strengthen external validity. But results from controlled experiments on groups of individuals are needed to provide more convincing evidence of treatment effectiveness and generalizability.

Scientists use different methods to study phenomena of interest to them. But all scientists share a skeptical, hard-nosed way of thinking called **critical thinking.** When thinking critically, we adopt a willingness to challenge the conventional wisdom that many of us take for granted. We find *reasons* to support beliefs rather than relying on feelings or gut impressions. We maintain an open mind and seek evidence to support or refute beliefs or claims. In the nearby "A Closer Look" section, we examine the features of critical thinking and how they can be applied to our study of abnormal psychology.

critical thinking Adoption of a questioning attitude and careful scrutiny of claims and arguments in the light of evidence.

CONTROVERSIES IN ABNORMAL PSYCHOLOGY

Psychoquackery: Discredited Psychological Treatments in Mental Health

—JOHN C. NORCROSS AND GERALD P. KOOCHER

Psychologists have an ethical commitment to offer treatments and relationships that work (Koocher & Keith-Spiegel, 2007). The *evidence-based practice* (EBP) movement in mental health attempts to identify, implement, and disseminate treatments that have been proven effective according to clinical and research evidence (APA Task Force, 2006). Although in principle all psychologists dedicate themselves to effective practice, the EBP movement has provoked enormous controversy on the decision rules to determine what works and what qualifies as evidence (Norcross, Beutler, & Levant, 2005). (See Chapter 4 for a discussion of evidence-based treatment.)

We believe that it might prove as useful and probably easier to establish what does *not* work—discredited psychological treatments. Or, as we prefer to call them, *psychoquackery.*

Pioneering efforts to identify pseudoscientific treatments (e.g., Della Sala, 1999; Eisner, 2000; Lilienfeld, Lynn, & Lohr, 2003) suffer from a prominent limitation. None of them systematically relied on expert consensus to determine which treatments to include. Instead, the authors selected ineffective treatments on the basis of their own opinions or assumed a professional consensus already existed. To remedy this problem, we conducted a poll of 101 mental health professionals to secure a professional consensus on what does not work (Norcross, Koocher, & Garofalo, 2006).

For the purpose of our expert poll, we defined *discredited treatments* as those unable to consistently produce success beyond that obtained by the passage of time alone, positive expectancies of change, or credible placebo. (The term *discredited* includes ineffective, detrimental, and disproven interventions.)

The experts showed considerable agreement in identifying a number of treatments they considered "certainly discredited." These included use of pyramid structures, the orgone accumulator, crystal healing, past lives therapy, future lives therapy, treatments for PTSD caused by alien abduction, rebirthing therapies, color therapy, primal scream therapy, chiropractic manipulation, thought field therapy, prefrontal lobotomy, and aroma therapy. A number of other treatments were designated as "probably discredited," including age-regression methods, sexual reorientation/reparative therapy for homosexuality, treatments for mental disorders resulting from Satanic ritual abuse, healing touch, and reparenting therapies.

Consider the discredited practice of using a device called the *orgone energy accumulator,* in which we sit in the accompanying photograph. Wilhelm Reich (1897–1957), an Austrian psychoanalyst who trained with Sigmund Freud, claimed to have discovered a physical form of energy he called *orgone,* which he believed is naturally present in all living things. Reich argued that orgone is the bio-energy basis for Freud's theory of neurosis. He claimed that traumatic experiences blocked the natural flow of this life-energy in the body, leading to physical and mental disease. In 1940, Reich constructed a device to accumulate orgone energy: a six-sided box constructed of alternating layers of organic materials (to attract the energy) and metallic materials (to radiate the energy toward the center of the box). Patients sit inside the accumulator and allegedly absorb orgone energy through the skin and lungs. Reich claimed that the accumulator had a healthy effect on blood and body tissue by improving the flow of life-energy and by releasing energy blocks. But the Food and Drug Administration (FDA), the U.S. government watchdog agency, thought otherwise. In 1954, the FDA sought an injunction against Reich, charging violation of the Food, Drug, and Cosmetic Act by selling misbranded and adulterated devices in interstate commerce and making false and misleading claims. The FDA called accumulators a sham and orgone energy nonexistent. A judge issued an injunction ordering all accumulators destroyed and prohibiting all labeling referring to orgone energy. The court ordered some of Reich's writings burned as well.

Experts widely consider orgone therapy, and the other psychological treatments previously mentioned, as discredited. We should interpret these results carefully, because consensus does not equal truth; even experts can be and have been wrong. A treatment considered discredited for one purpose might prove credible for another. We should take care not to threaten innovation and creativity in practice. And we must also avoid hubris by bearing in mind that contemporary therapies we consider effective today may be discredited at some point in the future.

At the same time, the consensus emerging from the poll leaves us feeling encouraged. Psychological science tends to behave in a self-correcting manner in that its foundation lies in empirical evidence. Mature professions

(continued)

should have the ability to publicly shun discredited practices. As a field, we are making progress in differentiating science from pseudoscience in the practice of psychology.

The listing of discredited practices offers a cogent first step in consensually identifying the psychoquackery of modern mental health. The President's New Freedom Commission on Mental Health (2003; www. mentalhealthcommission. gov) called attention to both the *underuse* of proven treatments and the *overuse* of treatments for which little evidence exists. We can simultaneously use (inclusively defined) evidence-based practices to promote what *does* work and avoid (consensually identified) discredited procedures to eradicate what does *not* work.

Critical Thinking

- How would you decide if a particular treatment method was effective? Would you base your decision on clinical experience, research evidence, and/or the patient's reports?
- If you were to publish a list of discredited or quack treatments, what would be the advantages and disadvantages of securing a group consensus on the list?
- The FDA regulates medications but does not regulate psychological treatments. Should they be legally regulated? Why or why not?

John C. Norcross, Ph.D., ABPP, is Professor of Psychology and Distinguished University Fellow at the University of Scranton, editor of *Journal of Clinical Psychology: In Session*, and a clinical psychologist in part-time independent practice. Gerald P. Koocher, Ph.D., ABPP, is Professor and Dean of the School for Health Studies at Simmons College, editor of the journal *Ethics & Behavior*, and 2006 President of the American Psychological Association. Together, they have published many articles and coedited the *Psychologists' Desk Reference*.

Warning! Warning!

"Warning - misuse of the Orgone Accumulator may lead to symptoms of orgone overdose. Leave the vicinity of the accumulator and call the 'Doctor' immediately!"
- Wilhelm Reich

Drs. John Norcross (top) and Gerald Koocher (bottom) are pictured here in an orgone accumulator. The identity of the parrot remains unknown.

SUMMING UP

How Do We Define Abnormal Behavior?

What criteria do mental health professionals use to determine that behavior is abnormal? Psychologists consider behavior abnormal when it meets some combination of the following criteria: when behavior is (a) unusual or statistically infrequent, (b) socially unacceptable or in violation of social norms, (c) fraught with misperceptions or misinterpretations of reality, (d) associated with states of severe personal distress, (e) maladaptive or self-defeating, or (f) dangerous. Psychological disorders are patterns of abnormal behavior associated with disturbances in states of emotional distress or impaired functioning.

How do views about abnormal behavior vary across cultures? Behaviors deemed normal in one culture may be considered abnormal in another. Concepts of health and illness are different in different cultures. Abnormal behavior patterns also take different forms in different cultures, and societal views or models explaining abnormal behavior also vary across cultures.

Historical Perspectives on Abnormal Behavior

How have views about abnormal behavior changed over time? Ancient societies attributed abnormal behavior to divine or supernatural forces. In medieval times, abnormal behavior was a sign of possession by the devil, and exorcism was intended to rid the possessed of the evil spirits that afflicted them. The 19th-century German physician Wilhelm Griesinger argued that abnormal behavior was caused by diseases of the brain. He and another German physician who followed him, Emil Kraepelin, were influential in the development of the modern medical model, which likens abnormal behavior patterns to physical illnesses.

How has the treatment of people with mental disorders changed over time? Asylums, or madhouses, arose throughout Europe in the late 15th and early 16th centuries. Conditions in these asylums were dreadful. With the rise of moral therapy in the 19th century, conditions in mental hospitals improved. Proponents of moral therapy believed that mental patients could be restored to functioning if they were treated with dignity and understanding. The decline of moral therapy in the latter part of the 19th century led to the belief that the "insane" could not be treated successfully. During this period of apathy, mental hospitals deteriorated, offering little more than custodial care. Not until the middle of the 20th century did public concern about the plight of mental patients lead to the development of community mental health centers as alternatives to long-term hospitalization.

What are the major contemporary models of abnormal behavior? The medical model conceptualizes abnormal behavior patterns, like physical diseases, in terms of clusters of symptoms, called syndromes, which have distinctive causes presumed to be biological in nature. Psychological models focus on the psychological roots of abnormal behavior and derive from psychoanalytic, behavioral, humanistic, and cognitive perspectives. The sociocultural model emphasizes a broader perspective that takes into account the social contexts in which abnormal behavior occurs. Today, many theorists subscribe to a biopsychosocial model that posits that multiple causes—representing biological, psychological, and sociocultural domains—interact in the development of abnormal behavior patterns.

Research Methods in Abnormal Psychology

What are the basic objectives of the scientific method, and what steps are involved in applying it? The scientific approach focuses on four general objectives: description, explanation, prediction, and control. There are four steps to the scientific method: formulating a research question, framing the research question in the form of a hypothesis, testing the hypothesis, and drawing conclusions about the correctness of

the hypothesis. Psychologists follow the ethical principles of the profession that govern research.

What are the methods psychologists use to study abnormal behavior? In naturalistic observation, the investigator carefully observes behavior under naturally occurring conditions. The correlational method of research explores relationships between variables, which may help predict future behavior and suggest possible underlying causes of behavior. However, correlational research cannot directly demonstrate cause-and-effect relationships. Longitudinal research is a correlational method in which a sample of subjects is repeatedly studied at periodic intervals over long periods of time, sometimes spanning decades.

In the experimental method, the investigator manipulates or controls the independent variable under controlled conditions to reveal cause-and-effect relationships. Experiments use random assignment as the basis for determining which subjects (called experimental subjects) receive an experimental treatment and which others (called control subjects) do not. Experiments are evaluated in terms of internal, external, and construct validity.

Epidemiological studies examine the rates of occurrence of abnormal behavior in various population groups or settings. Kinship studies, such as twin studies and adoptee studies, attempt to differentiate the contributions of environment and heredity.

Case studies provide rich material, but are limited by difficulties obtaining accurate and unbiased client histories, by possible therapist biases, and by the lack of control groups. Single-case experimental designs are intended to help researchers overcome some of the limitations of the case-study method.

KEY TERMS

psychological disorder *(p. 4)*
abnormal psychology *(p. 4)*
medical model *(p. 5)*
trephination *(p. 10)*
humors *(p. 11)*
dementia praecox *(p. 15)*
general paresis *(p. 16)*
psychodynamic model *(p. 17)*
biopsychosocial model *(p. 19)*
scientific method *(p. 19)*
theory *(p. 20)*
hypothesis *(p. 21)*
informed consent *(p. 21)*
confidentiality *(p. 22)*
naturalistic observation *(p. 22)*

correlational method *(p. 22)*
correlation coefficient *(p. 22)*
longitudinal study *(p. 23)*
experimental method *(p. 23)*
independent variables *(p. 23)*
dependent variables *(p. 23)*
experimental group *(p. 24)*
control group *(p. 24)*
random assignment *(p. 24)*
selection factor *(p. 24)*
blind *(p. 24)*
placebo *(p. 24)*
internal validity *(p. 25)*
external validity *(p. 26)*
construct validity *(p. 26)*

epidemiological studies *(p. 26)*
survey method *(p. 26)*
incidence *(p. 27)*
prevalence *(p. 27)*
random sample *(p. 27)*
genotype *(p. 27)*
phenotype *(p. 27)*
proband *(p. 28)*
adoptee studies *(p. 29)*
case study *(p. 29)*
single-case experimental designs *(p. 29)*
reversal design *(p. 29)*
critical thinking *(p. 32)*

MEDIA TOOLS

A variety of digital and online learning tools are avaiable to enrich your learning experience and help you succeed in the course. These resources include:

- **MYPSYCHLAB,** an online learning system for your course in abnormal psychology that allows you to test your mastery of concepts in the book by using chapter-by-chapter diagnostic tests. Results from the diagnostic tests help you build a customized study plan. To access **MyPsycLab,** visit www.prenhall.com/mypsychlab and follow the instructions on the site.

- **"SPEAKING OUT" PATIENT INTERVIEWS,** a set of video case examples of actual patients you can access on the companion CD-ROM included with the text. Icons in the margins of the chapter highlight the video case examples included on the CD-ROM.

- **COMPANION WEB SITE,** an online study center that offers computer-scored quizzes you can use to test your knowledge, along with other study tools and links to related sites to enhance your learning of abnormal psychology. To access the companion web site, visit www.prenhall.com/nevid and use the various tabs and links on the site to access these learning resources.

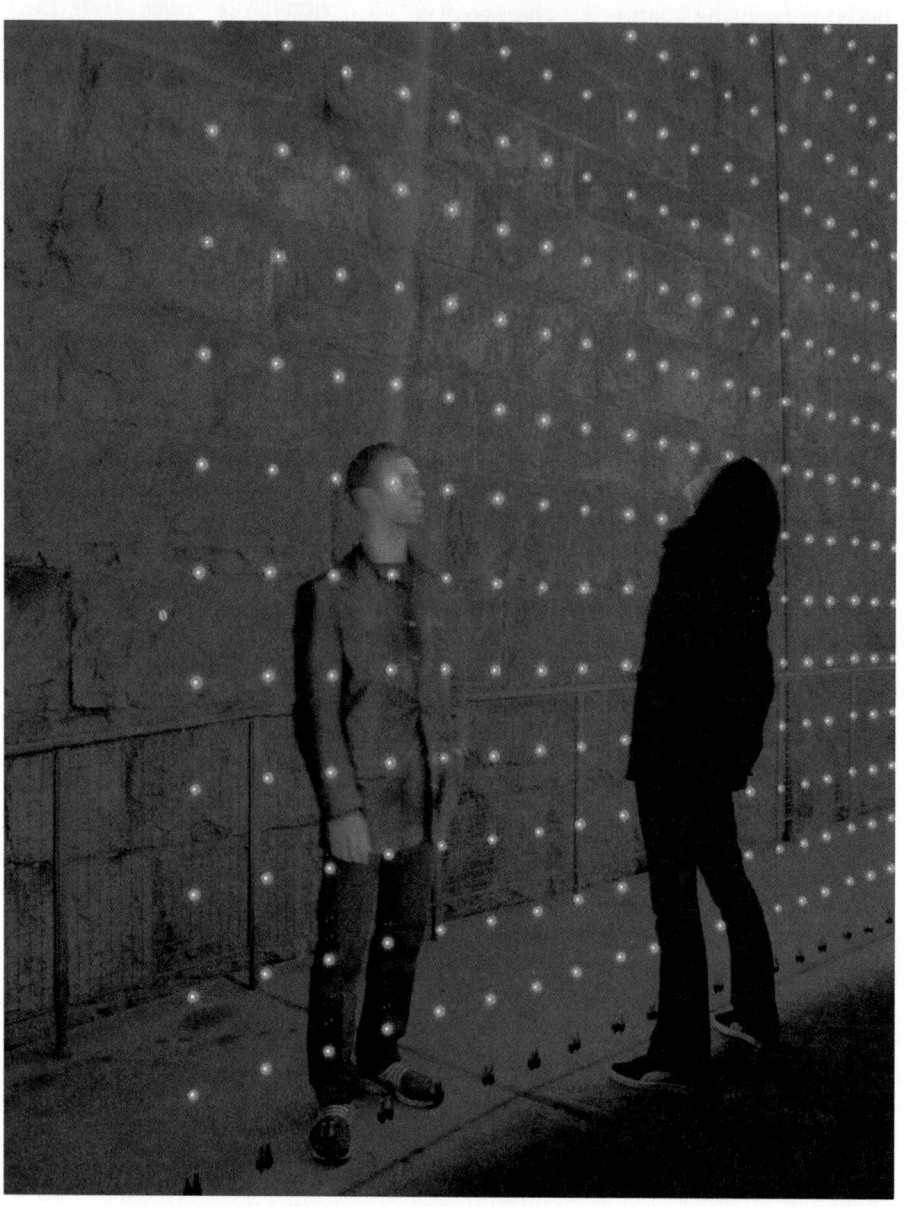

CHAPTER 2

Contemporary Perspectives on Abnormal Behavior

CHAPTER OUTLINE

THE BIOLOGICAL PERSPECTIVE 38–44

The Nervous System
Evaluating Biological Perspectives
  on Abnormal Behavior

THE PSYCHOLOGICAL PERSPECTIVE 45–60

Psychodynamic Models
Learning Models

Humanistic Models
Cognitive Models

**THE SOCIOCULTURAL PERSPECTIVE
60–63**

Ethnicity and Mental Health
Evaluating the Sociocultural Perspective

**THE BIOPSYCHOSOCIAL PERSPECTIVE
63–66**

The Diathesis–Stress Model
Evaluating the Biopsychosocial Perspective
The Case of Jessica—A Final Word

SUMMING UP 66–67

"I"

Jessica's "Little Secret"

I don't want Ken (her fiancé) to find out. I don't want to bring this into the marriage. I probably should have told him, but I just couldn't do it. Every time I wanted to I just froze up. I guess I figured I'd get over this before the wedding. I have to stop bingeing and throwing up. I just can't stop myself. You know, I want to stop, but I get to thinking about the food I've eaten and it sickens me. I picture myself getting all fat and bloated and I just have to rush to the bathroom and throw it up. I would go on binges, and then throw it all up. It made me feel like I was in control, but really I wasn't.

    I have this little ritual when I throw up. I go to the bathroom and run the water in the sink. Nobody ever hears me puking. It's my little secret. I make sure to clean up really well and spray some Lysol before leaving the bathroom. No one suspects I have a problem. Well, that's not quite true. The only one who suspects is my dentist. He said my teeth were beginning to decay from stomach acid. I'm only 20 and I've got rotting teeth. Isn't that awful?

    . . . Now I've started throwing up even when I don't binge. Sometimes just eating dinner makes me want to puke. I've just got to get the food out of my body—fast, you know. Right after dinner, I make some excuse about needing to go to the bathroom. It's not every time but at least several times a week. After lunch sometimes, too. I know I need help. It's taken me a long time to come here, but you know I'm getting married in three months and I've got to stop.

                    —Jessica, a 20-year-old communications major

Source: From the Author's Files

TRUTH or FICTION

T☐ F☐ Recent research shows that most psychological disorders are caused by defective genes. (p. 45)

T☐ F☐ Punishment does not eliminate undesirable behavior. (p. 55)

T☐ F☐ Children may acquire a distorted self-concept that mirrors what others expect them to be, but that does not reflect who they truly are. (p. 57)

T☐ F☐ According to a leading cognitive theorist, emotional distress is caused by beliefs people hold about negative life experiences, not by the experiences themselves. (p. 59)

T☐ F☐ Black Americans have higher rates of psychological disorders than White Europeans Americans, even when we account for income differences between these groups. (p. 62)

JESSICA EXCUSES HERSELF FROM THE DINNER TABLE, GOES TO THE BATHROOM, STICKS A FINGER down her throat to gag, and throws up her dinner. Sometimes she binges first and then forces herself to throw up. You'll recall that in Chapter 1 we described the criteria that mental health professionals generally use to classify behavior patterns as abnormal. Jessica's behavior clearly meets several of these criteria. Bingeing and throwing up is a source of personal distress and is maladaptive in the sense that it can lead to serious health consequences, such as decaying teeth (see Chapter 10), and social consequences (which is why she kept it a secret and feared it would damage her forthcoming marriage). It is also statistically infrequent, although perhaps not as infrequent as you might think. Jessica was diagnosed with *bulimia,* a type of eating disorder that we discuss in Chapter 10.

How can we understand such unusual and maladaptive behavior? In this chapter we examine contemporary approaches to understanding abnormal behavior from the vantage points offered by the biological, psychological, and sociocultural perspectives. Each perspective provides a window for examining abnormal behavior, but none captures a complete view of the subject. Many scholars today believe that abnormal behavior patterns are complex phenomena that are best understood by taking into account the contributions of multiple factors representing these different perspectives, rather than from any one causal factor.

Since earliest times, humans have sought explanations for strange or deviant behavior. As we saw in Chapter 1, through the Middle Ages, most people believed that abnormal behavior was caused by demons and other supernatural forces. But even in ancient times, some scholars, such as Hippocrates and Galen, looked for natural explanations of abnormal behavior. Today, of course, superstition and demonology have given way to theoretical models from the natural and social sciences. These approaches pave the way not only for a scientifically based understanding of abnormal behavior but also for ways of treating people with psychological disorders.

In this chapter we examine the biological, psychological, and sociocultural perspectives on abnormal behavior. Each perspective provides a window for examining abnormal behavior, but none captures a complete view of the subject. Many scholars today believe that abnormal behavior patterns are complex phenomena that are best understood by taking into account these multiple perspectives. As we shall see in Chapter 4, the major biological and psychological perspectives on abnormal behavior give rise to different ways of treating these problems.

THE BIOLOGICAL PERSPECTIVE

The *biological perspective,* inspired by scientists and physicians since the time of Hippocrates, focuses on the biological underpinnings of abnormal behavior and the use of biologically based approaches, such as drug therapy, to treat psychological disorders. The biological perspective gave rise to the development of the *medical model,* which remains today a powerful force in contemporary understandings of abnormal behavior. People who adopt the medical model subscribe to the belief that abnormal behaviors represent symptoms of underlying disorders or diseases, called *mental illnesses,* that have biological root causes. The medical model is not synonymous with the biological perspective, however. We can speak of biological perspectives without adopting the tenets of the medical model. For example, a behavior pattern such as shyness may have a strong genetic (biological) component but not be considered a "symptom" of any underlying "disorder" or illness.

Our understanding of the biological underpinnings of abnormal behavior has grown in recent years. In Chapter 1 we focused on the methods of studying the role of heredity or genetics. Genetics plays a role in many forms of abnormal behavior, as we shall see throughout the text.

We also know that other biological factors, especially the functioning of the nervous system, are involved in the development of abnormal behavior. To better understand the role of the nervous system in abnormal behavior patterns, we first need to learn how the nervous system is organized and how nerve cells communicate with each other. In Chapter 5 we examine another body system, the *endocrine system,* and the important roles that it plays in the body's response to stress.

The Nervous System

Perhaps if you did not have a nervous system, you would never feel nervous—but neither would you see, hear, or move. However, even calm people have nervous systems. The nervous system is made up of **neurons,** nerve cells that transmit signals or "messages" throughout the body. These messages allow us to sense an itch from a bug bite, coordinate our vision and muscles to ice skate, write a research paper, solve a math problem, and in the case of hallucinations, hear or see things that are not really there.

Every neuron has a cell body that contains the nucleus of the cell and metabolizes oxygen to carry out the work of the cell (see Figure 2.1). Short fibers called **dendrites** project from the cell body to receive messages from adjoining neurons. Each neuron has an **axon** that projects trunklike from the cell body. Axons can extend as long as several feet, if they are conveying messages between the toes and the spinal cord. Axons terminate in small branching structures that are aptly called **terminals.** Neurons convey messages in one direction, from the dendrites or cell body along the axon to the axon terminals. The messages are then conveyed from the terminals to other neurons, muscles, or glands.

Neurons transmit messages to other neurons by means of chemical substances called **neurotransmitters.** Neurotransmitters induce chemical changes in receiving neurons. These changes cause axons to conduct the messages in electrical form.

The junction or small gap between a transmitting neuron and a receiving neuron is termed a **synapse.** The message does not jump across the synapse like a spark. Instead, axon terminals release neurotransmitters into the cleft like myriad ships casting off into the seas (Figure 2.2).

neurons Nerve cells.

dendrites The rootlike structures at the ends of neurons that receive nerve impulses from other neurons.

axon The long, thin part of a neuron along which nerve impulses travel.

terminals The small branching structures at the tips of axons.

neurotransmitters Chemical substances that transmit messages from one neuron to another.

synapse The junction between one neuron and another through which nerve impulses pass.

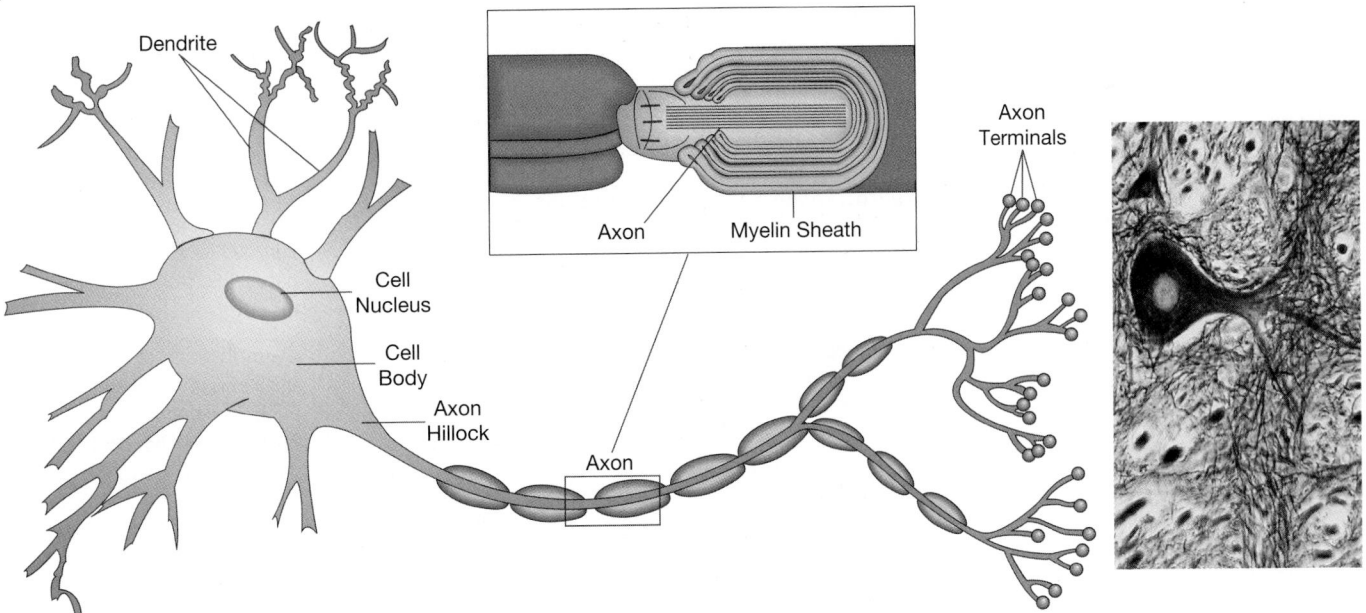

FIGURE 2.1 Anatomy of a neuron.
The three basic parts of the neuron are the cell body, the dendrites, and the axon. The axon of this neuron is wrapped in a myelin sheath, which insulates it from the bodily fluids surrounding the neuron and facilitates transmission of neural impulses (messages that travel within the neuron).

FIGURE 2.2 Transmission of neural impulses across the synapse.
The diagram here shows the structure of the neuron and the mode of transmission of neural impulses between neurons. Neurons transmit messages, or neural impulses, across synapses, which consist of the axon terminal of the transmitting neuron, the gap or synapse between the neurons, and the dendrite of the receiving neuron. The "message" is carried by neurotransmitters that are released into the synapse and taken up by receptor sites on the receiving neuron. Patterns of firing of many thousands of neurons give rise to psychological events such as thoughts and mental images. Different forms of abnormal behavior are associated with irregularities in the transmission or reception of neural messages.

TABLE 2.1

Neurotransmitter Functions and Relationships with Abnormal Behavior Patterns

Neurotransmitter	Functions	Associations with Abnormal Behavior
Acetylcholine (ACh)	Control of muscle contractions and formation of memories	Reduced levels found in patients with Alzheimer's disease (see Chapter 15)
Dopamine	Regulation of muscle contractions and mental processes involving learning, memory, and emotions	Overutilization of dopamine in the brain may be involved in the development of schizophrenia (see Chapter 12)
Norepinephrine	Mental processes involved in learning and memory	Irregularities linked with mood disorders such as depression (see Chapter 8)
Serotonin	Regulation of mood states, satiety, and sleep	Irregularities are implicated in depression and eating disorders (see Chapters 8 and 10)

receptor site A part of a dendrite on a receiving neuron that is structured to receive a neurotransmitter.

Each kind of neurotransmitter has a distinctive chemical structure. It will fit only into one kind of harbor, or **receptor site,** on the receiving neuron. Consider the analogy of a lock and key. Only the right key (neurotransmitter) operates the lock, causing the *postsynaptic* (receiving) neuron to forward the message.

When released, some molecules of a neurotransmitter reach port at receptor sites of other neurons. "Loose" neurotransmitters may be broken down in the synapse by enzymes, or be reabsorbed by the axon terminal (a process termed *reuptake*), to prevent the receiving cell from continuing to fire.

Psychiatric drugs, including drugs used to treat anxiety, depression, and schizophrenia, work by affecting the availability of neurotransmitters in the brain (Snyder, 2002). Consequently, many scientists suspect that irregularities in the workings of neurotransmitter systems in the brain play important roles in the development of these abnormal behavior patterns (see Table 2.1).

Depression is linked to chemical imbalances in the brain involving irregularities in the functioning of several neurotransmitters, especially serotonin (Bremner et al., 2003; Harmer et al., 2003; Meyer et al., 2003) (see Chapter 8). Serotonin is a key brain chemical involved in regulating moods, so it is not surprising that it would play a role in depression (Gupta, 2003). The most widely used antidepressant drugs—Prozac and Zoloft—belong to a class of drugs that increase the availability of serotonin in the brain. Serotonin is also linked to anxiety disorders, sleep disorders, and eating disorders.

Alzheimer's disease, a brain disease in which there is a progressive loss of memory and cognitive functioning, is associated with reductions in the levels of the neurotransmitter *acetylcholine* in the brain (see Chapter 15). Irregularities involving the neurotransmitter *dopamine* are implicated in the development of schizophrenia (see Chapter 12). Antipsychotic drugs used to treat schizophrenia apparently work by blocking dopamine receptors in the brain.

Although neurotransmitter systems are implicated in many psychological disorders, the precise causal mechanisms remain to be determined.

central nervous system The brain and spinal cord.

peripheral nervous system The somatic and autonomic nervous systems.

Parts of the Nervous System The nervous system consists of two major parts, the **central nervous system** and the **peripheral nervous system.** The central nervous system consists of the brain and spinal cord. The peripheral nervous system is made up of nerves that (a) receive and transmit sensory messages (messages from sense organs such as the eyes and ears) to the brain and spinal cord, and (b) transmit messages from the brain or

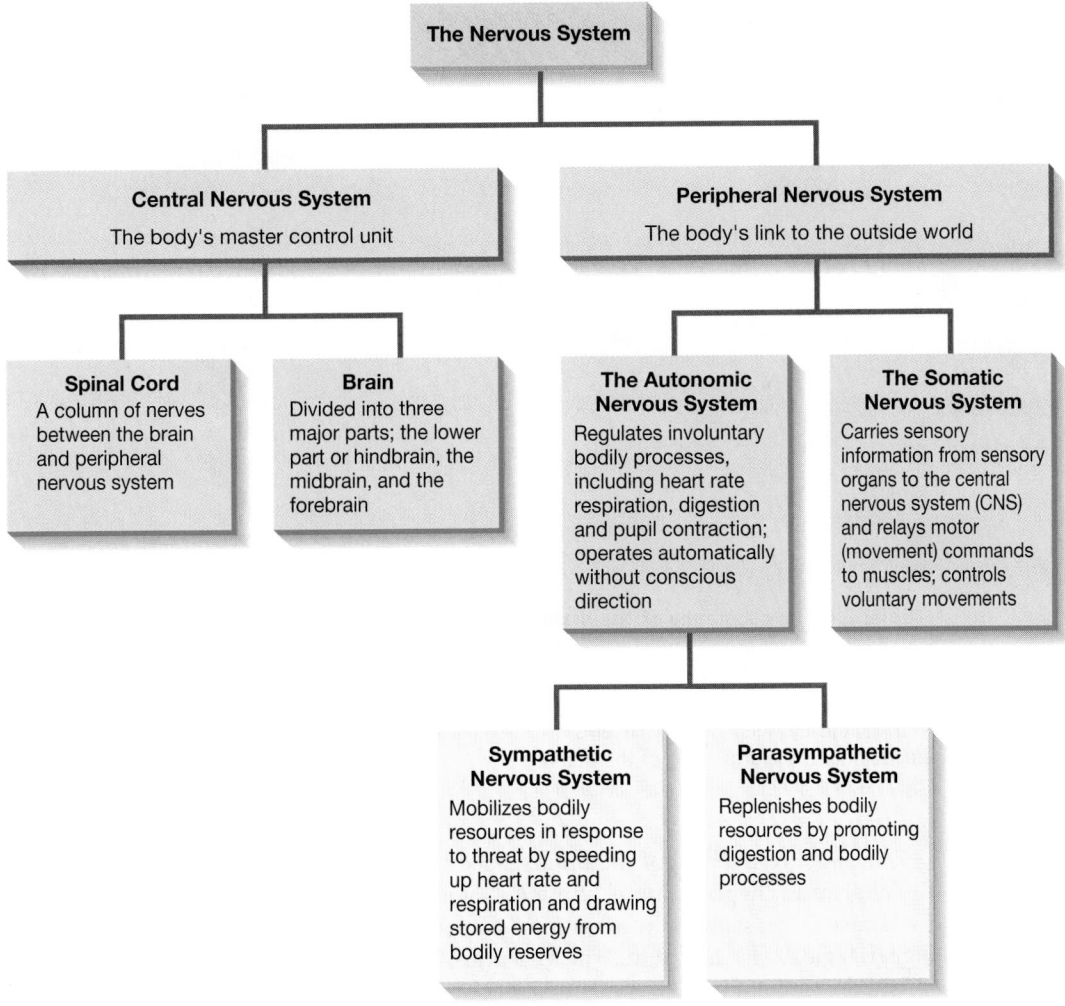

FIGURE 2.3 The organization of the nervous system.

Source: Adapted from J. S. Nevid, *Psychology: Concepts and Applications,* Second Edition (Boston: Houghton Mifflin Co., 2007), p. 56. Reprinted by permission.

spinal cord to the muscles, causing them to contract, and to glands, causing them to secrete hormones. The organization of the nervous system is represented in Figure 2.3.

Central Nervous System We begin our overview of the parts of the central nervous system with the back of the head, where the spinal cord meets the brain, and work forward (see Figure 2.4). The lower part of the brain, or hindbrain, consists of the *medulla, pons,* and *cerebellum.* The **medulla** plays roles in such vital life-support functions as heart rate, respiration, and blood pressure. The **pons** transmits information about body movement and is involved in functions related to attention, sleep, and respiration.

Behind the pons is the **cerebellum** (Latin for "little brain"). The cerebellum regulates balance and motor (muscle) behavior. Injury to the cerebellum can impair your ability to coordinate your movements, causing stumbling and loss of muscle tone.

The *midbrain* lies above the hindbrain and contains nerve pathways linking the hindbrain to the upper region of the brain, called the *forebrain.* The **reticular activating system** (RAS) starts in the hindbrain and rises through the midbrain into the lower part of the forebrain. The RAS is a weblike network of neurons (nerve cells) that play important roles in regulating sleep, attention, and states of arousal. Stimulation of the RAS heightens alertness. On the other hand, use of *depressant drugs,* such as alcohol, dampens central nervous system activity, which reduces RAS activity and can induce states of grogginess or even stupor. (Effects of depressants and other drugs are discussed further in Chapter 9.)

medulla An area of the hindbrain involved in regulation of heartbeat and respiration.

pons A structure in the hindbrain involved in respiration.

cerebellum A structure in the hindbrain involved in coordination and balance.

reticular activating system Brain structure involved in processes of attention, sleep, and arousal.

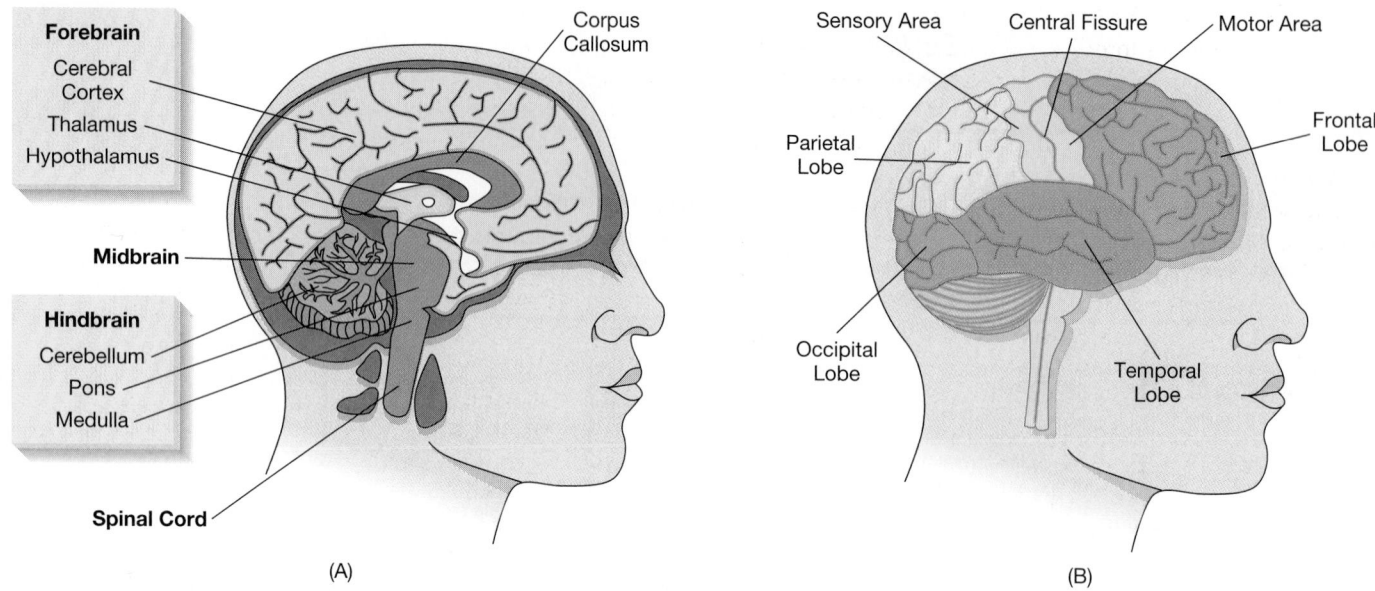

FIGURE 2.4 The geography of the brain.
Part A shows parts of the hindbrain, midbrain, and forebrain. Part B shows the four lobes of the cerebral cortex: frontal, parietal, temporal, and occipital. In B, the sensory (tactile) and motor areas lie across the central fissure from one another. Researchers are investigating the potential relationships between various patterns of abnormal behavior and irregularities in the formation or functioning of the structures of the brain.

thalamus A structure in the forebrain involved in relaying sensory information to the cortex and in processes related to sleep and attention.

hypothalamus A structure in the forebrain involved in regulating body temperature, emotion, and motivation.

limbic system A group of forebrain structures involved in learning, memory, and basic drives.

basal ganglia An assemblage of neurons located between the thalamus and cerebrum, involved in coordinating motor (movement) processes.

cerebrum The large mass of the forebrain, consisting of the two cerebral hemispheres.

cerebral cortex The wrinkled surface area of the cerebrum responsible for processing sensory stimuli and controlling higher mental functions, such as thinking and use of language.

The large frontal area of the brain, called the *forebrain,* includes such structures as the thalamus, hypothalamus, limbic system, basal ganglia, and cerebrum. The **thalamus** relays sensory information (such as tactile and visual stimulation) to the higher regions of the brain. The thalamus, in coordination with the RAS, is also involved in regulating sleep and attention.

The **hypothalamus** (hypo meaning "under") is a tiny, pea-sized structure located under the thalamus. Despite its small size (it weighs a mere four grams), the hypothalamus plays a key role in many vital bodily functions, including regulation of body temperature, concentration of fluids in the blood, and reproductive processes, as well as emotional and motivational states. By implanting electrodes in parts of the hypothalamus of animals and observing the effects when a current is switched on, researchers have found that the hypothalamus is involved in a range of motivational drives and behaviors, including hunger, thirst, sex, parenting behaviors, and aggression.

The hypothalamus, together with parts of the thalamus and other nearby interconnected structures, make up the brain's **limbic system.** The limbic system plays important roles in emotional processing and memory. It also serves important functions regulating more basic drives involving hunger, thirst, and aggression. The **basal ganglia** lie in front of the thalamus and are involved in regulating postural movements and coordination.

The **cerebrum** is the brain's crowning glory. It is responsible for higher mental functions, such as thinking and problem solving, and also accounts for the delightfully rounded shape of the human head. The surface of the cerebrum is convoluted with ridges and valleys. This surface area is called the **cerebral cortex.** It is the thinking, planning, and executive center of the brain, as well as the seat of consciousness and the sense of self.

Structural or functional abnormalities of brain structures are involved in various forms of abnormal behavior. For example, investigators find abnormalities in parts of the cerebral cortex and limbic system in schizophrenia patients (discussed in Chapter 12). The hypothalamus is implicated in certain types of sleep disorders (see Chapter 10), and deterioration of the basal ganglia is associated with Huntington's disease, a degenerative disease that can lead to disturbances of mood and paranoia and even to dementia (see Chapter 15). These are but a few of the brain-behavior relationships we shall discuss in later sections of this text.

Peripheral Nervous System   The peripheral nervous system is a network of neurons connecting the brain to our sense organs—our eyes, ears, and so on—as well as our glands and muscles. These neural pathways allows us to both sense the world around us and act upon it by using our muscles to move our limbs. The peripheral nervous system consists of two main parts or divisions, called the *somatic nervous system* and the *autonomic nervous system* (see Figure 2.3).

The **somatic nervous system** transmits messages from our sensory organs to the brain for processing, leading to the experience of visual, auditory, tactile, and other sensations. Commands emanating from the brain pass downward through the spinal cord to nerves of the somatic nervous system that connect to our muscles, allowing us to voluntarily control our movements, such as when raising an arm or walking.

Psychologists are especially interested in the workings of the **autonomic nervous system** (ANS) because of its role in emotional processing. *Autonomic* means "automatic." The ANS regulates the glands and involuntary processes such as heart rate, breathing, digestion, and dilation of the pupils of the eyes, even when we are sleeping.

The ANS has two branches, the **sympathetic nervous system** and the **parasympathetic nervous system.** These have mostly opposing effects. Many organs and glands are served by both branches of the ANS. The sympathetic division is most involved in processes that mobilize the body's resources in times of stress, such as drawing energy from stored reserves to prepare the person to deal with imposing threats or dangers (see Chapter 5). When we face a threatening or dangerous situation, the sympathetic branch of the ANS kicks in by accelerating our heart rate and breathing rate and thereby preparing our body to either fight or flee from a threatening stressor. Sympathetic activation in the face of a threatening stimulus is associated with emotional responses such as fear or anxiety. When we relax, the parasympathetic branch decelerates the heart rate. The parasympathetic division is most active during processes that replenish energy reserves, such as digestion. Because the sympathetic branch dominates when we are fearful or anxious, fear or anxiety can lead to indigestion because activation of the sympathetic nervous system curbs digestive activity.

The Cerebral Cortex   The parts of the brain responsible for higher mental functions, such as thought and use of language, are the two large masses of the cerebrum called the right and left *cerebral hemispheres*. The outer layer or covering of each hemisphere is called the cerebral cortex. (The word *cortex* literally means "bark" and is so used because the cerebral cortex can be likened to the bark of a tree.) Each hemisphere is divided into four parts, called *lobes*, as shown in Figure 2.4. The *occipital lobe* is primarily involved in processing visual stimuli; the *temporal lobe* is involved in processing sounds or auditory stimuli. The *parietal lobe* is involved in processing sensations of touch, temperature, and pain. The *sensory area* of the parietal lobe receives messages from receptors in the skin all over the body. Neurons in the motor area (or *motor cortex*) of the *frontal lobe* control muscular responses, enabling us to move our limbs. The *prefrontal cortex* (the part of the frontal lobe that lies in front of the motor cortex) regulates higher mental functions such as thinking, problem solving, and use of language.

Evaluating Biological Perspectives on Abnormal Behavior

Biological structures and processes are involved in many patterns of abnormal behavior, as we will see in later chapters. Genetic factors, as well as disturbances in neurotransmitter functioning and underlying brain abnormalities or defects, are implicated in many psychological disorders. For some disorders, such as Alzheimer's disease, biological processes play the direct causative role. (Even then, however, the precise causes remain unknown.) But for most disorders, we need to examine the interaction of biological and environmental factors.

Genes play important roles in determining our vulnerability or susceptibility to psychological disorders. But genes do not tell the whole story when it comes to understanding the origins of these disorders (Kendler, 2005; Plomin et al., 2003). Scientists today are moving past the old "nature–nurture" (gene vs. environment) debate to

somatic nervous system The division of the peripheral nervous system that relays information from the sense organs to the brain and transmits messages from the brain to the skeletal muscles.

autonomic nervous system The division of the peripheral nervous system that regulates the activities of the glands and involuntary functions.

sympathetic nervous system Pertaining to the division of the autonomic nervous system whose activity leads to heightened states of arousal.

parasympathetic nervous system Pertaining to the division of the autonomic nervous system whose activity reduces states of arousal and regulates bodily processes that replenish energy reserves.

CONTROVERSIES IN ABNORMAL PSYCHOLOGY

Is It All in the Genes?

It's not stretching a point to say that progress in genetic research in recent years has been nothing less than remarkable. The highlight of these achievements was the cracking of the human genome, the complete genetic blueprint of a human being. The genome consists of the precise chemical sequence in human DNA—a recipe for determining the features or traits of human beings (International Human Genome, 2001; Wade, 2003b). We are now able to read the coded instructions that comprise the genetic script of a human being. The genome has even been published on the Internet for scientists to use in their studies (Baltimore, 2000).

We each possess a unique genetic code and buried within that code are sequences of DNA that are believed to play important roles in determining our risks of developing many physical and mental disorders (Kendler, 2005). Evidence connects genetic factors to a wide range of psychological disorders, including schizophrenia, bipolar (manic–depressive) disorder, major depression, alcoholism, autism, dementia due to Alzheimer's disease, anxiety disorders, dyslexia, and antisocial personality disorder (Merikangas & Risch, 2003; NIMH, 2003; Plomin & McGuffin, 2003; Waterworth et al., 2002).

Just what it is we inherit that puts us at greater risk of developing psychological disorders is a question that continues to challenge researchers. We shouldn't think there is any one-to-one relationship between individual genes and the complex patterns of behavior we recognize as schizophrenia, bipolar disorder, or any other psychological disorders. No, there doesn't appear to be any one gene that causes schizophrenia or any other psychological disorder. Rather, multiple genes interact in complex ways, affecting underlying processes involved in brain chemistry and brain structures, which in turn affect the likelihood of developing psychological disorders.

Scientists are seeking to find particular genes involved in psychological disorders such as schizophrenia, depression, and autism (Bunney et al., 2003; Plomin, 2003; Plomin et al., 2003; Tecott, 2003). They hope that one day in the not-too-distant future, it will be possible to repair defective or harmful genes, perhaps by blocking their actions, as well as to enhance the actions of beneficial genes (Phillips et al., 2002; Plomin & McGuffin, 2003; Sapolsky, 2003).

Against the backdrop of increasing evidence of genetic contributions across a wide swath of abnormal behavior, the question remains, "Is it all in the genes?" More specifically, is the development of psychological disorders a matter of luck in the genetic draw?

These questions touch on a long-standing debate in psychology, arguably the longest debate—the so-called "nature versus nurture" debate. The debate has shifted to one pitting nature against nurture to one framed in terms of how much of our behavior is a product of nature (genes) and how much is a product of nurture (environment). As the long debate continues, let us offer a few key points to consider:

1. *Genes do not dictate behavioral outcomes.* Evidence of a genetic contribution in psychological disorders is arguably strongest in the case of schizophrenia. But as discussed in Chapter 12, even for monozygotic twins who share 100% genetic overlap, when scientists find one schizophrenic MZ twin, the chance of the other twin having schizophrenia is slightly less than 50%. In other words, genetics alone does not account for schizophrenia or any other psychological disorder. As Kenneth Kendler, a leading genetics researcher, explained it, "We do not have and are not likely to ever discover 'genes' for psychiatric illness" (Kendler, 2005, p. 1250).

2. *Genetic factors create a predisposition or likelihood—not a certainty—that certain behaviors or disorders will develop.* Genes do not directly cause psychological disorders. Rather, they create predispositions that raise the risk or likelihood of developing particular disorders. Our genes are carried in our chromosomes from the moment of conception and are not affected directly by the environment. However, the effects that genes

have on the body and mind may be influenced by many environmental factors such as life experiences, family relationships, and levels of life stress (Fraga et al., 2005; Kendler, 2005; Moffitt, Caspi, & Rutter, 2006). Even our ethnicity and gender influence how our genes operate in the body (Williams et al., 2003).

3. *Multigenic determinism affects psychological disorders.* We noted that for disorders in which genetic factors play a role, multiple genes are involved, not individual genes alone (Plomin, 2003; Uhl & Grow, 2004). We have yet to find any psychological disorder that can be explained by defects or variations on a single gene (USDHHS, 1999a).

4. *Genetic factors and environmental influence interact with each other in shaping our personalities and determining our vulnerability to a range of psychological disorders.* The contemporary view of the nature–nurture debate is best expressed in terms of nature *and* nurture acting together, not nature *versus* nurture (Angier, 2003 Andreasen, 2003; Plomin et al., 2003; Ridley, 2003).

Critical Thinking

- How might investigators determine the role of genetic factors in the development of psychological disorders? (Consider the research methods discussed in Chapter 1.)
- What would you say to someone who believes that genetics is destiny when it comes to determining one's risk of developing psychological disorders such as depression or schizophrenia?

A human being, decoded.
Here we see a portion of the human genome, the genetic code of a human being. Scientists recognize that genes play an important role in determining predispositions for many psychological traits and disorders. But whether these predispositions are expressed depends on the interactions of genetic and environmental influences.

study the complex interactions between genes and environmental factors to better understand the determinants of abnormal behavior patterns (Andreasen, 2003; Fraga et al., 2003; Kendler, 2005). (See *Controversies in Abnormal Psychology* on page 44.)

Although we continue to learn more about the biological foundations of abnormal behavior patterns, the interface between biology and behavior is a two-way street. Researchers have uncovered links between psychological factors and many physical disorders and conditions (see Chapter 5). Researchers are also investigating whether the combination of psychological and drug treatments for such problems as depression, anxiety disorders, and substance abuse disorders, among others, may increase the therapeutic benefits of either of the two approaches alone.

THE PSYCHOLOGICAL PERSPECTIVE

At about the time that biological models of abnormal behavior were becoming prominent in the late 19th century with the contributions of Kraepelin, Griesinger, and others, another approach to understanding abnormal behavior began to emerge. This approach emphasized the psychological roots of abnormal behavior and was most closely identified with the work of the Austrian physician Sigmund Freud. Over time other psychological models would emerge from the behaviorist, humanistic, and cognitivist traditions. Let us begin our study of psychological perspectives with Freud's contribution and the development of psychodynamic models.

Psychodynamic Models

Psychodynamic theory is based on the contributions of Sigmund Freud and his followers. Freud's **psychoanalytic theory** is based on the belief that the roots of psychological problems, such as hysteria, involve unconscious motives and conflicts that can be traced back to childhood. Freud put the study of the unconscious mind on the map (Lothane, 2006). To Freud, unconscious motives and conflicts revolve around primitive sexual and aggressive instincts and the need to keep these primitive impulses out of consciousness. But why must the mind keep impulses hidden from consciousness awareness? Because, in the Freudian view, were we to become fully aware of our most basic sexual and aggressive urges—which, according to Freud, include incestuous and violent impulses—our conscious self would be flooded with crippling anxiety. On the Freudian account, abnormal behavior patterns represent "symptoms" of these dynamic struggles taking place within the unconscious mind. In the case of hysteria, the "symptom" represents the *conversion* of an unconscious psychological conflict into a physical problem. The patient is aware of the symptom, but not the unconscious conflict that lies at its root. Let's take a closer look at the key elements in psychoanalytic theory.

The Structure of the Mind We can liken Freud's model of the mind to an iceberg with only the tip visible above the surface of awareness (Figure 2.5). Freud called this region "above the surface" the **conscious** part of the mind. It is the part of the mind that corresponds to our present awareness. The larger part of the mind remains below the surface of consciousness. The regions that lie beneath the surface of awareness were labeled the *preconscious* and the *unconscious.*

In the **preconscious** are memories that are not in awareness, but that can be brought into awareness by focusing on them. Your telephone number, for example, remains in the preconscious until you focus on it. The **unconscious,** the largest part of the mind, remains shrouded in mystery. Its contents can only be brought to awareness with great difficulty, if at all. Freud believed the unconscious is the repository of our basic biological impulses or drives, which he called instincts—primarily sexual and aggressive instincts.

psychoanalytic theory The theoretical model of personality developed by Sigmund Freud; also called psychoanalysis.

conscious To Freud, the part of the mind that corresponds to our present awareness.

preconscious To Freud, the part of the mind whose contents lie outside present awareness but can be brought into awareness by focusing attention.

unconscious To Freud, the part of the mind that lies outside the range of ordinary awareness and that contains instinctual urges.

FIGURE 2.5 The parts of the mind, according to Freud.
In psychodynamic theory, the mind is akin to an iceberg; only a small part of it rises to conscious awareness at any moment in time. Although material in the preconscious mind may be brought into consciousness by focusing our attention on it, the impulses and ideas in the unconscious tend to remain veiled in mystery.

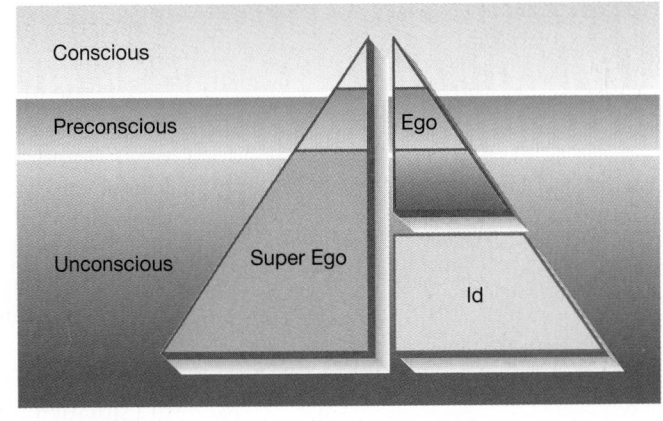

id The unconscious psychic structure, present at birth, that contains primitive instincts and is regulated by the pleasure principle.

pleasure principle The governing principle of the id, involving demands for immediate gratification of needs.

ego The psychic structure that corresponds to the concept of the self, governed by the reality principle and characterized by the ability to tolerate frustration.

reality principle The governing principle of the ego, which involves considerations of social acceptability and practicality.

superego The psychic structure that incorporates the values of the parents and important others and functions as a moral conscience.

defense mechanisms The reality-distorting strategies used by the ego to shield the self from awareness of anxiety-provoking materials.

The Structure of Personality According to Freud's structural hypothesis, the personality is divided into three mental entities, or psychic structures: the *id, ego,* and *superego.*

The **id** is the original psychic structure, present at birth. It is the repository of our baser drives and instinctual impulses, including hunger, thirst, sex, and aggression. The id, which operates completely in the unconscious, follows the **pleasure principle:** It demands instant gratification of instincts without consideration of social rules or customs or the needs of others.

During the first year of life, the child discovers that every demand is not instantly gratified. He or she must learn to cope with the delay of gratification. The **ego** develops during this first year to organize reasonable ways of coping with frustration. Standing for "reason and good sense" (Freud, 1933/1964, p. 76), the ego seeks to curb the demands of the id and to direct behavior in keeping with social customs and expectations. Gratification can thus be achieved, but not at the expense of social disapproval. Let's say the id floods your consciousness with hunger pangs. Were it to have its way, the id might prompt you to wolf down whatever food is at hand or even to swipe someone else's plate. But the ego creates the idea of walking to the refrigerator, making a sandwich, and pouring a glass of milk.

The ego is governed by the **reality principle.** It considers what is practical and possible, as well as the urgings of the id. The ego lays the groundwork for developing a conscious sense of ourselves as distinct individuals.

During middle childhood, the **superego** develops from the internalization of the moral standards and values of our parents and other key people in our lives. The superego serves as a conscience, or internal moral guardian, that monitors the ego and passes judgment on right and wrong. It metes out punishment in the form of guilt and shame when it finds that the ego has failed to adhere to the superego's moral standards. Ego stands between the id and the superego. It endeavors to satisfy the cravings of the id without offending the moral standards of the superego.

Defense Mechanisms Although part of the ego rises to consciousness, some of its activity is carried out unconsciously. In the unconscious, the ego serves as a kind of watchdog, or censor, which screens impulses from the id. It uses **defense mechanisms** (psychological defenses) to prevent socially unacceptable impulses from rising into consciousness. If not for these defense mechanisms, the darkest sins of our childhoods, the primitive demands of our ids, and the censures of our superegos might disable us psychologically. *Repression,* or motivated forgetting by which unacceptable wishes, urges, and impulses are banished to the unconscious, is the most basic of the defense mechanisms (Boag, 2006). Others are described in Table 2.2.

A dynamic unconscious struggle thus takes place between the id and the ego. Biological drives that are striving for expression (the id) are pitted against the ego, which seeks to restrain them or channel them into socially acceptable outlets. When these conflicts are not resolved smoothly, they can lead to the development of features associated with psychological disorders, such as hysterical symptoms, phobias, and behavioral problems. Because we cannot view the unconscious mind directly, Freud developed a method of mental detective work called *psychoanalysis,* which is described in Chapter 4.

The use of defense mechanisms to cope with feelings such as anxiety, guilt, and shame is considered normal. These mechanisms enable us to constrain impulses from the id as we go about our daily business. Freud believed that slips of the tongue and ordinary forgetfulness could represent hidden motives that are kept out of consciousness by repression. If a friend means to say, "I hear what you're saying," but it comes out, "I hate what you're saying," perhaps the friend is expressing a repressed hateful impulse. If a lover storms out in anger but forgets his umbrella, perhaps he is unconsciously creating an excuse for returning. Defense mechanisms may also give rise to abnormal behavior, however. The person who regresses to an infantile state under pressures of enormous stress is clearly not acting adaptively to the situation.

TABLE 2.2

Major Defense Mechanisms in Psychodynamic Theory

Type of Defense Mechanism	Description	Example
Repression	Expulsion from awareness of unacceptable ideas or motives	A person remains unaware of harboring hateful or destructive impulses toward others.
Regression	The return of behavior that is typical of earlier stages of development	Under stress, a college student starts biting his nails or becomes totally dependent on others.
Displacement	The transfer of unacceptable impulses away from their original objects onto safer or less-threatening objects	A worker slams a door after his boss chews him out.
Denial	Refusal to recognize a threatening impulse or desire	A person who nearly chokes someone to death acts afterward like it was "no big deal."
Reaction formation	Behaving in a way that is the opposite of one's true wishes or desires to keep these repressed	A sexually frustrated person goes on a personal crusade to stamp out pornography.
Rationalization	The use of self-justifications to explain away unacceptable behavior	When asked why she continues to smoke, a woman says, "Cancer doesn't run in my family."
Projection	Imposing one's own impulses or wishes onto another person	A sexually inhibited person misinterprets other people's friendly approaches as sexual advances.
Sublimation	The channeling of unacceptable impulses into socially constructive pursuits	A person channels aggressive impulses into competitive sports.

Source: From J. S. Nevid, *Psychology: Concepts and Applications,* Second Edition (Boston: Houghton Mifflin Co., 2007), p. 466. Reprinted with permission.

Regression? In Freudian theory, the ego may shield itself from anxiety or extreme stress by employing the defense mechanism of regression, which involves the return of behavior associated with an earlier stage of psychological development.

Stages of Psychosexual Development Freud argued that sexual drives are the dominant factors in the development of personality, even in childhood. Freud believed that the child's basic relationship to the world in its first several years of life is organized around the pursuit of sensual or sexual pleasure. In Freud's view, all activities that are physically pleasurable, such as eating or moving one's bowels, are in essence "sexual." (What Freud meant by *sexual* is probably closer in present-day meaning to the word *sensual.*)

The drive for sexual pleasure represents, in Freud's view, the expression of a major life instinct, which he called Eros—the basic drive to preserve and perpetuate life. He called the energy contained in Eros that allows it to fulfill its function *libido,* or sexual energy. Freud believed libidinal energy is expressed through sexual pleasure in different body parts, called *erogenous zones,* as the child matures. In Freud's view, the stages of human development are psychosexual in nature because they correspond to the transfer of libidinal energy from one erogenous zone to another. Freud proposed the existence of five psychosexual stages of development: oral (first year of life), anal

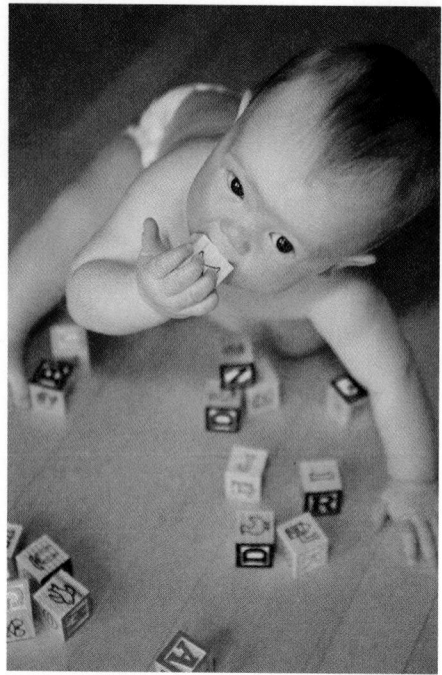

The oral stage of psychosexual development? According to Freud, the child's early encounters with the world are largely experienced through the mouth.

An Oral Fixation? Freud believed that too little or too much gratification at a particular stage of psychosexual development can lead to fixation, resulting in personality traits associated with that stage, such as exaggerated oral traits.

(second year of life), phallic (beginning during the third year of life), latency (from around age 6 to age 12), and genital (beginning in puberty).

In the first year of life, the *oral stage,* infants achieve sexual pleasure by sucking their mothers' breasts and by mouthing anything that happens to be nearby. Oral stimulation, in the form of sucking and biting, is a source of both sexual gratification and nourishment. During the *anal stage* of psychosexual development, the child experiences sexual gratification through contraction and relaxation of the sphincter muscles that control elimination of bodily waste.

The next stage of psychosexual development, the *phallic stage,* generally begins during the third year of life. The major erogenous zone during the stage is the phallic region (the penis in boys, the clitoris in girls). Perhaps the most controversial of Freud's beliefs was his suggestion that phallic-stage children develop unconscious incestuous wishes for the parent of the opposite gender and begin to view the parent of the same sex as a rival. Freud dubbed this conflict the *Oedipus complex,* after the legendary Greek king Oedipus, who unwittingly slew his father and married his mother. The female version of the Oedipus complex has been named by some followers (although not by Freud himself) the *Electra complex,* after the character of Electra, who, according to Greek legend, avenged the death of her father, King Agamemnon, by slaying her father's murderers—her own mother and her mother's lover. Freud believed the Oedipus conflict represents a central psychological conflict of early childhood and that failure to successfully resolve the conflict can set the stage for the development of psychological problems in later life.

Successful resolution of the Oedipus complex involves the boy repressing his incestuous wishes for his mother and identifying with his father. This identification leads to development of the aggressive, independent characteristics associated with the traditional masculine gender role. Successful resolution of the complex for the girl involves repression of the incestuous wishes for her father and identification with her mother, leading to the acquisition of the more passive, dependent characteristics traditionally associated with the feminine sex role.

The Oedipus complex comes to a point of resolution, whether fully resolved or not, by about the age of 5 or 6. From the identification with the parent of the same gender comes the internalization of parental values in the form of the superego. Children then enter the *latency stage* of psychosexual development, a period of late childhood during which sexual impulses remain in a latent state. Interests become directed toward school and play activities.

Sexual drives are once again aroused with the *genital stage,* beginning with puberty, which reaches fruition in mature sexuality, marriage, and the bearing of children. The sexual feelings toward the parent of the opposite gender that had remained repressed during the latency period emerge during adolescence but are displaced, or transferred, onto socially appropriate members of the opposite gender. In Freud's view, successful adjustment during the genital stage involves attaining sexual gratification through sexual intercourse with someone of the opposite gender, presumably within the context of marriage.

One of Freud's central beliefs is that the child may encounter conflict during each of the psychosexual stages of development. Conflict in the oral stage, for example, centers on whether or not the infant receives adequate oral gratification. Too much gratification could lead the infant to expect that everything in life is given with little or no effort on his or her part. In contrast, early weaning might lead to frustration. Too little or too much gratification at any stage could lead to **fixation** in that stage, which leads to the development of personality traits characteristic of that stage. Oral fixations could include an exaggerated desire for "oral activities," which could become expressed in later life in smoking, alcohol abuse, overeating, and nail biting. Like the infant who depends on the mother's breast for survival and gratification of oral pleasure, orally fixated adults may also become clinging and dependent in their interpersonal relationships. In Freud's view, failure to successfully resolve the conflicts of the phallic stage (i.e., the Oedipus complex) can lead to the rejection of the traditional masculine or feminine roles and to homosexuality.

Other Psychodynamic Theorists Psychodynamic theory has been shaped over the years by the contributions of psychodynamic theorists who shared certain central tenets in common with Freud, such as that behavior reflects unconscious motivation, inner conflict, and the operation of defensive responses to anxiety. However, many psychodynamic theorists deviated sharply from Freud's positions on many issues. For example, they tended to place less emphasis than Freud on basic instincts such as sex and aggression, and greater emphasis on conscious choice, self-direction, and creativity.

Swiss psychiatrist Carl Jung (1875–1961) was a member of Freud's inner circle. His break with Freud came when he developed his own psychodynamic theory, which he called *analytical psychology*. Jung believed that an understanding of human behavior must incorporate the facts of self-awareness and self-direction as well as the impulses of the id and the mechanisms of defense. He believed that not only do we have a *personal* unconscious, a repository of repressed memories and impulses, but we also inherit a collective unconscious. The collective unconscious contains primitive images, or **archetypes,** which reflect on the history of our species, including vague, mysterious mythical images like the all-powerful God, the fertile and nurturing mother, the young hero, the wise old man, and themes of rebirth or resurrection. Although archetypes remain unconscious, in Jung's view, they influence our thoughts, dreams, and emotions and render us responsive to cultural themes in stories and films. Alfred Adler (1870–1937), like Jung, held a place in Freud's inner circle, but broke away as he developed his own beliefs that people are basically driven by an inferiority complex, not by the sexual instinct, as Freud maintained. For some people, feelings of inferiority are based on physical deficits and the resulting need to compensate for them. But all of us, because of our small size during childhood, encounter feelings of inferiority to some degree. These feelings lead to a powerful drive for superiority, which motivates us to achieve prominence and social dominance. In the healthy personality, however, strivings for dominance are tempered by devotion to helping other people.

Adler, like Jung, believed self-awareness plays a major role in the formation of personality. Adler spoke of a *creative self,* a self-aware aspect of personality that strives to overcome obstacles and develop the individual's potential. With the hypothesis of the creative self, Adler shifted the emphasis of psychodynamic theory from the id to the ego. Because our potentials are uniquely individual, Adler's views have been termed *individual psychology.*

Some psychodynamic theorists, such as Karen Horney (1885–1952) (pronounced HORN-eye), stressed the importance of child–parent relationships in the development of emotional problems. She maintained that when parents are harsh or uncaring, children come to develop a deep-seated form of anxiety called *basic anxiety,* which she described as a feeling of "being isolated and helpless in a potentially hostile world" (cited in Quinn, 1987, p. 41). Children who harbor deep-seated resentment toward their parents may develop a form of hostility she labeled *basic hostility.* She shared with Freud the view that children repress their hostility toward their parents because of an underlying fear of losing them or of suffering reprisals or punishment from them. However, repressed hostility generates more anxiety and insecurity. With Horney and other psychodynamic theorists who followed Freud, the emphasis shifts from a focus on sexual and aggressive drives toward a closer examination of social influences on development.

More recent psychodynamic models also place a greater emphasis on the self or the ego and less emphasis on the sexual instinct than Freud. Today, most psychoanalysts see people as motivated on two tiers: by the growth-oriented, conscious pursuits of the ego as well as by the more primitive, conflict-ridden drives of the id. Heinz Hartmann (1894–1970) was one of the originators of **ego psychology,** which posits that the ego has energy and motives of its own. The choices to seek an education, dedicate oneself to art and poetry, and further humanity are not merely defensive forms of sublimation, as Freud had seen them.

Erik Erikson (1902–1994) was influenced by Freud but became an important theorist in this own right. He focused on psychosocial development in contrast to Freud's emphasis on psychosexual development. Erikson attributed more importance to social

fixation In Freudian theory, a constellation of personality traits associated with a particular stage of psychosexual development, resulting from either too much or too little gratification at the stage.

archetypes Primitive images or concepts that reside in the collective unconscious.

ego psychology Modern psychodynamic approach that focuses more on the conscious strivings of the ego than on the hypothesized unconscious functions of the id.

The power of archetypes. One reason adventure stories such as *Lord of the Rings* and the *Star Wars* saga are so compelling may be that they feature archetypes such as the struggle between good and evil characters.

Karen Horney

Erik Erikson

Margaret Mahler

object-relations theory The psychodynamic viewpoint that focuses on the influences of internalized representations of the personalities of parents and other strong attachment figures (called "objects").

relationships and formation of personal identity than unconscious processes. Whereas Freud's developmental theory ends with the genital stage, beginning in early adolescence, Erikson's developmental theory posits that our personalities continue to be shaped throughout adulthood as we deal with psychosocial challenges or crises we face during each period of life. In Erikson's view, for example, the major psychosocial challenge faced by adolescents is development of *ego identity,* a clearly defined sense of who they are and what they believe in.

One popular contemporary psychodynamic approach, **object-relations theory,** focuses on how children come to develop symbolic representations of important others in their lives, especially their parents. The object-relations theorist Margaret Mahler (1897–1985) saw the process of separating from the mother during the first 3 years of life as crucial to personality development (discussed further in Chapter 13).

According to psychodynamic theory, we introject, or incorporate, into our own personalities parts of parental figures in our lives. For example, you might introject your father's strong sense of responsibility or your mother's eagerness to please others. Introjection is more powerful when we fear losing others because of death or rejection. Thus we might be particularly apt to incorporate elements of people who *disapprove* of us or who see things differently.

In Mahler's view, these symbolic representations, which are formed from images and memories of others, come to influence our perceptions and behavior. We experience internal conflict as the attitudes of introjected people battle with our own. Some of our perceptions may be distorted or seem unreal to us. Some of our impulses and behavior may seem unlike us, as if they come out of the blue. With such conflict, we may not be able to tell where the influences of other people end and our "real selves" begin. The aim of Mahler's therapeutic approach was to help clients separate their own ideas and feelings from those of the introjected objects so they could develop as individuals—as their own persons.

Psychodynamic Views on Normality and Abnormality In the Freudian model, mental health is a function of the dynamic balance among the psychic structures of id, ego, and superego (USDHHS, 1999a). In mentally healthy people, the ego is strong enough to control the instincts of the id and to withstand the condemnation of the superego. The presence of acceptable outlets for the expression of some primitive impulses, such as the expression of mature sexuality in marriage, decreases the pressures within the id and, at the same time, lessens the burdens of the ego in repressing the remaining impulses. Being reared by reasonably tolerant parents might prevent the superego from becoming overly harsh and condemnatory.

In people with psychological disorders, the balance among the psychic structures is lopsided. Some unconscious impulses may "leak," producing anxiety or leading to psychological disorders, such as hysteria and phobias. The symptom expresses the conflict among the parts of the personality while it protects the self from recognizing the inner turmoil. A person with a fear of knives, for example, is shielded from becoming aware of her own unconscious aggressive impulses to use a knife to murder someone or attack herself. So long as the symptom is maintained (and the person avoids knives), the murderous or suicidal impulses are kept at bay. If the superego becomes overly powerful, it may create excessive feelings of guilt and lead to depression. People who intentionally hurt others without feeling guilty about it are believed to have an underdeveloped superego.

Freud believed that the underlying conflicts that give rise to psychological disorders originate in childhood and are buried in the depths of the unconscious. Through psychoanalysis, he sought to help people uncover and learn to deal with these underlying conflicts. This way, they can free themselves of the need to maintain the overt symptoms.

Perpetual vigilance and defense take their toll. The ego can weaken and, in extreme cases, lose the ability to keep a lid on the id. When the urges of the id spill forth, untempered by an ego that is either weakened or underdeveloped, the result is **psychosis.** Psychosis is characterized, in general, by bizarre behavior and thoughts and by faulty perceptions of reality such as hallucinations ("hearing voices" or seeing things that are not present). Speech may become incoherent; there may be bizarre posturing and gestures. Schizophrenia is the major form of psychosis (see Chapter 12).

Freud equated psychological health with the *abilities to love and to work.* The normal person can care deeply for other people, find sexual gratification in an intimate relationship, and engage in productive work. To accomplish these ends, sexual impulses must be expressed in a relationship with a partner of the opposite gender. Other impulses must be channeled (sublimated) into socially productive pursuits, such as work, enjoyment of art or music, or creative expression. Other psychodynamic theorists, such as Jung and Adler, emphasized the need to develop a differentiated self—the unifying force that provides direction to behavior and helps develop a person's potential. Adler also believed that psychological health involves efforts to compensate for feelings of inferiority by striving to excel in one or more of the arenas of human endeavor. For Mahler, similarly, abnormal behavior derives from failure to develop our distinctive and individual identity.

Evaluating Psychodynamic Models Psychodynamic theory has pervaded the general culture (Lothane, 2006). Even people who have never read Freud look for symbolic meanings in slips of the tongue and assume that abnormalities can be traced to early childhood. Terms such as *ego* and *repression* have become commonplace, although their everyday meanings do not fully overlap with those intended by Freud.

The psychodynamic model led us to recognize that we are not transparent to ourselves (Panek, 2002)—that our behavior may be driven by hidden drives and impulses of which we are unaware or only dimly aware. Moreover, Freud's beliefs about childhood sexuality were both illuminating and controversial. Before Freud, children were perceived as pure innocents, free of sexual desire. Freud recognized, however, that young children, even infants, seek pleasure through stimulation of the oral and anal cavities and the phallic region. Yet his beliefs that primitive drives give rise to incestuous desires, intrafamily rivalries, and conflicts remain sources of controversy, even within psychodynamic circles.

Many critics, including some of Freud's followers, believe he placed too much emphasis on sexual and aggressive impulses and underemphasized social relationships. Critics have also argued that the psychic structures—the id, ego, and superego—may be little more than useful fictions, poetic ways to represent inner conflict. Many critics argue that Freud's hypothetical mental processes are not scientific concepts because they cannot be directly observed or tested. Therapists can speculate, for example, that a client "forgot" about an appointment because "unconsciously" she or he did not want

psychosis A severe form of disturbed behavior characterized by impaired ability to interpret reality and difficulty meeting the demands of daily life.

B. F. Skinner

behaviorism The school of psychology that defines psychology as the study of observable behavior.

to attend the session. Such unconscious motivation may not be subject to scientific verification, however. On the other hand, psychodynamically oriented researchers have developed scientific approaches to test many of Freud's concepts. They believe that a growing body of evidence supports the existence of unconscious processes that lie outside ordinary awareness, including defense mechanisms such as repression (Cramer, 2000; Westen & Gabbard, 2002).

Learning Models

The psychodynamic models of Freud and his followers were the first major psychological theories of abnormal behavior. Other relevant psychologies also took shape early in the 20th century. The behavioral perspective is identified with the Russian physiologist Ivan Pavlov (1849–1936), the discoverer of the conditioned reflex, and the American psychologist John B. Watson (1878–1958), the father of **behaviorism.** The behavioral perspective focuses on the role of learning in explaining both normal and abnormal behavior. From a learning perspective, abnormal behavior represents the acquisition, or learning, of inappropriate, maladaptive behaviors.

From the medical and psychodynamic perspectives, abnormal behavior is *symptomatic*, respectively, of underlying biological or psychological problems. From the learning perspective, however, the abnormal behavior itself is the problem. In this perspective, abnormal behavior is learned in much the same way as normal behavior. Why do some people behave abnormally? It may be that their learning histories differ from most people's. For example, a person who was harshly punished as a child for masturbating might become anxious, as an adult, about sexuality. Poor child-rearing practices, such as capricious punishment for misconduct and failure to praise or reward good behavior, might lead to antisocial behavior. Children with abusive or neglectful parents might learn to pay more attention to inner fantasies than to the world outside and have difficulty distinguishing reality from fantasy.

Watson and other behaviorists, such as Harvard University psychologist B. F. Skinner (1904–1990), believed that human behavior is the product of our genetic inheritance and environmental or situational influences. Like Freud, Watson and Skinner discarded concepts of personal freedom, choice, and self-direction. But whereas Freud saw us as driven by irrational forces, behaviorists see us as products of environmental influences that shape and manipulate our behavior. Behaviorists also believed that we should limit the study of psychology to behavior itself rather than focus on underlying motivations. Therapy, in this view, consists of shaping behavior rather than seeking insight into the workings of the mind. Behaviorists focus on the roles of two forms of learning in shaping both normal and abnormal behavior, classical conditioning and operant conditioning.

FIGURE 2.6 The apparatus used in Ivan Pavlov's experiments on conditioning. Pavlov used an apparatus such as this to demonstrate the process of conditioning. To the left is a two-way mirror, behind which a researcher rings a bell. After the bell is rung, meat is placed on the dog's tongue. Following several pairings of the bell and the meat, the dog learns to salivate in response to the bell. The animal's saliva passes through the tube to a vial, where its quantity may be taken as a measure of the strength of the conditioned response.

Role of Classical Conditioning The Russian physiologist Ivan Pavlov discovered the conditioned reflex (now called a *conditioned response*) quite by accident. In his laboratory, he harnessed dogs to an apparatus like that in Figure 2.6 to study their salivary response to food. Along the way he observed that the animals would salivate and secrete gastric juices even before they started to eat. These responses appeared to be elicited by the sound of the food cart as it was wheeled into the room. So Pavlov undertook an experiment that showed that animals could learn to salivate in response to other stimuli, such as the sound of a bell, if these stimuli were *associated* with feeding.

Ivan Pavlov. Russian physiologist Ivan Pavlov (center, with white beard) demonstrates his apparatus for classical conditioning to students. How might the principles of classical conditioning explain the acquisition of excessive irrational fears that we refer to as phobias?

Because dogs don't normally salivate to the sound of bells, Pavlov reasoned that they had acquired this response. He called it a **conditioned response** (CR), or conditioned reflex, because it had been paired with what he called an **unconditioned stimulus** (US)—in this case, food—which naturally elicited salivation (see Figure 2.7). The salivation to food, an unlearned response, Pavlov called the **unconditioned response** (UR), and the bell, a previously neutral stimulus, he called the **conditioned stimulus** (CS).

Can you recognize examples of **classical conditioning** in your everyday life? Do you flinch in the waiting room at the sound of the dentist's drill? The sound of the drill may be a conditioned stimulus that elicits conditioned responses of fear and muscle tension.

Phobias or excessive fears may be acquired by classical conditioning. For instance, a person may develop a phobia for riding on elevators following a traumatic experience on an elevator. In this example, a previously neutral stimulus (elevator) becomes paired or associated with an aversive stimulus (trauma), which leads to the conditioned response (phobia).

conditioned response In classical conditioning, a learned response to a previously neutral stimulus.

unconditioned stimulus A stimulus that elicits an unlearned response.

unconditioned response An unlearned response.

conditioned stimulus A previously neutral stimulus that evokes a conditioned response after repeated pairings with an unconditioned stimulus that had previously evoked that response.

classical conditioning A form of learning in which a response to one stimulus can be made to occur to another stimulus by pairing or associating the two stimuli.

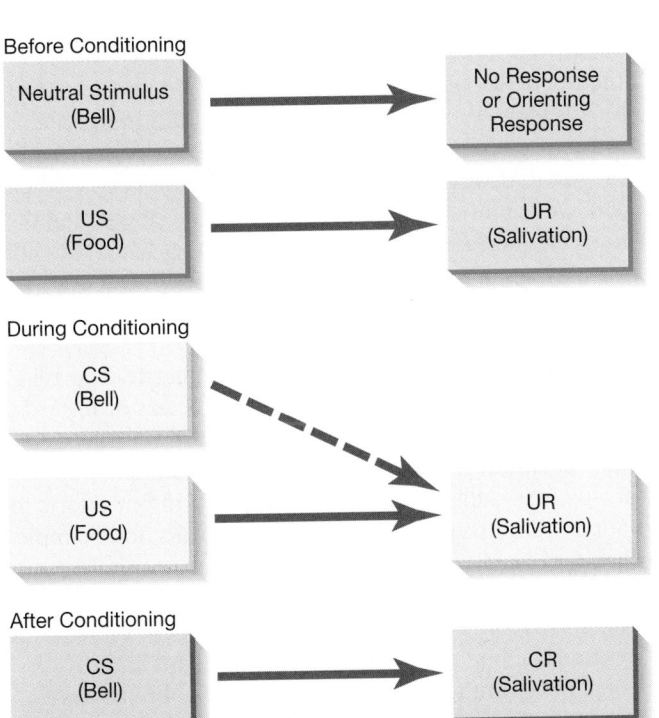

FIGURE 2.7 Schematic diagram of the process of classical conditioning. Before conditioning, food (an unconditioned stimulus, or US) placed on a dog's tongue will naturally elicit salivation (an unconditioned response, or UR). The bell, however, is a neutral stimulus that may elicit an orienting response but not salivation. During conditioning, the bell (the conditioned stimulus, or CS) is rung while food (the US) is placed on the dog's tongue. After several conditioning trials have occurred, the bell (the CS) will elicit salivation (the conditioned response, or CR) when it is rung, even though it is not accompanied by food (the US). The dog is said to have been conditioned, or to have learned to display the conditioned response (CR) in response to the conditioned stimulus (CS). Learning theorists have suggested that irrational excessive fears of harmless stimuli may be acquired through principles of classical conditioning.

Watson himself had demonstrated how a fear response could be acquired through classical conditioning. Together with his research assistant who was later to become his wife, Rosalie Rayner, Watson classically conditioned an 11-month-old boy, who is well known in the annals of psychology as "Little Albert," to develop a fear response to a white rat (Watson & Rayner, 1920). Prior to conditioning, the boy showed no fear of the rat and had actually reached out to stroke it. Then, as the boy reached for the animal, Watson banged a steel bar with a hammer just behind the boy's head, creating a loud, aversive sound. After repeated pairings of the jarring sound and the presence of the animal, Albert sure enough showed a conditioned response, displaying fear to the rat alone.

From the learning perspective, normal behavior involves responding adaptively to stimuli, including conditioned stimuli. After all, if we do not learn to be afraid of putting our hand too close to a hot stove after one or two experiences of being burned or nearly burned, we might repeatedly suffer unnecessary burns. On the other hand, acquiring inappropriate and maladaptive fears on the basis of conditioning may cripple our efforts to function in the world. Chapter 6 explains how conditioning may help explain anxiety disorders such as phobias and posttraumatic stress disorder.

Role of Operant Conditioning Classical conditioning can explain the development of simple, reflexive responses, such as salivating to cues associated with food, as well as the emotional response of fear to stimuli that have been paired with painful or aversive stimuli. But classical conditioning does not account for more complex behaviors, such as studying, working, socializing, or preparing meals. The behavioral psychologist B. F. Skinner (1938) called these types of complex behaviors *operant responses* because they operate on the environment to produce effects or consequences. In **operant conditioning,** responses are acquired and strengthened by their consequences.

We acquire responses or skills, such as raising our hand in class, that lead to **reinforcement.** Reinforcers are changes in the environment (stimuli) that increase the frequency of the preceding behavior.

Behaviors that lead to rewarding consequences are strengthened—that is, they are more likely to occur again. Over time, such behaviors become habits (Staddon & Cerutti, 2003). For example, you likely acquired the habit of raising your hand in class on the basis of experiences early in grade school when your teachers responded to you only if you first raised your hand.

Skinner identified two types of reinforcers. **Positive reinforcers,** which are commonly called *rewards*, boost the frequency of a behavior when they are introduced or presented. Most of Skinner's work focused on studying operant conditioning in animals, such as pigeons. If a pigeon gets food when it pecks a button, it will contine to peck a button until it has eaten its fill. If we get a friendly response from people when we hold the door open for them, we're more likely to develop the habit of opening the door for others. **Negative reinforcers** increase the frequency of behavior when they are *removed*. If picking up a crying child stops the crying, the behavior (picking up the child) is negatively reinforced (made stronger) by the removal of the negative reinforcer (the crying, an aversive stimulus).

Adaptive, normal behavior involves learning responses or skills that lead to reinforcement. We learn behaviors that allow us to obtain positive reinforcers or rewards, such as food, money, and approval, and that help us remove or avoid negative reinforcers, such as pain and disapproval. But if our early learning environments do not provide opportunities for learning new skills, we might be hampered in our efforts to develop the skills needed to obtain reinforcement. A lack of social skills, for example, may reduce our opportunities for social reinforcement (approval or praise from others), which may lead in turn to depression and social isolation. In Chapter 8, we examine links between changes in reinforcement levels and the development of depression. In Chapter 12, we examine how principles of reinforcement are incorporated in learning-based treatment programs to help people with schizophrenia develop more adaptive social behaviors.

---

operant conditioning A form of learning in which behavior is acquired and strengthened when it is reinforced.

reinforcement A stimulus or event that increases the frequency of the response that it follows.

positive reinforcers Reinforcers that, when introduced, increase the frequency of the preceding behavior.

negative reinforcers Reinforcers that, when removed, increase the frequency of the preceding behavior.

Punishment can be considered the flip side of reinforcement. Punishments are aversive stimuli that *decrease* the frequency of the behavior they follow. Punishment may take many forms, including physical punishment (spanking or use of other painful stimuli), removal of a reinforcing stimulus (turning off the TV), assessment of monetary penalties (parking tickets, etc.), taking away privileges ("You're grounded!"), or removal from a reinforcing environment ("time-out").

Before going further, let us distinguish between two terms that are often confused: *negative reinforcement* and *punishment.* The confusion arises from the fact that an aversive or painful stimulus can serve as either a negative reinforcer or a punishment, depending on the situation. With punishment, the *introduction* or application of the aversive or painful stimulus weakens the preceding behavior. With negative reinforcement, the removal of the aversive or painful stimulus strengthens the preceding behavior. A baby's crying can serve as a punishment (if it weakens the preceding behavior, such as turning your attention away from the baby) or a negative reinforcer (if it strengthens the behavior that leads to its removal, such as picking the baby up).

Punishment, especially physical punishment, may not eliminate undesirable behavior, although it may suppress it for the moment. The behavior may return when the punishment is withdrawn. Another limitation of punishment is that it does not lead to the development of more desirable alternative behaviors. It may also encourage people to withdraw from such learning situations. Punished children may cut classes, drop out of school, or run away. Moreover, punishment may generate anger and hostility rather than constructive learning and may cross the boundary into abuse, especially when it is repetitive and severe. Child abuse figures prominently in many abnormal behavior patterns, including some types of personality disorders (Chapter 13) and dissociative disorders (Chapter 7).

Psychologists recognize that reinforcement is more desirable than punishment. But rewarding good behavior requires paying attention to it, not just to misbehavior. Some children who develop conduct problems gain attention from others only when they misbehave. Consequently, other people may be inadvertently reinforcing these children for undesirable behavior. Learning theorists point out that adults need to teach children desirable behavior and regularly reinforce them for displaying it.

Let us now consider a contemporary model of learning, called *social-cognitive theory* (formerly called *social-learning theory*), which considers the role of cognitive factors in learning and behavior.

Social-Cognitive Theory **Social-cognitive theory** represents the contributions of theorists such as Albert Bandura (1925–), Julian B. Rotter (1916–), and Walter Mischel (1930–). Social-cognitive theorists expanded traditional learning theory by including roles for thinking, or cognition, and learning by observation, which is also called **modeling** (Bandura, 2004). A phobia for spiders, for example, may be learned by observing the fearful reactions of others in real life, on television, or in the movies.

Social-cognitive theorists believe that people have an impact on their environment, just as their environment has an impact on them (Bandura, 2001, 2004). Social-cognitive theorists agree with traditional behaviorists like Watson and Skinner that theories of human nature should be tied to observable behavior. However, they argue that factors *within* the person, such as **expectancies** and the values placed on particular goals, also need to be considered in explaining human behavior. For example, we will see in Chapter 9 that people who hold more positive expectancies about the effects of a drug are more likely to use the drug and to use larger quantities of the drug than are people with less positive expectancies.

Evaluating Learning Models Learning perspectives have spawned a model of therapy, called *behavior therapy* (also called *behavior modification*), that involves systematically applying learning principles to help people change their behavior (see Chapter 4). Behavior therapy techniques have helped people overcome a wide range of psychological problems, including phobias and other anxiety disorders, sexual

---

punishment Application of aversive or painful stimuli that reduces the frequency of the behavior it follows.

TRUTH or FICTION

Punishment does not eliminate undesirable behavior.

☑ **TRUE.** Punishment does not eliminate an undesirable behavior, but only suppresses it. The behavior may return when it is no longer punished.

social-cognitive theory A learning-based theory that emphasizes observational learning and incorporates roles for cognitive variables in determining behavior.

modeling Learning by observing and imitating the behavior of others.

expectancies Beliefs about expected outcomes.

Observational learning. According to social-cognitive theory, much human behavior is acquired through modeling, or observational learning.

self-actualization In humanistic psychology, the tendency to strive to become all that one is capable of being. The motive that drives one to reach one's full potential and express one's unique capabilities.

unconditional positive regard Valuing other people as having basic worth regardless of their behavior at a particular time.

conditional positive regard Valuing other people on the basis of whether their behavior meets one's approval.

Self-actualization. Humanistic theorists believe that there exists in each of us a drive toward self-actualization—to become all that we are capable of being. In the humanistic view, each of us, such as artist Geraldine Pitts, shown here with one of her paintings, is unique. No two people follow quite the same pathway toward self-actualization.

dysfunctions, and depression. Moreover, reinforcement-based programs are now widely used in helping parents learn better parenting skills and helping children learn in the classroom.

Critics contend that behaviorism alone cannot explain the richness of human behavior and that human experience cannot be reduced to observable responses. Many learning theorists, too—especially social-cognitive theorists—have been dissatisfied with the strict behavioristic view that environmental influences—rewards and punishments—mechanically control our behavior. Humans experience thoughts and dreams and formulate goals and aspirations; behaviorism does not seem to address much of what it means to be human. Social-cognitive theorists have broadened the scope of traditional behaviorism, but critics claim that social-cognitive theory places too little emphasis on genetic contributions to behavior and doesn't provide a full enough account of subjective experience, such as self-awareness and the flow of consciousness. As we'll see next, subjective experience takes center stage in humanistic models.

Humanistic Models

A "third force" in modern psychology emerged during the mid-20th century—humanistic psychology. American psychologists Carl Rogers (1902–1987) and Abraham Maslow (1908–1970) believed that people have an inborn tendency toward **self-actualization**—to strive to become all they are capable of being. Each of us possesses a singular cluster of traits and talents that gives us our own set of feelings and needs and our own perspective on life. By recognizing and accepting our genuine needs and feelings, by being true to ourselves, we live *authentically,* with meaning and purpose. We may not decide to act out every wish and fancy, but awareness of our authentic feelings and subjective experiences can help us make more meaningful choices.

To understand abnormal behavior, in the humanist's view, we need to understand the roadblocks that people encounter in striving for self-actualization and authenticity. To accomplish this, psychologists must learn to view the world from clients' own perspectives because clients' subjective views of their world lead them to interpret and evaluate their experiences in either self-enhancing or self-defeating ways. The humanistic viewpoint involves the attempt to understand the subjective experience of others, the stream of conscious experiences people have of "being in the world."

Humanistic Concepts of Abnormal Behavior Rogers held that abnormal behavior results from a distorted concept of the self. Parents can help children develop a positive self-concept by showing them **unconditional positive regard;** that is, by prizing them and showing them that they are worthy of love irrespective of their behavior at any given time. Parents may disapprove of a certain behavior but need to convey to their children that the behavior is undesirable, not the child. However, when parents show children **conditional positive regard**—accept them only when they behave in the way the parents want them to behave—the children may learn to disown all the thoughts, feelings, and behaviors their parents have rejected. Children will learn to develop *conditions of worth;* that is, they will think of themselves as worthwhile only if they behave in certain approved ways. For example, children whose parents seem to value them only when they are compliant may deny to themselves that they ever feel angry. Children in some families learn that it is unacceptable to hold their own ideas, lest they depart from their parents' views. Parental disapproval causes them to see themselves as "bad" and their feelings as wrong, selfish, or even evil. To retain their self-esteem, they may have to deny their genuine feelings or disown parts of themselves. The result can be a distorted *self-concept:* the children become strangers to their true selves.

Carl Rogers and Abraham Maslow. Two of the principal forces in humanistic psychology.

Rogers believed we become anxious when we sense that our feelings and ideas are inconsistent with a distorted self-concept that mirrors what others expect us to be—for example, if our parents expected us to be docile and obedient but we sense ourselves becoming angry or defiant. Because anxiety is unpleasant, we may deny to ourselves that these feelings and ideas even exist. And so the actualization of our authentic self is bridled. We channel our psychological energy not toward growth but toward continued denial and self-defense. Under such conditions, we cannot hope to perceive our genuine values or personal talents. The result is frustration and dissatisfaction, which set the stage for abnormal behavior.

According to the humanists, we cannot fulfill all the wishes of others and remain true to ourselves. This does not mean that self-actualization invariably leads to conflict. Rogers believed that people hurt one another or become antisocial in their behavior only when they are frustrated in their endeavors to reach their unique potentials. When parents and others treat children with love and tolerance for their differences, children, too, grow up to be loving—even if some of their values and preferences differ from their parents' choices.

In Rogers's view, the pathway to self-actualization involves a process of self-discovery and self-acceptance, of getting in touch with our true feelings, accepting them as our own, and acting in ways that genuinely reflect them. These are the goals of Rogers's method of psychotherapy, called *client-centered therapy* or *person-centered therapy.*

Evaluating Humanistic Models The strength of humanistic models in understanding abnormal behavior lies largely in their focus on conscious experience and their therapy methods that guide people toward self-discovery and self-acceptance. The humanistic movement brought concepts of free choice, inherent goodness, personal responsibility, and authenticity into modern psychology. Ironically, the primary strength of the humanistic approach—its focus on conscious experience—may also be its primary weakness. Conscious experience is private and subjective, which makes it difficult to quantify and study objectively. How can psychologists be certain they accurately perceive the world through the eyes of their clients? Humanists may counter that we should not shrink from the challenge of studying consciousness because to do so would deny an essential aspect of what it means to be human.

Critics also claim that the concept of self-actualization—which is so basic to Maslow and Rogers—cannot be proved or disproved. Like a psychic structure, a

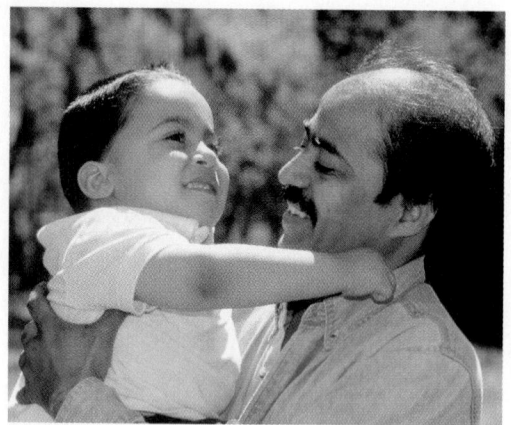

The makings of unconditional positive regard? Rogers believed that parents can help their children develop self-esteem and set them on the road toward self-actualization by showing them unconditional positive regard—prizing them on the basis of their inner worth, regardless of their behavior of the moment.

self-actualizing force is not directly measurable or observable. It is inferred from its supposed effects. Self-actualization also yields circular explanations for behavior. When someone is observed engaging in striving, what do we learn by attributing striving to a self-actualizing tendency? The source of the tendency remains a mystery. Similarly, when someone is observed *not* to be striving, what do we gain by attributing the lack of endeavor to a blocked or frustrated self-actualizing tendency? We must still determine the source of frustration.

Cognitive Models

The word *cognitive* derives from the Latin *cognitio,* meaning "knowledge." Cognitive theorists study the cognitions—the thoughts, beliefs, expectations, and attitudes—that accompany and may underlie abnormal behavior. They focus on how reality is colored by our expectations, attitudes, and so forth, and how inaccurate or biased processing of information about the world—and our places within it—can give rise to abnormal behavior. Cognitive theorists believe that our interpretations of the events in our lives, and not the events themselves, determine our emotional states.

Information-Processing Models Many cognitive psychologists apply concepts of computer science to human cognition. Computers process information to solve problems. Information is fed into the computer (encoded so that it can be accepted by the computer as input) and placed in *memory* while it is manipulated. You can also place the information permanently in *storage,* on a CD-ROM, a hard disk, or another device. Information-processing theorists discuss human cognition in terms such as *input* (based on perception), *manipulation* (interpreting or transforming information), *storage* (placing information in memory), *retrieval* (accessing information from memory), and *output* (acting on the information). Psychological disorders are seen as disturbances in these processes. The blocking or distortion of input or the faulty storage, retrieval, or manipulation of information can lead to distorted output (e.g., bizarre behavior). People with schizophrenia, for example, frequently jump from topic to topic in a disorganized fashion, which may reflect problems in retrieving and manipulating information. They also seem to have difficulty focusing their attention and filtering out extraneous stimuli, such as distracting noises, which may represent problems in the initial processing of input from their senses.

Manipulation of information may also be distorted by what cognitive therapists call *cognitive distortions,* or errors in thinking. For example, people who are depressed tend to develop an unduly negative view of their personal situation by exaggerating the importance of unfortunate events they experience, such as receiving a poor evaluation at work or being rejected by a dating partner. Cognitive theorists such as Albert Ellis (1913–2007) and Aaron Beck (1921–) have postulated that distorted or irrational thinking patterns can lead to emotional problems and maladaptive behavior.

Social-cognitive theorists, who share many basic ideas with the cognitive theorists, focus on the ways in which social information is encoded. For example, aggressive boys and adolescents are likely to incorrectly encode other people's behavior as threatening (see Chapter 14). They assume other people intend them ill when they do not. Aggressive children and adults may behave in ways that elicit coercive or hostile behavior from others, which serves to confirm their aggressive expectations (Meichenbaum, 1993). Rapists, especially date rapists, may misread a woman's expressed wishes. They may wrongly assume, for example, that the woman who says "no" really means yes and is merely playing "hard to get."

Albert Ellis Psychologist Albert Ellis (1977b, 1993), a prominent cognitive theorist, believed that troubling events in themselves do not lead to anxiety, depression, or disturbed behavior. Rather, it is the irrational beliefs we hold about unfortunate experiences that foster negative emotions and maladaptive behavior. Consider someone who loses a job and becomes anxious and despondent about it. It may seem that being fired is the direct cause of the person's misery, but the misery actually stems from the person's beliefs about the loss, not directly from the loss itself.

Ellis used an "ABC approach" to explain the causes of the misery. Being fired is an *activating event* (A). The ultimate outcome, or *consequence* (C), is emotional distress. But the activating event (A) and the consequences (C) are mediated by various *beliefs* (B). Some of these beliefs might include "That job was the major thing in my life," "What a useless washout I am," "My family will go hungry," "I'll never be able to find another job as good," "I can't do a thing about it." These exaggerated and irrational beliefs compound depression, nurture helplessness, and distract us from evaluating what to do.

The situation can be diagrammed like this:

ACTIVATING EVENT ⟶ BELIEF ⟶ CONSEQUENCES

Ellis pointed out that apprehension about the future and feelings of disappointment are perfectly normal when people face losses. However, the adoption of irrational beliefs leads people to catastrophize their disappointments, leading to profound distress and states of depression. Irrational beliefs—"I must have the love and approval of nearly everyone who is important to me or else I'm a worthless and unlovable person"—impair coping ability. In his later writings, Ellis emphasized the demanding nature of irrational or self-defeating beliefs—tendencies to impose "musts" and "shoulds" on ourselves (Ellis, 1993, 1997). Ellis noted that the desire for others' approval is understandable, but it is irrational to assume that one must have it to survive or to feel worthwhile. It would be marvelous to excel in everything we do, but it's absurd to demand it of ourselves or believe that we couldn't stand it if we failed to measure up. Ellis developed a model of therapy, called *rational-emotive behavior therapy* (REBT), to help people dispute these irrational beliefs and substitute more rational ones. Ellis admitted that childhood experiences are involved in the origins of irrational beliefs, but he maintained that it is repetition of these beliefs in the "here and now" that continues to make us miserable. For most people who are anxious and depressed, the key to greater happiness does not lie in discovering and liberating deep-seated conflicts, but in recognizing and modifying irrational self-demands.

Aaron Beck Another prominent cognitive theorist, psychiatrist Aaron Beck, proposes that depression may result from errors in thinking or "cognitive distortions," such as judging oneself entirely on the basis of one's flaws or failures and interpreting events in a negative light (through blue-colored glasses, as it were) (A. T. Beck et al., 1979). Beck stresses the four basic types of cognitive distortions that contribute to emotional distress:

1. *Selective abstraction.* People may *selectively abstract* (focus exclusively on) the parts of their experiences that reflect on their flaws and ignore evidence of their competencies. For example, a student may focus entirely on the one mediocre grade received on a math test and ignore all the higher grades.
2. *Overgeneralization.* People may *overgeneralize* from a few isolated experiences. For example, a person may believe he will never marry because he was rejected by a date.
3. *Magnification.* People may blow out of proportion, or *magnify,* the importance of unfortunate events. For example, a student may catastrophize a bad test grade by jumping to the conclusion that she will flunk out of college and her life will be ruined.
4. *Absolutist thinking.* Absolutist thinking is seeing the world in black-and-white terms, rather than in shades of gray. For example, an absolutist thinker may assume that a work evaluation less than a total rave is a total failure.

Like Ellis, Beck has developed a major model of therapy, called *cognitive therapy,* which focuses on helping individuals with psychological disorders identify and correct faulty ways of thinking.

Evaluating Cognitive Models As we'll see in later chapters, cognitive theorists have had an enormous impact on our understanding of abnormal behavior patterns and development of therapeutic approaches. The overlap between the learning-based and

Albert Ellis. Cognitive theorist Albert Ellis believed that negative emotions arise from the judgments we make about the events we experience, not from the events themselves.

TRUTH or FICTION

According to a leading cognitive theorist, emotional distress is caused by the beliefs people hold about negative life experiences, not by the experiences themselves.

☑ **TRUE.** Ellis believed that emotional distress is determined by the beliefs we hold about events we experience, not by the events themselves.

Aaron Beck. Aaron Beck, a leading cognitive theorist, focuses on how errors in thinking, or cognitive distortions, set the stage for negative emotional reactions in the face of unfortunate events.

cognitive approaches is best represented by the emergence of *cognitive-behavioral therapy* (CBT), a form of therapy that focuses on modifying self-defeating beliefs in addition to overt behaviors.

A major issue concerning cognitive perspectives is their range of applicability. Cognitive therapists have largely focused on emotional disorders relating to anxiety and depression. They have had less impact on the development of treatment approaches, or conceptual models, of more severe forms of disturbed behavior, such as schizophrenia. Moreover, in the case of depression, it remains unclear, as we see in Chapter 8, whether distorted thinking patterns are causes of depression or are themselves effects of depression.

THE SOCIOCULTURAL PERSPECTIVE

Does abnormal behavior arise from forces within the person, as the psychodynamic theorists propose, or from learned maladaptive behaviors, as the learning theorists suggest? Or, as the *sociocultural perspective* proposes, does a fuller accounting of abnormal behavior require that we consider the roles of social and cultural factors, including factors relating to ethnicity, gender, and social class? As we noted in Chapter 1, sociocultural theorists seek causes of abnormal behavior in the failures of society rather than in the person. Some of the more radical psychosocial theorists, like Thomas Szasz, even deny the existence of psychological disorders or mental illness. Szasz (1961, 2000) argues that "abnormal" is merely a label society attaches to people whose behavior deviates from accepted social norms. According to Szasz, this label is used to stigmatize social deviants.

Throughout the text we examine relationships between abnormal behavior patterns and sociocultural factors such as gender, ethnicity, and socioeconomic status. Here let us examine recent research on relationships between ethnicity and mental health.

Ethnicity and Mental Health

When Europeans first arrived on America's shores, the land was populated solely by Native Americans. By the time the United States achieved nationhood, the numbers of people of European descent were approaching those of Native Americans. During the 19th century, the nation became predominantly populated by people of European descent. Although Euro-Americans (also called European Americans or non-Hispanic White Americans) remain in the majority today, the nation is becoming increasingly ethnically diverse.

Presently, African Americans, whose ancestors were forcibly brought to this country and enslaved, represent about 12% of the population. Latinos (Hispanic Americans) account for about 13% of the population, whereas Asian Americans/Pacific Islanders account for about 4% and Native Americans for nearly 1%. The terms *Hispanic American* or *Latino(a)* refer to persons of Mexican, Puerto Rican, Cuban, or other Central and South American or Spanish origin.

The term *minority* is quickly becoming something of a misnomer, as traditionally identified minority groups now comprise the majority in many U.S. cities and in the nation's most populous state, California. White Euro-Americans are expected to become a minority in the nation at some point during this century. The largest anticipated increase among population groups will be among Latinos (Hispanic Americans), as their population ranks are expected to jump to about 24% by the year 2050. Latinos (Hispanics) now represent the nation's largest minority group, having surpassed African Americans for the first time in the nation's history.

Ethnic designations are general categories that encompass many different subgroups. For example, Latinos include Spanish-speaking people who may trace their heritage to Mexico, Puerto Rico, or Colombia. The population of Asian Americans/ Pacific Islanders includes people whose backgrounds and ancestries represent areas as diverse as China, Japan, Korea, Indochina, Thailand, the Philippines, India, and Pakistan. Asian Americans may perceive themselves as Filipino Americans or Chinese

Americans rather than Asian Americans per se. When considering racial or ethnic distinctions, we must take into account differences among cultural and ethnic subgroups within our own culture.

We also need to recognize that traditional racial or ethnic distinctions are becoming increasingly blurry as increasing numbers of people in the United States and Canada identify themselves as biracial, multiracial, or multiethnic. Individuals of multiracial background, such as golfer Tiger Woods, baseball player Derek Jeter, and singer Mariah Carey, cannot easily be classified according to traditional racial groupings. Nearly seven million U.S. residents described themselves as multiracial in the most recent population census (Schmitt, 2001a, 2001b). Young people today are twice as likely as their parents to consider themselves multiracial (Takahashi, 2001).

Given the increasing ethnic diversity of the population, researchers have begun to study ethnic group differences in the prevalence of psychological disorders. Knowing that a disorder disproportionately affects one group or another can help planners direct prevention and treatment programs to the groups that are most in need (Pole et al., 2005). Researchers recognize that income level or socioeconomic status must be considered when comparing rates of a given diagnosis across ethnic groups. We also need to account for differences among ethnic subgroups, such as differences among the various subgroups that comprise the Hispanic American and Asian American populations. We find, for example, higher levels of depression among Hispanic immigrants to the United States from Central America than from Mexico, even when considering differences in educational backgrounds (Salgado de Snyder, Cervantes, & Padilla, 1990).

We should be cautious—and think critically—when interpreting ethnic group differences in rates of diagnoses of psychological disorders. Might these differences reflect ethnic or racial differences, or differences in other factors on which groups may vary, such as socioeconomic level, living conditions, or cultural backgrounds?

A recent analysis of ethnic group differences in rates of mental disorders revealed an interesting pattern (Breslau et al., 2005). Using data from a nationally representative sample of adult Americans, investigators found that traditionally disadvantaged groups (non-Hispanic Black Americans and Hispanic Americans) had either significantly lower rates of psychological disorders or comparable rates, as compared to European Americans (non-Hispanic Whites) (see Figure 2.8). However, when the investigators looked at the persistence, or *chronicity*, of psychological disorders, they found that

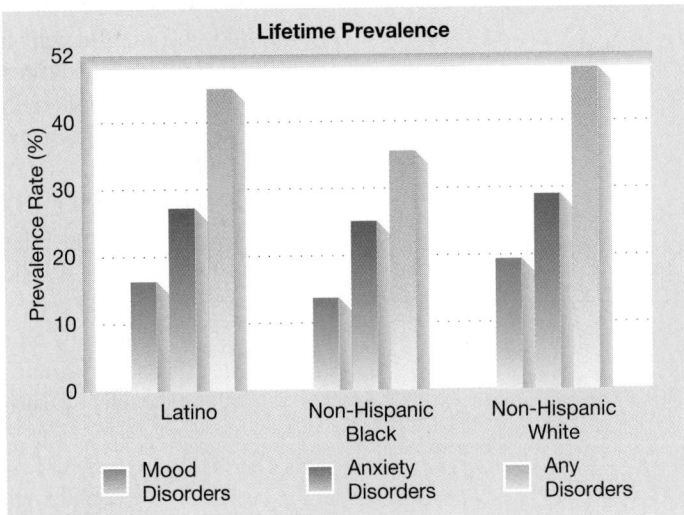

FIGURE 2.8 Ethnicity and psychological disorders in the United States.
We can see that European Americans (non-Hispanic Whites) tend to have higher prevalence rates of psychological disorders than either Hispanic Americans (Latinos) or (non-Hispanic) Black Americans. Though not all of these differences were statistically significant, in none of these comparisons were there significantly higher prevalence rates among Hispanic Americans and Black Americans than among European Americans.

Source: Breslau et al., 2005, based on data from the National Comordibity Survey (NCS).

TRUTH or FICTION

Hispanic Americans and Black Americans tended to experience more persistent mental disorders than European Americans.

What might we make of these findings on persistence of mental disorders? Additional analysis showed that differences in persistence were not a function of socioeconomic level. But might they reflect differences in access to quality care? The question needs to be addressed in further research, but it is conceivable that White European Americans benefit from better access to quality mental health care that shortens the length of psychological disorders they experience.

Native Americans are a traditionally disadvantaged minority group with high rates of mental disorders. They also happen to be among the most impoverished ethnic groups in both the United States and Canada. Native Americans suffer from a much greater prevalence of mental health problems than other ethnicities, most commonly alcohol dependence, posttraumatic stress disorder (PTSD), and depression (Beals et al., 2005). The rate of alcohol-related disorders among Native Americans is six times that of other Americans (Rabasca, 2000a). The death rate due to suicide among adolescents in the 10- to 14-year-old age range is about four times higher among Native Americans than among other ethnic groups. Male Native American adolescents and young adults have the highest suicide rates in the nation (USDHHS, 1999a).

Asian Americans typically show lower rates of psychological disorders than the general U.S. population (Chang, 2002). But there are exceptions. When you envision stereotypes such as hula dancing, luaus, and wide tropical beaches, you may assume that Native Hawaiians are a carefree people. Reality paints a different picture, however. One reason for studying the relationship between ethnicity and abnormal behavior is to debunk erroneous stereotypes. Native Hawaiians, like other Native American groups, are economically disadvantaged and suffer a disproportionate share of physical diseases and mental health problems. Native Hawaiians tend to die at a younger age than other residents of Hawaii, largely because they face an increased risk of serious diseases, including hypertension, cancer, and heart disease (Johnson et al., 2004). They also show increased rates of risk factors associated with these life-threatening diseases, such as smoking, alcohol abuse, and being overweight. Compared to other Hawaiians, Native Hawaiians also experience higher rates of mental health problems, including higher suicide rates among males, higher rates of alcoholism and drug abuse, and higher rates of antisocial behavior.

In addition to economic disadvantage, the mental health problems of Native Americans, including Native Hawaiians, may at least partly reflect alienation and disenfranchisement from the land and a way of life that resulted from colonization by European cultures (Rabasca, 2000a). Native peoples often attribute mental health problems, especially depression and alcoholism, to the collapse of their traditional culture brought about by colonization (Timpson et al., 1988). Researchers recount how a Native Canadian elder in northwestern Ontario explained depression in his people (Timpson et al., 1988, p. 6):

> Before the White Man came into our world we had our own way of worshipping the Creator. We had our own church and rituals. When hunting was good, people would gather together to give gratitude. This gave us close contact with the Creator. There were many different rituals depending on the tribe. People would dance in the hills and play drums to give recognition to the Great Spirit. It was like talking to the Creator and living daily with its spirit. Now people have lost this. They can't use these methods and have lost conscious contact with this high power. The more distant we are from the Creator the more complex things are because we have no sense of direction. We don't recognize where life is from.

The depression so common among indigenous or native peoples may reflect the loss of a relationship with the world that was based on maintaining harmony with nature. The description of the loss of this special relationship reminds us of the Western concept of alienation.

Whatever the underlying differences in psychopathology among ethnic groups, members of ethnic minority groups tend to underutilize mental health services compared to White European Americans (USDHHS, 1999a). Native Americans, for example, commonly seek help from traditional healers rather than mental health professionals (Beals et al., 2005). Members of other ethnic minority groups often turn to members of the clergy or to spiritualists. Those who do seek services are more likely to drop out prematurely from treatment. In Chapter 4 we consider barriers that limit the utilization of mental health services by various ethnic minority groups in our society.

Evaluating the Sociocultural Perspective

Lending support to the link between social class and psychological disturbance, a classic research study in New Haven, Connecticut, showed that people from the lower socioeconomic groups were more likely to be institutionalized for psychiatric problems (Hollingshead & Redlich, 1958). One reason may be that the poor have less access to private outpatient care.

An alternative view, the **social causation model,** holds that people from lower socioeconomic groups are at greater risk of severe behavior problems because living in poverty subjects them to a greater level of social stress than that faced by more well-to-do people (Costello et al., 2003; Wadsworth & Achenbach, 2005). Yet another view, the **downward drift hypothesis,** suggests that problem behaviors, such as alcoholism, lead people to drift downward in social status, thereby explaining the linkage between low socioeconomic status and severe behavior problems.

Investigators recently had an opportunity to put the social causation model to the test. They focused on mental health problems among children on a Native American (American Indian) reservation both before and after the introduction of a casino. The casino brought considerable wealth to the previously impoverished Indian community, helping many families to rise out of poverty. Prior to the casino, Indian children showed a high rate of problem behaviors and psychiatric symptoms of depression and anxiety. But four years after the money from the casino began to flow to the community, Indian children whose families were no longer below the poverty line showed a significant reduction in problem behaviors. However, levels of anxiety and depression were not reduced. This research lacked the experimental controls needed to firm up evidence of cause and effect, but it lends support to social causation model for at least some forms of problem behavior (Costello et al., 2003; Rutter, 2003).

Sociocultural theorists have focused much needed attention on the social stressors that can lead to abnormal behavior. Throughout the text we consider how sociocultural factors relating to gender, race, ethnicity, and lifestyle inform our understanding of abnormal behavior and our response to people deemed mentally ill. In Chapter 4, we consider how issues relating to race, culture, and ethnicity impact the therapeutic process.

THE BIOPSYCHOSOCIAL PERSPECTIVE

Contemporary views of abnormal behavior are informed by several different models or perspectives representing biological, psychological, and sociocultural perspectives. The fact that there are different ways of looking at the same phenomenon doesn't mean that one model must be right and the others wrong. No one theoretical perspective accounts for the many complex forms of abnormal behavior we encounter in this text. Each perspective contributes something to our understanding, but none offers a complete view. Table 2.3 presents an overview of these perspectives.

The final perspective we discuss, the *biopsychosocial perspective,* takes a broader view of abnormal behavior than the other models. It examines the contributions of multiple factors representing biological, psychological, and sociocultural domains, as well as their interactions, in the development psychological disorders. As we shall see in later chapters, most psychological disorders involve multiple causes, as well as the interactions among them. We are only beginning to unravel the complex web of factors that underlie many of the disorders we discuss in this text. Even disorders that are primarily biological may be influenced by psychological factors, or vice-versa. For example,

social causation model The belief that social stressors, such as poverty, account for the greater risk of severe psychological disorders among people of lower socioeconomic status.

downward drift hypothesis The theory that explains the linkage between low socioeconomic status and behavior problems by suggesting that problem behaviors lead people to drift downward in social status.

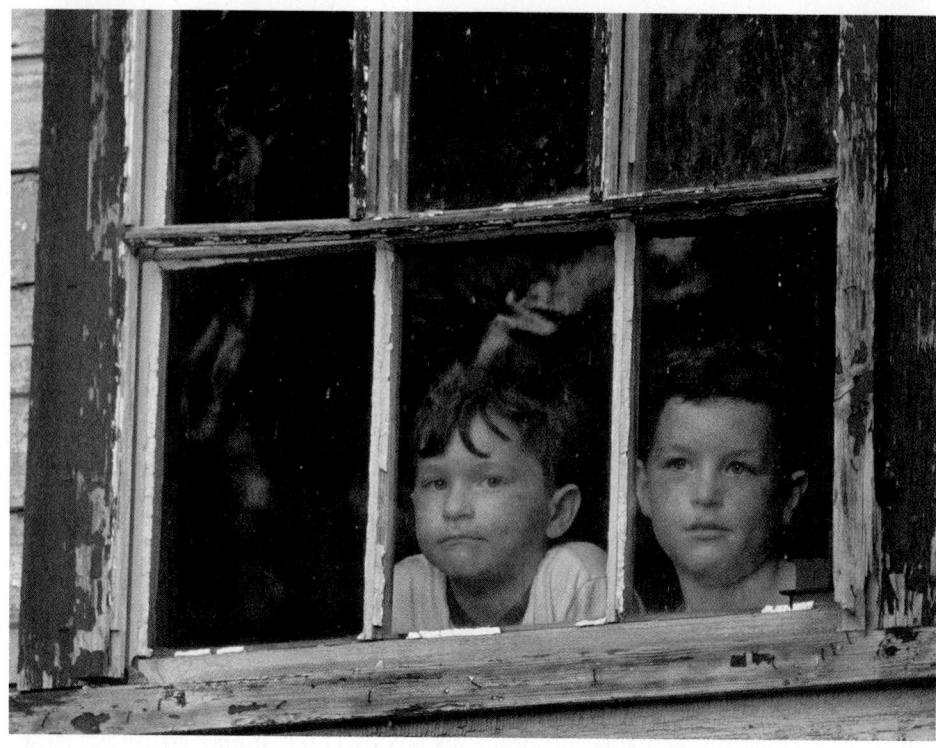

Roots of abnormal behavior? Sociocultural theorists believe that the roots of abnormal behavior are found not in the individual but in the social ills of society, such as poverty, social decay, discrimination based on race and gender, and lack of economic opportunity.

some phobias may be learned behaviors that are acquired through experiences in which particular objects became associated with traumatic or painful experiences (see Chapter 6). Yet, some people may inherit certain traits that make them susceptible to the development of acquired or conditioned phobias.

Here we take a closer look at one of the leading examples of a biopsychosocial model, the *diathesis–stress model*, which posits that psychological disorders arise from an interaction of vulnerability factors (primarily biological in nature) and stressful life experiences.

The Diathesis-Stress Model

The **diathesis–stress model** was originally developed as a framework for understanding schizophrenia (see Chapter 12). It has since been applied to other psychological disorders, including depression (Lewinsohn, Joiner, & Rohde, 2001). According to this view, psychological disorders, such as schizophrenia, arise from a combination or interaction of a **diathesis** (vulnerability or predisposition, usually genetic in nature) with life stress (see Figure 2.9). Whether the disorder actually develops depends on the type and severity of stressors the person experiences in life. The life stressors that may contribute to the development of disorders include birth complications, trauma or serious illness in childhood, childhood sexual or physical abuse, prolonged unemployment, loss of loved ones, or significant medical problems (Jablensky et al., 2005).

In some cases, people with a diathesis for a particular disorder, say schizophrenia, will remain free of the disorder or will develop a milder form of the disorder if the level of stress in their lives remains low or if they develop effective coping responses for handling the stress they encounter. However, the stronger the diathesis, the less stress is generally needed to trigger the disorder. In some cases the diathesis may be so strong that the disorder develops even under the most benign life circumstances.

Not all diatheses involve a biological vulnerability. A psychological diathesis may increase vulnerability to psychological disorders in the face of stress, such as maladaptive personality traits and dysfunctional thinking patterns that increase the risk of

diathesis–stress model A model that posits that abnormal behavior problems involve the interaction of a vulnerability or predisposition and stressful life events or experiences.

diathesis A vulnerability or predisposition to a particular disorder.

TABLE 2.3

Perspectives on Abnormal Behavior

	Model	Focus	Key Questions
Biological Perspective	Medical model	Biological underpinnings of abnormal behavior	What role is played by neurotransmitters in abnormal behavior? By genetics? By brain abnormalities?
Psychological Perspective	Psychodynamic models	Unconscious conflicts and motives underlying abnormal behavior	How do particular symptoms represent or symbolize unconscious conflicts? What are the childhood roots of a person's problem?
	Learning models	Learning experiences that shape the development of abnormal behavior	How are abnormal patterns of behavior learned? What role does the environment play in explaining abnormal behavior?
	Humanistic models	Roadblocks that block self-awareness and self-acceptance	How do a person's emotional problems reflect a distorted self-image? What roadblocks did the person encounter in the path toward self-acceptance and self-realization?
	Cognitive models	Faulty thinking underlying abnormal behavior	What styles of thinking characterize people with particular types of psychological disorders? What role do personal beliefs, thoughts, and ways of interpreting events play in the development of abnormal behavior patterns?
Sociocultural Perspective		Social ills, such as poverty, racism, and prolonged unemployment, contributing to the development of abnormal behavior; relationships between abnormal behavior and ethnicity, gender, culture, and socioeconomic level	What relationships exist between social-class status and risks of psychological disorders? Are there gender or ethnic group differences in various disorders? How are these explained? What are the effects of stigmatization of people who are labeled mentally ill?
Biopsychosocial Perspective		Interactions of biological, psychological, and sociocultural factors in the development of abnormal behavior	How might genetic or other factors predispose individuals to psychological disorders in the face of life stress? How do biological, psychological, and sociocultural factors interact in the development of complex patterns of abnormal behavior?

Source: From Nevid, J. S., *Psychology: Concepts and Applications.* Second Edition (Boston: Houghton Mifflin, 2007), p. 56. Reprinted by permission.

developing a particular disorder in the face of stress (Harris & Curtin, 2002; Zvolensky et al., 2005). For example, the tendency to blame oneself for negative life events, such as a divorce or job loss, may put a person at greater risk of developing depression when such events occur (see Chapter 8) (Just, Abramson, & Alloy, 2001).

Evaluating the Biopsychosocial Perspective

The strength of the biopsychosocial model—its very complexity—may also be its greatest weakness. The model holds the view that with few exceptions, psychological disorders or other patterns of abnormal behavior are complex phenomena that arise from multiple causes. We cannot pinpoint any one cause that leads to the development of schizophrenia or panic disorder, for example. In addition, different people may develop the same disorder based on different sets of causal influences. Yet the complexity of understanding the interplay of underlying causes of abnormal behavior patterns should not deter us from the effort. The accumulation of a body of knowledge is a continuing process. We know a great deal more today than we did a few short years ago. We will surely know more in the years ahead.

FIGURE 2.9 The diathesis–stress model.

The Case of Jessica—A Final Word

Let us briefly return to the case of Jessica, the young woman with bulimia whom we introduced at the beginning of the chapter. The biopsychosocial model leads us to consider the biological, psychological, and sociocultural factors that might account for bulimic behavior. As we shall consider further in Chapter 10, evidence points to biological influences, such as genetic factors and irregularities in neurotransmitter activity in the brain. Evidence also points to contributions of sociocultural factors, such as the social pressures imposed on young women in our society to adhere to unrealistic standards of thinness, as well as psychological influences such as body dissatisfaction, cognitive factors such as thinking in perfectionistic and dichotomous ("black or white") terms, and underlying emotional and interpersonal problems. In all likelihood, multiple factors interact in leading to bulimia and other eating disorders. For example, we might apply the diathesis–stress model to frame a potential causal model of bulimia. From this perspective, we can propose that a genetic predisposition (diathesis) affecting the regulation of neurotransmitters in the brain interacts in some cases with stress in the form of social and family pressures, leading to the development of eating disorders.

We will return to consider these causal influences in Chapter 10. For now, let us simply note that psychological disorders such as bulimia are complex phenomena that are best approached by considering the contributions and interactions of multiple factors.

SUMMING UP

The Biological Perspective

How is the nervous system organized? The nervous system consists of two major parts, the central nervous system and the peripheral nervous system. The central nervous system consists of the brain and spinal cord. The peripheral nervous system consists of two major divisions, the somatic nervous system, which transmits messages between the central nervous system and the sense organs and muscles, and the autonomic nervous system, which controls involuntary bodily processes. The autonomic nervous system has two branches or subdivisions, the sympathetic and the parasympathetic. The nervous system is composed of neurons, nerve cells that communicate with one another through chemical messengers, called neurotransmitters, that transmit nerve impulses across the tiny gaps, or synapses, between neurons.

What are the biological underpinnings of abnormal behavior?

Biological factors such as disturbances in neurotransmitter functioning in the brain, heredity, and underlying brain abnormalities are implicated in the development of abnormal behavior.

The Psychological Perspective

What are the major psychological models of abnormal behavior?
Psychodynamic perspectives reflect the views of Freud and his followers, who believed that abnormal behavior stemmed from psychological causes based on underlying psychic forces within the personality. Learning theorists posit that the principles of learning can be used to explain both abnormal and normal

behavior. Humanistic theorists believe it is important to understand the obstacles that people encounter as they strive toward self-actualization and authenticity. Cognitive theorists focus on the role of distorted and self-defeating thinking in explaining abnormal behavior.

The Sociocultural Perspective

What is the basic idea underlying the sociocultural perspective on abnormal behavior? Sociocultural theorists believe we need to broaden our outlook on abnormal behavior by taking into account the role of social ills, including poverty, racism, and lack of opportunity, in the development of abnormal behavior patterns.

The Biopsychosocial Perspective

What is the distinguishing feature of the biopsychosocial perspective? The biopsychosocial perspective seeks an understanding of abnormal behavior based on the interplay of biological, psychological, and sociocultural factors.

What is the diathesis–stress model? The diathesis–stress model holds that a person may have a predisposition, or diathesis, for a particular disorder, but whether the disorder actually develops depends on the interaction of the diathesis with stress-inducing life experiences.

KEY TERMS

neurons *(p. 38)*
dendrites *(p. 38)*
axon *(p. 38)*
terminals *(p. 38)*
neurotransmitters *(p. 38)*
synapse *(p. 38)*
receptor site *(p. 40)*
central nervous system *(p. 40)*
peripheral nervous system *(p. 40)*
medulla *(p. 41)*
pons *(p. 41)*
cerebellum *(p. 41)*
reticular activating system *(p. 41)*
thalamus *(p. 42)*
hypothalamus *(p. 42)*
limbic system *(p. 42)*
basal ganglia *(p. 42)*
cerebrum *(p. 42)*
cerebral cortex *(p. 42)*
somatic nervous system *(p. 43)*

autonomic nervous system *(p. 43)*
sympathetic *(p. 43)*
parasympathetic *(p. 43)*
psychoanalytic theory *(p. 45)*
conscious *(p. 45)*
preconscious *(p. 45)*
unconscious *(p. 45)*
id *(p. 46)*
pleasure principle *(p. 46)*
ego *(p. 46)*
reality principle *(p. 46)*
superego *(p. 46)*
defense mechanisms *(p. 46)*
fixation *(p. 48)*
archetypes *(p. 49)*
ego psychology *(p. 49)*
object-relations theory *(p. 50)*
psychosis *(p. 51)*
behaviorism *(p. 52)*
conditioned response *(p. 53)*

unconditioned stimulus *(p. 53)*
unconditioned response *(p. 53)*
conditioned stimulus *(p. 53)*
classical conditioning *(p. 53)*
operant conditioning *(p. 54)*
reinforcement *(p. 54)*
positive reinforcers *(p. 54)*
negative reinforcers *(p. 54)*
punishment *(p. 55)*
social-cognitive theory *(p. 55)*
modeling *(p. 55)*
expectancies *(p. 55)*
self-actualization *(p. 56)*
unconditional positive regard *(p. 56)*
conditional positive regard *(p. 56)*
social causation model *(p. 63)*
downward drift hypothesis *(p. 63)*
diathesis–stress model *(p. 64)*
diathesis *(p. 64)*

MEDIA TOOLS

A variety of digital and online learning tools are available to enrich your learning experience and help you succeed in the course. These resources include:

- **MyPsychLab,** an online learning system for your course in abnormal psychology that allows you to test your mastery of concepts in the book by using chapter-by-chapter diagnostic tests. Results from the diagnostic tests help you build a customized study plan. To access **MyPsychLab,** visit www.prenhall.com/mypsychlab and follow the instructions on the site.

- **"SPEAKING OUT" PATIENT INTERVIEWS,** a set of video case examples of actual patients you can access on the companion

CD-ROM included with the text. Icons in the margins of the chapter highlight the video case examples included on the CD-ROM.

- **COMPANION WEB SITE,** an online study center that offers computer-scored quizzes you can use to test your knowledge, along with other study tools and links to related sites to enhance your learning of abnormal psychology. To access the companion web site, visit www.prenhall.com/nevid and use the various tabs and links on the site to access these learning resources.

Classification and Assessment of Abnormal Behavior

CHAPTER OUTLINE

HOW ARE ABNORMAL BEHAVIOR PATTERNS CLASSIFIED? 70–77

The *DSM* and Models of Abnormal Behavior

STANDARDS OF ASSESSMENT 77–80

Reliability
Validity

METHODS OF ASSESSMENT 80–99

The Clinical Interview
Computerized Interviews
Psychological Tests
Neuropsychological Assessment
Behavioral Assessment

Cognitive Assessment
Physiological Measurement

SOCIOCULTURAL AND ETHNIC FACTORS IN ASSESSMENT 99–100

SUMMING UP 100–101

"I"

"Jerry Has a Panic Attack on the Interstate"

Interviewer: Can you tell me a bit about what it was that brought you to the clinic?

Jerry: Well, . . . after the first of the year, I started getting these panic attacks. I didn't know what the panic attack was.

Interviewer: Well, what was it that you experienced?

Jerry: Uhm, the heart beating, racing . . .

Interviewer: Your heart started to race on you.

Jerry: And then uh, I couldn't be in one place, maybe a movie, or a church . . . things would be closing in on me and I'd have to get up and leave.

Interviewer: The first time that it happened to you, can you remember that?

Jerry: Uhm, yeah I was . . .

Interviewer: Take me through that, what you experienced.

Jerry: I was driving on an interstate and, oh I might've been on maybe 10 or 15 minutes.

Interviewer: Uh huh.

Jerry: All of a sudden I got this fear. I started to . . . uh race.

Interviewer: So you noticed you were frightened?

Jerry: Yes.

Interviewer: Your heart was racing and you were perspiring. What else?

Jerry: Perspiring and uh, I was afraid of driving anymore on that interstate for the fear that I would either pull into a car head on, so uhm, I just, I just couldn't function. I just couldn't drive.

Interviewer: What did you do?

Jerry: I pulled, uh well at the nearest exit. I just got off . . . uh stopped and, I had never experienced anything like that before.

Interviewer: That was just a . . .

Jerry: Out of the clear blue . . .

Interviewer: Out of the clear blue? And what'd you think was going on?

Jerry: I had no idea.

Interviewer: You just knew you were . . .

Jerry: I thought maybe I was having a heart attack.

Interviewer: Okay.

Source: Exerpted from "Panic Disorder: The Case of Jerry," found on the *Videos in Abnormal Psychology* CD-ROM that accompanies this textbook.

JERRY BEGINS TO TELL HIS STORY, GUIDED BY THE INTERVIEWER. PSYCHOLOGISTS AND OTHER mental health professionals use clinical interviews and a variety of other means to assess abnormal behavior, including psychological testing, behavioral assessment, and physiological monitoring. The clinical interview is an important way of assessing abnormal behavior and arriving at a diagnostic impression—in this case, panic disorder. The clinician matches the presenting problems and associated features with a set of diagnostic criteria in forming a diagnostic impression.

The diagnosis of psychological or mental disorders represents a way of classifying patterns of abnormal behavior on the basis of their common features or symptoms. Abnormal behavior has been classified since ancient times. Hippocrates classified abnormal behaviors according to his theory of *humors* (vital bodily fluids). Although his theory proved to be flawed, Hippocrates' classification of some types of mental health problems generally correspond to diagnostic categories we use today. His description of melancholia, for example, is similar to our current conception of depression.

During the Middle Ages some "authorities" classified abnormal behaviors into two groups, those that resulted from demonic possession and those due to natural causes.

The 19th-century German psychiatrist Emil Kraepelin was the first modern theorist to develop a comprehensive model of classification based on the distinctive features, or symptoms, associated with abnormal behavior patterns (see Chapter 1). The most commonly used classification system today is largely an outgrowth and extension of Kraepelin's work: the *Diagnostic and Statistical Manual of Mental Disorders (DSM),* published by the American Psychiatric Association.

Why is it important to classify abnormal behavior? For one thing, classification is the core of science. Without labeling and organizing patterns of abnormal behavior, researchers could not communicate their findings to one another, and progress toward understanding these disorders would come to a halt. Moreover, important decisions are made on the basis of classification. Certain psychological disorders respond better to one therapy than another or to one drug than another. Classification also helps clinicians predict behavior: schizophrenia, for example, follows a more or less predictable course. Finally, classification helps researchers identify populations with similar patterns of abnormal behavior. By classifying groups of people as depressed, for example, researchers might be able to identify common factors that help explain the origins of depression.

This chapter reviews the classification and assessment of abnormal behavior, beginning with the *DSM*.

HOW ARE ABNORMAL BEHAVIOR PATTERNS CLASSIFIED?

The *DSM* was introduced in 1952. The latest version, published in 2000, is the *DSM-IV-TR,* the Text Revision (TR) of the Fourth Edition (*DSM-IV*) (APA, 2000). Another common system of classification, published by the World Health Organization, is used mainly for compiling statistics on the worldwide occurrence of disorders: the *International Statistical Classification of Diseases and Related Health Problems (ICD),* which is now in its tenth revision (the *ICD*-10). The *DSM-IV* is compatible with the *ICD,* so that *DSM* diagnoses could be coded in the *ICD* system as well. Thus the two systems can be used to share information about the prevalences and characteristics of particular disorders. The *DSM* has been widely adopted by mental health professionals. However, many psychologists and other professionals criticize the *DSM* on several grounds, such as relying too strongly on the medical model. Our focus on the *DSM* reflects recognition of its widespread use, not an endorsement.

In the *DSM,* abnormal behavior patterns are classified as "mental disorders." *Mental disorders* involve either emotional distress (typically depression or anxiety), significantly impaired functioning (difficulty meeting responsibilities at work, in the family, or in society at large), or behavior that places people at risk for personal suffering, pain, disability, or death (e.g., suicide attempts, repeated use of harmful drugs).

Let us also note that a behavior pattern that represents an expected or culturally appropriate response to a stressful event, such as signs of bereavement or grief following the death of a loved one, is not considered disordered within the *DSM,* even if behavior is significantly impaired. If a person's behavior remains significantly impaired over an extended period of time, however, a diagnosis of a mental disorder might become appropriate.

The *DSM* and Models of Abnormal Behavior

The *DSM* system, like the medical model, treats abnormal behaviors as signs or symptoms of underlying disorders or pathologies. However, the *DSM* does not assume that abnormal behaviors necessarily reflect biological causes or defects. It recognizes that the causes of most mental disorders remain uncertain: Some disorders may have purely biological causes, whereas others may have psychological causes. Still others, probably most, are best explained within a multifactorial model that takes into account the interaction of biological, psychological, social (socioeconomic, sociocultural, and ethnic), and physical environmental factors.

TABLE 3.1

Sample Diagnostic Criteria for Generalized Anxiety Disorder

1. Occurrence of excessive anxiety and worry on most days during a period of 6 months or longer.
2. Anxiety and worry are not limited to one or a few concerns or events.
3. Difficulty controlling feelings of worry.
4. The presence of a number of features associated with anxiety and worry, such as the following:
   a. experiencing restlessness or feelings of edginess
   b. becoming easily fatigued
   c. having difficulty concentrating or finding one's mind going blank
   d. feeling irritable
   e. having states of muscle tension
   f. having difficulty falling asleep or remaining asleep or having restless, unsatisfying sleep
5. Experiencing emotional distress or impairment in social, occupational, or other areas of functioning as the result of anxiety, worry, or related physical symptoms.
6. Worry or anxiety is not accounted for by the features of another disorder.
7. The disturbance does not result from the use of a drug of abuse or medication or a general medical condition and does not occur only in the context of another disorder.

Source: Adapted from *DSM-IV-TR* (APA, 2000).

The authors of the *DSM* recognize that their use of the term *mental disorder* is problematic because it perpetuates a long-standing but dubious distinction between mental and physical disorders (American Psychiatric Association, 1994, 2000). They point out that there is much that is "physical" in "mental" disorders and much that is "mental" in "physical" disorders. The diagnostic manual continues to use the term *mental disorder* because its developers have not been able to agree on an appropriate substitute. In this text we use the term *psychological disorder* in place of *mental disorder* because we feel it is more appropriate to place the study of abnormal behavior more squarely within a psychological context. Moreover, the term *psychological* has the advantage of encompassing behavioral patterns as well as strictly "mental" experiences, such as emotions, thoughts, beliefs, and attitudes.

We should also recognize that the *DSM* is used to classify disorders, not people. Rather than classify someone as a *schizophrenic* or a *depressive*, we refer to *an individual with schizophrenia* or *a person with major depression.* This difference in terminology is not simply a matter of semantics. To label someone a schizophrenic carries an unfortunate and stigmatizing implication that a person's identity is defined by the disorder he or she has.

Features of the *DSM* The *DSM* is descriptive, not explanatory. It describes the diagnostic features—or, in medical terms, symptoms—of abnormal behaviors; it does not attempt to explain their origins or adopt any particular theoretical framework, such as psychodynamic or learning theory. Using the *DSM* classification system, the clinician arrives at a diagnosis by matching a client's behaviors with the criteria that define particular patterns of abnormal behavior ("mental disorders"). Table 3.1 shows the diagnostic criteria for generalized anxiety disorder.

Abnormal behavior patterns are categorized according to the features they share. For example, abnormal behavior patterns chiefly characterized by anxiety, such as panic disorder or generalized anxiety disorder (see Table 3.1), are classified as anxiety disorders. Behaviors chiefly characterized by disruptions in mood are categorized as mood disorders. The *DSM* recommends that clinicians assess an individual's mental state according to five factors, or axes. Together the five axes provide a broad range of information about the individual's functioning, not just a diagnosis (see Table 3.2). The system contains the following axes.

1. *Axis I: Clinical Disorders and Other Conditions That May Be a Focus of Clinical Attention.* This axis incorporates a wide range of clinical syndromes, including anxiety disorders, mood disorders, schizophrenia and other psychotic disorders,

TABLE 3.2

The Multiaxial Classification System of the *DSM-IV-TR*

Axis	Type of Information	Brief Description
Axis I	Clinical disorders	The patterns of abnormal behavior ("mental disorders") that impair functioning and are stressful to the individual.
	Other conditions that may be a focus of clinical attention	Other problems that may be the focus of diagnosis or treatment but do not constitute mental disorders, such as academic, vocational, or social problems, and psychological factors that affect medical conditions (such as delayed recovery from surgery due to depressive symptoms).
Axis II	Personality disorders	Personality disorders involve excessively rigid, enduring, and maladaptive ways of relating to others and adjusting to external demands.
	Mental retardation	Mental retardation involves a delay or impairment in the development of intellectual and adaptive abilities.
Axis III	General medical conditions	Chronic and acute illnesses and medical conditions that are important to the understanding or treatment of the psychological disorder or that play a direct role in causing the psychological disorder.
Axis IV	Psychosocial and environmental problems	Problems in the social or physical environment that affect the diagnosis, treatment, and outcome of psychological disorders.
Axis V	Global assessment of functioning	Overall judgment of current functioning with respect to psychological, social, and occupational functioning; the clinician may also rate the highest level of functioning occurring for at least a few months during the past year.

Source: Adapted from the *DSM-IV-TR* (APA, 2000).

adjustment disorders, and disorders usually first diagnosed during infancy, childhood, or adolescence (except for mental retardation, which is coded on Axis II). Axis I also includes relationship problems, academic or occupational problems, and bereavement, conditions that may be the focus of diagnosis and treatment but that do not in themselves constitute definable psychological disorders. Also coded on Axis I are psychological factors that affect medical conditions, such as anxiety that exacerbates an asthmatic condition or depressive symptoms that delay recovery from surgery.

2. *Axis II: Personality Disorders and Mental Retardation.* Personality disorders are enduring and rigid patterns of maladaptive behavior that typically impair relationships with others and social functioning. These include antisocial, paranoid, narcissistic, and borderline personality disorders (see Chapter 13). Mental retardation, which is also coded on Axis II, involves pervasive intellectual impairment (see Chapter 14).

   People may be given either Axis I or Axis II diagnoses or a combination of the two when both apply. For example, a person may receive a diagnosis of an anxiety disorder (Axis I) *and* a second diagnosis of a personality disorder (Axis II).

3. *Axis III: General Medical Conditions.* All medical conditions and diseases that may be important to the understanding or treatment of an individual's mental disorders are coded on Axis III. For example, if *hypothyroidism* were a direct cause of an individual's mood disorder (such as major depression), it would be coded under Axis III. Medical conditions that affect the understanding or treatment of a mental disorder (but that are not direct causes of the disorder) are also listed on Axis III. For instance, the presence of a heart condition may determine whether a particular course of drug therapy should be used with a depressed person.

4. *Axis IV: Psychosocial and Environmental Problems.* The psychosocial and environmental problems that affect the diagnosis, treatment, or outcome of a mental disorder are placed on Axis IV. These include job loss, marital separation or divorce, homelessness or inadequate housing, lack of social support, the death or loss of a friend, or

TABLE 3.3

Psychosocial and Environmental Problems

Problem Categories	Examples
Problems with primary support group	Death of family members; health problems of family members; marital disruption in the form of separation, divorce, or estrangement; sexual or physical abuse within the family; child neglect; birth of a sibling
Problems related to the social environment	Death or loss of a friend; social isolation or living alone; difficulties adjusting to a new culture (acculturation); discrimination; adjustment to transitions occurring during the life cycle, such as retirement
Educational problems	Illiteracy; academic difficulties; problems with teachers or classmates; inadequate or impoverished school environment
Occupational problems	Work-related problems including stressful workloads and problems with bosses or coworkers; changes in employment; job dissatisfaction; threat of loss of job; unemployment
Housing problems	Inadequate housing or homelessness; living in an unsafe neighborhood; problems with neighbors or landlord
Economic problems	Financial hardships or extreme poverty; inadequate welfare support
Problems with access to health care services	Inadequate health care services or availability of health insurance; difficulties with transportation to health care facilities
Problems related to interaction with the legal system/crime	Arrest or imprisonment; becoming involved in a lawsuit or trial; being a victim of crime
Other psychosocial problems	Natural or human-made disasters; war or other hostilities; problems with caregivers outside the family, such as counselors, social workers, and physicians; lack of availability of social service agencies

Source: Adapted from the *DSM-IV-TR* (APA, 2000).

exposure to war or other disasters. Some positive life events, such as a job promotion, may also be listed on Axis IV, but only when they create problems for the individual, such as difficulties adapting to a new job. Table 3.3 lists other examples from this axis.

5. *Axis V: Global Assessment of Functioning.* The clinician rates the client's current level of psychological, social, and occupational functioning using a scale similar to that shown in Table 3.4. The clinician may also indicate the highest level of functioning achieved for at least a few months during the preceding year. The level of current functioning indicates the current need for treatment or intensity of care. The level of highest functioning is suggestive of the level of functioning that might be restored.

Table 3.5 shows an example of a diagnosis in the *DSM* multiaxial system for a hypothetical case. The person receives two diagnoses, an Axis I diagnosis of generalized anxiety disorder (discussed in Chapter 6) and an Axis II diagnosis of dependent personality disorder (discussed in Chapter 13). The person also has a medical disorder (hypertension) and several psychosocial/environmental problems, as noted by the listing on Axis IV of marital separation and unemployment. The clinician also gives the person an overall rating of 62 on the level of functioning scale (GAF) on Axis V, which indicates that although the person is presenting with a mild level of symptoms or impaired functioning, he or she is functioning fairly well.

Culture-Bound Syndromes Some patterns of abnormal behavior, called **culture-bound syndromes,** occur in some cultures but are rare or unknown in others.

Culture-bound syndromes may reflect exaggerated forms of common folk superstitions and belief patterns within a particular culture. For example, the psychiatric disorder *taijin-kyofu-sho* (TKS) is common among young men in Japan but rare elsewhere. The disorder is characterized by excessive fear of embarrassing or offending other people (Nakamura et al., 2002). People with TKS may dread blushing in front of

culture-bound syndromes Patterns of abnormal behavior found within only one or a few cultures.

TABLE 3.4

Global Assessment of Functioning (GAF) Scale

Code	Severity of Symptoms	Examples
91–100	Superior functioning across a wide variety of activities of daily life	Lacks symptoms Handles life problems without them "getting out of hand"
81–90	Absent or minimal symptoms, no more than everyday problems or concerns	Mild anxiety before exams Occasional argument with family members
71–80	Transient and predictable reactions to stressful events, OR no more than slight impairment in functioning	Difficulty concentrating after argument with family Temporarily falls behind in schoolwork
61–70	Some mild symptoms, OR some difficulty in social, occupational, or school functioning, but functioning pretty well	Feels down, mild insomnia Occasional truancy or theft within household
51–60	Moderate symptoms, OR moderate difficulties in social, occupational, or school functioning	Occasional panic attacks Few friends, conflicts with coworkers
41–50	Serious symptoms, OR any serious impairment in social, occupational, or school functioning	Suicidal thoughts, frequent shoplifting Unable to hold job, has no friends
31–40	Some impairment in reality testing or communication, OR major impairment in several areas	Speech illogical Depressed man or woman unable to work, neglects family, and avoids friends
21–30	Strong influence on behavior of delusions or hallucinations, OR serious impairment in communication or judgment, OR inability to function in almost all areas	Grossly inappropriate behavior, speech sometimes incoherent Stays in bed all day, no job, home, or friends
11–20	Some danger of hurting self or others, OR occasionally fails to maintain personal hygiene, OR gross impairment in communication	Suicidal gestures, frequently violent Smears feces
1–10	Persistent danger of severely hurting self or others, OR persistent inability to maintain minimal personal hygiene, OR seriously suicidal act	Largely incoherent or mute Serious suicidal attempt, recurrent violence

Source: Adapted from the *DSM-IV-TR* (APA, 2000).

TRUTH or FICTION

Some men in India have a psychological disorder characterized by anxiety over losing semen.

☑ **TRUE.** That disorder is a culture-bound syndrome found in India in which men develop intense fears over loss of semen.

others not because they are afraid of embarrassing themselves, but for fear of embarrassing others. People with TKS may also fear mumbling their thoughts aloud, lest they inadvertently offend others. The syndrome primarily affects young Japanese men and is connected with the emphasis in Japanese culture on not embarrassing others as well as deep cultural concerns over issues of shame (McNally et al., 1990).

Culture-bound syndromes in the United States include anorexia nervosa (discussed in Chapter 10) and dissociative identity disorder (formerly called *multiple personality disorder;* discussed in Chapter 7). These abnormal behavior patterns are essentially unknown in less-developed cultures. Table 3.6 lists some other culture-bound syndromes identified in the *DSM-IV-TR.*

TABLE 3.5

Example of a Diagnosis in the Multiaxial DSM System

Axis I	Generalized Anxiety Disorder
Axis II	Dependent Personality Disorder
Axis III	Hypertension
Axis IV	Problem with Primary Support Group (marital separation); Occupational Problem (unemployment)
Axis V	GAF = 62

Evaluating the *DSM* System To be useful, a diagnostic system such as the *DSM* must demonstrate **reliability** and **validity**. The *DSM* may be considered reliable, or consistent, if different evaluators using the system are likely to arrive at the same diagnoses when they evaluate the same cases. The system may be considered valid if diagnostic judgments correspond with observed behavior. For example, people diagnosed with social phobia should show abnormal levels of anxiety in social situations. Another form of validity is *predictive validity,* or ability to predict the course the disorder is likely to follow or its response to treatment. For example, people diagnosed with bipolar disorder typically respond to the drug lithium (see Chapter 8). Likewise, persons diagnosed with specific phobias (such as fear of heights) tend to be highly responsive to behavioral techniques for reducing fears (see Chapter 6).

Overall, evidence supports the reliability and validity of many *DSM* categories, including many anxiety and mood disorders, as well as alcohol and drug dependence disorders (Grant et al., 2006; Hasin et al., 2006). Yet questions about validity persist for some diagnostic classes, such as Axis II personality disorders, as well as Axis V, Global Assessment of Functioning (Moos, McCoy, & Moos, 2000; Widiger & Simonsen, 2005). Overall, it is fair to say that the validity of the *DSM* remains a subject of ongoing debate and study (Hummelen et al., 2006; Kendell & Jablensky, 2003; Watson & Clark, 2006).

Many observers have argued that the *DSM* should become more sensitive to cultural and ethnic diversity. The behaviors included as diagnostic criteria in the *DSM* are determined by consensus of mostly U.S.-trained psychiatrists, psychologists, and social workers. Had the American Psychiatric Association asked Asian-trained or Latin American–trained professionals to develop their diagnostic manual, for example, there might have been some different diagnostic criteria or even different diagnostic categories.

In fairness to the *DSM,* however, the latest edition does place greater emphasis than did earlier editions on weighing cultural factors when assessing abnormal behavior. It recognizes that clinicians unfamiliar with an individual's cultural background may incorrectly classify that individual's behavior as abnormal when it in fact falls within the normal spectrum in his or her culture. In Chapter 1 we noted that the same behavior might be deemed normal in one culture but abnormal in another. The *DSM-IV-TR* specifies that in order to make a diagnosis of a mental disorder, the behavior in question must not merely represent a culturally expectable and sanctioned response to a particular event, even though it may seem odd in the light of the examiner's own cultural standards. The *DSM-IV-TR* also recognizes that abnormal behaviors may take different forms in different cultures and that some abnormal behavior patterns are culturally specific (see Table 3.6).

All things considered, the current edition of the *DSM,* the *DSM-IV-TR,* is widely recognized as an improvement over previous editions, even though questions remain about the reliability and validity of certain diagnostic categories and about the specific criteria used to reach certain diagnoses (McGlinchey et al., 2006; Widiger & Clark, 2000; Zimmerman et al., 2006).

Advantages and Disadvantages of the *DSM* System The major advantage of the *DSM* may be its designation of specific diagnostic criteria. The *DSM* permits the clinician to readily match a client's complaints and associated features with specific standards to see which diagnosis best fits the case. For example, auditory hallucinations ("hearing voices") and delusions (fixed, but false beliefs, such as thinking that other people are devils) are characteristic symptoms of schizophrenia.

The multiaxial system paints a comprehensive picture of clients by integrating information concerning abnormal behaviors, medical conditions that affect abnormal behaviors, psychosocial and environmental problems that may be stressful to the individual, and level of functioning. The possibility of multiple diagnoses prompts clinicians to consider presenting

Assessment of level of functioning. The assessment of functioning takes into account the individual's ability to manage the responsibilities of daily living. Here we see a group home for people with mental retardation. The residents assume responsibility for household functions.

reliability In psychological assessment, the consistency of a measure or diagnostic instrument or system.

validity The degree to which a test or diagnostic system measures the traits or constructs it purports to measure.

Cultural underpinnings of abnormal behavior patterns. Culture-bound syndromes often represent exaggerated forms of cultural beliefs and values. TKS is characterized by excessive fear that one may embarrass or offend other people. The syndrome primarily affects young Japanese men and appears to be connected with the emphasis in Japanese culture on politeness and avoiding embarrassing other people.

TABLE 3.6

Examples of Culture-Bound Syndromes from Other Cultures

Culture-Bound Syndrome	Description
Amok	A disorder principally occurring in men in Southeastern Asian and Pacific Island cultures, as well as in traditional Puerto Rican and Navajo cultures in the West, it describes a type of dissociative episode (a sudden change in consciousness or self-identity) in which an otherwise normal person suddenly goes berserk and strikes out at others, sometimes killing them. During these episodes, the person may have a sense of acting automatically or robotically. Violence may be directed at people or objects and is often accompanied by perceptions of persecution. A return to the person's usual state of functioning follows the episode. In the West, we use the expression "running amuck" to refer to an episode of losing oneself and running around in a violent frenzy. The word *amuck* is derived from the Malaysian word *amoq*, meaning "engaging furiously in battle." The word passed into the English language during colonial times when British colonial rulers in Malaysia observed this behavior among the native people.
Ataque de nervios ("attack of nerves")	A way of describing states of emotional distress among Latin American and Latin Mediterranean groups, it most commonly involves features such as shouting uncontrollably, fits of crying, trembling, feelings of warmth or heat rising from the chest to the head, and aggressive verbal or physical behavior. These episodes are usually precipitated by a stressful event affecting the family (e.g., receiving news of the death of a family member) and are accompanied by feelings of being out of control. After the attack, the person returns quickly to his or her usual level of functioning, although there may be amnesia for events that occurred during the episode.
Dhat syndrome	A disorder (described further in Chapter 7) affecting males found principally in India that involves intense fear or anxiety over the loss of semen through nocturnal emissions, ejaculations, or excretion with urine (despite the folk belief, semen doesn't actually mix with urine). In Indian culture, there is a popular belief that loss of semen depletes the man of his vital natural energy.
Falling out or blacking out	Occurring principally among southern U.S. and Caribbean groups, the disorder involves an episode of sudden collapsing or fainting. The attack may occur without warning or be preceded by dizziness or feelings of "swimming" in the head. Although the eyes remain open, the individual reports an inability to see. The person can hear what others are saying and understand what is occurring but feels powerless to move.
Ghost sickness	A disorder occurring among American Indian groups, it involves a preoccupation with death and with the "spirits" of the deceased. Symptoms associated with the condition include bad dreams, feelings of weakness, loss of appetite, fear, anxiety, and a sense of foreboding. Hallucinations, loss of consciousness, and states of confusion may also be present, among other symptoms.
Koro	Found primarily in China and some other South and East Asian countries, the syndrome (also discussed further in Chapter 7) refers to an episode of acute anxiety involving the fear that one's genitals (the penis in men and the vulva and nipples in women) are shrinking and retracting into the body and that death may result.
Zar	A term used in a number of countries in North Africa and the Middle East to describe the experience of spirit possession. Possession by spirits is often used in these cultures to explain dissociative episodes (sudden changes in consciousness or identity) that may be characterized by periods of shouting, banging of the head against the wall, laughing, singing, or crying. Affected people may seem apathetic or withdrawn or refuse to eat or carry out their usual responsibilities.

Source: Adapted from the *DSM-IV-TR* (APA, 2000); Osborne, 2001; and other sources.

current problems (Axis I) along with the relatively long-standing personality problems (Axis II) that may contribute to them.

Criticisms are also leveled against the *DSM* system. Critics challenge the utility of particular symptoms or features associated with particular syndromes or of specified diagnostic criteria, such as the requirement that major depression be present for 2 weeks before a diagnosis is reached (Faraone et al., 2006; Zimmerman et al., 2006). Others challenge the reliance on the medical model. In the *DSM* system, problem behaviors are viewed as symptoms of underlying mental disorders in much the same way that physical symptoms are signs of underlying physical disorders. The very use of the term *diagnosis* presumes the medical model is an appropriate basis for classifying abnormal behaviors. But some clinicians feel that behavior, abnormal or otherwise, is too complex and meaningful to be treated as merely symptomatic. They assert that the medical model focuses too much on what may happen within the individual and not enough on external influences on behavior, such as social factors (socioeconomic, sociocultural, and ethnic) and physical environmental factors.

Another concern is that the medical model focuses on categorizing psychological (or mental) disorders rather than describing people's behavioral strengths and weaknesses. Similarly, many investigators question whether the diagnostic model should retain its categorical structure (a disorder is either present or not). Perhaps, they argue, it should be replaced with a dimensional approach in which abnormal behavior patterns such as anxiety, depression, and personality disorders, represent extreme variations of normally occurring emotional states and psychological traits (e.g., Akiskal & Benazzi, 2005; Cuthbert, 2005; First, 2005, 2006; Kupfer, 2005; Prisciandaro & Roberts, 2005).

To behaviorally oriented psychologists, the understanding of behavior, abnormal or otherwise, is best approached by examining the interaction between the person and the environment. The *DSM* aims to determine what "disorders" people "have"—not how well they can function in particular situations. The behavioral model, alternatively, focuses more on behaviors than on underlying processes—more on what people "do" than on what they "are" or "have." Behaviorists and behavior therapists also use the *DSM,* of course, in part because mental health centers and health insurance carriers require the use of a diagnostic code and in part because they want to communicate in a common language with other practitioners. Many behavior therapists view the *DSM* diagnostic code as a convenient means of labeling patterns of abnormal behavior, a shorthand for a more extensive behavioral analysis of the problem.

Critics also complain that the *DSM* system might stigmatize people by labeling them with psychiatric diagnoses. Our society is strongly biased against people who are labeled as mentally ill. They are often shunned by others, including even family members, and subjected to discrimination—or **sanism** (Perlin, 1994), the counterpart to other forms of prejudice, such as racism, sexism, and ageism—in housing and employment.

sanism The negative stereotyping of people who are identified as mentally ill.

The *DSM* system, despite its critics, has become part and parcel of the everyday practice of most U.S. mental health professionals. It may be the one reference manual found on the bookshelves of nearly all professionals and dog-eared from repeated use. Perhaps the *DSM* is best considered a work in progress, not a final product. Work on the fifth edition of the *DSM—the DSM-V—*was well underway at the time of this writing (Krueger & Markon, 2006; McGorry, 2007). In the nearby *Controversies in Abnormal Psychology* feature, a prominent investigator in the field, Thomas Widiger, shares his views on the *DSM,* or what he refers to as the "Bible of Psychiatry." Dr. Widiger also discusses the dimensional approach to assessing personality disorders such as antisocial personality disorder. (See Chapter 13 for a description of the features of antisocial personality disorder and other personality disorders).

Now let us consider various ways of assessing abnormal behavior. We begin by considering the basic requirements for methods of assessment—that they be reliable and valid.

STANDARDS OF ASSESSMENT

Important decisions are made on the basis of classification and assessment. For example, recommendations for specific treatment techniques vary according to our assessment of the problems clients exhibit. Therefore, methods of assessment, like diagnostic categories, must be *reliable* and *valid*.

Reliability

The reliability of a method of assessment, like that of a diagnostic system, refers to its consistency. A gauge of height would be unreliable if people looked taller or shorter at every measurement. A reliable measure of abnormal behavior must also yield the same results on different occasions. Also, different people should be able to check the yardstick and

CONTROVERSIES IN ABNORMAL PSYCHOLOGY

The Bible of Psychiatry

—THOMAS WIDIGER

If you are a clinical psychologist, there are probably many reasons to dislike the American Psychiatric Association's *Diagnostic and Statistical Manual of Mental Disorders* (*DSM*). First, it is under the control of a profession with which clinical psychologists are in professional and economic competition. Second, it can be perceived as being used by, or perhaps is in fact used by, insurance companies as a means of limiting coverage of clinical practice. For example, a managed care company might limit the number of sessions they will cover depending upon the patient's diagnosis (they might not even cover the treatment of some disorders). I am not too sure that these are necessarily valid reasons for disliking the *DSM*, but I do believe they contribute to some of the criticism that it receives. But, third, and most fundamentally important, it doesn't really work that well. A diagnosis of a disorder should lead to the identification of a specific disorder that has a specific pathology that accounts for it and a specific therapy that can be used to cure the patient of that pathology. That hasn't been the case for mental disorders diagnosed by the *DSM* system, not yet at least.

Despite its shortcomings, the *DSM* is a necessary document. Clinicians and researchers need a common language with which to communicate with each other about patterns of psychopathology, and that is the primary function of the *DSM*. Prior to its first edition, the clinical practice was awash with a confusing plethora of different names for the same thing and the same name for quite different things. It was, simply put, chaotic.

Many helping professionals are critical of the DSM for placing labels on persons. We work with our clients. We don't want to categorize or label them; however, labeling is a necessity. Persons who object to labeling must also use terms (e.g., categories) that describe the problems that clients present. It is not that labeling per se is the problem. It is perhaps in part the negative connotations of receiving a psychiatric diagnosis and the stereotyping of patients diagnosed with various disorders. Each of these concerns will be briefly discussed in turn.

Regrettably, many persons feel shame or embarrassment upon receiving a psychiatric diagnosis or undergoing psychological or psychiatric treatment. In part the embarrassment or shame reflects the myth that only a small minority of the population experiences psychological problems that warrant a diagnosis of a mental disorder. It's never been clear to me why we believe that we have not, do not, or will not suffer from a mental disorder. All of us have, do, and will suffer from quite a few physical disorders. Why should it be so different for mental disorders? It's not as if any of us are born with perfect genes, or are raised by perfect parents, or go through life untouched by stress, trauma, or psychological problems.

The difficulty with stereotyping is also problematic. People receiving psychiatric diagnoses are lumped into diagnostic categories that seem to treat all members of a particular diagnostic grouping as having the same characteristics. The diagnostic system fails to take individual profiles of psychopathology into account with respect to identifying the distinctive patterns of symptoms and presenting problems that particular individuals present.

Most (if not all) mental disorders appear to result from a complex array of interacting biological vulnerabilities and dispositions with a number of sig-

nificant environmental and psychosocial factors that often exert their effects over a period of time. The symptoms and pathologies of mental disorders appear to be influenced by a wide range of neurobiological, interpersonal, cognitive, and other factors, leading to the development of particular constellations of symptoms and complaints that characterize an individual's psychopathology profile. This complex web of causal factors and the distinctiveness of individual psychopathology profiles are unlikely to be captured by any single diagnostic category. I prefer the more individualized description of persons provided by dimensional models of classification, as for example, the *five-factor model* for the classification of personality disorders.

These five broad domains have been identified as extraversion, agreeableness versus antagonism, conscientiousness, neuroticism or emotional instability, and openness or unconventionality. Each of the five domains can also be differentiated into more specific facets. For example, the domain of agreeableness can be broken down into its underlying components of trust versus mistrust, straightforwardness versus deception, self-sacrifice versus exploitation, compliance versus aggression, modesty versus arrogance, and softheartedness versus callousness.

Most important for clinical psychology, all of the personality disorders are described well in terms of the domains and facets of the five-factor model. For example, antisocial personality disorder includes many of the facets of low conscientiousness (low deliberation, self-discipline, and dutifulness) and high antagonism (callous, exploitative, deceptive, and aggressive). The glib charm and fearlessness seen in the psychopath are represented by abnormally low levels of the neuroticism facets of self-consciousness, anxiousness, and vulnerability. This approach to describing patients provides a more individualized description of each patient, and it might even help somewhat with the stigmatization of a mental disorder diagnosis. All persons vary in the extent of their neuroticism, in the extent to which they are agreeable versus antagonistic, and in the extent to which they're conscientious. Persons with personality disorders would no longer be said to have disorders that are qualitatively distinct from normal psychological functioning but would instead be simply persons who have relatively extreme and maladaptive variants of the personality traits that are evident within all of us.

Critical Thinking

- Do we really need an authoritative diagnostic manual? Why or why not?
- How can we fix the problems of negative, pejorative connotations of diagnoses of mental disorders in our society?

Thomas A. Widiger is Professor of Psychology at the University of Kentucky. He received his Ph.D. in clinical psychology from Miami University (Ohio) and completed his internship at Cornell University Medical College. He currently serves as Associate Editor of *Journal of Abnormal Psychology* and *Journal of Personality Disorders*, as well as the *Annual Review of Clinical Psychology*. He was a member of the DSM-IV Task Force and served as the Research Coordinator for DSM-IV.

agree on the measured height of the subject. A yardstick that shrinks and expands with the slightest change in temperature will be unreliable. So will one that is difficult to read.

An assessment technique has *internal consistency* if the different parts of the test yield consistent results. For example, if responses to the different items on a depression scale are not highly correlated with each other, the items may not be measuring the same characteristic or trait—in this case, depression. On the other hand, some tests are designed to measure a set of different traits or characteristics. For example, the widely used personality test, the Minnesota Multiphasic Personality Inventory (MMPI), contains subscales measuring various traits related to abnormal behavior.

An assessment method has *test–retest reliability* if it yields similar results on separate occasions. We would not trust a bathroom scale that yielded different results each time we weighed ourselves—unless we had stuffed or starved ourselves between weighings. The same principle applies to methods of psychological assessment.

Finally, an assessment method that relies on judgments from observers or raters must show *interrater reliability*. That is, raters must show a high level of agreement in their ratings. For example, two teachers may be asked to use a behavioral rating scale to evaluate a child's aggressiveness, hyperactivity, and sociability. The scale would have good interrater reliability if both teachers rated the same children in similar ways.

Validity

Assessment techniques must also be valid; that is, instruments used in assessment must measure what they intend to measure. Suppose a measure of depression actually turned out to be measuring anxiety. Using such a measure may lead an examiner to a wrong diagnosis. There are different ways of measuring validity, including *content, criterion,* and *construct validity.*

The **content validity** of an assessment technique is the degree to which its content represents the behaviors associated with the trait in question. For example, depression includes features such as sadness and refusal to participate in activities the person once enjoyed. In order to have content validity, then, techniques that assess depression should include items that address these areas.

Criterion validity represents the degree to which the assessment technique correlates with an independent, external criterion (standard) of what the technique is intended to assess. *Predictive validity* is a form of criterion validity. A test or assessment technique shows good predictive validity if it can be used to predict future performance or behavior. For example, a test measuring antisocial behavior would show predictive validity if people scoring high on the measure later showed more evidence of delinquent or criminal behavior than did low scorers.

Another way of measuring criterion validity of a diagnostic test for a particular disorder is to see if it is able to identify people who meet diagnostic criteria for the disorder. Two related concepts are important here: sensitivity and specificity. *Sensitivity* refers to the degree to which a test correctly identifies people who have the disorder the test is intended to detect. Tests that lack sensitivity produce a high number of *false negatives*—individuals identified as not having the disorder who truly have the disorder. *Specificity* refers to the degree to which the test avoids classifying people as having a particular disorder who truly do not have the disorder. Tests that lack specificity produce a high number of *false positives*—people identified as having the disorder who truly do not have the disorder. By taking into account sensitivity and specificity of a given test, we can determine the ability of a test to classify individuals correctly.

Construct validity is the degree to which a test corresponds to the theoretical model of the underlying construct or trait it purports to measure. Let's say we have a test that purports to measure anxiety. Anxiety is not a concrete object or phenomenon. It can't be measured directly, counted, weighed, or touched. Anxiety is a theoretical construct that helps explain phenomena such as a pounding heart or the sudden inability to speak

Phrenology. In the 19th century, some people believed that mental faculties and abilities were based in certain parts of the brain and that people's acumen in such faculties could be assessed by gauging the protrusions and indentations of the skull.

content validity The degree to which the content of a test or measure represents the content domain of the construct it purports to measure.

criterion validity The degree to which a test correlates with an independent, external criterion or standard.

construct validity The degree to which a test measures the hypothetical construct that it purports to measure.

when you are asking someone out on a date. Anxiety may be indirectly measured by such means as self-report (the client rates the personal level of anxiety) and physiological techniques (measuring the level of sweat on the palms of the client's hands).

The construct validity of a test of anxiety requires the results of the test to predict other behaviors that would be expected, given your theoretical model of anxiety. Let's say your theoretical model predicts that socially anxious college students will have greater difficulties than calmer students in speaking coherently when asking someone for a date, but not when they are merely rehearsing the invitation in private. If the results of an experimental test of these predictions fit these predicted patterns, we could say the evidence supports the test's construct validity (Smith, 2005).

A test may be reliable (give you consistent responses) but still not measure what it purports to measure (be invalid). For example, 19th-century phrenologists believed they could gauge people's personalities by measuring the bumps on their heads. Their calipers provided reliable measures of their subjects' bumps and protrusions; the measurements, however, did not provide valid estimates of subjects' psychological traits. The phrenologists were bumping in the dark, so to speak.

METHODS OF ASSESSMENT

Clinicians use different methods of assessment to arrive at diagnoses, including interviews, psychological testing, self-report questionnaires, behavioral measures, and physiological measures. The role of assessment, however, goes further than classification. A careful assessment provides a wealth of information about clients' personalities and cognitive functioning. This information helps clinicians acquire a broader understanding of their clients' problems and recommend appropriate forms of treatment. In most cases, the formal assessment involves one or more clinical interviews with the client, leading to a diagnostic impression and a treatment plan. In some cases, more formal psychological testing probes the client's psychological problems and intellectual, personality, and neuropsychological functioning.

The Clinical Interview

The *clinical interview* is the most widely used means of assessment. The interview is usually the client's first face-to-face contact with a clinician. Clinicians often begin by asking clients to describe the presenting complaint in their own words, saying something like, "Can you describe to me the problems you've been having lately?" (Therapists learn not to ask, "What brings you here?" to avoid receiving such answers as, "A car," "A bus," or "My social worker.") The clinician will then usually probe aspects of the presenting complaint, such as behavioral abnormalities and feelings of discomfort, the circumstances regarding the onset of the problem, history of past episodes, and how the problem affects the client's daily functioning. The clinician may explore possible precipitating events, such as changes in life circumstances, social relationships, employment, or schooling. The interviewer encourages the client to describe the problem in her or his own words in order to understand it from the client's viewpoint. For example, the interviewer in the case vignette that opened the chapter asked Jerry to discuss the concerns that prompted him to seek help.

Although the format may vary, most interviews cover these topics:

1. *Identifying data.* Information regarding the client's sociodemographic characteristics: address and telephone number, marital status, age, gender, racial/ethnic characteristics, religion, employment, family composition, and so on.
2. *Description of the presenting problem(s).* How does the client perceive the problem? What troubling behaviors, thoughts, or feelings are reported? How do they affect the client's functioning? When did they begin?
3. *Psychosocial history.* Information describing the client's developmental history: educational, social, and occupational history; early family relationships.

Building rapport. By developing rapport and feelings of trust with a client, the skillful interviewer helps put the client at ease and encourages candid communication.

4. *Medical/psychiatric history.* History of medical and psychiatric treatment and hospitalizations: Is the present problem a recurrent episode of a previous problem? How was the problem handled in the past? Was treatment successful? Why or why not?

5. *Medical problems/medication.* Description of present medical problems and present treatment, including medication. The clinician is alert to ways in which medical problems may affect the presenting psychological problem. For example, drugs for certain medical conditions can affect people's moods and general levels of arousal.

The interviewer is attentive to the client's nonverbal as well as verbal behavior, forming judgments about the appropriateness of the client's attire and grooming, apparent mood, and ability to focus attention. Clinicians also judge the clarity or soundness of clients' thought and perceptual processes and level of orientation, or awareness of themselves and their surroundings (who they are, where they are, and what the present date is). These clinical judgments form an important part of the initial assessment of the client's mental state.

Interview Formats   There are three general types of clinical interviews. In an **unstructured interview,** the clinician adopts his or her own style of questioning rather than following a standard format. In a **semistructured interview,** the clinician follows a general outline of questions designed to gather essential information but is free to ask the questions in any particular order and to branch off into other directions to follow up on important information. In a **structured interview,** the interview follows a preset series of questions in a particular order.

The major advantage of the unstructured interview is its spontaneity and conversational style. Because the interviewer is not bound to follow any specific set of questions, there is an active give-and-take with the client. The major disadvantage is the lack of standardization. Different interviewers may ask questions in different ways. For example, one interviewer might ask, "How have your moods been lately?" whereas another might pose the question, "Have you had any periods of crying or tearfulness during the past week or two?" The clients' responses may depend to a certain extent on how the questions are asked. Also, the conversational flow of the interview may fail to touch on important clinical information needed to form diagnostic information, such as suicidal tendencies.

A semistructured interview provides more structure and uniformity, but at the expense of some spontaneity. Some clinicians prefer to conduct a semistructured interview in which they follow a general outline of questions but allow themselves the flexibility to depart from the interview protocol when they want to pursue issues that seem important.

Structured interviews (also called *standardized interviews*) provide the highest level of reliability and consistency in reaching diagnostic judgments, which is why they are used frequently in research settings. The Structured Clinical Interview for the *DSM* (SCID) includes closed-ended questions to determine the presence of behavior patterns that suggest specific diagnostic categories and open-ended questions that allow clients to elaborate their problems and feelings. The SCID guides the clinician in testing diagnostic hypotheses as the interview progresses. Evidence supports the reliability of the SCID across various clinical settings (J. B. Williams et al., 1992).

The interviewer arrives at a diagnostic impression by compiling all the information available: from the interview, from review of the client's background, and from the presenting problems.

Computerized Interviews

Do clinical interviews need to be conducted by a trained, live interviewer? Today, many of us do our banking by computer, order airline tickets over the Internet, and organize our schedules electronically. Might the clinical interviewer be replaced by a computer?

Computerized assessment protocols are becoming more widely used, although it is unlikely they will replace human interviewers anytime soon. In a computerized clinical interview, people respond to questions about their psychological symptoms and related concerns that are posed to them on a computer screen. Interestingly, evidence shows that people tend to reveal as much if not more personal information to a computer than

unstructured interview Interview in which the clinician adopts his or her own style of questioning rather than following any standard format.

semistructured interview Interview in which the clinician follows a general outline of questions designed to gather essential information but is free to ask them in any order and to branch off in other directions.

structured interview Interview that follows a preset series of questions in a particular order.

Computerized interview. Would you be more likely or less likely to tell your problems to a computer than to a person? Computerized clinical interviews have been used for more than 25 years, and some research suggests that the computer may be more sensitive than its human counterpart in teasing out problems.

they do to a human interviewer (Kobak et al., 1997). The computer interview may actually be more helpful in identifying problems that clients are embarrassed or unwilling to report to a live interviewer (Taylor & Luce, 2003). Perhaps people feel less self-conscious if someone isn't looking at them when they are interviewed. Or perhaps the computer seems more willing to take the time to note all complaints.

On the other hand, computers may lack the human touch needed to delve into sensitive concerns such as a person's deepest fears, relationship problems, sexual matters, and the like. A computer also lacks the means of judging the nuances in people's facial expressions that may reveal more about their innermost concerns than their typed or verbal responses. All in all, however, evidence shows that computer programs are as capable as skilled clinicians at obtaining information from clients and reaching an accurate diagnosis (Taylor & Luce, 2003). Computer programs are also less expensive and more time efficient than personal interviews.

Most clients and clinicians respond favorably to computerized assessment, but some do not (Richard & Bobicz, 2003). Most of the resistance to using computer interviews seems to come from clinicians rather than clients. Some clinicians believe that personal, eye-to-eye contact is necessary to tease out a client's underlying concerns. We should also recognize that since computer-administered diagnostic interviews sometimes yield misleading findings, computer assessments should be combined with clinical judgment by a trained clinician (Garb, 2007). Although the computer may never completely replace the human interviewer, a combination of computerized and interviewer-based assessment may strike the best balance of efficiency and sensitivity.

Another change in the offing is the development of online assessments. Some psychologists are now conducting psychological assessments via e-mail, videoconferencing, and the Internet (Naglieri et al., 2004; Shore et al., 2007).

Psychological Tests

A psychological test is a structured method of assessment used to evaluate reasonably stable traits, such as intelligence and personality. Tests are usually standardized on large numbers of subjects and provide norms that compare clients' scores with the average. By comparing test results from samples of people who are free of psychological disorders with those of people who have diagnosable psychological disorders, we may gain some insights into the types of response patterns that are indicative of abnormal behavior. Although we tend to think of medical tests as a "gold standard" of testing, a recent analysis showed that many psychological tests were on par with many medical tests in their ability to predict criterion variables, such as underlying conditions or future outcomes (Daw, 2001; Meyer et al., 2001).

Here we examine two major types of psychological tests: intelligence tests and personality tests.

Intelligence Tests The assessment of abnormal behavior often includes an evaluation of intelligence. Formal intelligence tests are used to help diagnose mental retardation (discussed in Chapter 14). They evaluate the intellectual impairment that may be caused by other disorders, such as organic mental disorders caused by damage to the brain. They also provide a profile of the client's intellectual strengths and weaknesses to help develop a treatment plan suited to the client's competencies.

Attempts to define intelligence continue to stir debate in the field. David Wechsler (1975), the originator of the most widely used intelligence tests, the Wechsler scales, defined intelligence as "capacity . . . to understand the world . . . and . . . resourcefulness to cope with its challenges." From his perspective, intelligence has to do with the ways in which we (a) mentally represent the world and (b) adapt to its demands.

The first formal intelligence test was developed by a Frenchman, Alfred Binet (1857–1911). In 1904, Binet was commissioned by school officials in Paris to develop a mental test to identify children who were unable to cope with the demands of regular classroom instruction and who required special classes to meet their needs. Binet and a colleague, Theodore Simon, developed an intelligence test consisting of memory tasks and other short tests of mental abilities that children were likely to encounter in daily life, such as counting. A later version of their test, called the Stanford-Binet Intelligence Scale, is still widely used to measure intelligence in children and young adults.

Intelligence, as given by a person's scores on intelligence tests, is usually expressed in the form of an intelligence quotient, or IQ. An IQ score is typically based on the relative difference (deviation) of a person's score on an intelligence test from the norms of the person's age group. A score of 100 is defined as the mean. People who answer more items correctly than the average obtain IQ scores above 100; those who answer fewer items correctly obtain scores of less than 100.

Wechsler's intelligence scales are today the most widely used intelligence tests. Different versions are used for different age groups. The Wechsler scales group questions into subtests or subscales, with each subscale measuring a different intellectual ability. (Table 3.7 shows examples from the adult version of the test.) The Wechsler scales are thus designed to offer insight into a person's relative strengths and weaknesses, and not simply yield an overall score.

Wechsler's scales include both *verbal* and *performance* subtests to compute verbal and performance IQs. Verbal subtests generally require knowledge of verbal concepts; performance subtests rely more on spatial relations skills. (Figure 3.1 shows items similar to those on the performance subscales of the Wechsler scales.)

Wechsler IQ scores are based on how respondents' answers deviate from those attained by their age-mates. The mean whole test score at any age is defined as 100. Wechsler distributed IQ scores so that 50% of the scores of the population would lie within a "broad average" range of 90 to 110.

Most IQ scores cluster around the mean (see Figure 3.2). Just 5% of them are above 130 or below 70. Wechsler labeled people who attained scores of 130 or above as "very superior" and those with scores below 70 as "intellectually deficient."

Clinicians use IQ scales to evaluate a client's intellectual resources and to help diagnose mental retardation. IQ scores below 70 are one of the criteria used in diagnosing mental retardation. Next we consider two major types of tests used to assess personality: *objective tests* and *projective tests*. Clinicians use personality tests to learn more about the client's underlying personality traits, needs, interests, and concerns.

TABLE 3.7

Examples of Items Similar to those on the Wechsler Adult Intelligence Scale

Verbal Subtests	Performance Subtests
Information Who wrote *Paradise Lost?*	**Digit Symbol** Given a key showing a set of symbols that correspond to particular numbers, fill in the correct symbols for a series of numbers.
Comprehension Why do people need to obey traffic laws? What does the saying "The early bird catches the worm" mean?	**Picture Completion** Identify the missing part from a picture, such as the picture of the watch in Figure 3.1.
Arithmetic John wanted to buy a shirt that cost $31.50, but only had 17 dollars. How much more money would he need to buy the shirt?	**Block Design** Using blocks such as those in Figure 3.1, match the design shown.
Similarities How are a stapler and a paper clip alike?	**Picture Arrangement** Arrange the pictures in the correct order to tell a story.
Digit Span (Forward order) Listen to this series of numbers and repeat them back to me in the same order: 6 4 5 2 7 3 (Backward order) Listen to this series of numbers and then repeat them backward: 9 4 2 5 8 7.	**Object Assembly** Arrange the pieces of the puzzle so that they form a meaningful object.
Vocabulary What does *capricious* mean?	

Source: Adapted from "Examples of Items Similar to Those on the WAIS-III" from Nevid, J.S. *Psychology: Concepts and Applications,* Second Edition, (Boston: Houghton Mifflin, 2007), p. 282. Reprinted by permission.

Picture Arrangement
These pictures tell a story but they are in the wrong order. Put them in the right order so that they tell a story.

Picture Completion
What part is missing from this picture?

  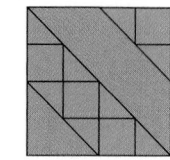

Block Design
Put the blocks together to make this picture.

Object Assembly
Put the pieces together as quickly as you can.

FIGURE 3.1 Items similar to those found on the performance subtests of the Wechsler Intelligence Scale (WAIS).
The Wechsler scales yield verbal and performance IQs that are based on the extent to which an individual's test scores deviate from the norm for her or his age group.

Source: From the Wechsler Intelligence Scales for Adults and Children. Copyright © 1949, 1955, 1974, 1981, 1991, 1997, 2003 by The Psychological Corporation, a Harcourt Assessment Company. Reproduced by permission. All rights reserved. Wechsler® is a trademark of The Psychological Corporation registered in the United States of America and/or other jurisdictions.

objective tests Self-report personality tests that can be scored objectively and that are based on a research foundation.

TRUTH or FICTION

An objective test of personality is one that does not require any subjective judgments on the part of the person taking the test.

☑**FALSE.** Objective personality tests are self-report instruments that rely on individuals providing subjective judgments about themselves. They are considered objective in the sense that they have limited response options that can be scored objectively.

Objective Tests Do you like automobile magazines? Are you easily startled by noises in the night? Are you bothered by periods of anxiety or shakiness? **Objective tests** are self-report personality inventories that use items similar to these to measure personality traits such as emotional instability, masculinity-femininity, and introversion. People are asked to respond to specific questions or statements about their feelings, thoughts, concerns, attitudes, interests, beliefs, and the like.

What makes personality tests *objective*? These tests are not objective in the sense that a bathroom scale is an objective measure of weight. After all, these tests rely on subjects giving subjective reports of their interests, feeling states, and so on. Rather, we consider these tests objective in the sense that they limit the range of possible responses and so can be scored objectively. They are also considered objective because they were developed based on empirical evidence supporting their validity. Subjects might be instructed to check adjectives that apply to them, to mark statements as true or false, to select preferred activities from lists, or to indicate whether items apply to them "always," "sometimes," or "never." For example, a test item may ask you to check either "true" or "false" to a statement like, "I feel uncomfortable in crowds." Here we focus on two of the more widely used objective personality tests in clinical settings, the Minnesota Multiphasic Personality Inventory (MMPI; now in a revised edition called the MMPI-2) and the Millon Clinical Multiaxial Inventory (MCMI).

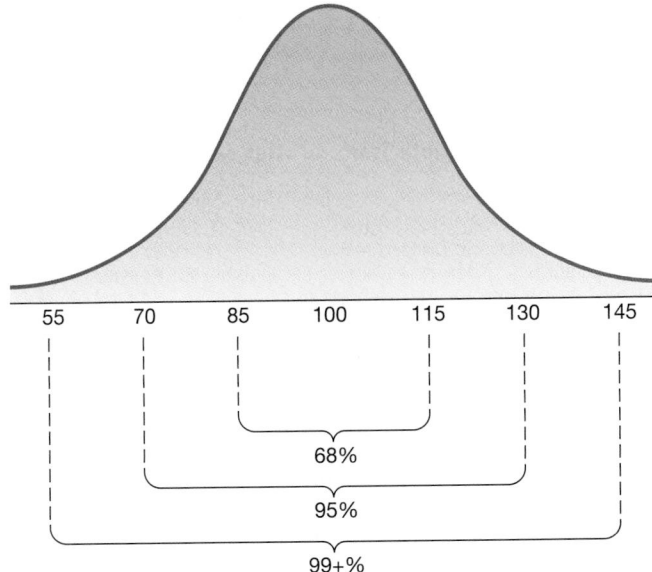

FIGURE 3.2 Normal distribution of IQ scores.
The distribution of IQ scores is based on a bell-shaped curve, which is referred to by psychologists as a normal curve. Wechsler defined the deviation IQ so that the average (mean) score was 100 and the standard deviation of scores was 15. A standard deviation is a statistical measure of the variability or dispersion of scores around the mean. Here we see the distribution of scores at one, two, and three standard deviations from the mean. Note also that 50% of the scores fall within the broad average range of 90 to 110.

Minnesota Multiphasic Personality Inventory (MMPI-2) The MMPI-2 contains more than 500 true-false statements that assess interests, habits, family relationships, physical (somatic) complaints, attitudes, beliefs, and behaviors characteristic of psychological disorders. It is widely used as a test of personality as well as to assist clinicians in diagnosing abnormal behavior patterns. The MMPI-2 consists of a number of individual scales comprised of items that tended to be answered differently by members of carefully selected diagnostic groups, such as patients diagnosed with schizophrenia or depression, than by members of reference groups.

Consider a hypothetical item: "I often read detective novels." If, for example, groups of depressed people tended to answer the item in a direction different from normal groups, the item would be placed on the depression scale. Many items that discriminate normal people from clinical groups are transparent in meaning, such as "I feel down much of the time." However, some items are more subtle in meaning or bear no obvious relationship to the measured trait. For example, a hypothetical item such as "I think people would be better off if they spent more time taking trains to flying whenever possible."

The items on the MMPI are divided into various clinical scales (see Table 3.8). A score of 65 or higher on a particular scale is considered clinically significant. The MMPI-2 also includes validity scales that assess tendencies to distort test responses in a favorable ("faking good") or unfavorable ("faking bad") direction. Other scales on the tests, called *content scales,* measure an individual's specific complaints and concerns, such as anxiety, anger, family problems, and problems of low self-esteem.

The MMPI-2 is interpreted according to individual scale elevations and interrelationships among scales. For example, a "2–7 profile," commonly found among people seeking therapy, refers to a test pattern in which scores for Scales 2 ("Depression") and 7 ("Psychasthenia") are clinically significant. Clinicians may refer to "atlases," or descriptions, of people who usually attain various profiles.

MMPI-2 scales are regarded as reflecting continua of personality traits associated with the diagnostic categories represented by the test. For example, a high score on Scale 4, psychopathic deviation, suggests that the respondent holds a higher-than-average number of nonconformist beliefs and may be rebellious, which are characteristics often found in people with antisocial personality disorder. However, because it is not tied specifically to *DSM* criteria, this score cannot be used to establish a diagnosis. The MMPI, which was originally developed in the 1930s and 1940s, cannot provide diagnostic judgments consistent with the current version of the *DSM* system. Even so, MMPI profiles may suggest possible diagnoses that can be considered in the light of other evidence. Moreover, many clinicians use the MMPI to gain general information

TABLE 3.8

Clinical Scales of the MMPI-2

Scale Number	Scale Label	Items Similar to Those Found on MMPI Scale	Sample Traits of High Scorers
1	Hypochondriasis	My stomach frequently bothers me. At times, my body seems to ache all over.	Many physical complaints, cynical defeatist attitudes, often perceived as whiny, demanding
2	Depression	Nothing seems to interest me anymore. My sleep is often disturbed by worrisome thoughts.	Depressed mood; pessimistic, worrisome, despondent, lethargic
3	Hysteria	I sometimes become flushed for no apparent reason. I tend to take people at their word when they're trying to be nice to me.	Naive, egocentric, little insight into problems, immature; develops physical complaints in response to stress
4	Psychopathic deviate	My parents often disliked my friends. My behavior sometimes got me into trouble at school.	Difficulties incorporating values of society, rebellious, impulsive, antisocial tendencies; strained family relationships; poor work and school history
5	Masculinity-Femininity	I like reading about electronics. (M) I would like to work in the theater. (F)	Males endorsing feminine attributes: have cultural and artistic interests, effeminate, sensitive, passive; Females endorsing male interests: Aggressive, masculine, self-confident, active, assertive, vigorous
6	Paranoia	I would have been more successful in life but people didn't give me a fair break. It's not safe to trust anyone these days.	Suspicious, guarded, blames others, resentful, aloof, may have paranoid delusions
7	Psychasthenia	I'm one of those people who have to have some thing to worry about. I seem to have more fears than most people I know.	Anxious, fearful, tense, worried, insecure, difficulties concentrating, obsessional, self-doubting
8	Schizophrenia	Things seem unreal to me at times. I sometimes hear things that other people can't hear.	Confused and illogical thinking, feels alienated and misunderstood, socially isolated or withdrawn, may have blatant psychotic symptoms such as hallucinations or delusional beliefs, or may lead detached, schizoid lifestyle
9	Hypomania	I sometimes take on more tasks than I can possibly get done. People have noticed that my speech is sometimes pressured or rushed.	Energetic, possibly manic, impulsive, optimistic, sociable, active, flighty, irritable, may have overly inflated or grandiose self-image or unrealistic plans
10	Social Introversion	I don't like loud parties. I was not very active in school activities.	Shy, inhibited, withdrawn, introverted, lacks self confidence, reserved, anxious in social situations

about respondents' personality traits and attributes that may underlie their psychological problems, rather than a diagnosis per se.

The validity of the MMPI-2 is supported by a large body of research findings (Garb, 2003; Kubisyzn et al., 2000). The test successfully discriminates between psychiatric patients and controls and between groups of people with different psychological disorders, such as anxiety versus depressive disorders (Ganellen, 1996; Graham, 2006). Moreover, the content scales of the MMPI-2 provide additional information to that provided by the clinical scales, which can help clinicians learn more about the client's specific problems (Graham, 2006; McGrath, Pogge, & Stokes, 2002; Sellbom, Graham, & Schenk, 2006).

The Millon Clinical Multiaxial Inventory (MCMI) The MCMI was developed to help the clinician make diagnostic judgments within the *DSM* system, especially for personality disorders found on Axis II (Millon, 2003). The MCMI (now in a third edition) is the only objective personality test that focuses specifically on personality disorders. The MMPI-2, by contrast, focuses on personality traits associated with Axis I diagnoses, such as mood disorders, anxiety disorders, and schizophrenic disorders. Some clinicians may use both instruments to capture a wider range of personality traits. Evidence indicates that the MCMI is useful in helping clinicians discriminate among various Axis I and Axis II disorders (Kubiszyn et al., 2000; Salekin et al., 2003). However, relationships between the MCMI and the underlying personality disorders it is intended to assess requires further study (Blais et al., 2003).

Evaluation of Objective Tests Objective or self-report tests are relatively easy to administer. Once the examiner has read the instructions to clients and made sure they can read and comprehend the items, clients can complete the tests unattended. Because the tests permit limited response options, such as marking items either true or false, they can be scored with high interrater reliability. Moreover, the accumulation of research findings on respondents provides a quantified basis for interpreting test responses. Such tests often reveal information that might not be revealed during a clinical interview or by observing the person's behavior. For example we might learn that a person harbors negative views of himself or herself—self-perceptions that may not be directly expressed in behavior or revealed during an interview. A disadvantage of self-rating tests is that they rely on individuals themselves as the sole source of information (Vazire, 2006). Test responses may therefore reflect underlying biases people may have when they evaluate themselves or their behavior, such as tendencies to give socially desirable responses that may not reflect their true feelings. For this reason, self-report inventories, such as the MMPI, contain validity scales to help ferret out response biases. Yet even these validity scales may not detect all sources of bias. Examiners may also look for corroborating information, such as interviewing others who are familiar with the client's behavior.

Tests are also only as valid as the criteria that were used to validate them. The original MMPI was limited in its role as a diagnostic instrument by virtue of the obsolete diagnostic categories that were used to classify the original clinical groups. Moreover, if a test does nothing more than identify people who are likely to have a particular disorder, its utility is usurped by more economical means of arriving at diagnoses, such as a structured clinical interview. We expect more from personality tests than diagnostic classification and the MMPI has shown its value in providing information about underlying personality traits and interest patterns. Psychodynamically oriented critics suggest that self-report instruments tell us little about possible unconscious processes. The use of such tests may also be limited to relatively high functioning individuals who can read well, respond to verbal material, and focus on a potentially tedious task. Clients who are disorganized, unstable, or confused may not be able to complete the tests.

Projective Tests A **projective test,** unlike an objective test, offers no clear, specified response options. Clients are presented with ambiguous stimuli, such as inkblots, and asked to respond to them. The word *projective* is used because these personality tests derive from the psychodynamic belief that people impose, or "project," their own psychological needs, drives, and motives, much of which lie in the unconscious, onto their interpretations of ambiguous stimuli.

The psychodynamic model holds that potentially disturbing impulses and wishes, often of a sexual or aggressive nature, are often hidden from consciousness by our defense mechanisms. Indirect methods of assessment, however, such as projective tests, may offer clues to unconscious processes. More behaviorally oriented critics contend, however, that the results of projective tests are based more on clinicians' subjective interpretations of test responses than on empirical evidence.

projective tests Psychological tests that present ambiguous stimuli onto which the examinee is thought to project his or her personality and unconscious motives.

One of the most widely used tests of personality asks people to interpret what they see in a series of inkblots.

☑ **TRUE.** The Rorschach is a widely used personality test in which a person's responses to inkblots are interpreted to reveal aspects of his or her personality.

Many projective tests have been developed, including tests based on how people fill in missing words to complete sentence fragments or how they draw human figures and other objects. The two most prominent projective techniques are the Rorschach Inkblot Test and the Thematic Apperception Test (TAT).

The Rorschach Test The Rorschach test was developed by a Swiss psychiatrist, Hermann Rorschach (1884–1922). As a child, Rorschach was intrigued by the game of dripping ink on paper and folding the paper to make symmetrical figures. He noted that people saw different things in the same blot, and he believed their "percepts" reflected their personalities as well as the stimulus cues provided by the blot. Rorschach's fraternity nickname was *Klex,* which means "inkblot" in German ("Time Capsule," 2000). As a psychiatrist, Rorschach experimented with hundreds of blots to identify those that could help in the diagnosis of psychological problems. He finally found a group of 15 blots that seemed to do the job and could be administered in a single session. Ten blots are used today because Rorschach's publisher did not have the funds to reproduce all 15 blots in the first edition of the text on the subject. Rorschach never had the opportunity to learn how popular and influential his inkblot test would become. Sadly, 7 months after the publication of the test that bears his name, Rorschach died at age 37 of complications from a ruptured appendix (Exner, 2002).

Five of the inkblots are black and white, and the other five have color (see Figure 3.3). Each inkblot is printed on a separate card, which is handed to subjects in sequence. Subjects are asked to tell the examiner what the blot might be or what it reminds them of. Then, they are asked to explain what features of the blot (its color, form, or texture) they used to form their perceptions.

Clinicians who use the Rorschach form interpretations based on the content and the form of the responses. For example, they may infer that people who use the entire blot in their responses show an ability to integrate events in meaningful ways. Those who focus on minor details of the blots may have obsessive–compulsive tendencies, whereas clients who respond to the negative (white) spaces may see things in their own idiosyncratic ways, suggesting underlying negativism or stubbornness.

reality testing The ability to perceive the world accurately and to distinguish reality from fantasy.

A response consistent with the form or contours of the blot is suggestive of adequate **reality testing.** People who see movement in the blots may be revealing intelligence and creativity. Content analysis may shed light on underlying conflicts. For example, adult clients who see animals but no people may have problems relating to people. Clients who appear confused about whether or not percepts of people are male or female may, according to psychodynamic theory, be in conflict over their own gender identity.

The Thematic Apperception Test (TAT) The Thematic Apperception Test (TAT) was developed by psychologist Henry Murray (1943) at Harvard University in the 1930s. *Apperception* is a French word that can be translated as "interpreting (new ideas or impressions) on the basis of existing ideas (cognitive structures) and past experience." The TAT consists of a series of cards, each depicting an ambiguous scene (see Figure 3.4). It is assumed that clients' responses to the cards will reflect their experiences and outlooks on life—and, perhaps, shed light on their deep-seated needs and conflicts.

Respondents are asked to describe what is happening in each scene, what led up to it, what the characters are thinking and feeling, and what will happen next. Psychodynamic theorists believe that people will identify with the protagonists in their stories and project underlying psychological needs and conflicts into their responses. More superficially, the stories suggest how respondents might interpret or behave in similar situations in their own lives. TAT results may also be suggestive of clients' attitudes toward others, particularly family members and lovers.

Evaluation of Projective Techniques The reliability and validity of projective techniques continues to be a subject of extensive research and ongoing debate. For one thing,

FIGURE 3.3 "What does this look like?"
In the Rorschach test, a person is presented with ambiguous stimuli in the form of inkblots and asked to describe what each of the blots looks like. Rorschach assumed that people project aspects of their own personalities into their responses, but controversy still whirls around the question of whether the test yields scientifically valid conclusions.

interpretation of a person's responses depends to some degree on the subjective judgment of the examiner. For example, two examiners may interpret the same Rorschach or TAT response differently.

Although more comprehensive scoring systems have improved standardization of scoring the Rorschach, the reliability of the test continues to be debated (see Acklin et al., 2000). Even if a Rorschach response can be scored reliably, the interpretation of the response—what it means—remains an open question (Garb et al., 2005).

Evidence supports the use of at least some limited uses of the Rorschach (e.g., Blais et al., 2001; G. J. Meyer, 2001). For example, Rorschach indicators may be useful in distinguishing between different types of psychological disorders (Dao & Prevatt, 2006; Kubiszyn et al., 2000), in detecting dependency behaviors and some forms of disturbed thinking (Lilienfeld, Fowler, & Lohr, 2003), and in predicting treatment outcomes in psychotherapy (G. J. Meyer, 2000).

Some reviewers find the overall validity of the Rorschach to be generally on par with that of other psychological tests, such as the MMPI (e.g., Meyer et al., 2001; Meyer & Archer, 2001; Weiner, Spielberger, & Abeles, 2002, 2003). However, other reviewers claim the Rorschach fails to meet overall tests of scientific utility or validity (Garb et al., 2002; Hamel et al., 2003; Hunsley & Bailey, 2001; Lilienfeld, Wood, & Garb, 2000). The debate over the validity and clinical utility of the Rorschach continues to rage between supporters and detractors with no clear resolution in sight.

One criticism of the TAT is that the stimulus properties of some of the cards, such as cues depicting sadness or anger, may exert too strong a "stimulus pull" on the subject. If so, clients' responses may represent reactions to the stimulus cues rather than projections of their personalities (Murstein & Mathes, 1996). The validity of the TAT in eliciting deep-seated material or tapping underlying psychopathology also remains to be demonstrated. However, evidence does indicate that it can discriminate between different types of Axis I and Axis II disorders (Kubiszyn et al., 2000).

Although many critics would like to see projective tests scrapped, others argue that in skilled hands, tests such as the TAT and the Rorschach can yield meaningful material that might not be revealed in interviews or by self-rating inventories (Stricker & Gold, 1999). Moreover, allowing subjects freedom of expression through projective testing reduces the tendency of individuals to offer socially desirable responses. George Stricker (2003) appraised the present standoff in the field as follows: "The field remains divided between believers and nonbelievers, and each is able to marshal considerable evidence and discount the evidence of their opponents to support their point of view" (p. 728).

FIGURE 3.4 "Tell me a story."
In the Thematic Apperception Test (TAT), the person is presented with a series of pictures, such as this one depicted here, and asked to tell a story about what is happening in the scene. The person is also asked to describe what events led up to the scene and how the story will turn out. How might the stories you tell reveal underlying aspects of your personality?

Reprinted by permission of the publishers from Henry A. Murray, THEMATIC APPERCEPTION TEST, Cambridge, Mass.: Harvard University Press, © 1943 by the President and Fellows of Harvard College, © 1971 by Henry A. Murray.

Neuropsychological Assessment

neuropsychological assessment
Measurement of behavior or performance that may be indicative of underlying brain damage or defects.

Neuropsychological assessment involves the use of tests to help determine whether psychological problems reflect underlying neurological impairment or brain damage. When neurological impairment is suspected, a neurological evaluation may be requested from a *neurologist*—a medical doctor who specializes in disorders of the nervous system. A clinical *neuropsychologist* may also be consulted to administer neuropsychological assessment techniques, such as behavioral observation and psychological testing, to reveal signs of possible brain damage. Neuropsychological testing may be used together with brain-imaging techniques such as the MRI and CT to shed light on relationships between brain function and underlying abnormalities (Fiez, 2001). The results of neuropsychological testing may not only suggest whether patients suffer from brain damage but also point to the parts of the brain that may be affected.

The Bender Visual Motor Gestalt Test One of the first neuropsychological tests to be developed and still one of the most widely used neuropsychological tests is the Bender Visual Motor Gestalt Test, now in a second edition, the Bender-Gestalt II (Brannigan & Decker, 2006; Raphael, Golden, & Cassidy-Feltgen, 2002). "The Bender" consists of geometric figures that illustrate various Gestalt principles of perception. The client is asked to copy geometric designs, and signs of possible brain damage include rotation of the figures, distortions in shape, and incorrect sizing of the figures in relation to one another (see Figure 3.5). The examiner then asks the client to reproduce the designs from memory, because neurological damage can impair memory functioning. Although the Bender remains a convenient and economical means of uncovering possible organic impairment, more sophisticated test batteries have been developed for this purpose, including the widely used Halstead-Reitan Neuropsychological Battery.

The Halstead-Reitan Neuropsychological Battery Psychologist Ralph Reitan developed the battery by adapting tests used by his mentor, Ward Halstead, an experimental psychologist, to study brain–behavior relationships among organically impaired individuals. The battery contains tests that measure perceptual, intellectual, and motor skills and performance. A battery of tests permits the psychologist to observe patterns of results, and various patterns of performance deficits are suggestive of certain kinds of brain defects, such as those occurring following head trauma (Loring & Larrabee, 2006; Reitan & Wolfson, 2000). The Halstead-Reitan test battery comprises a number of subtests, including the following:

1. *The Category Test.* This test measures abstract thinking ability, as indicated by the individual's proficiency at forming principles or categories that relate different stimuli to one another. A series of groups of stimuli that vary in shape, size, location, color, and other characteristics are flashed on a screen. The subject's task is to discern the principle that links them, such as shape or size, and to indicate which stimuli in each grouping represent the correct category by pressing a key. By analyzing the patterns of correct and incorrect choices, the subject normally learns to identify the principles that determine the correct choice. Performance on the test is believed to reflect functioning in the frontal lobe of the cerebral cortex.

2. *The Rhythm Test.* This is a test of concentration and attention. The subject listens to 30 pairs of tape-recorded rhythmic beats and indicates whether the beats in each pair are the same or different. Performance deficits are associated with damage to the right temporal lobe of the cerebral cortex.

3. *The Tactual Performance Test.* This test requires the blindfolded subject to fit wooden blocks of different shapes into corresponding depressions on a form board. Afterward, the subject draws the board from memory as a measure of visual memory.

(A)

(B)

FIGURE 3.5 The Bender Visual Motor Gestalt Test.
The "Bender" is intended to assess organic impairment. Part A shows the series of figures respondents are asked to copy. Part B shows the drawings of a person who is known to be brain damaged.

behavioral assessment The approach to clinical assessment that focuses on the objective recording and description of problem behavior.

Behavioral Assessment

Traditional personality tests such as the MMPI, Rorschach, and TAT were designed to measure underlying psychological traits and dispositions. Test responses are interpeted as *signs* of traits and dispositions believed to play important roles in determining people's behavior. For example, certain Rorschach responses are interpreted as revealing underlying traits, such as psychological dependency, that are believed to influence how people relate to others. In contrast, **behavioral assessment** treats test results as *samples* of behavior that occur in specific situations rather than as *signs* of underlying personality traits. According to the behavioral approach, behavior is primarily determined by environmental or situational factors, such as stimulus cues and reinforcement, not by underlying traits.

Behavioral assessment aims to sample an individual's behavior in settings as similar as possible to the real-life situation, thus maximizing the relationship between the testing situation and the criterion. Behavior may be observed and measured in such settings as the home, school, or work environment. The examiner may also try to simulate situations in the clinic or laboratory that serve as analogues of the problems the individual confronts in daily life.

The examiner may conduct a *functional analysis* of the problem behavior—an analysis of the problem behavior in relation to antecedents, or stimulus cues that trigger it, and consequences, or reinforcements that maintain it. Knowledge of the environmental conditions in which a problem behavior occurs may help the therapist work with the client and the family to change the conditions that trigger and maintain it. The examiner may conduct a *behavioral interview* by posing questions to learn more about the history and situational aspects of problem behavior. For example, if a client seeks help because of panic attacks, the behavioral interviewer might ask how the client

---

◆

Kerry, the "Royal Terror"

A 7-year-old boy, Kerry, is brought by his parents for evaluation. His mother describes him as a "royal terror." His father complains he won't listen to anyone. Kerry throws temper tantrums in the supermarket, screaming and stomping his feet if his parents refuse to buy him what he wants. At home, he breaks his toys by throwing them against the wall and demands new ones. Sometimes, though, he appears sullen and won't talk to anyone for hours. At school he appears inhibited and has difficulty concentrating. His progress at school is slow, and he has difficulty reading. His teachers complain he has a limited attention span and doesn't seem motivated.

—From the Author's Files

---

experiences these attacks—when, where, how often, under what circumstances. The interviewer looks for precipitating cues, such as thought patterns (e.g., thoughts of dying or losing control) or situational factors (e.g., entering a department store) that may provoke an attack. The interviewer also seeks information about reinforcers that may maintain the panic. Does the client flee the situation when an attack occurs? Is escape reinforced by relief from anxiety? Has the client learned to lessen anticipatory anxiety by avoiding exposure to situations in which attacks have occurred?

The examiner may also use observational methods to connect the problem behavior to the stimuli and reinforcements that help maintain it. Consider the case of Kerry. The psychologist may use direct home observation to assess the interactions between Kerry and his parents. Alternatively, the psychologist may observe Kerry and his parents through a one-way mirror in the clinic. Such observations may suggest interactions that explain the child's noncompliance. For example, Kerry's noncompliance may follow parental requests that are vague (e.g., a parent says, "Play nicely now," and Kerry responds by throwing toys) or inconsistent (e.g., a parent says, "Go play with your toys but don't make a mess," to which Kerry responds by scattering the toys). Observation may suggest ways in which Kerry's parents can improve communication and cue and reinforce desirable behaviors.

Direct observation, or behavioral observation, is the hallmark of behavioral assessment. Through direct observation, clinicians can observe and quantify problem behavior. Observations may be videotaped to permit subsequent analysis of behavioral patterns. Observers are trained to identify and record targeted patterns of behavior. Behavior coding systems have been developed that enhance the reliability of recording.

There are both advantages and disadvantages to direct observation. One advantage is that direct observation does not rely on the client's self-reports, which may be distorted by efforts to make a favorable or unfavorable impression. In addition to providing accurate measurements of problem behavior, behavioral observation can suggest strategies for intervention. A mother might report that her son is so hyperactive he cannot sit still long enough to complete homework assignments. By using a one-way mirror, the clinician may discover that the boy becomes restless only when he encounters a problem he cannot solve right away. The child may then be helped by being taught ways of coping with frustration and of solving certain kinds of academic problems.

Direct observation also has its drawbacks. One issue is the possible lack of consensus in defining problems in behavioral terms. In coding the child's behavior for hyperactivity, clinicians must agree on which aspects of the child's behavior represent hyperactivity. Another potential problem is a lack of reliability, or inconsistency, of measurement across time or between observers. Reliability is reduced when an observer is inconsistent in the coding of specific behaviors or when two or more observers code behavior inconsistently.

Observers may also show response biases. An observer who has been sensitized to expect that a child is hyperactive may perceive normal variations in behavior as subtle cues of hyperactivity and erroneously record them as instances of hyperactive behavior. We can help minimize these biases by keeping observers uninformed or "blind" about the target subject they are observing.

Reactivity is another potential problem. Reactivity refers to the tendency for the behavior being observed to be influenced by the way in which it is measured. For example, people may put their best feet forward when they know they are being observed. Using covert observation techniques, such as hidden cameras or one-way mirrors, may reduce reactivity. Covert observation may not be feasible, however, because of ethical concerns or practical constraints. Another approach is to accustom subjects to observation by watching them a number of times before collecting data. Another potential problem is *observer drift*—the tendency of observers, or groups of raters, to deviate from the coding system in which they were trained as time elapses. One suggestion to help control this problem is to regularly retrain observers to ensure continued compliance with the coding system (Kazdin, 1992). As time elapses, observers may also become fatigued or distracted. It may be helpful to limit the duration of observations and to provide frequent breaks.

Behavioral observation is limited to measuring overt behaviors. Many clinicians also wish to assess subjective or private experiences—for example, feelings of depression and anxiety or distorted thought patterns. Such clinicians may combine direct observation with forms of assessment that permit clients to reveal internal experiences. Staunch behavioral clinicians tend to consider self-reports unreliable and to limit their data to direct observation.

In addition to behavioral interviews and direct observation, behavioral assessment may involve the use of other techniques, such as self-monitoring, contrived or analogue measures, and behavioral rating scales.

Self-Monitoring Training clients to record or monitor the problem behavior in their daily lives is another method of relating problem behavior to the settings in which it occurs. In **self-monitoring,** clients assume the responsibility for assessing the problem behavior in the settings in which it naturally occurs.

self-monitoring The process of observing or recording one's own behaviors, thoughts, or emotions.

Behaviors that can be easily counted, such as food intake, cigarette smoking, nail biting, hair pulling, study periods, or social activities, are well suited for self-monitoring. Self-monitoring can produce highly accurate measurement, because the behavior is recorded as it occurs, not reconstructed from memory.

There are various devices for keeping track of the targeted behavior. A behavioral diary or log is a handy way to record calories ingested or cigarettes smoked. Such logs can be organized in columns and rows to track the frequency of occurrence of the problem behavior and the situations in which it occurs (time, setting, feeling state, etc.). A record of eating may include entries for the type of food eaten, the number of calories, the location in which the eating occurred, the feeling states associated with eating, and the consequences of eating (e.g., how the client felt afterward). In reviewing an eating diary with the clinician, a client can identify problematic eating patterns, such as eating when feeling bored or in response to TV food commercials, and devise better ways of handling these cues.

Today, clinicians are turning to the use of palmtop electronic devices, such as electronic diaries or personal digital assistants (PDAs) to help clients track specific behaviors. In one recent study, teenagers used palmtop devices to keep track of their smoking behavior and aggressive and depressive symptoms (Whalen et al., 2001).

Behavioral diaries can also help clients increase desirable but low-frequency behaviors, such as assertive behavior and dating behavior. Unassertive clients might track occasions that seem to warrant an assertive response and jot down their actual responses to each occasion. Clients and clinicians then review the log to highlight problematic situations and rehearse assertive responses. A client who is anxious about dating might record social contacts with the opposite gender. To measure the effects of treatment, clinicians may encourage clients to engage in a baseline period of self-monitoring before treatment is begun.

Self-monitoring, though, is not without its disadvantages. Some clients are unreliable and do not keep accurate records. They become forgetful or sloppy, or they underreport undesirable behaviors, such as overeating or smoking, because of embarrassment or fear of criticism. To offset these biases, clinicians may, with clients' consent, corroborate the accuracy of self-monitoring by gathering information from other parties, such as clients' spouses. (Achenbach et al., 2005). Private behaviors such as eating or smoking alone cannot be corroborated in this way, however. Sometimes other means of corroboration, such as physiological measures, are available. For example, blood alcohol levels can be used to verify self-reports of alcohol use, or analysis of carbon monoxide levels in clients' breath samples can be used to corroborate reports of abstinence from smoking.

Recording undesirable behaviors may make people more aware of the need to change them. Thus, self-monitoring can be put to therapeutic use if it leads to adaptive behavioral changes. In one weight-loss study, for example, the more consistently participants monitored what they ate, the more weight they lost (Baker & Kirschenbaum, 1993). This is not to imply that self-monitoring alone is sufficient to produce a desired behavior change. Motivation to change and skills needed to make behavior changes are also important.

Analogue Measures *Analogue measures* are intended to simulate the setting in which the behavior naturally takes place but are carried out in laboratory or controlled settings. Role-playing exercises are common analogue measures. For example, suppose a client has difficulty challenging authority figures, such as professors. The clinician might describe a scene to the client as follows: "You've worked very hard on a term paper and received a very poor grade, say a D or an F. You approach the professor, who asks, 'Is there some problem?' What do you do now?" The client's enactment of the scene may reveal deficits in self-expression that can be addressed in therapy or assertiveness training.

The Behavioral Approach Task, or BAT, is a widely used analogue measure of a phobic person's approach to a feared object, such as a snake. Approach behavior is broken down into levels of response, such as looking in the direction of the snake from about 20 feet, touching the box holding the snake, and touching the snake. The BAT provides direct

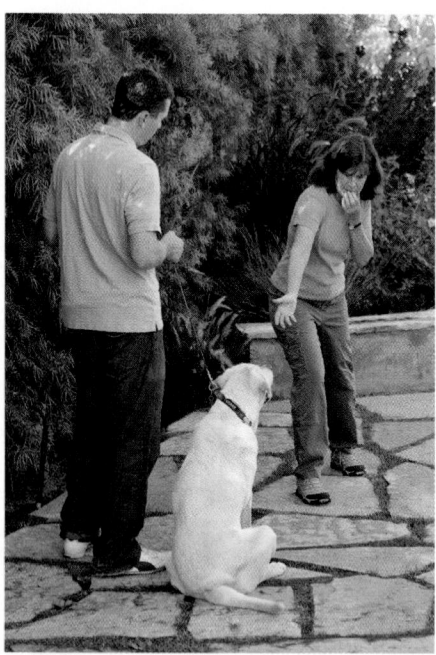

Behavioral approach task. One form of behavioral assessment of phobia involves measurement of the degree to which the person can approach or interact with the phobic stimulus. Here we see a woman with a dog phobia tentatively reaching out to pet a dog. Other people with snake phobias would not be able to touch the snake or even remain in its presence unless it was securely caged.

measurement of a response to a stimulus in a controlled situation. The subject's approach behavior can be quantified by assigning a score to each level of approach. In a recent treatment study of phobic children, the effectiveness of treatment was gauged in part by comparing the children's ability to approach the phobic stimulus (e.g., live animal, insect) after treatment with their performance before treatment (Öst et al., 2001).

Behavioral Rating Scales A *behavioral rating scale* is a checklist that provides information about the frequency, intensity, and range of problem behaviors. Behavioral rating scales differ from self-report personality inventories, in that items assess specific behaviors rather than personality characteristics, interests, or attitudes.

Behavioral rating scales are often used by parents to assess children's problem behaviors. The Child Behavior Checklist (CBCL) (Achenbach & Dumenci, 2001), for example, asks parents to rate their children on more than 100 specific problem behaviors, including the following:

- ❏ refuses to eat
- ❏ is disobedient
- ❏ hits
- ❏ is uncooperative
- ❏ destroys own things

The scale yields an overall problem-behavior score and subscale scores on dimensions such as delinquency, aggressiveness, and physical problems. The clinician can compare the child's score on these dimensions with norms based on samples of age-mates.

Cognitive Assessment

Cognitive assessment involves measurement of *cognitions*—thoughts, beliefs, and attitudes. Cognitive therapists believe that people who hold self-defeating or dysfunctional cognitions are at greater risk of developing emotional problems, such as depression, in the face of stressful or disappointing life experiences. They help clients replace dysfunctional thinking patterns with self-enhancing, rational thought patterns.

cognitive assessment Measurement of thoughts, beliefs, and attitudes that may be associated with emotional problems.

Several methods of cognitive assessment have been developed. One of the most straightforward is the thought record or diary. Depressed clients may carry such diaries to record dysfunctional thoughts as they arise. Aaron Beck (A. T. Beck et al., 1979) designed a thought diary or "Daily Record of Dysfunctional Thoughts" to help clients identify thought patterns connected with troubling emotional states. Each time the client experiences a negative emotion such as anger or sadness, entries are made to identify

1. The situation in which the emotional state occurred
2. The automatic or disruptive thoughts that passed through the client's mind
3. The type or category of disordered thinking that the automatic thought(s) represented (e.g., selective abstraction, overgeneralization, magnification, or absolutist thinking—see Chapter 2)
4. A rational response to the troublesome thought
5. The emotional outcome or final emotional response

A thought diary can become part of a treatment program in which the client learns to replace dysfunctional thoughts with rational alternative thoughts.

The Automatic Thoughts Questionnaire (ATQ-30; Hollon & Kendall, 1980) has clients rate the weekly frequency and degree of conviction associated with 30 automatic negative thoughts. (Automatic thoughts are thoughts that seem to just pop into our minds.) Sample items include the following:

- I don't think I can go on.
- I hate myself.
- I've let people down.

A total score is obtained by summing the frequencies of occurrence of each item. Higher scores are suggestive of depressive thought patterns. The 30-item ATQ has been statistically sorted into four categories or factors of related thoughts (see Table 3.9).

The ATQ successfully discriminates between depressed and nondepressed subjects, with higher scores indicative of more severe depressive symptoms (Blankstein & Segal, 2001). Recent evidence also suggests that in depressed patients who are treated with cognitive-behavioral therapy, reducing negative thinking as reflected in changes on the ATQ leads to reductions in depressive symptoms (Kaufman et al., 2005).

Another cognitive measure, the Dysfunctional Attitudes Scale (DAS; A. N. Weissman & Beck, 1978), consists of an inventory of a relatively stable set of underlying attitudes or assumptions associated with depression (Blankstein & Segal, 2001). Examples include, "I feel like I'm nothing if someone I love doesn't love me back." Subjects use a 7-point scale to rate the degree to which they endorse each belief. The DAS taps underlying assumptions believed to predispose individuals to depression, so it may be sensitive to detecting vulnerability to depression (DeRubeis, Tang, & Beck, 2001; Weich, Churchill, & Lewis, 2003).

Cognitive assessment opens a new domain to the psychologist in understanding how disruptive thoughts are related to abnormal behavior. Only in the past two decades or so have cognitive and cognitive-behavioral therapists begun to explore what B. F. Skinner labeled the "black box"—people's internal states—to learn how thoughts and attitudes influence emotional states and behavior.

The behavioral objection to cognitive techniques is that clinicians have no direct means of verifying clients' subjective experiences, their thoughts and beliefs. These are private experiences that can be reported but not observed and measured directly. However, even though thoughts remain private experiences, reports of cognitions in the form of rating scales or checklists can be quantified and validated by reference to external criteria.

Physiological Measurement

Physiological assessment is the study of people's physiological responses. Anxiety, for example, is associated with arousal of the sympathetic division of the autonomic nervous system (see Chapter 2). Anxious people therefore show elevated heart rates and blood pressure, which can be measured directly by means of the pulse and a blood pressure cuff. People also sweat more heavily when they are anxious. When we sweat, our skin becomes wet, increasing its ability to conduct electricity. Sweating can be measured by means of the *electrodermal response* or galvanic skin response (*GSR*). (*Galvanic* is named after the Italian physicist and physician Luigi Galvani, who was a pioneer in research in electricity.) Measures of the GSR assess the amount of electricity that passes through two points on the skin, usually of the hand. We assume the person's anxiety level correlates with the amount of electricity conducted across the skin.

The *GSR* is just one example of a physiological response measured through probes or sensors connected to the body. Another example is the *electroencephalograph* (EEG), which measures brain waves by attaching electrodes to the scalp (Figure 3.6).

Changes in muscle tension are also often associated with states of anxiety or tension. They can be detected through the *electromyograph* (EMG), which monitors muscle tension through sensors attached to targeted muscle groups. Placement of EMG probes on the forehead can indicate muscle tension associated with tension headaches.

Brain-Imaging and Recording Techniques   Advances in medical technology have made it possible to study the workings of the brain without the need for surgery. One of the most common is the *electroencephalograph* (EEG), which is a record of the electrical activity of the brain. The EEG detects minute amounts of electrical activity in the brain, or *brain waves,* which are conducted between electrodes placed on the scalp. Certain brain wave patterns are associated with mental states such as relaxation and with the different stages of sleep. The EEG is used to examine brain wave

physiological assessment Measurement of physiological responses that may be associated with abnormal behavior.

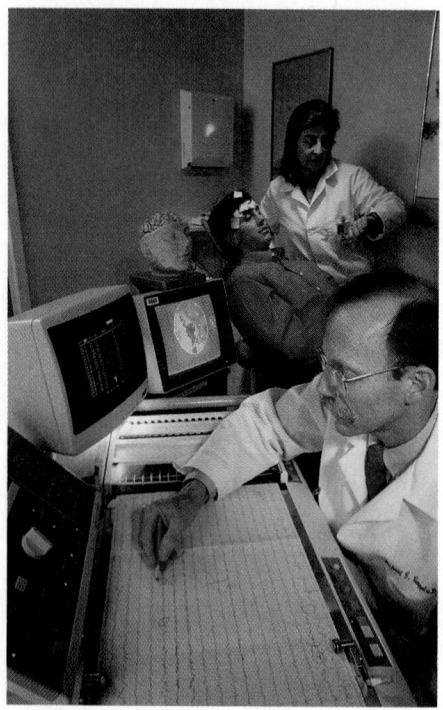

FIGURE 3.6 The electroencephalograph (EEG).
The EEG can be used to study differences in brain waves between groups of normal people and people with problems such as schizophrenia or organic brain damage.

TABLE 3.9

Items Defining Factors on the Automatic Thoughts Questionnaire

Factor 1: Personal maladjustment and desire for change	Something has to change. What's the matter with me? I wish I were a better person. What's wrong with me? I'm so disappointed in myself.
Factor 2: Negative self-concept and negative expectations	My future is bleak. I'm a failure. I'll never make it. My life's not going the way I wanted it to. I'm a loser. Why can't I ever succeed? I'm no good.
Factor 3: Low self-esteem	I'm worthless. I hate myself.
Factor 4: Giving up/helplessness	I can't finish anything. It's just not worth it.

Source: Adapted from Hollon & Kendall (1980).

patterns associated with psychological disorders, such as schizophrenia, and with brain damage. The EEG is also used by medical personnel to reveal brain abnormalities such as tumors.

Brain-imaging techniques generate images that reflect the structure and functioning of the brain. In a *computed tomography* (CT) scan, a narrow X-ray beam is aimed at the head (Figure 3.7). The radiation that passes through is measured from multiple angles. The CT scan (also called CAT scan for *computerized axial tomography*) reveals abnormalities in shape and structure that may be suggestive of lesions, blood clots, or tumors. The computer enables scientists to integrate the measurements into a three-dimensional picture of the brain. Evidence of brain damage that was once detectable only by surgery may now be displayed on a monitor.

FIGURE 3.7 The computed tomography (CT) scan.
The CT scan aims a narrow X-ray beam at the head, and the resultant radiation is measured from multiple angles as it passes through. The computer enables researchers to consolidate the measurements into a three-dimensional image of the brain. The CT scan reveals structural abnormalities in the brain that may be implicated in various patterns of abnormal behavior.

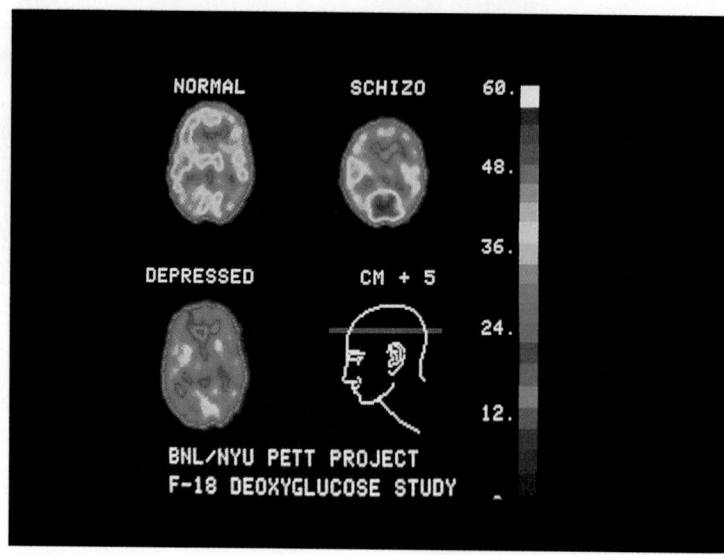

FIGURE 3.8 Positron emission tomography (PET) scan.
These PET scan images suggest differences in the metabolic processes of the brains of people with depression, schizophrenia, and controls who are free of psychological disorders.

Another imaging method, *positron emission tomography* (PET scan), is used to study the functioning of various parts of the brain (Figure 3.8). In this method, a small amount of a radioactive compound or tracer is mixed with glucose and injected into the bloodstream. When it reaches the brain, patterns of neural activity are revealed by measurement of the positrons—positively charged particles—emitted by the tracer. The glucose metabolized by parts of the brain generates a computer image of neural activity. Areas of greater activity metabolize more glucose. The PET scan has been used to learn which parts of the brain are most active (metabolize more glucose) when we are listening to music, solving a math problem, or using language. It can also be used to reveal abnormalities in brain activity in people with schizophrenia (see Chapter 12).

A third imaging technique is *magnetic resonance imaging* (MRI). In MRI, the person is placed in a donut-shaped tunnel that generates a strong magnetic field. The basic idea of the MRI, in the words of its inventor, is to stuff a human being into a large magnet (Weed, 2003). Radio waves of certain frequencies are then directed at the head. As a result, the brain emits signals that can be measured from several angles. As with the CT scan, the signals are integrated into a computer-generated image of the brain, which can reveal brain abnormalities associated with psychological disorders, such as schizophrenia and obsessive–compulsive disorder.

A new type of MRI, called *functional magnetic resonance imaging* (fMRI), is used to identify parts of the brain that become active when people engage in particular tasks,

FIGURE 3.9 Functional magnetic resonance imaging (fMRI). A fMRI is a specialized type of MRI that allows investigators to determine the parts of the brain that are activated during particular tasks. The areas depicted in red become activated when a person thinks about performing certain gestures (top), such as using a hammer or writing with a pen, and when the person actually performs these gestures (bottom). The right hemisphere is shown on the left side of the photographs, and the left hemisphere is shown on the right side.

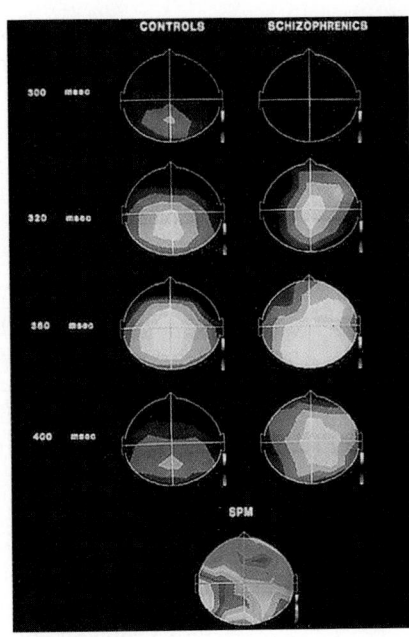

FIGURE 3.10 Brain electrical activity mapping (BEAM).
BEAM is a type of EEG in which electrodes are attached to the scalp (left) to measure electrical activity in various regions of the brain. The left column of the brain scans (right) shows the average level of electrical activity in the brains of 10 normal people ("controls") at 4 time intervals. The column to the right shows the average level of activity of subjects with schizophrenia during the same intervals. Higher activity levels are represented in increasing order by yellows, reds, and whites. The computer-generated image in the bottom center summarizes differences in activity levels between the brains of normal subjects and those with schizophrenia. Areas of the brain depicted in blue show small differences between the groups. White areas represent larger differences.

such as vision, memory, or use of speech (see Figure 3.9). In an illustrative example of an fMRI study, investigators found that that when cocaine-addicted subjects experienced cocaine cravings, their brains showed increased activity in the same areas that were engaged when healthy subjects watched depressing videotapes (Wexler et al., 2001). This suggests there may be a physiological link between depressive feelings and drug cravings.

Brain electrical activity mapping (BEAM), a sophisticated type of EEG, uses the computer to analyze brain wave patterns and reveal areas of relative activity and inactivity from moment to moment (Figure 3.10) (F. H. Duffy, 1994; Silberstein et al., 1998). Twenty or more electrodes are attached to the scalp and simultaneously feed information about brain activity to a computer. The computer analyzes the signals and displays the pattern of brain activity on a color monitor, providing a vivid image of the electrical activity of the brain at work. BEAM and other similar techniques have been helpful in studying the brain activity of people with schizophrenia and children with attention-deficit hyperactivity disorder, among other physical and psychological disorders. In later chapters we see how modern imaging techniques are furthering our understanding of various patterns of abnormal behavior.

SOCIOCULTURAL AND ETHNIC FACTORS IN ASSESSMENT

Researchers and clinicians must keep sociocultural and ethnic factors in mind when assessing personality traits and psychological disorders. When testing people from other cultures, careful translations are essential to capture the meanings of the original items (Butcher et al., 2002, 2003). However, assessment techniques that are reliable and valid within one culture may not be so in another, even when they are translated accurately (Bolton, 2001; Cheung et al., 2003).

For example, the Chinese version of the Beck Depression Inventory (BDI), a widely used inventory of depression in the United States, has shown good validity in distinguishing people with depression from people without depression (Chan, 1991;

TRUTH or FICTION

Cocaine cravings in people addicted to cocaine have been linked to parts of the brain that are normally activated during pleasant emotions.

☑ **FALSE.** Just the opposite was the case. Cravings were associated with activation of parts of the brain that normally become active when watching depressing videotapes.

Yeung et al., 2002). However, other investigators found that Chinese people in both Hong Kong and the People's Republic of China showed high levels of disturbed behavior when tested with a Chinese version of the MMPI (Cheung, Song, & Butcher, 1991). However, more careful analysis suggests that their test responses reflected cultural differences rather than greater psychopathology (Cheung, 1991; Cheung & Ho, 1997). In other words, researchers need to disentangle psychopathology from sociocultural factors. Translations of assessment instruments should not only translate words, but also provide instructions that encourage examiners to address the importance of cultural beliefs, norms, and values, so diagnosticians and interviewers will consider the client's background when making assessments of abnormal behavior patterns.

Studies in our own culture have put psychological instruments such as the BDI and MMPI-2 under a cultural microscope. Recently, investigators found that the BDI, now in a second edition called the BDI-II, works well in assessing depressive symptoms of African American medical patients (Grothe et al., 2005). Other investigators find no evidence of clinically significant cultural bias on the MMPI-2 in comparing groups of African American and European American (non-Hispanic White) patients in either outpatient or inpatient settings (Arbisi, Ben-Porath, & McNulty, 2002; McNulty et al., 1997). In yet other research, investigators found that the MMPI-2 was sensitive to detecting problem behaviors and symptoms in American Indian tribal members (Greene et al., 2003; Robin et al., 2003).

Interviewers must also recognize the importance of taking language preferences into account when conducting multicultural assessments. Meanings can get lost in translation, or worse, distorted. For example, Spanish-speakers are often judged to be more disturbed when interviewed in English than in Spanish (Fabrega, 1990). Interviewers, too, may fail to appreciate the idioms and subtleties of different languages. For instance, we recall one clinician, a foreign-born and -trained psychiatrist whose native language was not English, reporting that a patient had exhibited the delusional belief that he was outside his body. The interviewer based this assessment on the patient's response when asked if he was feeling anxious. "Yes, Doc," the patient replied, "I feel like I'm jumping out of my skin at times."

In conclusion, people's psychological problems, which are no less complex than people themselves, are assessed in many ways. Clients are asked to explain their problems as best they can; sometimes a computer does the asking. Psychologists can draw on batteries of tests that assess intelligence, personality, and neuropsychological integrity. Many psychologists prefer to observe people's behavior directly. Modern technology has provided several means of studying the structure and function of the brain. The methods of assessment clinicians select reflect the problems of their clients, their theoretical orientations, and their mastery of specialized technologies.

SUMMING UP

How Are Abnormal Behavior Patterns Classified?

What is the DSM and what are its major features? The *Diagnostic and Statistical Manual of Mental Disorders (DSM)* is the most widely accepted system for classifying mental disorders. The *DSM* uses specific diagnostic criteria to group patterns of abnormal behaviors that share common clinical features and a multiaxial system of evaluation.

Why is the DSM considered a multiaxial system? The *DSM* system consists of five axes of classification: Axis I (Clinical Disorders), Axis II (Personality Disorders and Mental Retardation), Axis III (General Medical Conditions), Axis IV (Psychosocial and Environmental Problems), and Axis V (Global Assessment of Functioning).

What are the major strengths and weaknesses of the DSM? Strengths of the *DSM* include its use of specified diagnostic criteria and a multiaxial system to provide a comprehensive picture of the person's functioning. Weaknesses include questions about reliability and validity of certain diagnostic categories and, to some, the adoption of a medical model framework for classifying abnormal behavior patterns.

Standards of Assessment

What are the standards by which methods of assessment are judged? Methods of assessment must be reliable and valid. Reliability of assessment techniques is shown in various ways, including internal consistency, test–retest reliability, and interrater reliability. Validity is measured by means of content validity, criterion validity, and construct validity.

Methods of Assessment

What is a clinical interview? A clinical interview involves the use of a set of questions designed to elicit relevant information from people seeking treatment.

What are the three major types of clinical interviews? The three major types of clinical interviews are unstructured interviews (clinicians use their own style of questioning rather than follow a particular script), semistructured interviews (clinicians follow a general outline in directing their questioning but are free to branch off in other directions), and structured interviews (clinicians strictly follow a preset order of questions).

What are psychological tests? Psychological tests are structured methods of assessment used to evaluate reasonably stable traits such as intelligence and personality.

What are the major types of psychological tests? Tests of intelligence, such as the Wechsler scales, are used for various purposes in clinical assessment, including determining evidence of mental retardation or cognitive impairment, and assessing strengths and weaknesses. Objective personality tests, such as the MMPI, use structured items to measure psychological characteristics or traits, such as anxiety, depression, and masculinity-femininity. These tests are considered objective in the sense that they make use of a limited range of possible responses to items and are based on an empirical, or objective, method of test construction. Projective personality tests, such as the Rorschach and TAT, require subjects to interpret ambiguous stimuli in the belief their answers may shed light on their unconscious processes.

What is neuropsychological assessment? Neuropsychological assessment involves the use of psychological tests to indicate possible neurological impairment or brain defects. The Halstead-Reitan Neuropsychological Battery uncovers skill deficits that are suggestive of underlying brain damage.

What are some of the methods used in behavioral assessment? In behavioral assessment, test responses are taken as samples of behavior rather than as signs of underlying traits or dispositions. The behavioral examiner may conduct a functional analysis, which relates the problem behavior to its antecedents and consequents. Methods of behavioral assessment include behavioral interviewing, self-monitoring, use of analogue or contrived measures, direct observation, and behavioral rating scales.

What is cognitive assessment? Cognitive assessment focuses on the measurement of thoughts, beliefs, and attitudes in order to help identify distorted thinking patterns. Specific methods of assessment include the use of a thought record or diary and the use of rating scales such as the Automatic Thoughts Questionnaire (ATQ) and the Dysfunctional Attitudes Scale (DAS).

How do clinicians and researchers study physiological functioning? Measures of physiological functioning include heart rate, blood pressure, galvanic skin response (GSR), muscle tension, and brain wave activity. Brain-imaging and recording techniques such as EEG, CT scans, PET scans, MRI, and BEAM probe the inner workings and structures of the brain.

Sociocultural and Ethnic Factors in Assessment

Why is it important to take cultural or ethnic factors into account in psychological assessment? We need to ensure that tests that are validated in one culture are reliable and valid when used with members of another culture.

KEY TERMS

culture-bound syndromes (*p. 73*)
reliability (*p. 75*)
validity (*p. 75*)
sanism (*p. 77*)
content validity (*p. 79*)
criterion validity (*p. 79*)

construct validity (*p. 79*)
unstructured interview (*p. 81*)
semistructured interview (*p. 81*)
structured interview (*p. 81*)
objective tests (*p. 84*)
projective tests (*p. 87*)

reality testing (*p. 88*)
neuropsychological assessment (*p. 90*)
behavioral assessment (*p. 92*)
self-monitoring (*p. 93*)
cognitive assessment (*p. 95*)
physiological assessment (*p. 96*)

MEDIA TOOLS

A variety of digital and online learning tools are avaiable to enrich your learning experience and help you succeed in the course. These resources include:

- MyPsychLab, an online learning system for your course in abnormal psychology that allows you to test your mastery of concepts in the book by using chapter-by-chapter diagnostic tests. Results from the diagnostic tests help you build a customized study plan. To access **MyPsychLab,** visit www.prenhall.com/mypsychlab and follow the instructions on the site.

- "SPEAKING OUT" PATIENT INTERVIEWS, a set of video case examples of actual patients you can access on the companion CD-ROM included with the text. Icons in the margins of the chapter highlight the video case examples included on the CD-ROM.

- COMPANION WEB SITE, an online study center that offers computer-scored quizzes you can use to test your knowledge, along with other study tools and links to related sites to enhance your learning of abnormal psychology. To access the companion web site, visit www.prenhall.com/nevid and use the various tabs and links on the site to access these learning resources.

CHAPTER 4

Methods of Treatment

CHAPTER OUTLINE

TYPES OF HELPING PROFESSIONALS 104

PSYCHOTHERAPY 104–125

Psychodynamic Therapy
Behavior Therapy
Humanistic Therapy
Cognitive Therapy
Cognitive-Behavioral Therapy
Eclectic Therapy
Group, Family, and Couple Therapy
Evaluating Methods of Psychotherapy
Multicultural Issues in Psychotherapy

BIOMEDICAL THERAPIES 126–130

Drug Therapy
Electroconvulsive Therapy
Psychosurgery
Evaluation of Biological Approaches

HOSPITALIZATION AND COMMUNITY-BASED CARE 131–137

Roles for Hospitalization
The Community Mental Health Center

Ethnic Group Differences in Use of Mental
  Health Services
Racial Stereotyping and the Mental
  Health System
Evaluation of Deinstitutionalization

SUMMING UP 137–138

"I"

Susanna—"A Girl, Interrupted"

Suicide is a form of murder—premeditated murder. It isn't something you do the first time you think of doing it. It takes getting used to. And you need the means, the opportunity, the motive. . . .

My motives were weak: an American-history paper I didn't want to write and the question I'd asked months earlier, Why not kill myself? Dead, I wouldn't have to write the paper. Nor would I have to keep debating the question. . . .

Anything I thought or did was immediately drawn into the debate. Made a stupid remark—why not kill myself? Missed the bus—better put an end to it all. Even the good got in there. I liked that movie—maybe I shouldn't kill myself.

Actually, it was only part of myself I wanted to kill: the part that wanted to kill herself, that dragged me into the suicide debate and made every window, kitchen implement, and subway station a rehearsal for tragedy.

I didn't figure this out, though, until after I'd swallowed the fifty aspirin.

I had a boyfriend named Johnny who wrote me love poems—good ones. I called him up, said I was going to kill myself, left the phone off the hook, took my fifty aspirin, and realized it was a mistake. Then I went out to get some milk, which my mother had asked me to do before I took the aspirin.

Johnny called the police. They went to my house and told my mother what I'd done. She turned up in the A&P on Mass. Ave, just as I was about to pass out over the meat counter.

As I walked the five blocks to the A&P I was gripped by humiliation and regret. I'd made a mistake and I was going to die because of it. I began to cry about my death. For a moment, I felt compassion for myself and all the unhappiness I contained. Then things started to blur and whiz. By the time I reached the store, the world had been reduced to a narrow, throbbing tunnel. I'd lost my peripheral vision, my ears were ringing, my pulse was pounding. The bloody chops and steaks straining against the plastic wrapping were the last things I saw clearly.

Having my stomach pumped brought me around. They took a long tube and put it slowly up my nose and down the back of my throat. That was like being choked to death. Then they began to pump. That was like having blood drawn on a massive scale—the suction, the sense of tissue collapsing and touching itself in a way it shouldn't, the nausea as all that was inside was pulled out. It was a good deterrent. Next time, I decided, I certainly wouldn't take aspirin.

But when they were done, I wondered if there would be a next time. I felt good. I wasn't dead, yet something was dead. Perhaps I'd managed my peculiar objective of partial suicide. I was lighter, airier than I'd been in years. . . .

The only odd thing was that suddenly I was a vegetarian. I associated meat with suicide, because of passing out at the meat counter. But I know there was more to it.

The meat was bruised, bleeding, and imprisoned in a tight wrapping. And, though I had a six-month respite from thinking about it, so was I.

—From *Girl, Interrupted* by Susanna Kaysen, copyright © 1993 by Susanna Kaysen.
Used by permission of Turtle bay Books, a division of Random House, Inc.

EIGHTEEN-YEAR-OLD SUSANNA KAYSEN SPENT TWO YEARS ON A PSYCHIATRIC WARD AFTER THIS halfhearted suicide attempt. Twenty-five years later she chronicled her experience as a psychiatric patient in her autobiographical book, *Girl, Interrupted*. Like Kaysen, many people who attempt or commit suicide have ambivalent feelings about taking their own lives. Kaysen called her boyfriend, giving him the opportunity to intervene. She survived, was able to get on with her life, and eventually wrote two novels and her memoir, which later became the subject of a motion picture of the same name. Unfortunately, many people who attempt suicide fail to get a second chance on life.

Girl, Interrupted. The memoir and movie of the same name chronicles the experiences of a young woman (played in the movie by actress Winona Ryder) who is hospitalized in a mental hospital after a halfhearted suicide attempt.

This chapter focuses on ways of helping people like Susanna who are struggling with psychological problems. Some forms of help involve outpatient treatment, such as psychotherapy or drug therapy. In more severe cases, such as with people who make suicide attempts or are suffering acute episodes of schizophrenia, treatment typically involves a period of inpatient care.

The treatment an individual receives depends not only on the particular problem but also on the therapeutic orientation and training of the helping professional. Consider someone suffering from depression. A psychiatrist might recommend a course of antidepressant medication, perhaps in combination with psychotherapy. A cognitively oriented psychologist might suggest cognitive therapy to help identify faulty thinking patterns that underlie depression, whereas a psychodynamic therapist might probe for unconscious conflicts believed to lie at the root of the person's problems.

In this chapter we focus on these and other ways of treating psychological disorders. About one out of seven people in the United States receives mental health treatment in any given year (USDHHS, 1999a). Yet, despite the widespread availability of mental health services, there remains a large unmet need, as most people with diagnosed mental disorders remain either untreated or undertreated (Kessler et al., 2005c; Wang et al., 2005).

In later chapters we examine the kinds of treatment approaches applied to particular disorders, but here we focus on the treatments themselves. We will see that the biological and psychological perspectives have spawned corresponding approaches to treatment. First, however, we consider the major types of mental health professionals who treat psychological or mental disorders and the different roles they play.

TYPES OF HELPING PROFESSIONALS

Many people are confused about the differences in qualifications and training of the various types of professionals who provide mental health care. It is little wonder people are confused, as there are different types of mental health professionals who represent a wide range of training backgrounds and areas of practice. For example, clinical psychologists and counseling psychologists have completed advanced graduate training in psychology and obtained a license to practice psychology. Psychiatrists are medical doctors who specialize in the diagnosis and treatment of emotional disorders. The major professional groupings of helping professionals, including clinical and counseling psychologists, psychiatrists, social workers, nurses, and counselors, are described in Table 4.1.

Unfortunately, many states do not limit the use of the titles *therapist* or *psychotherapist* to trained professionals. In such states, anyone can set up shop as a psychotherapist and practice "therapy" without a license. Thus, people seeking help are advised to inquire about the training and licensure of helping professionals. If you or someone you know should seek the services of a psychologist, how would you find one? The *A Closer Look* feature, "How Do I Find Help?," offers some suggestions.

We now consider the major types of psychotherapy and their relationships to the theoretical models from which they are derived.

PSYCHOTHERAPY

psychotherapy A structured form of treatment derived from a psychological framework that consists of one or more verbal interactions or treatment sessions between a client and a therapist.

Psychotherapy is a systematic interaction between a client and a therapist that draws on psychological principles to help bring about changes in the client's behaviors, thoughts, and feelings. Psychotherapy is used to help clients overcome abnormal

TABLE 4.1

Major Types of Helping Professionals

Type	Description
Clinical psychologists	Have earned a doctoral degree in psychology (either a Ph.D., or Doctor of Philosophy; a Psy.D., or Doctor of Psychology; or an Ed.D., or Doctor of Education) from an accredited college or university. Training in clinical psychology typically involves 4 years of graduate coursework, followed by a year-long internship and completion of a doctoral dissertation. Clinical psychologists specialize in administering psychological tests, diagnosing psychological disorders, and practicing psychotherapy. Until recently, they were not permitted to prescribe psychiatric drugs. However, as of this writing, two states (New Mexico and Louisiana) had enacted laws granting prescription privileges to psychologists who complete specialized training programs (Comas-Diaz, 2006; Practice Directorate Staff, 2005). Whether other states will follow suit remains to be seen. Moreover, the granting of prescription privileges to psychologists remains a hotly contested issue between psychologists and psychiatrists and within the field of psychology itself.
Counseling psychologists	Also hold doctoral degrees in psychology and have completed graduate training preparing them for careers in college counseling centers and mental health facilities. They typically provide counseling to people with psychological problems falling in a milder range of severity than those treated by clinical psychologists, such as difficulties adjusting to college or uncertainties regarding career choices.
Psychiatrists	Have earned a medical degree (M.D.) and completed a residency program in psychiatry. Psychiatrists are physicians who specialize in the diagnosis and treatment of psychological disorders. As licensed physicians, they can prescribe psychiatric drugs and may employ other medical interventions, such as electroconvulsive therapy (ECT). Many also practice psychotherapy based on training they receive during their residency programs or in specialized training institutes.
Clinical or psychiatric social workers	Have earned a master's degree in social work (M.S.W.) and use their knowledge of community agencies and organizations to help people with severe mental disorders receive the services they need. For example, they may help people with schizophrenia make a more successful adjustment to the community once they leave the hospital. Many clinical social workers practice psychotherapy or specific forms of therapy, such as marital or family therapy.
Psychoanalysts	Typically are either psychiatrists or psychologists who have completed extensive additional training in psychoanalysis. They are required to undergo psychoanalysis themselves as part of their training.
Counselors	Have typically earned a master's degree by completing a graduate program in a counseling field. Counselors work in many settings, including public schools, college testing and counseling centers, and hospitals and health clinics. Many specialize in vocational evaluation, marital or family therapy, rehabilitation counseling, or substance abuse counseling. Counselors may focus on providing psychological assistance to people with milder forms of disturbed behavior or those struggling with a chronic or debilitating illness or recovering from a traumatic experience. Some are clergy members who are trained in pastoral counseling programs to help parishioners cope with personal problems.
Psychiatric nurses	Typically are R.N.s who have completed a master's program in psychiatric nursing. They may work in a psychiatric facility or in a group medical practice where they treat people suffering from severe psychological disorders.

Source: Adapted from Nevid, J. S. (2007). *Psychology: Concepts and applications* (2nd ed.). Boston: Houghton Mifflin.

behavior, solve problems in living, or develop as individuals. Let us take a closer look at these features of psychotherapy:

1. *Systematic interaction.* "Systematic" means that therapists structure their interactions with clients in ways that reflect their theoretical points of view.
2. *Psychological principles.* Psychotherapists draw on psychological principles, research, and theory in their practice.

TRUTH or FICTION

Some psychologists have been trained to prescribe drugs.

☑ **TRUE.** Some psychologists have received specialized training that prepares them to prescribe psychiatric medications.

3. *Behavior, thoughts, and feelings.* Psychotherapy may be directed at behavioral, cognitive, and emotional domains to help clients overcome psychological problems and lead more satisfying lives.

4. *Abnormal behavior, problem solving, and personal growth.* At least three groups of people are assisted by psychotherapy. First are people with abnormal behavior problems such as mood disorders, anxiety disorders, or schizophrenia. Second are people who seek help for personal problems that are not regarded as abnormal, such as social shyness or confusion about career choices. Third are people who seek personal growth. For them, psychotherapy is a means of self-discovery that may help them reach their potentials as, for example, parents, creative artists, performers, or athletes.

Psychotherapies share other features as well. For one, they are all "talking therapies"—psychologically based treatment involving verbal interchanges between clients and therapists. In some cases, there is a continuous back-and-forth dialogue between the client and therapist. In others, such as traditional psychoanalysis, the client does virtually all the talking. Skillful therapists are also active listeners: They listen intently to what clients are saying to understand as clearly as possible what they are experiencing and attempting to convey. Therapists also express interest in what the client is saying through words as well as nonverbal gestures, such as establishing eye contact and leaning forward when the client is speaking. Skillful therapists are also sensitive to clients' nonverbal cues, such as gestures that may indicate underlying feelings or conflicts. Therapists also seek to convey empathy, or accurate understanding of the client's feelings and experiences. Therapist empathy is a consistent predictor of therapy outcome. Clients of therapists who are perceived as warmer and more empathic show greater improvement than clients of other therapists, regardless of the type of therapy.

TRUTH or FICTION

In many states people can set up shop as a psychotherapist without any kind of license or credentials.

☑ **TRUE.** It is legal in many states to use the title "psychotherapist" or to practice psychotherapy without a license or credentials.

A CLOSER LOOK

How Do I Find Help?

In most areas in the United States and Canada, there are pages upon pages of psychologists and other mental health professionals in the telephone directory. Many people have no idea whom to call for help. If you don't know where to go or whom to see, there are a number of steps you can take to ensure that you receive appropriate care:

1. *Seek recommendations from respected sources, such as your family physician, course instructor, clergyperson, or college health service.*

2. *Seek a consultation with your college counseling center or health services center.* Most colleges and universities offer psychological assistance to students, generally without charge.

3. *Seek a referral from a local medical center or local community mental health center.* When making inquiries, ask about the services that are available or about opportunities for referral to qualified treatment providers in the area.

4. *Contact professional organizations for recommendations.* Many local or national organizations maintain a referral list of qualified treatment providers in your area. If you would like to consult a psychologist, contact the American Psychological Association in Washington, DC, by telephone at 202-336-5650 or on the Internet at www.apa.org. At the Web site, click on the links to "Find a Psychologist" for a listing of psychologists in your particular area. Alternatively, you can call your local or state psychology association in the United States or your provincial or territorial psychological association in Canada.

5. *Let your fingers do the walking—but be careful!* Look under "Psychologists," "Physicians," "Social Workers," or "Social and Human Services" in your local Yellow Pages. However, be wary of professionals who take out large ads and claim to be experts in treating many different kinds of problems.

6. *Make sure the treatment provider is a licensed member of a recognized mental health profession, such as psychology, medicine, counseling, or social work.* In many states, anyone can set up practice as a "therapist," even as a "psychotherapist." These titles may not be limited by law to licensed practitioners. Licensed professionals clearly display their licenses and other credentials in their offices, usually in plain view. If you have any questions about the licensure status of a treatment provider, contact the licensing board in your state, province, or territory.

7. *Inquire about the type of therapy being provided (e.g., psychoanalysis, family therapy, behavior therapy).* Ask the treatment provider to explain how his or her particular type of therapy is appropriate to treating the problems you are having.

8. *Inquire about the treatment provider's professional background.* Ask about the person's educational background, supervised experience, and credentials. An ethical practitioner will not hesitate to provide this information.

9. *Inquire whether the treatment provider has had experience treating other people with similar problems.* Ask about their results and how they were measured.

10. *Once the treatment provider has had the opportunity to conduct a formal evaluation of your problem, discuss the diagnosis and treatment plan before making any commitments to undertake treatment.*

11. *Ask about costs and insurance coverage.* Ask what types of insurance the provider accepts and whether copayments are required on your part. Ask whether the provider will adjust his or her fees on a sliding scale that takes your income and family situation into account. If you are eligible for Medicaid or Medicare, inquire whether the treatment provider accepts these types of coverage. College students may also be covered by their parents' health insurance plans or by student plans offered by their colleges. Find out if the treatment provider participates in any health maintenance organization to which you may belong.

12. *Find out about the treatment provider's policies regarding charges for missed or canceled sessions.*

13. *If medication is to be prescribed, find out how long a delay is expected before it starts working.* Also inquire about possible side effects, and about

(continued)

which side effects should prompt you to call with questions. Don't be afraid to seek a second opinion before undergoing any course of medication.

14. *If the treatment recommendations don't sound quite right to you, discuss your concerns openly.* An ethical professional will be willing to address your concerns rather than feel insulted.

15. *If you still have any doubts, request a second opinion.* An ethical professional will support your efforts to seek a second opinion. Ask the treatment provider to recommend other professionals—or select your own.

Source: Adapted from Nevid, J. S., *Psychology: Concepts and Applications,* Second Edition (Boston: Houghton Mifflin, 2007), p. 56. Reprinted by permission.

Another common feature among different psychotherapies is the instilling in clients of a sense of hope of improvement. Clients generally enter therapy with expectations of receiving help to overcome their problems. Responsible therapists do not promise results or guarantee cures; however, they do instill hope that they can help clients deal with their problems. Positive expectancies can become a type of self-fulfilling prophecy by leading clients to mobilize their efforts toward overcoming their problems. Responses to positive expectancies are termed *placebo effects* or *expectancy effects.*

These common features that cut across different approaches to psychotherapy, such as the encouragement of hope and the display of empathy and attentiveness on the part of the therapist, are called **nonspecific treatment factors.** These factors may have therapeutic benefits in themselves, quite apart from the specific benefits associated with particular forms of therapy. We will discuss these factors in greater detail in the section on evaluating psychotherapy.

nonspecific treatment factors Factors not specific to any one form of psychotherapy, such as therapist attention and support, and creating positive expectancies of change.

psychoanalysis The method of psychotherapy developed by Sigmund Freud.

psychodynamic therapy Therapy that helps individuals gain insight into, and resolve, unconscious conflicts.

free association The method of verbalizing thoughts as they occur without a conscious attempt to edit or censure them.

Psychodynamic Therapy

Sigmund Freud was the first theorist to develop a psychological model—the *psychodynamic model*—of abnormal behavior (see Chapter 2). He was also the first to develop a model of psychotherapy, which he called **psychoanalysis,** to help people who suffered from psychological disorders. Psychoanalysis was the first **psychodynamic therapy.** Psychodynamic therapy helps individuals gain insight into, and resolve, the unconscious conflicts believed to lie at the root of abnormal behavior. Working through these conflicts, the ego would be freed of the need to maintain defensive behaviors—such as phobias, obsessive–compulsive behaviors, hysterical complaints, and the like—that shield it from recognition of inner turmoil.

Freud summed up the goal of psychoanalysis by saying, "Where id was, there shall ego be." This meant, in part, that psychoanalysis could help shed the light of awareness, represented by the conscious ego, on the inner workings of the id. Through this process a man might come to realize that unresolved anger toward his dominating or rejecting mother has sabotaged his intimate relationships with women during his adulthood. A woman with a loss of sensation in her hand that could not be explained medically might come to see that she harbored guilt over urges to masturbate. The loss of sensation might have prevented her from acting on these urges. Through confronting hidden impulses and the conflicts they produce, clients learn to sort out their feelings and find more constructive and socially acceptable ways of handling their impulses and wishes. The ego is then freed to focus on more constructive interests.

The major methods that Freud used to accomplish these goals were free association, dream analysis, and analysis of the transference relationship.

Free Association **Free association** is the process of uttering uncensored thoughts as they come to mind. Free association is believed to gradually break down the defenses that block awareness of

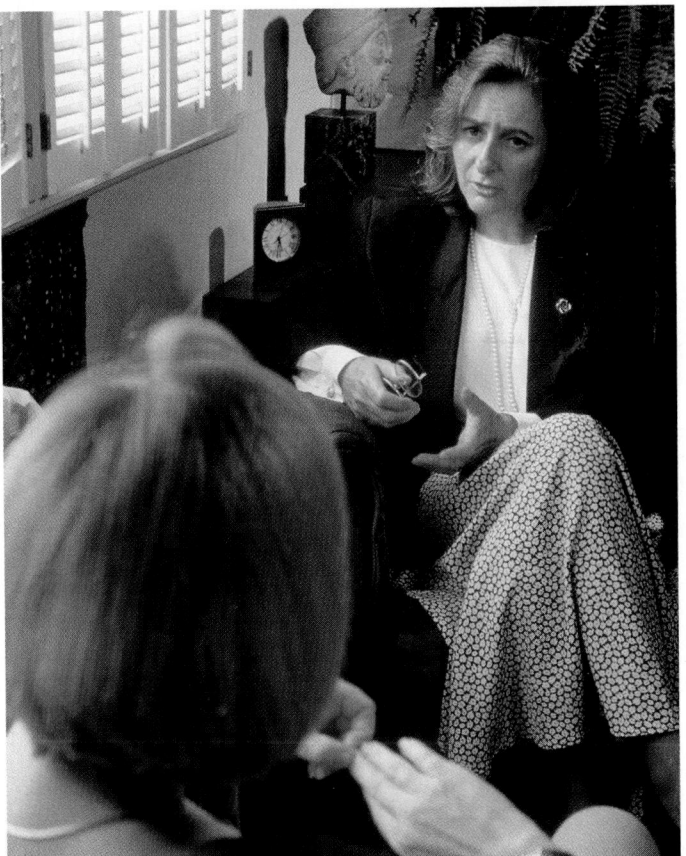

The therapeutic relationship. In the course of successful psychotherapy, a therapeutic relationship is forged between the therapist and patient. Therapists use attentive listening to understand as clearly as possible what the client is experiencing and attempting to convey. Skillful therapists are also sensitive to clients' nonverbal cues, such as gestures and posture, that may indicate underlying feelings or conflicts.

unconscious processes. Clients are told not to censor or screen out thoughts, but to let their minds wander "freely" from thought to thought. Psychoanalysts do not believe that the process of free association is truly free. Repressed impulses press for expression or release, leading to a *compulsion to utter*. Although free association may begin with small talk, the compulsion to utter eventually leads the client to disclose more meaningful material.

The ego, however, continues to try to avert the disclosure of threatening impulses and conflicts. Consequently, clients may show *resistance,* an unwillingness or inability to recall or discuss disturbing or threatening material. Clients may report that their minds suddenly go blank when they venture into sensitive areas, such as hateful feelings toward family members or sexual yearnings. They may switch topics abruptly or accuse the analyst of trying to pry into material that is too personal or embarrassing to talk about. Or they may conveniently "forget" the next appointment after a session in which sensitive material is touched upon. The analyst monitors the dynamic conflict between the compulsion to utter and resistance. Signs of resistance are often suggestive of meaningful material. Now and then, the analyst brings interpretations of this material to the attention of the client to help the client gain better insight into deep-seated feelings and conflicts.

Dream Analysis   To Freud, dreams represented the "royal road to the unconscious." During sleep, the ego's defenses are lowered and unacceptable impulses find expression in dreams. Because the defenses are not completely eliminated, the impulses take a disguised or symbolized form. In psychoanalytic theory, dreams have two levels of content:

1. *Manifest content:* the material of the dream the dreamer experiences and reports
2. *Latent content:* the unconscious material the dream symbolizes or represents

A man might dream of flying in an airplane. Flying is the apparent or manifest content of the dream. Freud believed that flying may symbolize erection, so perhaps the latent content of the dream reflects unconscious issues related to fears of impotence. Because such symbols may vary from person to person, analysts ask clients to free-associate to the manifest content of the dream to provide clues to the latent content. Although dreams may have a psychological meaning, as Freud believed, there remains no independent way of determining what dreams mean (Squier & Domhoff, 1998).

Transference   Freud found that clients responded to him not only as an individual but also in ways that reflected their feelings and attitudes toward other important people in their lives. A young female client might respond to him as a father figure, displacing, or transferring, onto Freud her feelings toward her own father. A man might also view him as a father figure, responding to him as a rival in a manner that Freud believed might reflect the man's unresolved Oedipus complex.

The process of analyzing and working through the **transference relationship** is considered an essential component of psychoanalysis. Freud believed that the transference relationship provides a vehicle for the reenactment of childhood conflicts with parents. Clients may react to the analyst with the same feelings of anger, love, or jealousy they felt toward their own parents. Freud termed the enactment of these childhood conflicts the *transference neurosis.* This "neurosis" had to be successfully analyzed and worked through for clients to succeed in psychoanalysis.

Childhood conflicts usually involve unresolved feelings of anger, rejection, or need for love. For example, a client may interpret any slight criticism by the therapist as a devastating blow, transferring feelings of self-loathing that the client had repressed from childhood experiences of parental rejection. Transference may also distort or color the client's relationships with others, such as a spouse or employer. A client might relate to a spouse as to a parent, perhaps demanding too much or unjustly accusing the spouse of being insensitive or uncaring. Or a client who had been mistreated by a past lover might not give new friends or lovers the benefit of a fair chance. The analyst helps the client recognize transference relationships, especially the therapy transference, and work through the residues of childhood feelings and conflicts that lead to self-defeating behavior in the present.

According to Freud, transference is a two-way street. Freud felt he transferred his underlying feelings onto his clients, perhaps viewing a young man as a competitor or a woman as a rejecting love interest. Freud referred to the feelings that he projected onto clients as **countertransference.** Psychoanalysts in training are expected to undergo

transference relationship In psychoanalysis, the client's transfer or generalization to the analyst of feelings and attitudes the client holds toward important figures in his or her life.

countertransference In psychoanalysis, the transfer of feelings or attitudes that the analyst holds toward other persons in her or his life onto the client.

Dream analysis. Freud believed that dreams represent the "royal road to the unconscious." Dream interpretation was one of the principal techniques that Freud used to uncover unconscious material.

psychoanalysis themselves to help them uncover motives that might lead to countertransferences in their therapeutic relationships. In their training, psychoanalysts learn to monitor their own reactions in therapy, so as to become better aware of when and how countertransferences intrude on the therapy process.

Although the analysis of transference is a crucial element of psychoanalytic therapy, it generally takes months or years for a transference relationship to develop and be resolved. This is one reason why psychoanalysis is typically a lengthy process.

Modern Psychodynamic Approaches Although some psychoanalysts continue to practice traditional psychoanalysis in much the same manner as Freud, briefer and less-intensive forms of psychodynamic treatment have emerged. They are able to reach clients who are seeking briefer and less costly forms of treatment, perhaps once or twice a week (Grossman, 2003).

Like Freudian psychoanalysis, the newer psychodynamic approaches aim to uncover unconscious motives and break down resistances and psychological defenses. Yet they focus more on the client's present relationships and encourage the client to make adaptive behavior changes. Many contemporary psychodynamic therapists draw more heavily on the ideas of Erik Erikson, Karen Horney, and other theorists than on Freud's ideas. Treatment entails a more open dialogue and direct exploration of the client's defenses and transference relationships than was traditionally the case (Messer, 2001b). The client and therapist generally sit facing each other, and the therapist engages in more frequent verbal give-and-take with the client, as in the following vignette. Note how the therapist uses interpretation to help the client, Mr. Arianes, achieve insight into how his relationship with his wife involves a transference of his childhood relationship with his mother:

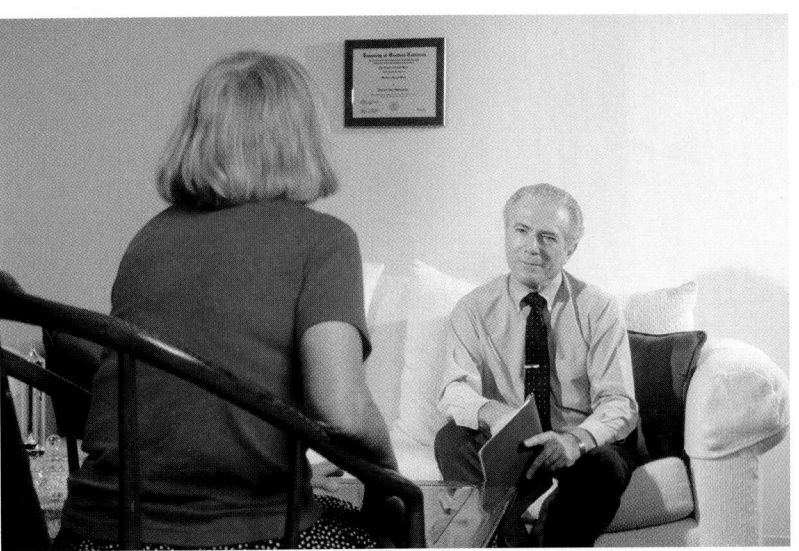

Modern psychodynamic psychotherapy. Modern psychodynamic therapists engage in more direct, face-to-face interactions with clients than do traditional Freudian psychoanalysts. Modern psychodynamic approaches are also generally briefer and focus more on the direct exploration of clients' defenses and transference relationships.

Offering an Interpretation

MR. ARIANES: *I think you've got it there, Doc. We weren't communicating. I wouldn't tell her [his wife] what was wrong or what I wanted from her. Maybe I expected her to understand me without saying anything.*

THERAPIST: *Like the expectations a child has of its mother.*

MR. ARIANES: *Not my mother!*

THERAPIST: *Oh?*

MR. ARIANES: *No, I always thought she had too many troubles of her own to pay attention to mine. I remember once I got hurt on my bike and came to her all bloodied up. When she saw me she got mad and yelled at me for making more trouble for her when she already had her hands full with my father.*

THERAPIST: *Do you remember how you felt then?*

MR. ARIANES: *I can't remember, but I know that after that I never brought my troubles to her again.*

THERAPIST: *How old were you?*

MR. ARIANES: *Nine. I know that because I got that bike for my ninth birthday. It was a little too big for me still, that's why I got hurt on it.*

THERAPIST: *Perhaps you carried this attitude into your marriage.*

MR. ARIANES: *What attitude?*

THERAPIST: *The feeling that your wife, like your mother, would be unsympathetic to your difficulties. That there was no point in telling her about your experiences because she was too preoccupied or too busy to care.*

MR. ARIANES: *But she's so different from my mother. I come first with her.*

THERAPIST: *On one level you know that. On another, deeper level there may well be the fear that people—or maybe only women, or maybe only women you're close to—are all the same, and you can't take a chance at being rejected again in your need.*

MR. ARIANES: *Maybe you're right, Doc, but all that was so long ago, and I should be over that by now.*

THERAPIST: *That's not the way the mind works. If a shock or a disappointment is strong enough, it can permanently freeze our picture of ourselves and our expectations of the world. The rest of us grows up—that is, we let ourselves learn about life from experience and from what we see, hear, or read of the experiences of others, but that one area where we really got hurt stays unchanged. So what I mean when I say you might be carrying that attitude into your relationship with your wife is that when it comes to your hopes of being understood and catered to when you feel hurt or abused by life, you still feel very much like that nine-year-old boy who was rebuffed in his need and gave up hope that anyone would or could respond to him.*

—Offering an Interpretation, from M. F. Basch, *Doing Psychotherapy* (Basic Books, 1980), pp. 29–30. Reprinted by permission of Basic Books, a member of Perseus Books Group.

Some modern psychodynamic therapists focus more on the role of the ego and less on the role of the id. These therapists, such as Heinz Hartmann, are generally described as *ego analysts*. Other modern psychoanalysts, such as Margaret Mahler, are identified with *object-relations* approaches to psychodynamic therapy. They focus on helping people separate their own ideas and feelings from the elements of others they have incorporated or *introjected* within themselves. Clients can then develop more as individuals—as their own persons, rather than trying to meet the expectations they believe others have of them.

Though psychodynamic therapy is no longer the dominant force in the field that it once was, it is still practiced widely. A recent survey of 177 practicing psychologists found that nearly half (45%) reported using psychodynamic techniques along with cognitive–behavioral techniques in their practice (Holloway, 2003; PracticeNet, 2003). Let's now turn to other forms of therapy, beginning with behavior therapy.

Behavior Therapy

behavior therapy The therapeutic application of learning-based techniques.

Behavior therapy is the systematic application of the principles of learning to the treatment of psychological disorders. Because the focus is on changing behavior—not on personality change or deep probing into the past—behavior therapy is relatively brief, lasting typically from a few weeks to a few months. Behavior therapists, like other therapists, seek to develop warm therapeutic relationships with clients, but they believe the special efficacy of behavior therapy derives from the learning-based techniques rather than from the nature of the therapeutic relationship.

Behavior therapy first gained widespread attention as a means of helping people overcome fears and phobias, problems that had proved resistant to insight-oriented therapies. Among the methods used are systematic desensitization, gradual exposure, and modeling. **Systematic desensitization** involves a therapeutic program of exposure (in imagination or by means of pictures or slides) to progressively more fearful stimuli while one remains deeply relaxed. First the person uses a relaxation technique, such as progressive relaxation (discussed in Chapter 5), to become deeply relaxed. The client is then instructed to imagine (or perhaps view, as through a series of slides) progressively more anxiety-arousing scenes. If fear is evoked, the client focuses on restoring relaxation. The process is repeated until the client can tolerate the scene without anxiety. The client then progresses to the next scene in the *fear-stimulus hierarchy*. The procedure is continued until the person can remain relaxed while imagining the most distressing scene in the hierarchy.

systematic desensitization A behavior therapy technique for overcoming phobias by means of exposure to progressively more fearful stimuli while one remains deeply relaxed.

gradual exposure A behavior therapy technique for overcoming fears through direct exposure to increasingly fearful stimuli.

In **gradual exposure** (also called in vivo, meaning "in life," exposure), people troubled by phobias purposely expose themselves to the stimuli that evoke their fear. Like systematic desensitization, the person progresses at his or her own pace through a hierarchy of progressively more anxiety-evoking stimuli. The person with a fear of snakes, for example, might first look at a harmless, caged snake from across the room and then gradually approach and interact with the snake in a step-by-step process, progressing to each new step only when feeling completely calm at the prior step. Gradual exposure is often combined with cognitive techniques that focus on replacing anxiety-arousing irrational thoughts with calming rational thoughts.

In **modeling,** individuals learn desired behaviors by observing others perform them (Braswell & Kendall, 2001). For example, the client may observe and then imitate others who interact with fear-evoking situations or objects. After observing the model, the client may be assisted or guided by the therapist or the model in performing the target behavior. The client receives ample reinforcement from the therapist for each attempt. Modeling approaches were pioneered by Albert Bandura and his colleagues, who had remarkable success using modeling techniques with children to treat various phobias, especially fears of animals, such as snakes and dogs (Bandura, Jeffery, & Wright, 1974; Braswell & Kendall, 2001).

Behavior therapists also use reinforcement techniques based on operant conditioning to shape desired behavior. For example, parents and teachers may be trained to systematically reinforce children for appropriate behavior by showing appreciation and to extinguish inappropriate behavior by ignoring it. In institutional settings, **token economy** systems seek to increase adaptive behavior by rewarding patients with tokens for performing appropriate behaviors, such as self-grooming and making their beds. The tokens can eventually be exchanged for desired rewards. Token systems have also been used to treat children with conduct disorders.

Other techniques of behavior therapy discussed in later chapters include *aversive conditioning* (used in the treatment of substance abuse problems such as smoking and alcoholism), and *social skills training* (used in the treatment of social anxiety and skills deficits associated with schizophrenia).

Humanistic Therapy

Psychodynamic therapists tend to focus on unconscious processes, such as internal conflicts. By contrast, humanistic therapists focus on clients' subjective, conscious experiences. Like behavior therapists, humanistic therapists also focus more on what clients are experiencing in the present—the here and now—than on the past. But there are also similarities between the psychodynamic and humanistic therapies. Both assume that the past affects present behavior and feelings and both seek to expand clients' self-insight. The major form of humanistic therapy is **person-centered therapy** (also called *client-centered therapy*), which was developed by the psychologist Carl Rogers.

Person-Centered Therapy Rogers (1951) believed that people have natural motivational tendencies toward growth, fulfillment, and health. In Rogers's view, psychological disorders develop largely from the roadblocks that other people place in the path toward self-actualization. When others are selective in their approval of our childhood feelings and behavior, we may disown the criticized parts of ourselves. To earn social approval, we may don social masks or facades. We learn "to be seen and not heard" and may become deaf even to our own inner voices. Over time, we may develop distorted self-concepts that are consistent with others' views of us but are not of our own making and design. As a result, we may become poorly adjusted, unhappy, and confused as to who and what we are.

Well-adjusted people make choices and take actions consistent with their personal values and needs. Person-centered therapy creates conditions of warmth and acceptance in the therapeutic relationship that help clients become more aware and accepting of their true selves. Rogers did not believe therapists should impose their own goals or values on their clients. His focus of therapy, as the name implies, is the person.

Person-centered therapy is *nondirective.* The client, not the therapist, takes the lead and directs the course of therapy. The therapist uses *reflection*—the restating or paraphrasing of the client's expressed feelings without interpreting them or passing judgment on them. This encourages the client to further explore his or her feelings and get in touch with deeper feelings and parts of the self that had become disowned because of social condemnation.

modeling A behavior therapy technique for helping an individual acquire a new behavior by means of having a therapist or another individual demonstrate a target behavior that is then imitated by the client.

token economy Behavioral treatment program in which a controlled environment is constructed such that people are reinforced for desired behaviors by receiving tokens that may be exchanged for desired rewards.

person-centered therapy The establishment of a warm, accepting therapeutic relationship that frees clients to engage in self-exploration and achieve self-acceptance.

"You say 'off with her head,' but what I'm hearing is, 'I feel neglected.'"

Drawing by Mike Ewers. Reprinted by permission.

Rogers stressed the importance of creating a warm therapeutic relationship that would encourage the client to engage in self-exploration and self-expression. The effective therapist should possess four basic qualities or attributes: *unconditional positive regard, empathy, genuineness,* and *congruence.* First, the therapist must be able to express **unconditional positive regard** for clients. In contrast to the conditional approval the client may have received from parents and others in the past, the therapist must be unconditionally accepting of the client as a person, even if the therapist sometimes objects to the client's choices or behaviors. Unconditional positive regard provides clients with a sense of security that encourages them to explore their feelings without fear of disapproval. As clients feel accepted or prized for themselves, they are encouraged to accept themselves in turn. To Rogers, every human being has intrinsic worth and value. Rogers believed that people are basically good and are motivated to pursue *pro*social goals.

Therapists who display **empathy** are able to reflect or mirror accurately their clients' experiences and feelings. Therapists try to see the world through their clients' eyes or frames of reference. They listen carefully to clients and set aside their own judgments and interpretations of events. Showing empathy encourages clients to get in touch with feelings of which they may be only dimly aware.

Genuineness is the ability to be open about one's feelings. Rogers admitted he had negative feelings at times during therapy sessions, typically boredom, but he attempted to express these feelings openly rather than hide them (Bennett, 1985).

Congruence refers to the fit between one's thoughts, feelings, and behavior. The congruent person is one whose behavior, thoughts, and feelings are integrated and consistent. Congruent therapists serve as models of psychological integrity to their clients.

Here Rogers (C. R.) uses reflection to help a client focus more deeply on her inner feelings:

Rogers Demonstrates Reflection

JILL: *I'm having a lot of problems dealing with my daughter. She's 20 years old; she's in college; I'm having a lot of trouble letting her go. And I have a lot of guilt feelings about her; I have a real need to hang on to her.*

C.R.:   *A need to hang on so you can kind of make up for the things you feel guilty about. Is that part of it?*

JILL: *There's a lot of that. Also, she's been a real friend to me, and filled my life. And it's very hard . . . a lot of empty places now that she's not with me.*

C.R.:   *The old vacuum, sort of, when she's not there.*

JILL: *Yes. Yes. I also would like to be the kind of mother that could be strong and say, you know, "Go and have a good life," and this is really hard for me, to do that.*

C.R.:   *It's very hard to give up something that's been so precious in your life, but also something that I guess has caused you pain when you mentioned guilt.*

JILL: *Yeah. And I'm aware that I have some anger toward her that I don't always get what I want. I have needs that are not met. And, uh, I don't feel I have a right to those needs. You know . . . she's a daughter; she's not my mother. Though sometimes I feel as if I'd like her to mother me . . . it's very difficult for me to ask for that and have a right to it.*

C.R.:   *So, it may be unreasonable, but still, when she doesn't meet your needs, it makes you mad.*

JILL: *Yeah I get very angry, very angry with her.*

C.R.:   *(Pause) You're also feeling a little tension at this point, I guess.*

JILL: *Yeah. Yeah. A lot of conflict . . . (C.R.: M-hm.). A lot of pain.*

C.R.:   *A lot of pain. Can you say anything more about what that's about?*

—From Farber, Brink, & Raskin, 1996, *The psychotherapy of Carl Rogers: Cases and commentary*, pp. 74–75. Reprinted with permission of The Guilford Press.

unconditional positive regard The expression of unconditional acceptance of another person's basic worth as a person.

empathy The ability to understand someone's experiences and feelings from that person's point of view.

genuineness The ability to recognize and express one's true feelings.

congruence The fit between one's thoughts, behaviors, and feelings.

Cognitive Therapy

There is nothing either good or bad, but thinking makes it so.

—Shakespeare, Hamlet

In these words, Shakespeare did not mean to imply that misfortunes or ailments are painless or easy to manage. His point, rather, was that the ways in which we evaluate upsetting events can heighten or diminish our discomfort and affect our ability to cope. Several hundred years later, cognitive therapists such as Aaron Beck and Albert Ellis adopted this simple but elegant expression as a kind of motto for their approach to therapy.

Cognitive therapists focus on helping clients identify and correct faulty thinking, distorted beliefs, and self-defeating attitudes that create or contribute to emotional problems. They argue that negative emotions such as anxiety and depression are caused by interpretations we place on troubling events, not on events themselves. Here we focus on two prominent types of **cognitive therapy:** Albert Ellis's rational emotive behavior therapy and Aaron Beck's cognitive therapy.

Rational Emotive Behavior Therapy Albert Ellis (1977b, 1993, 2001; Dryden & Ellis, 2001) believed that negative emotions such as anxiety and depression are caused by the irrational ways in which we interpret or judge negative events, not by negative events themselves. Consider the irrational belief that we must have the approval almost all the time of the people who are important to us. Ellis finds it understandable to want other people's approval and love, but he argues that it is irrational to believe we cannot survive without it. Another irrational belief is that we must be thoroughly competent and achieving in virtually everything we seek to accomplish. We are doomed to eventually fall short of these irrational expectations, and when we do, we may experience negative emotional consequences, such as depression and lowered self-esteem. Emotional difficulties such as anxiety and depression are not directly caused by negative events, but rather by how we distort their meaning by viewing them through the dark-colored glasses of self-defeating beliefs. In Ellis's **rational emotive behavior therapy (REBT)**, therapists actively *dispute* clients' irrational beliefs and the premises on which they are based and help clients to develop alternative, adaptive beliefs in their place.

Ellis and Dryden (1987) describe the case of a 27-year-old woman, Jane, who was socially inhibited and shy, particularly with attractive men. Through REBT, Jane identified some of her underlying irrational beliefs, such as "I must speak well to people I find attractive" and "When I don't speak well and impress people as I should, I'm a stupid, inadequate person!" (p. 68). REBT helped Jane discriminate between these irrational beliefs and rational alternatives, such as "If people do reject me for showing them how anxious I am, that will be most unfortunate, but I can stand it" (p. 68). REBT encouraged Jane to debate or dispute irrational beliefs by posing challenging questions to herself: (1) "*Why* must I speak well to people I find attractive?" and (2) "When I don't speak well and impress people, how does that make me a *stupid and inadequate person?*" (p. 69). Jane learned to form rational responses to her self-questioning. For example, (1) "There is no reason I must speak well to people I find attractive, but it would be desirable if I do so, so I shall make an effort—but not kill myself—to do so," and (2) "When I speak poorly and fail to impress people, that only makes me a *person who spoke unimpressively this time*—not a *totally stupid or inadequate person*" (p. 69). After 9 months of REBT, Jane was able to talk comfortably to men she found attractive and was preparing to take a job as a teacher, a position she had previously avoided due to fear of facing a class.

Rational emotive behavior therapists help clients substitute more effective interpersonal behavior for self-defeating or maladaptive behavior. Ellis often gave clients specific tasks or homework assignments, such as disagreeing with an overbearing relative or asking someone for a date. He assisted them in practicing or rehearsing adaptive behaviors.

cognitive therapy A form of therapy that helps clients identify and correct faulty cognitions (thoughts, beliefs, and attitudes) believed to underlie their emotional problems and maladaptive behavior.

rational emotive behavior therapy (REBT) A therapeutic approach that focuses on helping clients replace irrational, maladaptive beliefs with alternative, more adaptive beliefs.

Beck's Cognitive Therapy Psychiatrist Aaron Beck and his colleagues (Beck et al., 1979; DeRubeis, Tang, & Beck, 2001) developed cognitive therapy, which, like REBT, focuses on people's faulty thoughts and beliefs. Cognitive therapists encourage clients to recognize and change errors in their thinking, called *cognitive distortions,* such as tendencies to magnify negative events and minimize personal accomplishments, that affect their moods and impair their behavior.

Cognitive therapists have clients record the thoughts that are prompted by upsetting events and note the connections between their thoughts and their emotional responses. They then help clients to dispute distorted thoughts and replace them with rational alternatives. Therapists also use behavioral homework assignments, such as encouraging depressed clients to fill their free time with structured activities, such as gardening or completing work around the house. Carrying out such tasks counteracts the apathy and loss of motivation that often characterize depression and may also provide concrete evidence of competence, which helps combat self-perceptions of helplessness and inadequacy.

Another type of homework assignment involves *reality testing,* whereby clients are asked to test their negative beliefs in the light of reality. For example, a depressed client who feels unwanted by everyone might be asked to call two or three friends on the phone to gather data about the friends' reactions to the calls. The therapist might then ask the client to report on the assignment: "Did they immediately hang up the phone, or did they seem pleased you called? Did they express any interest at all in talking to you again or getting together sometime? Does the evidence support the conclusion that *no one* has any interest in you?" Such exercises help clients replace distorted beliefs with rational alternatives.

Consider this case in which a depressed man was encouraged to test his belief that he was about to be fired from his job. The case also illustrates several cognitive distortions or errors in thinking, such as selectively perceiving only one's flaws (in this case, self-perceptions of laziness) and expecting the worst (expectations of being fired).

Kyle Tests His Beliefs

Kyle, a 35-year-old frozen foods distributor, had suffered from chronic depression since his divorce 6 years earlier. During the past year the depression had worsened, and he found it increasingly difficult to call upon customers or go to the office. Each day that he avoided working made it more difficult for him to go to the office and face his boss. He was convinced that he was in imminent danger of being fired because he had not made any sales calls for more than a month. Because he had not earned any commissions in a while, he felt he was not adequately supporting his two daughters and was concerned that he wouldn't have the money to send them to college. He was convinced that his basic problem was laziness, not depression. His therapist pointed out the illogic in his thinking. First of all, there was no real evidence that his boss was about to fire him. His boss had actually encouraged him to get help and was paying for part of the treatment. His therapist also pointed out that judging himself as lazy was unfair because it overlooked the fact that he had been an industrious, successful salesman before he became depressed. Although not fully persuaded, the client agreed to a homework assignment in which he was to call his boss and also make a sales call to one of his former customers. His boss expressed support and reassured him that his job was secure. The customer ribbed him about "being on vacation" during the preceding 6 weeks but placed a small order. The client discovered that the small unpleasantness he experienced in facing the customer and being teased paled in comparison to the intense depression he felt at home while he was avoiding work. Within the next several weeks he gradually worked himself back to a normal routine, calling upon customers and making future plans. This process of viewing himself and the world from a fresh perspective led to a general improvement in his mood and behavior.

—Adapted from Burns & Beck, 1978, pp. 124–126

TABLE 4.2 Overview of Major Types of Psychotherapy

TYPE OF THERAPY	Major Figure(s)	Goal	Length of Treatment	Therapist's Approach	Major Techniques
Classical psychoanalysis	Sigmund Freud	Gaining insight and resolving unconscious psychological conflicts	Lengthy, typically lasting several years	Passive, interpretive	Free association, dream analysis, interpretation
Modern psychodynamic approaches	Erik Erikson Harry Stack Sullivan Heinz Hartmann Melanie Klein Margaret Mahler	Focus on developing insight, but with greater emphasis on ego functioning, current interpersonal relationships, and adaptive behavior than traditional psychoanalysis	Briefer than traditional psychoanalysis	More direct probing of client defenses; more back-and-forth discussion	Direct analysis of client's defenses and transference relationships
Behavior therapy	Various	Directly changing problem behavior through use of learning-based techniques	Relatively brief, typically lasting 10 to 20 sessions	Directive, active problem solving	Systematic desensitization, gradual exposure, modeling, reinforcement techniques
Humanistic, client-centered therapy	Carl Rogers	Self-acceptance and personal growth	Varies, but briefer than traditional psychoanalysis	Nondirective, allowing client to take the lead, with therapist serving as an empathic listener	Use of reflection, creation of a warm, accepting therapeutic relationship
Ellis's rational emotive behavior therapy	Albert Ellis	Replacing irrational beliefs with rational alternative beliefs; making adaptive behavioral changes	Relatively brief, typically lasting 10 to 20 sessions	Direct, sometimes confrontational challenging of client's irrational beliefs	Identifying and challenging irrational beliefs, behavioral homework assignments
Beck's cognitive therapy	Aaron Beck	Identify and correcting distorted or self-defeating thoughts and beliefs; making adaptive behavioral changes	Relatively brief, typically lasting 10 to 20 sessions	Collaboratively engaging client in process of logically examining thoughts and beliefs and testing them out	Identifying and correcting distorted thoughts; behavioral homework including reality testing
Cognitive-behavioral therapy	Various	Use of cognitive and behavioral techniques to change maladaptive behaviors and cognitions	Relatively brief, typically lasting 10 to 20 sessions	Direct, active problem solving	Combination of cognitive and behavioral techniques

REBT and Beck's cognitive therapy have much in common, especially the focus on helping clients replace self-defeating thoughts and beliefs with more rational ones. Perhaps the major difference between the two approaches is therapeutic style. REBT therapists tend to be more confrontational and forceful in their approach to disputing clients' irrational beliefs. Cognitive therapists tend to adopt a more gentle, collaborative approach in helping clients discover and correct the distortions in their thinking.

The therapies developed by Beck and Ellis can be classified as forms of *cognitive-behavioral therapy*, which is the treatment approach we turn to next. We will then turn to consider a growing movement among therapists toward incorporating principles and techniques derived from different schools of therapy. Before reading further, you may wish to review Table 4.2, which summarizes the major approaches to psychotherapy.

cognitive-behavioral therapy (CBT)
A learning-based approach to therapy incorporating cognitive and behavioral techniques.

Cognitive-Behavioral Therapy

Today, most behavior therapists identify with a broader model of behavior therapy called **cognitive-behavioral therapy** (CBT) (also called *cognitive-behavior therapy*). Cognitive-behavioral therapy attempts to integrate therapeutic techniques that help individuals make changes not only in their overt behavior but also in their underlying thoughts, beliefs, and attitudes. Cognitive-behavioral therapy draws on the assumption that thinking patterns and beliefs affect behavior and that changes in these cognitions can produce desirable behavioral and emotional changes (Dobson & Dozois, 2001; McGinn & Sanderson, 2001). Cognitive-behavioral therapists focus on helping clients identify and correct the maladaptive beliefs and negative, automatic thoughts that may underlie their emotional problems.

Cognitive-behavioral therapists use an assortment of cognitive techniques and behavioral techniques. The following case illustration shows how behavioral techniques (exposure to fearful situations) and cognitive techniques (changing maladaptive thoughts) were used in the treatment of a case of *agoraphobia*, a type of anxiety disorder characterized by excessive fears of venturing out in public.

Mrs. X Uses CBT to Overcome Agoraphobia

Mrs. X was a 41-year-old woman with a 12-year history of agoraphobia. She feared venturing into public places alone and required her husband or children to accompany her from place to place. In vivo (actual) exposure sessions were arranged in a series of progressively more fearful encounters (a fear-stimulus hierarchy). The first step in the hierarchy, for example, involved taking a shopping trip while accompanied by the therapist. After accomplishing this task, Mrs. X gradually moved upward in the hierarchy. By the third week of treatment, she was able to complete the last step in her hierarchy: shopping by herself in a crowded supermarket.

Cognitive restructuring was conducted along with the exposure training. Mrs. X was asked to imagine herself in various fearful situations and to report the self-statements she experienced. The therapist helped her identify disruptive self-statements, such as, "I am going to make a fool of myself." The therapist questioned this particular self-statement by asking whether it was realistic to believe that she would actually lose control and, secondly, by disputing the belief that the consequences of losing control, were it to happen, would truly be disastrous. Mrs. X progressed rapidly with treatment and became capable of functioning more independently, but she still worried about future relapses. The therapist focused at this point on deeper cognitive structures involving her fears of abandonment by the people she loved if she were to relapse and be unable to attend to their needs. In challenging these beliefs, the therapist helped Mrs. X realize that she was not as helpless as she perceived herself to be and that she was loved for other reasons than her ability to serve others. She also explored the question, "Who am I improving for?" She realized that she needed to find reasons to overcome her phobia that were related to meeting her own personal needs, not simply the needs of her loved ones. At a follow-up interview 9 months after treatment, she was functioning independently, which allowed her to pursue her own interests, such as taking night courses and seeking a job.

—*Adapted from Biran, 1988, pp. 173–176*

Cognitive-behavioral therapy has produced impressive results in treating a wide range of emotional disorders, including depression, panic disorder, generalized anxiety disorder, social phobia, posttraumatic stress disorder, agoraphobia, and obsessive-compulsive disorder, as well as other disorders such as bulimia and personality disorders (e.g., Bockting et al., 2005; Butler et al., 2006; DeRubeis et al., 2005; Heimberg, Turk, & Mennin, 2004; Hollon et al., 2005, 2006; Lilienfeld, 2007; Norton & Price, 2007). Yet, like other forms of treatment, including drug therapy, CBT is not effective in all cases; perhaps as many 30–40% of patients fail to respond to treatment (David & Szentagotaia, 2006).

Eclectic Therapy

Each of the major psychological models of abnormal behavior—the psychodynamic, behaviorist, humanistic, and cognitive approaches—has spawned its own approaches to psychotherapy. Although many therapists identify with one or another of these schools of therapy, an increasing number of therapists practice **eclectic therapy,** in which they draw on techniques and teachings of multiple therapeutic approaches. Eclectic therapists seek to enhance their therapeutic effectiveness by incorporating principles and techniques from different therapeutic orientations. An eclectic therapist might use behavior therapy techniques to help a client change specific maladaptive behaviors, for example, along with psychodynamic techniques to help the client gain insight into the childhood roots of the problem.

A greater percentage of clinical and counseling psychologists identify with an eclectic or integrative orientation than any other therapeutic orientation (Bechtoldt et al., 2001; see Figure 4.1). Therapists who adopt an eclectic approach tend to be older and more experienced (Beitman, Goldfried, & Norcross, 1989). Perhaps they have learned through experience of the value of drawing on diverse contributions to the practice of therapy.

Eclecticism has different meanings for different therapists. Some therapists are *technical eclectics*. They draw on techniques from different schools of therapy without necessarily adopting the theoretical positions that spawned the techniques (Beutler, Harwood, & Caldwell, 2001; Lazarus, 1992). They assume a pragmatic approach in using techniques from different therapeutic approaches that they believe are most likely to work with a given client.

Other eclectic therapists are *integrative eclectics*. They attempt to synthesize and integrate diverse theoretical approaches—to bring together different theoretical concepts and therapeutic approaches under the roof of one integrated model of therapy (Beutler, Harwood, & Caldwell, 2001; Stricker & Gold, 2001). Although various approaches to integrative psychotherapy have been proposed, there is as yet no clear agreement as to the principles and practices that constitute therapeutic integration (Garfield, 1994). Perhaps multiple approaches are needed (Safran & Messer, 1997).

Not all therapists subscribe to the view that therapeutic integration is a desirable or achievable goal. They believe that combining elements of different therapeutic approaches will lead to a hodgepodge of techniques that lack a cohesive conceptual framework. Still, interest in the professional community in therapeutic integration is growing, and we expect to see new models emerging that aim to tie together the contributions of different approaches.

eclectic therapy An approach to psychotherapy that incorporates principles or techniques from various systems or theories.

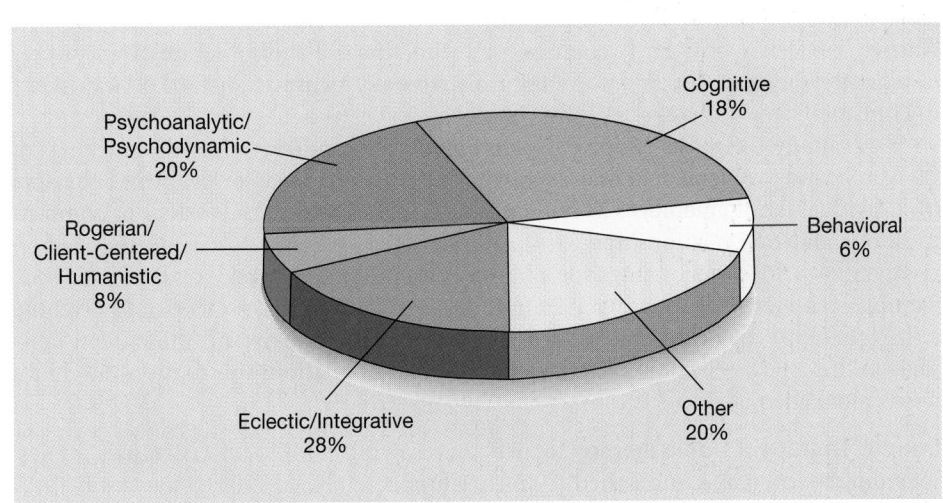

FIGURE 4.1 Therapeutic orientations of clinical and counseling psychologists. An eclectic/integrative orientation is the most widely endorsed therapeutic orientation among clinical and counseling psychologists today.

Source: Adapted from Bechtoldt et al. (2001).

Group, Family, and Couple Therapy

Some approaches to therapy expand the focus of treatment to include groups of people, families, and couples.

Group Therapy In **group therapy,** a group of clients meets together with a therapist or a pair of therapists. Group therapy has several advantages over individual treatment. For one, group therapy is less costly to individual clients, because several clients are treated at the same time. Many clinicians also believe that group therapy is more effective in treating groups of clients who have similar problems, such as complaints relating to anxiety, depression, lack of social skills, or adjustment to divorce or other life stresses. Clients learn how people with similar problems cope and receive social support from the group as well as the therapist. Group therapy also provides members with opportunities to work through their problems in relating to others. For example, the therapist or other members may point out to a particular member patterns of behavior that mirror the client's behavior outside the group. Group members may also rehearse social skills with one another in a supportive atmosphere.

Despite these advantages, clients may prefer individual therapy for various reasons. For one, clients might not wish to disclose their problems in a group. Some clients prefer the individual attention of the therapist. Others are too socially inhibited to feel comfortable in a group setting. Because of such concerns, group therapists require that group disclosures be kept confidential, that group members relate to each other supportively and nondestructively, and that group members receive the attention they need.

Family Therapy In **family therapy,** the family, not the individual, is the unit of treatment. Family therapy aims to help troubled families resolve their conflicts and problems so the family functions better as a unit and individual family members are subjected to less stress from family conflicts. In family therapy, family members learn to communicate more effectively and to air their disagreements constructively. Family conflicts often emerge at transitional points in the life cycle, when family patterns are altered by changes in one or more members. Conflicts between parents and children, for example, often emerge when adolescent children seek greater independence or autonomy. Family members with low self-esteem may be unable to tolerate different attitudes or behaviors from other members of the family and may resist their efforts to change or become more independent. Family therapists work with families to resolve these conflicts and help them adjust to life changes.

Family therapists are sensitive to tendencies of families to scapegoat one family member as the source of the problem, or the "identified client." Disturbed families seem to adopt a sort of myth: Change the identified client, the "bad apple," and the "barrel," or family, will once again become functional. Family therapists encourage families to work together to resolve their disputes and conflicts, instead of scapegoating one member.

Many family therapists adopt a *systems approach* to understanding the workings of the family and problems that may arise within the family. They see problem behaviors of individual family members as representing a breakdown in the system of communications and role relationships within the family. For example, a child may feel in competition with other siblings for a parent's attention and develop enuresis, or bedwetting, as a means of securing attention. Operating from a systems perspective, the family therapist may focus on helping family members understand the hidden messages in the child's behavior and make changes in their relationships to meet the child's needs more adequately.

Couple Therapy **Couple therapy** focuses on resolving conflicts in distressed couples, including married and unmarried couples (Christensen et al., 2004). Like family therapy, couple therapy focuses on improving communication and analyzing role relation-

Group therapy. What are some of the advantages of group therapy over individual therapy? What are some of its disadvantages?

group therapy A form of therapy in which a group of clients meets together with a therapist.

Family therapy. In family therapy, the family, not the individual, is the unit of treatment. Family therapists help family members communicate more effectively with one another, for example, to air their disagreements in ways that are not hurtful to individual members. Family therapists also try to prevent one member of the family from becoming the scapegoat for the family's problems.

family therapy A form of therapy in which the family, not the individual, is the unit of treatment.

couple therapy A form of therapy that focuses on resolving conflicts in distressed couples.

CONTROVERSIES IN ABNORMAL PSYCHOLOGY

Online Therapy: A New Therapeutic Tool, or Pandora's Box?

You can do almost anything on the Internet these days, from ordering concert tickets to downloading music (legally, of course) or whole books. You can also receive counseling or therapy services from an online therapist. As the numbers of online counseling services continues to increase, so does the controversy concerning their use.

When we last commented upon the use of Internet-based psychological services in the last edition of this textbook, we noted that many professionals had voiced significant concerns about the clinical, ethical, and legal issues of these treatments. These concerns remain. One problem is that although psychologists are licensed in particular states, Internet communications easily cross state and international borders. It remains unclear whether psychologists or other mental health professionals can legally provide online services to residents of states in which they are not licensed. Ethical problems and liability issues arise when psychologists and other helping professionals offer services to clients they never meet in person. Many therapists also express concerns that interacting with a client only by computer would prevent them from evaluating nonverbal cues and gestures that might signal deeper levels of distress than are verbally reported or typed on a keyboard.

Yet another problem is that online therapists living at great distances from their clients may not be able to provide the more intensive services clients need during times of emotional crisis. Professionals also express concern about the potential for unsuspecting clients to be victimized by unqualified practitioners or "quacks." We don't yet have a system to ensure that only licensed and qualified practitioners offer online therapeutic services.

On the other hand, many professionals argue that online consultation and counseling services can have therapeutic value (e.g, Chang & Yeh, 2003; Taylor & Luce, 2003). One advantage of these Internet-based services is that they require fewer therapist resources than standard face-to-face therapy (Litz et al., 2005). They may also be able to reach people who have avoided seeking help because of shyness or embarrassment. Online consultation may also make people feel more comfortable about receiving help, making it a first step toward meeting a therapist in person. Online therapy may also provide treatment services people might not otherwise receive because they lack mobility or live in remote areas.

Far from writing off so-called e-therapy, psychologists are seeking responsible ways of using the Internet and other forms of electronically delivered psychological services, or *psychotechnology*, as this new field was recently called (Comas-Diaz, 2006). Evidence is mounting that Internet-based treatments can yield therapeutic benefits in treating anxiety disorders such as posttraumatic stress disorder (PTSD), panic disorder, and social phobia, as well as helping people quit smoking and overcome insomnia and even test anxiety (Andersson et al., 2006; Carlbring et al., 2006; Litz et al., 2005;

Orbach, Lindsay, & Grey, 2007; Walters, Wright, & Shegog, 2006). Online support groups may also be helpful to people who are depressed and have few social outlets (Houston et al., 2002).

We should also note that other technologies hold great promise for expanding services and for training opportunities. For example, teleconferencing is being used to help rural clinicians further develop their skills by providing them access to training and consultation with specialists (Schopp, Johnstone, & Reid-Arndt, 2005). In other cases, investigators report significant improvements in depression among patients who participated in a cognitive-behavioral treatment program administered by telephone (Mohr et al., 2005). Added to the mix are computerized versions of cognitive-behavioral therapy designed to increase access to therapy and reduce costs associated with traditional therapy (McCrone et al., 2004; Proudfoot et al., 2004). In one recent example, investigators found that a computer-assisted cognitive therapy program produced effects that were comparable to standard cognitive therapy in treating depression (Wright et al., 2005).

Critical Thinking

- What ethical and practical problems do therapists who offer online therapy face?
- What are the potential benefits of online therapy? What are the potential risks?

Internet Therapy. Online therapeutic services are popping up on the Internet. Although Internet-based counseling or therapy services may have therapeutic benefits, many mental health professionals express concerns about potential clinical, ethical, and legal issues associated with these services.

ships. For example, one partner may play a dominant role and resist any request to share power. The couple therapist helps bring these role relationships into the open, so that partners can explore alternative ways of relating to one another that would lead to a more satisfying relationship.

Evaluating Methods of Psychotherapy

What, then, of the effectiveness of psychotherapy? Does psychotherapy work? Are some forms of therapy more effective than others? Are some forms of therapy more effective for some types of clients or for some types of problems than for others?

The effectiveness of psychotherapy receives strong support from the research literature. Reviews of the scientific literature often utilize a statistical technique called *meta-analysis*, which averages the results of a large number of studies to determine an overall level of effectiveness.

In the most frequently cited meta-analysis of psychotherapy research, M. L. Smith and Glass (1977) analyzed the results of some 375 controlled studies comparing various types of therapies (psychodynamic, behavioral, humanistic, etc.) against control groups. The results of their analyses showed that the average psychotherapy client in these studies was better off than 75% of the clients who remained untreated. A larger analysis based on 475 controlled outcome studies showed the average person who received therapy was better off at the end of treatment than 80% of those who did not (M. L. Smith, Glass, & Miller, 1980).

Other meta-analyses also show positive outcomes for psychotherapy, including analyses of cognitive-behavioral therapy, brief psychodynamic therapy, child and adolescent psychotherapy, group psychotherapy, and behavioral marital therapy (e.g., Butler et al., 2006; McDermut, Miller, & Brown, 2001; McLeod & Weisz, 2004; Shadish & Baldwin, 2005). Psychotherapy is effective not only in the confines of clinical research centers, but also in settings that are more typical of ordinary clinical practice (Shadish et al., 2000).

The greatest gains in psychotherapy typically occur in the first several months of treatment (Barkham et al., 1996). At least 50% of patients in controlled research studies show clinically significant improvement in about 13 treatment sessions; by 26 sessions, this figure rises to more than 80% (E. M. Anderson & Lambert, 2001; Hanson et al., 2002; Messer, 2001a). Yet we should recognize that many clients drop out prematurely, before therapeutic benefits are achieved.

Studies using the technique of meta-analysis show that different forms of therapy produce about the same size or magnitude of effects when they are compared to control groups (Wampold, 2001). This suggests that the effectiveness of different forms of psychotherapy may have more to do with nonspecific factors they have in common than with the specific techniques that set them apart. Nonspecific or common factors include expectations of improvement and features of the therapist–client relationship, including the following: (1) empathy, support, and attention shown by the therapist; (2) *therapeutic alliance,* or the attachment the client develops toward the therapist and the therapy process; and (3) the *working alliance,* or the development of an effective working relationship in which the therapist and client work together to identify and confront the important issues and problems the client faces (Busseri & Tyler, 2003; Klein et al., 2003; Westra, Dozois, & Marcus, 2007).

Should we conclude that different therapies are about equally effective? Not necessarily. Different therapies may be more or less equivalent in their effects overall, but some may be more effective for some patients or some types of problems. We should also allow that the effectiveness of therapy may have more to do with effectiveness of the therapist than with the particular form of therapy (Wampold, 2001).

All in all, the question of whether some forms of therapy are more effective than others remains unresolved. Perhaps the time has come for investigators to turn more of their attention to examining the active ingredients that make some therapists more effective than others, such as interpersonal skills, empathy, and ability to develop a good therapeutic relationship or alliance (Hanna, 2003; Karver et al., 2006). A stronger therapeutic alliance, especially an alliance formed early in therapy, is associated with better treatment outcomes (Constantino et al., 2005; Loeb et al., 2005; Strauss et al., 2006; Zuroff, & Blatt, 2006). The personal qualities that therapists bring to the therapeutic relationship, such as flexibility, honesty, warmth, and trustworthiness, impact their ability to form effective therapeutic alliances (Ackerman & Hilsenroth, 2003).

Another approach to determining which therapies are effective in treating which particular problems is the effort undertaken by a task force of psychologists to designate evidence-based practices (EBPs), which are also called *empirically supported treatments* or ESTs (APA Presidential Task Force on Evidence-Based Practice, 2006; Deegear & Lawson, 2003; Wells & Miranda, 2006). ESTs are specific psychological treatments that have demonstrated their effectiveness in treating specific problem behaviors or disorders in carefully designed clinical studies (see the listing in Table 4.3) (Chambless & Ollendick, 2001). We should note that the designation of empirically supported treatments is a work in progress, as other treatments may eventually be

TABLE 4.3

Examples of Empirically Supported Treatments (ESTs)

Treatment	Conditions for Which Treatment Is Effective
Cognitive therapy	(Chapter in text where treatment is discussed is shown in parentheses.) Headache (Chapter 5) Depression (Chapter 8)
Behavior therapy or behavior modification	Depression (Chapter 8) Persons with developmental disabilities (Chapter 14) Enuresis (Chapter 14)
Cognitive-behavioral therapy	Panic disorder with and without agoraphobia (Chapter 6) Generalized anxiety disorder (Chapter 6) Bulimia (Chapter 10)
Exposure treatment	Agoraphobia and specific phobia (Chapter 6)
Exposure and response prevention	Obsessive–compulsive disorder (Chapter 6)
Interpersonal psychotherapy	Depression (Chapter 8)
Parent training programs	Children with oppositional behavior (Chapter 14)

added to the list as scientific evidence of their efficacy in treating specific types of problems becomes available.

The attempt to designate evidence-based treatments may help address the problem of clients receiving mental health treatments that are not known to be effective (Thase, 2006). We should caution, however, that the inclusion of a particular treatment does not guarantee it is effective in every case. We also need to point out that methods and criteria used to determine which treatments are considered empirically supported remains a point of controversy in the field (see Crits-Christoph, Wilson, & Hollon, 2005; Weisz, Weersing, & Henggeler, 2005; Westen, Novotny, & Thompson-Brenner, 2004, 2005). This topic is explored further in the accompanying *Controversies in Abnormal Psychology* feature.

Let us conclude by noting that it is thus insufficient to ask which therapy works best. Instead, we must ask, Which therapy works best for which type of problem? Which clients are best suited for which type of therapy? What are the advantages and limitations of particular therapies? Although the effort to identify empirically supported treatments moves us in the direction of matching treatments to particular disorders, the process of determining which treatment, practiced by whom, and under what conditions is most effective for a given client remains a challenge.

CONTROVERSIES IN ABNORMAL PSYCHOLOGY

The Controversy Over Evidence-Based Practice: Repairing the Rift

—WILLIAM C. SANDERSON

When you make a visit to your physician with a particular ailment, it is safe to assume that whatever treatment you are given is the one most likely to be effective. You expect that the doctor's decision about which treatment approach to use is guided by clinical evidence, rather than personal preference. Increasingly, medical professionals are drawing upon *evidence-based treatments* as the basis for making treatment choices.

Is the same process used by psychologists in selecting a particular psychotherapy approach? Let's say a person suffering from panic disorder

consults a psychologist for treatment. What is the likelihood the person will receive the therapeutic intervention having the most supporting evidence for its efficacy? Unfortunately, the fact is that most people receiving treatment for panic disorder fail to receive the particular treatment that has received the strongest support in the research literature—cognitive-behavioral therapy. (See Chapter 6 for further discussion of cognitive-behavioral treatment of panic disorder.) Let us consider some of the reasons why evidence-based practices are not used more widely. But first, what do we mean by the term *evidence-based practices*?

(continued)

(continued)

WHAT ARE EVIDENCE-BASED PRACTICES?

Evidence-based practices (EBPs) (also called *empirically supported treatments* or ESTs) are treatments that have been shown to be effective in well-conducted controlled research trials (that is, in trials that randomize participants to treatment conditions, use a control or comparison group, and rely on a treatment manual that specifically describes the treatment protocol). The initial, and perhaps the most influential, effort to identify EBPs was undertaken in 1993 by a task force commissioned by The Society of Clinical Psychology (Division 12) of the American Psychological Association (APA). For a treatment to be considered evidence-based, the task force determined that it must have been shown to be either (a) equivalent to an already established treatment, or (b) superior to a placebo drug or psychotherapy placebo condition in at least two separate well-controlled studies. The task force was transformed into a standing committee of the division in 1999 (i.e., the Committee on Science and Practice) and continues its efforts today.

WHY IS THERE CONTROVERSY OVER EBPs?

In principle, psychologists are likely to agree on the necessity of providing empirical support for treatment interventions they use. It is also reasonable to assume that consumers of mental heath treatment expect to receive a treatment whose effectiveness has been proven when one is available. Therefore, one would expect clinicians to embrace EBPs. However, psychologists are split on the EBP movement. I believe that with the possible exception of the controversy over prescription privileges for psychologists, there is probably no issue more hotly debated among practicing psychologists today. Why? I will briefly summarize the main arguments against the use of EBPs.

First, many clinicians claim that EBPs essentially favor cognitive-behavioral therapies because these represent the kinds of standardized treatments that can be tested more readily in controlled clinical trials. As a result, they believe that viable alternative treatments (e.g., psychodynamic therapy), which cannot be as easily standardized, will fail to measure up to the EBP criteria, even though they may be effective in clinical practice. Second, it has been argued that most studies supportive of EBPs fail to capture the complexity and uniqueness of patients seen in "actual" practice. Consequently, these clinicians question the applicability of these manualized treatments to patients seen in the community. Third, many clinicians have a negative reaction to being "told what to do" by researchers who generate these data. This is part of an ongoing tension between scientists and practitioners as to who "knows best" about treatment decisions—those who generate the research findings or those who provide clinical treatment in actual practice?

FUTURE DIRECTIONS

Division 12's interest in identifying EBPs is part of a larger worldwide movement to make findings from applied medical research more available to clinicians in practice, a movement generally known as *evidence-based medicine*. The basic aim of this effort is to improve the quality of patient care by making it easier for practitioners to use empirical evidence to inform their choice of medical services. As a result, the issue of EBPs in psychology will need to be resolved if psychologists expect to have their roles as health-care providers taken seriously within the health-care community.

In my opinion, the future of the EBP movement will primarily be focused on repairing the rift between scientists and practitioners so they can work together to deal with this important issue. In particular, researchers must address the concerns of clinicians, noted briefly before. First, treatments clinicians believe are effective must be subject to empirical investigations to support their legitimacy. Second, more attention needs to be paid to evaluating EBPs in true clinical settings (known as *effectiveness research*) rather than only in clinical research centers. Third, researchers should work with clinicians to form a collaborative effort in disseminating EBPs in clinical practice, rather than having one group impose them on another. I believe that these issues are beginning to be addressed in the psychology community and am confident that psychologists will move together toward acceptance and dissemination of evidence-based practices.

William C. Sanderson, Ph.D., is Professor of Psychology at Hofstra University and Editor of the APA Division 12 publication, *The Clinical Psychologist*. Dr. Sanderson was a member of the original Division 12 Task Force on evidence-based treatment and served as Chair of the committee for several years.

Critical Thinking

- Evidence-based treatments exist for many, but not all, psychological disorders. What do you think a clinician should do if no evidence-based guidance exits for a particular disorder?
- Demonstrating that evidence-based treatments work in actual clinical settings is an essential area of future research. What may be some reasons for concern that these treatments may not be as effective as those tested in clinical trials in research centers or universities?

(For further information of the present status of EBPs in psychology, see the following publication: Bruce, T. J., & Sanderson, W. C. (2004). Evidence-based psychosocial practices: The past, present, and future. In C. Stout & R. Hayes (Eds.), *Evidence-based practice: Methods, models and tolls for mental health professionals* (pp. 220–243). New York: John Wiley and Sons.)

All in all, psychotherapy is a complex process that incorporates common features along with specific techniques that foster adaptive change. We need to take into account the contributions to therapeutic change of both specific and nonspecific factors, as well as their interactions.

Managed Care or Managed Costs? This is an appropriate juncture to note that the practice of psychotherapy has been influenced by changes in the general health-care environment in recent years, especially the increasing role of **managed care systems,** such as health maintenance organizations (HMOs). Managed care systems typically impose limits on the number of treatment sessions they will approve for payment and the fees they will allow for reimbursement. Consequently, there is greater emphasis today on briefer, more direct forms of treatment, including cognitive-behavioral therapy and shorter-term psychodynamic therapies. Moreover, managed care has curbed costly inpatient mental health treatment, primarily through limiting the lengths of stay of patients in psychiatric hospitals (USDHHS, 1999a).

managed care systems Health care delivery systems that impose limits on the number of treatment sessions they will approve for payment and the fees they will allow for reimbursement.

Though managed care may help trim costs, many people express concerns about the risks of sacrificing quality of care in the interests of cutting costs. A recent study found that quality of mental health care is lacking in many HMOs (Druss et al., 2002). Consumers rank autonomy in treatment decisions (not having a particular treatment turned down for reimbursement by a managed care company), choice of therapists, copayment amounts, limits to confidentiality, and ease of access to care as the most important elements of psychotherapy service plans offered by managed care companies (Kremer & Gesten, 2003).

Though health-care providers understand the need to curtail the spiraling costs of care, they are understandably concerned that the cost-cutting emphasis of managed care plans may discourage people with identifiable psychological disorders from seeking help or receiving adequate care (Landerman et al., 1994). According to a Surgeon General's report, "Excessively restrictive cost-containment strategies and financial incentives to providers and facilities to reduce specialty referrals, hospital admissions, or length or amount of treatment may ultimately contribute to lowered access and quality of care" (cited in USDDHS, 1999a).

Overzealous cost-cutting policies may also be financially shortsighted because the failure to provide adequate mental health care when problems arise may lead to a need for more expensive care later. Evidence shows that for people with severe psychological disorders, such as schizophrenia, bipolar disorder, and borderline personality disorder, psychotherapy actually reduces health-care costs by reducing the need for hospitalization and work impairment (Fraser, 1996; Gabbard et al., 1997).

"IT'S YOUR INSURANCE COMPANY, THEY SAY YOU'RE CURED."

Managed care or managed costs?

From the Wall Street Journal—permission, Cartoon Features Syndicate.

Multicultural Issues in Psychotherapy

We live in an increasingly diverse, multicultural society in which people bring to therapy not only their personal backgrounds and individual experiences but also their cultural learning, norms, and values. Normal and abnormal behaviors occur in a context of culture and community. Clearly, therapists need to be culturally competent to provide appropriate services to people of varied backgrounds (Hall, 2005; Stuart, 2004).

Therapists need to be sensitive to cultural differences and how they affect the therapeutic process. Cultural sensitivity involves more than good intentions. Therapists must also have accurate knowledge of cultural factors, as well as the ability to use that knowledge effectively in developing culturally sensitive approaches to treatment (Cardemil & Battle, 2003; Muñoz & Mendelson, 2005). Moreover, they need to avoid ethnic stereotyping and demonstrate sensitivity to the values, languages, and cultural beliefs of members of racial or ethnic groups that are different than their own. Perhaps it shouldn't surprise us that clients who rate their therapists high on multicultural competence also tend to perceive them as having skills of empathy and general competence (Fuertes & Brobst, 2002). However, a recent survey of professional psychologists showed that they applied relatively few of the recommended multicultural psychotherapy competencies in their practices (Hansen et al., 2006).

We must also recognize that just because a given therapy works with one population does not mean that it will necessarily work with another population (Hwang, 2006). We need evidence that speaks directly to whether particular therapies are effective with different populations (Muñoz, & Mendelson, 2005). We also need to learn more about how racial and gender differences between patients and therapists affect the development of the therapeutic alliance (Karlsson, 2005; Wintersteen, Mensinger, & Diamond, 2005).

Let us touch on some of the issues involved in treating members of the major ethnic minority groups in our society: African Americans, Asian Americans, Hispanic Americans, and Native Americans.

Cultural sensitivity. Therapists need to be sensitive to cultural differences and how they may affect the therapeutic process. They also need to avoid ethnic stereotyping and to demonstrate sensitivity to the values, languages, and cultural beliefs of members of racial or ethnic groups that are different than their own. Clients who are not fluent in English profit from having therapists who can conduct therapy in their own languages.

African Americans The cultural history of African Americans must be understood in the context of extreme racial discrimination (Boyd-Franklin, 1989; Greene, 1990). African Americans have needed to develop coping mechanisms for managing the pervasive racism they encounter in such areas as employment, housing, education, and access to health care (Greene, 1993a, 1993b). For example, the sensitivity of many African Americans to the potential for maltreatment and exploitation is a survival tool and may take the form of a heightened level of suspiciousness or reserve (Greene, 1986). Therapists need to be aware of the tendency of African American clients to minimize their vulnerability by being less self-disclosing, especially in early stages of therapy (Ridley, 1984). Therapists should not confuse such suspiciousness with paranoia (Boyd-Franklin, 1989; Greene, 1986).

In addition to whatever psychological problems African American clients may present, therapists often need to help their clients develop coping mechanisms to deal with racial barriers they encounter in daily life. Therapists also need to be attuned to tendencies of some African Americans to internalize the negative stereotypes about Blacks that are perpetuated in the dominant culture (Greene, 1985, 1992a, 1992b; Nickerson, Helms, & Terrell, 1994; Pinderhughes, 1989).

To be culturally competent, therapists not only must understand the cultural traditions and languages of the groups with which they work, but also must recognize their own racial and ethnic attitudes and how these underlying attitudes affect their clinical practice (Greene, 1985, 1992a, 1992b; Nickerson, Helms, & Terrell, 1994; Pinderhughes, 1989). Therapists are exposed to the same negative stereotypes about African Americans as other people in society and must recognize how these stereotypes, if left unexamined, can become destructive to the therapeutic relationships they form with African American clients. In effect, therapists must be willing to confront their own racism and prejudices and replace these attitudes with more realistic appraisals of African Americans (Mays, 1985).

Therapists must also be aware of the cultural characteristics of African American families, such as strong kinship bonds, often including people who are not biologically related (for example, a close friend of a parent may have some parenting role and may be addressed as "aunt"), strong religious and spiritual orientation, multigenerational households, adaptability and flexibility of gender roles (African American women have a long history of working outside the home), and distribution of child-care responsibilities among different family members (Boyd-Franklin, 1989; Collins, 1990; Ferguson-Peters, 1985; Greene, 1990; USDHHS, 1999a).

Asian Americans Culturally sensitive therapists not only understand the beliefs and values of other cultures but also integrate this knowledge within the therapy process. Generally speaking, Asian cultures, including Japanese culture, value restraint in talking about oneself and one's feelings. Public expression of emotions is also discouraged in Asian cultures, which may inhibit Asian clients from revealing their feelings in therapy. In traditional Asian cultures, the failure to keep one's feelings to oneself, especially negative feelings, may be perceived as reflecting poorly on one's upbringing. Asian clients who appear passive or emotionally restrained when judged by Western standards may be responding in ways that are culturally appropriate and should not be judged as shy, uncooperative, or avoidant by therapists (Hwang, 2006).

Clinicians also note that Asian clients often express psychological complaints in terms of physical symptoms. However, this tendency to *somaticize* emotional problems may be attributed in part to differences in communication styles (Zane & Sue, 1991). That is, Asians may use somatic terms to convey emotional distress.

In some cases, the goals of therapy may conflict with the values of a particular culture. Therapists need to recognize that the individualism of American society, which is expressed in therapeutic interventions that focus on development of the self, may conflict with the group- and family-centered values of Asian cultures. Framing the therapy process in culturally appropriate terms may help build bridges, such as by emphasizing the strong links in Asian cultures between mind, body, and spirit (Hwang, 2006).

Hispanic Americans Although Hispanic American subcultures differ in various respects, many share certain cultural values and beliefs, such as adherence to a strong patriarchal (male-dominated) family structure and strong kinship ties. De la Cancela and Guzman (1991) identify some other values shared by many Hispanic Americans:

> One's identity is in part determined by one's role in the family. The male, or *macho*, is the head of the family, the provider, the protector of the family honor, and the final decision maker. The woman's role (*marianismo*) is to care for the family and the children. Obviously, these roles are changing, with women entering the work force and achieving greater educational opportunities. Cultural values of *respeto* (respect), *confianza* (trust), *dignidad* (dignity), and *personalismo* (personalism) are highly esteemed and are important factors in working with many [Hispanic Americans] (p. 60).

Therapists need to recognize that the traditional Hispanic American value of interdependency within the family may conflict with the values of independence and self-reliance that are stressed in the mainstream U.S. culture (De la Cancela & Guzman, 1991). Psychotherapeutic interventions should respect differences in values rather than attempt to impose values of majority cultures. Therapists should also be trained to reach beyond the confines of their offices to work within the Hispanic American community itself, in settings that have an impact on the daily lives of Hispanic Americans, such as social clubs, *bodegas* (neighborhood groceries), and neighborhood beauty and barber shops. We can further break down barriers that may impede utilization of mental health services by Hispanic Americans by recruiting bicultural/bilingual staff and creating a welcoming therapeutic atmosphere that is accepting of Hispanic American cultural values (Guarnaccia & Rodriguez, 1996).

Native Americans Traditionally underserved groups, including people of color, have the greatest unmet needs for mental health treatment services (Wang et al., 2005). A case in point are Native Americans, who are underserved by mental health professionals partly as the result of the cultural gap between providers and recipients (Duran et al., 2005). Commenting upon this gap, Kahn (1982) suggests that if mental health professionals are to be successful in helping Native Americans, they must do so within a context that is relevant and sensitive to Native Americans' customs, culture, and values. For example, many Native Americans expect the therapist will do most of the talking and they will play a passive role in treatment. These expectations are in keeping with the traditional healer role but conflict with the client-focused approach of many forms of conventional therapy. There may yet be other differences in gestures, eye contact, facial expression, and other modes of nonverbal expression that can impede effective communication between therapist and client (Renfrey, 1992).

Psychologists recognize the importance of bringing elements of tribal culture into mental health programs for Native Americans (Rabasca, 2000a). For example, therapists can use indigenous ceremonies that are part of the client's cultural or religious traditions. Purification and cleansing rites are therapeutic for many Native American peoples in the United States and elsewhere, as *Santeria* is among the African Cuban community, *umbanda* for the Brazilian community, and *vodoun* in the Haitian community (Lefley, 1990). Cleansing rites are often sought by people who believe their problems are caused by failure to placate malevolent spirits or to perform mandatory ritual.

Respect for cultural differences is a key feature of culturally sensitive therapies. Training in multicultural therapy is becoming more widely integrated into training programs for therapists. Culturally sensitive therapies adopt a respectful attitude that encourages people to tell their own personal story as well as the story of their culture (Coronado & Peake, 1992).

psychopharmacology The field of study that examines the effects of therapeutic or psychiatric drugs.

BIOMEDICAL THERAPIES

There is a growing emphasis in American psychiatry on biomedical therapies, especially the use of *psychotropic drugs* (also called psychiatric drugs). Biomedical therapies are generally administered by medical doctors, many of whom have specialized training in psychiatry or **psychopharmacology.** Many family physicians or general practitioners also prescribe psychotherapeutic drugs for their patients.

Biomedical approaches have had dramatic success in treating some forms of abnormal behavior, although they also have their limitations. For one, drugs may have unwelcome or dangerous side effects. There is also the potential for abuse. One of the most commonly prescribed minor tranquilizers, Valium, has become a major drug of abuse among people who become psychologically and physiologically dependent on it. Psychosurgery has been all but eliminated as a form of treatment because of serious harmful effects of earlier procedures.

Drug Therapy

Different classes of psychotropic drugs are used in treating many types of psychological disorders. But all the drugs in these classes act on neurotransmitter systems in the brain, affecting the delicate balance of chemicals that ferry nerve impulses from neuron to neuron (Snyder, 2002). The major classes of psychiatric drugs are antianxiety drugs, antipsychotic drugs, and antidepressants, as well as lithium, which is used to treat mood swings in people with bipolar disorder. The use of other psychotropic drugs, such as stimulants, will be discussed in later chapters.

antianxiety drugs Drugs that combat anxiety and reduce states of muscle tension.

Antianxiety Drugs **Antianxiety drugs** (also called *anxiolytics,* from the Greek *anxietas,* meaning "anxiety," and *lysis,* meaning "bringing to an end") combat anxiety and reduce states of muscle tension. They include mild tranquilizers, such as those of the *benzodiazepine* class of drugs, including *diazepam* (Valium) and *alprazolam* (Xanax), as well as hypnotic-sedatives, such as *triazolam* (Halcion) and *flurazepam* (Dalmane).

Antianxiety drugs depress the level of activity in certain parts of the central nervous system (CNS). In turn, the CNS decreases the level of sympathetic nervous system activity, reducing the respiration rate and heart rate and lessening states of anxiety and tension. Mild tranquilizers such as Valium grew in popularity when physicians became concerned about the use of more potent depressants, such as barbiturates, which are highly addictive and extremely dangerous when taken in overdoses or mixed with alcohol. Unfortunately, it has become clear that these tranquilizers also can, and often do, lead to physiological dependence (addiction). People who are dependent on Valium may go into convulsions when they abruptly stop taking it. Deaths have been reported among people who mix mild tranquilizers with alcohol or who are unusually sensitive to them.

tolerance Physical habituation to use of a drug.

Side effects of using antianxiety drugs include fatigue, drowsiness, and impaired motor coordination that can impair the ability to function or to operate an automobile. Regular usage of these drugs can also produce **tolerance,** a physiological sign of dependence, which refers to the need over time for increasing dosages of a drug to achieve the same effect. When used on a short-term basis, antianxiety drugs can be safe and effective in treating anxiety and insomnia. Yet drugs by themselves do not teach people more adaptive ways of solving their problems and may encourage them to rely on a chemical agent to cope with stress rather than to develop active means of coping. Drug therapy is thus often combined with psychotherapy to help people with anxiety complaints. However, combining drug therapy and psychotherapy may present special problems and challenges. For one, drug-induced relief from anxiety may reduce clients' motivation to try to solve their problems. For another, medicated clients who develop skills for coping with stress in psychotherapy may fail to retain what they have learned once the tranquilizers are discontinued or find themselves too tense to employ their newly acquired skills.

Rebound anxiety is another problem associated with regular use of tranquilizers. Many people who regularly use antianxiety drugs report that anxiety or insomnia returns in a more severe form once they discontinue them. For some, this may represent a fear of not having the drugs to depend on. For others, rebound anxiety might reflect changes in biochemical processes that are not well understood at present.

rebound anxiety The experiencing of strong anxiety following withdrawal from a tranquilizer.

Antipsychotic Drugs **Antipsychotic drugs,** also called *neuroleptics,* are commonly used to treat the more flagrant features of schizophrenia and other psychotic disorders, such as hallucinations, delusions, and states of confusion. Introduced during the 1950s, many of these drugs, including *chlorpromazine* (Thorazine), *thioridazine* (Mellaril), and *fluphenazine* (Prolixin), belong to the *phenothiazine* class of chemicals. Phenothiazines appear to control psychotic features by blocking the action of the neurotransmitter dopamine at receptor sites in the brain. Although the underlying causes of schizophrenia remain unknown, researchers suspect an irregularity in the dopamine system in the brain may be involved (see Chapter 12). *Clozapine* (Clozaril), a neuroleptic of a different chemical class than the phenothiazines, is effective in treating many people with schizophrenia whose symptoms were unresponsive to other neuroleptics (see Chapter 12). The use of clozapine must be carefully monitored, however, because of potentially dangerous side effects.

antipsychotic drugs Drugs used to treat schizophrenia or other psychotic disorders.

The use of neuroleptics has greatly reduced the need for more restrictive forms of treatment for severely disturbed patients, such as physical restraints and confinement in padded cells, and has lessened the need for long-term hospitalization. The introduction of the first generation of antipsychotic drugs in the mid-1950s was one of the major factors that led to a massive exodus of chronic mental patients from state institutions. Many formerly hospitalized patients have been able to resume family life and hold jobs while continuing to take their medications.

Neuroleptics are not without their problems, including potential side effects such as muscular rigidity and tremors. Although these side effects are generally controllable by use of other drugs, long-term use of antipsychotic drugs (possibly excepting *clozapine*) can produce a potentially irreversible and disabling motor disorder called *tardive dyskinesia* (see Chapter 12), which is characterized by uncontrollable eye blinking, facial grimaces, lip smacking, and other involuntary movements of the mouth, eyes, and limbs. Researchers are experimenting with lowered dosages, intermittent drug regimens, and new medications to reduce the risk of such complications.

Antidepressants We have three major classes of **antidepressants** in use today: *tricyclics (TCAs), monoamine oxidase (MAO) inhibitors,* and *selective serotonin-reuptake inhibitors (SSRIs).* Tricyclics and MAO inhibitors increase the availability of the neurotransmitters norepinephrine and serotonin in the brain. Some of the more common tricyclics are *imipramine* (Tofranil), *amitriptyline* (Elavil), and *doxepin* (Sinequan). The MAO inhibitors include such drugs as *phenelzine* (Nardil). Tricyclic antidepressants (TCAs) are favored over MAO inhibitors because they cause fewer potentially serious side effects.

antidepressants Drugs used to treat depression that affect the availability of neurotransmitters in the brain.

The third class of antidepressants, selective serotonin-reuptake inhibitors, or SSRIs, have more specific effects on serotonin function in the brain. Drugs in this class include *fluoxetine* (Prozac) and *sertraline* (Zoloft). They increase the availability of serotonin in the brain by interfering with its reuptake by the transmitting neuron.

Slightly more than half of depressed patients treated with antidepressants of the tricyclic class respond favorably (Depression Guideline Panel, 1993b). Bear in mind that a favorable response to treatment does not mean depression is relieved, however. Overall, the effects of antidepressants appear to be modest at best, with full remission of symptoms in only about one in three patients treated in the first round of antidepressant medication (Lespérance et al., 2007; Rush et al., 2006). Perhaps another 5% to 10% of patients will show remission if then switched to other antidepressant drugs (Nelson, 2006). Nor is any particular antidepressant clearly more effective than any other (Depression Guideline Panel, 1993b). Even Prozac, which some hailed as a

TRUTH or FICTION

Antidepressants are used only to treat depression.

☑ **FALSE.** Antidepressants have many psychiatric uses, including treatment of many anxiety disorders and bulimia.

Electroconvulsive therapy (ECT). ECT is helpful in many cases of severe or prolonged depression that do not respond to other forms of treatment. Still, its use remains controversial.

electroconvulsive therapy (ECT) A method of treating severe depression by administering electrical shock to the head.

"wonder drug," produces about the same level of therapeutic benefit as the older generation of antidepressants, the TCAs. Prozac and other SSRIs may be preferred, however, because they are associated with fewer side effects, such as weight gain, and have a lower risk of lethal overdoses than the older tricyclics.

Antidepressants also have beneficial effects in treating a wide range of psychological disorders, including panic disorder, social phobia, obsessive–compulsive disorder (see Chapter 6), and bulimia, a type of eating disorder (see Chapter 10). As research into the underlying causes of these disorders continues, we may find that irregularities of neurotransmitter functioning in the brain plays a key role in their development.

Lithium Lithium carbonate, a salt of the metal lithium in tablet form, helps stabilize the dramatic mood swings in many cases of people with bipolar disorder (formerly *manic depression*) (see Chapter 8). People with bipolar disorder may have to continue using lithium indefinitely to control the disorder. Because of potential toxicity associated with lithium, the blood levels of patients maintained on the drug must be carefully monitored.

Table 4.4 lists psychotropic drugs according to their drug class and category.

Electroconvulsive Therapy

In 1939, the Italian psychiatrist Ugo Cerletti introduced the technique of **electroconvulsive therapy (ECT)** in psychiatric treatment. Cerletti had observed the practice in some slaughterhouses of using electric shock to render animals unconscious. He observed that the shocks also produced convulsions. Cerletti incorrectly believed, as did other researchers in Europe at the time, that convulsions of the type found in epilepsy were incompatible with schizophrenia and that a treatment method that induced convulsions might be used to cure schizophrenia.

After the introduction of the phenothiazines in the 1950s, the use of ECT became generally limited to the treatment of severe depression. The introduction of antidepressants has limited the use of ECT even further today. However, evidence indicates that many people with major depression who have failed to respond to antidepressants do show significant improvement following ECT (Ebmeier, Donaghey, & Steele, 2006; UK ECT Review Group, 2003).

ECT remains a source of controversy for several reasons. First, many people, including many professionals, are uncomfortable about the idea of passing an electric shock through a person's head, even if the level of shock is closely regulated and the convulsions are controlled by drugs. Second, ECT carries potential side effects, including some memory loss. Permanent loss of memory may occur for events that happen during the months that precede ECT and for several weeks afterwards (Glass, 2001). Third, the relative effectiveness of ECT, as compared to antidepressant drugs and to alternative treatments, such as cognitive-behavioral therapy, remains under study. Fourth, no one yet knows why ECT works, although it is suspected that it might help correct neurotransmitter imbalances in the brain. Finally, ECT is associated with a high rate of relapse following treatment (Sackeim et al., 2001, 2004).

Although controversies concerning the use of ECT persist, increasing evidence supports its effectiveness in helping people with severe depression, including cases in which depressed people fail to respond to psychotherapy or antidepressant medication (Sackeim et al., 2001). ECT is generally considered a treatment of last resort, after less-intrusive methods have been tried and failed.

TABLE 4.4

Major Psychotropic Drugs

	Generic Name	Brand Name	Clinical Uses	Possible Side Effects or Complications
Antianxiety Drugs	Diazepam Chlordiazepoxide Lorazepam Alprazolam	Valium Librium Ativan Xanax	Treatment of anxiety and insomnia	Drowsiness, fatigue, impaired coordination, nausea
Antidepressant Drugs	**Tricyclics**			
	Imipramine Desipramine Amitriptyline Doxepin	Tofranil Norpramin Elavil Sinequan	Depression, bulimia, panic disorder	Changes in blood pressure, heart irregularities, dry mouth, confusion, skin rash
	MAO Inhibitors			
	Phenelzine	Nardil	Depression	Dizziness, headache, sleep disturbance, agitation, anxiety, fatigue
	Selective Serotonin-Reuptake Inhibitors			
	Fluoxetine Sertraline Paroxetine Citalopram	Prozac Zoloft Paxil Celexa	Depression, bulimia, panic disorder, obsessive-compulsive disorder, posttraumatic stress disorder (Zoloft), social anxiety (Paxil)	Nausea, diarrhea, anxiety, insomnia, sweating, dry mouth, dizziness, drowsiness
	Other Antidepressant Drugs			
	Bupropion	Wellbutrin, Zyban	Depression, nicotine dependence	Dry mouth, insomnia, headaches, nausea, constipation, tremors
	Venlafaxine	Effexor	Depression	Nausea, constipation, dry mouth, drowsiness, insomnia, dizziness, anxiety
Antipsychotic Drugs	**Phenothiazines**			
	Chlorpromazine Thioridazine Trifluoperazine Fluphenazine	Thorazine Mellaril Stelazine Prolixin	Schizophrenia and other psychotic disorders	Movement disorders (e.g., tardive dyskinesia), drowsiness, restlessness, dry mouth, blurred vision, muscle rigidity
	Other Antipsychotic Drugs			
	Haloperidol	Haldol	Schizophrenia and other psychotic disorders	Similar to phenothiazines
	Clozapine	Clozaril	Schizophrenia and other psychotic disorders	Potentially lethal blood disorder, seizures, fast heart rate, drowsiness, dizziness, nausea
	Risperidone	Risperdal	Schizophrenia and other psychotic disorders	Feeling unable to sit still, constipation, dizziness, drowsiness, weight gain
	Olanzapine	Zyprexa	Schizophrenia and other psychotic disorders	Low blood pressure, dizziness, drowsiness, heart palpitations, fatigue, constipation, weight gain
Antimanic Drugs	Lithium carbonate	Eskalith	Manic episodes and stabilization of mood swings associated with bipolar disorder	Tremors, thirst, diarrhea, drowsiness, weakness, lack of coordination
	Divalproex sodium	Depakote		Nausea, vomiting, dizziness, abdominal cramps, sleeplessness
Stimulant Drugs	Methylphenidate	Ritalin Concerta	Childhood hyperactivity	Nervousness, insomnia, nausea, dizziness, heart palpitations, headache; may temporarily retard growth
	Amphetamine with dextroamphetamine	Adderall		

Source: From Nevid, J. S., *Psychology: Concepts and Applications,* Second Edition (Boston: Houghton Mifflin, 2007), p. 574. Reprinted by permission.

Psychosurgery

Psychosurgery is yet more controversial than ECT and is rarely practiced today. Although no longer performed today, the most common form of psychosurgery was the *prefrontal lobotomy*. This procedure involved surgical severing of nerve pathways linking the thalamus to the prefrontal lobes of the brain. The operation was based on the theory that extremely disturbed patients suffer from overexcitation of emotional impulses emanating from lower brain centers, such as the thalamus and hypothalamus. It was believed that by severing the connections between the thalamus and the higher brain centers in the frontal lobe of the cerebral cortex, the patient's violent or aggressive tendencies could be controlled. The prefrontal lobotomy was developed by the Portuguese neurologist António Egas Moniz and was introduced to the United States in the 1930s. More than 1,000 mental patients received the operation by 1950. Although the operation did reduce violent and agitated behavior in many cases, it was not always successful. In a cruel ironic twist, a patient whom Moniz had treated later shot him, leaving him paralyzed from a bullet that lodged in his spine. The procedure was abandoned, in large part because it often produced serious complications and even deaths, and also because of the advent in the 1950s of psychiatric drugs that could be used to control violent or disruptive behavior.

Today, more sophisticated psychosurgery techniques have been introduced. Guided by a better understanding of brain circuitry involved in certain disorders, such as obsessive–compulsive disorder, these surgical techniques target smaller parts of the brain and produce less damage than the prefrontal lobotomy (Wichmann & Delong, 2005). These techniques have been used in treating some patients with severe forms of obsessive-compulsive disorder, bipolar disorder, and major depression that have not responded to other treatments (Kopell, Machado, & Rezai, 2005). Yet a debate continues over both the safety and efficacy of these procedures, so it is best to continue to classify them as experimental treatments (Anderson & Booker, 2006; Bejerot, 2003). Before leaving this topic, let us underscore that psychosurgery should only be considered as a treatment of last resort.

Evaluation of Biological Approaches

There is little doubt that biological treatments have helped many people with severe psychological problems. Many thousands of people with schizophrenia who were formerly hospitalized are able to function in the community because of antipsychotic drugs. Antidepressant drugs have helped relieve depression in many cases and have shown therapeutic benefits in treating other disorders, such as panic disorder, obsessive–compulsive disorder, and eating disorders. ECT is helpful in relieving depression in many people who have been unresponsive to other treatments.

On the other hand, some forms of psychotherapy may be as effective as drug therapy in treating anxiety disorders and depression (see Chapters 6 and 8). Moreover, problems such as side effects persist. In addition, antianxiety drugs, such as Valium, often become drugs of abuse among people who become dependent on them for relieving the effects of stress. Medical practitioners have often been too quick to use their prescription pads to help people with anxiety complaints, rather than to help them examine their lives or refer them for psychological treatment. Physicians often feel pressured, of course, by patients who seek a chemical solution to their life problems.

Although we continue to learn more about the biological foundations of abnormal behavior patterns, the interface between biology and behavior can be construed as a two-way street. Researchers have uncovered links between psychological factors and many physical disorders and conditions (see Chapter 5). Researchers are also investigating whether the combination of psychological and drug treatments for such problems as depression, anxiety disorders, and substance abuse disorders, among others, may increase the therapeutic benefits of either of the two approaches alone.

HOSPITALIZATION AND COMMUNITY-BASED CARE

People receive mental health services within various settings, including hospitals, outpatient clinics, community mental health centers, and private practices. In this section we explore the purposes of hospitalization and the movement toward community-based care. Due to **deinstitutionalization**—the policy of shifting the burden of care from state hospitals to community-based treatment settings—an exodus has taken place from state mental hospitals. We will see that deinstitutionalization has had a profound impact on the delivery of mental health services as well as on the larger community.

deinstitutionalization The policy of shifting care for patients with severe or chronic mental health problems from inpatient facilities to community-based facilities.

Roles for Hospitalization

Different types of hospitals provide different types of mental health treatment. State mental hospitals provide care to people with severe psychological problems. Municipal and community-based hospitals tend to focus on short-term care for people with serious psychological problems who need a structured hospital environment to help them through a crisis. In these kinds of cases, psychotropic drugs and other biological treatments, such as ECT for severe cases of depression, are often used in combination with short-term psychotherapy. Hospitalization may be followed by outpatient treatment. Many private psychiatric hospitals provide longer-term care or are specialized to help people withdraw safely from alcohol or drugs. Susanna, whose case opened this chapter, was treated in such a hospital for nearly two years.

Most state hospitals today are better managed and provide more humane care than those of the 19th and early 20th centuries, but here and there deplorable conditions persist. Today's state hospital is generally more treatment oriented and focuses on preparing residents to return to community living. State hospitals today often function as part of an integrated, comprehensive approach to treatment. They provide a structured environment for people who are unable to function in a less-restrictive community setting. When hospitalization restores patients to a higher level of functioning, the patients are reintegrated in the community and given follow-up care and transitional residences, if needed, to help them adjust to community living. Patients may be rehospitalized as needed in a state hospital if a community-based hospital is not available or if they require more extensive care. For younger and less intensely disturbed people, the state hospital stay is typically briefer than it was in the past, lasting only until their condition allows them to reenter society. Older chronic patients may be unprepared to handle the most rudimentary tasks (shopping, cooking, cleaning, and so on) of independent life, however—in part because the state hospital may be the only home such patients have known as adults.

The Community Mental Health Center

Community mental health centers (CMHCs) perform many functions in the effort to reduce the need for hospitalization of new patients and rehospitalization of formerly hospitalized patients. A primary function of the CMHC is to help discharged mental patients adjust to the community by providing continuing care and closely monitoring their progress. Unfortunately, not enough CMHCs have been established to serve the needs of the hundreds of thousands of formerly hospitalized patients and to prevent the need to hospitalize new patients by providing intervention services and day hospital programs. Patients in *day hospitals* attend structured therapy and vocational rehabilitation programs in a hospital setting during the day, but are returned to their families or homes at night. Many CMHCs also administer transitional treatment facilities in the community, such as *halfway houses*. Halfway houses provide a sheltered living environment to help discharged mental patients gradually adjust to the community as well as to offer people in crisis an alternative to hospitalization. CMHCs also provide consultative services to other professionals, such as training police officers to handle disturbed people. One of the major functions of the community mental health center is

The Mental hospital. Under the policy of deinstitutionalization, mental hospitals today provide a range of services, including short-term treatment of people in crisis or in need of a secure treatment setting. They also provide long-term treatment in a structured environment for people who are unable to function in less-restrictive community settings.

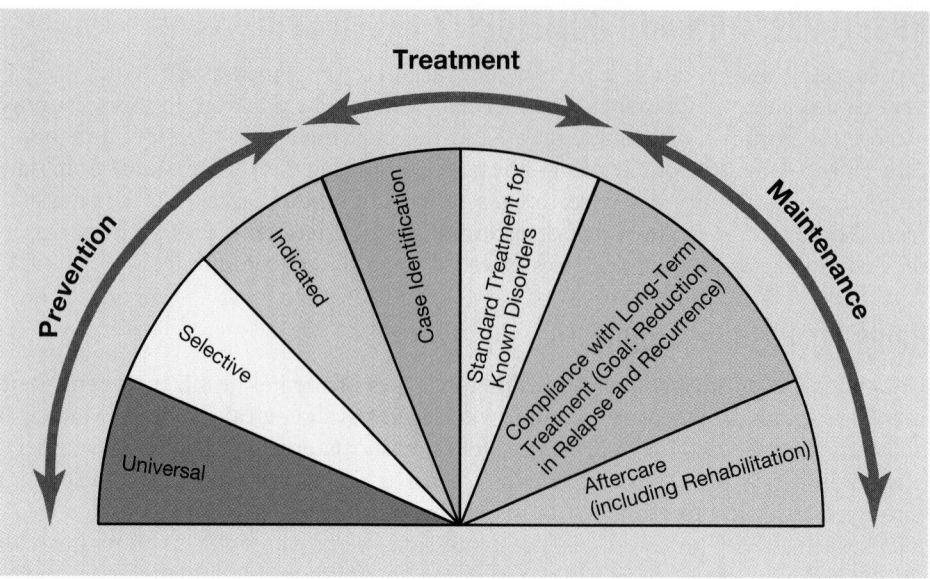

FIGURE 4.2 The mental health intervention spectrum for mental disorders.

Source: Mazrek, P. J., & Haggerty, R. J., *Reducing risks for mental disorders: Frontiers for preventive intervention research.* Copyright © 1994 by the National Academy of Sciences. Courtesy of the National Academy Press, Washington, DC. Reprinted with permission.

prevention. "An ounce of prevention is worth a pound of cure," so goes the saying. In medical science, vaccines prevent people from contracting such diseases as smallpox and polio. In the mental health system, however, resources are generally directed toward treating mental health problems rather than attempting to prevent them from developing. However, a report by the prestigious Institute of Medicine (IOM) called for increased support for research on prevention and for programs to promote psychological well-being and reduce the risks of mental health disorders (Muñoz, Mrazek, & Haggerty, 1996).

The Spectrum of Prevention Traditionally, the term *prevention* has been applied to interventions that run the gamut from programs designed to prevent the onset of mental disorders to those that attempt to reduce the impact of disorders once they develop. The IOM report limits the term *prevention* to interventions that occur before the onset of a diagnosable disorder. Interventions focusing on lessening the impact of already developed disorders are classified as *treatment interventions* rather than prevention.

The IOM report conceptualizes a mental health spectrum of interventions ranging from prevention efforts through treatment and maintenance interventions (see Figure 4.2). Three categories of prevention programs are identified: universal, selective, and indicated.

Universal preventive interventions are targeted toward the whole population or general public, and include programs designed to enhance prenatal health or childhood nutrition. *Selective preventive interventions* are targeted toward individuals or groups known to be at higher than average risk of developing mental disorders, such as children of schizophrenic parents. **Primary prevention** efforts—programs designed to prevent problems from arising—can be either universal or selective, depending on whether they are focused on the general population or "at-risk" groups.

Indicated preventive interventions are directed toward individuals with early signs or symptoms that foreshadow the development of a mental disorder but don't yet meet diagnostic criteria for the particular disorder. This form of prevention, commonly called **secondary prevention,** attempts to nip in the bud developing problems. For example, secondary preventive programs aimed at changing the drinking habits of

primary prevention Efforts designed to prevent problems from arising.

secondary prevention Efforts to ameliorate existing problems at an early stage.

high-risk drinkers or early problem drinkers may forestall the onset of more severe alcohol-related problems or alcohol dependence (Botelho & Richmond, 1996; Marlatt et al., 1998).

We now have ample evidence supporting the effectiveness of prevention interventions across a range of problem outcomes of concern to society (Barrer & Sandler, 2006; Cuijpers, Van Straten, & Smit, 2005). For example, evidence supports the benefits of prevention interventions in the following:

- Reducing depression in at-risk teens (Lynch et al., 2005);
- Preventing problems in children from divorced families (Tein et al., 2004)
- Reducing risks of eating disorder in college-age women (Stice et al., 2007; Taylor et al., 2006)
- Reducing risk of HIV transmission in at-risk population groups (Albarracín, Durantini, & Ear, 2006; DiClemente et al., 2004; Durantini et al., 2006)

Psychologist Martin Seligman and his colleagues have shown that teaching cognitive skills involved in disputing catastrophic, negative thoughts reduced the risk of depression in both college students and school-age children (Jaycox et al., 1994; Seligman, 1998). Still, we have much to learn about developing effective prevention programs to prevent psychological disorders. To develop effective preventive programs we must expand our knowledge of the underlying causes of these disorders as well as mount controlled investigations to examine ways of preventing them.

The challenge of preventing psychological disorders is before us. The question is whether the nation can muster the political will and financial resolve to meet the challenge.

Ethnic Group Differences in Use of Mental Health Services

A report by the U.S. Surgeon General concluded that members of racial and ethnic minority groups typically have less access to mental health care and receive lower-quality care than do other Americans (USDHHS, 2001; see Table 4.5). A major reason for this disparity is that a disproportionate number of minority group members remain

An ounce of prevention. Obtaining good prenatal care can help prevent health problems in both the mother and the fetus. Mental health professionals face the challenge of developing programs to reduce the risks of psychological disorders.

TABLE 4.5

Culture, Race, Ethnicity, and Mental Health: Major Findings of the Surgeon General's Report

- The percentage of African Americans receiving needed care for mental health problems is only half that of non-Hispanic Whites. African Americans have less access to mental health care than Whites, partly because a greater percentage of African Americans lack health insurance.

- Of all American ethnic groups, Hispanic Americans are the least likely to have health insurance. Moreover, the limited availability of Spanish-speaking mental health professionals means that many Hispanic Americans who speak little or no English lack the opportunity to receive care from linguistically similar treatment providers.

- Largely because of lingering stigma and shame associated with mental illness, Asian Americans/Pacific Islanders often fail to seek care until their problems are more advanced than is the case with other groups. Moreover, accessibility is limited by scarcity of treatment providers with appropriate language skills.

- American Indians/Alaska Natives have a suicide rate that is 50% higher than the national average, but little is known about how many people within these groups receive needed care. In addition, the rural, isolated locations in which many Native Americans live places a severe constraint on the availability of mental health services.

Source: Adapted from Stenson, 2001a; USDHHS, 2001.

uninsured or underinsured, leaving them unable to afford mental health care. Consequently, minorities shoulder a greater burden of mental health problems that go undiagnosed and untreated (Neighbors et al., 2007; Stenson, 2001a).

Cultural factors are yet another reason for underutilization of mental health services by minority groups (Sanders Thompson et al., 2004). Mental health clinics are not typically the first places where African Americans go for help for emotional problems. They are more likely to turn first to the church and second to the emergency room of the local general hospital (Lewis-Hall, 1992). The National Survey of African Americans found that slightly more than half (54%) of those who reported experiencing feelings of a "nervous breakdown" failed to consult any type of professional for help with their problems (Neighbors, 1992). Another study found that only about 1 in 10 African Americans in a community-based sample who experienced major depression consulted a mental health professional (D. R. Brown, Ahmed, Gary, & Milburn, 1995).

Latinos who encounter emotional problems are more likely to seek assistance from friends and relatives or from spiritualists than to reach out to mental health facilities, which they perceive as cold and impersonal (De La Cancela & Guzman, 1991). Latinos are also more likely to seek assistance for emotional problems from primary-care physicians than from psychologists or psychiatrists, in part to avoid the perceived stigma of consulting a mental health provider (Kouyoumdjian, Zamboanga, & Hansen, 2003). Asian Americans/Pacific Islanders are also less likely than Euro Americans to seek help from mental health providers (Breaux, Matsuoka, & Ryujin, 1995).

We may better understand low rates of utilization of outpatient mental health services by ethnic minorities by examining the barriers that exist to receiving treatment, which include the following (adapted from Cheung, 1991; USDHHS, 1999a; Woodward, Dwinell, & Arons, 1992):

1. *Cultural mistrust.* People from minority groups often fail to use mental health services because of a lack of trust (Sanders Thompson et al., 2004). Mistrust may stem from a cultural or personal history of oppression, discrimination, or experiences in which service providers were unresponsive to their needs. When ethnic minority clients perceive majority therapists and the institutions in which they work to be cold or impersonal, they are less likely to place their trust in them.

2. *Institutional barriers.* Facilities may be inaccessible to minority group members because they are located at a considerable distance from their homes or because of lack of public transportation. Most facilities operate only during daytime work hours, which means they are inaccessible to working people. Moreover, minority group members feel staff members often make them feel stupid for not being familiar with clinic procedures, and their requests for assistance often become tangled in red tape.

3. *Cultural barriers.* Many recent immigrants, especially those from Southeast Asian countries, have had little, if any, previous contact with mental health professionals. They may hold different conceptions of mental health problems or view mental health problems as less severe than physical problems. In some ethnic minority subcultures, the family is expected to take care of members who have psychological problems and may resist seeking outside assistance. Other cultural barriers include cultural differences between typically lower socioeconomic strata minority group members and mostly White, middle-class staff members and incongruence between the cultural practices of minority group members and techniques used by mental health professionals. For example, Asian immigrants may find little value in talking about their problems or may be uncomfortable expressing their feelings to strangers. In many ethnic minority groups, personal and interpersonal problems are brought to trusted elders in the family or religious leaders, not to outside professionals. In light of these fac-

tors, it is not surprising to find evidence that East Asian immigrants who are willing to seek psychological treatment tend to be older, more assimilated, and have better proficiency in English than their peers (Barry & Grilo, 2002).

4. *Language barriers.* Differences in language make it difficult for minority group members to describe their problems or obtain needed services. Many mental health facilities lack staff members who can communicate in the languages used by ethnic minority residents in their communities (Biever et al., 2002).

5. *Economic and accessibility barriers.* As mentioned earlier, financial burdens are often a major barrier to utilization of mental health services by ethnic minorities, many of whom live in economically distressed areas (Sanders Thompson et al., 2004). Moreover, many minority group members live in rural or isolated areas where mental health services may be lacking or inaccessible (USDHHS, 2001).

Cheung (1991) concludes that greater utilization of mental health services will depend to a great extent on the ability of the mental health system to develop programs that take cultural factors into account and build staffs that consist of culturally sensitive providers, including minority mental health professionals and paraprofessionals. Cultural mistrust of the mental health system among minority group members may be grounded in the perception that many mental health professionals are racially biased in how they evaluate and treat members of minority groups. Let's take a closer look at whether the evidence bears out this perception.

Racial Stereotyping and the Mental Health System

If you are African American, you are more likely to be admitted to a mental hospital and more likely to be involuntarily committed than if you are White (Lindsey & Paul, 1989). You are also more likely to be diagnosed with schizophrenia (Coleman & Baker, 1994; USDHHS, 1999a). The question is, *why?*

Relationships between ethnicity and diagnostic and admission practices are complex. They depend in part on differences in rates of mental disorders among different ethnic groups. If the rate of a given disorder is higher in a particular group, then it stands to reason that more members of the group will be diagnosed with the disorder. We know that African Americans as a group are no more likely to develop schizophrenia, a severe psychological disorder that often leads to hospitalization, than are Euro Americans of the same socioeconomic level (USDHHS, 1999a). However, we also know that African Americans are overrepresented among lower socioeconomic groups in our society, and people in the lower strata on the socioeconomic ladder are more likely to have severe psychological disorders, such as schizophrenia. Thus, differences in socioeconomic backgrounds offer at least a partial explanation of ethnic/racial differences in diagnostic practices and rates of psychiatric hospitalization.

Ethnic stereotyping by mental health professionals may also contribute to an overdiagnosis of severe psychological problems requiring hospitalization. For example, although African Americans and Hispanic Americans are more likely than Euro Americans to be diagnosed with schizophrenia, independent assessment of patients does not justify such differences in rates of diagnosis (Garb, 1997; Lawson et al., 1994). This evidence strongly suggests that bias comes into play in diagnosing members of ethnic minority groups. African Americans are also more likely than Euro Americans to receive psychiatric medication, including antipsychotic medication (Segal, Bola, & Watson, 1996). Investigators believe that clinician biases rather than clinical criteria may account for differences in prescription patterns (Frackiewicz et al., 1999).

How might bias affect a clinician's clinical judgments? As the Surgeon General's report on mental health points out, diagnostic and treatment decisions in mental health settings are based more on behavioral signs and patient reporting of symptoms than on more objective laboratory tests (USDHHS, 1999a). Consequently, clinician judgment plays an important role in determining whether someone receives a schizophrenia diagnosis and is deemed to be in need of hospitalization or antipsychotic medication.

Evaluation of Deinstitutionalization

Let us return to the issue of deinstitutionalization. Has this policy achieved its goal of successfully reintegrating mental patients into society, or does it remain a promise that is largely unfulfilled? Deinstitutionalization has often been criticized for failing to live up to its expectations. The criticism seems to be well founded. Among the most frequent criticisms is the charge that many hospital patients were merely dumped into the community and not provided with the community-based services they needed to adjust to demands of community living. A 1998 national study found that fewer than half of patients with schizophrenia were receiving adequate care (Winerip, 1999).

Though the community mental health movement has had some successes, a great many patients with severe and persistent mental health problems fail to receive the range of mental health and social services they need to adjust to life in the community (Jacobs, Newman, & Burns, 2001). One of the major challenges facing the community mental system is the problem of psychiatric homelessness (Folsom et al., 2005).

Deinstitutionalization and the Psychiatric Homeless Population The federal government estimates that about one-third of homeless adults in the United States suffer from severe psychological disorders (NIH, 2003). Many formerly hospitalized mental patients were essentially dumped into local communities after discharge and left with little if any support. Lacking adequate support, they often face more dehumanizing conditions on the street, under deinstitutionalization, than they did in the hospital. Many compound their problems by turning to illegal street drugs such as crack. Also, some of the younger psychiatric homeless population might have been hospitalized in earlier times but are now, in the wake of deinstitutionalization, directed toward community support programs when they are available.

The lack of available housing and transitional care facilities and effective case management plays an important role in homelessness among people with psychiatric problems (Folsom et al., 2005). Some homeless people with severe psychiatric problems are repeatedly hospitalized for brief stays in community-based hospitals during acute episodes. They move back and forth between the hospital and the community as though caught in a revolving door. Frequently, they are released from the hospital with inadequate arrangements for housing and community care. Some are left essentially to fend for themselves. Although many state hospitals closed their doors and others slashed the number of beds, the states never funded the support services in the community that were supposed to replace the need for long-term hospitalization (Winerip, 1999).

Problems of homelessness are especially severe for children. Not surprisingly, homeless children tend to have more behavior problems than housed children (Schteingart et al., 1995). The problem of psychiatric homelessness is not limited to urban areas, although it is on our city streets that the problem is most visible. The pattern in rural areas tends to be one of inconsistent housing and unstable living arrangements, rather than outright homelessness (Drake et al., 1991).

The mental health system alone does not have the resources to resolve the multifaceted problems faced by the psychiatric homeless population. Helping the psychiatric

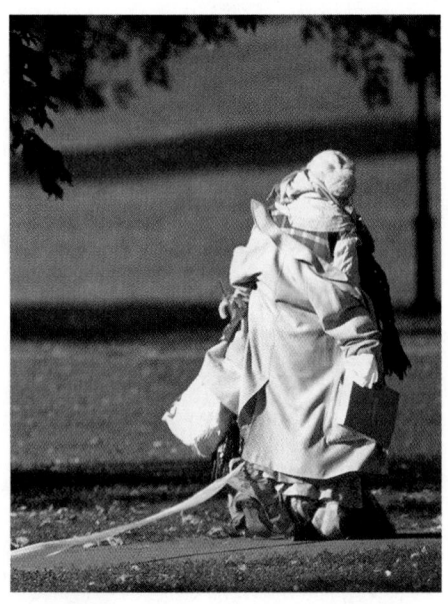

The problem of psychiatric homelessness. Many homeless people have severe psychological problems but fall through the cracks of the mental health and social service systems.

homeless escape from homelessness requires an integrated effort involving mental health and alcohol and drug abuse programs; access to decent, affordable housing; and provision of other social services (Rosenheck, Kasprow et al., 2003). It also requires effective means of evaluating the mental health needs of homeless people and matching services to their specific needs (Jacobs, Newman, & Burns, 2001; Tolomiczenko, Sota, & Goering, 2000).

Another difficulty in meeting the challenge of psychiatric homelessness is that homeless people with severe psychological problems typically do not seek out mental health services. More intensive outreach and intervention efforts that focus on helping homeless people connect with the services they need are likely to produce the best outcomes (Coldwell & Bender, 2007; Rosenheck, 2000). All in all, the problems of the psychiatric homeless population remain complex, vexing problems for the mental health system and society at large.

Deinstitutionalization: A Promise as Yet Unfulfilled Although the net results of deinstitutionalization may not yet have lived up to expectations, a number of successful community-oriented programs are available. However, they remain underfunded and unable to reach many people needing ongoing community support. If deinstitutionalization is to succeed, patients need continuing care and opportunities for decent housing, gainful employment, and training in social and vocational skills.

New, promising services exist to improve community-based care for people with chronic psychological disorders—for example, psychosocial rehabilitation centers, family psychoeducational groups, supportive housing and work programs, and social skills training. Unfortunately, too few of these services exist to meet the needs of many patients who might benefit from them. The community mental health movement continues to need expanded community support and adequate financial resources if it is to succeed in fulfilling its original promise.

SUMMING UP

Types of Helping Professionals

How do the three major groups of mental health professionals—clinical psychologists, psychiatrists, and psychiatric social workers—differ in their training backgrounds? Clinical psychologists complete graduate training in clinical psychology, typically at the doctoral level. Psychiatrists are medical doctors who specialize in psychiatry. Psychiatric social workers are trained in graduate schools of social work or social welfare, generally at the master's level.

Psychotherapy

What is psychotherapy? Psychotherapy involves a systematic interaction between a therapist and clients that incorporates psychological principles to help clients overcome abnormal behavior, solve problems in living, or develop as individuals.

What is psychodynamic therapy? Psychodynamic therapy originated with psychoanalysis, the approach to treatment developed by Freud. Psychoanalysts use techniques such as free association and dream analysis to help people gain insight into their unconscious conflicts and work through them in the light of their adult personalities. Contemporary psychodynamic therapy is typically briefer and more direct in its approach to exploring the patient's defenses and transference relationships.

What is behavior therapy? Behavior therapy applies the principles of learning to help people make adaptive behavioral changes. Behavior therapy techniques include systematic desensitization, gradual exposure, modeling, operant conditioning approaches, and social skills training. Cognitive-behavioral therapy integrates behavioral and cognitive approaches in treatment.

What is humanistic therapy? Humanistic therapy focuses on the client's subjective, conscious experience in the here and now. Rogers's person-centered therapy helps people increase their awareness and acceptance of inner feelings that had met with social condemnation and been disowned. The effective person-centered therapist possesses the qualities of unconditional positive regard, empathy, genuineness, and congruence.

What are two major approaches to cognitive therapy? Cognitive therapy focuses on modifying the maladaptive cognitions believed to underlie emotional problems and self-defeating behavior. Ellis's rational emotive behavior therapy focuses on disputing irrational beliefs that occasion emotional distress and substituting adaptive beliefs and behavior. Beck's cognitive therapy focuses on helping clients identify, challenge, and replace distorted cognitions, such as tendencies to magnify negative events and minimize personal accomplishments.

What is cognitive-behavioral therapy? Cognitive-behavioral therapy is a broader form of behavior therapy that integrates cognitive and behavioral techniques in treatment.

What are the two major forms of eclectic therapy? These are technical eclecticism, a pragmatic approach that draws on techniques from different schools of therapy without necessarily subscribing to the theoretical positions represented by these schools, and integrative eclecticism, an approach that attempts to synthesize and integrate diverse theoretical approaches in an integrative model of therapy.

What are the general aims of group therapy, family therapy, and couple therapy? Group therapy provides opportunities for mutual support and shared learning experiences within a group setting to help individuals overcome psychological difficulties and develop more adaptive behaviors. Family therapists work with conflicted families to help them resolve their differences. Family therapists focus on clarifying family communications, resolving role conflicts, guarding against scapegoating individual members, and helping members develop greater autonomy. Couple therapists focus on helping couples improve their communications and resolve their differences.

Does psychotherapy work? Evidence from meta-analyses of psychotherapy outcome studies that compare psychotherapy with control groups supports the value of various approaches to psychotherapy. The question of whether there are differences in the effectiveness of different types of psychotherapy remains under study.

Biomedical Therapies

What are the major biomedical approaches to treating psychological disorders, and how effective are they? The major biomedical therapies are drug therapy and electroconvulsive therapy (ECT). Antianxiety drugs, such as Valium, may relieve short-term anxiety but do not directly help people solve their problems or cope with stress. Antipsychotic drugs help control flagrant psychotic symptoms, but regular use of these drugs is associated with the risk of serious side effects. Antidepressants can help relieve depression, and lithium is helpful in many cases in stabilizing mood swings in people with bipolar disorder. ECT often leads to dramatic relief from severe depression. Psychosurgery has all but disappeared as a form of treatment because of adverse consequences.

Hospitalization and Community-Based Care

What roles do mental hospitals and community mental health centers play in the mental health system? Mental hospitals provide structured treatment environments for people in acute crisis and for those who are unable to adapt to community living. Community mental health centers seek to prevent the need for psychiatric hospitalization by providing intervention services and alternatives to full hospitalization.

What factors account for underutilization of mental health services by racial or ethnic minorities in the United States? These include cultural factors regarding preferences for other forms of help, cultural mistrust of the mental health system, cultural barriers, linguistic barriers, and economic and accessibility barriers.

How successful is the policy of deinstitutionalization? Deinstitutionalization has greatly reduced the population of state mental hospitals, but it has not yet fulfilled its promise of providing the quality of care needed to restore discharged patients to a reasonable quality of life in the community. One example of the challenges yet to be met are the many homeless people with severe psychological problems who are not receiving adequate care in the community.

KEY TERMS

psychotherapy (p. 104)
nonspecific treatment factors (p. 107)
psychoanalysis (p. 107)
psychodynamic therapy (p. 107)
free association (p. 107)
transference relationship (p. 108)
countertransference (p. 108)
behavior therapy (p. 110)
systematic desensitization (p. 110)
gradual exposure (p. 110)
modeling (p. 111)
token economy (p. 111)
person-centered therapy (p. 111)

unconditional positive regard (p. 112)
empathy (p. 112)
genuineness (p. 112)
congruence (p. 112)
cognitive therapy (p. 113)
rational emotive behavior therapy (REBT) (p. 113)
cognitive-behavioral therapy (CBT) (p. 116)
eclectic therapy (p. 117)
group therapy (p. 118)
family therapy (p. 118)
couple therapy (p. 118)

managed care systems (p. 122)
psychopharmacology (p. 126)
antianxiety drugs (p. 126)
tolerance (p. 126)
rebound anxiety (p. 127)
antipsychotic drugs (p. 127)
antidepressants (p. 127)
electroconvulsive therapy (ECT) (p. 128)
deinstitutionalization (p. 131)
primary prevention (p. 132)
secondary prevention (p. 132)

MEDIA TOOLS

A variety of digital and online learning tools are available to enrich your learning experience and help you succeed in the course. These resources include:

• **MyPsychLab,** an online learning system for your course in abnormal psychology that allows you to test your mastery of concepts in the book by using chapter-by-chapter diagnostic tests. Results from the diagnostic tests help you build a customized study plan. To access **MyPsychLab,** visit www.prenhall.com/mypsychlab and follow the instructions on the site.

• **"Speaking Out" Patient Interviews,** a set of video case examples of actual patients you can access on the companion CD-ROM included with the text. Icons in the margins of the chapter highlight the video case examples included on the CD-ROM.

• **Companion Web site,** an online study center that offers computer-scored quizzes you can use to test your knowledge, along with other study tools and links to related sites to enhance your learning of abnormal psychology. To access the companion Web site, visit www.prenhall.com/nevid and use the various tabs and links on the site to access these learning resources.

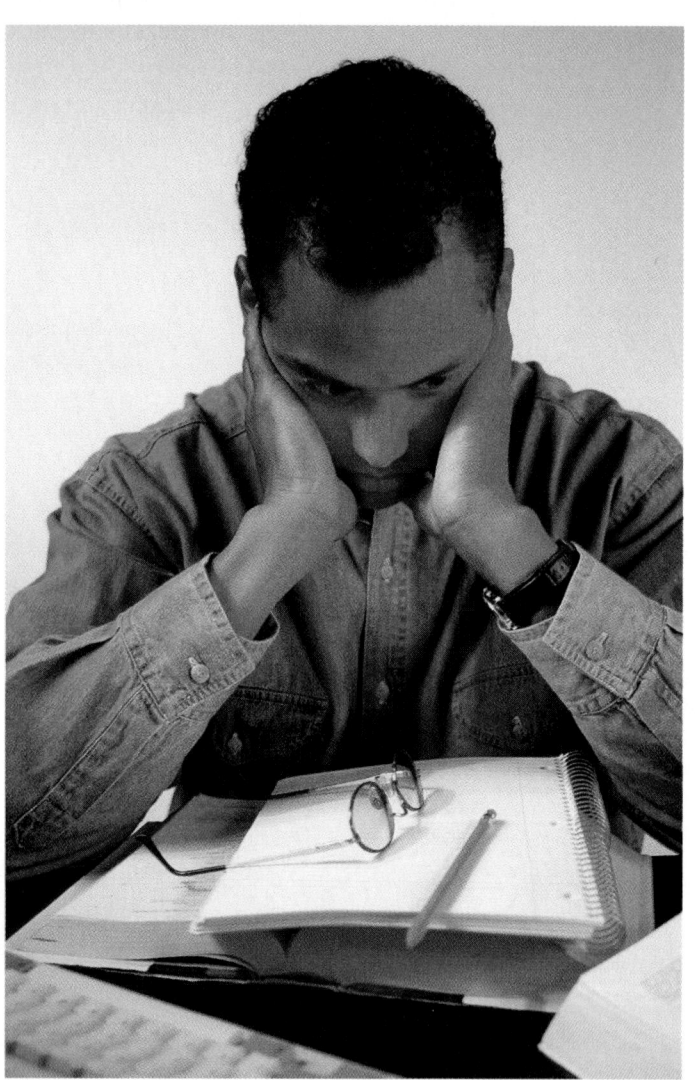

CHAPTER 5

Stress, Psychological Factors, and Health

CHAPTER OUTLINE

ADJUSTMENT DISORDERS 142–143

STRESS AND ILLNESS 144–156

Stress and the Endocrine System
Stress and the Immune System
Terrorism-Related Trauma
The General Adaptation Syndrome
Stress and Life Changes

Acculturative Stress: Making It in America
Psychological Factors That Moderate Stress

PSYCHOLOGICAL FACTORS AND PHYSICAL DISORDERS 156–167

Headaches
Cardiovascular Disease

Asthma
Cancer
Acquired Immunodeficiency Syndrome (AIDS)

SUMMING UP 168

"Is there a problem?" I (J.S.N.) asked as I entered my classroom at St. John's University in Queens, New York, on the morning of September 11, 2001. The students were gathered around the window. None replied, but one pointed out the window with a pained expression on her face that I'll never forget. Moments later, I saw for myself the smoke billowing out of one of the towers of the World Trade Center, clearly visible some 15 miles to the west. Then the second tower suddenly burst into flames. We watched in stunned silence. Then the unthinkable occurred. Suddenly one tower was gone and then the other. A student who had come into the room asked, "Where are they?" Another answered that they were gone. The first replied, "What do you mean, gone?"

We watched from a distance the horror that we knew was unfolding. But many other New Yorkers experienced the World Trade Center disaster firsthand, including thousands like New York City police officer Terri Tobin, who risked their lives to save others. Here, Officer Tobin tells of her experience:

"I"

"Go! Go! It's Coming Down!"

Then I saw people running toward me, and they were screaming. "Go! Go! It's coming down!" Just for a second, I looked up and saw it. I thought, *I'm not going to outrun this.* But then I thought, *Maybe I can make it back to my car and jump in the back seat.* Before I could make a move, the force of the explosion literally blew me out of my shoes. It lifted me up and propelled me out, over a concrete barrier, all the way to the other side of the street. I landed face-first on a grassy area outside the Financial Center, and after I landed there, I just got pelted with debris coming out of this big black cloud.

And then I felt it, but what sticks with me is hearing it: The whomp of my helmet when I got hit in the head. The helmet literally went crack, split in half, and fell off my head. I realized then that I'd just taken a real big whack in the head. I felt blood going down the back of my neck, and when I was able to reach around, I felt this chunk of cement sticking out three or four inches from the back of my head. It was completely embedded in my skull.

Then it got pitch black, and I thought, *I must have been knocked unconscious, because it's totally black.* But then I thought, *I wouldn't be thinking about how black it is if I'm unconscious.* And it was really hard to breathe. All I heard were people screaming. Screaming bloody murder. All sorts of cries. At that moment, I thought, *This is it. We're all going to die on the street.*

—*From Hagen & Carouba, 2002,* Women at Ground Zero: Stories of Courage and Compassion

TRUTH or FICTION

T☐ F☐ If concentrating on your schoolwork has become difficult because of the breakup of a recent romance, you could be experiencing a psychological disorder. (p. 143)

T☐ F☐ Your body continually conducts search-and-destroy missions to find and eradicate foreign invaders. (p. 145)

T☐ F☐ Surprisingly, stress makes you more resistant to the common cold. (p. 146)

T☐ F☐ Writing about traumatic experiences may be good for your physical and emotional health. (p. 146)

T☐ F☐ Immigrants show better psychological adjustment when they forsake their cultural heritage and adopt the values of the host culture. (p. 152)

T☐ F☐ Pregnant women with more optimistic attitudes tend to have higher birth-weight babies. (p. 155)

T☐ F☐ People can relieve the pain of migraine headaches by raising the temperature in a finger. (p. 160)

T☐ F☐ Compelling evidence now exists that psychotherapy can increase survival rates in cancer patients. (p. 165)

EXPOSURE TO STRESS, ESPECIALLY TRAUMATIC STRESS LIKE THAT EXPERIENCED BY MANY thousands of people on 9/11, can have profound and enduring effects on our mental and physical health. This chapter focuses on the psychological and physical effects of stress. In the next chapter, we discuss the types of psychological disorders that can arise from exposure to traumatic stress.

The effects of psychological forms of stress bring into context the age-old debate about the relationship between the mind and the body. The 17th-century French philosopher René Descartes (1596–1650) influenced modern thinking with his belief in *dualism*, or separateness, between the mind and body. Today, scientists recognize that mind and body are much more closely intertwined than Descartes would have imagined. Psychological factors both influence and are influenced by physical functioning (Jones, 2006; Ryffa et al., 2006). Psychologists who study the interrelationships between psychological factors and physical health are called **health psychologists.**

The study of the relationships between mind and body bring us to examining the role of stress in both mental and physical functioning. The term *stress* refers to pressure or

health psychologist A psychologist who studies the role of psychological factors in physical illness.

stress A demand made on an organism to adapt or adjust.

stressor A source of stress.

force placed on a body. In the physical world, tons of rocks that crash to the ground in a landslide cause stress on impact, forming indentations or craters when they land. In psychology, we use the term **stress** to refer to a pressure or demand that is placed on an organism to adapt or adjust. A **stressor** is a source of stress. Stressors (or stresses) include psychological factors, such as examinations in school and problems in social relationships, and life changes, such as the death of a loved one, divorce, or a job termination. They also include daily hassles, such as traffic jams, and physical environmental factors, such as exposure to extreme temperatures or noise levels. The term *stress* should be distinguished from *distress*, which refers to a state of physical or mental pain or suffering. Some amount of stress is probably healthy for us; it helps keep us active and alert. But stress that is prolonged or intense can overtax our coping ability and lead to states of emotional distress, such as anxiety or depression, and to physical complaints, such as fatigue and headaches. A recent survey by the American Psychological Association showed that 43% of adult Americans report suffering adverse health effects from stress (American Psychological Association, 2006).

Stress is implicated in a wide range of physical and psychological problems. We begin our study of the effects of stress by discussing a category of psychological disorders called *adjustment disorders,* which involve maladaptive reactions to stress. We then consider the role of stress and other psychological and sociocultural factors in physical disorders.

ADJUSTMENT DISORDERS

adjustment disorder A maladaptive reaction to an identified stressor, characterized by impaired functioning or emotional distress that exceeds what would normally be expected.

Adjustment disorders are the first psychological disorders we discuss in this book, and they are among the mildest. An **adjustment disorder** is a maladaptive reaction to an identified stressor that develops within a few months of the onset of the stressor. According to the *DSM,* the maladaptive reaction is characterized by significant impairment in social, occupational, or academic functioning or by states of emotional distress that exceed those normally induced by the stressor. Prevalence estimates of the rates of the disorder in the population vary widely. However, the disorder is common among people seeking outpatient mental health care, with estimates indicating that between 5% and 20% of people receiving outpatient mental health services present with a diagnosis of adjustment disorder (APA, 2000).

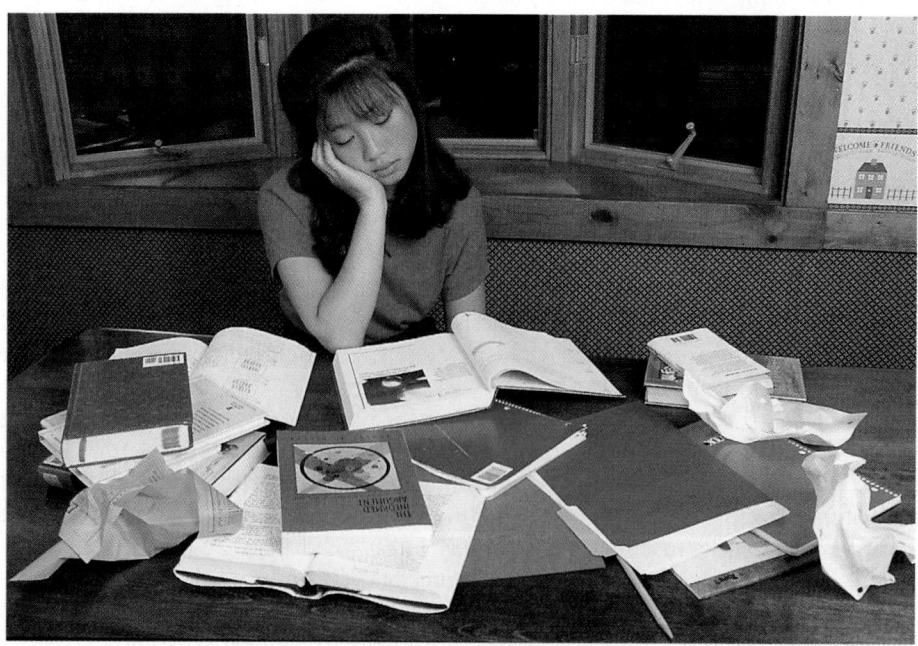

Difficulty in concentrating or adjustment disorder? An adjustment disorder is a maladaptive reaction to a stressor that may take the form of impaired functioning at school or at work, such as having difficulties keeping one's mind on one's studies.

TABLE 5.1

Subtypes of Adjustment Disorders

Disorder	Chief Features
Adjustment Disorder with Depressed Mood Adjustment Disorder with Anxiety	Sadness, crying, and feelings of hopelessness Worrying, nervousness, and jitters (or in children, separation fears from primary attachment figures)
Adjustment Disorder with Mixed Anxiety and Depressed Mood	A combination of anxiety and depression
Adjustment Disorder with Disturbance of Conduct	Violation of the rights of others or violation of social norms appropriate for one's age. Sample behaviors include vandalism, truancy, fighting, reckless driving, and defaulting on legal obligations (e.g., stopping alimony payments)
Adjustment Disorder with Mixed Disturbance	Both emotional disturbance, such as depression or anxiety, and conduct disturbance (as described above)
Adjustment Disorder Unspecified	A residual category that applies to cases not classifiable in one of the other subtypes

Source: Adapted from the *DSM-IV-TR* (APA, 2000).

If your relationship with someone comes to an end (an identified stressor) and your grades are falling off because you are unable to keep your mind on schoolwork, you may fit the bill for an adjustment disorder. If Uncle Harry has been feeling down and pessimistic since his divorce from Aunt Jane, he too may be diagnosed with an adjustment disorder. So too might Cousin Billy if he has been cutting classes and spraying obscene words on the school walls or showing other signs of disturbed conduct. There are several subtypes of adjustment disorders that vary in terms of the type of maladaptive reaction (see Table 5.1).

The concept of "adjustment disorder" as a *mental disorder* highlights some of the difficulties in attempting to define what is normal and what is not. When something important goes wrong in life, we should feel bad about it. If there is a crisis in business, if we are victimized by a crime, or if there is a flood or a devastating hurricane, it is understandable that we might become anxious or depressed. There might, in fact, be something more seriously wrong with us if we did not react in a "maladaptive" way, at least temporarily. However, if our emotional reaction exceeds an expected response, or our ability to function is impaired (e.g., avoidance of social interactions, difficulty getting out of bed, or falling behind in schoolwork), then a diagnosis of adjustment disorder may be indicated. Thus, if you are having trouble concentrating on your schoolwork following the breakup of a romantic relationship and your grades are slipping, you may have an adjustment disorder.

For the diagnosis to apply, the stress-related reaction must not be sufficient to meet the diagnostic criteria for other clinical syndromes, such as anxiety disorders or mood disorders (see Chapters 6 and 8). The maladaptive reaction may be resolved if the stressor is removed or the individual learns to cope with it. If the maladaptive reaction lasts for more than 6 months after the stressor (or its consequences) have been removed, the diagnosis may be changed. Although the *DSM* system distinguishes adjustment disorder from other clinical syndromes, it may be difficult to identify distinguishing features of adjustment disorders that are distinct from other disorders, such as depression (Casey et al., 2006).

TRUTH or FICTION

If concentrating on your schoolwork has become difficult because of the breakup of a recent romance, you could be experiencing a psychological disorder.

☑ **TRUE.** If you have trouble concentrating on your schoolwork following the breakup of a romantic relationship, you may have a mild type of psychological disorder called an adjustment disorder.

STRESS AND ILLNESS

Psychological sources of stress not only diminish our capacity for adjustment, but also may adversely affect our health. Many visits to physicians, perhaps even most, can be traced to stress-related illness. Stress is associated with an increased risk of various types of physical illness, ranging from digestive disorders to heart disease.

The field of *psychoneuroimmunology* studies relationships between psychological factors, especially stress, and the workings of the endocrine system, the immune system, and the nervous system (Kiecolt-Glaser et al., 2002). Here we examine what we've learned about these relationships.

Stress and the Endocrine System

endocrine system The system of ductless glands that secrete hormones directly into the bloodstream.

hormones Substances secreted by endocrine glands that regulate body functions and promote growth and development.

Stress has a domino effect on the **endocrine system,** the body's system of glands that release their secretions, called **hormones,** directly into the bloodstream. (Other glands, such as the salivary glands that produce saliva, release their secretions into a system of ducts.) The endocrine system consists of glands distributed throughout the body. Figure 5.1 shows the major endocrine glands in the body.

Several endocrine glands are involved in the body's response to stress. First, the hypothalamus, a small structure in the brain, releases a hormone that stimulates the nearby pituitary gland to secrete *adrenocorticotrophic hormone* (ACTH). ACTH, in turn, stimulates the adrenal glands, which are located above the kidneys. Under the influence of ACTH, the outer layer of the adrenal glands, called the *adrenal cortex,* releases a group of hormones called *cortical steroids* (cortisol and cortisone are examples). Cortical steroids (also called *corticosteroids*) have a number of functions in the body. They boost resistance to stress, foster muscle development, and induce the liver to

FIGURE 5.1 Major glands of the endocrine system.
The glands of the endocrine pour their secretions—called hormones—directly into the bloodstream. Although hormones may travel throughout the body, they act only on specific receptor sites. Many hormones are implicated in stress reactions and various patterns of abnormal behavior.

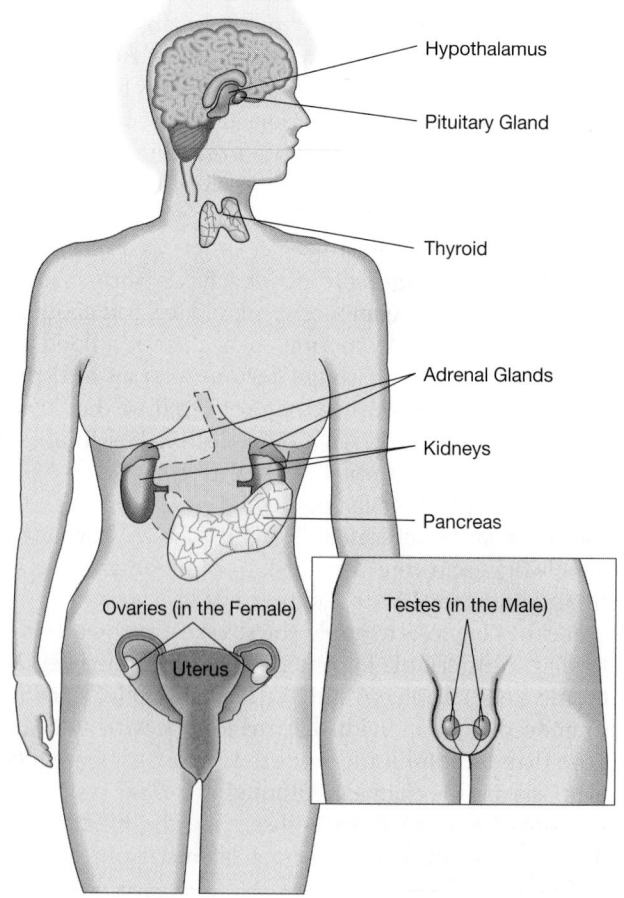

release sugar, which provides needed bursts of energy for responding to a threatening stressor (for example, a lurking predator or assailant) or an emergency situation. They also help the body defend against allergic reactions and inflammation.

The sympathetic branch of the autonomic nervous system, or ANS, stimulates the inner layer of the adrenal glands, called the *adrenal medulla,* to release a mixture of epinephrine (adrenaline) and norepinephrine (noradrenaline). These chemicals function as hormones when released into the bloodstream. Norepinephrine is also produced in the nervous system, where it functions as a neurotransmitter. Together epinephrine and norepinephrine mobilize the body to deal with a threatening stressor by accelerating the heart rate and by also stimulating the liver to release stored glucose (sugar), making energy available where it can be of use in protecting ourselves in a threatening situation.

The stress hormones produced by the adrenal glands help the body prepare to cope with an impending threat or stressor. Once the stressor has passed, the body returns to a normal state. This is perfectly normal and adaptive. However, when stress is enduring or recurring, the body regularly pumps out stress hormones and mobilizes other systems, which over time can tax the body's resources and impair health (Gabb et al., 2006; Kemeny, 2003). Chronic or repetitive stress can damage many bodily systems, including the cardiovascular system (heart and arteries) and the immune system.

Stress and the Immune System

Given the intricacies of the human body and the rapid advance of scientific knowledge, we might consider ourselves dependent on highly trained medical specialists to contend with illness. Actually our bodies cope with most diseases on their own, through the functioning of the immune system.

The **immune system** is the body's system of defense against disease. It combats disease in a number of ways (Jiang & Chess, 2006). Your body is constantly engaged in search-and-destroy missions against invading microbes, even as you're reading this page. Millions of white blood cells, or *leukocytes,* are the immune system's foot soldiers in this microscopic warfare. Leukocytes systematically envelop and kill pathogens such as bacteria, viruses, and fungi, worn-out body cells, and cells that have become cancerous.

Leukocytes recognize invading pathogens by their surface fragments, called *antigens,* literally *anti*body *gene*rators. Some leukocytes produce *antibodies,* specialized proteins that lock into position on an antigen, marking them for destruction by specialized "killer" lymphocytes that act like commandos on a search-and-destroy mission (Greenwood, 2006; Kay, 2006).

Special "memory lymphocytes" (lymphocytes are a type of leukocyte) are held in reserve rather than marking foreign bodies for destruction or going to war against them. They can remain in the bloodstream for years and form the basis for a quick immune response to an invader the second time around.

Although occasional stress may not impair our health, chronic or repetitive stress can eventually weaken the body's immune system (Epstein, 2003; Kemeny, 2003). A weakened immune system increases our susceptibility to many illnesses, including the common cold and the flu, and may increase the risk of developing chronic diseases, including cancer.

Psychological stressors can dampen the response of the immune system, especially when the stress is intense or prolonged (Segerstrom & Miller, 2004). Even relatively brief periods of stress, such as final exam time, can weaken the immune system, although these effects are more limited than those associated with chronic or prolonged stress. The kinds of life stressors that can take a toll on the immune system and leave us more vulnerable to disease include marital conflict, divorce, and chronic unemployment (e.g., Kiecolt-Glaser et al., 2002). Traumatic stress,

immune system The body's system of defense against disease.

T R U T H or F I C T I O N

Your body continually conducts search-and-destroy missions to find and eradicate foreign invaders.

☑ **TRUE.** Your immune system is always on guard against invading microbes and continuously dispatches specialized white blood cells to identify and eliminate infectious organisms.

The war within. White blood cells, shown here (colored purple) attacking and engulfing a pathogen, form the major part of the body's system of defense against bacteria, viruses, and other invading organisms.

Stress and the common cold. Are you more likely to develop a cold during stressful times in your life? Investigators find that people under severe stress are more likely to become sick after exposure to cold viruses.

TRUTH or FICTION

Surprisingly, stress makes you more resistant to the common cold.

☑ **FALSE.** Stress increases the risk of developing a cold.

TRUTH or FICTION

Writing about traumatic experiences may be good for your physical and emotional health.

☑ **TRUE.** Talking or writing about your feelings can help enhance both psychological and physical well-being.

such as exposure to earthquakes, hurricanes, or other natural or technological disasters, or to terrorist attacks or other forms of violence, can also impair immunological functioning (Solomon et al., 1997).

Scientists recently discovered that one way chronic stress damages the body's immune system is by increasing levels of a chemical in the body called *interleukin-6* (Kiecolt-Glaser et al., 2003). Sustained high levels of this chemical are linked to inflammation, which in turn can contribute to the development of many disorders, including cardiovascular disease, cancer, and arthritis.

Social support appears to moderate the harmful effects of stress on the immune system. For example, investigators in two landmark studies found that medical and dental students with large numbers of friends showed better immune functioning than students with fewer friends (Jemmott et al., 1983; Kiecolt-Glaser et al., 1984). Consider too the results of a classic study reporting that lonely students showed greater suppression of immune responses than did students with more social support (Glaser et al., 1985).

Exposure to stress is also linked to greater risk of developing the common cold. In another landmark study in this field, people who reported high levels of daily stress, such as pressures at work, showed low blood levels of antibodies that fend off cold viruses (Stone et al., 1994). A later study by the same research group showed that more sociable people had greater resistance to developing the common cold than their less sociable peers after these groups voluntarily received injections of a cold virus (Cohen et al., 2003). These results point to a possible role of socialization or social support in buffering the effects of stress.

We should caution that much of the research in the field of psychoneuroimmunology is correlational. Researchers examine immunological functioning in relation to different indices of stress, but do not (nor would they!) directly manipulate stress to observe its effect on subjects' immune systems or general health. Correlational research helps us better understand relationships between variables and may point to possible underlying causal factors, but does not in itself demonstrate causal connections.

Investigators have learned that expressing emotions through writing about stressful or traumatic events has positive effects on both psychological and physical health and well-being (Frattaroli, 2006). Evidence shows that people assigned to an expressive writing program show fewer psychological and physical symptoms than do control participants (Low, Stanton, & Danoff-Burg, 2006; Sloan & Marx, 2005; Sloan et al., 2007; Smyth & Pennebaker, 2001). In addition, terminally ill cancer patients asked to write about their cancer had less sleep disturbance than did control patients who wrote about neutral topics (de Moor et al., 2003).

Why might expressive writing produce such beneficial effects? One possibility is that keeping thoughts and feelings about traumatic events tightly under wraps places a stressful burden on the autonomic nervous system, which in turn may weaken the immune system and thereby increase susceptibility to stress-related disorders. We should caution, however, that more research is needed before we can reach any definite conclusions about the effects of writing or other psychological interventions on the workings of the immune system (Miller & Cohen, 2001).

Terrorism-Related Trauma

The September 11, 2001 terrorist attacks on America changed everything. Before 9/11 we may have felt secure in our homes, offices, and other public places from the threat of terrorism. But now, terrorism looms as a constant threat to our safety and sense of security. Still, we endeavor to maintain a sense of normalcy in our lives. We travel and attend public gatherings, although the ever-present security regulations are a constant reminder of the heightened concern about terrorism. Many of us who were directly affected by 9/11 or lost friends or loved ones may still be trying to cope with the emotional consequences of that day. Many survivors, like survivors of other forms of trauma, such as floods and tornadoes, may experience prolonged, maladaptive stressful reactions, such as posttraumatic stress disorder (PTSD) (discussed in Chapter 6).

TABLE 5.2

Stress-Related Symptoms Reported by Americans in the Week Following the Terrorists Attacks of September 11, 2001

	Depression	Lack of Focus (difficulty concentrating)	Insomnia
Men	62	44	26
Women	79	53	40
Genders combined	71	49	33

Source: Pew Research Center. (2002, September 20). *American psyche reeling from terror attacks.* www.people-press.org/terroist01rpt.htm.

Evidence from a recent community-based study in Michigan shows that the number of suicide attempts jumped in the months following the 9/11 attacks (Starkman, 2006). But even those free of serious mental health problems may be emotionally affected in one way or another by the events of 9/11 (Galea et al., 2002).

Most Americans reported feeling depressed in the immediate aftermath of 9/11, and a substantial proportion reported difficulty concentrating or suffered from insomnia (see Table 5.2). Not surprisingly, factors such as direct exposure to the attacks in New York City and Washington, D.C., and time spent viewing TV coverage of the attacks were linked to higher levels of posttraumatic stress disorder (PTSD) symptoms (Schlenger et al., 2002). Although most people exposed to traumatic events do not develop PTSD, many do experience symptoms associated with the disorder, such as difficulties concentrating and high levels of arousal. In more than 60% of households in New York City, parents reported that their children were upset by the attacks. Since 9/11, many of us have become sensitized to the emotional consequences of traumatic stress. The accompanying *A Closer Look* feature focuses on the warning signs of trauma-related stress.

People vary in their reactions to traumatic stress. Investigators trying to pinpoint factors that account for resiliency in the face of stress suggest that positive emotions can play an important role. Evidence gathered since 9/11 shows that experiencing positive emotions such as feelings of gratitude and love, helped buffer the effects of stress (Fredrickson et al., 2003).

The General Adaptation Syndrome

Stress researcher Hans Selye (1976) coined the term **general adaptation syndrome (GAS)** to describe a common biological response pattern to prolonged or excessive stress. Selye pointed out that our bodies respond similarly to many kinds of unpleasant stressors, whether the source of stress is an invasion of microscopic disease organisms, a divorce, or the aftermath of a flood. The GAS model suggests that our bodies, under stress, are like clocks with alarm systems that do not shut off until their energy is perilously depleted.

general adaptation syndrome (GAS) The body's three-stage response to states of prolonged or intense stress.

The GAS consists of three stages: the alarm reaction, the resistance stage, and the exhaustion stage. Perception of an immediate stressor (for example, a car that swerves in front of your own on the highway) triggers the **alarm reaction.** The alarm reaction mobilizes the body to prepare for challenge or stress. We can think of it as the body's first line of defense against a threatening stressor. The body reacts with a complex, integrated response involving both the central nervous system and endocrine system (Ellis, Jackson, & Boyce, 2006).

alarm reaction The first stage of the GAS, characterized by heightened sympathetic activity.

In 1929, Harvard University physiologist Walter Cannon termed this response pattern the **fight-or-flight reaction.** We noted earlier how the endocrine system responds to stress. During the alarm reaction, the adrenal glands, under control by the pituitary

fight-or-flight reaction The inborn tendency to respond to a threat by either fighting or fleeing.

IN THE BLEACHERS ©2006 Steve Moore. Reprinted with permission of UNIVERSAL PRESS SYNDICATE. All rights reserved.

TABLE 5.3
Stress-Related Changes in the Body Associated with the Alarm Reaction
Corticosteroids are released.
Epinephrine and norepinephrine are released.
Heart rate, respiration rate, and blood pressure increase.
Muscles tense.
Blood shifts from the internal organs to the skeletal muscles.
Digestion is inhibited.
Sugar is released by the liver.
Blood-clotting ability is increased.
Stress triggers the alarm reaction. The reaction is defined by secretion of corticosteroids, catecholamines, and activity of the sympathetic branch of the ANS. The reaction is defined by secretion of stress hormones and increased activity of the sympathetic branch of the ANS.

gland in the brain, pump out cortical steroids and stress hormones that help mobilize the body's defenses (see Table 5.3).

The fight-or-flight reaction most probably helped our early ancestors cope with the many perils they faced. The reaction may have been provoked by the sight of a predator or by a rustling sound in the undergrowth. But our ancestors usually did not experience prolonged activation of the alarm reaction. Once a threat was eliminated, the body reinstated a lower level of arousal. Our ancestors fought off predators or fled quickly; then their bodies returned to the normal, nonaroused state. Sensitive alarm reactions increased their chances of survival. Yet our ancestors did not remain for long in a state of heightened arousal after the immediate danger was past. In contrast, people today are continually bombarded with stressors—everything from battling traffic in the morning to balancing school and work, or rushing from job to job. Consequently, our alarm system is turned on much of the time, which may eventually increase the likelihood of developing stress-related disorders.

When a stressor is persistent, we progress to the **resistance stage,** or adaptation stage, of the GAS. Endocrine and sympathetic system responses (release of stress hormones,

resistance stage The second stage of the GAS, involving the body's attempt to withstand prolonged stress and preserve resources.

A CLOSER LOOK

Warning Signs of Trauma-Related Stress

People normally experience psychological distress in the face of trauma. If anything it would be abnormal to remain blasé at a time of crisis or disaster. But stress reactions that linger beyond a month and affect an individual's ability to function in everyday life can be a cause for concern. The American Psychological Association lists the following symptoms as warning signs of traumatic stress reactions.

• Recurring thoughts or nightmares about the event
• Having trouble sleeping or changes in appetite
• Experiencing anxiety and fear, especially when exposed to events or situations reminiscent of the trauma
• Being on edge, being easily startled, or becoming overly alert
• Feeling depressed, sad, and having low energy
• Experiencing memory problems including difficulty in remembering aspects of the trauma
• Feeling "scattered" and unable to focus on work or daily activities
• Having difficulty making decisions
• Feeling irritable, easily agitated, or angry and resentful

• Feeling emotionally "numb," withdrawn, disconnected or different from others
• Spontaneously crying, feeling a sense of despair and hopelessness
• Feeling extremely protective of, or fearful for, the safety of loved ones
• Not being able to face certain aspects of the trauma, and avoiding activities, places, or even people that remind you of the event

If you or a loved one has experienced these symptoms for more than a month, it would be worthwhile to seek professional mental health assistance. Assistance is available through your college health services (for registered students) or through networks of trained professionals. For more information or a referral, you may contact your local American Red Cross chapter or the American Psychological Association at 202-336-5800. Also see A Closer Look in Chapter 4 for guidelines to follow in choosing a mental health professional.

Reprinted from Nevid & Rathus, 2005, with permission of Wiley & Sons, Inc. Source: American Psychological Association. Warning Signs of Trauma-Related Stress. Web posting, http://www.apa.org/practice/ptsd.html. Copyright 2002 by American Psychological Association. Reprinted by permission.

for example) remain at high levels, but not quite as high as during the alarm reaction. During this stage the body tries to renew spent energy and repair damage. But when stressors continue or new ones enter the picture, we may progress to the final stage of the GAS, which is called the **exhaustion stage.** Although there are individual differences in capacity to resist stress, all of us will eventually exhaust our bodily resources. The exhaustion stage is characterized by dominance of the parasympathetic branch of the ANS. Consequently, our heart and respiration rates decelerate. Do we benefit from the respite? Not necessarily. If the source of stress persists, we may develop what Selye termed "diseases of adaptation." These range from allergic reactions to heart disease—and, at times, even death. The lesson is clear: Chronic stress can damage our health, leaving us more vulnerable to a range of diseases and other physical health problems.

Cortical steroids are perhaps one reason that persistent stress may eventually lead to health problems. Although cortical steroids help the body cope with stress, they also suppress the activity of the immune system. Cortical steroids have negligible effects when they are only released periodically. Continuous secretion, however, weakens the immune system by disrupting the production of antibodies, which can over time increase vulnerability to colds and other infections.

Although Selye's model speaks to the general response pattern of the body under stress, different biological processes may respond to particular kinds of stressors. For example, persistent exposure to excessive noise may invoke different bodily processes than other sources of stress, such as overcrowding, or psychological sources of stress, such as divorce or separation.

exhaustion stage The third stage of the GAS, characterized by lowered resistance, increased parasympathetic activity, and eventual physical deterioration.

Stress and Life Changes

Researchers have investigated the stress–illness connection by quantifying life stress in terms of life changes (also called *life events*). Life changes are sources of stress because they force us to adjust. They include both positive events, such as getting married, and negative events, such as the death of a loved one. You can gain insight into the level of stressful life changes you may have experienced during the past year by completing the College Life Stress Inventory on page 150.

Evidence shows that people who experience greater numbers of life changes are more likely to suffer from psychological and physical health problems (Dohrenwend, 2006). Again, we need to be cautious when interpreting these findings. The reported links are correlational and not experimental. In other words, researchers did not (and would not!) assign subjects to conditions in which they were exposed to either a high or low level of life changes to see what effects these conditions might have on their health over time. Rather, existing data are based on observations of relationships, say, between life changes on the one hand and physical health problems on the other. Such relationships are open to other interpretations. It could be that physical symptoms are sources of stress in themselves and lead to more life changes. Physical illness may cause disruptions of sleep or financial burdens, and so forth. Hence, in some cases at least, the causal direction may be reversed: Health problems may lead to life changes. We can't yet tease out the possible cause-and-effect relationships.

Although both positive and negative life changes can be

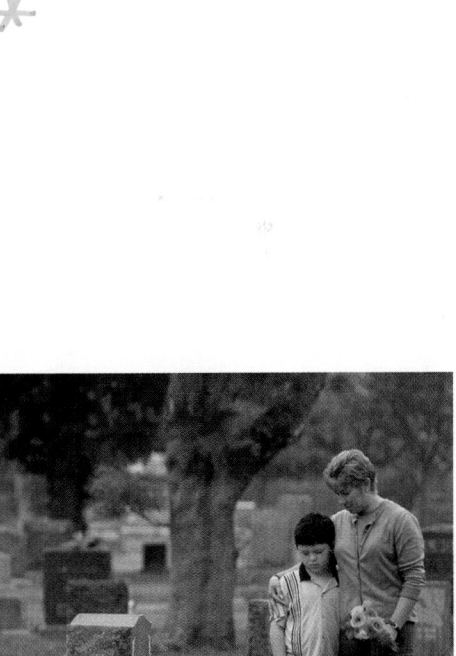

For better or for worse. Life changes such as marriage and the death of loved ones are sources of stress that require adjustment. The death of a spouse may be one of the most stressful life changes that people ever face.

QUESTIONNAIRE
Going Through Changes

How stressful has your life been lately? The College Life Stress Inventory contains a listing of stressful events that college students may face. Circle each of the events that you have experienced in the past year. Then compute your total, and look at the guide at the end of the chapter to interpret your score.

905 total

EVENT	STRESS RATING	EVENT	STRESS RATING
Being raped	100	Drunk driving	82
Finding out that you are HIV-positive	100	Sense of overload in school or work	(82)
Depression or crisis in your best friend	73	Two exams in one day	(80)
Difficulties with parents	(73)	Cheating on your boyfriend or girlfriend	77
Talking in front of a class	(72)	Getting married	76
Lack of sleep	(69)	Negative consequences of drinking or drug use	75
Change in housing situation (hassles, moves)	(69)	Declaring a major or concerns about future plans	65
Competing or performing in public	69	A class you hate	(62)
Getting in a physical fight	66	Drinking or use of drugs	61
Difficulties with a roommate	66	Confrontations with professors	60
Job changes (applying, new job, work hassles)	(65)	Starting a new semester	58
Being accused of rape	98	Going on a first date	57
Death of a close friend	97	Registering for classes	(55)
Death of a close family member	96	Maintaining a steady dating relationship	(55)
Contracting a sexually transmitted disease (other than AIDS)	94	Commuting to campus or work, or both	54
Concerns about being pregnant	91	Peer pressures	53
Finals week	(90)	Being away from home for the first time	53
Concerns about your partner being pregnant	90	Getting sick	52
Oversleeping for an exam	89	Concerns about your appearance	52
Flunking a class	89	Getting straight As	51
Having a boyfriend or girlfriend cheat on you	85	A difficult class that you love	48
Ending a steady dating relationship	85	Making new friends; getting along with friends	(47)
Serious illness in a close friend or family member	85	Fraternity or sorority rush	47
Financial difficulties	(84)	Falling asleep in class	40
Writing a major term paper	83	Attending an athletic event (e.g., football game)	20
Being caught cheating on a test	83		

522

Source: Renner, M. J., & Mackin, R. S. (1998). "A life stress instrument for classroom use." *Teaching of Psychology, 25,* 46–48. Reprinted with permission.

381

stressful, it is reasonable to assume that positive life changes are generally less disruptive than negative life changes. In other words, marriage tends to be less stressful than divorce or separation. Or to put it another way, a change for the better may be a change, but it is less of a hassle.

Acculturative Stress: Making It in America

Should Hindu women who immigrate to the United States give up the sari in favor of California casuals? Should Russian immigrants continue to teach their children Russian in the home? Should African American children be acquainted with the music and art of African peoples? Should women from traditional Islamic societies remove the veil and enter the competitive workplace? How do the stresses of acculturation affect the psychological well-being of immigrants and their families?

Sociocultural theorists have alerted us to the importance of accounting for social stressors in explaining abnormal behavior. One of the primary sources of stress imposed on immigrant groups, or on native groups living in the larger mainstream culture, is the need to adapt to a new culture. We can define *acculturation* as the process of adaptation by which immigrants, native groups, and ethnic minority groups adjust to the new culture or majority culture through making behavioral and attitudinal changes. **Acculturative stress** is pressure that results from the demands placed on immigrant, native, and ethnic minority groups to adjust to life in the mainstream culture.

acculturative stress Pressure to adjust to a host or mainstream culture.

Consider the challenges faced by Hispanic Americans. There are two general theories of the relationships between acculturation and adjustment. One theory, dubbed the *melting pot theory,* holds that acculturation helps people adjust to living in the host culture. From this perspective, Hispanic Americans might adjust better by replacing Spanish with English and adopting the values and customs associated with mainstream American culture. A competing theory, the *bicultural theory,* holds that psychosocial adjustment is fostered by identification with both traditional and host cultures. That is, the ability to adapt to the ways of the new society, combined with a supportive cultural tradition and a sense of ethnic identity, may predict good adjustment. From a bicultural perspective, immigrants maintain their ethnic identity and traditional values while learning to adapt to the language and customs of the host culture.

If we are to investigate acculturation and its relationship to mental health we first must be able to measure it. Measures of acculturation vary. In assessing acculturation among Hispanic Americans, for example, researchers assess variables such as the degree to which people favor English or Spanish in social situations, when reading, or while watching TV; preferences for types of food and styles of clothing; and self-perceptions of ethnic identity.

We've learned that relationships between acculturation and psychological adjustment are complex. Some research links higher acculturation status to a greater likelihood of developing psychological problems, whereas other research shows the opposite to be the case. First, let us note some findings from research with Hispanic (Latino) Americans that highlight psychological risks associated with acculturation.

- *Increased risk of heavy drinking among women.* Evidence shows that highly acculturated Hispanic American women are more likely than relatively unacculturated Hispanic American women to become heavy drinkers (Caetano, 1987). In Latin American cultures, men tend to drink much more alcohol than women, largely because gender-based cultural prohibitions against drinking constrain alcohol use among women. These constraints appear to have loosened among Hispanic American women who adopt "mainstream" U.S. attitudes and values.

- *Increased risk of delinquency, smoking, and sexual intercourse among adolescents.* Third-generation Mexican American male adolescents—who are more likely to be acculturated than first- or second-generation Mexican Americans—were at higher risk of delinquency (Buriel, Calzada, & Vasquez, 1982). Higher levels of acculturation are also linked to increased risks of smoking (Ribisl et al., 2000; Unger, Cruz, & Rohrbach, 2000) and participation in sexual intercourse among Latino teens (Adam et al., 2005).

- *Increased risk of disturbed eating behaviors.* Highly acculturated Hispanic American high school girls were more likely than their less-acculturated counterparts to show test scores associated with anorexia (an eating disorder characterized by excessive weight loss and fears of becoming fat—see Chapter 10) on an eating attitudes questionnaire (Pumariega, 1986). Acculturation apparently made these girls more vulnerable to the demands of striving toward the contemporary American ideal of the (very!) slender woman.

From this evidence, we might gather that acculturation has a negative influence on psychological adjustment. Acculturation may contribute to an erosion of traditional family networks and values, which in turn may increase susceptibility to psychological disorders in the face of stress (Ortega et al., 2000). On the other hand, we also have evidence of psychological benefits of a pattern of bicultural identification in which the individual makes efforts to adjust to the host culture while also maintaining an identity with the traditional culture. Consider a study of Mexican American elders (Zamanian et al., 1992). Those who were minimally acculturated showed higher levels of depression than did those who were either acculturated or bicultural. The bicultural and highly acculturated groups were similar in levels of depression, whereas those who were minimally acculturated had a greater risk of depression. However, people with a bicultural identity in which they maintained identification with their original culture, while also adapting to the new one, experienced no greater vulnerability to depression.

Why would low acculturation status be linked to increased risk of depression? The answer may be that low acculturation status is often a marker for low socioeconomic

Maintaining ethnic identity. Some studies point to psychological benefits in immigrant groups that adapt to the host culture while maintaining ethnic identity.

status (SES). People who are minimally acculturated often face economic hardship and occupy the lower strata of socioeconomic status. Social stress resulting from financial difficulties, lack of proficiency in the host language, and limited economic opportunities add to the stress of adapting to the host culture, all of which may contribute to increased risk of depression and other psychological problems (Ryder, Alden, & Paulhus, 2000; Yeh, 2003). Not surprisingly, evidence shows that Mexican Americans who were more proficient in English generally had fewer signs of depression and anxiety than did their less English-proficient counterparts (Salgado de Snyder, 1987; Warheit et al., 1985). Yet socioeconomic status and language proficiency are not the only, nor necessarily the most important, determinants of mental health among immigrant groups. Consider the findings from a northern California sample that showed better mental health profiles among Mexican immigrants than among people of Mexican descent born in the United States, despite the greater socioeconomic disadvantages faced by the immigrant group (Vega et al., 1998). It appears that "Americanization" may have damaging effects on mental health of Mexican Americans and that retention of cultural traditions may have a protective or "buffer" effect (Escobar, 1998).

In sum, the erosion of traditional family networks and traditional values that may accompany acculturation among immigrant groups might increase the risk of psychological problems (Ortega et al., 2000). Studies with other ethnic groups also point to the benefits of adapting to the host culture while maintaining ties to the traditional culture. Among Asian Americans, for example, investigators find that establishing contacts with the majority culture while maintaining traditional ethnic identity appears to generate less stress than withdrawal and separation from the host culture (Huang, 1994). Maintaining one's ethnic identity also seems to hold a psychological benefit. Studies with Asian American adolescents show that those who with a strong ethnic identity are better adjusted psychologically and have higher self esteem than others who are less strongly identified with their traditional culture (Huang, 1994; Phinney & Alipuria, 1990). Let us also note that a recent study of Asian immigrant adolescents in the United States showed that feelings of being alienated from both cultures or feeling caught between the two—the United States and the traditional culture—can lead to mental health problems (Yeh, 2003).

Moreover, some outcomes need careful interpretation. For example, does the finding that highly acculturated Hispanic American women are more likely to drink heavily argue in favor of placing greater social constraints on women? Perhaps a loosening of restraints is a double-edged sword, and all people—male and female, Hispanic and non-Hispanic—encounter adjustment problems when they gain new freedoms.

Finally, we need to consider gender differences in acculturation. In one study, female immigrants showed higher levels of depression than male immigrants (Salgado de Snyder, Cervantes, & Padilla, 1990). Their higher levels of depression may be linked to the greater level of stress women typically encounter in adjusting to changes in family patterns and personal issues, such as the greater freedom of gender roles for men and women in U.S. society. Because they were reared in cultures in which men are expected to be breadwinners and women homemakers, immigrant women may encounter more family and internal conflict when they enter the workforce, regardless of whether they work because of economic necessity or personal choice. Given these factors, we shouldn't be surprised that wives in more acculturated Mexican American couples tend to report greater marital distress than those in less-acculturated couples (Negy & Snyder, 1997). The lead author of this study, psychologist Charles Negy of the University of Central Florida, explores the role of acculturation among Latinos in the *Controversies in Abnormal Psychology* feature on page 153.

CONTROVERSIES IN ABNORMAL PSYCHOLOGY

Coming to America: The Case of Latinos

—CHARLES NEGY

As a young man of part Mexican American heritage, I worked in a grocery store in East Los Angeles and was intrigued by the wide range of people of Mexican ancestry I encountered. Many recent immigrants from Mexico seemed eager to practice the little English they knew and were interested in learning more about mainstream American culture. I also knew many immigrants, including many who had lived in California for more than 20 years, who spoke barely any English and hardly ever ventured beyond the local community.

When I entered graduate school it seemed natural for me to study acculturation among Latino or Hispanic Americans. Acculturation refers to adopting the values, attitudes, and behaviors of a host culture. In my early studies, I quickly observed what other researchers had already discovered; namely, that Latinos in the United States varied greatly in their degree of acculturation toward the U.S. culture. In general, the longer time they had lived in the United States, the more acculturated they tended to be, and the more acculturated they were, the more they resembled non-Hispanic Whites in their values, attitudes, and customs.

In my early studies (e.g., Negy & Woods, 1992a; 1993), I found that the more acculturated Mexican American college students were, the more similar their scores were to those of non-Hispanic Whites on standardized personality tests. I wasn't surprised to find that those who were more acculturated tended to come from higher socioeconomic backgrounds (Negy & Woods, 1992b). I also found that among lower-income Mexican American adolescents who showed signs of depression, the more acculturated they were, the more likely they were to have experienced thoughts of committing suicide (Rasmussen, Negy, Carlson, & Burns, 1997).

I later began a line of research examining ethnic differences in marital relationships by comparing Mexican American couples to (non-Hispanic) White couples and Mexican couples (Negy, & Snyder, 1997; Negy, Snyder, & Diaz-Loving, 2004). As a group, Mexican couples reported more verbal and/or physical aggression in their relationships than did Mexican American couples, who in turn reported more aggression in their relationships than did White couples. We also observed that Mexican American couples had more egalitarian (equal) relationships and higher levels of marital satisfaction than Mexican couples (Negy & Snyder, 2004). We learned from these findings that living in the United States was associated with relationship patterns among Mexican Americans that were closer to the Americanized ideal of mutual respect and shared decision-making. Our more recent research showed that the more acculturated Cuban Americans and Puerto Ricans were, the more positive attitudes they held toward mental illness (in terms of being treatable and being associated with less social stigma) and the more open they were to seeking professional therapy for themselves (Rojas-Vilches & Negy, in preparation).

Taken together, my research suggests that more highly acculturated Hispanic couples have less conflicted, more egalitarian, and more satisfying marriages. On the other hand, acculturation is also linked to some mental health problems, such as increased likelihood of suicidal thinking as a way of dealing with depression. This mixed picture of acculturation among Latinos is similar to the complex and sometimes conflicting results from studies examining relationships between acculturation and mental health reported in this chapter.

We also observed in our study of Mexican American couples that more highly acculturated women reported less satisfaction with the sexual component of their relationships than did less well acculturated women. These findings lead us to wonder whether American culture imparts greater expectations of female sexual satisfaction in marriages that translate into lower satisfaction when these expectations are not fulfilled.

There are important issues to keep in mind when interpreting our research findings. For starters, the research is correlational in nature. As you may recall about correlational data, we cannot say whether one variable causes another variable. For example, based on the findings from my study of marital couples, I cannot conclude that acculturation is causally related to the development of more egalitarian marriages. It is possible that causation works in the opposite direction—that having an egalitarian marriage influences acculturation. How? We can speculate that Mexican Americans with more egalitarian relationships may be more accepted by mainstream society, and the more interactions they have within the general society, the more opportunities they have to acculturate. It may also be the case that having egalitarian marriages tends to be associated (correlated) with acculturation, but there is no causal link between the two.

Learning more about Hispanics' relationships, particularly in the context of acculturation and mental health, is important because for many Latinos, the family, including the marital relationship, is the cornerstone of their identity and functioning. Our research may help inform the treatment interventions clinicians can offer to Hispanic couples and families struggling with adjustment and acculturation challenges.

Critical Thinking

- Do you believe that it desirable for recent immigrants to balance assimilation into mainstream society and ethnic identity? Why or why not?
- How strong an influence is your own cultural or ethnic heritage in your life? Explain.

Charles Negy, Ph.D., is Associate Professor of Psychology at the University of Central Florida and is a licensed psychologist in the state of Florida. His research primarily focuses on the acculturation of Hispanic Americans.

Psychological Factors That Moderate Stress

Stress may be a fact of life, but the ways in which we handle stress help determine our ability to cope with it. Individuals react differently to stress depending on psychological factors such as the meaning they ascribe to stressful events. For example, whether a major life event, such as pregnancy, is a positive or negative stressor depends on a couple's desire for a child and their readiness to care for one. We can say the stress of pregnancy is moderated by the perceived value of children in a couple's eyes and their self-efficacy—their confidence in their ability to raise a child. As we see next, psychological factors such as coping styles, self-efficacy expectancies, psychological hardiness, optimism, social support, and ethnic identity may moderate or buffer the effects of stress.

Styles of Coping What do you do when faced with a serious problem? Do you pretend it does not exist? Like Scarlett O'Hara in the classic film *Gone With the Wind*, do you say to yourself, "I'll think about it tomorrow," and then banish it from your mind? Or do you take charge and confront it squarely?

Pretending that problems do not exist is a form of denial. Denial is an example of **emotion-focused coping** (Lazarus & Folkman, 1984). In emotion-focused coping, people take measures that immediately reduce the impact of the stressor, such as denying its existence or withdrawing from the situation. Emotion-focused coping, however, does not eliminate the stressor (a serious illness, for example) or help the individual develop better ways of managing it. In **problem-focused coping,** by contrast, people examine the stressors they face and do what they can to change them or modify their own reactions to render stressors less harmful. These basic styles of coping—emotion-focused and problem-focused—have been applied to ways in which people respond to illness.

Denial of illness can take various forms, including the following.

1. Failing to recognize the seriousness of the illness
2. Minimizing the emotional distress the illness causes
3. Misattributing symptoms to other causes (for example, assuming the appearance of blood in the stool represents nothing more than a local abrasion)
4. Ignoring threatening information about the illness

Denial can be dangerous to your health, especially if it leads to avoidance of, or noncompliance with, needed medical treatment. Avoidance is another form of emotion-based coping. Like denial, avoidance may deter people from complying with medical treatments, which can lead to a worsening of their medical conditions. Evidence supports the negative consequences of avoidant coping. In one study, people who had an avoidant style of coping with cancer (for example, by trying not to think or talk about it) showed greater disease progression when evaluated a year later than did people who more directly confronted the illness (Epping-Jordan, Compas, & Howell, 1994). Other investigators link avoidance coping to the later development of depression and to PTSD among combat veterans (Holahan et al., 2005; Stein et al., 2005).

Another form of emotion-focused coping, the use of wish-fulfillment fantasies, is also linked to poor adjustment in coping with serious illness. Examples of wish-fulfillment fantasies include ruminating about what might have been had the illness not occurred and longing for better times. Wish-fulfillment fantasy offers the patient no means of coping with life's difficulties other than an imaginary escape.

Does this mean that people are invariably better off when they know all the facts concerning their illnesses? Not necessarily. Whether you will be better off knowing all the facts may depend on your preferred style of coping. A mismatch between the individual's style of coping and the amount of information provided may hamper recovery. In one study, cardiac patients with a repressive style of coping (relying on denial) who received information about their conditions showed a higher incidence of medical complications than repressors who were largely kept in the dark (Shaw et al., 1985). Sometimes ignorance helps people manage stress—at least temporarily.

Problem-focused coping involves strategies that address the source of stress, such as seeking information about the illness through self-study and medical consultation. Information seeking may help the individual maintain a more optimistic frame of mind by creating an expectancy that the information will prove to be useful.

Self-Efficacy Expectancies **Self-efficacy expectancies** refer to our expectations regarding our abilities to cope with the challenges we face, to perform certain behaviors skillfully, and to produce positive changes in our lives (Bandura, 1982, 1986).

emotion-focused coping A coping style that attempts to minimize emotional responsiveness rather than deal with the stressor directly.

problem-focused coping A coping style that attempts to confront the stressor directly.

self-efficacy expectancies Beliefs in one's ability to accomplish particular tasks.

We may be better able to manage stress, including the stress of coping with illness, if we feel confident (have higher self-efficacy expectancies) in our ability to cope effectively. A forthcoming exam may be more or less stressful depending on your confidence in your ability to achieve a good grade.

In a classic study, psychologist Albert Bandura and colleagues found that spider-phobic women showed high levels of the stress hormones epinephrine and norepinephrine when they interacted with the phobic object, such as by allowing a spider to crawl on their laps (Bandura et al., 1985). However, as their confidence or self-efficacy expectancies for coping with these tasks increased, the levels of these stress hormones declined. Epinephrine and norepinephrine arouse the body by way of the sympathetic branch of the ANS. They make us feel shaky, have "butterflies in the stomach," and generally feel nervous. Because high self-efficacy expectancies appear to be associated with lower secretion of these stress hormones, people who believe they can cope with their problems may be less likely to feel nervous.

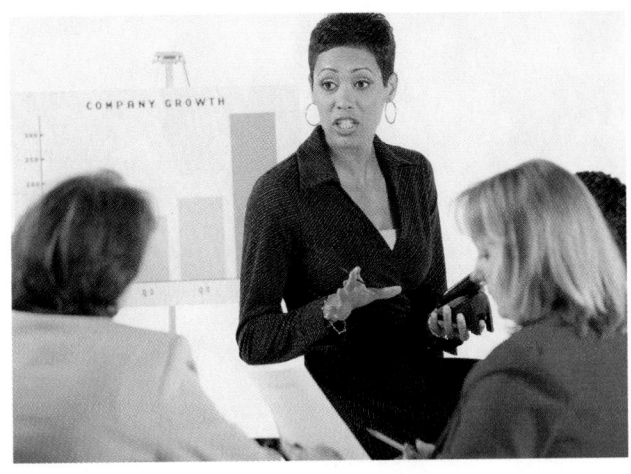

Coping with stress. Psychologically hardy people appear to cope more effectively with stress by adopting active, problem-solving approaches and by perceiving themselves as choosing high-stress situations.

Psychological Hardiness **Psychological hardiness** refers to a cluster of traits that may help people manage stress. Suzanne Kobasa (1979) and her colleagues investigated business executives who resisted illness despite heavy burdens of stress. Three key traits distinguished the psychologically hardy executives (Kobasa, Maddi, & Kahn, 1982, pp. 169–170):

psychological hardiness A cluster of stress-buffering traits characterized by commitment, challenge, and control.

1. *Commitment.* Rather than feeling alienated from their tasks and situations, hardy executives involved themselves fully. That is, they believed in what they were doing.
2. *Challenge.* Hardy executives believed change was the normal state of things, not sterile sameness or stability for the sake of stability.
3. *Control over their lives* (Maddi & Kobasa, 1984). Hardy executives believed and acted as though they were effectual rather than powerless in controlling the rewards and punishments of life. In terms suggested by social-cognitive theorist Julian Rotter (1966), psychologically hardy individuals have an *internal locus of control.*

Psychologically hardy people appear to cope more effectively with stress by using more active, problem-solving approaches. They are also likely to report fewer physical symptoms and less depression in the face of stress than nonhardy people (Ouellette & DiPlacido, 2001; Pengilly & Dowd, 2000). Kobasa suggests that hardy people are better able to handle stress because they perceive themselves as *choosing* their stress-creating situations. They perceive the stressors they face as making life more interesting and challenging, not as simply burdening them with additional pressures. A sense of control is a key factor in psychological hardiness.

Optimism Seeing the proverbial glass as half full rather than half empty is linked to better outcomes in terms of both physical and psychological health. Among heart disease patients, optimistic attitudes are associated with less emotional distress; among cancer patients, optimism is associated with lower levels of emotional distress, better psychological adjustment, and lower levels of reported pain; and among pregnant women, it is linked to better birth outcomes, such as higher infant birth weights (Bjerklie, 2005; Carver et al., 2005; Shnek et al., 2001; Trunzo & Pinto, 2003).

Among pain patients, those expressing more pessimistic thoughts during flare-ups of pain tended to report more severe pain and distress (Gil et al., 1990). The pessimistic thoughts included, "I can no longer do anything," "No one cares about my pain," and "It isn't fair I have to live this way." Research to date shows only correlational links between optimism and health. Perhaps we shall soon learn whether learning to alter attitudes—to learn to see the glass as half filled—plays a causal role in maintaining or

TRUTH or FICTION

Pregnant women with more optimistic attitudes tend to have higher birth-weight babies.

☑ **TRUE.** Yes, optimism in the mother is associated with better birth outcomes, including higher infant birth weights.

Ethnic pride as a moderator of the effects of stress. Pride in one's racial or ethnic identity may help the individual withstand the stress imposed by racism and intolerance.

positive psychology A growing contemporary movement within psychology that focuses on the positive attributes of human behavior.

restoring health. You can evaluate your own level of optimism by completing the Life Orientation Test in this section.

The study of optimism falls within a broader contemporary movement in psychology called **positive psychology.** The developers of this movement believe that psychology should focus more of its efforts on the positive aspects of the human experience, rather than just the deficit side of the human equation, such as problems of emotional disorders, drug abuse, and violence (Gable & Haidt, 2005; Lyubomirsky, Sheldon, & Schkade, 2005; Seligman et al., 2005; Simonton & Baumeister, 2005; Vallea, Huebner, & Suldo, 2006). Although we shouldn't turn away from the study of emotional problems, we need to explore how positive attributes, such as optimism, love, and hope, affect our ability to lead satisfying and fulfilling lives. Another positive aspect of the human experience is the ability to help others in need and be helped by others in turn, as in the case of social support.

Social Support The role of social support as a buffer against stress is well documented (e.g., Wills & Filer Fegan, 2001). In one study, having a broad network of social contacts was associated with greater resistance to developing an infection following exposure to a common cold virus (Cohen & Mannarino, 1997). The investigators believe that having a wide range of social contacts may help protect the body's immune system by serving as a buffer against stress.

Ethnic Identity African Americans, on the average, stand a greater risk than Euro Americans of suffering chronic health problems, such as obesity, hypertension, heart disease, diabetes, and certain types of cancer (Brown, 2006; "CDC Finds," 2005; Shields, Lerman, & Sullivan, 2005). The particular stressors that African Americans often face, such as racism, poverty, violence, and overcrowded living conditions, may contribute to their heightened risks of serious health-related problems. Yet African Americans often demonstrate a high degree of resilience in coping with stress (Cutrona et al., 2000). Among the factors that help buffer stress among African Americans are strong social networks of family and friends, beliefs in one's ability to handle stress (self-efficacy), coping skills, and ethnic identity. Interestingly, African Americans in a recent study who reported more active attempts to seek social support showed less physiological responsiveness to the effects of perceived racism, a significant life stressor, than did those who were low in support seeking (Clark, 2006).

Ethnic identity is associated with perceptions of a better quality of life among African Americans (Utsey et al., 2002) and appears to be more strongly related to psychological well-being among African Americans than among White Americans (Gray-Little & Hafdahl, 2000). Acquiring and maintaining pride in one's racial identity and cultural heritage may help African Americans and other ethnic minorities withstand stresses imposed by racism. Although more research is needed to elucidate the links among racial identity, self-esteem, and tolerance of stress, the available evidence suggests that African Americans who become alienated from their culture develop more negative self-images and stand a greater risk of developing not only physical and psychological disorders, but also academic underachievement and marital conflicts (Anderson, 1991).

PSYCHOLOGICAL FACTORS AND PHYSICAL DISORDERS

We noted at the start of the chapter that psychological factors can influence physical functioning. Here we take a closer look at the role of psychological factors in physical disorders.

◆

QUESTIONNAIRE
The Life Orientation Test

 Do you see the glass as half full or half empty? Do you expect bad things to happen or do you find the silver lining in every cloud? The Life Orientation Test can afford you insight as to how optimistic or pessimistic you are.

Directions: Indicate whether or not each of the items represents your feelings by writing a number in the blank space according to the following code. Then turn to the scoring key at the end of the chapter.

4 = strongly agree
3 = agree
2 = neutral
1 = disagree
0 = strongly disagree

1. _____ In uncertain times, I usually expect the best.

2. _____ It's easy for me to relax.

3. _____ If something can go wrong for me, it will.

4. _____ I always look on the bright side of things.

5. _____ I'm always optimistic about my future.

6. _____ I enjoy my friends a lot.

7. _____ It's important for me to keep busy.

8. _____ I hardly ever expect things to go my way.

9. _____ Things never work out the way I want them to.

10. _____ I don't get upset too easily.

11. _____ I'm a believer in the idea that "every cloud has a silver lining."

12. _____ I rarely count on good things happening to me.

Source: Questionnaire—The Life Orientation Test, from Scheier, M. F., & Carver, C. S., "Optimism, Coping, and Health: Assessment and implication of Generalized Outcome Expectancies," Health Psychology, 4, 1985, pp. 219–247. Reproduced with permission of Lawrence Erlbaum Associates Inc. in the format Textbook via Copyright Clearance Center.

A CLOSER LOOK

Psychological Methods for Lowering Arousal

Stress induces bodily responses such as excessive levels of sympathetic nervous system arousal, which if persistent may impair our ability to function optimally and possibly increase the risk of stress-related illnesses. Psychological treatments have been shown to lower states of bodily arousal that may be prompted by stress. In this feature, we consider two widely used psychological methods of lowering arousal: meditation and progressive relaxation.

MEDITATION

Meditation comprises several ways of narrowing consciousness to moderate the stressors of the outer world. Yogis (adherents to Yoga philosophy) study the design on a vase or a mandala. The ancient Egyptians riveted their attention on an oil-burning lamp, which is the inspiration for the tale of Aladdin's lamp. In Turkey, Islamic mystics called whirling dervishes fix on their motion and the cadences of their breathing. We've learned that meditation has measurable benefits in treating many psychological and physical disorders, especially those in which stress plays a contributing role, such as cardiovascular disorders (Walsh & Shapiro, 2006). For example, a recent clinical trial showed improvements in coronary heart disease risk factors, including lower blood pressure, among heart patients who practiced meditation (Paul-Labrador et al., 2006).

There are many meditation methods, but they share the common thread of narrowing one's attention by focusing on repetitive stimuli. Through passive observation, the regular person–environment connection is transformed. Problem solving, worry, planning, and routine concerns are suspended, and consequently, levels of sympathetic nervous system arousal are reduced.

Many thousands of Americans regularly practice *transcendental meditation (TM)*, a simplified kind of Indian meditation brought to the United States in 1959 by Maharishi Mahesh Yogi. Practitioners of TM repeat *mantras*—relaxing sounds such as *ieng* and *om*.

Benson (1975) studied TM practitioners ages 17 to 41—students, businesspeople, artists. His subjects included relative novices and veterans of 9 years of practice. Benson found that TM yields a *relaxation response* in many people. The relaxation response is characterized by reduced heart rate and metabolic rate and by lower blood pressure in people with hypertension (Benson, Manzetta, & Rosner, 1973; Gatchel, 2001). Meditators also tend to produce more alpha waves, which are brain waves connected with relaxation. Critics of meditation do not argue that meditation is without value; they suggest, instead, that meditation may have no distinct effects when compared to other forms of relaxation or even taking a restful break from a stressful routine.

In *mindfulness meditation,* a form of meditation practiced by Tibetan Buddhists, the person focuses on conscious experience (thoughts, feelings,

(continued)

(continued)

and sensations) on a moment-to-moment basis, without judging or evaluating the experience (Baer, 2003; Kabat-Zinn, 2003). This practice has been likened to observing the flow of a river. Mindfulness meditation shows promise in treating various physical and mental health problems, including chronic pain and stress, as well as improving psychological well-being and reducing relapse rates in depressed patients (Baer, 2003; Logsdon-Conradsen, 2002; Ma & Teasdale, 2004; Roemer & Orsillo, 2003).

Although there are differences among meditative techniques, the following suggestions illustrate some general guidelines.

1. Try meditation once or twice a day for 10 to 20 minutes at a time.
2. When you meditate, what you *don't* do is more important than what you do. So embrace a passive attitude: Tell yourself, "What happens, happens." In meditation, you take what you get. You don't *strive* for more. Striving of any kind hinders meditation.
3. Place yourself in a hushed, calming environment. For example, don't face a light directly.
4. Avoid eating for an hour before you meditate. Avoid caffeine (found in coffee, tea, many soft drinks, and chocolate) for at least 2 hours before meditation.
5. Get into a relaxed position. Modify it as needed. You can scratch or yawn if you feel the urge.
6. For a focusing device, you can concentrate on your breathing or sit in front of a serene object, such as a plant or incense. Benson suggests "perceiving" (not "mentally saying") the word *one* each time you breathe out. That is, think the word, but "less actively" than you normally would. Other researchers suggest thinking the word *in* as you breathe in and *out,* or *ah-h-h,* as you breathe out. They also suggest mantras, such as *ah-nam, rah-mah,* and *shi-rim.*
7. When preparing for meditation, repeat your mantra aloud many times—if you're using a mantra. Enjoy it. Then say it progressively more softly. Close your eyes. Focus on the mantra. Allow thinking the mantra to become more and more "passive" so you "perceive" rather than think it. Again, embrace your "what happens, happens" attitude. Keep on focusing on the mantra. It may become softer or louder, or fade and then reappear.
8. If unsettling thoughts drift in while you're meditating, allow them to "pass through." Don't worry about squelching them, or you may become tense.
9. Remember to take what comes. Meditation and relaxation cannot be forced. You cannot force the relaxing effects of meditation. Like sleep, you can only set the stage for it and then permit it to happen.
10. Let yourself drift. (You won't get lost.) What happens, happens.

Going with the flow.
Meditation is a popular method of managing the stresses of the outside world by reducing states of bodily arousal. This young woman practices yoga, a form of meditation. She "goes with the flow," allowing the distractions of her environment to, in a sense, "pass through." Contrast her meditative state with the apparently stressful features of the young man sitting behind her.

PROGRESSIVE RELAXATION

Progressive relaxation was originated by University of Chicago physician Edmund Jacobson in 1938. Jacobson noticed that people tense their muscles under stress, intensifying their uneasiness. They tend to be unaware of these contractions, however. Jacobson reasoned that if muscle contractions contributed to tension, muscle relaxation might reduce tension. But clients who were asked to focus on relaxing muscles often had no idea what to do.

Jacobson's method of progressive relaxation teaches people how to monitor muscle tension and relaxation. With this method, people first tense, then relax, selected muscle groups in the arms; facial area; the chest, stomach, and lower back muscles; the hips, thighs, and calves; and so on. The sequence heightens awareness of muscle tension and helps people differentiate feelings of tension from relaxation. The method is progressive in that people progress from one group of muscles to another in practicing the technique. Since the 1930s, progressive relaxation has been used by a number of behavior therapists, including Joseph Wolpe and Arnold Lazarus (1966).

The following instructions from Wolpe and Lazarus (1966, pp. 177–178) illustrate how the technique is applied to relaxing the arms. Relaxation should be practiced in a favorable setting. Settle back on a recliner, a couch, or a bed with a pillow. Select a place and time when you're unlikely to be disturbed. Make the room warm and comfortable. Dim sources of light. Loosen tight clothing. Tighten muscles about two thirds as hard as you could if you were trying your hardest. If you sense that a muscle could have a spasm, you are tightening too much. After tensing, let go of tensions completely.

Relaxation of Arms (time: 4–5 minutes)

Settle back as comfortably as you can. Let yourself relax to the best of your ability. . . . Now, as you relax like that, clench your right fist, just clench your fist tighter and tighter, and study the tension as you do so. Keep it clenched and feel the tension in your right fist, hand, forearm . . . and now relax. Let the fingers of your right hand become loose, and observe the contrast in your feelings. . . . Now let yourself go and try to become more relaxed all over. . . . Once more, clench your right fist really tight . . . hold it, and notice the tension again. . . . Now let go, relax; your fingers straighten out, and you notice the difference once more. . . . Now repeat that with your left fist. Clench your left fist while the rest of your body relaxes; clench that fist tighter and feel the tension . . . and now relax. Again enjoy the contrast. . . . Repeat that once more, clench the left fist, tight and tense. . . . Now do the opposite of tension—relax and feel the difference. Continue relaxing like that for a while. . . . Clench both fists tighter and together, both fists tense, forearms tense, study the sensations . . . and relax; straighten out your fingers and feel that relaxation. Continue relaxing your hands and forearms more and more. . . . Now bend your elbows and tense your biceps, tense them harder and study the tension feelings . . . all right, straighten out your arms, let them relax and feel that difference again. Let the relaxation develop. . . . Once more, tense your biceps; hold the tension and observe it carefully. . . . Straighten the arms and relax; relax to the best of your ability. . . . Each time, pay close attention to your feelings when you tense up and when you relax. Now straighten your arms, straighten them so that you feel most tension in the triceps muscles along the back of your arms; stretch your arms and feel that tension. . . . And now relax. Get your arms back into a comfortable position. Let the relaxation proceed on its own. The arms should feel comfortably heavy as you allow them to relax. . . . Straighten the arms once more so that you feel the tension in the triceps muscles; straighten them. Feel that tension . . . and relax. Now let's concentrate on pure relaxation in the arms without any tension. Get your arms comfortable and let them relax further and further. Continue relaxing your arms even further. Even when your arms seem fully relaxed, try to go that extra bit further; try to achieve deeper and deeper levels of relaxation.

Physical disorders in which psychological factors are believed to play a causal or contributing role have traditionally been termed **psychosomatic** disorders. The term *psychosomatic* is derived from the Greek roots *psyche*, meaning "soul" or "intellect," and *soma*, which means "body." Disorders such as asthma and headaches have traditionally been labeled as psychosomatic because of the belief that psychological factors play an important role in their development.

Ulcers are another ailment traditionally identified as a psychosomatic disorder. Ulcers affect about 1 in 10 people in the United States. However, their status as a psychosomatic disorder has been reevaluated in the light of recent landmark research showing that a bacterium, *H. pylori*, not stress or diet, is the major cause of the types of ulcers called *peptic ulcers*, which are sores in the lining of the stomach or upper part of the small intestine (Jones, 2006). Ulcers may arise when the bacterium damages the protective lining of the stomach or intestines. Treatment with a regimen of antibiotics may cure ulcers by attacking the bacterium directly. We don't yet know why some people who harbor the bacterium develop ulcers and others do not. The virulence of the particular strain of *H. pylori* may determine whether infected people develop peptic ulcers. Stress may also play a role, although we lack definitive evidence that stress contributes to vulnerability (Jones, 2006).

The field of psychosomatic medicine explores health-related connections between the mind and the body. Today, evidence points to the importance of psychological factors in a much wider range of physical disorders than those traditionally identified as psychosomatic. In this section we discuss several traditionally identified psychosomatic disorders as well as other diseases in which psychological factors may play a role in the course or treatment of the disease—cardiovascular disease, cancer, and HIV/AIDS.

psychosomatic Pertaining to a physical disorder in which psychological factors play a causal or contributing role.

Headaches

Headaches are symptoms of many medical disorders. When they occur in the absence of other symptoms, however, they may be classified as stress-related. By far the most frequent kind of headache is the *tension headache*. Stress can lead to persistent contractions of the muscles of the scalp, face, neck, and shoulders, giving rise to periodic or chronic tension headaches. Such headaches develop gradually and are generally characterized by dull, steady pain on both sides of the head and feelings of pressure or tightness.

Most other headaches, including the severe migraine headache, appear to involve changes in the blood flow to the brain (Durham, 2004; Linde et al., 2005). Migraine headaches affect more than 28 million Americans. Typical migraines last for hours or days. They may occur as often as daily or as seldom as every other month. They are characterized by piercing or throbbing sensations on one side of the head only or centered behind an eye. They can be so intense that they seem intolerable. Sufferers may experience an *aura*, or cluster of warning sensations that precedes the attack. Auras are typified by perceptual distortions, such as flashing lights, bizarre images, or blind spots. Coping with the misery of brutal migraine attacks can take its toll, impairing the quality of life and leading to disturbances of sleep, mood, and thinking processes.

Theoretical Perspectives The underlying causes of headaches remain unclear and subject to continued study. One factor contributing to tension headaches may be increased sensitivity of the neural pathways that send pain signals to the brain from the face and head (Holroyd, 2002). Migraines headaches may involve an underlying central nervous system disorder involving nerves and blood vessels in the brain. The neurotransmitter serotonin is also implicated. Falling levels of serotonin may cause blood vessels in the brain to contract (narrow) and then dilate (expand). This stretching stimulates sensitized nerve endings that give rise to the throbbing, piercing

Migraine! Migraine headaches involve intense throbbing pain on one side of the head. They may be triggered by many factors, such as hormonal changes, exposure to strong light, changes in barometric pressure; hunger, exposure to pollen, red wine, and use of certain drugs and even monosodium glutamate (MSG).

biofeedback training (BFT) A method of feeding back to the individual information about bodily functions so that the person can gain some degree of control over these functions.

cardiovascular disease A disease or disorder of the cardiovascular system, such as coronary heart disease or hypertension.

TRUTH or FICTION

People can relieve the pain of migraine headaches by raising the temperature in a finger.

☑ **TRUE.** Some people have relieved migraine headaches by raising the temperature in a finger. This biofeedback technique modifies patterns of blood flow in the body.

sensations associated with migraines. Evidence also points to a strong genetic contribution to migraine ("Scientists Discover," 2003).

Many factors may trigger a migraine attack. These include stress; stimuli such as bright lights; changes in barometric pressure; pollen; certain drugs; the chemical monosodium glutamate (MSG), which is often used to enhance the flavor of food; red wine; and even hunger. Hormonal changes of the sort that affect women prior to and during menstruation can also trigger attacks, and the incidence of migraines among women is about twice that among men.

Treatment Commonly available pain relievers, such as aspirin, ibuprofen, and acetaminophen, may reduce or eliminate pain associated with tension headaches. Drugs that constrict dilated blood vessels in the brain or help regulate serotonin activity are used to treat the pain from migraine headache (Brandes, 2006; Silberstein et al., 2000).

Psychological treatment can also help relieve tension or migraine headache pain in many cases. These treatments include training in biofeedback, relaxation, coping-skills training, and some forms of cognitive therapy (Gatchel, 2001; Holroyd, 2002). **Biofeedback training (BFT)** helps people gain control over various bodily functions, such as muscle tension and brain waves, by giving them information (feedback) about these functions in the form of auditory signals (e.g., "bleeps") or visual displays. People learn to make the signal change in the desired direction. Training people to use relaxation skills combined with biofeedback has also been shown to be effective. *Electromyographic* (EMG) biofeedback is a form of BFT that involves relaying information about muscle tension in the forehead. EMG biofeedback thus heightens awareness of muscle tension in this region and provides cues that people can use to learn to reduce it.

Some people have relieved the pain of migraine headaches by raising the temperature in a finger. This biofeedback technique, called *thermal BFT*, modifies patterns of blood flow throughout the body, including blood flow to the brain, to help control migraine headaches (Blanchard et al., 1990; Gauthier, Ivers, & Carrier, 1996). One way of providing thermal feedback is by attaching a temperature-sensing device to a finger. A console "bleeps" more slowly or rapidly as the temperature in the finger rises. The temperature rises when more blood flows to the fingers and away from the head. The client can imagine the finger growing warmer to bring about these desirable changes in the flow of blood in the body.

Cardiovascular Disease

Your cardiovascular system, the network that connects your heart and blood vessels, is your highway of life. Unfortunately, there are accidents along this highway in the form of **cardiovascular disease** (CVD, or heart and artery disease). CVD is the leading cause of death in the United States, claiming about 1 million lives annually and accounting for about 4 in 10 deaths, most often as the result of heart attacks or strokes (Hu & Willett, 2002; Nabel, 2003). *Coronary heart disease* (CHD) is the major form of cardiovascular disease, accounting for about 700,000 deaths annually, mostly from heart attacks. CVD is the leading cause of death for both men and women, claiming even more women's lives than breast cancer.

In coronary heart disease, the flow of blood to the heart is insufficient to meet the heart's needs. The underlying disease process in CHD is called *arteriosclerosis*, or "hardening of the arteries," a condition in which artery walls become thicker, harder, and less elastic, which makes it more difficult for blood to flow freely. The major underlying cause of arteriosclerosis is *atherosclerosis*, a process involving the buildup of fatty deposits along artery walls that leads to the formation of artery-clogging plaque. If a blood clot should form in an artery narrowed by plaque, it may nearly or completely block the flow of blood to the heart. The result is a heart attack (also called a *myocardial infarction*), a life-threatening event in which heart tissue dies due to a lack of oxygen-rich blood. When a blood clot blocks the supply of blood in an artery serving the brain, a *stroke* can occur, leading to death of brain tissue that can result in loss of function controlled by that part of the brain, coma, or even death.

The good news is that CHD is largely preventable (Nabel, 2003). How? By reducing the risk factors we can control. Some risk factors we can't control, such as age and family history. But a number of risk factors can be controlled through medical treatment or lifestyle changes—factors such as high blood cholesterol, hypertension (high blood pressure), smoking, overeating, heavy drinking, consuming a high-fat diet, and leading a sedentary lifestyle (e.g., Mendelsohn & Karas, 2005; Panagiotakos et al., 2005; Pickering, 2003). Unfortunately, many of these factors remain uncontrolled. For example, only about one in four adults with hypertension take medications to control blood pressure (Chobanian, 2001; Hyman & Pavlik, 2001).

Adopting healthier behaviors can have beneficial effects on the heart. For example, evidence shows that even seasoned couch potatoes can reduce their risk of cardiovascular disease by becoming more physically active (Blumenthal et al., 2005; Borjesson & Dahlof, 2005).

Negative Emotions Might your emotions be putting you at risk of coronary heart disease? It appears so. Frequent emotional distress in the form of anger, anxiety, and depression can have damaging effects on the cardiovascular system (Frasure-Smith & Lespérance, 2005; Geipert, 2007; Orth-Gomér et al., 2000).

Researchers highlight the toxic effects of chronic anger on the heart. Occasional feelings of anger may not damage the heart in healthy people, but chronic anger—the type you see in people who seem angry all of the time—is linked to increased risk of CHD (Kiecolt-Glaser et al., 2002; Pressman, & Cohen, 2005; Rutledge & Hogan, 2002; Steptoe, Wardle, & Marmot, 2005).

Anger is closely associated with hostility—a personality trait characterized by quickness to anger and by tendencies to blame others and to perceive the world in negative terms. Hostility is a component of the **Type A behavior pattern (TABP),** a style of behavior that characterizes people who are hard driving, ambitious, impatient, and highly competitive. Although earlier research had linked the Type A pattern to a higher risk of CHD, more recent research casts doubts on the relationship between this personality pattern and coronary risk (Geipert, 2007). However, we have more consistent evidence linking the trait of hostility, a component of the Type A pattern, to increased risks of heart disease and other negative health outcomes (Geipert, 2007; Mathews, 2005; Olson et al., 2006). Hostile people tend to have "short fuses" and are prone to get angry easily.

How might anger and other negative emotions contribute to heart disease? Although we can't be sure, investigators suspect that the stress hormones epinephrine and norepinephrine play significant roles (Januzzi & DeSanctis, 1999; Melani, 2001). Anxiety and anger trigger the release of these stress hormones by the adrenal glands. These hormones increase heart rate, breathing rate, and blood pressure, which results in pumping more oxygen-rich blood to the muscles to enable them to prepare for defensive action—to either fight or flee—in the face of a threatening stressor. In people who frequently experience strong negative emotions such as anger or anxiety, the body may repeatedly pump out these stress hormones, eventually damaging the heart and blood vessels.

Evidence indicates that episodes of acute anger can actually trigger heart attacks and sudden cardiac death in some people with established heart disease (Clay, 2001a). We have also learned that people who are higher in hostility tend to have more cardiovascular risk factors, such as obesity and smoking, than do less hostile people (Bunde & Suls, 2006). Anxiety and anger may also compromise the cardiovascular system by increasing blood levels of cholesterol, the fatty substance that clogs arteries and increases the risk of heart attacks (Suinn, 2001).

Type A behavior pattern (TABP) A behavior pattern characterized by a sense of time urgency, competitiveness, and hostility.

Emotions and the heart. Emotional stress in the form of persistent negative emotions, such as anxiety and anger, is a risk factor in heart-related problems.

A CLOSER LOOK

Dying of a Broken Heart

The patient's heart was failing (Sanders, 2006). She was only 45, but showed all the signs of having a heart attack. But it wasn't a heart attack. Were it a heart attack, there would have been blockage of blood flow through the arteries that service the heart. However, blood flowed freely to her heart. No, in this case, the woman's heart was failing because of the emotional shock of losing her husband in a car crash two days earlier. She had rushed to the crash site and collapsed next to his body, crying inconsolably and trying desperately but unsuccessfully to wake him. Two days later she was rushed to the hospital complaining of chest pains and difficulty breathing. The doctors realized she was a victim of "broken-heart syndrome," a potentially life threatening condition. Under high emotional stress, the body releases large amounts of the epinephrine and norepinephrine into the blood stream.

Physicians suspect that in broken-heart syndrome, these hormones effectively "stun" the heart, preventing it from pumping normally (Wittstein et al., 2006). This woman's heart was pumping only a fraction of the expected amount of blood. Fortunately, the woman survived, as the levels of stress hormones receded and the heart returned to pumping at a nearly normal level. Later, she told a reporter, "If anyone had told me that you could die of a broken heart . . . I'd never have believed it. But I almost did" (Sanders, 2006, p. 28). Fortunately, broken-heart syndrome is a rare occurrence, but it may explain cases of people who suddenly die a few days or weeks following an emotional shock, such as the sudden death of a spouse. Patients with established coronary heart disease may be especially susceptible to coronary events in response to strong emotional stress (Strike et al., 2006).

Helping angry people learn to remain calm in provocative situations may have beneficial effects on the heart as well as the mind. Cognitive-behavioral therapies are available to help chronically angry people better control their emotional responses to anxiety-provoking or angering situations (e.g., Deffenbacher et al., 2000). Along these lines, men with CHD who received a hostility-reduction program showed less hostility and lower blood pressures after treatment than did controls (Gidron, Davidson, & Bata, 1999).

Investigators find additional links between coronary heart disease and other forms of emotional stress, including depression (Carney, Freedland, & Jaffe, 2001; Miller & Blackwell, 2006). In one research example, people without established heart disease who suffered from major depression were nearly four times more likely than nondepressed people to die from heart-related causes over a 4-year study period (Penninx et al., 2000). All in all, taking care of our emotional health may have additional benefits for our physical health.

Social Environmental Stress *Social environmental stress* also appears to heighten the risk of CHD (Krantz et al., 1988). Such factors as overtime work, assembly-line labor, and exposure to conflicting demands are linked to increased risk of CHD (C. D. Jenkins, 1988). The stress–CHD connection is not straightforward, however. For example, the effects of demanding occupations may be moderated by factors such as psychological hardiness and whether or not people find their work meaningful (Krantz et al., 1988).

Other forms of stress are also linked to increased cardiovascular risk. Researchers in Sweden, for example, find that among women, marital stress triples the risk of recurrent cardiac events, including heart attacks and cardiac death (Foxhall, 2001; Orth-Gomér et al., 2000).

Ethnicity and CHD Coronary heart disease is not an equal opportunity destroyer. European Americans (non-Hispanic Whites) and African Americans (non-Hispanic Blacks) have the highest rates of death due to coronary heart disease (see Figure 5.2). Factors such as obesity, smoking, diabetes, and hypertension play important roles in determining relative risks of CHD and the rate of CHD-related deaths. For example, African Americans have higher rates of hypertension relative to other U.S. population groups (see Figure 5.3) as well as higher rates of obesity and diabetes. Moreover, a dual standard of care limits access to quality health care for minority group members. Black Americans with CHD who suffer heart attacks typically receive less aggressive and potentially lifesaving treatments than do Whites with CHD, which likely contributes to their higher death rates (Chen et al., 2001; Stolberg, 2001). This dual standard of care may reflect discrimination as well as cultural factors limiting utilization of services, such as African Americans' cultural mistrust toward the medical establishment.

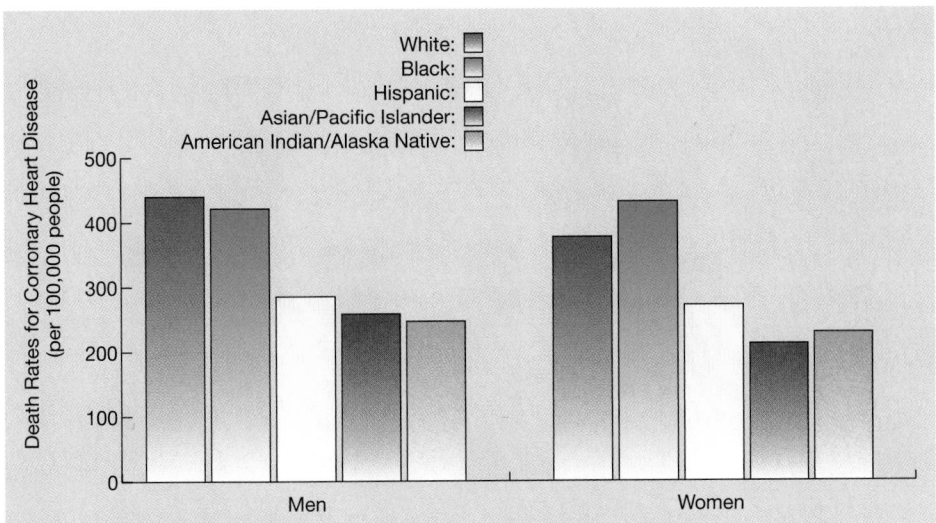

FIGURE 5.2 Coronary heart disease death rates in relation to race and ethnicity.
Deaths due to CHD in our society fall disproportionately on White men and on Black (non-Hispanic) men and women.

Source: Morbidity and Mortality Weekly Report, Centers for Disease Control, February 16, 2001, *50*(006), 90–93.

We finish this section with encouraging news. Americans have begun to take better care of their cardiovascular health. The incidence of CHD and deaths from heart disease have been declining steadily during the past 50 years, thanks largely to reductions in smoking, to improved treatment for coronary heart disease, and perhaps to other lifestyle changes, such as reduced intake of dietary fat. Better-educated people are also more likely to modify unhealthful behavior patterns and reap the benefits of change. Is there a message here for you?

Asthma

Asthma is a respiratory disorder in which the main tubes of the windpipe—the bronchi—constrict and become inflamed, and large amounts of mucus are secreted. During asthma attacks, people wheeze, cough, and struggle to breathe in enough air. They may feel as though they are suffocating.

According to the Centers for Disease Control (CDC), an estimated 14 million adults and 5 million children in the United States are affected by asthma (CDC, 2001b, 2004a). Rates of asthma are on the rise, having more than doubled over the past thirty years. Attacks can last from just a few minutes to several hours and vary notably in intensity. Series of attacks can harm the bronchial system, causing mucus to collect and muscles to lose their elasticity. Sometimes the bronchial system is weakened to the point where a subsequent attack is lethal.

Theoretical Perspectives Many causal factors are implicated in asthma, including allergic reactions; exposure to environmental pollutants, including cigarette smoke and smog; and genetic and immunological factors (Giembycz & O'Connor, 2000; Van Eerdewegh et al., 2002). Asthmatic reactions in susceptible people can be triggered by exposure to allergens such as pollen, mold spores, and animal dander; by cold, dry air; and by emotional responses such as anger or even laughing too hard. Psychological factors such as stress, anxiety, and depression can increase susceptibility to asthmatic attacks (Greengrass, 2002; Lehrer et al., 2002). Asthma, moreover, has psychological consequences. Some sufferers avoid strenuous activity, including exercise, for fear of increasing their demand for oxygen and tripping attacks.

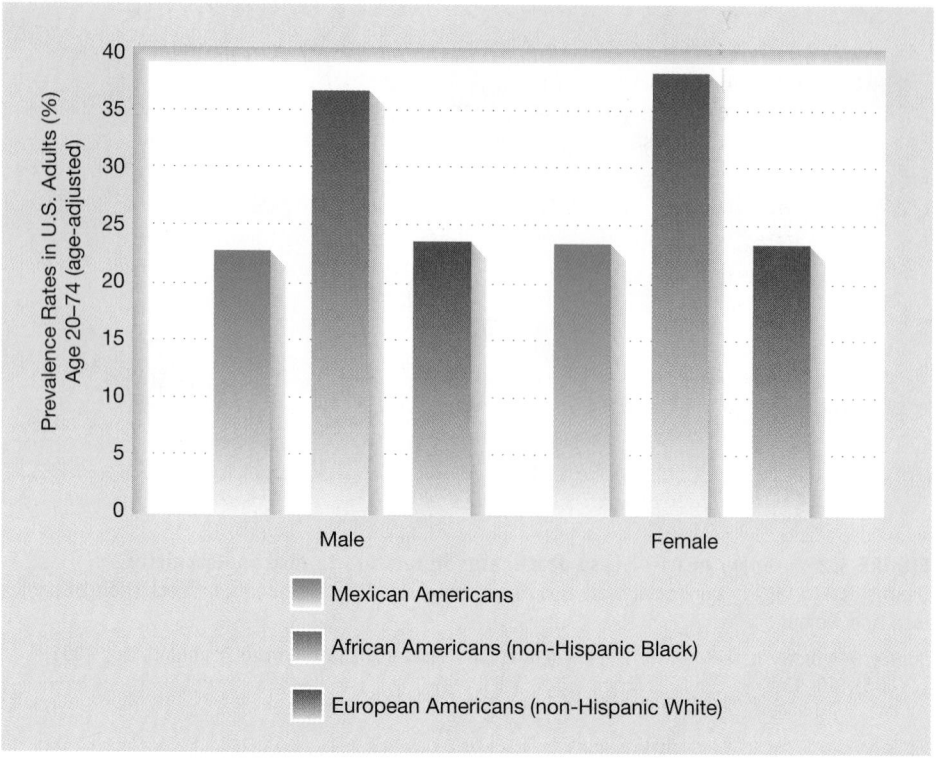

FIGURE 5.3 Ethnicity and Hypertension.
African Americans have higher rates of hypertension, one of the key risk factors for heart attacks and strokes.

Source: Adapted from *Heart Disease and Stroke Statistics—2005 Update.* American Heart Association, 2005.

Treatment Although asthma cannot be cured, it can be controlled by reducing exposure to allergens, by desensitization therapy ("allergy shots") to help the body acquire more resistance to allergens, by use of inhalers, and by drugs that open bronchial passages during asthma attacks (called *bronchodilators)* and others (called *anti-inflammatories)* that reduce future attacks by helping to keep bronchial tubes open (Sears et al., 2003; Sin et al., 2004). Psychological treatment may also help asthma sufferers apply the skills of muscle relaxation to improve their breathing (Lehrer et al., 1994), and for asthmatic children, family therapy that helps reduce family conflict (Lehrer et al., 1992). Family conflict is linked to increased rates of hospitalization for asthmatic children (Chen et al., 2003).

Cancer

The word *cancer* is arguably the most feared word in the English language, and rightly so: One of every four deaths in the United States is caused by cancer. Cancer claims about half a million lives in the United States annually, one every 90 seconds or so. Men have a one in two chance of developing cancer at some point in their lives; for women the odds are one in three. Yet there is good news to report: The cancer death rate has been inching downward in recent years, in large part due to better screening and treatment (Jemal et al., 2007).

Cancer involves the development of aberrant, or mutant, cells that form growths (tumors) that spread to healthy tissue. Cancerous cells can take root anywhere—the blood, the bones, lungs, digestive tract, and reproductive organs. When it is not contained early, cancer may *metastasize,* or establish colonies throughout the body, leading to death.

There are many causes of cancer, including genetic factors, exposure to cancer-causing chemicals, and even exposure to some viruses (Godtfredsen, Prescott, & Osler, 2005; Samuels et al., 2004; Walsh et al., 2006). Unhealthy behavior patterns also contribute to the development of cancer, including dietary practices (high fat intake), heavy alcohol consumption, smoking, and excessive sun exposure (ultraviolet light causes skin cancer). On the other hand, daily intake of fruits and vegetables may lower the risk of some forms of cancer. Death rates from cancer are lower in Japan than in the United States, where people ingest more fat, especially animal fat. The difference is not genetic or racial, however, because Japanese Americans whose fat intake approximates that of other Americans show similar death rates from cancer.

Stress and Cancer A weakened or compromised immune system may increase susceptibility to cancer. We've seen that psychological factors, such as exposure to stress, may affect the immune system. So it stands to reason that exposure to stress might increase a person's risk of developing cancer. However, evidence linking stress to cancer is inconclusive and requires further study (Delahanty & Baum, 2001; Dougall & Baum, 2001).

On the other hand, we have learned that psychological interventions that focus on helping cancer patients cope with the disease, such as group support programs, can improve their psychological adjustment and well-being (Helgeson, 2005; Taylor et al., 2003). It remains to be seen whether psychological interventions actually increase the length of survival of patients suffering from cancer.

Cancer patients may benefit from training programs that focus on developing coping skills, such as relaxation, stress management, and coping thoughts, to help relieve the stress and pain of coping with cancer. Coping-skills training may also help cancer patients deal with the unpleasant side effects of chemotherapy. Cues associated with chemotherapy, such as the hospital environment itself, may become conditioned stimuli that elicit nausea and vomiting even before the drugs are administered. Pairing relaxation, pleasant imagery, and attentional distraction with these cues can help reduce nausea and vomiting associated with chemotherapy (Redd & Jacobsen, 2001).

Acquired Immunodeficiency Syndrome (AIDS)

Acquired immunodeficiency syndrome (AIDS) is a disease caused by the *human immunodeficiency virus* (HIV). HIV attacks the immune system, leaving it helpless to fend off diseases it normally would hold in check. HIV/AIDS is one of history's worst epidemics. Worldwide, more than 40 million people are infected with HIV (Hammer et al., 2006). HIV/AIDS has claimed more than 430,000 lives in the United States and some 25 million lives worldwide.

There are two primary reasons for including HIV/AIDS in our discussion of psychological factors in physical illness. First, people living with HIV/AIDS often develop significant psychological problems in adjusting to living with the disease. Second, behavioral patterns such as unsafe sexual and injection practices play the dominant role in determining the risk of contracting and transmitting the virus.

HIV can be transmitted by sexual contact (vaginal and anal intercourse; oral–genital contact); direct infusion of contaminated blood, as from transfusions of contaminated blood, accidental pricks from needles used previously on an infected person, or needle sharing among injecting drug users; and from an infected mother to a child during pregnancy or childbirth or through breast-feeding. AIDS is not contracted by donating blood; by airborne germs; by insects; or by casual contact, such as using public toilets, holding or hugging infected people, sharing eating utensils with them, or living or going to school with them. Routine screening of the blood supply for HIV has reduced the risk of infection from blood transfusions to virtually nil. The majority of cases of HIV transmission worldwide involve heterosexual intercourse; in the United States, heterosexual intercourse accounts for 35% of new cases of HIV infections (CDC, 2004b).

TRUTH or FICTION

Compelling evidence now exists that psychotherapy can increase survival rates in cancer patients.

☑ **FALSE.** Evidence has not demonstrated—not yet at least—that psychological treatments increase survival rates of cancer patients. However, evidence does show that psychological treatment in the form of group therapy improves the emotional well-being of cancer patients.

There is no cure or vaccine for HIV infection, but the introduction of highly effective antiretroviral drugs has revolutionized treatment of the disease, raising hopes that it can become a chronic but manageable disease. However, hopes are tempered by the fact that many patients fail to benefit fully from antiviral drug combinations and by the emergence of some drug-resistant strains of the virus. The lack of a cure or effective vaccine means that prevention programs focusing on reducing or eliminating risky sexual and injection practices represent our best hope for controlling the epidemic.

Adjustment of People with HIV and AIDS Given the nature of the disease and the stigma suffered by people with HIV and AIDS, it is not surprising that many people with HIV, although certainly not all, develop psychological problems, most commonly anxiety and depression (Heckman et al., 2004; Morrison et al., 2002).

Psychologists and other mental health professionals are involved in providing treatment services to people affected by HIV/AIDS. Coping-skills training and cognitive-behavioral therapy can help improve psychological functioning, ability to handle stress, and quality of life among patients with HIV/AIDS and reduce their feelings of depression and anxiety (Lechner et al, 2003; Lutgendorf et al., 1997). Treatment may incorporate training in stress-management techniques, such as self-relaxation and positive mental imagery, and cognitive strategies to control intrusive negative thoughts and preoccupations. The importance of stress management skills is highlighted by findings that stressful life events and passive coping (use of denial) were associated with faster progression to AIDS in HIV-infected men (Leserman et al., 2000).

Antidepressant medication may also help patients with HIV/AIDS cope with a frequent emotional consequence of living with the disease—depression. Whether treatment of depression or stress management training can improve immunological functioning or prolong life in people with HIV and AIDS remains an open question.

Psychological Interventions to Reduce Risky Behaviors Providing information about risk reduction alone is not sufficient to induce widespread changes in sexual behavior. Despite awareness of the dangers, many people continue to practice unsafe sexual and injection behaviors. Fortunately, psychological interventions are effective in helping people alter these risky behaviors (e.g., Albarracín, Durantini, & Ear, 2006; Carey et al., 2004). These programs raise people's awareness about risky behaviors and help them develop more adaptive behaviors, such as learning how to refuse invitations

AIDS support group. AIDS support groups offer emotional support and assistance to people with HIV/AIDS, their families, and their friends.

to engage in unsafe sex and how to communicate effectively with one's partner(s) about safer sex. The likelihood of engaging in safer sex practices is also linked to the avoidance of alcohol and drugs before sex and to the perception that safer sex practices represent the social norm (expected behavior) within one's peer group.

Preventing AIDS For the first time, a generation of young people has come of age at a time when the threat of HIV/AIDS hangs over every sexual encounter. People may decrease the risk of being infected by HIV and other sexually transmitted diseases (STDs) by taking the following measures. Only the first two are sure paths to avoiding the sexual transmission of HIV. The others reduce the risk of infection, but cannot be certified as perfectly safe. For those who are going to be sexually active without knowing (not guessing) whether their partner(s) are infected with HIV or some other STD, we can speak only of safe(r) sex—not of perfectly safe sex.

1. *Maintaining lifelong celibacy.*
2. *Remaining in a lifelong monogamous relationship with an uninfected person who is doing the same thing.* Although these first two sexual career paths guarantee safety, they are not followed by the majority of students or other Americans.
3. *Being discerning in one's choice of sex partners.* Get to know another person before engaging in sexual activity. Still, getting to know a person is no guarantee the person is uninfected with HIV. Avoid contact with multiple partners or with people who are likely to have multiple partners.
4. *Being assertive with sex partners.* It is important to communicate concerns about AIDS clearly and assertively with sex partners.
5. *Inspecting one's partner's sex organs.* There are no obvious signs of HIV infection, but people who are infected with HIV are often infected by other sexually transmitted diseases as well. It may be feasible to visually inspect your partner's sex organs for rashes, chancres, blisters, discharges, warts, and lice during foreplay. Consider any disagreeable odor a warning sign.
6. *Using latex condoms.* Condoms protect men from infected vaginal fluids and stop infected semen from entering women. All condoms (including so-called natural condoms made of animal intestines or "skins") act as barriers to sperm, but only latex condoms can prevent transmission of HIV.
7. *Using spermicides.* Spermicides containing the ingredient nonoyxnol-9 kill HIV as well as sperm. Spermicides should be used along with latex condoms, not as a substitute for condoms.
8. *Consulting a physician following suspected exposure to a sexually transmitted disease (STD).* Antibiotics following unprotected sex may guard against bacterial STDs, but they are of no use against viral STDs, such as genital herpes and HIV/AIDS. Consult with a physician before using any medications, including medications you may have stored away in your medicine cabinet.
9. *Seeking regular medical checkups.* Checkups and appropriate laboratory tests enable you to learn about and treat disorders that might have gone unnoticed.
10. *Avoiding sexual activity if there are doubts about safety.* None of the safer sex practices listed guarantees protection. Why not avoid sexual activity when doubts of safety exist?

In this chapter we focused on relationships between stress and health and on the psychological factors involved in health. Psychology has much to offer in the understanding and treatment of physical disorders. Psychological approaches may help in the treatment of such physical disorders as headaches and coronary heart disease. Psychologists also help people reduce the risks of contracting health problems such as cardiovascular disorders, cancer, and AIDS. Emerging fields such as psychoneuroimmunology promise to further enhance our knowledge of the intricate relationships between mind and body.

SUMMING UP

Adjustment Disorders

What are adjustment disorders? Adjustment disorders are maladaptive reactions to identified stressors.

What are their features? Adjustment disorders are characterized by emotional reactions that are greater than normally expected given the circumstances or by evidence of significant impairment in functioning. Impairment usually takes the form of problems at work or school, or in social relationships or activities.

Stress and Illness

How is stress linked to physical illness? Evidence links exposure to stress to weakened immune system functioning, which in turn can increase vulnerability to physical illness. However, because this evidence is correlational, questions of cause and effect remain.

What is the general adaptation syndrome? This is the name given by Hans Selye to the generalized pattern of response of the body to persistent or enduring stress, as characterized by three stages: the alarm reaction, the resistance stage, and the exhaustion stage.

How are life changes related to physical health problems? Again, links are correlational, but evidence shows that people who experience more life stress in the form of life changes and daily hassles are at an increased risk of developing physical health problems.

What psychological factors buffer the effects of stress? These factors include coping styles, self-efficacy expectancies, psychological hardiness, optimism, and social support.

Psychological Factors and Physical Disorders

What roles do psychological factors play in the onset of headaches and their treatment? The most common headache is the muscle-tension headache, which is often stress related. Behavioral methods of relaxation training and biofeedback are of help in treating various types of headaches.

What behavioral or lifestyle factors increase the risk of coronary heart disease? Psychological factors that increase the risk of coronary heart disease include patterns of consumption, leading a sedentary lifestyle, and persistent negative emotions.

What role do psychological factors play in asthma? Psychological factors such as stress, anxiety, and depression may trigger asthma attacks in susceptible individuals.

What role do psychological factors play in the development of cancer and its treatment? Although relationships between stress and risk of cancer remain under study, behavioral risk factors for cancer include dietary practices (espe-

cially high fat intake), heavy alcohol use, smoking, and excessive sun exposure. Psychological interventions help cancer patients cope better with the symptoms of the disease and its treatment.

What roles do psychologists play in the prevention of HIV/AIDS and treatment of people with HIV? Our behavior patterns influence our risk for contracting HIV. Psychologists have become involved in the prevention and treatment of AIDS because AIDS, like cancer, can have devastating psychological effects on victims, their families and friends, and society at large, and because AIDS can be prevented through reducing risky behavior.

Scoring Key for The College Life Stress Inventory. Although we have no national norms by which to compare your score, the test developers obtained an average (mean) score of 1,247 based on a sample of 257 introductory psychology students. About two of three students obtained scores in the range of 806 to 1,688.

Computing your total score helps you gauge how you compare to the students in the original study sample in terms of your overall stress level. Bear in mind, however, that the same level of stress may affect different people differently. Your ability to cope with stress depends on many factors, including your coping skills and the level of social support you have available. If you are experiencing a high level of stress, you may wish to examine the sources of stress in your life. Perhaps you can reduce the level of stress you experience or learn more effective ways of handling the sources of stress you can't avoid.

Scoring Key for The Life Orientation Test. To arrive at your total score for the test, first *reverse* your score on items 3, 8, 9, and 12. That is,

    4 is changed to 0
    3 is changed to 1
    2 remains the same
    1 is changed to 3
    0 is changed to 4

Now add the numbers of items 1, 3, 4, 5, 8, 9, 11, and 12. (Items 2, 6, 7, and 10 are "fillers"; that is, your responses are not scored as part of the test.) Your total score can vary from 0 to 32.

Scheier and Carver (1985) provide the following norms for the test, based on administration to 357 undergraduate men and 267 undergraduate women. The average (mean) score for men was 21.03 (standard deviation = 4.56), and the mean score for women was 21.41 (standard deviation = 5.22). All in all, approximately 2 out of 3 undergraduates obtained scores between 16 and 26. Scores above 26 may be considered quite optimistic, and scores below 16 quite pessimistic. Scores between 16 and 26 are within a broad average range, and higher scores within this range are relatively more optimistic.

KEY TERMS

health psychologist *(p. 141)*
stress *(p. 142)*
stressor *(p. 142)*
adjustment disorder *(p. 142)*
endocrine system *(p. 144)*
hormones *(p. 144)*
immune system *(p. 145)*
general adaptation syndrome (GAS) *(p. 147)*

alarm reaction *(p. 147)*
fight-or-flight reaction *(p. 147)*
resistance stage *(p. 148)*
exhaustion stage *(p. 149)*
acculturative stress *(p. 150)*
emotion-focused coping *(p. 154)*
problem-focused coping *(p. 154)*
self-efficacy expectancies *(p. 154)*
psychological hardiness *(p. 155)*

positive psychology *(p. 156)*
psychosomatic *(p. 159)*
biofeedback training (BFT) *(p. 160)*
cardiovascular disease *(p. 160)*
Type A behavior pattern (TABP) *(p. 161)*

MEDIA TOOLS

A variety of digital and online learning tools are available to enrich your learning experience and help you succeed in the course. These resources include:

- **MyPsychLab,** an online learning system for your course in abnormal psychology that allows you to test your mastery of concepts in the book by using chapter-by-chapter diagnostic tests. Results from the diagnostic tests help you build a customized study plan. To access **MyPsychLab,** visit www. prenhall.com/mypsychlab and follow the instructions on the site.

- **"Speaking Out" Patient Interviews,** a set of video case examples of actual patients you can access on the companion CD-ROM included with the text. Icons in the margins of the chapter highlight the video case examples included on the CD-ROM.

- **Companion Web site,** an online study center that offers computer-scored quizzes you can use to test your knowledge, along with other study tools and links to related sites to enhance your learning of abnormal psychology. To access the companion web site, visit www. prenhall. com/nevid and use the various tabs and links on the site to access these learning resources.

Anxiety Disorders

CHAPTER OUTLINE

**OVERVIEW OF ANXIETY DISORDERS
171–172**

PANIC DISORDER 172–179

Theoretical Perspectives
Treatment Approaches

PHOBIC DISORDERS 179–193

Types of Phobic Disorders
Theoretical Perspectives
Treatment Approaches

**OBSESSIVE–COMPULSIVE DISORDER
194–198**

Theoretical Perspectives
Treatment Approaches

**GENERALIZED ANXIETY DISORDER
198–200**

Theoretical Perspectives
Treatment Approaches

**ACUTE STRESS DISORDER AND
POSTTRAUMATIC STRESS DISORDER
200–204**

Features of Traumatic Stress Disorders
Theoretical Perspectives
Treatment Approaches

**ETHNIC DIFFERENCES IN ANXIETY
DISORDERS 204–205**

SUMMING UP 206–207

"I Felt Like I Was Going to Die Right Then and There"

I never experienced anything like this before. It happened while I was sitting in the car at a traffic light. I felt my heart beating furiously fast, like it was just going to explode. It just happened, for no reason. I started breathing really fast but couldn't get enough air. It was like I was suffocating and the car was closing in around me. I felt like I was going to die right then and there. I was trembling and sweating heavily. I thought I was having a heart attack. I felt this incredible urge to escape, to just get out of the car and get away.

I somehow managed to pull the car over to the side of the road but just sat there waiting for the feelings to pass. I told myself if I was going to die, then I was going to die. I didn't know whether I'd survive long enough to get help. Somehow—I can't say how—it just passed and I sat there a long time, wondering what had just happened to me. Just as suddenly as the panic overcame me, it was gone. My breathing slowed down and my heart stopped thumping in my chest. I was alive. I was not going to die. Not until the next time, anyway.

—*"The Case of Michael," from the Author's Files*

T❏ F❏ People who experience a panic attack often think they are having a heart attack. (p. 173)

T❏ F❏ The same drugs used to treat schizophrenia are also used to control panic attacks. (p. 177)

T❏ F❏ Some people are so fearful of leaving their homes that they are unable to venture outside even to mail a letter. (p. 183)

T❏ F❏ We may be genetically predisposed to acquire fears of objects that posed a danger to ancestral humans. (p. 187)

T❏ F❏ Therapists have used virtual reality to help people overcome phobias. (p. 192)

T❏ F❏ Obsessional thinking helps relieve anxiety. (p. 195)

T❏ F❏ Exposure to combat is the most common trauma linked to posttraumatic stress disorder (PTSD). (p. 203)

WHAT IS IT LIKE TO HAVE A PANIC ATTACK? PEOPLE TEND TO USE THE WORD *PANIC* LOOSELY, AS when they say, "I panicked when I couldn't find my keys." Clients in therapy often speak of having panic attacks, although what they describe often falls in a milder spectrum of anxiety reactions. During a true panic attack, like the one Michael describes, the level of anxiety rises to the point of sheer terror. Unless you have suffered one, it is difficult to appreciate just how intense panic attacks can be. People who suffer them describe them as the most frightening experiences of their lives. Panic attacks are a feature of a severe form of anxiety disorder called *panic disorder.*

There is much to be anxious about—our health, social relationships, examinations, careers, international relations, and the condition of the environment are but a few sources of possible concern. It is normal, even adaptive, to be somewhat anxious about these aspects of life. **Anxiety** is a generalized state of apprehension or foreboding. Anxiety is useful because it prompts us to seek regular medical checkups or motivates us to study for tests. Anxiety is therefore a normal response to threats, but anxiety becomes abnormal when its level is out of proportion to a threat, or when it seems to come out of the blue—that is, when it is not in response to environmental changes. In Michael's case, panic attacks began spontaneously, without any warning or trigger. This kind of maladaptive anxiety reaction, which can cause significant emotional distress or impair the person's ability to function, is labeled an **anxiety disorder.** Anxiety, the common thread that connects the various types of anxiety disorders, can be experienced in different ways, from the intense fear associated with a panic attack to the generalized sense of foreboding or worry we find in generalized anxiety disorder.

anxiety An emotional state characterized by physiological arousal, unpleasant feelings of tension, and a sense of apprehension or foreboding.

anxiety disorder A class of psychological disorders characterized by excessive or maladaptive anxiety reactions.

OVERVIEW OF ANXIETY DISORDERS

Anxiety is characterized by a wide range of symptoms that cut across physical, behavioral, and cognitive domains:

a) *Physical features* may include jumpiness, jitteriness, trembling or shaking, tightness in the pit of the stomach or chest, heavy perspiration, sweaty palms, light-headedness or faintness, dryness in the mouth or throat, shortness of breath, heart pounding or racing, cold fingers or limbs, and upset stomach or nausea, among other physical symptoms.

b) *Behavioral features* may include avoidance behavior, clinging or dependent behavior, and agitated behavior.

c) *Cognitive features* may include worry, a nagging sense of dread or apprehension about the future, preoccupation or keen awareness of bodily sensations, fear of losing control, thinking the same disturbing thoughts over and over, jumbled or confused thoughts, difficulty concentrating or focusing one's thoughts, and thinking that things are getting out of hand.

Although people with anxiety disorders don't necessarily experience all of these features, it is easy to see why anxiety is distressing. The *DSM* recognizes the following specific types of anxiety disorders we discuss in this chapter: panic disorder, phobic disorders, obsessive–compulsive disorder, generalized anxiety disorder, and acute stress disorder and posttraumatic stress disorder. Table 6.1 provides an overview of the anxiety disorders we discuss in this chapter. The anxiety disorders are not mutually exclusive. People frequently meet diagnostic criteria for more than one of them. Moreover, many people with anxiety disorders also have other types of disorders, especially mood disorders.

The anxiety disorders, along with dissociative disorders and somatoform disorders (see Chapter 7), were classified as neuroses throughout most of the 19th century. The term *neurosis* derives from roots meaning "an abnormal or diseased condition of the nervous system." The Scottish physician William Cullen coined the term "neurosis" in the 18th century. As the derivation implies, it was assumed that neurosis had biological origins. It was seen as an affliction of the nervous system.

At the beginning of the 20th century, Cullen's organic assumptions were largely replaced by Sigmund Freud's psychodynamic views. Freud maintained that neurotic behavior stems from the threatened emergence of unacceptable anxiety-evoking ideas into conscious awareness. According to Freud, disorders involving anxiety (as well as the dissociative and somatoform disorders discussed in Chapter 7) represent ways in which the ego attempts to defend itself against anxiety. Freud's views on the origins of these problems united them under the general category of neuroses. Freud's concepts were so widely accepted in the early 1900s that they formed the basis for the classification systems found in the first two editions of the *Diagnostic and Statistical Manual of Mental Disorders (DSM)*.

Since 1980, the *DSM* has not contained a category termed *neuroses*. The *DSM* today is based on similarities in observable behavior and distinctive features rather than on causal assumptions. Many clinicians continue to use the terms *neurosis* and *neurotic* in the manner in which Freud described them, however. Some clinicians use the term "neuroses" to group milder behavioral problems in which people maintain relatively good contact with reality. "Psychoses," such as schizophrenia, are typified by loss of touch with reality and by the appearance of bizarre behavior, beliefs, and hallucinations.

Anxiety is not limited to the diagnostic categories traditionally termed "neuroses," moreover. People with adjustment problems, depression, and psychotic disorders may also encounter problems with anxiety. Let us now consider the major types of anxiety disorders in terms of their features or symptoms, causes, and ways of treating them.

PANIC DISORDER

Panic disorder is characterized by the occurrence of repeated, unexpected *panic attacks*. Panic attacks are intense anxiety reactions accompanied by physical symptoms such as a pounding heart; rapid respiration, shortness of breath, or difficulty breathing; heavy perspiration; and weakness or dizziness (Glass, 2000). There is a stronger bodily component to panic attacks than to other forms of anxiety. The attacks are accompanied by feelings of sheer terror and a sense of imminent danger or impending doom and by an urge to escape the situation. They are usually accompanied by thoughts of losing control, going crazy, or dying.

People who experience panic attacks tend to be keenly aware of changes in their heart rates and may think they are having a heart attack, even though there is nothing

panic disorder A type of anxiety disorder characterized by repeated episodes of intense anxiety or panic.

Panic. Panic attacks have stronger physical components—especially cardiovascular symptoms—than other types of anxiety reactions.

TABLE 6.1 Overview of Anxiety Disorders

TYPE OF DISORDER	Lifetime Prevalence in Population (approx.)	Description	Associated Features
Panic Disorder	a) Overall: 5.1% b) With agoraphobia: 1.1% c) Without agoraphobia: 4%	Repeated panic attacks (episodes of sheer terror accompanied by strong physiological symptoms, thoughts of imminent danger or impending doom, and an urge to escape)	Fears of recurring attacks may prompt avoidance of situations associated with the attacks or in which help might not be available; attacks begin unexpectedly but may become associated with certain cues or specific situations; may be accompanied by agoraphobia, or general avoidance of public situations
Generalized Anxiety Disorder	4%	Persistent anxiety that is not limited to particular situations	Excessive worrying; heightened states of bodily arousal, tenseness, being "on edge"
Specific Phobia	9%	Excessive fears of particular objects or situations	Avoidance of phobic stimulus or situation; examples include acrophobia, claustrophobia, and fears of blood, small animals, or insects
Social Phobia	5%	Excessive fear of social interactions	Characterized by an underlying fear of rejection, humiliation, or embarrassment in social situations
Agoraphobia (without Panic Disorder)	0.17%	Fear and avoidance of open, public places	May occur secondarily to losses of supportive others to death, separation, or divorce
Obsessive–Compulsive Disorder	2% to 3%	Recurrent obsessions (recurrent, intrusive thoughts) and/or compulsions (repetitive behaviors the person feels compelled to perform)	Obsessions generate anxiety that may be at least partially relieved by performance of the compulsive rituals
Acute Stress Disorder	Unknown	Acute maladaptive reaction in the days or weeks following a traumatic event	Similar features as PTSD, but characterized more by dissociation or feelings of detachment from oneself or one's environment—being in a "daze"
Posttraumatic Stress Disorder	8%	Prolonged maladaptive reaction to a traumatic event	Reexperiencing the traumatic event, avoidance of cues or stimuli associated with the trauma; general or emotional numbing, hyperarousal, emotional distress, and impaired functioning

Sources: APA, 2000; Conway et al., 2006; Grant et al., 2005a; Grant et al., 2006b, 2006c; Kessler et al., 1995, 2005a; Ozer & Weiss, 2004.

wrong with their hearts. But because symptoms of panic attacks can mimic those of heart attacks or even severe allergic reactions, a thorough medical evaluation should be performed.

As in the case of Michael, panic attacks began suddenly and spontaneously, without any warning or clear triggering event. The attack builds to a peak of intensity within 10 to 15 minutes (USDHHS, 1999a). Attacks usually last for minutes, but can extend to hours and are associated with a strong urge to escape the situation in which they occur. For the diagnosis of panic disorder to be made, there must be the presence

TRUTH or FICTION

People who experience a panic attack often think they are having a heart attack.

☑ **TRUE.** People experiencing a panic attack may believe they are having a heart attack, even though their hearts are perfectly healthy.

TABLE 6.2

Diagnostic Features of Panic Attacks

A panic attack involves an episode of intense fear or discomfort in which at least four of the following features develop suddenly and reach a peak within 10 minutes:

1. Heart palpitations, pounding heart, tachycardia (rapid heart rate)
2. Sweating
3. Trembling or shaking
4. Shortness of breath or smothering sensations
5. Choking sensations
6. Chest pains or discomfort
7. Feelings of nausea or other signs of abdominal distress
8. Feelings of dizziness, unsteadiness, light-headedness, or faintness
9. Feelings of strangeness or unreality about one's surroundings (derealization) or detachment from oneself (depersonalization)
10. Fear of losing control or going crazy
11. Fear of dying
12. Numbness or tingling sensations
13. Chills or hot flashes

Source: Adapted from the *DSM-IV-TR* (APA, 2000).

agoraphobia Excessive, irrational fear of open or public places.

Agoraphobia. People with agoraphobia fear venturing into open or crowded places. In extreme cases, they may become literally housebound out of fear of venturing away from the security of their home.

of recurrent panic attacks that begin unexpectedly—attacks that are not triggered by specific objects or situations. They seem to come out of the blue. Although the first attacks occur spontaneously or unexpectedly, over time they may become associated with certain situations or cues, such as entering a crowded department store or boarding a train or airplane. The person may associate these situations with panic attacks in the past or may perceive them as difficult to escape from in the event of another attack.

People often describe panic attacks as the worst experiences of their lives. Their coping abilities are overwhelmed. They may feel they must flee. If flight seems useless, they may freeze. There is a tendency to cling to others for help or support. Some people with panic attacks fear going out alone. Recurrent panic attacks may become so difficult to cope with that sufferers become suicidal. In many cases, people who experience panic attacks limit their activities to avoid places in which they fear attacks may occur or they are cut off from their usual supports. Consequently, panic disorder can lead to **agoraphobia**—an excessive fear of being in public places in which escape may be difficult or help unavailable (White et al., 2006). That said, panic disorder *without* accompanying agoraphobia is much more prevalent (lifetime rate of 4%) than panic disorder *with* agoraphobia (lifetime rate of 1.1%) (Grant et al., 2006b).

Table 6.2 lists the diagnostic features of panic attacks. Not all of these features need to be present. Not all panic attacks are signs of panic disorder; about 10% of otherwise healthy people may experience an isolated attack in a given year (USDHHS, 1999a). For a diagnosis of panic disorder to be made, the person must have experienced repeated, unxpected panic attacks, and at least one of the attacks must be followed by one of the following (American Psychiatric Association, 2000):

a) At least a month of persistent fear of subsequent attacks
b) Worry about the implications or consequences of the attack (e.g., fear of losing one's mind or "going crazy" or having a heart attack)
c) Significant change in behavior (e.g., refusing to leave the house or venture into public for fear of having another attack).

According to recent nationally representative survey, 5.1% of the general U.S. population develops panic disorder at some point in their lives (Grant et al., 2006b).

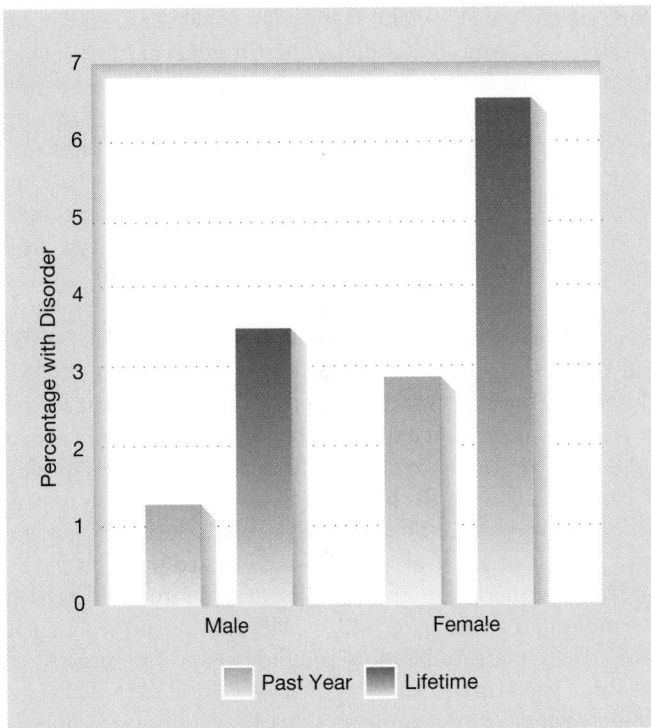

FIGURE 6.1 Prevalence of panic disorder by gender.
Panic disorder affects about two times as many women as men.
Source: Grant et al., 2006b.

Panic disorder usually begins in late adolescence through the mid-30s and occurs about twice as often among women than men (Grant et al., 2006b; Katon, 2006) (see Figure 6.1).

Theoretical Perspectives

The prevailing view of panic disorder reflects a combination of cognitive and biological factors, of misattributions (misperceptions of underlying causes) on the one hand and physiological reactions on the other. Like Michael, who feared that his physical symptoms were signs of a beginning heart attack, panic-prone individuals tend to misattribute minor changes in internal bodily sensations to underlying dire causes. For example, internal sensations such as momentary dizziness, light-headedness, or heart palpitations may be taken as signs of an impending heart attack, loss of control, or "going crazy." Perceiving these bodily sensations as dire threats induces anxiety, which is accompanied by activation of the sympathetic nervous system. Under control of the sympathetic nervous system, the adrenal glands release the stress hormones epinephrine (adrenaline) and norepinephrine (noradrenaline). These hormones intensify physical sensations by inducing accelerated heart rate, rapid breathing, and sweating. These changes in bodily sensations, in turn, become misinterpreted as evidence of an impending panic attack or, worse, as a catastrophe in the making ("My God, I'm having a heart attack!"). Catastrophic misattributions of bodily sensations reinforce perceptions of threat, which intensifies anxiety, leading to more anxiety-related bodily symptoms and yet more catastrophic misinterpretations in a vicious cycle that can quickly spiral into a full-fledged panic attack.

The changes in bodily sensations that trigger a panic attack may result from many factors, such as unrecognized *hyperventilation* (rapid breathing), exertion, changes in temperature, or reactions to certain drugs or medications. Or they may be fleeting, normally occurring changes in bodily states that typically go unnoticed. But in panic-prone individuals, these bodily cues may be misattributed to dire causes, setting in motion a vicious cycle that can bring on a full-fledged attack.

Why are some people prone to develop panic disorder? Here again, a combination of biological and cognitive factors come into play.

Biological Factors Evidence suggests that genetic factors are at work in explaining proneness to panic disorder (Hettema, Neale, & Kendler, 2001; Straub et al., 2002). Bear in mind, however, that genes may create a predisposition or likelihood, not a certainty, that a psychological disorder will develop under certain conditions. Other factors are also involved, including cognitive factors (Casey, Oei, & Newcombe, 2004). For example, people with panic disorder are more likely than other people to misinterpret bodily sensations as signs of impending catastrophe (Clark et al., 1997). Panic-prone people also show greater awareness of, and sensitivity to, their own internal physiological cues, such as heart palpitations (Pauli et al., 1997; Richards, Edgar, & Gibbon, 1996).

The biological underpinnings of panic attacks may involve an unusually sensitive alarm system or fear network in the brain involving the limbic system and frontal lobes that normally respond to cues of threat or danger (Glass, 2000; Katon, 2005). Psychiatrist Donald Klein (1994) proposed a variation of the alarm model called the *suffocation false alarm theory*. He postulated that a defect in the brain's respiratory alarm system triggers a false alarm in response to minor cues of suffocation. In Klein's model, small changes in the level of carbon dioxide in the blood, perhaps resulting from hyperventilation, produce sensations of suffocation. These respiratory sensations trigger the respiratory alarm, leading to a cascade of physical symptoms associated with the classic panic attack: shortness of breath, smothering sensations, dizziness, faintness, increased heart rate or palpitations, trembling, sensations of hot or cold flashes, and feelings of nausea. Klein's intriguing proposal remains to be more fully tested and has received at best mixed support in the research literature to date (e.g., Vickers & McNally, 2005).

We also need to consider the role of neurotransmitters, especially *gamma-aminobutyric acid* (GABA). GABA is an *inhibitory* neurotransmitter, which means that it tones down excess activity in the nervous system and helps quell stress responses. When the action of GABA is inadequate, neurons can fire excessively, possibly bringing about seizures. In less dramatic cases, inadequate action of GABA may heighten states of anxiety. This view of the role of GABA is supported by findings that people with panic disorder show low levels of GABA in some parts of the brain (Goddard et al., 2001). Also, we know that the group of antianxiety drugs called *benzodiazepines*, which include the well-known Valium and Xanax, specifically work on GABA receptors, making them more sensitive and thereby enhancing the calming effects of the neurotransmitter.

Other neurotransmitters, especially serotonin, also appear to be important in regulating anxiety (Weisstaub et al., 2006). Serotonin's role is supported by evidence that antidepressant drugs that specifically target serotonin activity in the brain have therapeutic effects in treating certain anxiety disorders, as we shall discuss later in the chapter.

Further evidence of biological factors in panic disorder comes from studies which compare the responses of people with panic disorder and control subjects to certain biological challenges that produce changes in bodily sensations (e.g., dizziness), such as infusion of the chemical *sodium lactate* or manipulation of carbon dioxide (CO_2) levels in the blood. CO_2 levels may be changed either by intentional hyperventilation (which reduces levels of CO_2 in the blood) or inhalation of carbon dioxide (which increases CO_2 levels). Studies show that panic disorder patients are more likely than nonpatient controls to experience anxious, panicky symptoms in response to these biological challenges (Coryell et al., 2006; Gorman et al., 2001).

Cognitive Factors In referring to the anxiety facing the nation in the wake of the economic depression of the 1930s, President Franklin Roosevelt said in his 1932 inaugural address, "We have nothing to fear but fear itself." These words echo today in research examining the role of fear of fear, or *anxiety sensitivity* (AS), in determining proneness to anxiety disorders, especially panic disorder (Hinton et al., 2006; Zvolensky et al., 2003). AS appears to magnify fear reactions to cues of bodily arousal (Schmidt & Mallott, 2006). People with high levels of AS fear their emotions or associated bodily states of arousal will get out of control, leading to harmful or dire consequences, such as heart attacks (Olatunjia et al., 2005). When they experience bodily signs of anxiety, such as a racing heart or shortness of breath, they may take these symptoms to be signs of an impending catastrophe, which in turn intensifies their anxiety reactions and makes them more vulnerable to suffering a full-blown panic attack. Anxiety sensitivity may also lead to avoidance of situations in which anxiety is experienced, a pattern we often see in people with panic disorder accompanied by agoraphobia (Wilson & Hayward, 2006).

We've learned that ethnicity can play a role in anxiety sensitivity. In the study of high school students, Asian and Hispanic students reported higher levels of anxiety sensitivity on the average than did Caucasian adolescents (Weems et al., 2002). However, anxiety sensitivity was less strongly connected to panic attacks in the Asian and Hispanic groups than the Caucasian group. Other investigators find higher levels of anxiety sensitivity among American Indian and Alaska Native college students than among Caucasian college students (Zvolensky et al., 2001). These findings remind us to be mindful of the need to consider ethnic differences when exploring the roots of abnormal behavior.

We shouldn't overlook the role that cognitive factors may play in determining oversensitivity of panic-prone people to biological challenges, such as manipulation of carbon dioxide levels in the blood. These challenges produce intense physical sensations that panic-prone people may misinterpret as signs of an impending heart attack or loss of control. Perhaps these misinterpretations—not any underlying biological sensitivities per se—are responsible for inducing panic. In support of the cognitive perspective, we have evidence that cognitive-behavioral therapy focused on changing faulty interpretations of bodily sensations can eliminate CO_2–induced panicky symptoms in most panic disorder patients (Schmidt, Trakowski, & Staab, 1997). In another study, having a helper or supportive person nearby during a CO_2 infusion reduced panicky symptoms in panic-prone individuals to the same level as healthy controls (Carter et al., 1995). Having a supportive person available may enable the panic-prone person to appraise the situation as less threatening, which may avert the spiraling of anxiety leading to panic attacks.

The fact that panic attacks often seem to come out of the blue seems to support the belief that the attacks are biologically triggered. However, the cues that set off many panic attacks may be internal, involving changes in bodily sensations, rather than external stimuli. Changes in internal (physical) cues, combined with catastrophic thinking, may lead to a spiraling of anxiety that culminates in a full-blown panic attack.

Treatment Approaches

The most widely used forms of treatment for panic disorder are drug therapy and cognitive-behavioral therapy. Drugs commonly used to treat depression, called *antidepressant drugs,* also have antianxiety and antipanic effects. The term "antidepressants" may be something of a misnomer since these drugs have broader effects than treating just treating depression.

Antidepressants help counter anxiety by normalizing activity of neurotransmitters in the brain. Antidepressants used for treating panic disorder include the tricyclics *imipramine* (brand name Tofranil) and *clomipramine* (brand name Anafranil) and the SSRIs *paroxetine* (brand name Paxil) and *sertraline* (brand name Zoloft) (Hicks et al., 2005; Katon, 2005; Katon et al., 2006). However, some troublesome side effects may occur with these drugs, such as heavy sweating and heart palpitations, leading many patients to prematurely stop using the drugs. The high-potency antianxiety drug *alprazolam* (Xanax), a type of benzodiazepine, is also helpful in treating panic disorder, social phobia, and generalized anxiety disorder.

A potential problem with drug therapy is that patients may attribute clinical improvement to the drugs and not their own resources. Let us also note that psychiatric drugs help control symptoms, but do not produce cures and that relapses are common after patients discontinue medication. Reemergence of panic is likely unless cognitive-behavioral treatment is provided to help panic patients modify their cognitive overreactions to their bodily sensations (Clark, 1986).

Cognitive-behavioral therapists use a variety of techniques in treating panic disorder, including coping skills for handling panic attacks, breathing retraining and relaxation training to reduce states of heightened bodily arousal, and exposure to situations linked to panic attacks and bodily cues associated with panicky symptoms. The therapist may help clients think differently about changes in bodily cues, such as sensations of

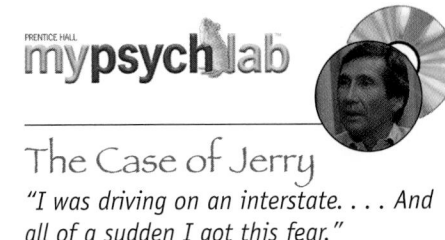

PRENTICE HALL
mypsychlab

The Case of Jerry

"I was driving on an interstate. . . . And all of a sudden I got this fear."

T R U T H or FICTION

The same drugs used to treat schizophrenia are also used to control panic attacks.

☑ **FALSE.** Drugs used to treat schizophrenia are not used to treat panic disorder. However, antidepressants have shown therapeutic benefits in helping to control panic attacks.

TABLE 6.3

Elements of Cognitive-Behavioral Programs for Treatment of Panic Disorder

Self-monitoring	Keeping a log of panic attacks to help determine situational stimuli that might trigger them.
Exposure	A program of gradual exposure to situations in which panic attacks have occurred. During exposure trials, the person engages in self-relaxation and rational self-talk to prevent anxiety from spiraling out of control. In some programs, participants learn to tolerate changes in bodily sensations associated with panic attacks by experiencing these sensations within a controlled setting of the treatment clinic. The person may be spun around in a chair to induce feelings of dizziness, learning in the process that such sensations are not dangerous or signs of imminent harm.
Development of Coping Responses	Developing coping skills to interrupt the vicious cycle in which overreactions to anxiety cues or cardiovascular sensations culminate in panic attacks. Behavioral methods focus on deep, regular breathing and relaxation training. Cognitive methods focus on modifying catastrophic misinterpretations of bodily sensations. Breathing retraining may be used to help the individual avoid hyperventilation during panic attacks.

dizziness or heart palpitations. By recognizing that these cues are fleeting sensations rather than signs of an impending heart attack or other catastrophe, clients learn to cope with them without panicking. Clients learn to replace catastrophizing thoughts and self-statements ("I'm having a heart attack") with calming, rational alternatives ("Calm down. These are panicky feelings that will soon pass."). Panic attack sufferers may also be reassured by having a medical examination to ensure that they are physically healthy and their physical symptoms are not signs of heart disease.

Breathing retraining is a technique that aims at restoring a normal level of carbon dioxide in the blood by having clients breathe slowly and deeply from the abdomen, avoiding the shallow, rapid breathing that leads to breathing off too much carbon dioxide. In some treatment programs, people with panic disorder are encouraged to intentionally induce panicky symptoms in order to learn how to cope with them, such as by hyperventilating in the controlled setting of the treatment clinic or spinning around in a chair (Antony et al., 2006; Katon, 2005). Through firsthand experiences with panicky symptoms, patients learn to calm themselves down and cope with these sensations rather than overreacting. Some commonly used elements in cognitive-behavioral therapy (CBT) for panic disorder are shown in Table 6.3.

Michael, whom we introduced at the beginning of the chapter, was 30 when he suffered his first panic attack. Michael first sought a medical consultation with a cardiologist to rule out any underlying heart condition. He was relieved when he received a clean bill of health. Although the attacks continued for a time, Michael learned to gain a better sense of control over them. Here he describes what the process was like:

The Case of Michael

For me, it came down to not fearing them. Knowing that I was not going to die gave me confidence that I could handle them. When I began to feel an attack coming on, I would practice relaxation and talk myself through the attack. It really seemed to take the steam out of them. At first I was having an attack every week or so, but after a few months, they whittled down to about one a month, and then they were gone completely. Maybe it was how I was coping with them, or maybe they just disappeared as mysteriously as they began. I'm just glad they're gone.

—*From the Author's Files*

A CLOSER LOOK

Coping with a Panic Attack

People who have panic attacks usually feel their hearts pounding such that they are overwhelmed and unable to cope. They typically feel an urge to flee the situation as quickly as possible. If escape is impossible, however, they may become immobilized and "freeze" until the attack dissipates. What can you do if you suffer a panic attack or an intense anxiety reaction? Here are a few coping responses.

- Don't let your breathing get out of hand. Breathe slowly and deeply.
- Try breathing into a paper bag. The carbon dioxide in the bag may help you calm down by restoring a more optimal balance between oxygen and carbon dioxide.
- Talk yourself down: Tell yourself to relax. Tell yourself you're not going to die. Tell yourself no matter how painful the attack is, it is likely to pass soon.

- Find someone to help you through the attack. Telephone someone you know and trust. Talk about anything at all until you regain control.
- Don't fall into the trap of making yourself housebound to avert future attacks.
- If you are uncertain about whether or not sensations such as pain or tightness in the chest have physical causes, seek immediate medical assistance. Even if you suspect your attack may "only" be one of anxiety, it is safer to have a medical evaluation than to diagnose yourself.

You need not suffer recurrent panic attacks and fears about loss of control. If your attacks are persistent or frightening, consult a professional. When in doubt, see a professional.

A number of well-controlled studies attest to the effectiveness of CBT in treating panic disorder (e.g., Addis et al., 2004; Kenardy et al, 2003; Roy-Byrne et al., 2005; Tsao et al., 2002). In one study, for example, nearly 90% of panic patients treated with CBT were free of panic attacks when evaluated at a follow-up assessment (Stuart et al., 2000). Despite the common belief that panic disorder is best treated with psychiatric drugs, CBT produces about as good short-term results and even better long-term results than pharmacological approaches (Barlow et al., 2000; Otto, Pollack, & Maki, 2000).

Why does CBT produce longer-lasting results? The answer seems to be that CBT helps people learn skills they can use once treatment has ended (Glass, 2000). Taking psychiatric drugs can help quell panicky symptoms, but does not help patients develop any new skills they can use once the drugs are withdrawn. In some cases, however, the effectiveness of psychological treatment may be enhanced by the addition of antidepressant drugs. Let us also note that other psychological treatments may prove to have therapeutic benefits. A recent study showed evidence of treatment benefits from a particular form of psychodynamic therapy specifically designed to treat panic symptoms (Milrod et al., 2007).

PHOBIC DISORDERS

The word **phobia** derives from the Greek *phobos,* meaning "fear." The concepts of fear and anxiety are closely related. *Fear* is anxiety experienced in response to a particular threat. A phobia is a fear of an object or situation that is disproportionate to the threat it poses. To experience a sense of gripping fear when your car is about to go out of control is not a phobia, because you truly are really in danger. In phobic disorders, however, the fear exceeds any reasonable appraisal of danger. People with a driving phobia, for example, might become fearful even when they are driving well below the speed limit on a sunny day and an uncrowded highway. Or they might be so afraid that they will not drive or even ride in a car. People with phobic disorders are not out of touch with reality; they generally recognize their fears are excessive or unreasonable.

A curious thing about phobias is that they usually involve fears of the ordinary events in life, such as taking an elevator or driving on a highway, not the extraordinary. Phobias can become disabling when they interfere with such daily tasks as taking buses, planes, or trains; driving; shopping; or even leaving the house.

Different types of phobias usually appear at different ages, as noted in Table 6.4. The ages of onset appear to reflect levels of cognitive development and life experiences. Fears of animals are frequent subjects of children's fantasies, for example. Agoraphobia, in contrast, often follows the development of panic attacks beginning in adulthood.

phobia An excessive, irrational fear.

TABLE 6.4

Typical Age of Onset for Various Phobias

	Mean Age of Onset
Animal phobia	7
Blood phobia	9
Injection phobia	8
Dental phobia	12
Social phobia	15
Claustrophobia	20
Agoraphobia	28

Source: Adapted from Grant et al., 2006c; Öst, 1987, 1992.

Types of Phobic Disorders

The *DSM* recognizes three distinct phobic disorders: *specific phobia*, *social phobia*, and *agoraphobia*.

specific phobia A phobia that is specific to a particular object or situation.

Specific Phobias A **specific phobia** is a persistent, excessive fear of a specific object or situation, such as fear of heights (*acrophobia*), fear of enclosed spaces (*claustrophobia*), or fear of small animals such as mice or snakes and various other "creepy-crawlies." The person experiences high levels of fear and physiological arousal when encountering the phobic object, which prompts strong urges to avoid or escape the situation or avoid the feared stimulus, as in the following case.

Carla Passes the Bar but Not the Courthouse Staircase: A Case of Specific Phobia

Passing the bar exam was a significant milestone in Carla's life, but it left her terrified at the thought of entering the county courthouse. She wasn't afraid of encountering a hostile judge or losing a case, but of climbing the stairs leading to a second floor promenade where the courtrooms were located. Carla, 27, suffered from acrophobia, or fear of heights. "It's funny, you know," Carla told her therapist. "I have no problem flying or looking out the window of a plane at 30,000 feet. But the escalator at the mall throws me into a tailspin. It's just any situation where I could possibly fall, like over the side of a balcony or banister."

People with anxiety disorders try to avoid situations or objects they fear. Carla scouted out the courthouse before she was scheduled to appear. She was relieved to find a service elevator in the rear of the building she could use instead of the stairs. She told her fellow attorneys with whom she was presenting the case that she suffered from a heart condition and couldn't climb stairs. Not suspecting the real problem, one of the attorneys said, "This is great. I never knew this elevator existed. Thanks for finding it."

—From the Author's Files

Three types of phobic disorder. The man in photo directly above has a specific phobia for dogs, a common phobia that may have an evolutionary origin. The young woman in the top-right photo would like to join others but keeps to herself because of social phobia, an intense fear of social criticism and rejection. The woman in the bottom-right photo has a specific phobia for injections. She does not fear the potential pain of the injection; rather, she cannot tolerate the idea of the needle sticking her.

To rise to the level of a diagnosable disorder, the phobia must significantly affect the person's lifestyle or functioning or cause significant distress. You may have a fear of snakes, but unless your fear interferes with your daily life or causes you significant emotional distress, it would not warrant a diagnosis of phobic disorder.

Specific phobias often begin in childhood. Many children develop passing fears of specific objects or situations. Some, however, go on to develop chronic clinically significant phobias (Merckelbach et al., 1996). Claustrophobia seems to develop later than most other specific phobias, with a mean age of onset of 20 years (see Table 6.4).

Specific phobias are among the most common psychological disorders, affecting about 9% of the general population at some point in their lives (Conway et al., 2006). Specific phobias tend to persist for years or decades unless they are treated successfully (USDHHS, 1999a). Women are about twice as likely as men to develop specific phobias. This gender difference may to a certain extent reflect cultural influences that socialize women into more dependent roles in society. Examiners also need to be aware of cultural factors when making diagnostic judgments. Fears of magic or spirits are common in some cultures and should not be considered a sign of a phobic disorder unless the fear is excessive in the culture in which it occurs and leads to significant emotional distress or impaired functioning (APA, 2000).

People with specific phobias will often recognize that their fears are exaggerated or unfounded. But they still are afraid, as in the case of this young woman whose fear of medical injections almost prevented her from getting married.

"This Will Sound Crazy, But . . ."

This will sound crazy, but I wouldn't get married because I couldn't stand the idea of getting the blood test. [Blood tests for syphilis were required at the time.] I finally worked up the courage to ask my doctor if he would put me out with ether or barbiturates— taken by pills—so that I could have the blood test. At first he was incredulous. Then he became sort of sympathetic but said that he couldn't risk putting me under any kind of general anesthesia just to draw some blood. I asked him if he would consider faking the report, but he said that administrative procedures made that impossible.

Then he got me really going. He said that getting tested for marriage was likely to be one of my small life problems. He told me about minor medical problems that could arise and make it necessary for blood to be drawn, or to have an IV in my arm, so his message was I should try to come to grips with my fear. I nearly fainted while he was talking about these things, so he gave it up.

The story has half a happy ending. We finally got married in [a state] where we found out they no longer insisted on blood tests. But if I develop one of those problems the doctor was talking about, or if I need a blood test for some other reason, even if it's life-threatening, I really don't know what I'll do. But maybe if I faint when they're going to [draw blood], I won't know about it anyway, right?

People have me wrong, you know. They think I'm scared of the pain. I don't like pain—I'm not a masochist—but pain has nothing to do with it. You could pinch my arm till I turned black and blue and I'd tolerate it. I wouldn't like it, but I wouldn't start shaking and sweating and faint on you. But even if I didn't feel the needle at all—just the knowledge that it was in me is what I couldn't take.

—From the Author's Files

Social Phobia It is not abnormal to experience some degree of fear in social situations such as dating, attending parties or social gatherings, or giving a talk or presentation to a class or group. Yet people with **social phobia** (also called *social anxiety disorder*) have such an intense fear of social situations that they may avoid them altogether or endure them only with great distress. The underlying problem is an excessive fear of negative evaluations from others. People with social phobia fear doing

social phobia Excessive fear of social interactions or situations.

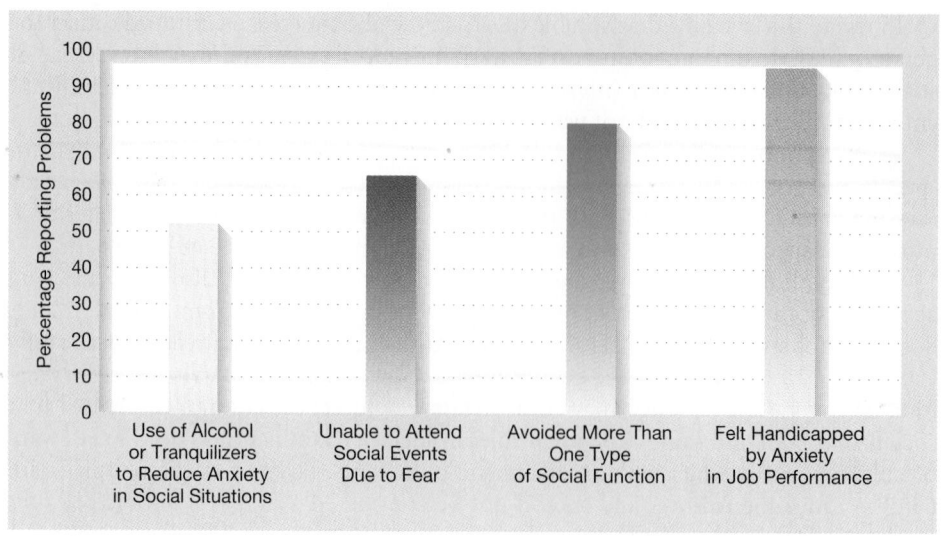

FIGURE 6.2 Percentage of people with social phobia reporting specific difficulties associated with their fears of social situations.
More than 90% of people with social phobia feel handicapped by anxiety in their jobs.
Source: Adapted from Turner & Beidel, 1989.

SOCIAL PHOBIA
(SOCIAL ANXIETY
DISORDER):

The Case of Steve
"I imagine that people are watching me . . . stumble."

or saying something humiliating or embarrassing. They may feel as if a thousand eyes are scrutinizing their every move. They tend to be severely critical of their social skills and become focused on evaluating their own performance in social interactions. Some even experience full-fledged panic attacks in social situations.

Stage fright, speech anxiety, and dating fears are common forms of social phobia. People with social phobias may find excuses for declining social invitations. They may lunch at their desks to avoid socializing with coworkers and avoid situations in which they might meet new people. Or they may find themselves in social situations and attempt a quick escape at the first sign of anxiety. Relief from anxiety negatively reinforces escape behavior, but escape prevents learning how to cope with fear-evoking situations. Leaving the scene while the person still feels anxious only serves to strengthen the link between the social situation and anxiety. Some people with social phobia are unable to order food in a restaurant for fear the server or their companions might make fun of the foods they order or how they pronounce them.

Social phobias can severely impair a person's daily functioning and quality of life. Fear may prevent people from completing educational goals, advancing in their careers, or even holding a job in which they need to interact with others. The greater the number of feared situations, the greater the level of impairment tends to be (Stein, Torgrud, & Walker, 2000). People with social phobias often turn to tranquilizers or try to "medicate" themselves with alcohol when preparing for social interactions (see Figure 6.2). In extreme cases, they may become so fearful of interacting with others that they become essentially housebound.

Findings from nationally representative samples showed that about 5% of U.S. adults were affected by social phobia or social anxiety disorder at some point in their lives (Conway et al., 2006; Grant et al., 2006c). The disorder is more common among women than men, perhaps because of the greater social or cultural pressures placed on young women to please others and earn their approval.

The average age of onset of social phobia is about 15 years (Grant et al., 2006c). Social phobia is strongly associated with a history of childhood shyness (Cox, MacPherson, & Enns, 2005). Consistent with the *diathesis–stress model* (see Chapter 2), shyness may represent a diathesis or predisposition that makes one more vulnerable to develop social phobia in the face of stressful experiences, such as traumatic social encounters (e.g., being embarrassed in front of others). Social phobia tends to be a chronic, persistent disorder, lasting about 16 years on the average (Grant et al., 2006c). Yet despite its early development and the many negative effects it has on the person's social functioning, people with social phobia first receive help at an average age of 27 (Grant et al., 2006c).

Agoraphobia   The word *agoraphobia* is derived from Greek words meaning "fear of the marketplace," which suggests a fear of being out in open, busy areas. People with agoraphobia develop a fear of places and situations from which it might be difficult or embarrassing to escape in the event of panicky symptoms or a full-fledged panic attack or of situations in which help may be unavailable if such problems should occur. People with agoraphobia may fear shopping in crowded stores; walking through crowded streets; crossing a bridge; traveling on a bus, train, or car; eating in restaurants; or even leaving the house. They may structure their lives around avoiding exposure to fearful situations and in some cases become housebound for months or even years, even to the extent of being unable to venture outside to mail a letter. Agoraphobia has the potential of becoming the most incapacitating type of phobia.

Agoraphobia is more common in women than men (Grant et al., 2006b). Frequently it begins in late adolescence or early adulthood. It may occur either with or without accompanying panic disorder. *Panic disorder with agoraphobia* (PDA) affects an estimated 1.1% of adult Americans at some point in their lives (Grant et al., 2006b). The person with PDA may live in fear of recurrent attacks and avoid public places where attacks have occurred or might occur. Because panic attacks can descend from nowhere, some people restrict their activities for fear of making public spectacles of themselves or finding themselves without help. Others venture outside only with a companion. Still others forge ahead despite intense anxiety.

People with agoraphobia who have no history of panic disorder may experience mild panicky symptoms, such as dizziness, that lead them to avoid venturing away from places where they feel safe or secure. They too tend to become dependent on others for support. A recent nationwide survey reported a very low lifetime prevalence of agoraphobia without panic disorder (0.17%, or 17 people in 10,000) (Grant et al., 2006b). The following case of agoraphobia without a history of panic disorder illustrates the dependencies often associated with agoraphobia.

TRUTH or FICTION

Some people are so fearful of leaving their homes that they are unable to venture outside even to mail a letter.

☑ **TRUE.** Some people with agoraphobia become literally housebound and unable to venture outside even to mail a letter.

Helen: A Case of Agoraphobia

Helen, a 59-year-old widow, became increasingly agoraphobic after the death of her husband 3 years earlier. By the time she came for treatment, she was essentially housebound, refusing to leave her home except under the strongest urging of her daughter, Mary, age 32, and only if Mary accompanied her. Her daughter and 36-year-old son, Pete, did her shopping for her and took care of her other needs as best they could. However, the burden of caring for their mother, on top of their other responsibilities, was becoming too great for them to bear. They insisted that Helen begin treatment, and Helen begrudgingly acceded to their demands.

Helen was accompanied to her evaluation session by Mary. She was a frail-looking woman who entered the office clutching Mary's arm and insisted that Mary stay throughout the interview. Helen recounted that she had lost her husband and mother within 3 months of one another; her father had died 20 years earlier. Although she had never experienced a panic attack, she always considered herself an insecure, fearful person. Even so, she had been able to function in meeting the needs of her family until the deaths of her husband and mother left her feeling abandoned and alone. She had now become afraid of "just about everything" and was terrified of being out on her own, lest something bad would happen and she wouldn't be able to cope with it. Even at home, she was fearful that she might lose Mary and Pete. She needed continual reassurance from them that they too wouldn't abandon her.

—From the Author's Files

Theoretical Perspectives

Theoretical approaches to understanding the development of phobias have a long history in psychology, beginning with the psychodynamic perspective.

Psychodynamic Perspectives From the psychodynamic perspective, anxiety is a danger signal that threatening impulses of a sexual or aggressive (murderous or suicidal) nature are nearing the level of awareness. To fend off these threatening impulses, the ego mobilizes its defense mechanisms. In phobias, the Freudian defense mechanism of *projection* comes into play. A phobic reaction is a projection of the person's own threatening impulses onto the phobic object. For instance, a fear of knives or other sharp instruments may represent the projection of one's own destructive impulses onto the phobic object. The phobia serves a useful function. Avoiding contact with sharp instruments prevents these destructive wishes toward the self or others from becoming consciously realized or acted upon. The threatening impulses remain safely repressed. Similarly, people with acrophobia may harbor unconscious wishes to jump that are controlled by avoiding heights. The phobic object or situation symbolizes or represents these unconscious wishes or desires. The person is aware of the phobia, but not of the unconscious impulses it symbolizes.

Learning Perspectives The classic learning perspective on phobias was offered by psychologist O. Hobart Mowrer (1948). Mowrer's **two-factor model** incorporated roles for both classical and operant conditioning in the development of phobias. The fear component of phobia is believed to be acquired through classical conditioning, as previously neutral objects and situations gain the capacity to evoke fear by being paired with noxious or aversive stimuli. A child who is frightened by a barking dog may acquire a phobia for dogs. A child who receives a painful injection may develop a phobia for hypodermic syringes. Consistent with this model, evidence shows that many cases of acrophobia, claustrophobia, and blood and injection phobias involve earlier pairings of the phobic object with aversive experiences (e.g., Kendler et al., 1992a; Merckelbach et al., 1996).

Consider the case of Phyllis, a 32-year-old writer and mother of two sons. Phyllis had not used an elevator in 16 years. Her life revolved around finding ways to avoid appointments and social events on high floors. She had suffered from a fear of elevators since the age of 8, when she had been stuck between floors with her grandmother. In conditioning terms, the unconditioned stimulus was the unpleasant experience of being stuck on the elevator, the conditioned stimulus the elevator itself.

As Mowrer pointed out, the avoidance component of phobias is acquired and maintained by operant conditioning, specifically by *negative reinforcement*. That is, relief from anxiety *negatively reinforces* the avoidance of fearful stimuli, which thus serves to

two-factor model A theoretical model that accounts for the development of phobic reactions on the basis of classical and operant conditioning.

Unconscious defense mechanisms? For psychodynamic theorists, phobias represent the operation of unconscious defense mechanisms such as projection. In their view, a fear of heights may represent the ego's attempt to defend itself against the emergence of threatening self-destructive impulses, such as an impulse to jump from a dangerous height. By avoiding heights, the person can maintain a safe distance from such threatening impulses. Because this process occurs unconsciously, the person may be aware of the phobia, not of the unconscious impulses that it symbolizes.

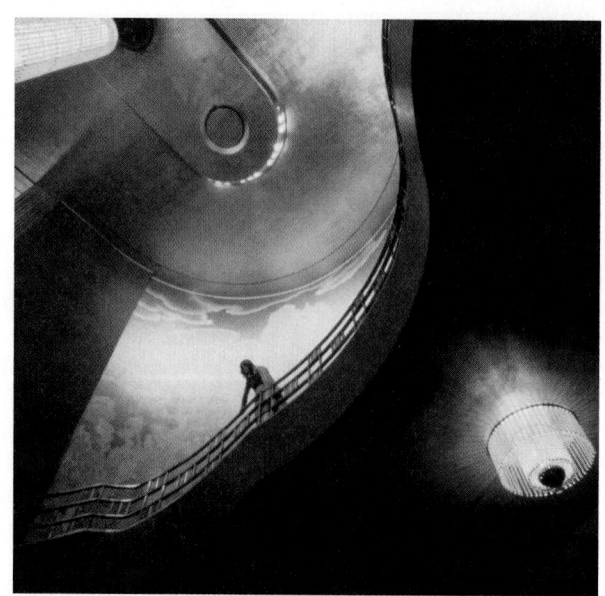

strengthen the avoidance response. Phyllis learned to relieve her anxiety over riding the elevator by opting for the stairs instead. Avoidance works to relieve anxiety, but at a significant cost. By avoiding the phobic stimulus (e.g., elevators), the fear may persist for years, even a lifetime. On the other hand, fear can be weakened and even eliminated by repeated, uneventful encounters with the phobic stimulus. In classical conditioning terms, *extinction* is the weakening of the conditioned response (e.g., the fear component of phobia) when the conditioned stimulus (the phobic object or stimulus) is repeatedly presented in the absence of the unconditioned stimulus (an aversive or painful stimulus).

Conditioning accounts for some, but certainly not all, phobias. In many cases, perhaps even most, people with specific phobias can't recall any aversive experiences with the objects they fear (USDHHS, 1999a). Learning theorists might counter that memories of conditioning experiences may be blurred by the passage of time or that the experience occurred too early in life to be recalled verbally. But contemporary learning theorists highlight the role of another form of learning—*observational learning*—that does not require direct conditioning of fears. In this form of learning, observing parents or significant others model a fearful reaction to a stimulus that can lead to the acquisition of a fearful response. In an illustrative study of 42 people with severe phobias for spiders, observational learning apparently played a more prominent role in fear acquisition than did conditioning (Merckelbach, Arnitz, & de Jong, 1991). Moreover, simply receiving information from others, such as hearing others speak about the dangers posed by a particular stimulus—spiders, for example—can also lead to the development of phobias (Merckelbach et al., 1996).

Learning models help account for the development of phobias (Field, 2006). But why do some people seem to acquire fear responses more readily than others? The biological and cognitive perspectives may offer some insights.

Biological Perspectives Genetic factors can predispose individuals to develop anxiety disorders, including panic disorder and phobic disorders (Coryell et al., 2006; Gelernter et al., 2004; Hamilton et al., 2004; Kendler, 2005). But how might genes affect the likelihood of developing fear responses?

A recent study suggests one possible mechanism. Investigators showed links between variations of a particular gene and different patterns of brain activity when people were exposed to fearful stimuli (Hariri et al., 2002). Individuals with a particular form of the gene showed greater neuronal activity in response to fearful stimuli in the *amygdala*, an almond-shaped structure in the limbic system of the brain. Located below the cerebral cortex, the limbic system consists of a set of interconnected structures involved in such functions as memory formation and processing of emotional responses. The amygdala is a kind of "emotional computer" for evaluating whether stimuli represent a threat or danger (Davidson, 2000; Öhman & Mineka, 2001) (see Figure 6.3).

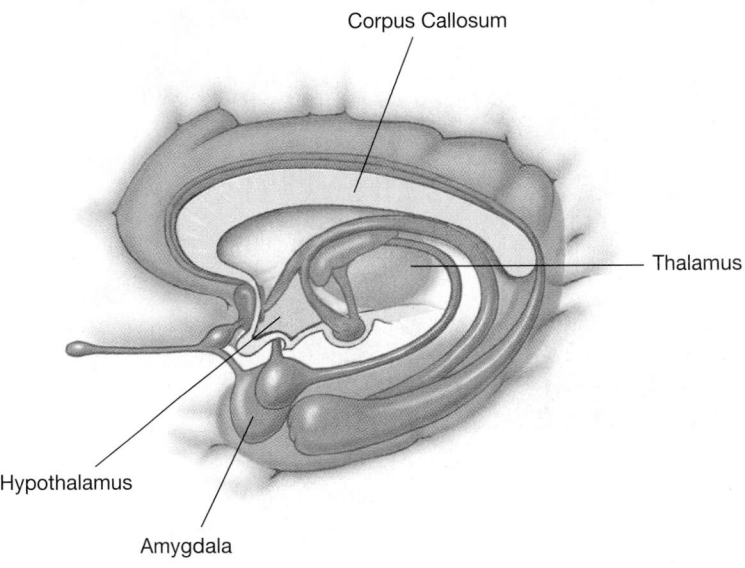

Corpus Callosum

Thalamus

Hypothalamus

Amygdala

FIGURE 6.3 The amygdala and limbic system.
The amygdala is part of the limbic system, a set of interconnected structures in the brain involved in forming memories and processing emotional responses. The limbic system, which also consists of specific parts of the thalamus and hypothalamus and other nearby structures, is located in the forebrain below the cerebral cortex.

FIGURE 6.4 The "all-clear" signal quells fear in rats.

Evidence shows that "all-clear" signals from the prefrontal cortex to the amygdala inhibit fear in rats. This discovery may lead to treatments that can help quell fear reactions in humans.

Source: Milad & Quirk, 2002. Figure reprinted from "Mimicking brain's 'all clear' quells fear in rats," *NIH News Release,* Posted 11/06/2002.

Greater excitability of the amygdala may help explain why some people experience more fear and anxiety in response to threatening environmental cues. Researchers also find increased activation of the amygdala in people with social phobia in response to faces showing expressions of anger or contempt (M. B. Stein et al., 2002). This research suggests that under genetic control, the amygdala may be especially reactive to cues of threat or rejection in people with phobic disorders.

Investigators also find that a part of the prefrontal cortex in the rat's brain sends a kind of "all-clear" signal to the amygdala, quelling fearful reactions (see Figure 6.4) (Milad & Quirk, 2002). As noted in Chapter 2, the prefrontal cortex, which lies in the frontal lobes, is responsible for many higher mental functions, such as thinking, problem solving, reasoning, and decision making. The investigators first conditioned rats to respond with fear to a tone by repeatedly pairing the tone with shock. The rats froze whenever they heard the tone. The investigators then extinguished the fear response by presenting the tone repeatedly without the shock. Following extinction, neurons in the middle of the prefrontal cortex fired up whenever the tone was sounded, sending signals through neural pathways to the amygdala. The more of these neurons that fired, the less the rats froze (NIH, 2002). The discovery that the prefrontal cortex sends a safety signal to the amygdala may eventually lead to new treatments of people with phobias that work by turning on the brain's "all-clear" signal.

Might we be genetically predisposed to acquire phobic responses to some classes of stimuli rather than others? People appear to be more likely have fears of snakes and spiders than rabbits, for example. This belief in a biological predisposition to acquire fears of certain types of objects or situations, called *prepared conditioning,* suggests that evolution favored the survival of human ancestors who were genetically predisposed to develop fears of potentially threatening objects, such as large animals, snakes, spiders, and other "creepy-crawlers;" of heights; of enclosed spaces; and even of strangers. This model may explain why we are more likely to develop fears of spiders or heights than of objects that appeared much later on the evolutionary scene, such as guns or knives, although these later-appearing objects pose more direct threats today to our survival.

Cognitive Perspectives Recent research highlights the importance of cognitive factors in determining proneness to phobias, including factors such as oversensitivity to threatening cues, overpredictions of dangerousness, and self-defeating thoughts and

Snakes and spiders. According to the concept of prepared conditioning, we are genetically predisposed to more readily acquire fears of the types of stimuli that would have threatened the survival of ancestral humans—stimuli such as large animals, snakes, and other creepy-crawlers.

irrational beliefs (e.g., Armfield, 2006; Kamphuis, Emmelkamp, & Krijn, 2002; Wenzel et al., 2005):

1. *Oversensitivity to threatening cues.* People with phobias tend to perceive danger in situations that most people consider safe, such as riding on elevators or driving over bridges. We all possess an internal alarm system that is sensitive to cues of threat. The amygdala in the brain's limbic system plays a key role in this brain's early warning system to threatening cues. This system may have had evolutionary advantages to ancestral humans by increasing the chances of survival in a hostile environment. Early humans who responded quickly to signs of threat, such as a rustling sound in the bush that may have indicated a lurking predator about to pounce, may have been better prepared to take defensive action (to fight or flee) than those with less-sensitive alarm systems.

    The emotion of fear is a key element in this alarm system and may have motivated our early ancestors to take defensive action, which in turn may have helped them survive. People today who have specific phobias and other anxiety disorders may have inherited an acutely sensitive internal alarm that leads them to become overly sensitive to threatening cues. To cope more effectively, they may need to learn to change how they appraise cues that do not objectively pose any real danger.

2. *Overprediction of danger.* Phobic individuals tend to overpredict how much fear or anxiety they will experience in the fearful situation. The person with a snake phobia, for example, may expect to tremble when he or she encounters a snake in a cage. People with dental phobia tend to hold exaggerated expectations of the pain they will experience during dental visits (Marks & De Silva, 1994). Typically speaking, the actual fear or pain experienced during exposure to the phobic stimulus is a good deal less than what people expect. Yet the tendency to expect the worst encourages avoidance of feared situations, which in turn prevents the individual from learning to manage and overcome anxiety.

    Overprediction of dental pain and fear may also lead people to postpone or cancel regular dental visits, which can contribute to more serious dental problems down the road. On the other hand, actual exposure to fearful situations tends to promote more accurate predictions of fear levels (Rachman & Bichard, 1988). A clinical implication is that with repeated exposure, people with anxiety disorders may come to anticipate their responses to fear-inducing stimuli more accurately, leading to reductions of fear expectancies. This in turn may reduce avoidance tendencies.

3. *Self-defeating thoughts and irrational beliefs.* Self-defeating thoughts can heighten and perpetuate anxiety and phobic disorders. When faced with fear-evoking stimuli, the person may think, "I've got to get out of here," or "My heart is going to leap out of my chest." Thoughts like these intensify autonomic arousal, disrupt planning, magnify the aversiveness of stimuli, prompt avoidance behavior, and decrease self-efficacy expectancies concerning one's ability to control the situation. Similarly, people with social phobia may think, "I'll sound stupid," whenever they have an opportunity to speak in front of a group of people (Hoffmann et al., 2004). Such self-defeating thoughts about the self may stifle social participation.

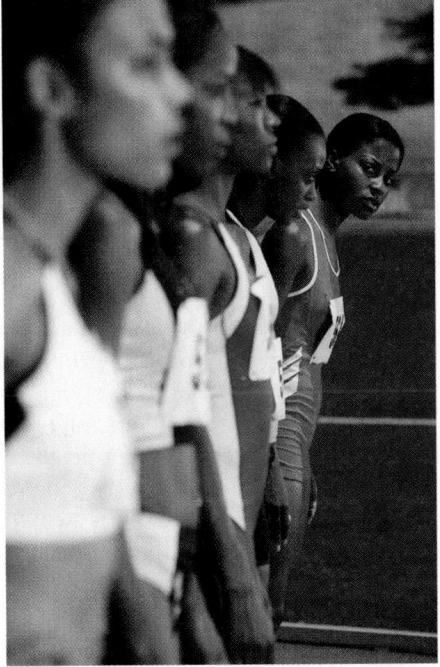

We may be genetically predisposed to acquire fears of objects that posed a danger to ancestral humans.

☑ **TRUE.** Some theorists believe that we are genetically predisposed to acquire certain fears, such as fears of large animals and snakes. The ability to readily acquire these fears may have had survival value to ancestral humans.

How do self-doubts affect our performance? We are likely to feel more anxious in situations in which we doubt our ability to perform competently. Anxiety may hamper our performance, making it more difficult for us to perform successfully. Even accomplished athletes may be seized with anxiety when they are under extreme pressure, as during slumps or when competing in championship games.

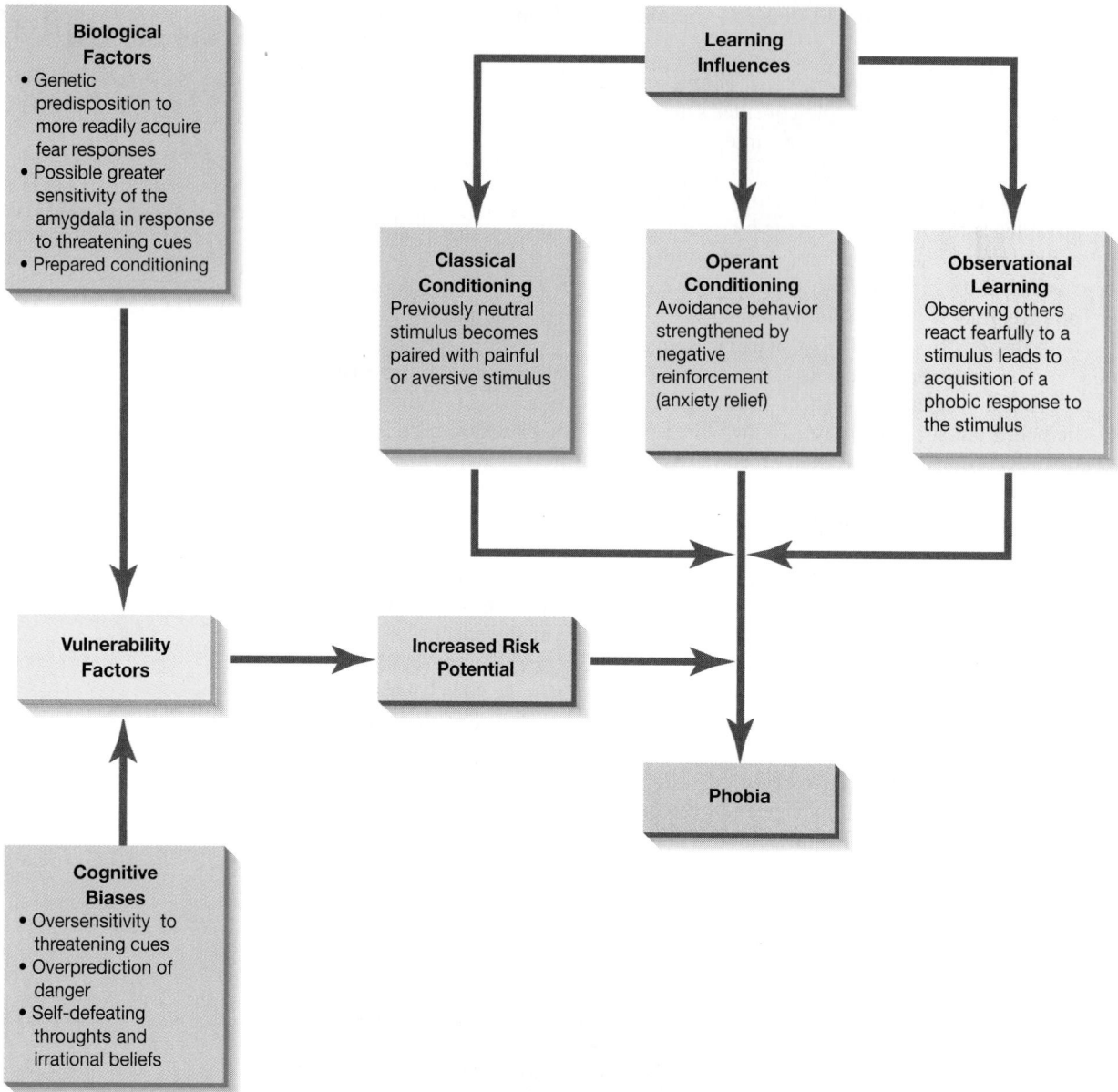

FIGURE 6.5 A multifactorial model of phobia.
Learning influences play a key role in the acquisition of many phobias. But whether these learning experiences lead to the development of phobias may also depend on vulnerability factors, such as a genetic predisposition and cognitive factors.

People with phobias also display more irrational beliefs of the type catalogued by Albert Ellis than do nonfearful people. These irrational beliefs may involve exaggerated needs to be approved of by everyone one meets and to avoid any situation in which negative appraisal from others might arise. Consider these beliefs: "What if I have an anxiety attack in front of other people? They might think I was crazy. I couldn't stand it if they looked at me that way." The results of an early study may hit close to home: College men who believed it was awful (not just unfortunate) to be turned down when requesting a date showed more social anxiety than those who were less likely to catastrophize rejection (Gormally et al., 1981).

Before going on, you may wish to review Figure 6.5, which illustrates a conceptual model for understanding phobias in terms of roles of learning influences and vulnerability factors such as a genetic predisposition and cognitive factors.

Treatment Approaches

Traditional psychoanalysis fosters awareness of how clients' fears symbolize their inner conflicts, so the ego can be freed from expending its energy on repression. Modern psychodynamic therapies also foster clients' awareness of inner sources of conflict. They focus to a greater extent than do traditional approaches on exploring sources of anxiety that arise from current rather than past relationships, however, and they encourage clients to develop more adaptive behaviors. Such therapies are briefer and more directed toward specific problems than traditional psychoanalysis. Although psychodynamic therapies may prove to be helpful in treating anxiety disorders, there is little compelling empirical support documenting their effectiveness (USDHHS, 1999a).

The major contemporary treatment approaches to specific phobias, as also for other anxiety disorders, derive from the learning, cognitive, and biological perspectives.

Learning-Based Approaches   A substantial body of research demonstrates the effectiveness of learning-based approaches in treating a range of anxiety disorders. At the core of these approaches is the effort to help individuals cope more effectively with anxiety-provoking objects and situations. Examples of learning-based approaches include *systematic desensitization, gradual exposure,* and *flooding.*

Adam Learns to Overcome His Fear of Injections

Adam has a phobia for receiving injections. His behavior therapist treats him as he reclines in a comfortable padded chair. In a state of deep muscle relaxation, Adam observes slides projected on a screen. A slide of a nurse holding a needle has just been shown three times, 30 seconds at a time. Each time Adam has shown no anxiety. So now a slightly more discomforting slide is shown: one of the nurse aiming the needle toward someone's bare arm. After 15 seconds, our armchair adventurer notices twinges of discomfort and raises a finger as a signal (speaking might disturb his relaxation). The projector operator turns off the light, and Adam spends two minutes imagining his "safe scene"—lying on a beach beneath the tropical sun. Then the slide is shown again. This time Adam views it for 30 seconds before feeling anxiety.

—From Essentials of Psychology *(6th ed.) by S. A. Rathus, p. 537 Copyright © 2001. Reprinted with permission of Brooks/Cole, an imprint of Wadsworth Group, a division of Thomson Learning.*

Adam is undergoing **systematic desensitization,** a fear-reduction procedure originated by psychiatrist Joseph Wolpe (1958) in the 1950s. Systematic desensitization is a gradual process in which clients learn to handle progressively more disturbing stimuli while they remain relaxed. About 10 to 20 stimuli are arranged in a sequence or hierarchy—called a **fear-stimulus hierarchy**—according to their capacity to evoke anxiety. By using their imagination or by viewing photos, clients are exposed to the items in the hierarchy, gradually imagining themselves approaching the target behavior—be it ability to receive an injection or remain in an enclosed room or elevator—without undue anxiety.

Systematic desensitization is based on the assumption that phobias are learned or conditioned responses that can be unlearned by substituting an incompatible response to anxiety in situations that usually elicit anxiety (Rachman, 2000). Muscle relaxation is generally used as the incompatible response, and followers of Wolpe usually use the method of progressive relaxation (described in Chapter 5) to help clients acquire relaxation skills. For this reason, Adam's therapist is teaching Adam to experience relaxation in the presence of (otherwise) anxiety-evoking slides of needles.

Systematic desensitization creates a set of conditions that can lead to extinction of fear responses. The technique fosters extinction by providing opportunities for repeated exposure to phobic stimuli in imagination without aversive consequences.

systematic desensitization A behavior therapy technique for overcoming phobias by means of exposure to progresively more fearful stimuli (in imagination or by viewing slides) while remaining deeply relaxed.

fear-stimulus hierarchy An ordered series of increasingly fearful stimuli.

gradual exposure In behavior therapy, a method of overcoming fears through a stepwise process of exposure to increasingly fearful stimuli in imagination or in real-life situations.

Gradual exposure uses a stepwise approach in which phobic individuals gradually confront the objects or situations they fear. Repeated exposure to a phobic stimulus in the absence of any aversive event ("nothing bad happening") can lead to extinction, or gradual weakening of the phobic response, even to the point that it is eliminated. Gradual exposure also leads to cognitive changes. The person comes to perceive the previously feared object or situation as harmless and perceives him or herself as capable of handling the situation more effectively.

Exposure therapy can take several forms, including *imaginal exposure* (imagining oneself in the fearful situation) and *in vivo exposure* (actual encounters with phobic stimuli in real life). In vivo exposure may be more effective than imaginal exposure, but both techniques are often used in therapy. The effectiveness of exposure therapy for phobias is well established, making it the treatment of choice for many types of specific phobia (e.g., Choy, Fyer, & Lipsitz, 2006; Hoffman et al., 2006; Kamphuis, Emmelkamp, & Krijn, 2002).

In exposure therapy for social phobia, for example, clients are instructed to enter increasingly stressful social situations (e.g., eating and conversing with coworkers in the cafeteria) and to remain in those situations until the anxiety and urge to escape lessens. The therapist may help guide them during exposure trials, gradually withdrawing direct support so that clients become capable of handling the situations on their own. Exposure therapy for agoraphobia generally follows a stepwise course in which the client is exposed to increasingly fearful stimulus situations, such as walking through congested streets or shopping in department stores. A trusted companion or perhaps the therapist may accompany the person during the exposure trials. The eventual goal is for the person to be able to handle each situation alone and without discomfort or an urge to escape. Gradual exposure was used in the following case of claustrophobia.

Gradual exposure. In gradual exposure, the client is exposed to a fear-stimulus hierarchy in real-life situations, often with a therapist or companion serving in a supportive role. To encourage the person to accomplish the exposure tasks increasingly on his or her own, the therapist or companion gradually withdraws direct support. Gradual exposure is often combined with cognitive techniques that focus on helping the client replace anxiety-producing thoughts and beliefs with calming, rational alternatives.

◇

Kevin Combats His Fear of Elevators: A Case of Claustrophobia

Claustrophobia (fear of enclosed spaces) is not very unusual, although Kevin's case was. Kevin's claustrophobia took the form of a fear of riding on elevators. What made his case so unusual was his occupation: He worked as an elevator mechanic. Kevin spent his work days repairing elevators. Unless it was absolutely necessary, however, Kevin managed to complete the repairs without riding in the elevator. He would climb the stairs to the floor where an elevator was stuck, make repairs, and hit the down button. He would then race downstairs to see that the elevator had operated correctly. When his work required an elevator ride, panic would seize him as the doors closed. Kevin tried to cope by praying for divine intervention to prevent him from passing out before the doors opened.

Kevin related the origin of his phobia to an accident three years earlier in which he had been pinned in his overturned car for nearly an hour. He remembered feelings of helplessness and suffocation. Kevin developed claustrophobia—a fear of situations from which he could not escape, such as flying on an airplane, driving in a tunnel, taking public transportation, and of course, riding in an elevator. Kevin's fear had become so incapacitating that he was seriously considering switching careers, although the change would require considerable financial sacrifice. Each night he lay awake wondering whether he would be able to cope the next day if he were required to test-ride an elevator.

Kevin's therapy involved gradual exposure in which he followed a stepwise program of exposure to increasingly fearful stimuli. A typical anxiety hierarchy for helping people overcome a fear of riding on elevators might include the following steps:

1. Standing outside the elevator
2. Standing in the elevator with the door open
3. Standing in the elevator with the door closed
4. Taking the elevator down one floor
5. Taking the elevator up one floor

6. *Taking the elevator down two floors*
7. *Taking the elevator up two floors*
8. *Taking the elevator down two floors and then up two floors*
9. *Taking the elevator down to the basement*
10. *Taking the elevator up to the highest floor*
11. *Taking the elevator all the way down and then all the way up*

Clients begin at step 1 and do not progress to step 2 until they are able to remain calm on the first. If they become bothered by anxiety, they remove themselves from the situation and regain calmness by practicing muscle relaxation or focusing on soothing mental imagery. The encounter is then repeated as often as necessary to reach and sustain feelings of calmness. They then proceed to the next step, repeating the process.

Kevin was also trained to practice self-relaxation and talk calmly and rationally to himself to help himself remain calm during his exposure trials. Whenever he began to feel even slightly anxious, he would tell himself to calm down and relax. He was able to counter the disruptive belief that he was going to fall apart if he was trapped in an elevator with rational self-statements such as, "Just relax. I may experience some anxiety, but it's nothing that I haven't been through before. In a few moments I'll feel relieved."

Kevin slowly overcame his phobia but still occasionally experienced some anxiety, which he interpreted as a reminder of his former phobia. He did not exaggerate the importance of these feelings. Now and then it dawned on him that an elevator he was servicing had once occasioned fear. One day following his treatment, Kevin was repairing an elevator, which serviced a bank vault 100 feet underground. The experience of moving deeper and deeper underground aroused fear, but Kevin did not panic. He repeated to himself, "It's only a couple of seconds and I'll be out." By the time he took his second trip down, he was much calmer.

—From the Author's Files

Flooding is a form of exposure therapy in which subjects are exposed to *high levels* of fear-inducing stimuli either in imagination or real-life situations. *Why?* The belief is that anxiety represents a conditioned response to a phobic stimulus and should dissipate if the individual remains in the phobic situation for a long enough period of time without harmful consequences. Most individuals with phobias avoid confronting phobic stimuli or beat a hasty retreat at the first opportunity if they cannot avoid them. Consequently, they lack the opportunity to unlearn the fear response. In flooding, the person purposely engages a highly feared situation, such as in the case of a person with social phobia sitting down at a lunch table where people have already gathered and remaining there for a long enough period of time for anxiety to dissipate. Flooding has been used effectively in treating various anxiety disorders, including social phobia and PTSD (Moulds & Nixon, 2006).

flooding A behavior therapy technique for overcoming fears by means of exposure to high levels of fear-inducing stimuli.

Virtual Therapy, the Next Best Thing to Being There In the movie the *Matrix*, the lead character played by Keanu Reeves comes to realize that the world he believes is real is merely an illusion, a complex virtual environment so lifelike that people cannot tell it isn't real. The *Matrix* is science fiction, but the use of virtual reality as a therapeutic tool is science fact.

Virtual reality therapy (VRT) is a behavior therapy technique that uses computer-generated simulated environments as therapeutic tools. By donning a specialized helmet and gloves that are connected to a computer, a person with a fear of heights, for example, can encounter frightening stimuli in this virtual world, such as riding a glass-enclosed elevator to the top floor of an imaginary hotel, peering over a railing on a balcony on the 20th floor, or crossing a virtual Golden Gate Bridge. By a process of exposure to a series of increasingly frightening virtual stimuli, while progressing only when fear at each step diminishes, people can learn to overcome fears in virtual reality in much the same way they would had they followed a program of gradual exposure in real-life situations (Winerman, 2005).

virtual reality therapy A form of exposure therapy involving the presentation of phobic stimuli in a virtual reality environment.

Overcoming fears with virtual reality. Virtual reality technology can be used to help people overcome phobias. Here we see a woman wearing a virtual reality helmet while participating in a fear of flying therapy program.

Virtual therapy has been used successfully in helping people overcome various types of phobias, including fear of heights and fear of flying (Kamphuis, Emmelkamp, & Krijn, 2002; Rothbaum et al., 2002). In one research example, virtual reality was just as effective as real-life exposure in treating fear of flying, with both treatments showing better results than an untreated (waiting list) control condition (Rothbaum et al., 2002). Ninety-two percent of VRT participants succeeded in flying on a commercial airliner in the year following treatment.

Virtual reality therapy offers some advantages over traditional exposure-based treatments. For one thing, it is often difficult or impossible to arrange in real life the types of exposure experiences that can be simulated in virtual reality, such as repeated airplane takeoffs and landings (Yancey, 2000). Virtual therapy also allows for greater control over the stimulus environment, as when the participant controls the intensity and range of stimuli used during virtual exposure sessions (Zimand et al., 2003). Individuals may also be more willing to perform certain fearful tasks in virtual reality than in real life.

In order for virtual therapy to be effective, says psychologist Barbara Rothbaum, who was an early pioneer in the use of the technique, the person must become immersed in the experience and believe at some level it is real and not like watching a videotape. "If the first person had put the helmet on and said, 'This isn't scary,' it wouldn't have worked," Dr. Rothbaum said. "But you get the same physiological changes—the racing heart, the sweat—that you would in the actual place" (cited in Goleman, 1995b, p. C11). Today, with advances in virtual reality technology, the simulated virtual environment is convincing enough to evoke intense anxiety in fearful people (Lubell, 2004).

We have only begun to explore the potential therapeutic uses of this new technology. Therapists are experimenting with virtual therapy to help people overcome many types of fears, such as fear of public speaking and agoraphobia. Therapists are experimenting with virtual bars and crack houses to help substance abusers learn to resist drugs (Lubell, 2004). In other applications, virtual therapy may help clients work through unresolved conflicts with significant figures in their lives by allowing them to confront these "people" in a virtual environment. A family therapist envisions virtual family sessions in which participants can see things from the emotional and physical vantage points of each other member of the family (Steven, 1995).

Self-help "therapy" modules, consisting of compact discs and virtual reality helmets and gloves, may even begin to appear on the shelves of your neighborhood computer software store in the not-too-distant future. With these self-help modules, people may be able in their own living rooms to confront objects or situations they fear, or learn to stop smoking or lose weight, all with the help and guidance of a "virtual therapist."

Cognitive Therapy Through rational emotive behavior therapy, Albert Ellis might have shown people with social phobias how irrational needs for social approval and perfectionism produce unnecessary anxiety in social interactions. Eliminating exaggerated needs for social approval is apparently a key therapeutic factor.

Cognitive therapists seek to identify and correct dysfunctional or distorted beliefs. For example, people with social phobias might think no one at a party will want to talk with them and that they will wind up lonely and isolated for the rest of their lives. Cognitive therapists help clients recognize the logical flaws in their thinking and to view situations rationally. Clients may be asked to gather evidence to test out their beliefs, which may lead them to alter beliefs they find are not grounded in reality. Therapists may encourage clients with social phobias to test their beliefs that they are bound to be ignored, rejected, or ridiculed by others in social gatherings by attending a party, initiating conversations, and monitoring other people's reactions. Therapists may also help clients develop social skills to improve their interpersonal effectiveness and teach them how to handle social rejection, if it should occur, without catastrophizing. A recent clinical trial showed that cognitive therapy outperformed a combined treatment consisting of drug therapy (Prozac) and self-administered exposure training in treating the generalized form of social phobia (Clark et al., 2003).

One example of a cognitive technique is **cognitive restructuring,** a method in which therapists help clients pinpoint self-defeating thoughts and generate rational alternatives they can use to cope with anxiety-provoking situations. For example, Kevin learned to replace self-defeating thoughts with rational alternatives and to practice speaking rationally and calmly to himself during his exposure trials.

Cognitive-behavioral therapy (CBT) is the general term used to apply to therapeutic approaches that combine behavioral and cognitive therapy techniques. CBT practitioners incorporate behavioral techniques, such as exposure, along with techniques drawn from the cognitive therapies of Ellis, Beck, and others. For example, in treating social phobia, therapists often combine exposure treatment with cognitive restructuring techniques that help clients replace anxiety-inducing thoughts with more adjustive thoughts (Mörtberg et al., 2006; Stangier et al., 2003). Recent studies support the effectiveness of CBT in treating both social phobia and claustrophobia (Choy, Fyer, & Lipsitz, 2006; Garcia-Lopez et al., 2006; Schneier, 2006).

Drug Therapy Evidence supports the use of antidepressant drugs, including *sertraline* (brand name Zoloft) and *paroxtine* (trade name Paxil), in treating social phobia (Liebowitz, Gelenberg, & Munjack, 2005; Schneier, 2006). A combination of psychotherapy and drug therapy may be more effective in some cases than either treatment approach alone (Feldman & Rivas-Vazquez, 2003).

Psychiatric drugs may also facilitate progress in exposure therapy for phobias (Munsey, 2006). Investigators used a drug that works on receptors in the amygdala, the part of the brain that first reacts to fearful stimuli (Davis et al., 2005). In this study, people with a fear of heights either received the active drug or a placebo drug before participating in exposure sessions using a virtual reality simulation of height situations. Participants who received the active drug showed greater symptom improvement than did those who received the placebo. Studies like this highlight the potential benefits of combining psychological and biomedical therapies.

cognitive restructuring A cognitive therapy method that involves replacing irrational thoughts with rational alternatives.

obsessive–compulsive disorder (OCD)
A type of anxiety disorder characterized by recurrent obsessions, compulsions, or both.

obsession A recurring thought or image that the individual cannot control.

compulsion A repetitive or ritualistic behavior that the person feels compelled to perform.

OBSESSIVE-COMPULSIVE DISORDER

People with **obsessive–compulsive disorder** (OCD) are troubled by recurrent obsessions, compulsions, or both obsessions and compulsions to the extent that they cause marked distress, occupy more than an hour a day, or significantly interfere with normal routines or occupational or social functioning (APA, 2000). An **obsession** is an intrusive and recurrent thought, idea, or urge that seems beyond the person's ability to control. Obsessions can be potent and persistent enough to interfere with daily life and can engender significant distress and anxiety. They include doubts, impulses, and mental images. One may wonder endlessly whether or not one has locked the doors and shut the windows, for example. One may be obsessed with the impulse to do harm to one's spouse. One can have intrusive mental images or fantasies, such as the recurrent fantasy of a young mother that her children had been run over by traffic on the way home from school.

A **compulsion** is a repetitive behavior (e.g., hand washing or checking door locks) or mental act (e.g., praying, repeating certain words, or counting) the person feels compelled or driven to perform (APA, 2000). Compulsions typically occur in response to obsessional thoughts and are frequent and forceful enough to interfere with daily life or cause significant distress. Table 6.5 shows some relatively common obsessions and compulsions. In the following first-person account, a man describes his obsessive concerns about having caused harm to other people (and even insects) as the result of his actions.

"Tormenting Thoughts and Secret Rituals"

My compulsions are caused by fears of hurting someone through my negligence. It's always the same mental rigmarole. Making sure the doors are latched and the gas jets are off. Making sure I switch off the light with just the right amount of pressure, so I don't cause an electrical problem. Making sure I shift the car's gears cleanly, so I don't damage the machinery. . . .

I fantasize about finding an island in the South Pacific and living alone. That would take the pressure off; if I would harm anyone it would just be me. Yet even if I were alone, I'd still have my worries, because even insects can be a problem. Sometimes when I take the garbage out, I'm afraid that I've stepped on an ant. I stare down to see if there is an ant kicking and writhing in agony. I took a walk last week by a pond, but I couldn't enjoy it because I remembered it was spawning season, and I worried that I might be stepping on the eggs of bass or bluegill.

I realize that other people don't do these things. Mainly, it's that I don't want to go through the guilt of having hurt anything. It's selfish in that sense. I don't care about them as much as I do about not feeling the guilt.

—*From Osborn, 1998*

TABLE 6.5

Examples of Obsessive Thoughts and Compulsive Behaviors

Obsessive Thought Patterns	Compulsive Behavior Patterns
Thinking that one's hands remain dirty despite repeated washing	Rechecking one's work time and time again
Difficulty shaking the thought that a loved one has been hurt or killed	Rechecking the doors or gas jets before leaving home
Repeatedly thinking that one has left the door to the house unlocked	Constantly washing one's hands to keep them clean and germ free
Worrying constantly that the gas jets in the house were not turned off	
Repeatedly thinking that one has done terrible things to loved ones	

Most compulsions fall into two categories: cleaning rituals and checking rituals. Rituals can become the focal point of life. A compulsive hand washer, Corinne, engaged in elaborate hand-washing rituals. She spent 3 to 4 hours daily at the sink and complained, "My hands look like lobster claws." Some people literally take hours checking and rechecking that all the appliances are off before they leave home, and still remain in doubt. In this first-person account of a checking compulsion, a woman with OCD describes the elaborate ritual she insisted her husband perform to complete the simple act of taking out the garbage. The couple lived in an apartment and deposited their garbage in a common dumpster. The ritual was intended to keep the neighbors' germs out of her apartment:

"I" Just Checking

First the water had to be turned on and left that way because if he touched the garbage and then the spigot, the spigot would get contaminated. . . . He'd take the bag down, stand a few feet from the dumpster to be sure not to touch it, and throw the bag in. Then he'd unlock the door, open it, slip his shoes off, come inside, and wash his hands. He used a pump soap so that he could use his clean wrist to pump some in the palm of his hand and not contaminate the dispenser. . . . He went through this procedure twenty times, once for each bag, until they were gone. If contamination occurred at any point during the process, say some brown liquid was on the outside of one of the bags and it got on his shirt, and I saw it, I would not be happy. I'd have to go over the scene again and again in my mind until I could find the way to convince myself that I wasn't really in danger of getting a disease. . . . If I couldn't shake the fear, I'd ask my husband to go through the discarded trash to find the contaminated bag and try to identify the liquid. He was usually pretty against this, so I had to beg. It was all I'd talk about for hours, and I guess in an effort to just shut me up he'd relent.
Source: Colas, 1998

Compulsions often accompany obsessions and may at least partially relieve the anxiety created by obsessional thinking. By washing one's hands 40 or 50 times in a row each time a public doorknob is touched, the compulsive hand washer may experience some relief from the anxiety engendered by the obsessive thought that germs or dirt still linger in the folds of skin. The person may believe that the compulsive ritual will help prevent a dreaded event, such as germ contamination. However, the repetitive nature of the compulsive behavior far exceeds any reasonable steps one can take as a precaution. In effect, the solution (i.e., performing the compulsive ritual) becomes the problem (Salkovskis et al., 2003). The person becomes trapped in a vicious pattern of worrisome intrusive thoughts leading to compulsive rituals. People with OCD generally recognize that their obsessive concerns are excessive or irrational, but feel incapable of stopping them (Belkin, 2005).

Obsessive–compulsive disorder affects between 2% and 3% of the general population at some point in their lives (APA, 2000; Taylor, 1995). A Swedish study found that although most OCD patients eventually showed some improvement, most also continued to have some symptoms of the disorder over the course of their lifetimes (Skoog & Skoog, 1999). The disorder occurs about equally often in men and women (APA, 2000; USDHHS, 1999a). The case example below illustrates a checking compulsion.

Theoretical Perspectives

Within the psychodynamic tradition, obsessions represent leakage of unconscious impulses into consciousness, and compulsions are acts that help keep these impulses repressed. Obsessive thoughts about contamination by dirt or germs may represent the threatened emergence of unconscious infantile wishes to soil oneself and play with feces. The compulsion (in this case, cleanliness rituals) helps keep such wishes at bay. The psychodynamic model remains largely speculative, in large part because of the difficulty (some would say impossibility) of arranging scientific tests to determine the existence of unconscious impulses and conflicts.

TRUTH or FICTION

Obsessional thinking helps relieve anxiety.

☑ **FALSE.** Obsessional thinking actually engenders anxiety. However, performing compulsive rituals may partially reduce the anxiety associated with obsessional thinking, thereby creating a cycle in which obsessional thinking prompts ritualistic behavior, which is reinforced by anxiety relief.

An obsessive thought? One type of obsession involves recurrent, intrusive images of a calamity occurring as the result of one's own carelessness. For example, a person may not be able to shake the image of his or her house catching fire due to an electrical short in an appliance inadvertently left on.

We also have evidence pointing to a genetic contribution in determining vulnerability to the disorder (Leckman & Kim, 2006; Pato, Pato, & Pauls, 2002). We also know that many people with OCD, especially those who developed the disorder during childhood, have a history of tic disorders. Investigators suspect there may be a genetic link between tic disorders and OCD, or at least in cases of OCD that develop in childhood (Eichstedt & Arnold, 2001; Stewart et al., 2007).

Just what genes are involved remains an active area of study, but evidence points to a possible role for a gene that works to tune-down the actions of *glutamate*, a neurotransmitter in the brain that is implicated in OCD (Arnold et al., 2006; Dickel et al., 2006; Leckman & Kim, 2006). Another possibility is that the actions of particular genes affect chemical balances that lead to overarousal of a particular brain circuit, called the *worry circuit*, which normally signals danger and that becomes active during states of worry. In cases of OCD, the brain may be constantly sending messages through this worry circuit that something is wrong and requires immediate attention, leading to obsessional worrisome thoughts and repetitive compulsive behaviors. Parts of the worry circuit incorporate structures in the limbic system, including the amygdala. We noted earlier that the amygdala is a brain structure involved in processing threatening stimuli.

Let us consider other intriguing possibilities regarding the biological underpinnings of OCD. One possibility requiring further study is that the compulsive aspects of OCD result from abnormalities in brain circuits that normally suppress repetitive behaviors. These abnormalities may lead people to feel compelled to perform repetitive behaviors as though they were "stuck in gear" (Leocani et al., 2001).

The frontal lobes in the cerebral cortex regulate brain centers in the lower brain that control bodily movements. Brain imaging studies implicate abnormal patterns of activation of brain circuits involving the frontal lobes in OCD patients (Mataix-Cols et al., 2004; Szeszko et al., 2005). Perhaps a disruption in these neural pathways explains the failure of people with compulsive behavior to inhibit repetitive, ritualistic behaviors. Changes in patterns of frontal lobe activation are also

PRENTICE HALL
mypsychlab
OBSESSIVE/
COMPULSIVE DISORDER:
The Case of Dave
"I knew in my heart of hearts that the water was turned off, but I had to go back and check it anyway."

Jack's "Little Behavioral Quirks:" A Case of Obsesssive–Compulsive Disorder

Jack, a successful chemical engineer, was urged by his wife Mary, a pharmacist, to seek help for "his little behavioral quirks," which she had found increasingly annoying. Jack was a compulsive checker. When they left the apartment, he would insist on returning to check that the lights or gas jets were off, or that the refrigerator doors were shut. Sometimes he would apologize at the elevator and return to the apartment to carry out his rituals. Sometimes the compulsion to check struck him in the garage. He would return to the apartment, leaving Mary fuming. Going on vacation was especially difficult for Jack. The rituals occupied the better part of the morning of their departure. Even then, he remained plagued by doubts.

Mary had also tried to adjust to Jack's nightly routine of bolting out of bed to recheck the doors and windows. Her patience was running thin. Jack realized that his behavior was impairing their relationship as well as causing himself distress. Yet he was reluctant to enter treatment. He gave lip service to wanting to be rid of his compulsive habits, but he also feared that surrendering his compulsions would leave him defenseless against the anxieties they helped ease.

—From the Author's Files

Is this as good as it gets? In the movie, *As Good as It Gets,* Jack Nicholson plays a character with many features of OCD, including such obsessive concerns about cleanliness that he brings his own plastic utensils to dine in restaurants.

found among patients who respond favorably to cognitive-behavioral treatment, which suggests that CBT may directly affect parts of the brain implicated in OCD (Ingram & Siegle, 2001).

Other parts of the brain, including the basal ganglia, may also be involved in OCD (Baxter, 2003). The basal ganglia are involved in controlling body movements, so it is conceivable that a dysfunction in this region might help explain the ritualistic behaviors seen in OCD patients.

Psychological models of OCD emphasize cognitive and learning-based factors. People with OCD tend to be overly focused on their thoughts (Janeck et al., 2003). They can't seem to break the mental loop in which the same intrusive, negative thoughts keep reverberating in their minds. They also tend to exaggerate the risk that unfortunate events will occur (Bouchard, Rhéaume, & Ladouceur, 1999). Because they expect terrible things to happen, people with OCD engage in rituals to prevent them. An accountant who imagines awful consequences for slight mistakes on a client's tax forms may feel compelled to repeatedly check her or his work.

Another cognitive factor linked to the development of OCD is perfectionism, or belief that one must perform flawlessly (Shafran & Mansell, 2001). People who hold perfectionist beliefs exaggerate the consequences of turning in less-than-perfect work and may feel compelled to redo their efforts until every detail is flawless.

From the learning perspective, compulsive behaviors are viewed as operant responses that are negatively reinforced by relief of anxiety engendered by obsessional thoughts. Put simply, "Obsessions give rise to anxiety/distress and compulsions reduce it" (Franklin, Abramowitz et al., 2002, p. 283). If a person obsesses that dirt or foreign bodies contaminate other people's hands, shaking hands or turning a doorknob may evoke powerful anxiety. Compulsive hand washing following exposure to a perceived contaminant provides some degree of relief from anxiety. Reinforcement, whether positive or negative, strengthens the behavior that precedes it. Thus, the person becomes more likely to repeat the compulsive ritual the next time he or she is exposed to anxiety-evoking cues, such as shaking hands or touching doorknobs.

The question remains why some people develop obsessive thoughts whereas others do not. Perhaps people who develop obsessive–compulsive disorder are physiologically sensitized to overreact to minor cues of danger. We can speculate that the brain's worry circuit may be unusually sensitive to cues of danger. Memory impairment may also play a role. Compulsive checkers may have difficulty remembering whether they have completed the task correctly, such as turning off the toaster oven before leaving for the day. Evidence shows that compulsive checkers tend to perform more poorly than others on many types of memory tasks (Woods et al., 2002). The degree to which impaired memory accounts for compulsive checking remains to be seen, however.

OBSESSIVE/
COMPULSIVE DISORDER:

The Case of Ed

"It was . . . awful . . . at that time . . . when the OCD started to show itself."

generalized anxiety disorder (GAD)
A type of anxiety disorder characterized by general feelings of dread and foreboding and heightened states of bodily arousal.

Treatment Approaches

Behavior therapists have achieved impressive results in treating obsessive–compulsive disorder with the technique of *exposure with response prevention* (Abramowitz et al., 2003; Anderson & Rees, 2006; Whittal, Thordarson, & McLean, 2005). The *exposure* component involves having clients intentionally place themselves in situations that evoke obsessive thoughts. For many people, such situations are hard to avoid. Leaving the house, for example, may trigger obsessive thoughts about whether the gas jets are turned off or the windows and doors are locked. Or clients may be instructed to purposely induce obsessive thoughts by leaving the house messy or rubbing their hands in dirt. *Response prevention* is the effort to prevent the compulsive behavior from occurring. Clients who rub their hands in dirt must avoid washing them for a designated period of time. The compulsive lock checker must avoid checking to see that the door was locked.

Through *exposure with response prevention* (ERP), people with OCD learn to tolerate the anxiety triggered by their obsessive thoughts while they are prevented from performing their compulsive rituals. With repeated exposure trials, the anxiety eventually subsides, and the person feels less compelled to perform the accompanying rituals. The underlying principle, yet again, is extinction. When cues that trigger obsessive thoughts and accompanying anxiety are repeatedly presented but the person sees that nothing bad happens, the bonds between these cues and the anxiety response should weaken. Cognitive techniques are often combined with ERP within a cognitive–behavioral treatment program (Anderson & Rees, 2006; Clark, 2004). The cognitive component involves correcting distorted ways of thinking (cognitive distortions), such as tendencies to overestimate the likelihood and severity of feared consequences.

SSRI-type antidepressant drugs also have therapeutic benefits in treating OCD (Saxena et al., 2003). This class of drugs includes *fluoxetine* (Prozac), *paroxetine* (Paxil), and *clomipramine* (Anafranil). These drugs increase the availability in the brain of the neurotransmitter serotonin (Riddle et al., 2001). The effectiveness of these drugs leads researchers to suspect that problems with serotonin transmission play an important role in the development of OCD in some cases (Franklin, Abramowitz et al., 2002). Bear in mind, however, that some people with OCD fail to respond to these drugs, and among those who do respond, many experience only partial relief (Franklin, Abramowitz et al., 2002; Riddle et al., 2001). We should also note that many patients also fail to respond fully to cognitive-behavioral therapy (Fisher & Wells, 2005).

Studies directly comparing cognitive–behavioral therapy (CBT) with drug therapy using SSRI-type antidepressants find that CBT produces at least as much benefit and may lead to more lasting results (Franklin, Rynn et al., 2002; Rauch & Jenike, 1998). As with other forms of anxiety disorder, some people with OCD may benefit from a combination of psychological and pharmacological treatment.

GENERALIZED ANXIETY DISORDER

Generalized anxiety disorder (GAD) is characterized by persistent feelings of anxiety that are not triggered by any specific object, situation, or activity, but rather seems to be what Freud labeled "free floating." The disorder is characterized by persistent feelings of anxiety that are not triggered by any specific object, situation, or activity. The central feature of GAD is worry (Ruscio, Borkovec, & Ruscio, 2001). People with GAD tend to be chronic worriers—even lifelong worriers (Fricchione, 2004). They may worry about many things, including the state of their finances, the well-being of their children, their social relationships, and so on. They tend to worry excessively about everyday, minor things, such as getting stuck in traffic, and about unlikely future events, such as going bankrupt (Dugas, 2002). Children with generalized anxiety tend to worry about academics, athletics, and social aspects of school life.

The emotional distress associated with GAD interferes significantly with the person's daily life. GAD frequently occurs together with other disorders, including depression or other anxiety disorders such as agoraphobia and obsessive–compulsive disorder. Other related features include restlessness; feeling tense, "keyed up," or "on edge"; becoming easily fatigued; having difficulty concentrating or finding one's mind going blank; irritability, muscle tension; and disturbances of sleep, such as difficulty falling asleep, staying asleep, or having restless and unsatisfying sleep (APA, 2000).

GAD tends to be a stable disorder that initially arises in the mid-teens to mid-20s and then typically follows a lifelong course. The lifetime prevalence of GAD in the general U.S. population is estimated to be around 4% overall, but is about twice as common in women as men (Conway et al., 2006). About 2% of adults are affected by GAD in any given year (Grant et al., 2005). In the following case, we find a number of features of generalized anxiety disorder:

◇

"Worrying About Worrying:" A Case of Generalized Anxiety Disorder

Earl was a 52-year-old supervisor at the automobile plant. His hands trembled as he spoke. His cheeks were pale. His face was somewhat boyish, making his hair seem grayed with worry.

He was reasonably successful in his work, although he noted that he was not a "star." His marriage of nearly three decades was in "reasonably good shape," although sexual relations were "less than exciting—I shake so much that it isn't easy to get involved." The mortgage on the house was not a burden and would be paid off within 5 years, but "I don't know what it is; I think about money all the time." The three children were doing well. One was employed, one was in college, and one was in high school. But "With everything going on these days, how can you help worrying about them? I'm up for hours worrying about them."

"But it's the strangest thing," Earl shook his head. "I swear I'll find myself worrying when there's nothing in my head. I don't know how to describe it. It's like I'm worrying first and then there's something in my head to worry about. It's not like I start thinking about this or that and I see it's bad and then I worry. And then the shakes come, and then, of course, I'm worrying about worrying, if you know what I mean. I want to run away; I don't want anyone to see me. You can't direct workers when you're shaking."

Going to work had become a major chore. "I can't stand the noises of the assembly lines. I just feel jumpy all the time. It's like I expect something awful to happen. When it gets bad like that I'll be out of work for a day or two with shakes."

Earl had been worked up "for everything; my doctor took blood, saliva, urine, you name it. He listened to everything, he put things inside me. He had other people look at me. He told me to stay away from coffee and alcohol. Then from tea. Then from chocolate and Coca-Cola, because there's a little bit of caffeine [in them]. He gave me Valium [an antianxiety drug or minor tranquilizer] and I thought I was in heaven for a while. Then it stopped working, and he switched me to something else. Then that stopped working, and he switched me back. Then he said he was 'out of chemical miracles' and I better see a shrink or something. Maybe it was something from my childhood."

—*From the Author's Files*

Theoretical Perspectives

From a psychodynamic perspective, generalized anxiety represents the threatened leakage of unacceptable sexual or aggressive impulses or wishes into consious awareness. The person is aware of the anxiety but not its underlying source. The problem with speculating about unconscious origins of anxiety is that they lie beyond the reach of direct scientific tests. We cannot directly observe or measure unconscious impulses.

From a learning perspective, generalized anxiety is precisely that: generalization of anxiety across many situations. People concerned about broad life themes, such as finances, health, and family matters, are likely to experience apprehension or worry in a variety of settings. Anxiety would thus become connected with almost any environment or situation.

The cognitive perspective on GAD emphasizes the role of exaggerated or distorted thoughts and beliefs, especially beliefs that underlie worry. People with GAD tend to worry about just about everything. They tend to perceive danger at every turn and to anticipate calamitous consequences. Consequently, they feel continually on edge, as their nervous systems respond to the perception of threat or danger with activation of the sympathetic nervous system, leading to increased states of bodily arousal and the accompanying feelings of anxiety.

Although we lack a clear biological model of GAD, it is reasonable to suspect irregularities in neurotransmitter activity. We mentioned earlier that antianxiety drugs such as the benzodiazepines *diazepam* (Valium) and *alprazolam* (Xanax) increase the effects of GABA, an inhibitory neurotransmitter that tones down central nervous system arousal. Similarly, irregularities of the neurotransmitter serotonin are implicated in GAD based on evidence that GAD responds favorably to the antidepressant drug *paroxetine* (Paxil), which specifically targets serotonin (Sheehan & Mao, 2003). Neurotransmitters work on brain structures that regulate emotional states such as anxiety and worry, so it is possible that an overreactivity of these brain structures (the amygdala for example) may also be involved.

Treatment Approaches

The major forms of treatment of generalized anxiety disorder are psychiatric drugs and cognitive-behavioral therapy (Mitte, 2005). Antidepressant drugs, such as *sertraline* (Zoloft) and *paroxetine* (Paxil) can help relieve anxiety symptoms (Allgulander et al., 2004; Liebowitz et al., 2002). Bear in mind, however, that although psychiatric drugs may help relieve anxiety, they do not cure the underlying problem. Once the drugs are discontinued, the symptoms often return.

Cognitive-behavioral therapists use a combination of techniques in treating GAD, including training in relaxation skills; learning to substitute calming, adaptive thoughts for intrusive, worrisome thoughts; and learning skills of decatastrophizing (avoiding tendencies to think the worst). Evidence from controlled studies shows substantial therapeutic benefits of CBT in treating GAD (Dugas et al., 2003; Heimberg, Turk, & Mennin, 2004). The efficacy of CBT is comparable to drug therapy, but with lower dropout rates, which indicates that the psychological treatment is better tolerated by patients (Mitte, 2005). In one illustrative study, the great majority of GAD patients treated with either behavioral or cognitive methods, or the combination of these methods, no longer met diagnostic criteria for the disorder following treatment (Borkovec et al., 2002).

ACUTE STRESS DISORDER AND POSTTRAUMATIC STRESS DISORDER

In adjustment disorders (discussed in Chapter 5), people have difficulty adjusting to life stressors, such as business or marital problems, chronic illness, or bereavement over a loss. Here we focus on two types of anxiety disorders that occur in response to traumatic events: *acute stress disorder* and *posttraumatic stress disorder*.

Acute stress disorder (ASD) is a maladaptive reaction that occurs during the initial month following the traumatic experience. It may occur in the context of combat or exposure to natural or technological disasters. A soldier may come through a horrific battle not remembering important features of the battle and feeling numb and detached from the environment. People who are injured or who nearly lose their lives in a hurricane may walk around "in a fog" for days or weeks afterward; be bothered by intrusive images, flashbacks, and dreams of the disaster; or relive the experience as though it were happening again.

Posttraumatic stress disorder (PTSD) is a prolonged maladaptive reaction to a traumatic experience. In contrast to ASD, PTSD may persist for months, years, or even decades and may not develop until many months or even years after the traumatic event.

Many people with ASD, but certainly not all, go on to develop PTSD (Harvey & Bryant, 2002; Kangas, Henry, & Bryant, 2005). We find both types of stress disorders in soldiers

acute stress disorder (ASD) A traumatic stress reaction occurring during the month following exposure to a traumatic event.

posttraumatic stress disorder (PTSD) A prolonged maladaptive reaction to a traumatic event.

Trauma. Trauma associated with the development of PTSD may involve combat, acts of terrorism, or violent crimes, including crimes such as the mass murders at Virginia Tech. However, the most frequent source of traumas linked to PTSD are serious motor vehicle accidents.

exposed to combat and among rape survivors, victims of motor vehicle and other accidents, and people who have witnessed the destruction of their homes and communities by natural disasters such as floods, earthquakes, or tornadoes, or technological disasters such as railroad or airplane crashes. For Margaret, the trauma involved a horrific truck accident.

◆

"I Thought the World Was Coming to an End:" A Case of PTSD

Margaret was a 54-year-old woman who lived with her husband, Travis, in a small village in the hills to the east of New York's Hudson River. Two winters earlier, in the middle of the night, a fuel truck had skidded down one of the icy inclines that led into the village center. Two blocks away, Margaret was shaken from her bed by the explosion ("I thought the world was coming to an end") when the truck slammed into the general store. The store and the apartments above were immediately engulfed in flames. The fire spread to the church next door. Margaret's first and most enduring visual impression was of shards of red and black that rose into the air in an eerie ballet. On their way down, they bathed the centuries-old tombstones in the church graveyard in hellish light. A dozen people died, mostly those who had lived above and in back of the general store. The old caretaker of the church and the truck driver were lost as well.

Margaret shared the village's loss, took in the temporarily homeless, and did her share of what had to be done. Months later, after the general store had been leveled to a memorial park and the church was on the way toward being restored, Margaret started to feel that life was becoming strange, that the world outside was becoming a little unreal. She began to withdraw from her friends, and scenes of the night of the fire would fill her mind. At night she now and then dreamt the scene. Her physician prescribed a sleeping pill, which she discontinued because "I couldn't wake up out of the dream." Her physician turned to Valium, to help her get through the day. The pills helped for a while, but "I quit them because I needed more and more of the things and you can't take drugs forever, can you?"

Over the next year and a half, Margaret tried her best not to think about the disaster, but the intrusive recollections and the dreams came and went, apparently on their own. By the time Margaret sought help, her sleep had been seriously distressed for nearly two months and the recollections were as vivid as ever.

—From the Author's Files

In ASD and PTSD, the traumatic event involves either actual or threatened death or serious physical injury, or threat to one's own or another's physical safety. The person's response to the threat involves feelings of intense fear, helplessness, or a sense of horror. Children with PTSD may experience the threat differently, such as by showing confused or agitated behavior.

Traumatic events are actually quite common, as more than two-thirds of people suffer a traumatic experience at some point in their lives (Galea, Nandi, & Vlahov, 2005). Yet, perhaps only about 8% of U.S. adults ever develop PTSD and only about 2% are presently affected by the disorder (Kessler et al., 1995; Ozer & Weiss, 2004). Although men more often encounter traumatic experiences, women are about twice as likely to develop PTSD (Tolin & Foa, 2006). Women's greater vulnerability to PTSD may have more to do with such factors as their greater incidence of sexual victimization and with their younger age at the time of the trauma than with their gender itself (Cortina & Kubiak, 2006; Olff et al., 2007). The prevalence of ASD in the general population remains unknown.

Since not all people exposed to significant trauma develop PTSD, investigators have turned to examine factors that increase the risk among trauma survivors. A listing of these risk factors is shown in Table 6.6. Note that some factors relate to the event itself, such as the degree of exposure to the trauma. For example, the more directly one is exposed to the trauma, the greater the likelihood of developing PTSD. Child survivors of Hurricane Katrina who experienced more hurricane exposure events suffered more PTSD symptoms on the average than did those with less direct exposure (Weems et al., 2007). People who were in the buildings that were struck in the 9/11 terrorist attack were nearly twice as likely to develop PTSD as those who personally witnessed the attacks but were outside the buildings at the time (Bonanno et al., 2006).

Although exposure to combat or terrorist attacks may be most strongly linked in the public's mind to PTSD (Pitman, 2006), the traumas most often associated with PTSD are motor vehicle accidents (Blanchard & Hickling, 2004). More than 1% of the population in the United States experience a serious motor vehicle accident resulting in personal injury each year. However, traumas involving violent acts, particularly rape and assault, are more likely to lead to PTSD than are other forms of trauma (Norris et al., 2003). For example, women who are raped are more likely to suffer PTSD than are survivors of natural disasters (Gray & Acierno, 2002). In another study, survivors of terrorist acts had double the rate of PTSD as did survivors of motor vehicle accidents, 38% versus 19%, respectively (Shalev & Freedman, 2005). The prevalence of PTSD among U.S. soldiers who served in the

TABLE 6.6

Factors Predictive of PTSD in Trauma Survivors

Factors Relating to the Event	Factors Relating to the Person or Social Environment
Degree of exposure to trauma	History of childhood sexual abuse
Severity of the trauma	Lack of social support
Exposure to violence	Lack of active coping responses in dealing with the traumatic stressor
	Feelings of shame
	Symptoms of detachment or "dissociation" shortly following the trauma

Sources: Brewin, Andrews, & Valentine, 2000; Koenen et al., 2003; Nishith, Mechanic, & Resick, 2000; Norris et al., 2003; Ozer et al., 2003; Prigerson et al., 2001; Regehr, Hill, & Glancy, 2000; Sharkansky et al., 2000; Silva et al., 2000.

Vietnam War was pegged at about one in five (19%) (Dohrenwend et al., 2006; McNally, 2006).

Other vulnerability factors relate to personal characteristics. For example, people with a history of childhood sexual abuse, those lacking social support, and with limited coping skills are at greater risk of suffering PTSD in response to trauma. Personality factors such as lack of self-efficacy and hostility are also linked to greater risk (Heinrichs et al., 2005). People who experience unusual symptoms during or immediately after the trauma, such as feeling that things are not real or feeling as though one were watching oneself in a movie as the events unfold, stand a greater risk of developing PTSD than do other trauma survivors (Ozer & Weiss, 2004). (These unusual reactions are called *dissociative* experiences; see Chapter 7). On the other hand, finding a sense of purpose or meaning in the traumatic experience, such as believing that the war one is fighting is just, may bolster the person's ability to cope with the stressful circumstances and reduce the risk of PTSD (Sutker et al., 1995).

Although the symptoms of PTSD often diminish within a few months, they may last for years, even decades. Many World War II and Korean War veterans, for example, were found to meet diagnostic criteria for PTSD when evaluated decades after their combat experience ended (Schnurr, Ford, & Friedman, 2000). Veterans with PTSD often have other problem behaviors, including substance abuse, marital problems, and poor work histories.

The *DSM-IV* loosened the criteria for PTSD to include reactions to a wide range of traumatic stressors, including receiving a diagnosis of a life-threatening illness. In breast cancer survivors, PTSD symptoms appear to be more common than would be expected in the general population (Bayer et al., 2002; Cordova et al., 1995). A study of patients who had experienced severe traumatic brain injuries showed a 27% rate of PTSD (Harvey & Bryant 2000).

Counseling veterans with posttraumatic stress disorder. Storefront counseling centers have been established across the country to provide supportive services to combat veterans suffering from PTSD.

TRUTH or FICTION

Exposure to combat is the most common trauma linked to posttraumatic stress disorder (PTSD).

☑ **FALSE.** Motor vehicle accidents are the most common trauma linked to PTSD.

Features of Traumatic Stress Disorders

The symptoms or features of ASD and PTSD include the following:

- *Avoidance behavior.* People may avoid cues or situations associated with the trauma. A rape survivor will avoid traveling to the part of town where she was attacked. A combat veteran will avoid reunions with soldiers or watching movies or feature stories about war or combat.
- *Reexperiencing the trauma.* The trauma may be reexperienced in the form of intrusive memories, recurrent disturbing dreams, even momentary flashbacks of feeling like one is again on the battlefield or being pursued by an attacker.
- *Impaired functioning.* PTSD is often associated with psychological problems such as depression, anxiety, or alcohol or substance abuse that can make it difficult for the person to function effectively in meeting daily responsiblities.
- *Heightened arousal.* PTSD patients may be unusually tense or feel "on edge" or "keyed up" much of the time. They may become hypervigilant (always on guard) and may complain of disturbed sleep, irritability and angry outbursts, and difficulty concentrating. They may show an exaggerated startle response, such as jumping at any sudden noise.
- *Emotional numbing.* People with PTSD may feel "numb" inside and lose the ability to enjoy activities they formerly took pleasure in or to have loving feelings.

The major difference in the features of ASD and PTSD is the emphasis in ASD on *dissociation*—feelings of detachment from oneself or one's environment (Bryant, 2001; Harvey & Bryant, 2002; USDHHS, 1999a). People with acute stress disorder may feel they are "in a daze" or that the world seems like a dreamlike or unreal place. People with ASD may also be unable to perform necessary tasks, such as obtaining needed medical or legal assistance (APA, 2000).

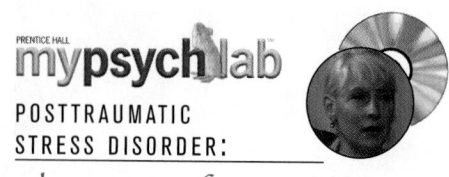

Theoretical Perspectives

The major conceptual understanding of PTSD derives from the behavioral or learning perspective. Within a classical conditioning framework, traumatic experiences are unconditioned stimuli that become paired with neutral (conditioned) stimuli such as the sights, sounds, and even smells associated with the trauma—for example, the battlefield or the neighborhood in which a person has been raped or assaulted. Consequently, anxiety becomes a conditioned response that is elicited by exposure to trauma-related stimuli.

Cues that reactivate negative arousal or anxiety are associated with thoughts, memories, or even dream images of the trauma, with overhearing someone talking about the trauma, or with visiting the scene of the trauma. Through operant conditioning, the person may learn to avoid any contact with trauma-related stimuli. Avoidance behaviors are operant responses that are negatively reinforced by relief from anxiety. Unfortunately, by avoiding trauma-related cues, the person also avoids opportunities to overcome the underlying fear. Extinction (gradual weakening or elimination) of conditioned anxiety can occur only when the person encounters the conditioned stimuli (the cues associated with the trauma) in the absence of any troubling unconditioned stimuli.

Treatment Approaches

Cognitive-behavioral therapy has produced impressive results in treating PTSD (Bradley et al., 2005; McDonagh et al., 2005; Monson et al., 2006; Sijbrandij et al., 2007). The basic treatment component is repeated exposure to cues and emotions associated with the trauma. In CBT, the person gradually reexperiences the anxiety associated with the traumatic event in a safe setting, thereby allowing extinction to take its course. The PTSD patient may be encouraged to repeatedly talk about the traumatic experience, reexperience the emotional aspects of the trauma in imagination, view related slides or films, or visit the scene of the traumatic event. Survivors of serious motor-vehicle crashes who have avoided driving since the accident might be instructed to make short driving trips around the neighborhood (Gray & Acierno, 2002). They might also be asked to repeatedly describe the incident and their emotional reactions they experienced. For combat-related PTSD, exposure-based homework assignments might include visiting war memorials or viewing war movies.

For rape survivors, exposure may take the form of recounting the horrifying ordeal within the supportive therapeutic setting. Evidence also shows that supplementing exposure with cognitive restructuring (challenging and replacing distorted thoughts or beliefs with rational alternatives) can enhance treatment gains (Bryant et al., 2003). Training in stress-management skills, such as self-relaxation, can also improve the client's ability to cope with troubling symptoms of PTSD, such as heightened arousal and the desire to run away from trauma-related stimuli. Training in anger-management skills may also be helpful, especially for combat veterans with PTSD. Treatment with antidepressant drugs, such as *sertraline* (Zoloft) may help reduce the anxiety components of PTSD.

The *Controversies in Abnormal Psychology* feature discusses a controversial form of treatment for PTSD, eye movement desensitization and reprocessing (EMDR). What is EMDR? Does it work? And if it does work, why does it work?

ETHNIC DIFFERENCES IN ANXIETY DISORDERS

Although anxiety disorders have been the subject of extensive study, little attention has been directed toward examining ethnic differences in the prevalence of these disorders. Are anxiety disorders more common in certain racial or ethnic groups? We might think that stressors that African Americans in our society are more likely

CONTROVERSIES IN ABNORMAL PSYCHOLOGY

EMDR: Fad or Find?

A new and controversial technique has emerged in the treatment of PTSD—**eye movement desensitization and reprocessing (EMDR)** treatment (Shapiro, 1995, 2001). In EMDR, the client is asked to form a mental picture of an image associated with the trauma while the therapist rapidly moves a finger back and forth in front of the client's eyes for about 20 to 30 seconds. While holding the image in mind, the client is asked to move his or her eyes to follow the therapist's finger. The client then relates to the therapist the images, feelings, bodily sensations, and thoughts that were experienced during the procedure. The procedure is then repeated until the client becomes desensitized to the emotional impact of this disturbing material.

Evidence from carefully controlled studies supports the therapeutic benefits of using EMDR in treating PTSD (e.g., Power et al., 2002; S. Taylor et al., 2003) and helping people who suffered emotional consequences in the aftermath of the 9/11 attacks in New York City (Silver et al., 2005). The controversy relates to why it works and whether the key feature of the technique—the eye movements themselves—are a necessary factor in explaining its effects.

We lack a compelling theoretical model explaining why rapid eye movements would relieve symptoms of PTSD. Critics contend that the therapeutic effects of EMDR may have nothing to do with eye movements per se (Devilly, 2002; May, 2005). Perhaps EMDR is effective because of nonspecific factors it shares with therapies, such as positive expectancies of improvement or attention from a therapist (Goldstein et al., 2000; Herbert et al., 2000).

Or perhaps EMDR works because it is a form of exposure therapy (Taylor et al., 2003). In this view, the effective ingredient in EMDR is repeated exposure to traumatic mental imagery, not the rapid eye movements. Although the controversy over EMDR is not yet settled, the technique may turn out to be nothing more than a novel way of conducting exposure-based therapy. Meanwhile, we have evidence from another study showing that more traditional exposure therapy worked better and faster in reducing avoidance behaviors than did EMDR, at least among people who completed treatment (Taylor et al., 2003).

As the debate over EMDR continues, it is worthwhile to consider the famous dictum known as *Occam's razor,* or the principle of parsimony. In its most widely used form today, the principle holds that "the simpler the explanation, the better" (Carroll, 2002). In other words, if we can explain the effects of EMDR on the basis of exposure, then there is no need to posit more complex explanations involving effects of eye movements in helping the individual become desensitized to traumatic images.

Critical Thinking

- Why is it important to determine why a treatment works, not simply whether it works?
- What types of research studies would be needed to determine whether rapid eye movements are needed to account for the benefits of EMDR?

to encounter, such as racism and economic hardship, might contribute to a higher rate of anxiety disorders in this population group. On the other hand, an alternative argument is that African Americans, by dint of having to cope with these hardships in early life, develop resiliency in the face of stress that shields them from anxiety disorders. Evidence from large epidemiological surveys lends support to this alternative argument.

According to the best available evidence drawn from a large national survey, the National Comorbidity Survey Replication (NCS-R), showed that African Americans (or non-Hispanic Blacks) and Latinos have lower rates of social anxiety disorder and generalized anxiety disorder than do European Americans (non-Hispanic Whites) (Breslau et al., 2006). We also have evidence from yet another large national survey showing higher lifetime rates of panic disorder (PD) in European Americans than Latinos, African Americans or Asian Americans (Grant et al., 2006b).

Let us also note that anxiety disorders are not unique to our culture. Panic disorder, for example, is known to occur in many countries, perhaps even universally. However, the specific features of panic attacks, such as shortness of breath or fear of dying, may vary from culture to culture. Some culture-bound syndromes have features similar to panic attacks, such as *ataque de nervios* (see Chapter 3).

PTSD is also found in many cultures. High rates of PTSD were found in a southwestern U.S. Indian tribe and among earthquake survivors in China, hurricane survivors in Nicaragua, Khmer refugees who survived the "killing fields" of the 1970s Pol Pot war in Cambodia, tortured Bhutanese refugees, and survivors of the Balkan conflicts of the 1990s. Cultural factors may play a role in determining how people manage and cope with trauma as well as in their vulnerability to traumatic stress reactions and the specific form such a disorder might take.

eye movement desensitization and reprocessing (EMDR) A controversial form of therapy for PTSD that involves eye tracking of a visual target while holding images of the traumatic experience in mind.

TYING IT TOGETHER

Many psychologists believe that the origins of anxiety disorders involve a complex interplay of environmental, physiological, and psychological factors. Complicating matters further is that different causal pathways may be at work in different cases. Given that multiple causes are at work, it is not surprising that different approaches to treating anxiety disorders have emerged.

To illustrate, let us offer a possible causal pathway for panic disorder, which is also diagrammed in the nearby *Concept Map for Abnormal Psychology*. Some people may inherit a genetic predisposition, or diathesis, that makes them overly sensitive to minor changes in bodily sensations. Cognitive factors may also be involved. Physical sensations associated with changing carbon dioxide levels, such as dizziness, tingling, or numbness, may be misconstrued as signs of an impending disaster—suffocation, heart attack, or loss of control. This in turn may lead, like dominoes falling in line, to an anxiety reaction that quickly spirals into a full-fledged panic attack.

Whether this happens may depend on another vulnerability factor, the individual's level of anxiety sensitivity. People with high levels of anxiety sensitivity may be more likely to panic in response to changes in their physical sensations. In some cases, a person's anxiety sensitivity may be so high that panic ensues, even without a genetic predisposition. Over time, panic attacks may come to be triggered by exposure to internal or external cues (conditioned stimuli) that have been associated with panic attacks in the past, such as heart palpitations or boarding a train or elevator. As we saw in the case of Michael at the beginning of the chapter, changes in physical sensations may be misconstrued as signs of an impending heart attack, setting the stage for a cycle of physiological responses and catastrophic thinking that can result in a full-blown panic attack. Helping panic sufferers develop more effective coping skills for handling anxiety symptoms without catastrophizing can help break this vicious cycle.

SUMMING UP

Overview of Anxiety Disorders

What are anxiety disorders? Anxiety, a generalized sense of apprehension or fear, is normal and desirable under some conditions, but it can become abnormal when it is excessive or inappropriate. Disturbed patterns of behavior in which anxiety is the most prominent feature are labeled anxiety disorders.

Panic Disorder

What is panic disorder? Panic disorder is characterized by often immobilizing, repeated panic attacks, which involve intense physical features, notably cardiovascular symptoms, that may be accompanied by sheer terror and fears of losing control, losing one's mind, or dying. Panic attack sufferers often limit their outside activity in fear of recurrent attacks. This can lead to agoraphobia, the fear of venturing into public places.

How is panic disorder understood in contemporary views? The predominant model conceptualizes panic disorder in terms of a combination of biological factors (e.g., genetic proneness, increased sensitivity to bodily cues) and cognitive factors (e.g., catastrophic misinterpretation of bodily sensations, anxiety sensitivity). In this view, panic disorder involves physiological and psychological factors interacting in a vicious cycle that can spiral into a full-blown panic.

What are the major treatment approaches for panic disorder? Cognitive-behavioral treatment of panic disorder incorporates self-monitoring, exposure to panic-related cues, including bodily sensations, and development of coping responses for handling panic attacks without catastrophic misinterpretations of bodily cues. Biomedical approaches incorporate use of antidepressant drugs, which have antianxiety and antipanic effects as well as antidepressant effects.

Phobic Disorders

What are phobic disorders? Phobias are excessive irrational fears of specific objects or situations. Phobias involve a behavioral component, avoidance of the phobic stimulus, in addition to physical and cognitive features. Specific phobias are excessive fears of particular objects or situations, such as mice, spiders, tight places, or heights. Social phobia involves an intense fear of being judged negatively by others. Agoraphobia involves fears of venturing into public places. Agoraphobia may occur with, or in the absence of, panic disorder.

How do phobias develop? Learning theorists explain anxiety disorders through conditioning and observational learning. Mowrer's two-factor model incorporates classical and operant conditioning in the explanation of phobias. Phobias, however, appear to be moderated by cognitive factors, such as oversensitivity to threatening cues, overpredictions of dangerousness, and self-defeating thoughts and irrational beliefs. Genetic factors also appear to increase proneness to development of phobias. Some investigators believe we are genetically predisposed to acquire certain types of phobias that may have had survival value for our prehistoric ancestors.

How are phobias treated? The major forms of treatment are learning-based approaches, such as systematic desensitization and gradual exposure, cognitive therapy, and drug therapy.

Obsessive–Compulsive Disorder

What is obsessive–compulsive disorder? Obsessive–compulsive disorder, or OCD, involves recurrent patterns of obsessions, compulsions, or a combination of the two. Obsessions are nagging, persistent thoughts that create anxiety and seem beyond the person's ability to control. Compulsions are apparently irresistible repetitive urges to perform certain behaviors, such as repeated elaborate washing after using the bathroom.

How is obsessive–compulsive disorder understood? Within the psychodynamic tradition, obsessions represent leakage of unconscious impulses into consciousness, and compulsions are acts that help keep these impulses repressed. Research on biological factors highlights roles for genetics and for brain mechanisms involved in signaling danger and controlling repetitive behaviors. Research evidence shows roles for cognitive factors, such as overfocusing on one's thoughts, exaggerated perceptions of risk of unfortunate events, and perfectionism, Learning theorists view compulsive behaviors as operant responses that are negatively reinforced by relief of anxiety produced by obsessional thinking.

How is obsesssive–compulsive disorder treated? The major contemporary treatment approaches include learning-based models (exposure with response prevention), cognitive therapy (correction of cognitive distortions), and use of SSRI-type antidepressants.

Generalized Anxiety Disorder

What is generalized anxiety disorder? Generalized anxiety disorder is a type of anxiety disorder involving persistent anxiety that seems to be "free floating" or not tied to specific situations.

How is generalized anxiety disorder understood? Psychodynamic theorists view anxiety disorders as attempts by the ego to control the conscious emergence of threatening impulses. Feelings of anxiety are seen as warning signals that threatening impulses are nearing awareness. Learning-based models focus on the generalization of anxiety across stimulus situations. Cognitive theorists seek to account for generalized anxiety in terms of faulty thoughts or beliefs that underlie worry. Biological models focus on irregularities in neurotransmitter functioning in the brain.

How is generalized anxiety disorder treated? The two major treatment approaches are cognitive-behavioral therapy (CBT) and drug therapy (typically *paroxetine*).

Acute Stress Disorder and Posttraumatic Stress Disorder

What are the two types of traumatic stress disorders? The two types of stress disorders are acute stress disorder and posttraumatic stress disorder. Both involve maladaptive reactions to traumatic stress. Acute stress disorder occurs in the days and weeks following exposure to a traumatic event. Posttraumatic stress disorder persists for months or even years or decades after the traumatic experience and may not begin until months or years after the event.

How might we understand the development of PTSD? Learning theory provides a framework for understanding the conditioning of fear to trauma-related stimuli and the role of negative reinforcement in maintaining avoidance behavior. However, other factors come into play in determining vulnerability to PTSD, including degree of exposure to the trauma and personal characteristics, such as a history of childhood sexual abuse and lack of social support.

How is PTSD treated? The major treatment approach is cognitive-behavioral therapy that focuses on repeated exposure to cues associated with the trauma and may be combined with cognitive restructuring and training in stress management and anger management techniques.

Ethnic Differences in Anxiety Disorders

What relationships exist between ethnicity and the prevalence of anxiety disorders? Evidence from nationally representative samples of U.S. adults showed generally lower rates of some anxiety disorders among ethnic minorities.

KEY TERMS

anxiety (*p. 171*)
anxiety disorder (*p. 171*)
panic disorder (*p. 172*)
agoraphobia (*p. 174*)
phobia (*p. 179*)
specific phobia (*p. 180*)
social phobia (*p. 181*)
two-factor model (*p. 184*)

systematic desensitization (*p. 189*)
fear-stimulus hierarchy (*p. 189*)
gradual exposure (*p. 190*)
flooding (*p. 191*)
virtual reality therapy (*p. 191*)
cognitive restructuring (*p. 193*)
obsessive–compulsive disorder (OCD) (*p. 194*)

obsession (*p. 194*)
compulsion (*p. 194*)
generalized anxiety disorder (GAD) (*p. 198*)
acute stress disorder (ASD) (*p. 200*)
posttraumatic stress disorder (PTSD) (*p. 200*)
eye movement desensitization and reprocessing (EMDR) (*p. 205*)

MEDIA TOOLS

A variety of digital and online learning tools are available to enrich your learning experience and help you succeed in the course. These resources include:

- **MyPsychLab,** an online learning system for your course in abnormal psychology that allows you to test your mastery of concepts in the book by using chapter-by-chapter diagnostic tests. Results from the diagnostic tests help you build a customized study plan. To access **MyPsychLab,** visit www. prenhall.com/mypsychlab and follow the instructions on the site.

- **"Speaking Out" Patient Interviews,** a set of video case examples of actual patients you can access on the companion CD-ROM included with the text. Icons in the margins of the chapter highlight the video case examples included on the CD-ROM.

- **Companion Web site,** an online study center that offers computer-scored quizzes you can use to test your knowledge, along with other study tools and links to related sites to enhance your learning of abnormal psychology. To access the companion web site, visit www. prenhall. com/nevid and use the various tabs and links on the site to access these learning resources.

Anxiety Disorders

are characterized by

Maladaptive behavior patterns involving different forms of anxiety

and include such types as

• Panic Disorder
• Phobic Disorders
• Generalized Anxiety Disorder
• Obsessive-Compulsive Disorder
• Acute Stress Disorder
• Posttraumatic Stress Disorder

and may be explained by

MODEL SPOTLIGHT

Multiple factors interacting in complex ways, as represented in this model of panic disorder:

and may be treated by

• Cognitive-behavioral therapy to develop more adaptive thoughts and behaviors
• Psychodynamic therapy to gain insight into underlying psychological issues or conflicts
• Humanistic therapy to enhance self-awareness and acceptance of genuine feelings and needs
• Drug therapy to control anxiety symptoms

Cognitive-Biological Model of Panic Disorder

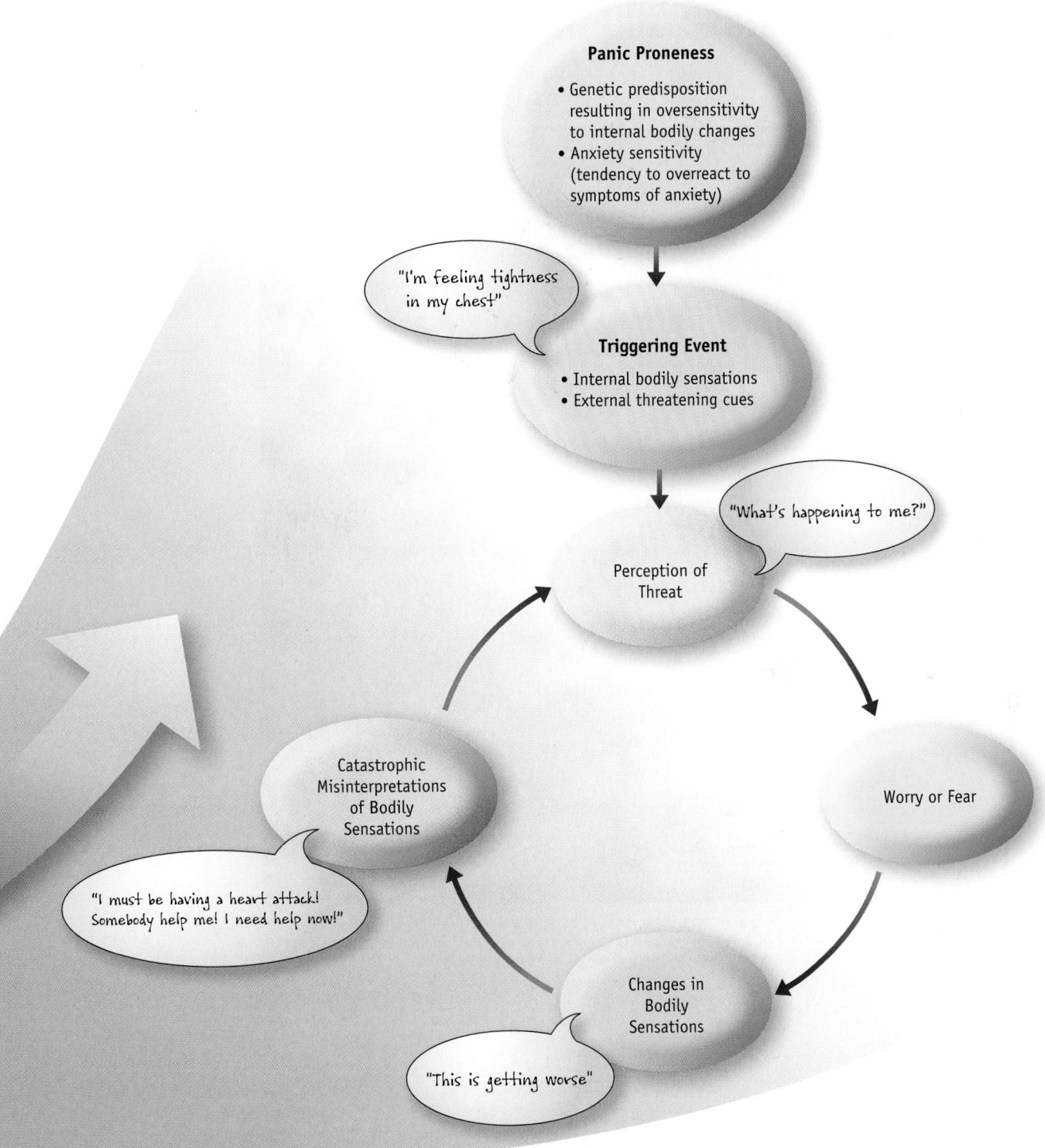

In panic-prone people, perceptions of threat from internal or external cues lead to feelings of worry or fear, which are accompanied by changes in bodily sensations (for example, heart racing or palpitations). Exaggerated, catastrophic interpretations of these sensations intensify perceptions of threat, which further heightens the perception of threat, resulting in yet more anxiety, more changes in bodily sensations, and so on in a vicious cycle that can culminate in a full-blown panic attack. Anxiety sensitivity increases the likelihood that people will overreact to bodily cues or symptoms of anxiety. Panic attacks may prompt avoidance of situations in which attacks have occurred or in which help might not be available.

Source: Adapted from Clark, 1986, and other sources.

Dissociative and Somatoform Disorders

Jean Metzinger (1883–1956), "Woman, frontal and profile". 1917. Musee National d'Art Moderne. Centre National d'Art et de Culture. Georges Pompidou. Reunion des Musees Nationaux/Art Resource, NY. ©2009 Artist Rights Society (ARS), NY.

CHAPTER OUTLINE

DISSOCIATIVE DISORDERS 212–227

Dissociative Identity Disorder
Dissociative Amnesia
Dissociative Fugue
Depersonalization Disorder
Culture-Bound Dissociative Syndromes
Theoretical Perspectives
Treatment of Dissociative Disorders

SOMATOFORM DISORDERS 227–241

Conversion Disorder
Hypochondriasis
Body Dysmorphic Disorder
Pain Disorder
Somatization Disorder

Koro and Dhat Syndromes: Far Eastern
  Somatoform Disorders?
Theoretical Perspectives
Treatment of Somatoform Disorders

SUMMING UP 241–242

"I" "We Share a Single Body"

Elaina is a licensed clinical therapist. Connie is a nurse. Sydney is a delightful little girl who likes to collect bugs in an old mayonnaise jar. Lynn is shy and has trouble saying her l's, and Heather—Heather is a teenager trying hard to be grown-up. We are many different people, but we have one very important thing in common: We share a single body. . . .

We have dozens of different people living inside us, each with our own memories, talents, dreams, and fears. Some of us "come out" to work or play or cook or sleep. Some of us only watch from inside. Some of us are still lost in the past, a tortured past full of incest and abuse. And there are many who were so damaged by this past and who have fled so deep inside, we fear we may never reach them. . . .

Many of our Alter personalities were born of abuse. Some came because they were needed, others came to protect.

Leah came whenever she heard our father say, "Come lay awhile with me." If she came, none of our other Alters would have to do those things he wanted. She could do them for us, and protect us from that part of our childhood.

Source: From "Quiet Storm," a pseudonym used by a woman who claims to have several personalities residing within herself.

TRUTH or FICTION

T☐ F☐ The term *split personality* refers to schizophrenia. (p. 214)

T☐ F☐ People who present with multiple personalities generally show two or perhaps three alternate personalities. (p. 215)

T☐ F☐ Very few of us have episodes in which we feel strangely detached from our own bodies or thought processes. (p. 221)

T☐ F☐ Most people who show multiple personalities do not report any history of physical or sexual abuse during childhood. (p. 224)

T☐ F☐ Some people show up repeatedly at hospital emergency rooms, feigning illness and seeking treatment for no apparent reason. (p. 230)

T☐ F☐ Some people who have lost their ability to see or move their legs become strangely indifferent toward their physical condition. (p. 232)

T☐ F☐ In China in the 1980s, more than 2,000 people fell prey to the belief that their genitals were shrinking and retracting into their bodies. (p. 236)

T☐ F☐ The term *hysteria* derives from the Greek word for *testicle*. (p. 237)

THIS IS A FIRST-HAND DESCRIPTION OF A PERSONALITY SO FRACTURED BECAUSE OF SEVERE childhood abuse that it splinters into many different pieces. Some of the pieces bear memories of the abuse, whereas others go about their business unaware of the pain and trauma. Now imagine that these separate parts develop their own unique characteristics. Imagine too that these alter personalities become so compartmentalized that they don't know of each other's existence. Even the core personality may not know of the existence of the others.

This is a description of *dissociative identity disorder*, known popularly as "multiple personality," perhaps the most perplexing and intriguing of all psychological disorders. The diagnosis is officially recognized in the *DSM* system, although it remains controversial, with many professionals doubting its existence or ascribing it to a form of role-playing. Dissociative identity disorder is classified as a type of *dissociative disorder*, a grouping of psychological disorders characterized by changes or disturbances in the functions of self—identity, memory, or consciousness—that make the personality whole.

Normally speaking, we know who we are. We may not be certain of ourselves in an existential, philosophical sense, but we know our names, where we live, and what we do for a living. We also tend to remember the salient events of our lives. We may not recall every detail, and we may confuse what we had for dinner on Tuesday with what we had on Monday, but we generally know what we have been doing for the past days, weeks, and years. Normally speaking, there is a unity to consciousness that gives rise to a sense of self. We perceive ourselves as progressing through space and time. In people with dissociative disorders, one or more of these aspects of daily living is disturbed—sometimes bizarrely so.

In this chapter we explore the dissociative disorders as well as another class of puzzling disorders, the *somatoform disorders*. People with somatoform disorders have physical complaints that defy any medical explanation and so are believed to involve underlying psychological conflicts or issues. People with these disorders may report blindness or numbness, although no organic basis can be detected. In other cases, people with somatoform disorders may hold exaggerated beliefs about the seriousness of their physical symptoms, such as taking them to be signs of life-threatening illnesses despite medical reassurances to the contrary.

In early versions of the *DSM*, dissociative and somatoform disorders were classified with the anxiety disorders under the general category of "neurosis." This grouping was based on the psychodynamic model, which holds that dissociative and somatoform disorders, as well as the anxiety disorders discussed in Chapter 6, involve maladaptive ways of managing anxiety. In the anxiety disorders, the appearance of disturbing levels of anxiety is expressed directly in behavior, such as in a phobic reaction to an object or situation. In contrast, the role of anxiety in the dissociative and somatoform disorders is inferred rather than expressed overtly in behavior. Persons with dissociative disorders manifest psychological problems, such as loss of memory or changes in identity, that, according to the psychodynamic model, keep the underlying sources of anxiety out of awareness, such as conflicts over sexual or aggressive impulses. Likewise, people with some somatoform disorders often show a strange indifference to physical problems, such as loss of vision, that would greatly concern most of us. Here, too, it was theorized that the "symptoms" mask unconscious sources of anxiety. Some theorists interpret indifference to symptoms to mean that those symptoms have an underlying benefit; that is, they help prevent anxiety from intruding into consciousness.

The *DSM* now separates the anxiety disorders from the other categories of neuroses—the dissociative and somatoform disorders—with which they were historically linked. Yet many practitioners continue to use the broad conceptualization of neuroses as a useful framework for classifying the anxiety, dissociative, and somatoform disorders.

DISSOCIATIVE DISORDERS

dissociative disorder A disorder characterized by disruption, or dissociation, of identity, memory, or consciousness.

The major **dissociative disorders** include *dissociative identity disorder, dissociative amnesia, dissociative fugue,* and *depersonalization disorder*. In each case, there is a disruption or dissociation ("splitting off") of the functions of identity, memory, or consciousness that normally make us whole. Table 7.1 presents an overview of the dissociative disorders discussed in the text.

Dissociative Identity Disorder

The Ohio State campus dwelled in terror as four college women were seized, coerced to cash checks or get money from automatic teller machines, then raped. A cryptic phone call led to the capture of Billy Milligan, a 23-year-old drifter who had been dishonorably discharged from the Navy.

◆

Not the Boy Next Door

Billy wasn't quite the boy next door. He tried twice to commit suicide while he was awaiting trial, so his lawyers requested a psychiatric evaluation. The psychologists and psychiatrists who examined Billy deduced that ten personalities dwelled inside of him. Eight were male and two were female. Billy's personality had been fractured by a brutal childhood. The personalities displayed diverse facial expressions, memories, and vocal patterns. They performed in dissimilar ways on personality and intelligence tests.

Arthur, a sensible but phlegmatic personality, conversed with a British accent. Danny, 14, was a painter of still lifes. Christopher, 13, was normal enough, but somewhat anxious. A 3-year-old English girl went by the name of Christine. Tommy, a 16-year-old, was an antisocial personality and escape artist. It was Tommy who had enlisted in the Navy. Allen was an 18-year-old con artist. Allen also smoked. Adelena was a 19-year-old introverted lesbian. It was she who had committed the rapes. It was probably David who had made the mysterious phone call. David was an anxious 9-year-old who wore the anguish of early childhood trauma on his sleeve. After his second suicide attempt, Billy had been placed in a straitjacket. When the guards checked his cell, however, he was sleeping with the straitjacket as a pillow. Tommy later explained that he was responsible for Billy's escape.

The defense argued that Billy was afflicted with multiple personality disorder. Several alternate personalities resided within him. The alternate personalities knew about Billy, but Billy was unaware of them. Billy, the core or dominant personality, had learned as a child that he could sleep as a way of avoiding the sexual and physical abuse of his father. A psychiatrist claimed that Billy had likewise been "asleep"—in a sort of "psychological coma"—when the crimes were committed. Therefore, Billy should be judged innocent by reason of insanity.

Billy was decreed not guilty by reason of insanity. He was committed to a mental institution. In the institution, 14 additional personalities emerged. Thirteen were rebellious and labeled "undesirables" by Arthur. The fourteenth was the "Teacher," who was competent and supposedly represented the integration of all the other personalities. Billy was released six years later.

—*Adapted from Keyes, 1982*

Table 7.1 Overview of Dissociative Disorders

TYPE OF DISORDER	Lifetime Prevalence in Population (approx.)	Description	Associated Features
Dissociative Identity Disorder	Unknown	Emergence of two or more distinct personalities	• Alternates may vie for control • May represent a psychological defense against severe childhood abuse or trauma
Dissociative Amnesia	Unknown	Inability to recall important personal material that cannot be accounted for by medical causes	• Information lost to memory is usually of traumatic or stressful experiences • Subtypes include localized amnesia, selective amnesia, and generalized amnesia
Dissociative Fugue	0.2% (2 people in 1,000)	Amnesia "on the run"; the person travels to a new location and is unable to remember personal information or reports a past filled with false information not recognized as false	• Person may be confused about his or her personal identity or assumes a new identity • Person may start a new family or business
Depersonalization Disorder	Unknown	Episodes of feeling detached from one's self or one's body or having a sense of unreality about one's surroundings (derealization)	• Person may feel as if he or she were living in a dream or acting like a robot • Episodes of depersonalization are persistent or recurrent and cause significant distress

Source: APA, 2000.

The Three Faces of Eve. In the classic film *The Three Faces of Eve*, a timid housewife, Eve White (left) harbors two alter personalities: Eve Black (middle), a libidinous and antisocial personality, and Jane (right), an integrated personality who can accept her sexual and aggressive urges but still engage in socially appropriate behavior. In the film, the three personalities are successfully integrated. In real life, however, the person depicted in the film reportedly split into 22 personalities later on.

dissociative identity disorder A dissociative disorder in which a person has two or more distinct, or alter, personalities.

Billy was diagnosed with multiple personality disorder, which is now called **dissociative identity disorder.** In dissociative identity disorder, two or more personalities—each with well-defined traits and memories—"occupy" one person. They may or may not be aware of one another. In some isolated cases, alternate personalities (also called *alter personalities*) may even show different EEG records, allergic reactions, responses to medication, and even different eyeglass prescriptions (Birnbaum, Martin, & Thomann, 1996; S. D. Miller et al., 1991; S. D. Miller & Triggiano, 1991). Or one personality may be color blind, whereas others are not (Braun, 1986). These findings are based on isolated case reports; if they stand up to further scientific scrutiny, they would offer a remarkable illustration of the diversity of physiological patterns that are possible within the same person.

Dissociative identity disorder, which is often called "multiple personality" or "split personality" by laypeople, should not be confused with schizophrenia. Schizophrenia (which comes from roots that mean "split brain") occurs much more commonly than multiple personality and involves the "splitting" of cognition, affect, and behavior. In a person with schizophrenia, there may be little agreement between thoughts and emotions, or between perceptions of reality and what is truly happening. The person with schizophrenia may become giddy when told of disturbing events or may experience hallucinations or delusions (see Chapter 12). In people with multiple personality, the personality apparently divides into two or more personalities, but each of them usually shows more integrated functioning on cognitive, affective, and behavioral levels than is true of people with schizophrenia.

Celebrated cases of multiple personality have been depicted in the popular media. One became the subject of the 1950s film *The Three Faces of Eve*. In the film, Eve White is a timid housewife who harbors two other personalities: Eve Black, a sexually provocative, antisocial personality, and Jane, a balanced, developing personality who could balance her sexual needs with the demands of social acceptability. The three faces eventually merged into one—Jane, providing a "happy ending." The real-life Eve, whose name was Chris Sizemore, failed to maintain this integrated personality. Her personality reportedly split into 22 subsequent personalities. A second well-known case is that of Sybil. Sybil was played by Sally Field in the film of the same name and reportedly had 16 personalities.

Features In some cases, the host (main) personality is unaware of the existence of the other identities, whereas the other identities are aware of the existence of the host (Dorahy, 2001). In other cases, the different personalities are completely unaware of one another. Sometimes two personalities vie for control of the person. Sometimes there is one dominant or core personality and several subordinate personalities. Some of the more common alter personalities include children of various ages, adolescents of the opposite gender, prostitutes, and gay males and lesbians. Some of the personalities may show psychotic symptoms—a break with reality expressed in the form of hallucinations and delusional thinking.

All in all, the clusters of alter personalities serve as a microcosm of conflicting urges and cultural themes. Themes of sexual ambivalence (sexual openness vs. restrictiveness) and shifting sexual orientations are particularly common. It is as if conflicting internal impulses cannot coexist or achieve dominance. As a result, each is expressed as the cardinal or steering trait of an alternate personality. The clinician can sometimes elicit alternate personalities by inviting them to make themselves known, as in asking, "Is there another part of you that wants to say something to me?" The following case illustrates the emergence of an alternate personality.

PRENTICE HALL
mypsych lab
DISSOCIATIVE IDENTITY:
The Three Faces
of Eve
"Let us hear the various personalities speak . . ."

Harriet Emerges: A Case of Dissociative Identity Disorder

[Margaret explained that] she often "heard a voice telling her to say things and do things." It was, she said, "a terrible voice" that sometimes threatened to "take over completely." When it was finally suggested to [Margaret] that she let the voice "take over," she closed her eyes, clenched her fists, and grimaced for a few moments during which she was out of contact with those around her. Suddenly she opened her eyes and one was in the presence of another person. Her name, she said, was "Harriet." Whereas Margaret had been paralyzed, and complained of fatigue, headache and backache, Harriet felt well, and she at once proceeded to walk unaided around the interviewing room. She spoke scornfully of Margaret's religiousness, her invalidism, and her puritanical life, professing that she herself liked to drink and "go partying" but that Margaret was always going to church and reading the Bible. "But," she said impishly and proudly, "I make her miserable—I make her say and do things she doesn't want to." At length, at the interviewer's suggestion, Harriet reluctantly agreed to "bring Margaret back," and after more grimacing and fist clenching, Margaret reappeared, paralyzed, complaining of her headache and backache, and completely amnesiac for the brief period of Harriet's release from prison.

—From Nemiah, 1978, pp. 179–180

Like Billy Milligan, Chris Sizemore, and Margaret, the dominant personality is often unaware of the existence of the alter personalities. The alter personalities may also lack any memory of the events experienced by other alters (Huntjens et al., 2005). It thus seems that unconscious processes control the underlying mechanism that results in dissociation, or splitting off of awareness. There may even be "interpersonality rivalry" in which one personality aspires to do away with another, usually in ignorance of the fact that murdering an alternate would result in the death of all.

Although women constitute the majority of cases of multiple personality, the proportion of males diagnosed with the disorder has been on the rise (Goff & Summs, 1993). Women with the disorder tend to have more alternate identities, averaging 15 or more, than do men, who average about 8 alter identities (APA, 2000). The reasons for this difference remain unknown.

The diagnostic features of dissociative identity disorder are listed in Table 7.2.

Controversies Although multiple personality is generally considered rare, the very existence of the disorder continues to arouse debate. Many professionals express profound doubts about the diagnosis (Pope et al., 1999).

TRUTH or FICTION

People who present with multiple personalities generally show two or perhaps three alternate personalities.

☑ **FALSE.** Men with the disorder typically show about 8 alternate personalities, where women average 15 or more.

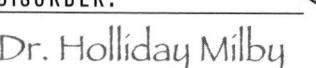

mypsych lab

DISSOCIATIVE IDENTITY
DISORDER:

Dr. Holliday Milby

TABLE 7.2
Features of Dissociative Identity Disorder (Formerly Multiple Personality Disorder)
1. At least two distinct personalities exist within the person, with each having a relatively enduring and distinct pattern of perceiving, thinking about, and relating to the environment and the self.
2. Two or more of these personalities repeatedly take complete control of the individual's behavior.
3. There is a failure to recall important personal information too substantial to be accounted for by ordinary forgetfulness.
4. The disorder cannot be accounted for by the effects of a psychoactive substance or a general medical condition.

Source: Adapted from the *DSM-IV-TR* (APA, 2000).

Only a handful of cases worldwide were reported from 1920 to 1970, but since then the number of reported cases has skyrocketed into the thousands (Spanos, 1994). This may indicate that multiple personality is more common than was earlier believed. However, it is also possible that the disorder has been overdiagnosed in highly suggestible people who might simply be following suggestions that they might have the disorder (APA, 2000). Increased public attention paid to the disorder in recent years may also account for the perception that its prevalence is greater than was commonly believed.

The disorder does appear to be culture-bound and largely restricted to North America (Spanos, 1994). Relatively few cases have been reported elsewhere, even in such Western countries as Great Britain and France. A recent survey in Japan failed to find even one case, and in Switzerland, 90% of the psychiatrists polled had never seen a case of the disorder (Modestin, 1992; Spanos, 1994). Even in North America, few psychologists and psychiatrists have ever encountered a case of multiple personality. Most cases are reported by a relatively small number of investigators and clinicians who strongly believe in the existence of the disorder. Critics wonder if they may be helping to manufacture that which they are seeking.

Some leading authorities, such as the late psychologist Nicholas Spanos, believe so. Spanos and others have challenged the existence of dissociative identity disorder (Reisner, 1994; Spanos, 1994). To Spanos, dissociative identity is not a distinct disorder, but a form of role-playing in which individuals first come to construe themselves as having multiple selves and then begin to act in ways that are consistent with their conception of the disorder. Eventually their role-playing becomes so ingrained that it becomes a reality to them. Perhaps their therapists or counselors unintentionally planted the idea in their minds that their confusing welter of emotions and behaviors may represent different personalities at work. Impressionable people may have learned how to enact the role of persons with the disorder by watching others on television and in the movies. Films such as *The Three Faces of Eve* and *Sybil* have given detailed examples of the behaviors that characterize multiple personalities. Or perhaps therapists provided cues about the features of multiple personality.

Once the role is established, it may be maintained through social reinforcement, such as attention from others and avoidance of accountability for unacceptable behavior. This is not to suggest that people with multiple personalities are "faking," any more than you are faking when you perform different daily roles as student, spouse, or worker. You may enact the role of a student (e.g., sitting attentively in class, raising your hand when you wish to talk) because you have learned to organize your behavior according to the nature of the role and because you have been rewarded for doing so. People with multiple personalities may have come to identify so closely with the role that it becomes real for them.

Relatively few cases of multiple personality involve criminal behavior, so the incentives for enacting a multiple personality role do not often relieve individuals of criminal responsibility for their behavior. But there still may be benefits to enacting the role of a multiple personality, such as a therapist's expression of interest and excitement at discovering a multiple personality. People with multiple personalities were often highly imaginative during childhood. Accustomed to playing games of "make believe," they may readily adopt alternate identities, especially if they learn how to enact the multiple personality role and there are external sources of validation, such as a clinician's interest and concern.

The social reinforcement model may help to explain why some clinicians seem to "discover" many more cases of multiple personality than others. These clinicians may unknowingly cue clients to enact the multiple personality role and then reinforce the performance with extra attention and concern. With the right set of cues, certain clients may adopt the role of a multiple personality to please their clinicians. Some authorities have challenged the role-playing model (e.g., Gleaves, 1996), and it remains to be seen how many cases of the disorder in clinical practice the model can explain.

Whether dissociative identity disorder is a real phenomenon or a form of role-playing, there is no question that people who display this behavior have serious emotional and behavioral difficulties. Moreover, the diagnosis may not be all that unusual among some subgroups in the population, such as psychiatric inpatients. In one study of 484 adult psychiatric inpatients, at least 5% showed evidence of multiple personality (Ross et al., 1991). We have noted a tendency for claims of multiple personality to spread on inpatient units. In one case, Susan, a prostitute admitted for depression and suicidal thoughts, claimed that she could only exchange sex for money when "another person" inside her emerged and took control. Upon hearing this, another woman, Ginny—a child abuser who had been admitted for depression after her daughter had been removed from her home by social services—claimed that she only abused her daughter when another person inside of her assumed control of her personality. Susan's chart recommended that she be evaluated further for multiple personality disorder (the term used at the time to refer to the disorder), but Ginny was diagnosed with a depressive disorder and a personality disorder, not with multiple personality disorder.

Suicidal behavior is common among people with multiple personalities. Seventy-two percent of the cases in a Canadian study (Ross et al., 1989) had attempted suicide, and about 2% had succeeded.

Dissociative Amnesia

Dissociative amnesia is believed to be the most common type of dissociative disorder (Maldonado, Butler, & Spiegel, 1998). *Amnesia* derives from the Greek roots *a-*, meaning "not," and *mnasthai*, meaning "to remember." In **dissociative amnesia** (formerly called *psychogenic amnesia*), the person becomes unable to recall important personal information, usually involving traumatic or stressful experiences, in a way that cannot be accounted for by simple forgetfulness. Nor can the memory loss be attributed to a particular organic cause, such as a blow to the head or a particular medical condition, or to the direct effects of drugs or alcohol. Unlike some progressive forms of memory impairment (such as dementia associated with Alzheimer's disease; see Chapter 15), the memory loss in dissociative amnesia is reversible, although it may last for days, weeks, or even years. Recall of dissociated memories may happen gradually but often occurs suddenly and spontaneously, as when the soldier who has no recall of a battle for several days afterward suddenly remembers being transported to a hospital away from the battlefield.

Memories of childhood sexual abuse are sometimes recovered during the course of psychotherapy or hypnosis. The sudden emergence of such memories has become a source of major controversy within the field and the general community, as we explore in the *Controversies in Abnormal Psychology* feature.

dissociative amnesia A dissociative disorder in which a person experiences memory loss without any identifiable organic cause.

"Jane Doe." This woman, called "Jane Doe" by rescue workers, was found wandering in a Florida park in a dazed state. She reported she had no memory of her background or even who she was. Her parents recognized her after she appeared on a national TV program. She reportedly never regained her memory.

Amnesia is not ordinary forgetfulness, such as forgetting someone's name or where you left your car keys. Memory loss in amnesia is more profound or wide ranging. Dissociative amnesia is divided into five distinct types of memory problems.

1. *Localized amnesia.* Most cases take the form of *localized amnesia* in which events occurring during a specific time period are lost to memory. For example, the person cannot recall events for a number of hours or days after a stressful or traumatic incident, such as a battle or car accident.

2. *Selective amnesia.* In *selective amnesia,* people forget only the disturbing particulars that take place during a certain period of time. A person may recall the period of life during which he conducted an extramarital affair, but not the guilt-arousing affair itself. A soldier may recall most of the battle, but not the death of his buddy.

3. *Generalized amnesia.* In *generalized amnesia,* people forget their entire lives—who they are, what they do, where they live, whom they live with. This form of amnesia is very rare, although you wouldn't think so if you watch daytime soap operas. Persons with generalized amnesia cannot recall personal information, but they tend to retain their habits, tastes, and skills. If you had generalized amnesia, you would still know how to read, although you would not recall your elementary school teachers. You would still prefer French fries to baked potatoes—or vice versa.

4. *Continuous amnesia.* In this form of amnesia, the person forgets everything that occurred from a particular point in time up to and including the present.

5. *Systematized amnesia.* Finally, in systematized amnesia, the memory loss is specific to a particular category of information, such as memory about one's family or particular people in one's life.

People with dissociative amnesia usually forget events or periods of life that were traumatic—that generated strong negative emotions, such as horror or guilt. Consider the case of Rutger.

Rutger: A Case of Dissociative Amnesia

He was brought to the emergency room of a hospital by a stranger. He was dazed and claimed not to know who he was or where he lived, and the stranger had found him wandering in the streets. Despite his confusion, it did not appear that he had been drinking or abusing drugs or that his amnesia could be attributed to physical trauma. After staying in the hospital for a few days, he awoke in distress. His memory had returned. His name was Rutger and he had urgent business to attend to. He wanted to know why he had been hospitalized and demanded to leave. At the time of admission, Rutger appeared to be suffering from generalized amnesia: He could not recall his identity or the personal events of his life. But now that he was requesting discharge, Rutger showed localized amnesia for the period between entering the emergency room and the morning he regained his memory for prior events.

Rutger provided information about the events prior to his hospitalization that was confirmed by the police. On the day when his amnesia began, Rutger had killed a pedestrian with his automobile. There had been witnesses, and the police had voiced the opinion that Rutger—although emotionally devastated—was blameless in the incident. Rutger was instructed, however, to fill out an accident report and to appear at the inquest. Still nonplussed, Rutger filled out the form at a friend's home. He accidentally left his wallet and his identification there. After placing the form in a mailbox, Rutger became dazed and lost his memory.

Although Rutger was not responsible for the accident, he felt awful about the pedestrian's death. His amnesia was probably connected with feelings of guilt, the stress of the accident, and concerns about the inquest.

—Adapted from Cameron, 1963, pp. 355–356

CONTROVERSIES IN ABNORMAL PSYCHOLOGY

Are Recovered Memories Credible?

A high-level business executive's comfortable life fell apart one day when his 19-year-old daughter accused him of having repeatedly molested her throughout her childhood. The executive lost his marriage as well as his $400,000-a-year job. But he fought back against the allegations, which he insisted were untrue. He sued his daughter's therapists, who had helped her recover these memories. A jury sided with the businessman, awarding him $500,000 in damages from the two therapists.

This case is but one of many involving adults who claim to have only recently become aware of memories of childhood sexual abuse. Hundreds of people throughout the country have been brought to trial on the basis of recovered memories of childhood abuse, with many of these cases resulting in convictions and long jail sentences, even in the absence of corroborating evidence. Such recovered memories often occur following suggestive probing by a therapist or hypnotist (Loftus, 1993). The issue of recovered memories continues to be hotly debated in psychology and the broader community. At the heart of the debate is the question, "Are recovered memories believable?" No one doubts that childhood sexual abuse is a major problem confronting our society. But should recovered memories be taken at face value?

Several lines of evidence lead us to question the validity of recovered memories. Experimental evidence shows that false memories can be created, especially under the influence of leading or suggestive questioning (Begley, 2001b; Gleaves et al., 2004; Kihlstrom, 2004; Loftus, 1997; Zoellner et al., 2000). Memory for events that never happened may be created; they may seem just as genuine as memories of real events (Zola, 1999). Moreover, although people who have experienced actual abuse in childhood may be somewhat sketchy on the details, total amnesia concerning the trauma is rare (Wakefield & Underwager, 1996). A leading memory expert, psychologist

Elizabeth Loftus (1996, p. 356), writes of the dangers of taking recovered memories at face value:

After developing false memories, innumerable "patients" have torn their families apart, and more than a few innocent people have been sent to prison. This is not to say that people cannot forget horrible things that have happened to them; most certainly they can. But there is virtually no support for the idea that clients presenting for therapy routinely have extensive histories of abuse of which they are completely unaware, and that they can be helped only if the alleged abuse is resurrected from their unconscious.

Should we conclude, then, that recovered memories are bogus? Not necessarily. Both false memories and recovered true memories may exist (Gleaves et al., 2004). It is possible for adults to suddenly recover memories of long-forgotten childhood experiences (Melchert, 1996), including memories of abuse (Chu et al., 1999). All in all, some recovered memories may be true; others may not be (Brown, 1997; Rubin, 1996).

In sum, we shouldn't think of the brain as a kind of mental camera that stores snapshots of events as they actually happened in the form of memories. Memory is more of a reconstructive process in which bits of information are pieced together in ways that can sometimes lead to a distorted recollection of events, although the person may be convinced the memory is accurate. Unfortunately we don't have the tools to distinguish the true memory from the false one (Cloitre, 2004; Loftus, 1993).

Critical Thinking

- Why should we not accept claims of recovered memories at face value?
- How does human memory work differently than a camera in recording events and experiences?

People sometimes claim they cannot recall certain events of their lives, such as criminal acts, promises made to others, and so forth. Falsely claiming amnesia as a way of escaping responsibility is called *malingering,* which refers to faking symptoms or making false claims for personal gain. We don't have any guaranteed methods for distinguishing people with dissociative amnesia from malingerers. But experienced clinicians can make reasonably well-educated guesses.

Dissociative Fugue

Fugue derives from the Latin *fugere,* meaning "flight." The word *fugitive* has the same origin. Fugue is like amnesia "on the run." In **dissociative fugue** (formerly called *psychogenic fugue*), the person travels suddenly and unexpectedly from his or her home or place of work, is unable to recall past personal information, and either becomes confused about his or her identity or assumes a new identity (either partially or completely) (APA, 2000). Despite these odd behaviors, the person may appear "normal" and show no other signs of mental disturbance (Maldonado et al., 1998). The person may not think about the past, or may report a past filled with false memories without recognizing them as false.

Whereas people with amnesia appear to wander aimlessly, people in a fugue state act more purposefully. Some stick close to home. They spend the afternoon in the park or in a theater, or they spend the night at a hotel under another name, usually avoiding contact with others. But the new identity is incomplete and fleeting, and the individual's former sense of self returns in a matter of hours or a few days. Less common is a pattern in which the fugue state lasts for months or years and involves travel to distant

dissociative fugue A dissociative disorder in which one suddenly flees from one's life situation, travels to a new location, assumes a new identity, and has amnesia for personal material.

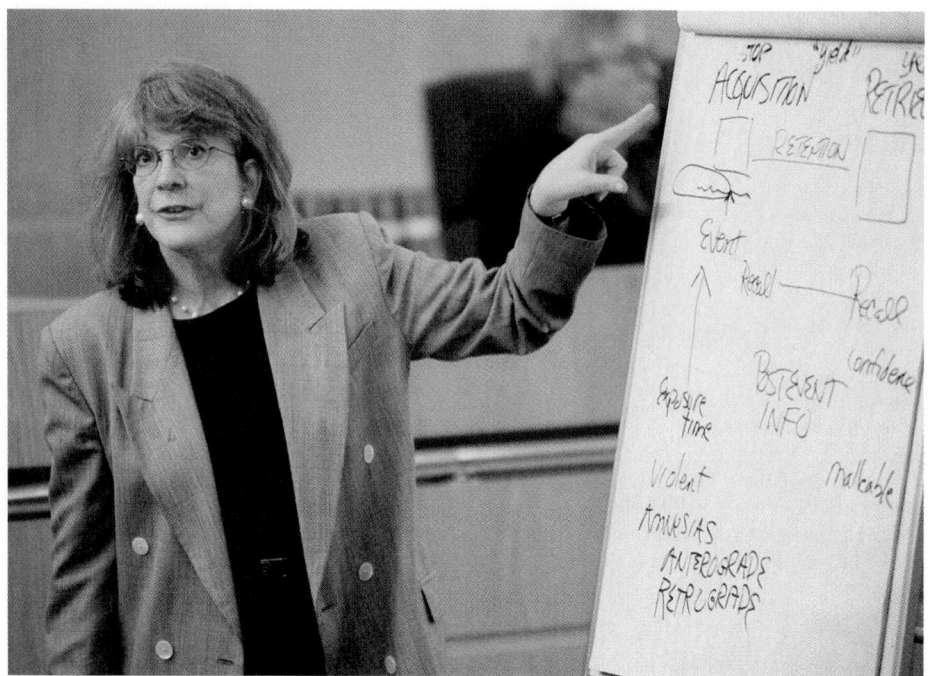

Elizabeth Loftus. Research by Loftus and others has demonstrated that false memories of events that never actually occurred can be induced experimentally. This research calls into question the credibility of reports of recovered memories.

places and assumption of a new identity. These individuals may assume an identity that is more spontaneous and sociable than their former selves, which were typically "quiet" and "ordinary." They may establish new families and successful businesses. Although these events sound rather bizarre, the fugue state is not considered psychotic because people with the disorder can think and behave quite normally—in their new lives, that is. Then one day, quite suddenly, awareness of their past identity returns to them, and they are flooded with old memories. Now they typically do not recall the events that occurred during the fugue state. The new identity, the new life—including all its involvements and responsibilities—vanish from memory.

Fugue, like amnesia, is relatively rare and is believed to affect only about 2 people in 1,000 within the general population (APA, 2000). It is most likely to occur in wartime or in the wake of another kind of disaster or extremely stressful event. The underlying notion is that dissociation in the fugue state protects one from traumatic memories or other sources of emotionally painful experiences or conflict (Maldonado et al., 1998).

Fugue can also be difficult to distinguish from malingering. That is, persons who were dissatisfied with their former lives could claim to have amnesia when they are discovered in their new locations and new identities. Let us consider a case that could lead to varying interpretations (Spitzer et al., 1989).

◆

Burt or Gene? A Case of Dissociative Fugue?

The man told the police that his name was Burt Tate. "Burt," a 42-year-old white male, had gotten into a fight at the diner where he worked. When the police arrived, they found that he carried no identification. He told them he had drifted into town a few weeks earlier, but could not recall where he had lived or worked before arriving in town. Although no charges were pressed against him, the police prevailed upon him to come to the emergency room for evaluation. "Burt" knew the town he was in and the current date and recognized that it was somewhat unusual that he couldn't remember his past, but he didn't seem concerned about it. There was no evidence of any physical injuries, head trauma, or drug or alcohol abuse. The police made some inquiries and discovered that "Burt" fit the profile of a missing person, Gene Saunders, who had disappeared a month earlier from a city some 2,000 miles away. Mrs. Saunders was called in and confirmed that "Burt" was indeed her husband. She reported that her husband, who had worked in middle-level management in a manufacturing company, had been having difficulty at work before his disappearance. He was passed over for promotion and his supervisor was highly critical of his work. The job stress apparently affected his behavior at home. Once easygoing and sociable, he withdrew into himself and began to criticize his wife and children. Then, just before his disappearance, he had a violent argument with his 18-year-old son. His son called him a "failure" and stormed out the door. Two days later, the man disappeared. When he came face to face with his wife again, he claimed he didn't recognize her, but appeared visibly nervous.

—Adapted from Spitzer et al., 1994, pp. 254–255

Although the presenting evidence supported a diagnosis of dissociative fugue, clinicians can find it difficult to distinguish true amnesia from amnesia that is faked to allow a person to start a new life.

Depersonalization Disorder

Depersonalization is a temporary loss or change in the usual sense of our own reality. In a state of depersonalization, people feel detached from themselves and their surroundings. They may feel as if they are dreaming or acting like a robot (Guralnik, Schmeidler, & Simeon, 2000; Sierra et al., 2006).

Derealization—a sense of unreality about the external world involving odd changes in the perception of one's surroundings or in the passage of time—may also be present. People and objects may seem to change in size or shape and sounds may seem different. All these feelings can be associated with feelings of anxiety, including dizziness and fears of going insane, or with depression.

Although these sensations are strange, people with depersonalization maintain contact with reality. They can distinguish reality from unreality, even during the depersonalization episode. In contrast to generalized amnesia and fugue, they know who they are. Their memories are intact and they know where they are—even if they do not like their present state. Feelings of depersonalization usually come on suddenly and fade gradually.

Note that we have thus far described only normal feelings of depersonalization. Healthy people frequently experience transient episodes of depersonalization and derealization (Hunter et al., 2003). According to the *DSM*, about half of all adults experience single brief episodes of depersonalization, usually during times of extreme stress (APA, 2000). About 80% to 90% of people in the general population have dissociative experiences at one time or another (Gershuny & Thayer, 1999).

Given the commonness of occasional dissociative symptoms, Richie's experience is not atypical.

depersonalization Feelings of unreality or detachment from one's self or one's body.

derealization A sense of unreality about the outside world.

Very few of us have episodes in which we feel strangely detached from our own bodies or thought processes.

☑ **FALSE.** About half of all adults, according to the *DSM*, at some time experience an episode of depersonalization in which they feel detached from their own bodies or mental processes.

"I" Depersonalization at Disney World

We went to Orlando with the children after school let out. I had also been driving myself hard, and it was time to let go. We spent three days "doing" Disney World, and it got to the point where we were all wearing shirts with mice and ducks on them and singing Disney songs. On the third day I began to feel unreal and ill at ease while we were watching these middle-American Ivory-soap teenagers singing and dancing in front of Cinderella's Castle. The day was finally cooling down, but I broke into a sweat. I became shaky and dizzy and sat down on the cement next to the 4-year-old's stroller without giving [my wife] an explanation. There were strollers and kids and [adults'] legs all around me, and for some strange reason I became fixated on the pieces of popcorn strewn on the ground. All of a sudden it was like the people around me were all silly mechanical creatures, like the dolls in the "It's a Small World" [exhibit] or the animals on the "Jungle Cruise." Things sort of seemed to slow down, the way they do when you've smoked marijuana, and there was this invisible wall of cotton between me and everyone else.

Then the concert was over and my wife was like "What's the matter?" and did I want to stay for the Electrical Parade and the fireworks or was I sick? Now I was beginning to wonder if I was going crazy and I said I was sick, that my wife would have to take me by the hand and drive us back to the Sonesta Village [motel]. Somehow we got back to the monorail and turned in the strollers. I waited in the herd [of people] at the station like a dead person, my eyes glazed over, looking out over kids with Mickey Mouse ears and Mickey Mouse balloons. The mechanical voice on the monorail almost did me in and I got really shaky.

I refused to go back to the Magic Kingdom. I went with the family to Sea World, and on another day I dropped [my wife] and the kids off at the Magic Kingdom and picked them up that night. My wife thought I was goldbricking or something, and we had a helluva fight about it, but we had a life to get back to and my sanity had to come first.

—*From the Author's Files*

Depersonalization. Episodes of depersonalization are characterized by feelings of detachment from oneself. During an episode, it may feel as if one were walking through a dream or observing the environment or oneself from outside one's body.

> ## TABLE 7.3
> ### Diagnostic Features of Depersonalization Disorder
>
> 1. Recurrent or persistent experiences of depersonalization, which are characterized by feelings of detachment from one's mental processes or body, as if one were an outside observer of oneself. The experience may have a dreamlike quality.
> 2. The individual is able to maintain reality testing (i.e., distinguish reality from unreality) during the depersonalization state.
> 3. The depersonalization experiences cause significant personal distress or impairment in one or more important areas of functioning, such as social or occupational functioning.
> 4. Depersonalization experiences cannot be attributed to other disorders or to the direct effects of drugs, alcohol, or medical conditions.
>
> Source: Adapted from the *DSM-IV-TR* (APA, 2000).

depersonalization disorder A disorder characterized by persistent or recurrent episodes of depersonalization.

Richie's depersonalization experience was limited to the one episode and would not qualify for a diagnosis of **depersonalization disorder.** Depersonalization disorder is diagnosed only when such experiences are persistent or recurrent and cause marked distress. The *DSM* diagnoses depersonalization disorder according to the criteria shown in Table 7.3. Note the following case example.

A Case of Depersonalization Disorder

A 20-year-old college student feared that he was going insane. For two years, he had increasingly frequent experiences of feeling "outside" himself. During these episodes, he experienced a sense of "deadness" in his body, and felt wobbly, frequently bumping into furniture. He was more apt to lose his balance during episodes that occurred when he was out in public, especially when he was feeling anxious. During these episodes, his thoughts seemed "foggy," reminding him of his state of mind when he was given shots of a pain-killing drug for an appendectomy five years earlier. He tried to fight off these episodes when they occurred, by saying "stop" to himself and by shaking his head. This would temporarily clear his head, but the feeling of being outside himself and the sense of deadness would shortly return. The disturbing feelings would gradually fade away over a period of hours. By the time he sought treatment, he was experiencing these episodes about twice a week, each one lasting from three to four hours. His grades remained unimpaired, and had even improved in the past several months, because he was spending more time studying. However, his girlfriend, in whom he had confided his problem, felt that he had become totally absorbed in himself and threatened to break off their relationship if he didn't change. She had also begun to date other men.

—Adapted from Spitzer et al., 1994, pp. 270–271

In terms of observable behavior and associated features, depersonalization may be more closely related to anxiety disorders such as phobias and panic disorder than to dissociative disorders. Unlike other forms of dissociative disorders that seem to protect the self from anxiety, depersonalization can lead to anxiety and in turn to avoidance behavior, as we saw in the case of Richie.

Cultural influences have an important bearing on the development and expression of abnormal behavior patterns, including dissociative syndromes such as depersonalization disorder. For example, evidence suggests that depersonalization experiences may be more common in individualistic cultures that emphasize

QUESTIONNAIRE
The Dissociative Experiences Scale

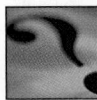 Brief dissociative experiences, such as momentary feelings of depersonalization, are quite common. Most of us experience them at least some of the time (Gershuny & Thayer, 1999). Dissociative disorders, by contrast, involve more persistent and severe dissociative experiences. Researchers have developed a measure, the Dissociative Experiences Scale (DES), to offer clinicians a way of measuring dissociative experiences that occur in both the general population and among people with dissociative disorders (Putnam & Carlson, 1994; Sanders & Green, 1995; Sar et al., 1996). Fleeting dissociative experiences are quite common, but those reported by people with dissociative disorders are more frequent and problematic than those in the general population (Waller & Ross, 1997).

The following is a listing of some of the types of dissociative experiences drawn from the Dissociative Experiences Scale that many people encounter from time to time. Bear in mind that transient experiences like these are reported in varying frequencies by both normal and abnormal groups. Let us also suggest that if these experiences become persistent or commonplace or cause you concern or distress, then it might be worthwhile to discuss them with a professional.

HAVE YOU EVER EXPERIENCED THE FOLLOWING?

1. Suddenly realizing, when you are driving the car, that you don't remember what has happened during all or part of the trip.
2. Suddenly realizing, when you are listening to someone talk, that you did not hear part or all of what the person said.
3. Finding yourself in a place and having no idea how you got there.
4. Finding yourself dressed in clothes that you don't remember putting on.
5. Experiencing a feeling that seemed as if you were standing next to yourself or watching yourself do something and actually seeing yourself as if you were looking at another person.
6. Looking in a mirror and not recognizing yourself.
7. Feeling sometimes that other people, objects, and the world around you are not real.
8. Remembering a past event so vividly that it seems like you are reliving it in the present.
9. Having the experience of being in a familiar place but finding it strange and unfamiliar.
10. Becoming so absorbed in watching television or a movie that you are unaware of other events happening around you.
11. Becoming so absorbed in a fantasy or daydream that it feels as if it were really happening to you.
12. Talking out loud to yourself when you are alone.
13. Finding that you act so differently in a particular situation compared with another that it feels almost as if you were two different people.
14. Finding that you cannot remember whether or not you have just done something or perhaps had just thought about doing it (for example, not knowing whether you have just mailed a letter or have just thought about mailing it).
15. Feeling sometimes as if you were looking at the world through a fog such that people and objects appear faraway or unclear.

Source: Bernstein, E. M., & Putnam, F. W. (1986). "Development, reliability, and validity of a dissociation scale." *Journal of Nervous and Mental Disease, 174,* 727–735. Copyright © Williams & Wilkins, 1986.

individualism or self-identity, such as the United States, than in collectivistic cultures, which emphasize group identity and responsibility to one's social roles and obligations (Sierra et al, 2006). As we explore next, dissociative disorders may also take very different forms in different cultures.

Culture-Bound Dissociative Syndromes

Similarities exist between the Western concept of dissociative disorder and certain culture-bound syndromes found in other parts of the world. For example, *amok* is a culture-bound syndrome occurring primarily in southeast Asian and Pacific Island cultures that describes a trancelike state in which a person suddenly becomes highly excited and violently attacks other people or destroys objects (see Chapter 3). People who "run amuck" may later claim to have no memory of the episode or recall feeling as if they were acting like a robot. Another example is *zar,* a term used in countries in North Africa and the Middle East to describe spirit possession in people who experience dissociative states. During these states, individuals engage in unusual behavior, ranging from shouting to banging their heads against the wall.

Theoretical Perspectives

The dissociative disorders are fascinating and perplexing phenomena. How can one's sense of personal identity become so distorted that one develops multiple personalities, blots out large chunks of personal memory, or develops a new identity? Although these disorders remain in many ways mysterious, some clues provide insights into their origins.

Games of make-believe. It is normal for children to play games of make-believe and even to have imaginary playmates. In the case of multiple personalities, however, games of make-believe and the invention of imaginary playmates may be used as psychological defenses against abuse. Research suggest that most people who develop multiple personalities where abused as children.

TRUTH or FICTION

Most people who show multiple personalities do not report any history of physical or sexual abuse during childhood.

☑**FALSE.** The great majority of people with multiple personalities report being physically or sexually abused as children.

Psychodynamic Views To psychodynamic theorists, dissociative disorders involve the massive use of repression, resulting in the "splitting off" from consciousness of unacceptable impulses and painful memories. Dissociative amnesia may serve an adaptive function of disconnecting or dissociating one's conscious self from awareness of traumatic experiences or other sources of psychological pain or conflict (Dorahy, 2001). In dissociative amnesia and fugue, the ego protects itself from anxiety by blotting out disturbing memories or by dissociating threatening impulses of a sexual or aggressive nature. In dissociative identity disorder, people may express these unacceptable impulses through the development of alternate personalities. In depersonalization, people stand outside themselves—safely distanced from the emotional turmoil within.

Social-Cognitive Theory From the standpoint of social-cognitive theory, we can conceptualize dissociation in the form of dissociative amnesia or dissociative fugue as a learned response involving the behavior of psychologically distancing oneself from disturbing memories or emotions. The habit of psychologically distancing oneself from these matters, such as by splitting them off from consciousness, is negatively reinforced by relief from anxiety or removal or of feelings of guilt or shame. As for example, shielding oneself from memories or emotions associated with past physical or sexual abuse by disconnecting (dissociating) them off from ordinary consciousness avoids anxiety or misplaced guilt these experiences may engender.

Some social-cognitive theorists, such as the late Nicholas Spanos, believe that dissociative identity disorder is a form of role-playing acquired through observational learning and reinforcement. This is not quite the same as pretending or malingering; people can honestly come to organize their behavior patterns according to particular roles they have observed. They might also become so absorbed in role-playing that they "forget" they are enacting a role.

Brain Dysfunction Might dissociative behavior be connected with underlying brain dysfunction? Research along these lines is still in its infancy, but preliminary evidence shows structural differences in brain areas involved in memory and emotion between patients with dissociative identity disorder (DID) and healthy controls (Vermetten et al., 2006). Although intriguing, the significance of these differences in explaining DID remains to be determined. Another study showed differences in brain metabolic activity between people with depersonalization disorder and healthy subjects (Simeon et al., 2000). These findings, which point to a possible dysfunction in parts of the brain involved in body perception, may help account for the feeling of being disconnected from one's body that is associated with depersonalization.

Diathesis–Stress Model Despite widespread evidence of severe physical or sexual abuse in childhood in the great majority of cases of dissociative identity disorder (Foote et al., 2005; Spiegel, 2006), very few severely abused children develop multiple personalities. Consistent with the diathesis–stress model, certain personality traits, such as proneness to fantasize, high ability to be hypnotized, and openness to altered states of consciousness, may predispose individuals to develop dissociative experiences in the face of extreme stress, such as traumatic abuse in childhood. (See the *Tying it Together* section on page 226.) These personality traits in themselves do not lead to dissociative disorders (Rauschenberger & Lynn, 1995). They are actually quite common in the population. However, they may increase the risk that people who experience severe trauma will develop dissociative phenomena as a survival mechanism (Butler et al., 1996). People who are low in fantasy proneness or hypnotizability may experience the kinds of anxious, intrusive thoughts characteristic of posttraumatic stress disorder (PTSD) in the aftermath of traumatic stress, rather than dissociative experiences (Kirmayer, Robbins, & Paris, 1994).

Perhaps most of us can divide our consciousness so that we become unaware of—at least temporarily—those events we normally focus on. Perhaps most of us can thrust the unpleasant from our minds and enact various roles—parent, child, lover, businessperson, and soldier—that help us meet the requirements of our situations. Perhaps the marvel is *not* that attention can be splintered, but that human consciousness is normally integrated into a meaningful whole.

Treatment of Dissociative Disorders

Dissociative amnesia and fugue are usually fleeting experiences that end abruptly. Episodes of depersonalization can be recurrent and persistent, and they are most likely to occur when people are undergoing periods of mild anxiety or depression. In such cases, clinicians usually focus on managing the anxiety or depression. Much of the attention in the research literature has focused on dissociative identity disorder and specifically on integrating the alter personalities into a cohesive personality structure (Burton & Lane, 2001).

Psychoanalysts seek to help people with dissociative identity disorder uncover and learn to cope with early childhood traumas. They often recommend establishing direct contact with alter personalities (Burton & Lane, 2001). The therapist may ask the client to close his or her eyes and wait for the alter personalities to emerge (Krakauer, 2001). Wilbur (1986) points out that the analyst can work with whatever personality dominates the therapy session. The therapist asks any and all personalities that come out to talk about their memories and dreams and assures them that the therapist will help them make sense of their anxieties, safely "relive" traumatic experiences, and make them conscious. The disclosure of abuse is considered essential to the therapeutic process (Krakauer, 2001). Wilbur notes that anxiety experienced during a therapy session may lead to a switch in personalities, because alter personalities were presumably developed as a means to cope with intense anxiety. But if therapy is successful, the self will be able to work through the traumatic memories and will no longer need to escape into alternate "selves" to avoid the anxiety associated with the trauma. Thus, reintegration of the personality becomes possible.

Through the process of integration, the disparate elements or "alters" are woven into a cohesive self. Here a patient speaks about this process of "making mine" those parts of the self that had been splintered off.

"I" "Everybody's Still Here"

. . . Integration made me feel alive for the first time. When I feel things now, I know I feel them. I'm slowly learning it's okay to feel all feelings, even unpleasant ones. The bonus is, I get to feel pleasurable feelings as well. I also don't worry about my sanity anymore.

It's difficult to explain even to people who try to understand what integration means to someone who has been "in parts" for a lifetime. I still talk in a "we" way sometimes. Some of my "before integration" friends assume I can now just get back to being "me"—whatever that is. They don't realize integration is like being three all over again. I don't know how to act in certain situations because "I" never did it before. Or I only know how to respond in fragmented ways. What does "sadness" mean to someone who doesn't feel it continually? I don't know sometimes when I feel sad if I really should. It's confusing and scary being responsible for me all by myself now.

The most comforting aspect of integration for me, and what I especially want other multiples to know is: Nobody died. Everybody's still here inside me, in their correct place without controlling my body independently. There was not a scene where everybody left except one. I am a remarkably different "brand new" person. I've spent months learning how to access my alters' skills and emotions—and they are mine now. I have balance and perspective that never existed before. I'm happy and content. This isn't about dying. It's about celebrating living to the fullest extent possible.

—From Olson, 1997

TYING IT TOGETHER

Although we have different conceptualizations of dissociative phenomena, evidence points to a history of childhood abuse in a great many cases. The most widely held view of dissociative identity disorder is that it represents a means of coping with and surviving severe, repetitive childhood abuse, generally beginning before the age of 5 (Burton & Lane, 2001; Foote, 2005). The severely abused child may retreat into alter personalities as a psychological defense against unbearable abuse. The construction of these alter personalities allows these children to psychologically escape or distance themselves from their suffering. In the "I" case example in the opening of the chapter, one alter personality, Leah, bore the worst of the abuse for all the others. Dissociation may offer a means of escape when no other is available. In the face of continued abuse, these alter personalities may become stabilized, making it difficult for the person to maintain a unified personality. In adulthood, people with multiple personalities may use their alter personalities to block out traumatic childhood memories and their emotional reactions to them, thus wiping the slate clean and beginning life anew in the guise of alter personalities. The alter identities or personalities may also help the person cope with stressful situations or express deep-seated resentments that the individual is unable to integrate within his or her primary personality.

Compelling evidence indicates that exposure to childhood trauma, usually by a relative or caretaker, is involved in the development of dissociative disorders, especially dissociative identity disorder. The great majority of people with dissociative identity disorder report being physically or sexually abused as children (Lewis et al., 1997; Weaver & Clum, 1995). In some samples, rates of reported childhood physical or sexual abuse have ranged from 76% to 95% (Ross et al., 1990; Scroppo et al., 1998). Evidence of cross-cultural similarity comes from a study in Turkey, which showed that the great majority of dissociative identity disorder patients in one research sample reported sexual or physical abuse in childhood (Sar et al., 1996). Childhood trauma or abuse is also reported more often in cases of dissociative amnesia and depersonalization disorder than in control groups (e.g., Simeon et al., 1997, 2001).

Childhood abuse is not the only source of trauma linked to dissociative disorders. Exposure to the trauma of warfare among both civilians and soldiers plays a part in some cases of dissociative fugue and dissociative amnesia. In fugue, the stress of combat and the secondary gain of leaving the battlefield seem to be important contributors (Loewenstein, 1991). The stress of coping with severe financial problems and the wish to avoid punishment for socially unacceptable behavior are other possible antecedents to episodes of fugue (Riether & Stoudemire, 1988). High levels of stress may also be linked to depersonalization disorder (Kluft, 1988).

The *Concept Map for Abnormal Psychology* at the end of the chapter depicts the causal factors in dissociative disorders and approaches to treating these intriguing yet puzzling disorders. Here, in Figure 7.1, you will find an illustration of a conceptual model of dissociative identity disorder based on the diathesis–stress framework.

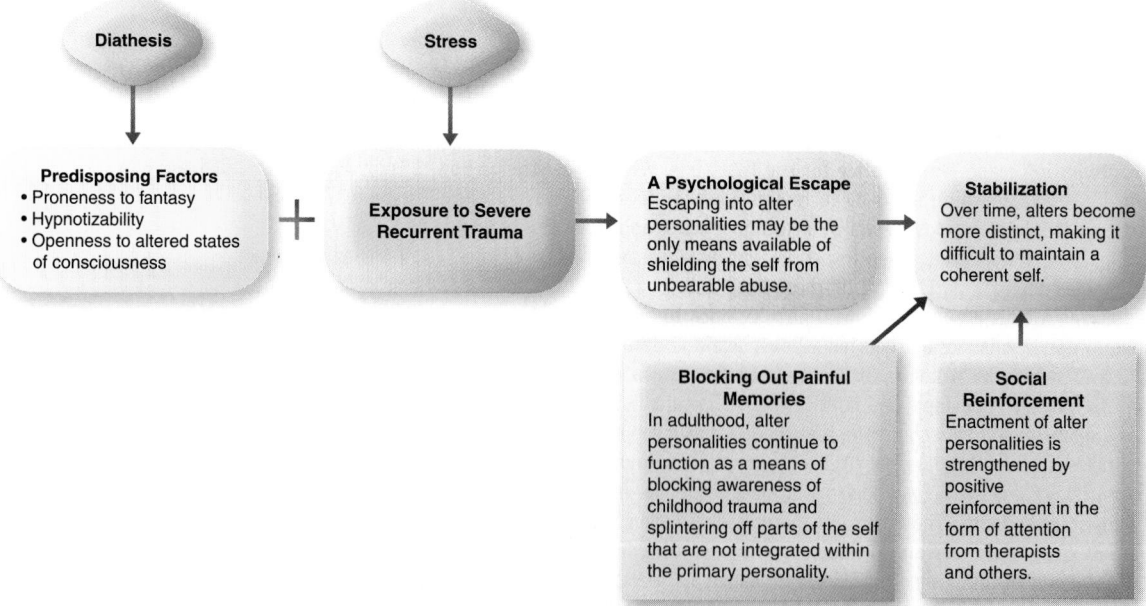

FIGURE 7.1 Diathesis–stress model of dissociative identity disorder.
In this model, exposure to severe, recurrent trauma (stress), together with certain predisposing factors (diathesis), leads in some few cases to the development of alter personalities, which over time become stabilized and strengthened by social reinforcement and blocking out of disturbing memories.

Wilbur describes the formation of another treatment goal in the case of a woman with dissociative identity disorder.

◇

The "Children" Should Not Feel Ashamed

A 45-year-old woman had suffered from dissociative identity disorder throughout her life. Her dominant personality was timid and self-conscious, rather reticent about herself. But soon after she entered treatment, a group of "little ones" emerged, who cried profusely. The therapist asked to speak with someone in the personality system who could clarify the personalities that were present. It turned out that they included several children, all of whom were under 9 years of age and had suffered severe, painful sexual abuse at the hands of an uncle, a great-aunt, and a grandmother. The great-aunt was a lesbian with several voyeuristic lesbian friends. They would watch the sexual abuse, generating fear, pain, rage, humiliation, and shame.

It was essential in therapy for the "children" to come to understand that they should not feel ashamed because they had been helpless to resist the abuse.

—Adapted from Wilbur, 1986, pp. 138–139

Does therapy work? Coons (1986) followed 20 "multiples" aged from 14 to 47 at time of intake for an average of 3-1/4 years. Only 5 of the subjects showed a complete reintegration of their personalities. Other therapists report significant improvement in measures of dissociative symptoms and depressive symptoms in treated patients, even in those who failed to achieve integration. However, greater symptom improvement was reported for those who achieved integration (Ellason & Ross, 1997).

Reports of the effectiveness of psychoanalytic and other forms of therapy, such as behavior therapy, rely on uncontrolled case studies. Controlled studies of treatments of dissociative identity disorder or other forms of dissociative disorder are yet to be reported (Maldonado et al., 1998). The relative infrequency of the disorder has hampered efforts to conduct controlled experiments that compare different forms of treatment with each other and with control groups. Nor do we have evidence showing psychiatric drugs or other biological approaches to be effective in bringing about an integration of various alternate personalities. Psychiatric drugs, such as the antidepressant Prozac, have also failed to produce therapeutic benefits in treating depersonalization disorder beyond those effects associated with placebos (Simeon et al., 2004). This lack of responsiveness is suggestive that depersonalization disorder is not secondary to depression.

SOMATOFORM DISORDERS

The word *somatoform* derives from the Greek *soma*, meaning "body." In the **somatoform disorders,** people have physical ("somatic") symptoms without an identifiable physical cause (De Gucht & Maes, 2006; Stotland, 2004). The symptoms significantly interfere with the person's life and often lead the person to go doctor shopping in the hope of finding a medical practitioner who could explain and treat their ailments (Rief & Sharpe, 2004). Or they may hold the belief that they are gravely ill, despite reassurances from their doctors to the contrary.

The concept of somatoform disorder presumes that the physical symptoms reflect psychological factors or conflicts. For example, some people complain of problems in breathing or swallowing, or of a "lump in the throat." Problems such as these can

somatoform disorders A disorder characterized by complaints of physical problems or symptoms that cannot be explained by physical causes.

Table 7.4 Overview of Somatoform Disorders

TYPE OF DISORDER	Lifetime Prevalence in Population (approx.)	Description	Associated Features
Conversion Disorder	Reported rates vary, from 1.1 in 10,000 people to 1 in 200 people	Change or loss of a physical function without medical cause	• Emerges in context of conflicts or stressful experiences, which lends credence to its psychological origins • May be associated with la belle indifférence (indifference to symptoms)
Hypochondriasis	1% to 5%	Preoccupation with the belief that one is seriously ill	• Fear persists despite medical reassurance • Tendency to interpret physical sensations or minor aches and pains as signs of serious illness
Somatization Disorder	0.2%–2% in women, less than 0.2% in men	Recurrent, multiple complaints about physical symptoms that have no clear organic basis	• Recurrent, multiple complaints about physical symptoms that have no clear organic basis
Body Dysmorphic Disorder	Unknown	Preoccupation with an imagined or exaggerated physical defect	• Person may believe that others think less of them as a person because of the perceived defect. • Person may engage in compulsive behaviors, such as excessive grooming, that aim to correct the perceived defect
Pain Disorder	Unknown	Persistent physical pain believed to be associated with psychological factors	• Pain severe and persistent enough to interfere with daily functioning; medical conditions and psychological factors may play important roles in accounting for the pain

Source: APA, 2000.

reflect overactivity of the sympathetic branch of the autonomic nervous system, which might result from anxiety. All in all, at least 20% of doctor visits involve complaints that cannot be explained medically (Rief & Sharpe, 2004).

There are several distinct types of somatoform disorders. In *conversion disorder,* a person may experience "paralysis" of a hand or leg that cannot be explained medically or that is inconsistent with the workings of the nervous system. In *hypochondriasis,* people misinterpret their physical symptoms, believing them to be signs of a serious illness, despite the fact that thorough medical evaluations fail to support their concerns. In *body dysmorphic disorder,* the person either has an imagined defect in appearance or exaggerates a minor physical flaw. In *pain disorder,* the person experiences pain in which psychological factors are held to play a prominent role. In *somatization disorder,* people present with many recurring physical complaints that cannot be fully explained by any known medical condition. Table 7.4 provides an overview of the somatoform disorders discussed in the text.

malingering Faking illness in order to avoid work or duty.

Somatoform disorders are not the same as **malingering,** or purposeful fabrication of symptoms for obvious gain (such as avoiding work). Feigning physical illness to avoid work or to qualify for disability benefits may be deceitful or even dishonest, but

Is this patient really sick? Münchausen syndrome is characterized by the fabrication of medical complaints for no other apparent purpose than to gain admission to hospitals. Some Münchausen patients may produce life-threatening symptoms in their attempts to deceive doctors.

it is not a psychological disorder. Somatoform disorders also need to be distinguished from **factitious disorders,** in which people fake or manufacture their symptoms, without any apparent motive.

Because malingering is motivated by external incentives, it is not considered a mental disorder within the *DSM* framework. But in factitious disorders, the symptoms do not bring about obvious gains. The absence of external incentives in these disorders suggests that they serve a psychological need; hence, they are classified as psychological or mental disorders.

The most common form of factitious disorder is **Münchausen syndrome,** a form of feigned illness in which the person either fakes being ill or makes himself or herself ill (by ingesting toxic substances, for example) (Huffman & Stern, 2003). Although people with somatoform disorders may benefit from having physical symptoms, they do not purposefully produce them. Even if there is no medical basis to their symptoms, they do not set out to deceive others. But Münchausen syndrome is not a somatoform disorder. It is a factitious disorder involving the deliberate fabrication of seemingly plausible physical complaints for no obvious gain.

Münchausen syndrome was named after Baron Karl von Münchausen, one of history's great fibbers. The good baron, an 18th-century German army officer, entertained friends with tales of outrageous adventures. In the vernacular, *Münchausenism* describes tellers of tall tales. In clinical terms, Münchausen syndrome refers to patients who tell tall tales or outrageous lies to their doctors. People who have Münchausen syndrome usually suffer deep anguish as they bounce from hospital to hospital and subject themselves to unnecessary, painful, and, sometimes risky medical treatments, even surgery. The *A Closer Look* feature explores this curious disorder in more depth.

factitious disorder A disorder characterized by intentional fabrication of psychological or physical symptoms for no apparent gain.

Münchausen syndrome A type of factitious disorder characterized by the fabrication of medical symptoms.

A CLOSER LOOK

Münchausen Syndrome

A woman staggered into the emergency room of a New York City hospital bleeding from the mouth, clutching her stomach and wailing with pain. Even in that setting, forever serving bleeders and clutchers and wailers, there was something about her, some terrible star quality that held center stage. Her pain was larger than life.

She told a harrowing story: A man had seduced her, then tied her up, beaten her, forced her to surrender money and jewelry on threat of death. She had severe pain in her lower left side, and an unbearable headache.

She was admitted, and exhaustively tested. Nothing could be found; no reason for the bleeding or the pain; the specialists were left scratching their heads.

Then, one day, a hospital aide came upon these items in her bedside table: a needle, syringe, and a blood thinner called heparin. Eureka. Inject yourself with enough blood thinner and you, too, can take stage center in an emergency room.

Confronted, she denied all charges. The stuff was not hers; someone was trying to frame her; if nobody believed her, she would check out of the place and find doctors who really cared. And off she went. Later, it was learned that she had recently been in two other hospitals: The same story, same symptom and same sequence of events.

Diagnosis: Münchausen syndrome.

Lear, 1988, p. 21. Copyright © 1988 by
The New York Times Company. *Reprinted by permission.**

Münchausen patients may go to great lengths to seek a confirmatory diagnosis, such as agreeing to exploratory surgery, even though they know there is nothing wrong with them. Some inject themselves with drugs to produce symptoms such as skin rashes. When confronted with evidence of their deception, they may turn nasty and stick to their guns. They are also skillful enough actors to convince others that their complaints are genuine.

Why do patients with Münchausen syndrome fake illness or put themselves at risk by making themselves to be sick or injured? Perhaps enacting the sick role in the protected hospital environment provides a sense of security that was lacking in childhood. Perhaps the hospital becomes a stage on which they can act out resentments against doctors and parents that have been brewing since childhood. Perhaps they are trying to identify with a parent who was often sick. Or perhaps they learned to enact a sick role in childhood to escape from repeated sexual abuse or other traumatic experiences and continue to enact the role to escape stressors in their adult lives (Trask & Sigmon, 1997). No one is really sure, and the disorder remains one of the more puzzling forms of abnormal behavior.

TRUTH or FICTION

Some people show up repeatedly at hospital emergency rooms, feigning illness and seeking treatment for no apparent reason.

☑ **TRUE.** People with Münchausen syndrome may show up repeatedly at emergency rooms, feigning illness and demanding treatment. Their motives remain a mystery.

MÜNCHAUSEN SYNDROME BY PROXY

In her memoir entitled *Sickened,* Julie Gregory recounts how she was subjected to numerous X-rays and operations as a child, not because there was anything wrong with her, but to find the cause of an illness that existed only in her mother's mind (Gregory, 2003). At age 13, Gregory underwent an invasive medical procedure, a heart catheterization, which her mother insisted upon to "get to the bottom of this thing." When the cardiologist informed Julie's mother that the test results were within normal limits, her mother argued for an even more invasive test involving open-heart surgery. When the doctor refused, Julie's mother confronted him in Julie's presence.

"I" Sickened

"I can't believe it? I cannot believe this! You're not going to dig into this and do the open-heart? I thought we had agreed to follow this through to the end, Michael. I thought you said you were committed to me on this."

"I'm committed to finding Julie's illness, Ms. Gregory, but Julie doesn't need heart surgery. Usually parents are thrilled to—"

"Oh, that's just it? That's all you're going to do? Just drop me like a hot potato? I mean, for crying out loud, why can't I just have a normal kid like other mothers? I mean I'm a good mom . . ."

I'm standing behind my mother's left leg, my eyes glued to the doctor, boring an SOS into his eyes: "Don't make me go, don't let her take me."

"Ms. Gregory, I didn't say you weren't a good mother. But I can't do anything else here. You need to drop the heart procedures. Period." And with that he turned on his heels.

"Well, you're the one who's going to be sorry," Mom screeches, "When this kid dies on you. That's what. 'Cause you're going to get sued out the ying-yang for being such an incompetent idiot. Can't even find out what's wrong with a thirteen-year-old girl! You are insane! This kid is sick, you hear me? She's sick!"

Source: Gregory, 2003.

Julie's case highlights a most pernicious form of child maltreatment called *Münchausen syndrome by proxy* (Rosenberg, 2003; Stutts, Hickey, & Kasdan, 2003), in which people intentionally falsify or induce physical or emotional illness or injury in a child or dependent person (Feldman, 2003).

Parents or caregivers who induce illness in their children may be trying to gain sympathy or experience the sense of control made possible by attending to a sick child. The disorder is controversial and remains under study by the psychiatric community. The controversy arises in large part because it appears to put a diagnostic label on abusive behavior. What is clear is that the disorder is linked to heinous crimes against children (Mart, 2003). In one sample case, a mother was suspected of purposely causing her 3-year-old's repeated bouts of diarrhea (Schreier & Ricci, 2002). Sadly, the child died before authorities could intervene. In another case, a foster mother is alleged to have brought about the deaths of three children by giving them overdoses of medicines containing potassium and sodium. The chemicals induced suffocation or heart attacks.

A review of 451 cases of Münchausen syndrome by proxy reported in the scientific literature showed that 6% of the victims died (Sheridan, 2003). Typical victims were 4 years of age or under. Mothers were perpetrators in three of four cases. Cases of Münchausen syndrome by proxy often involve mysterious high fevers in children, seizures of unknown origin, and similar symptoms. Doctors typically find the illnesses to be unusual, prolonged, and unexplained. They require some medical sophistication on the part of the perpetrator.

---

* Martha Weinman Lear is a former staff writer for The New York Times Magazine and author of the books *Heartsounds* and *Where Did I Leave My Glasses?: The What, When and Why of Normal Memory Loss.*

> **TABLE 7.5**
>
> ### Diagnostic Features of Conversion Disorder
>
> 1. At least one symptom or deficit involving voluntary motor or sensory functions that suggests the presence of a physical disorder.
> 2. Psychological factors are judged to be associated with the disorder because the onset or exacerbation of the physical symptom is linked to the occurrence of psychosocial stressors or conflict situations.
> 3. The person does not purposefully produce or fake the physical symptom.
> 4. The symptom cannot be explained as a cultural ritual or response pattern, nor can it be explained by any known physical disorder on the basis of appropriate testing.
> 5. The symptom causes significant emotional distress, impairment in one or more important areas of functioning, such as social or occupational functioning, or is sufficient to warrant medical attention.
> 6. The symptom is not restricted to complaints of pain or problems in sexual functioning, nor can it be accounted for by another mental disorder.
>
> *Source:* Adapted from the *DSM-IV-TR* (APA, 2000).

Let us now proceed to discuss several major types of somatoform disorder: conversion disorder, hypochondriasis, body dysmorphic disorder, pain disorder, and somatization disorder.

Conversion Disorder

Conversion disorder is characterized by a major change in or loss of physical functioning, although no medical findings are found to account for the physical symptoms or deficits (see Table 7.5). The symptoms are not intentionally produced. The person is not malingering. The physical symptoms usually come on suddenly in stressful situations. A soldier's hand may become "paralyzed" during intense combat, for example. The fact that conversion symptoms first appear in the context of, or are aggravated by, conflicts or stressors suggest a psychological connection (APA, 2000). Reported rates of the disorder in the general population range from as few as 1.1 in 10,000 people to perhaps as many as 1 in 200 people (APA, 2000). Like dissociative identity disorder, conversion disorder has been linked to childhood traumatization. A recent study found a higher frequency of childhood physical and sexual abuse among conversion disorder patients than among comparison patients diagnosed with mood disorders (Roelofs et al., 2002).

Conversion disorder is so named because of the psychodynamic belief that it represents the channeling, or *conversion,* of repressed sexual or aggressive energies into physical symptoms. Conversion disorder was formerly called *hysteria* or *hysterical neurosis,* and it played an important role in Freud's development of psychoanalysis (see Chapter 1). Hysterical or conversion disorders seem to have been more common in Freud's day than they are today.

According to the *DSM,* conversion symptoms mimic neurological or general medical conditions involving problems with voluntary motor (movement) or sensory functions. Some classic symptom patterns take the form of paralysis, epilepsy, problems in coordination, blindness and tunnel vision, loss of the sense of hearing or of smell, or loss of feeling in a limb (anesthesia). The bodily symptoms found in conversion disorders often do not match the medical conditions they suggest. For example, conversion epileptics, unlike true epileptic patients, may maintain control over their bladders during an attack. People whose vision is supposedly impaired may walk through the physician's office without bumping into the furniture. People who become "incapable" of standing or walking may nevertheless perform other leg movements normally. Nonetheless, hysteria and conversion symptoms are sometimes incorrectly diagnosed in people who turn out to have underlying medical conditions (Stone et al., 2005).

conversion disorder A somatoform disorder characterized by loss or impairment of physical function in the absence of any apparent organic cause.

TABLE 7.6

Diagnostic Features of Hypochondriasis

1. The person is preoccupied with a fear of having a serious illness or with the belief that one has a serious illness. The person interprets bodily sensations or physical signs as evidence of physical illness.
2. Fears of physical illness, or beliefs of having a physical illness, persist despite medical reassurances.
3. The preoccupations are not of a delusional intensity (the person recognizes the possibility that these fears and beliefs may be exaggerated or unfounded) and are not restricted to concerns about appearance.
4. The preoccupations cause significant emotional distress or interfere with one or more important areas of functioning, such as social or occupational functioning.
5. The disturbance has persisted for 6 months or longer.
6. The preoccupations do not occur exclusively within the context of another mental disorder.

Source: Adapted from the *DSM-IV-TR* (APA, 2000).

TRUTH or FICTION

Some people who have lost their ability to see or move their legs become strangely indifferent toward their physical condition.

☑ **TRUE.** Some people with conversion disorder show a remarkable lack of concern about their symptoms (*la belle indifférence*).

---

hypochondriasis A somatoform disorder characterized by misinterpretation of physical symptoms as signs of underlying serious disease.

mypsychlab

HYPOCHONDRIASIS:

The Case of Henry

"I had a growth that I was worried about on my face."

If you suddenly lost your vision, or if you could no longer move your legs, you would probably show understandable concern. But some people with conversion disorders, like those with dissociative amnesia, show a remarkable indifference to their symptoms, a phenomenon termed *la belle indifférence* ("beautiful indifference") (Stone et al., 2006). The *DSM* advises against relying on indifference to symptoms as a factor in making the diagnosis, however, because many people cope with real physical disorders by denying or minimizing their pain or concerns, which relieves anxieties—at least temporarily.

Hypochondriasis

The core feature of **hypochondriasis** is a preoccupation or fear that one's physical symptoms are due to a serious, underlying illness, such as cancer or heart disease. The fear persists despite medical reassurances that it is groundless (see Table 7.6). Hypochondriasis is believed to affect about 1% to 5% of the general population and about 5% of patients seeking medical care (APA, 2000; Barksy & Ahern, 2004).

People with hypochondriasis do not consciously fake their physical symptoms. They generally experience physical discomfort, often involving the digestive system or an assortment of aches and pains. Unlike conversion disorder, hypochondriasis does not involve the loss or distortion of physical function. Unlike people with conversion disorder, who are often indifferent toward their symptoms, people with hypochondriasis are very concerned, indeed unduly concerned, about their symptoms and what they fear they may mean. The disorder appears to be about equally common in men and women. It most often begins between the ages of 20 and 30, although it can begin at any age.

People with hypochondriasis may be overly sensitive to benign changes in physical sensations, such as slight changes in heartbeat and minor aches and pains (Barsky et al., 2001). Anxiety about physical symptoms can produce its own physical sensations, however—for example, heavy sweating and dizziness, even fainting. Thus, a vicious cycle may ensue. People with hypochondriasis may become resentful when their doctors tell them that their own fears may be causing their physical symptoms. They frequently go "doctor shopping" in the hope that a competent and sympathetic physician will heed them before it is too late. Physicians, too, can develop hypochondriasis, as we see in the following case example.

◆

The Doctor Feels Sick: A Case of Hypochondriasis

Robert, a 38-year-old radiologist, has just returned from a 10-day stay at a famous diagnostic center where he has undergone extensive testing of his entire gastrointestinal tract. The evaluation proved negative for any significant physical illness, but rather than feel relieved, the radiologist appeared resentful and disappointed with the findings. The radiologist has been bothered for several months with various physical symptoms, which he describes as symptoms of mild abdominal pain, feelings of "fullness," "bowel rumblings," and a feeling of a "firm abdominal mass." He has become convinced that his symptoms are due to colon cancer and has become accustomed to testing his stool for blood on a weekly basis and carefully palpating his abdomen for "masses" while lying in bed every several days. He has also secretly performed X-ray studies on himself. There is a history of a heart murmur that was detected when he was 13, and his younger brother died of congenital heart disease in early childhood. When the evaluation of his murmur proved it to be benign, he nonetheless began to worry that something might have been overlooked. He developed a fear that something was actually wrong with his heart, and while the fear eventually subsided, it has never entirely left him. In medical school he worried about the diseases that he learned about in pathology. Since graduating, he has repeatedly experienced concerns about his health that follow a typical pattern: noticing certain symptoms, becoming preoccupied with what the symptoms might mean, and undergoing physical evaluations that proved negative. His decision to seek a psychiatric consultation was prompted by an incident with his 9-year-old son. His son accidentally walked in on him while he was palpating his abdomen and asked, "What do you think it is this time, Dad?" He becomes tearful as he relates this incident, describing his feelings of shame and anger—mostly at himself.

—Adapted from Spitzer et al., 1994, pp. 88–90

body dysmorphic disorder (BDD)
A somatoform disorder characterized by preoccupation with an imagined or exaggerated physical defect of appearance.

People who develop hypochondriasis have more health worries, have more psychiatric symptoms, and perceive their health to be worse than do other people (Noyes et al., 1993). They are also more likely than other psychiatric patients to report having been sick as children, having missed school because of health reasons, and having experienced childhood trauma, such as sexual abuse or physical violence (Barsky et al., 1994). Most people who meet diagnostic criteria for hypochondriasis continue to show evidence of the disorder when reinterviewed 5 years later (Barsky et al., 1998). Most also have other psychological disorders, especially major depression and anxiety disorders (Barsky, Wyshak, & Klerman, 1992; Noyes et al., 1993).

Body Dysmorphic Disorder

People with **body dysmorphic disorder (BDD)** are preoccupied with an imagined or exaggerated physical defect in their appearance. They may spend hours examining themselves in the mirror and go to extreme measures to correct the perceived defect, even undergoing invasive or unpleasant medical procedures, including unnecessary plastic surgery (Crerand et al., 2005). Others remove all mirrors from their homes so as not to be reminded of the glaring flaw in their appearance. People with BDD may believe that others view them as ugly or deformed and that their unattractive physical appearance leads others to think negatively of them.

Although BDD is believed to be relatively common, we don't have specific data on the rates of the disorder because many people with the disorder fail to

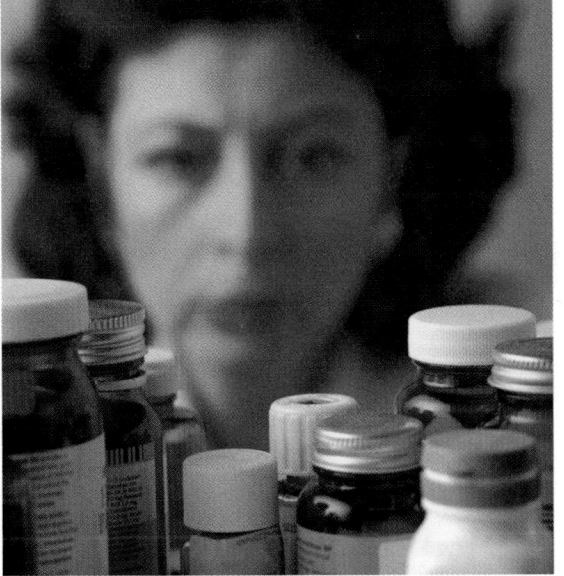

What to take? Hypochondriasis is a persistent concern or fear that one is seriously ill, although no organic basis can be found to account for one's physical complaints. People with this disorder frequently medicate themselves with over-the-counter medications and find little if any reassurance in doctors' assertions that their health is not in jeopardy.

Can't you see it? A person with body dysmorphic disorder may spend hours in front of a mirror obsessing about an imagined or exaggerated physical defect in appearance.

seek help or try to keep their symptoms a secret (Cororve & Gleaves, 2001; Phillips et al., 2006). We should not underplay the emotional distress associated with BDD, as evidence shows high rates of suicidal thinking and suicide attempts among people with the disorder (Phillips & Menard, 2006).

People with BDD often show a pattern of compulsive grooming, washing, or styling their hair in an attempt to correct the perceived defect, as in the following case example.

◆

"When My Hair Isn't Right . . . I'm Not Right": A Case of Body Dysmorphic Disorder

For Claudia, a 24-year-old legal secretary, virtually every day was a bad hair day. She explained to her therapist, "When my hair isn't right, which is like every day, I'm not right." "Can't you see it," she went on to explain, "It's so uneven. This piece should be shorter and this one just lies there. People think I'm crazy but I can't stand looking like this. It makes me look like I'm deformed. It doesn't matter if people can't see what I'm talking about. I see it. That's what counts." Several months earlier Claudia had a haircut she described as a disaster. Shortly thereafter, she had thoughts of killing herself: "I wanted to stab myself in the heart. I just couldn't stand looking at myself."

Claudia checked her hair in the mirror innumerable times during the day. She would spend two hours every morning doing her hair and still wouldn't be satisfied. Her constant pruning and checking had become a compulsive ritual. As she told her therapist, "I want to stop pulling and checking it, but I just can't help myself."

—*From the Author's Files*

Having a "bad hair day" for Claudia meant that she would not go out with her friends and would spend every second examining herself in the mirror and fixing her hair. Occasionally she would cut pieces of her hair herself in an attempt to correct the mistakes of her last haircut. But cutting it herself inevitably made it even worse, in her view. Claudia was forever searching for the perfect haircut that would correct defects only she could perceive. Several years earlier she had what she described as a perfect haircut. "It was just right. I was on top of the world. But it began to look crooked when it grew in." Forever in search of the perfect haircut, Claudia had obtained a hard-to-get appointment with a world-renowned hair stylist in Manhattan, whose clientele included many celebrities. "People wouldn't understand paying this guy $375 for a haircut, especially on my salary, but they don't realize how important it is to me. I'd pay any amount I could." Unfortunately even this celebrated hair stylist disappointed her: "My $25 haircut from my old stylist on Long Island was better than this."

Claudia reported other fixations about her appearance earlier in life: "In high school, I felt my face was like a plate. It was just too flat. I didn't want any pictures taken of me. I couldn't help thinking what people thought of me. They won't tell you, you know. Even if they say there's nothing wrong, it doesn't mean anything. They were just lying to be polite." Claudia related that she was taught to equate physical beauty with happiness: "I was told that to be successful you had to be beautiful. How can I be happy if I look this way?"

Pain Disorder

pain disorder A somatoform disorder in which psychological factors are presumed to play a significant role in the development, severity, or course of chronic pain.

The major feature of somatoform **pain disorder** is pain associated with psychological factors, such as stressful life events. The psychological factors may contribute to the development, severity, or maintenance of the pain. The pain is severe enough and persistent enough to interfere with the person's daily functioning. For example, the pain may make it difficult for the person to attend school or go to work. The pain can become the major focus of the person's life and lead to disruption of normal family life. Pain disorder appears to be relatively common, although precise estimates of its prevalence are lacking (APA, 2000).

The *DSM* system does not exclude the possibility that medical conditions may help explain somatoform pain disorder; both medical conditions and psychological factors can play important roles in the disorder. But when psychological factors play little if any role in the development of pain, the condition is not classified as somatoform pain disorder.

However, the distinction between medical pain and psychiatric pain presents a problem for clinicians (Sharpe & Williams, 2002). The underlying medical cause of pain is often difficult to ascertain. Because they cannot find a physical cause, clinicians may assume that psychological factors play a prominent role. On the other hand, separating "medical pain" from "psychiatric pain" may discount the important role of psychological factors, such as coping responses, in cases of pain that involve obvious medical disease. In sum, the problem of chronic pain is widespread and involves both psychological and medical factors. However, there remains a debate in the field with respect to whether somatoform pain disorder should stand on its own as a diagnosable psychological disorder (Sullivan, 2000).

Somatization Disorder

Somatization disorder, formerly known as Briquet's syndrome, is characterized by multiple and recurrent somatic complaints that begin prior to the age of 30 (but usually during the teen years). These complaints persist for at least several years, and result either in the seeking of medical attention or in significant impairment in fulfilling social or occupational roles.

somatization disorder A somatoform disorder characterized by repeated multiple complaints that cannot be explained by physical causes.

Somatization disorder frustrates patients, their families, and their physicians (Holder-Perkins & Wise, 2002). Complaints usually involve different organ systems. Patients' complaints cannot be explained by physical causes or exceed what would be expected from a known physical problem. Complaints seem vague or exaggerated, and the person frequently receives medical care from a number of physicians, sometimes at the same time. Seldom does a year pass without some physical complaint that prompts a trip to the doctor, or generally, to many doctors. A study that tracked medical-care utilization of somatizing patients found them to be heavy users of medical services (Barsky, Orav, & Bates, 2005).

The essential feature of hypochondriasis is fear of disease, of what bodily symptoms may portend. Persons with somatization disorder, by contrast, are pestered by the symptoms themselves. Both diagnoses may be given to the same individual if the diagnostic criteria for both disorders are met.

Reported rates of somatization disorder vary from 0.2% to 2% in women to less than 0.2% in men (APA, 2000). The disorder is also four times more likely to occur among African Americans than other ethnic or racial groups (Swartz et al., 1991). Yet, like pain disorder, somatization disorder is controversial. Many patients, especially female patients, are misdiagnosed with psychological disorders, including somatization disorder, because modern medicine fails to identify the underlying medical basis of their physical complaints (Klonoff & Landrine, 1997).

Somatization disorder usually begins in adolescence or young adulthood and appears to be a chronic or even lifelong disorder. Although not much is known about the childhood backgrounds of people with somatization disorder, a recent study characterized the family environments in which many somatization disorder patients were raised as emotionally cold, distant, and unsupportive and wracked by a pattern of chronic emotional and physical abuse (Brown, Schrag, & Trimble, 2005).

koro syndrome A culture-bound somatoform disorder, found primarily in China, in which people fear that their genitals are shrinking.

In China in the 1980s, more than 2,000 people fell prey to the belief that their genitals were shrinking and retracting into their bodies.

✓ **TRUE.** An epidemic was reported in China in which some 2,000 people fell prey to the belief that their genitals were shrinking and retracting into their bodies. This condition, called koro, is classified by the *DSM* system as a culture-bound syndrome.

dhat syndrome A culture-bound somatoform disorder, found primarily among Asian Indian males, characterized by excessive fears over the loss of seminal fluid.

Koro and Dhat Syndromes: Far Eastern Somatoform Disorders?

In the United States, it is common for people who develop hypochondriasis to be troubled by the idea that they have serious illnesses, such as cancer. The koro and dhat syndromes of the Far East share some clinical features with hypochondriasis. Although these syndromes may seem foreign to North American readers, each is connected with the folklore of its own culture.

Koro syndrome is a culture-bound syndrome found primarily in China and some other Far Eastern countries (Sheung-Tak, 1996). People with koro syndrome fear that their genitals are shrinking and retracting into their body, which they believe will result in death (Fabian, 1991; Goetz & Price, 1994; Tseng et al., 1992). Koro is considered a culture-bound syndrome, although some cases have been reported outside China and the Far East (e.g., Chowdhury, 1996). The syndrome has been identified mainly in young men, although some cases have also been reported in women (Tseng et al., 1992). Koro syndrome tends to be short-lived and to involve episodes of acute anxiety that one's genitals are retracting. Physiological signs of anxiety that approach panic are common, including profuse sweating, breathlessness, and heart palpitations. Men who suffer from koro have been known to use mechanical devices, such as chopsticks, to try to prevent the penis from retracting into the body (Devan, 1987).

Koro syndrome has been traced within Chinese culture as far back as 3000 B.C.E. Epidemics involving hundreds or thousands of people have been reported in China, Singapore, Thailand, and India (Tseng et al., 1992). In Guangdong Province in China, an epidemic of koro involving more than 2,000 persons occurred during the 1980s (Tseng et al., 1992). Guangdong residents who developed koro tended to be more superstitious, lower in intelligence, and more accepting of koro-related folk beliefs (such as the belief that shrinkage of the penis will be lethal) than those who did not fall victim to the epidemic (Tseng et al., 1992). Medical reassurance that such fears are unfounded often quells koro episodes (Devan, 1987). Koro episodes among those who do not receive corrective information tend to pass with time but may recur. A number of investigators would like to see the koro syndrome incorporated into the *DSM* as a somatoform disorder (Bernstein & Gaw, 1990; Fishbain, 1991).

Dhat syndrome, found among young Asian Indian males, involves excessive fears over the loss of seminal fluid during nocturnal emissions (Akhtar, 1988). Some men with this syndrome also believe (incorrectly) that semen mixes with urine and is excreted through urination. Men with dhat syndrome may roam from physician to physician seeking help to prevent nocturnal emissions or the (imagined) loss of semen mixed with excreted urine. There is a widespread belief within Indian culture (and other Near and Far Eastern cultures) that the loss of semen is harmful because it depletes the body of physical and mental energy (Chadda & Ahuja, 1990). Like other culture-bound syndromes, dhat must be understood within its cultural context:

> In India, attitudes toward semen and its loss constitute an organized, deep-seated belief system that can be traced back to the scriptures of the land ... [even as far back as the classic Indian sex manual, the Kama Sutra, which was believed to be written by the sage Vatsayana between the third and fifth centuries A.D.].... Semen is considered to be the elixir of life, in both a physical and mystical sense. Its preservation is supposed to guarantee health and longevity.
>
> —From Akhtar, 1988, p. 71

It is a commonly held Hindu belief that it takes "forty meals to form one drop of blood; forty drops of blood to fuse and form one drop of bone marrow, and forty drops of this to produce one drop of semen" (Akhtar, 1988, p. 71). Based on the

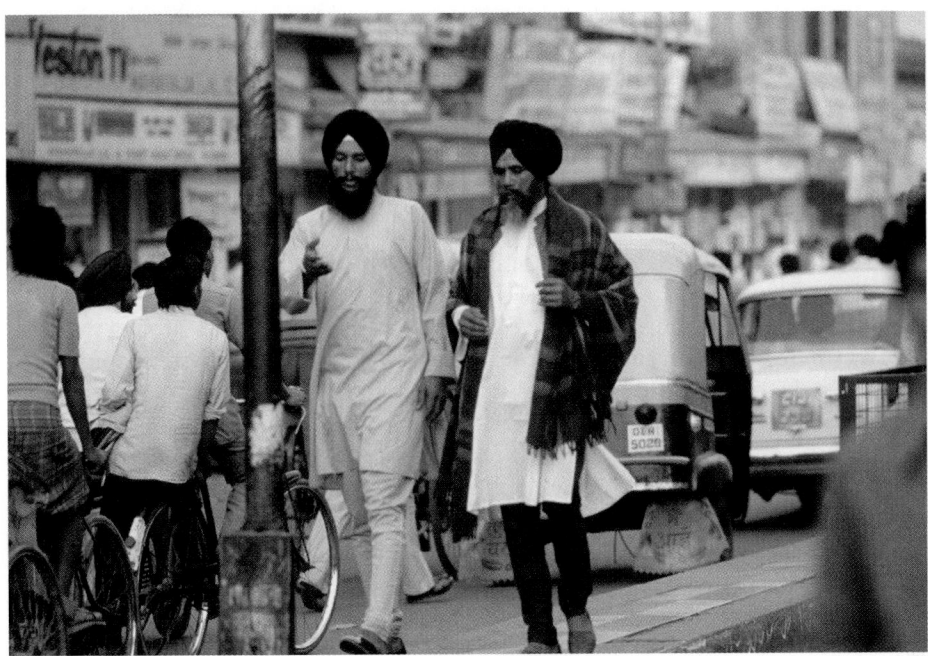

Dhat syndrome. Found principally in India, dhat syndrome describes men with an intense fear or anxiety over the loss of semen.

cultural belief in the life-preserving nature of semen, it is not surprising that some Indian males experience extreme anxiety over the involuntary loss of the fluid through nocturnal emissions (Akhtar, 1988). Dhat syndrome has also been associated with difficulty in achieving or maintaining erection, apparently due to excessive concern about loss of seminal fluid through ejaculation (Singh, 1985).

Theoretical Perspectives

Conversion disorder, or "hysteria," was known to the great physician of ancient Greece, Hippocrates, who attributed the strange bodily symptoms to a wandering uterus (*hystera* in Greek) creating internal chaos. Hippocrates noticed that these complaints were less common among married than unmarried women. He prescribed marriage as a "cure" on the basis of these observations and also on the theoretical assumption that pregnancy would satisfy uterine needs and fix the organ in place. Pregnancy fosters hormonal and structural changes that are of benefit to some women with menstrual complaints, but Hippocrates's mistaken belief in the "wandering uterus" has contributed throughout the centuries to degrading interpretations of complaints by women of physical problems. Despite Hippocrates's belief that hysteria is exclusively a female concern, it also occurs in men.

Not much is known about the biological underpinnings of somatoform disorders. However, a genetic link to somatization disorder is suggested by evidence that the disorder tends to run in families, primarily among female members (Guze, 1993). However, we cannot rule out the possibility that social influences play a part in explaining this familial association.

Brain-imaging studies of patients with hysterical paralysis (a limb the person claims to be unable to move, despite healthy muscles and nerve) points to possible disruptions occurring in brain circuitry responsible for controlling movement and emotional responses (Kinetz, 2006). These imaging studies suggest that normal control

The wandering uterus. The ancient Greek physician Hippocrates believed that hysterical symptoms were exclusively a female problem caused by a wandering uterus. Might he have changed his mind had he the opportunity to treat male aviators during World War II who developed "hysterical night blindness" that prevented them from carrying out dangerous nighttime missions?

of movement may be inhibited by activation of brain circuits involved in processing emotions. We should caution that we are only at the beginning stages of understanding the biological bases of conversion disorder and much remains unknown. Like the dissociative disorders, the scientific study of conversion disorder and other forms of somatoform disorder has been largely approached from the psychological perspective, which is our focus here.

Psychodynamic Theory Hysterical disorders provided an arena for some of the debate between the psychological and biological theories of the 19th century. The alleviation—albeit often temporarily—of hysterical symptoms through hypnosis by Charcot, Breuer, and Freud contributed to the belief that hysteria was rooted in psychological rather than physical causes and led Freud to the development of a theory of the unconscious mind (see Chapter 1). Freud held that the ego manages to control unacceptable or threatening sexual and aggressive impulses arising from the id through defense mechanisms such as repression. Such control prevents the anxiety that would occur if the person were to become aware of these impulses. In some cases, the leftover emotion that is "strangulated," or cut off, from the threatening impulses, becomes *converted* into a physical symptom, such as hysterical paralysis or blindness. Although the early psychodynamic formulation of hysteria is still widely held, empirical evidence has been lacking. One problem with the Freudian view is that it does not explain how energies left over from unconscious conflicts become transformed into physical symptoms (E. Miller, 1987).

According to psychodynamic theory, hysterical symptoms are functional: They allow the person to achieve *primary gains* and *secondary gains.* The primary gain of the symptoms is to allow the individual to keep internal conflicts repressed. The person is aware of the physical symptom but not of the conflict it represents. In such cases, the "symptom" is symbolic of, and provides the person with a "partial solution" for, the underlying conflict. For example, the hysterical paralysis of an arm might symbolize and also prevent the individual from acting out on repressed unacceptable sexual (e.g., masturbatory) or aggressive (e.g., murderous) impulses. Repression occurs unconsciously, so the individual remains unaware of the underlying conflicts. *La belle indifférence,* first noted by Charcot, is believed to occur because the physical symptoms help relieve rather than cause anxiety. From the psychodynamic perspective, conversion disorders, like dissociative disorders, serve a purpose.

Secondary gains from the symptoms are those that allow the individual to avoid burdensome responsibilities and to gain the support—rather than condemnation—of those around them. For example, soldiers sometimes experience sudden "paralysis" of their hands, which prevents them from firing their guns in battle. They may then be sent to recuperate at a hospital rather than face enemy fire. The symptoms in such cases are not considered contrived, as would be the case in malingering. A number of bomber pilots during World War II suffered hysterical "night blindness" that prevented them from carrying out dangerous nighttime missions. In the psychodynamic view, their "blindness" may have achieved a primary gain of shielding them from guilt associated with dropping bombs on civilian areas. It may also have achieved a secondary purpose of helping them avoid dangerous missions.

Learning Theory Theoretical formulations including both psychodynamic theory and learning theory, focus on the role of anxiety in explaining conversion disorders. Psychodynamic theorists, however, seek the causes of anxiety in unconscious conflicts. Learning theorists focus on the more direct reinforcing properties of the symptom and its secondary role in helping the individual avoid or escape anxiety-evoking situations.

From the learning perspective, the symptoms in conversion and other somatoform disorders may also carry the benefits, or reinforcing properties, of the "sick role." Persons with conversion disorders may be relieved of chores and responsibilities such as going to work or performing household tasks (Miller, 1987). Being sick also usually earns sympathy and support. See *Tying it Together* on page 226 for a schematic representation of the psychodynamic and learning theory conceptualizations of conversion disorder.

Differences in learning experiences may explain why conversion disorders were historically more often reported among women than men. It may be that women in Western culture are more likely than men to be socialized to cope with stress by enacting a sick role (Miller, 1987). We are not suggesting that people with conversion disorders are fakers. We are merely pointing out that people may learn to adopt roles that lead to reinforcing consequences, regardless of whether they deliberately seek to enact these roles.

Some learning theorists link hypochondriasis and body dysmorphic disorder to obsessive–compulsive disorder (OCD; see Chapter 6) (e.g., Barsky et al., 1992; Buhlmann et al., 2002; Cororve & Gleaves, 2001). In hypochondriasis, people are bothered by obsessive, anxiety-inducing thoughts about their health. Running from doctor to doctor may be a form of compulsive behavior that is reinforced by the temporary relief from anxiety that patients experience when doctors assure them that their fears are unwarranted. Yet the troublesome thoughts eventually return, prompting repeated consultations. The cycle then repeats. Similarly, with body dysmorphic disorder, the constant grooming and pruning in the attempt to "fix" the perceived physical defect may offer partial relief from anxiety, but the "fix" is never quite good enough to completely erase the underlying concerns.

Cognitive Theory Cognitive theorists have speculated that some cases of hypochondriasis may represent a type of self-handicapping strategy, a way of blaming poor performance on failing health (Smith, Snyder, & Perkins, 1983). In other cases, diverting attention to physical complaints can serve as a means of avoiding thinking about other life problems.

Another cognitive explanation focuses on the role of distorted thinking. People who develop hypochondriasis have a tendency to exaggerate the significance of minor physical complaints (Barsky et al., 2001). They misinterpret benign symptoms as signs of a serious illness, which creates anxiety, which leads them to chase down one doctor after another in an attempt to uncover the dreaded disease they fear they have. The anxiety itself may lead to unpleasant physical symptoms, which are likewise exaggerated in importance, leading to more worrisome cognitions.

Cognitive theorists speculate that hypochondriasis and panic disorder, which often occur together, may share a common cause: a distorted way of thinking that leads the person to misinterpret minor changes in bodily sensations as signs of pending catastrophe (Salkovskis & Clark, 1993). Differences between the two disorders may hinge on whether the misinterpretation of bodily cues carries a perception of an imminent threat that leads to a rapid spiraling of anxiety (panic disorder) or of a longer-range threat that leads to a fear of an underlying disease process (hypochondriasis).

Given the role of anxiety in hypochondriasis and somatization disorder, investigators question whether these disorders should continue to be classified as distinct forms of somatoform disorders (Creed & Barsky, 2004). Evidence shows a high rate of co-occurrence (*comorbidity*) of hypochondriasis and somatization disorder with both anxiety and depressive disorders (Creed & Barsky, 2004; de Waal et al., 2004; Holder-Perkins & Wise, 2002). As the DSM-V is taking shape, some investigators are calling for a reconsideration of how the somatoform disorders are classified (e.g., De Gucht & Maes, 2006; Mayou et al., 2005).

Figure 7.2 provides a visual representation of the two leading concept models of conversion disorder (psychodynamic theory and learning theory).

Treatment of Somatoform Disorders

The treatment approach that Freud pioneered, psychoanalysis, began with the treatment of hysteria, which is now termed conversion disorder. Psychoanalysis seeks to uncover and bring unconscious conflicts that originated in childhood into conscious awareness. Once the conflict is aired and worked through, the symptom is no longer needed and should disappear. The psychoanalytic method is supported by case studies, some reported by Freud and others by his followers. However, the infrequent occurrence of conversion disorders in contemporary times has made it difficult to mount controlled studies of the psychoanalytic technique.

The behavioral approach to treating conversion disorders and other somatoform disorders focuses on removing sources of secondary reinforcement (or secondary gain) that may become connected with physical complaints. Family members and others, for example, often perceive individuals with somatization disorder as sickly and incapable of carrying normal responsibilities. This reinforces dependent and complaining behaviors. The behavior therapist may teach family members to reward attempts to assume responsibility and to ignore nagging and complaining. The behavior therapist may also work directly with patients, helping them learn more adaptive ways of handling stress or anxiety (through relaxation and cognitive restructuring, for example).

Cognitive-behavioral therapy has achieved good results in treating several types of somatoform disorders, including hypochondriasis and body dysmorphic disorder

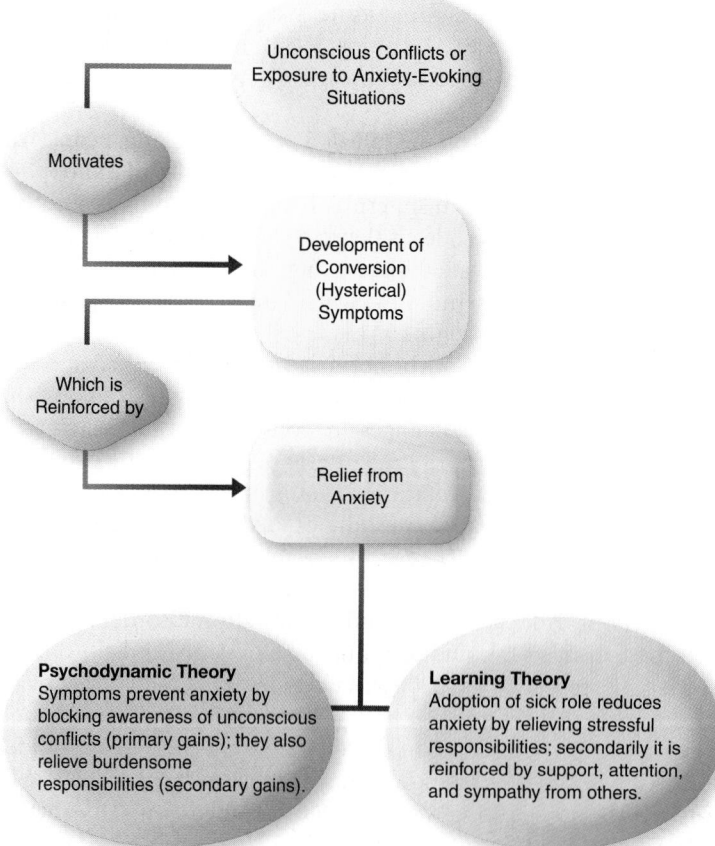

FIGURE 7.2 Conceptual models of conversion disorder.
Psychodynamic and learning theory offer conceptual models of conversion disorder that emphasize the role of conversion symptoms leading to escape or relief from anxiety.

(Barksy & Ahern, 2004; Looper & Kirmayer, 2002; Visser & Bouman, 2001; Williams, Hadjistavropoulos, & Sharpe, 2006). In treating hypochondriasis, for example, the cognitive technique of restructuring distorted beliefs helps people replace exaggerated illness-related beliefs with rational alternatives. The behavioral technique of *exposure with response prevention,* which is discussed in Chapter 6, can help hypochondriasis patients people break the cycle of running to doctors for reassurance whenever they experience some worrisome, health-related concerns. People with hypochondriasis can also benefit from breaking problem habits, such as repeatedly checking the Internet for illness-related information and reading newspaper obituaries (Barksy & Ahern, 2004; "Study Finds," 2004). Unfortunately, many hypochondriasis patients drop out of treatment when they are told that their problems are psychological in nature, not physical. As one leading expert, Dr. Arthur Barksy, put it, "They'll say, 'I don't need to talk about this, I need somebody to stick a biopsy needle in my liver, I need that CAT scan repeated.'" ("Therapy and Hypochondriacs," 2004, p. A19.)

In treating body dysmorphic disorder (BDD), exposure can take the form of intentionally revealing the perceived defect in public, rather than concealing it with makeup or clothing (Cororve & Gleaves, 2001). Response prevention may involve efforts to avoid mirror checking (for example, by covering mirrors at home) and excessive grooming. In cognitive restructuring, therapists challenge clients' distorted beliefs about their physical appearance by encouraging them to evaluate these beliefs in the light of evidence.

Attention has recently turned to the use of antidepressants, especially fluoxetine (Prozac), in treating some types of somatoform disorder (Rief & Sharpe, 2004). However, there remains little research involving controlled drug-placebo studies to present firm conclusions regarding the efficacy of drug therapy for somatoform disorders. We do have a recent finding that the antidepressant drug *fluvoxamine* (brand name Luvox) showed therapeutic benefits in treating somatoform pain disorder (Turkington et al., 2002). We also have learned that the drug Prozac was significantly more effective than placebo in treating factitious disorder (Münchausen syndrome) (Phillips, Albertini, & Rasmussen, 2002).

Before moving on, you may wish to review the *Concept Map for Abnormal Psychology,* shown on page 244–245, which depicts the causal factors and treatments of dissociative disorders and somatoform disorders. All in all, the dissociative and somatoform disorders remain among the most intriguing and least understood patterns of abnormal behavior.

SUMMING UP

Dissociative Disorders

What are dissociative disorders? Dissociative disorders involve changes or disturbances in identity, memory, or consciousness that affect the ability to maintain an integrated sense of self. Thus, the symptoms are theorized to reflect psychological rather than organic factors.

What is dissociative identity disorder? In dissociative identity disorder, two or more distinct personalities, each possessing well-defined traits and memories, exist within the person and repeatedly take control of the person's behavior.

What is dissociative amnesia? In dissociative amnesia, the person experiences a loss of memory for personal information that cannot be accounted for by organic causes.

What is dissociative fugue? In dissociative fugue, the person suddenly travels away from home or place of work, shows a loss of memory for his or her personal past, and experiences identity confusion or takes on a new identity.

What is depersonalization disorder? In depersonalization disorder, the person experiences persistent or recurrent episodes of depersonalization of sufficient severity to cause significant distress or impairment in functioning.

How do theorists explain the development of dissociative disorders? Psychodynamic theorists view dissociative disorders as a form of psychological defense by which the ego defends itself against troubling memories and unacceptable impulses by blotting them out of consciousness. There is increasing documentation of a link between dissociative disorders and early childhood trauma, which lends support to the view that dissociation may serve to protect the self from troubling memories. To learning and cognitive theorists, dissociative experiences involve ways of learning not to think about certain troubling behaviors or thoughts that might lead to feelings of guilt or shame. Relief from anxiety negatively reinforces this pattern of dissociation. Some social-cognitive theorists suggest that multiple personality may represent a form of role-playing behavior.

How is dissociative identity disorder treated? The major form of treatment is psychotherapy aimed at achieving a reintegration of the personality by focusing on helping persons with dissociative identity disorder uncover and integrate dissociated painful experiences from childhood.

Somatoform Disorders

What are somatoform disorders? In somatoform disorders, there are physical complaints that cannot be accounted for by organic causes. Thus, the symptoms are theorized to reflect psychological rather than organic factors. Three major types of somatoform disorders are conversion disorder, hypochondriasis, and somatization disorder.

What is Münchausen syndrome? Münchausen syndrome, a type of factitious disorder, is characterized by the deliberate fabrication of physical symptoms for no apparent reason, other than to assume a patient role.

What is conversion disorder? In conversion disorder, symptoms or deficits in voluntary motor or sensory functions occur that suggest an underlying physical disorder, but no apparent medical basis for the condition can be found to account for the condition.

What is hypochondriasis? Hypochondriasis is a preoccupation with the fear of having, or the belief that one has, a serious medical illness, although no medical basis for the complaints can be found, and fears of illness persist despite medical reassurances.

What is pain disorder? Pain disorder is a type of somatoform disorder in which psychological factors are presumed to play important roles in explaining symptoms of pain.

What is body dysmorphic disorder? In body dysmorphic disorder, people are preoccupied with an imagined or exaggerated defect in their physical appearance.

What is somatization disorder? People with somatization disorder have multiple and recurrent complaints of physical symptoms that have persisted for many years and that cannot be accounted for by organic causes.

How are somatoform disorders conceptualized within the major theoretical perspectives? The psychodynamic view holds that conversion disorders represent the conversion into physical symptoms of the leftover emotion or energy cut off from unacceptable or threatening impulses that the ego has prevented from reaching awareness. The symptom is functional, allowing the person to achieve both primary gains and secondary gains. Learning theorists focus on reinforcements that are associated with conversion disorders, such as the reinforcing effects of adopting a "sick role." One learning-theory model likens hypochondriasis to obsessive–compulsive behavior. Cognitive factors in hypochondriasis include possible self-handicapping strategies and cognitive distortions.

What are the major approaches to treating somatoform disorders? Psychodynamic therapists attempt to uncover and bring to the level of awareness the unconscious conflicts, originating in childhood, believed to be at the root of the problem. Once the conflict is uncovered and worked through, the symptoms should disappear because they are no longer needed as a partial solution to the underlying conflict. Behavioral approaches focus on removing underlying sources of reinforcement that may be maintaining the abnormal behavior pattern. More generally, behavior therapists assist people with somatoform disorders to learn to handle stressful or anxiety-arousing situations more effectively. In addition, a combination of cognitive-behavioral techniques, such as exposure with response prevention and cognitive restructuring, may be used in treating hypochondriasis and body dysmorphic disorder. Antidepressant medication may prove to be helpful in treating some forms of somatoform disorders.

KEY TERMS

dissociative disorder *(p. 212)*
dissociative identity disorder *(p. 214)*
dissociative amnesia *(p. 217)*
dissociative fugue *(p. 219)*
depersonalization *(p. 221)*
derealization *(p. 221)*

depersonalization disorder *(p. 222)*
somatoform disorders *(p. 227)*
malingering *(p. 228)*
factitious disorder *(p. 229)*
Münchausen syndrome *(p. 229)*
conversion disorder *(p. 231)*

hypochondriasis *(p. 232)*
body dysmorphic disorder (BDD) *(p. 233)*
pain disorder *(p. 234)*
somatization disorder *(p. 235)*
koro syndrome *(p. 236)*
dhat syndrome *(p. 236)*

MEDIA TOOLS

A variety of digital and online learning tools are available to enrich your learning experience and help you succeed in the course. These resources include:

- **MyPsychLab,** an online learning system for your course in abnormal psychology that allows you to test your mastery of concepts in the book by using chapter-by-chapter diagnostic tests. Results from the diagnostic tests help you build a customized study plan. To access **MyPsychLab,** visit www.prenhall.com/mypsychlab and follow the instructions on the site.

- **"Speaking Out" Patient Interviews,** a set of video case examples of actual patients you can access on the companion CD-ROM included with the text. Icons in the margins of the chapter highlight the video case examples included on the CD-ROM.

- **Companion Web site,** an online study center that offers computer-scored quizzes you can use to test your knowledge, along with other study tools and links to related sites to enhance your learning of abnormal psychology. To access the companion web site, visit www.prenhall.com/nevid and use the various tabs and links on the site to access these learning resources.

Dissociative Disorders

are characterized by

Disruption or dissociation of identity, memory, or consciousness

and include such types as

- Dissociative Identity Disorder
- Dissociative Amnesia
- Dissociative Fugue
- Depersonalization Disorder

and may be explained by causal factors including

• Psychotherapy aimed at reintegration of the personality in cases of dissociative identity disorder. However, studies of treatment effectiveness have been limited to isolated case examples.

and may be treated by

- Social-environmental factors, such as severe childhood sexual or physical abuse (in dissociative identity disorder) or exposure to traumatic experiences (in dissociative amnesia and dissociative fugue)
- Social-cognitive factors, such as positive reinforcement (attention) for enacting the role of a multiple personality and negative reinforcement in the form of anxiety relief from splitting off disturbing memories (in dissociative amnesia and dissociative fugue)
- Possible biological factors, such as abnormalities in parts of the brain involved in regulating memory and emotion

Somatoform Disorders

are characterized by

Physical complaints not accounted for by organic causes or exaggerated concerns about physical complaints or perceived physical defects

and include such types as

- Conversion Disorder
- Hypochondriasis
- Body Dysmorphic Disorder
- Pain Disorder
- Somatization Disorder

and may be explained by causal factors including

- Possible genetic factors (somatization disorder)
- Social-environmental factors, such as socialization into dependent (sick) roles
- Learning factors, such as positive reinforcement (for enacting sick role) and negative reinforcement (relief from anxiety by avoiding or escaping anxiety-evoking or burdensome situations)
- Cognitive factors, such as misinterpretations of physical symptoms
- In Freudian theory, conversion of psychic energy into physical symptoms (conversion disorder)
- Interactions among multiple factors

and may be treated by

- Cognitive-behavioral techniques to promote more adaptive ways of handling stress and anxiety and correct distorted beliefs about health or appearance
- Psychodynamic therapy to gain insight into underlying unconscious conflicts
- Limited uses of drug therapy in treating some types of somatoform disorder

Mood Disorders and Suicide

CHAPTER OUTLINE

TYPES OF MOOD DISORDERS 248–259

Major Depressive Disorder
Dysthymic Disorder
Bipolar Disorder
Cyclothymic Disorder

CAUSAL FACTORS IN DEPRESSIVE DISORDERS 259–269

Stress and Depression
Psychodynamic Theories
Humanistic Theories

Learning Theories
Cognitive Theories
Learned Helplessness (Attributional) Theory
Biological Factors

CAUSAL FACTORS IN BIPOLAR DISORDERS 269–270

TREATMENT OF MOOD DISORDERS 270–278

Treating Depression
Biological Approaches

Treating Bipolar Disorder

SUICIDE 278–285

Who Commits Suicide?
Why Do People Commit Suicide?
Theoretical Perspectives on Suicide
Predicting Suicide

SUMMING UP 285–286

William Styron (1925–2006), the celebrated author of *The Confessions of Nat Turner* and *Sophie's Choice*, suffered at age 60 from depression that was so severe that he planned to commit suicide. In a 1990 memoir he speaks about this personal darkness and about reclaiming his commitment to life.

"I"
Darkness Visible

I watched myself in mingled terror and fascination as I began to make the necessary preparation: going to see my lawyer in the nearby town—there rewriting my will—and spending part of a couple of afternoons in a muddled attempt to bestow upon posterity a letter of farewell. It turned out that putting together a suicide note, which I felt obsessed with a necessity to compose, was the most difficult task of writing that I had ever tackled. . . .

But even a few words came to seem to me too longwinded, and I tore up all my efforts, resolving to go out in silence. Late one bitterly cold night, when I knew that I could not possibly get myself through the following day, I sat in the living room of the house bundled up against the chill; something had happened to the furnace. My wife had gone to bed, and I had forced myself to watch the tape of a movie in which a young actress, who had been in a play of mine, was cast in a small part. At one point in the film, which was set in late–nineteenth-century Boston, the characters moved down the hallway of a music conservatory, beyond the walls of which, from unseen musicians, came a contralto voice, a sudden soaring passage from the *Brahms Alto Rhapsody*.

This sound, which like all music—indeed, like all pleasure—I had been numbly unresponsive to for months, pierced my heart like a dagger, and in a flood of swift recollection I thought of all the joys the house had known: the children who had rushed through its rooms, the festivals, the love and work, the honestly earned slumber, the voices and the nimble commotion, the perennial tribe of cats and dogs and birds. . . . All this I realized was more than I could ever abandon, even as what I had set out so deliberately to do was more than I could inflict on those memories, and upon those, so close to me, with whom the memories were bound. And just as powerfully I realized I could not commit this desecration on myself. I drew upon some last gleam of sanity to perceive the terrifying dimensions of the mortal predicament I had fallen into. I woke up my wife and soon telephone calls were made. The next day I was admitted to the hospital.

—*From* Darkness Visible *by* William Styron

A DISTINGUISHED AUTHOR STANDS AT THE PRECIPICE OF TAKING HIS OWN LIFE. THE depression that enshrouded him and that nearly cost him his life—this *darkness visible*—is an unwelcome companion for millions of people. Depression is a disturbance of mood that casts a long, deep shadow over many facets of life.

Moods are feeling states that color our psychological lives. Most of experience changes in mood. We feel elated when we have earned high grades, a promotion, or the affections of Ms. or Mr. Right. We feel down or depressed when we are rejected by a date, flunk a test, or suffer financial reverses. It is normal and appropriate to be happy about uplifting events. It is just as normal, just as appropriate, to feel depressed by dismal events. It might very well be abnormal if we did not feel down or depressed in the face of tragic or deeply disappointing events or circumstances. But people with **mood disorders** experience disturbances in mood that are unusually severe or prolonged and impair their ability to function in meeting their normal responsibilities. Some people become severely depressed even when things appear to be going well or when they encounter mildly upsetting events that others take in stride. Still others experience extreme mood swings. They ride an emotional roller coaster with dizzying

T☐ F☐ Feeling sad or depressed is abnormal. (p. 249)

T☐ F☐ The economic toll of depression is about half that of heart disease or diabetes. (p. 251)

T☐ F☐ Most people who experience a major depressive episode never have another one. (p. 252)

T☐ F☐ Men are about twice as likely as women to develop major depression. (p. 252)

T☐ F☐ The bleak light of winter casts some people into a diagnosable state of depression. (p. 253)

T☐ F☐ The ancient Greeks and Romans used a chemical to curb turbulent mood swings that is still used today. (p. 276)

T☐ F☐ Placing a powerful electromagnet on the scalp can help relieve depression. (p. 278)

T☐ F☐ People who threaten suicide are basically attention seekers. (p. 282)

mood disorders Psychological disorders characterized by disturbances of mood.

247

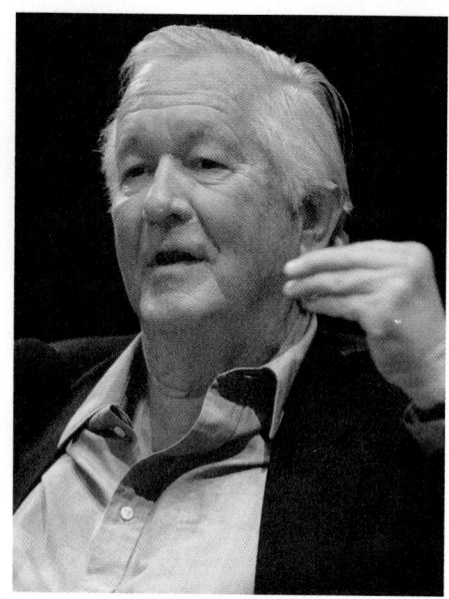

William Styron. The celebrated author William Styron suffered from severe depression—a "darkness visible" that led him to the precipice of suicide.

heights and abysmal depths when the world around them remains largely on an even keel. Let us begin our study of these types of emotional problems by examining the different types of mood disorders.

TYPES OF MOOD DISORDERS

This chapter explores major forms of mood disorder: depressive disorders and bipolar disorders (mood swing disorders). We will see that there are two major types of depressive disorders that vary in severity: *major depressive disorder,* the more severe type, and *dysthymic disorder* (also called *dysthymia*), the milder type. Similarly, bipolar or mood swing disorders vary in terms of severity—the more severe disorder is called *bipolar disorder,* whereas the milder disorder is termed *cyclothymic disorder* (also called *cyclothymia*). Note that depressive disorders are also called *unipolar* disorders, because the mood disturbance is in only one emotional direction or pole: down. By contrast, mood swing disorders are labeled *bipolar* disorders because they involve states of both depression and elation, which often appear in an alternating pattern. Table 8.1 provides an overview of these disorders. A convenient way of conceptualizing differences in mood states corresponding to these disorders is shown in the form of a mood thermometer in Figure 8.1.

Many of us, probably most of us, have periods of sadness from time to time. We may feel down in the dumps, cry, lose interest in things, find it hard to concentrate, expect the worst to happen, or even consider suicide. For most of us, mood changes pass

Table 8.1 Overview of Mood Disorders

TYPE OF DISORDER		Lifetime Prevalence (approx.)	Primary Features or Symptoms	Related Features
Depressive Disorders	Major depression	12% in men; 21% in women; 16.5% overall	Episodes of severe depression characterized by downcast mood, feelings of hopelessness and worthlessness, changes in sleep patterns or appetite, loss of motivation, loss of pleasure in pleasant activities	Following a depressive episode, the person may return to his or her usual state of functioning, but recurrences are common. Seasonal affective disorder (SAD) is a type of major depression.
	Dysthymic disorder	4.3%	A chronic pattern of mild depression	Person feels "down in the dumps" most of the time, but is not as severely depressed as in major depression.
Bipolar Disorders	Bipolar disorder	0.4% to 1.6% (4 to 16 people in 1,000) for bipolar I disorder; 0.5% for bipolar disorder II	Periods of shifting moods between mania and depression, perhaps with intervening periods of normal mood; two general subtypes are bipolar I disorder (history of manic episode and possible major depressive episode) and bipolar II disorder (major depressive episode and hypomanic episode)	Manic episodes are characterized by pressured speech, flight of ideas, poor judgment, high levels of restlessness and excitability, and inflated mood and sense of self.
	Cyclothymic disorder (cyclothymia)	0.4% to 1% (4 to 10 people in 1,000)	Mood swings that are milder in severity than those in bipolar disorder	Cyclothymia usually begins in late adolescence or early adulthood and tends to persist for years.

Source: Adapted from J. S. Nevid, *Psychology: Concepts and Applications,* Second Edition (Boston: Houghton Mifflin Co., 2007), p. 527. Reprinted with permission.

Severe mania

Hypomania (mild to moderate mania)

Normal/balanced mood

Mild to moderate depression

Severe depression

FIGURE 8.1 A mood thermometer.
Mood states can be conceptualized as varying along a spectrum or continuum. One end represents severe depression and the other end severe mania, which is a cardinal feature of bipolar disorder. Mild or moderate depression is often called "the blues" but is classified as "dysthymia" when it becomes chronic. In the middle of the spectrum is normal or balanced mood. Mild or moderate mania is called hypomania, which characterizes cyclothymic disorder.
Source: NIMH, 2001.

quickly or are not severe enough to interfere with our lifestyle or ability to function. Among people with mood disorders, including depressive disorders and bipolar disorders, mood changes are more severe or prolonged and affect daily functioning.

Major Depressive Disorder

The diagnosis of **major depressive disorder** (also called *major depression*) is based on the occurrence of one or more *major depressive episodes* in the absence of a history of **mania** or **hypomania**. In a major depressive episode, the person experiences either a depressed mood (feeling sad, hopeless, or "down in the dumps") or loss of interest or pleasure in all or virtually all activities for a period of at least 2 weeks (APA, 2000). Table 8.2 lists some of the common features of depression. The diagnostic criteria for a major depressive episode are listed in Table 8.3.

T R U T H or F I C T I O N

Feeling sad or depressed is abnormal.

☑ **FALSE.** Feeling depressed is not abnormal in the context of depressing events or circumstances.

major depressive disorder A severe mood disorder characterized by major depressive episodes.

mania A state of unusual elation, energy, and activity.

hypomania A relatively mild state of mania.

TABLE 8.2

Common Features of Depression

Changes in Emotional States	• Changes in mood (persistent periods of feeling down, depressed, sad, or blue) • Evidence of tearfulness or crying • Increased irritability, jumpiness, or loss of temper
Changes in Motivation	• Feeling unmotivated, or having difficulty getting going in the morning or even getting out of bed • Reduced level of social participation or interest in social activities • Loss of enjoyment or interest in pleasurable activities • Reduced interest in sex • Failure to respond to praise or rewards
Changes in Functioning and Motor Behavior	• Moving about or talking more slowly than usual • Changes in sleep habits (sleeping too much or too little, awakening earlier than usual and having trouble getting back to sleep in early morning hours—so-called early morning awakening) • Changes in appetite (eating too much or too little) • Changes in weight (gaining or losing weight) • Functioning less effectively at work or school; failing to meet responsibilities and neglecting one's physical appearance
Cognitive Changes	• Difficulty concentrating or thinking clearly • Thinking negatively about oneself and one's future • Feeling guilty or remorseful about past misdeeds • Lack of self-esteem or feelings of inadequacy • Thinking of death or suicide

TABLE 8.3

Diagnostic Features of a Major Depressive Episode

A major depressive episode is denoted by the occurrence of five or more of the following features or symptoms during a 2-week period, which represents a change from previous functioning. At least one of the features must involve either (1) depressed mood, or (2) loss of interest or pleasure in activities. Moreover, the symptoms must cause either clinically significant levels of distress or impairment in at least one important area of functioning, such as social or occupational functioning, and must not be due directly to the use of drugs or medications, to a medical condition, or be accounted for by another psychological disorder.* Further, the episode must not represent a normal grief reaction to the death of a loved one—that is, bereavement.

1. Depressed mood during most of the day, nearly every day. Can be irritable mood in children or adolescents.
2. Greatly reduced sense of pleasure or interest in all or almost all activities, nearly every day for most of the day.
3. A significant loss or gain of weight (more than 5% of body weight in a month) without any attempt to diet, or an increase or decrease in appetite.
4. Daily (or nearly daily) insomnia or hypersomnia (oversleeping).
5. Excessive agitation or slowing down of movement responses nearly every day.
6. Feelings of fatigue or loss of energy nearly every day.
7. Feelings of worthlessness or misplaced or excessive or inappropriate guilt nearly every day.
8. Reduced ability to concentrate or think clearly or make decisions nearly every day.
9. Recurrent thoughts of death or suicide without a specific plan, or occurrence of a suicidal attempt or specific plan for committing suicide.

*The *DSM* includes separate diagnostic categories for mood disorders due to medical conditions or use of substances such as drugs of abuse.

Source: Adapted from the *DSM-IV-TR* (APA, 2000).

mypsychlab

MAJOR DEPRESSION:

The Case of Everett

"You feel absolute worthlessness."

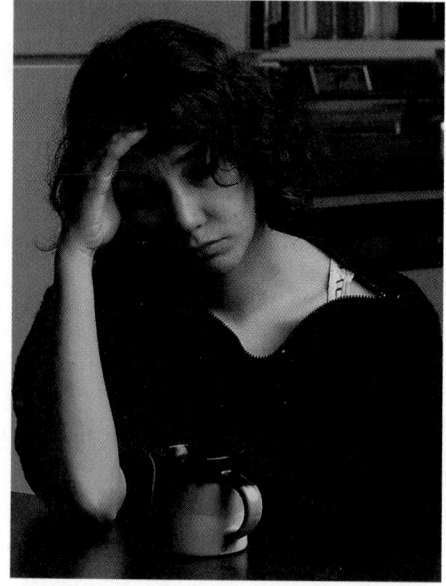

When are changes in mood considered abnormal? Although changes in mood in response to the ups and downs of everyday life may be quite normal, persistent or severe changes in mood, or cycles of extreme elation and depression, may suggest the presence of a mood disorder.

Major depression is not simply a state of sadness or "the blues." People with major depressive disorder (MDD) may have poor appetite, lose or gain substantial amounts of weight, have trouble sleeping or sleep too much, and become physically agitated or—at the other extreme—show a marked slowing down in their motor activity. Here, a woman recounts how depression—the "Beast" as she calls it—affects every fiber of her being.

"The Beast Is Back"

My body aches intermittently, in waves, as if I had malaria. I eat with no appetite, simply because the taste of food is one of my dwindling number of pleasures. I am tired, so tired. Last night I lay like a pile of old clothes, and when David came to bed I did not stir. Sex is a foreign notion. At work today I am forgetful; I have trouble forming sentences, I lose track of them halfway through, and my words keep getting tangled. I look at my list of things to do today, and keep on looking at it; nothing seems to be happening. Things are sad to me. This morning I thought of the woman who used to live in my old house, who told me she went to Sears to buy fake lace curtains. It seemed a forlorn act—having to save your pennies, not being able to afford genuine lace. (Why? A voice in my head asks. The curtains she bought looked perfectly nice.) I feel as if my brain were a lump of protoplasm with tiny circuits embedded in it, and some of the wires keep shorting out. There are tiny little electrical fires up there, leaving crispy sections of neurons smoking and ruined. . . .

I don't even know when this current siege began—a week ago? A month ago? The onset is so gradual, and these things are hard to tell. All I know is, the Beast is back.

It is called depression, and my experiences with it have shaped my life—altered my personality, affected my most intimate relationships, changed the course of my career—in ways I will probably never be fully aware of.

—*From Thompson, 1995*

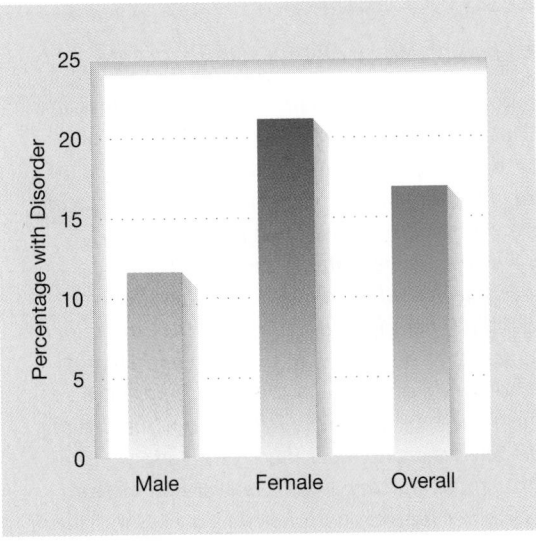

FIGURE 8.2 Lifetime prevalence rates for major depressive disorder.
Major depressive episodes affect about twice as many women as men.

Source: Conway et al., 2006.

Major depression impairs people's ability to meet the ordinary responsibility of everyday life. People with major depression may lose interest in most of their usual activities and pursuits, have difficulty concentrating and making decisions, have pressing thoughts of death, and attempt suicide. They even show impaired driving skills in driving simulation tests (Bulmash et al., 2006).

Many people don't seem to understand that people who are clinically depressed can't simply "shake it off" or "snap out of it." Many people still view depression as a sign of weakness, not a diagnosable disorder. Even many people with major depression believe they can handle the problem themselves. These attitudes may explain why, despite the availability of safe and effective treatments, only about half of people with diagnosable major depression in a recent nationwide survey received any treatment during the preceding year, and fewer than one-third of these received treatment from a mental health specialist (Kessler et al., 2003). All told, only about one in five people with major depressive disorder in the nationwide survey received adequate treatment. One factor explaining the lack of adequate care is that many depressed patients seek help from their family physicians, who often fail to treat depression aggressively (Duenweld, 2003; Simon et al., 2004).

Major depressive disorder or MDD is the most common type of diagnosable mood disorder. According to a recent nationally representative survey, lifetime prevalence for major depression is about 12% for men, 21% for women, and 16.5% overall (Conway et al., 2006) (see Figure 8.2). About 7% of U.S. adults suffer from the disorder in any given year (Kessler et al., 2003). An estimated 120 million people worldwide suffer from depression (E. Olson, 2001).

The economic costs of depression are staggering, amounting to an estimated $44 billion annually in the United States in lost productive time (Stewart et al., 2003). The average worker with major depression loses 27.2 workdays to the disorder per year—for bipolar disorder, 65.5 days are lost (Kessler et al., 2006). The economic toll of depression is as great if not greater than the costs of major medical illnesses, such as heart disease and diabetes (Druss, Rosenheck, & Sledge, 2000; Stewart et al., 2003). On the other hand, effective treatment for depression leads not only to psychological improvement but also to more stable employment and increased income, as people return to a more productive level of functioning (Wells et al., 2000).

Major depression, particularly in more severe episodes, may be accompanied by psychotic features, such as delusions that one's body is rotting from illness. People with severe depression may also experience hallucinations, such as "hearing" voices condemning them for perceived misdeeds.

The following case illustrates the range of features connected with major depressive disorder.

TRUTH or FICTION

The economic toll of depression is about half that of heart disease or diabetes.

☑ **FALSE.** Actually, the economic burden to the nation of depression is estimated to be as great if not greater than that for heart disease or diabetes.

Slowly Killing Herself: A Case of Major Depressive Disorder

A 38-year-old female clerical worker has suffered from recurrent bouts of depression since she was about 13 years of age. Most recently, she has been troubled by crying spells at work, sometimes occurring so suddenly she wouldn't have enough time to run to the ladies room to hide her tears from others. She has difficulty concentrating at work and feels a lack of enjoyment from work she used to enjoy. She harbors severe pessimistic and angry feelings, which have been more severe lately because she has been putting on weight and has been neglectful in taking care of her diabetes. She feels guilty that she may be slowly killing herself by not taking better care of her health. She sometimes feels that she deserves to be dead. She has been bothered by excessive sleepiness for the past year and a half, and her driving license has been suspended due to an incident the previous month in which she fell asleep while driving, causing her car to hit a telephone pole. She wakes up most days feeling groggy and just "out of it," and remains sleepy throughout the day. She has never had a steady boyfriend, and lives quietly at home with her mother, with no close friends outside of her family. During the interview, she cried frequently and answered questions in a low monotone, staring downward continuously.

—Adapted from Spitzer et al., 1989, pp. 59–62

Major depressive episodes may resolve in a matter of months or last for a year or more (APA, 2000; USDHHS, 1999a). Some people experience a single episode with a full return to previous levels of functioning. However, the great majority of people with major depression eventually have repeated occurrences (Kanai et al., 2003; Kennedy et al., 2003). Over the course of a lifetime, the average person with major depression can expect to have four episodes (Judd, 1997). Relapses tend to be more frequent in people who continue to have some leftover depressive symptoms following a first depressive episode (Judd, Paulus et al., 2000). Given a pattern of repeated occurrences and long-lasting symptoms, many professionals view major depression as a chronic disorder. However, the longer the period of recovery from major depression, the lower the risk of eventual relapse (Solomon et al., 2000).

Risk Factors in Major Depression   Factors that place people at increased risk of developing major depression include age (initial onset is most common among young adults); socioeconomic status (people lower down the socioeconomic ladder are at greater risk than those who are better off); and marital status (people who are separated or divorced have higher rates than married or never-married people).

Women are nearly twice as likely as men to be diagnosed with major depressive disorder (major depression) (Hasin et al., 2005). The difference in relative risk between males and females begins in early adolescence and persists through at least the mid-50s (Barefoot et al., 2001; Kessler et al., 1993). Noting the existence of a gender gap in the diagnosis of depression is one thing; explaining it is quite another (see *Controversies in Abnormal Psychology*).

Seasonal Affective Disorder   Are you glum on gloomy days? Is your temper short during the brief days of winter? Are you dismal during the long, dark winter nights and sunny when spring and summer return?

Many people report that their moods do vary with the weather. For some people, the changing of the seasons from summer into fall and winter leads to a type of major depression called *seasonal affective (mood) disorder* (SAD). SAD is not a diagnostic category in its own right in the *DSM-IV* but is a specifier or subcategory of a mood disorder involving major depression. For example, major depressive disorder that occurs seasonally would be diagnosed as major depressive disorder with seasonal pattern. Although the causes of SAD remain unknown, one possibility is that seasonal changes in light may alter the body's underlying biological rhythms that regulate such processes as body temperature and sleep–wake cycles (Lewy et al., 2006). Another possibility is that some parts of the central nervous system may have deficiencies in transmission of

---

mypsych lab

DEPRESSION:

The Case of Helen

"I had electroshock treatments every other day for two weeks."

CONTROVERSIES IN ABNORMAL PSYCHOLOGY

Why Are More Women Depressed?

Evidence shows that women are about twice as likely as men to suffer from clinical depression (NIMH, 2000). The gender gap is found in many other countries, including Canada, Brazil, Germany, and Japan (Gilbert, 2004). The question is, *why*?

Professionals continue to debate the issue. Might the gender gap be a function of biological differences between men and women? Some professionals argue that biological factors, such as hormonal fluctuations, may contribute to depression in women (Cyranowski et al., 2000).

Might the gender difference be explained, at least in part, by a reporting bias that leads men to underreport depression? In our culture, men are expected to be tough and resilient. Consequently, they are less likely to report depression or seek treatment for it. Even physicians are not immune from these social expectations. As one male physician put it, "I'm the John Wayne generation. . . I thought depression was a weakness—there was something disgraceful about it. A real man would just get over it" (cited in Wartik, 2000). The stigma associated with depression shows signs of lessening, but not disappearing. Although depression was long viewed by men as a sign of personal weakness, more men are coming forward to get help. The male ego has been battered by assaults from corporate downsizing and growing financial insecurity.

An expert panel convened by the American Psychological Association (APA) debated the question of gender differences in depression and concluded that they are largely the result of the greater amount of stress that women encounter in contemporary life (McGrath et al., 1990). The panel recognized that women are more likely than men to encounter such stressful life factors as physical and sexual abuse, poverty, single parenthood, and sexism.

More recently, psychologist Janet Nolen-Hoeksema proposed that differences in coping styles may also underlie women's greater proneness toward depression. Regardless of whether the factors that precipitate depression are

biological, psychological, or social, one's coping responses may either exacerbate or reduce the severity and duration of depressive episodes. Nolen-Hoeksema and her colleagues (1991; Nolen-Hoeksema, Morrow, & Fredrickson, 1993) proposed that women are more likely to amplify depression by sitting at home when they are depressed and ruminating about their feelings or trying to understand the reasons they feel the way they do, whereas men are more likely to distract themselves by doing something they enjoy, such as going to a favorite hangout to get their mind off their feelings. On the other hand, men often turn to alcohol as a form of self-medication, which can lead to another set of psychological and social problems (Nolen-Hoeksema et al., 1993). We shouldn't think that rumination is limited to women, however (Treynor, Gonzalez, & Nolen-Hoeksema, 2003). Evidence shows that both men and women who ruminate more following the loss of loved ones or when feeling down or sad are more likely to become depressed and to suffer longer and more severe depression than those who ruminate less (Just & Alloy, 1997; Nolen-Hoeksema, 2000).

More research is needed to fully understand the gender gap in depression. Hopefully, research into factors such as hormonal influences, stress burdens, and ruminative styles will lead to the development of more specifically targeted interventions for treating depression in women. Likewise, by understanding men's culturally instilled resistance to reporting depression, we can help destigmatize the disorder so that men suffering from depression will seek help rather than suffer in silence (Cochran & Rabinowitz, 2003).

Critical Thinking

- How might a theorist in the biopsychosocial tradition account for gender differences in depression?
- Give an example of how more knowledge about the causes of gender differences in depression can lead to improved treatment approaches.

the mood-regulating neurotransmitter serotonin during the winter months (Schwartz et al., 1997). Cognitive factors may play a part: People with seasonal affective disorder report more automatic negative thoughts throughout the year than do nondepressed controls (Rohan, Sigmon, & Dorhofer, 2003).

Whatever the underlying cause, the therapeutic use of bright artificial light, called *phototherapy,* often helps relieve depression in cases of SAD (Lam et al., 2006; Rohan et al., 2007). The artificial light apparently supplements the meager sunlight the person otherwise receives. Patients can generally carry out some daily activities (for example, eating, reading, or writing) during phototherapy sessions. Improvement typically occurs within several days of beginning treatment, but treatment often needs to be continued throughout the winter season. Antidepressant drugs, such as Prozac, may also help relieve depression in patients with seasonal affective disorder (Lam et al., 2006).

Postpartum Depression Many, perhaps even most, new mothers experience mood changes, periods of tearfulness, and irritability following the birth of a child. These mood changes are commonly called the "maternity blues," "postpartum blues," or "baby blues." They usually last for a couple of days and are believed to be a normal response to hormonal changes that attend childbirth. Given these turbulent hormonal shifts, it would be "abnormal" for most women *not* to experience some changes in feeling states shortly following childbirth.

Some mothers, however, undergo severe mood changes that persist for months or even a year or more. These problems in mood are referred to as **postpartum depression (PPD).** *Postpartum* derives from the Latin roots *post,* meaning "after," and *papere,* meaning "to bring forth." PPD is often accompanied by disturbances in appetite and sleep, low self-esteem, and difficulties in maintaining concentration or attention. An estimated 13% of mothers suffer from some form of postpartum depression (O'Hara, 2003).

TRUTH or FICTION

The bleak light of winter casts some people into a diagnosable state of depression.

☑ **TRUE.** The changing of the seasons does lead to a major depressive disorder in some people.

postpartum depression (PPD) Persistent and severe mood changes that occur after childbirth.

QUESTIONNAIRE
Are You Depressed?

This test, offered by the organizers of the National Depression Screening Day, can help you assess whether you are suffering from a depression. It is not intended for you to diagnose yourself, but rather to raise your awareness of concerns you may want to discuss with a professional.

	YES	NO
1. I feel downhearted, blue, and sad.	___	___
2. I don't enjoy the things that I used to.	___	___
3. I feel that others would be better off if I were dead.	___	___
4. I feel that I am not useful or needed.	___	___
5. I notice that I am losing weight.	___	___
6. I have trouble sleeping through the night.	___	___
7. I am restless and can't keep still.	___	___
8. My mind isn't as clear as it used to be.	___	___
9. I get tired for no reason.	___	___
10. I feel hopeless about the future.	___	___

Rating your responses: If you agree with at least five of the statements, including either item 1 or 2, and if you have had these complaints for at least 2 weeks, professional help is strongly recommended. If you answered "yes" to statement 3, seek consultation with a professional immediately. If you don't know whom to turn to, contact your college counseling center, neighborhood mental health center, or health care provider.

Source: Adapted from J. E. Brody, "Myriad masks hide an epidemic of depression," *The New York Times,* September 30, 1992, p. C12.

dysthymic disorder A mild but chronic type of depressive disorder.

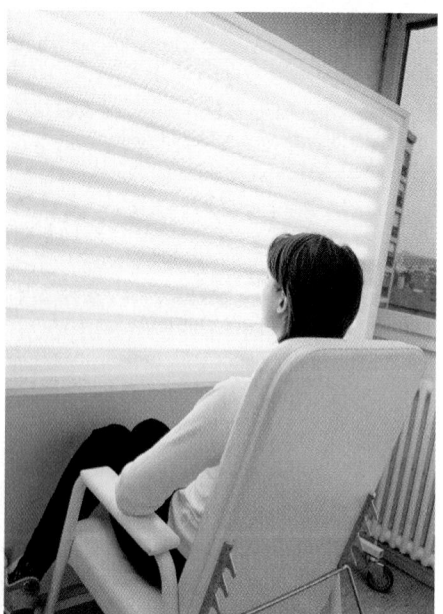

Light therapy. Exposure to bright artificial light for a few hours a day during the fall and winter months can often bring relief from seasonal affective disorder.

Postpartum depression is a form of major depression in which the onset of the depressive episode begins within 4 weeks after childbirth (APA, 2000). A major review article of studies on postpartum depression reported that 7.1% of women experienced an episode of major depression during the first 3 months postpartum (Gavin et al., 2005).

Postpartum depression typically is less severe than other forms of major depression and lifts relatively sooner than most (Whiffen & Gotlib, 1993). Yet some suicides are linked to postpartum depression. Factors associated with a heightened risk of PPD include stress, single or first-time motherhood, financial problems, a troubled marriage, social isolation, lack of support from partners and family members, a history of depression, or having an unwanted, sick, or temperamentally difficult infant (Forman et al., 2000; Ritter et al., 2000; Swendsen & Mazure, 2000). Having PPD also increases the risk that the woman will suffer future depressive episodes. Fortunately, there are effective treatments available, including different forms of psychotherapy and antidepressant drugs (e.g., Cooper et al., 2003; Murray et al., 2003; Stuart et al., 2003). Much less common than PPD are psychotic reactions following childbirth involving a loss of contact with reality. These reactions, labeled *post-partum psychosis,* usually involve manic episodes of bipolar disorder rather than schizophrenia or another form of psychotic disorder (Blackmore et al., 2006; Stotland, 2006).

Postpartum depression is not limited to our culture. A study in an urban area in Portugal reported a similar prevalence rate (13%) (Augusto et al., 1996). Researchers have found high rates of PPD among South African women (Cooper et al., 1999) and Chinese women from Hong Kong (D. T. S. Lee et al., 2001). In the South African sample, a lack of psychological and financial support from the baby's father was associated with an increased risk of the disorder in this sample, mirroring findings with U.S. samples.

Dysthymic Disorder

Major depressive disorder is severe and marked by a relatively abrupt change from one's preexisting state. A milder form of depression seems to follow a chronic course of development that often begins in childhood or adolescence (Klein, Keller et al., 2000; Klein, Schwartz et al., 2000). Earlier diagnostic formulations of this type of chronic sadness were labeled "depressive neurosis" or "depressive personality." It was so labeled in an effort to account for several features traditionally identified with neurosis, such as early childhood origins, a chronic course, and generally mild levels of severity. The *DSM* classifies this form of depression **dysthymic disorder,** or *dysthymia,* which derives from Greek roots *dys-,* meaning "bad" or "hard" and *thymos,* meaning "spirit."

Persons with dysthymic disorder do feel "bad spirited" or "down in the dumps" most of the time, but they are not so severely depressed as those with major depressive disorder. Whereas major depressive disorder tends to be severe and time limited, dysthymic disorder is relatively mild and nagging, typically lasting for years (Klein, Schwartz et al., 2000). Feelings of depression and social difficulties continue even after the person makes an apparent recovery (USDHHS, 1999a). The risk of relapse is quite high (Keller et al., 2000), as is the risk of major depressive disorder: 90% of people with dysthmia eventually develop major depression (Friedman, 2002).

Dysthymia affects about 4% of the general population at some point in their lifetimes (APA, 2000; Conway et al., 2006). Like major depressive disorder, dysthymic disorder is more common in women than men (see Figure 8.3).

In dysthymic disorder, complaints of depression may become such a fixture of people's lives that they seem to be intertwined with the personality structure.

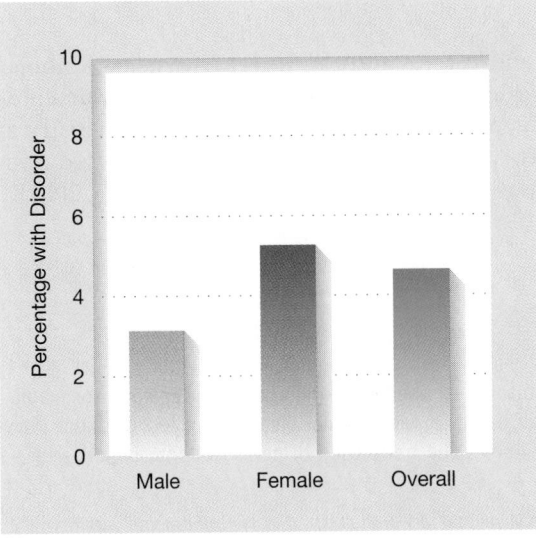

FIGURE 8.3 Lifetime prevalence rates for dysthymic disorder. Like major depression, dysthymic disorder occurs in about twice as many women as men.

Source: Conway et al., 2006.

The persistence of complaints may lead others to perceive the person as whining and complaining. Although dysthymic disorder is less severe than major depressive disorder, persistent depressed mood and low self-esteem can affect the person's occupational and social functioning, as we see in the following case.

◆

A Case of Dysthymic Disorder

The woman, a 28-year-old junior executive, complained of chronic feelings of depression since the age of 16 or 17. Despite doing well in college, she brooded about how other people were "genuinely intelligent." She felt she could never pursue a man she might be interested in dating because she felt inferior and intimidated. Although she had extensive therapy through college and graduate school, she could never recall a time during those years when she did not feel somewhat depressed. She got married shortly after college graduation to the man she was dating at the time, although she didn't think that he was anything "special." She just felt she needed to have a husband for companionship, and he was available. But they soon began to quarrel, and she's lately begun to feel that marrying him was a mistake. She has had difficulties at work, turning in "slipshod" work and never seeking anything more than what was basically required of her and showing little initiative. Although she dreams of acquiring status and money, she doesn't expect that she or her husband will rise in their professions because they lack "connections." Her social life is dominated by her husband's friends and their spouses, and she doesn't think that other women would find her interesting or impressive. She lacks interest in life in general and expresses dissatisfaction with all facets of her life—her marriage, her job, her social life.

—*Adapted from Spitzer et al., 1994, pp. 110–112*

double depression Concurrent major depressive disorder and dysthymic disorder.

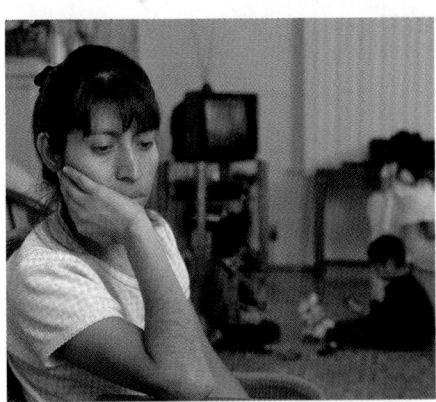

Women and depression. Women are more likely to suffer from major depression than men. A panel convened by the American Psychological Association attributed the higher rates of depression among women to factors such as unhappy marriages, physical and sexual abuse, impoverishment, single parenthood, sexism, hormonal changes, childbirth, and excessive caregiving burdens. APA panel member Bonnie Strickland expressed surprise that even more women were not clinically depressed, because they are treated as second-class citizens.

Some people are affected by both dysthymic disorder and major depression at the same time. The term **double depression** applies to those who have a major depressive episode superimposed on a longer-standing dysthymic disorder. People suffering from double depression generally have more severe depressive episodes than do people with major depression alone (Klein, Schwartz et al., 2000).

We have noted that major depressive disorder and dysthymic disorder are depressive disorders in the sense that the disturbance of mood is only in one direction—down. Yet people with mood disorders may have fluctuations in mood in both directions that exceed the usual ups and downs of everyday life. These types of disorders are called bipolar disorders. Here we focus on the major types of mood-swing disorders: (1) bipolar disorder and (2) cyclothymic disorder.

Carrie Fisher. The actress Carrie Fisher, who starred as Princess Leia in the early *Star Wars* movies, was diagnosed with bipolar disorder in her 20s.

bipolar disorder A psychological disorder characterized by mood swings between states of extreme elation and depression.

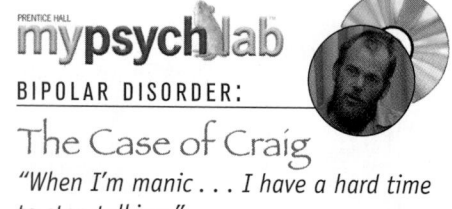

BIPOLAR DISORDER:

The Case of Craig

"When I'm manic . . . I have a hard time to stop talking."

Bipolar Disorder

Kay Redfield Jamison, a psychologist and leading authority on the treatment of **bipolar disorder,** herself suffers from the disorder. Within 3 months of beginning her first professional appointment as an assistant professor in the Department of Psychiatry at UCLA, she became, in her own words, "ravingly psychotic." Jamison has suffered from bipolar disorder since her teens but wasn't diagnosed until she was 28 (Ballie, 2002).

"I" An Unquiet Mind

In her 1995 memoir, *An Unquiet Mind*, Jamison described her early and milder episodes of mania as "absolutely intoxicating states that gave rise to great personal pleasure, an incomparable flow of thoughts, and a ceaseless energy that allowed the translation of new ideas into papers and projects" (p. 5). "But then

> . . . as night inevitably goes after the day, my mood would crash, and my mind again would grind to a halt. I lost all interest in my schoolwork, friends, reading, wandering, or daydreaming. I had no idea of what was happening to me, and I would wake up in the morning with a profound sense of dread that I was going to have to somehow make it through another entire day. I would sit for hour after hour in the undergraduate library, unable to muster up enough energy to go to class. I would stare out the window, stare at my books, rearrange them, shuffle them around, leave them unopened, and think about dropping out of college. . . . I understood very little of what was going on, and I felt as though only dying would release me from the overwhelming sense of inadequacy and blackness that surrounded me.

> —*From Jamison, 1995*

People with bipolar disorder ride an emotional roller coaster, swinging from the heights of elation to the depths of depression without external cause. The first episode may be either manic or depressive. Manic episodes, typically lasting from a few weeks to several months, are generally shorter in duration and end more abruptly than major depressive episodes. Some people with recurring bipolar disorder attempt suicide "on the way down" from the manic phase (Baldessarini & Tondo, 2003). They report that they would do nearly anything to escape the depths of depression they know lie ahead.

The *DSM* distinguishes between two general types of bipolar disorder, *bipolar I disorder* and *bipolar II disorder*. The distinction can be confusing, so let us try to clarify. The distinction is made on the basis of whether the person has suffered a full-blown manic episode. For bipolar I disorder to be diagnosed, the person must have experienced at least one *full manic episode* at some point in life. Typically, bipolar I disorder involves extreme mood swings between mania and depression with intervening periods of normal mood. However, some cases present with no history of major depressive episodes. In such cases, however, we assume that major depression may either have been overlooked in the past or will develop in the future.

Bipolar II disorder involves less severe forms of mania, but more frequent major depressive episodes (Judd et al., 2003a, 2003b; Kupfer, 2005b). For bipolar II disorder to be diagnosed, the person must have experienced one or more major depressive episodes and at least one *hypomanic episode* (a mild form of mania). But unlike bipolar I disorder, the person has never had a full-blown manic episode.

The question that remains to be determined is whether bipolar I and bipolar II disorders are actually two qualitatively different disorders or simply different points along a continuum of severity of bipolar disorder. We may very well see a clarification of the distinction between these two forms of bipolar disorder when the next edition of the *DSM*, the *DSM-V* is published.

Bipolar disorder is relatively uncommon, with reported lifetime prevalence rates of about 0.4% to 1.6% for bipolar I disorder and about 0.5% for bipolar II disorder (APA, 2000; Kupfer, 2005b; USDHHS, 1999a). Bipolar disorder typically develops around age 20 in both men and women and becomes a chronic, recurring condition requiring long-term treatment (Frank & Kupfer, 2003; Tohen, Zarate et al., 2003).

Unlike major depression, rates of bipolar I disorder appear about equal in men and women. In men, however, the onset of bipolar I disorder typically begins with a manic episode, whereas with women, it usually begins with a major depressive episode. The underlying reason for this gender difference remains unknown. Bipolar II disorder appears to be more common in women (APA, 2000).

In some cases, a pattern of "rapid cycling" occurs in which the individual experiences two or more full cycles of mania and depression within a year without any intervening normal periods. Rapid cycling is relatively uncommon, but occurs more often among women than men (Schneck et al., 2004). It is usually limited to a year or less, but is associated with a more severe form of the disorder and more serious suicide attempts (Coryell et al, 2003; Schneck et al., 2004).

Many observers have noted connections between mood disorders, especially bipolar disorder, and creativity (e.g., McDermott, 2001; Nettle, 2001). Many distinguished writers, artists, and composers seemed to have suffered from major depression or bipolar disorder. The list of luminaries who suffered from mood disorders stretches from artists Michelangelo and Vincent van Gogh, to composers William Schumann and Peter Tchaikovsky, to novelists Virginia Woolf and Ernest Hemingway, and to poets Alfred Lord Tennyson, Emily Dickinson, Walt Whitman, and Sylvia Plath. Perhaps some creative people are able to channel the seemingly boundless energy and rapid stream of thoughts associated with manic periods to enhance their productivity and ability to express themselves in novel ways. However, the great majority of writers and artists do not suffer from mood disorders, nor does creativity typically spring from psychological disturbance. Moreover, not all studies find links between psychological disorders and creativity, so it's best to reserve judgment on the nature of the relationship (Bailey, 2003).

Manic Episode Manic episodes, or periods of mania, typically begin abruptly, gathering force within days. During a manic episode, the person experiences a sudden elevation or expansion of mood and feels unusually cheerful, euphoric, or optimistic. The person seems to have boundless energy and is extremely sociable, although perhaps to the point of becoming overly demanding and overbearing toward others. Other people recognize the sudden shift in mood to be excessive in the light of the person's circumstances. It is one thing to feel elated if one has just won the state lottery. It is another to feel euphoric because it's Wednesday. Here, a young man with bipolar disorder describes what a manic episode is like for him (Behrman, 2002).

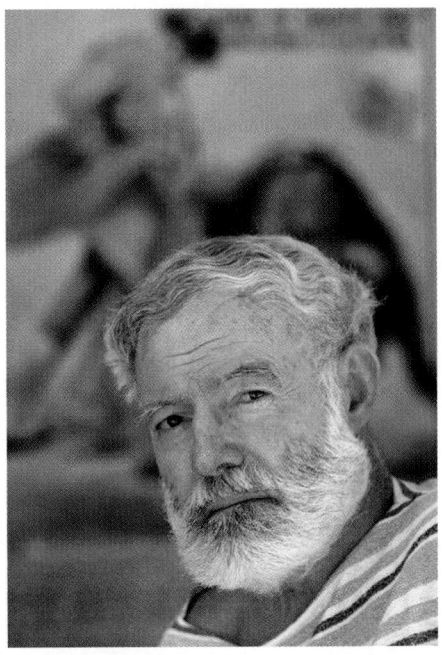

Is there a thin line between genius and madness? Many creative individuals, including the famed novelist Ernest Hemingway who is pictured here and the artist Vincent van Gogh, suffered from mood disorders. Whatever the links between creativity and mood disorders may be, we should bear in mind that the great majority of creative writers and artists do not suffer from serious mood disturbances.

manic episode A period of unrealistically heightened euphoria, extreme restlessness, and excessive activity characterized by disorganized behavior and impaired judgment.

"I" Electroboy

Manic depression is about buying a dozen bottles of Heinz ketchup and all eight bottles of Windex in stock at the Food Emporium on Broadway at 4 A.M., flying from Zurich to the Bahamas and back to Zurich in three days to balance the hot and cold weather (my "sweet and sour" theory of bipolar disorder), carrying $20,000 in $100 bills in your shoes into the country on your way back to Tokyo, and picking out the person sitting six seats away at the bar to have sex with only because he or she happens to be sitting there. It's about blips and burps of madness, moments of absolute delusion, bliss, and irrational and dangerous choices made in order to heighten pleasure and excitement and to ensure a sense of control. The symptoms of manic depression come in different strengths and sizes. Most days I need to be as manic as possible to come as close as I can to destruction, to get a real good high—a $25,000 shopping spree, a four-day drug binge, or a trip around the world. Other days a simple high from a shoplifting excursion at Duane Reade for a toothbrush or a bottle of Tylenol is enough. I'll admit it: There's a great deal of pleasure to mental illness, especially to the mania associated with manic depression. It's an emotional state similar to Oz, full of excitement, color, noise, and speed—an overload of sensory stimulation— whereas the sane state of Kansas is plain and simple, black and white, boring and flat. Mania has such a dreamlike quality that often I confuse my manic episodes with dreams I've had. . . .

Mania is about desperately seeking to live life at a more passionate level, taking second and sometimes third helpings on food, alcohol, drugs, sex, and money, trying to live a whole life in one day. Pure mania is as close to death as I think I have ever come. The euphoria is both pleasurable and frightening. My manic mind teems with rapidly changing ideas and needs; my head is cluttered with vibrant colors, wild images, bizarre thoughts, sharp details, secret codes, symbols, and foreign languages. I want to devour everything—parties, people, magazines, books, music, art, movies, and television.

—*From* Electroboy *by* Andy Behrman

People in a manic episode tend to show poor judgment and to become argumentative, sometimes going so far as destroying property. Roommates may find them abrasive and avoid them. They may become extremely generous and make large charitable contributions they can ill afford or give away costly possessions.

People in a manic episode tend to speak very rapidly (with *pressured speech*). Their thoughts and speech may jump from topic to topic in a *rapid flight of ideas.* Others find it difficult to get a word in edgewise. They typically experience an inflated sense of self-esteem that may range from extreme self-confidence to wholesale delusions of grandeur (Schulze et al., 2005). They may feel capable of solving the world's problems or of composing symphonies, despite a lack of any special knowledge or talent. They may spout off about matters on which they know little, such as how to eliminate world hunger or create a new world order. It soon becomes clear that they are disorganized and incapable of completing their projects. They also become highly distractible. Their attention is easily diverted by irrelevant stimuli like the sounds of a ticking clock or people talking in the next room. They tend to take on multiple tasks, more than they can handle. They may suddenly quit their jobs to enroll in law school, wait tables at night, organize charity drives on weekends, and work on the great American novel in their "spare time." They may not be able to sit still or sleep restfully. They almost always show decreased need for sleep. They tend to awaken early yet feel well rested and full of energy. They sometimes go for days without sleep and without feeling tired. Although they may have abundant stores of energy, they seem unable to organize their efforts constructively. Their elation impairs their ability to work and to maintain normal relationships.

People in manic episodes tend to exercise poor judgment and fail to weigh the consequences of their actions. They may get into trouble as a result of lavish spending, reckless driving, or sexual escapades. In severe cases, they may experience hallucinations or become grossly delusional, believing, for example, that they have a special relationship with God.

Cyclothymic Disorder

Cyclothymia is derived from the Greek *kyklos,* which means "circle," and *thymos,* meaning "spirit." The notion of a circular-moving spirit is an apt description, because this disorder represents a chronic cyclical pattern of mood disturbance characterized by mild mood swings lasting at least 2 years (1 year for children and adolescents). **Cyclothymic disorder** usually begins in late adolescence or early adulthood and persists for years. Few, if any, periods of normal mood last for more than a month or two. However, neither the periods of elevated or depressed mood are severe enough to warrant a diagnosis of bipolar disorder. Estimates from community studies indicate lifetime prevalence rates for cyclothymic disorder of between 0.4% to 1% (4 to 10 people in 1,000), with men and women about equally likely to be affected (APA, 2000).

The periods of elevated mood are called *hypomanic* episodes (from the Greek prefix *hypo-,* meaning "under" or "less than"). They are less severe than manic episodes and are not accompanied by the severe social or occupational problems associated with full-blown manic episodes. During hypomanic episodes, people may have an inflated sense of self-esteem, may feel unusually charged with energy, and may be more alert, restless, and irritable than usual. They may be able to work long hours with little fatigue or need for sleep. Their projects may be left unfinished when their moods reverse, however. Then they enter a mildly depressed mood state and feel lethargic and depressed, but not to the extent typical of a major depressive episode. Social relationships

cyclothymic disorder A mood disorder characterized by a chronic pattern of less-severe mood swings than are found in bipolar disorder.

may become strained by shifting moods, and work may suffer. Sexual interest waxes and wanes with the person's moods.

The boundaries between bipolar disorder and cyclothymic disorder are not yet clearly established. Some forms of cyclothymic disorder may represent a mild, early type of bipolar disorder. Approximately 33% of people with cyclothymic disorder eventually develop bipolar disorder, a figure that is about 33 times higher than the general population (USDHHS, 1999a). We presently lack the ability to distinguish persons with cyclothymia who are likely to develop bipolar disorder. The following case presents an example of the mild mood swings that typify cyclothymic disorder.

"Good Times and Bad Times": A Case of Cyclothymic Disorder

The man, a 29-year-old car salesman, reports that since the age of 14 he has experienced alternating periods of "good times and bad times." During his "bad" periods, which generally last between 4 and 7 days, he sleeps excessively and feels a lack of confidence, energy, and motivation, as if he were "just vegetating." Then his moods abruptly shift for a period of three or four days, usually upon awakening in the morning, and he feels aflush with confidence and sharpened mental ability. During these "good periods" he engages in promiscuous sex and uses alcohol, in part to enhance his good feelings and in part to help him sleep at night. The good periods may last upwards of 7 to 10 days at times, before shifting back into the "bad" periods, generally following a hostile or irritable outburst.

—*Adapted from Spitzer et al., 1994, pp. 155–157*

CAUSAL FACTORS IN DEPRESSIVE DISORDERS

Mood disorders are best understood in terms of complex interactions of biological and psychosocial influences (Kendler, Gardner, & Prescott, 2002; NIMH, 2003). Although a full understanding of the causes of mood disorders presently lies beyond our grasp, we have begun to identify many of the important contributors to mood disorders, especially depression. In the next sections, we examine contemporary understandings of the causal factors in both depressive disorders and bipolar disorders. Many factors are implicated in the development of these disorders, including stressful life events as well as psychological and biological factors.

Stress and Depression

Stress plays an important role in determining vulnerability in bipolar disorder and even more strongly in major depression. Sources of stress may include the loss of a loved one, the breakup of a romantic relationship, prolonged unemployment, physical illness, marital or relationship problems, economic hardship, pressure at work, exposure to racism and discrimination, or living in an unsafe, distressed neighborhood (Cutrona, Wallace, & Wesner, 2006; Drieling, Calker, & Hecht, 2006; Kendler et al., 2004). For reasons that remain to be studied further, major stressful events in life are more strongly connected to the initial onset of major depression than to subsequent episodes (Monroe et al., 2007). People are also more likely to become depressed when they experience humiliating events involving key life roles (as parents, for example) and when they hold themselves responsible for undesirable events, such as school problems, financial difficulties, unwanted pregnancy, interpersonal problems, and legal problems (e.g., Kendler, Hettema et al., 2003).

Yet the relationship between stress and depression may cut both ways: Stressful life events may contribute to depression, and depressive symptoms in themselves may be stressful or lead to additional sources of stress, such as divorce or loss of employment.

"Gotta have friends." Social support from friends and family members appears to buffer the effects of stress and may reduce the risk of depression. People who lack important relationships and who rarely join in social activities are more likely to suffer from depression.

When you're depressed, for example, you may find it more difficult to keep up with work, which can lead to more stress as your work backs up. The stress of unemployment and financial hardship may lead to depression, but depression may also lead to unemployment and lower income (Whooley et al., 2002). Stressful events, especially severe negative events, may also trigger depressive episodes in bipolar patients (Johnson, 2005). However, many depressive episodes in bipolar patients appear unrelated to negative life events.

Although stress is often implicated in depression, not everyone who encounters stress becomes depressed. Factors such as coping skills, genetic endowment, and availability of social support may all contribute to the likelihood of depression in the face of stressful events (USDHHS, 1999a). Increased vulnerability to depression is associated with adverse experiences in early life, including parental divorce and physical abuse (Wainwright & Surtees, 2002). Consistent with the *diathesis–stress model* (see Chapter 2), researchers find that young women are more likely to develop depression in the face of stressful life events if they possessed a diathesis in the form of exposure to childhood adversities such as family violence or having parents with a psychological disorder or alcoholism (Hammen, Henry, & Daley, 2000). Moreover, physical or sexual abuse in childhood can disrupt the development of early attachment bonds to parents, setting the stage for later relationship problems and emotional disorders involving depression and anxiety (USDHHS, 1999a).

A strong marital relationship may provide a source of support during times of stress. Not surprisingly, people who are divorced or separated have higher rates of depression and suicide attempts than those who are married (Weissman et al., 1991). People with major depression often lack skills needed to solve interpersonal problems they have with friends, coworkers, or supervisors (Marx, Williams, & Claridge, 1992). But those who take an active approach to solving their interpersonal problems tend to have better clinical outcomes than depressed people who assume a passive style of coping (Sherbourne, Hays, & Wells, 1995).

Psychodynamic Theories

The classic psychodynamic theory of depression of Freud (1917/1957) and his followers (e.g., Abraham, 1916/1948) holds that depression represents anger directed inward rather than against significant others. Anger may become directed against the self following either the actual or threatened loss of these important others.

Freud believed that mourning, or normal bereavement, is a healthy process by which one eventually comes to separate oneself psychologically from a person who is lost through death, separation, divorce, or other reason. Pathological mourning, however, does not promote healthy separation. Rather, it fosters lingering depression. Pathological mourning is likely to occur in people who hold powerful ambivalent feelings—a combination of positive (love) and negative (anger, hostility) feelings—toward the person who has departed or whose departure is feared. Freud theorized that when people lose, or even fear losing, an important figure about whom they feel ambivalent, their feelings of anger turn to rage. Yet rage triggers guilt, which in turn prevents the person from venting anger directly at the lost person (called an "object").

To preserve a psychological connection to the lost object, people *introject,* or bring inward, a mental representation of the object. They thus incorporate the other person into the self. Now anger is turned inward, against the part of the self that represents the inward representation of the lost person. This produces self-hatred, which in turn leads to depression.

From the psychodynamic viewpoint, bipolar disorder represents shifting dominance of the individual's personality between the ego and superego. In the depressive phase, the superego is dominant, producing exaggerated notions of wrongdoing and flooding the individual with feelings of guilt and worthlessness. After a time, the ego rebounds and asserts supremacy, producing feelings of elation and self-confidence that characterize the manic phase. The excessive display of ego eventually triggers a return of guilt, once again plunging the individual into depression.

While also emphasizing the importance of loss, more recent psychodynamic models shift the focus toward the individual's sense of self-worth or self-esteem. One model, called the *self-focusing model,* considers how people allocate their attentional processes after a loss, such as the death of a loved one or a personal failure or significant disappointment (Pyszczynski & Greenberg, 1987). In this view, depressed people have difficulty thinking about anything other than themselves and the loss they experienced.

Consider a person who must cope with the termination of a failed romantic relationship. The depression-prone individual gets wrapped up in thinking about the relationship and hopes of restoring it, rather than recognizing the futility of the effort and getting on with life. Moreover, the lost partner was a source of emotional support on whom the depression-prone individual had relied to maintain self-esteem. Following the loss, the depression-prone individual feels stripped of hope and optimism because these positive feelings had depended on the lost object. The loss of self-esteem and of feelings of security, not of the relationship per se, precipitates depression. Similarly, loss of a specific occupational goal may trigger self-focusing and consequent depression. Only by surrendering the object or lost goal and fostering alternate sources of identity and self-worth can the cycle be broken.

Research Evidence Psychodynamic theorists focus on the role of loss in depression. Research does show that loss of significant others (through death or divorce, for example) is often associated with the development of depression (Kendler et al., 2002; Kendler, Hettema et al., 2003). Such a loss may also lead to other psychological disorders, however. There is yet a lack of research to support Freud's view that repressed anger toward the departed loved one is turned inward in depression.

Evidence supports the view that a self-focusing style—an inward or self-absorbed focus of attention—is associated with depression, especially in women (Mor & Winquist, 2002; Muraven, 2005). Yet self-focused attention is not limited to depression; it is also linked to other disorders, including anxiety disorders, alcoholism, mania, and schizophrenia (Ingram, 1991). Thus, the general linkage between self-focused attention and psychopathology may limit the model's value as an explanation of depression.

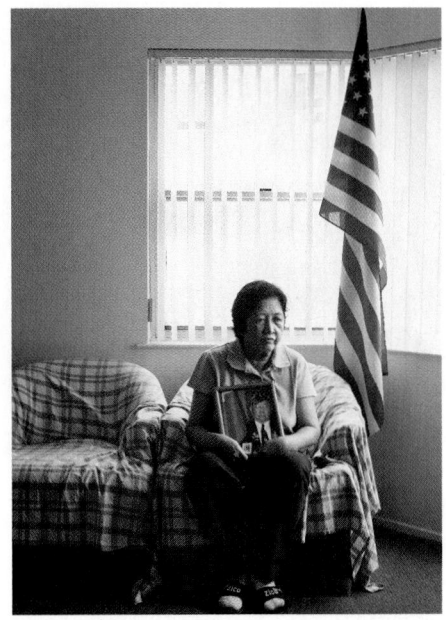

Loss and depression. Psychodynamic theorists focus on the important role of loss in the development of depression.

Humanistic Theories

From the humanistic framework, people become depressed when they cannot imbue their existence with meaning and make authentic choices that lead to self-fulfillment. The world is then a drab place. People's search for meaning gives color and substance to their lives. Guilt may arise when people believe they have not lived up to their potential. Humanistic psychologists challenge us to take a long hard look at our lives. Are they worthwhile and enriching? Or are they drab and routine? If the latter, perhaps we have frustrated our needs for self-actualization. We may be settling, coasting through life. Settling can give rise to a sense of dreariness that becomes expressed in depressive behavior—lethargy, sullen mood, and withdrawal.

Like psychodynamic theorists, humanistic theorists focus on the loss of self-esteem that can arise when people lose friends or family members or suffer occupational setbacks. We tend to connect our personal identity and sense of self-worth with our social roles as parents, spouses, students, or workers. When these role identities are lost, through the death of a spouse, the departure of children to college, or loss of a job, our sense of purpose and self-worth can be shattered. Depression is a frequent consequence of such losses. It is especially likely when we base our self-esteem on our occupational role or success. The loss of a job, a demotion, or a failure to achieve a promotion are common precipitants of depression, especially for individuals who value themselves on the basis of occupational success.

Learning Theories

Whereas the psychodynamic perspectives focus on inner, often unconscious, causes, learning theorists emphasize situational factors, such as the loss of positive reinforcement. We perform best when levels of reinforcement are commensurate with our efforts.

Changes in the frequency or effectiveness of reinforcement can shift the balance so that life becomes unrewarding.

The Role of Reinforcement Learning theorist Peter Lewinsohn (1974) proposed that depression results from an imbalance between behavior and reinforcement. A lack of reinforcement for one's efforts can sap motivation and induce feelings of depression. Inactivity and social withdrawal reduce opportunities for reinforcement; lack of reinforcement exacerbates withdrawal.

Working out to work it out. Recent evidence suggests that regular physical activity or exercise may be helpful in combating depression, especially in people facing significant life stressors.

The low rate of activity typical of depressed individuals may also be a source of secondary reinforcement. Family members and other people may rally around people suffering from depression and release them from their responsibilities. Sympathy may thus become a source of reinforcement that helps maintain depressed behavior.

Reduction in reinforcement levels can occur for many reasons. A person who is recuperating at home from a serious illness or injury may find little that is reinforcing to do. Social reinforcement may plummet when people close to us, who were suppliers of reinforcement, die or leave us. People who suffer social losses are more likely to become depressed when they lack the social skills to form new relationships. Some first-year college students are homesick and depressed because they lack the skills to form rewarding new relationships. Widows and widowers may be at a loss as to how to start a new relationship.

Changes in life circumstances may also alter the balance of effort and reinforcement. A prolonged layoff may reduce financial reinforcement, which may in turn force painful cutbacks in lifestyle. A disability or an extended illness may also impair one's ability to ensure a steady flow of reinforcements. Lewinsohn's model is supported by research findings that connect depression to a low level of positive reinforcement, and importantly, to evidence that encouraging depressed patients to participate in rewarding activities and goal-oriented behaviors can help alleviate depression (Otto, 2006). Encouraging depressed patients to engage in regular physical activity or regular exercise may also have direct benefits in combating depression, especially in the face of major life stressors (Harris, Cronkite, & Moos, 2006).

Interactional Theory Difficulties in social interactions may help explain the lack of positive reinforcement. Interactional theory, developed by psychologist James Coyne (1976), proposes that the adjustment to living with a depressed person can become so stressful that the partner or family member becomes progressively less reinforcing.

Interactional theory is based on the concept of *reciprocal interaction.* People's behavior influences and, in turn, is influenced by the behavior of others. The theory holds that depression-prone people react to stress by demanding greater reassurance and social support from significant others. At first people who become depressed may succeed in garnering support. Over time, however, their demands and behavior begin to elicit anger or annoyance. Although loved ones may keep their negative feelings to themselves, these feelings may surface in subtle ways that spell rejection. Depressed people may react to rejection with deeper depression and greater demands, triggering a vicious cycle of further rejection and more profound depression. They may also feel guilty about distressing their family members, which can exacerbate their negative feelings about themselves.

Family members may find it stressful to adjust to the depressed person's behavior, especially withdrawal, lethargy, despair, and constant requests for reassurance. People whose spouses are being treated for depression tend to report higher-than-average levels of emotional distress (Benazon, 2000). Research evidence generally supports Coyne's belief that people who suffer from depression elicit rejection from others. But investigators suspect that a lack of social skills may best explain this rejection (Segrin & Abramson, 1994). Depressed people tend to be unresponsive, uninvolved, and even impolite when they interact with others. For example, they tend to gaze very little at the other person, to take an excessive amount of time to respond, to show very little approval or validation of the other person, and to dwell on their problems and negative feelings. They even dwell on negative feelings when interacting with strangers. In effect, they turn other people off, setting the stage for rejection.

Cognitive Theories

Cognitive theorists relate the origin and maintenance of depression to the ways in which people see themselves and the world around them. One of the most influential cognitive theorists, psychiatrist Aaron Beck (Beck, 1976; Beck et al., 1979), relates the development of depression to the adoption early in life of a negatively biased or distorted way of thinking—the **cognitive triad of depression** (see Table 8.4). The cognitive triad includes negative beliefs about oneself ("I'm no good"), the environment or the world at large ("This school is awful"), and the future ("Nothing will ever turn out right for me"). Cognitive theory holds that people who adopt this negative way of thinking are at greater risk of becoming depressed in the face of stressful or disappointing life experiences, such as getting a poor grade or losing a job.

cognitive triad of depression The view that depression derives from adopting negative views of oneself, the environment or world at large, and the future.

Beck views these negative concepts of the self and the world as mental templates that are adopted in childhood on the basis of early learning experiences. Children may find that nothing they do is good enough to please their parents or teachers. As a result, they come to regard themselves as basically incompetent and to perceive their future prospects as dim. These beliefs may sensitize them later in life to interpret any failure or disappointment as a reflection of something basically wrong or inadequate about themselves. Even a minor disappointment becomes a crushing blow or a total defeat that can quickly lead to states of depression.

The tendency to magnify the importance of minor failures is an example of an error in thinking that Beck labels a *cognitive distortion.* He believes cognitive distortions set the stage for depression in the face of personal losses or negative life events. Psychiatrist David Burns (1980) enumerated a number of the cognitive distortions associated with depression:

1. *All-or-nothing thinking.* Seeing events as either all good or all bad, or as either black or white with no shades of gray. For example, one may perceive a relationship that ended in disappointment as a totally negative experience, despite any positive feelings or experiences that may have occurred along the way. Perfectionism is an example of all-or-nothing thinking. Perfectionists judge any outcome other than perfect success to be complete failure. They may consider a grade of B or even A- to be tantamount to an F. Perfectionism is connected with an increased vulnerability to depression as well as to poor treatment outcomes (Blatt et al., 1998; Minarik & Ahrens, 1996).
2. *Overgeneralization.* Believing that if a negative event occurs, it is likely to occur again in similar situations in the future. One may interpret a single negative event as foreshadowing an endless series of negative events. For example, receiving a letter of rejection from a potential employer leads one to assume that all other job applications will be similarly rejected.

TABLE 8.4
The Cognitive Triad of Depression

Negative View of Oneself	Perceiving oneself as worthless, deficient, inadequate, unlovable, and as lacking the skills necessary to achieve happiness.
Negative View of the Environment	Perceiving the environment as imposing excessive demands and/or presenting obstacles that are impossible to overcome, leading continually to failure and loss.
Negative View of the Future	Perceiving the future as hopeless and believing that one is powerless to change things for the better. One expects of the future only continuing failure and unrelenting misery and hardship.

Note: According to Aaron Beck, depression-prone people adopt a habitual style of negative thinking—the so-called cognitive triad of depression.

Source: Adapted from Beck & Young, 1985; Beck et al., 1979.

3. *Mental filter.* Focusing only on negative details of events, thereby rejecting the positive features of one's experiences. Like a droplet of ink that spreads to discolor an entire beaker of water, focusing only on a single negative detail can darken one's vision of reality. Beck called this cognitive distortion *selective abstraction,* meaning the individual selectively abstracts the negative details from events and ignores the events' positive features. One thus bases one's self-esteem on perceived weaknesses and failures, rather than on positive features or on a balance of accomplishments and shortcomings. For example, a person receives a job evaluation that contains both positive and negative comments but focuses only on the negative ones.

4. *Disqualifying the positive.* This refers to the tendency to snatch defeat from the jaws of victory by neutralizing or denying one's accomplishments. An example is dismissal of congratulations for a job well done by thinking and saying, "Oh, it's no big deal. Anyone could have done it." By contrast, taking credit where credit is due may help people overcome depression by increasing their belief that they can make changes that will lead to a positive future (Needles & Abramson, 1990).

5. *Jumping to conclusions.* Forming a negative interpretation of events, despite a lack of evidence. Two examples of this style of thinking are "mind reading" and "the fortune teller error." In *mind reading,* a person arbitrarily jumps to the conclusion that others don't like or respect him or her, as in interpreting a friend's not calling for a while as a rejection. The *fortune teller error* is the prediction that something bad is always about to happen. The person believes the prediction of calamity is factually based, even though there is no evidence to support it. For example, the person concludes that a passing tightness in the chest *must* be a sign of heart disease, discounting the possibility of more benign causes.

6. *Magnification and minimization.* Magnification, or *catastrophizing,* refers to the tendency to make mountains out of molehills—to exaggerate the importance of negative events, personal flaws, fears, or mistakes. Minimization is the mirror image, a type of cognitive distortion in which one minimizes or underestimates one's good points.

7. *Emotional reasoning.* Basing reasoning on emotions—for example, thinking, "If I feel guilty, it must be because I've done something really wrong." One interprets feelings and events based on emotions rather than on fair consideration of evidence.

8. *"Should" statements.* Creating personal imperatives or self-commandments—"shoulds" or "musts." For example, "I *should* always get my first serve in!" or "I *must* make Chris like me!" By creating unrealistic expectations, *musterbation*—the label given this form of thinking by Albert Ellis—can lead one to become depressed when one falls short.

9. *Labeling and mislabeling.* Explaining behavior by attaching negative labels to oneself and others. You may explain a poor grade on a test by thinking you were "lazy" or "stupid" rather than simply unprepared for the specific exam or, perhaps, ill. Labeling other people as "stupid" or "insensitive" can engender hostility toward them. Mislabeling involves the use of labels that are emotionally charged and inaccurate, such as calling yourself a "pig" because of a minor deviation from your usual diet.

10. *Personalization.* Assuming that one is responsible for other people's problems and behavior. For example, an individual may feel blame if his or her partner or spouse is crying, rather than recognizing that other causes may be involved.

"How could I have missed that tackle?" This football player missed a crucial tackle and is rehashing it. He is putting himself down and telling himself that there is nothing he can do to improve his performance. Cognitive theorists believe that a person's self-defeating or distorted interpretations of negative events can set the stage for depression.

Consider the errors in thinking illustrated in the following case example.

Distorted thinking tends to be experienced as automatic, as if the thoughts had just popped into one's head. Automatic

---

Christie's Errors in Thinking

Christie was a 33-year-old real estate sales agent who suffered from frequent episodes of depression. Whenever a deal fell through, she would blame herself: "If only I had worked harder . . . negotiated better . . . talked more persuasively . . . the deal would have been done." After several successive disappointments, each one followed by self-recriminations, she felt like quitting altogether. Her thinking became increasingly dominated by negative thoughts, which further depressed her mood and lowered her self-esteem: "I'm a loser. . . . I'll never succeed. . . . It's all my fault. . . . I'm no good and I'm never going to succeed at anything."

Christie's thinking included cognitive errors such as the following: (1) personalization (believing herself to be the sole cause of negative events); (2) labeling and mislabeling (labeling herself to be a loser); (3) overgeneralization (predicting a dismal future on the basis of a present disappointment); and (4) mental filter (judging her personality entirely on the basis of her disappointments). In therapy, Christie learned to think more realistically about events and not to jump to conclusions that she was automatically at fault whenever a deal fell through, or to judge her whole personality on the basis of disappointments or perceived flaws in herself. In place of this self-defeating style of thinking, she began to think more realistically when disappointments occurred, like telling herself, "Okay, I'm disappointed. I'm frustrated. I feel lousy. So what? It doesn't mean I'll never succeed. Let me discover what went wrong and try to correct it the next time. I have to look ahead, not dwell on disappointments in the past."

—From the Author's Files

---

thoughts are likely to be accepted as statements of fact rather than as opinions or habitual ways of interpreting events.

Beck and his colleagues formulated a **cognitive-specificity hypothesis,** which proposes that different disorders are characterized by different types of automatic thoughts. Beck and his colleagues showed some interesting differences in the types of automatic thoughts people with depressive and anxiety disorders reported (Beck et al., 1987) (see Table 8.5).

cognitive-specificity hypothesis
The belief that different emotional disorders are linked to particular kinds of automatic thoughts.

TABLE 8.5

Automatic Thoughts Associated with Depression and Anxiety

Common Automatic Thoughts Associated with Depression	Common Automatic Thoughts Associated with Anxiety
1. I'm worthless.	1. What if I get sick and become an invalid?
2. I'm not worthy of other people's attention or affection.	2. I am going to be injured.
3. I'll never be as good as other people are.	3. What if no one reaches me in time to help?
4. I'm a social failure.	4. I might be trapped.
5. I don't deserve to be loved.	5. I am not a healthy person.
6. People don't respect me anymore.	6. I'm going to have an accident.
7. I will never overcome my problems.	7. Something will happen that will ruin my appearance.
8. I've lost the only friends I've had.	8. I am going to have a heart attack.
9. Life isn't worth living.	9. Something awful is going to happen.
10. I'm worse off than they are.	10. Something will happen to someone I care about.
11. There's no one left to help me.	11. I'm losing my mind.
12. No one cares whether I live or die.	
13. Nothing ever works out for me anymore.	
14. I have become physically unattractive.	

Source: Adapted from Beck et al., 1987.

People with diagnosable depression more often reported automatic thoughts concerning themes of loss, self-deprecation, and pessimism. People with anxiety disorders more often reported automatic thoughts concerning physical danger and other threats.

Research Evidence on Cognitions and Depression Evidence that depressed people show higher levels of distorted or dysfunctional thinking than nondepressed controls supports Beck's model (e.g., Clark, Cook, & Snow, 1998; Riso et al., 2003). Yet more recent evidence links cognitive errors and depression among African American, Caucasian, and Hispanic adolescents (Kennard et al., 2006). We also find that dysfunctional attitudes (above a certain threshold) increase vulnerability to depression in the face of negative life events (Lewinsohn, Joiner, & Rohde, 2001). Lending support to the cognitive-specificity hypothesis, investigators also find that thoughts relating to loss or personal failure were strongest predictors of depressive symptoms among a sample of children and adolescents, whereas thoughts relating to social threat were strongest predictors of anxiety symptoms (Schniering & Rapee, 2004).

Although dysfunctional cognitions (negative, distorted, or pessimistic thoughts) are more common among people who are depressed, the causal pathways remain unclear. We can't yet say whether dysfunctional or negative thinking causes depression or is merely a feature of depression. Thus the central theme of cognitive theory, that negative, distorted thoughts are causally related to depression, is yet to be confirmed (e.g., Oei, Bulbeck, & Campbell, 2006).

The causal linkages may work both ways. In other words, thoughts may affect moods, and moods may affect thoughts. For example, depressed mood may induce negative, distorted thinking. The more negative and distorted depressed individuals' thinking becomes, the more depressed they may feel, and the more depressed they feel, the more dysfunctional their thinking becomes. However, it is equally possible that dysfunctional thinking comes first in the cycle, perhaps in response to a disappointing life experience, which then leads to a downcast mood. This in turn may accentuate negative thinking, and so on. We are still faced with the old "chicken or the egg" dilemma of determining which comes first in the causal sequence, distorted thinking or depressed mood. Future research may help tease out these causal pathways. Even if it becomes clear that distorted cognitions play no direct role in causing depression, the mutual interaction between thoughts and moods may contribute to the maintenance of depressive episodes and increase the likelihood of their recurrence (Kwon & Oei, 1994). We know, for example, that people who recover from depression but continue to hold distorted cognitions tend to be at greater risk of relapse (Rush & Weissenburger, 1994). Fortunately, evidence shows that dysfunctional attitudes tend to decrease with effective treatment for depression (Fava et al., 1994).

Learned Helplessness (Attributional) Theory

learned helplessness A behavior pattern characterized by passivity and perceptions of lack of control.

The **learned helplessness** model proposes that people may become depressed because they learn to view themselves as helpless to change their lives for the better. The originator of the learned helplessness concept, Martin Seligman (1973, 1975), suggests that people learn to perceive themselves as helpless because of their experiences. The learned helplessness model therefore straddles the behavioral and the cognitive: Situational factors foster attitudes that lead to depression.

Seligman and his colleagues based the learned helplessness model on early laboratory studies of animals. In these studies, dogs exposed to an inescapable electric shock showed the "learned helplessness effect" by failing to learn to escape when escape became possible (Overmier & Seligman, 1967; Seligman & Maier, 1967). Exposure to uncontrollable forces apparently taught the animals they were helpless to change their situation. Animals who developed learned helplessness showed behaviors that were similar to those of people with depression, including lethargy, lack of motivation, and difficulty acquiring new skills (Maier & Seligman, 1976).

Seligman (1975, 1991) proposed that some forms of depression in humans might result from exposure to apparently uncontrollable situations. Such experiences can instill the expectation that future reinforcements will also be beyond the individual's control. A cruel vicious cycle may come into play in many cases of depression. A few failures may produce feelings of helplessness and expectations of further failure. Perhaps you know people who have failed certain subjects, such as mathematics. They may come to believe themselves incapable of succeeding in math. They may thus decide that studying for the quantitative section of the Graduate Record Exam is a waste of time. They then perform poorly, completing the self-fulfilling prophecy, which further intensifies feelings of helplessness, leading to lowered expectations, and so on, in a vicious cycle.

"Is it me?" According to reformulated helplessness theory, the kinds of attributions we make concerning negative events can make us more or less vulnerable to depression. Attributing the breakup of a relationship to internalizing ("It's me"), globalizing ("I'm totally worthless"), and stabilizing ("Things are always going to turn out badly for me") causes can lead to depression.

Although it stimulated much interest, Seligman's model failed to account for the low self-esteem typical of people who are depressed. Nor did it explain why depression persists in some people but not in others. Seligman and his colleagues (Abramson, Seligman, & Teasdale, 1978) offered a reformulation of the theory to meet such shortcomings. The revised theory held that perception of lack of control over reinforcement alone did not explain the persistence and severity of depression. It was also necessary to consider cognitive factors, especially the ways in which people explain their failures and disappointments to themselves.

Seligman and his colleagues recast helplessness theory in terms of the social psychology concept of *attributional style.* An attributional style is a personal style of explanation. When disappointments or failures occur, we may explain them in various characteristic ways. We may blame ourselves (an internal attribution), or we may blame the circumstances we face (an external attribution). We may see bad experiences as typical events (a stable attribution) or as isolated events (an unstable attribution). We may see them as evidence of broader problems (a global attribution) or as evidence of precise and limited shortcomings (a specific attribution). The reformulated helplessness theory holds that people who explain the causes of negative events (such as failure in work, school, or romantic relationships) according to the following three types of attributions are most vulnerable to depression:

1. Internal factors, or beliefs that failures reflect their personal inadequacies, rather than external factors, or beliefs that failures are caused by environmental factors
2. Global factors, or beliefs that failures reflect sweeping flaws in personality rather than specific factors, or beliefs that failures reflect limited areas of functioning
3. Stable factors, or beliefs that failures reflect fixed personality factors rather than unstable factors, or beliefs that the factors leading to failures are changeable

Let us illustrate these attributional styles with the example of a college student who goes on a disastrous date. Afterward he shakes his head in wonder and tries to make sense of his experience. An internal attribution for the calamity is characterized by self-blame, as in "I really messed it up." An external attribution would place the blame elsewhere, as in "Some couples just don't hit it off," or "She must have been in a bad mood." A stable attribution would suggest a problem that cannot be changed, as in "It's my personality." An unstable attribution, on the other hand, would suggest a transient condition, as in "It was probably the head cold." A global attribution for failure magnifies the extent of the problem, as in "I really have no idea what I'm doing when I'm with people." A specific attribution, in contrast, chops the problem down to size, as in "My problem is how to make small talk to get a relationship going."

The revised theory holds that each attributional dimension makes a specific contribution to feelings of helplessness. Internal attributions for negative events are linked to lower self-esteem. Stable attributions help explain the persistence—or, in medical terms, the chronicity—of helplessness cognitions. Global attributions are associated with the generality or pervasiveness of feelings of helplessness following negative events. Attributional style should be distinguished from negative thinking (Gotlib et al., 1993). Whether you think negatively (pessimistically) or positively (optimistically), you may still hold yourself to blame for your perceived failures.

Depressed people are more likely than nondepressed people to have a negative attributional style (attributing negative life events to internal, stable, and global factors) (Riso et al., 2003; Seligman et al., 1988). Further support for the model comes from findings that negative attributional styles and dysfunctional attitudes predict higher lifetime rates of major depression (Alloy et al., 2000). However, attributional style may have a stronger relationship to depression in people who tend to think more about the causes of events (Haaga, 1995).

Biological Factors

Biological factors, especially genetics and neurotransmitter functioning, play important roles in depressive disorders.

Genetic Factors   Genetic factors play a significant role in determining proneness to mood disorders, including major depression and bipolar disorder (Holmans et al., 2007; Levinson et al., 2007; McGuffin et al., 2003). Let us look more closely at the evidence for genetic factors in major depression. Not only does major depression tend to run in families, but the closer the genetic relationship people share, the more likely they are to share a depressive disorder (e.g., Klein et al., 2001). Yet families share environmental as well as genetic similarities. To better tease out the effects of genetic factors, investigators have turned to studies of twins. They examine the relative percentages of cases in which MZ or identical twins share a common trait or disorder, as compared to DZ or fraternal twins. The percentage of cases in which the twin of a person who is identified as having a given trait or disorder also has the trait or disorder is called the concordance (agreement) rate. Because MZ twins have 100% of these in common, as compared to 50% among DZ twins, evidence of a higher concordance rate among MZ twins provides strong support for a genetic contribution. Evidence shows more than double the concordance rate for major depression among MZ twins than DZ twins (Kendler et al., 1992b, 1993). This provides strong support for a genetic component, but is short of the 100% concordance we would expect if genetics were solely responsible for these disorders. Although heredity appears to plays an important role in major depression, it isn't the only determinant, nor is it necessarily the most important one. Environmental factors, such as exposure to stressful life events, appear to play at least as great a role—if not a greater role—than genetics (Kendler & Prescott, 1999).

An emerging model in the field focuses on interactions of genetic and environmental factors in the development of major depression and other mood disorders (Jokela et al., 2007). For example, investigators recently discovered that people who inherit a variation of a particular gene stand more than double the chance of developing major depression following stressful life events than those who have another version of the gene (Caspi et al., 2003; NIMH, 2003). The gene regulates production of a protein that plays a key role in transmission of serotonin, the neurotransmitter targeted by antidepressants such as Prozac and Zoloft. More work examining the relationship between genetics and depression is needed.

Biochemical Factors and Brain Abnormalities   Research on the biological underpinnings of mood disorders has largely focused on abnormalities in neurotransmitter activity in the brain. Early research more than 50 years ago showed that drugs we now call *antidepressants,* which increase levels in the brain of the neurotransmitters norepinephrine and serotonin, often helped relieve depression (Berton & Nestler, 2006; Mann, 2005). Might depression be caused simply by a lack of key neurotransmitters in the brain? Investigators discount this view, in part because antidepressants boost levels of neurotransmitters in the brain within a few days or even hours of use, but it usually takes a week or more before a therapeutic benefit is achieved (Jacobs, 2004; Taylor et al., 2006). Therefore, it is unlikely that these drugs work by simply boosting levels of neurotransmitters in the brain.

We are still learning more about how antidepressants work. More complex views of the role of neurotransmitters are evolving (Andreasen, 2003). Several intriguing possibilities drawing attention among scientists involve irregularities in the numbers of

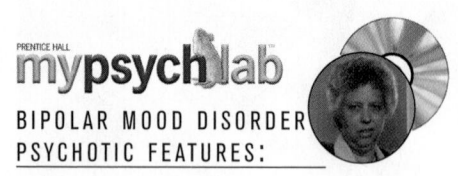

PRENTICE HALL
mypsych lab

BIPOLAR MOOD DISORDER
PSYCHOTIC FEATURES:

The Case of Ann

"When you're racing at that level you tend to alienate people."

A CLOSER LOOK

Something Fishy About This

You may have heard that high concentrations in the diet of certain types of fish oil, especially *omega-3 fatty acids*, are linked to lower rates of cardiovascular disease. But you may not know that scientists suspect that high dietary levels of fish oil are also linked to lower risks of major depression and bipolar disorder (Yager, 2003). Some scientists believe that omega-3 fatty acids are essential nutrients the brain needs to function optimally (Kalb, 2002). Early evidence points to therapeutic benefits of using omega-3 fatty acids in supplement form in treating depressed and bipolar patients (Frangou, Lewis, & McCrone, 2006; Warner, 2002; Roy-Byrne, 2006). Although these results are promising, we need additional research to determine whether omega-3 fatty acids have a part to play in the treatment of depression (Williams et al., 2006).

Several cross-cultural studies show links between high consumption of seafood, rich in omega-3 fatty acids, and low rates of mood disorders (Parker et al., 2006). In one study, the country consuming the most seafood, Iceland, showed low rates of bipolar disorder, whereas countries with lower levels of seafood consumption, such as Germany, Switzerland, Italy, and Israel, showed higher rates (Noaghiul & Hibbeln, 2003).

We should caution that causal linkages cannot be ascertained from observed relationships between eating fish and lower risks of mood disorders. Nevertheless, these linkages encourage researchers to explore further whether a dietary supplement may indeed live up to its popular billing as good brain food. In the meantime, anyone for salmon?

receptors on receiving neurons where neurotransmitters dock (having either too many or too few), abnormalities in the sensitivity of receptors to particular neurotransmitters, or irregularities in the process by which these chemicals bind to receptors (Oquendo et al., 2007; Sharp, 2006). Perhaps, then, antidepressants work by altering the number of these receptors or their sensitivity to these chemical messengers, a process that takes time to occur. Complicating matters further, we need to recognize that several different types of receptors exist for each neurotransmitter along with different subtypes for each type. The actions of particular antidepressants may be specific to certain types or subtypes of receptors. Antidepressants possibly also perform therapeutic actions on more than one neurotransmitter system (USDHHS, 1999a). Complicated indeed.

Another avenue of research into the biological underpinnings of mood disorders focuses on abnormalities in certain areas of the brain. Brain-imaging studies show lower metabolic activity in the *prefrontal cortex* of clinically depressed people as compared to healthy controls (Davidson et al., 2002; Schatzberg, 2002). The prefrontal cortex lies in the frontal lobes of the cerebral cortex and is the area of the brain responsible for higher mental functions, such as thinking, problem solving and decision making, and organizing thoughts and behaviors. The neurotransmitters serotonin and norepinephrine play important roles in regulating nerve impulses in the prefrontal cortex, so it is not surprising that evidence points to irregularities in this region of the brain. Other research reveals brain abnormalities in people with mood disorders (major depression and bipolar disorder) in parts of the brain involved in governing emotions (Parsey et al., 2006; Raeburn, 2005; Society for Neuroscience, 2005; Steele et al., 2007).

As research using brain-imaging techniques continues, we will likely develop a clearer picture of how the brains of people with mood disorders differ from those of healthy individuals and perhaps even ways of better diagnosing these disorders and treating them. Other systems in the body, such as the endocrine system, may also play a role in the development of mood disorders in ways that future research may help clarify.

CAUSAL FACTORS IN BIPOLAR DISORDERS

Most investigators suspect that multiple causes acting together contribute to the development of bipolar disorder. Genetic factors play a major role. In a large population-based study in Finland, investigators found the concordance rate to be seven times greater among MZ twins than DZ twins (43% versus 6%, respectively) (Kieseppä et al., 2004). Genetics appears to play an even stronger role in bipolar disorder that it does in major depressive disorder (McGuffin et al., 2003). Scientists are actively involved in tracking down specific genes implicated in bipolar disorder (Baum et al., 2007; Schulze et al., 2005). However, genes don't tell the whole story. If bipolar disorder were caused entirely by heredity, then an identical twin of someone having the disorder would always develop the disorder, but this isn't the case (NIMH, 2001). Consistent with the diathesis–stress model, stressful life factors and other biological influences may interact with a genetic predisposition to increase vulnerability to the disorder. Moreover, we have learned that stressful life events can trigger mood episodes in people with bipolar disorder (Alloy et al., 2005).

We continue to learn more about the role of psychosocial factors in bipolar disorders. For example, recent evidence suggests that the social support from family members and friends can enhance functioning of bipolar patients by providing a buffer against the negative effects of stress (Alloy et al., 2005). Moreover, the availability of social support appears to play a role in helping speed recoveries from mood episodes and reducing the likelihood of recurrent episodes (Alloy et al., 2005; Johnson, Winett et al., 1999).

TREATMENT OF MOOD DISORDERS

Just as different theoretical perspectives point to many factors that may be involved in the development of mood disorders, these models have spawned different approaches to treatment. Here we focus on the leading contemporary approaches.

Treating Depression

Depressive disorders are typically treated with psychotherapy, such as in the form of psychodynamic therapy, behavior therapy, or cognitive therapy, or with biomedical approaches, such as antidepressant medication or electroconvulsive therapy (ECT). Sometimes a combination of treatment approaches is used.

Psychodynamic Approaches Traditional psychoanalysis aims to help people who become depressed understand their ambivalent feelings toward important people (objects) in their lives they have lost or whose loss was threatened. By working through feelings of anger toward these lost objects, people can turn anger outward—through verbal expression of feelings, for example—rather than leave it to fester and turn inward.

Traditional psychoanalysis can take years to uncover and deal with unconscious conflicts. Modern psychoanalytic approaches also focus on unconscious conflicts, but they are more direct, relatively brief, and focus on present as well as past conflicted relationships. Some psychodynamic therapists also use behavioral methods to help clients acquire the social skills needed to develop a broader social network.

A newer psychodynamic model, called *interpersonal psychotherapy* (IPT), is a relatively brief form of therapy (usually no more than 9 to 12 months) that focuses on the client's current interpersonal relationships (Klerman et al., 1984). The developers of IPT believe that depression occurs within an interpersonal context and that relationship issues should be emphasized in treatment. IPT has been shown to be an effective treatment for major depression and shows promise in treating other psychological disorders, including dysthymic disorder, bulimia, and posttraumatic stress disorder (PTSD) (Bleiberg & Markowitz, 2005; Frank et al., 2007; Weissman, 2007). Investigators find IPT effective in treating depressed patients from other parts of the world, including sub-Saharan Africa (Bolton et al., 2003).

Although IPT shares some features with traditional psychodynamic approaches (principally the belief that early life experiences and rigid personality features affect psychological adjustment), it differs from traditional psychodynamic therapy by focusing on clients' current relationships rather than on unconscious internal conflicts of childhood origins.

Interpersonal psychotherapy (IPT). IPT is usually a brief, psychodynamically oriented therapy that focuses on issues in the person's current interpersonal relationships. Like traditional psychodynamic approaches, IPT assumes that early life experiences are key issues in adjustment, but IPT focuses on the present—the here and now.

IPT helps clients deal with unresolved or delayed grief reactions following the death of a loved one as well as with role conflicts in present relationships (Weissman & Markowitz, 1994). The therapist also helps clients identify areas of conflict in their present relationships, understand the issues that underlie them, and consider ways of resolving them. If the problems in a relationship are beyond repair, the therapist helps the client consider ways of ending it and establishing new relationships. Take the case of 31-year-old Sal D., whose depression was associated with marital conflict.

◇

Interpersonal Psychotherapy in a Case of Depression

Sal began to explore his marital problems in the fifth therapy session, becoming tearful as he recounted his difficulty expressing his feelings to his wife because of feelings of being "numb." He felt that he had been "holding on" to his feelings, which was causing him to become estranged from his wife. The next session zeroed in on the similarities between himself and his father, in particular how he was distancing himself from his wife in a similar way to how his father had kept a distance from him. By session 7, a turning point had been reached. Sal expressed how he and his wife had become "emotional" and closer to one another during the previous week and how he was able to talk more openly about his feelings, and how he and his wife had been able to make a joint decision concerning a financial matter that had been worrying them for some time. When later he was laid off from his job, he sought his wife's opinion, rather than picking a fight with her as a way of thrusting his job problems on her. To his surprise he found that his wife responded positively—not "violently," as he had expected—to times when he expressed his feelings. In his last therapy session (session 12), Sal expressed how therapy had led to a "reawakening" within himself with respect to the feelings he had been keeping to himself—an openness that he hoped to create in his relationship with his wife.

—Adapted from Klerman et al., 1984, pp. 111–113

Behavioral Approaches Behavior therapists generally focus on helping depressed patients develop more effective social or interpersonal skills and increasing their participation in pleasurable or rewarding activities. Evidence shows that behavioral techniques can produce substantial benefits in treating depression in both adults and adolescents (Cuijpers, van Straten, & Warmerdam, 2007). In fact, this model of therapy, generally called *behavioral activation*, produced higher rates of remission in treating severely depressed patients in one recent study than did alternative forms of treatment (Dimidjian et al., 2006). Let's now turn to cognitive therapy, which is perhaps the most widely used form of psychological treatment for depression.

Cognitive Therapy Cognitive therapists believe that distorted thinking (cognitive distortions) play a key role in the development of depression. Depressed people typically focus on how they are feeling rather than on the thoughts that may underlie their feeling states. That is, they usually pay more attention to how bad they feel than to the thoughts that may trigger or maintain their depressed moods. Aaron Beck and his colleagues have developed a multicomponent treatment approach, called *cognitive therapy*, that focuses on helping people with depression learn to recognize and correct their dysfunctional thinking patterns. Table 8.6 shows some common examples of distorted, automatic thoughts, the types of cognitive distortions they represent, and rational alternative responses that can be used to replace these distorted thoughts.

Cognitive therapy, like behavior therapy, is relatively brief, lasting perhaps 14 to 16 weekly sessions. Therapists use a combination of behavioral and cognitive techniques to help clients identify and change dysfunctional thoughts and develop more adaptive behaviors. For example, they help clients connect thought patterns to negative moods by having them monitor the automatic negative thoughts they experience throughout

TABLE 8.6

Cognitive Distortions and Rational Responses

Automatic Thought	Kind of Cognitive Distortion	Rational Response
I'm all alone in the world.	All-or-nothing thinking	It may feel like I'm all alone, but there are some people who care about me.
Nothing will ever work out for me.	Overgeneralization	No one can look into the future. Concentrate on the present.
My looks are hopeless.	Magnification	I may not be perfect looking, but I'm far from hopeless.
I'm falling apart. I can't handle this.	Magnification	Sometimes I just feel overwhelmed. But I've handled things like this before. I'll just take it a step at a time and I'll be okay.
I guess I'm just a born loser.	Labeling and mislabeling	Nobody is destined to be a loser. Stop talking yourself down.
I've only lost 8 pounds on this diet. I should just forget it. I can't succeed.	Negative focusing/Minimization/ Disqualifying the positive/Jumping to conclusions/All-or-nothing thinking	Eight pounds is a good start. I didn't gain all this weight overnight, and I have to expect that it will take time to lose it.
I know things must really be bad for me to feel this awful.	Emotional reasoning	Feeling something doesn't make it so. If I'm not seeing things clearly, my emotions will be distorted too.
I know I'm going to flunk this course.	Fortune teller error	Give me a break! Just focus on getting through this course, not on jumping to negative conclusions.
I know John's problems are really my fault.	Personalization	Stop blaming yourself for everyone else's problems. There are many reasons why John's problems have nothing to do with me.
Someone my age should be doing better than I am.	Should statements	Stop comparing yourself to others. All anyone can be expected to do is their best. What good does it do to compare myself to others? It only leads me to get down on myself rather than get motivated.
I just don't have the brains for college.	Labeling and mislabeling	Stop calling yourself names like "stupid." I can accomplish a lot more than I give myself credit for.
Everything is my fault.	Personalization	There you go again. Stop playing this game of pointing blame at yourself. There's enough blame to go around. Better yet, forget placing blame and try to think through how to solve this problem.
It would be awful if Sue turns me down.	Magnification	It might be upsetting, but it needn't be awful unless I make it so.
If people really knew me, they would hate me.	Mind reader	What evidence is there for that? More people who get to know me like me than don't like me.
If something doesn't get better soon, I'll go crazy.	Jumping to conclusions/Magnification	I've dealt with these problems this long without falling apart. I just have to hang in there. Things are not as bad as they seem.
I can't believe I have another pimple on my face. This is going to ruin my whole weekend.	Mental filter	Take it easy. A pimple is not the end of the world. It doesn't have to spoil my whole weekend. Other people get pimples and seem to have a good time.

the day using a thought diary or daily record. They note when and where negative thoughts occur and how they feel at the time. Then the therapist helps the client challenge the negative thoughts and replace them with more adaptive thoughts. The following case example shows how a cognitive therapist works with a client to challenge the validity of thoughts that reflect the cognitive distortion called *selective abstraction* (the tendency to judge oneself entirely on the basis of specific weaknesses or flaws in character). The client judged herself to be totally lacking in self-control because she ate a single piece of candy while she was on a diet.

Cognitive Therapy for Depression

CLIENT: *I don't have any self-control at all.*

THERAPIST: *On what basis do you say that?*

C: *Somebody offered me candy and I couldn't refuse it.*

T: *Were you eating candy every day?*

C: *No, I just ate it this once.*

T: *Did you do anything constructive during the past week to adhere to your diet?*

C: *Well, I didn't give in to the temptation to buy candy every time I saw it at the store. . . . Also, I did not eat any candy except that one time when it was offered to me and I felt I couldn't refuse it.*

T: *If you counted up the number of times you controlled yourself versus the number of times you gave in, what ratio would you get?*

C: *About 100 to 1.*

T: *So if you controlled yourself 100 times and did not control yourself just once, would that be a sign that you are weak through and through?*

C: *I guess not—not through and through (smiles).*

—Adapted from Beck et al., 1979, p. 68

Cognitive therapy and other forms of cognitive-behavioral therapy have produced impressive results in treating major depression and reducing the risks of recurrent episodes (e.g, DeRubeis et al., 2005; Hamilton & Dobson, 2002; Hollon, Stewart, & Strunk, 2006; Merrill, Tolbert, & Wade, 2003; Miranda et al., 2006). The benefits of cognitive therapy appear to be at least equal to those of antidepressant medication in treating depression, even moderate to severe depression, at least when practiced by experienced cognitive therapists (DeRubeis et al., 1999, 2005).

Might the combination of drugs and therapy be more effective still? A recent review of scientific evidence showed that the combination of antidepressant medication and psychotherapy produced slightly better outcomes as compared to either psychotherapy or medication alone (Friedman et al., 2004). Combined treatment might be especially beneficial in cases of more severe, recurrent depression (Mann, 2005).

Biological Approaches

The most common biological approaches to treating mood disorders are the use of antidepressant drugs and electroconvulsive therapy for depression and lithium carbonate for bipolar disorder.

Antidepressant Drugs Today, we have three major classes of antidepressants that increase the availability of key neurotransmitters in the brain: (1) *tricyclic antidepressants* (TCAs), *monoamine oxidase (MAO) inhibitors*, and *selective serotonin-reuptake inhibitors* (SSRIs) (Berton & Nestler, 2006; Mann, 2005). All antidepressants increase availability of neurotransmitters, but they do so in different ways (see Figure 8.4).

The tricyclics, which include *imipramine* (trade name Tofranil), *amitriptyline* (Elavil), *desipramine* (Norpramin), and *doxepin* (Sinequan), are so named because of their three-ringed molecular structure. They increase brain levels of the neurotransmitters norepinephrine and serotonin by interfering with the reuptake (reabsorption by the transmitting cell) of these chemical messengers. The SSRIs, such as *fluoxetine* (trade name Prozac) and *sertraline* (trade name Zoloft), work in a similar fashion but have more specific effects on raising the levels of serotonin in the brain. The MAO inhibitors, such as *phenelzine* (trade name Nardil), increase the availability of neurotransmitters by inhibiting the action of monoamine oxidase, an enzyme that normally breaks down or degrades neurotransmitters in the synapse. MAO inhibitors are used less widely than other antidepressants because of potentially serious interactions with certain foods and alcoholic beverages.

We understand how antidepressants affect neurotransmitter levels, but as noted earlier, we don't clearly understand the underlying mechanisms explaining how they work to

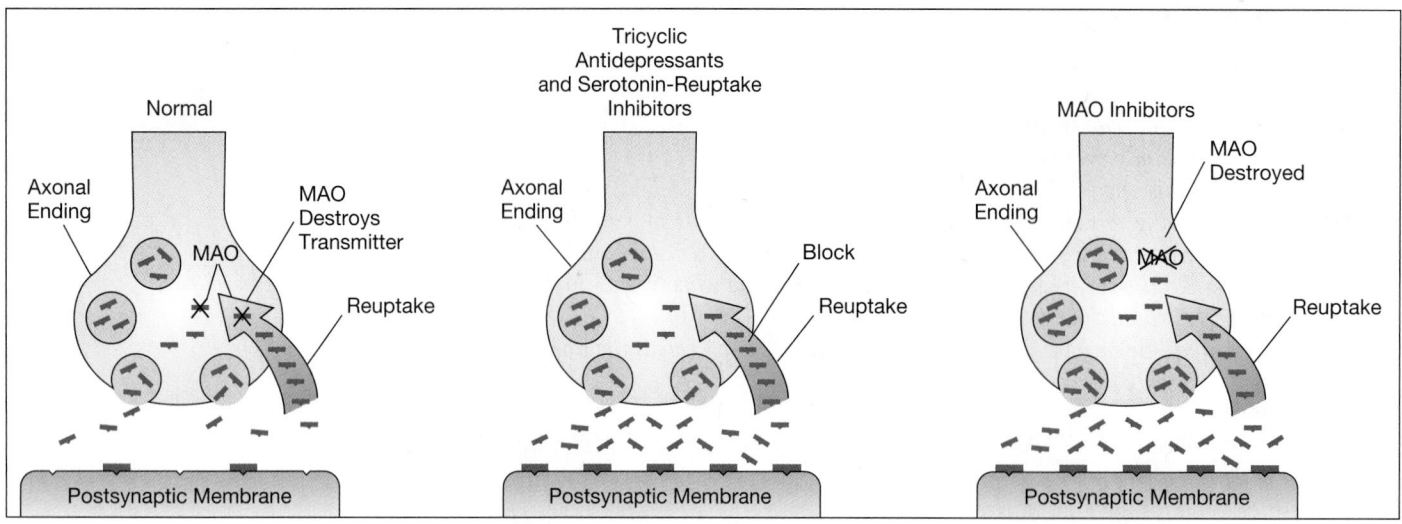

FIGURE 8.4 The actions of various types of antidepressants at the synapse.
Tricyclic antidepressants and serotonin-reuptake inhibitors both increase the availability of neuro-transmitters by preventing their reuptake by the presynaptic neuron. Tricyclic antidepressants impede the reuptake of both norepinephrine and serotonin. MAO inhibitors work by inhibiting the action of monoamine oxidase, an enzyme that normally breaks down neurotransmitters in the synaptic cleft.

relieve depression. The potential side effects of tricyclics and MAO inhibitors include dry mouth, a slowing down of motor responses, constipation, blurred vision, sexual dysfunction, and less frequently, urinary retention, paralytic ileus (a paralysis of the intestines, which impairs the passage of intestinal contents), confusion, delirium, and cardiovascular complications, such as reduced blood pressure. Tricyclics are also highly toxic, which raises the prospect of suicidal overdoses if the drugs are used without close supervision.

Antidepressants help relieve symptoms of depression and help prevent recurrent episodes when patients continue taking them (Lépine et al., 2004; Reynolds et al., 2006). However, clinical trials typically show that only 30% or less of patients treated with antidepressants achieve complete symptom relief or remission (Menza, 2006; Trivedi et al., 2006). Moreover, despite dramatic responses to antidepressants shown in drug company commercials, antidepressants produce only modestly stronger effects overall than placebo (inert) drugs (Boyles, 2002; Kirsch et al., 2002). However, among patients who fail to respond to one antidepressant, about one in four experience complete symptom relief when switched to another one (Rush et al., 2006).

There is little difference in levels of effectiveness among the different SSRIs or between SSRIs and the older generation of tricyclic antidepressants (Mann, 2005; Serrano-Blanco et al., 2006). Yet because they hold two major advantages, the SSRIs have largely replaced the earlier drugs. The first advantage is that they are less toxic and so are less dangerous in overdose. Secondly, they have fewer cardiovascular effects and other common side effects (such as dry mouth, constipation, and weight gain) associated with the tricyclics and MAO inhibitors. Still, Prozac and other SSRIs may produce side effects such as upset stomach, headaches, agitation, insomnia, lack of sexual drive, and delayed orgasm (Michelson et al., 2000). Another significant concern is that use of antidepressants appears to be connected with increased suicidal thinking in some children, and adolescents, and young adults—an important issue discussed further in Chapter 14.

Another concern with psychiatric drugs is the high rate of relapse in patients who are withdrawn from active medication and even in those who continue to take antidepressant medication (Kellner et al., 2006; McGrath et al., 2006; Yager, 2006). Cognitive-behavioral therapies provide greater protection against relapse than antidepressant medication, perhaps because patients learn skills in therapy they can then use to handle life stressors and disappointments that patients receiving only medication do not (Bockting et al., 2005; Hollon, Stewart, & Strunk, 2006; Tang et al., 2007). Adding cognitive-behavioral therapy to pharmacological treatment may also help reduce the risk of relapse after psychiatric drugs are withdrawn (Friedman et al., 2004).

Overall, about 50% to 70% of depressed patients treated on an outpatient basis respond favorably to either psychotherapy or antidepressant medication (USDHHS, 1999a). Some people who fail to respond to psychotherapy respond to antidepressants. The opposite is also true: Some people who fail to respond to drug therapy respond to psychotherapy.

St. John's Wort—A Natural "Prozac"? Might a humble herb be a remedy for depression? The herb, called St. John's wort, or *Hypericum perforatum,* has been used for centuries to help heal wounds. Now, people are using it to relieve depression. The herb appears to increase levels of serotonin in the brain by interfering with reabsorption of the neurotransmitter, as does Prozac. Although people seeking help for depression may be attracted to the idea of using a natural product such as St. John's wort, the results of outcome studies are mixed (Kalb, 2002). Hopes were lowered by the results of a study showing that St. John's wort worked no better than a placebo in treating major depression (Shelton et al., 2001). However, other evidence suggests that the herb may have therapeutic benefits in treating milder forms of depression (Lecrubier et al., 2002).

Electroconvulsive Therapy *Electroconvulsive therapy* (ECT), more commonly called *shock therapy,* continues to evoke controversy. The idea of passing an electric current through someone's brain may seem barbaric. Yet ECT is a generally safe and effective treatment for severe depression, and it can help relieve major depression in many cases in which alternative treatments have failed (UK ECT Review Group, 2003).

In ECT, an electrical current of between 70 and 130 volts is applied to the head to induce a convulsion that is similar to a *grand mal* epileptic seizure. ECT is usually administered in a series of 6 to 12 treatments, given three times per week over several weeks (USDHHS, 1999a). The patient is put to sleep with a brief-acting general anesthetic and given a muscle relaxant to avoid wild convulsions that might result in injury. As a result, spasms may be barely perceptible to onlookers. The patient awakens soon after the procedure and generally remembers nothing. Although ECT had earlier been used in the treatment of a wide variety of psychological disorders, including schizophrenia and bipolar disorder, the American Psychiatric Association recommends that ECT only be used to treat major depressive disorder in people who do not respond to antidepressant medication.

ECT leads to significant improvement in a majority of people with major depression who have failed to respond to antidepressant medication (Ebmeier, Donaghey, & Steele, 2006; Prudic et al., 2004; Reifler, 2006). It can also have dramatic effects on relieving suicidal thinking (Kellner et al., 2005). Although no one knows exactly how ECT works, one possibility is that ECT normalizes neurotransmitter activity in the brain.

Although ECT can be an effective short-term treatment of severe depression, it too is no panacea. There is an understandable concern among patients, relatives, and professionals themselves about possible risks, especially memory loss for events occurring around the time of treatment (Glass, 2001). As noted in Chapter 4, another nagging problem with ECT is a high rate of relapse following treatment (Sackeim et al., 2001). In one recent study, about two-thirds of patients whose depression had remitted following ECT experienced a relapse within 6 months (Prudic et al., 2004). Depression often returns even among patients who continue to be treated with antidepressant medication (Sackeim et al., 1994). All in all, many professionals view ECT as a treatment of last resort, to be considered only after other treatment approaches have been tried and failed.

Clinical Practice Guidelines for Depression A government-sponsored expert panel set up to develop guidelines for treating depression found the following treatments to be effective (Depression Guideline Panel, 1993b):

- Antidepressant medication (tricyclics or selective serotonin-reuptake inhibitors)
- Three specific forms of psychotherapy: cognitive therapy, behavioral therapy, and interpersonal psychotherapy
- A combination of one of the recommended forms of psychotherapy and antidepressant medication
- Other specified forms of treatment, including ECT and phototherapy for seasonal depression

Treating Bipolar Disorder

Bipolar disorder is most commonly treated with drugs that aim to stabilize mood swings.

Lithium and Other Mood Stabilizers It could be said that the ancient Greeks and Romans were among the first to use lithium as a form of chemotherapy. They prescribed mineral water that contained lithium for people with turbulent mood swings. Today, the drug *lithium carbonate,* a powdered form of the metallic element lithium, is widely used in treating bipolar disorder.

Lithium, the most widely used and widely studied drug for bipolar disorder, is effective in stabilizing moods in bipolar patients and reducing the risk of recurrent manic episodes as well as suicides (Bowden et al., 2003; Cipriani et al., 2005; López-Muñoza et al., 2006). However, we don't yet know whether lithium reduces the risk of recurrent depressive episodes (Geddes et al., 2004).

People with bipolar disorder may need to use lithium indefinitely to control their mood swings, just as diabetics use insulin continuously to control their illness. Despite more than 40 years of use as a therapeutic drug, we still can't say how lithium works.

Despite its benefits, lithium is no panacea. At least 30% to 40% of patients with mania either fail to respond to the drug or cannot tolerate it (Dubovsky, 2000). Lithium treatment must be closely monitored because of potential toxic effects and other side effects. Lithium can also lead to mild memory problems, which may lead people to stop taking it. The drug can lead to weight gain, lethargy, and grogginess, and to a general slowing down of motor functioning. It can also produce gastrointestinal distress and lead to liver problems over the long term.

Although lithium is still widely used, the drug's limitations have prompted efforts to find alternative treatments. Investigators find that anticonvulsant drugs used in the treatment of epilepsy, including *carbamazepine* (brand name Tegretol), *divalproex* (brand name Depakote), and *lamotrigine* (brand name Lamictal), can reduce manic symptoms and may help stabilize moods in people with bipolar disorder (Nasrallah, Ketter, & Kalali, 2006; "New Studies," 2006; Nierenberg et al., 2006). Anticonvulsant drugs may benefit people with bipolar disorder who either do not respond to lithium or cannot tolerate the drug because of side effects. Anticonvulsant drugs usually cause fewer or less severe side effects than lithium. However, some patients have only a partial response to lithium or anticonvulsant drugs, and some fail to respond at all. Recent evidence points to therapeutic benefits of combining mood stabilizers with a class of antipsychotic drugs, called *atypical antipsychotics,* which are generally used to treat schizophrenia (see Chapter 12) (Scherk, Pajonk, & Leucht, 2007).

For Kay Jamison, managing manic depression involved both medication (lithium) and psychotherapy.

"I" "Leading a Normal Life"

At this point in my existence, I cannot imagine leading a normal life without both taking lithium and having had the benefits of psychotherapy. Lithium prevents my seductive but disastrous high, diminishes my depressions, clears out the wool and webbing from my disordered thinking,

---

TRUTH or FICTION

The ancient Greeks and Romans used a chemical to curb turbulent mood swings that is still used today.

☑ **TRUE.** The ancient Greeks and Romans did use a chemical substance to control mood swings that is still widely used today. It is called lithium.

slows me down, gentles me out, keeps me from ruining my career and relationships, keeps me out of a hospital, alive, and makes psychotherapy possible. But, ineffably, psychotherapy heals. It makes some sense of the confusion, reins in the terrifying thoughts and feelings, returns some control and hope and possibility of learning from it all.

—From Jamison, 1995

Psychological Approaches Large-scale investigations of the effects of psychological treatments for bipolar disorder are underway. Early studies suggest that psychosocial treatments, such as cognitive-behavioral therapy, interpersonal therapy, and family therapy, may be helpful adjunctive therapies when used along with drug therapy in the treatment of bipolar disorder (Alloy et al., 2005; Frank et al., 2005; Miklowitz et al., 2007). We also have evidence that psychological treatment can improve the level of functioning and adherence to a medication regimen in bipolar patients (Johnson & Leahy, 2003; Miklowitz et al., 2003; Rougeta & Aubry, 2007). Moreover, a recent randomized controlled study showed that cognitive therapy reduced the rate of relapse in bipolar patients (Lam et al., 2003).

TYING IT TOGETHER

Mood disorders involve the interplay of multiple factors (see the accompanying *Concept Map for Abnormal Psychology*). Consistent with the *diathesis–stress model,* depression may reflect an interaction of biological factors (such as genetic factors, neurotransmitter irregularities, or brain abnormalities), psychological factors (such as cognitive distortions or learned helplessness), and social and environmental stressors (such as divorce or loss of a job).

The concept map illustrates a possible causal pathway based on the diathesis–stress model. Stressful life events, such as prolonged unemployment or a divorce, may have a depressing effect by reducing neurotransmitter activity in the brain. These biochemical effects may be more likely to occur or may be more pronounced in people with a genetic predisposition, or diathesis, for depression. However, a depressive disorder may not develop, or may develop in a milder form, in people with more effective coping resources for handling stressful situations. For example, people who receive emotional support from others may be better able to withstand the effects of stress than those who have to go it alone. So, too, for people who make active coping efforts to meet the challenges they face in life.

Sociocultural factors can be sources of stress that influence the development or recurrence of mood disorders (Ostler et al., 2001). These factors include poverty; overcrowding; exposure to racism, sexism, and prejudice; violence in the home or community; unequal stressful burdens placed on women; and family disintegration. Other sources of stress that can contribute to mood disorders include negative life events such as the loss of a job, the development of a serious illness, the breakup of a romantic relationship, and the loss of a loved one.

The diathesis for depression may take the form of a psychological vulnerability involving a depressive thinking style, one characterized by tendencies to exaggerate the consequences of negative events, to heap blame on oneself, and to perceive oneself as helpless to effect positive change. This cognitive diathesis may increase the risk of depression in the face of negative life events. These cognitive influences may also interact with a genetically based diathesis to further increase the risk of depression following stressful life events. Then, too, the availability of social support from others may help bolster a person's resistance to stress during difficult times. People with more effective social skills may be better able to garner and maintain social reinforcement from others and thus be better able to resist depression than people lacking social skills. But biochemical changes in the brain might make it more difficult for the person to cope effectively and bounce back from stressful life events. Lingering biochemical changes and feelings of depression may exacerbate feelings of helplessness, compounding the effects of the initial stressor.

Gender-related differences in coping styles may also come into play. According to Nolen-Hoeksema, women are more likely to ruminate when facing emotional problems, and men are more likely to abuse alcohol. These or other differences in coping styles may propel women into longer and more severe bouts of depression while setting the stage for the development of drinking problems in men. As you can see, a complex web of contributing factors is likely involved in the development of mood disorders.

A CLOSER LOOK

Magnetic Stimulation Therapy for Depression

Mesmer would be proud. Franz Friedrich Mesmer (1734–1815) was the 18th-century Austrian physician from whose name the term *mesmerism* is derived (we still sometimes speak of people being "mesmerized" by things). He believed that hysteria was caused by an underlying imbalance in the distribution of a magnetic fluid in the body—a problem he believed he could correct by prodding the body with metal rods. A scientific commission of the time debunked Mesmer's claims and attributed any cures he obtained to the effects of natural recovery or self-delusion (what we might today call the power of suggestion). The chairperson of the commission was none other than our own Benjamin Franklin, who served at the time as ambassador to France from the newly independent United States. Although Mesmer's theories and practices were discredited, recent evidence into the therapeutic use of magnetism suggests that he might have been on to something.

Fast forward 200 years. Australian doctors identified 60 patients with major depression who had failed to respond to different types of antidepressants (Fitzgerald et al., 2003). In a double-blind controlled design, they treated these patients with either strong magnetic stimulation to the head (called *transcranial magnetic stimulation,* or TMS) or a fake treatment that had all the trappings of the active treatment except that the magnet was angled away to prevent magnetic stimulation of the brain. With TMS, a powerful electromagnet placed on the scalp generates a strong magnetic field that passes through the skull and affects the electrical activity of the brain.

After 2 weeks of treatment, patients receiving TMS showed clinical improvement in depression as opposed to the minimal change found in the sham group. Improvement was modest and did not occur in all patients. The investigators believe that longer treatment (at least 4 weeks) may be necessary to produce more meaningful therapeutic benefits. This study adds to a growing body of evidence supporting the antidepressant effects of TMS (e.g., Avery et al., 2006; Herwig et al., 2003; Mantovani et al., 2007). The specific form and intensity of TMS needed to produce therapeutic effects remains under study. We should also note that TMS carries some potential risks, such as the possibility of seizures. However, the risk of seizures may be reduced by using low-frequency stimulation.

In sum, TMS shows promise as a new form of treatment for moderate depression (Gershon, Dannon, & Grunhaus, 2003). Although it has been approved for medical use in Canada, it is still experimental in the United States (Dubovsky, 2006). It also appears promising as an alternative to ECT in cases of major depression that fail to respond to pharmacological treatment. TMS may be particularly helpful in treating depression because the prefrontal cortex in the left cerebral hemisphere becomes less active in depressed patients, and this part of the brain can be directly affected by TMS (Henry, Pascual-Leone, & Cole, 2003). Yet investigators caution that more evidence is needed to support its efficacy and safety before it can be recommended for general use in treating depression (Aarre et al., 2003; Martin et al., 2003). TMS may also have therapeutic benefits in treating other disorders, such as posttraumatic stress disorder (Cohen et al., 2004).

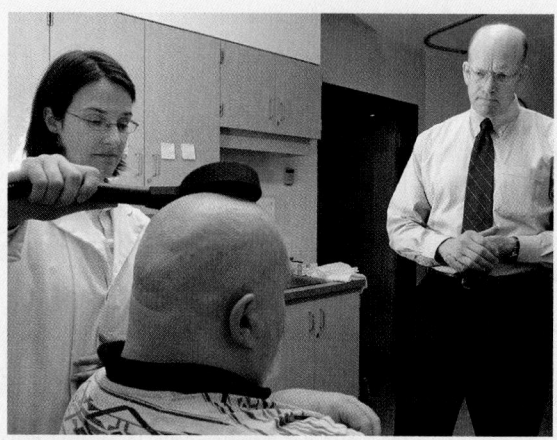

Transcranial magnetic stimulation therapy. TMS is a promising therapeutic approach in which powerful magnets are used to help relieve depression.

TRUTH or FICTION

Placing a powerful electromagnet on the scalp can help relieve depression.

☑ **TRUE.** In a number of research studies magnetic stimulation of the head has been shown to have antidepressant effects.

SUICIDE

Suicidal thoughts are common enough. At times of great stress, many, if not most, people have considered suicide. A nationally representative survey found that 13% of U.S. adults reported having experienced suicidal thoughts, and 4.6% reported making a suicide attempt (Kessler, Borges, & Walters, 1999). It is fortunate that most people who have suicidal thoughts do not act on them. Still, each year in the United States some 500,000 people are treated in hospital emergency rooms for attempted suicide, and more than 30,000 "succeed" in taking their lives (Lemonick, 2003a; Mokdad et al., 2004; National Strategy for Suicide Prevention, 2001). There are twice as many deaths from suicide as from HIV/AIDS (NIMH, 2003). Suicide exacts a heavy toll on the nation, as you can see in statistics reported by the U.S. Surgeon General (see Table 8.7).

Suicidal behavior is not a psychological disorder in itself. But it is often a feature or symptom of an underlying psychological disorder, usually a mood disorder (Bernal et al., 2007), which is the reason we discuss it in this chapter. The federal government estimates that about 60% of people who commit suicide suffer from a mood disorder (National Strategy for Suicide Prevention, 2001).

TABLE 8.7

U.S. Surgeon General's Report on Suicide: Cost to the Nation

- Every 17 minutes another life is lost to suicide. Every day, 86 Americans take their own lives and over 1,500 attempt suicide.
- Suicide is now the eighth leading cause of death in Americans.
- For every two victims of homicide in the United States, there are three deaths from suicide.
- There are now twice as many deaths due to suicide than due to HIV/AIDS.
- Between 1952 and 1995, the incidence of suicide among adolescents and young adults nearly tripled.
- In the month prior to their suicide, 75% of elderly persons had visited a physician.
- Over half of all suicides occur in adult men, ages 25 to 65.
- Many who make suicide attempts never seek professional care immediately after the attempt.
- Males are four times more likely to commit suicide than are females.
- More teenagers and young adults die from suicide than from cancer, heart disease, AIDS, birth defects, stroke, pneumonia and influenza, and chronic lung disease, combined.
- Suicide takes the lives of more than 30,000 Americans every year.

Source: Center for Mental Health Services, 2001.

Who Commits Suicide?

What do you think is the second leading cause of death among college students, after motor vehicle accidents? Drugs? Homicide? The answer is suicide, with an estimated 1,000 suicides and 24,0000 suicide attempts annually among the nation's college students age 18 to 24 (Lamberg, 2006; Rawe & Kingsbury, 2006). Although attention is focused on the tragedy of youthful suicide, as well it should be, suicide rates are actually highest among adults age 65 and older, especially older White males (Bruce et al., 2004; Joe et al., 2006; see Figure 8.5). (We discuss youth suicide further in Chapter 14.)

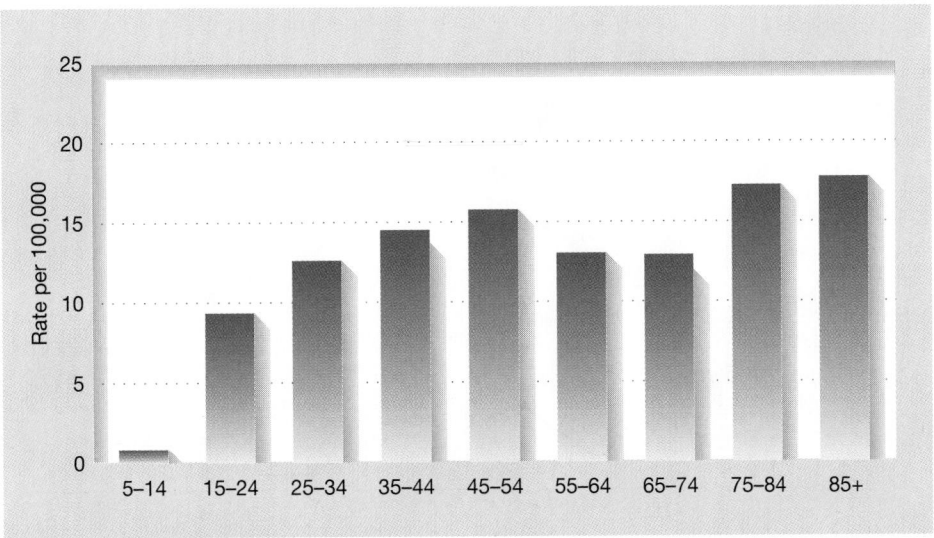

FIGURE 8.5 Suicide rates according to age.
Although adolescent suicides may be more highly publicized, adults, especially older adults, have higher suicide rates.

Source: WISQARS Injury Mortality Reports 1999–2003, Centers for Disease Control and Prevention, National Center for Injury Prevention, published online January 2006.

Suicide in Older Adults Despite life-extending advances in medical care, some older adults find the quality of their lives less than satisfactory. Older people are more susceptible to diseases such as cancer and Alzheimer's, which can leave them with feelings of helplessness and hopelessness that, in turn, can give rise to depression and suicidal thinking (Starkstein et al., 2005).

Many older adults also suffer a mounting accumulation of losses of friends and loved ones, leading to social isolation (Stroebe, Stroebe, & Abakoumkin, 2005). These losses, as well as the loss of good health and of a responsible role in the community, may wear down the will to live. Not surprisingly, the highest suicide rates in older men are among those who are widowed or socially isolated. Society's increased acceptance of suicide in older people may also play a part. Whatever the causes, suicide has become an increased risk for elderly people. Perhaps society should focus its attention on the quality of life that is afforded our elderly, in addition to providing them the medical care that helps make longer life possible.

Gender and Ethnic/Racial Differences More women attempt suicide, but more men "succeed" (Houry, 2004; Miller et al., 2004). For every female suicide, there are four male suicides. More males "succeed" in large part because they tend to choose quicker-acting and more lethal means, such as handguns.

Suicides are more common among (non-Hispanic) White Americans and Native Americans than African Americans, Asian Americans, or Hispanic Americans (Garlow, Purselle, & Heninger, 2005; Gone, 2004; see Figure 8.6). White Americans are more than twice as likely to take their own lives as African Americans (Joe et al., 2006). Yet the highest suicide rates in the nation are found among Native American adolescent and young adult males (Meyers, 2007).

Hopelessness and exposure to others who have attempted or committed suicide may contribute to the increased risk of suicide among Native American youth. Native American youth at greatest risk tend to be reared in communities that are largely isolated from U.S. society at large. They perceive themselves as having relatively few opportunities to gain the skills necessary to join the workforce in the larger society and are also relatively more prone to substance abuse, including alcohol abuse. Knowledge that peers have attempted or completed suicide renders suicide a highly visible escape from psychological pain.

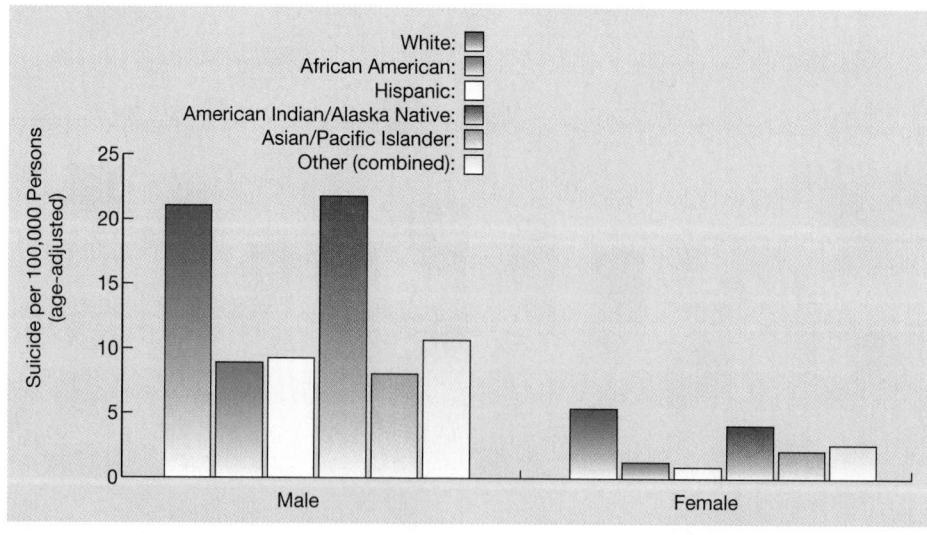

FIGURE 8.6 Ethnicity and suicide rates.
Suicide rates are higher among males than females, and higher among White (European) Americans and Native Americans than other ethnicities.

Source: WISQARS Injury Mortality Reports 1999–2003, Centers for Disease Control and Prevention, National Center for Injury Prevention, published online January 2006.

Why Do People Commit Suicide?

To many lay observers, suicide seems so extreme an act that they believe only "insane" people (meaning people who are out of touch with reality) would commit suicide. However, suicidal thinking does not necessarily imply loss of touch with reality, deep-seated unconscious conflict, or a personality disorder. Having thoughts about suicide generally reflects a narrowing of the range of options people think are available to them to deal with their problems. That is, they are discouraged by their problems and see no other way out.

The risk of suicide is much higher among people with severe mood disorders, such as major depression and bipolar disorder (Bruce et al., 2004). As many as one in five people with bipolar disorder eventually commit suicide (Cowan & Kandel, 2001). Attempted or completed suicide is also linked to many other psychological disorders, including alcoholism and drug dependence, anorexia, schizophrenia, panic disorder, personality disorders, posttraumatic stress disorder, and borderline personality disorder (e.g., Franko & Keel, 2006; McGirra et al., 2006; Moran et al., 2003; Walker et al., 2004).

Past suicidal behavior plays an important role in later suicidal behavior (Joiner et al., 2005). Sadly, people who fail on a first attempt often complete suicide on a subsequent attempt. Those who survive an attempt but express to others that they wished they had died are more likely to go on to eventually complete suicide than are those who expressed ambivalence about the attempt (Henriques et al., 2005). Adolescents who have a history of attempted suicide stand a risk of a later completed suicide that is 14 times higher in females and 22 times higher in males as compared to the general adolescent population (Olfson et al., 2005).

Not all suicides are connected with psychological disorders. Some people suffering from painful and hopeless physical illness seek to escape further suffering by taking their own lives. These suicides are sometimes labeled "rational suicides" in the belief that they are based on a rational decision that life is no longer worth living in the light of continual suffering. However, in perhaps many of these cases the person's judgment and reasoning ability may be colored by an underlying and potentially treatable psychological disorder, such as depression. Other suicides are motivated by deep-seated religious or political convictions, such as in the case of people who sacrifice themselves in acts of protest against their governments or who kill themselves and others in suicide bombings in the belief that their acts will be rewarded in an afterlife.

Suicide attempts often occur in response to highly stressful life events, especially "exit events," such as the death of a spouse, close friend, or relative; divorce or separation; a family member's leaving home; or the loss of a close friend. People who consider suicide in times of stress may lack problem-solving skills and be unable to find alternative ways of coping with stressors. Underscoring the psychological impact of severe stress, researchers find suicides to be more common among survivors of natural disasters, especially severe floods (Krug et al., 1998).

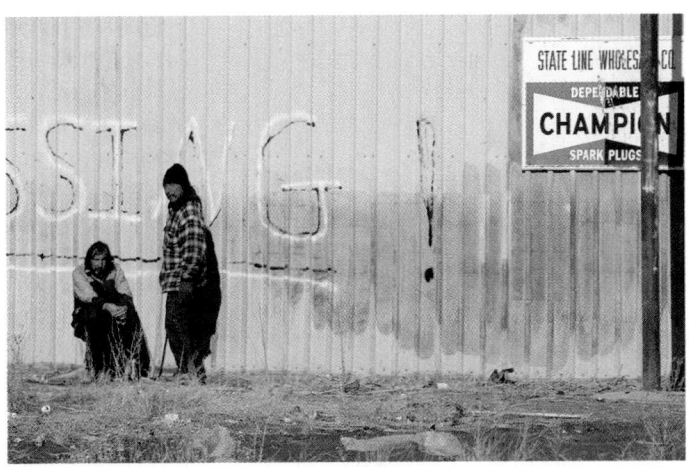

Seeds of hopelessness. Suicide rates are higher among Native Americans than other groups. Many Native Americans living in depressed areas see a bleak future ahead that offers few, if any, promising opportunities.

DEPRESSION/DELIBERATE
SELF HARM:

The Case of Sarah

"I ended up starting to cut because the depression was so bad."

Theoretical Perspectives on Suicide

The classic psychodynamic model views depression as the turning inward of anger against the internal representation of a lost love object. Suicide then represents inward-directed anger that turns murderous. Suicidal people, then, do not seek to destroy themselves. Instead, they seek to vent their rage against the internalized representation of the love object. In so doing, they destroy themselves as well, of course. In his later writings, Freud speculated that suicide may be motivated by the "death instinct," a tendency to return to the tension-free state that preceded birth. Existential and humanistic theorists relate suicide to the perception that life is meaningless and hopeless. Suicidal people report they find life duller, emptier, and more boring than nonsuicidal people (Mehrabian & Weinstein, 1985).

In the 19th century, social thinker Emile Durkheim (1897/1958) noted that people who experienced *anomie*—who feel lost, without identity, rootless—are more likely to commit suicide. Sociocultural theorists likewise believe that alienation may play a role in suicide. In our modern, mobile society, people frequently move hundreds or thousands of miles to schools and jobs. Executives and their families may be relocated every 2 years or so. Military personnel and their families may be shifted about yet more rapidly. Many people are thereby socially isolated or cut off from their support groups. Moreover, city dwellers tend to limit or discourage informal social contacts because of crowding, overstimulation, and fear of crime. It is thus understandable that many people find few sources of support in times of crisis. In some cases, the family support is available but not helpful. Family members may be perceived as part of the problem, not part of the solution.

Learning theorists focus largely on the lack of problem-solving skills for handling significant life stress. According to Shneidman (1985), those who attempt suicide wish to escape unbearable psychological pain and may perceive no other way out. People who threaten or attempt suicide may also receive sympathy and support from loved ones and others, perhaps making future—and more lethal—attempts more likely. This is not to suggest that suicide attempts or gestures should be ignored. People who threaten suicide are *not* merely seeking attention. Although those who threaten suicide may not carry out the act, they should be taken seriously. People who commit suicide often tell others of their intentions or provide clues. Moreover, many people make aborted suicide attempts before they go on to make actual suicide attempts.

Social-cognitive theorists suggest that suicide may be motivated by personal expectancies, such as beliefs that one will be missed by others or that survivors will feel guilty for having mistreated the person, or that suicide will solve one's own problems or even other people's problems (e.g., "He won't have to worry about me any longer") in one fell swoop.

Social-cognitive theorists also focus on the potential modeling effects of observing suicidal behavior in others, especially among teenagers who feel overwhelmed by academic and social stressors. A *social contagion*, or spreading of suicide in a community, may occur in the wake of suicides that receive widespread publicity. Teenagers, who seem to be especially vulnerable to these modeling effects, may even romanticize the suicidal act as one of heroic courage. The incidence of suicide among teenagers sometimes rises markedly in the period following news reports about suicide. Copycat suicides may be more likely to occur when reports of suicides are sensationalized, so that other teenagers expect their deaths to have a meaningful impact on their communities (Kessler et al., 1990).

Biological factors are also implicated in suicide, including reduced utilization or availability of the mood-regulating chemical serotonin (Joiner, Brown, & Wingate, 2005; Malone et al., 2003). Because serotonin is linked to depression, the relationship with suicide is not surprising. Yet serotonin also acts to curb or inhibit nervous system activity, so perhaps lowered serotonin activity leads to *disinhibition*, or release, of impulsive behavior that takes the form of a suicidal act in vulnerable individuals. Suicide also tends to run in families, which hints at genetic factors. Genes may influence susceptibility to suicide by affecting the regulation of serotonin in the brain (Lemonde et al., 2003; Zhou et al., 2005).

Mood disorders in family members and parental suicide are also connected with suicide risk (Brent et al., 2002). But what are the causal connections? Do people who attempt suicide inherit vulnerabilities to mood disorders that are connected with suicide? Does the family atmosphere promote feelings of hopelessness? Does the suicide of one family member give others the idea of doing the same thing? Does one suicide create the impression that other family members are destined to kill themselves? These are all questions researchers need to address.

TRUTH or FICTION

People who threaten suicide are basically attention seekers.

☑ **FALSE.** Although people who threaten suicide may not carry out the act, their threats should be taken seriously. Most people who do commit suicide had told others of their intentions or had left clues.

Starry, Starry Night. The famed artist Vincent van Gogh suffered from severe bouts of depression and eventually took his own life at the age of 37, dying of a self-inflicted gunshot wound. In this self-portrait, van Gogh strikes a melancholy pose that allows the viewer to sense the deep despair he had endured.

Suicide is often motivated by the desire to escape from unbearable emotional pain. Here, the celebrated actress Patty Duke, who rose to acclaim in childhood by playing the role of Helen Keller in the movie *The Miracle Worker* and who battled bipolar disorder throughout much of her life, expresses how the desire to escape pain motivated many of the suicide attempts she had made in her life:

"I" Please Make This Stop

I can't even remember how many times I tried to kill myself. Not all of them got as far as actually taking the pills or digesting the pills. And it was almost always pills, although I did make a show sometimes of trying to use razors. But I always chickened out. A couple of times I tried to jump out of a moving car. But I didn't seem willing to inflict physical pain on myself. Some of the attempts continued to be attention-getting devices. Others came out of so much pain. I just wanted it to stop. I wish I had a more colorful, more profound way to describe it, but the only thoughts that went through my head were "Please make this stop. Please make be brave enough to die so that this anguish will stop."

Source: *Duke & Hochman, 1992*

Suicide is connected with a complex web of factors, and its prediction is not simple. Moreover, many myths about suicide abound (see Table 8.8). Yet it is clear that many suicides could be prevented if people with suicidal feelings received treatment for underlying disorders, including depression, bipolar disorder, schizophrenia, and alcohol and substance abuse. We also need strategies that emphasize the maintenance of hope during times of severe stress.

TABLE 8.8
Myths About Suicide

Myth	Fact
People who threaten suicide are only seeking attention.	Not so. Researchers report that most people who commit suicide gave prior indications of their intentions or consulted a health provider beforehand (Luoma, Martin, & Pearson, 2002).
A person must be insane to attempt suicide.	Most people who attempt suicide may feel hopeless, but they are not insane (i.e., out of touch with reality).
Talking about suicide with a depressed person may prompt the person to attempt it.	An open discussion of suicide with a depressed person does not prompt the person to attempt it. In fact, extracting a promise that the person will not attempt suicide before calling or visiting a mental health worker may well *prevent* a suicide.
People who attempt suicide and fail aren't serious about killing themselves.	Most people who commit suicide have made previous unsuccessful attempts.
If someone threatens suicide, it is best to ignore it so as not to encourage repeated threats.	Although some people do manipulate others by making idle threats, it is prudent to treat every suicidal threat as genuine and to take appropriate action.

Source: Adapted from J. S. Nevid, *Psychology: Concepts and Applications,* Second Edition (Boston: Houghton Mifflin Co., 2007), p. 529. Reprinted by permission.

Predicting Suicide

"I don't believe it. I just saw him last week and he looked fine."

"She sat here just the other day, laughing with the rest of us. How were we to know what was going on inside her?"

"I knew he was depressed, but I never thought he'd do something like this. I didn't have a clue."

"Why didn't she just call me?"

Friends and family members often respond to news of a suicide with disbelief or guilt that they failed to pick up signs of the impending act. Yet even trained professionals find it difficult to predict who is likely to commit suicide.

Evidence points to the pivotal role of hopelessness about the future in predicting suicidal thinking and suicide attempts (Kaslow et al., 2002; Malone et al., 2000). But *when* does hopelessness lead to suicide?

People who commit suicide tend to signal their intentions, often quite explicitly, such as by telling others about their suicidal thoughts. In fact, most people who commit suicide make contact beforehand with a health-care provider (Luoma, Martin, & Pearson, 2002). Yet some cloak their intentions. However, behavioral clues may still reveal suicidal intent. Edwin Shneidman, a leading researcher on suicide, found that 90% of the people who committed suicide had left clear clues, such as disposing of their possessions (Gelman, 1994). People contemplating suicide may also suddenly try to sort out their affairs, as in drafting a will or buying a cemetery plot. They may purchase a gun despite lack of prior interest in firearms. When troubled people decide to commit suicide, they may seem to be suddenly at peace; they feel relieved because they no longer have to contend with life problems. This sudden calm may be misinterpreted as a sign of hope.

The prediction of suicide is not an exact science, even for experienced professionals. Many observable factors, such as hopelessness, do seem to be connected with suicide, but we cannot accurately predict *when* a hopeless person will attempt suicide, if at all.

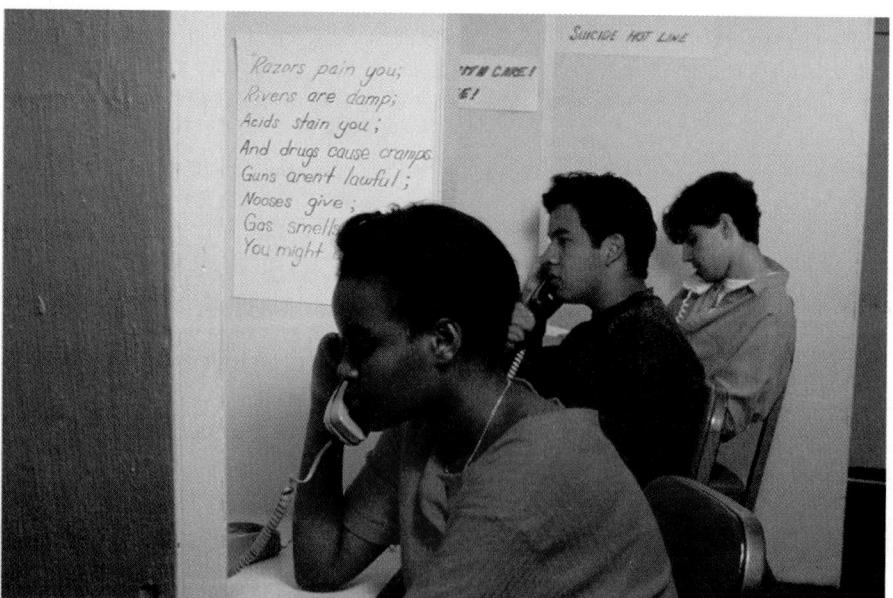

Suicide hotlines. Telephone hotlines provide emergency assistance and referral services to people experiencing suicidal thoughts or impulses. If you know someone experiencing suicidal thoughts or threatening suicide, speak to a mental health professional or call a suicide hotline in your community for advice.

A CLOSER LOOK

Suicide Prevention

Imagine yourself having an intimate conversation with a close campus friend, Chris. You know that things have not been good. Chris's grandfather died 6 weeks ago, and the two were very close. Chris's grades have been going downhill, and Chris's romantic relationship also seems to be coming apart at the seams. Still, you are unprepared when Chris says very deliberately, "I just can't take it anymore. Life is just too painful. I don't feel like I want to live anymore. I've decided that the only thing I can do is to kill myself."

When somebody discloses that he or she is contemplating suicide, you may feel bewildered and frightened, as if a great burden has been placed on your shoulders. It has. If someone confides suicidal thoughts to you, your goal should be to persuade him or her to see a professional, or to get the advice of a professional yourself as soon as you can. But if the suicidal person declines to talk to another person and you sense you can't break away for such a conference, here are some things you can do then and there:

1. *Draw the person out.* Shneidman advises framing questions such as "What's going on?" "Where do you hurt?" "What would you like to see happen?" (1985, p. 11). Such questions may prompt people to verbalize thwarted psychological needs and offer some relief. They also grant you the time to appraise the risk and contemplate your next move.
2. *Be sympathetic.* Show that you fathom how troubled the person is. Don't say something like, "You're just being silly. You don't really mean it."

3. *Suggest that means other than suicide can be discovered to work out the person's problems, even if they are not apparent at the time.* Shneidman (1985) notes that suicidal people can usually see only two solutions to their predicaments—suicide or some kind of magical resolution. Professionals try to broaden the available alternatives.
4. *Ask how the person expects to commit suicide.* People with explicit methods who also possess the means (for example, a gun or drugs) are at greatest risk. Ask if you may hold on to the gun, drugs, or whatever, for a while. Sometimes the person agrees.
5. *Propose that the person accompany you to consult a professional right away.* Many campuses, towns, and cities have hotlines that you or the suicidal individual can call anonymously. Other possibilities include the emergency room of a general hospital, a campus health center or counseling center, or the campus or local police. If you are unable to maintain contact with the suicidal person, get professional assistance as soon as you separate.
6. *Don't say something like "You're talking crazy."* Such comments are degrading and injurious to the individual's self-esteem. Don't press the suicidal person to contact specific people, such as parents or a spouse. Conflict with these people may have given rise to the suicidal thoughts.

Above all, keep in mind that your primary goal is to confer with a helping professional. Don't go it alone any longer than you have to.

SUMMING UP

Types of Mood Disorders

What are mood disorders? Mood disorders are disturbances in mood that are unusually prolonged or severe and serious enough to impair daily functioning.

What are the major types of mood disorders? There are various kinds of mood disorders, including depressive (unipolar) disorders, such as major depressive disorder and dysthymic disorder, and disorders involving mood swings, such as bipolar disorder and cyclothymic disorder.

What is major depressive disorder? In major depression, people experience a profound change in mood that impairs their ability to function. There are many associated features of major depressive disorder, including downcast mood; changes in appetite; difficulty sleeping; reduced sense of pleasure in formerly enjoyable activities; feelings of fatigue or loss of energy; sense of worthlessness; excessive or misplaced guilt; difficulties concentrating, thinking clearly, or making decisions; repeated thoughts of death or suicide; attempts at suicide; and even psychotic behaviors (hallucinations and delusions).

What is dysthymic disorder? Dysthymic disorder is a form of chronic depression that is milder than major depressive disorder but may nevertheless be associated with impaired functioning in social and occupational roles.

What is bipolar disorder? In bipolar disorder, people experience fluctuating mood states that interfere with the ability to function. Bipolar I disorder is identified by one or more manic episodes and typically, by alternating episodes of major depression. Bipolar II is characterized by the occurrence of at least one major depressive episode and one hypomanic episode, but without any full-blown manic episodes.

What are the features of a manic episode? Manic episodes are characterized by sudden elevation or expansion of mood and sense of self-importance, feelings of almost boundless energy, hyperactivity, and extreme sociability, which often takes a demanding and overbearing form. People in manic episodes tend to exhibit pressured or rapid speech, rapid "flight of ideas," and decreased need for sleep.

What is cyclothymic disorder? Cyclothymic disorder is a type of bipolar disorder characterized by a chronic pattern of mild mood swings that sometimes progresses to bipolar disorder.

Causal Factors in Depressive Disorders

How is stress related to mood disorders? Exposure to life stress is associated with an increased risk of development and recurrence of mood disorders, especially major depression. Yet some people are more resilient in the face of stress, perhaps because of psychosocial factors such as social support.

How do psychodynamic theorists conceptualize mood disorders?

In classic psychodynamic theory, depression is viewed in terms of inward-directed anger. People who hold strongly ambivalent feelings toward people they have lost, or whose loss is threatened, may direct unresolved anger toward the inward representations of these people that they have incorporated or introjected within themselves, producing self-loathing and depression. Bipolar disorder is understood within psychodynamic theory in terms of the shifting balances between the ego and superego. More recent psychodynamic models, such as the self-focusing model, incorporate both psychodynamic and cognitive aspects in explaining depression in terms of self-absorption with the lost love object.

How do humanistic theorists view depression? Theorists working within the humanistic framework view depression as reflecting a lack of meaning and authenticity in a person's life.

How do learning theorists view depression? Learning perspectives explain depression by focusing on situational factors, such as changes in the level of reinforcement. When reinforcement is reduced, the person may feel unmotivated and depressed, which can occasion inactivity and further reduce opportunities for reinforcement. Coyne's interactional theory focuses on the negative family interactions that can lead the family members of people with depression to become less reinforcing toward them.

What are two major cognitive models of depression? Beck's cognitive model focuses on the role of negative or distorted thinking in depression. Depression-prone people hold negative beliefs toward themselves, the environment, and the future. This cognitive triad of depression leads to specific errors in thinking, or cognitive distortions, in response to negative events, which, in turn, lead to depression.

The learned helplessness model is based on the belief that people may become depressed when they come to view themselves as helpless to control the reinforcements in their environment or to change their lives for the better. A reformulated version of the theory held that the ways in which people explain events—their attributions—determine their proneness toward depression in the face of negative events. The combination of internal, global, and stable attributions for negative events renders one most vulnerable to depression.

What role do biological factors play in depression? Genetics appears to play a role in explaining major depressive disorder, as does imbalances in neurotransmitter activity in the brain. The diathesis-stress model is an explanatory framework that illustrates how biological or psychological diatheses may interact with stress in the development of mood disorders such as major depression.

Causal Factors in Bipolar Disorders

What causal factors are implicated in bipolar disorders? Genetics appears to play an important role, but stressful life experiences also contribute. Bipolar disorders are perhaps best explained in terms of multiple causes acting together within a diathesis–stress framework. Social support may be important in speeding recovery from mood episodes and reducing the risks of recurrences.

Treatment of Mood Disorders

What approaches to treatment are represented by each of the major theoretical perspectives? Psychodynamic treatment of depression has traditionally focused on helping the depressed person uncover and work through ambivalent feelings toward the lost object, thereby lessening the anger directed inward. Modern psychodynamic approaches tend to be more direct and briefer and focus more on developing adaptive means of achieving self-worth and resolving interpersonal conflicts. Learning theory approaches have focused on helping people with depression increase the frequency of reinforcement in their lives through such means as increasing the rates of pleasant activities in which they participate and assisting them in developing more effective social skills to increase their ability to obtain social reinforcements from others. Cognitive therapists focus on helping the person identify and correct distorted or dysfunctional thoughts and learn more adaptive behaviors. Biological approaches have focused on the use of antidepressant drugs and other biological treatments, such as electroconvulsive therapy (ECT). Antidepressant drugs may help normalize neurotransmitter functioning in the brain. Bipolar disorder is commonly treated with either lithium or anticonvulsant drugs.

Suicide

What factors are linked to suicide? Mood disorders are often linked to suicide. Although women are more likely to attempt suicide, more men actually succeed, probably because they select more lethal means. The elderly—not the young—are more likely to commit suicide. People who attempt suicide are often depressed, but they are generally in touch with reality. They may, however, lack effective problem-solving skills and see no other way of dealing with life stress than suicide. A sense of hopelessness also figures prominently in suicides.

What are the major theoretical approaches to understanding suicide? These draw on the classic psychodynamic model of anger turned inward; the role of social alienation; and learning, social-cognitive, and biologically based perspectives.

Why should you never ignore a person's threat to commit suicide? Although certainly not all people who threaten suicide go on to commit the act, many do. People who commit suicide often signal their intentions, such as by telling others about their suicidal thoughts.

KEY TERMS

mood disorders *(p. 247)*
major depressive disorder *(p. 249)*
mania *(p. 249)*
hypomania *(p. 249)*
postpartum depression (PPD) *(p. 253)*

dysthymic disorder *(p. 254)*
double depression *(p. 255)*
bipolar disorder *(p. 256)*
manic episode *(p. 257)*
cyclothymic disorder *(p. 258)*

cognitive triad of depression *(p. 263)*
cognitive-specificity hypothesis *(p. 265)*
learned helplessness *(p. 266)*

MEDIA TOOLS

A variety of digital and online learning tools are available to enrich your learning experience and help you succeed in the course. These resources include:

- **MYPSYCHLAB,** an online learning system for your course in abnormal psychology that allows you to test your mastery of concepts in the book by using chapter-by-chapter diagnostic tests. Results from the diagnostic tests help you build a customized study plan. To access **MyPsychLab,** visit www.prenhall.com/mypsychlab and follow the instructions on the site.

- **"SPEAKING OUT" PATIENT INTERVIEWS,** a set of video case examples of actual patients you can access on the companion

CD-ROM included with the text. Icons in the margins of the chapter highlight the video case examples included on the CD-ROM.

- **COMPANION WEB SITE,** an online study center that offers computer-scored quizzes you can use to test your knowledge, along with other study tools and links to related sites to enhance your learning of abnormal psychology. To access the companion web site, visit www.prenhall.com/nevid and use the various tabs and links on the site to access these learning resources.

Mood Disorders

are characterized by

Disturbances of mood states and related behaviors

and include such types as

- Major Depressive Disorder
- Dysthymic Disorder
- Bipolar Disorder
- Cycloythmic Disorder

and may be explained by causal factors including

- Biological factors, including genetic influences, neurotransmitter irregularities, and brain abnormalities
- Social-environmental factors, such as stressful life events or losses
- Cognitive factors, such as a biased or distorted way of thinking or a depressive attributional style
- Interaction of multiple factors, as represented in this diathesis-stress model of depression:

and may be treated by

- Biomedical therapies, such as antidepressant medication, mood stabilizers, phototherapy, and electroconvulsive therapy
- Cognitive-behavioral therapy to correct distorted thinking and increase opportunities for positive reinforcement
- Interpersonal psychotherapy to resolve interpersonal problems and lingering grief reactions

MODEL SPOTLIGHT

Diathesis–Stress Model of Depression

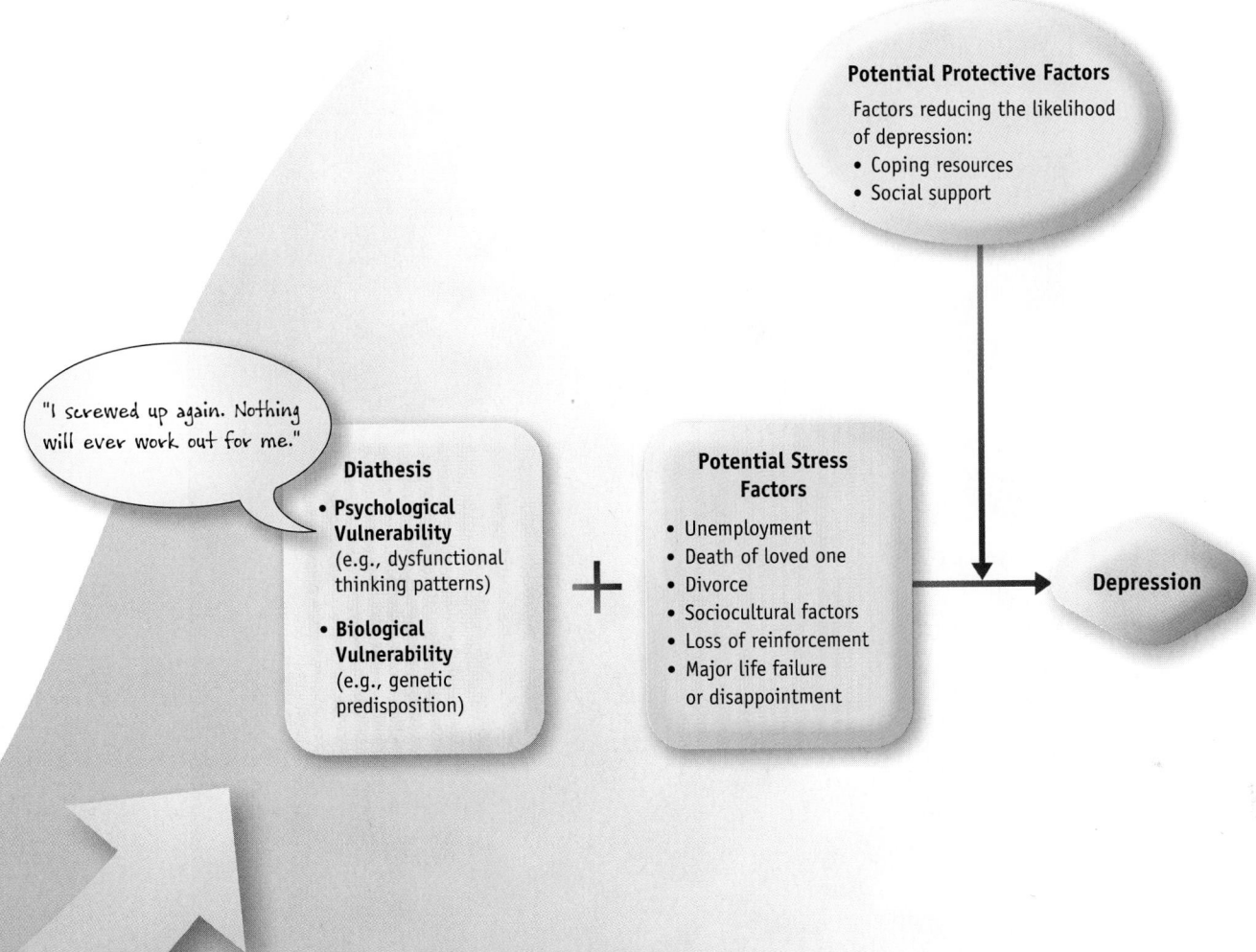

Substance Abuse and Dependence

CHAPTER OUTLINE

CLASSIFICATION OF SUBSTANCE-RELATED DISORDERS 291–296

Substance Abuse and Dependence
Addiction and Other Forms of Compulsive
 Behavior
Racial and Ethnic Differences in Substance
 Use Disorders
Pathways to Drug Dependence

DRUGS OF ABUSE 296–310

Depressants
Stimulants
Hallucinogens

THEORETICAL PERSPECTIVES 310–316

Biological Perspectives
Learning Perspectives
Cognitive Perspectives
Psychodynamic Perspectives
Sociocultural Perspectives

**TREATMENT OF SUBSTANCE ABUSE
AND DEPENDENCE 316–325**

Biological Approaches
Culturally Sensitive Treatment
 of Alcoholism
Nonprofessional Support Groups

Residential Approaches
Psychodynamic Approaches
Behavioral Approaches
Relapse-Prevention Training

SUMMING UP 325–326

"Nothing and Nobody Comes Before My Coke"

She had just caught me with cocaine again after I had managed to convince her that I hadn't used in over a month. Of course I had been tooting (snorting) almost every day, but I had managed to cover my tracks a little better than usual. So she said to me that I was going to have to make a choice—either cocaine or her. Before she finished the sentence, I knew what was coming, so I told her to think carefully about what she was going to say. It was clear to me that there wasn't a choice. I love my wife, but I'm not going to choose anything over cocaine. It's sick, but that's what things have come to. Nothing and nobody comes before my coke.

—From Weiss & Mirin, 1987, p. 55

T□ F□ Heroin accounts for more deaths than any other drug. (p. 291)

T□ F□ You cannot be psychologically dependent on a drug without also being physically dependent on it. (p. 295)

T□ F□ More teenagers and young adults die from alcohol-related motor vehicle accidents than from any other cause. (p. 297)

T□ F□ It is safe to let someone who has passed out from drinking just "sleep it off." (p. 301)

T□ F□ Even moderate use of alcohol increases the risk of heart attacks. (p. 303)

T□ F□ Coca-Cola originally contained cocaine. (p. 306)

T□ F□ Breast cancer is the leading cause of cancer deaths among U.S. women. (p. 307)

T□ F□ People who can "hold their liquor" better than most stand a lower risk of becoming problem drinkers. (p. 312)

T□ F□ A widely used treatment for heroin addiction involves substituting another addictive drug. (p. 318)

THESE COMMENTS FROM EUGENE, A 41-YEAR-OLD ARCHITECT, UNDERSCORE THE POWERFUL effects that drugs like cocaine can have on people's lives. Our society is flooded with psychoactive substances that alter the mood and twist perceptions—substances that lift you up, calm you down, and turn you upside down. Many young people start using these substances because of peer pressure or because their parents and other authority figures tell them not to. For Eugene, as for many others who become addicted to drugs, the pursuit and use of drugs takes center stage in their lives and becomes even more important than family, work, or their own welfare.

In this chapter we examine the physiological and psychological effects of the major classes of drugs. We explore how mental health professionals classify substance-related disorders and where we draw the line between use and abuse. We then examine contemporary understandings of the origins of these disorders and how mental health professionals help people who struggle to combat them.

CLASSIFICATION OF SUBSTANCE-RELATED DISORDERS

Under certain conditions, the use of substances that affect mood and behavior is normal, at least as gauged by statistical frequency and social standards. It is normal to start the day with caffeine in the form of coffee or tea, to take wine or coffee with meals, to meet friends for a drink after work, and to end the day with a nightcap. Many of us take prescription drugs that calm us down or ease our pain. Flooding the bloodstream with nicotine by means of smoking is normal in the sense that about 1 in 5 Americans do it. However, some psychoactive substances, such as cocaine, marijuana, and heroin, are illegal and are used illicitly. Others, such as antianxiety drugs (such as Valium and Xanax) and amphetamines (such as Ritalin), are available by prescription for legitimate medical uses. Still others, such as tobacco (which contains nicotine, a mild stimulant) and alcohol (a depressant), are available without prescription, or over-the-counter. Ironically, the most widely and easily accessible substances—tobacco and alcohol—cause more deaths through sickness and accidents than all illicit drugs combined.

The classification of substance-related disorders in the *DSM* system is not based on whether a drug is legal or not, but rather on how drug use impairs the person's physiological and psychological functioning. The *DSM-IV* classifies substance-related disorders into two major categories: substance use disorders and substance-induced disorders.

Substance-induced disorders are disorders induced by using psychoactive substances, such as intoxication, withdrawal syndromes, mood disorders, delirium, dementia, amnesia, psychotic disorders, anxiety disorders, sexual dysfunctions, and sleep disorders. Different substances have different effects, so some of these disorders may be induced by one, a few, or nearly all substances. Let us consider the example of intoxication.

Heroin accounts for more deaths than any other drug.

☑ **FALSE.** Two legally available substances, alcohol and tobacco, cause far more deaths.

substance-induced disorders Disorders, such as intoxication, that can be induced by using psychoactive substances.

Two of the many faces of alcohol use—and abuse. Alcohol is our most widely used—and abused—drug. Many people use alcohol to celebrate achievements and happy occasions, as in the photograph on the left. Unfortunately, like the man in the photograph on the right, some people use alcohol to drown their sorrows, which may only compound their problems. Where exactly does substance use end and abuse begin? According to the *DSM,* use becomes abuse when it leads to damaging consequences.

intoxication A state of drunkenness.

Substance **intoxication** refers to a state of drunkenness or being "high." This effect largely reflects the chemical actions of the psychoactive substances. The particular features of intoxication depend on which drug is ingested, the dose, the user's biological reactivity, and—to some degree—the user's expectations. Signs of intoxication often include confusion, belligerence, impaired judgment, inattention, and impaired motor and spatial skills. Extreme intoxication from use of alcohol, cocaine, opioids, (narcotics) and PCP can even result in death (yes, you can die from alcohol overdoses), either because of the substance's biochemical effects or because of behavior patterns—such as suicide—that are connected with psychological pain or impaired judgment brought on by use of the drug.

substance use disorders Disorders chararacterized by maladaptive use of psychoactive substances (e.g., substance dependence).

Substance use disorders are patterns of maladaptive use of psychoactive substances. These disorders, which include *substance abuse* and *substance dependence,* are the major focus of our study.

Substance Abuse and Dependence

substance abuse The continued use of a psychoactive drug despite the knowledge that it is causing a social, occupational, psychological, or physical problem.

Where does substance use end and abuse begin? According to the *DSM,* **substance abuse** is a pattern of recurrent use that leads to damaging consequences. Damaging consequences may involve failure to meet one's major role responsibilities (e.g., as student, worker, or parent), putting oneself in situations where substance use is physically dangerous (e.g., mixing driving and substance use), encountering repeated problems with the law arising from substance use (e.g., multiple arrests for substance-related behavior), or having recurring social or interpersonal problems because of substance use (e.g., repeatedly getting into fights when drinking).

When people repeatedly miss school or work because they are drunk or "sleeping it off," their behavior may fit the definition of substance abuse. A single incident of excessive drinking at a friend's wedding would not qualify. Nor would regular consumption of low to moderate amounts of alcohol be considered abusive so long as it is not connected with any impairment in functioning. Neither the amount nor the type of drug ingested, nor whether the drug is illicit, is the key to defining substance abuse according to the *DSM.* Rather, the determining feature of substance abuse is whether a pattern of drug-using behavior becomes repeatedly linked to damaging consequences.

substance dependence Impaired control over the use of a psychoactive substance; often characterized by physiological dependence.

Substance abuse may continue for a long period of time or progress to **substance dependence,** a more severe disorder associated with physiological signs of dependence (tolerance or withdrawal syndrome) *or* compulsive use of a substance. People who

> ### TABLE 9.1
> ## Diagnostic Features of Substance Dependence
>
> Substance dependence is defined as a maladaptive pattern of use that results in significant impairment or distress, as shown by the following features occurring within the same year:
>
> 1. Tolerance for the substance, as shown by either
>   a. the need for increased amounts of the substance to achieve the desired effect or intoxication, or
>   b. marked reduction in the effects of continuing to ingest the same amounts.
> 2. Withdrawal symptoms, as shown by either
>   a. the withdrawal syndrome that is considered characteristic for the substance, or
>   b. the taking of the same substance (or a closely related substance, as when methadone is substituted for heroin) to relieve or to prevent withdrawal symptoms.
> 3. Taking larger amounts of the substance or for longer periods of time than the individual intended (e.g., person had desired to take only one drink, but after taking the first, continues drinking until severely intoxicated).
> 4. Persistent desire to cut down or control intake of substance or lack of success in trying to exercise self-control.
> 5. Spending a good deal of time in activities directed toward obtaining the substance (e.g., visiting several physicians to obtain prescriptions or engaging in theft), in actually ingesting the substance, or in recovering from its use. In severe cases, the individual's daily life revolves around substance use.
> 6. The individual has reduced or given up important social, occupational, or recreational activities due to substance use (e.g., person withdraws from family events in order to indulge in drug use).
> 7. Substance use is continued despite evidence of persistent or recurrent psychological or physical problems either caused or exacerbated by its use (e.g., repeated arrests for driving while intoxicated).
>
> *Note:* Not all of these features need be present for a diagnosis to be made.
> *Source:* Adapted from the *DSM-IV-TR* (APA, 2000).

become compulsive users lack control over their drug use. They may be aware of how their drug use is disrupting their lives or damaging their health, but feel helpless or powerless to stop using drugs, even though they may want to. By the time they become dependent on a given drug, they've given over much of their lives to obtaining and using it. The cocaine user whose words opened this chapter would certainly fit this definition. The diagnostic features of substance dependence are listed in Table 9.1.

Repeated use of a substance may alter the body's physiological reactions, leading to the development of tolerance or a physical withdrawal syndrome (see Table 9.1). **Tolerance** is a state of physical habituation to a drug, resulting from frequent use, such that higher doses are needed to achieve the same effect. A **withdrawal syndrome** (also called an *abstinence syndrome*) is a cluster of symptoms that occur when a dependent person abruptly stops using a particular substance following heavy, prolonged use. People who experience a withdrawal syndrome often return to using the substance to relieve the discomfort associated with withdrawal, which thus serves to maintain the addictive pattern. Withdrawal symptoms vary with the particular type of drug. With alcohol dependence, typical withdrawal symptoms include dryness in the mouth, nausea or vomiting, weakness, increased heart rate, anxiety, depression, headaches, insomnia, elevated blood pressure, and fleeting hallucinations.

In some cases of chronic alcoholism, withdrawal produces a state of *delirium tremens*, or DTs. DTs are usually limited to chronic, heavy users of alcohol who dramatically lower their intake of alcohol after many years of heavy drinking. DTs involve intense autonomic hyperactivity (profuse sweating and tachycardia) and *delirium*—a state of mental confusion characterized by incoherent speech, disorientation, and extreme restlessness. Terrifying hallucinations—frequently of creepy, crawling animals—may also be present.

Substances that may lead to withdrawal syndromes include—in addition to alcohol—opioids, cocaine, amphetamines, sedatives and barbiturates, nicotine, and

tolerance Physical habituation to a drug such that with frequent use, higher doses are needed to achieve the same effects.

withdrawal syndrome A characteristic cluster of symptoms following the sudden reduction or cessation of use of a psychoactive substance after physiological dependence has developed.

FIGURE 9.1 Lifetime prevalence of drug dependence disorder by type of illicit drug. Drug dependence disorders involving illicit drugs affect nearly 3 in 100 adults in the United States. Marijuana (cannabis) dependence is the most common type.

Source: Conway et al., 2006.

antianxiety agents (minor tranquilizers). Marijuana and hallucinogens such as LSD are not recognized as producing a withdrawal syndrome, because abrupt withdrawal from these substances does not produce clinically significant withdrawal effects (APA, 2000).

Substance dependence is often, but not always, associated with the development of physiological dependence. It sometimes involves a pattern of compulsive use without physiological or chemical dependence. For example, people may become compulsive users of marijuana, especially when they rely on the drug to help them cope with the stresses of daily life. Yet they may not require larger amounts of the substance to get "high" or experience distressing withdrawal symptoms when they cease using it. In most cases, however, substance dependence and physiological features of dependence occur together. Despite the fact that the *DSM* considers substance abuse and dependence to be distinct diagnostic categories, the borderline between the two is not always clear.

Unfortunately, substance abuse and dependence disorders are common problems in our society (Adelson, 2006). An estimated 10.3% of adults in the United States develop drug (substance) use disorders on an illicit drug at some point in their lives, with about 7.7% developing a drug abuse disorder and about 2.5% developing a drug dependence disorder (Compton et al., 2005). About 8% of adult Americans develop alcohol abuse or dependence disorders (Lemonick, 2007). People with one drug use disorder, such as alcohol dependence disorder, often present with another, such as cocaine dependence disorder (Stinson et al., 2005). In Figure 9.1 we see the percentages of U.S. adults who develop drug dependence disorders on various types of illicit drugs.

Addiction and Other Forms of Compulsive Behavior

The *DSM* uses the terms *substance abuse* and *substance dependence* as categories of substance use disorders. It does not use the term *addiction* to describe these problems. Yet the concept of addiction is widespread among professionals and laypeople alike. Even some leading professionals believe the word "addiction" should replace the word "dependence" in the diagnostic manual (O'Brien, Volkow, & Li, 2006). But what does the term "addiction" mean? Before we proceed to discuss drugs of abuse, let us define the terms we will be using.

We lack any universally accepted definition of addiction. For our purposes, we define **addiction** as compulsive use of a drug accompanied by signs of physiological dependence. People become compulsive users when they have impaired control over their use of a drug. In effect, they feel compelled to continue using the drug despite the negative consequences that continued use of the drug entails. By **physiological dependence,** we mean that a person's body has changed as a result of the regular use of a psychoactive drug in such a way that it comes to depend on having a steady supply of the substance. The major signs of physiological dependence are the development of tolerance and a withdrawal syndrome.

addiction Impaired control over the use of a chemical substance, accompanied by physiological dependence.

physiological dependence A condition in which the drug user's body comes to depend on a steady supply of the substance.

People can also develop **psychological dependence** on a drug without becoming physiologically or chemically dependent. These individuals come to compulsively use a drug to meet psychological needs. We can think of someone who compulsively uses marijuana to cope with daily stress, but is not physiologically dependent on the drug. On the other hand, a person may become physiologically dependent on a drug but not become a compulsive user. For example, people recuperating from surgery are often given narcotics derived from opium as painkillers. Some develop signs of physiological dependence, such as tolerance and a withdrawal syndrome, but do not develop impaired control over the use of these drugs.

Other forms of compulsive behavior, such as compulsive gambling, shopping, or even Internet use, can be likened to forms of nonchemical addiction. Whether we label such behavioral patterns as addictions depends on how we define the concept of addiction (see Chapter 13 for a discussion of compulsive gambling). In this chapter, we focus on chemical forms of dependence.

psychological dependence Compulsive use of a substance to meet a psychological need.

TRUTH or FICTION

You cannot be psychologically dependent on a drug without also being physically dependent on it.

☑ **FALSE.** You can become psychologically dependent on a drug without developing a physiological dependence.

Racial and Ethnic Differences in Substance Use Disorders

Despite the popular stereotype that drug dependence is more frequent among ethnic minorities, this belief is not supported by evidence. To the contrary, African Americans and Latinos have comparable or even lower rates of substance use disorders than do European Americans (non-Hispanic Whites) (Breslau et al., 2005; Compton et al., 2005). Moreover, African American adolescents are much less likely than European American adolescents to develop substance abuse or dependence problems (Kilpatrick et al., 2000). In a later section we shall examine evidence on racial/ethnic group differences in alcohol use and abuse.

Pathways to Drug Dependence

Although the progression to substance dependence varies from person to person, one common pathway involves a progression through the following stages (Weiss & Mirin, 1987):

1. *Experimentation.* During the stage of experimentation, or occasional use, the drug temporarily makes users feel good, even euphoric. Users feel in control and believe they can stop at any time.
2. *Routine use.* During the next stage, a period of routine use, people begin to structure their lives around the pursuit and use of drugs. Denial plays a major role at this stage, as users mask the negative consequences of their behavior to themselves and others. Values change. What had formerly been important, such as family and work, comes to matter less than the drugs.

   The following clinical interview illustrates how denial can mask reality. This 48-year-old executive was brought for a consultation by his wife. She complained his once-successful business was jeopardized by his erratic behavior, he was grouchy and moody, and he had spent $7,000 in the previous month on cocaine.

CLINICIAN: Have you missed many days at work recently?
EXECUTIVE: Yes, but I can afford to, since I own the business. Nobody checks up on me.
CLINICIAN: It sounds like that's precisely the problem. When you don't go to work, the company stays open, but it doesn't do very well.
EXECUTIVE: My employees are well trained. They can run the company without me.
CLINICIAN: But that's not happening.
EXECUTIVE: Then there's something wrong with them. I'll have to look into it.
CLINICIAN: It sounds as if there's something wrong with you, but you don't want to look into it.
EXECUTIVE: Now you're on my case. I don't know why you listen to everything my wife says.
CLINICIAN: How many days of work did you miss in the last two months?
EXECUTIVE: A couple.
CLINICIAN: Are you saying that you missed only two days of work?
EXECUTIVE: Maybe a few.

CLINICIAN: Only three or four days?

EXECUTIVE: Maybe a little more.

CLINICIAN: Ten? Fifteen?

EXECUTIVE: Fifteen.

CLINICIAN: All because of cocaine?

EXECUTIVE: No.

CLINICIAN: How many were because of cocaine?

EXECUTIVE: Less than fifteen.

CLINICIAN: Fourteen? Thirteen?

EXECUTIVE: Maybe thirteen.

CLINICIAN: So you missed thirteen days of work in the last two months because of cocaine. That's almost two days a week.

EXECUTIVE: That sounds like a lot but it's no big deal. Like I say, the company can run itself.

CLINICIAN: How long have you been using cocaine?

EXECUTIVE: About three years.

CLINICIAN: Did you ever use drugs or alcohol before that in any kind of quantity?

EXECUTIVE: No.

CLINICIAN: Then let's think back five years. Five years ago, if you had imagined yourself missing over a third of your workdays because of a drug, and if you had imagined yourself spending the equivalent of $84,000 a year on that same drug, and if you saw your once-successful business collapsing all around you, wouldn't you have thought that that was indicative of a pretty serious problem?

EXECUTIVE: Yes, I would have.

CLINICIAN: So what's different now?

EXECUTIVE: I guess I just don't want to think about it.

—From Weiss & Mirin, 1987, pp. 79–80

As routine drug use continues, problems mount. Users devote more resources to drugs. They ravage family bank accounts, seek "temporary" loans from friends and family for trumped-up reasons, and sell family heirlooms and jewelry for a fraction of their value. Lying and manipulation become a way of life to cover up the drug use. The husband sells the TV set and forces the front door open to make it look like a burglary. The wife claims to have been robbed at knifepoint to explain the disappearance of a gold chain or engagement ring. Family relationships become strained as the mask of denial shatters and the consequences of drug abuse become apparent: days lost from work, unexplained absences from home, rapid mood shifts, depletion of family finances, failure to pay bills, stealing from family members, and missing family gatherings or children's birthday parties.

3. *Addiction or dependence.* Routine use becomes addiction or dependence when users feel powerless to resist drugs, either because they want to experience their effects or to avoid the consequences of withdrawal. Little or nothing else matters at this stage, as we saw in the case of Eugene with which we opened the chapter.

Now let us examine the effects of different types of drugs of abuse and the consequences associated with their use and abuse.

DRUGS OF ABUSE

Drugs of abuse are generally classified within three major groupings: (a) depressants, such as alcohol and opioids; (b) stimulants, such as amphetamines and cocaine; and (c) hallucinogens.

Depressants

depressant A drug that lowers the level of activity of the central nervous system.

A **depressant** is a drug that slows down or curbs the activity of the central nervous system. It reduces feelings of tension and anxiety, slows movement, and impairs cognitive processes. In high doses, depressants can arrest vital functions and cause death.

The most widely used depressant, alcohol, can cause death when taken in large amounts because of its depressant effects on breathing. Other effects are specific to the particular kind of depressant. For example, some depressants, such as heroin, produce a "rush" of pleasure. Here let us consider several major types of depressants.

Alcohol Alcohol is the most widely abused substance in the United States and worldwide You might not think of alcohol as a drug, perhaps because it is so common, or perhaps because it is ingested by drinking rather than by smoking or injection. But alcoholic beverages—such as wine, beer, and hard liquor—contain a depressant drug called *ethyl alcohol* (or *ethanol*). The concentration of the drug varies with the type of beverage (wine and beer have less pure alcohol per ounce than distilled spirits such as rye, gin, or vodka). Alcohol is classified as a depressant because it has biochemical effects similar to those of a class of antianxiety agents or minor tranquilizers, the *benzodiazepines*, which includes the well-known drugs *diazepam* (Valium) and *chlordiazepoxide* (Librium). We can think of alcohol as an over-the-counter tranquilizer.

Most American adults drink alcohol at least occasionally and do so in moderation. But many people develop significant problems with alcohol. Many lay and professional people use the terms **alcoholism** and alcohol dependence interchangeably, as we will. We use either term to refer to a pattern of impaired control over the use of alcohol in someone who has become physiologically dependent on the drug. An estimated eight million U.S. adults suffer from alcholism (Kranzler, 2006).

The most widely held view of alcoholism is the disease model, the belief that alcoholism is a medical illness or disease. From this perspective, once a person with alcoholism takes a drink, the biochemical effects of the drug on the brain create an irresistible physical craving for more. The disease model holds that alcoholism is a chronic, permanent condition. The peer-support group Alcoholics Anonymous (AA) subscribes to this view, which is expressed in their slogan, "Once an alcoholic, always an alcoholic." AA views people suffering from alcoholism as either drinking or "recovering," never "cured." However, later in this chapter we shall see that some professionals, including the psychologists Linda and Mark Sobell, adopt a different perspective. Their research shows that some alcohol abusers can learn skills of controlled social drinking that enables them to drink moderately without "falling off the wagon." The contention that some people with alcohol problems can learn to drink moderately remains controversial.

The personal and social costs of alcoholism exceed those of all illicit drugs combined. Alcohol abuse is connected with lower productivity, loss of jobs, and downward movement in socioeconomic status. Alcohol plays a role in many violent crimes, including assaults and homicides, and more than 180,000 rapes and sexual attacks annually in the United States (Bartholow & Heinz, 2006; Buddie & Testa, 2005; O'Farrell, Fals-Stewart, & Murphy, 2005). About 1 in 3 suicides in this country and about the same proportion of deaths due to unintentional injury (such as from motor vehicle accidents) are linked to alcohol use (Dougherty et al., 2004; Sher, 2005; Shneidman, 2005). More teenagers and young adults die from alcohol-related motor vehicle accidents than from any other cause. Despite increased awareness about the risks of drinking and driving, fatal alcohol-related motor vehicle accidents are on the rise (O'Donnell, 2003). All told, an estimated 100,000 people in the United States die from alcohol-related causes each year, mostly from motor vehicle crashes and alcohol-related diseases (Society for Neuroscience, 2005b).

Despite the popular image of the person who develops alcoholism as a skid-row drunk, only a small minority of people with alcoholism fit the stereotype. The great majority of people with alcoholism are quite ordinary—your neighbors, coworkers, friends, and members of your own family. They are found in all walks of life and every social and economic class. Many have families, hold good jobs, and live fairly comfortably. Yet alcoholism can have just as devastating an effect on the well-to-do as on the indigent, leading to wrecked careers and marriages, to motor vehicle and other accidents, and to severe, life-threatening physical disorders, as well as exacting an enormous emotional toll. Alcoholism is also linked to higher levels of domestic violence and greater risk of divorce (Marshal, 2003).

alcoholism An alcohol dependence disorder or addiction that results in serious personal, social, occupational, or health problems.

T R U T H or F I C T I O N

More teenagers and young adults die from alcohol-related motor vehicle accidents than from any other cause.

☑ **TRUE.** Alcohol-related motor vehicle accidents are the leading cause of death among teenagers and young adults.

QUESTIONNAIRE
Are You Hooked?

Are you dependent on alcohol? If you shake and shiver and undergo the tortures of the darned (our editor insisted on changing this word to maintain the decorum of a textbook) when you go without a drink for a while, the answer is clear enough. However, sometimes the clues are more subtle.

The following questions, adapted from the National Council on Alcoholism's self-test, can shed some light on the question. Simply place a check mark in the "yes" or "no" column for each item. Then check the key at the end of the chapter.

	YES	NO
1. Do you sometimes go on drinking binges?		
2. Do you tend to keep away from your family or friends when you are drinking?		
3. Do you become irritated when your family or friends talk about your drinking?		
4. Do you feel guilty now and then about your drinking?		
5. Do you often regret the things you have said or done when you have been drinking?		
6. Do you find that you fail to keep the promises you make about controlling or cutting down on your drinking?		
7. Do you eat irregularly or not at all when you are drinking?		
8. Do you feel low after drinking?		
9. Do you sometimes miss work or appointments because of drinking?		
10. Do you drink more and more to get drunk?		

Source: Adapted from *Newsweek*, February 20, 1989, p. 52.

No single drinking pattern is exclusively associated with alcoholism. Some people with alcoholism drink heavily every day; others binge only on weekends. Others can abstain for lengthy periods of time, but periodically "go off the wagon" and engage in episodes of binge drinking that last for weeks or months.

Alcohol, not cocaine or other drugs, is the drug of choice among young people today and the leading drug of abuse. Drinking has become so integrated into college life that it is essentially normative, as much a part of the college experience as attending a weekend football or basketball game. Alcohol, not cocaine, heroin, or marijuana, is the BDOC—big drug on campus (Johnston et al., 2004). Yet drinking often begins before young people reach college age. About 1 in 5 eighth-graders report having had a drink within the past month, along with more than 1 in 3 tenth graders and about half of twelfth graders (The Center on Alcohol Marketing and Youth, 2005).

Drinking among college students tends to be limited to weekends and to be heavier early in the semester when academic requirements are relatively light (Del Boca et al., 2004). As a group, young adults in the 18- to 24-year age range show the highest rates of alcohol use and the highest proportions of problem drinking (Ham & Hope, 2003). College students drink more than their peers who do not attend college (Slutske, 2005). Researchers describe a continuum of alcohol-related problems among college students, ranging from mild problems, such as missing class, to extreme problem behaviors, such as arrests resulting from drinking (Ham & Hope, 2003). In the *A Closer Look* section, we focus on a particular form of problem drinking that has become a leading problem on college campuses today—binge drinking.

Risk Factors for Alcoholism A number of factors place people at increased risk for developing alcoholism and alcohol-related problems. These include the following:

1. *Gender.* Men are more than twice as likely as women to develop alcoholism (Hasin et al., 2007). One possible reason for this gender difference is sociocultural; perhaps tighter cultural constraints are placed on women. Yet it may also be that alcohol hits women harder, and not only because women usually weigh less than men. Alcohol seems to "go to women's heads" more rapidly than men's. This is apparently because women have less of an enzyme that metabolizes alcohol in the stomach than men do (Lieber, 1990). Ounce for ounce, women absorb more alcohol into their bloodstreams than do men. As a result, they are likely to become inebriated on less alcohol than men. Consequently, women's bodies may put the brakes on excessive drinking more quickly than men's.

2. *Age.* The great majority of cases of alcohol dependence develop in young adulthood, typically between the ages of 20 and 40. Although alcohol use disorders tend to develop somewhat later in women than in men, women who develop these problems experience similar health, social, and occupational problems by middle age as their male counterparts.

3. *Antisocial personality disorder.* Antisocial behavior in adolescence or adulthood increases the risk of later alcoholism. On the other hand, many people with alcoholism showed no antisocial tendencies in adolescence, and many antisocial adolescents do not abuse alcohol or other drugs as adults.

4. *Family history.* The best predictor of problem drinking in adulthood appears to be a family history of alcohol abuse. Family members who drink may act as models ("set a poor example"). Moreover, the biological relatives of people with alcohol dependence may also inherit a predisposition that makes them more likely to develop problems with alcohol.

Women and alcohol. Women are less likely to develop alcoholism, in part because of greater cultural constraints on excessive drinking by women, and perhaps because women absorb more pure alcohol into the bloodstream than men, making them more biologically sensitive to the effects of alcohol at the same level of intake as men.

5. *Sociodemographic factors.* Alcohol dependence is generally more common among people of lower income and educational levels, as well as among people living alone (Anthony et al., 1994).

Ethnicity and Alcohol Use and Abuse Rates of alcohol use and alcoholism vary among American ethnic and racial groups. Some groups—Jews, Italians, Greeks, and Asian—have relatively low rates of alcoholism, largely as the result of tight social controls placed on excessive and underage drinking. Asian Americans, in general, drink less heavily than other population groups (Adelson, 2006; Wong, Klingle, & Price, 2004). Not only do Asian families place strong cultural constraints on excessive drinking, but an underlying biological factor may be at work in curbing alcohol use. Asian Americans are more likely than other groups to show a flushing response to alcohol. Flushing is characterized by redness and feelings of warmth on the face, and, at higher doses, nausea, heart palpitations, dizziness, and headaches. Genes that control the metabolism of alcohol are believed to be responsible for the flushing response (Luczak, Glatt, & Wall, 2006). Because people like to avoid these unpleasant experiences, flushing may serve as a natural defense against alcoholism by curbing excessive alcohol intake.

Hispanic American men and non-Hispanic White men have similar rates of alcohol consumption and alcohol-related physical problems. Hispanic American women, however, are much less likely to use alcohol and to develop alcohol use disorders than non-Hispanic White women. *Why?* An important factor may be cultural expectations. Traditional Hispanic American cultures place severe restrictions on the use of alcohol by women, especially heavy drinking. However, with increasing acculturation, Hispanic American women in the United States apparently are becoming more similar to Euro American women with respect to alcohol use and abuse.

Alcohol abuse is taking a heavy toll on African Americans. For example, the prevalence of *cirrhosis*, a degenerative, potentially fatal liver disease, is nearly twice as high in African Americans as in non-Hispanic White Americans. Yet African Americans are much less likely than non-Hispanic White Americans to develop alcohol abuse or dependence (Grant et al., 1994). Why, then, do African Americans suffer more from alcohol-related problems?

Socioeconomic factors may help explain these differences. African Americans are more likely to encounter the stresses of unemployment and economic hard-

"I'm the gene that causes alcoholism. I figured I'd cut out the middle man."

Alcohol and ethnic diversity. The damaging effects of alcohol abuse appear to be taking the heaviest toll on African Americans and Native Americans. The prevalence of alcohol-related cirrhosis of the liver is nearly twice as high among African Americans than among White Americans, even though African Americans are less likely to develop alcohol abuse or dependence disorders. Jewish Americans have relatively low incidences of alcohol-related problems, perhaps because they tend to expose children to the ritual use of wine in childhood and impose strong cultural restraints on excessive drinking. Asian Americans tend to drink less heavily than most other Americans, in part because of cultural constraints and possibly because they have less biological tolerance of alcohol, as shown by a greater flushing response to alcohol.

ship, and stress may compound the damage to the body caused by heavy alcohol consumption. African Americans also tend to lack access to medical services and may be less likely to receive early treatment for the medical problems caused by alcohol abuse.

Although rates of alcohol abuse and dependence vary from tribe to tribe, Native American overall have high rates of alcoholism and suffer more from alcohol-related problems than any other ethnic group—problems such as cirrhosis of the liver, fetal abnormalities, and automobile and other accident-related fatalities (Hasin et al., 2007; Hawkins et al., 2004; Mitchell et al., 2006).

Many Native Americans believe the loss of their traditional culture is largely responsible for their high rates of drinking-related problems (Beauvais, 1998). The disruption of traditional Native American culture caused by the appropriation of Indian lands and by attempts by European American society to sever Native Americans from their cultural traditions while denying them full access to the dominant culture resulted in severe cultural and social disorganization (Kahn, 1982). Beset by such problems, Native American adults are also prone to child abuse and neglect. Abuse and neglect contribute to feelings of hopelessness and depression among adolescents, who may seek escape from their feelings by using alcohol and other drugs.

Psychological Effects of Alcohol The effects of alcohol or other drugs vary from person to person. By and large they reflect the interaction of (a) the physiological effects of the substances, and (b) our interpretations of those effects. What do most people expect from alcohol? People frequently hold stereotypical expectations that alcohol will reduce tension, enhance pleasurable experiences, wash away worries, and enhance social skills. But what *does* alcohol actually do?

At a physiological level, alcohol appears to work like the benzodiazepines (a family of antianxiety drugs), by heightening activity of the neurotransmitter GABA (see Chapter 6). Because GABA is an inhibitory neurotransmitter (it tones down nervous system activity), increasing GABA activity produces feelings of

ALCOHOLISM:
The Case of Chris
"Toughest thing I ever did was admitting I had a problem."

A CLOSER LOOK

Binge Drinking, a Dangerous College Pastime

A major problem receiving a great deal of attention on college campuses today is binge drinking. About 4 in 10 college students today report engaging in binge drinking (Ham & Hope, 2003)—drinking 5 or more drinks (for men) or 4 or more drinks (for women) on a single occasion.

Concerns about binge drinking are well placed. Binge drinking is linked to increased risks of serious motor vehicle and other accidents, violent and aggressive behavior, poor grades, sexual promiscuity, and development of substance abuse and dependence (Chassin et al., 2002; Naimi et al., 2003; Sink, 2004). Consider the tragic case of Leslie, a young college student at the University of Virginia. An art major whose work her professors found promising, Leslie had maintained a 3.67 GPA and was completing her senior essay on a Polish-born sculptor (Winerip, 1998). But she never finished it, because one day after binge drinking, she fell down a flight of stairs and died. We may hear more about the deaths of young people due to heroin or cocaine overdoses, but hundreds of college students, like Leslie, die from alcohol-related causes such as overdoses and accidents each year (Li et al., 2001).

In a recent review article, Lindsay Ham and Debra Hope (2003) identified two general subtypes of college students who appear most clearly at risk of becoming problem drinkers. The first type includes students who drink mostly for social or enjoyment purposes. They tend to be male, Anglo-American, and participate in Greek organizations or other social organizations in which heavy drinking is socially acceptable. The second type includes students who drink due to pressures to conform or who use alcohol to soothe negative feelings. They more often tend to be female and to be troubled by problems with anxiety or depression. Generating these profiles may help counselors and health-care providers identify young people at increased risk of developing problem drinking patterns.

Binge drinking and related drinking games (beer chugging) can place people at significant risk of death from alcohol overdose. Many students who play these games don't stop until they become too drunk or too sick to continue (Johnson, 2002). What should you do if you see a friend or acquaintance become incapacitated or pass out from heavy drinking? Should you just let the person sleep it off? Can you tell whether a person has had too much to drink? Should you just mind your own business or turn to others for help?

You cannot tell simply by looking at a person whether the person has overdosed on alcohol. But a person who becomes unconscious or unresponsive is in need of immediate medical attention. Don't assume that the person will simply "sleep it off": He or she may never wake up. Be aware of the signs of potential overdose, such as the following (adapted from Nevid & Rathus, 2007).

- Nonresponsive when talked to or shouted at
- Nonresponsive to being pinched, shaken, or poked

- Unable to stand up on his or her own
- Failure to wake up or gain consciousness
- Purplish color or clammy-feeling skin
- Rapid pulse rate or irregular heart rhythms, low blood pressure, or difficulty breathing.

If you suspect an overdose, do not leave the person alone. Summon medical help or emergency assistance and remain with the person until help arrives. If possible place the person on the side or have the person sit up with his or her head bowed. Do not give the person any food or drink or induce vomiting. If the person is responsive, find out if he or she had taken any medication or other drugs that might be interacting with the effects of the alcohol. Also, find out whether the person has an underlying illness that may contribute to the problem, such as diabetes or epilepsy.

It may be easier to just pass by without taking action. But ask yourself what you would like someone else to do if you showed signs of overdosing on alcohol. Wouldn't you want one of your friends to intervene to save your life?

A dangerous pastime. Beer chugging and binge drinking can quickly lead to an alcohol overdose, a medical emergency that can have lethal consequences. Many college officials cite binge drinking as *the* major drug problem on campus.

relaxation. As people drink, their senses become clouded, and balance and coordination suffer. Still higher doses act on the parts of the brain that regulate involuntary vital functions, such as heart rate, respiration rate, and body temperature.

People may do many things when drinking that they would not do when sober, in part because of expectations concerning the drug, in part because of the drug's effects on the brain. For example, they may become more flirtatious or sexually aggressive or say or do things they later regret. Their behavior may reflect their expectation that alcohol has liberating effects and provides an external excuse for questionable behavior. Later, they can claim, "It was the alcohol, not me." The drug may also impair the brain's ability to curb impulsive, risk-taking, or violent behavior, perhaps by interfering with information-processing functions. Investigators find strong links between alcohol use and violent behavior (Boles & Miottoa,

TRUTH or FICTION

It is safe to let someone who has passed out from drinking just "sleep it off."

☑ **FALSE.** Sadly, the person may never wake up. Passing out from drinking needs to be treated as a medical emergency.

2003), including domestic violence and sexual assaults (Abbey et al., 2004; Fals-Stewart, 2003; Marshal, 2003).

Although alcohol makes people feel more relaxed and self-confident, it also impairs judgment, which can lead them to make choices they would ordinarily reject, such as engaging in risky sex. Chronic alcohol abuse can impair cognitive abilities, such as memory, problem solving, and attention (Ratti et al., 2002).

One of the lures of alcohol is that it induces short-term feelings of euphoria and elation that can drown self-doubts and self-criticism. Alcohol also makes people less capable of perceiving the unfortunate consequences of their behavior.

Alcohol use can dampen sexual arousal or excitement and impair sexual performance. As an intoxicant, alcohol also hampers coordination and motor ability. These effects help explain why alcohol use is implicated in about one in three accidental deaths in the United States.

Physical Health and Alcohol Chronic, heavy alcohol use affects virtually every organ and body system, either directly or indirectly. Heavy alcohol use is linked to increased risk of many serious health concerns, including liver disease, increased risk of some forms of cancer, coronary heart disease, and neurological disorders. Two of the major forms of alcohol-related liver disease are *alcoholic hepatitis,* a serious and potentially life-threatening inflammation of the liver, and *cirrhosis of the liver,* a potentially fatal disease in which healthy liver cells are replaced with scar tissue.

Habitual drinkers tend to be malnourished, which can put them at risk of complications arising from nutritional deficiencies. Chronic drinking is thus associated with such nutritionally linked disorders as cirrhosis of the liver (linked to protein deficiency) and *alcohol-induced persisting amnestic disorder* (connected with vitamin B deficiency). This condition, also known as *Korsakoff's syndrome,* is characterized by glaring confusion, disorientation, and memory loss for recent events (see Chapter 15).

Mothers who drink during pregnancy place their fetuses at risk for infant mortality, birth defects, central nervous system dysfunctions, and later academic problems. Children whose mothers drink during pregnancy may develop *fetal alcohol syndrome* (FAS), a syndrome characterized by facial features such as a flattened nose, widely spaced eyes, and underdeveloped upper jaw, as well as mental retardation and social skills deficits (Carroll, 2003; O'Connor et al., 2006). FAS affects from 1 to 3 of every 1,000 live births.

We don't know whether a minimum amount of alcohol is needed to produce FAS. Although the risk is greater among women who drink heavily during pregnancy, FAS has been found among children of mothers who drank as little as a drink and a half per week (Carroll, 2003). Although the question of whether there is any safe dose of alcohol during pregnancy continues to be debated, the fact remains that FAS is an entirely preventable birth defect. The safest course for women who know or suspect they are pregnant is not to drink. *Period.*

Moderate Drinking: Is There a Health Benefit? Despite this list of adverse effects associated with heavy drinking, evidence shows that moderate use of alcohol (1 to 2 drinks per day for women, 2 to 4 drinks for men) is linked to lower risks of heart attacks and strokes, as well as lower death rates overall (Di Castelnuovo et al., 2006; Mukamal et al., 2003; Reynolds et al., 2003). Higher doses of alcohol are associated with higher mortality (death) rates. Researchers suspect that alcohol may help prevent the formation of blood clots that can clog arteries and lead to heart attacks. Alcohol also appears to increase the levels of HDL cholesterol, the so-called good cholesterol that sweeps away fatty deposits along artery walls (Goldberg et al., 2001). Although moderate use of alcohol may have a protective effect on the heart and circulatory system, public health officials have not endorsed using alcohol for this reason, based largely on concerns that such an endorsement may increase the risks of problem drinking. Health promotion efforts might be better directed toward finding safer ways of achieving the health benefits associated with moderate drinking than by encouraging alcohol consumption, such as by quitting smoking, lowering dietary intake of fat and cholesterol, and exercising more regularly.

Barbiturates   About 1% of adult Americans develop a substance abuse or dependence disorder involving the use of barbiturates, sleep medication (hypnotics), or antianxiety agents at some point in their lives. **Barbiturates** such as *amobarbital, pentobarbital, phenobarbital,* and *secobarbital* are depressants, or *sedatives.* These drugs have several medical uses, including easing anxiety and tension, dulling pain, and treating epilepsy and high blood pressure. Barbiturate use quickly leads to psychological dependence and physiological dependence in the form of both tolerance and development of a withdrawal syndrome.

Barbiturates are also popular street drugs because they are relaxing and produce a mild state of euphoria, or "high." High doses of barbiturates, like alcohol, produce drowsiness, slurred speech, motor impairment, irritability, and poor judgment—a particularly deadly combination of effects when their use is combined with operation of a motor vehicle. The effects of barbiturates last from 3 to 6 hours.

Because of synergistic effects, a mixture of barbiturates and alcohol is about 4 times as powerful as either drug used by itself. A combination of barbiturates and alcohol is implicated in the deaths of the entertainers Marilyn Monroe and Judy Garland. Even such widely used antianxiety drugs as Valium and Librium, which have a wide margin of safety when used alone, can be dangerous and lead to overdoses when combined with alcohol (APA, 2000).

Physiologically dependent people need to be withdrawn carefully, and only under medical supervision, from sedatives, barbiturates, and antianxiety agents. Abrupt withdrawal can produce states of delirium that may involve visual, tactile, or auditory hallucinations and disturbances in thinking processes and consciousness. The longer the period of use and the higher the doses used, the greater the risk of severe withdrawal effects. Epileptic (grand mal) seizures and even death may occur if the individual undergoes untreated, abrupt withdrawal.

Opioids   Opioids are classified as **narcotics**—addictive drugs that have pain-relieving and sleep-inducing properties. Opioids include both naturally occurring opiates (morphine, heroin, codeine) derived from the juice of the poppy plant and synthetic drugs (e.g., Demerol, Darvon) that have opiatelike effects. The ancient Sumerians named the poppy plant *opium,* meaning "plant of joy."

Opioids produce a *rush,* or intense feelings of pleasure, which is the primary reason for their popularity as street drugs. They also dull awareness of one's personal problems, which is attractive to people seeking a mental escape from stress. Their pleasurable effects derive from their ability to directly stimulate the brain's pleasure circuits—the same brain networks responsible for feelings of sexual pleasure or pleasure from eating a satisfying meal (Begley, 2001b).

The major medical application of opioids—natural or synthetic—is the relief of pain, or *analgesia.* Medical use of opioids, however, is carefully regulated because overdoses can lead to coma and even death. Street use of opioids is associated with many fatal overdoses and accidents. In a number of American cities, young men are more likely to die of a heroin overdose than in an automobile accident (Alter, 2001).

About 3 million Americans have used heroin and nearly 1 million are believed to be addicted to the drug (Krantz & Mehler, 2004). Once dependence sets in, it usually becomes chronic, relieved by brief periods of abstinence (APA, 2000).

Adding to the problem is that prescription opioids too, used medically for pain relief, can become drugs of abuse when they are used illicitly as street drugs (Friedman, 2006). Recent estimates indicate that about 7% of college students have used the prescription opioid Vicodin without a prescription (Whitten, 2006). Among twelfth graders, about 5.5% report using another opioid, OxyContin, and 9.5% report taking

barbiturates Sedative drugs which are depressants with high addictive potential.

narcotics Drugs that are used medically for pain relief but that have strong addictive potential.

Vicodin (MTF Survey, 2006). Eric, an 18-year-old living in San Francisco, explains how he is able to get Vicodin so easily, although he underestimates its risks:

"I can get prescription drugs from different places and don't ever have to see a doctor. . . . I have friends whose parents are pill addicts, and we 'borrow' from them. Other times I have friends who have ailments who get lots of pills and sell them for cheap. As long as prescription pills are taken right, they're much safer than street drugs."

—*Cited in Friedman, 2006, p. 1148*

endorphins Natural substances that function as neurotransmitters in the brain and are similar in their effects to morphine.

Two discoveries made in the 1970s show that the brain produces chemicals of its own that have opiatelike effects. One was that neurons in the brain have receptor sites that opiates fit like a key in a lock. The second was that the human body produces its own opiatelike substances that dock at the same receptor sites as opiates do. These natural substances, or **endorphins,** play important roles in regulating natural states of pleasure and pain. Opioids mimic the actions of endorphins by docking at receptor sites intended for them, which in turn stimulates the brain centers that produce pleasurable sensations.

The withdrawal syndrome associated with opioids can be severe. It begins within 4 to 6 hours of the last dose. Flulike symptoms are accompanied by anxiety, feelings of restlessness, irritability, and cravings for the drug. Within a few days, symptoms progress to rapid pulse, high blood pressure, cramps, tremors, hot and cold flashes, fever, vomiting, insomnia, and diarrhea, among others. Although these symptoms can be uncomfortable, they are usually not devastating, especially when other drugs are prescribed to relieve them. Moreover, unlike withdrawal from barbiturates, the withdrawal syndrome rarely results in death.

morphine A strongly addictive narcotic derived from the opium poppy that relieves pain and induces feelings of well-being.

heroin A narcotic derived from morphine that has strong addictive properties.

Morphine Morphine—which receives its name from Morpheus, the Greek god of dreams—was introduced at about the time of the U.S. Civil War. Morphine, a powerful opium derivative, was used liberally to deaden pain from wounds. Physiological dependence on morphine became known as the "soldier's disease." There was little stigma attached to dependence until morphine became a restricted substance.

Heroin Heroin, the most widely used opiate, is a powerful depressant that can create a euphoric rush. Users of heroin claim that it is so pleasurable it can eradicate any thought of food or sex. Heroin was developed in 1875 during a search for a drug that would relieve pain as effectively as morphine, but without causing addiction. Chemist Heinrich Dreser transformed morphine into a drug believed to have "heroic" effects in relieving pain without addiction, which is why it was called *heroin.* Unfortunately, heroin does lead to physiological dependence.

Estimates are that some 3 million Americans have used heroin, which is the most widely used and abused opioid, and nearly 1 million are addicted (Krantz & Mehler, 2004). Heroin is usually injected either directly beneath the skin (skin popping) or into a vein (mainlining). The positive effects are immediate. There is a powerful rush that lasts from 5 to 15 minutes and a state of satisfaction, euphoria, and well-being that lasts from 3 to 5 hours. In this state, all positive drives seem satisfied. All negative feelings of guilt, tension, and anxiety disappear. With prolonged usage, addiction can develop. Many physiologically dependent people support their habits through dealing (selling heroin), prostitution, or selling stolen goods. Heroin is a depressant, however, and its chemical effects do not directly stimulate criminal or aggressive behavior.

Shooting up. Heroin users often inject the substance directly into their veins. Heroin is a powerful depressant that provides a euphoric rush. Users often claim that heroin is so pleasurable that it obliterates any thought of food or sex.

Stimulants

Stimulants are psychoactive substances that increase the activity of the central nervous system, which enhances states of alertness and can produce feelings of pleasure or even euphoric highs. The effects vary with the particular drug.

Amphetamines The **amphetamines** are a class of synthetic stimulants. Street names for stimulants include speed, uppers, bennies (for *amphetamine sulfate;* trade name Benzedrine), "meth" (for *methamphetamine;* trade name Methedrine), and dexies (for *dextroamphetamine;* trade name Dexedrine).

Amphetamines are used in high doses for their euphoric rush. They are often taken in pill form or smoked in a relatively pure form called "ice" or "crystal meth." The most potent form of amphetamine, liquid methamphetamine, is injected directly into the veins and produces an intense and immediate rush. Some users inject methamphetamine for days on end to maintain an extended high. Eventually such highs come to an end. People who have been on extended highs sometimes "crash" and fall into a deep sleep or depression. Some people commit suicide on the way down. High doses can cause restlessness, irritability, hallucinations, paranoid delusions, loss of appetite, and insomnia.

Almost 3 times as many people have used "meth" as have used heroin (Bonné, 2001). About 5% of Americans age 12 or older report using "meth" and about 0.2% (2 in a thousand) report current (past-month) use (SAMHSA, 2006). This amounts to more than 12 million Americans who have used "meth" at some point in their lives (Jefferson, 2005). Physiological dependence can develop from using amphetamines, leading to an abstinence syndrome characterized by depression and fatigue, as well as by unpleasant, vivid dreams, insomnia or hypersomnia (excessive sleeping), increased appetite, and either a slowing down of motor behavior or agitation (APA, 2000). Psychological dependence is seen most often in people who use amphetamines as a way of coping with stress or depression.

Methamphetamine abuse can cause brain damage, producing deficits in learning and memory in addition to other effects (Thompson et al., 2004; Toomey et al., 2003; Volkow et al., 2001). Violent behavior may also occur, especially when the drug is smoked or injected intravenously. The hallucinations and delusions of **amphetamine psychosis** mimic those of paranoid schizophrenia, which has encouraged researchers to study the chemical changes induced by amphetamines as possible clues to the underlying causes of schizophrenia.

Ecstasy The drug *ecstasy,* or MDMA (3,4-methylenedioxymethamphetamine) is a designer drug, a chemical knockoff similar in chemical structure to amphetamine. It produces mild euphoria and hallucinations and has become especially popular on college campuses and in clubs and "raves" in many cities (Hernandez, 2000; Strote & Wechsler, 2002). On the other hand, teen use of ecstasy dropped significantly in the early years of the new millennium ("Fewer Teens," 2004). Perhaps the message about the dangers of ecstasy are beginning to get across to young people.

Ecstasy can produce adverse psychological effects, including depression, anxiety, insomnia, and even paranoia and psychosis. The drug may also impair cognitive functioning, including learning ability and attention, and may have long-lasting effects on memory (Reneman, et al., 2001). Scientists suspect that the drug may kill dopamine-using neurons in the brain, which can have long-lasting effects on the ability to experience pleasure in everyday life experiences (Ricaurte et al., 2002). Physical side effects include higher heart rate and blood pressure, a tense or chattering jaw, and body warmth and/or chills (Braun, 2001). The drug can be lethal when taken in high doses. Despite its risks, many users—including most teens—believe (mistakenly) that it is relatively safe ("Teens See Little Risk," 2003).

Cocaine It might surprise you to learn that the original formula for Coca-Cola contained an extract of **cocaine.** In 1906, however, the company withdrew cocaine

stimulants Psychoactive substances that increase the activity of the nervous system.

amphetamines A class of stimulants that activate the central nervous system, producing heightened states of arousal and feelings of pleasure.

amphetamine psychosis A psychotic state induced by ingestion of amphetamines.

cocaine A stimulant derived from the leaves of the coca plant.

Ecstasy. Recreational use of the drug ecstasy has become popular in many clubs catering to young people. Yet even occasional use of the drug may affect cognitive functioning, such as learning, memory, and attention. High doses can be lethal.

crack The hardened, smokable form of cocaine.

from its secret formula. The drink was originally described as a "brain tonic and intellectual beverage," in part because of its cocaine content. Cocaine is a natural stimulant extracted from the leaves of the coca plant—the plant from which the soft drink obtained its name. Coca-Cola is still flavored with an extract from the coca plant, one that is not known to be psychoactive.

It was long believed that cocaine was not physically addicting. However, the drug produces a tolerance effect and an identifiable withdrawal syndrome, which is characterized by depressed mood and disturbances in sleep and appetite (APA, 2000). Intense cravings for the drug and loss of ability to experience pleasure may also be present. Withdrawal symptoms are usually brief in duration and may involve a "crash," or period of intense depression and exhaustion, following abrupt withdrawal.

Cocaine is usually snorted in powder form or smoked in the form of **crack,** a hardened form of cocaine that may be more than 75% pure. Crack "rocks"—so called because they look like small white pebbles—are available in small ready-to-smoke amounts and considered to be the most habit-forming street drug available. Crack produces a prompt and potent rush that wears off in a few minutes. The rush from snorting powdered cocaine is milder and takes a while to develop, but it tends to linger longer than the rush of crack.

Freebasing also intensifies the effects of cocaine. In freebasing, cocaine in powder form is heated with ether, freeing the psychoactive chemical base of the drug, and then smoked. Ether, however, is highly flammable.

Next to marijuana, cocaine is the most widely used illicit drug in the United States. Nearly 14% of Americans age 12 and older have used cocaine and about 0.8% are current (past-month) users (SAMHSA, 2006).

Effects of Cocaine Like heroin, cocaine directly stimulates the brain's reward or pleasure circuits. It also produces a sudden rise in blood pressure and an accelerated heart rate that can cause potentially dangerous, even fatal, irregular heart rhythms. Overdoses can produce restlessness, insomnia, headaches, nausea, convulsions, tremors, hallucinations, delusions, and even sudden death due to respiratory or cardiovascular collapse. Regular snorting of cocaine can lead to serious nasal problems, including ulcers in the nostrils.

Repeated use and high-dose use of cocaine can lead to depression and anxiety. Depression may be severe enough to prompt suicidal behavior. Both initial and routine users report episodes of "crashing" (feelings of depression after a binge), although crashing is more common among long-term high-dose users. Psychotic behaviors, which can be induced by cocaine use as well as by use of amphetamines, tend to become more severe with continued use. Cocaine psychosis is usually preceded by a period of heightened suspiciousness, depressed mood, compulsive behavior, faultfinding, irritability, and increasing paranoia. The psychosis may also include intense visual and auditory hallucinations and delusions of persecution.

Nicotine Habitual smoking is not merely a bad habit: It is also a physical addiction to a stimulant drug, nicotine, found in tobacco products including cigarettes, cigars, and smokeless tobacco (American Cancer Society, 2004). Smoking is also deadly, claiming more than 400,000 lives in the United States alone, most from lung cancer and other lung diseases, as well as cardiovascular (heart and artery) disease (Teo et al., 2006; Zickler, 2004). Smoking doubles the risk of dying in midlife (prior to age 70) (Doll et al., 2004; Vollset, Tverdal, & Gjessing, 2006). Figure 9.2 shows the percentages of deaths due to smoking associated with several of the leading causes of death.

The World Health Organization estimates that 1 billion people worldwide smoke and more than 3 million die each year from smoking-related causes. The good news is that the percentage of Americans who smoke declined from 42% in 1966 to about 21% today (CDC, 2005; TIPS, 2005). The bad news is that 21% of Americans still smoke and that rates of teenage smoking are on the rise, portending increased rates of adult smoking and premature deaths in the years ahead.

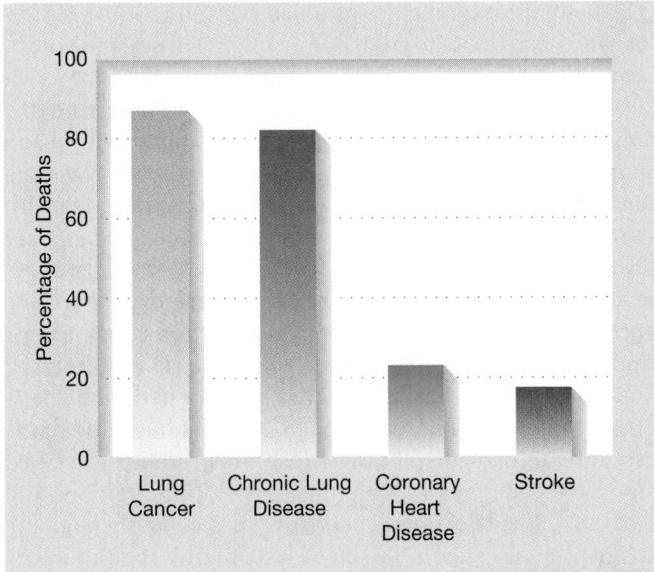

FIGURE 9.2 Smoking-related causes of death, by type of disease.
Cigarette smoking accounts for nearly 90% of deaths due to lung cancer, about 80% of deaths due to chronic lung diseases, especially emphysema, and about 20% of deaths due to coronary heart disease and stroke.

Sources: U.S. Department of Health and Human Services. Reducing the Health Consequences of Smoking: 25 Years of Progress. A Report of the Surgeon General. Public Health Service, Centers for Disease Control, DHHS Publication No. (CDC) 89-8411, 1989; and Smoking. American Lung Association of Texas. http://www.texaslung.org, updated May 2004.

It may surprise you to learn that more women die of lung cancer than any other type of cancer, including breast cancer (Springen, 2004). Although quitting smoking clearly has health benefits for women and men, it unfortunately does not reduce the risks to normal (nonsmoking) levels. The lesson is clear: If you don't smoke, don't start; if you do smoke, quit.

Ethnic differences in smoking rates are shown in Figure 9.3. With the exception of Native Americans (American Indian/Alaskan Native), women in each ethnic group are less likely to smoke than their male counterparts. Smoking is also becoming increasingly concentrated among people at lower income and educational levels.

TRUTH or FICTION

Breast cancer is the leading cause of cancer deaths among U.S. women.

☑ **FALSE.** Lung cancer has surpassed breast cancer as the leading cancer killer among women. It is also the leading cancer killer among men. Cigarette smoking is the culprit in the great majority of cases.

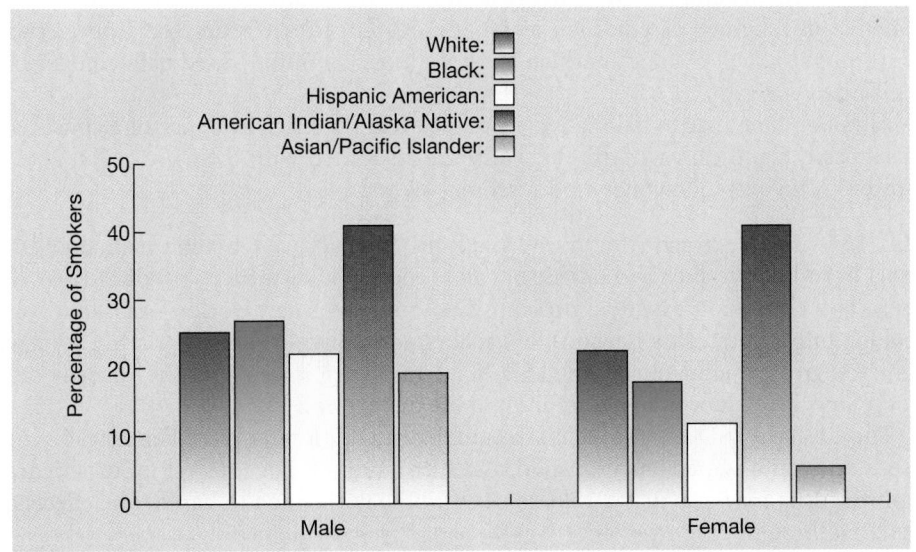

FIGURE 9.3 Ethnic and gender differences in rates of cigarette smoking among U.S. adults.
Smoking rates are higher among Native Americans (American Indian and Alaska Native) than other major racial/ethnic groups in the United States. Women in each ethnic group (with the exception of Native Americans) are less likely to smoke than their male counterparts.

Source: Cigarette Smoking Among Adults—United States, 2004. *Morbidity and mortality weekly report, 54* (November 11, 2005).

Nicotine is delivered to the body through the use of tobacco products. As a stimulant it increases alertness but can also give rise to cold, clammy skin, nausea and vomiting, dizziness and faintness, and diarrhea—all of which account for the discomforts of novice smokers. Nicotine also stimulates the release of epinephrine, a hormone that generates a rush of autonomic nervous system activity, including rapid heartbeat and release of stores of sugar into the blood. Nicotine quells the appetite and provides a psychological "kick." Nicotine also leads to the release of endorphins, the opiatelike hormones produced in the brain. This may account for the pleasurable feelings associated with tobacco use.

Habitual use of nicotine leads to physiological dependence on the drug. Nicotine dependence is associated with both tolerance (intake rises to a level of a pack or two a day before leveling off) and a characteristic withdrawal syndrome. The withdrawal syndrome for nicotine includes such features as lack of energy, depressed mood, irritability, frustration, nervousness, impaired concentration, lightheadedness and dizziness, drowsiness, headaches, fatigue, irregular bowels, insomnia, cramps, lowered heart rate, heart palpitations, increased appetite, weight gain, sweating, tremors, and craving for cigarettes (APA, 2000). It is nicotine dependence, not cigarette smoking per se, that is classifiable as a mental disorder in the *DSM* system. The great majority of regular smokers (80% to 90%) meet diagnostic criteria for nicotine dependence (APA, 2000).

Hallucinogens

hallucinogens Substances that cause hallucinations.

Hallucinogens, also known as *psychedelics,* are a class of drugs that produce sensory distortions or hallucinations, including major alterations in color perception and hearing. Hallucinogens may also have additional effects, such as relaxation and euphoria or, in some cases, panic.

Hallucinogens include lysergic acid diethylamide (LSD), psilocybin, and mescaline. Psychoactive substances that are similar in effect to psychedelic drugs are marijuana (*cannabis*) and *phencyclidine* (PCP). Mescaline is derived from the peyote cactus and has been used for centuries by Native Americans in the Southwest, Mexico, and Central America in religious ceremonies, as has psilocybin, which is derived from certain mushrooms. LSD, PCP, and marijuana are the most commonly used hallucinogens in the United States.

Although tolerance to hallucinogens may develop, we lack evidence of a consistent or clinically significant withdrawal syndrome associated with their use (APA, 2000). However, cravings following withdrawal may occur.

LSD LSD is the acronym for *lysergic acid diethylamide,* a synthetic hallucinogenic drug. In addition to the vivid parade of colors and visual distortions produced by LSD, users have claimed it "expands consciousness" and opens new worlds—as if they were looking into some reality beyond the usual reality. Sometimes they believe they have achieved great insights during the LSD "trip," but when it wears off they usually cannot follow through or even summon up these discoveries.

The effects of LSD are unpredictable and depend on the amount taken as well as the user's expectations, personality, mood, and surroundings. The user's prior experiences with the drug may also play a role, as users who have learned to handle the effects of the drug through past experience may be better prepared than new users.

Some users have unpleasant experiences with the drug, or "bad trips." Feelings of intense fear or panic may occur. Users may fear losing control or sanity. Some experience terrifying fears of death. Fatal accidents have sometimes occurred during LSD trips. *Flashbacks,* typically involving a reexperiencing of some of the perceptual distortions of the "trip," may occur days, weeks, or even years afterward. Flashbacks tend to occur suddenly and often without warning. Perceptual distortions may involve geometric forms, flashes of color, intensified colors, afterimages, or appearances of halos around objects, among others (APA, 2000). They may stem from chemical changes in the brain caused by the prior use of the drug. Triggers for flashbacks include entry into darkened environments, drug use, anxiety or fatigue states, or stress. Psychological factors, such as underlying personality problems, may also explain why some users experience flashbacks. In some cases, a flashback may involve an imagined reenactment of the LSD experience.

Phencyclidine (PCP) *Phencyclidine,* or PCP—which is referred to as "angel dust" on the streets—was developed as an anesthetic in the 1950s but was discontinued as such when its hallucinatory side effects were discovered. A smokable form of PCP became popular as a street drug in the 1970s. However, its popularity has since waned, largely because of its unpredictable effects.

The effects of PCP, like most drugs, are dose related. In addition to causing hallucinations, PCP accelerates the heart rate and blood pressure and causes sweating, flushing, and numbness. PCP is classified as a *deliriant*—a drug capable of producing states of delirium. It also has dissociating effects, causing users to feel as if there is some sort of invisible barrier between themselves and their environments. Dissociation can be experienced as pleasant, engrossing, or frightening, depending on the user's expectations, mood, setting, and so on. Overdoses can give rise to drowsiness and a blank stare, convulsions, and, now and then, coma; paranoia and aggressive behavior; and tragic accidents resulting from perceptual distortion or impaired judgment during states of intoxication.

Marijuana **Marijuana** is derived from the *Cannabis sativa* plant. Marijuana is generally classified as a hallucinogen because it can produce perceptual distortions or mild hallucinations, especially in high doses or when used by susceptible individuals. The psychoactive substance in marijuana is *delta-9-tetrahydrocannabinol,* or, thankfully, THC for short. THC is found in branches and leaves of the plant but is highly concentrated in the resin of the female plant. *Hashish,* or "hash," also derived from the resin, is more potent than marijuana but has similar effects.

marijuana A hallucinogenic drug derived from the leaves and stems of the plant *Cannabis sativa.*

Use of marijuana exploded throughout the so-called swinging 1960s and the 1970s, but the drug then lost some (but not all) of its cachet. Still, marijuana remains our most widely used illegal drug, and abuse of marijuana is the most common of all the substance abuse disorders involving illicit drugs (Compton et al., 2004). That said, the prevalence of use and abuse of marijuana doesn't compare with that of alcohol.

About 40% of Americans 12 years of age and older report having used marijuana or hashish in their lives, and about 6% are current (past-month) users (SAMHSA, 2006). About 1.5% of the U.S. adult population suffers from a marijuana abuse or dependence disorder (Compton et al., 2004). Males are more likely than females to develop a marijuana abuse or dependence disorder, and rates of these disorders are greatest among people age 18 to 30 (APA, 2000).

Low doses of the drug can produce relaxing feelings similar to drinking alcohol. Some users report that at low doses the drug makes them feel more comfortable in social gatherings. Higher doses, however, often lead users to withdraw into themselves. Some users believe the drug increases their capacity for self-insight or creative thinking, although the insights achieved under its influence may not seem so insightful once the drug's effects have passed. People may turn to marijuana, as to other drugs, to help them cope with life problems or to help them function when they are under stress. Strongly intoxicated people perceive time as passing more slowly. A song of a few minutes may seem to last an hour. There is increased awareness of bodily sensations, such as heartbeat. Smokers also report that strong intoxication heightens sexual sensations. Visual hallucinations may occur.

Strong intoxication can cause smokers to become disoriented. If their moods are euphoric, disorientation may be construed as harmony with the universe. Yet some smokers find strong intoxication disturbing. An accelerated heart rate and sharpened awareness of bodily sensations cause some smokers to fear their hearts will "run away" with them. Some smokers are frightened by disorientation and fear they will not "come back." High levels of intoxication now and then induce nausea and vomiting.

Cannabis dependence is associated more with patterns of compulsive use or psychological dependence than with physiological dependence. Although tolerance to many of the drug's effects may occur with chronic use, some users report reverse tolerance, or *sensitization*. Although a clear-cut withdrawal syndrome has not been reliably demonstrated, recent evidence identified a definable withdrawal syndrome among long-term, heavy users who stopped using the drug abruptly (Budney et al., 2004). We have also learned that long-term use can lead to problems with both learning and memory (Messinis et al., 2006; Solowij et al., 2002).

Evidence also links marijuana use to later use of harder drugs such as heroin and cocaine (Kandel, 2002, 2003). Whether marijuana use is a causal factor leading to use of harder drugs remains unclear. We do know that marijuana impairs perception and motor coordination and thus makes driving and the operation of other heavy machinery dangerous. Although marijuana use induces positive mood changes in many users, some people report anxiety and confusion; there are also occasional reports of paranoia or psychotic reactions (Johns, 2001). Marijuana elevates heart rate and blood pressure and is linked to an increased risk of heart attacks in people with heart disease. And like cigarettes, smoking marijuana can cause respiratory diseases, including chronic bronchitis (Zickler, 2006).

THEORETICAL PERSPECTIVES

People begin using psychoactive substances for various reasons. Some adolescents start using drugs because of peer pressure or because they believe drugs make them seem more sophisticated or grown up. Some use drugs as a way of rebelling against their parents or society at large. Regardless of why people get started with drugs, they continue to use them because drugs produce pleasurable effects or because they find it difficult to stop. Most adolescents drink alcohol to "get high," not to establish that they are adults. Many people smoke cigarettes for the pleasure they provide. Others smoke to help them relax when they are tense and, paradoxically, to give them a kick or a lift when they are tired. Many would like to quit but find it difficult to break their addiction.

People who are anxious about their jobs or social lives may be drawn to the calming effects of alcohol, marijuana (in certain doses), tranquilizers, and sedatives. People with low self-confidence and self-esteem may be drawn to the ego-bolstering effects of amphetamines and cocaine. Many poor young people attempt to escape the poverty, anguish, and tedium of inner-city life through using heroin and similar drugs. More well-to-do adolescents may rely on drugs to manage the transition from dependence to independence and major life changes concerning jobs, college, and lifestyles.

In the next sections we consider several major theoretical perspectives on substance abuse and dependence.

Biological Perspectives

We are beginning to learn more about the biological underpinnings of drug use and addiction. Much of the recent research has focused on neurotransmitters, especially dopamine, and on the role of genetic factors.

Neurotransmitters Many psychoactive drugs, including nicotine, alcohol, heroin, marijuana, and especially cocaine and amphetamines, increase levels of the neurotransmitter dopamine in the brain's pleasure or reward circuits—the networks of neurons responsible for producing feelings of pleasure or states of euphoria (Nestler, 2005; Pierce & Kumaresan, 2006; Society for Neuroscience, 2005c; Volkow et al., 2005; Zangen et al., 2006). Over time, regular use of these drugs reduces the brain's own production of dopamine. Consequently, the brain's natural reward system—the "feel good" circuitry that produces states of pleasure associated with the ordinarily rewarding activities of life, such as consuming a satisfying meal and engaging in pleasant activities—becomes blunted (Dubovsky, 2006). In effect, the addict's brain comes to depend on having the drug available to produce feelings of pleasure or satisfaction (Denizet-Lewis, 2006). Without drugs, life may not seem to be worth living.

PRENTICE HALL
mypsychlab

SUBSTANCE ABUSE:

Therapist Jean
Obert

"Being addicted to heroin is one of the most difficult things to kick."

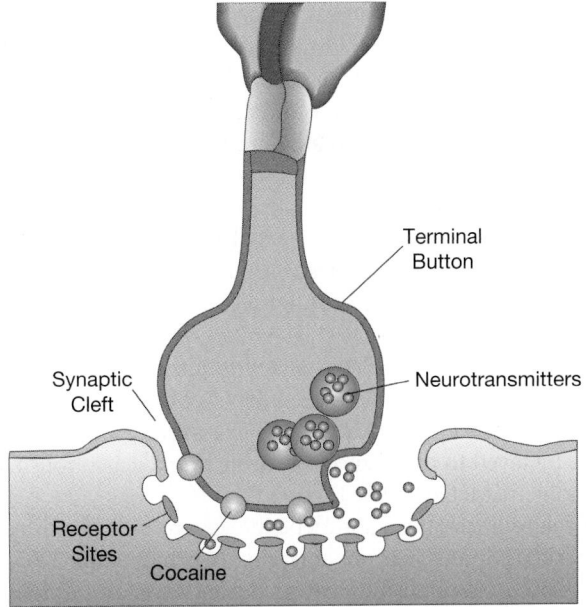

FIGURE 9.4 Cocaine's effects in the brain. Neurotransmitters are released into the synapse (synaptic cleft or gap) from terminal buttons at the end of axons. Normally, excess molecules of neurotransmitters are reabsorbed by the terminal buttons of the transmitting neuron in a process called *reuptake*. Cocaine, as represented here by the orange circles, blocks this process of reuptake, allowing more neurotransmitter molecules to remain in the synapse, which creates a euphoric high by overstimulating receiving neurons in brain networks regulating feelings of pleasure.

Changes in the dopamine system may help explain the intense cravings and anxiety that accompany drug withdrawal and the difficulty people have maintaining abstinence. Although investigators highlight the role of dopamine in helping us understand the biochemical bases of substance abuse and dependence, they recognize that other neurotransmitters, including serotonin and endorphins, also play a role (Addolorato et al., 2005; Buchert et al., 2004).

Figure 9.4 shows the effects of cocaine in the brain. Use of the drug increases the availability of neurotransmitters norepinephrine and dopamine by interfering with the process by which excess molecules of these chemicals are reabsorbed by the transmitting neuron through a process called *reuptake*. High levels of these neurotransmitters therefore remain active in the synaptic gaps between neurons within brain networks that control feelings of pleasure, thereby magnifying and extending feelings the pleasurable effects of the drug (see Figure 9.4).

Endorphins are a class of neurotransmitters that have pain-blocking properties similar to those of opioids such as heroin. Endorphins and opiates dock at the same receptor sites in the brain. Normally, the brain produces a certain level of endorphins that maintains a psychological steady state of comfort and potential to experience pleasure. However, when the body becomes habituated to a supply of opioids, it may stop producing endorphins. This makes the user dependent on opiates for comfort, relief from pain, and pleasure. When the habitual user stops using heroin or other opiates, feelings of discomfort and little aches and pains may be magnified until the body resumes adequate production of endorphins. This discomfort may account, at least in part, for the unpleasant withdrawal symptoms that opiate addicts experience. However, this model remains speculative, and more research is needed to document direct relationships between endorphin production and withdrawal symptoms.

Genetic Factors Evidence links genetic factors to various forms of substance use and abuse, including alcohol abuse and dependence, heroin dependence, and even cigarette smoking (nicotine dependence) (Feng et al., 2004; Hampton, 2006; Liu et al., 2004; Xu et al., 2004). Investigators have begun the hunt for specific genes involved in alcohol and drug abuse and dependence (e.g., Audrain-McGovern et al., 2004; Drakenberg et al., 2006). We focus on alcohol dependence, because this has been the area of greatest research interest.

Alcoholism tends to run in families (APA, 2000). The closer the genetic relationship, the greater the risk. Familial patterns provide only suggestive evidence of genetic factors, because families share a common environment as well as common genes. More definitive evidence comes from twin and adoptee studies.

Monozygotic (MZ) twins have identical genes, whereas fraternal or dizygotic (DZ) twins share only half of their genes. If genetic factors are involved, we would expect MZ twins to have higher concordance (agreement) rates for alcoholism than DZ twins. Evidence of higher concordance rates for alcoholism is found among MZ twins than DZ twins, although the results are more consistent for male samples than female samples (Wood et al., 2001).

A limitation of twin studies is that MZ twins may share more environmental as well as genetic similarity than DZ twins. That is, they may be treated more alike than DZ twins. However, evidence also shows that male adoptees whose biological parents suffered from alcoholism have an increased risk of developing alcoholism themselves, even if they are raised in nondrinking homes (Gordis, 1995). Among women, however, the rate of alcoholism in adopted-away daughters of parents with alcoholism is only slightly higher than that for adopted-away daughters of nonalcoholics, thus casting doubt on a strong genetic linkage to alcoholism in women (Svikis, Velez, & Pickens, 1994). All in all, genetic factors are believed to play a moderate role in male alcoholism and a modest role in female alcoholism (McGue, 1993).

If alcoholism or other forms of substance abuse and dependence are influenced by genetic factors, what exactly is inherited? Some clues are emerging (Corbett et al., 2005; Edenberg et al., 2005; Radel et al., 2005). Alcoholism, nicotine dependence, and opioid addiction are linked to genes that determine the structure of dopamine receptors in the brain. As we've noted, dopamine is involved in regulating states of pleasure, so one possibility is that genetic factors enhance feelings of pleasure derived from alcohol. The genetic vulnerability to alcoholism most probably involves a combination of factors, such as reaping greater pleasure from alcohol and a capacity for greater biological tolerance for the drug. People who can tolerate larger doses of alcohol without incurring upset stomachs, dizziness, and headaches may have difficulty knowing when to stop drinking. Thus people who are better able to "hold their liquor" may thus be at greater risk of developing drinking problems. They may need to rely on other cues, such as counting their drinks, to limit their drinking. Other people whose bodies more readily "put the brakes" on excess drinking may be less likely to develop problems in moderating their drinking.

Whatever the role of heredity in alcohol dependence and other forms of substance dependence, genes do not dictate behavior; they interact with environmental factors (Kendler, Jacobson et al., 2003). For example, being raised in an environment free of parental alcoholism is associated with a lower risk of alcohol-related disorders in people at high genetic risk of these disorders (Jacob et al., 2003). In sum, addiction experts believe that multiple genes acting together with social, cultural, and psychological factors contribute to the the development of alcoholism and other forms of substance dependence (e.g., Dick et al., 2001).

TRUTH or FICTION

People who can "hold their liquor" better than most stand a lower risk of becoming problem drinkers.

☑ **FALSE.** A high physical tolerance for liquor may lead a person to drink excessively, which may set the stage for problem drinking.

Learning Perspectives

Learning theorists propose that substance-related behaviors are largely learned and can, in principle, be unlearned. They focus on the roles of operant and classical conditioning and observational learning. Substance abuse problems are not regarded as symptoms of disease but rather as problem habits. Although learning theorists do not deny that genetic or biological factors may increase susceptiblity to substance abuse problems, but they emphasize the role of learning in the development and maintenance of these problem behaviors (McCrady, 1993, 1994). They also recognize that people who suffer from depression or anxiety may turn to alcohol as a way of relieving these troubling emotional states, however briefly. Evidence shows that emotional stress, such as anxiety or depression, often sets the stage for the development of substance abuse (Dixit & Crum, 2000; McGue, Slutske, & Iaono, 1999).

Drug use may become habitual because of the pleasure (positive reinforcement) or temporary relief (negative reinforcement) from negative emotions, such as anxiety and depression, which drugs can produce. With drugs like cocaine, which appear capable of directly stimulating pleasure mechanisms in the brain, the positive reinforcement is direct and powerful.

Operant Conditioning People may initially use a drug because of social influence, trial and error, or social observation. In the case of alcohol, they learn that the drug can produce reinforcing effects, such as feelings of euphoria, and reductions in anxiety and tension. Alcohol may also reduce behavioral inhibitions. Alcohol can thus be reinforcing when it is used to combat depression (by producing euphoric feelings, even if short lived), to combat tension (by functioning as a tranquilizer), or to help people sidestep moral conflicts (for example, by dulling awareness of moral prohibitions). Substance abuse may also provide social reinforcers, such as the approval of drug-abusing companions and, in the cases of alcohol and stimulants, the (temporary) overcoming of social shyness.

Alcohol and Tension Reduction Learning theorists have long maintained that one of the primary reinforcers for using alcohol is relief from states of tension or unpleasant states of arousal. According to the *tension-reduction theory,* the more often one drinks to reduce tension or anxiety, the stronger or more habitual the habit becomes. We can think of some uses of alcohol and other drugs as forms of *self-medication*—as a means of using the pill or the bottle to ease psychological pain, at least temporarily (Bolton et al., 2006; Tomlinson et al., 2006). We can see this pattern of negative reinforcement (relief from psychological pain) in the following case example.

"Taking Away the Hurt I Feel"

"I use them (the pills and alcohol) to take away the hurt I feel inside." Joceyln, a 36-year-old mother of two, was physically abused by her husband, Phil. "I have no self-esteem. I just don't feel I can do anything," she told her therapist. Jocelyn had escaped from an abusive family background by getting married at age 17, hoping that marriage would offer her a better life. The first few years were free of abuse, but things changed when Phil lost his job and began to drink heavily. By then, Jocelyn had two young children and felt trapped. She blamed herself for her unhappy family life, for Phil's drinking, for her son's learning disability. "The only thing I can do is drink or do pills. At least then I don't have to think about things for awhile." Although drug use temporarily dulled her emotional pain, it came with a greater long-term cost in terms of the burden of addiction.

—From the Author's Files

Although nicotine, alcohol, and other drugs may temporarily alleviate emotional distress, they cannot resolve underlying personal or emotional problems. Rather than learning to resolve these problems, people who turn to alcohol or other drugs as forms of self-medication often find themselves facing additional substance-related problems.

Self-medication? People who turn to other drugs or alcohol to quell disturbing emotions can compound their problems by developing a substance use disorder.

Negative Reinforcement and Withdrawal Once people become physiologically dependent, negative reinforcement comes into play in maintaining the drug habit. In other words, people may resume using drugs to gain relief from unpleasant withdrawal symptoms. In operant conditioning terms, relief from unpleasant withdrawal symptoms is a negative reinforcer for resuming drug use (Higgins, Heil, & Lussier, 2004). For example, the addicted smoker who quits cold turkey may shortly return to smoking to fend off the discomfort of withdrawal.

The Conditioning Model of Cravings Classical conditioning may help explain drug cravings. In this view, cravings reflect the body's need to restore high blood levels of the addictive substance and thus have a biological basis. But they also come to be associated with environmental cues associated with prior use of the substance (Kilts et al., 2004). These cues, such as the sight or aroma of an alcoholic beverage or the sight of a needle and syringe, become conditioned stimuli that elicit a conditioned response: strong cravings for the drug. For example, socializing with certain companions ("drinking buddies") or even passing a liquor store may elicit conditioned cravings for alcohol. In support of this theory, alcoholic subjects show distinctive changes in brain activity in areas of the brain that regulate emotion, attention, and appetitive behavior when shown pictures of alcoholic beverages (George et al., 2001). Social drinkers, by comparison, do not show this pattern of brain activation.

Sensations of anxiety or depression that are paired with the use of alcohol or drugs may also elicit cravings. The following case illustrates conditioned cravings to environmental cues.

A Case of Conditioned Drug Cravings

A 29-year-old man was hospitalized for the treatment of heroin addiction. After 4 weeks of treatment, he returned to his former job, which required him to ride the subway past the stop at which he had previously bought his drugs. Each day, when the subway doors opened at this location, [he] experienced enormous craving for heroin, accompanied by tearing, a runny nose, abdominal cramps, and gooseflesh. After the doors closed, his symptoms disappeared, and he went on to work.

—*From Weiss & Mirin, 1987, p. 71*

Similarly, some people are primarily "stimulus smokers." They reach for a cigarette in the presence of smoking-related stimuli, such as seeing someone smoke or smelling smoke. Smoking becomes a strongly conditioned habit because it is paired repeatedly with many situational cues—watching TV, finishing dinner, driving in the car, studying, drinking or socializing with friends, sex, and, for some, using the bathroom.

The conditioning model of craving receives support from research showing that people with alcoholism tend to salivate more than others at the sight and smell of alcohol (Monti et al., 1987). Pavlov's classic experiment conditioned a salivation response in dogs by repeatedly pairing the sound of a bell (a conditioned stimulus) with the presentation of food powder (an unconditioned stimulus). Salivation among people who develop alcoholism can also be viewed as a conditioned response to alcohol-related cues. People with drinking problems who show the greatest salivary response to alcohol cues may be at highest risk of relapse. They may also profit from conditioning-based treatments designed to extinguish responses to alcohol-related cues.

In one treatment occurring over a series of sessions, called *cue exposure training*, the person is seated in front of alcohol-related cues, such as open alcoholic beverages, but prevented from imbibing (Dawe et al., 2002). The pairing of the cue (alcohol bottle) with nonreinforcement (by dint of preventing drinking) may lead to extinction of the conditioned craving. However, cravings can, and often do, return after treatment when people go back to their usual environments (Collins & Brandon, 2002; Havermans & Jansen, 2003).

Observational Learning Modeling or observational learning plays an important role in determining risk of substance abuse problems. Parents who model inappropriate or excessive drinking or use of illicit drugs may set the stage for maladaptive drug use in their children (Kirisci, Vanyukov, & Tarter, 2005). Evidence shows that adolescents who have a parent who smokes face a substantially higher risk of smoking than do their peers in families where neither parent smokes (Peterson et al., 2006). Other investigators find that having friends who smoke influences adolescents to begin smoking (Bricker et al., 2006).

Cognitive Perspectives

Evidence supports the role of cognitive factors in substance abuse and dependence, especially the role of expectancies. Expectancies about the perceived benefits of using alcohol or other drugs and smoking cigarettes clearly influence the decision to use these substances (Cable & Sacker, 2006; Mitchell et al., 2006; Park, 2004). Outcome expectancies in teens—what they expect a drug's effects will be—are strongly influenced by the beliefs of their peers. The degree to which friends hold positive attitudes toward alcohol use is thus an important factor in alcohol use in adolescents (Wood et al., 2001). Public health campaigns appear to be having some impact in changing attitudes of young people toward cigarette smoking. Adolescents in a Midwestern community showed more negative attitudes toward smoking than did adolescents a generation earlier (Chassin et al., 2003).

Alcohol or other drug use may also boost *self-efficacy expectations*—personal expectancies we hold about our ability to successfully perform tasks. If we believe we need a drink or two (or more) to "get out of our shell" and relate socially to others, we may come to depend on alcohol in social situations.

Expectancies may account for the "one-drink effect"—the tendency of chronic alcohol abusers to binge once they have a drink. Psychologist G. Alan Marlatt (1978) explained the one-drink effect as a type of self-fulfilling prophecy. If people with alcohol-related problems believe that just one drink will cause a loss of control, they may perceive the outcome as predetermined when they drink. Having even one drink may thus escalate into a binge. This type of expectation is an example of what Aaron Beck calls *absolutist thinking*. When we insist on seeing the world in black and white rather than shades of gray—as either complete successes or complete failures—we may interpret one bite of dessert as proof we are off our diets, or one cigarette as proof we are hooked again. Rather than telling ourselves, "Okay, I goofed, but that's it. I don't have to have more," we encode our lapses as catastrophes and transform them into relapses. Still, alcohol-dependent people who believe they may go on a drinking binge if they have just one drink are well advised to abstain.

Psychodynamic Perspectives

According to traditional psychodynamic theory, alcoholism reflects an *oral-dependent personality*. Psychodynamic theory also associates excessive alcohol use with other oral traits, such as dependence and depression, and traces the origins of these traits to fixation in the oral stage of psychosexual development. Excessive drinking or smoking in adulthood symbolizes an individual's efforts to attain oral gratification.

Research support for these psychodynamic concepts is mixed. Although people who develop alcoholism often show dependent traits, it is unclear whether dependence contributes to or stems from problem drinking. Chronic drinking, for example, is connected with loss of employment and downward movement in social status, both of which would render drinkers more reliant on others for support. Moreover, an empirical connection between dependence and alcoholism does not establish that alcoholism represents an oral fixation that can be traced to early development.

Then too, many—but certainly not all—people who suffer from alcoholism have antisocial personalities characterized by independence seeking as expressed through rebelliousness and rejection of social and legal codes. All in all, there doesn't appear to be any single alcoholic personality (Wood et al., 2001).

Sociocultural Perspectives

Drinking is determined, in part, by where we live, whom we worship with, and the social or cultural norms that regulate our behavior. Cultural attitudes can encourage or discourage problem drinking. As we have already seen, rates of alcohol abuse vary across ethnic and religious groups. Let us note some other sociocultural factors. Church attendance, for example, is generally connected with abstinence from alcohol. Perhaps people who are more willing to engage in culturally sanctioned activities, such as churchgoing, are also more likely to adopt culturally sanctioned prohibitions against excessive drinking. Rates of alcohol use also vary across cultures.

Peer pressure and exposure to a drug subculture are important influences in determining substance use among adolescents and young adults (Dishion & Owen, 2002; Hu, Davies, & Kandel, 2006). Kids who start drinking before age 15 stand a fivefold higher risk of developing alcohol dependence in adulthood than do teens who began drinking at a later age (Kluger, 2001). Yet studies of Hispanic and African American adolescents show that support from family members can reduce the negative influence of drug-using peers on the adolescent's use of tobacco and other drugs (Farrell & White, 1998; Frauenglass et al., 1997).

TREATMENT OF SUBSTANCE ABUSE AND DEPENDENCE

There is a vast array of nonprofessional, biological, and psychological approaches to substance abuse and dependence. However, treatment has often been a frustrating endeavor. In many, perhaps most, cases, people with drug dependencies really do not want to stop and do not seek treatment on their own. When people do come for treatment, helping them through the withdrawal syndrome is usually straightforward enough, as we shall see. However, helping them pursue a life devoid of their preferred substances is more problematic. Treatment takes place in a setting—such as the therapist's office, a support group, a residential center, or a hospital—in which abstinence is valued and encouraged. Then the individual returns to the work, family, or street settings in which abuse and dependence were instigated and maintained. The problem of relapse can thus be more troublesome than the problems involved in initial treatment.

Peer pressure. Peer pressure is a major influence on alcohol and drug use among adolescents.

Another complication is that many people with substance abuse problems have other psychological disorders as well. However, most clinics and treatment programs focus on the drug or alcohol problem, or the other psychological disorders, rather than treating all these problems simultaneously. This narrow focus results in poorer treatment outcomes, including more frequent rehospitalizations among those with these *dual diagnoses.*

Biological Approaches

An increasing range of biological approaches is used in treating problems of substance abuse and dependence. For people with chemical dependencies, biological treatment typically begins with **detoxification**—that is, helping them through withdrawal from addictive substances.

detoxification The process of ridding the system of alcohol or other drugs under supervised conditions.

Detoxification Detoxification is often more safely carried out in a hospital setting. In the case of addiction to alcohol or barbiturates, hospitalization allows medical personnel to monitor and treat potentially dangerous withdrawal symptoms such as convulsions. Antianxiety drugs, such as the benzodiazepines Librium and Valium, may help block severe withdrawal symptoms such as seizures and delirium tremens. Detoxification to alcohol takes about a week. Detoxification is an important step toward staying clean, but it is only a start. Approximately half of all drug abusers relapse within a year of detoxification (Cowley, 2001b). Continuing support and structured therapy, such as behavioral counseling, plus possible use of therapeutic drugs, increase the chances of long-term success.

A number of therapeutic drugs are used in treating people with chemical dependencies, and more chemical compounds are in the testing stage. Here we survey some of the major drugs in use today.

Disulfiram The drug *disulfiram* (brand name Antabuse) discourages alcohol consumption because the combination of the two produces a violent response consisting of nausea, headache, heart palpitations, and vomiting. In some extreme cases, combining disulfiram and alcohol can produce such a dramatic drop in blood pressure that the individual goes into shock or even dies. Although disulfiram has been used widely in alcoholism treatment, its effectiveness is limited because many patients who want to continue drinking simply stop using the drug. Others stop taking the drug because they believe that they can remain abstinent without it. Unfortunately, many return to uncontrolled drinking. Another drawback is that the drug has toxic effects in people with liver disease, a frequent ailment of people who suffer from alcoholism. Little evidence supports the efficacy of the drug in the long run.

Antidepressants Antidepressants may help reduce cravings for cocaine following withdrawal. These drugs stimulate neural processes that promote feelings of pleasure derived from everyday experiences. If cocaine users can feel pleasure from non–drug-related activities, they may be less likely to return to using cocaine. However, antidepressants have yet to produce consistent results in reducing relapse rates for cocaine dependence, so it is best to withhold judgment concerning their efficacy. The antidepressant drug *bupropion* (trade name Zyban) is used to blunt cravings for nicotine in much the same way that other antidepressants are being used to reduce cocaine cravings. The drug has a modest benefit in helping people quit smoking successfully (Croghan et al., 2007). Another drug, *varenicline*, may be more effective than bupropion for smoking cessation (Barclay & Vega, 2006). Several recent controlled studies show that varenicline produces significant benefits in aiding smokers in quitting relative to placebo (Gonzales et al., 2006; Jorenby et al., 2006; Klesges, Johnson, & Somes, 2006; Tonstad et al., 2006). The drug works by binding to nicotine receptors in the brain to blunt the reward value of smoking and to prevent withdrawal symptoms.

Nicotine Replacement Therapy Most regular smokers, perhaps the great majority, are nicotine dependent. The use of nicotine replacements in the form of prescription gum (brand name Nicorette), transdermal (skin) patches, and nasal sprays can help smokers avoid unpleasant withdrawal symptoms and cravings for cigarettes (Strasser

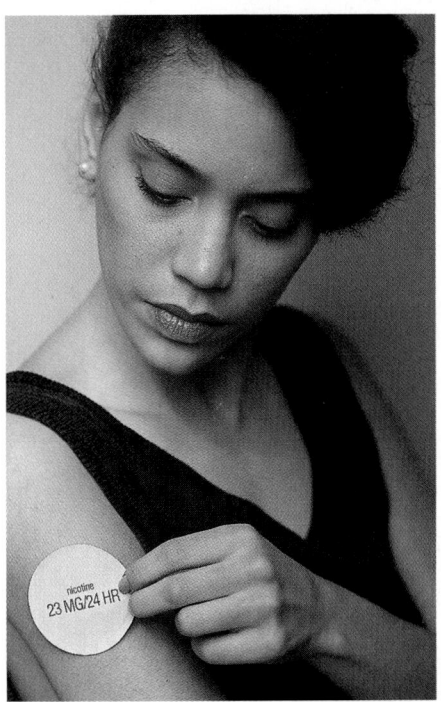

Is the path to abstinence from smoking skin deep? Forms of nicotine replacement therapy, such as nicotine transdermal (skin) patches and chewing gum that contains nicotine, allow people to continue to take in nicotine when they quit smoking. Although nicotine replacement therapy is more effective than a placebo in helping people quit smoking, it does not address the behavioral components of addiction to nicotine, such as the habit of smoking while drinking alcohol. For this reason, nicotine replacement therapy may be more effective if it is combined with behavior therapy that focuses on changing smoking habits.

et al., 2005; Shiffman et al., 2002). After quitting smoking, ex-smokers can gradually wean themselves from the nicotine replacement. Evidence supports the therapeutic benefits of nicotine replacement therapy, although men seem to benefit more from treatment than women (Cepeda-Benito, Reynoso, & Erath, 2004; Strasser et al., 2005).

Although nicotine replacement can help quell the physiological components of withdrawal, it has no effect on the behavioral patterns of addiction, such as the habit of smoking while drinking alcohol or socializing. As a result, nicotine replacement may be ineffective in promoting long-term changes unless it is combined with behavioral therapy that focuses on fostering adaptive behavioral changes.

Methadone Maintenance Programs Methadone is a synthetic opiate that blunts cravings for heroin and helps curb the unpleasant symptoms that accompany withdrawal. Because methadone in normal doses does not produce a high or leave the user feeling drugged, it can help heroin addicts hold jobs and get their lives back on track (Schwartz et al., 2006). However, like other opioids, methadone is highly addictive. For this reason, people treated with methadone are, in effect, substituting dependence on one drug for dependence on another. Yet because most methadone programs are publicly financed, they relieve people addicted to heroin of the need to engage in criminal activity to support their drug habit. Methadone programs need to be strictly monitored because overdoses can be lethal, and the drug can become abused as a street drug (Belluck, 2003). Some 200,000 heroin addicts in the United States participate in methadone programs (Markel, 2002).

Since the introduction of methadone treatment, the annual death rate from opioid dependence declined from 21 per 1,000 to 13 per 1,000 (Krantz & Mehler, 2004). One frequent criticism of methadone treatment is that many participants continue to take the drug indefinitely, potentially even for a lifetime, rather than be weaned from it. However, proponents of methadone treatment point out that the measure of success should be whether people are able to take care of themselves and their families and act responsibly, not how long they continue to receive treatment (Marion, 2005). Even so, not everyone succeeds in treatment. Some patients turn to other drugs, such as cocaine, to get high or return to using heroin. Others drop out of methadone programs.

Still another synthetic opiate drug that is chemically similar to morphine, *buprenorphine,* blocks withdrawal symptoms and cravings without producing a strong narcotic high (Fiellin et al., 2006). Many treatment providers prefer buprenorphine to methadone because it produces less of a sedative effective and can be taken in pill form only three times a week, whereas methadone is given in liquid form daily. Another synthetic antiopiate, *levomethadyl,* also lasts longer than methadone and can be dispensed three times a week (Krantz & Mehler, 2004). For maximum effectiveness, pharmacotherapy with methadone or similar drugs should be combined with psychological counseling and psychosocial rehabilitation (P.G. O'Connor, 2000; E. O'Connor, 2001a).

Naltrexone Naltrexone is a drug that blocks the high produced by alcohol and by opioids, such as heroin. The drug doesn't prevent the person from taking a drink or using heroin, but seems to blunt cravings for these drugs. Evidence shows that naltrexone and similar drugs are useful in treating alcohol and opiate dependence (Anton et al., 2006; Comer et al., 2006; Garbutt et al, 2005a, 2005b; Kranzler, 2006). By blocking the pleasure produced by alcohol, the drug can help break the vicious cycle in which one drink creates a desire for another, leading to episodes of binge drinking.

A nagging problem with drugs such as naltrexone, disulfiram, and methadone is that people with substance abuse problems may simply stop using them and return to their substance-abusing behavior. Nor do such drugs provide alternative sources of positive reinforcement that can replace the pleasurable states produced by drugs of abuse. These drugs are effective only in the context of a broader treatment program consisting of psychological counseling and life-skills components, such as job training, and stress-management training. These treatments provide people with the skills they need to embark on a life in the mainstream culture and to find drug-free outlets for coping with stress (Fouquereau et al., 2003; Miller & Brown, 1997).

---

methadone An artificial narcotic that is used to help people who are addicted to heroin to abstain from it without a withdrawal syndrome.

TRUTH or FICTION

A widely used treatment for heroin addiction involves substituting another addictive drug.

✓ **TRUE.** Methadone, a synthetic narcotic, is widely used in treating heroin addiction.

naltrexone A drug that blocks the high from alcohol as well as from opiates.

Culturally Sensitive Treatment of Alcoholism

Members of ethnic minority groups may resist traditional treatment approaches because they feel excluded from full participation in society. Native American women, for example, tend to respond less favorably to traditional alcoholism counseling than White women (Rogan, 1986). Hurlburt and Gade (1984) attribute this difference to the resistance of Native American women to "White man's" authority. They suggest that Native American counselors might be more successful in overcoming this resistance.

The use of counselors from the client's own ethnic group is an example of a *culturally sensitive treatment approach.* Culturally sensitive programs address all facets of the human being, including racial and cultural identity, that nurture pride and help people resist the temptation to cope with stress through chemicals (Rogan, 1986). Culturally sensitive treatment approaches have been extended to other forms of drug dependence, including programs for smoking cessation (Nevid & Javier, 1997; Nevid, Javier, & Moulton, 1996).

Treatment providers may also be more successful if they recognize and incorporate indigenous forms of healing into treatment. For example, spirituality is an important aspect of traditional Native American culture, and spiritualists have played important roles as natural healers. Seeking the assistance of a spiritualist may improve the counseling relationship. Likewise, given the importance of the church in African American and Hispanic American cultures, counselors working with people with alcohol use disorders from these groups may be more successful when they draw on clergy and church members as resources.

Nonprofessional Support Groups

Despite the complexity of the factors contributing to substance abuse and dependence, these problems are frequently handled by laypeople or nonprofessionals. Such people often have or had the same problems themselves. For example, self-help group meetings are sponsored by organizations such as Alcoholics Anonymous, Narcotics Anonymous, and Cocaine Anonymous. These groups promote abstinence and provide members an opportunity to discuss their feelings and experiences in a supportive group setting. More experienced group members (sponsors) support newer members during periods of crisis or potential relapse. The meetings are sustained by nominal voluntary contributions.

The most widely used nonprofessional program, Alcoholics Anonymous (AA), is based on the belief that alcoholism is a disease, not a sin. The AA philosophy holds that that people suffering from alcoholism will never be cured, regardless of how long they abstain from alcohol, rather, people with alcoholism who remain "clean and sober" are seen as "recovering alcoholics." It is also assumed that people who suffer from alcoholism cannot control their drinking and need help to stop drinking. AA has more than 50,000 chapters in North America. AA is so deeply embedded in the consciousness of helping professionals that many of them automatically refer newly detoxified people to AA as the follow-up agency. About half of AA members have problems with illicit drugs as well as alcohol.

The AA experience is in part spiritual, in part group supportive, in part cognitive. AA follows a 12-step approach that focuses on accepting one's powerlessness over alcohol and turning one's will and life over to a higher power. This spiritual component may be helpful to some participants but distasteful to others. (Other lay organizations, such as Rational Recovery, adopt a nonspiritual approach.) The later steps focus on examining one's character flaws, admitting one's wrongdoings, being open to a higher power for help to overcome one's character defects, making amends to others, and, in step 12, bringing the AA message to other people suffering from alcoholism. Members are urged to pray or meditate to help them get in touch with their higher power. The meetings themselves provide group support. So does the buddy, or sponsor, system, which encourages members to call each other for support when they feel tempted to drink.

The success rate of AA remains in question, in large part because AA does not keep records of its members, but also because of an inability to conduct randomized clinical

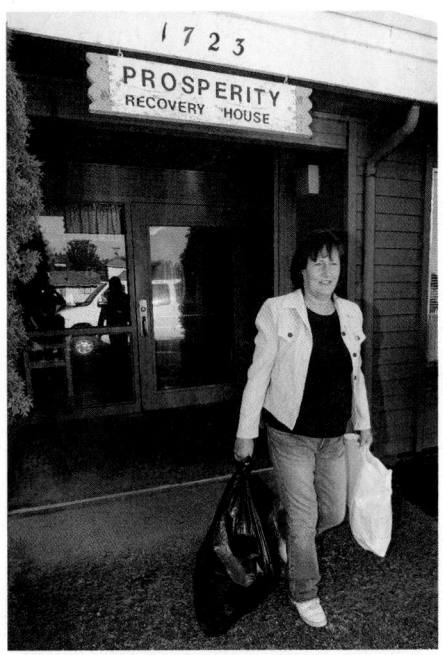

Culturally sensitive treatment. Culturally sensitive therapy or treatment addresses all aspects of the person, including ethnic factors and the nurturance of pride in one's cultural identity. Ethnic pride may help people resist the temptation to cope with stress through alcohol and other substances.

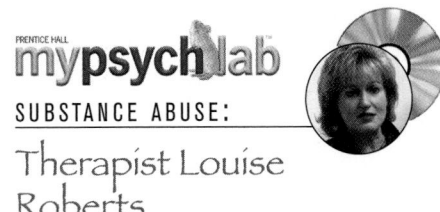

mypsychlab
SUBSTANCE ABUSE:
Therapist Louise Roberts
"You try to make sense out of an addiction that doesn't make sense."

trials in AA settings. However, we do have evidence that participation in AA is linked to lower frequency and intensity of drinking (Ferri et al., 2006). However, many people drop out of AA, as well as from other treatment programs. People who are more likely to do well with AA tend to be those who make a commitment to abstinence, who express intentions to avoid high-risk situations associated with alcohol use, and who stay longer with the program (McKellar, Stewart, & Humphreys, 2003; Moos & Moos, 2004; Morgenstern et al., 2002).

Al-Anon, begun in 1951, is a spin-off of AA that supports the families and friends of people suffering from alcoholism. Another spin-off of AA, Alateen, provides support to children whose parents have alcoholism, helping them see that they are not to blame for their parents' drinking and are thus undeserving of the guilt they may feel.

Residential Approaches

A residential approach to treatment requires a stay in a hospital or therapeutic residence. Hospitalization is recommended when substance abusers cannot exercise self-control in their usual environments, cannot tolerate withdrawal symptoms, or behave self-destructively or dangerously. Less-costly outpatient treatment is indicated when withdrawal symptoms are less severe, clients are committed to changing their behavior, and support systems, such as families, can help clients make the transition to a drug-free lifestyle. The great majority of alcohol-dependent patients are treated on an outpatient basis.

Most inpatient programs use an extended 28-day detoxification period. For the first few days, treatment focuses on helping clients with withdrawal symptoms. Then the emphasis shifts to counseling about the destructive effects of alcohol and combating distorted ideas or rationalizations. Consistent with the disease model, abstinence is the goal.

Most people with alcohol use disorders do not require hospitalization. A classic review article showed that outpatient and inpatient programs achieved about the same relapse rates (Miller & Hester, 1986). However, because medical insurance does not always cover outpatient treatment, many people who might benefit from outpatient treatment admit themselves for inpatient treatment instead.

A number of residential therapeutic communities are also in use. Some have part- or full-time professional staffs. Others are run entirely by laypeople. Residents are expected to remain free of drugs and take responsibility for their actions. They are often challenged to take responsibility for themselves and to acknowledge the damage caused by their drug abuse. They share their life experiences to help one another develop productive ways of handling stress.

As with AA, we lack evidence from controlled studies demonstrating the efficacy of residential-treatment programs. Also like AA, therapeutic communities have high numbers of early dropouts. Moreover, many residents relapse upon returning to the world outside.

Psychodynamic Approaches

Psychoanalysts view substance abuse and dependence as symptoms of conflicts rooted in childhood experiences. The therapist attempts to resolve the underlying conflicts, assuming that abusive behavior will then subside as the client seeks more mature forms of gratification. Although there are many successful psychodynamic case studies of people with substance abuse problems, there is a dearth of controlled and replicable research studies. The effectiveness of psychodynamic methods for treating substance abuse and dependence thus remains unsubstantiated.

Behavioral Approaches

Behavioral approaches to treating substance abuse and dependence focus on modifying abusive and dependent behavior patterns. The key question to behaviorally oriented therapists is not whether substance abuse and dependence are diseases but whether abusers can learn to change their behavior when they are faced with temptation.

Self-Control Strategies *Self-control training* helps abusers develop skills they can use to change their abusive behavior. Behavior therapists focus on three components—the "ABCs"— of substance abuse:

1. The *antecedent* cues or stimuli (As) that prompt or trigger abuse
2. The abusive *behaviors* (Bs) themselves
3. The reinforcing or punishing *consequences* (Cs) that maintain or discourage abuse

Table 9.2 shows the kinds of strategies used to modify the ABCs of substance abuse.

TABLE 9.2

Self-Control Strategies for Modifying the "ABCs" of Substance Abuse

1. Controlling the As (Antecedents) of Substance Abuse

People who abuse or become dependent on psychoactive substances become conditioned to a wide range of external (environmental) and internal stimuli (bodily states). They may begin to break these stimulus-response connections by:

- Removing drinking and smoking paraphernalia from the home—including all alcoholic beverages, beer mugs, carafes, ashtrays, matches, cigarette packs, lighters, etc.
- Restricting the stimulus environment in which drinking or smoking is permitted by using, the substance only in a stimulus-deprived area of their homes, such as the garage, bathroom, or basement. All stimuli that might be connected to using the substance are removed from this area—e.g., there is no TV, reading materials, radio, or telephone. In this way, substance abuse becomes detached from many controlling stimuli.
- Not socializing with others with substance abuse problems, by avoiding situations linked to abuse—bars, the street, bowling alleys, etc.
- Frequenting substance-free environments—lectures or concerts, a gym, museums, evening classes; and by socializing with nonabusers, eating in restaurants without liquor licenses.
- Managing the internal triggers for abuse. This can be done by practicing self-relaxation or meditation and not taking the substance when tense; by expressing angry feelings by writing them down or self-assertion, not by taking the substance; by seeking counseling not alcohol, pills, or cigarettes, for prolonged feelings of depression.

2. Controlling the Bs (Behaviors) of Substance Abuse

People can prevent and interrupt substance abuse by:

- Using response prevention—breaking abusive habits by physically preventing them from occurring or making them more difficult (e.g., by not bringing alcohol home or keeping cigarettes in the car).
- Using competing responses when tempted; by being prepared to handle substance-related situations with appropriate ammunition—mints, sugarless chewing gum, etc.; by taking a bath or shower, walking the dog, walking around the block, taking a drive, calling a friend, spending time in a substance-free environment, practicing meditation or relaxation, or exercising when tempted, rather than using the substance.
- Making abuse more laborious—buying one can of beer at a time; storing matches, ashtrays, and cigarettes far apart; wrapping cigarettes in foil to make smoking more cumbersome; pausing for 10 minutes when struck by the urge to drink, smoke, or use another substance and asking oneself, "Do I really need *this* one?"

3. Controlling the Cs (Consequences) of Substance Abuse

Substance abuse has immediate positive consequences such as pleasure, relief from anxiety and withdrawal symptoms, and stimulation. People can counter these intrinsic rewards and alter the balance of power in favor of nonabuse by:

- Rewarding themselves for nonabuse and punishing themselves for abuse.
- Switching to brands of beer and cigarettes they don't like.
- Setting gradual substance-reduction schedules and rewarding themselves for sticking to them.
- Punishing themselves for failing to meet substance-reduction goals. People with substance abuse problems can assess themselves, say, 10 cents for each slip and donate the cash to an unpalatable cause, such as a brother-in-law's birthday present.
- Rehearsing motivating thoughts or self-statements—such as writing reasons for quitting smoking on index cards. For example:
  - Each day I don't smoke adds another day to my life.
  - Quitting smoking will help me breathe deeply again.
  - Foods will smell and taste better when I quit smoking.
  - Think how much money I'll save by not smoking.
  - Think how much cleaner my teeth and fingers will be by not smoking.
  - I'll be proud to tell others that I kicked the habit.
  - My lungs will become clearer each and every day I don't smoke.

Smokers can carry a list of 20 to 25 such statements and read several of them at various times throughout the day. They can become parts of one's daily routine, a constant reminder of one's goals.

Contingency Management Programs Learning theorists believe that our behavior is shaped by rewards and punishments. Consider how virtually everything you do, from attending class to stopping at red lights to working for a paycheck, is influenced by the flow of reinforcements or rewards (money, praise, approval) and punishments (traffic tickets, rebukes). *Contingency management* (CM) programs provide reinforcements (rewards) contingent on performing desirable behaviors, such as producing drug-negative urine samples (Petry et al., 2005; Poling et al., 2006; Roll et al., 2006). In one example, one group of patients had the opportunity to draw from a bowl and win monetary rewards or prize money (rewards) ranging from $1 to $100 in value (Petry & Martin, 2002). The monetary reward was contingent on submitting clean urine samples for cocaine and opioids. On average, the contingency management (reward) group achieved longer periods of continual abstinence than the standard methadone treatment group. Investigators are finding that even modest rewards for abstinence can help improve therapeutic outcomes in treating substance abusers (Higgins, Heil, & Lussier, 2004; Higgins, 2006).

Aversive Conditioning In *aversive conditioning,* painful or aversive stimuli are paired with substance abuse or abuse-related stimuli to condition a negative emotional response to drug-related stimuli. In the case of problem drinking, tasting alcoholic beverages is usually paired with drugs that cause nausea and vomiting or with electric shock. As a consequence, alcohol may come to elicit an unpleasant emotional or physical reaction. Unfortunately, aversive conditioning effects are often temporary and fail to generalize to real-life settings in which aversive stimuli are no longer administered. However, it may be useful as a treatment component in a broader-based treatment program.

Social Skills Training Social skills training helps people develop effective interpersonal responses in social situations that prompt substance abuse. Assertiveness training, for example, may be used to train alcohol abusers to fend off social pressures to drink. Behavioral marital therapy seeks to improve marital communication and problem-solving skills with the goal of relieving marital stresses that can trigger abuse. Couples may learn how to use written behavioral contracts. For example, the person with a substance abuse problem might agree to abstain from drinking or to take Antabuse, while the spouse agrees to refrain from commenting on past drinking and the probability of future lapses. Evidence suggests that social skills training and behavioral marital therapy are useful in treating alcoholism (Finney & Monahan, 1996; O'Farrell et al., 1996).

Controlled Drinking: A Viable Goal? According to the disease model of alcoholism, people who suffer from the disease who have just one drink will lose control and go on a binge. Some professionals argue that behavior modification self-control techniques can teach many people with alcohol abuse or dependence to engage in *controlled drinking*—to have a drink or two without necessarily falling off the wagon (Sobell & Sobell, 1973a, 1973b, 1984). This contention remains controversial. The proponents of the disease model of alcoholism, who wield considerable political strength, strongly oppose attempts to teach controlled social drinking.

Controlled drinking programs may represent a pathway to abstinence for people who would not otherwise enter abstinence-only treatment programs (Marlatt et al., 1993). That is, a controlled drinking program can be a first step toward giving up drinking completely. By offering moderation as a treatment goal, controlled drinking programs may reach many people who refuse to participate in abstinence-only treatment programs (Marlatt et al., 1993). In the accompanying *Controversies in Abnormal Psychology*, Mark and Linda Sobell speak about what it was like to be in the eye of the storm of controversy over the issue of controlled drinking.

Relapse-Prevention Training

The word *relapse* derives from Latin roots meaning "to slide back." Between 50% to 90% of people who are successfully treated for substance abuse problems eventually relapse (Leary, 1996). Because of the prevalence of relapse, cognitive-behavioral therapists have devised a number of methods referred to as *relapse-prevention training.* This training is designed to help substance abusers identify high-risk situations and learn effective coping for handling

CONTROVERSIES IN ABNORMAL PSYCHOLOGY

In the Eye of the Storm: The Controlled Drinking Controversy

MARK AND LINDA SOBELL, IN THEIR OWN WORDS

Our careers began before we had our doctorates. In 1969, we began summer jobs at Patton State Hospital (CA). Within weeks, that evolved into an unusual opportunity to conduct federally funded alcohol research. We were in the right place at the right time. The field of behavioral therapy was in its infancy and witnessing some exciting advances. The scientific study of alcohol problems was also in its infancy. Early research at the hospital had demonstrated that severely dependent alcohol abusers could limit their drinking (e.g., drink just 1 to 3 drinks) in a supervised hospital environment. Furthermore, we found several published studies that suggested that some alcohol abusers could learn to drink moderately without losing control of their drinking. This led us to conduct our highly controversial study, "Individualized Behavior Therapy for Alcoholics" (Sobell & Sobell, 1973b).

Patients were evaluated for their eligibility for a moderate drinking goal, and those who qualified were randomly assigned either to an inpatient-based, broad-spectrum behavioral treatment program that had a controlled drinking goal or to a control group (i.e., standard hospital treatment with an abstinence goal). Those ineligible for a moderation goal were randomized to the behavioral treatment or the standard hospital treatment, both with an abstinence goal. Follow-up was conducted for 2 years (Sobell & Sobell, 1976); an independent double-blind third-year follow-up was also conducted (Caddy, Addington, & Perkins, 1978). Although both experimental groups had superior outcomes relative to their control groups, the moderate drinking group's superiority was maintained over a 3-year period, whereas differences between the abstinence goal groups were no longer significant after the 1-year follow-up. The moderate drinking group had more than twice as many "functioning well" days (i.e., not drinking or drinking just a few drinks) and twice as many abstinent days as their control group. The findings of our rigorous study challenged, as no other study had, the traditional view that only abstinence goals were effective.

In 1982 our careers almost ended when the journal *Science* published an article challenging the study's findings. Although the allegations were veiled in the article, in media interviews the authors claimed we had falsified our data (Marlatt, 1983). Fortunately, we had retained our original data (e.g., drivers' records, arrest records, tape-recorded interviews with clients). When the allegations were released, they triggered a media frenzy tantamount to a witch hunt. Several investigations eventually vindicated us. The first, a blue ribbon committee in Toronto, where we were employed, examined our data and concluded, "The Committee finds the Sobell's published data to be accurate, and concludes unequivocally that there is no evidence of fraud, deception, dishonesty or unethical behavior" (Dickens et al., 1982, p. 9). Shortly thereafter, there was a congressional investigation followed by an investigation by the National Institutes of Health and two ethics investigations by the American Psychological Association. In all instances, we were vindicated, as no investigation found evidence of fraud or deception. Nevertheless, the allegations traveled fast among traditional alcohol treatment programs and the public, leading many to the unquestioning assumption that controlled drinking had been "debunked." Unfortunately, because vindications are not as newsworthy as are allegations of fraud, many still are not aware of our vindication.

Why did the attack happen? In our published response to the attack (Sobell & Sobell, 1984) we interpreted what had occurred as a reflection of a scientific revolution. The alcohol field's prevailing view that abstinence was the only legitimate treatment goal was seriously threatened, and it was defended at all costs. Our accusers' objective, as stated in media interviews, was to expunge our work from the literature. Although this did not occur, it was clear that those pursuing moderate-drinking research did so at their own professional peril.

Replication is at the core of the scientific process. In the intervening years between the attack and now, many studies have demonstrated that low-risk or moderate drinking can be achieved in treating many problem drinkers (persons with low- to moderate-severity alcohol problems) (Sobell & Sobell, 1995). Research also shows that even chronic alcohol abusers treated with behavior therapy and a moderate drinking goal did better than control patients who were treated in a traditional abstinence-oriented program (Caddy et al., 1978; Sobell & Sobell, 1973a, 1973b, 1976). That's not to say that chronic alcohol abusers treated in moderate-drinking programs are problem free. Rather, we think of the outcomes of these programs in terms of *harm reduction*, meaning that participants suffer fewer negative consequences than control patients treated in traditional abstinence programs. An important legacy of our work was that it raised serious questions about the efficacy of traditional treatments, questions that remain largely unanswered.

Critical Thinking

- Do you believe that chronic alcohol abusers can learn to drink responsibly? Why or why not?
- What is the basis for determining when alcohol use becomes abuse or dependence? Have you or someone you know crossed the line between use and abuse?

Mark B. Sobell, Ph.D., ABPP, is Professor at the Center for Psychological Studies at Nova Southeastern University and Past-Editor of the *Journal of Consulting and Clinical Psychology* of the American Psychological Association.

Linda Sobell, Ph.D., ABPP, is Professor and Associate Director of Clinical Training at the Center for Psychological Studies at Nova Southeastern University and Past-President of the Association for Advancement of Behavior Therapy and of the Society of Clinical Psychology, American Psychological Association.

these situations without turning to alcohol or drugs skills (Witkiewicz & Marlatt, 2004). High-risk situations include negative mood states, such as depression, anger, or anxiety; interpersonal conflict (e.g., marital problems or conflicts with employers); and socially conducive situations such as "the guys getting together" (Chung & Maisto, 2006). Participants learn to cope with these situations, for example, by learning relaxation skills to counter anxiety and by learning to resist social pressures to drink. They also learn to avoid practices that might prompt a relapse, such as keeping alcohol on hand for friends.

Relapse prevention training also focuses on preventing *lapses* from turning into full-blown *relapses*. Clients learn about the importance of their *interpretations* of any lapses or slips that may occur, such as smoking a first cigarette or taking a first drink following quitting. They are taught not to overreact to a lapse by changing how they think about lapses. For example, they learn that people who lapse are more likely to relapse if they attribute their slip to personal weakness, and experience shame and guilt, than if they attribute the slip to an external or transient event. For example, consider a skater who slips on the ice (Marlatt & Gordon, 1985). Whether the skater gets back up and continues to perform depends largely on whether the skater sees the slip as an isolated and correctable event or as a sign of complete failure. Because lapses in ex-smokers often occur in response to withdrawal symptoms, it is important to help smokers develop ways of coping with these symptoms without resuming smoking (Piasecki et al., 2003). Participants in relapse-prevention training programs learn to view lapses as temporary setbacks that provide opportunities to learn what kinds of situations lead to temptation and to either avoid them or learn to cope with them. If they can learn to think, "Okay, I had a slip, but that doesn't mean all is lost unless I believe it is," they are less likely to relapse.

All in all, efforts to treat people with substance abuse and dependence problems have had mixed results at best. Many abusers really do not want to discontinue use of these substances, although they would prefer, if possible, to avoid their negative consequences. Yet many treatment approaches, including 12-step and cognitive-behavioral approaches, can work well when they are well delivered and when individuals desire change (Miller & Brown, 1997; Moos & Moos, 2005; Project MATCH Research Group, 1997).

Effective treatment programs include multiple approaches that match the needs of substance abusers and the range of problems with which they often present, including co-occurring psychiatric problems, such as depression and personality disorders (Grant et al., 2004; Nunes & Levin, 2004). *Comorbidity* (co-occurrence) of substance use disorders and other psychological disorders, especially mood disorders, have become the rule in treatment facilities rather than the exception (Morris, Stewart, & Ham, 2005; Quello, Brady, & Sonne, 2005). Not surprisingly, drug abuse treatment is often complicated by the presence of other serious psychological problems. As noted in this first-person narrative, the co-occurrence of substance abuse greatly complicates the treatment of other psychological disorders.

"I" "Surely They Can't Mean Beer!"

Six years ago, at the age of 24, I was diagnosed with manic-depression. Learning to live with this mental illness has been extremely difficult. I have been in a series of different hospitals. After suffering a manic episode and being hospitalized, I would attempt to recover, but within 90 days or so I would end up in a hospital again. I never really had a fair chance of recovering from my manic depression because I had been suffering from alcoholism, another illness, at the same time. The alcoholism wasn't being treated. After being discharged from hospitals I would resume drinking and then within a matter of a few months I would be back in another hospital having suffered another manic episode. It was strongly suggested to me when I was first diagnosed with manic depression that I should stop drinking. I remember my response clearly. "Surely they can't mean beer!"

My drinking escalated when I first joined a program known as Alcoholics Anonymous. During those years I was in complete denial of what alcohol was doing to the chemical make-up of my body. I drank in order to suppress the negative feelings of mania and depression. I had to live with double trouble and the more I drank the sicker I became. I simply refused to address my alcoholism problem because alcohol had become my best friend. Denial runs deep!

It took a family crisis where my parents told me they would no longer support me emotionally or financially if I ended up in the hospital and alcohol was involved. This scared me to the point where I called Alcoholics Anonymous and began attending AA meetings. It takes time but AA seems to be working for me. I have arrested my drinking problem through total abstinence. Now the medication I take has a chance to work the way it was intended. Stopping drinking alcohol is only part of the solution. For me, working with doctors who understand my manic depressive illness and getting the proper medication is the key to a successful recovery.

—*From Adam White, reprinted with permission of* New York City Voices

TYING IT TOGETHER

Substance abuse and dependence are complex patterns of behavior that reflect the interplay of biological, psychological, and environmental factors. These problems are best approached by investigating the distinctive constellation of factors that apply to each individual case. No single model or set of factors will explain each case, which is why we need to understand each individual's unique characteristics and personal history and direct treatment accordingly. The accompanying *Concept Map for Abnormal Psychology* illustrates key causal factors and major treatment approaches, along with a conceptual model for understanding how these causal factors interact.

Genetic factors can create a predisposition or diathesis for substance abuse and dependence. Some people may be born with a greater tolerance for alcohol, which can make it difficult for them to regulate use of alcohol—to know "when to say when." Others have genetic tendencies that can lead them to become unusually tense or anxious. Perhaps they turn to alcohol or other drugs to quell their nervousness. Genetic predispositions can interact with environmental factors to increase the potential for drug abuse and dependence—factors such as pressure from peers to use drugs, parental modeling of excessive drinking or drug use, and family disruption that results in a lack of effective guidance or support. Cognitive factors, especially positive drug expectancies (e.g., beliefs that using drugs will enhance one's social skills or sexual prowess), raise the potential for alcohol or drug use problems. In adolescence and adulthood, these positive expectations, together with social pressures and a lack of cultural constraints, affect the young person's decision to begin using drugs and to continue to use them. Patterns of regular use can lead to abuse and dependence. Once physiological dependence develops, people use the substance to avoid withdrawal symptoms.

Sociocultural and biological factors are also included in this matrix of factors: the availability of alcohol and other drugs; the presence or absence of cultural constraints; the glamorizing of drug use in popular media; and genetic tendencies (such as among Asians) to "flush" more readily following alcohol intake (Luczak, Glatt, & Wall, 2006).

Learning factors also play important roles. Drug use may be *positively* reinforced by pleasurable effects (mediated perhaps by release of dopamine in the brain or by activation of endorphin receptors). It may also be *negatively* reinforced by the reduction of tension and anxiety that depressant drugs such as alcohol, heroin, and tranquilizers can produce. In a sad but ironic twist, people who become dependent on drugs may continue to use them solely because of the relief from withdrawal symptoms and cravings they encounter when they go without the drug.

Although effective treatment programs are available, only a minority of people with alcohol dependence ever receive treatment, even when we define treatment broadly enough to include AA (Kranzler, 2006). A recent study in Canada echoed these findings. In a sample of more than 1,000 people in Ontario, Canada, with alcohol abuse or dependence disorders, only about one in three had ever received any treatment for their disorder (Cunningham & Breslin, 2004). Clearly more needs to be done to help people whose use of alcohol and other drugs puts them at risk.

In the case of inner-city youth who have become trapped within a milieu of street drugs and hopelessness, culturally sensitive drug counseling and job training would be of considerable benefit in helping them assume more productive social roles. The challenge is clear: to develop cost-effective ways of helping people recognize the negative effects of substances and forgo the powerful and immediate reinforcements they provide.

SUMMING UP

Classification of Substance-Related Disorders

How does the* DSM *distinguish between substance abuse disorders and substance dependence disorders? According to the *DSM*, a substance abuse disorder is a pattern of recurrent use of a substance that repeatedly leads to damaging consequences. Substance dependence disorders involve impaired control over use of a substance and often include features of physiological dependence on the substance, as manifest by the development of tolerance or an abstinence syndrome.

What do we mean by the terms "addiction" and "psychological dependence"? Although different people use the term *addiction* differently, it is used here to refer to the habitual or compulsive use of a substance combined with the development of physiological dependence. Psychological dependence is the *compulsive* use of a substance, with or without the development of physiological dependence.

Drugs of Abuse

What are depressants? Depressants are drugs that depress or slow down nervous system activity. They include alcohol, sedatives and minor tranquilizers, and opioids. Their effects include intoxication, impaired coordination, slurred speech, and impaired intellectual functioning. Chronic alcohol abuse is linked to alcohol-induced persisting amnestic disorder (Korsakoff's syndrome), cirrhosis of the liver, fetal alcohol syndrome, and other physical health problems. Barbiturates are depressants or sedatives that have been used medically for short-term relief of anxiety and treatment of epilepsy, among other uses. Opioids such as morphine and heroin are derived from the opium poppy. Others are synthesized. Opioids are used medically for relief of pain and are strongly addictive.

What are stimulants? Stimulants increase the activity of the central nervous system. Amphetamines and cocaine are stimulants that increase the availability of neurotransmitters in the brain, leading to heightened states of arousal and pleasurable feelings. High doses can produce psychotic reactions that mimic features of paranoid schizophrenia. Habitual cocaine use can lead to a variety of health problems, and an overdose can cause sudden death. Repeated use of nicotine, a mild stimulant found in cigarette smoking, leads to physiological dependence.

What are hallucinogens? Hallucinogens are drugs that distort sensory perceptions and can induce hallucinations. They include LSD, psilocybin, and mescaline. Other drugs with similar effects are cannabis (marijuana) and phencyclidine (PCP). Althoug these drugs may not lead to physiological dependence, psychological dependence may occur.

Theoretical Perspectives

How do the major theoretical perspectives view the causes of substance abuse and dependence? The biological perspective focuses on uncovering the biological pathways that may explain mechanisms of physiological dependence. The biological perspective spawns the disease model, which posits that alcoholism and other forms of substance dependence are disease processes. Learning perspectives view substance abuse disorders as learned patterns of behavior, with roles for classical and operant conditioning and observational learning. Cognitive perspectives focus on roles of attitudes, beliefs, and expectancies in accounting for substance use and abuse. Sociocultural perspectives emphasize the cultural, group, and social factors that underlie drug-use patterns, including the role of peer pressure in determining adolescent drug use. Psychodynamic theorists view problems of substance abuse, such as excessive drinking and habitual smoking, as signs of an oral fixation.

Treatment of Substance Abuse and Dependence

What treatment approaches are used to help people overcome problems of substance abuse and dependence? Biological approaches to substance abuse disorders include detoxification; the use of drugs such as disulfiram, methadone, naltrexone, and antidepressants; and nicotine replacement therapy. Residential treatment approaches include hospitals and therapeutic residences. Nonprofessional support groups, such as Alcoholics Anonymous, promote abstinence within a supportive group setting. Psychodynamic therapists focus on uncovering the inner conflicts originating in childhood that they believe lie at the root of substance abuse problems. Behavior therapists focus on helping people with substance-related problems change problem behaviors through such techniques as self-control training, aversive conditioning, and skills training approaches. Regardless of the initial success of a treatment technique, relapse remains a pressing problem in treating people with substance abuse problems. Relapse-prevention training employs cognitive-behavioral techniques to help recovering substance abusers cope with high-risk situations and prevent lapses from becoming relapses by interpreting lapses in less damaging ways.

KEY TERMS

substance-induced disorders (p. 291)
intoxication (p. 292)
substance use disorders (p. 292)
substance abuse (p. 292)
substance dependence (p. 292)
tolerance (p. 293)
withdrawal syndrome (p. 293)
addiction (p. 294)
physiological dependence (p. 294)

psychological dependence (p. 295)
depressant (p. 296)
alcoholism (p. 297)
barbiturates (p. 303)
narcotics (p. 303)
endorphins (p. 304)
morphine (p. 304)
heroin (p. 304)
stimulants (p. 305)

amphetamines (p. 305)
amphetamine psychosis (p. 305)
cocaine (p. 305)
crack (p. 306)
hallucinogens (p. 308)
marijuana (p. 309)
detoxification (p. 317)
methadone (p. 318)
naltrexone (p. 318)

KEY FOR "ARE YOU HOOKED?" QUESTIONNAIRE

Any yes answer suggests you may be dependent on alcohol. If you have answered any of these questions in the affirmative, we suggest you seriously examine what your drinking means to you.

MEDIA TOOLS

A variety of digital and online learning tools are available to enrich your learning experience and help you succeed in the course. These resources include:

- **MyPsychLab,** an online learning system for your course in abnormal psychology that allows you to test your mastery of concepts in the book by using chapter-by-chapter diagnostic tests. Results from the diagnostic tests help you build a customized study plan. To access **MyPsychLab,** visit www.prenhall.com/mypsychlab and follow the instructions on the site.

- **"SPEAKING OUT" PATIENT INTERVIEWS,** a set of video case examples of actual patients you can access on the companion CD-ROM included with the text. Icons in the margins of the chapter highlight the video case examples included on the CD-ROM.

- **COMPANION WEB SITE,** an online study center that offers computer-scored quizzes you can use to test your knowledge, along with other study tools and links to related sites to enhance your learning of abnormal psychology. To access the companion web site, visit www.prenhall.com/nevid and use the various tabs and links on the site to access these learning resources.

Substance-Related Disorders

are characterized by

Drug use leading to impaired physiological or psychological functioning

and are classified within two major categories of

- Substance Use Disorders (substance abuse and substance dependence disorders)
- Substance-Induced Disorders (including intoxication and delirium)

and involve multiple causes including

- Biological factors, such as genetic predispositions
- Learning factors, such as positive and negative reinforcement for using drugs, modeling influences, and conditioned cravings
- Cognitive factors, such as positive expectancies and enhanced self-efficacy associated with using drugs
- Sociocultural factors, such as peer pressure and exposure to a drug subculture
- Multiple factors acting together, as in this example of a potential causal pathway for substance abuse and dependence:

and may be treated by

- Cognitive-behavioral therapy to change drug-using behavior patterns and strengthen adaptive behaviors
- Biomedical therapies such as detoxification, antidepressant medication to curb drug cravings, chemical substitutes for addictive drugs, and drugs that block the effects of addictive substances
- Psychodynamic therapy aimed at identifying and resolving psychological conflicts underlying drug-using behavior
- Peer support groups and residential treatment programs

MODEL SPOTLIGHT

A Biopsychosocial Model of Substance Abuse and Dependence

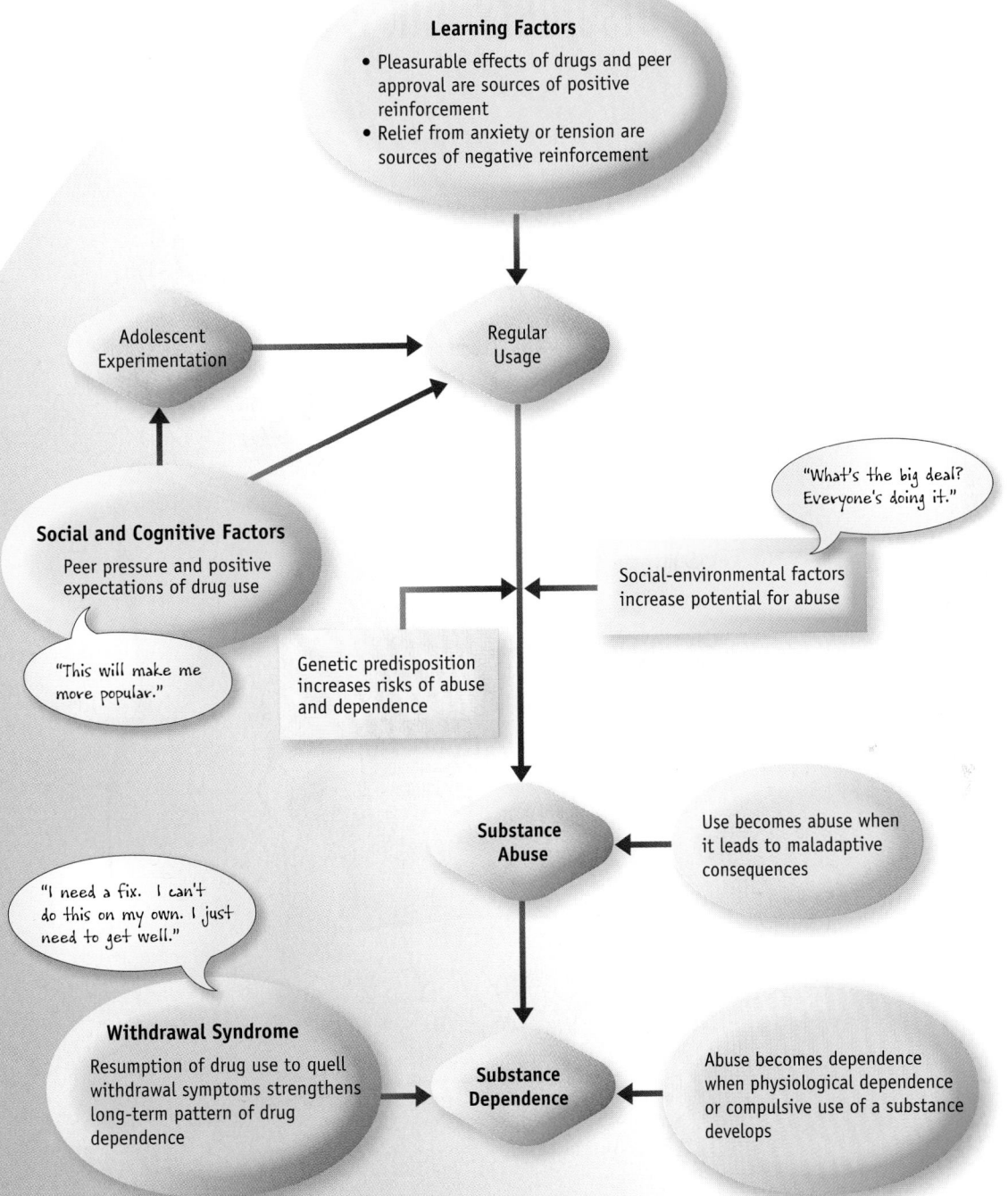

Eating Disorders and Sleep Disorders

CHAPTER OUTLINE

EATING DISORDERS 332–345

Anorexia Nervosa
Bulimia Nervosa
Causes of Anorexia and Bulimia
Treatment of Eating Disorders
Binge-Eating Disorder

Facing the Challenge of Obesity

SLEEP DISORDERS 345–354

Dyssomnias
Parasomnias
Treatment of Sleep Disorders

SUMMING UP 354–355

"I" "What's Up with That?"

Every night that I throw up I can't help but be afraid that my heart might stop or something else will happen. I just pray and hope I can stop this throwing up before it kills me. I hate this bulimia and I won't stop. It's hard for me to binge and throw up now (refrigerator is locked) and I just can't do it anymore. I just can't race through so much food so fast and then throw it up. I don't really want to. There are times that I do but not often. My new pattern is sure leaving me with an awful feeling in the morning. I eat dinner and kind of keep eating (snacking) afterwards to the point where I either feel too full or think (know) I've eaten too much, then I fall asleep (one hour or so) wake up and think I have to throw up. Half of me doesn't want to, the other half does and I always find myself throwing up. I try falling back asleep but it always seems like eventually sometime during the night I always throw up.

I feel crazy when I have a panic attack because someone I'm with is eating totally sugary foods, as though I'm afraid just being near it will somehow allow the food, or the fat, or the calories to attack me. Julie picked me up from class the other day, and she was eating dry sugar cookie mix from a bowl with a huge spoon. I panicked. I shook, perspired, had trouble taking full breaths, and couldn't focus or concentrate with all the thoughts rushing through my head. I wasn't eating it, but I could smell it and see it and heard the sugar crystals crunch as she chewed big mouthfuls of it. Then she started eating a cupcake. I couldn't handle it. She offered me some and I became severely nauseated by the mere thought of her offer. When she dropped me off, I raced into the house to gain control of this incredible binge. I was horrified and sick, saw myself gaining weight through my distorted vision, and immediately took laxatives to rid myself of all that forbidden food I felt inside, even though I hadn't eaten a thing.

After I calmed down, I realized the reality of the situation, and I felt stupid and crazy and like a total failure. Not only do I not need anyone else to abuse me, now I can do that myself. I don't even need a binge to have my purging cycle triggered to an intense degree. What's up with that?

—Costin, 1997, pp. 62–63

TRUTH or FICTION

T❑ F❑ Although others see them as extremely thin, young women with anorexia nervosa still see themselves as too fat. (p. 334)

T❑ F❑ Dieting is an abnormal eating pattern among American women. (p. 337)

T❑ F❑ Bulimic women induce vomiting only after binges. (p. 338)

T❑ F❑ Drugs used to treat depression may also help curb binge eating in bulimic women. (p. 340)

T❑ F❑ Obesity is one of the most common psychological disorders in the United States. (p. 344)

T❑ F❑ After Santa Claus, the most recognizable figure to children is Ronald McDonald. (p. 345)

T❑ F❑ Many people suffer from sleep attacks in which they suddenly fall asleep without any warning. (p. 349)

T❑ F❑ Some people literally gasp for breath hundreds of times during sleep without realizing it. (p. 349)

THE YOUNG WOMAN WHO WROTE THIS VIGNETTE HAS *BULIMIA NERVOSA*, AN EATING DISORDER characterized by repeated episodes of binge eating and purging. How can we explain eating disorders like *bulimia nervosa* and *anorexia nervosa*, a psychological disorder of self-starvation that can lead to serious medical consequences, even death? Eating disorders primarily affect young people of high school or college age, especially young women. Even if you don't know anyone with a diagnosable eating disorder, chances are you know people with disturbed eating behaviors such as occasional binge eating and excessive dieting. You probably also know people who suffer from obesity, a major health problem that affects increasing numbers of Americans.

This chapter explores the eating disorders of anorexia and bulimia as well as a newly proposed disorder, binge-eating disorder. We also examine factors that contribute to obesity, a health problem that has reached epidemic proportions in our society. Our focus in this chapter also extends to another set of problems that commonly affects young adults: sleep disorders. The most common form of sleep disorder, chronic insomnia, affects many young people who are making their way in the world and tend to bring their worries and concerns to bed with them.

EATING DISORDERS

anorexia nervosa An eating disorder characterized by maintenance of an abnormally low body weight, a distorted body image, intense fears of gaining weight, and in females, amenorrhea.

bulimia nervosa An eating disorder characterized by recurrent binge eating followed by self-induced purging, accompanied by overconcern with body weight and shape.

eating disorder A psychological disorder characterized by disturbed patterns of eating and maladaptive ways of controlling body weight.

In a nation of plenty, some people literally starve themselves—sometimes to death. They are obsessed with their weight and desire to achieve an exaggerated image of thinness. Others engage in repeated cycles in which they binge on food and then attempt to purge their excess eating, such as by inducing vomiting. These dysfunctional patterns are, respectively, the two major types of eating disorders, **anorexia nervosa** and **bulimia nervosa.**

Eating disorders are characterized by disturbed patterns of eating and maladaptive ways of controlling body weight. Like many other psychological disorders, anorexia and bulimia are often accompanied by other forms of psychopathology, including depression, anxiety disorders, and substance abuse disorders. Table 10.1 provides an overview of the eating disorders we examine in this chapter.

The great majority of cases of anorexia and bulimia occur among young women. Although eating disorders may develop in middle or even late adulthood, they typically begin during adolescence or early adulthood when the pressures to be thin are the strongest. As these social pressures have increased, so too have rates of eating disorders. An estimated 2 million college women in the United States are believed to be affected by diagnosable eating disorders (González et al., 2003). Results of a large, population-based survey indicate that anorexia affects about 0.9% of women in our society (about 9 in 1,000) (Hudson et al., 2006). Bulimia is believed to affect about 1% to 3% of women (APA, 2000).

Rates of anorexia and bulimia among men are estimated at about 0.3% (3 in 1,000) for anorexia and 0.1% 0.3% (1 to 3 in a thousand) for bulimia (APA, 2000; Hudson et al., 2006). Many men with anorexia participate in sports, such as wrestling, that impose pressures on maintaining weight within a narrow range.

Many women show anorexic or bulimic behaviors but not to the point that they would warrant a diagnosis of an eating disorder. Studies of college women indicate that perhaps 1 in 2 have binged and purged at least once (Fairburn & Wilson, 1993).

Table 10.1 Overview of Eating Disorders

TYPE OF DISORDER	Lifetime Prevalence in Population (approx.)	Description	Associated Features
Anorexia Nervosa	0.9%, or 9 in 1,000 women; about 0.3%, or 3 in 1,000 men	Self-starvation, resulting in a minimal weight for one's age and height or dangerously unhealthy weight	• Strong fears of gaining weight or becoming fat • Distorted self-image (perceiving oneself as fat despite extreme thinness) • Two general subtypes: binge-eating/purging type and restrictive type • Potentially serious, even fatal medical complications • Typically affects young, European American women
Bulimia Nervosa	1%–3% in women; about 0.1%–0.3% in men	Recurrent episodes of binge eating followed by purging	• Weight is usually maintained within a normal range • Overconcern about body shape and weight • Binge–purge episodes may result in serious medical complications • Typically affects young, European American women
Binge-Eating Disorder (a proposed diagnosis requiring further study)	3% in women; 2% in men	Recurrent binge eating without compensatory purging	• Individuals with BED frequently are described as compulsive overeaters • Typically affects obese women who are older than those affected by anorexia or bulimia

Source: APA, 2000; Hudson et al., 2006.

Anorexia Nervosa

◇

The Case of Karen

Karen was the 22-year-old daughter of a renowned English professor. She had begun her college career full of promise at the age of 17, but two years ago, after "social problems" occurred, she had returned to live at home and taken progressively lighter course loads at a local college. Karen had never been overweight, but about a year ago her mother noticed that she seemed to be gradually "turning into a skeleton."

Karen spent literally hours every day shopping at the supermarket, butcher, and bakeries conjuring up gourmet treats for her parents and younger siblings. Arguments over her lifestyle and eating habits had divided the family into two camps. The camp led by her father called for patience; that headed by her mother demanded confrontation. Her mother feared that Karen's father would "protect her right into her grave" and wanted Karen placed in residential treatment "for her own good." The parents finally compromised on an outpatient evaluation.

At an even 5 feet, Karen looked like a prepubescent 11-year-old. Her nose and cheekbones protruded crisply. Her lips were full, but the redness of the lipstick was unnatural, as if too much paint had been dabbed on a corpse for the funeral. Karen weighed only 78 pounds, but she had dressed in a stylish silk blouse, scarf, and baggy pants so that not one inch of her body was revealed.

Karen vehemently denied that she had a problem. Her figure was "just about where I want it to be" and she engaged in aerobic exercise daily. A deal was struck in which outpatient treatment would be tried as long as Karen lost no more weight and showed steady gains back to at least 90 pounds. Treatment included a day hospital with group therapy and two meals a day. But word came back that Karen was artfully toying with her food—cutting it up, sort of licking it, and moving it about her plate—rather than eating it. After 3 weeks Karen had lost another pound. At that point, her parents were able to persuade her to enter a residential treatment program, where her eating behavior could be more carefully monitored.

—From the Author's Files

The word *anorexia* derives from the Greek roots *an-*, meaning "without," and *orexis*, meaning "a desire for." *Anorexia* thus means "without desire for [food]," which is something of a misnomer, because people with anorexia nervosa rarely lose their appetite. However, they may be repelled by food and refuse to eat more than is absolutely necessary to maintain a minimal weight for their ages and heights. Often, they starve themselves to the point where they become dangerously emaciated. Anorexia nervosa usually develops between the ages of 12 and 18, although earlier and later onsets are sometimes found.

Table 10.2 shows the clinical features used to diagnose anorexia nervosa. Although reduced body weight is the most obvious sign, the most prominent

TABLE 10.2

Diagnostic Features of Anorexia Nervosa

A. Refusal to maintain weight at or above the minimal normal weight for one's age and height; for example, a weight more than 15% below normal.

B. Strong fear of putting on weight or becoming fat, despite being thin.

C. A distorted body image in which one's body—or part of one's body—is perceived as fat, although others perceive the person as thin.

D. In case of females who have had menarche, absence of three or more consecutive menstrual periods.

Source: Adapted from the *DSM-IV-TR* (APA, 2000).

ANOREXIA NERVOSA–
BINGE-EATING/PURGING
TYPE:

The Case of Jessica

"The diet started being my only way of getting control."

TRUTH or FICTION

Although others see them as extremely thin, young women with anorexia nervosa still see themselves as too fat.

☑**TRUE.** Others may see them as nothing but "skin and bones," but anorexic women have a distorted body image and may still see themselves as too fat.

How do I see myself? A distorted body image is a key component of eating disorders.

clinical feature is an intense fear of obesity. One common pattern of anorexia begins after menarche when the girl notices added weight and insists it must come off. The addition of body fat is normal in adolescent females: in an evolutionary sense, fat is added in preparation for childbearing and nursing. But anorexic women seek to rid their bodies of any additional weight and so turn to extreme dieting and, often, excessive exercise. However, these efforts continue unabated after the initial weight-loss goal is achieved even after family and friends express concern. Another common pattern occurs when young women leave home to attend college and encounter difficulties adjusting to the demands of college life and independent living. Anorexia is also common among young women involved in ballet or modeling, both fields that place strong emphasis on maintaining an unrealistically thin body shape.

Adolescent girls and women with anorexia almost always deny that they are losing too much weight. They may argue that their ability to engage in stressful exercise demonstrates their fitness. Women with eating disorders are more likely than normal women to have a distorted body image. Other people may see them as nothing but "skin and bones," but anorexic women still see themselves as too fat. Although they literally starve themselves, they may spend much of the day thinking and talking about food and even preparing elaborate meals for others.

Subtypes of Anorexia There are two general subtypes of anorexia, a *binge-eating/purging type* and a *restrictive type*. The first type is characterized by frequent episodes of binge eating and purging; the second type is not. Although repeated cycles of binge eating and purging occur in bulimia, bulimic individuals do not reduce their weight to anorexic levels. The distinction between the subtypes of anorexia is supported by differences in personality patterns. Individuals with the eating/purging type tend to have problems relating to impulse control, which in addition to binge-eating episodes may involve substance abuse or stealing. They tend to alternate between periods of rigid control and impulsive behavior. Those with the restrictive type tend to rigidly, even obsessively, control their diet and appearance.

Medical Complications of Anorexia Anorexia can lead to serious medical complications that in extreme cases can be fatal. Losses of as much as 35% of body weight may occur, and anemia may develop. Females suffering from anorexia are also likely to encounter dermatological problems such as dry, cracking skin; fine, downy hair; even a yellowish discoloration of the skin that may persist for years after weight is regained. Cardiovascular complications include heart irregularities, hypotension (low blood pressure), and associated dizziness upon standing, sometimes causing blackouts. Decreased food ingestion can cause gastrointestinal problems such as constipation, abdominal pain, and obstruction or paralysis of the bowels or intestines. Menstrual irregularities are common, and amenorrhea (absence or suppression of menstruation) is part of the clinical definition of anorexia in females. Muscular weakness and abnormal growth of bones may occur, causing loss of height and osteoporosis. High rates of suicide are also reported for patients with anorexia (Franko & Keel, 2006).

Bulimia Nervosa

The Case of Nicole

Nicole has only opened her eyes, but already she wishes it was time for bed. She dreads going through the day, which threatens to turn out like so many other recent days. Each morning she wonders if this will be the day that she will be able to get by without being obsessed by thoughts of food. Or will she spend the day gorging herself? Today is the day she will get off to a new start, she promises herself. Today she will begin to live like a normal person. Yet she is not convinced that it is really up to her.

Nicole starts the day with eggs and toast. Then she goes to work on cookies; doughnuts; bagels smothered with butter, cream cheese, and jelly; granola; candy bars; and bowls of cereal and milk—all within 45 minutes. Then she cannot take in any more food and turns her attention to purging what she has eaten. She goes to the bathroom, ties back her hair, turns on the shower to mask any noise she will make, drinks a glass of water, and makes herself vomit. Afterward she vows, "Starting tomorrow, I'm going to change." But she suspects that tomorrow may be just another chapter of the same story.

—*Adapted from Boskind-White & White, 1983, p. 29*

mypsych lab
BULIMIA:
The Case of Ann
"I was just afraid to go home and be around food."

Nicole suffers from bulimia nervosa. *Bulimia* derives from the Greek roots *bous,* meaning "ox" or "cow," and *limos,* meaning "hunger." The unpretty picture inspired by the origin of the term is one of continuous eating, like a cow chewing its cud. Bulimia nervosa is an eating disorder characterized by recurrent episodes of gorging on large quantities of food, followed by use of inappropriate ways to prevent weight gain. These may include purging by means of self-induced vomiting; use of laxatives, diuretics, or enemas; or fasting or engaging in excessive exercise (see Table 10.3). A person with bulimia may use two or more strategies for purging, such as vomiting and laxatives. Although people with anorexia are extremely thin, bulimic individuals are usually of normal weight. However, they have an excessive concern about their shape and weight.

Bulimic individuals typically gag themselves to induce vomiting. Most attempt to conceal their behavior. Fear of gaining weight is a constant factor. Although an overconcern with body shape and weight is a cardinal feature of bulimia and anorexia, bulimic individuals do not pursue the extreme thinness characteristic of anorexia. Their ideal weights are similar to those of women who do not suffer from eating disorders.

The binge itself usually occurs in secret, most commonly at home during unstructured afternoon or evening hours (Drewnowski, 1997; Guertin, 1999). A binge typically lasts from 30 to 60 minutes and involves consumption of forbidden foods that are generally sweet and rich in fat. Binge eaters typically feel they lack control over their bingeing and may consume 5,000 to 10,000 calories at a sitting. One young woman described eating everything available in the refrigerator, even to the point of scooping out margarine from its container with her finger. The episode continues until the binger is spent or exhausted, suffers painful stomach distension, induces vomiting, or runs out of food. Drowsiness, guilt, and depression usually ensue, but bingeing is initially pleasant because of release from dietary constraints.

Bulimia nervosa typically affects women in late adolescence or early adulthood, when concerns about dieting and dissatisfaction with body shape or weight are at their height (APA, 2000). Despite the widespread belief that eating disorders, especially anorexia nervosa, are most common among affluent people, available evidence shows

TABLE 10.3

Diagnostic Features of Bulimia Nervosa

A. Recurrent episodes of binge eating (gorging) as shown by both:
  1. Eating an unusually high quantity of food during a 2-hour period, and
  2. Sense of loss of control over food intake during the episode.

B. Regular inappropriate behavior to prevent weight gain, such as self-induced vomiting; abuse of laxatives, diuretics, or enemas; or fasting or excessive exercise.

C. A minimum average of two episodes a week of binge eating and inappropriate compensatory behavior to prevent weight gain over a period of at least 3 months.

D. Persistent overconcern with the shape and weight of one's body.

Source: Adapted from the *DSM-IV-TR* (APA, 2000).

no strong linkage between socioeconomic status and eating disorders (Wakeling, 1996). Beliefs that eating disorders are associated with high socioeconomic status may reflect the tendency for affluent patients to obtain treatment. Alternatively, it may be that the social pressures on young women to strive to achieve an ultrathin ideal have now generalized across all socioeconomic levels.

Medical Complications of Bulimia Like anorexia, bulimia is associated with many medical complications. Many of these stem from repeated vomiting: skin irritation around the mouth due to frequent contact with stomach acid, blockage of salivary ducts, decay of tooth enamel, and dental cavities. The acid from the vomit may damage taste receptors on the palate, making the person less sensitive to the taste of vomit with repeated purging. Decreased sensitivity to the aversive taste of vomit may help maintain the purging behavior. Cycles of bingeing and vomiting may cause abdominal pain, hiatal hernia, and other abdominal complaints, as well as disturbed menstrual functioning. Stress on the pancreas may produce pancreatitis (inflammation), which is a medical emergency. Excessive use of laxatives may cause bloody diarrhea and laxative dependency, so the person cannot have normal bowel movements without laxatives. In extreme cases, the bowel can lose its reflexive eliminatory response to pressure from waste material. Bingeing on large quantities of salty food may cause convulsions and swelling. Repeated vomiting or abuse of laxatives can lead to potassium deficiency, producing muscular weakness, cardiac irregularities, even sudden death—especially when diuretics are used. As with anorexia, menstruation may come to a halt. Although patients with bulimia do not appear to have elevated risks of completed suicide, a very high percentage, estimated at 25% to 35%, make suicide attempts (Franko & Keel, 2006).

Causes of Anorexia and Bulimia

Like other psychological disorders, anorexia and bulimia involve a complex interplay of factors (Polivy & Herman, 2002). Most significant are social pressures that lead young women to base their self-worth on their physical appearance, especially their weight.

Sociocultural Factors Sociocultural theorists point to social pressures and expectations placed on young women in our society as contributing factors in eating disorders (Mendez, 2005; The McKnight Investigators, 2003). The pressure to achieve an unrealistic standard of thinness, combined with the importance attached to appearance in defining the female role in society, can lead young women to become dissatisfied with their bodies (Stice, 2001). These pressures are underscored by findings that among college women in one sample, 1 in 7 (14%) reported that buying a single chocolate bar in a store would cause them to feel embarrassed (Rozin, Bauer, & Catanese, 2003). In another study, peer pressure to adhere to a thin body shape emerged as a strong predictor of bulimic behavior in young women (Young, McFatter, & Clopton, 2001).

Exposure to media images of ultrathin women can lead to the internalization of a thin ideal, setting the stage for body dissatisfaction (Blowers et al., 2003; Cafri et al., 2005). Even in children as young as eight, girls express more dissatisfaction with their bodies than do boys (Ricciardelli & McCabe, 2001). Body dissatisfaction in young women may lead to excessive dieting and to the development of disturbed eating behaviors. Even on laboratory tasks, women with high levels of bulimic symptoms show greater attention to cues relating to body size than do other women (Viken et al., 2002). Although eating disorders in men are much less common, investigators link body dissatisfaction to symptoms of eating disorders in college men (Olivardia et al., 2004).

The idealization of thinness in women can be illustrated in the changes in the **body mass index (BMI)** of winners of the Miss America pageant (Rubinstein & Caballero, 2000) (see Figure 10.1). BMI is a measure of height-adjusted weight. Notice the downward trend. What messages about feminine beauty might this be conveying to young women and young men?

body mass index (BMI) A standard measure of overweight and obesity that takes both body weight and height into account.

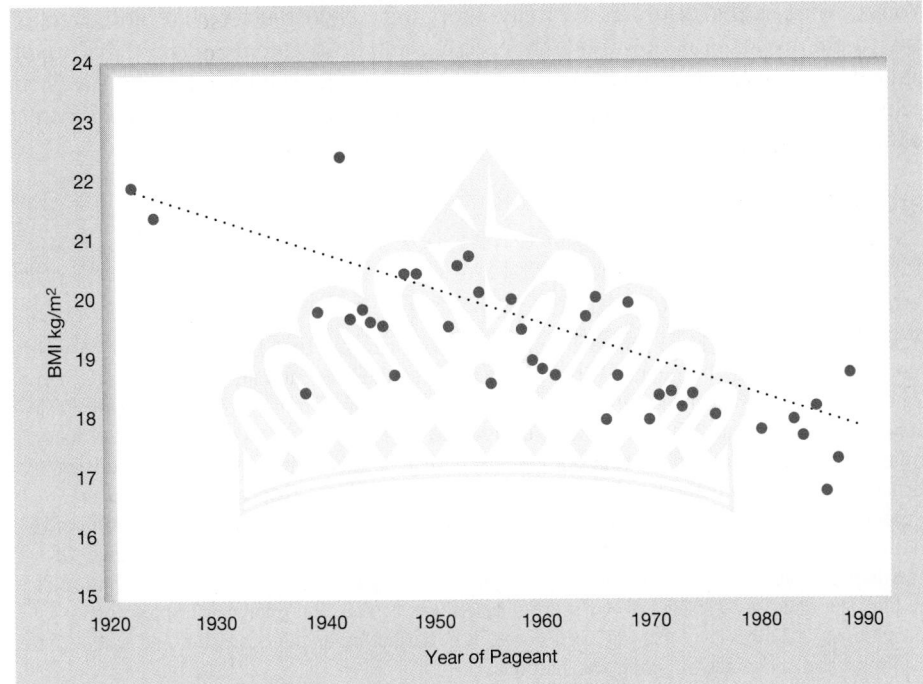

FIGURE 10.1 Thinner and thinner.
Note the downward trend in the body mass index levels (BMIs) of Miss America contest winners over time. What might these data suggest about changes in society's view of the ideal female form?

Source: Rubinstein & Caballero (2000).

The pressure to be thin is so prevalent that dieting has become the normative pattern of eating among young American women. Four out of five young women in the United States have gone on a diet by the time they reach their 18th birthdays. A recent survey of a sample of college women showed that regardless of how much they weighed, the great majority, about 80%, reported dieting (Malinauskas et al., 2006). Concerns about social pressures to be thin bring to light the idealized body images to which girls are exposed, including perhaps the most famous of all ultrathin ideals—Barbie (see the nearby *Controversies in Abnormal Psychology* feature).

In support of the sociocultural model, eating disorders are less common, even rare, in non-Western countries (Stice, 1994; Wakeling, 1996). Even in non-Western countries, such as in East Africa, the level of exposure to media and Western contact (e.g., travel abroad) is associated with a higher rate of eating disorder symptoms in young women (Eddy, Hennessey, & Thompson-Brenner, 2007).

Eating disorders in developing countries may be linked to factors other than obsessive concerns about weight. For example, among young women in the African country of Ghana, researchers found that extreme thinness was linked to fasting for religious reasons rather than weight concerns (Bennett et al., 2004). Rates of disordered eating behaviors and eating disorders also vary in the United States among ethnic groups, with higher rates found among Euro American adolescents than among African American and other ethnic minority adolescents (Lamberg, 2003; Striegel-Moore et al., 2003). One likely reason for this discrepancy is that body image and body dissatisfaction are less closely tied to body weight among minority women (Angier, 2000b). That said, investigators expect that the prevalence of eating disorders in young women of color will rise with increased exposure to Eurocentric concepts of feminine beauty (Gilbert, 2003).

Disturbed eating behaviors may also be more common among ethnic minority groups, including Native Americans, than is commonly believed (Shaw et al., 2004; Smith & Krejci, 1991). Likewise, investigators caution that body dissatisfaction may be more prevalent among Hispanic and Asian girls than is generally recognized and that this may set the stage for distorted eating behaviors in these groups (Robinson et al., 1996).

Psychosocial Factors Although cultural pressures to conform to an ultrathin female ideal play a major role in eating disorders, the great majority of young women exposed to these pressures do not develop eating disorders. Other factors must be involved. A pattern of overly restricted dieting is common to women with bulimia and anorexia.

TRUTH or FICTION

Dieting is an abnormal eating pattern among American women.

☑ **FALSE.** Dieting has become such a common pattern that it is now essentially the normative pattern of eating among American women.

Women with eating disorders typically adopt very rigid dietary rules and practices about what they can eat, how much they can eat, and how often they can eat. It's important to recognize, however, that eating disorders involve deeper emotional issues involving feelings of insecurity, body dissatisfaction, and use of food for emotional gratification, as illustrated in this woman's first-hand account.

"I"
My Voice, My Cry for Help

I started dieting when I was 13. As I look back now, I can see that I had feelings of insecurity that were surfacing as I struggled with relationships, my identity, and my sexuality. Back then it just felt like I was too fat. As my body began to change from a normal undeveloped child to a rounder, curvier woman, I held on to the ideals I saw in the media of the very thin, tall, hard bodies that defined beauty. My body was wrong. All my emotional struggles and insecurities became placed on my body. The first day I put myself on a diet, I stopped listening to the wisdom and truth of my own body. I began instead the pattern of forcing myself to conform to cultural standards that were impossible for me to obtain. My soul was crying out for love, for reassurance, security, and emotional soothing during a very overwhelming, confusing period in my life. The only way I knew how to soothe myself was to eat. The only way I knew how to be accepted was to diet. My voice, my cry for help was buried under the obsession and compulsion of dieting and bingeing, bingeing and purging.

Source: Normandi & Rorak, 1998

Death by Starvation. A leading fashion model, Brazilian Ana Carolina Reston, was just 21 when she died in 2006 from complications due to anorexia. At the time of her death, the 5'7" Reston weighed only 88 pounds. Anorexia is a widespread problem among fashion models today, as it is among people in other occupations in which great emphasis is put on unrealistic standards of thinness.

From a learning perspective, we can conceptualize eating disorders as a type of weight phobia. In this model, relief from anxiety acts as negative reinforcement. Bulimic women tend to have been slightly overweight before they developed bulimia, and the binge–purge cycle usually begins after a period of strict dieting to lose weight. In a typical scenario, the rigid dietary controls fail, leading to a loss of inhibitions (disinhibition), which prompts a binge-eating episode. The binge eating induces fear of weight gain, which in turn prompts self-induced vomiting or excessive exercise. Some bulimic women even resort to vomiting after every meal. Purging is negatively reinforced because it produces relief, or at least partial relief, from anxiety over gaining weight. Similarly for women with anorexia, food-rejecting behavior (and purging in cases of the binge-eating/purging subtype) is negatively reinforced by relief from anxiety about weight gain.

Body dissatisfaction is also an important factor in eating disorders. Body dissatisfaction may lead to maladaptive attempts—through self-starvation and purging—to attain a desired body weight or shape. Bulimic and anorexic women tend to be extremely concerned about their body weight and shape (Jacobi et al., 2004). Even many normal-weight children express concerns about their weight—concerns that may set the stage for the development of disturbed eating behaviors in adolescence ("Nutrition, Obesity and Perception," 2001).

Cognitive factors are also important. Young women with anorexia often hold perfectionistic attitudes (Bardone-Cone et al., 2006; Lilenfeld et al., 2006; Pearson & Gleaves, 2006). They may impose unreasonable pressures on themselves to achieve a "perfect body" and get down on themselves when they fail to meet their impossibly high standards. Their extreme dieting may give them a sense of control and independence that they feel they lack in other aspects of their lives.

Bulimic women also tend to think in dichotomous or "black or white" terms. Thus, they expect to adhere perfectly to their rigid dietary rules and judge themselves as complete failures when they deviate even slightly. They also judge themselves harshly for episodes of binge eating and purging. They may also hold exaggerated beliefs about the negative consequences of gaining weight, which further contributes to disordered eating. Recent evidence shows that women with eating disorders tend to heap blame on themselves for negative events in general, and self-blame most probably contributes to maintaining their disordered eating behavior (Morrison, Waller, & Lawson, 2006).

CONTROVERSIES IN ABNORMAL PSYCHOLOGY

Should Barbie Be Banned?

We're not suggesting that Barbie and her entourage be thrown overboard in some modern-day version of the Boston Tea Party, or that stores be prohibited from selling the popular toys. But by raising such a provocative question we hope to encourage you to think critically about the effects that these anatomically incorrect figurines may have on the psyches of young women. As writer Laura Vanderkam (2003) notes in her article, "Barbie and Fat as a Feminist Issue," Barbie was designed to fit the idealized male fantasy of a bosomy but impossibly thin female form, and then sold to girls who grew up wanting to look like her. Social worker Abigail Natenshon, author of *When Your Child Has an Eating Disorder*, argues that images of Barbie and ultrathin female models and actresses create expectations in the minds of young women about how they are supposed to look. Though many factors undoubtedly contribute to eating disorders, should parents keep Barbie at bay and not bring the doll into their homes? Or should they welcome Barbie but help their daughters see that her ultrathin form is not a female ideal, and help them understand that self-esteem should not be measured by a bathroom scale?

For that matter, should parents inform their sons that bulked-up wrestlers, muscularized movie heroes, and even action figures in video games are not exemplars of what they should aspire to? Even GI Joe–type action figures (i.e., dolls) appear more muscular today than in earlier versions.

Exposure to overly masculinized male images may create pressures on boys that can lead to disturbed eating behaviors, just as young women feel pressured to look like ultrathin magazine models ("Male Eating Disorders," 2004). Evidence shows that many men express dissatisfaction with their bodies (Tiggemann, Martins, & Kirkbride, 2007). For either gender, regular exposure to "perfect" bodies may reinforce the idea that "normal" bodies are not acceptable.

On the other hand, Vanderkam cautions us not to the throw the "Barbie" out with the bathwater (apologies for the pun). In light of the epidemic of obesity facing our society, perhaps we should champion the active, energetic lifestyle that Barbie embodies. What do you think?

Critical Thinking

- Assume you are a parent of a young boy or girl. Would you restrict the kinds of toys you buy based on considerations of appropriate body size and weight? Why or why not?
- What messages should parents convey to children regarding the overly slenderized and masculinized images that children regularly see?

To be like Barbie. The Barbie doll has long represented a symbol of the buxom but thin feminine form that has become idealized in our culture. If women were to be proportioned like the classic Barbie doll, they would resemble the woman in the photograph on the right. To achieve this idealized form, the average woman would need to grow nearly a foot in height, reduce her waist by 5 inches, and add 4 inches to her bustline. What message do you think the Barbie-doll figure conveys to young girls?

Is this normal? Body dissatisfaction is not limited to young women. Regular exposure to overly muscularized masculine images may reinforce the idea that "normal" bodies are not acceptable.

Although anorexia is far more common in women than in men, an increasing number of young men are presenting with disturbed eating behavior, even anorexia. Many of the factors associated with disturbed eating behavior in young men parallel those in young women, such as perfectionism, perceived pressures from others to lose weight, and participation in sports that place a strong value on leanness (Ricciardelli & McCabe, 2004).

Psychodynamically oriented writers believe that girls with anorexia have difficulty separating from their families and consolidating separate, individuated identities (e.g., Bruch, 1973; Minuchin, Rosman, & Baker, 1978). Perhaps anorexia represents the girl's unconscious effort to remain a prepubescent child. By maintaining the veneer of childhood, pubescent girls may avoid dealing with such adult issues as increased independence and separation from their families, sexual maturation, and assumption of adult responsibilities.

Bulimia is also linked to problems in interpersonal relationships. Bulimic women tend to be shy and to have few if any close friends (Fairburn et al., 1997). Enhancing the social skills of women with bulimia may increase the quality of their relationships and perhaps reduce their tendencies to use food in maladaptive ways.

Young women with bulimia tend to have more emotional problems and lower self-esteem than other dieters (Jacobi et al., 2004). We often find that bulimia is accompanied by other diagnosable disorders, such as depression, obsessive–compulsive disorder, and substance-related disorders (O'Brien & Vincent, 2003; Stice, Burton, & Shaw, 2004). This suggests that some forms of binge eating represent attempts at coping with emotional distress (Sherwood et al., 2000). Unfortunately, cycles of bingeing and purging exacerbate emotional problems rather than relieve them. We also have learned that bulimic women are more likely than other women to have experienced childhood sexual and physical abuse (Kent & Waller, 2000). In some cases, bulimia may develop as an ineffective means of coping with abuse.

Family Factors Eating disorders frequently develop against a backdrop of family problems and conflicts. Some theorists focus on the brutal effect of self-starvation on parents. They suggest that some adolescents refuse to eat to punish their parents for feelings of loneliness and alienation they experience in the home. One study compared the mothers of adolescent girls with eating disorders to the mothers of other girls. Mothers of adolescents with eating disorders were more likely to be unhappy about their families' functioning, to have their own problems with eating and dieting, to believe their daughters ought to lose weight, and to regard their daughters as unattractive (Pike & Rodin, 1991). Is binge eating, as suggested by Humphrey (1986), a metaphoric effort to gain the nurturance and comfort that the mother is denying her daughter? Does purging represent the symbolic upheaval of negative feelings toward the family?

Families of young women with eating disorders tend to be more often conflicted, less cohesive and nurturing, yet more overprotective and critical than those of reference groups (Fairburn et al., 1997). The parents seem less capable of promoting independence in their daughters. Conflicts with parents over issues of autonomy are often implicated in the development of both anorexia nervosa and bulimia (Ratti, Humphrey, & Lyons, 1996). Yet it remains uncertain whether these family patterns contribute to the eating disorders or whether eating disorders disrupt family life. The truth probably lies in an interaction between the two.

From the systems perspective, families are systems that regulate themselves in ways that minimize the open expression of conflict and reduce the need for change. Within this perspective, girls who develop anorexia may be seen as helping maintain the shaky balances and harmonies found in dysfunctional families by displacing attention from family conflicts and marital tensions onto themselves. The girl may become the *identified patient,* although actually it is the family unit that is dysfunctional.

Regardless of the factors that initiate eating disorders, social reinforcers may maintain them. Children with eating disorders may quickly become the focus of attention of their families, receiving attention from their parents that is otherwise lacking.

Biological Factors Scientists suspect that abnormalities in brain mechanisms controlling hunger and satiety are involved in bulimia, most probably involving the brain chemical serotonin. Serotonin plays a key role in regulating mood and appetite, especially appetite for carbohydrates. Low levels of the chemical, or lack of sensitivity of serotonin receptors in the brain, may prompt binge-eating episodes, especially carbohydrate bingeing (Levitan et al., 1997). This line of thinking is buttressed by evidence that antidepressants, such as Prozac, which increases serotonin activity, can decrease binge-eating episodes in bulimic women (Walsh et al., 2004). We also know that many women with eating disorders are depressed or have a history of depression, and imbalances of serotonin are implicated in depressive disorders.

Genetic factors appear to play a role in the development of eating disorders (Bulik et al., 2006; Lamberg, 2003). Eating disorders tend to run in families, which is suggestive of a genetic component (Hitti, 2006). But stronger evidence comes from an important early study of more than 2,000 female twins, which showed a much higher concordance rate for bulimia, 23% versus 9%, among monozygotic (MZ) twins than dizygotic (DZ) twins (Kendler et al., 1991). A greater concordance for anorexia was also found among MZ than DZ twins, 50% versus 5% (Holland, Sicotte, & Treasure, 1988). Nonetheless, genetic factors cannot fully account for the development of eating disorders. Consistent with the diathesis–stress model, perhaps a genetic predisposition affecting the regulation of neurotransmitter activity in the brain interacts with stress associated with social and family pressures to increase the risk of eating disorders.

Treatment of Eating Disorders

Eating disorders are difficult to treat (Yager, 2005). People with anorexia may be hospitalized, especially when weight loss is severe or body weight is falling rapidly (Lindblad, Lindberg, & Hjern, 2006; Willer, Thuras, & Crow, 2005). In the hospital they are usually placed on a closely monitored refeeding regimen. Behavioral therapy is also commonly used, with rewards made contingent on adherence to the refeeding protocol. Commonly used reinforcers include ward privileges and social opportunities.

Psychodynamic therapy is sometimes combined with behavior therapy to probe for psychological conflicts. Family therapy may also be employed to help resolve underlying family conflicts. Continuing therapy following hospitalization, generally in the form of individual or family therapy, is recommended to provide continuing care.

Hospitalization may also be helpful in breaking the binge–purge cycle in bulimia, but it appears to be necessary only where eating behaviors are clearly out of control and outpatient treatment has failed, or where there are severe medical complications, suicidal thoughts or attempts, or substance abuse.

Cognitive-behavioral therapy (CBT) has emerged as an effective treatment approach for bulimia and is currently recognized as the treatment of choice for this disorder (Ghaderi, 2006; Schmidt et al., 2007; Wilson, Grilo, & Vitousek, 2007). Although specific techniques vary, CBT helps bulimic women challenge self-defeating thoughts and beliefs, such as unrealistic, perfectionistic expectations regarding dieting and body weight. Another common dysfunctional thinking pattern is dichotomous (all-or-nothing) thinking, which predisposes them to purge when they slip even a little from their rigid diets. CBT also challenges tendencies to overemphasize appearance in determining self-worth. To eliminate self-induced vomiting, therapists may use the behavioral technique of *exposure with response prevention*, which was developed for treatment of people with obsessive–compulsive disorder. In this technique, the bulimic patient is exposed to eating forbidden foods while the therapist stands by to prevent vomiting until the urge to purge passes. Bulimic individuals thus learn to tolerate violations of their rigid dietary rules without resorting to purging.

Interpersonal psychotherapy (IPT), a structured form of psychodynamic therapy, has also been used effectively in treating bulimia. IPT focuses on resolving interpersonal problems in the belief that more effective interpersonal functioning will lead to healthier food habits and attitudes. Although CBT appears to produce stronger and faster treatment effects (Agras et al., 2000a), IPT may be useful in cases where CBT proves unsuccessful (Wilson & Fairburn, 1998).

Antidepressant drugs, such as Prozac, have demonstrated therapeutic benefits in treating bulimia (Walsh et al., 2004). These drugs decrease the urge to binge by normalizing levels of serotonin—the brain chemical involved in regulating appetite. On the other hand, antidepressant drugs have yielded mixed results in treating anorexia (Walsh et al., 2006).

QUESTIONNAIRE
The Fear of Fat Scale

The fear of becoming fat is a prime factor underlying eating disorders such as anorexia and bulimia. The Goldfarb Fear of Fat Scale measures the degree to which people fear becoming fat. The scale may help identify individuals at risk of developing eating disorders. It differentiates between anorexic and normal women, and between bulimic and nonbulimic women. Dieters, however, also score higher on the scale than nondieters.

To complete the Fear of Fat Scale, read each of the following statements and write in the number that best represents your own feelings and beliefs. Then check the key at the end of the chapter.

1 = very untrue
2 = somewhat untrue
3 = somewhat true
4 = very true

1. ———— My biggest fear is of becoming fat.
2. ———— I am afraid to gain even a little weight.
3. ———— I believe there is a real risk that I will become overweight someday.
4. ———— I don't understand how overweight people can live with themselves.
5. ———— Becoming fat would be the worst thing that could happen to me.
6. ———— If I stopped concentrating on controlling my weight, chances are I would become very fat.
7. ———— There is nothing that I can do to make the thought of gaining weight less painful and frightening.
8. ———— I feel like all my energy goes into controlling my weight.
9. ———— If I can eat even a little, I may lose control and not stop eating.
10. ———— Staying hungry is the only way I can guard against losing control and becoming fat.

Source: From L. A. Goldfarb, E. M. Dykens, & M. Gerrard, "The Goldfarb Fear of Fat Scale," in *Journal of Personality Assessment*, 49, 1985 pp. 329–332. Reproduced with permission of Lawrence Erlbaum Associates Inc. in the format Textbook via Copyright Clearance Center.

Although progress has been made in treating eating disorders, there is considerable room for improvement (McIntosh et al., 2005). Even CBT, which is recognized as the most effective form of treatment for bulimia, fails to succeed with a substantial proportion of bulimic patients (Thompson-Brenner, Glass, & Westen, 2003; Wilson, Grilo, & Vitousek, 2007). Drug therapy sometimes proves helpful in bulimic patients who fail to respond to cognitive-behavioral treatment (Walsh et al., 2000). We can't yet say whether a combination CBT/medication approach is more effective than either component alone.

Eating disorders can be tenacious and enduring problems, especially when excessive fears of body weight and distortions in body image continue beyond active treatment (Fairburn et al., 2003). Investigators in one study reported that 10 years after women in their treatment program presented with bulimia, approximately 30% still showed recurrent binge-eating or purging behaviors (Keel et al., 1999). Recovery from anorexia also tends to be a long and uncertain process (Steinhausen, 2002).

Difficulties in treating eating disorders only buttress the need to develop effective prevention programs. Recently, investigators showed positive results from an Internet-based intervention that focused on changing disordered eating behaviors and attitudes and reducing body dissatisfaction in a sample of college women (Celio et al., 2000). The intervention had a significant impact on reducing risk factors for eating disorders (i.e., disordered attitudes and behaviors) as compared to a no-treatment control condition.

Binge-Eating Disorder

binge-eating disorder (BED) A disorder characterized by recurrent eating binges without purging; classified as a potential disorder requiring further study.

People with **binge-eating disorder (BED)** have recurrent eating binges but do not purge themselves of the excess food afterward. Binge-eating disorder is classified in the *DSM* manual as a potential disorder requiring further study. Too little is known about the characteristics of people with BED to include it as an official diagnostic category. However, we do know that BED is more common than either anorexia or bulimia, affecting about 3% of women and 2% of men at some point in their lives (Hudson et al., 2006).

Although the final set of criteria that might be used in the diagnostic manual to identify the disorder remains under review, the present criteria require evidence of bingeing at least 2 days a week for a period of 3 months (Stotland, 2000). During a binge, people with this disorder continue to eat despite feeling uncomfortably full. They are embarrassed to be seen during a binge and feel guilty afterward.

Unlike bulimia, BED is closely associated with obesity, especially severe obesity (Hudson et al., 2005). BED is also linked to depression and a history of unsuccessful attempts at losing excess weight and keeping it off. People with BED also tend to be older than those with anorexia or bulimia. Like other eating disorders, it is found more frequently among women.

People with BED are often described as "compulsive overeaters." During a binge they feel a loss of control over their eating. BED may fall within a broader domain of compulsive behaviors characterized by impaired control over maladaptive behaviors, such as pathological gambling and substance abuse disorders. A history of dieting may play a role in some cases of BED, although it appears to be a less important factor in BED than in bulimia (Howard & Porzelius, 1999). Some forms of BED may be related to the actions of particular genes (Branson et al., 2003; Farooqi et al., 2003).

Cognitive-behavioral therapy (CBT) has shown therapeutic benefits in treating binge-eating disorder and is now recognized as the treatment of choice (Grilo & Masheb, 2005; Wilson, Grilo, & Vitousek, 2007). Antidepressants, especially those of the SSRI family, may also reduce the frequency of binge-eating episodes by normalizing serotonin levels in the brain (Apopolinario et al., 2003; Stotland, 2000). Appetite-suppressant drugs that curb food cravings also show promise in treating binge eating in obese individuals (McElroy et al., 2003). This brings us to the problem that is closely identified with binge-eating disorder: obesity.

TYING IT TOGETHER

We can conceptualize eating disorders within a multifactorial framework in which psychosocial and biological influences underlie the development of disturbed eating behaviors. Negative reinforcement in the form of relief from anxiety about gaining weight plays a pivotal role in strengthening and maintaining maladaptive ways of controlling body weight through food-rejecting behavior and purging. The Concept Map for Abnormal Psychology *at the end of the chapter illustrates the multifaceted causes in eating disorders and contemporary approaches to treating these challenging problems.*

obesity A condition of excess body fat; generally defined by a BMI of 30 or higher.

TRUTH or FICTION

Obesity is one of the most common psychological disorders in the United States.

☑ **FALSE.** Obesity is a medical disorder, not a psychological disorder.

A CLOSER LOOK

Obesity: A National Epidemic

The problem of **obesity** once again brings into context the complex interrelationships between mind and body. Obesity is classified as a medical condition, not a psychological disorder, but psychological factors play important roles in its development and treatment, which is why it is the focus of our attention here.

Obesity has reached epidemic proportions not only in the United States, but throughout the world ("Curbing the Obesity Epidemic," 2006; Vastag, 2004). More than 120 million Americans are either overweight or obese (Hellmich, 2003). Worldwide, 1 in 4 people are overweight (Lamberg, 2006). For the first time in human history, there are as many people in the world who are overweight as there are people who are underfed (Bazell, 2002). Consider these other disturbing statistics:

- More Americans are overweight today than at any time since the government started tracking obesity in the 1960s. Nearly two-thirds of Americans are overweight, and nearly one-third are clinically obese (Howard et al., 2006; Manson & Bassuk, 2003; Vastag, 2004).
- Obesity in children and adolescents is also on the upswing, having doubled over the past 25 years (Connelly, 2003; Dietz, 2004; Hedley et al., 2004). All told, 1 in 3 children is overweight or at risk of becoming overweight.

Health officials are rightly concerned about obesity because it is a major risk factor in many chronic and potentially life-threatening diseases, including heart disease, stroke, diabetes, respiratory disease, and some forms of cancer (Gregg et al., 2005; Mokdad et al., 2003; Yan et al, 2006). All told, obesity accounts for more than 100,000 excess deaths in the United States every year and shaves 6 or 7 years off the average person's life expectancy (Fontaine et al., 2003; Flegal et al., 2005). Even people who are overweight but not obese are at increased risk of premature death (Adams et al., 2006; Jee et al., 2006; NCI, 2006).

Despite all the money and effort spent on weight-loss products and programs, our collective waistlines are getting larger—a result, health experts believe, of consuming too many calories and exercising too little (Lamberg, 2006; Pollan, 2003). Americans today average 530 more calories per day than they did 30 years ago (Gorman, 2003). The reasons? A diet containing too much high-fat, high-calorie food and super-sized portions that are growing ever larger (Lamberg, 2006; Mitka, 2003).

What causes obesity? Body weight varies as a function of energy balance. When caloric intake exceeds energy output, the excess calories are stored in the body in the form of fat, leading to obesity (Pi-Sunyer, 2003) (see Figure 10.2). The key to preventing obesity is to bring energy expenditure in line with energy

(caloric) intake. Unfortunately, this is easier said than done. Research suggests that a number of factors contribute to the imbalance between energy intake and expenditure that underlies obesity, including genetics, metabolic factors, lifestyle factors, psychological factors and socioeconomic factors.

Genetic Factors

Obesity is partly determined by genetics, but genes don't tell the whole story (Couzin, 2006; Farooqi et al., 2003; Herbert et al., 2006). Environmental

FIGURE 10.2 Weight: A balancing act.
Body weight is determined by the balance between energy consumed in the form of food calories and energy used in the course of the day through physical activity and maintenance of bodily processes. When calories consumed in food exceed calories used, we gain weight. To lose weight, we need to take in fewer calories than we expend. Weight control involves a balance between calories consumed with calories used.

Source: Physical Activity and Weight Control, National Institutes of Diabetes and Digestive and Kidney Diseases (NIDDK), http://win.niddk.nih.gov/publications/physical.htm.

(continued)

(continued)

factors (diet and exercise patterns) are also important contributors (Wing & Polley, 2001).

Metabolic Factors

Genetic differences in *metabolic rate* (the rate at which the body burns calories) may play an important role in determining risk of obesity. Moreover, when we lose weight, especially significant amounts of weight, the body reacts as if it were starving. It responds to falling weight by slowing the metabolic rate (Pinel et al., 2000; Woods et al., 2000). This makes it difficult to continue losing more weight or even maintain the weight that was lost. Some theorists believe that mechanisms in the brain control the body's metabolism to keep body weight around a genetically determined *set point* (Keesey & Powley, 1986). The ability of the body to adjust the metabolic rate downward when calorie intake declines may have helped ancestral humans survive times of famine (Grady, 2002). However, this mechanism is a bane to dieters today trying to lose weight and keep it off.

People may be able to offset this metabolic adjustment by losing weight more gradually and by following a more vigorous exercise regimen. Vigorous exercise burns calories directly and may increase the metabolic rate by replacing fat tissue with muscle, especially if the exercise program involves weight-bearing activity. Also, ounce for ounce, muscle tissue burns more calories than fat tissue. Before starting an exercise regimen, check with your physician to determine which types of activity are best suited to your overall health condition.

Fat Cells

Fat cells, which are cells that store fat, comprise the fatty tissue in the body (also called *adipose tissue*). Obese people have more fat cells than people who are not obese. Severely obese people may have some 200 billion fat cells, as compared to 25 or 30 billion in normal-weight individuals. Why does this matter? As time passes after eating, the blood sugar level declines, drawing out fat from these cells to supply more nourishment to the body. The hypothalamus in the brain triggers hunger when it detects depletion of fat in these cells. Hunger is a drive that motivates eating, which thereby replenishes the fat cells.

People with more fatty tissue send more signals of fat depletion to the brain than people who are equal in weight but who have fewer fat cells; as a result, they feel food deprived sooner. Sad to say, dieters do not expel fat cells; instead, they shrink them. Many dieters who are markedly obese, even successful dieters, thus complain they are constantly hungry as they struggle to maintain normal weights. People with high levels of adipose tissue are doubly beset, because fatty tissue metabolizes food more slowly than muscle.

How is the number of fat cells in our bodies determined? Unfortunately, heredity seems to play a role. However, excessive food intake in early childhood may also have an influence (Brownell & Wadden, 1992).

Lifestyle Factors

Eating habits are changing, and not for the better. The constant bombardment of food-related cues in television commercials, print advertising, and the like, can take a toll on our individual and collective waistlines. Restaurants today are competing with each other in terms of who can pile the most food on ever-larger dinner plates. Pizzerias are using larger pans and fast-food restaurants are supersizing meals—all of which takes a toll on the waistline. That "big gulp" 64-ounce soft drink packs an incredible 800 calories! (Smith, 2003). And guess which character, after Santa Claus, children recognize the most often? The answer: Ronald McDonald (Parloff, 2003).

Another contributing factor to our expanding waistlines is America's growing suburbs and the car-dependent culture this entails (McKee, 2003). City dwellers may burn off some extra calories hiking around town, but suburbanites must rely on their cars to get from place to place in spread-out communities in the suburban sprawl (Ewing et al., 2003).

Psychological Factors

According to psychodynamic theory, eating is the cardinal oral activity. Psychodynamic theorists believe that people who were fixated in the oral stage by conflicts concerning dependence and independence are likely to regress in times of stress to excessive oral activities such as overeating. Other psychological factors connected with overeating and obesity include low self-esteem, lack of self-efficacy expectancies, family conflicts, and negative emotions. Emotions such as anger, fear, and sadness can prompt excessive eating.

Socioeconomic Factors

Obesity is more prevalent among people of lower income levels. Because people of color in our society are as a group lower in socioeconomic status than (non-Hispanic) White Americans, we should not be surprised that rates of obesity are higher among people of color, at least among women of color (see Figure 10.3).

Why are people on the lower rungs of the socioeconomic ladder at greater risk of obesity? For one thing, more affluent people have greater access to information about nutrition and health and more likely to take health education courses. They also have greater access to health-care providers. Poorer people also exercise less regularly than more affluent people do. More affluent people are more likely to have the time, the income, and the space to exercise. Many poor people in the inner city also turn to food as a way of coping with the stresses of poverty, discrimination, crowding, and crime.

Acculturation may also contribute to obesity, at least when it involves adopting the unhealthful dietary practices of the host culture. Consider that Japanese American men living in California and Hawaii eat a higher-fat diet than Japanese men do. Not surprisingly, the prevalence of obesity is 2 to 3 times higher among Japanese American men than among men living in Japan (Curb & Marcus, 1991).

Hazardous waist. Obesity is indeed a hazard to health and longevity.

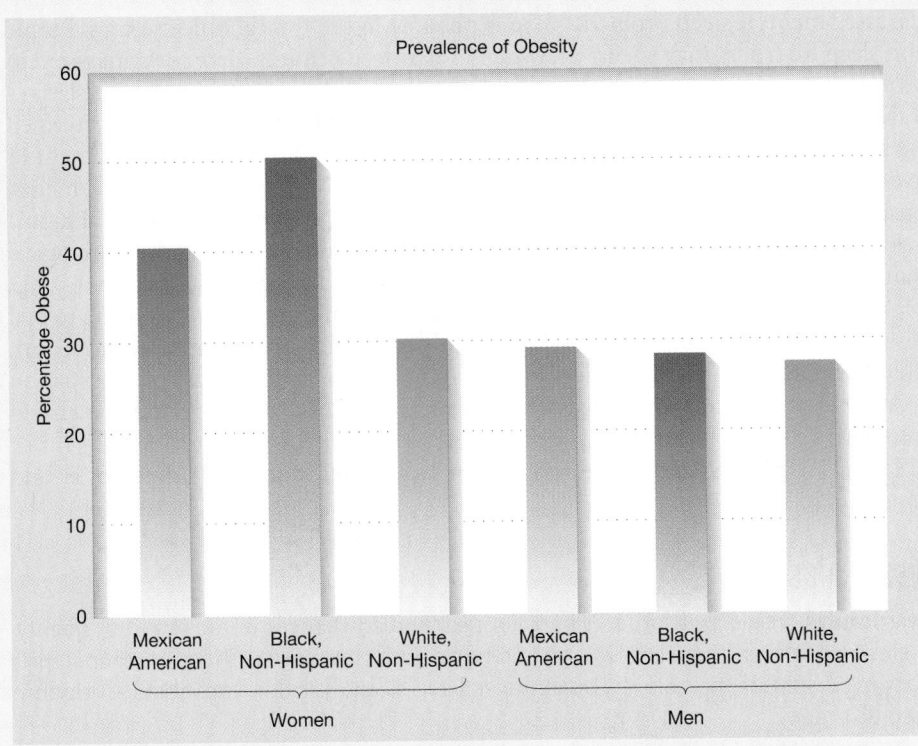

FIGURE 10.3 Rates of obesity (age 20 or higher).
This figure shows the rates of obesity among U.S. adults in relation to race and ethnicity.
Source: Health, United States, 2003, Centers for Disease Control and Prevention, National Center for Health Statistics, National Health and Nutrition Examination Survey.

Facing the Challenge of Obesity

Despite their appeal, quickie diets don't work. The great majority of people who diet, perhaps more than 9 out of 10 people, regain any weight they lose. Nor are antiobesity or diet drugs the answer, as they offer at best a temporary benefits and can carry significant side effects. However, weight medication may be used as a supplement to behavioral modification programs designed to help participants make lasting changes in diet and exercise habits (Wadden et al., 2005).

Long-term success in the "battle of the bulge" requires a continuing commitment to following a sensible, lower-calorie, lower-fat diet combined with regular exercise (Irwin et al., 2002; Manson et al., 2004; Wing & Polley, 2001). Even people whose heredity may work against them can control their weight within some broad limits through adopting a sensible diet, increasing activity and exercise levels, and developing healthier eating habits.

SLEEP DISORDERS

Sleep is a biological function that remains in many ways a mystery. We know that sleep is restorative and that most of us need 7 or more hours of sleep a night to function at our best. Yet we cannot identify the specific biochemical changes occurring during sleep that account for its restorative function. We also know that many of us are troubled by sleep problems, although the causes of some of these problems remain obscure. Sleep problems of sufficient severity and frequency that they lead to significant personal distress or impaired functioning in social, occupational, or other roles are classified in the *DSM* system as **sleep disorders.** Table 10.4 provides an overview of the sleep disorders discussed in the chapter.

sleep disorders Persistent or recurrent sleep-related problems that cause distress or impaired functioning.

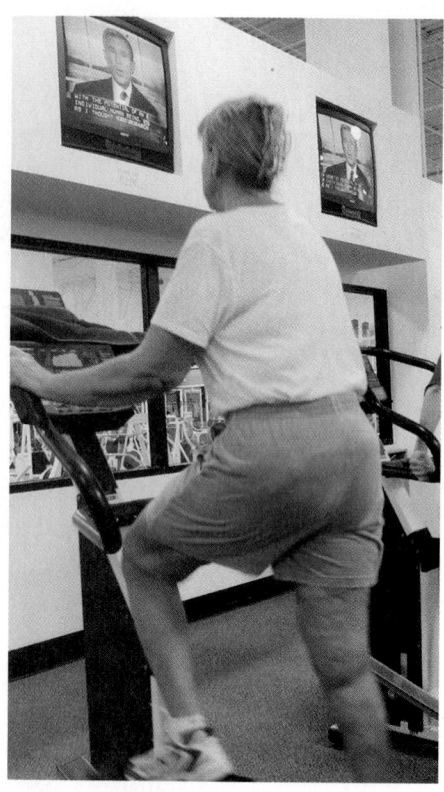

Taking it off and keeping it off. Health experts recognize that losing excess weight and keeping if off requires a lifelong commitment to adopting a sensible diet and engaging in regular exercise.

dyssomnias Sleep disorders involving disturbances in the amount, quality, or timing of sleep.

insomnia Difficulties falling asleep, remaining asleep, or achieving restorative sleep.

primary insomnia A sleep disorder characterized by chronic or persistent insomnia not caused by another psychological or physical disorder or by the effects of drugs or medications.

Highly specialized diagnostic facilities, called sleep disorders centers, have been established throughout the United States and Canada to provide a more comprehensive assessment of sleep problems than is possible in the typical office setting. People with sleep disorders may spend a few nights at a sleep center, where they are wired to devices that track their physiological responses during sleep or attempted sleep—brain waves, heart and respiration rates, and so on. This form of assessment is termed *polysomnographic (PSG) recording* because it involves simultaneous measurement of diverse physiological response patterns, including brain waves, eye movements, muscle movements, and respiration. Information obtained from physiological monitoring of sleep patterns is combined with that obtained from medical and psychological evaluations, subjective reports of sleep disturbance, and sleep diaries (i.e., daily logs compiled by the problem sleeper that track the length of time between retiring to bed and falling asleep, number of hours slept, nightly awakenings, daytime naps, and so on). Multidisciplinary teams of physicians and psychologists sift through this information to arrive at a diagnosis and suggest treatment approaches to address the presenting problem.

The *DSM* groups sleep disorders within two major categories: *dyssomnias* and *parasomnias*.

Dyssomnias

Dyssomnias are sleep disorders characterized by disturbances in the amount, quality, or timing of sleep. There are five specific types of dyssomnias: primary insomnia, primary hypersomnia, narcolepsy, breathing-related sleep disorder, and circadian rhythm sleep disorder.

Insomnia The term **insomnia** derives from the Latin *in-*, meaning "not" or "without," and, of course, *somnus*, meaning "sleep." Occasional bouts of insomnia, especially during times of stress, are not abnormal. But persistent insomnia characterized by recurrent difficulty getting to sleep or remaining asleep is an abnormal behavior pattern. An estimated 10% of U.S. adults suffer from the most commonly occurring sleep disorder—**primary insomnia** (Smith & Perlis, 2006). Chronic insomnia lasting a month or longer is often a sign of an underlying physical problem or a psychological disorder, such as depression, substance abuse, or physical illness. If the underlying problem is treated successfully, chances are that normal sleep patterns will be restored. Chronic insomnia that is not accounted for by another psychological or physical disorder or by the effects of drugs or medications is classified as primary insomnia (Silber, 2005).

Primary insomnia mostly affects people over age 40 (Nagourney, 2001b). But many college students and other young adults are also affected. People with primary insomnia have persistent difficulty falling asleep, remaining asleep, or achieving restorative sleep (sleep that leaves the person feeling refreshed and alert) for a period of a month or longer (Pallesen et al., 2001). Young people with primary insomnia usually complain it takes too long to get to sleep. Older people are more likely to complain of waking frequently during the night or of waking too early in the morning.

Primary insomnia leads to daytime fatigue and causes significant levels of personal distress or difficulties performing usual social, occupational, student, or other roles. Not surprisingly, people with the disorder often have other psychological problems as well, especially anxiety and depression.

Psychological factors clearly contribute to primary insomnia. People troubled by chronic insomnia tend to bring their anxieties and worries to bed with them, which raises their bodily arousal to a level that prevents natural sleep. Then they worry about not getting enough sleep, which only compounds their sleep difficulties. They may try to force themselves to sleep, which tends to backfire by creating more anxiety and tension, making sleep even less likely. You cannot force yourself to fall asleep. However, you can set the scene for sleep by going to bed when you are tired and relaxed and allowing sleep to occur naturally.

Table 10.4 **Overview of Sleep Disorders**

TYPE OF DISORDER	Lifetime Prevalence in Population (approx.)	Description
Dyssomnias, which are disturbances in the amount, quality, or timing of sleep		
Insomnia	10%	Persistent difficulty falling asleep, remaining asleep, or getting enough restful sleep
Hypersomnia	Unknown	Excessive daytime sleepiness
Narcolepsy	.02% (2 in 10,000) to 0.16% (16 in 10,000)	Sudden attacks of sleep during the day
Breathing-Related Sleep Disorder	1%–10%	Sleep repeatedly interrupted due to difficulties breathing
Circadian Rhythm Sleep Disorder	Unknown	Disruption of the internal sleep–wake cycle due to time changes in sleep patterns
Parasomnias, which are sleep disturbances occurring either during sleep or at the threshold between sleep and wakefulness		
Nightmare Disorder	Unknown	Repeated awakenings due to nightmares
Sleep Terror Disorder	Unknown	Repeated experiences of sleep terrors resulting in abrupt awakenings
Sleepwalking Disorder	Estimated 1%–5% in children	Repeated episodes of sleepwalking

Source: APA, 2000; Smith & Perlis, 2006.

The principles of classical conditioning help explain the development of chronic insomnia (Pollack, 2004b). After pairing a few anxious, sleepless nights with stimuli associated with the bedroom, simply entering the bedroom for the night may be sufficient to elicit bodily arousal that impairs sleep onset. Thus, states of heightened arousal become conditioned responses elicited by the conditioned stimuli in the bedroom.

Hypersomnia The word *hypersomnia* is derived from the Greek *hyper,* meaning "over" or "more than normal," and the Latin *somnus,* meaning "sleep." Primary **hypersomnia** is a pattern of excessive sleepiness during the day that continues for a month or longer. The excessive sleepiness (sometimes referred to as "sleep drunkenness") may take the form of difficulty awakening following a prolonged sleep period (typically 8 to 12 hours). Or there may be a pattern of daytime sleep episodes, occurring virtually every day, in the form of intended or unintended napping (such as inadvertently falling asleep while watching TV). Despite the fact that daytime naps often last an hour or more, the person does not feel refreshed upon awakening. The disorder is considered primary because it cannot be accounted for by inadequate amounts of sleep during the night, by another psychological or physical disorder, or by drug or medication use.

Although many of us feel sleepy during the day from time to time, and may even drift off occasionally while reading or watching TV, the person with primary hypersomnia has persistent and severe periods of sleepiness that typically lead to difficulties in daily functioning, such as missing important meetings. Although the prevalence of the disorder is unknown, daytime sleepiness affects 0.5% to 5% of the adult population (APA, 2000).

Narcolepsy The word **narcolepsy** derives from the Greek *narke,* meaning "stupor" and *lepsis,* meaning "an attack." People with narcolepsy experience sleep attacks in which they suddenly fall asleep without warning at various times during the day. They remain asleep for about 15 minutes. The person can be in the midst of a conversation at one moment and slump to the floor fast asleep a moment later. The diagnosis is made when sleep attacks occur

hypersomnia A pattern of excessive sleepiness during the day.

narcolepsy A sleep disorder characterized by sudden, irresistible episodes of sleep.

Sleep center. People with sleep disorders are often evaluated in sleep centers, where their physiological responses can be monitored as they sleep.

daily for a period of 3 months or longer and occur in conjunction with one or both of the following conditions: (a) *cataplexy* (a sudden loss of muscular control); and (b) intrusions of *REM sleep* in the transitional state between wakefulness and sleep (APA, 2000). REM, or rapid eye movement, sleep is the stage of sleep associated with dreaming. It is so named because the sleeper's eyes tend to dart about rapidly under the closed lids. Narcoleptic attacks are associated with an almost immediate transition into REM sleep from a state of wakefulness. In normal sleep, REM typically follows several stages of non-REM sleep.

Cataplexy typically follows a strong emotional reaction such as joy or anger. It can range from a mild weakness in the legs to a complete loss of muscle control resulting in the person suddenly collapsing (Siegel, 2004). People with narcolepsy may also experience *sleep paralysis,* a temporary state following awakening in which the person feels incapable of moving or talking. The person may also report frightening hallucinations, called *hypnagogic hallucinations,* which occur just before the onset of sleep and tend to involve visual, auditory, tactile, and kinesthetic (body movement) sensations.

Narcolepsy affects men and women equally and is a relatively uncommon disorder, affecting an estimated 0.02% (2 in 10,000) to 0.16% (16 in 10,000) of the general adult population (APA, 2000; Dauvilliers, Arnulf, & Mignot, 2007). Unlike hypersomnia, in which daytime sleep episodes follow a period of increasing sleepiness, narcoleptic attacks occur abruptly, and the person awakes feeling refreshed. The attacks can be dangerous and frightening, especially if they occur when the person is driving or using heavy equipment or sharp implements. About 2 of 3 people with narcolepsy have fallen asleep while driving, and 4 of 5 have fallen asleep on the job (Aldrich, 1992). Household accidents resulting from falls are also common. Not surprisingly, the disorder is associated with a lower quality of life in terms of general health and daily functioning (Ferrans, Cohen, & Smith, 1992). The cause or causes of narcolepsy remain unknown, but suspicion focuses on the loss of brain cells in the hypothalamus that produce a sleep-regulating chemical (Bazell, 2000; Mignot & Thorsby, 2001).

Breathing-Related Sleep Disorder People with a **breathing-related sleep disorder** experience repeated disruptions of sleep due to respiratory problems (APA, 2000). These frequent disruptions of sleep result in insomnia or excessive daytime sleepiness.

The subtypes of the disorder are distinguished in terms of the underlying causes of the breathing problem. The most common type is *obstructive sleep apnea,* which involves

breathing-related sleep disorder A sleep disorder in which sleep is repeatedly disrupted by difficulty with breathing normally.

repeated episodes of either complete or partial obstruction of breathing during sleep. Obstructive sleep apnea is a relatively common problem, with estimates indicating that the disorder affects approximately 1% to 10% of the adult population and perhaps an even higher percentage of older adults (APA, 2000). The disorder is most common in middle age and affects men more frequently up to about the age of 50, at which point the rates are similar for men and women (Bardwell et al., 2003; Tishler et al., 2003). The disorder is more common among people who are obese, apparently because of a narrowing of the upper airways due to an enlargement of soft tissue (APA, 2000; Haynes, 2005).

The word *apnea* derives from the Greek prefix *a-*, meaning "not, without," and *pneuma*, meaning "breath." The breathing difficulty results from the blockage of airflow in the upper airways, which is often caused by a structural defect, such as an overly thick palate or enlarged tonsils or adenoids. In cases of complete obstruction, the sleeper may literally stop breathing for periods of 15 to 90 seconds as many as 500 times during the night! When these lapses of breathing occur, the sleeper may suddenly sit up, gasp for air, take a few deep breaths, and fall back asleep without awakening or realizing that breathing was interrupted.

Although a biological reflex kicks in to force a gasping breath after these brief interruptions of breathing, the frequent disruptions of normal sleep resulting from apneas can leave people feeling sleepy the following day, making it difficult for them to function effectively.

Not surprisingly, people who have sleep apnea generally report an impaired quality of life. They also tend to have higher levels of depression than nonaffected individuals (Peppard et al., 2006). Sleep apnea is also a health concern because of its association with an increased risk of hypertension, a major risk factor for heart attacks and strokes (Arnulf et al., 2002; Shahar, Whitney, & Redline, 2002). Unfortunately, about three of four cases remain untreated (Minerd & Jasmer, 2006).

Circadian Rhythm Sleep Disorder Most bodily functions follow a cycle or an internal rhythm—called a circadian rhythm—that lasts about 24 hours. Even when people are relieved of scheduled activities and work duties and placed in environments where they are not aware of the time of day, they usually follow relatively normal sleep–wake schedules.

In **circadian rhythm sleep disorder,** this rhythm becomes grossly disturbed because of a mismatch between the sleep schedule demands imposed on the person and the person's internal sleep–wake cycle. The disruption in normal sleep patterns can lead to insomnia or hypersomnia. For the disorder to be diagnosed, the mismatch must be persistent and severe enough to cause significant levels of distress or to impair the person's ability to function in social, occupational, or other roles. The jet lag that accompanies travel between time zones does not qualify because it is usually transient. However, frequent changes of time zones and frequent changes of work shifts (as encountered, for example, by nursing personnel) can induce more persistent or recurrent problems, resulting in a circadian rhythm sleep disorder. Treatment may include a program of gradual adjustments in the sleep schedule to allow the person's circadian system to become aligned with changes in the sleep–wake schedule.

Parasomnias

The **parasomnias** are abnormal behavioral patterns or physiological events that take place during sleep or at the threshold between wakefulness and sleep. Among the more common parasomnias are nightmare disorder, sleep terror disorder, and sleepwalking disorder.

Nightmare Disorder **Nightmare disorder** involves recurrent awakenings from sleep because of frightening dreams (nightmares). The nightmares typically involve lengthy storylike dreams that include threats of imminent physical danger to the individual, such as being chased, attacked, or injured. The person usually recalls the nightmare vividly upon awakening. Although the person becomes alert quickly after awakening, anxiety and fear may linger and prevent a return to sleep. Perhaps half the adult population occasionally experiences nightmares, although the percentages of people having the intense, recurrent nightmares that would lead to a diagnosis of nightmare disorder remains unknown.

circadian rhythm sleep disorder A sleep disorder characterized by a mismatch between the body's normal sleep–wake cycle and the demands of the environment.

parasomnias Sleep disorders involving abnormal behaviors or physiological events that occur during sleep or while falling asleep.

nightmare disorder A sleep disorder characterized by recurrent awakenings due to frightening nightmares.

Sleep apnea. Loud snoring may be a sign of obstructive sleep apnea, a breathing-related sleep disorder in which the person may temporarily stop breathing as many as 500 times during a night's sleep. Loud snoring, described by bed partners as reaching levels of industrial noise pollution, may alternate with momentary silences when breathing is suspended.

Nightmares are often associated with traumatic experiences and generally occur most often when the individual is under stress. Supporting the general link between trauma and nightmares, researchers report that the incidence of nightmares was greater among survivors of the 1989 San Francisco earthquake in the weeks following the quake than among comparison groups (Wood et al., 1992). An increased frequency of nightmares was also observed among children who experienced the 1994 Los Angeles earthquake (Kolbert, 1994).

Nightmares generally occur during rapid-eye movement or REM sleep, the stage of sleep in which most dreams occur. Periods of REM sleep tend to become longer and the dreams occurring during REM more intense in the latter half of nightly sleep, so nightmares usually occur late at night or toward morning. Although nightmares may involve a great deal of agitated movement in the dream itself, as in nightmares of fleeing from an assailant, dreamers show little muscle activity. The biological processes that activate dreams—including nightmares—inhibit body movement, causing a type of paralysis. This is indeed fortunate, as it prevents the dreamer from jumping out of bed and running into a dresser or a wall in the attempt to elude the pursuing assailants from the dream.

Sleep Terror Disorder It typically begins with a loud, piercing cry or scream in the night. Even the most soundly sleeping parent will be summoned to the child's bedroom as if shot from a cannon. The child (most cases involve children) may be sitting up, appearing frightened and showing signs of extreme arousal—profuse sweating with rapid heartbeat and respiration. The child may start talking incoherently or thrash about wildly but remain asleep. If the child awakens fully, he or she may not recognize the parent or may attempt to push the parent away. After a few minutes the child falls back into a deep sleep and upon awakening in the morning remembers nothing of the experience. These terrifying attacks, called *sleep terrors,* are more intense than ordinary nightmares. Unlike nightmares, sleep terrors tend to occur during the first third of nightly sleep and during deep, non-REM sleep (Dahl, 1992).

Sleep terror disorder is characterized by repeated episodes of sleep terrors resulting in abrupt awakenings that begin with a panicky scream (APA, 2000). If awakening occurs during a sleep terror episode, the person will usually appear confused and disoriented for a few minutes. The person may feel a vague sense of terror and report some fragmentary dream images, but not the sort of detailed dreams typical of nightmares. Most of the time the person falls back asleep and remembers nothing of the experience the following morning.

Children with sleep terror disorder typically outgrow the disorder during adolescence. More boys than girls are affected, but among adults the gender ratio is about even. In adults, the disorder tends to follow a chronic course during which the frequency and intensity of the episodes waxes and wanes over time. Prevalence data on the disorder are lacking, but episodes of sleep terror are estimated to occur in 1% to 6% of children and in less than 1% of adults (APA, 2000). The cause of sleep terror disorder remains a mystery.

Sleepwalking Disorder In **sleepwalking disorder,** there are repeated episodes in which the sleeper arises from bed and walks about the house while remaining fully asleep. Because these episodes tend to occur during the deeper stages of sleep in which there is an absence of dreaming, sleepwalking episodes do not seem to involve the enactment of a dream. In sleepwalking disorder, the person experiences repeated episodes of sleepwalking that are of sufficient severity to cause significant levels of personal distress or impaired functioning. Sleepwalking disorder is most common in children, affecting between 1% and 5% of children, according to some estimates (APA, 2000). Between 10% and 30% of children are believed to have had at least one episode of sleepwalking. The prevalence of the disorder among adults is unknown, as are its causes. However, perhaps as many as 7% of adults have experienced occasional sleepwalking episodes (APA, 2000). Here, a man recounts an episode of sleepwalking from his childhood, which was one of many such incidents:

"He's Only Sleepwalking"

All five of my sisters remember me as the family sleepwalker. [My sister] Shannon recalls helping Mom fold clothes in the den late one night when I appeared. Perhaps it was the fragrant smell of laundry, like incense, that drew me. I stopped in front of the TV in my pj's, eyes open, and began yelling. It was gibberish, Shannon remembers, but the choking anger behind it was alarming. While that behavior alone is odd, the aspect of her story I find most fascinating is my mother's reaction: unfazed, "He's only sleepwalking," she murmured, as though it were as common as the evening paperboy's late delivery. I imagine her then saying calmly, "Okay, Shannon, let's start on the towels."
—From Hayes, 2001

The causes of sleepwalking remain obscure, although both genetic and environmental factors appear to be involved (Hublin et al., 1997). Although sleepwalkers typically avoid walking into things, accidents occasionally happen. Sleepwalkers tend to have a blank stare on their faces during these episodes. They are generally unresponsive to others and difficult to awaken. When they do awaken the following morning, they typically have little, if any, recall of the experience. If they are awakened during the episode, they may be disoriented or confused for a few minutes (as is the case with sleep terrors), but full alertness is soon restored. There is no basis to the belief that it is harmful to sleepwalkers to awaken them during episodes. Isolated incidents of violent behavior have been associated with sleepwalking, but these are rare and may well involve other forms of psychopathology.

Treatment of Sleep Disorders

The most common method for treating sleep disorders in the United States is the use of sleep medications. However, because of problems associated with these drugs, non-pharmacological treatment approaches, principally cognitive-behavioral therapy, have come to the fore.

sleep terror disorder A sleep disorder characterized by recurrent episodes of sleep terror resulting in abrupt awakenings.

sleepwalking disorder A sleep disorder involving repeated episodes of sleepwalking.

Biological Approaches Antianxiety drugs are among the drugs often used to treat insomnia, including the class of antianxiety drugs called *benzodiazepines* (for example, Valium and Ativan). (These drugs are also widely used in the treatment of anxiety disorders, as we saw in Chapter 6.) Another widely used drug, *zolpidem* (trade name Ambien), has also been effective in both reducing the length of time it takes people with insomnia to fall asleep and increasing sleep duration (Roth et al., 2006).

When used for the short-term treatment of insomnia, sleep medications generally reduce the time it takes to get to sleep, increase total length of sleep, and reduce nightly awakenings. They work by reducing arousal and inducing feelings of calmness, thereby making the person more receptive to sleep. Sleep medications primarily work by increasing the activity of GABA, a neurotransmitter that dampens the activity of the central nervous system (see Chapter 6) (Pollack, 2004a).

Despite the benefits, there are significant problems associated with using drugs to combat insomnia (Kryger, Roth, & Dement, 2000). Sleep-inducing drugs tend to suppress REM sleep, which may interfere with some of the restorative functions of sleep. They can also lead to a carryover or "hangover" the following day, which is associated with daytime sleepiness and reduced performance. Rebound insomnia can also follow discontinuation of the drug, causing worse insomnia than was originally the case. Rebound insomnia may be lessened, however, by tapering off the drug rather than abruptly discontinuing it. These drugs quickly lose their effectiveness at a given dosage level, so progressively larger doses must be used to achieve the same effect. High doses can be dangerous, especially if they are mixed with alcoholic beverages at bedtime.

Sleep medications can also produce chemical dependence if used regularly over time and can lead to tolerance (Pollack, 2004a). Once dependence is established, people experience withdrawal symptoms when they stop using the drugs, including agitation, tremors, nausea, headaches, and in severe cases, delusions or hallucinations.

Users can also become *psychologically* dependent on sleeping pills. That is, they can develop a psychological need for the medication and assume they will not be able to get to sleep without it. Because worry heightens bodily arousal, such self-doubts are likely to become self-fulfilling prophecies. Moreover, users may attribute their success in falling asleep to the pill and not to themselves, which strengthens reliance on the drugs and makes it harder to forgo using them.

Evidence supporting long-term benefits of drug therapy remains lacking. This should not be surprising, since reliance on sleeping pills does nothing to resolve the underlying cause of the problem or help the person learn more effective ways of coping. If drugs such as benzodiazepines are prescribed for sleep problems, they should be used only for a brief period of time (a few weeks at most) and at the lowest possible dosage level (Kupfer & Reynolds, 1997). The aim should be to provide a temporary respite so the therapist can help the client find more effective ways of handling sources of stress and anxiety that contribute to insomnia.

Antianxiety drugs of the benzodiazepine family and tricyclic antidepressants are also used to treat the deep-sleep disorders—sleep terrors and sleepwalking. They seem to have a beneficial effect by decreasing the length of deep sleep and reducing partial arousals between sleep stages. As with primary insomnia, use of sleep medications for these disorders incurs the risk of physiological and psychological dependence. Therefore, sleep medications should be used only in severe cases and only as a temporary means of "breaking the cycle." Other psychoactive drugs, such as stimulants, are sometimes used to help maintain wakefulness in people with narcolepsy and to combat daytime sleepiness in people with hypersomnia. Daily naps of 10 to 60 minutes and coping support from mental health professionals or self-help groups may also be of help in treating narcolepsy.

The first-line treatment for sleep apnea is use of mechanical devices that help maintain breathing during sleep, such as a nose mask that exerts pressure to keep the upper airway passages open (Haynes, 2005). Surgery may be used to widen the upper airways in some cases.

Psychological Approaches Psychological approaches have by and large been limited to treatment of primary insomnia. Cognitive-behavioral techniques are short term in emphasis and focus on directly lowering states of physiological arousal, modifying maladaptive sleeping habits, and changing dysfunctional thoughts (Bastien et al., 2004; McCurry et al., 2007; Silber, 2005). Cognitive-behavioral therapists typically use a combination of techniques, including stimulus control, establishment of a regular sleep–wake cycle, relaxation training, and rational restructuring.

Stimulus control involves changing the environment associated with sleeping. Under normal conditions, we learn to associate stimuli relating to lying down in bed with sleeping, so that exposure to these stimuli induces feelings of sleepiness. But when people use their beds for many other activities—such as eating, reading, and watching television—the bed may lose its association with sleepiness. Moreover, the longer the person with insomnia lies in bed tossing and turning, the more the bed becomes associated with cues related to anxiety and frustration. Stimulus control techniques strengthen the connection between the bed and sleep by restricting as much as possible the activities spent in bed to sleeping. Typically, the person is instructed to limit the time spent in bed trying to fall sleep to 10 or 20 minutes at a time. If sleep does not occur within the designated time, the person leaves the bed and goes to another room to restore a relaxed frame of mind before returning to bed—for example, by sitting quietly, reading, watching TV, or practicing relaxation exercises. Moreover, the person is encouraged to establish a regular sleep–wake cycle by adopting more consistent sleeping and waking times, including on weekends and holidays, so as to program the body with a predictable sleep–wake cycle (Brody, 2006). Practicing relaxation techniques before bedtime (such as the Jacobson progressive relaxation approach described in Chapter 5), may reduce the level of physiological arousal.

Rational restructuring involves substituting rational alternatives for self-defeating, maladaptive thoughts or beliefs (see the accompanying *A Closer Look* section for examples). The belief that failing to get a good night's sleep will lead to unfortunate, even disastrous, consequences the next day reduces the chances of falling asleep because it raises the level of anxiety. Most of us function reasonably well if we lose sleep or even miss a night of sleep.

Cognitive-behavioral therapy (CBT) has emerged as the treatment of choice for chronic insomnia (Smith & Perlis, 2006). CBT yields substantial therapeutic benefits, as measured by both reductions in the time it takes to get to sleep and improved sleep quality (Irwin, Cole, & Nicassio, 2006; Rybarczyk et al., 2005; Sivertsen et al., 2006). CBT produces better results in the long term than sleep medications (Wu et al., 2006). After all, taking a pill does not help people with insomnia learn more adaptive sleep habits. Charles Morin, a leading expert on the treatment of insomnia, notes that sleep medication may produce faster results, but behavioral treatment produces longer-lasting results (cited in Pollack, 2004a, 2004b). Although CBT methods have been proposed for treating parasomnias, we have little evidence to date of the effectiveness of these interventions (Sadeh, 2005).

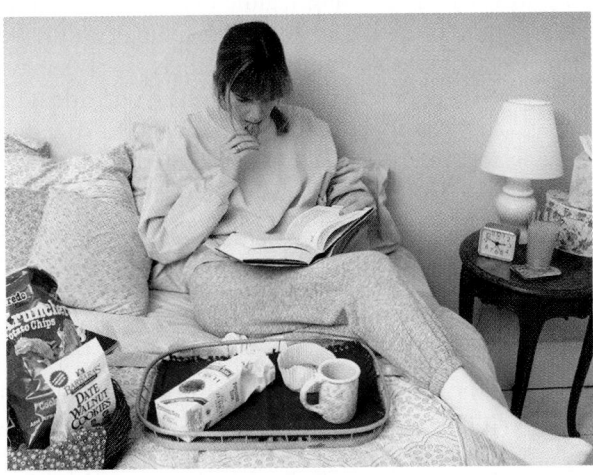

What's wrong with this picture? People who use their beds for many other activities besides sleeping, including eating, reading, and watching television, may find that lying in bed loses its value as a cue for sleeping. Behavior therapists use stimulus control techniques to help people with insomnia create a stimulus environment associated with sleeping.

A CLOSER LOOK

To Sleep, Perchance to Dream

Many of us have difficulty from time to time falling asleep or remaining asleep. Although sleep is a natural function and cannot be forced, we can develop more adaptive sleep habits that help us become more receptive to sleep. However, if insomnia or other sleep-related problems persist or become associated with difficulties functioning during the day, it is worthwhile to have a professional evaluate the problem. Here are some techniques to help you acquire more adaptive sleep habits.

1. Go to bed only when you feel sleepy.
2. Limit your activities in bed as much as possible to sleeping. Avoid watching TV or reading in bed.
3. If after 10 to 20 minutes of lying in bed you are unable to fall asleep, get out of bed, go to another room, and put yourself in a relaxed mood by reading, listening to calming music, or practicing self-relaxation.
4. Establish a regular routine. Sleeping late to make up for lost sleep can throw off your body clock. Set your alarm for the same time each morning and get up, regardless of how many hours you have slept.
5. Avoid naps during the daytime. You'll feel less sleepy at bedtime if you catch *z*'s during the afternoon.
6. Avoid ruminating in bed. Don't focus on problems as you attempt to sleep. Tell yourself that you'll think about tomorrow, tomorrow. Help yourself enter a more sleepful frame of mind by engaging in a mental fantasy or mind trip, or just let all thoughts slip away from consciousness. If an important idea comes to you, don't rehearse it in your mind. Jot it down on a handy pad so you won't lose it. But if thoughts persist, get up and follow them elsewhere.
7. Put yourself in a relaxed frame of mind before sleep. Some people unwind before bed by reading; others prefer watching TV or just resting quietly. Do whatever you find most relaxing. You may find it helpful to

incorporate within your regular bedtime routine the techniques for lowering your level of arousal discussed earlier in this text, such as meditation or progressive relaxation.
8. Establish a regular daytime exercise schedule. Regular exercise during the day (not directly before bedtime) can help induce sleepiness upon retiring.
9. Avoid use of caffeinated beverages, such as coffee and tea, in the evening or late afternoon. Also, avoid drinking alcoholic beverages. Alcohol can interfere with normal sleep patterns (reduced total sleep, REM sleep, and sleep efficiency), even when consumed upwards of 6 hours before bedtime.
10. Practice rational restructuring. Substitute rational alternatives for self-defeating thoughts. Here are some examples:

SELF-DEFEATING THOUGHTS	RATIONAL ALTERNATIVES
"I must fall asleep right now or I'll be a wreck tomorrow."	"I may feel tired, but I've been able to get by with little sleep before. I can make up for it tomorrow by getting to bed early."
"What's the matter with me that I can't seem to fall sleep?"	"Stop blaming yourself. You can't control sleep. Just let whatever happens, happen."
"If I don't get to sleep right now, I won't be able to concentrate on the exam (conference, meeting, etc.) tomorrow."	"My concentration may be off a bit, but I'm not going to fall apart. There' no point blowing things out of proportion. I might as well get up for a while and watch a little TV rather than lie here dwelling on this."

SUMMING UP

Eating Disorders

What are the major types of eating disorders? Two major types of eating disorders are included in the *DSM:* anorexia nervosa and bulimia nervosa. Anorexia nervosa, which is characterized by self-starvation and failure to maintain normal body weight, intense fears of becoming overweight, distorted body image, and in females, amenorrhea. Bulimia nervosa involves preoccupation with weight control and body shape, repeated binges, and regular purging to keep weight down. Another type of eating disorder, binge-eating disorder (BED), is presently classified as a potential disorder requiring further study.

What factors are implicated in the development of eating disorders? Eating disorders typically begin in adolescence and affect more females than males. Anorexia and bulimia are linked to preoccupations with weight control and maladaptive ways of trying to keep weight down. Many other factors are implicated in their development, including social pressures on young women to adhere to unrealistic standards of thinness, issues of control, underlying psychological problems, and conflict within the family, especially over issues of autonomy. People with BED

tend to be older than those with anorexia or bulimia and to suffer from obesity.

What are the major forms of treatment for eating disorders? Severe cases of anorexia are often treated in an inpatient setting where a refeeding regimen can be closely monitored. Behavior modification and other psychological interventions, including psychotherapy and family therapy, also may be helpful. Most cases of bulimia are treated on an outpatient basis, with evidence supporting the therapeutic benefits of cognitive-behavioral therapy, interpersonal psychotherapy, and antidepressant medication. Cognitive-behavioral therapy and antidepressant medication have shown positive effects in treating binge-eating disorder.

Sleep Disorders

What are the major types of sleep disorders? Sleep disorders are classified in two major categories, dyssomnias and parasomnias. Dyssomnias are disturbances in the amount, quality, or timing of sleep. They include five specific types: primary insomnia, primary hypersomnia, narcolepsy, breathing-related sleep disorder, and circadian rhythm sleep disorder. Parasomnias are disturbed behaviors or abnormal physiological responses occurring either during sleep or at the threshold between wakefulness and sleep. Parasomnias include three major types: nightmare disorder, sleep terror disorder, and sleepwalking disorder.

What are the major forms of treatment for sleep disorders?
The most common form of treatment of sleep disorders involves the use of antianxiety drugs. However, use of these drugs should be time limited because of the potential for psychological and/or physical dependence, among other problems associated with their use. Cognitive-behavioral interventions have produced substantial benefits in helping people with chronic insomnia.

Norms for the Fear of Fat Scale

First add up your scores on the 10-item Fear of Fat scale. You may compare your own score on the scale to those obtained by the groups listed below. However, the comparative scores given below are limited to female samples.

Group	Number of Respondents	Average (Mean) Scores
Nondieting college women (women satisfied with their weight)	49	17.30
General female college population	73	18.33
College women who are dissatisfied with their weight and have been on three or more diets during the past year	40	23.90
Bulimic college women (actively bingeing and purging)	32	30.00
Anorexic women in treatment	7	35.00

Source: Goldfarb, L. A., Dykens, E. M., & Gerrard, M. (1985). The Goldfarb Fear of Fat scale, *Journal of Personality Assessment, 49,* 329–332.

Keep the following in mind as you interpret your score:
1. The Goldfarb samples are quite small.
2. A score at a certain level does not place you in that group; it merely means that you report an equivalent fear of fat. In other words, a score of 33.00 does not indicate you have bulimia or anorexia. It means that your self-reported fear of fat approximates those reported by bulimic and anorexic women in the Goldfarb study.

KEY TERMS

anorexia nervosa *(p. 332)*
bulimia nervosa *(p. 332)*
eating disorder *(p. 332)*
body mass index (BMI) *(p. 336)*
binge-eating disorder (BED) *(p. 342)*
obesity *(p. 343)*

sleep disorders *(p. 345)*
dyssomnias *(p. 346)*
insomnia *(p. 346)*
primary insomnia *(p. 346)*
hypersomnia *(p. 347)*
narcolepsy *(p. 347)*

breathing-related sleep disorder *(p. 348)*
circadian rhythm sleep disorder *(p. 349)*
parasomnias *(p. 349)*
nightmare disorder *(p. 349)*
sleep terror disorder *(p. 351)*
sleepwalking disorder *(p. 351)*

MEDIA TOOLS

A variety of digital and online learning tools are available to enrich your learning experience and help you succeed in the course. These resources include:

- **MYPSYCHLAB,** an online learning system for your course in abnormal psychology that allows you to test your mastery of concepts in the book by using chapter-by-chapter diagnostic tests. Results from the diagnostic tests help you build a customized study plan. To access **MyPsychLab,** visit www.prenhall.com/mypsychlab and follow the instructions on the site.
- **"SPEAKING OUT" PATIENT INTERVIEWS,** a set of video case examples of actual patients you can access on the companion

CD-ROM included with the text. Icons in the margins of the chapter highlight the video case examples included on the CD-ROM.

- **COMPANION WEB SITE,** an online study center that offers computer-scored quizzes you can use to test your knowledge, along with other study tools and links to related sites to enhance your learning of abnormal psychology. To access the companion web site, visit www.prenhall.com/nevid and use the various tabs and links on the site to access these learning resources.

Eating Disorders

are characterized by

Disturbed eating behaviors and maladaptive ways of controlling body weight

and include such types as

- Anorexia Nervosa
- Bulimia Nervosa
- Binge-Eating Disorder (proposed disorder requiring further study)

and may be explained by causal factors including

- Sociocultural factors, such as pressures to achieve unrealistic standards of thinness
- Psychosocial factors, such as rigid dieting, body dissatisfaction, and perfectionistic and dichotomous thinking
- Biological factors, such as disturbed neurotransmitter functioning and genetic influences
- Conflicts with parents over autonomy
- Multiple causes as represented in this potential causal pathway in bulimia:

and may be treated by

- Biomedical therapies such as antidepressant drugs for bulimia and hospitalization in severe cases
- Psychotherapy to explore and resolve underlying psychological issues and conflicts
- Cognitive-behavioral therapy to correct self-defeating beliefs and develop healthier eating behaviors
- Family therapy to reduce conflicts and improve communication within the family

MODEL SPOTLIGHT

A Potential Causal Pathway in Bulimia

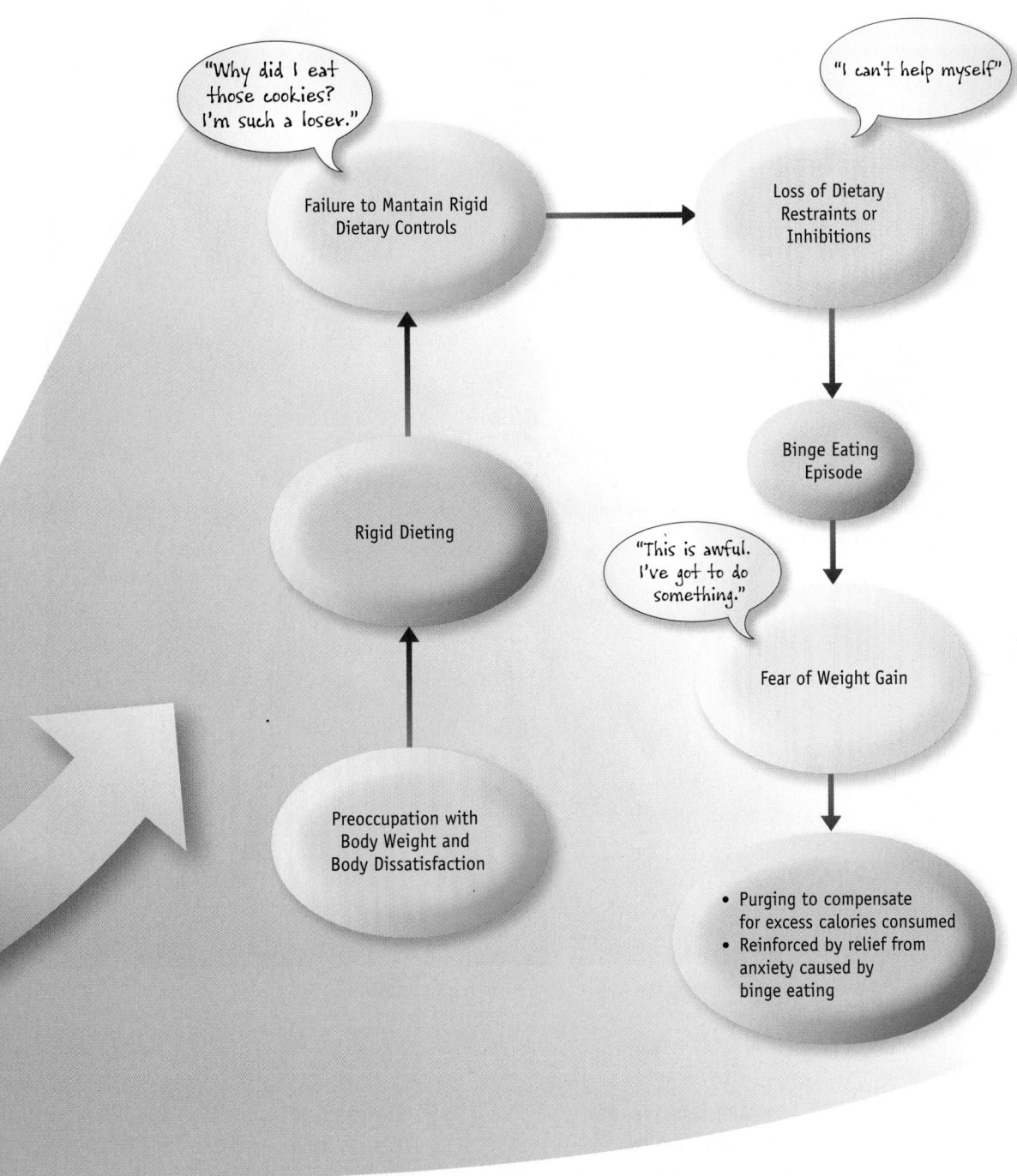

Note that negative reinforcement in the form of temporary relief from anxiety about gaining weight strengthens food-rejecting behavior in anorexia nervosa and purging in bulimia nervosa, but at the cost of maintaining these maladaptive behaviors.

Disorders Involving Gender and Sexuality

Eric Fischel, "The Bed, The Chair, The Sitter." 78" x 93". Oil on Linen. 1999–2000. Courtesy: Mary Boone Gallery, New York.

CHAPTER OUTLINE

GENDER IDENTITY DISORDER 360–364

Theoretical Perspectives

SEXUAL DYSFUNCTIONS 365–376

Types of Sexual Dysfunctions
Theoretical Perspectives
Treatment of Sexual Dysfunctions

PARAPHILIAS 376–387

Types of Paraphilias
Theoretical Perspectives
Treatment of Paraphilias

RAPE 387–391

Types of Rape
Theoretical Perspectives

SUMMING UP 391–392

"I" "I Know Something None of You Will Ever Know"

Gender identity disorder (GID) is defined by the American Psychiatric Association (2000) as a "strong and persistent cross-gender identification [accompanied by] a persistent discomfort with his or her sex or sense of appropriateness in the gender role of that sex." All of my life, I harbored the strongest conviction that I was inappropriately assigned to the wrong [sex]—that of a man—when inside I knew myself to be a woman. Even so (and like so many other GIDs) I continued a lifelong struggle with this deeply felt mistake. I was successful in school, became a national swimming champion, received my college degrees, married twice (fathering children in both marriages), and was respected as a competent and good man in the workplace. However, the persistently unrelenting wrongfulness of my life continued. Not until my fourth decade was I truly able to address my gender issue.

Jay Thomas, Ph.D., underwent gender reassignment and officially became Jayne Thomas, Ph.D., in November of 1985, and what has transpired in the ensuing years has been the most enlightening of glimpses into the plight of humankind. . . .

Iconoclastically, I try to challenge both the masculine and feminine. "I know something none of you women know or will ever know in your lifetime." I can provocatively address the females in my audiences as Jayne. "I once lived as a man and have been treated as an equal. You never have nor will you experience such equality." Or, when a male student once came to my assistance in a classroom, fixing an errant video playback device and then strutting peacock-like back to his seat as only a satisfied male can, I teasingly commented to a nearby female student, "I used to be able to do that."

Having once lived as a man and now as a woman, I can honestly state that I see profound differences in our social/psychological/biological being as man and woman. I have now experienced many of the ways in which women are treated as less than men. Jay worked as a consultant to a large banking firm in Los Angeles and continued in that capacity as a woman following her gender shift. Amazingly the world presented itself in a different perspective. As Jay, technical presentations to management had generally been received in a positive manner and credit for my work fully acknowledged. Jayne now found management less accessible, credit for her efforts less forthcoming and, in general, found herself working harder to be well prepared for each meeting than she ever had as a male. As a man, her forceful and impassioned presentations were an asset; as a woman they definitely seemed a liability.

On one occasion, as Jayne, when I passionately asserted my position regarding what I felt to be an important issue, my emotion and disappointment in not getting my point across (my voice showed my frustration) was met with a nearby colleague (a man) reaching to touch my arm with words of reassurance, "There, there, take it easy, it will be all right." Believe me, that never happened to Jay. There was also an occasion when I had worked most diligently on a presentation to management only to find the company vice president more interested in the fragrance of my cologne than my technical agenda.

Certainly there are significant differences in the treatment of men and women, and yet I continue to be impressed with how similar we two genders really are. Although I have made this seemingly enormous change in lifestyle (and it is immense in so many ways), I continue as the same human being, perceiving the same world through these same sensory neurons. The difference—I now find myself a more comfortable and serene being than the paradoxical woman in a man's body, with anatomy and gender that have attained congruence. . . .

Having lived as man and woman in the same lifetime, one personal truth seems clear. Rather than each gender attempting to change and convert the other to its own side, as I often see couples undertaking to accomplish (women need be more logical and men

TRUTH or FICTION

T❑ F❑ Gay males and lesbians have the gender identity of the other sex. (p. 363)

T❑ F❑ Orgasm is a reflex. (p. 367)

T❑ F❑ Wearing revealing bathing suits is a form of exhibitionism. (p. 378)

T❑ F❑ People who become sexually aroused while watching their partners disrobe are voyeurs. (p. 380)

T❑ F❑ Some people cannot become sexually aroused unless they are subjected to pain or humiliation. (p. 382)

T❑ F❑ College women are more likely to be raped by strangers than by men they know. (p. 389)

T❑ F❑ Deep down, most women desire to be raped. (p. 390)

T❑ F❑ Rapists are mentally ill. (p. 390)

359

Dr. Jayne Thomas

more sharing of their emotions), we might more productively come together in our relationships building upon our gender uniqueness and strengths. Men and women have different perspectives, which can be used successfully to address life's issues.

—Dr. Jayne Thomas, *in her own words*[1]

[1]*Dr. Thomas taught psychology at Mission College in California. Sadly, she passed away in 2002, a personal loss to your authors and to the general community.*

JAY THOMAS WAS SO UNCOMFORTABLE WITH HIS ANATOMICAL GENDER THAT HE UNDERWENT a sex reassignment procedure. Imagine what it must be like to be living in a body that feels alien to you by dint of the sex to which you were born. When children are born, even before fingers and toes are counted, the obstetrician will announce, "It's a girl" (or a boy). In this chapter we explore a wide range of psychological disorders involving not only sexual identity, but also deviant or atypical patterns of sexual attraction and problems relating to lack of sexual interest or response. We will also consider a form of abnormal behavior that is not classified as a psychological disorder but that can have devastating emotional and physical effects on people it victimizes: rape.

In sexual behavior, as in other types of behavior, the lines between the normal and the abnormal are not always agreed upon or drawn precisely. Sex, like eating, is a natural function. Also like eating, sexual behavior varies greatly among individuals and cultures. Our sexual behavior is profoundly affected by cultural, religious, and moral beliefs, custom, folklore, and superstition. In the realm of sexual behavior, our conceptions of what is normal or abnormal are influenced by cultural learning imparted through the family, school, and religious institutions.

Many patterns of sexual behavior, such as masturbation, premarital intercourse, and oral–genital sex are normal in contemporary American society, if frequency of occurrence is any indication. But frequency is not the only yardstick of normal behavior. Behavior is frequently labeled abnormal when it deviates from the norms of one's society. For example, kissing is highly popular in Western cultures but is consider deviant behavior in some preliterate societies in South America and Africa (Rathus, Nevid, & Fichner-Rathus, 2008). Members of the Thonga tribe of Africa were shocked when they first observed European visitors kissing. One man exclaimed, "Look at them—they eat each other's saliva and dirt." We will see that some sex-related activities are considered as abnormal in the eyes of mental health professionals as kissing seemed to the Thonga—for example, feeling that one is trapped in the body of the wrong sex, being more sexually aroused by articles of clothing than by one's partner, or losing interest in sex or being unable to become sexually aroused despite adequate stimulation.

We may also consider behavior to be abnormal when it is self-defeating, harms others, or causes personal distress. We shall see how psychological disorders discussed in this chapter meet one or more of these standards of abnormality. In exploring these disorders, we touch on questions that probe the boundaries between abnormality and normality. For example, is it abnormal to have difficulty becoming sexually aroused or reaching orgasm? How do mental health professionals define exhibitionism and voyeurism? When is it normal to watch another person disrobe, and when is it abnormal? Where do we draw the lines?

We begin with gender identity disorder, a disorder that touches on the most basic part of our experience as sexual beings—our sense of being male or female.

GENDER IDENTITY DISORDER:

The Case of Denise

"My earliest memories, back when I was about 4 years old . . . I remember cross-dressing back then, all the way until really around my puberty."

gender identity One's psychological sense of being female or being male.

gender identity disorder (GID) A type of psychological disorder characterized by conflict between one's anatomic sex and one's gender identity.

GENDER IDENTITY DISORDER

Gender identity is the psychological sense of being male or female. For most people, gender identity is consistent with a person's anatomic sex. In **gender identity disorder (GID)**, however, there is a conflict between one's anatomic sex and one's gender identity that is associated with serious emotional distress or impaired functioning.

TABLE 11.1
Clinical Features of Gender Identity Disorder

A. A strong, persistent identification with the other gender. At least four of the following features are required to make the diagnosis in children:

1. Repeated expression of the desire to be a member of the other sex (or expression of the belief that one actually belongs to the other sex).

2. Preference for wearing clothing stereotypical of members of the other sex.

3. Persistent fantasies about being a member of the other sex, or assumption of roles played by members of the other sex in make-believe play.

4. Desire to participate in activities and games considered stereotypical of the other sex.

5. Preference for playmates that belong to the other sex at ages when children typically prefer playmates of their own sex.
Adolescents and adults typically express the wish to be of the other sex, frequently "pass" as a member of the other sex, or believe that their emotions and behavior typify the other sex.

B. A strong, persistent sense of discomfort with one's anatomic sex or with the stereotypical gender role of one's sex.

In children, these features are commonly present: Boys state that their external genitals are repugnant or that it would be better not to have them, show aversion to masculine-typed toys, games, and rough-and-tumble play. Girls prefer not to urinate while sitting, express the wish not to grow breasts or to menstruate, or show an aversion to feminine-typed clothing.

Adolescents and adults typically state that they were born the wrong sex and express the wish for medical intervention (e.g., hormone treatments, surgery, or both) to rid them of their own sex characteristics and simulate the characteristics of the other sex.

C. There is no "intersex condition," such as ambiguous sexual anatomy, that might give rise to the individual's feelings.

D. The features cause serious distress or impair key areas of occupational, social, or other functioning.

Source: Adapted from the *DSM-IV-TR* (APA, 2000).

Gender identity disorder (also referred to as *transsexualism*) may begin in childhood. Some children with the disorder find their anatomic sex to be a source of persistent and intense distress. The diagnosis is not used simply to label "tomboyish" girls and "sissyish" boys. It is applied to children who persistently repudiate their anatomic traits or who are preoccupied with clothing or activities that are stereotypical of the other sex (see Table 11.1). The diagnosis of GID applies to both children and adults who perceive themselves psychologically as members of the other sex and who show persistent discomfort with their anatomic sex.

Although the prevalence rate of GID is unknown, the disorder is certainly uncommon. It is believed to occur about five times more often in boys than girls (Jones & Hill, 2002). GID takes many paths. It can end by adolescence, with the child's becoming more accepting of her or his gender identity, or it may persist into adolescence or adulthood (Cohen-Kettenis, 2001). The child sometimes develops a gay male or lesbian sexual orientation (Bailey, 2003a, 2003b).Transsexual adults typically showed cross-gender preferences in play and dress in early childhood. Some report that they felt they belonged to the other sex as long as they can remember (Zucker, 2005a, 2005b). Some male transsexuals recall that, as children, they preferred playing with dolls, enjoyed wearing frilly dresses, and disliked rough-and-tumble play. Some female transsexuals report that as children they disliked dresses and acted like tomboys. They preferred playing "boys' games" and playing with boys. Female transsexuals may have an easier time adjusting than male transsexuals (Selvin, 1993). Tomboys generally find acceptance more easily than "sissy boys." Even in adulthood, it may be easier for a female transsexual to wear male clothes and "pass" as a slightly built man than it is for a brawny man to pass for a large woman.

Not all people with GID seek reassignment surgery. Fewer than 20,000 people are known to have undergone sex-reassignment surgery (Jones & Hill, 2002). For those who do, surgeons attempt to construct external genital organs that closely resemble those of the opposite sex. Male-to-female surgery is generally more successful than female-to-male. Hormone treatments promote the development of secondary sex characteristics of the reassigned sex, such as growth of fatty tissue in the breasts in male-to-female cases and the growth of the beard and body hair in female-to-male cases.

What is normal and what is abnormal? The cultural context must be considered in defining what is normal and what is abnormal in the realm of sexual and sexually related behavior. The people in these photographs—and the ways in which they cloak or expose their bodies—would be quite out of place in one another's societies.

People who undergo sex-reassignment surgery can participate in sexual activity and even reach orgasm, but they cannot conceive or bear children because they lack the internal reproductive organs of their newly reconstructed sex. Investigators generally find positive postoperative adjustment of transsexuals (Smith et al., 2005). In one study, none of 20 adolescents who underwent sex reassignment surgery later expressed regrets (Smith et al., 2001). In another recent survey, 85% of male-to-female transsexuals were able to achieve orgasm during sexual activity after reassignment surgery (Lawrence, 2005).

Postoperative adjustment tends to be more favorable for female-to-males. One reason may be that society is more accepting of women who desire to become men (Smith et al., 2005). Female-to-male transsexuals also may be better adjusted before surgery, so their superior postoperative adjustment may represent a selection factor.

Dr. Jayne Thomas, whom we introduced at the beginning of the chapter, spoke about the psychological adjustment and shift in gender roles she experienced following sex reassignment surgery.

"Everybody Is Born Unique, but Most of Us Die Copies"

Does the shifting of gender role create difficulties in the GID's life? Most assuredly it does. Family and intimate relationships rank highest among those issues most problematic for the transitioning individual to resolve. When one shifts gender role the effects of such a change are global; as ripples in a pond, the transformation radiates outward impacting all that have significantly touched the GID's life. My parents had never realized that their eldest son was dealing with such a lifelong problem. Have they accepted or do they fully understand the magnitude of my issue? I fear not. After almost 15 years of having lived as a female, my father continues to call me by my male name. I do not doubt my parents' or children's love for me, but so uninformed are we of the true significance of gender identity that a clear understanding seems light-years away. Often I see my clients losing jobs, closeness with family members, visitation rights with children, and generally becoming relegated to the role of societal outcast. Someone once stated that "Everybody is born unique, but most of us die copies"—a great price my clients often pay for personal honesty and not living their lives as a version of how society deems they should.

—Dr. Jayne Thomas

Men seeking sex-reassignment outnumber women by perhaps 3 or 4 to 1. Most female-to-male individuals with GID do not seek complete sex-reassignment surgery. Instead, they may remove their internal sex organs (ovaries, fallopian tubes, uterus) along with the fatty tissue in their breasts (Bockting & Fung, 2006). Testosterone (male sex hormone) treatments increase muscle mass and growth of the beard. But only a few female-to-male transsexuals have the series of operations necessary to construct an artificial penis, largely because the constructed penises do not work very well, and the surgery is expensive. Therefore, most female-to-male transsexuals limit their physical alteration to hysterectomies, mastectomies, and testosterone treatment (Bailey, 2003b).

Gender identity should not be confused with sexual orientation. Gay males and lesbians have erotic interests in members of their own sex, but their gender identity (sense of being male or female) is consistent with their anatomic sex. They do not desire to become members of the other sex or despise their own genitalia, as we find in many people with GID.

You'll recall from Chapter 1 that homosexuality is no longer classified as a mental or psychological disorder. However, some authorities have argued that *homophobia*, or hatred and fear of gay men and lesbians, should be recognized as a form of abnormal behavior or psychopathology (see the *A Closer Look* feature).

It is important to note that the GID diagnosis remains controversial, especially within the transgender community. People with gender identities that don't match their anatomic sex may show no signs of psychological disturbance other than their discomfort with their anatomic sex. They may consider themselves to have a *transgender* identity, not a psychological disorder. They may regard the mismatch between their gender identity as a mistake of nature. Or if they do have psychological problems, they may argue that it is because of how society mistreats people who are different.

Theoretical Perspectives

The origins of GID remain unclear (van Goozen et al., 2002). Psychodynamic theorists point to extremely close mother–son relationships, empty relationships with parents, and fathers who were absent or detached (Stoller, 1969). These family circumstances may foster strong identification with the mother in young males, leading to a reversal of expected gender roles and identity. Girls with weak, ineffectual mothers and strong masculine fathers may overly identify with their fathers and develop a psychological sense of themselves as "little men."

Learning theorists similarly point to father absence in the case of boys—to the unavailability of a strong male role model. Children who were reared by parents who had wanted children of the other gender and who strongly encouraged cross-gender dressing and patterns of play may learn socialization patterns and develop a gender identity associated with the opposite sex.

TRUTH or **FICTION**

Gay males and lesbians have the gender identity of the other sex.

☑ **FALSE.** Gender identity should not be confused with sexual orientation. Gay males and lesbians have erotic interest in members of their own gender but their gender identity is consistent with their anatomic sex.

A CLOSER LOOK

Homophobia: Social Prejudice or Personal Psychopathology?

George Weinberg (1972) coined the term **homophobia** to describe the persistent, irrational fear of lesbians and gay men. Recent evidence suggests that in some cases homophobia is grounded in an aversion to homosexuality, rather than the underlying attraction. Homophobia is deemed irrational because it is usually based on beliefs that are of questionable validity or have been overwhelmingly disputed. For example, homophobes may believe, falsely, that gay men are more likely to become child molesters than heterosexual men, that lesbians and gay men wish to be members of the other gender, that they do not make good parents, that their children will become lesbian or gay, that they are sexually promiscuous or indiscriminate in their sexual attractions, that their relationships are transitory and focused only on sex, that they are responsible for the AIDS epidemic, and so on. People who hold such beliefs may use them to justify prejudicial acts against lesbians and gay men, ranging from personal rudeness or hostility to vandalism, harassment, and even violent physical attacks (Freiberg, 1995; Katz, 1995). As these attacks have become commonplace in many parts of the United States, they have created a climate of terror for lesbians and gay men.

But do the roots of homophobia lie within the individual or the society? Many theoreticians use the term **heterosexism** (Herek, 1996) to describe a broader cultural ideology and resulting pattern of institutional discrimination against lesbians and gay men. They suggest that the antigay feelings of individuals are only part of a broader pattern that is based on a cultural assumption that reproductive sexuality is the only outcome of healthy and morally correct psychosexual development. They go on to suggest that antigay sentiments are rewarded in our society more than they are punished and so are not widely considered to be abnormal or pathological.

Others believe that homophobia represents a form of personal psychopathology because it involves irrational beliefs that persist in the face of evidence to the contrary. Marvin Kantor (1998) views homophobia as a psychological disorder in which the false beliefs about lesbians and gay men and the anxiety associated with them resemble a paranoid delusion. In this view, homophobic beliefs represent people's underlying fears or anxieties about their own underlying homosexual attractions or insecurity about their own

masculinity or femininity. Evidence on whether homophobes harbor underlying homosexual attractions remains inconclusive, however (Meier et al., 2006).

Violent physical and verbal attacks against lesbians and gay men are referred to as gay bashing and are considered a form of hate crime. According to Kantor, many people who engage in gay bashing are really attempting to reassure themselves that they do not have such feelings or attractions. By punishing those who express these forbidden wishes, the gay basher may be seeking to prove to himself and others that he is not one of them.

Research on people with homophobia portrays them as having rigid personalities and intolerance of anything that deviates from their personal view of appropriate behavior (Kantor, 1998). Although many report having not had contact with gay males or lesbians, at least to their knowledge, they harbor intensely hostile attitudes toward them (Herek, 1996). Their beliefs are selectively drawn from a larger culture that has historically created demeaning images of lesbians and gay men, depicting them as dangerous, perverted, depressed, or comical. Ignorance about lesbians and gay men, maintained by negative portrayals in the media, fuels homophobic attitudes.

Because of the harm that homophobia and heterosexism do to lesbians and gay men and because of adverse effects on their mental health, these phenomena are worthy of our serious attention and understanding. The question remains, do heterosexism and homophobia constitute a form of social or personal pathology, or both?

Gay bashing. In a heinous case that brought gay bashing into the national spotlight in 1998, a gay 21-year-old University of Wyoming student, Matthew Shepard, was pistol-whipped, tied to a fencepost, and left to die by a group of assailants.

---

homophobia Hatred and fear of lesbians and gay males.

heterosexism The culturally based belief system that holds that only reproductive sexuality between men and women is psychologically healthy and morally correct.

Nonetheless, the great majority of people with the types of family histories described by psychodynamic and learning theorists do not develop GID. Perhaps these family factors play a role in combination with a biological predisposition. We know that many adults with a transgender identity showed cross-gender preferences in toys, games, and clothing very early in childhood. If critical early learning experiences play a part, they most probably occurred very early in life.

GID may develop as the result of an interaction *in utero* between the developing brain and the release of male sex hormones (Dennis, 2004). Investigators suspect that the release of male sex hormones during prenatal development has an organizing effect on the brain, sculpting it in a masculine direction if sufficient amounts of the hormone are present, or in a feminine direction if the hormone is absent (as is normally the case with female fetuses) (van Goozen et al., 2002). Perhaps a disturbance in the endocrine (hormonal) environment during gestation leads the brain to become differentiated with respect to gender identity in one direction while the genitals develop normally in the other direction. However, we lack direct evidence of abnormal hormonal balances during prenatal development that could explain the development of GID (Gooren & Kruijver, 2002). Even if such hormonal factors were demonstrated, they are unlikely to be the sole cause.

Investigators are also actively exploring possible genetic underpinnings (Dennis, 2004). As with many psychological disorders, biological factors, such as genetic and hormonal influences, may create a disposition that interacts with early life experiences to result in the development of GID. Yet speculations about the origins of gender identity disorder remain unsubstantiated by hard evidence.

SEXUAL DYSFUNCTIONS

Sexual dysfunctions are persistent problems with sexual interest, arousal, or response. Table 11.2 provides an overview of the sexual dysfunctions reviewed in this chapter.

Reports of sexual problems are widespread in our society. The estimates of prevalence rates of sexual problems reported in Table 11.2 are drawn from two large-scale surveys, the National Health and Social Life Survey or NHSLS (Laumann et al., 1994 Laumann, Paik, & Rosen, 1999; Rosen & Laumann, 2003) and the Men's Attitudes to Life Events and Sexuality (MALES) Study (Rosen et al., 2004). Women more often report problems regarding painful sex, inability to attain orgasm, and lack of sexual desire. Men were more likely to report reaching orgasm too quickly (premature ejaculation). We should note that reports of sexual problems shown in the table don't necessarily mean that a diagnosable disorder is present. We lack clear evidence of the underlying rates of diagnosable sexual dysfunctions in the general community.

Sexual dysfunctions may be classified according to two general categories, lifetime versus acquired and situational versus generalized. Cases of sexual dysfunction that have existed for the individual's lifetime are called *lifetime dysfunctions. Acquired dysfunctions* begin following a period of normal functioning. In *situational dysfunctions,* the problems occur in some situations (for example, with one's spouse), but not in others (for example, with a lover or when masturbating), or at some times but not others. *Generalized dysfunctions* occur in all situations and at every time the individual engages in sexual activity.

Despite the fact that sexual dysfunctions are believed to be widespread, relatively few people seek treatment for these problems (Nicolosi et al., 2006). People may not know that effective treatments are available or where to obtain help, or they may avoid seeking help because of the long-standing stigma attached to admitting a sexual difficulty.

sexual dysfunctions Persistent or recurrent problems with sexual interest, arousal, or response.

TABLE 11.2 **Overview of Sexual Dysfunctions**

TYPE OF DISORDER	Prevalence in Population (approx.)	Description
SEXUAL DESIRE DISORDERS Disorders involving lack of sexual interest or aversion to genital contact		
Hypoactive sexual desire disorder	32% women, 15% men	Lack of sexual interest or desire
Sexual aversion disorder	Unknown	Aversion to, and avoidance of, genital sexual contact
SEXUAL AROUSAL DISORDERS Disorders involving lack of sexual excitement or arousal		
Female sexual arousal disorder	21%*	Difficulty becoming aroused or maintaining sexual arousal or excitement during sexual activity
Male erectile disorder	10%–22%	Difficulty achieving or maintaining erection during sexual activity
ORGASM DISORDERS Disorders involving impaired orgasmic response		
Female orgasmic disorder	26%	Difficulty achieving orgasm
Male orgasmic disorder	8%	Difficulty achieving orgasm
Premature ejaculation	30%**	Climaxing (ejaculating) too early
SEXUAL PAIN DISORDERS Disorders in women involving pain during intercourse or penetration		
Dyspareunia	2%***	Pain during or following sexual intercourse not explainable by an underlying medical condition
Vaginismus	Unknown	Involuntary contractions of the vaginal musculature, making penile penetration painful or impossible

Sources: Laumann, Paik, & Rosen, 1999; Rosen & Laumann, 2003; Rosen et al., 2004.

Note: Prevalence rates reflect percentages of adults reporting problems and may not correspond to clinical diagnosis of sexual dysfunctions. Reports of sexual pain and climaxing too early were based on individuals who were sexually active during the past 12-month period.

*having trouble lubricating

**climaxing too early

***experienced pain during sex

Types of Sexual Dysfunctions

The *DSM-IV-TR* groups most sexual dysfunctions within the following categories:

1. Sexual desire disorders
2. Sexual arousal disorders
3. Orgasm disorders
4. Sexual pain disorders

hypoactive sexual desire disorder
Persistent or recurrent lack of sexual interest or sexual fantasies.

Sexual Desire Disorders Sexual desire disorders are disturbances in sexual appetite or an aversion to genital sexual activity. People with **hypoactive sexual desire disorder** have an absence or lack of sexual interest or desire. Typically there is either a virtual or complete absence of sexual fantasies. A recent study of women with the disorder found that they generally have a less active sex life and experience less satisfaction with sexual relationships (Leiblum et al., 2006). Lack of desire is more common among women than men (Goldstein et al., 2006). Nevertheless, the belief that men are always eager for sex is a myth.

Clinicians do not necessarily agree on criteria for determining the level of sexual desire considered "normal." They may weigh various factors in reaching a diagnosis of hypoactive sexual desire disorder, such as the client's lifestyle (for example, parents contending with the demands of young children may lack energy for interest in sex), sociocultural factors (culturally restrictive attitudes may restrain sexual desire or interest), the quality of the relationship (problems in a relationship may contribute to lack of interest in sex), and the client's age (desire normally declines with age) (Ghizzani, 2003; McCarthy et al., 2006).

The literature on sex differences supports the view that women are generally less interested in sex than are men (Peplau, 2003). Sex researchers continue to debate how to define sexual dysfunctions, especially in women (McCarthy et al., 2006). For example, some researchers argue that labeling a lack of sexual desire among women as a dysfunction imposes a male model of what is normal on women (Bean, 2002). Researchers also debate whether to diagnose female sexual dysfunction on the basis of a lack of desire or difficulty achieving orgasm or by the woman's own perceptions of these experiences as causing distress (Smith, 2003b). Keep in mind that lack of desire usually does not come to the health practitioner's attention unless one partner is more interested in sex than the other. That is when the less-interested partner may be labeled with a dysfunction. But questions remain about where to draw the line between "normal" and "abnormal" levels of sexual drive or interest.

sexual aversion disorder A type of sexual dysfunction characterized by aversion to, and avoidance, of genital sexual contact.

People with **sexual aversion disorder** have a strong aversion to genital sexual contact and avoid all or nearly all genital contact with a partner. They may, however, desire and enjoy affectionate contact or nongenital sexual contact. Deep aversion to any form of genital contact, especially in women, may stem from childhood sexual abuse, rape, or other traumatic experiences (Firestone, Firestone, & Catlett, 2006; Najman et al., 2005). In other cases, deep-seated feelings of sexual guilt or shame may impair sexual response. In men, the diagnosis is often connected with a history of erectile failure, which may lead men to associate sexual opportunities with feelings of failure and shame (Bancroft et al., 2005a, 2005b). Their partners may also develop aversions to sexual contact because their sexual contacts have been so frustrating or emotionally painful.

female sexual arousal disorder A type of sexual dysfunction in women involving difficulty becoming sexually aroused or lack of sexual excitement or pleasure during sexual activity.

male erectile disorder A sexual dysfunction in males characterized by difficulty in achieving or maintaining erection during sexual activity.

Sexual Arousal Disorders Disorders of sexual arousal are characterized by an inability to achieve or maintain the physiological responses involved in sexual arousal or excitement—vaginal lubrication in the woman or erection in the man—that are needed to complete sexual activity to the point of genital intercourse.

In women, sexual arousal is accompanied by lubrication of the vaginal walls that makes entry by the penis possible. In men, sexual arousal is characterized by erection. Almost all women now and then have difficulty becoming or remaining lubricated. Almost all men have occasional difficulty attaining or maintaining an erection through intercourse. The diagnoses of **female sexual arousal disorder** and **male erectile disorder** (also called erectile dysfunction, or ED) apply to persistent or recurrent problems in becoming genitally aroused. People with sexual arousal disorders may also lack the feelings of sexual pleasure or excitement that normally accompany sexual arousal (APA, 2000).

Occasional problems in achieving or maintaining erection are common enough, due to factors such as fatigue, alcohol, or anxiety with a new partner. The more concerned the man becomes about his sexual ability, the more likely he is to suffer *performance anxiety.* As we will explore further, performance anxiety can contribute to repeated failure, and a vicious cycle of anxiety and failure may develop (Bancroft et al., 2005a; McCabe, 2005).

The risks of erectile disorder increase with age (Ghizzani, 2003). Approximately 50% of men in the 40- to 70-year age range experience some degree of erectile dysfunction (Saigal, 2004).

Orgasm Disorders Orgasm or sexual climax is an involuntary reflex that results in rhythmic contractions of the pelvic muscles and is usually accompanied by feelings of intense pleasure. In men, these contractions are accompanied by expulsion of semen. There are three types of disorders involving problems with achieving orgasm: **female orgasmic disorder, male orgasmic disorder,** and **premature ejaculation.**

In male and female orgasmic disorder, there is a persistent or recurrent delay in reaching orgasm, or the absence of orgasm, following a normal level of sexual interest and arousal. The clinician needs to make a judgment about whether there is an "adequate" amount and type of stimulation needed to achieve orgasm, taking into consideration the wide variation in normal sexual response. Might a woman's difficulty achieving orgasm with her partner result from a lack of effective stimulation rather than an orgasmic disorder? Many women, for example, require direct clitoral stimulation (by their own hand or their partner's) in order to achieve orgasm during vaginal intercourse. This should not be considered abnormal because it is the *clitoris,* not the *vagina,* which is the woman's most erotically sensitive organ.

Male orgasmic disorder has received little attention in the clinical literature (Dekker, 1993; Rosen & Leiblum, 1995). Men with this problem can usually reach orgasm through masturbation but not through intercourse.

Premature ejaculation, the most common form of sexual dysfunction in men (Patrick et al., 2005), is defined as a recurrent or persistent pattern of ejaculation with minimal sexual stimulation. Most men with the disorder ejaculate either just prior to or immediately upon penetration or following a few penile thrusts (Byers & Grenier, 2003). In making the diagnosis, the clinician weighs the man's age, the novelty of the partner, and the frequency of sexual activity. Occasional experiences of rapid ejaculation, such as when the man is with a new partner, has had infrequent sexual contacts, or is very highly aroused, are not considered abnormal.

Sexual Pain Disorders In **dyspareunia,** sexual intercourse is associated with recurrent pain in the genital region. The pain cannot be explained fully by an underlying medical condition and so is believed to have a psychological component. The pain may stem from underlying physical causes, emotional factors, or a combination of the two (Goldstein et al., 2006). However, because many if not most cases of pain during intercourse are traceable to an underlying medical condition, such as insufficient lubrication or a urinary tract infection, controversy persists over whether dyspareunia should be classified as a mental disorder (Binik, 2005; Spitzer, 2005). Presently, the *DSM* classifies cases of clear medical origin under a different diagnostic label, "Sexual Dysfunction Due to Medical Condition."

Vaginismus is the involuntary spasm of the muscles surrounding the vagina when vaginal penetration is attempted, making sexual intercourse painful or impossible. Vaginismus is not a medical condition, but a conditioned response in which penile contact with the woman's genitals elicits an involuntary response of the vaginal musculature, preventing penetration.

Theoretical Perspectives

Many factors are implicated in the development of sexual dysfunctions, including factors representing psychological, biological, and sociocultural perspectives.

female orgasmic disorder A type of sexual dysfunction involving persistent difficulty achieving orgasm despite adequate stimulation.

male orgasmic disorder Persistent or recurrent delay in achieving orgasm or inability to achieve orgasm despite a normal level of sexual interest and arousal.

premature ejaculation A type of sexual dysfunction involving a pattern of unwanted rapid ejaculation during sexual activity.

T R U T H or F I C T I O N

Orgasm is a reflex.

☑ **TRUE.** People cannot will or force an orgasm. Nor can they will or force other sexual reflexes, such as erection and vaginal lubrication. Trying to force these responses generally backfires and only increases anxiety.

dyspareunia Persistent or recurrent pain experienced during or following sexual intercourse.

vaginismus The involuntary spasm of the muscles surrounding the vagina when vaginal penetration is attempted, making sexual intercourse difficult or impossible.

Psychological Perspectives The major contemporary psychological views of sexual dysfunctions emphasize the roles of anxiety, lack of sexual skills, irrational beliefs, perceived causes of events, and relationship problems. Here we consider several potential causal pathways.

Physically or psychologically painful sexual experiences may lead the person to respond to sexual contact with anxiety rather than arousal or pleasure. Conditioned anxiety resulting from a history of sexual trauma or rape plays a role in many women with sexual arousal disorder, sexual aversion disorder, orgasmic disorder, and vaginismus (Bean, 2002; Najman et al., 2005). Women with problems becoming sexually aroused may harbor deep-seated anger and resentment toward their partners (Moore & Heiman, 2006). Other psychologically based causes of sexual arousal disorder, especially in women, include guilt about sex and ineffective stimulation by the partner (Goldstein et al., 2006).

Sexual trauma early in life may make it difficult for men or women to respond sexually when they develop intimate relationships. People with a history of sexual trauma may be flooded with feelings of helplessness, unresolved anger, or misplaced guilt. They may also experience flashbacks of the abusive experiences when they engage in sexual relations, preventing them from becoming sexually aroused or achieving orgasm. Other psychological problems, such as depression, can also result in impaired sexual interest, arousal, or response.

Another principal form of anxiety in sexual dysfunctions is *performance anxiety,* which represents an excessive concern about the ability to perform successfully. Performance anxiety can develop when people experience problems performing sexually and begin to doubt their abilities. People troubled by performance anxiety become spectators during sex, rather than performers. Their attention is focused on how their bodies are responding (or not responding) to sexual stimulation. They are plagued by disruptive thoughts about the anticipated negative consequences of failing to perform adequately ("What will she think of me?") rather than focusing on their erotic experiences. Men with performance anxiety may have difficulty achieving or maintaining an erection or may ejaculate prematurely; women may fail to become adequately aroused or have difficulty achieving orgasm (Goldstein et al., 2006). A vicious cycle may ensue in which each failure experience instills deeper doubts, which leads to more anxiety during sexual encounters, which occasions repeated failure, and so on.

In Western cultures, there is a deeply ingrained connection between a man's sexual performance and his sense of manhood. The man who repeatedly fails to perform sexually may suffer a loss of self-esteem, become depressed, or feel he is no longer a man. He may see himself as a total failure, despite other accomplishments in life. Sexual opportunities are construed as tests of his manhood, and he may respond to them by bearing down and trying to will (force) an erection. Willing an erection may backfire because erection is a reflex that cannot be forced. With so much of his self-esteem on the line whenever he makes love, it is little wonder that performance anxiety may mount to a point that it inhibits erection. The erectile reflex is controlled by the parasympathetic branch of the autonomic nervous system. Activation of the sympathetic nervous system, which occurs when we are anxious or under stress, can block parasympathetic control, preventing the erectile reflex from occurring. Ejaculation, in contrast, is under sympathetic nervous system control, so heightened levels of arousal, as in the case of performance anxiety, can trigger premature ejaculation (Hellstrom et al., 2006; Janssen & Bancroft, 2006). The relationship between performance anxiety and sexual dysfunction can become a vicious cycle:

> One client who suffered from erectile dysfunction described his feelings of sexual inadequacy this way: I always felt inferior, like I was on probation, having to prove myself. I felt like I was up against the wall. You can't imagine how embarrassing this was. It's like you walk out in front of an audience that you think is a nudist convention and it turns out to be a tuxedo convention.

—The Author's Files

Another client described how performance anxiety led him to prepare for sexual relations as though he were psyching himself up for a big game:

"I"
"Paralyzed with Anxiety"

At work I have control over what I do. With sex, you don't have control over your sex organ. I know that my mind can control what my hands do. But the same is not true of my penis. I had begun to view sex as a basketball game. I used to play in college. When I would prepare for a game, I'd always be thinking, "Who was I guarding that night?" I'd try to psych myself up, sketching out in my mind how to play this guy, thinking through all possible moves and plays. I began to do the same thing with sex. If I were dating someone, I'd be thinking the whole evening about what might happen in bed. I'd always be preparing for the outcome. I'd sketch out in my mind how I was going to touch her, what I'd ask her to do. But all the time, right through dinner or the movies, I'd be worrying that I wouldn't get it up. I kept picturing her face and how disappointed she'd be. By the time we did go to bed, I was paralyzed with anxiety.

—*The Author's Files*

Women, too, may equate their self-esteem with their ability to reach frequent and intense orgasms. Yet when men and women try to will arousal or lubrication, or to force an orgasm, they may find that the harder they try, the more these responses elude them. Several generations ago the pressures concerning sex often revolved around the issue "Should I or shouldn't I?" Today, however, the pressures for both men and women are often based more on achieving performance goals relating to reaching orgasm and satisfying one's partner's sexual needs.

Sexual fulfillment is also based on learning sexual skills. Sexual skills or competencies, like other types of skills, are acquired through opportunities for new learning. We learn about how our and our partner's bodies respond sexually in various ways, including trial and error with our partners, by learning about our own sexual response through self-exploration (as in masturbation), by reading about sexual techniques, and perhaps by talking to others or viewing sex films or videotapes. Yet children who are raised to feel guilty or anxious about sex may have lacked opportunities to develop sexual knowledge and skills and so remain ignorant of the types of stimulation they need to achieve sexual gratification. They may also respond to sexual opportunities with feelings of anxiety and shame rather than arousal and pleasure.

Cognitive theorists, such as Albert Ellis (1977b), point out that underlying irrational beliefs and attitudes can contribute to sexual dysfunctions. Consider two such irrational beliefs: (a) we must have the approval at all times of everyone who is important to us; and (b) we must be thoroughly competent at everything we do. If we cannot accept the occasional disappointment of others, we may catastrophize the significance of a single frustrating sexual episode. If we insist that every sexual experience be perfect, we set the stage for inevitable failure.

How we appraise situations in terms of the perceived causes of events also plays a role. Attributing the cause for erectile difficulty to oneself ("What's wrong with me?") rather than to the situation ("It was the alcohol. . . . I was tired. . . .") can undermine future sexual functioning (Weisberg et al., 2001).

Relationship problems can also contribute to sexual dysfunctions, especially when they involve long-simmering resentments and conflicts (Moore & Heiman, 2006). The quality of sexual relations is usually no better than other facets of relationships or marriages. Couples who harbor resentments toward one another may choose the sexual arena for combat. Communication problems, moreover, are linked to general marital dissatisfaction. Couples who find it difficult to communicate their sexual desires may lack the means to help each other become more effective lovers.

When a source of pleasure becomes a source of misery. Sexual dysfunctions can be a source of intense personal distress and lead to friction between partners. Lack of communication is a major contributor to the development and maintenance of sexual dysfunctions.

The following case illustrates how sexual arousal disorder may be connected with problems in the relationship.

The Case of Paul and Petula

After living together for 6 months, Paul and Petula are contemplating marriage. But a problem has brought them to a sex therapy clinic. As Petula puts it, "For the last 2 months he hasn't been able to keep his erection after he enters me." Paul is 26 years old, a lawyer; Petula, 24, is a buyer for a large department store. They both grew up in middle-class, suburban families, were introduced through mutual friends and began having intercourse, without difficulty, a few months into their relationship. At Petula's urging, Paul moved into her apartment, although he wasn't sure he was ready for such a step. A week later he began to have difficulty maintaining his erection during intercourse, although he felt strong desire for his partner. When his erection waned, he would try again, but would lose his desire and be unable to achieve another erection. After a few times like this, Petula would become so angry that she began striking Paul in the chest and screaming at him. Paul, who at 200 pounds weighed more than twice as much as Petula, would just walk away, which angered Petula even more. It became clear that sex was not the only trouble spot in their relationship. Petula complained that Paul preferred to spend time with his friends and go to baseball games than to spend time with her. When together at home, he would become absorbed in watching sports events on television, and showed no interest in activities she enjoyed—attending the theater, visiting museums, etc. Because there was no evidence that the sexual difficulty was due to either organic problems or depression, a diagnosis of male erectile disorder was given. Neither Paul nor Petula was willing to discuss their nonsexual problems with a therapist. Although the sexual problem was treated successfully with a form of sex therapy modeled after techniques developed by Masters and Johnson, and the couple later married, Paul's ambivalences continued, even well into their marriage, and there were future recurrences of sexual problems as well.

—Adapted from Spitzer et al., 1994, pp. 198–200

Biological Perspectives Biological factors such as low testosterone levels and disease can dampen sexual desire and reduce responsiveness. The male sex hormone testosterone plays a pivotal role in energizing sexual desire and sexual activity in both men and women (Davis et al., 2005). Both men and women produce testosterone in their bodies, although women produce smaller amounts. In men, a decline in testosterone production can lead to a loss of sexual interest and even a loss of the capacity to achieve erections. The adrenal glands and ovaries are the sites where testosterone is produced in women. Women who have these organs surgically removed because of invasive disease no longer produce testosterone and may gradually lose sexual interest and the capacity for sexual response. However, most men and women with sexual dysfunctions have normal hormone levels (Spark, 1991).

Cardiovascular problems involving impaired blood flow both to and through the penis can cause erectile disorder—a problem that becomes more common as men age. Erectile disorder may share common risk factors with cardiovascular disorders (heart and artery diseases) (Rosen et al., 2004; Sun & Swindle, 2005), which should alert physicians that erectile dysfunction may be a sign of underlying cardiovascular disorders that need to be medically evaluated (Thompson et al., 2005). Erectile dysfunction is also more common in obese men (as are cardiovascular problems) (Saigal, 2004) and in men with prostate and urinary problems (Shabsigh et al., 2005). The good news is that obese men who lose weight and increase their activity levels may experience improved erectile functioning (Esposito et al., 2004).

Men with *diabetes mellitus* also stand an increased risk of ED (Rosen et al., 2004). Diabetes can damage blood vessels and nerves, including those serving the penis. Recent evidence shows that men with erectile disorder are more than twice as likely to have diabetes as men without erectile disorder (Sun et al., 2006).

Erectile disorder and male orgasmic disorder may also result from *multiple sclerosis* (MS), a disease in which nerve cells lose the protective coatings that facilitate transmission of neural messages (Rees, Fowler, & Maas, 2007). Chronic kidney disease, cancer, and emphysema can also impair erectile response, as can endocrine disorders that impair testosterone production (Ralph & McNicholas, 2000).

Eric Rimm (2000) of the Harvard School of Public Health studied 2,000 men and found that erectile dysfunction was associated with having a large waist, physical inactivity, and drinking too much alcohol (or not drinking at all). The common link among these factors may be high levels of cholesterol. Cholesterol can impede blood flow to the penis, just as it can impede blood flow to the heart. Exercise, weight loss, and moderate alcohol intake all help lower cholesterol levels, but we are not recommending that abstainers begin drinking to avert or treat erectile problems. However, the findings of the Massachusetts Male Aging Study suggest that regular exercise may reduce the risk of erectile dysfunction (Derby, 2000). In this study, men who burned 200 calories or more a day in physical activity, an amount that can be achieved by taking a brisk walk for two miles, had about half the risk of erectile dysfunction than did more sedentary men. Exercise may help prevent clogging of arteries, keeping them clear for the flow of blood into the penis.

Women also develop vascular or nervous disorders that impair genital blood flow, reducing lubrication and sexual excitement, rendering intercourse painful, and reducing their ability to reach orgasm. As with men, these problems become more likely as women age.

Before we move on to discuss psychological factors, we need to note that prescription drugs and psychoactive drugs, including antidepressants and antispsychotics, can impair erectile functioning and cause orgasmic disorders (Olfson et al., 2005; Taylor, Rudkin, & Hawton, 2005). Tranquilizers such as Valium and Xanax may cause orgasmic disorder in either men or women. Some medicinal drugs used to treat high blood pressure and other conditions, such as high blood cholesterol levels, can also interfere with erectile response.

Depressant drugs such as alcohol, heroin, and morphine can reduce sexual desire and impair sexual arousal. Narcotics, such as heroin, also depress testosterone production, which can diminish sexual desire and lead to erectile failure. Regular use of cocaine can cause erectile disorder or male orgasmic disorder and reduce sexual desire in both women and men (Rawson et al., 2002). Some people report increased sexual pleasure from initial use of cocaine, but repeated use can lead to dependency on the drug for sexual arousal, and long-term use may lessen sexual pleasure.

Sociocultural Perspectives At around the turn of the 20th century, an Englishwoman was quoted as saying she would "close her eyes and think of England" when her husband approached her to perform her marital duties. This old-fashioned stereotype suggests how sexual pleasure was once considered exclusively a male preserve—that sex, for women, was primarily a duty. Mothers usually informed their daughters of the conjugal duties before the wedding, and girls encoded sex as just one of the ways in which women serviced the needs of others. Women who harbor such stereotypical attitudes toward female sexuality are unlikely to become aware of their sexual potentials. In addition, sexual anxieties may transform negative expectations into self-fulfilling prophecies. Sexual dysfunctions in men, too, may be linked to extremely strict sociocultural beliefs and sexual taboos.

Our colleague, psychologist Rafael Javier (1993), takes note of the idealization within many Hispanic cultures of the *marianismo* stereotype, which derives its name from the Virgin Mary. From this sociocultural perspective, the ideal virtuous woman "suffers in silence" as she submerges her needs and desires to those of her husband and children. She is the provider of joy, even in the face of her own pain or frustration.

Masters & Johnson. Sex therapists William Masters and Virginia Johnson.

It is not difficult to imagine that women who adopt these stereotypical expectations find it difficult to assert their own needs for sexual gratification or express resistance to this cultural ideal by becoming sexually unresponsive.

Sociocultural factors play an important role in erectile dysfunction as well. Investigators find a greater incidence of erectile dysfunction in cultures with more restrictive sexual attitudes toward premarital sex among females, toward sex in marriage, and toward extramarital sex (Welch & Kartub, 1978). Men in these cultures may be prone to develop sexual anxiety or guilt that interferes with sexual performance.

In India, cultural beliefs that link the loss of semen to a draining of the man's life energy underlie the development of Dhat syndrome, an irrational fear of loss of semen (discussed in Chapter 7). Men with this condition sometimes develop erectile dysfunction because their fears about wasting precious seminal fluid interfere with their ability to perform sexually (Shukla & Singh, 2000).

Treatment of Sexual Dysfunctions

Until the groundbreaking research of the famed sex researchers William Masters and Virginia Johnson in the 1960s, there was no effective treatment for most sexual dysfunctions. Psychoanalytic therapy approached sexual dysfunctions indirectly. It was assumed that sexual dysfunctions represented underlying conflicts, so treatment focused on resolving those conflicts through psychoanalysis. A lack of evidence about the efficacy of this approach led to development of methods that focus more directly on the sexual problems.

Most contemporary sex therapists assume sexual dysfunctions can be treated by directly modifying the couple's sexual interactions. Pioneered by Masters and Johnson (1970), sex therapy uses cognitive-behavioral techniques in a brief therapy format to help individuals enhance their sexual competencies (sexual knowledge and skills) and relieve performance anxiety. When feasible, both partners are involved in therapy. In some cases, however, individual therapy may be preferable, as we shall see.

Before we turn to consider these specific methods, we should note that because sexual problems are often embedded in a context of troubled relationships, therapists may also use couple therapy to help couples share power in their relationships, improve communication skills, and negotiate differences (Coyle, 2006; McCarthy, Ginsberg, & Fucito, 2006). Let us also note that significant changes have occurred in the treatment of sexual dysfunctions in the past 25 years. Clinicians increasingly emphasize the role of biological or organic factors in the development of sexual problems and the use of medical treatments, such as the drug *sildenafil* (Viagra), to treat male erectile dysfunction (Saigal, 2004). But even men with biologically based erectile problems can benefit from sex therapy as an adjunct to medical treatment. Let us survey some of the more common sex therapy techniques for particular types of disorders.

Sexual Desire Disorders Sex therapists may try to help people with low sexual desire kindle their sexual appetite through the use of self-stimulation (masturbation) exercises together with erotic fantasies. When working with couples, therapists prescribe mutual pleasuring exercises the couple can perform at home or encourage them to expand their sexual repertoire to add novelty and excitement to their sex life. When a lack of sexual desire is connected with depression, the treatment focuses on treating the underlying depression. Lack of sexual desire may reflect problems in the relationship, in which case couple therapy might be in order. When problems of low sexual desire or sexual aversion appear to stem from deep-seated causes, some sex therapists use insight-oriented (psychodynamic) approaches to help uncover and resolve underlying issues.

Some cases of hypoactive sexual desire in men and women are associated with hormonal deficiencies, especially lack of the male sex hormone testosterone. Treatment with testosterone shows promise in heightening sexual desire in such cases (Munarriz et al., 2002; Brown & Haaser, 2005). Recently, the use of a testosterone gel patch attached to the skin for administering the hormone has increased both sexual desire and sexual function in men with testosterone deficiency (Wang et al., 2004).

Disorders of Arousal Sexual arousal results in the pooling of blood in the genital region, causing erection in the male and vaginal lubrication in the female. These changes in blood flow occur as a reflexive response to sexual stimulation; they cannot be willed. Women who have difficulty becoming sexually aroused and men with erectile problems are first educated to the fact that they need not "do" anything to become aroused. As long as their problems are psychological, not organic, they need only expose themselves to sexual stimulation under relaxed, unpressured conditions, so that disruptive thoughts and anxiety do not inhibit reflexive responses.

Masters and Johnson have a couple counter performance anxiety by engaging in *sensate focus exercises.* These are nondemand sexual contacts—sensuous exercises that do not demand sexual arousal in the form of vaginal lubrication or erection. Partners begin by massaging one another without touching the genitals. The partners learn to "pleasure" each other and to "be pleasured" by following and giving verbal instructions and by guiding each other's hands. The method fosters both communication and sexual skills and countermands anxiety because there is no demand for sexual arousal. After several sessions, direct massage of the genitals is included in pleasuring. Even when obvious signs of sexual excitement are produced (lubrication or erection), the couple does not straightaway engage in intercourse, because intercourse might create performance demands. After excitement is achieved consistently, the couple engages in a relaxed sequence of other sexual activities, culminating eventually in intercourse.

Success rates in treating individual cases of erectile disorder with sex therapy techniques are variable, and we still lack methodologically sound studies that support the overall effectiveness of the technique (Leiblum & Rosen, 2000; O'Donohue et al., 1999). The following case example illustrates sex therapy techniques for treating erectile dysfunction.

A Case of Erectile Dysfunction

Victor P., a 44-year-old concert violinist, was eager to show the therapist reviews of his concert tour. A solo violinist with a distinguished orchestra, Victor's life revolved around practice, performances, and reviews. He dazzled audiences with his technique and the energy of his performance. As a concert musician, Victor had exquisite control over his body, especially his hands. Yet he could not control his erectile response in the same way. Since his divorce seven years earlier, Victor had been troubled by recurrent episodes of erectile failure. Time and time again he had become involved in a new relationship, only to find himself unable to perform sexually. Fearing repetition, he would sever the relationship. He was unable to face an audience of only one. For a while he dated casually, but then he met Michelle.

Michelle was a writer who loved music. They were a perfect match because Victor, the musician, loved literature. Michelle, a 35-year-old divorcée, was exciting, earthy, sensual, and accepting. The couple soon grew inseparable. He would practice while she would write—poetry mostly, but also short magazine pieces. Unlike some women Victor met who did not know Bach from Bartok, Michelle held her own in conversations with Victor's friends and fellow musicians over late night dinner at Sardi's, a famous New York restaurant. They kept their own apartments; Victor needed his own space and solitude for practice.

In the 9 months of their relationship, Victor was unable to perform on the stage that mattered most to him—his canopied bed. It was just so frustrating, he said. "I would become erect and then just as I approach her to penetrate, pow! It collapses on me." Victor's history of nocturnal erections and erections during light petting suggested that he was basically suffering from performance anxiety. He was bearing down to force an erection, much as he might try to learn the fingering of a difficult

(continued)

violin piece. Each night became a command performance in which Victor served as his own severest critic. Rather than focus on his partner, his attention was riveted on the size of his penis. As noted by the late great pianist Vladimir Horowitz, the worst thing a pianist can do is watch his fingers. Perhaps the worst thing a man with erectile problems can do is watch his penis.

To break the vicious cycle of anxiety, erectile failure, and more anxiety, Victor and Michelle followed a sex therapy program (Rathus & Nevid, 1977) modeled after the Masters and Johnson treatment. The aim was to restore the pleasure of sexual activity, unfettered by anxiety. The couple was initially instructed to abstain from attempts at intercourse to free Victor from any pressure to perform. The couple progressed through a series of steps:

1. *Relaxing together in the nude without any touching, such as when reading or watching TV together.*
2. *Sensate focus exercises.*
3. *Genital stimulation of each other manually or orally to orgasm.*
4. *Nondemand intercourse (intercourse performed without any pressure on the man to satisfy his partner). The man may afterward help his partner achieve orgasm by using manual or oral stimulation.*
5. *Resumption of vigorous intercourse (intercourse involving more vigorous thrusting and use of alternative positions and techniques that focus on mutual satisfaction). The couple is instructed not to catastrophize occasional problems that may arise.*

The therapy program helped Victor overcome his erectile disorder. Victor was freed of the need to prove himself by achieving erection on command. He surrendered his post as critic. Once the spotlight was off the bed, he became a participant and not a spectator.

—From the Author's Files

Disorders of Orgasm Women with orgasmic disorder often harbor underlying beliefs that sex is dirty or sinful. They may have been taught not to touch themselves. They feel anxious about sex and have not learned, through trial and error, what kinds of sexual stimulation will arouse them and help them reach orgasm. Treatment in these cases includes modification of negative attitudes toward sex. When orgasmic disorder reflects the woman's feelings about or relationship with her partner, treatment also involves enhancing the relationship.

In either case, Masters and Johnson worked with the couple and first used sensate focus exercises to lessen performance anxiety, open channels of communication, and help the couple acquire sexual skills. The woman directs her partner to use caresses and techniques that stimulate her. By taking charge, the woman becomes psychologically freed from the stereotype of the passive, submissive female role.

Masters and Johnson preferred working with the couple in cases of female orgasmic dysfunction, but other sex therapists prefer to work with the woman individually by directing her to practice masturbation in private (Leiblum & Rosen, 2000). Directed masturbation provides women opportunities to learn about their own bodies at their own pace and has a success rate of 70% to 90% (Leiblum & Rosen, 2000). It frees women of the need to rely on or please partners. Once women can reliably masturbate to orgasm, couple-oriented treatment may facilitate transfer of training to orgasm with a partner.

Little attention has focused on male orgasmic disorder in the scientific literature. The standard treatment, barring underlying organic problems, focuses on increasing sexual stimulation and reducing performance anxiety (Leiblum & Rosen, 2000).

The most widely used behavioral approach to treating premature ejaculation, called the *stop-start* or *stop-and-go* technique, was introduced in 1956 by a urologist with the intriguing name of James Semans. The partners suspend sexual activity when the man is about to ejaculate and then resume stimulation when his sensations subside.

Repeated practice enables him to regulate ejaculation by sensitizing him to the cues that precede the ejaculatory reflex, making him more aware of his "point of no return," the point at which the ejaculatory reflex is triggered. Therapists have reported success rates as high as 95% in treating premature ejaculation with the stop-start method, but relapse rates tend to be high (Segraves & Althof, 1998).

Vaginismus and Dyspareunia Vaginismus is a conditioned reflex involving the involuntary constriction of the vaginal opening. It represents a psychologically based fear of penetration, rather than a medical problem. Treatment for vaginismus may include a combination of relaxation techniques, cognitive techniques, and use of methods of gradual exposure in order to desensitize the vaginal musculature to penetration, such as finger insertion of first one and then two fingers by the woman and her partner and use of vaginal dilators (plastic rods) that are inserted, like a tampon, in the vagina by the woman (ter Kuile et al., 2006). Through therapy is often successful, more research is needed to further improve therapeutic effectiveness (Van Lankveld et al., 2006). Because many women with vaginismus and dyspareunia have histories of rape or sexual abuse, psychotherapy may be part of the treatment program in order to deal with the psychological consequences of traumatic experiences.

Biological Treatments of Sexual Dysfunction Erectile disorder frequently has organic causes, so it is not surprising that treatment is becoming increasingly medicalized.

Sexual arousal in both men and women depends on engorgement of blood in the genitals. Drugs that increase blood flow to the penis, such as Viagra, are successful in producing erections in a majority of men suffering from erectile disorder (Naughton, 2004; Walker, 2004). In some cases of erectile disorder, surgical insertion of a penile implant may be performed if drugs or other less invasive techniques fail.

Investigators are actively exploring biomedical therapies for female sexual dysfunctions, including use of Viagra and similar drugs (Berman et al., 2003; Kleinplatz, 2003). For example, Viagra appears to increase sexual arousal in women (O'Connor, 2004). Many women also report greater vaginal lubrication and stronger orgasms after using Viagra (e.g., Berman et al., 2001).

The male sex hormone testosterone has also been used successfully to increase sexual drive in both premenopausal women (Goldstat et al., 2003) and older women

Viagra. Viagra and other erectile disorder drugs are advertised widely on television and even on billboards. Do you believe these drugs should be advertised so heavily in popular media? Why or why not?

(Munarriz et al., 2002). A cream form of testosterone is applied to the thighs. However, questions remain about the safety and side effects of these hormonal treatments, such as possible growth of facial hair and acne.

Testosterone treatment may also help men with low levels of male sex hormones (Brown & Haaser, 2005). Yet testosterone treatments can have side effects, such as liver damage and prostate cancer, they are undertaken cautiously. Surgery may be effective in rare cases in which blocked blood vessels prevent blood flow to the penis, or in which the penis is structurally defective. Selective serotonin reuptake inhibitors (SSRIs), such as the antidepressants *fluoxetine* (Prozac), *paroxetine* (Paxil), and *sertraline* (Zoloft), work by increasing the action of the neurotransmitter serotonin. Increased availability of serotonin in the brain can have the side effect of delaying ejaculation, which can be helpful to men with premature ejaculation (Bancroft et al., 2005a; Waldinger et al., 2002).

The medicalization of treatments for sexual dysfunctions holds great promise, but no pill or biomechanical device will enhance the quality of a relationship. If people have serious problems with their partners, popping a pill or applying a cream is unlikely to solve them. All in all, the success rates reported for treating sexual dysfunctions through psychological or biological approaches are quite encouraging, especially when we remember that only a few generations ago, there were no effective treatments.

Before moving on, you may wish to review the types of sexual dysfunctions, as well as the causal factors involved in the development of these problems and ways treating them, as represented in the *Concept Map for Abnormal Psychology* at the end of the chapter.

PARAPHILIAS

The word *paraphilia* was coined from the Greek roots *para,* meaning "to the side of," and *philos,* meaning "loving." People with **paraphilias** show sexual arousal ("loving") in response to atypical stimuli ("to the side of" normally arousing stimuli). According to the *DSM-IV-TR,* paraphilias are recurrent, powerful sexual urges and fantasies lasting 6 months or longer that center on either (a) nonhuman objects such as underwear, shoes, leather, or silk; (b) humiliation or experience of pain in oneself or one's partner; or (c) children and other persons who do not or cannot grant consent. Diagnosis of a paraphilia may be given even in the absence of overt paraphiliac behavior. In these cases, there must be evidence that the urges are a source of personal distress or cause other significant problems.

Some persons who receive the diagnosis can function sexually in the absence of paraphiliac stimuli or fantasies. Others resort to deviant stimuli under stress. Still others cannot become sexually aroused unless these stimuli are used, in actuality or in fantasy. For some individuals, engaging in paraphiliac acts is the exclusive means of attaining sexual gratification. Though the prevalence rates of paraphilias are unknown, we do know that these disorders are almost never diagnosed in women with the exception of some cases of sexual masochism and some isolated cases of other disorders (Seligman & Hardenburg, 2000). Even with masochism, it is estimated that men are perhaps twenty times more likely to receive the diagnosis than women (APA, 2000).

Types of Paraphilias

Some paraphilias are relatively harmless and victimless. Among these are fetishism and transvestic fetishism. Others, such as exhibitionism, pedophilia, and voyeurism have unwilling victims. A most harmful paraphilia is sexual sadism when acted out with a nonconsenting partner.

Exhibitionism Exhibitionism—or "flashing"—involves recurrent, powerful urges to expose one's genitals to an unsuspecting stranger to surprise, shock, or sexually arouse the victim. The person may masturbate while fantasizing about or actually exposing himself (almost all cases involve men). The victims are almost always women. Relatively few cases are reported to the police.

paraphilias Sexual deviations or types of sexual disorders in which the person experiences recurrent sexual urges and sexually arousing fantasies involving nonhuman objects (such as articles of clothing), inappropriate or nonconsenting partners (for example, children), or situations producing humiliation or pain to oneself or one's partner.

exhibitionism A type of paraphilia almost exclusively occurring in males, in which the man experiences persistent and recurrent sexual urges and sexually arousing fantasies involving the exposure of his genitals to a stranger and either has acted upon these urges or feels strongly distressed by them.

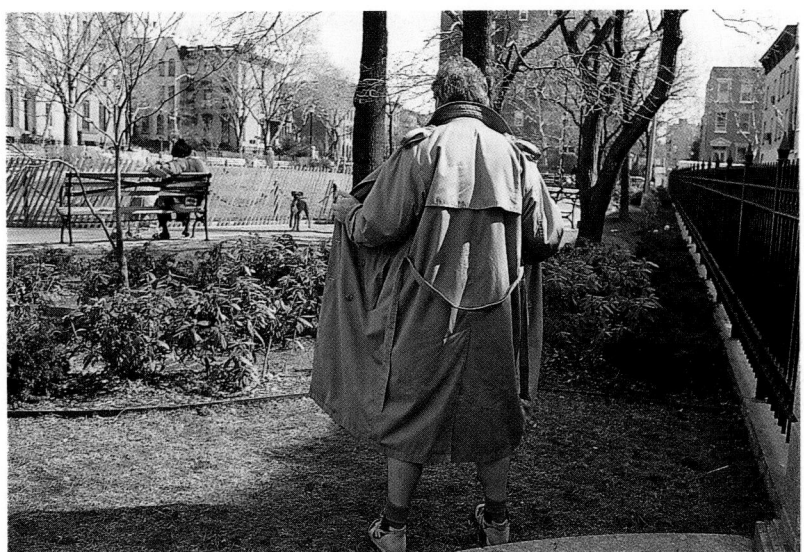

Exhibitionism. Exhibitionism is a type of paraphilia that characterizes people who seek sexual arousal or gratification through exposing themselves to unsuspecting victims. People with this disorder are usually not interested in actual sexual contact with their victims.

The person diagnosed with exhibitionism usually does not seek sexual contact with the victim. Nevertheless, some exhibitionists progress to more serious crimes of sexual aggression (Price et al., 2002). Whether or not the exhibitionist seeks physical contact, the victim may believe herself to be in danger and be traumatized by the act. Victims are probably best advised to show no reaction to exhibitionists, but to just continue on their way, if possible. It would be unwise to insult the exhibitionist, lest it provoke a violent reaction. Nor do we recommend an exaggerated show of shock or fear, which tends to reinforce the behavior.

Some researchers view exhibitionism as a means of indirectly expressing hostility toward women, perhaps because of perceptions of having been wronged by women in the past or of not being noticed or taken seriously by them (Geer, Heiman, & Leitenberg, 1984). Men with this disorder tend to be shy, dependent, lacking in social and sexual skills, and socially inhibited. Some doubt their masculinity and harbor feelings of inferiority. Their victims' revulsion or fear boosts their sense of mastery of the situation and heightens their sexual arousal. Consider the following case example of exhibitionism.

The Case of Michael

Michael was a 26-year-old, handsome, boyish-looking married male with a 3-year-old daughter. He had spent about one quarter of his life in reform schools and in prison. As an adolescent he had been a fire-setter. As a young adult, he had begun to expose himself. He came to the clinic without his wife's knowledge because he was exposing himself more and more often—up to three times a day—and he was afraid that he would eventually be arrested and thrown into prison again.

Michael said he liked sex with his wife, but it wasn't as exciting as exposing himself. He couldn't prevent his exhibitionism, especially now, when he was between jobs and worried about where the family's next month's rent was coming from. He loved his daughter more than anything and couldn't stand the thought of being separated from her.

(continued)

Michael's method of operation was as follows: He would look for slender adolescent females, usually near the junior high school and the senior high school. He would take his penis out of his pants and play with it while he drove up to a girl or a small group of girls. He would lower the car window, continuing to play with himself, and ask them for directions. Sometimes the girls didn't see his penis. That was okay. Sometimes they saw it and didn't react. That was okay, too. When they saw it and became flustered and afraid, that was best of all. He would start to masturbate harder, and now and then he managed to ejaculate before the girls had departed.

Michael's history was unsettled. His father had left home before he was born, and his mother had drunk heavily. He was in and out of foster homes throughout his childhood. Before he was 10 years old he was involved in sexual activities with neighborhood boys. Now and then the boys also forced neighborhood girls into petting, and Michael had mixed feelings when the girls got upset. He felt bad for them, but he also enjoyed it. A couple of times girls seemed horrified at the sight of his penis, and it made him "really feel like a man. To see that look, you know, with a girl, not a woman, but a girl—a slender girl, that's what I'm after."

—*The Author's Files*

fetishism A type of paraphilia in which a person uses an inanimate object as a focus of sexual interest and as a source of arousal.

transvestic fetishism A type of paraphilia in heterosexual males involving sexual urges and sexually arousing fantasies involving dressing in female clothing. Also termed *transvestism*.

Although some cases are reported among women, virtually all people diagnosed with exhibitionism are men (Hugh-Jones, Gough, & Littlewood 2005). Exhibitionists are motivated by the wish to shock and dismay unsuspecting observers, not to show off the attractiveness of their bodies. Therefore, wearing skimpy bathing suits or other revealing clothing is not a form of exhibitionism in the clinical sense of the term. Nor do professional strippers typically meet the clinical criteria for exhibitionism. They are generally not motivated by the desire to expose themselves to unsuspecting strangers in order to arouse them or shock them. The chief motive of the exotic dancer is usually to earn a living (Philaretou, 2006).

Fetishism The French word *fétiche* is thought to derive from the Portuguese *feitico*, referring to a "magic charm." In this case, the "magic" lies in the object's ability to arouse sexually. The chief feature of **fetishism** is recurrent, powerful sexual urges and arousing fantasies involving inanimate objects, such as an article of clothing (bras, panties, hosiery, boots, shoes, leather, silk, and the like). It is not abnormal for men to become sexually aroused by the sight, feel, and smell of their lovers' undergarments. Men with fetishism, however, may prefer the object to the person and may not be able to become sexually aroused without it. They often experience sexual gratification by masturbating while fondling the object, rubbing it, or smelling it; or by having their partners wear it during sexual activity.

The origins of fetishism can be traced to early childhood in many cases. Most individuals with a rubber fetish in one early research sample were able to recall first experiencing a fetishistic attraction to rubber sometime between the ages of 4 and 10 (Gosselin & Wilson, 1980).

Transvestic Fetishism The most prominent feature of **transvestic fetishism** ("transvestism") is recurrent, powerful urges and related fantasies involving cross-dressing for purposes of sexual arousal. Most all transvestites are men (Långström & Zucker, 2005). Although other men with fetishes can be satisfied by handling objects such as women's clothing while they masturbate; transvestite men want to wear them. They may wear full feminine attire and makeup or favor one particular article of clothing, such as women's stockings. Although some transvestite men are gay, the disorder is usually found among heterosexual men (Taylor & Rupp, 2004). The man typically cross-dresses in private and imagines himself to be a woman whom he is stroking as he masturbates. Some frequent transvestite clubs or become involved in a transvestic subculture. Some transvestite men are sexually stimulated by fantasies that their own bodies are female (Bailey, 2003b).

Men with GID may cross-dress to "pass" as women or because they are not comfortable dressing in male clothing. Some gay men also cross-dress, perhaps to make a statement about overly rigid gender roles, but not because they seek to become sexually aroused. Because cross-dressing among gay men and men with GID is performed for reasons other than sexual arousal or gratification, their behavior is not classified as transvestic fetishism. Nor are female impersonators who cross-dress for theatrical purposes considered to have a form of transvestism.

Most men with transvestic fetishism are married and engage in sexual activity with their wives, but they seek additional sexual gratification through dressing as women, as in the following case.

A Case of Transvestic Fetishism

Archie was a 55-year-old plumber who had been cross-dressing for many years. There was a time when he would go out in public as a woman, but as his prominence in the community grew, he became more afraid of being discovered. His wife Myrna knew of his "peccadillo," especially because he borrowed many of her clothes, and she also encouraged him to stay at home, offering to help him with his "weirdness." For many years his paraphilia had been restricted to the home.

The couple came to the clinic at the urging of the wife. Myrna described how Archie had imposed his will on her for 20 years. Archie would wear her undergarments and masturbate while she told him how disgusting he was. (The couple also regularly engaged in "normal" sexual intercourse, which Myrna enjoyed.) The cross-dressing situation had come to a head because a teenaged daughter had almost walked into the couple's bedroom while they were acting out Archie's fantasies.

With Myrna out of the consulting room, Archie explained that he grew up in a family with several older sisters. He described how underwear had been perpetually hanging all around the one bathroom to dry. As an adolescent, Archie experimented with rubbing against articles of underwear, then with trying them on. On one occasion a sister walked in while he was modeling panties before the mirror. She told him he was a "dredge to society" and he straightaway experienced unparalleled sexual excitement. He masturbated when she left the room, and his orgasm was the strongest of his young life.

Archie did not think that there was anything wrong with wearing women's undergarments and masturbating. He was not about to give it up, regardless of whether his marriage was destroyed as a result. Myrna's main concern was finally separating herself from Archie's "sickness." She didn't care what he did anymore, so long as he did it by himself. "Enough is enough," she said.

That was the compromise the couple worked out in marital therapy. Archie would engage in his fantasies by himself. He would choose times when Myrna was not at home, and she would not be informed of his activities. He would also be very, very careful to choose times when the children were not around.

Six months later the couple were together and content. Archie had replaced Myrna's input into his fantasies with transvestic-sadomasochistic magazines. Myrna said, "I see no evil, hear no evil, smell no evil." They continued to have sexual intercourse. After a while, Myrna even forgot to check to see which underwear had been used.

—The Author's Files

Voyeurism The chief feature of **voyeurism** is either acting on or being strongly distressed by recurrent, powerful sexual urges and fantasies of watching unsuspecting people, generally strangers, who are undressed, disrobing, or engaging in sexual activity. The purpose of watching, or "peeping," is to attain sexual excitement. The person

voyeurism A type of paraphilia involving sexual urges and sexually arousing fantasies focused on acts of watching unsuspecting others who are naked, in the act of undressing, or engaging in sexual activity.

frotteurism A type of paraphilia involving sexual urges or sexually arousing fantasies involving bumping and rubbing against nonconsenting persons for sexual gratification.

pedophilia A type of paraphilia involving sexual attraction to children.

who engages in voyeurism does not typically seek sexual activity with the person or persons being observed.

Are acts of watching your partner disrobe or viewing sexually explicit films forms of voyeurism? The answer is no. The people who are observed know they are being observed by their partners or will be observed by film audiences. Nor is attending a strip club for purposes of sexual stimulation considered abnormal, as it does not involve seeking sexual arousal by watching unsuspecting persons. People may also frequent strip clubs for other reasons than sexual gratification, such as bonding experiences with friends (Montemurro et al., 2003).

The voyeur usually masturbates while watching or while fantasizing about watching. Peeping may be the voyeur's only sexual outlet. Some people engage in voyeuristic acts in which they place themselves in risky situations. The prospects of being discovered or injured apparently heighten their excitement.

Frotteurism The French word *frottage* refers to the artistic technique of making a drawing by rubbing against a raised object. The chief feature of the paraphilia of **frotteurism** is recurrent, powerful sexual urges and related fantasies involving rubbing against or touching a nonconsenting person. Frotteurism, also called "mashing," often occurs in crowded places, such as subway cars, buses, or elevators. The rubbing or touching, not the coercive aspect of the act, sexually arouses the man. He may imagine himself enjoying an exclusive, affectionate sexual relationship with the victim. Because the physical contact is brief and furtive, people who commit frotteurism stand only a small chance of being caught by authorities. Even victims may not realize at the time what has happened or register much protest. In the following case, a man victimized about 1,000 women over several years but was arrested only twice.

A Case of Frotteurism

A 45-year-old man was seen by a psychiatrist following his second arrest for rubbing against a woman in the subway. He would select as his target a woman in her 20s as she entered the subway station. He would then position himself behind her on the platform and wait for the train to arrive. He would then follow her into the subway car and when the doors closed would begin bumping against her buttocks, while fantasizing that they were enjoying having intercourse in a loving and consensual manner. About half of the time he would reach orgasm. He would then continue on his way to work. Sometimes when he hadn't reached orgasm, he would change trains and seek another victim. While he felt guilty for a time after each episode, he would soon become preoccupied with thoughts about his next encounter. He never gave any thought to the feelings his victims might have about what he had done to them. Although he was married to the same woman for 25 years, he appears to be rather socially inept and unassertive, especially with women.

—Adapted from Spitzer et al., 1994, pp. 164–165

Pedophilia The word **pedophilia** derives from the Greek *paidos*, meaning "child." The chief feature of pedophilia is recurrent, powerful sexual urges and related fantasies involving sexual activity with prepubescent children (typically 13 years old or younger). Molestation of children may or may not occur. To be diagnosed with pedophilia, the person must be at least 16 years of age and at least 5 years older than the child or children toward whom the person is sexually attracted or has victimized. In some cases of pedophilia, the person is attracted only to children. In other cases, the person is attracted to adults as well.

Even though they may attempt to conceal their sexual attraction to children, men with pedophilia show deviant sexual responses to child stimuli when tested with more subtle methods that do not require verbal reports of arousal (Gray et al., 2005). Some pedophiles restrict their deviant activities to looking at or undressing children, whereas others engage in exhibitionism, kissing, fondling, oral sex, and anal intercourse and, in the case of girls, vaginal intercourse. Not being worldly wise, children are often taken advantage of by molesters, who inform them they are "educating" them, "showing them something," or doing something they will "like."

Some men with pedophilia limit their sexual activity with children to incestuous relations with family members; others only molest children outside the family. Not all child molesters have pedophilia, however. The clinical definition of pedophilia is brought to bear only when sexual attraction to children is recurrent and persistent. Some molesters engage in these acts or experience pedophilic urges only occasionally or during times of opportunity.

Despite the stereotype, most cases of pedophilia do not involve "dirty old men" who hang around schoolyards in raincoats. Men with this disorder (virtually all cases involve men) are usually (otherwise) law-abiding, respected citizens in their 30s or 40s. Most are married or divorced and have children of their own. They are usually well acquainted with their victims, who are typically either relatives or friends of the family. Many cases of pedophilia are not isolated incidents. They often begin when children are very young and continue for years until they are discovered or the relationship is broken off.

The origins of pedophilia are complex and varied. Some cases fit the stereotype of the weak, shy, socially inept, and isolated man who is threatened by mature relationships and turns to children for sexual gratification because children are less critical and demanding. In other cases, it may be that childhood sexual experiences with other children were so enjoyable that the man, as an adult, is attempting to recapture the excitement of earlier years. In some cases, men who were sexually abused in childhood reverse the situation in an effort to establish feelings of mastery. Men whose pedophilic acts involve incestuous relationships with their own children tend to fall at one extreme or the other on the dominance spectrum, either being very dominant or very passive (Ames & Houston, 1990).

Effects of Sexual Abuse on Children An estimated 50,000 children in the United States suffer sexual abuse each year (Villarosa, 2002). The typical abuser is not the proverbial stranger lurking in the shadows, but a relative or step-relative of the child, a family friend, or a neighbor—someone who has held and then abused the child's trust. Sexual abuse can inflict great psychological harm, whether it is perpetrated by a family member, acquaintance, or stranger. Abused children may suffer from a litany of short- and long-term psychological problems, including anger, anxiety, depression, eating disorders, inappropriate sexual behavior, aggressive behavior, drug abuse, suicide attempts, posttraumatic stress disorder, low self-esteem, sexual dysfunction, and feelings of detachment (Edwards et al., 2003). But the psychological effects of sexual abuse on children are variable, and no one single pattern emerges (Resick, 2003; Saywitz et al., 2000). Sexual abuse may also cause genital injuries and psychosomatic problems such as stomachaches and headaches.

Younger children sometimes react with tantrums or aggressive or antisocial behavior. Older children often develop substance abuse problems. Some abused children become socially withdrawn and retreat into fantasy or refuse to leave the house. Abused children may also show regressive behaviors, such as thumb sucking, fear of the dark, and fear of strangers. Many survivors of childhood sexual abuse develop posttraumatic stress disorder (see Chapter 6). They suffer flashbacks, nightmares, emotional numbing, and feel alienated from other people (Herrera & McCloskey, 2003).

The sexual development of abused children may veer off in dysfunctional directions. For example, abused children may become prematurely sexually active or promiscuous in adolescence and adulthood (Browning, 2002; Herrera & McCloskey, 2003). Adolescent girls who have been sexually abused tend to be more sexually active than their peers.

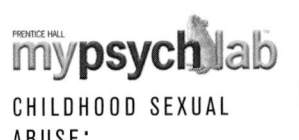

CHILDHOOD SEXUAL ABUSE:

The Case of Karen

"He started when I was six years old. . . . He would always get one bed in motel rooms because he said he needed to save money."

The effects of childhood sexual abuse tend to be similar in boys and girls (Edwards et al., 2003). Both tend to become fearful and have trouble sleeping. But there are some sex differences. The most pronounced is that boys more often externalize their problems, often through physical aggression. Girls more often internalize their difficulties, as by becoming depressed (Edwards et al., 2003).

Psychological problems may continue into adulthood in the form of PTSD, anxiety, depression, substance abuse, and relationship problems. Late adolescence and early adulthood are particularly difficult times for survivors of child sexual abuse, because unresolved feelings of anger and guilt and a deep sense of mistrust can prevent the development of intimate relationships. Evidence shows that women who blame themselves for the abuse show relatively lower self-esteem and greater depression than those who do not (Edwards et al., 2003). Childhood sexual abuse is also linked to later development of borderline personality disorder, a psychological disorder discussed in Chapter 13.

sexual masochism A type of paraphilia characterized by sexual urges and sexually arousing fantasies involving receiving humiliation or pain.

TRUTH or FICTION

Some people cannot become sexually aroused unless they are subjected to pain or humiliation.

☑ **TRUE.** These people have a form of paraphilia called sexual masochism.

Sexual Masochism Sexual masochism derives its name from the Austrian novelist Ritter Leopold von Sacher Masoch (1835–1895), who wrote stories and novels about men who sought sexual gratification from women by inflicting pain on them, often in the form of flagellation (being beaten or whipped). Sexual masochism involves strong, recurrent urges and fantasies relating to sexual acts that involve being humiliated, bound, flogged, or made to suffer in other ways. The urges are either acted on or cause significant personal distress. In some cases of sexual masochism, the person cannot attain sexual gratification in the absence of pain or humiliation.

In some cases, sexual masochism involves binding or mutilating oneself during masturbation or sexual fantasies. In others, a partner is engaged to restrain (bondage), blindfold (sensory bondage), paddle, or whip the person. Some partners are prostitutes; others are consensual partners who are asked to perform the sadistic role. In some cases, the person may desire, for purposes of sexual gratification, to be urinated or defecated upon or subjected to verbal abuse.

A most dangerous expression of masochism is **hypoxyphilia,** in which participants are sexually aroused by being deprived of oxygen—for example, by using a noose, plastic bag, chemical, or pressure on the chest during a sexual act, such as masturbation. The oxygen deprivation is usually accompanied by fantasies of asphyxiating or being asphyxiated by a lover. People who engage in this activity generally discontinue it before they lose consciousness, but occasional deaths due to suffocation occur.

hypoxyphilia A paraphilia in which a person seeks sexual gratification by being deprived of oxygen by means of using a noose, plastic bag, chemical, or pressure on the chest.

sexual sadism A type of paraphilia or sexual deviation characterized by recurrent sexual urges and sexually arousing fantasies involving inflicting humiliation or physical pain on sex partners.

Sexual Sadism Sexual sadism is named after the infamous Marquis de Sade, the 18th-century Frenchman who wrote stories about the pleasures of achieving sexual gratification by inflicting pain or humiliation on others. Sexual sadism is the flip side of sexual masochism. It is characterized by recurrent, powerful urges and related fantasies to engage in acts in which the person is sexually aroused by inflicting physical suffering or humiliation on another person. People with this paraphilia either act out their fantasies with nonconsenting others, or the urges and related fantasies cause significant personal distress or difficulties with others. People with sexually sadistic fantasies do sometimes recruit consenting partners, who may be lovers or wives with masochistic interests, or prostitutes, who are paid to play a masochistic role. But some sexual sadists stalk and assault nonconsenting victims and become aroused by inflicting pain or suffering on them. Sadistic rapists fall into this last group. Let us note, however, that most rapists do not become sexually aroused by inflicting pain; many even lose sexual interest when they see their victims in pain.

sadomasochism Sexual activities between partners involving the attainment of gratification by means of inflicting and receiving pain and humiliation.

Many people have occasional sadistic or masochistic fantasies or engage in sex play involving simulated or mild forms of **sadomasochism** (or S&M) with their partners. Sadomasochism refers to a practice of mutually gratifying sexual interactions involving both sadistic and masochistic acts. Stimulation may take the form of using a feather brush to strike one's partner, so that no actual pain is administered. Rituals, such as the "master and slave" game are staged, as though they were scenes in a play (Gross, 2006). People who engage in sadomasochism frequently switch roles. The clinical diagnosis of sexual masochism or sadism is not brought to bear unless such people become distressed by their behavior or fantasies, or these urges and fantasies lead to problems with other people.

Other Paraphilias There are many other paraphilias. These include making obscene phone calls ("telephone scatologia"), necrophilia (sexual urges or fantasies involving contact with corpses), partialism (sole focus on part of the body, such as the breasts), zoophilia (sexual urges or fantasies involving contact with animals), and sexual arousal associated with feces (coprophilia), enemas (klismaphilia), and urine (urophilia).

In the *Controversies in Abnormal Psychology* feature, we discuss what may be a new psychological disorder—cybersex addiction.

Theoretical Perspectives

As in the case of so many psychological disorders, approaches to understanding the causes of paraphilias emphasize psychological and biological factors.

Psychological Perspectives Psychodynamic theorists see many of the paraphilias as defenses against leftover *castration anxiety* from the phallic period of psychosexual development (see Chapter 2). In Freudian theory, the young boy develops a sexual desire for his mother and perceives his father as a rival. Castration anxiety— the unconscious fear that the father will retaliate by removing the organ that has become associated with sexual pleasure through masturbation—motivates the boy to give up his incestuous yearnings for his mother and identify with the aggressor, his father. But a failure to successfully resolve the conflict may lead to leftover castration anxiety in adulthood. The adult man now unconsciously equates the disappearance of the penis during genital intercourse with adult women with the risk of castration. Castration anxiety motivates the man to displace his sexual arousal onto sexual activities that are unconsciously perceived as safer, such as sexual contact with undergarments, viewing others, or having sex with children. Psychodynamic views of the origins of paraphilias remain speculative and controversial. We lack any direct evidence that men with paraphilias are handicapped by unresolved castration anxiety.

Learning theorists explain paraphilias in terms of conditioning and observational learning. Some object or activity becomes inadvertently associated with sexual arousal. The object or activity then gains the capacity to elicit sexual arousal. For example, sex researcher June Reinisch (1990) speculates that the earliest awareness of sexual arousal or response (such as erection) may have been connected with rubber pants or diapers. The person makes an association between the two, setting the stage for the development of a rubber fetish. Or a boy who glimpses his mother's stockings on the towel rack while he is masturbating goes on to develop a fetish for stockings (Breslow, 1989). Orgasm in the presence of the object reinforces the erotic connection, especially when it occurs repeatedly. Yet if fetishes were acquired by mechanical association, we might expect people to develop fetishes to stimuli that are inadvertently and repeatedly connected with sexual activity, such as bed sheets, pillows, even ceilings. But they do not. The *meaning* of the stimulus plays a primary role. The development of fetishes may depend on eroticizing certain types of stimuli (like women's undergarments) by incorporating them within sexual fantasies and masturbation rituals.

Family relationships may play a role. Some transvestite men report a history of "petticoat punishment" during childhood. That is, they were humiliated by being dressed

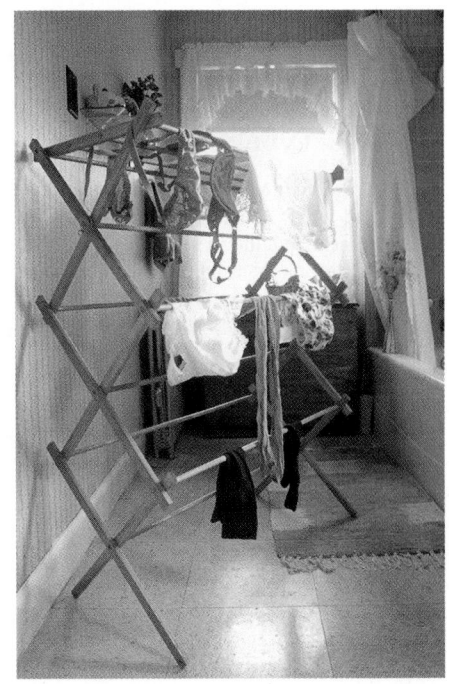

Origins of fetishism? The conditioning model of the origins of fetishism suggests that men who develop fetishisms involving women's undergarments may have had experiences in childhood in which sexual arousal was paired with exposure to their mother's undergarments. The developing fetish may have been strengthened by eroticizing the meaning of these stimuli by incorporating them within erotic fantasies or masturbatory activity.

CONTROVERSIES IN ABNORMAL PSYCHOLOGY

"Cybersex Addiction"—A New Psychological Disorder?

Internet use has exploded in recent years, and cybersex is a major factor accounting for this growth. People are logging on to view adult sites on the Internet, engaging in online sex with people in Internet chat rooms, and sometimes progressing to real-life sexual encounters with people they meet online. Estimates are that at least a third of Web visits involve sexually oriented sites, chat rooms, and news groups (Cooper et al., 2000, 2004).

For some, the attraction to cybersex may be relatively harmless recreational pursuit. But experts express concern that for others, easy access to cybersex is feeding a new type of psychological disorder called *cybersex addiction* (Gerevich et al., 2005; Philaretou et al., 2005). An estimated 6% of adult users of the Internet show evidence of sexual compulsiveness in their online behavior, such as experiencing withdrawal symptoms when they are away from the Internet for a length of time (Bailey, 2003a).

Cybersex compulsives can be likened to drug addicts, using the Internet for gratification in much the same way that a drug addict uses a drug of choice (Brody, 2000; Cooper, 2004; Schneider, 2005). Based on a survey of 9,265 men and women who admitted surfing the 'Net for sex, psychologist Al Cooper and his colleagues (1999, 2000) concluded that the 'Net is "the crack cocaine of sexual compulsivity," with at least 1% of respondents strongly addicted to online sex. Although some studies find that men who become addicted to online sex have ample sexual opportunities in the real world, other studies find them to be lonelier than other men (Yoder et al., 2005).

Physician Jennifer Schneider (2003, 2004) conducted a survey of 94 family members affected by cybersex addiction and found that it can arise even among people in good relationships and having an abundance of sexual opportunities. "Sex on the 'Net is just so seductive and it's so easy to stumble upon it [that] people who are vulnerable can get hooked before they know it" (cited in Brody, 2000).

Schneider (2005) defends the view that cybersex addiction is a true addiction, characterized by "loss of control, continuation of the behavior despite significant adverse consequences, and preoccupation or obsession with obtaining the drug or pursuing the behavior." Although behavioral addictions do not involve taking drugs, they may cause changes in the brain, such as releasing endorphins—brain chemicals whose actions mimic those of the narcotic morphine—that maintain the behavior (Plant & Plant, 2003).

Sexual arousal and orgasm also reinforce the behavior. As researcher Mark Schwartz noted: "Intense orgasms from the minimal investment of a few keystrokes are powerfully reinforcing. Cybersex affords easy, inexpensive access to a myriad of ritualized encounters with idealized partners" (cited in Brody, 2000).

As with other addictions, tolerance to cybersex stimulation can develop, prompting the person to take more and more risks to recapture the initial high. Online viewing that began as a harmless recreation can become all-consuming and even lead to real sexual encounters with people met online. Cybersex compulsives sometimes ignore their partners and children and risk their jobs. Many companies monitor employees' online activities, and visits to sexual sites can cost employees their jobs. Schneider reports other adverse consequences, including broken relationships. Partners often report feeling betrayed, ignored, and unable to compete with the online fantasies.

A 34-year-old woman married 14 years to a minister told Schneider, "How can I compete with hundreds of anonymous others who are now in our bed, in his head? Our bed is crowded with countless faceless strangers, where once we were intimate" (cited in Brody, 2000).

Cybersex addiction is not yet recognized as an official diagnostic category. Nor can we clearly determine where recreational use of sexual material on the Internet ends and sexual compulsion begins. Yet the problem of cybersex compulsion continues to grow, especially now that broadband availability allows for the streaming of explicit sexual video programming to computer screens around the world.

Critical Thinking

- What criteria would you apply to determine that pursuit of sexual explicit content on the Internet represents a psychological disorder?
- What the similarities between cybersex addiction and drug addiction? What are the differences?

Source: From Rathus, S. A., Nevid, J. S., & Fichner-Rathus, L. *Human Sexuality In A World of Diversity*, 6e. Published by Allyn and Bacon, Boston, MA. Copyright © 2004 by Pearson Education. Reprinted by permission of the publisher.

Cybersex addiction. Easy access to cybersex may be feeding a new psychological disorder called cybersex addiction. Many compulsive users of online sexual content deny that they have a problem, even though their behavior can seriously disrupt their work and home lives.

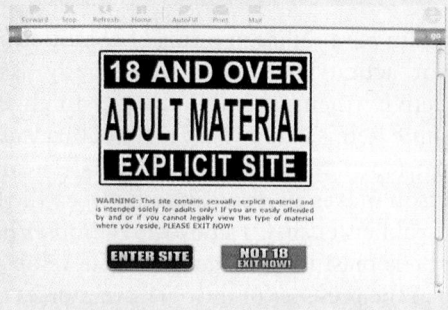

in girl's attire. Perhaps the adult transvestite male is attempting psychologically to convert humiliation into mastery by achieving an erection and engaging in sexual activity despite being attired in female clothing.

Biological Perspectives Researchers are investigating the possible role of biological factors in paraphiliac behavior. Investigators find evidence of higher-than-average sex drives in men with paraphilias, as evidenced by a higher frequency of sexual fantasies and urges and a shorter *refractory period* after orgasm by masturbation (i.e., length of time needed to become rearoused) (Haake et al., 2003; Kafka, 2003). Kafka (2003) refers to this heightened sex drive as *hypersexual desire*—the opposite of hypoactive sexual desire disorder (see the section on sexual dysfunctions). Other investigators find differences between paraphiliac men and male control subjects in the electrical response patterns in the brain to paraphiliac (fetishistic and sadomasochistic) images and control images (nude women, genital intercourse, oral sex) (Waismann et al., 2003). The meaning of these differences is not yet clear, but they suggest that the brains of paraphiliacs and other men may respond differently to different types of sexual stimuli.

Psychologist J. Michael Bailey (2003a) believes that with time, we will learn more about the biological underpinnings of paraphiliac behavior. Like other sexual patterns, paraphilias may have multiple biological, psychological, and sociocultural origins. Might our understanding of them thus be best approached from a theoretical framework that incorporates multiple perspectives? Sex researcher John Money (2000), for example, traced the origins of paraphilias to childhood. He suggested that childhood experiences etch a pattern in the brain, which he called a *lovemap*. A lovemap determines the types of stimuli and activities that become sexually arousing. In the paraphilias, lovemaps may become distorted or "vandalized" by early traumatic experiences. Evidence does tie early childhood emotional or sexual trauma to later development of paraphilias in many cases (Lee et al., 2002).

Treatment of Paraphilias

A major problem with treating paraphilias is that many people who engage in these behaviors are not motivated to change. They may not want to alter their behavior unless they believe that treatment will relieve them from serious punishment, such as imprisonment or loss of a family life. Consequently, they don't typically seek treatment on their own. They usually receive treatment in prison after they have been convicted of a sexual offense, such as exhibitionism, voyeurism, or child molestation. Or they are referred to a treatment provider by the courts. Under these circumstances it is not surprising that sex offenders resist treatment. Therapists recognize that treatment may be futile when clients lack the motivation to change their behavior. Nonetheless, some forms of treatment, principally cognitive-behavioral therapy, may be helpful to sex offenders who seek to change their behavior (Abracen & Looman, 2004).

Psychoanalysis Psychoanalysts attempt to bring childhood sexual conflicts (typically of an Oedipal nature) into awareness so they can be resolved in the light of the individual's adult personality (Laws & Marshall, 2003). Favorable results from individual case studies appear in the literature from time to time, but there is a dearth of controlled investigations to support the efficacy of psychodynamic treatment of paraphilias.

Cognitive-Behavioral Therapy Traditional psychoanalysis involves a lengthy process of exploration of the childhood roots of the problem. Cognitive-behavioral therapy is briefer and focuses directly on changing problem behavior. Cognitive-behavioral therapy includes a number of specific techniques, such as aversion therapy, covert sensitization, and social skills training, to help eliminate paraphiliac behaviors and strengthen appropriate sexual behaviors (Krueger & Kaplan, 2002). In many cases a combination of methods is used.

The goal of *aversion therapy* is to induce a negative emotional response to paraphiliac stimuli or fantasies. In this technique, a stimulus that elicits sexual arousal (for example, a mental image of a nude child) is paired repeatedly with an aversive stimulus (for example, electric shock) in the hope that the person will develop a conditioned aversion toward the paraphiliac stimulus.

Covert sensitization is a variation of aversion therapy in which paraphiliac fantasies are paired with an aversive stimulus in imagination. In one study of 38 pedophiles and 62 exhibitionists, more than half of whom were court-referred, subjects paired imagined aversive stimuli with deviant fantasies (Maletzky, 1980). First, they were instructed to fantasize pedophiliac or exhibitionistic scenes. Then,

> At a point . . . when sexual pleasure is aroused, aversive images are presented. . . . Examples might include a pedophiliac fellating a child, but discovering a festering sore on the boy's penis, an exhibitionist exposing to a woman but suddenly being discovered by his wife or the police, or a pedophiliac laying a young boy down in a field, only to lie next to him in a pile of dog feces (Maletzky, 1980, p. 308).

In a 25-year follow-up study of 7,275 sex offenders who received similar treatment, Maletzky and Steinhauser (2002) found that benefits were maintained for many men with exhibitionism but few with pedophilia. However, fewer than 50% of the original participants could be contacted after this amount of time elapsed.

Social skills training helps the individual improve his ability to develop and maintain relationships with adult partners. The therapist might first model a desired behavior, such as asking a woman out on a date or handling rejection. The client might then rehearse the behavior with the therapist playing the woman's role. The therapist provides feedback and additional guidance and modeling to help the client further improve his social skills.

Research on the effectiveness of cognitive-behavioral techniques is limited by the absence of untreated control groups. Consequently, we cannot discount the possibility that other factors, such as fears of legal consequences, influenced the outcomes.

Biomedical Therapies There is no magic pill or other medical cure for paraphilias. Yet progress has been made in treating exhibitionism, voyeurism, and fetishism with selective serotonin reuptake inhibitor (SSRI) antidepressants, such as Prozac (Bradford, 2001; Roesler & Witztum, 2000). Why SSRIs? We noted in Chapter 6 that SSRIs are often helpful in treating obsessive–compulsive disorder, a psychological disorder characterized by recurrent obsessions and compulsions. Paraphilias appear to mirror these behavioral patterns, which suggests that they may fall within an obsessive–compulsive spectrum of behaviors. People with paraphilias often experience obsessive thoughts or images of the paraphiliac object or stimulus, such as intrusive and recurrent mental images of young children. Many also feel compelled to repeatedly carry out the paraphiliac acts.

Antiandrogen drugs reduce levels of testosterone in the bloodstream (Bradford, 2001). Testosterone energizes sexual drives, so use of antiandrogens can reduce sexual desires, including paraphiliac urges and fantasies. The most widely used antiandrogen is *medroxyprogesterone acetate* (MPA) (trade name Depo-Provera), which is usually administered in weekly injections. Antiandrogens do not completely eliminate paraphiliac urges, nor do they change the types of erotic stimuli to which the man is attracted. Yet they may help curb impulses to act out on these urges. Evidence suggests that antiandrogens are helpful in controlling paraphiliac urges, especially when they are used in combination with psychological treatment (Roesler & Witztum, 2000).

Before moving on, you may want to review Table 11.3, which provides an overview of paraphilias.

TABLE 11.3 **Overview of Paraphilias**

Major Types Of Paraphilias	Atypical or deviant patterns of sexual gratification; excepting masochism, these disorders occur almost exclusively among males
Exhibitionism	Sexual gratification from exposing one's genitals in public
Voyeurism	Sexual gratification from observing unsuspecting others who are naked, undressing, or engaging in sexual arousal
Sexual Masochism	Sexual gratification associated with the receipt of humiliation or pain
Fetishism	Sexual attraction to inanimate objects or particular body parts
Frotteurism	Sexual gratification associated with acts of bumping or rubbing against nonconsenting strangers
Sexual Sadism	Sexual gratification associated with inflicting humiliation or pain on others
Transvestic Fetishism	Sexual gratification associated with cross-dressing
Pedophilia	Sexual attraction to children

Causal Factors	Multiple causes may be involved
Learning Perspective	• Atypical stimuli become conditioned stimuli for sexual arousal as the result of prior pairing with sexual activity • Atypical stimuli may become eroticized by incorporating them within erotic and masturbatory fantasies
Psychodynamic Perspective	• Unresolved castration anxiety from childhood leads to sexual arousal being displaced onto safer objects or activities
Multifactorial Perspective	• Sexual or physical abuse in childhood may corrupt normal sexual arousal patterns

Treatment Approches	Results remain questionable
Biomedical Treatment	• Drugs to help individuals control deviant sexual urges or reduce sexual drives
Cognitive-Behavioral Therapy	• Including aversive conditioning (pairing deviant stimuli with aversive stimuli), covert sensitization (pairing the undesirable behavior with an aversive stimulus in imagination), and nonaversive methods that help individuals acquire more adaptive behaviors

RAPE

Ann, a college student who met a young man at a party, offered the following account of a rape.

"I Never Thought It Would Happen to Me"

I first met him at a party. He was really good looking and he had a great smile. I wanted to meet him but I wasn't sure how. I didn't want to appear too forward. Then he came over and introduced himself. We talked and found we had a lot in common. I really liked him. When he asked me over to his place for a drink, I thought it would be OK. He was such a good listener, and I wanted him to ask me out again.

When we got to his room, the only place to sit was on the bed. I didn't want him to get the wrong idea, but what else could I do? We talked for a while and then he made his move. I was so startled. He started by kissing. I really liked him so the kissing was nice. But then he pushed me down on the bed. I tried to get up and I told him to stop. He was so much bigger and stronger. I got scared and I started to cry. I froze and he raped me.

It took only a couple of minutes and it was terrible, he was so rough. When it was over he kept asking me what was wrong, like he didn't know. He had just forced himself on me and he thought that was OK. He drove me home and said he wanted to see me again. I'm so afraid to see him. I never thought it would happen to me.

—*The Author's Files*

Rape, especially date rape, is a pressing concern on college campuses, where thousands of women have been raped by dates or acquaintances. College men frequently perceive their dates' protests as part of an adversarial sex game. Consider the comments of Jim, the man who raped Ann.

"Why Did She Put Up Such a Big Struggle?"

I first met her at a party. She looked really hot, wearing a sexy dress that showed off her great body. We started talking right away. I knew that she liked me by the way she kept smiling and touching my arm while she was speaking. She seemed pretty relaxed so I asked her back to my place for a drink. . . . When she said yes, I knew that I was going to be lucky!

When we got to my place, we sat on the bed kissing. At first, everything was great. Then, when I started to lay her down on the bed, she started twisting and saying she didn't want to. Most women don't like to appear too easy, so I knew that she was just going through the motions. When she stopped struggling, I knew that she would have to throw in some tears before we did it.

She was still very upset afterwards, and I just don't understand it! If she didn't want to have sex, why did she come back to the room with me? You could tell by the way she dressed and acted that she was no virgin, so why she had to put up such a big struggle I don't know.

—The Author's Files

rape Forced sexual intercourse with a nonconsenting person. Note that the legal definition of rape varies from state to state.

Rape is not classified as a mental disorder in the *DSM* system, and rapists do not necessarily suffer from any diagnosable disorder. However, its violent nature and the often devastating effects it has on its victims place rape and other forms of sexual assault squarely within the framework of abnormal behavior. Moreover, rape survivors often experience a range of health problems, both psychological and physical.

Many survivors are traumatized by the experience (Kaczmarek, LeVine, & Segal, 2006; Koss et al., 2002, 2003). They have trouble sleeping and cry frequently. They report eating problems, cystitis, headaches, irritability, mood changes, anxiety and depression, and menstrual irregularity. Survivors may become withdrawn, sullen, and mistrustful. Women who are raped may at least partly blame themselves, which can lead to feelings of guilt and shame. Emotional distress tends to peak by about 3 weeks following the attack and generally remains high for a month or so, before beginning to decline (Koss et al., 2002, 2003). But many survivors encounter lasting problems. A study of women in the military who had survived rape and physical abuse found psychological and health-related problems a decade after the assault (Sadler et al., 2000). Some survivors suffer physical injuries and sexually transmitted infections, even HIV/AIDS.

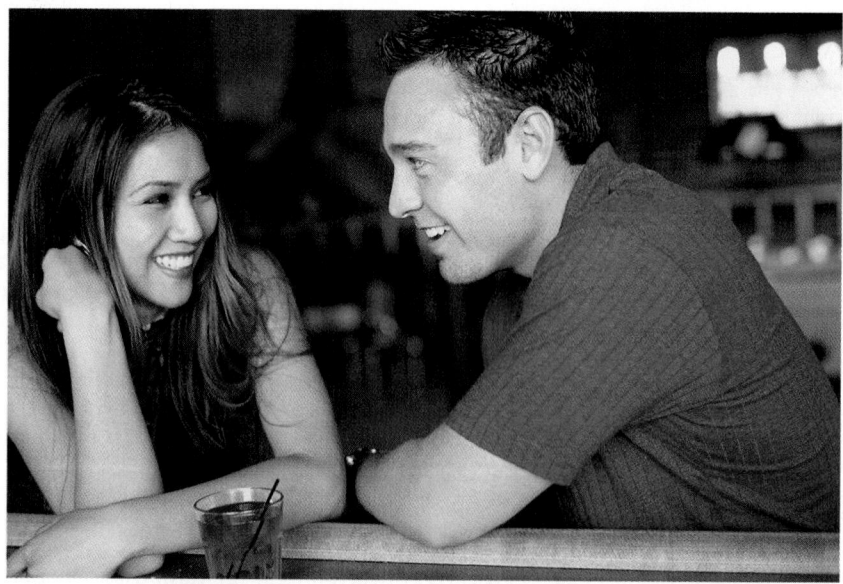

Misreading cues? Many date rapists misperceive social cues, such as assuming that women who frequent singles bars and similar places are signaling their willingness to have sex.

The government's National Crime Victimization Survey estimates, according to the most recent statistics available, that more than 190,000 women are sexually assaulted each year (U.S. Department of Justice, 2006). This figure includes some 72,000 rapes and another 40,000 attempted rapes. About 10% of rapes involve cases of men being raped. However, crime statistics underreport the actual incidence of rape, because the majority of rapes are not reported to authorities or prosecuted (Fisher et al., 2003). Many women do not report rape because they fear being humiliated by the criminal justice system. Some fear reprisal from their families or the rapist himself. Many women mistakenly believe that coercive sex is rape only when the rapist is a stranger or uses a weapon (Watts & Zimmerman, 2002). In sum, the weight of the evidence indicates that as many as one in four women in the United States is raped during her lifetime (Campbell & Wasco, 2005). Though women of all ages are at risk of being raped, young women ages 16 to 24 stand the greatest risk ((Burgess & Morgenbesser, 2005; U.S. Department of Justice, 2006).

Types of Rape

The main types of rape include stranger rape, acquaintance rape, marital rape, and male rape. *Stranger rape* is committed by an assailant (or assailants) who is not acquainted with the victim. The stranger rapist tends to select targets who appear to be vulnerable—women who live alone, who are walking deserted or dimly lit streets, or who are asleep or drugged.

According to the U.S. Department of Justice (2006), more than four of five rapes are *acquaintance rapes*—rapes committed by people known by the victim. Survivors of rape may not perceive sexual assaults by acquaintances as rapes. Even if a police report is filed, it may be treated as "misunderstanding" or "lovers' quarrel," rather than a violent crime (Campbell, 2006; Logan et al., 2006). Only about one-quarter of the women in a large-scale national college survey who were sexually assaulted saw themselves as victims of rape (Koss & Kilpatrick, 2001; Rozee & Koss, 2001).

Figure 11.1 shows the relationship patterns of rapist and victim based on the same national survey of college women. This survey revealed a disturbingly high percentage of college women reporting they had experienced either rape (15.4%) or attempted rape. In nearly 90% of the rapes in the college sample, the woman was acquainted with the assailant. In any given year, about 3% of college women in the United States suffer a rape or attempted rape (Fisher et al., 2003).

T R U T H or F I C T I O N

College women are more likely to be raped by strangers than by men they know.

☑ **FALSE.** According to a large-scale college survey, most rapes of college women are committed by men with whom they are acquainted.

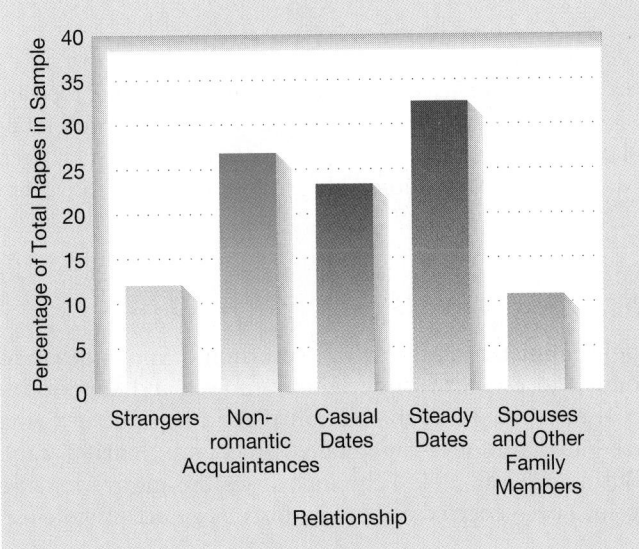

FIGURE 11.1 Relative percentages of stranger rapes and acquaintance rapes.
According to a large-scale survey of more than 3,000 college women at 32 colleges, the great majority of rapes of college women were committed by men whom the women were acquainted with, including dates, nonromantic acquaintances, and family members.

Date rape is a kind of acquaintance rape. Date rape is more likely to occur when the couple has been drinking and then park in the man's car or return to his room. Men tend to perceive a date's willingness to go home with him as a sign of willingness to have sexual relations. Most men who engage in date rape overcome the women's protests by force.

Some date rapists believe that acceptance of a date implies willingness to engage in sexual relations. They may believe that a woman they take out to dinner should pay with sex. Men may think that women who frequent singles bars and similar places are automatically willing to have sex. Some date rapists believe that women who resist advances are simply trying not to look "easy." These men misinterpret resistance as a ploy in the "battle of the sexes." Like Jim, who raped Ann in his dorm room, they may believe that when a woman says no, she means yes, especially when a sexual relationship has already begun.

Marital rapes may be even more common than date rapes because the sexual relationship has already been established in the context of marriage (Monson et al., 2000; Osman, 2003). Investigators report that 10% to 14% of all married women suffer marital rape (Martin, Taft, & Resick, 2007). A traditional-minded husband may think he is entitled to have sex with his wife whenever he wishes. He may see sex as his wife's duty, even when she is unwilling. But rape is rape, regardless of the woman's marital status. Men who are better educated and less accepting of traditional stereotypes about relationships between men and women are less likely to commit marital rape (Basile, 2002).

Gang rapists seek to exercise power over their victims and typically try to impress their friends by conforming to the stereotype of the tough "he-man." Consider the case of Kurt, who committed multiple rapes with his friend, Pete.

"I Couldn't Chicken Out"

I always looked up to Pete and felt second-class to him. I felt I owed him and couldn't chicken out on the rapes. I worshiped him. He was the best fighter, lover, water-skier, motorcyclist I knew. Taking part in the sexual assaults made me feel equal to him. . . . I didn't have any friends and felt like a nobody. . . . He brought me into his bike club. He made me a somebody.

I'd go to a shopping center and find a victim. I'd approach her with a knife or a gun and then bring her to him. He'd rape her first and then I would. . . . We raped about eight girls together over a four-month period.

—*Groth & Birnbaum, 1979, p. 113*

About one in ten rape survivors are men. Most men who engage in *male rape* are heterosexual. Their motives often include domination and control, revenge and retaliation, sadism and degradation, and—when the rape is carried out by a gang member—status and affiliation (Krahe, Waizenhofer, Moller, 2003). Sexual motives are often minimal or absent.

Theoretical Perspectives

Many motives underlie rape. Feminists see rape as an expression of men's desire to dominate and degrade women, to establish unquestioned power and superiority over them. Other theorists argue that sexual motivation plays a key role in many kinds of rape, particularly acquaintance rape, date rape, and marital rape (Baumeister et al., 2002; Bushman et al., 2003). In such cases the motive may be largely sexual, but make no mistake—coerced sex in any form is an act of violence.

For some rapists, violent cues appear to enhance sexual arousal, so they are motivated to combine sex with aggression. College men who report having used force or threat of force to gain sexual favors showed greater penile arousal in a laboratory study in response to depictions of rape scenes than did noncoercive men (Lohr, Adams, & Davis, 1997). Some rapists who were abused as children may humiliate women as a way of expressing anger and power over women and of taking revenge.

Social attitudes, myths, and cultural factors also contribute to the high incidence of rape. Many people believe myths about rape, such as "Women say no when they mean yes." Yet another myth is that deep down inside, women want to be raped. Certainly the popular media contribute to this belief when they portray a woman as first resisting a man's advances but then yielding to his overpowering masculinity. These myths have the effect of blaming the victim for the assault and legitimizing rape in the eyes of the public. Although both women and men believe some rape myths, researchers find that college men are more likely than college women to do so (Maxwell et al., 2003; Osman, 2003). The nearby questionnaire will afford you insight as to whether you believe in myths that have the effect of legitimizing rape.

Although some rapists show evidence of psychopathology on psychological tests, especially antisocial or psychopathic traits, many do not (Lalumière et al., 2005a). The very normality of many rapists on psychological instruments suggests that socialization of young men plays an important role in creating a climate of sexual aggression.

Perhaps, as some researchers contend, our society breeds rapists by socializing men into socially and sexually dominant roles (Davis & Liddell, 2002; Malamuth, Huppin, & Paul, 2005). Males are often reinforced from childhood for aggressive and competitive behavior. They may learn to "score" at all costs, whether they are on the ball field or in the bedroom. Such socialization influences may also lead men to reject "feminine" traits such as tenderness and empathy that might restrain aggression. Adding alcohol to the mix further increases the risk of sexual assault (Cole, 2006). A rapist may be just like the boy next door; in fact, he may be the boy next door. We end with two questions that we hope will provoke some thoughtful discussion: What are we teaching our sons? How can we teach them differently?

QUESTIONNAIRE
Cultural Myths That Create a Climate That Supports Rape

 Read each of the following statements and indicate whether you believe it to be true or false by circling the T or the F. Then look at the scoring key at the end of the chapter to evaluate your beliefs.

1. T   F   Women who dress provocatively in public places are just "asking for it."
2. T   F   A woman who accompanies a man home from a club or a bar deserves whatever she gets.
3. T   F   Women who claim they were raped are just looking for excuses for having engaged in sex.
4. T   F   Any physically healthy woman could resist a man's advances if she really wanted to.
5. T   F   If a woman allows a man to touch her in a sexual way, it means she wants to have intercourse.
6. T   F   Most women who are raped probably did something to lead the man on.
7. T   F   If a woman initiates touching or petting with a man, it's her own fault if things go too far.
8. T   F   Women may not admit it, but they truly want to be overpowered by men.
9. T   F   If a woman has too much to drink at a party, it's her fault if men take advantage of her.
10. T   F   Rape results from a misunderstanding that gets out of hand.

Source: Adapted from *Psychology and the Challenges of Life*, 9th Edition, by Rathus and Nevid, (John Wiley & Sons, 2005).

SUMMING UP

Gender Identity Disorder

What is gender identity disorder? People with GID find their anatomic gender to be a source of persistent and intense distress. People with the disorder may seek to change their sex organs to resemble those of the other sex, and many undergo hormone treatments and/or surgery to achieve this end.

How does gender identity disorder differ from homosexuality? In GID, as defined in the *DSM* system, there is a mismatch between one's psychological sense of being male or female and one's anatomic sex. Sexual orientation relates to the direction of one's sexual attraction—toward members of one's own sex or the other sex. Unlike people with GID, the great majority of people with a gay male or lesbian sexual orientation have a gender identity that is consistent with their anatomic sex.

Sexual Dysfunctions

What are sexual dysfunctions? Sexual dysfunctions involve persistent or recurrent patterns of lack of sexual desire, problems in becoming sexually aroused, and/or problems in reaching orgasm.

What types of sexual dysfunctions are there? Sexual dysfunctions include sexual desire disorders (hypoactive sexual desire disorder and sexual aversion disorder), sexual arousal disorders (female sexual arousal disorder and male erectile disorder), orgasm disorders (female and male orgasmic disorders and premature ejaculation), and sexual pain disorders (dyspareunia and vaginismus).

What are the causes of sexual dysfunctions? Sexual dysfunctions can stem from biological factors (such as fatigue, disease, the effects of aging, or the effects of alcohol and other drugs), psychological factors (such as performance anxiety, lack of sexual skills, disruptive cognitions, relationship problems), and sociocultural factors (such as sexually restrictive cultural learning).

What is sex therapy? Sex therapy is a cognitive-behavioral approach that helps people overcome sexual dysfunctions by enhancing self-efficacy expectancies, teaching sexual skills, improving communication, and reducing performance anxiety.

What biologically based treatments are available to help treat sexual dysfunctions? These include hormone treatments, penile implants, and most commonly, the use of drugs to facilitate blood flow to the genital region (Viagra and its cousins) or delay ejaculation (SSRIs).

Paraphilias

What are paraphilias? Paraphilias are sexual deviations involving patterns of arousal to stimuli such as nonhuman objects (for example, shoes or clothes), humiliation or the experience of pain in oneself or one's partner, or children.

What are the major types of paraphilia? Paraphilias include exhibitionism, fetishism, transvestic fetishism, voyeurism, frotteurism, pedophilia, sexual masochism, and sexual sadism. Although some paraphilias are essentially harmless (such as fetishism), others, such as pedophilia and sexual sadism, often harm nonconsenting victims.

What are the causes of paraphilias? Psychoanalysts see many paraphilias as defenses against castration anxiety. Learning theorists attribute paraphilias to early learning experiences. Biological factors may also be implicated, such as higher-than-normal sex drives in people with paraphilias.

Rape

What are the effects of rape? Many survivors of rape suffer physical and/or psychological trauma, such as PTSD. They have trouble sleeping, cry frequently, may become sullen and mistrustful, and may blame themselves. There may be injuries to the genital organs and other parts of the body, and the victim may be infected with sexually transmitted diseases.

What are the major types of rape? The main types of rape include stranger rape, acquaintance rape, date rape, marital rape, and male rape.

What motivates rape? Men rape women as a way of dominating them and as a way of coercing them into sexual activity. Cultural myths about rape have the effects of blaming the victim and creating a climate that legitimizes rape. For some rapists, sexual arousal and violence become fused together.

Scoring the Rape Myths Scale

Each of the items on this scale represents a rape myth. For example, a rapist who believes that women truly desire to be overpowered by men may think he was just giving the woman what she wanted. But how can anyone know what someone else truly wants unless that person reveals it? Such beliefs are often used as self-serving justifications to explain away unacceptable behavior. Let's be entirely clear about this: When it comes to sex, *no* means *no*. Not *maybe*. Not *sometimes*. Not *in a few minutes*. Just *no*. Moreover, consenting to one sexual act (fondling, kissing, oral sex, etc.) does not imply consent for any other sexual act. Anyone has a right to say *no* at any time or to place limits on what they are willing to do. If you endorsed any of these items, apply your critical-thinking skills to reexamine your beliefs.

KEY TERMS

gender identity *(p. 360)*
gender identity disorder (GID) *(p. 360)*
homophobia *(p. 364)*
heterosexism *(p. 364)*
sexual dysfunctions *(p. 365)*
hypoactive sexual desire
disorder *(p. 366)*
sexual aversion disorder *(p. 366)*
female sexual arousal disorder *(p. 366)*

male erectile disorder *(p. 366)*
female orgasmic disorder *(p. 367)*
male orgasmic disorder *(p. 367)*
premature ejaculation *(p. 367)*
dyspareunia *(p. 367)*
vaginismus *(p. 367)*
paraphilias *(p. 376)*
exhibitionism *(p. 376)*
fetishism *(p. 378)*

transvestic fetishism *(p. 378)*
voyeurism *(p. 379)*
frotteurism *(p. 380)*
pedophilia *(p. 380)*
sexual masochism *(p. 382)*
hypoxyphilia *(p. 382)*
sexual sadism *(p. 382)*
sadomasochism *(p. 382)*
rape *(p. 388)*

MEDIA TOOLS

A variety of digital and online learning tools are available to enrich your learning experience and help you succeed in the course. These resources include:

- **MyPsychLab,** an online learning system for your course in abnormal psychology that allows you to test your mastery of concepts in the book by using chapter-by-chapter diagnostic tests. Results from the diagnostic tests help you build a customized study plan. To access **MyPsychLab,** visit www. prenhall.com/mypsychlab and follow the instructions on the site.
- **"SPEAKING OUT" PATIENT INTERVIEWS,** a set of video case examples of actual patients you can access on the companion

CD-ROM included with the text. Icons in the margins of the chapter highlight the video case examples included on the CD-ROM.

- **COMPANION WEB SITE,** an online study center that offers computer-scored quizzes you can use to test your knowledge, along with other study tools and links to related sites to enhance your learning of abnormal psychology. To access the companion Web site, visit www.prenhall.com/nevid and use the various tabs and links on the site to access these learning resources.

Sexual Dysfunctions

are characterized by

Disturbances of sexual interest, arousal, or response

and are classified within diagnostic categories of

- Sexual Desire Disorders, including hypoactive sexual desire disorder and sexual aversion disorder
- Sexual Arousal Disorders, including female sexual arousal disorder and male erectile disorder
- Orgasm Disorders, including female orgasmic disorder, male orgasmic disorder, and premature ejaculation
- Sexual Pain Disorders, including dyspareunia and vaginismus

- Sex therapy and/or couple therapy to improve communication skills, enhance sexual competencies, and reduce performance anxiety
- Biomedical therapies, including drugs to enhance erectile response or curb premature ejaculation

and may be treated by

and involve such causal influences as

- Biological factors, such as physical illness, hormonal deficiencies, and drug side-effects
- Psychosocial factors, such as performance anxiety, sexual trauma or abuse, lack of sexual skills, and negative attitudes toward sexuality
- Cognitive factors, such as disruptive or interfering thoughts
- A combination of factors leading to a vicious cycle, as in this diagram:

MODEL SPOTLIGHT

Performance Anxiety and Sexual Dysfunctions:
A Vicious Cycle

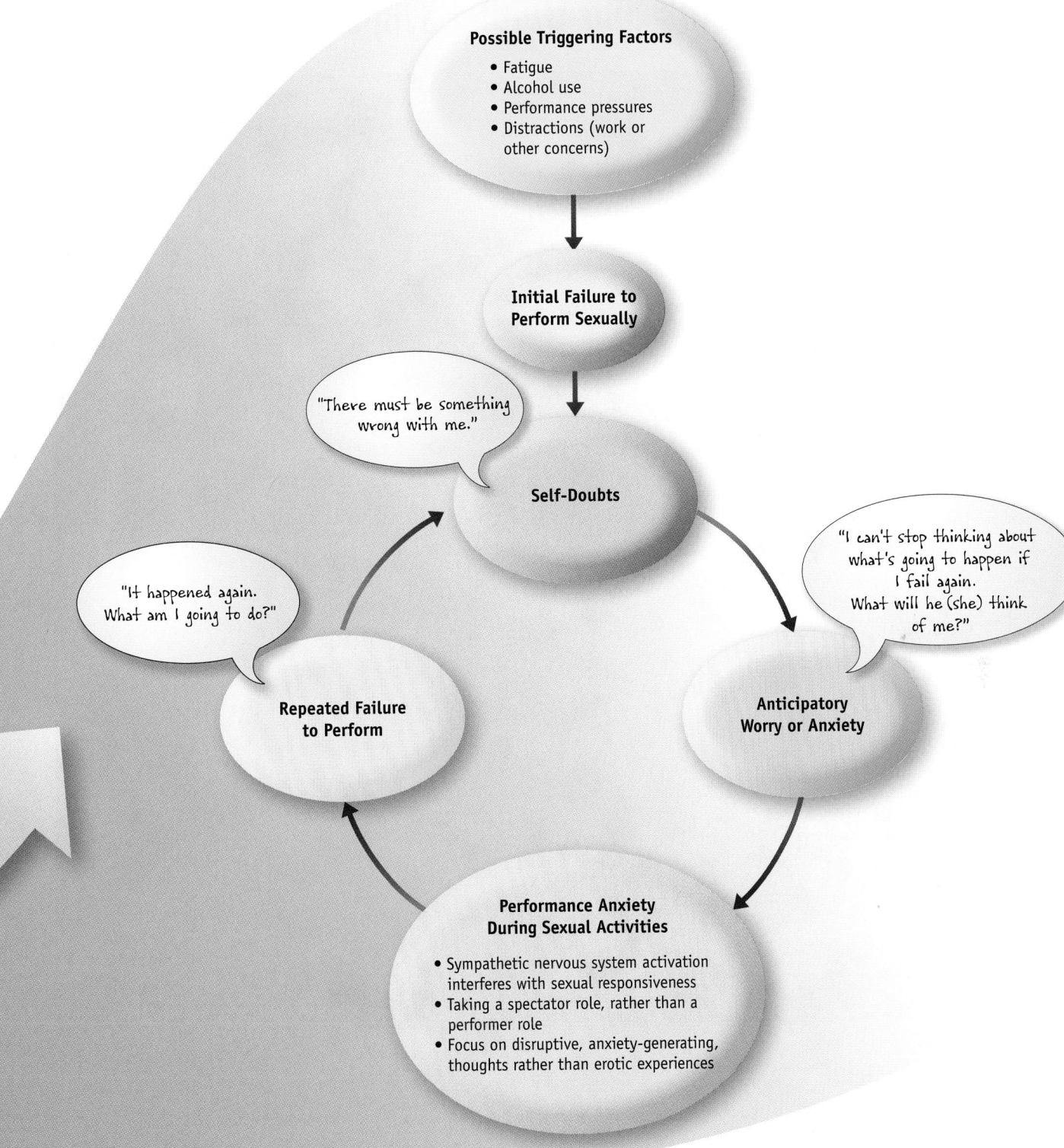

Schizophrenia and Other Psychotic Disorders

CHAPTER OUTLINE

SCHIZOPHRENIA 397–426

Course of Development
Prevalence
Diagnostic Features
Perceptual Disturbances

Subtypes of Schizophrenia
Theoretical Perspectives
Treatment Approaches

OTHER FORMS OF PSYCHOSIS 426–429

Brief Psychotic Disorder

Schizophreniform Disorder
Delusional Disorder
Schizoaffective Disorder

SUMMING UP 429–430

Schizophrenia typically develops in late adolescence or early adulthood, at the very time that young people are making their way from the family into the outside world. For Lori Schiller, an active speaker who shares her personal experience with schizophrenia, the first psychotic episode ("first break") came during her last year at summer camp.

"I" "I Hear Something You Can't Hear"

It was a hot night in August 1976, the summer of my seventeenth year, when, uninvited and unannounced, the Voices took over my life.

I was going into my senior year in high school, so this was to be my last year at summer camp. College, a job, adulthood, responsibility—they were all just around the corner. But for the moment I wasn't prepared for anything more than a summer of fun. I certainly wasn't prepared to have my life change forever. . . .

"You must die!" Other Voices joined in. "You must die! You will die!"

At first I didn't realize where I was. Was I at the lake? Was I asleep? Was I awake? Then I snapped back to the present. I was here at camp, alone. My summertime fling was long gone, two years gone. That long-ago scene was being played out in my mind, and in my mind alone. But as soon as I realized that I was in my bunk, and awake—and that my roommate was still sleeping peacefully—I knew I had to run. I had to get away from these terrible, evil Voices. . . .

Since that time, I have never been completely free of those Voices. At the beginning of that summer, I felt well, a happy, healthy girl—I thought—with a normal head and heart. By summer's end, I was sick, without any clear idea of what was happening to me or why. And as the Voices evolved into a full-scale illness, one that I only later learned was called schizophrenia, it snatched from me my tranquility, sometimes my self-possession, and very nearly my life.

Along the way I have lost many things: the career I might have pursued, the husband I might have married, the children I might have had. During the years when my friends were marrying, having their babies and moving into the houses I once dreamed of living in, I have been behind locked doors, battling the Voices who took over my life without even asking my permission.

—*From Schiller & Bennett, 1994*

TRUTH or FICTION

T□ F□ Schizophrenia exists in the same form in every culture that has been studied. (p. 401)

T□ F□ Visual hallucinations ("seeing things") are the most common type of hallucinations in people with schizophrenia. (p. 405)

T□ F□ It is normal for people to hallucinate nightly. (p. 406)

T□ F□ If you have two parents with schizophrenia, it's nearly certain that you will develop schizophrenia yourself. (p. 412)

T□ F□ Although schizophrenia is widely believed to be a brain disease, evidence of abnormalities in the brains of schizophrenia patients remains lacking. (p. 416)

T□ F□ We now have drugs that not only treat schizophrenia but also can cure it in many cases. (p. 422)

T□ F□ Some people have delusions that they are loved by a famous person. (p. 427)

SCHIZOPHRENIA IS PERHAPS THE MOST PUZZLING AND DISABLING PSYCHOLOGICAL DISORDER. It is the condition that best corresponds to popular conceptions of madness or lunacy. Although researchers are probing the psychological and biological foundations of schizophrenia, the disorder remains largely a mystery. In this chapter we consider what we know about schizophrenia and what remains to be learned. But schizophrenia is not the only type of psychotic disorder in which the person experiences a break with reality. In this chapter we also consider other psychotic disorders, including brief psychotic disorder, schizophreniform disorder, schizoaffective disorder, and delusional disorder. But we begin with the most common of these disorders, schizophrenia.

SCHIZOPHRENIA

Schizophrenia is a chronic, debilitating disorder that touches every facet of the affected person's life. People who develop schizophrenia become increasingly disengaged from society. They fail to function in the expected roles of student, worker, or spouse, and their families and communities grow intolerant of their deviant behavior. Acute episodes

schizophrenia A chronic psychotic disorder characterized by disturbed behavior, thinking, emotions, and perceptions.

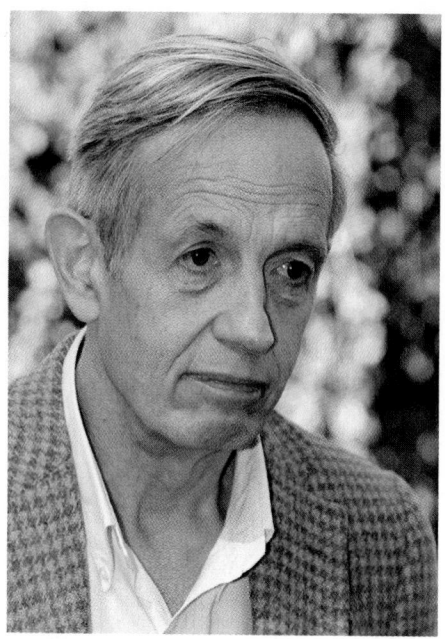

A beautiful mind. In the movie *A Beautiful Mind*, Russell Crowe portrayed Nobel Prize winner John Nash (shown here), a brilliant mathematician whose mind captured the beautiful intricacies of mathematical formulations but was also twisted by the delusions and hallucinations of schizophrenia.

of schizophrenia are characterized by delusions, hallucinations, illogical thinking, incoherent speech, and bizarre behavior. Between acute episodes, people with schizophrenia may still be unable to think clearly, may speak in a flat tone, may have difficulty perceiving emotions in other people's facial expressions, and may show little if any facial expressions of emotions themselves (Gur et al., 2002; Kohler et al., 2003; Schneider et al., 2006). Their clinical symptoms and cognitive impairment make it difficult for them to function in daily life, including being able to hold a job (Rosenheck et al., 2006).

Schizophrenia often elicits fear, misunderstanding, and condemnation rather than sympathy and concern. It strikes at the heart of the person, stripping the mind of the intimate connections between thoughts and emotions, and filling it with distorted perceptions, false ideas, and illogical conceptions, as in the following case example.

◇

Angela's "Hellsmen"

Angela, 19, was brought to the emergency room by her boyfriend, Jaime, because she had cut her wrists. When she was questioned, her attention wandered. She seemed transfixed by creatures in the air, or by something she might be hearing. It seemed as if she had an invisible earphone.

Angela explained that she had slit her wrists at the command of the "hellsmen." Then she became terrified. Later she related that the hellsmen had cautioned her not to disclose their existence. Angela feared that the hellsmen would punish her for her indiscretion.

Jaime related that Angela and he had been living together for nearly a year. They had initially shared a modest apartment in town. But Angela did not like being around other people and persuaded Jaime to rent a cottage in the country. There Angela spent much of her days making fantastic sketches of goblins and monsters. She occasionally became agitated and behaved as if invisible beings were issuing directions. Her words would become jumbled.

Jaime would try to persuade her to go for help, but she would resist. Then, about nine months ago, the wrist-cutting began. Jaime believed that he had made the bungalow secure by removing all knives and blades. But Angela always found a sharp object.

Then he would bring Angela to the hospital against her protests. Stitches would be put in, she would be held under observation for a while, and she would be medicated. She would recount that she cut her wrists because the hellsmen had informed her that she was bad and had to die. After a few days in the hospital, she would disavow hearing the hellsmen and insist on discharge.

Jaime would take her home. The pattern would repeat.

—From the Author's Files

Course of Development

Schizophrenia typically develops during a person's late teens or early 20s, a time when the brain is reaching full maturation (Cowan & Kandel, 2001; Harrop & Trower, 2001). In about three of four cases, the first signs of schizophrenia appear by the age of 25. In some cases, the onset of the disorder is acute, as it was in the case of Lori Schiller. It occurs suddenly, within a few weeks or months. The individual may have been well adjusted and shown few signs of behavioral disturbance. Then a rapid transformation in personality and behavior leads to an acute psychotic episode.

In most cases, there is a slower, more gradual decline in functioning, as was the case with Ian Chovil, a young man who has been living with schizophrenia since the age of 17. He shares his story with the hope that the next generation of people affected by this debilitating disorder will be spared some of the experiences he has endured.

"I and I, Dancing Fool, Challenge You the World to a Duel"

Insidious is an appropriate word to describe the onset of schizophrenia I experienced. I gradually lost all my human relationships, first my girlfriend, then my immediate family, then friends and coworkers. I experienced a lot of emotional turmoil and social anxiety. Somehow I graduated from Trent University in Peterborough, Ontario, Canada, but the last year I was smoking marijuana almost every day. I was creative but found it increasingly difficult to actually read anything. My career aspirations were to become a Rastafarian sociobiologist. I had become incapable of long-term romantic relationships after the demise of my first one. At graduate school in Halifax I was hospitalized for a couple for weeks, a nervous breakdown I thought. Although I was prescribed *chlorpromazine* and then *trifluoperazine* [two types of antipsychotic drugs], no one mentioned schizophrenia to me or my father, a family physician. I tried to complete my year, but some courses went unfinished and I was kicked out of graduate school.

Within two years I was one of the homeless in Calgary, sleeping in a city park or the single men's hostel, hungry because I didn't get to eat very often. A World War II hero wanted to hurt me because I had discovered the war was caused by the influenza of 1918. Tibetan Buddhists read my mind everywhere I went because I had caused the Mount Saint Helens eruption for them earlier that year with my natural tantric abilities. For 10 years I lived more or less like that, in abject poverty, without any friends, quite delusional. At first I was going to be a Buddhist saint, then I was a pawn in a secret war between the sexuals and the antisexuals that would determine the fate of humanity, then I realized I was in contact with aliens of the future. There was going to be a nuclear holocaust that would break up the continental plates, and the oceans would evaporate from the lava. The aliens had come to collect me and one woman. All life here was about to be destroyed. My future wife and I were going to become aliens and have eternal life.

My actual situation by then was a sharp contrast. I was living in a downtown Toronto rooming house with only cockroaches for friends, changing light bulbs as they burnt out in a large department store. It was a full time job I could do, but I hated it intensely. I worried about my enemies who were trying to turn me into a homosexual, and I was in constant telepathic conversation with my future wife, listening to rock and roll songs for messages from aliens in my spare time. I ran into trouble with the law one night after becoming furious with the aliens for not transferring my mind to another body. The judge sentenced me to 3 years of probation with the condition I see a psychiatrist for that time.

. . . I wrote a poem as an undergraduate that was published in the student newspaper. The first line was "I and I, dancing fool, challenge you the world to a duel." I intend to challenge the world to the best of my ability, until people like me have the quality of life possible with the most effective treatment strategies available.

From Chovil, 2000 Reprinted with permission of the National Institute of Mental Heath

As in this case, psychotic behaviors may emerge gradually over several years, although early signs of deterioration may be observed. This period of deterioration is called the **prodromal phase.** It is characterized by waning interest in social activities and increasing difficulty in meeting the responsibilities of daily living. At first, such people seem to take less care of their appearance. They fail to bathe regularly or they wear the same clothes repeatedly. Over time, their behavior may become increasingly odd. There are lapses in job performance or schoolwork. Their speech becomes vague and rambling. At first these changes in personality may be so gradual that they raise little concern among friends and families. They may be attributed to "a phase" that the person is passing through. But as behavior becomes more bizarre—such as hoarding food, collecting garbage, or talking to oneself on the street—the acute phase of the disorder begins. Frankly psychotic symptoms develop, such as wild hallucinations, delusions, and increasingly bizarre behavior.

prodromal phase In schizophrenia, the period of decline in functioning that precedes the first acute psychotic episode.

residual phase In schizophrenia, the phase that follows an acute phase, characterized by a return to the level of functioning of the prodromal phase.

Following acute episodes, some people with schizophrenia enter the **residual phase,** in which their behavior returns to the level of the prodromal phase. Flagrant psychotic behaviors are absent, but the person is still impaired by significant cognitive, social, and emotional deficits, such as a deep sense of apathy and difficulties thinking or speaking clearly, and by harboring unusual ideas, such as beliefs in telepathy or clairvoyance (Docherty et al., 2003; Messias et al., 2005; Roth et al., 2004). These cognitive and social deficits can impede the ability of schizophrenia patients to function effectively in social and occupational roles even more severely than the severe hallucinations and delusions of the psychotic episode (Barch, 2003). Here, in his first-person account, Ian Chovil observes that despite improvement following treatment with the antipsychotic drug *olanzapine,* his functioning was still impaired by these deficits—the "poverties" as he calls them.

"I" "The Poverties"

My life has been improving a little each year, and noticeably on *olanzapine,* but I am still quite unsure of myself. I still have what I call "the poverties," like poverty of thought, emotion, friends, and hard cash. My social life seems to be the slowest to improve. I have three or four recreational friends, only one without a mental illness, only one that I see fairly often. I lived for awhile with Rosemary, whom I still see often, in a two bedroom apartment until the government changed its regulations on cohabitation and we had to separate or lose almost $400 a month in income. Now I'm in a very nice subsidized apartment, fairly happy on my own for the first time thanks to *olanzapine* and my position at the Homewood, which brings me into contact with a lot of people.

From Chovil, 2000 Reprinted with permission of the National Institute of Mental Health

Although schizophrenia is a chronic disorder, as many as one half to two thirds of schizophrenia patients improve significantly over time (USDHHS, 1999a). Full return to normal behavior is uncommon but does occur in some cases. Typically, patients develop a chronic pattern characterized by occasional acute episodes and continued cognitive, emotional, and motivational impairment between psychotic episodes (Walker et al., 2004).

Prevalence

About 1% of the adult population in the United States is affected by schizophrenia, more than 2 million people in total (Freedman, 2003; Perälä et al., 2007). According to the results of a World Health Organization (WHO) multinational study, the rate of schizophrenia appears to be similar in both developed and developing cultures (Jablensky et al., 1992). The WHO estimates that about 24 million people worldwide suffer from schizophrenia (Olson, 2001). Nearly 1 million people in the United States receive treatment for schizophrenia each year, with about a third of these requiring hospitalization.

Men tend to have a slightly higher risk of developing schizophrenia than women (Aleman, Kahn, & Selten, 2003; NCA, 2005). Women tend to develop the disorder somewhat later than men do, with onset occurring most commonly between age 25 and the mid-30s in women and between age 18 and 25 in men (APA, 2000). Women also tend to achieve a higher level of functioning before the onset of the disorder and to have a less severe course of illness than do men.

Although we believe schizophrenia occurs universally across cultures, the course of the disorder and its particular symptoms can vary from culture to culture. For example, visual hallucinations appear to be most common in some non-Western cultures (Ndetei & Singh, 1983). In a study conducted in an English hospital in Kenya, researchers found that people of African, Asian, or Jamaican background with schizophrenia were about twice as likely to experience visual hallucinations as those of European background (Ndetei & Vadher, 1984).

TABLE 12.1 Overview of Schizophrenia

Clinical Features of Schizophrenia

Disturbed Thought Processes	Delusions (fixed false ideas) and thought disorder (disorganized thinking and incoherent speech)
Attentional Deficiencies	Difficulty attending to relevant stimuli and screening out irrelevant stimuli
Perceptual Disturbances	Hallucinations (sensory perceptions in the absence of external stimulation)
Emotional Disturbances	Flat (blunted) or inappropriate emotions
Other Types of Impairment	Confusion about personal identity, lack of volition, excitable behavior or states of stupor, odd gestures or bizarre facial expressions, and impaired ability to relate to others

Major Subtypes of Schizophrenia

Disorganized Type	Confused and bizarre behavior, incoherent speech, vivid hallucinations, flat or inappropriate affect, and disorganized delusions
Catatonic Type	Gross disturbances in motor activity in which behavior may slow to a stupor but abruptly shift to a highly agitated state
Paranoid Type	Delusions (typically of themes of grandeur, persecution, or jealousy) and frequent auditory hallucinations

Source: APA, 2000.

Note: Lifetime prevalence of schizophrenia is estimated to be about 1% of the adult population.

Diagnostic Features

Schizophrenia is a pervasive disorder that affects a wide range of psychological processes involving cognition, affect, and behavior. The *DSM-IV* criteria for schizophrenia require that psychotic behaviors be present at some point during the course of the disorder and that signs of the disorder be present for at least 6 months. People with briefer forms of psychosis receive other diagnoses, such as brief psychotic disorder (discussed later in the chapter). Table 12.1 provides an overview of schizophrenia. Table 12.2 lists the major diagnostic criteria for schizophrenia.

People with schizophrenia show a marked decline in occupational and social functioning. They may have difficulty holding a conversation, forming friendships, holding a job, or taking care of their personal hygiene. Yet no one behavior pattern is unique to schizophrenia. People with schizophrenia may exhibit delusions, problems with associative thinking, and hallucinations at one time or another, but not necessarily all at once. There are also different kinds or types of schizophrenia, characterized by different behavior patterns.

TRUTH or FICTION

Schizophrenia exists in the same form in every culture that has been studied.

☑ **FALSE.** Both the course of schizophrenia and its features can vary among cultures.

TABLE 12.2

Major Diagnostic Features of Schizophrenia

A. Two or more of the following must be present for a significant portion of time over the course of a 1-month period:
  1. Delusions
  2. Hallucinations
  3. Speech that is either incoherent or characterized by marked loosening of associations
  4. Disorganized or catatonic behavior
  5. Negative features (e.g., flattened affect)

B. Functioning in such areas as social relations, work, or self-care during the course of the disorder is markedly below the level achieved prior to the onset of the disorder. If the onset develops during childhood or adolescence, there is a failure to achieve the expected level of social development.

C. Signs of the disorder have occurred continuously for a period of at least 6 months. This 6-month period must include an active phase lasting at least a month in which psychotic symptoms (listed in A), which are characteristic of schizophrenia, occur.

D. The disorder cannot be attributed to the effects of a substance (e.g., substance abuse or prescribed medication) or to a general medical condition.

Source: Adapted from the *DSM-IV-TR* (APA, 2000).

As we noted, men and women with schizophrenia differ in several ways. Men tend to show an earlier age of onset, have a poorer level of adjustment before showing signs of the disorder, and also tend to have more cognitive impairment, behavioral deficits, and a poorer response to drug therapy than do women (Gorwood et al., 1995; Ragland et al., 1999). These differences have led researchers to speculate that men and women may tend to develop different forms of schizophrenia. Perhaps schizophrenia affects different areas of the brain in men and women, which may explain differences in the form or features of the disorder.

Schizophrenia affects a wide range of behaviors, including thinking, speech, attentional and perceptual processes, emotional processes, and voluntary behavior. One way of grouping symptoms of schizophrenia is to distinguish between positive and negative symptoms:

- **Positive symptoms** represent more flagrant abnormal thoughts and behaviors, such as hallucinations, delusions, disturbed thinking and disorganized speech, disorganized or aberrant behavior, and agitation.
- **Negative symptoms** involve loss or reduction of normal functions, such as attentional deficiencies, lack of emotions or of emotional expression, loss of motivation, loss of pleasure in normally pleasant activities, social withdrawal, and impoverished speech ("poverty of speech").

Here we take a closer look at several key features or symptoms associated with schizophrenia.

Disturbed Thought and Speech Schizophrenia is characterized by positive symptoms involving disturbances in thinking and expression of thoughts through coherent, meaningful speech. Aberrant thinking may be found in both the content and form of thought.

Aberrant Content of Thought Delusions represent disturbed content of thought. These are false beliefs that remain fixed in the person's mind despite their illogical bases and lack of evidence to support them. They tend to remain unshakable even in the face of disconfirming evidence. Delusions may take many forms. Some of the most common types are:

- *Delusions of persecution* (e.g., "The CIA is out to get me")
- *Delusions of reference* ("People on the bus are talking about me," or "People on TV are making fun of me," or "The neighbors hear everything I say. They've put bugs in the walls of my house")
- *Delusions of being controlled* (believing that one's thoughts, feelings, impulses, or actions are controlled by external forces, such as agents of the devil)
- *Delusions of grandeur* (believing oneself to be Jesus or believing one is on a special mission, or having grand but illogical plans for saving the world)

Other delusions include beliefs that one has committed unpardonable sins, is rotting away from a horrible disease, that the world or oneself does not really exist, or, as in the following case, that one desperately needs to help people.

positive symptoms Flagrant symptoms of schizophrenia, such as hallucinations, delusions, bizarre behavior, and thought disorder.

negative symptoms Behavioral deficiencies associated with schizophrenia, such as social skills deficits, social withdrawal, flattened affect, poverty of speech and thought, psychomotor retardation, and failure to experience pleasure.

The Hospital at the North Pole

Although people with schizophrenia may feel hounded by demons or earthly conspiracies, Mario's delusions had a messianic quality. "I need to get out of here," he said to his psychiatrist. "Why do you need to leave?" the psychiatrist asked. Mario responded, "My hospital. I need to get back to my hospital." "Which hospital?" he was asked. "I have this hospital. It's all white and we find cures for everything wrong with people." Mario was asked where his hospital was located. "It's all the way up at the North Pole," he responded. His psychiatrist asked, "But how do you get there?" Mario responded, "I just get there. I don't know how. I just get there. I have to do my work. When will you let me go so I can help the people?"

—From the Author's Files

Other commonly occurring delusions include *thought broadcasting* (believing one's thoughts are somehow transmitted to the external world so that others can overhear them), *thought insertion* (believing one's thoughts have been planted in one's mind by an external source), and *thought withdrawal* (believing that thoughts have been removed from one's mind). Mellor (1970) offers the following examples:

- *Thought Broadcasting:* A 21-year-old student reported, "As I think, my thoughts leave my head on a type of mental ticker tape. Everyone around has only to pass the tape through their mind and they know my thoughts."
- *Thought Insertion:* A 29-year-old housewife reported that when she looks out of the window, she thinks, "The garden looks nice and the grass looks cool, but the thoughts of [a man's name] come into my mind. There are no other thoughts there, only his. . . . He treats my mind like a screen and flashes his thoughts on it like you flash a picture."
- *Thought Withdrawal:* A 22-year-old woman experienced the following: "I am thinking about my mother, and suddenly my thoughts are sucked out of my mind by a phrenological vacuum extractor, and there is nothing in my mind, it is empty."

Aberrant Forms of Thought Unless we are engaged in daydreaming or purposefully letting our thoughts wander, our thoughts tend to be tightly knit together. The connections (or associations) between our thoughts tend to be logical and coherent. In contrast, people with schizophrenia tend to think in a disorganized, illogical fashion. In schizophrenia, the form or structure of thought processes as well as their content is often disturbed. Clinicians label this type of disturbance a **thought disorder.**

Thought disorder is recognized by the breakdown in the organization, processing, and control of thoughts. Looseness of associations is a cardinal sign of thought disorder. The speech pattern of people with schizophrenia is often disorganized or jumbled, with parts of words combined incoherently or words strung together to make meaningless rhymes. Their speech may jump disconnectedly from one topic to another. People with thought disorder are usually unaware that their thoughts and behavior appear abnormal. In severe cases their speech may become completely incoherent or incomprehensible.

Another common sign of thought disorder is *poverty of speech* (speech that is coherent but so slow, limited in production, or vague that little information is conveyed). Less commonly occurring signs include *neologisms* (made-up words that have little or no meaning to others), *perseveration* (inappropriate but persistent repetition of the same words or train of thought), *clanging* (stringing together of words or sounds on the basis of rhyming, such as, "I know who I am but I don't know Sam"), and *blocking* (involuntary, abrupt interruption of speech or thought). Disconnected speech is more common and more severe among younger patients, whereas poverty of speech is found more often and is more severe among older patients (Harvey et al., 1997).

Many schizophrenia patients, but not all, show evidence of thought disorder. Some appear to think and speak coherently but have disordered content of thought, as seen by the presence of delusions. Nor is disordered thought unique to schizophrenia; it is even found in milder form among people without psychological disorders, especially when they are tired or under stress. Disordered thought is also found among other diagnostic groups, such as persons with mania. Thought disorders in people experiencing a manic episode tend to be short lived and reversible, however. In those with schizophrenia, thought disorder tends to be more persistent or recurrent. Thought disorder occurs most often during acute episodes, but may linger into residual phases.

Attentional Deficiencies To read this book you must screen out background noises and other environmental stimuli. Attention, the ability to focus on relevant stimuli and ignore irrelevant ones, is basic to learning and thinking. People with

thought disorder A disturbance in thinking characterized by the breakdown of logical associations between thoughts.

Filtering out extraneous stimuli. You probably have little difficulty filtering out unimportant stimuli, such as street sounds. But people with schizophrenia may be distracted by irrelevant stimuli and be unable to filter them out. Consequently, they may have difficulty focusing their attention and organizing their thoughts.

schizophrenia often have difficulty filtering out irrelevant stimuli, making it nearly impossible for them to focus their attention, organize their thoughts, and filter out unessential information. The mother of a son who had schizophrenia described her son's difficulties in filtering out extraneous sounds:

> His hearing is different when he's ill. One of the first things we notice when he's deteriorating is his heightened sense of hearing. He cannot filter out anything. He hears each and every sound around him with equal intensity. He hears the sounds from the street, in the yard, and in the house, and they are all much louder than normal.

Anonymous, 1985, p. 1; as cited in Freedman et al., 1987, p. 670

People with schizophrenia also appear to be *hypervigilant,* or acutely sensitive to extraneous sounds, especially during the early stages of the disorder. During acute episodes, they may become flooded by these stimuli, overwhelming their ability to make sense of their environments. Through measuring brain waves, researchers find that the brains of people with schizophrenia are less able than those of other people to inhibit or screen out responses to distracting sounds (Braff, 1993). Scientists suspect there may be a "gating" mechanism in the brain for filtering extraneous stimuli (Leonard et al., 2002). Researchers have discovered a genetic defect tied to a brain abnormality that may explain this filtering deficit (Grady, 1997).

Links between attentional deficits and schizophrenia are supported by various studies focusing on the psychophysiological aspects of attention. Here we review some of this research.

Eye Movement Dysfunction About one in three chronic schizophrenia patients shows evidence of *eye movement dysfunction* (Ross, 2000). Patients with this dysfunction (also called *eye tracking dysfunction*) have abnormal movements of the eyes when they track a moving target across their field of vision. Rather than steadily tracking the target, the eyes fall back and then catch up in a kind of jerky movement. Eye movement dysfunctions appear to involve a defect in the brain's involuntary attentional processes responsible for visual attention.

Eye movement dysfunctions are common among people with schizophrenia and among their first-degree relatives (parents, children, and siblings), which suggests it might be a genetically transmitted trait, or *marker,* associated with genes involved in the development of schizophrenia (Ross, 2000). The role of eye movement dysfunction as a biological marker for schizophrenia is clouded, however, because it is not unique

mypsychlab
The Case of Larry
"I have all kinds of voices."

A painting by a schizophrenia patient. Paintings or drawings by schizophrenia patients often express the bizarre quality of their thought patterns.

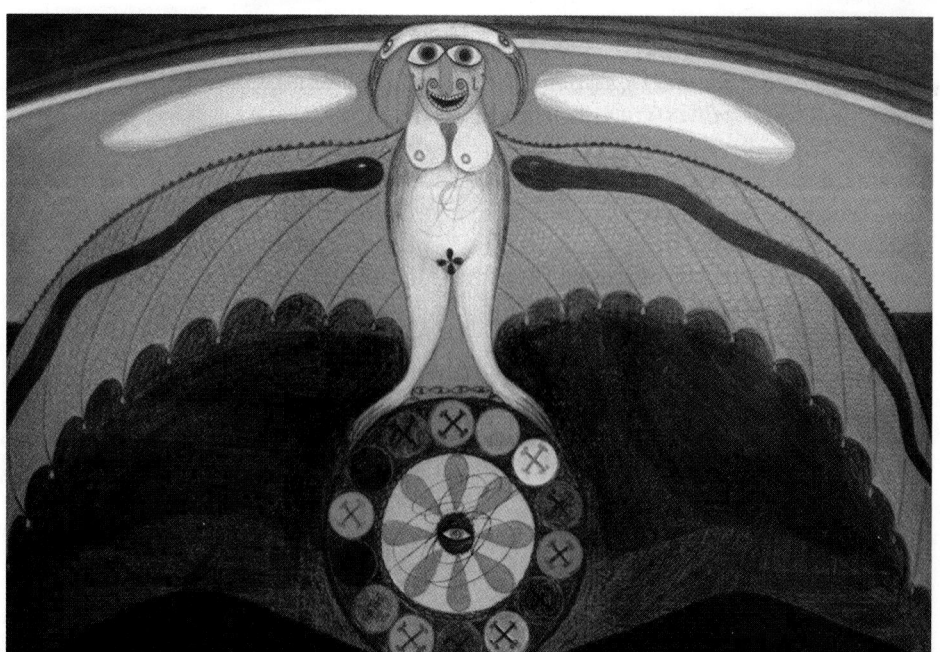

to schizophrenia. People with other psychological disorders, such as bipolar disorder, sometimes show the dysfunction. Nor do all people with schizophrenia or their family members show eye movement dysfunctions. In sum, eye movement dysfunction may be a marker for one of many different genetic pathways leading to of schizophrenia.

Abnormal Event-Related Potentials   Researchers have also studied brain wave patterns, called *event-related potentials,* or ERPs, that occur in response to external stimuli like sounds and flashes of light. ERPs can be broken down into various components that emerge at different intervals following the presentation of a stimulus. Normally, the brain suppresses ERPs to repeated stimuli, which allows us to disregard irrelevant stimuli, like the sound of a ticking clock. But schizophrenia patients often show an inability to suppress ERPs that occur in the first few hundred milliseconds in response to a repeated stimulus (Dubovsky, 2006b; Hall et al., 2007). As a result, unusually high levels of sensory information may reach the higher brain centers, producing a condition called *sensory overload.* This deficiency in the sensory gating mechanism may explain why schizophrenia patients have difficulty filtering out distracting stimuli.

Schizophrenia patients also show reduced levels of later-occurring ERPs (e.g., van der Stelt et al., 2004; Winterer et al., 2004). These later-occurring ERPs are believed to be involved in the process of focusing attention on a stimulus in order to extract meaningful information. Consequently, schizophrenia patients may have difficulty extracting meaningful information from stimuli such as lights, sounds, and touch.

Studies of ERPs are consistent with the view that schizophrenia patients are flooded with high levels of sensory information and have great difficulty extracting useful information from it. As a result, they may become confused and find it difficult to filter out distracting stimuli.

Perceptual Disturbances

Voices, Devils, and Angels

Every so often during the interview, Sally would look over her right shoulder in the direction of the office door and smile gently. When asked why she kept looking at the door, she said that the voices were talking about the two of us just outside the door and she wanted to hear what they were saying. "Why the smile?" Sally was asked. "They were saying funny things," she replied, "like maybe you thought I was cute or something."

Tom was flailing his arms wildly in the hall of the psychiatric unit. Sweat seemed to pour from his brow, and his eyes darted about with agitation. He was subdued and injected with haloperidol (brand name Haldol) to reduce his agitation. When he was about to be injected he started shouting, "Father, forgive them for they know not . . . forgive them . . . father . . ." His words became jumbled. Later, after he had calmed down, he reported that the ward attendants had looked to him like devils or evil angels. They were red and burning, and steam issued from their mouths.

—From the Author's Files

Hallucinations   The most common form of perceptual disturbance in schizophrenia are **hallucinations,** which are sensory perceptions experienced in the absence of external stimulation. They are difficult to distinguish from reality. For Sally, the voices coming from outside the consulting room were real enough, although no one was there. Hallucinations can involve any of the senses. Auditory hallucinations ("hearing voices") are most common, affecting about three of four schizophrenia patients (Goode, 2003b). Tactile hallucinations (such as tingling, electrical, or burning sensations) and somatic hallucinations (such as feeling like snakes are crawling inside one's belly) are also common. Visual hallucinations (seeing things that are not there), gustatory hallucinations (tasting things that are not present), and olfactory hallucinations (sensing odors that are not present) are rarer.

hallucinations Perceptions occurring in the absence of external stimuli that become confused with reality.

T R U T H or F I C T I O N

Visual hallucinations ("seeing things") are the most common type of hallucination in people with schizophrenia.

☑ **FALSE.** Auditory, not visual, hallucinations are the most common type of hallucinations among people with schizophrenia.

People with schizophrenia may experience auditory hallucinations as female or male voices and as originating inside or outside their head (Asaad & Shapiro, 1986). Hallucinators may hear voices conversing about them in the third person, debating their virtues or faults. Some voices are experienced as supportive and friendly, but most are critical or even terrorizing.

Some people with schizophrenia experience *command hallucinations,* voices that instruct them to perform certain acts, such as harming themselves or others (Braham, Trower, & Birchwood, 2004). Angela, for example, was instructed by the "hellsmen" to commit suicide. People with schizophrenia who experience command hallucinations are often hospitalized for fear they may harm themselves or others. There is a good reason for this, as evidence shows that some individuals who hear commands to do harm act upon them (Braham, Trower, & Birchwood, 2004). Yet command hallucinations often go undetected by professionals, because patients deny them or are unwilling to discuss them.

Hallucinations are not unique to schizophrenia. People with major depression and mania sometimes experience hallucinations. Nor are hallucinations invariably a sign of psychopathology. They are common and socially valued in some cultures (Bentall, 1990). Even in developed countries like the United States, about 5% of respondents in nonpatient samples report experiencing hallucinations during the preceding year, mostly auditory hallucinations (Honig et al., 1998). Hallucinations in people without psychiatric conditions are often triggered by unusually low levels of sensory stimulation (lying in the dark in a soundproof room for extended time) or low levels of arousal (Teunisse et al., 1996). Unlike psychotic individuals, these people realize that their hallucinations are not real and feel in control of them.

People who are free of psychological disorders sometimes experience hallucinations during the course of religious experiences or rituals. Participants in such experiences may report fleeting trancelike states with visions or other perceptual aberrations. All of us hallucinate nightly, if we consider dreams to be a form of hallucination (perceptual experience in the absence of external stimuli).

Hallucinations during waking states can also occur in response to hallucinogenic drugs, such as LSD, and can occur during grief reactions, when images of the deceased may appear, and in other stressful conditions. The hallucinations of psychiatric patients are different from those of mourners because those with psychiatric disorders typically cannot distinguish between real and imaginary events (Bentall, 1990).

Drug-induced hallucinations tend to be visual and often involve abstract shapes such as circles or stars or flashes of light. Schizophrenic hallucinations, in contrast, tend to be more fully formed and complex. Hallucinations (for example, of bugs crawling on one's skin) may also arise during *delirium tremens* (the DTs), which often occur as part of the withdrawal syndrome for chronic alcoholism. Hallucinations may also occur as side effects of medications or in neurological disorders, such as Parkinson's disease.

The causes of psychotic hallucinations remain unknown, but speculations abound. Disturbances in brain chemistry are suspected. The neurotransmitter dopamine is implicated, largely because antipsychotic drugs that block dopamine activity also tend to reduce hallucinations. Conversely, drugs that lead to increased production of dopamine, such as cocaine, can induce hallucinations. Because hallucinations resemble dreamlike states, they may be connected to a failure of brain mechanisms that normally prevent dream images from intruding on waking experiences.

Hallucinations may also represent a type of inner speech (silent self-talk) (Jones & Fernyhough, 2007). Many of us, perhaps even all of us, talk to ourselves from time to time, although we usually keep our mutterings beneath our breaths (subvocal) and recognize the voice we "hear" as our own. Might auditory hallucinations in schizophrenia be a projection of the patient's own internal voice, or self-speech, onto external sources?

Investigators suspect that in auditory hallucinations, the auditory cortex (the part of the brain that processes auditory stimulation) becomes spontaneously active despite the absence of external sounds (Hunter et al., 2006). It is conceivable that the auditory cortex is responding to inner speech that it somehow mistakes for external sounds. Similar electrical activity occurs in the auditory cortex of the brain during auditory

T R U T H or F I C T I O N

It is normal for people to hallucinate nightly.

☑ **TRUE.** Hallucinations—perceptual experiences such as visual images, smells, etc., in the absence of external stimulation—occur nightly in the form of dreams.

hallucinations and in response to hearing real sounds (Tiihonen et al., 1992). This supports the view that auditory hallucinations may be a form of inner speech that for unknown reasons is attributed to external sources rather than to one's own thoughts (Ford et al., 2001; Jones & Fernyhough, 2006). This line of research has led to treatments in which cognitive-behavioral therapists attempt to teach hallucinators to reattribute their voices to themselves. Hallucinators are also trained to recognize the situational cues associated with their hallucinations. For example:

> . . . one patient . . . recognized that her voices tended to become worse following family arguments. She became aware that the content of her voices reflected the things that she was feeling and thinking about her family but that she was unable to express. Specific targets and goals were then set to allow her to address these difficulties with her family, and techniques such as rehearsal, problem solving and cognitive restructuring were employed to help her work towards these goals.
>
> —*Bentall, Haddock, & Slade, 1994, p. 58*

Cognitive-behavioral therapy has become a helpful adjunct to drug therapy in controlling hallucinations (e.g., Messari & Hallam, 2003; Pfammatter, Junghan, & Brenner, 2006). But even if theories linking inner speech to auditory hallucinations stand up to further scientific inquiry, they cannot account for hallucinations in other sensory modalities, such as visual, tactile, or olfactory hallucinations.

The brain mechanisms responsible for hallucinations probably involve a number of interconnected systems. One intriguing possibility is that defects in deeper brain structures may lead the brain to create its own reality. This alternative reality goes unchecked because the higher thinking centers in the brain, located in the frontal lobes of the cerebral cortex, may fail to perform a "reality check" on these images to determine whether they are real, imagined, or hallucinated. Consequently, people may misattribute their own internally generated voices to outside sources. As we'll see later, evidence from other brain-imaging studies points to abnormalities in the frontal lobes in people with schizophrenia.

The Case of Georgiana

"Then it got out of hand, where I couldn't control coming and going, back and forth, and in my body, out of my body, it was no longer under my control."

Emotional Disturbances Disturbances of affect or emotional response in schizophrenia may involve negative symptoms, such as a loss of normal affect or emotional expression, which is labeled blunted affect or *flat affect*. Flat affect is inferred from the absence of emotional expression in the face and voice. People with schizophrenia may speak in a monotone and maintain an expressionless face, or "mask." They may not experience a normal range of emotional response to people and events. We may also find positive symptoms, which involve exaggerated or inappropriate affect. For example, the person may laugh for no reason or giggle at bad news.

It is not clear, however, whether emotional blunting in people with schizophrenia is a disturbance in their ability to express emotions, to report the presence of emotions, or to actually experience emotions. Laboratory-based evidence shows that schizophrenia patients experience more intense negative emotions, but less intense positive emotions, than controls (Myin-Germeys, Delespaul, & deVries, 2000). In other words, schizophrenia patients may experience strong emotions (especially negative emotions), even if their experiences are not communicated to the world outside through their facial expressions or behavior. People with schizophrenia may lack the capacity to express their emotions outwardly.

Other Types of Impairment People who suffer from schizophrenia may become confused about their personal identities—the cluster of attributes and characteristics that define themselves as individuals and give meaning and direction to their lives. They may fail to recognize themselves as unique individuals and be unclear about how much of what they experience is part of themselves. In psychodynamic terms, this phenomenon is sometimes referred to as loss of *ego boundaries*. They may also have difficulty adopting a third-party perspective: they fail to perceive their own behavior and verbalizations as socially inappropriate in a given situation because they cannot see things from another person's point of view (Carini & Nevid, 1992). They also have difficulty recognizing or perceiving emotions in others (Penn et al., 2000).

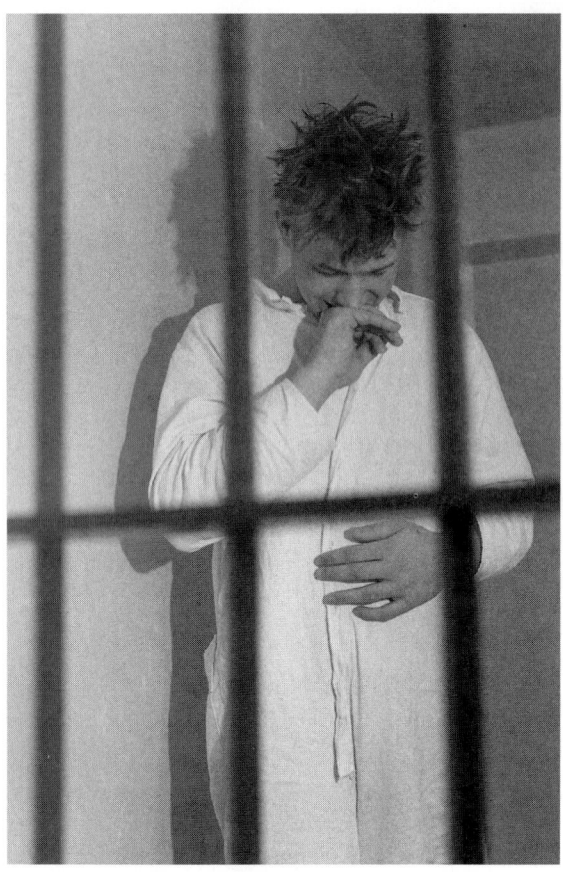

A young man diagnosed with disorganized schizophrenia. One of the characteristic features of disorganized schizophrenia is grossly inappropriate affect, as shown by this patient, who continually giggles and laughs for no apparent reason.

disorganized type The subtype of schizophrenia characterized by disorganized behavior, bizarre delusions, and vivid hallucinations.

Disturbances of volition are most often seen in the residual or chronic state. These negative symptoms are characterized by loss of initiative to pursue goal-directed activities. People with schizophrenia may be unable to carry out plans and may lack interest or drive. Apparent ambivalence toward choosing courses of action may block goal-directed activities.

People with schizophrenia may show highly excited or wild behavior or may slow to a state of *stupor*. They may exhibit odd gestures and bizarre facial expressions or become unresponsive and curtail spontaneous movement. In extreme cases, as in catatonic schizophrenia, the person seems unaware of the environment or maintains a rigid posture. Or the person moves about in an excited but seemingly purposeless manner.

People with schizophrenia also show significant impairment in interpersonal relationships. They withdraw from social interactions and become absorbed in private thoughts and fantasies. Or they cling so desperately to others that they make them uncomfortable. They may become so dominated by their own fantasies that they essentially lose touch with the outside world. They also tend to have been introverted and peculiar even before the appearance of psychotic behavior. These early signs may be associated with a vulnerability to schizophrenia, at least in people with a genetic risk of developing the disorder.

Subtypes of Schizophrenia

The *DSM-IV* lists three specific types of schizophrenia: *disorganized, catatonic,* and *paranoid.* People with schizophrenia who display active psychotic features, such as hallucinations, delusions, incoherent speech, or confused or disorganized behavior, but who do not meet the specifications of the other types, are considered to be of an *undifferentiated type.* Others who have no prominent psychotic features at the time of evaluation but have some residual features (for example, social withdrawal, peculiar behavior, blunted or inappropriate affect, strange beliefs or thoughts) would be classified as having a *residual type* of schizophrenia.

Here let us consider the specific types of schizophrenia recognized by the *DSM* system.

Disorganized Type The **disorganized type** of schizophrenia is associated with such features as confused behavior, incoherent speech, silly irrelevant laughter, vivid and frequent hallucinations, flattened or inappropriate affect, and disorganized delusions that often involve sexual or religious themes. Social impairment is common. People with disorganized schizophrenia display silliness and giddiness of mood, giggling and talking nonsensically. They often neglect their appearance and hygiene and lose control of their bladders and bowels. Consider the following case example.

A Case of Schizophrenia, Disorganized Type

A 40-year-old man who looks more like 30 is brought to the hospital by his mother, who reports that she is afraid of him. It is his twelfth hospitalization. He is dressed in a tattered overcoat, baseball cap, and bedroom slippers, and sports several medals around his neck. His affect ranges from anger (hurling obscenities at his mother) to giggling. He speaks with a childlike quality and walks with exaggerated hip movements and seems to measure each step very carefully. Since stopping his medication about a month ago, his mother reports, he had been hearing voices and looking and acting more bizarrely. He tells the interviewer he has been "eating wires" and lighting fires. His speech is generally incoherent and frequently falls into rhyme and clanging associations. His history reveals a series of hospitalizations since the age of 16.

Between hospitalizations, he lives with his mother, who is now elderly, and often disappears for months at a time, but is eventually picked up by the police for wandering in the streets.

—Adapted from Spitzer et al., 1994, pp. 189–190

Catatonic Type The **catatonic type** of schizophrenia is characterized by markedly impaired motor behavior and a slowing down of activity that progresses to a stupor but may switch abruptly into an agitated phase. People with catatonic schizophrenia may show unusual mannerisms or grimacing or maintain bizarre, apparently strenuous postures for hours, although their limbs become stiff or swollen. A striking but less common feature is *waxy flexibility,* which involves adopting a fixed posture into which they have been positioned by others. They will not respond to questions or comments during these periods, which can last for hours. Later they may report they heard what others were saying at the time, however.

catatonic type The subtype of schizophrenia characterized by gross disturbances in motor activity, such as catatonic stupor.

A Case of Schizophrenia, Catatonic Type

A 24-year-old man had been brooding about his life. He professed that he did not feel well but could not explain his bad feelings. While hospitalized, he initially sought contact with people but a few days later was found in a statuesque position, his legs contorted awkwardly. He refused to talk to anyone and acted as if he couldn't see or hear. His face was an expressionless mask. A few days later, he began to talk, but in an echolalic or mimicking way. For example, he would respond to the question, "What is your name?" by saying, "What is your name?" He could not care for his needs and had to be fed.

—Adapted from Arieti, 1974, p. 40

Catatonia is not unique to schizophrenia. It occurs in other disorders, including brain disorders, drug intoxication, and metabolic disorders. In fact, it is found more often in people with mood disorders than those with schizophrenia (Taylor & Fink, 2003).

Paranoid Type The **paranoid type** of schizophrenia is characterized by preoccupations with one or more delusions or with the presence of frequent auditory hallucinations (APA, 2000). The behavior and speech of someone with paranoid schizophrenia does not show the marked disorganization typical of the disorganized type, nor is there a prominent display of flattened or inappropriate affect or catatonic behavior. The delusions often involve themes of grandeur, persecution, or jealousy. The patient may believe, for example, that the spouse or lover is unfaithful despite a lack of evidence. Patients may become highly agitated, confused, and fearful.

paranoid type The subtype of schizophrenia characterized by hallucinations and systematized delusions, commonly involving themes of persecution.

A Case of Schizophrenia, Paranoid Type

The 25-year-old woman was visibly frightened. She was shaking badly and had the look of someone who feared that she might be attacked at any moment. The night before she had been found cowering in a corner of the local bus station, mumbling incoherently to herself, having arrived in town minutes earlier on a bus from Philadelphia. The station manager had called the police, who took her to the hospital. She told the interviewer that she had to escape Philadelphia because the Mafia was closing in on her. She was a schoolteacher, she explained, at least until the voices started bothering her. The voices would tell her she was bad and had to be punished. Sometimes the voices were in her head, sometimes they spoke to her through the electrical wires in her apartment. The voices told her how someone from the Mafia

(continued)

would come to kill her. She felt that one of her neighbors, a shy man who lived down the hall, was in league with the Mafia. She felt the only hope she had was to escape. To go somewhere, anywhere. So she hopped on the first bus leaving town, heading nowhere in particular, except away from home.

—From the Author's Files

Type I versus Type II Schizophrenia Some investigators go beyond the *DSM* typology in proposing other ways of typing schizophrenia. One alternative typology distinguishes between two basic types of schizophrenia, Type 1 and Type II (Crow, 1980a, 1980b, 1980c). Type I schizophrenia is characterized by the more flagrant or positive symptoms of schizophrenia we describe earlier, such as hallucinations, delusions, and looseness of associations, as well as by an abrupt onset, preserved intellectual ability, and a more favorable response to antipsychotic medication (Roth et al., 2004; Walker et al., 2004). Type II schizophrenia corresponds to a pattern consisting largely of the deficit or negative symptoms of schizophrenia, such as lack of emotional expression, low or absent levels of motivation, loss of ability to experience pleasure, social withdrawal, and poverty of speech, as well as by a more gradual onset, intellectual impairment, and poorer response to antipsychotic drugs (USDHHS, 1999a).

One intriguing possibility is that Type I and Type II schizophrenia represent different pathological processes. The Type I pattern may involve a defect in the inhibitory (blocking) mechanisms in the brain that normally control excessive or distorted behaviors. Underlying this malfunction may be a disturbance in the supply or regulation of dopamine in the brain, because antipsychotic drugs that regulate dopamine levels generally have a favorable impact on positive symptoms. The negative symptoms associated with Type II schizophrenia represent the more enduring or persistent characteristics of schizophrenia. The Type II pattern is associated with poorer functioning before the person developed schizophrenia (*premorbid functioning*) and with a more progressive decline in functioning leading to more enduring disability (Earnst & Kring, 1997). One possibility is that the negative symptoms associated with Type II schizophrenia are caused by structural damage in the brain.

The Type I–Type II distinction remains controversial, as evidence remains unclear how many schizophrenia patients can be classified as having predominantly positive or negative symptoms. Positive and negative symptoms may not define distinct subtypes of schizophrenia but rather separate dimensions that can coexist in the same individual.

Theoretical Perspectives

Schizophrenia has been approached from each of the major theoretical perspectives. Although the underlying causes of schizophrenia remain elusive, they are presumed to involve brain abnormalities in combination with psychological, social, and environmental influences (USDHHS, 1999a).

Psychodynamic Perspectives Within the psychodynamic perspective, schizophrenia represents the overwhelming of the ego by primitive sexual or aggressive drives or impulses arising from the id. These impulses threaten the ego and give rise to intense intrapsychic conflict. Under such a threat, the person regresses to an early period in the oral stage, referred to as *primary narcissism*. In this period, the infant has not yet learned that the world is distinct from itself. Because the ego mediates the relationship between the self and the outer world, this breakdown in ego functioning accounts for the detachment from

A person diagnosed with catatonic schizophrenia. People with catatonic schizophrenia remain in unusual, difficult positions that can last for hours, even though their limbs become stiff or swollen. They seem oblivious to their environment during these episodes, even to people who are talking about them. Some sufferers later say that they heard what was being said. Periods of stupor commonly alternate with periods of agitation.

reality that is typical of schizophrenia. Input from the id causes fantasies to become mistaken for reality, giving rise to hallucinations and delusions. Primitive impulses may also carry more weight than social norms and be expressed in bizarre, socially inappropriate behavior.

Freud's followers, such as Harry Stack Sullivan, placed more emphasis on interpersonal than intrapsychic factors. Sullivan (1962), for example, who devoted much of his life's work to schizophrenia, emphasized that impaired mother–child relationships can set the stage for gradual withdrawal from other people. In early childhood, anxious and hostile interactions between the child and parent lead the child to take refuge in a private fantasy world. A vicious cycle ensues: The more the child withdraws, the less opportunity there is to develop a sense of trust in others and the social skills necessary to establish intimacy. Then the weak bonds between the child and others prompt social anxiety and further withdrawal. This cycle continues until young adulthood. Then, faced with increasing demands at school or work and in intimate relationships, the person becomes overwhelmed with anxiety and withdraws completely into a world of fantasy.

Critics of Freud's views point out that schizophrenic behavior and infantile behavior are different, so schizophrenia cannot be explained by regression. Critics of Freud and modern psychodynamic theorists note that psychodynamic explanations are post hoc, or retrospective. Early child–adult relationships are recalled from the vantage point of adulthood rather than observed longitudinally. Psychoanalysts have not been able to demonstrate that hypothesized early childhood experiences or family patterns lead to schizophrenia.

Learning Perspectives Although learning theory does not offer a complete explanation of schizophrenia, the development of some forms of schizophrenic behavior can be understood in terms of the principles of conditioning and observational learning. From this perspective, people with schizophrenia learn to exhibit certain bizarre behaviors when these are more likely to be reinforced than normal behaviors.

Consider a classic case study of operant conditioning. Haughton and Ayllon (1965) conditioned a 54-year-old woman with chronic schizophrenia to cling to a broom. A staff member first gave her the broom to hold, and when she did, another staff member gave her a cigarette (a reinforcement). This pattern was repeated several times. Soon the woman could not be parted from the broom. But the fact that reinforcement can influence people to engage in peculiar behavior does not demonstrate that the bizarre behaviors characteristic of schizophrenia are shaped by reinforcement.

Social-cognitive theorists suggest that modeling of schizophrenic behavior can occur within the mental hospital, where patients may begin to model themselves after fellow patients who act strangely. Hospital staff may also inadvertently reinforce schizophrenic behavior by paying more attention to patients who exhibit bizarre behavior. This understanding is consistent with the observation that schoolchildren who disrupt the class garner more attention from their teachers than well-behaved children do.

Perhaps some types of of schizophrenic behavior can be explained by the principles of modeling and reinforcement. However, many people display schizophrenic behavior patterns without prior exposure to other people with schizophrenia. In fact, the onset of schizophrenic behavior patterns is more likely to lead to hospitalization than to result from hospitalization.

Biological Perspectives Although we still have much to learn about the biological underpinnings of schizophrenia, most investigators today recognize that biological factors play a determining role.

Genetic Factors A wealth of evidence supports the important role of genetics in the development of schizophrenia (Braff, Schork, &. Gottesman, 2007; Gottesman & Hanson, 2005; Gur et al., 2007; Hall et al., 2007; Ho et al., 2006; Reiss, 2005). For example, the closer the genetic relationship between schizophrenia patients and their family members, the greater the likelihood (or *concordance rate*) that the relatives will also

Paranoid schizophrenia. People with paranoid schizophrenia hold systematized delusions that commonly involve themes of persecution and grandeur. They usually do not show the degree of confusion, disorganization, or disturbed motor behavior seen in people with catatonic or disorganized schizophrenia. Unless they are discussing the areas in which they are delusional, their thought processes can appear to be relatively intact.

Withdrawing into oneself? Harry Stack Sullivan and some other psychodynamic theorists see individuals with schizophrenia as withdrawing into private fantasy worlds, largely because of severely disturbed relationships with their mothers.

TRUTH or FICTION

If you have two parents with schizophrenia, it's nearly certain that you will develop schizophrenia yourself.

☑ **FALSE.** Children of parents who both have schizophrenia have about a 45% chance of developing the disorder.

have schizophrenia (Gottesman, 2001). Overall, first-degree relatives of people with schizophrenia (parents, children, or siblings) have about a tenfold greater risk of developing schizophrenia than do members of the general population (APA, 2000; Kendler & Diehl, 1993).

Figure 12.1 shows the pooled results of European studies on family incidence of schizophrenia conducted from 1920 to 1987. However, the fact that families share common environments as well as common genes requires that we dig deeper to examine the genetic underpinnings of schizophrenia.

More direct evidence of a genetic factor to schizophrenia comes from twin studies showing concordance rates for the disorder among identical or monozygotic (MZ) twins of about 48%, or more than twice the rate found among fraternal or dizygotic (DZ) twins (about 17%) (Gottesman, 1991; Plomin et al., 1994). A twins study in Norway found an even greater spread: 48% concordance in MZ twins versus 3.6% in DZ twins (Onstad et al., 1991).

We should be cautious, however, not to overinterpret the results of twin studies. MZ twins not only share 100% genetic similarity, but they may also be treated more alike than DZ twins. Thus environmental factors may help explain the higher concordance rates found among MZ twins. To help sort out environmental from genetic factors, investigators have turned to adoption studies in which high-risk (HR) children (children of one or more biological parents with schizophrenia) were adopted away shortly after birth and reared apart from their biological parents.

Adoption studies provide the strongest evidence to date for a genetic contribution to schizophrenia. In perhaps the best-known example, researchers in Denmark examined official registers and found 39 HR adoptees who had been reared apart from their biological mothers who had schizophrenia (Rosenthal et al., 1968, 1975). Three of the 39 HR adoptees (8%) were diagnosed with schizophrenia, as compared to 0% of a reference group of 47 adoptees whose biological parents had no psychiatric history.

Other investigators have approached the question of heredity from the opposite direction. U.S. researcher Seymour Kety and Danish colleagues (Kety et al., 1975, 1978) used official records to find 33 index cases of children in Copenhagen, Denmark, who had been adopted early in life and were later diagnosed with schizophrenia. They compared the rates of diagnosed schizophrenia in the biological and adoptive relatives of the index cases with those of the relatives of a matched reference group of adoptees with no psychiatric history. The results strongly supported the genetic explanation. The incidence of diagnosed schizophrenia was greater among biological relatives of adoptees who had schizophrenia than among biological relatives of control adoptees. Adoptive relatives of both the index cases and control cases showed similar, *low* rates of schizophrenia. Similar results were found in later research that extended the scope of the investigation to the rest of Denmark (Kety et al., 1994). It thus appears that family linkages in schizophrenia follow shared genes, not shared environments (Kinney et al., 1997; Moldin, 1994).

In another approach to teasing out genetic from environmental influences, called the *cross-fostering study,* we compare the incidence of schizophrenia among children whose biological parents either had or didn't have schizophrenia and who were reared by adoptive parents who either had or didn't have schizophrenia. In a classic study conducted in Denmark, Wender and his colleagues (Wender et al., 1974) found the risk of schizophrenia related to the presence of schizophrenia in the children's biological parents, but not in their adoptive parents. High-risk children (children whose biological parents had schizophrenia) were almost twice as likely to develop schizophrenia as those of nonschizophrenic biological parents, regardless of whether they were reared by a parent with schizophrenia. It is also notable that adoptees whose biological

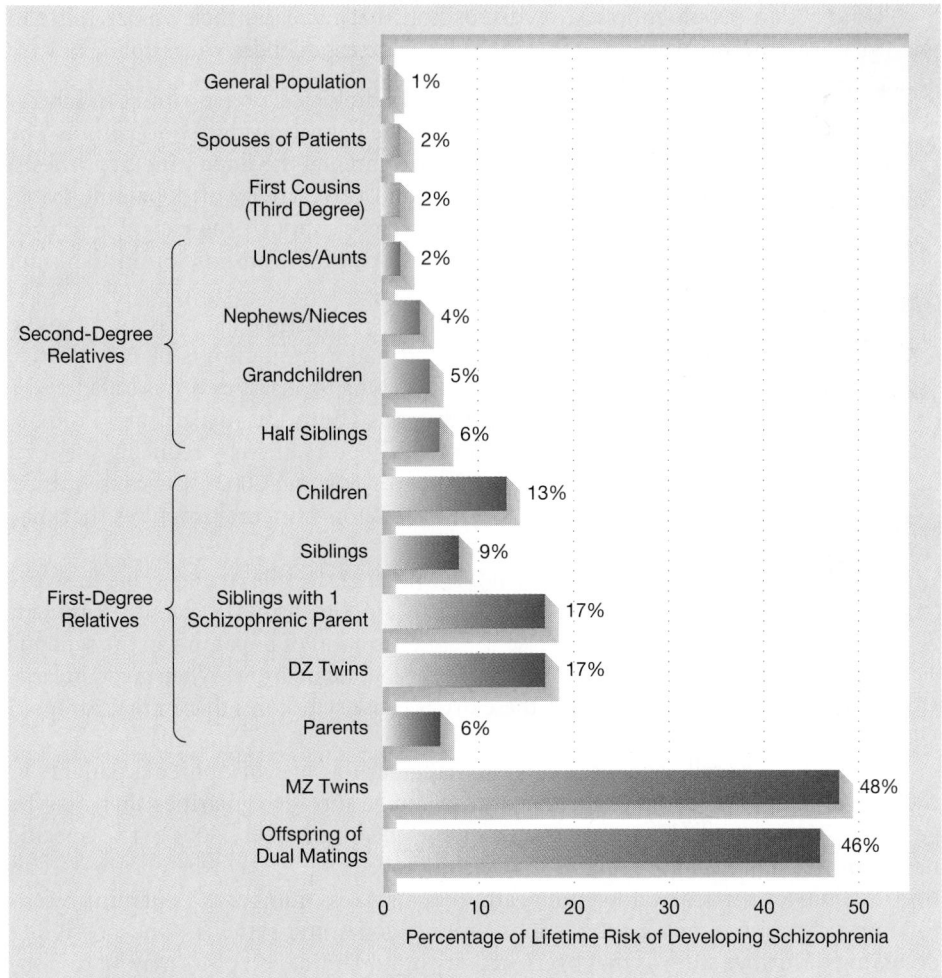

FIGURE 12.1 The familial risk of schizophrenia.
Generally speaking, the more closely one is related to people who have developed schizophrenia, the greater the risk of developing schizophrenia for oneself. Monozygotic (MZ) twins, whose genetic heritages are identical, are much more likely than dizygotic (DZ) twins, whose genes overlap by 50%, to be concordant for schizophrenia.

Source: Adapted from Gottesman et al. (1987).

parents did not suffer from schizophrenia were placed at no greater risk of developing schizophrenia by being reared by an adoptive parent with schizophrenia than by a non-schizophrenic parent. In sum, a genetic relationship with a person with schizophrenia seems to be the most prominent risk factor for developing the disorder.

Although we understand that genetics plays an important role in schizophrenia, we haven't yet discovered particular genes that are involved in the disorder. Scientists today believe that multiple genes are involved in creating a predisposition or susceptibility to schizophrenia (e.g., DeRosse et al., 2006; Fanous et al., 2005; Ho et al., 2006; Peirce et al., 2005). A number of research teams are actively trying to track down these genes (e.g., Gurling et al., 2006). Each of these genes may have but a small effect on its own, but probably influence each other in raising the overall risk of the disorder.

We need to recognize that genetics alone does not determine a person's risk of developing schizophrenia. Environmental influences also play an important role (Sullivan, Kendler, & Neale, 2003). People who carry a high genetic risk of schizophrenia don't necessarily develop the disorder. In fact, the rate of concordance among MZ twins, as noted earlier, is well below 100%, although identical twins carry identical genes. The prevailing view of schizophrenia, the diathesis–stress model (discussed later in the chapter) holds

The Genain quadruplets. Schizophrenia is more likely to affect individuals who have family members with the disorder. Here we see a photo of the Genain quadruplets, each of whom developed schizophrenia.

dopamine hypothesis The prediction that schizophrenia involves overactivity of dopamine receptors in the brain.

that people inherit a predisposition that increases their vulnerability to schizophrenia in the face of stressful life experiences.

Biochemical Factors Contemporary biological investigations of schizophrenia have focused on the role of the neurotransmitter dopamine. The leading biochemical model of schizophrenia, the **dopamine hypothesis,** posits that schizophrenia involves an overreactivity of dopamine transmission in the brain. Increasing evidence supports the view that schizophrenia involves an irregularity in dopamine transmission in the brain (McGowan et al., 2004).

The major source of evidence for the dopamine model is found in the effects of antipsychotic drugs called major tranquilizers or *neuroleptics.* The most widely used neuroleptics belong to a class of drugs called *phenothiazines,* which includes such drugs as Thorazine, Mellaril, and Prolixin. Neuroleptic drugs block dopamine receptors, thereby reducing the level of dopamine activity (Gründer, Carlsson, & Wong, 2002). As a consequence, neuroleptics inhibit excessive transmission of neural impulses that may give rise to schizophrenic behavior.

Another source of evidence supporting the role of dopamine in schizophrenia is based on the actions of amphetamines, a class of stimulant drugs. These drugs increase the concentration of dopamine in the synaptic cleft by blocking its reuptake by presynaptic neurons. When given in large doses to normal people, these drugs cause symptoms that mimic paranoid schizophrenia.

Overall, evidence points to irregularities in schizophrenia patients in the neural pathways in the brain that utilize dopamine—irregularities that may be genetically influenced (Hirvonen et al., 2006; McGowan et al., 2004). The specific nature of this abnormality remains under study. We can't yet say whether there is an overreactivity of particular dopamine pathways, an excess number of dopamine receptors, or yet more complex interactions among dopamine systems. One possibility deserving of further study is that overreactivity of dopamine receptors may be responsible for positive symptoms, whereas decreased dopamine reactivity may be involved in negative symptoms (Earnst & Kring, 1997). Other neurotransmitters, such as norepinephrine, serotonin, and GABA, also appear to be involved in schizophrenia (Walker et al., 2004).

Viral Infections Might schizophrenia be caused by a slow-acting virus that attacks the developing brain of a fetus or newborn child? Prenatal rubella (German measles), a viral infection, is a cause of later mental retardation. Could another virus give rise to schizophrenia? The answer is that we don't yet know, but intriguing evidence points to a possible link (Babulas et al., 2006). Results from one recent study showed a sevenfold greater risk of schizophrenia in individuals exposed to the influenza virus (the "flu" virus) during the first trimester of pregnancy (Brown et al., 2004). If this link is confirmed by other findings, it would suggest that viral agents may act on the developing brain in the early stages of prenatal development in ways to increase the risk of developing schizophrenia later in life. But even if a viral basis for schizophrenia were discovered, it would probably account for but a small fraction of cases.

Brain Abnormalities Using modern brain-imaging techniques, investigators are trying to track down the abnormalities in the brain that may result in schizophrenia. We have compelling evidence of both structural changes (loss of brain tissue) and functional disturbance (abnormalities of functioning) in the brains of schizophrenia patients (e.g., Bagary et al., 2003; Hong et al., 2007; Onitsuka et al., 2006; Vidal et al., 2006). However, we have yet to discover any one source of pathology in the brain that is specific to schizophrenia or present in all cases of schizophrenia (Walker et al., 2004).

The most prominent finding of structural changes is the loss of brain tissue (gray matter) of about 5% on the average in schizophrenia patients as compared to normal controls (Cowan & Kandel, 2001). In Figure 12.2 we see a visual representation of the loss of brain tissue in the brains of adolescents with early-onset (childhood) schizophrenia (Thompson et al., 2001). We have evidence of a loss of brain tissue in perhaps three of four adult schizophrenia patients as shown by the presence of enlarged brain ventricles (hollow spaces in the brain) (see Figure 12.3) (Coursey, Alford, & Safarjan, 1997). Enlarged ventricles are signs of loss of brain tissue (cell loss).

What is the underlying cause of the loss of brain tissue? Scientists can't yet say, but they suspect that the brains of schizophrenia patients may have been damaged or failed to develop normally as the result of early influences such as prenatal factors (e.g., viral infections, inadequate fetal nutrition, genetic defects) or birth traumas or complications (Sørensen et al., 2003; Wahlbeck et al., 2001; Walker et al., 2004). Bear in mind, however, that not all people with schizophrenia show evidence of structural damage to brain tissue. This finding leads researchers to suspect that there may be several forms of schizophrenia that have different causal processes.

One area of the brain showing prominent signs of both abnormal functioning and loss of brain tissue is the *prefrontal cortex* (Cannon et al., 2005; Winterer et al., 2006). The prefrontal cortex is the thinking and organizing center of the brain. It is the area of the frontal lobes of the cerebral cortex that lies in front of the motor cortex (the part of the brain that controls voluntary body movements).

Evidence of functional impairment comes from studies showing reduced neural activity in the prefrontal cortex of schizophrenia patients (Callicott et al., 2003; Ragland et al., 2004; Snitz et al., 2005) (see Figure 12.4). For example, schizophrenia patients show less activation in this part of the brain than do healthy controls during mental arithmetic tasks (Hugdahl et al., 2004). Functional impairment may result from underlying structural damage (loss of brain tissue) (Karp et al., 2001; Selemon et al., 2002).

The prefrontal cortex controls many cognitive and emotional functions, the kinds of functions that are often impaired in people with schizophrenia. The prefrontal cortex serves as a kind of mental clipboard for holding information needed to guide organized behavior. Prefrontal abnormalities may explain why people with schizophrenia have difficulty with working memory—the ability to temporarily hold information in mind and mull it over (Barch & Csernansky, 2007; Lee & Park, 2005; McClure et al., 2007). The prefrontal cortex is also responsible for other higher-order (or "executive")

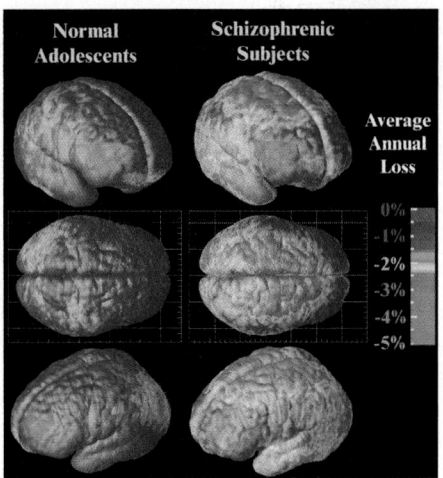

FIGURE 12.2 Loss of brain tissue in adolescents with early-onset schizophrenia. The brains of adolescents with early-onset schizophrenia (right image) show a substantial loss of gray matter. Some shrinkage of gray matter occurs normally during adolescence (left image), but the loss is more pronounced in adolescents with schizophrenia.

Source: Thompson et al. (2001).

FIGURE 12.3 Structural changes in the brain of a person with schizophrenia as compared with that of a normal subject.
The magnetic resonance imaging (MRI) of the brain of a person with schizophrenia (left) shows a relatively shrunken hippocampus (yellow) and relatively enlarged, fluid-filled ventricles (grey) when compared to the structures of the normal subject (right). The MRI was conducted by schizophrenia researcher Nancy C. Andreasen. Photos by Nancy C. Andreasen, M.D./University of Iowa Hospitals & Clinics.

Source: Gershon, E. S., & Rieder, R. O. (1992). Major disorders of mind and brain. *Scientific American, 267*(No. 3), p. 128.

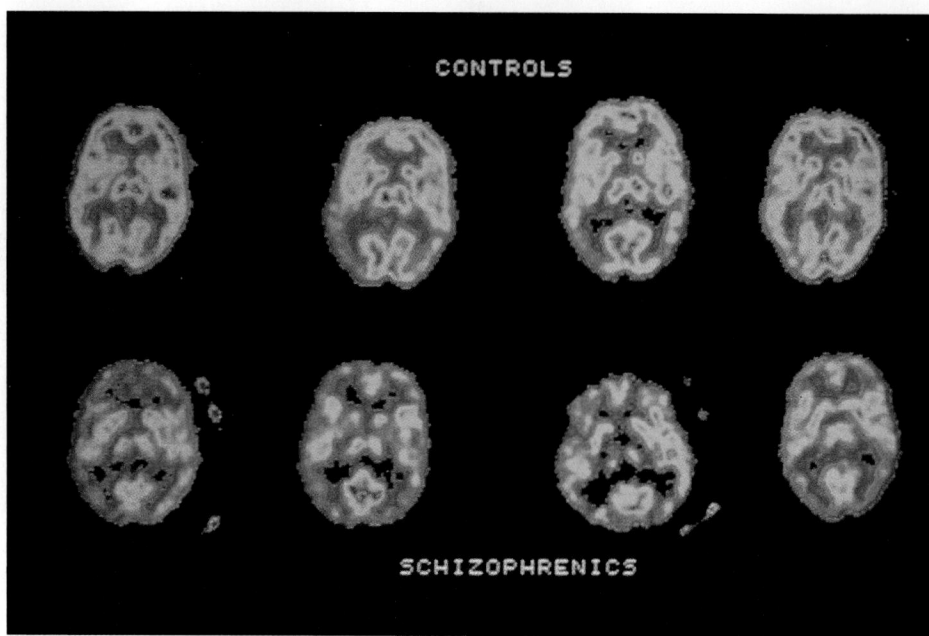

FIGURE 12.4 PET scans of people with schizophrenia versus normals.
Positron emission tomography (PET) scan evidence of the metabolic processes of the brain shows relatively less metabolic activity (indicated by less yellow and red) in the frontal lobes of the brains of people with schizophrenia. PET scans of the brains of four normal people are shown in the top row, and PET scans of the brains of four people with schizophrenia are shown below.

functions, such as as regulating attention, organizing thoughts and behavior, prioritizing information, and formulating goals—the very types of deficits often found in people with schizophrenia (Barch, 2003; Goldberg et al., 2003). These are intriguing findings that may provide clues as to the biological bases of schizophrenia as well as lead to new treatment approaches. For example, cognitive training efforts have recently been found to help schizophrenia patients improve their working memory (Bell et al., 2003).

We have yet other evidence of structural differences in the brains of schizophrenia patients in the limbic system and other subcortical structures in the brain involved in regulating emotions, attention, and memory formation (e.g., Csernansky et al., 2004; Gaser et al., 2004). Disturbances in brain physiology in these subcortical regions, perhaps involving neurotransmitter imbalances or faulty connections (wiring) between neurons, may contribute to disturbances in thinking, attention, and emotions associated with schizophrenia (Hazlett et al., 2004). Investigators also suspect that schizophrenia involves disturbances in the working connections between these subcortical brain structures and the prefrontal cortex needed to perform complex mental functions (Ragland et al., 2004).

Though evidence of the biological underpinnings of schizophrenia continues to mount, a long-standing debate is whether disordered behavior of the kind we see in schizophrenia patients is necessarily a sign of a biological disease process. We review this controversy in the *Controversies in Abnormal Psychology* feature, "Is Mental Illness a Myth?" on page 417.

Family Theories What role do disturbed family relationships play in the development and course of schizophrenia? An early, but since discredited theory, focused on the role of the *schizophrenogenic mother* (Fromm-Reichmann, 1948, 1950). In what some feminists view as historic psychiatric sexism, the schizophrenogenic mother was described as cold, aloof, overprotective, and domineering. She was characterized as stripping her children of self-esteem, stifling their independence, and forcing them into dependency on her. Children reared by such mothers were believed to be at special risk for developing schizophrenia if their fathers were passive and failed to counteract the mother's pathogenic influences. Thankfully, the concept of the "schizophrenogenic mother" was discredited as investigators showed that mothers of people who develop schizophrenia do not fit this stereotypical pattern (e.g., Hirsch & Leff, 1975).

T R U T H or F I C T I O N

Although schizophrenia is widely believed to be a brain disease, evidence of abnormalities in the brains of schizophrenia patients remains lacking.

☑ **FALSE.** Mounting evidence points to both structural and functional abnormalities in the brains of many schizophrenia patients.

CONTROVERSIES IN ABNORMAL PSYCHOLOGY

Is Mental Illness a Myth?

In 1961 the psychiatrist Thomas Szasz shocked the psychiatric establishment by making a bold claim that mental illness does not exist. In his controversial book, *The Myth of Mental Illness,* Szasz argued that mental illness is a myth, a convenient fiction society uses to stigmatize and subjugate people whose behavior it finds to be deviant, odd, or bizarre. To Szasz, "mental illnesses" are really "problems in living," not diseases in the same sense that influenza, hypertension, and cancer are diseases. Szasz does not dispute that the behavior of people diagnosed with schizophrenia or other mental disorders is peculiar or disturbed. Nor does he deny that these individuals suffer emotional problems or have difficulties adjusting to society. But he challenges the conventional view that strange or eccentric behavior is a product of an underlying disease. Szasz argues that treating problems as "diseases" empowers psychiatrists to put socially deviant people away in medical facilities. To Szasz, involuntary hospitalization is a form of tyranny disguised as therapy. It deprives people of human dignity and strips them of the most essential human right—liberty.

Are the myriad problems of people with schizophrenia—the deluded thoughts and hallucinations and incoherent speech—merely "problems in living," or are they symptoms of an underlying disease process? The belief that mental illness is a myth or a social construction is difficult to reconcile with a large body of evidence showing structural and functional differences in the brains of schizophrenia patients and of genetic factors that increase the risk of developing the disorder.

We've learned a great deal about the biological underpinnings of mental or psychological disorders since Szasz claimed that mental illness doesn't exist, although we still have much to learn. Our knowledge of the causes of many diseases, including cancer and Alzheimer's disease, is also incomplete, but a lack of knowledge does not make them any less of a disease. Many professionals believe that radical theorists like Szasz go too far in arguing that mental illness is merely a fabrication invented by society to stigmatize social deviants.

Evidence supports a prominent role for biological factors in many abnormal behavior patterns, including schizophrenia, mood disorders, and autism. But how far should we extend the disease model? Is antisocial personality disorder an illness? Or attention-deficit hyperactivity disorder? Or specific phobias, such as fear of flying? What are the implications of treating abnormal behavioral patterns as diseases versus viewing them as problems in living?

The *DSM* itself does not take a position on which mental disorders, if any, are biologically based. It recognizes that causes of most mental disorders remain uncertain: Some disorders may have purely biological causes. Some may have psychological causes. Still others, probably most, involve an interaction of biological, psychological, and social/environmental causes.

All in all, the views of Szasz and other critics of the mental health establishment have helped bring about much needed improvements in the protection of the rights of mental patients in psychiatric institutions. They have also directed our attention to the social and political implications of our responses to deviant behavior. Perhaps most importantly, they have challenged us to examine our assumptions when we label and treat undesirable behaviors as signs of illness rather than as problems of adjustment.

Thomas Szasz. Psychiatrist Thomas Szasz has waged a long-standing battle with institutional psychiatry. Arguing that mental illness is a myth, Szasz believes that mental health problems are problems in living, not medical diseases.

Critical Thinking

- What would it mean to say that schizophrenia is a problem of living rather than a disease? What would be the implications for treatment? For the way society responds to people who behave in unusual ways?
- Based on knowledge that has accumulated since Szasz wrote his book, which mental illnesses should be classified as problems of living? Which as diseases?

Today, investigators interested in family influences have turned to consider the effects of deviant patterns of communication within the family as well as intrusive, negative comments directed toward the schizophrenic family member.

Communication Deviance Communication deviance (CD) is a pattern of unclear, vague, disruptive, or fragmented communication that is often found among parents and family members of schizophrenia patients. CD is speech that is hard to follow and from which it is difficult to extract any shared meaning (Wahlberg et al., 2001). High CD parents often have difficulty focusing on what their children are saying. They verbally attack their children rather than offer constructive criticism. They may also interrupt the child with intrusive, negative comments. They are prone to telling the child what she or he "really" thinks rather than allowing the child to formulate her or his own thoughts and feelings. We have evidence showing that parents of schizophrenia patients tend to have higher levels of communication deviance than do parents in families without any schizophrenic member (Docherty et al., 2004).

We should note that the causal pathway between CD and schizophrenia may work in both directions. On the one hand, CD may increase the risk of schizophrenia in genetically vulnerable individuals. But CD may be a parental reaction to the behavior of disturbed children. Parents may learn to use odd language as a way of coping with children who continually interrupt and confront them.

Expressed Emotion Another form of disturbed family communication, *expressed emotion* (EE), is a pattern of responding to the schizophrenic family member in hostile, critical, and unsupportive ways (Barrowclough & Hooley, 2003; Weisman et al., 2006). Schizophrenia patients from high EE families stand a higher risk of relapsing than those with low EE (more supportive) families (Kopelowicz et al., 2006; Van Humbeeck et al., 2002). High EE relatives typically show less empathy, tolerance, and flexibility than low EE relatives (Hooley & Hiller, 2000). They also tend to believe that schizophrenia patients can exercise greater control over their behavior than do low EE relatives of the same patients (Weisman et al., 2000). Expressed emotion in relatives is also associated with a greater risk of relapse from other disorders, such as major depression and eating disorders (Van Humbeeck et al., 2002). It is also associated with a higher level of communication deviance in family members (Kymalainen et al., 2006).

Low EE families may actually protect, or buffer, the family member with schizophrenia from the adverse impact of outside stressors and help prevent recurrent episodes (see Figure 12.5). Yet family interactions are a two-way street. Family members and patients influence each other and are influenced in turn. Disruptive behaviors by the schizophrenic family member frustrate other members of the family, prompting them to respond to the person in a less-supportive and more critical and hostile way. This in turn can exacerbate the schizophrenia patient's disruptive behavior.

We need to take a close look at cultural differences in both the frequency of EE in family members of schizophrenia patients and the effects these behaviors have on patients. Investigators find high EE families to be more common in industrialized countries, such as the United States and Canada, than in developing countries, such as India (Barrowclough & Hooley, 2003).

Cross-cultural evidence shows that Mexican American, Anglo American, and Chinese families with high levels of expressed emotion are more likely than low EE families to view the psychotic behavior of a schizophrenic family member as within the person's control (Weisman et al., 1998; Yang et al., 2004). The anger and criticism

FIGURE 12.5 Relapse rates of people with schizophrenia in high and low EE families. People with schizophrenia whose families are high in expressed emotion (EE) are at greater risk of relapse than those whose families are low in EE. Whereas low-EE families may help protect the family member with schizophrenia from environmental stressors, high-EE families may impose additional stress.

Source: Adapted from King & Dixon, 1999, based upon data provided in two seminal British studies.

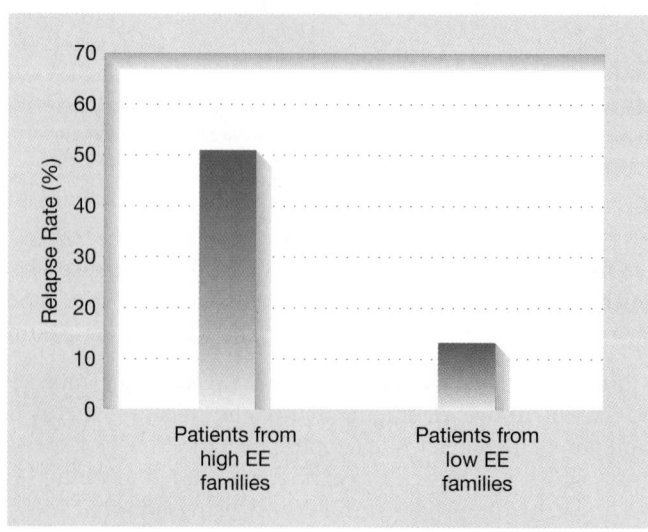

of high EE family members may stem from the perception that patients can and should exert greater control over their aberrant behavior.

Results of a recent study linked high levels of EE in family members to more negative outcomes in schizophrenia patients among Anglo American families, but no such link was found for Mexican American families (Lopez et al., 2004). Rather, for Mexican American families, the degree of family warmth, not EE per se, was related to a more positive course of schizophrenia in the affected family members, whereas for Anglo American patients, family warmth did not relate to such outcomes. In another study, investigators reported that among African American patients, high levels of EE were actually associated with better outcomes (Rosenfarb, Bellack, & Aziz, 2006). What might be the reason for this apparent contradiction? The study investigators suggested that for African Americans, intrusive critical comments during family interactions may be perceived as signs of caring and concern rather than rejection. Other investigators concur, finding relationships between how much relatives criticize patients and patients' perceptions of their relatives' criticism only among white and Latino patients, but not among African American patients (Weisman et al., 2006). These studies underscore the important of looking at abnormal behavior patterns through a cultural lens.

Families of people with schizophrenia typically have little if any preparation for coping with the stress of caring for them. Rather than focusing so much attention on the negative influence of high EE family members, perhaps we should seek to help family members learn more constructive ways of relating to one another. Evidence shows that families can be helped to reduce their level of expressed emotion (Dixon, Adams, & Lucksted, 2000).

Family Factors in Schizophrenia: Causes or Sources of Stress? No evidence supports the belief that family factors, such as negative family interactions, lead to schizophrenia in children who do not have a genetic vulnerability. Rather, a genetic vulnerability to schizophrenia renders individuals more susceptible to troubled family and social relationships (Reiss, 2005; Tienari et al., 2004).

Within the diathesis–stress model, disturbed patterns of family interaction and communication represent sources of life stress that increase the risks of developing schizophrenia among people with a genetic predisposition for the disorder. These increased risks might be minimized or even eliminated if families learn to handle stress and to become less critical and more supportive of the schizophrenia family member. Family intervention programs have been developed to help family members develop more cooperative, less-confrontational ways of relating to their family members with schizophrenia.

How families conceptualize mental disorders also has a bearing on how they relate to relatives who suffer from them. For example, the term *schizophrenia* carries a stigma in our society and comes with the expectation that the disorder is enduring (Jenkins & Karno, 1992). In contrast, to many Mexican Americans, a person with schizophrenia is perceived as suffering from *nervios* ("nerves"), a cultural label attached to a wide range of troubled behaviors, including anxiety, schizophrenia, and depression, and one that carries less stigma and more positive expectations than the label of schizophrenia (Jenkins & Karno, 1992). The label *nervios* may have the effect of destigmatizing family members with schizophrenia.

Family members may respond differently to relatives who have schizophrenia if they ascribe aspects of their behavior to a temporary or curable condition, which they believe can be altered by willpower, than if they believe the behavior is caused by a permanent brain abnormality. The degree to which relatives perceive family members with schizophrenia as having control over their disorders may be a critical factor in how they respond to them. Families may cope better with a family member with schizophrenia if they take a balanced view, believing on the one hand that people with schizophrenia can maintain some control over their behavior, while allowing that some of their odd or disruptive behavior is a product of their underlying disorder (Weisman et al., 1993). It remains to be seen whether these different ways in which family members conceptualize schizophrenia are connected with differences in the rates of recurrence of the disorder among affected family members.

TYING IT TOGETHER

THE DIATHESIS–STRESS MODEL

In 1962, psychologist Paul Meehl proposed an integrative model for schizophrenia that led to the development of the diathesis–stress model. Meehl suggested that certain people possess a genetic predisposition to schizophrenia that is expressed behaviorally only if they are reared in stressful environments (Meehl, 1962, 1972).

Later, Zubin and Spring (1977) formulated the diathesis–stress model, which views schizophrenia in terms of the interaction or combination of a *diathesis,* in the form of a genetic predisposition to develop the disorder, with environmental stress that exceeds the individual's stress threshold or coping resources. Environmental stressors may include psychological factors, such as family conflict, child abuse, emotional deprivation, or loss of supportive figures, as well as physical environmental influences, such as early brain trauma or injury. On the other hand, if environmental stress remains below the person's stress threshold, schizophrenia may never develop, even in persons at genetic risk. But what is the biological basis for the diathesis?

Hunting for Endophenotypes

Endophenotypes? Although still in its infancy, the scientific search for **endophenotypes** in mental disorders has begun (Bedwell, Kamath, & Baksh, 2006; Dingfelder, 2006; Hirvonen et al., 2006). An endophenotype is a measurable process or mechanism, unseen by the unaided human eye, which explains how genetic instructions encoded in an organism's DNA influence an observable characteristic of the organism, or *phenotype* (Gottesman & Gould, 2003). Phenotypes are outward expressions of traits, such as eye color or observed behavior. Think of endophenotypes as the mechanisms or critical links by which genes become expressed in behavioral or physical traits or disorders.

Investigators are investigating a number of possible endophenotypes in schizophrenia, including disturbances in brain circuitry, deficits in working memory and cognitive abilities, and abnormalities of neurotransmitter functioning (Braff, Schork, &. Gottesman, 2007; Gur et al., 2007; Hall et al., 2007). Consider, for example, disturbances in brain circuitry as a possible endophenotype for schizophrenia. Brain circuits between the prefrontal cortex and lower brain regions, including the limbic system, are involved in organizing our thoughts, perceptions, emotions, and attentional processes. Defects in this circuitry may lead to a breakdown in these processes, resulting in positive features of schizophrenia such as hallucinations, delusions, and thought disorder. To better understand how schizophrenia develops, we need to dig under the surface to see how genes affect underlying processes, and how these processes in turn contribute to the development of the disorder.

Figure 12.6 shows a model representing links between candidate genes and potential endophenotypes, leading to increased vulnerability to schizophrenia. The *Concept Map for Abnormal Psychology*

endophenotypes Measurable processes or mechanisms not apparent to the naked eye, which are the means by which an organism's genetic code comes to affect its observable characteristics or phenotypes.

FIGURE 12.6 From genes to vulnerabilty.

Source: Adapted from Gottesman & Gould, 2003.

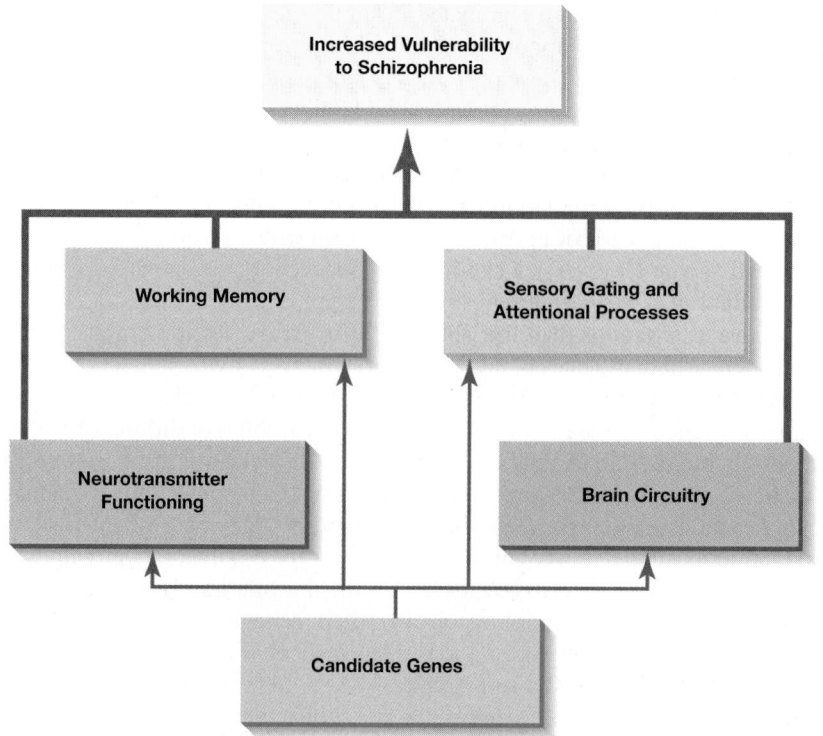

at the end of the chapter depicts the diathesis–stress model of schizophrenia, whereby increased vulnerability—a diathesis—interacts with life stress in leading to the disorder.

While the search for these hidden mechanisms in schizophrenia is well underway, we should understand that scientists haven't found any one brain abnormality that is present in every schizophrenia patient. Perhaps it shouldn't surprise us that a "one-size-fits-all" model doesn't apply. Schizophrenia is a complex disorder characterized by different subtypes and symptom complexes. Different causal processes in the brain may explain different forms of schizophrenia. What we now call *schizophrenia* may actually turn out to be more than one disorder.

Research Evidence Supporting the Diathesis–Stress Model Several lines of evidence support the diathesis-stress model. One is the fact that schizophrenia tends to develop in late adolescence or early adulthood, around the time that young people typically face the increased stress associated with establishing independence and finding a role in life. Other evidence shows that psychosocial stress, such as expressed emotion (harping criticisms from family members), worsens symptoms in people with schizophrenia and increases risks of relapse. However, the question of whether stress directly triggers the initial onset of schizophrenia in genetically vulnerable individuals still remains open to debate (Walker & Diforio, 1997). Other stressors, such as economic hardship and living in distressed neighborhoods may also interact with genetic vulnerability in the casual matrix leading to schizophrenia.

More direct support for the diathesis–stress model comes from longitudinal studies of high-risk (HR) children who are at increased genetic risk of developing the disorder by virtue of having one or both parents with schizophrenia. Longitudinal studies of HR children support the central tenet of the diathesis–stress model that heredity interacts with environmental influences in determining vulnerability to schizophrenia. Longitudinal studies track individuals over extended periods of time. Ideally they begin before the emergence of the disorder or behavior pattern in question and follow its course. In this way, investigators may identify early characteristics that predict the later development of a disorder. These studies require a commitment of many years and substantial cost. Because schizophrenia occurs in only about 1% of the general adult population, researchers have focused on HR children. Children with one parent with schizophrenia have about a 10% to 25% chance of developing schizophrenia, and those with two parents have about a 45% risk (Erlenmeyer-Kimling et al., 1997; Gottesman, 1991).

The best-known longitudinal study of HR children was undertaken by Sarnoff Mednick and his colleagues in Denmark. In 1962, the Mednick group identified 207 HR children (children whose mothers had schizophrenia) and 104 reference subjects who were matched for such factors as gender, social class, age, and education but whose mothers did not have schizophrenia (Mednick, Parnas, & Schulsinger, 1987). The children from both groups ranged in age from 10 to 20 years, with a mean of 15 years. None showed signs of disturbance when first interviewed.

Five years later, at an average age of 20, the children were reexamined. By then 20 of the HR children were found to have demonstrated abnormal behavior, although not necessarily a schizophrenic episode (Mednick & Schulsinger, 1968). The children who showed abnormal behavior, referred to as the HR "sick" group, were then compared with a matched group of 20 HR children from the original sample who remained well functioning (an HR "well" group) and a matched group of 20 low-risk (LR) subjects. It turned out that the mothers of the HR "well" offspring had experienced easier pregnancies and deliveries than those of the HR "sick" group or the LR group. Seventy percent of the mothers of the HR "sick" children had serious complications during pregnancy or delivery. Perhaps, consistent with the diathesis--stress model, stressful factors such as complications during pregnancy, childbirth, or shortly after birth may cause brain damage that, in combination with a genetic vulnerability, leads to severe mental disorders in later life.

Finnish researchers also find links between fetal and postnatal abnormalities and the development of schizophrenia in adulthood (Jones et al., 1998). The low rate of complications during pregnancy and birth in the HR "well" group in the Danish study suggests that normal pregnancies and births may actually help protect HR children from developing abnormal behavior patterns (Mednick et al., 1987).

Protective factors in high-risk children. A supportive and nurturing environment may reduce the likelihood of developing schizophrenia among high-risk children.

Certain environmental factors, such as good parenting, may help prevent the disorder in people at increased genetic risk. In support of the role of early environmental influences, Mednick and his colleagues found that HR children who later developed schizophrenia had poorer relationships with their parents than did HR children who did not (Mednick et al., 1987). The presence of childhood behavior problems may also be a marker for the later development of schizophrenia-related disorders in HR children (Amminger et al., 1999).

Treatment Approaches

There is no cure for schizophrenia. Treatment is generally multifaceted, incorporating pharmacological, psychological, and rehabilitative approaches. Most people treated for schizophrenia in organized mental health settings receive some form of antipsychotic medication, which is intended to control symptoms such as hallucinations and delusions and decrease the risk of recurrent episodes.

Biological Approaches The advent in the 1950s of antipsychotic drugs—also referred to as major tranquilizers or neuroleptics—revolutionized the treatment of schizophrenia and provided the impetus for large-scale releases of mental patients to the community (deinstitutionalization). Antipsychotic medication helped control the more flagrant behavior patterns of schizophrenia and reduced the need for long-term hospitalization when taken on a maintenance or continuing basis after an acute episode (Kane, 1996). Yet for many patients with chronic schizophrenia, entering a hospital is like going through a revolving door: they are repeatedly admitted and discharged. Many are simply discharged to the streets once they are stabilized on medication and receive little if any follow-up care. This often leads to a pattern of chronic homelessness punctuated by brief stays in the hospital.

Commonly used antipsychotic drugs include the phenothiazines *chlorpromazine* (Thorazine), *thioridazine* (Mellaril), *trifluoperazine* (Stelazine), and *fluphenazine* (Prolixin). *Haloperidol* (Haldol), which is chemically distinct from the phenothiazines, produces similar effects.

Although we can't say with certainty how these drugs work, it appears they derive their therapeutic effect from blocking dopamine receptors in the brain. This reduces dopamine activity, which seems to quell symptoms such as hallucinations and delusions. The effectiveness of antipsychotic drugs has been repeatedly demonstrated in double-blind, placebo-controlled studies (Kane, 1996). Yet, a substantial minority of people with schizophrenia receives little benefit from traditional neuroleptics, and no clear-cut factors exist to help clinicians determine who will best respond (Kane & Marder, 1993).

The major risk of long-term treatment with neuroleptic drugs is a potentially disabling side effect called **tardive dyskinesia (TD)**. TD can take different forms, the most common of which is frequent eye blinking. Common signs of the disorder include involuntary chewing and eye movements, lip smacking and puckering, facial grimacing, and involuntary movements of the limbs and trunk. In some cases, the movement disorder is so severe that patients have difficulty breathing, talking, or eating. In many cases the disorder persists even when the neuroleptic medication is withdrawn.

TD is most common among older people and among women. Although TD tends to improve gradually or stabilize over a period of years, many people with TD remain persistently and severely disabled. We presently lack an effective and safe treatment for this very troubling side effect, although some promising treatments are being tested (e.g. Richardson et al., 2003).

The risk of this potentially disabling side effect requires physicians to weigh carefully the risks and benefits of long-term drug treatment. Investigators have altered drug regimens in the attempt to reduce the risk of TD, such as by reducing dosages, switching medications, or stopping medication altogether in stable outpatients and starting it again when early symptoms reappear (Kane, 2006).

A second generation of antipsychotic drugs, referred to as *atypical antipsychotic drugs* (*clozapine, risperidone,* and *olanzapine* are examples) has largely replaced the earlier generation of antipsychotics (Heres et al., 2006). The atypical antipsychotics are at least as effective as the first generation antipsychotics but have the advantage of carrying fewer neurological side effects (Kane, 2006; Lieberman, 2006; Rosenheck et al., 2006). One of these drugs, *clozapine*, has also been shown to be superior to first generation drugs in treating patients who had failed to respond to other drugs (Lewis et al., 2006; Schooler et al., 2005). However, we can't say with certainty whether these second generation drugs reduce the risk of tardive dyskinesia relative to first generation drugs (Rosenheck, 2006). It also remains to be seen whether the atypical drugs improve negative symptoms better than conventional antipsychotics (Artaloytia et al., 2006).

TRUTH or FICTION

We now have drugs that not only treat schizophrenia but also can cure it in many cases.

☑ **FALSE.** Antipsychotic drugs help control the symptoms of schizophrenia but cannot cure the disorder.

tardive dyskinesia (TD) A disorder characterized by involuntary movements of the face, mouth, neck, trunk, or extremities and caused by long-term use of antipsychotic medication.

For Lori Schiller, the woman who experienced her first psychotic break during summer camp, the voices became softer when she was treated with *clozapine*.

"I" The Voices Grow Softer

It was as if it [my brain] were draining out from the inside. My head had been filled with sticky stuff, like melted rubber or motor oil. Now all that sticky stuff was dripping out, leaving only my brain behind. Slowly I was beginning to think more clearly.

And the Voices? The Voices were growing softer. Were the Voices growing softer? They were growing softer! They began moving around, from outside my skull, to inside, to outside again. But their decibel level was definitely falling.

It was happening. I was being set free. I had prayed to find some peace, and my prayers were finally being answered. . . . I want to live. I want to live.

—*From Schiller & Bennett, 1994*

Over time the voices receded into the background and then disappeared. Lori needed to learn to live without the voices and to build a life for herself. She began venturing beyond the confines of the hospital. She entered a halfway house and began to move toward a more independent life. Lori spent 3½ years at a halfway house and is now living independently.

Antipsychotic drugs help control the more flagrant or bizarre features of schizophrenia but are not a cure. People with chronic schizophrenia typically receive maintenance doses of antipsychotic drugs once their acute symptoms abate. However, many patients relapse even if they keep taking medication. The risk of relapse is even greater for those patients who stop taking medication. Still, not all people with schizophrenia require antipsychotic medication to live independently. Unfortunately, no one can yet predict which patients can manage effectively without continued medication.

We need to note that atypical antipsychotics carry risks of troubling side effects and medical complications, including substantial weight gain and potentially serious metabolic problems that can double or even triple the likelihood of death due to cardiovascular disease (Kane, 2006; Lamberti et al., 2006; McGlashan et al., 2006; Newcomer, 2005; Remington, 2006). Partly as the result of side effects, the majority of patients in recent studies discontinued using these drugs within the first 18 months of treatment (Bruce & Alahi, 2006). One of the leading atypicals, *clozapine,* is also associated with risk of a potentially lethal disorder in which the body produces inadequate supplies of white blood cells. Because of this risk, patients receiving the drug must receive frequent blood monitoring. In sum, physicians today face a difficult choice, having to balance the benefits of treatment with the attendant risks (Friedman, 2005).

Whatever the benefits of antipsychotic medication may be, these drugs are insufficient to meet the multifaceted needs of people with schizophrenia. For example, a recent drug trial failed to find any substantial benefit from the antipsychotic drug *clozapine* in improving either social skills or problem-solving ability of schizophrenia patients (Bellack et al., 2004). Drug therapy needs to be supplemented with psychological treatment, rehabilitation, and social services to help schizophrenia patients adjust to demands of community living (Briand et al., 2006; Swartz et al., 2007). A wide array of treatment components are needed within a comprehensive model of care, including the use of antipsychotic medication, medical care, psychological treatment, family therapy, social skills training, crisis intervention, rehabilitation services, and housing and other social services. Treatment programs must also ensure a continuity of care between the hospital and the community.

Sociocultural Factors in Treatment Investigators find that response to psychiatric medications and dosage levels varies with patient ethnicity (USDHHS, 1999a). Asians and Hispanics, for example, may require lower doses of neuroleptics than do

European Americans. Asians also tend to experience more side effects from the same dosage. But racial disparities also exist in how schizophrenia patients are treated. For example, African American patients are less likely to receive the newer generation of atypical antipsychotics than are European American patients (Kuno & Rothbard, 2002).

Ethnicity may also play a role in the family's involvement in treatment. In a study of 26 Asian Americans and 26 non-Hispanic White Americans with schizophrenia, family members of the Asian American patients were more frequently involved in the treatment program (Lin et al., 1991). For example, family members were more likely to accompany the Asian American patients to their medication evaluation sessions. The authors believe that the greater family involvement among Asian Americans represents the relatively stronger sense of family responsibility in Asian cultures. Non-Hispanic White Americans are more likely to emphasize individualism and self-responsibility.

Maintaining connections between the person with schizophrenia and the family and larger community is part of the cultural tradition in many Asian cultures, as well as in other parts of the world, such as Africa. The seriously mentally ill of China, for instance, retain strong supportive links to their families and workplaces, which helps increase their chances of being reintegrated into community life (Liberman, 1994). In traditional healing centers for the treatment of schizophrenia in Africa, the strong support that patients receive from the family and community members, together with a community centered lifestyle, are important elements of successful care (Peltzer & Machleidt, 1992).

Psychodynamic Therapy Freud did not believe that traditional psychoanalysis was well suited to the treatment of schizophrenia. The withdrawal into a fantasy world that typifies schizophrenia prevents the individual with schizophrenia from forming a meaningful relationship with the psychoanalyst. The techniques of classical psychoanalysis, Freud wrote, must "be replaced by others; and we do not know yet whether we shall succeed in finding a substitute" (as cited in Arieti, 1974, p. 532).

Other psychoanalysts, such as Harry Stack Sullivan and Frieda Fromm-Reichmann, adapted psychoanalytic techniques specifically for the treatment of schizophrenia. However, research has failed to demonstrate the effectiveness of psychoanalytic or psychodynamic therapy for schizophrenia. However, promising results are reported for a form of individual psychotherapy called *personal therapy* that is grounded in the diathesis–stress model. Personal therapy helps patients cope with stress and helps them build social skills, such as learning how to deal with criticism from others. Preliminary evidence suggests that personal therapy may reduce relapse rates and improve social functioning, at least among schizophrenia patients living with their families (Bustillo et al., 2001; Hogarty et al., 1997a, 1997b).

Learning-Based Therapies Although few behavior therapists believe that faulty learning causes schizophrenia, learning-based interventions have been shown to be effective in modifying schizophrenic behavior and helping people with the disorder develop behaviors that can help them adjust more effectively to living in the community. Therapy methods include the following:

1. *Selective reinforcement of behavior,* such as providing attention for appropriate behavior and extinguishing bizarre verbalizations through withdrawal of attention;
2. *Token economy,* in which individuals on inpatient units are rewarded for appropriate behavior with tokens, such as plastic chips, that can be exchanged for tangible reinforcers such as desirable goods or privileges; and
3. *Social skills training,* in which clients are taught conversational skills and other appropriate social behaviors through coaching, modeling, behavior rehearsal, and feedback.

Although token economies can help increase desirable behaviors of psychiatric inpatients, they have largely fallen out of favor in mental hospitals in recent years (Dickerson, Tenhula, & Green-Paden, 2005). Part of the problem is that they are time- and staff-intensive. To be successful, they must have strong administrative support, skilled treatment leaders, extensive staff training, and continuous quality control, all of which can limit their practicality.

Social skills training (SST) programs help individuals acquire a range of social and vocational skills. People with schizophrenia are often deficient in basic social skills needed for community living, such as assertiveness, interviewing skills, and general conversational skills. SST can help them improve their social skills and general level of social functioning (Granholm et al., 2005; Kopelowicz, Liberman, & Zarate, 2006; Pfammatter, Junghan, & Brenner, 2006). However, it remains unclear whether SST helps reduce relapse rates or improves community functioning of schizophrenia patients once they leave the hospital (Walker et al., 2004).

The basic model for social skills training uses role-playing exercises within a group format. Participants practice skills such as starting or maintaining conversations with new acquaintances and receive feedback and reinforcement from the therapist and other group members. The first step might be a dry run in which the participant role-plays the targeted behavior, such as asking strangers for bus directions. The therapist and other group members then praise the effort and provide constructive feedback. Role-playing is augmented by techniques such as modeling (observation of the therapist or other group members enacting the desired behavior), direct instruction (specific directions for enacting the desired behavior), shaping (reinforcement for successive approximations to the target behavior), and coaching (use of verbal or nonverbal prompts to elicit a particular desired behavior in the role play). Participants are given homework assignments to practice the behaviors in the settings in which they live, such as on the hospital ward or in the community. The aim is to generalize the training or transfer it to other settings. Training sessions may also be run in stores, restaurants, schools, and other real-life settings.

Another learning-based approach coming into wider practice in treating schizophrenia is cognitive-behavioral therapy (CBT). CBT shows promise as an adjunct to drug therapy, not only for reducing hallucinations, but also for helping patients adjust more effectively to community living (e.g., Bechdolf et al., 2004; Morrison et al., 2004; Penn et al., 2005; Tarrier & Wykesm 2004; Turkington, Kingdon, & Weiden, 2006). This brings us to consider the importance of psychosocial rehabilitation as part of a multi-faceted treatment approach.

Psychosocial Rehabilitation People with schizophrenia typically have difficulties functioning in social and occupational roles and performing work that depends upon basic cognitive abilities involving attention and memory. These problems limit their ability to adjust to community life, even in the absence of overt psychotic behavior. Recently, promising results were reported for cognitive rehabilitation training to help schizophrenia patients strengthen such basic cognitive skills as attention and memory (Hogarty et al., 2004; Penadés et al., 2006).

A number of self-help clubs (commonly called clubhouses) and rehabilitation centers have sprung up to help people with schizophrenia find a place in society. Many centers were launched by nonprofessionals or by people with schizophrenia themselves, largely because mental health agencies often failed to provide comparable services. A "clubhouse" is not a home; rather, it serves as a self-contained community that provides members with social support and help in finding educational opportunities and paid employment.

Multiservice rehabilitation centers typically offer housing as well as job and educational opportunities. These centers often make use of skills-training approaches to help clients learn how to handle money, resolve disputes with family members, develop friendships, take buses, cook their own meals, shop, and so on.

Family Intervention Programs Family conflicts and negative family interactions can heap stress on family members with schizophrenia, increasing the risk of recurrent episodes. Researchers and clinicians have worked with families of people with schizophrenia to help them cope with the burdens of care and assist them in developing more cooperative, less-confrontational ways of relating to others. The specific components of family interventions vary, but they usually share some common features, such as a focus on the practical aspects of everyday living, educating family members about schizophrenia, teaching them how to relate in a less-hostile way to family members with schizophrenia, improving communication, and fostering effective problem-solving and coping skills. Structured family intervention programs can reduce friction in the family, improve social functioning in schizophrenia patients, and even reduce relapse rates (Mueser et al., 2001; Pfammatter, Junghan, & Brenner, 2006; Pilling et al., 2002). However, the benefits appear to be relatively modest, and questions remain about whether relapses are prevented or merely delayed.

In sum, no single treatment approach meets all the needs of people with schizophrenia. The conceptualization of schizophrenia as a lifelong disability underscores the need for long-term treatment interventions that incorporate antipsychotic medication, family therapy, supportive or cognitive-behavioral forms of therapy, vocational training, and housing and other social support services. To help the individual reach maximal social adjustment, these interventions should be coordinated and integrated within a comprehensive model of treatment.

OTHER FORMS OF PSYCHOSIS

DSM-IV recognizes several other types of psychotic disorders beside schizophrenia. Here we focus on several of these disorders: brief psychotic disorder, schizophreniform disorder, delusional disorder, and schizoaffective disorder.

Brief Psychotic Disorder

Some brief psychotic episodes do not progress to schizophrenia. The *DSM-IV* category of **brief psychotic disorder** applies to a psychotic disorder that lasts from a day to a month and is characterized by at least one of the following features: delusions, hallucinations, disorganized speech, or disorganized or catatonic behavior. Eventually there is a full return to the individual's prior level of functioning. Brief psychotic disorder is often linked to a significant stressor or stressors, such as the loss of a loved one or exposure to brutal traumas in wartime. Women sometimes experience the disorder after childbirth.

Schizophreniform Disorder

Schizophreniform disorder consists of abnormal behaviors identical to those in schizophrenia that have persisted for at least 1 month but less than 6 months. They thus do not yet justify the diagnosis of schizophrenia. Although some cases have good outcomes, in others the disorder persists beyond 6 months and may be reclassified as schizophrenia or perhaps another form of psychotic disorder, such as schizoaffective disorder. Questions remain about the validity of the diagnosis, however. It may be more appropriate to diagnose people who show psychotic features of recent origin with a classification such as *psychotic disorder of an unspecified type* until additional information clearly indicates the specific type of disorder involved.

Delusional Disorder

Many of us, perhaps even most of us, feel suspicious of other people's motives at times. We may feel others have it in for us or believe others are talking about us behind our backs. For most of us, however, paranoid thinking does not take the form of outright delusions. The diagnosis of **delusional disorder** applies to people who hold persistent, clearly delusional beliefs, often involving paranoid themes (Sammons, 2005). Delusional disorder is uncommon, affecting an estimated 5 to 10 people in 10,000 during their lifetimes (APA, 2000).

brief psychotic disorder A psychotic disorder lasting from a day to a month that often follows exposure to a major stressor.

schizophreniform disorder A psychotic disorder lasting less than 6 months in duration, with features that resemble schizophrenia.

delusional disorder A type of psychosis characterized by persistent delusions, often of a paranoid nature, that do not have the bizarre quality of the type found in paranoid schizophrenia.

Is someone out to get you? People with delusional disorder often weave paranoid fantasies in their minds such that they confuse with reality.

A CLOSER LOOK

The Love Delusion

Erotomania, or the love delusion, is a rare delusional disorder in which the individual believes he or she is loved by someone else, usually someone famous or of high social status. In reality, the individual has only a passing or nonexistent relationship with the alleged lover. People with erotomania are often unemployed and socially isolated (Kennedy et al., 2002). Although the love delusion was once thought to be predominantly a female disorder, recent reports suggest it may not be a rarity among men. Although women with erotomania may have a potential for violence when their attentions are rebuffed, men with this condition appear more likely to threaten or commit acts of violence in the pursuit of the objects of their unrequited desires (Goldstein, 1986). Antipsychotic medications may reduce the intensity of the delusion but do not appear to eliminate it (Kelly, Kennedy, & Shanley, 2000). Nor do we have evidence that psychotherapy helps people with erotomania. The prognosis is thus bleak, and people with erotomania may harass their love objects for many years. Mental health professionals need to be aware of the potential for violence in the management of people who possess these delusions of love. The following cases provide some examples of the love delusion.

T R U T H or F I C T I O N

Some people have delusions that they are loved by a famous person.

☑ **TRUE.** Some people do suffer from the delusion that they are loved by a famous person. They are said to have a delusional disorder, erotomanic type.

Three Cases of Erotomania

Mr. A., a 35-year-old man, was described as a "love-struck" suitor of a daughter of a former President of the United States. He was arrested for repeatedly harassing the woman in an attempt to win her love, although they were actually perfect strangers. Refusing to adhere to the judge's warnings to stop pestering the woman, he placed numerous phone calls to her from prison and was later transferred to a psychiatric facility, still declaring they were very much in love.

Mr. B. was arrested for breaching a court order to stop pestering a famous pop singer. A 44-year-old farmer, Mr. B. had followed his love interest across the country, constantly bombarding her with romantic overtures. He was committed to a psychiatric hospital, but maintained the belief that she'd always wait for him.

Then there was Mr. C., a 32-year-old businessman, who believed a well-known woman lawyer had fallen in love with him following a casual meeting. He constantly called and sent flowers and letters, declaring his love. While she repeatedly rejected his advances and eventually filed criminal charges for harassment, he felt that she was only testing his love by placing obstacles in his path. He abandoned his wife and business and his functioning declined. When the woman continued to reject him, he began sending her threatening letters and was committed to a psychiatric facility.

—*Adapted from Goldstein, 1986, p. 802*

erotomania A delusional disorder characterized by the belief that one is loved by someone of high social status.

In delusional disorders, the delusional beliefs concern events that may possibly occur, such as the infidelity of a spouse, persecution by others, or attracting the love of a famous person. The apparent plausibility of these beliefs may lead others to take them seriously and check them out before concluding they are unfounded. Apart from the delusion, the individual's behavior does not show evidence of obviously bizarre or odd behavior, as we see in the following case example.

Mr. Polsen's Hit Men

Mr. Polsen, a married 42-year-old postal worker, was brought to the hospital by his wife because he had been insisting that there was a contract out on his life. Mr. Polsen told the doctors that the problem had started some four months ago when his supervisor accused him of tampering with a package, an offense that could have cost him his job. When he was exonerated at a formal hearing, his supervisor was "furious" and felt publicly humiliated, according to Mr. Polsen. Shortly afterwards, Mr. Polsen reported, his coworkers began avoiding him, turning away from him when he

(continued)

walked by, as if they didn't want to see him. He then began to think that they were talking about him behind his back, although he could never clearly make out what they were saying. He gradually became convinced that his coworkers were avoiding him because his boss had put a contract on his life. Things remained about the same for two months, when Mr. Polsen began to notice several large white cars cruising up and down the street where he lived. This frightened him, and he became convinced there were hit men in these cars. He then refused to leave his home without an escort and would run home in panic when he saw one of these cars approaching. Other than the reports of his belief that his life was in danger, his thinking and behavior appeared entirely normal on interview. He denied experiencing hallucinations and showed no other signs of psychotic behavior, except for the queer beliefs about his life being in danger. The diagnosis of Delusional Disorder, Persecutory type seemed the most appropriate, because there was no evidence that a contract had been taken on his life (hence, a persecutory delusion) and there were no other clear signs of psychosis that might support a diagnosis of a schizophrenic disorder.

—*Adapted from Spitzer et al., 1994, pp. 177–179*

Mr. Polsen's delusional belief that "hit teams" were pursuing him was treated with antipsychotic medication in the hospital and faded in about 3 weeks. His belief that he had been the subject of an attempted "hit" stuck in his mind, however. A month following admission, he stated, "I guess my boss has called off the contract. He couldn't get away with it now without publicity" (Spitzer et al., 1994, p. 179).

Although delusions frequently occur in schizophrenia, delusional disorder is believed to be distinct from schizophrenia. Persons with delusional disorder do not exhibit confused or jumbled thinking. Hallucinations, when they occur, are not as prominent. Delusions in schizophrenia are embedded within a larger array of disturbed thoughts, perceptions, and behavior. In delusional disorders, the delusion itself may be the only clear sign of abnormality.

Delusional disorder is relatively uncommon and should also be distinguished from another disorder in which paranoid thinking is present—*paranoid personality disorder* (discussed in Chapter 13). People with paranoid personality disorder may hold exaggerated or unwarranted suspicions of others, but not the outright delusions that are found among people with delusional disorders or paranoid schizophrenia.

Various types of delusional disorder are described in Table 12.3. Like other forms of psychosis, delusional disorders often respond to antipsychotic medication (Morimoto et al., 2002; Sammons, 2005). However, once the delusion is established, it may persevere, although the individual's concern about it may wax and wane over the years. In other cases, the delusion may disappear entirely for periods of time and then recur. Sometimes the disorder permanently disappears.

Schizoaffective Disorder

schizoaffective disorder A type of psychotic disorder in which individuals experience both severe mood disturbance and features associated with schizophrenia.

Schizoaffective disorder is sometimes referred to as a "mixed bag" of symptoms because it includes psychotic features such as hallucinations and delusions along with disturbances of mood, such as mania or major depression. Like schizophrenia, schizoaffective disorder tends to follow a chronic course that is characterized by persistent difficulties adjusting to the demands of adult life (Marneros, 2003). Also like schizophrenia, the psychotic features of schizoaffective disorder often respond to antipsychotic drugs (Jaffe & Levine, 2003; Woerner et al., 2003).

Schizoaffective disorder and schizophrenia appear to share a genetic link (Bramon & Sham, 2001). Consistent with a common genetic basis, researchers find a greater than average incidence of schizoaffective disorders among the relatives of people with schizophrenia and a greater than average incidence of schizophrenia among the

TABLE 12.3

Types of Delusional Disorder

Type	Description
Erotomanic Type	Delusional beliefs that someone else, usually someone of higher social status, such as a movie star or political figure, is in love with you; also called *erotomania*.
Grandiose Type	Inflated beliefs about your worth, importance, power, knowledge, or identity, or beliefs that you hold a special relationship to a deity or a famous person. Cult leaders who believe they have special mystical powers of enlightenment may have delusional disorders of this type.
Jealous Type	Delusions of jealousy in which the person may become convinced, without due cause, that his or her lover is unfaithful. The delusional person may misinterpret certain clues as signs of unfaithfulness, such as spots on the bedsheets.
Persecutory Type	The most common type of delusional disorder, persecutory delusions involve themes of being conspired against, followed, cheated, spied upon, poisoned or drugged, or otherwise maligned or mistreated. Persons with such delusions may repeatedly institute court actions, or even commit acts of violence, against those who they perceived are responsible for their mistreatment.
Somatic Type	Delusions involving physical defects, disease, or disorder. Persons with these delusions may believe that foul odors are emanating from their bodies, or that internal parasites are eating away at them, or that certain parts of their body are unusually disfigured or ugly, or not functioning properly despite evidence to the contrary.
Mixed Type	Delusions typify more than one of the other types; no single theme predominates.

Source: Adapted from *DSM-IV-TR* (APA, 2000).

relatives of people with schizoaffective disorder (Kendler, Gruenberg, & Tsuang, 1985; Maj et al., 1991). If schizoaffective disorders and schizophrenia share a common genetic substrate, we need to discover why this genetic predisposition leads to one disorder and not the other.

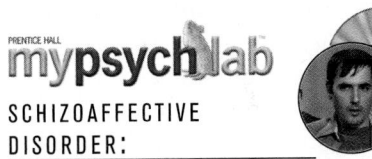

SUMMING UP

Schizophrenia

What is schizophrenia and how prevalent is it? Schizophrenia is a chronic psychotic disorder characterized by acute episodes involving a break with reality, as manifested by such features as delusions, hallucinations, illogical thinking, incoherent speech, and bizarre behavior. Residual deficits in cognitive, emotional, and social areas of functioning persist between acute episodes. Schizophrenia is believed to affect about 1% of the adult population.

What are the major phases of schizophrenia? Schizophrenia usually develops in late adolescence or early adulthood. Its onset may be abrupt or gradual. Gradual onset is preceded by a prodromal phase, a period of gradual deterioration that precedes the onset of acute symptoms. Acute episodes, which may occur periodically throughout life, are typified by clear psychotic symptoms, such as hallucinations and delusions. Between acute episodes the disorder is characterized by a residual phase in which the person's level of functioning is similar to that which was present during the prodromal phase.

What are the most prominent features of schizophrenia? Among the more prominent features of schizophrenia are disorders in the content of thought (delusions) and the form of thought (thought disorder), as well as the presence of often severe perceptual distortions (hallucinations) and emotional disturbances (flattened or inappropriate affect). There are also dysfunctions in brain processes regulating attention to the external world.

What are the specific subtypes of schizophrenia? The disorganized type is associated with grossly disorganized behavior and thought processes. The catatonic type is associated with grossly impaired motor behaviors, such as maintenance of fixed postures and muteness for long periods. The paranoid type is characterized by paranoid delusions and frequent auditory hallucinations. The undifferentiated type is a catchall category applying to cases in which schizophrenic episodes don't clearly fit the other types. The residual type applies to individuals with schizophrenia who do not have prominent psychotic behaviors at the time of evaluation. Researchers have also distinguished between two general types of schizophrenia: Type I, characterized by positive symptomatology, more abrupt onset, better response to antipsychotic medication, and better preserved intellectual ability, and Type II, characterized by negative symptomatology, more gradual onset, poorer response to antipsychotic medication, and greater cognitive impairment.

How is schizophrenia conceptualized within traditional psychodynamic theory and learning perspectives? In the traditional psychodynamic model, schizophrenia represents a regression to a psychological state corresponding to early infancy in which the proddings of the id produce bizarre, socially deviant behavior and give rise to hallucinations and delusions. Learning theorists propose that some form of schizophrenic behavior may result from lack of social reinforcement, which leads to gradual detachment from the social environment and increased attention to an inner world of fantasy. Modeling and selective reinforcement of bizarre behavior may explain some schizophrenic behaviors in the hospital setting.

What do we know about the biological bases of schizophrenia? Compelling evidence for a strong genetic component in schizophrenia comes from studies of family patterns of schizophrenia, twin studies, and adoption studies. The mode of genetic transmission remains unknown. Most researchers believe the neurotransmitter dopamine plays a role in schizophrenia, especially in the more flagrant features of the disorder. Viral factors may also be involved, but definite proof of viral involvement is lacking. Evidence of brain abnormalities and structural damage in schizophrenia is accumulating.

How is schizophrenia conceptualized within the diathesis-stress model? The diathesis-stress model posits that schizophrenia results from an interaction of a genetic predisposition (the diathesis) and environmental stressors (e.g., family conflict, child abuse, emotional deprivation, loss of supportive figures, early brain trauma).

How are family factors related to the development and course of schizophrenia? Family factors such as communication deviance and expressed emotion may act as sources of stress that increase the risk of development or recurrence of schizophrenia among people with a genetic predisposition.

How does the treatment of schizophrenia involve a multifaceted approach? Contemporary treatment approaches tend to be multifaceted, incorporating pharmacological and psychosocial approaches. Antipsychotic medication is not a cure but tends to stem the more flagrant aspects of the disorder and to reduce the need for hospitalization and the risk of recurrent episodes.

What types of psychosocial interventions have shown promising results? These are principally learning-based approaches, such as token economy systems and social skills training. They help increase adaptive behavior of schizophrenia patients. Psychosocial rehabilitation approaches help people with schizophrenia adapt more successfully to occupational and social roles in the community. Family intervention programs help families cope with the burdens of care, communicate more clearly, and learn more helpful ways of relating to the patient.

Other Forms of Psychosis

What are other forms of psychotic disorders besides schizophrenia? These include brief psychotic disorder (a psychotic disorder lasting less than a week that may be reactive to a significant stressor), schizophreniform disorder (symptoms identical to those of schizophrenia that lasting for a month to less than 6 months), delusional disorder (denoted by delusions that are apparently plausible and less bizarre than those in schizophrenia), and schizoaffective disorder (combination of psychotic symptoms and significant mood disturbance).

KEY TERMS

schizophrenia *(p. 397)*
prodromal phase *(p. 399)*
residual phase *(p. 400)*
positive symptoms *(p. 402)*
negative symptoms *(p. 402)*
thought disorder *(p. 403)*

hallucinations *(p. 405)*
disorganized type *(p. 408)*
catatonic type *(p. 409)*
paranoid type *(p. 409)*
dopamine hypothesis *(p. 414)*
endophenotypes *(p. 420)*

tardive dyskinesia (TD) *(p. 422)*
brief psychotic disorder *(p. 426)*
schizophreniform disorder *(p. 426)*
delusional disorder *(p. 426)*
erotomania *(p. 427)*
schizoaffective disorder *(p. 428)*

MEDIA TOOLS

A variety of digital and online learning tools are available to enrich your learning experience and help you succeed in the course. These resources include:

- **MyPsychLab,** an online learning system for your course in abnormal psychology that allows you to test your mastery of concepts in the book by using chapter-by-chapter diagnostic tests. Results from the diagnostic tests help you build a customized study plan. To access **MyPsychLab,** visit www. prenhall.com/mypsychlab and follow the instructions on the site.

- **"SPEAKING OUT" PATIENT INTERVIEWS,** a set of video case examples of actual patients you can access on the companion CD-ROM included with the text. Icons in the margins of the chapter highlight the video case examples included on the CD-ROM.

- **COMPANION WEB SITE,** an online study center that offers computer-scored quizzes you can use to test your knowledge, along with other study tools and links to related sites to enhance your learning of abnormal psychology. To access the companion Web site, visit www.prenhall.com/nevid and use the various tabs and links on the site to access these learning resources.

Schizophrenia

is characterized by

Severely disturbed behavior, thinking, emotions, and perceptions involving a break with reality (psychosis)

and can be classified within such types as

- Disorganized Type
- Catatonic Type
- Paranoid Type

and involve interactions of multiple factors such as

MODEL SPOTLIGHT

- Biological factors, including genetic factors, neurotransmitter irregularities, and brain abnormalities
- Psychosocial factors interacting with genetic factors as represented by the diathesis-stress model:

and may be treated with

- Antipsychotic drugs
- Learning-based treatments, such as the token economy and social skills training
- Psychosocial rehabilitation services, such as residential treatment facilities
- Family intervention programs to improve communication and reduce conflicts

Diathesis-Stress Model

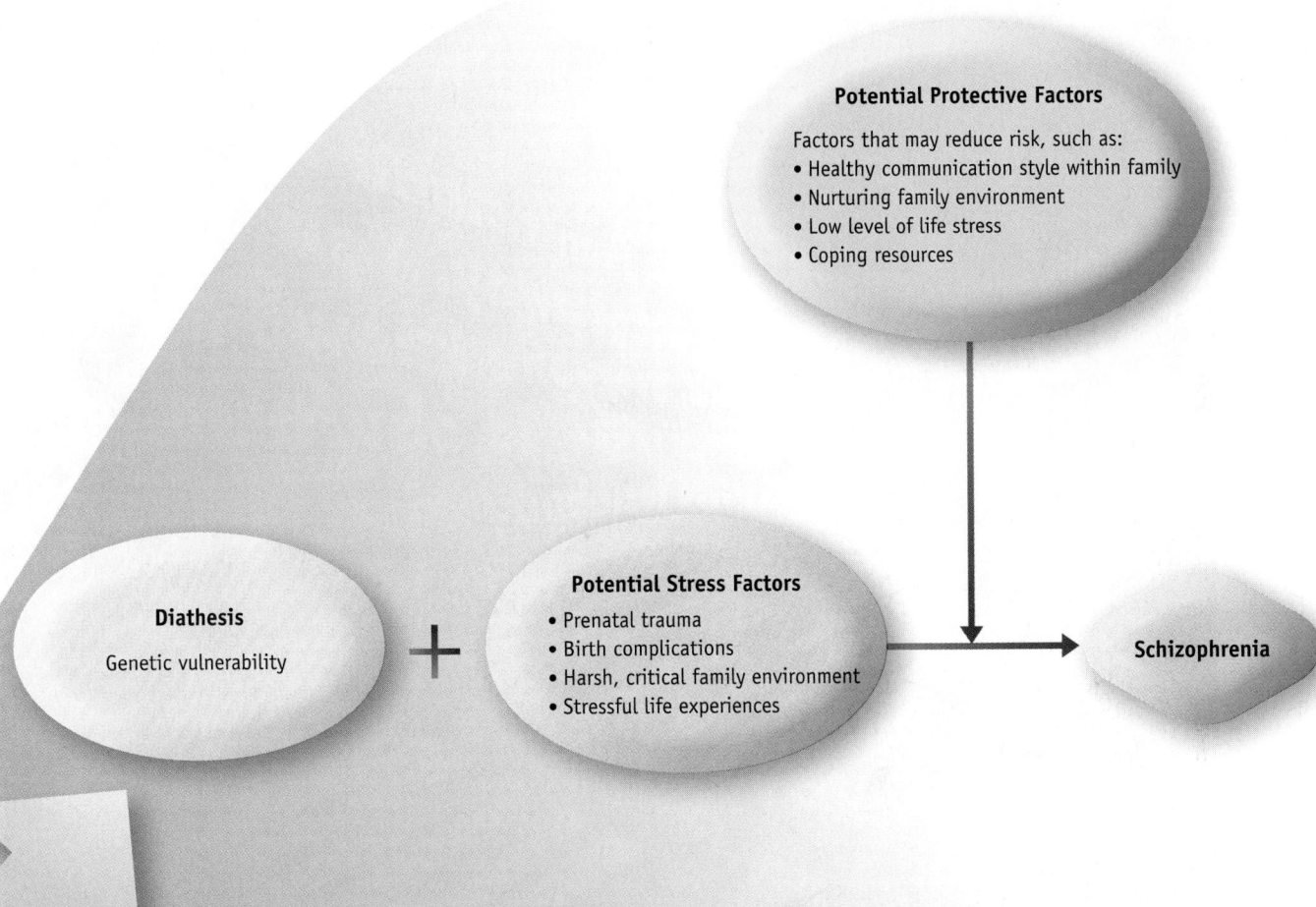

Potential Protective Factors

Factors that may reduce risk, such as:
- Healthy communication style within family
- Nurturing family environment
- Low level of life stress
- Coping resources

Diathesis

Genetic vulnerability

+

Potential Stress Factors
- Prenatal trauma
- Birth complications
- Harsh, critical family environment
- Stressful life experiences

Schizophrenia

Personality Disorders and Impulse Control Disorders

Barbara Kruger, "Power Pleasure Desire Disgust". Installation: November 1997. Courtesy: Mary Boone Gallery, New York.

CHAPTER OUTLINE

TYPES OF PERSONALITY DISORDERS 435–454

Personality Disorders Characterized by Odd or Eccentric Behavior
Personality Disorders Characterized by Dramatic, Emotional, or Erratic Behavior
Personality Disorders Characterized by Anxious or Fearful Behavior
Problems with the Classification of Personality Disorders

THEORETICAL PERSPECTIVES 454–463

Psychodynamic Perspectives
Learning Perspectives
Family Perspectives
Biological Perspectives
Sociocultural Perspectives

TREATMENT OF PERSONALITY DISORDERS 463–465

Psychodynamic Approaches
Behavioral Approaches
Biological Approaches

IMPULSE CONTROL DISORDERS 465–469

Pathological Gambling
Kleptomania

SUMMING UP 469–470

"I" "My Dark Place"

There are times in my life when I go to a dark place. I find it hard to run or hide from this symptom that feels like it controls my life. It's called self-mutilation or cutting. It's part of my . . . diagnosis called borderline personality disorder (BPD). Cutting is when you feel an urge to cut different places on your body. In my case, it's my arms and legs. I remember being depressed at a very young age. At age eight-years-old, I cut myself for the first time. I was very alone in my pain and no one noticed my scar. But, even at that very young age, after I cut, I felt a sense of relief. For a while I was able to block out everything and just feel free. Even today, I still feel a need to comfort myself. Now that I'm older I must find other outlets for my pain. It's something that's going to take a lot of work and therapy.

Source: New York City Voices. *Reprinted with permission*

LIKE THIS PERSON, PEOPLE WITH BORDERLINE PERSONALITY DISORDER ARE OFTEN SEVERELY depressed and turn to self-mutilation in a twisted attempt to escape from emotional pain. But their problems lie deeper than depression. They involve the kinds of rigid, inflexible and maladaptive behavior patterns that clinicians classify as *personality disorders.* These maladaptive patterns of behavior have far-reaching consequences for the person's psychological adjustment and relationships with others.

All of us have particular styles of behavior and ways of relating to others. Some of us are orderly, others sloppy. Some of us prefer solitary pursuits; others are more social. Some of us are followers; others are leaders. Some of us seem immune to rejection by others, whereas others avoid social initiatives for fear of getting shot down. When behavior patterns become so inflexible or maladaptive that they cause significant personal distress or impair people's social or occupational functioning, they may be classified as personality disorders.

Later in the chapter we discuss another class of disorders, called *impulse control disorders,* which are also characterized by maladaptive patterns of behavior. With impulse control disorders, such as *pathological (compulsive) gambling* and *kleptomania,* the maladaptive behaviors take the form of failure to resist impulses that lead to harmful consequences. Another feature that personality disorders and impulse disorders have in common is that people diagnosed with these disorders often fail to see how their own behaviors are seriously disrupting their lives.

TYPES OF PERSONALITY DISORDERS

> In most of us by the age of thirty, the character has set like plaster, and will never soften again.
>
> —William James

Personality disorders are excessively rigid patterns of behavior or ways of relating to others. The rigidity prevents people from adjusting to external demands; thus the patterns ultimately become self-defeating. The disordered personality traits or characteristics become evident by adolescence or early adulthood and continue through much of adult life, becoming so deeply ingrained that they are highly resistant to change. The warning signs of personality disorders may be detected during childhood, even in the troubled behavior of preschoolers. Children with psychological disorders or problem behaviors in childhood, such as conduct disorder, depression, anxiety, and immaturity, are at greater than average risk of later developing personality disorders (Kasen et al., 2001). Personality disorders appear to be quite common, not only here in

personality disorders Excessively rigid behavior patterns, or ways of relating to others, that ultimately become self-defeating.

ego syntonic Referring to behaviors or feelings that are perceived as natural parts of the self.

ego dystonic Referring to behaviors or feelings that are perceived to be alien to one's self-identity.

the United States, but elsewhere in the world. For example, a community survey of adults in Oslo, Norway, found that 13.4% of community residents showed evidence of having one or more personality disorders (Torgersen, Kringlen, & Cramer, 2001).

Despite the self-defeating consequences of their behavior, people with personality disorders do not generally perceive a need to change. Using psychodynamic terms, the *DSM* notes that people with personality disorders tend to perceive their traits as **ego syntonic**—as natural parts of themselves. Consequently, people with personality disorders are more likely to be brought to the attention of mental health professionals by others than to seek services themselves. In contrast, people with anxiety disorders (Chapter 6) or mood disorders (Chapter 8) tend to view their disturbed behaviors as **ego dystonic.** They do not see their behaviors as parts of their self-identities and are thus more likely to seek help to relieve the distress caused by them.

The *DSM* groups clinical syndromes (such as mood disorders and anxiety disorders) on Axis I and personality disorders on Axis II. The personality disorders are classified separately from the clinical syndromes because they typically involve more enduring and rigid patterns of behavior. But clinical syndromes and personality disorders often occur together, or *comorbidly.* For example, a person may have an Axis I mood disorder, such as major depression, as well as an Axis II personality disorder, such as borderline personality disorder.

The *DSM* groups personality disorders into three clusters:

Cluster A: People who are perceived as odd or eccentric. This cluster includes paranoid, schizoid, and schizotypal personality disorders.
Cluster B: People whose behavior is overly dramatic, emotional, or erratic. This grouping consists of antisocial, borderline, histrionic, and narcissistic personality disorders.
Cluster C: People who often appear anxious or fearful. This cluster includes avoidant, dependent, and obsessive–compulsive personality disorders.

Table 13.1 provides an overview of the personality disorders discussed in this chapter.

TABLE 13.1 Overview of Personality Disorders

Disorder	Lifetime Prevalence in Population (approx.)	Description
Personality Disorders Characterized by Odd or Eccentric Behavior		
Paranoid Personality Disorder	0.5%–2.5%	Pervasive suspiciousness of the motives of others but without outright paranoid delusions
Schizoid Personality Disorder	Unknown	Social aloofness and shallow or blunted emotions
Schizotypal Personality Disorder	3%	Persistent difficulty forming close social relationships and odd or peculiar beliefs and behaviors without clear psychotic features
Personality Disorders Characterized by Dramatic, Emotional, or Erratic Behavior		
Antisocial Personality Disorder	3%–6% in men, 1% in women	Chronic antisocial behavior, callous treatment of others, irresponsible behavior, and lack of remorse for wrongdoing
Borderline Personality Disorder	2%	Tumultuous moods and stormy relationships with others, unstable self-image, and lack of impulse control
Histrionic Personality Disorder	Est. 2%–3%	Overly dramatic and emotional behavior; demands to be the center of attention; excessive needs for reassurance, praise, and approval
Narcissistic Personality Disorder	Under 1%	Grandiose sense of self; extreme needs for admiration
Personality Disorders Characterized by Anxious or Fearful Behavior		
Avoidant Personality Disorder	.05%–1%	Chronic pattern of avoiding social relationships due to fears of rejection
Dependent Personality Disorder	Unknown	Excessive dependence on others and difficulty making independent decisions
Obsessive–Compulsive Personality Disorder	1%	Excessive needs for orderliness and perfectionism, excessive attention to detail, rigid ways of relating to others

Sources: APA, 2000; Kessler et al., 1994.

Personality Disorders Characterized by Odd or Eccentric Behavior

This group of personality disorders includes paranoid, schizoid, and schizotypal disorders. People with these disorders often have difficulty relating to others or show little or no interest in developing social relationships.

Paranoid Personality Disorder   The defining trait of the **paranoid personality disorder** is pervasive suspiciousness—the tendency to interpret other people's behavior as deliberately threatening or demeaning. People with the disorder are excessively mistrustful of others, and their relationships suffer for it. Although they may be suspicious of coworkers and supervisors, they can generally maintain employment.

The following case illustrates the unwarranted suspicion and reluctance to confide in others that typifies people with paranoid personalities.

paranoid personality disorder A personality disorder characterized by undue suspiciousness of others' motives, but not to the point of delusion.

A Case of Paranoid Personality Disorder

An 85-year-old retired businessman was interviewed by a social worker to determine health care needs for himself and his wife. The man had no history of treatment for a mental disorder. He appeared to be in good health and mentally alert. He and his wife had been married for 60 years, and it appeared that his wife was the only person he'd ever really trusted. He had always been suspicious of others. He would not reveal personal information to anyone but his wife, believing that others were out to take advantage of him. He had refused offers of help from other acquaintances because he suspected their motives. When called on the telephone, he would refuse to give out his name until he determined the nature of the caller's business. He'd always involved himself in "useful work" to occupy his time, even during his 20 years of retirement. He spent a good deal of time monitoring his investments and had altercations with his stockbroker when errors on his monthly statement prompted suspicion that his broker was attempting to cover up fraudulent transactions.

—Adapted from Spitzer et al., 1994, pp. 211–213

People who have paranoid personality disorder tend to be overly sensitive to criticism, whether real or imagined. They take offense at the smallest slight. They are readily angered and hold grudges when they think they have been mistreated. They are unlikely to confide in others because they believe that personal information may be used against them. They question the sincerity and trustworthiness of friends and associates. A smile or a glance may be viewed with suspicion. As a result, they have few friends and intimate relationships. When they do form an intimate relationship, they may suspect infidelity, even without evidence. They tend to remain hypervigilant, as if they must be on the lookout against harm. They deny blame for misdeeds, even when warranted, and are perceived by others as cold, aloof, scheming, devious, and humorless. They tend to be argumentative and may launch repeated lawsuits against those who they believe have mistreated them.

Clinicians need to weigh cultural and sociopolitical factors when arriving at a diagnosis of paranoid personality disorder. For example, members of immigrant or ethnic minority groups, political refugees, or people from other cultures may seem guarded or defensive, but this behavior may reflect unfamiliarity with the language, customs, or rules and regulations of the majority culture or cultural mistrust arising from a history of neglect or oppression. Such behavior should not be confused with paranoid personality disorder.

Although people with paranoid personality disorder harbor exaggerated and unwarranted suspicions, they do not have the outright paranoid delusions that characterize the thought patterns of people with paranoid schizophrenia (for example, believing the FBI is out to get them). People who have paranoid personalities are

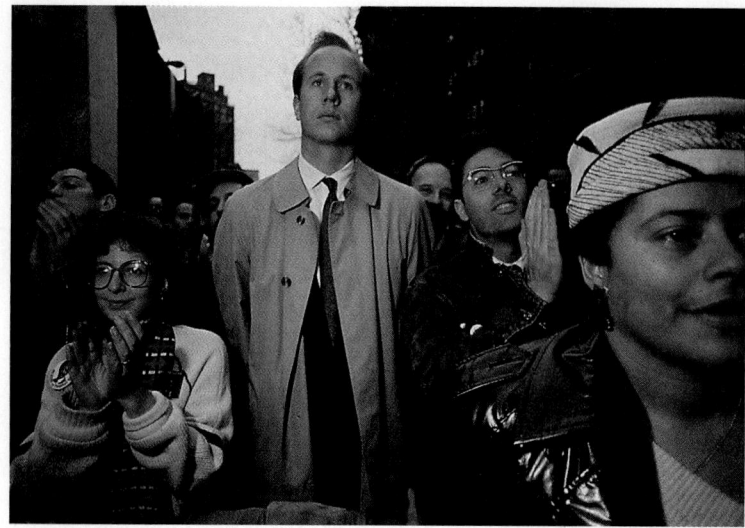

Schizoid personality. It is normal to be reserved about displaying one's feelings, especially when one is among strangers. But people with schizoid personalities rarely express emotions and are distant and aloof. Yet the emotions of people with schizoid personalities are not as shallow or blunted as they are in people with schizophrenia.

schizoid personality disorder A personality disorder characterized by persistent lack of interest in social relationships, flattened affect, and social withdrawal.

schizotypal personality disorder A personality disorder characterized by eccentricities of thought and behavior, but without clearly psychotic features.

unlikely to seek treatment; they see others as causing their problems. The reported prevalence of paranoid personality disorder in the general population ranges from 0.5% to 2.5% (APA, 2000). The disorder is diagnosed in people receiving mental health treatment more often in men than women.

Schizoid Personality Disorder Social isolation is the cardinal feature of **schizoid personality disorder.** Often described as a loner or an eccentric, the person with a schizoid personality lacks interest in social relationships. The person's emotions usually appear shallow or blunted, but not to the degree found in schizophrenia (see Chapter 12). People with this disorder rarely, if ever, experience strong anger, joy, or sadness. They look distant and aloof. Their faces tend to show no emotional expression, and they rarely exchange social smiles or nods. They seem indifferent to criticism or praise and appear to be wrapped up in abstract ideas rather than in thoughts about people. Although they prefer to remain distant from others, they maintain better contact with reality than do people with schizophrenia. The prevalence of the disorder in the general population remains unknown. Men with this disorder rarely date or marry. Women with the disorder are more likely to accept romantic advances passively and to marry, but they seldom initiate relationships or develop strong attachments to their partners.

We may find inconsistencies between outer appearances and the inner lives of people with schizoid personalities (Akhtar, 2003). Although they may appear to have little appetite for sex, for example, they may harbor voyeuristic wishes and become attracted to pornography. The distance and social aloofness of people with schizoid personalities may be somewhat superficial, however. They may also harbor exquisite sensitivity, deep curiosities about people, and wishes for love that they cannot express. In some cases, sensitivity is expressed in deep feelings for animals rather than people.

◆

A Case of Schizoid Personality Disorder

John, a 50-year-old retired police officer, sought treatment a few weeks after his dog was hit by a car and died. Since the dog's death, John has felt sad and tired. He has had difficulty concentrating and sleeping. He lives alone and prefers to be by himself, limiting his contacts with others to a passing "Hello" or "How are you?" He feels that social conversation is a waste of time and feels awkward when others try to initiate a friendship. Although he avidly reads newspapers and keeps abreast of current events, he has no real interest in people. He works as a security guard and is described by his coworkers as a "loner" and a "cold fish." The only relationship he had was with his dog, with which he felt he could exchange more sensitive and loving feelings than he could share with people. At Christmas, he would "exchange gifts" with his dog, buying presents for the dog and wrapping a bottle of Scotch for himself as a gift from the animal. The only event that ever saddened him was the loss of his dog. In contrast, the loss of his parents failed to evoke an emotional response. He considers himself to be different from other people and is bewildered by the displays of emotionality that he sees in others.

—Adapted from Spitzer et al., 1989, pp. 249–250

Schizotypal Personality Disorder The diagnosis of **schizotypal personality disorder** applies to people who have difficulties forming close relationships and whose behavior, mannerisms, and thought patterns seem peculiar or odd, but not disturbed enough to merit a diagnosis of schizophrenia. They may be especially anxious in social situations, even when interacting with familiar people. Their social anxieties seem to be associated with paranoid thinking (e.g., fears that others mean them harm) rather than with concerns about being rejected or evaluated negatively by others (APA, 2000).

Schizotypal personality disorder may be slightly more common in males than in females and is believed to affect about 3% of the general population (APA, 2000). Investigators also find higher rates of the disorder among African Americans than among Caucasians or Hispanic Americans (Chavira et al., 2003). However, clinicians need to be careful not to label as schizotypal certain behavior patterns that reflect culturally determined beliefs or religious rituals, such as beliefs in voodoo and other magical beliefs.

The eccentricity associated with the schizoid personality is limited to a lack of interest in social relationships. In paranoid personality disorder, unusual beliefs are limited to undue suspiciousness of others. But in schizotypal personality disorder, there is a wider range of odd behaviors, beliefs, and perceptions. Persons with the disorder may experience unusual perceptions or illusions, such as feeling the presence of a deceased family member in the room. They realize, however, that the person is not actually there. They may become unduly suspicious of others or paranoid in their thinking. They may develop *ideas of reference,* such as the belief that other people are talking about them. They may engage in *magical thinking,* such as believing they possess a "sixth sense" (i.e., can foretell the future) or that others can sense their feelings. They may attach unusual meanings to words. Their own speech may be vague or unusually abstract, but it is not incoherent or filled with the loose associations that characterize schizophrenia. They may appear unkempt, display unusual mannerisms, and engage in unusual behaviors, such as talking to themselves in the presence of others. Their faces may register little emotion. Like people with schizoid personalities, they may fail to exchange smiles with, or nod at, others. Or they may appear silly and smile and laugh at the wrong times. They tend to be socially withdrawn and aloof, with few if any close friends or confidants. They seem to be especially anxious around unfamiliar people. We can see evidence of the social aloofness and illusions that are often associated with schizotypal personality disorder in this case.

◆

A Case of Schizotypal Personality Disorder

Jonathan, a 27-year-old auto mechanic, had few friends and preferred science fiction novels to socializing with other people. He seldom joined in conversations. At times, he seemed to be lost in his thoughts, and his coworkers would have to whistle to get his attention when he was working on a car. He often showed a "queer" expression on his face. Perhaps the most unusual feature of his behavior was his reported intermittent experience of "feeling" his deceased mother standing nearby. These illusions were reassuring to him, and he looked forward to their occurrence. Jonathan realized they were not real. He never tried to reach out to touch the apparition, knowing it would disappear as soon as he drew closer. It was enough, he said, to feel her presence.

—From the Author's Files

Despite the *DSM's* grouping of "schizotypal" behaviors with personality disorders, the schizotypal behavior pattern may fall within a spectrum of schizophrenia-related disorders that includes paranoid and schizoid personality disorders and schizoaffective disorder (discussed in Chapter 12) as well as schizophrenia itself. Schizotypal personality disorder may share a common genetic basis with schizophrenia (Bedwell, Kamath, & Baksh, 2006; Siever & Davis, 2004). Supporting this genetic link, evidence from a recent brain imaging study showed brain abnormalities in patients with schizotypal personality disorder similar to those found in schizophrenia patients (Dickey et al., 2006, 2007).

Let us also note that relatively few people diagnosed with schizotypal personality disorder go on to develop schizophrenia or other psychotic disorders (APA, 2000).

Antisocial personality. Mass murderer Henry Lee Lucas, a drifter and violent career criminal, fits the stereotype of an antisocial personality.

antisocial personality disorder A personality disorder characterized by antisocial and irresponsible behavior and lack of remorse for misdeeds.

T R U T H (or) FICTION

People we call psychopaths are psychotic.

☑ **FALSE.** People we call psychopaths have psychopathic personalities. They may be diagnosed with antisocial personality disorder, but do not suffer from psychosis (manifest by a break with reality, as in schizophrenia).

Perhaps the emergence of schizophrenia in persons with this shared genetic predisposition is determined by such factors as stressful life experiences.

Personality Disorders Characterized by Dramatic, Emotional, or Erratic Behavior

This cluster of personality disorders includes the antisocial, borderline, histrionic, and narcissistic types. People with these disorders exhibit behavior patterns that are excessive, unpredictable, or self-centered; they also have difficulty forming and maintaining relationships and show antisocial behavior.

Antisocial Personality Disorder People with **antisocial personality disorder** are *antisocial* in the sense that they often violate the rights of others, disregard social norms and conventions, and, in some cases, break the law. They are not "antisocial" in the colloquial sense of seeking to avoid people. People with antisocial personalities also tend to be impulsive and fail to live up to their commitments to others. Yet they often show a superficial charm and possess at least average intelligence. They frequently show low levels of anxiety when faced with threatening situations and lack feelings of guilt or remorse following wrongdoing (Goldstein et al., 2006; Kiehl, 2006). Punishment may have little or no effect on their behavior. Although parents and others have usually punished them for their misdeeds, they persist in leading irresponsible and impulsive lives.

Men are more likely than women to be diagnosed with antisocial personality disorder (Cale & Lilienfeld, 2002). The prevalence rates for the disorder in community samples range from about 1% in women to 3% to 6% in men (APA, 2000; Kessler et al., 1994; see Figure 13.1). The person must be at least 18 years of age to receive a diagnosis of antisocial personality disorder. An alternative diagnosis of conduct disorder may be used with younger people who show similar characteristics (see Chapter 14).

Clinicians once used terms such as *psychopath* and *sociopath* to refer to people who today are classified as having antisocial personalities, people whose behavior is amoral and asocial, impulsive, and lacking in remorse and shame. Some clinicians continue to use these terms interchangeably with *antisocial personality*. The roots of the word *psychopath* focus on the idea that there is something amiss (pathological) in the individual's psychological functioning. The roots of *sociopath* center on the person's social deviance.

FIGURE 13.1 Lifetime prevalences of antisocial personality disorder by gender. Antisocial personality disorder is more than five times as common among men than women. However, the disorder has been rising more rapidly among women in recent years.

Source: National Comorbidity Survey (Kessler et al., 1994).

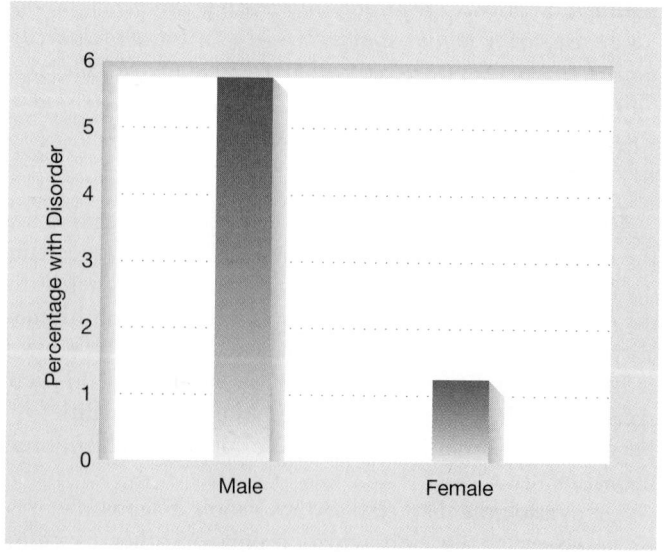

The pattern of behavior that characterizes antisocial personality disorder begins in childhood or adolescence and extends into adulthood (e.g., Blonigen et al., 2006; Lahey et al., 2005). However, the antisocial and criminal behavior associated with the disorder tends to decline with age and may disappear by the time the person reaches the age of 40. Not so for the underlying personality traits associated with the disorder—traits such as egocentricity; manipulativeness; lack of empathy, guilt, or remorse; and callousness toward others. These appear to be relatively stable even with increasing age (Harpur & Hare, 1994).

Much of our attention in this chapter focuses on antisocial personality disorder. Historically it is the personality disorder that has been most extensively studied by scholars and researchers.

Sociocultural Factors and Antisocial Personality Disorder

Antisocial personality disorder cuts across all racial and ethnic groups. The disorder is most common, however, among people in lower socioeconomic groups. One explanation is that people with antisocial personality disorder drift downward occupationally, perhaps because their antisocial behavior makes it difficult for them to hold steady jobs or progress upward. People from lower socioeconomic levels may also be more likely to have parents who modeled antisocial behavior. However, the diagnosis may also be misapplied to people living in hard-pressed communities who engage in seemingly antisocial behaviors as a survival strategy (APA, 2000).

Criminality or antisocial personality disorder? It is likely that many prison inmates could be diagnosed with antisocial personality disorder; however, people may become criminals or delinquents not because of a disordered personality but because they were raised in environments or exposed to subcultures that both encouraged and rewarded criminal behavior.

Antisocial Behavior and Criminality

We tend to think of antisocial behavior as synonymous with criminal behavior. Although it is the case that antisocial personality disorder is associated with an increased risk of criminality (e.g., Kosson, Lorenz, & Newman, 2006), not all criminals have antisocial personalities nor do all people with antisocial personality disorder become criminals. Many people with antisocial personality disorders are law abiding and successful in their careers, even though they may treat others in a callous and insensitive manner.

Investigators have begun to view antisocial personality as composed of two somewhat independent dimensions. The first is a *personality dimension*. It consists of such traits as superficial charm, selfishness, lack of empathy, callous and remorseless use of others, and disregard for their feelings and welfare. This type of psychopathic personality applies to people who have these kinds of psychopathic traits but don't become lawbreakers.

The second dimension is a *behavioral dimension*. It is characterized by the adoption of a generally unstable and antisocial lifestyle, including frequent problems with the law, poor employment history, and unstable relationships. These two dimensions are not entirely separate; many antisocial individuals show evidence of both sets of traits.

We should also note that some people do not become criminals or delinquents because of a disordered personality but because they were reared in environments or subcultures that rewarded criminal behavior. Although criminal behavior is deviant to society at large, it is normal by the standards of the subculture. Also, lack of remorse, which is a cardinal feature of antisocial personality disorder, does not characterize all criminals. Some criminals regret their crimes, and judges and parole boards consider evidence of remorse when passing sentence or recommending a prisoner for parole.

Only about half of prison inmates could be diagnosed with antisocial personality disorder (Robins et al., 1991). Moreover, only a minority of people with antisocial personality disorder run afoul of the law. Many fewer still fit (thankfully!) the stereotype of the psychopathic killer popularized in such films as *The Silence of the Lambs*.

Profile of the Antisocial Personality

In a classic work in the field, Hervey Cleckley (1941) argued that the characteristics that define the psychopathic or antisocial personality—self-centeredness, irresponsibility, impulsivity, and insensitivity to the

T R U T H or F I C T I O N

People with antisocial personalities inevitably run afoul of the law.

☑ **FALSE.** Not all criminals show signs of psychopathy and not all people with psychopathic personalities become criminals.

mypsychlab
PRENTICE HALL

ANTISOCIAL PERSONALITY DISORDER:

The Case of Paul

"I went to prison for kicking down my wife's door."

TABLE 13.2

Diagnostic Features of Antisocial Personality Disorder

A. The person is at least 18 years old.

B. There is evidence of a conduct disorder prior to the age of 15, as shown by such behavior patterns as truancy, running away, initiating physical fights, use of weapons, forcing someone into sexual activities, physical cruelty to people or animals, deliberate destruction of property or fire setting, lying, stealing, or mugging.

C. Since the age of 15, there has been general indifference to and violation of the rights of other people, as shown by several of the following:

1. Lack of conformity to social norms and legal codes, as shown by law-breaking behavior that may or may not result in arrest, such as destruction of property, engaging in unlawful occupations, stealing, or harassing others.

2. Aggressive and highly irritable style of relating to others, as shown by repeated physical fights and assaults with others, possibly involving abuse of one's spouse or children.

3. Consistent irresponsibility, as shown by failure to maintain employment due to chronic absences, lateness, abandonment of job opportunities or extended periods of unemployment despite available work; and/or by failure to honor financial obligations, such as failing to maintain child support or defaulting on debts; and/or by lack of a sustained monogamous relationship.

4. Failure to plan ahead or impulsivity, as shown by traveling around without prearranged employment or clear goals.

5. Disregard for the truth, evidenced by repeated lying, conning others, or use of aliases for personal gain or pleasure.

6. Recklessness with regard to personal safety or the safety of other people, as shown by driving while intoxicated or repeated speeding.

7. Lack of remorse for misdeeds, as shown by indifference to the harm done to others, and/or by rationalizing that harm.

Source: Adapted from the *DSM-IV-TR* (APA, 2000).

needs of others—exist not only among criminals but also among many respected members of the community, including doctors, lawyers, politicians, and business executives. Other common traits of people with antisocial personality disorder include failure to conform to social norms, irresponsibility, aimlessness and lack of long-term goals or plans, impulsive behavior, outright lawlessness, violence, chronic unemployment, marital problems, lack of remorse or empathy, substance abuse or alcoholism, and a disregard for the truth and for the feelings and needs of others (Patrick, Cuthbert, & Lang, 1994; Robins et al., 1991).

Irresponsibility, a common trait among people with antisocial personalities, may be seen in a personal history dotted by repeated, unexplained absences from work, abandonment of jobs without having other job opportunities to fall back on, or long stretches of unemployment. Irresponsibility often extends to financial matters, where there may be repeated failure to repay debts, to pay child support, or to meet other financial responsibilities to one's family and dependents. The diagnostic features of antisocial personality disorder, as defined in the *DSM*, are shown in Table 13.2.

The following case represents a number of antisocial characteristics.

A Case of Antisocial Behavior

The 19-year-old male is brought by ambulance to the hospital emergency room in a state of cocaine intoxication. He's wearing a T-shirt with the imprint "Twisted Sister" on the front, and he sports a punk-style haircut. His mother is called and sounds groggy and confused on the phone; the doctors must coax her to come to the hospital. She later tells the doctors that her son has arrests for shoplifting and for driving while intoxicated. She suspects that he takes drugs, although she has no direct evidence. She believes that he is performing fairly well at school and has been a star member of the basketball team.

A CLOSER LOOK

"In Cold Blood:" Peering into the Minds of Psychopathic Murderers

The popular image we hold of the psychopathic murderer is of a "cold-blooded" killer, someone motivated by external goals in carrying out calculating, premeditated murder. But is this image supported by hard evidence?

Canadian researchers compared homicides committed by psychopathic offenders with those committed by nonpsychopathic offenders in a sample of 125 incarcerated murderers (Woodworth & Porter, 2002). They expected that the homicides committed by the psychopathic offenders would fit the profile of a cold-blooded killing, whereas those committed by nonpsychopathic offenders would be "crimes of passion" (impulsive, "hot-headed," angry reactions to provocative situations).

The sample was drawn from two Canadian federal institutions, one in British Columbia and the other in Nova Scotia. The investigators administered a widely used and well-validated measure of psychopathy to classifying offenders as psychopathic. The results supported the hypothesis that psychopathic offenders were more likely to have committed cold-blooded homicides—intentional acts motivated by such goals as obtaining drugs, money, sex or revenge without any emotional triggering situation. More than 90% (93%) of the homicides committed by the psychopathic offenders fit this profile, as compared to 48% of the murders committed by offenders who were not psychopathic.

Interestingly, the image of the "cold-blooded" psychopathic killer does not square with the long-recognized belief that psychopathic personalities often engage in impulsive, acting-out behavior. The investigators suggest that psychopathic offenders may engage in *selective impulsivity* by constraining their impulses to perform such an extreme act as murder. With such high stakes involved (e.g., lifetime incarceration if convicted), the psychopathic offender may adopt a more calculated role when carrying out these acts.

However chilling the results of this study, they help us better understand the psychological aspects of homicide. In that respect, they may help homicide investigators narrow the scope of their investigations by focusing on personality profiles of offenders who are likely to commit particular types of crimes.

TRUTH or FICTION

Recent research findings support the popular image of psychopathic murderers as "cold-blooded" killers.

☑ **TRUE.** Canadian researchers found that psychopathic murderers incarcerated for homicide were more likely than other incarcerated murderers to have committed cold-blooded homicides.

It turns out that her son has been lying to her. In actuality, he never completed high school and never played on the basketball team. A day later, his head cleared, the patient tells his doctors, almost boastfully, that his drug and alcohol use started at the age of 13, and that by the time he was 17, he was regularly using a variety of psychoactive substances, including alcohol, speed, marijuana, and cocaine. Lately, however, he has preferred cocaine. He and his friends frequently participate in drug and alcohol binges. At times they each drink a case of beer in a day along with downing other drugs. He steals car radios from parked cars and money from his mother to support his drug habit, which he justifies by adopting a (partial) "Robin Hood" attitude—that is, taking money only from people who have lots of it.

—Adapted from Spitzer et al., 1994, pp. 81–83

PRENTICE HALL
mypsych lab

BORDERLINE
PERSONALITY DISORDER:

The Case of Liz
"I have problems with anger management."

Although this case is suggestive of antisocial personality disorder, the diagnosis was maintained as provisional because the interviewer could not determine that the deviant behavior (lying, stealing, skipping school) began before the age of 15.

Borderline Personality Disorder Borderline personality disorder (BPD) is characterized by a range of behavioral, emotional, and personality features (Sanislow, Grilo, & McGlashan, 2000). At the core is a pervasive pattern of instability in relationships, self-image, and mood, along with a lack of control over impulses. People with borderline personality disorder tend to be uncertain about their personal identities—their values, goals, careers, and perhaps even their sexual orientations. This instability in self-image or personal identity leaves them with nagging feelings of emptiness and boredom. They cannot tolerate being alone and will make desperate attempts to avoid feelings of abandonment. Fear of abandonment renders them clinging and demanding in their social relationships, but their clinging often pushes away the people on whom they depend. Signs of rejection may enrage them, straining their relationships further. Their feelings toward others are consequently intense and shifting. They alternate between extremes of adulation (when their needs are met) and loathing (when they feel scorned). They tend to

borderline personality disorder (BPD)
A personality disorder characterized by abrupt shifts in mood, lack of a coherent sense of self, and unpredictable, impulsive behavior.

Cutting. People with borderline personalities may engage in impulsive acts of self-mutilation, such as cutting themselves, perhaps as a means of temporarily blocking or escaping from deep, emotional pain.

TRUTH or FICTION

Many notable figures in history, from Lawrence of Arabia to Adolf Hitler and even Marilyn Monroe, showed signs of borderline personality.

☑ **TRUE.** Many notable public figures have shown personality traits associated with borderline personality disorder.

view other people as all good or all bad, shifting abruptly from one extreme to the other. As a result, they may flit from partner to partner in a series of brief and stormy relationships. People they had idealized are treated with contempt when relationships end or when they feel the other person fails to meet their needs (Gunderson, 2001).

BPD is believed to occur in about 2% of the general population (APA, 2000). Although it is diagnosed more often (about 75% of the time) in women, gender differences in prevalence rates for BPD in the general population remain undetermined. Recent evidence indicates higher rates of the disorder among Hispanics than among Caucasians and African Americans (Chavira et al., 2003). The factors accounting for these differences require further investigation. Many notable figures have been described as having personality features associated with borderline personality disorder, including Marilyn Monroe, Lawrence of Arabia, Adolf Hitler, and the philosopher Sören Kierkegaard.

The term *borderline personality* was originally used to refer to individuals whose behavior appeared on the border between neuroses and psychoses. People with borderline personality disorder generally maintain better contact with reality than people with psychoses, although they may show fleeting psychotic behaviors during times of stress. Generally speaking, they are more severely impaired than most people with neuroses but not as dysfunctional as those with psychotic disorders. People with BPD tend to harbor intense psychological pain (Conklin & Westen, 2005) and may exhibit other features such as chronic anger, feelings of loneliness and boredom, a deep sense of emptiness, and impulsivity (Bagge et al., 2004; Zanarini et al., 2003).

People with BPD have difficulty regulating their emotions (Gratz et al., 2006). Unstable and turbulent moods are a central characteristic of the disorder (Fertuck et al., 2006). Their moods may run the gamut from anger and irritability to depression and anxiety (Koenigsberg et al., 2002). Mood shifts tend to be frequent and abrupt. People with BPD often have difficulty controlling anger and are prone to fights or smashing things.

People with borderline personalities may fly into a rage at but the slightest sign of rejection or for little or no reason at all, as this woman recounts about her husband:

"I" Walking on Eggshells

Living with my borderline husband is heaven one minute and hell the next. I call his personalities Jovial Jekyll and Horrible Hyde. I walk on eggshells trying to please someone who blows up just because I spoke too soon, too quickly, in the wrong tone, with the wrong facial motions—whatever!

From the perspective of someone with borderline personality, the rage masks deeper emotional pain and fears:

Jeremy: When I feel I cannot control my surroundings, I become nervous and angry. It gets much worse when I am under stress. Everything negative comes in full blast and overwhelms me. When triggered, I can go from perfectly calm to full-blown, white-hot rage within a fraction of a second. . . .

I think that my temper comes from the abuse I suffered when I was a child. At some point, I decided that I didn't have to take my parents' abuse anymore. Raging back became a matter of survival.

So now, it's hard for me to feel concerned about the other person's feelings—in fact, I want them to hurt because they've hurt me.

Laura: . . . No borderline will admit that the anger is really fear of being hurt. When I'm mad, all the intellectual understanding in the world doesn't help. The only thing that helps is when my husband says to me, "I know you are scared and not angry." At that moment my anger melts away and I can feel my fear again."

Source: Mason & Kreger, 1998, pp. 39–41

Borderline personalities often act on impulse, such as eloping with someone they have just met. This impulsive and unpredictable behavior is often self-destructive, involving behaviors such as self-mutilation and suicidal gestures and actual attempts (Fertuck et al., 2006; Oldham, 2006). Women with BPD tend to show more inwardly directed aggression, such as cutting or self-mutilation. Men with BPD tend to show more outward expressions of aggression (Schmahl & Bremner, 2006). Suicide attempts and nonsuicidal self-injuries may be motivated by the desire to escape from troubling emotions (Brown, Comtois, & Linehan, 2002).

Impulsive behavior in BPD patients may also include spending sprees, gambling, drug abuse, unsafe sexual activity, reckless driving, binge eating, or shoplifting. Among young adults, borderline personality features such as emotional instabilty and impulsivity are associated with poor performance in school and social maladjustment (Bagge et al., 2004). A saving grace perhaps is that impulsivity tends to "burn out" with age, as investigators find that impulsivity decreases among older BPD patients (Stevenson et al., 2003). Impulsive acts of self-mutilation, such as the self-inflicted cutting described at the opening of this chapter, may also involve scratching the wrists or even touching burning cigarettes on the arms. The following dialogue illustrates this type of behavior.

> CLIENT: I've got such repressed anger in me; what happens is . . . I can't *feel* it; I get anxiety attacks. I get very nervous, smoke too many cigarettes. So what happens to me is I tend to *explode*. Into tears or hurting myself or whatever . . . because I don't know how to contend with all those mixed up feelings.
>
> INTERVIEWER: What was the more recent example of such an "explosion"?
>
> CLIENT: I was alone at home a few months ago; I was frightened! I was trying to get in touch with my boyfriend and I couldn't . . . He was nowhere to be found. All my friends seemed to be busy that night and I had no one to talk to. . . . I just got more and more nervous and more and more agitated. Finally, *bang!* . . . I took out a cigarette and lit it and stuck it into my forearm. I don't know why I did it because I didn't really care for him all that much. I guess I felt I had to do something dramatic. . . .
>
> —*Adapted from Stone, 1980, p. 400*

Self-mutilation is sometimes an expression of anger or a means of manipulating others. Such acts may be intended to counteract self-reported feelings of "numbness," particularly in times of stress. Individuals with BPD often have very troubled relationships with their families and others (Johnson et al., 2006; Liotti et al., 2000). They often had troubling childhood experiences, such as parental losses or separations, harsh punishment or abuse, parental neglect or lack of nurturing, or witnessing violence. They tend to view their relationships as rife with hostility and to perceive others as rejecting and abandoning. They also tend to be difficult to work with in psychotherapy, demanding a great deal of support from therapists, calling them at all hours or acting suicidally to elicit support, or dropping out of therapy prematurely. Their feelings toward therapists, as toward other people, undergo rapid alterations between idealization and outrage. Psychoanalysts interpret these abrupt shifts in feelings as signs of **splitting,** or inability to reconcile the positive and negative aspects of one's experience of oneself and others.

Histrionic Personality Disorder

Histrionic personality disorder is characterized by excessive emotionality and an overwhelming need to be the center of attention. The term is derived from the Latin *histrio,* which means "actor." People with histrionic personality disorder tend to be dramatic and emotional, but their emotions seem shallow, exaggerated, and volatile. The disorder was formerly called *hysterical personality.* The following case example illustrates the excessively dramatic behaviors typical of someone with histrionic personality disorder.

splitting An inability to reconcile the positive and negative aspects of the self and others, resulting in sudden shifts between positive and negative feelings.

histrionic personality disorder A personality disorder characterized by excessive need for attention, praise, reassurance, and approval.

Over the top? Not all people who dress outrageously or flamboyantly have histrionic personalities. What other personality features characterize people with histrionic personality disorder?

A Case of Histrionic Personality Disorder

Marcella was a 36-year-old, attractive, but overly made up woman who was dressed in tight pants and high heels. Her hair was in a bird's nest of the type that had been popular when she was a teenager. Her social life seemed to bounce from relationship to relationship, from crisis to crisis. Marcella sought help from the psychologist at this time because her 17-year-old daughter, Nancy, had just been hospitalized for cutting her wrists. Nancy lived with Marcella and Marcella's current boyfriend, Morris, and there were constant arguments in the apartment. Marcella recounted the disputes that took place with high drama, waving her hands, clanging the bangles that hung from her bracelets, and then clutching her breast. It was difficult having Nancy live at home because Nancy had expensive tastes, was "always looking for attention," and flirted with Morris as a way of "flaunting her youth." Marcella saw herself as a doting mother and denied any possibility that she was in competition with her daughter.

Marcella came for a handful of sessions, during which she basically ventilated her feelings and was encouraged to make decisions that might lead to a reduction of some of the pressures on herself and her daughter. At the end of each session she said, "I feel so much better" and thanked the psychologist profusely. At termination of "therapy," she took the psychologist's hand and squeezed it endearingly. "Thank you so much, Doctor," she said and made her exit.

—From the Author's Files

The supplanting of *hysterical* with *histrionic* and the associated exchange of the roots *hystera* (meaning "uterus") and *histrio* allow professionals to distance themselves from the notion that the disorder is intricately bound up with being female. The disorder is diagnosed more frequently in women than men (Hartung & Widiger, 1998), although some studies using structured interview methods find similar rates of occurrence among men and women (APA, 2000). Whether the gender discrepancy in clinical practice reflects true differences in the underlying rates of the disorder, diagnostic biases, or unseen factors remains an open question.

People with histrionic personalities may become unusually upset by news of a sad event and exude exaggerated delight at a pleasant occurrence. They may faint at the sight of blood or blush at a slight faux pas. They tend to demand that others meet their needs for attention and play the victim when others fall short. They also tend to be self-centered and intolerant of delays of gratification: They want what they want when they want it. They grow quickly restless with routine and crave novelty and stimulation. They are drawn to fads. Others may see them as putting on airs or playacting, although they may evince a certain charm. They tend to be flirtatious and seductive but are too wrapped up in themselves to develop intimate relationships or have deep feelings toward others. As a result, their associations tend to be stormy and ultimately ungratifying. They tend to use their physical appearance as a means of drawing attention to themselves. Men with the disorder may act and dress in an overly "macho" way, and women may choose very frilly, feminine clothing. Glitter supercedes substance.

People with histrionic personalities may be attracted to professions like modeling or acting, where they can hog the spotlight. Despite outward successes, they lack self-esteem and strive to impress others to boost their self-worth. If they suffer setbacks or lose their place in the limelight, depressing inner doubts may emerge.

Narcissistic Personality Disorder *Narkissos* was a handsome youth who, according to Greek myth, fell in love with his reflection in a spring. Because of his excessive self-love, the gods transformed him into the flower we know as the narcissus.

A narcissistic personality? People with narcissistic personalities are often preoccupied with fantasies of success and power, ideal love, or recognition for their brilliance or beauty. They may pursue careers that provide opportunities for public recognition and adulation, such as acting, modeling, or politics. They may become deeply wounded by any hint that they are not as special as they believe themselves to be.

TABLE 13.3

Features of Normal Self-Interest Compared with Self-Defeating Narcissism

Normal Self-Interest	Self-Defeating Narcissism
Appreciating acclaim, but not requiring it in order to maintain self-esteem.	Craving adoration insatiably; requiring acclaim in order to feel momentarily good about oneself
Being temporarily wounded by criticism.	Being inflamed or crushed by criticism and brooding about it extensively
Feeling unhappy but not worthless following failure.	Having enduring feelings of mortification and worthlessness triggered by failure
Feeling "special" or uncommonly talented in some way.	Feeling incomparably better than other people, and insisting upon acknowledgment of that preeminence
Feeling good about oneself, even when other people are being critical.	Needing constant support from other people in order to maintain one's feelings of well-being
Being reasonably accepting of life's setbacks, even though they can be painful and temporarily destabilizing.	Responding to life's wounds with depression or fury
Maintaining self-esteem in the face of disapproval or denigration.	Responding to disapproval or denigration with loss of self-esteem
Maintaining emotional equilibrium despite lack of special treatment.	Feeling entitled to special treatment and becoming terribly upset when one is treated in an ordinary manner
Being empathic and caring about the feelings of others.	Being insensitive to other people's needs and feelings; exploiting others until they become fed up

Source: Based on Goleman, 1988, p. C1.

Persons with **narcissistic personality disorder** have an inflated or grandiose sense of themselves and an extreme need for admiration. They brag about their accomplishments and expect others to shower them with praise. They expect others to notice their special qualities, even when their accomplishments are ordinary, and they enjoy basking in the light of adulation. They are self-absorbed and lack empathy for others. Although they share certain features with histrionic personalities, such as demanding to be the center of attention, they have a much more inflated view of themselves and are less melodramatic than people with histrionic personality disorder. As compared to people with borderline personality disorder (BPD), those with narcissistic personality disorder are generally better able to organize their thoughts and actions. They tend to be more successful in their careers and are better able to rise to positions of status and power. Their relationships also tend to be more stable than those of people with BPD.

Narcissistic personality disorder is found among less than 1% of the general population (APA, 2000). Although more than half of the people diagnosed with the disorder are men, we cannot say whether there is an underlying gender difference in prevalence rates in the general population. A certain degree of narcissism may represent a healthful adjustment to insecurity, a shield from criticism and failure, or a motive for achievement. Excessive narcissistic qualities can become unhealthful, especially when the cravings for adulation are insatiable. Table 13.3 compares "normal" self-interest with self-defeating extremes of narcissism. Up to a point, self-interest fosters success and happiness. In more extreme cases, as with narcissism, it can compromise relationships and careers.

People with narcissistic personalities tend to be preoccupied with fantasies of success and power, ideal love, or recognition for brilliance or beauty. Like people with histrionic personalities, they may gravitate toward careers in modeling, acting, or politics. Although they tend to exaggerate their accomplishments and abilities, many people with narcissistic personalities are quite successful in their occupations. But they envy those who achieve even greater success. Insatiable ambition may prompt them to

narcissistic personality disorder
A personality disorder characterized by adoption of an inflated self-image and demands for attention and admiration.

devote themselves tirelessly to work. They are driven to succeed, not so much for money as for the adulation that attends success.

People with narcissistic personalities are extremely sensitive to the slightest hint of rejection or criticism. These *narcissistic injuries,* as they are called, hurt so deeply because they reopen very old psychological wounds. Even a seemingly trivial comment can throw the person into a tailspin, as in the following example of a woman, Stephanie, whose husband's criticism exposed old wounds of inadequacy. Moreover, instead of making the pain go away, his mild rebuke added insult to injury:

"I" Rubbing Salt into a Wound

"Watch the ball," she told herself [during a game of tennis], "get sideways, hit through, finish up" . . . For a few precious moments, she was in that "zone" that athletes cherish when everything comes together and there are no mistakes.

She was smiling secretly, enjoying an illicit high, wondering if her husband, Doug, had also noticed how well she was hitting today, when a heavily underspun return angled into her backhand. She lunged, stabbed, and caught the ball on her racquet rim, sending it flying out of the court. "You never read that spin," Doug scolded from the far court." Never," Stephanie echoed, suddenly feeling as though she had just blown an internal tire. Pain washed over her and settled in the middle of her chest. . . . "I'll never be any good at this game," she thought miserably, smashing the next three balls into the net. The elation of only moments before had evaporated, replaced by a hopeless feeling of ineptitude. Stephanie swallowed the tears rising in her throat and gave herself a mental kick in the backside. "You're such a baby," she muttered to herself as she prepared to pack up and go home. "You wimping out on me again?" Doug called out. He was only teasing, trying to goad her back into the drill, but his words were like salt on a fresh abrasion. There would be no more tennis this day.

Source: Hotchkiss, 2002

Interpersonal relationships are invariably strained by the demands that people with narcissistic personality impose on others and by their lack of empathy with, and concern for, other people. They seek the company of flatterers and, although they are often superficially charming and friendly, their interest in people is one-sided: They seek people who will serve their interests and nourish their sense of self-importance. They have feelings of entitlement that lead them to exploit others. They tend to adopt a game-playing style in romantic relationships rather than seek true intimacy, apparently because of their needs for power and autonomy (Campbell, Foster, & Finkel, 2002). They treat sex partners as devices for their own pleasure or to brace their self-esteem, as in the case of Bill.

A Case of Narcissistic Personality Disorder

Most people agreed that Bill, a 35-year-old investment banker, had a certain charm. He was bright, articulate, and attractive. He possessed a keen sense of humor that drew people to him at social gatherings. He would always position himself in the middle of the room, where he could be the center of attention. The topics of conversation invariably focused on his "deals," the "rich and famous" people he had met, and his outmaneuvering of opponents. His next project was always bigger and more daring than the last. Bill loved an audience. His face would light up when others responded to him with praise or admiration for his business successes, which were always inflated beyond their true measure. But when the conversation shifted to other people, he would lose interest and excuse himself to make a drink or to call his answering machine. When hosting a party, he would urge guests to stay late and feel hurt if they had to leave early; he showed no sensitivity to, or awareness of, the needs of his friends.

The few friends he had maintained over the years had come to accept Bill on his own terms. They recognized that he needed to have his ego fed or that he would become cool and detached.

Bill had also had a series of romantic relationships with women who were willing to play the adoring admirer and make the sacrifices that he demanded—for a time. But they inevitably tired of the one-sided relationship or grew frustrated by Bill's inability to make a commitment or feel deeply toward them. Lacking empathy, Bill was unable to recognize other people's feelings and needs. His demands for constant attention from willing admirers did not derive from selfishness, but from a need to ward off underlying feelings of inadequacy and diminished self-esteem. It was sad, his friends thought, that Bill needed so much attention and adulation from others and that his many achievements were never enough to calm his inner doubts.

—From the Author's Files

Personality Disorders Characterized by Anxious or Fearful Behavior

This cluster of personality disorders includes the avoidant, dependent, and obsessive–compulsive types. Although the features of these disorders differ, they share a component of fear or anxiety.

Avoidant Personality Disorder   Persons with **avoidant personality disorder** are so terrified of rejection and criticism that they are generally unwilling to enter relationships without ardent reassurances of acceptance. As a result, they may have few close relationships outside their immediate families. They also tend to avoid group occupational or recreational activities for fear of rejection. They prefer to lunch alone at their desks. They shun company picnics and parties, unless they are perfectly sure of acceptance. Avoidant personality disorder, which appears to be equally common in men and women, is believed to affect between 0.5% and 1.0% of the general population (APA, 2000).

Unlike people with schizoid qualities, with whom they share the feature of social withdrawal, individuals with avoidant personalities have interest in, and feelings of warmth toward, other people. However, fear of rejection prevents them from striving to meet their needs for affection and acceptance. In social situations, they tend to hug the walls and avoid conversing with others. They fear public embarrassment, the thought that others might see them blush, cry, or act nervously. They tend to stick to their routines and exaggerate the risks or effort involved in trying new things. They may refuse to attend a party that is an hour away on the pretext that the late drive home would be too taxing. Consider the following case example.

avoidant personality disorder A personality disorder characterized by avoidance of social relationships due to fears of rejection.

◆

A Case of Avoidant Personality Disorder

Harold, a 24-year-old accounting clerk, had dated but a few women, and he had met them through family introductions. He never felt confident enough to approach a woman on his own. Perhaps it was his shyness that first attracted Stacy, a 22-year-old secretary who worked alongside Harold and asked him if he would like to get together sometime after work. At first Harold declined, claiming some excuse, but when Stacy asked again a week later, Harold agreed, thinking she must really like him if she were willing to pursue him. The relationship developed quickly, and soon they were dating virtually every night. The relationship was strained, however. Harold interpreted any slight hesitation in her voice as a lack of interest. He repeatedly requested reassurance that she cared about him, and he evaluated every word and gesture for evidence of her feelings. If Stacy said that she could not see him because of fatigue or illness, he assumed she was rejecting him and sought further reassurance. After several months, Stacy decided she could no longer accept Harold's nagging, and the relationship ended. Harold assumed that Stacy had never truly cared for him.

—From the Author's Files

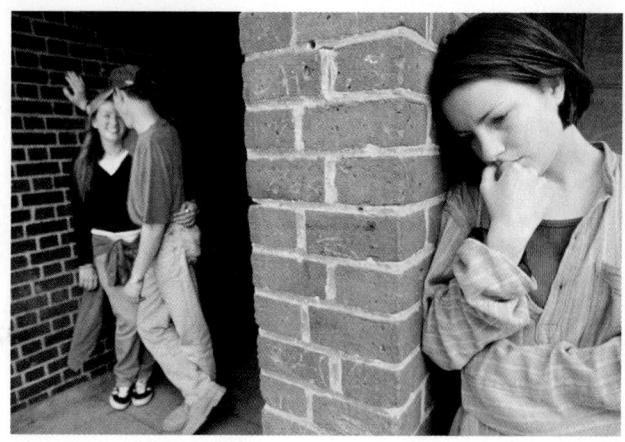

An avoidant personality? People with avoidant personalities often keep to themselves because of fear of rejection.

dependent personality disorder A personality disorder characterized by difficulty making independent decisions and overly dependent behavior.

![TRUTH or FICTION]

People with dependent personality disorder have so much difficulty making independent decisions that they may allow their parents to decide whom they will marry.

☑ **TRUE.** People with dependent personality disorder in our culture may be so dependent on others for making decisions that they allow their parents to determine whom they will marry.

There is a good deal of overlap between avoidant personality disorder and social phobia, particularly a severe subtype of social phobia involving a generalized pattern of social phobia (excessive, irrational fear of most social situations). Although many cases of generalized social phobia occur in the absence of avoidant personality disorder, relatively fewer cases of avoidant personality occur in the absence of generalized social phobia (Widiger, 1992). Thus avoidant personality disorder may represent a more severe form of social phobia. Still, the scientific jury is out on the question of whether avoidant personality disorder should be considered a severe form of generalized social phobia or a distinct diagnostic category.

Dependent Personality Disorder Dependent personality disorder describes people who have an excessive need to be taken care of by others. This leads them to be overly submissive and clinging in their relationships and extremely fearful of separation. People with this disorder find it very difficult to do things on their own. They seek advice in making even the smallest decision. Children or adolescents with the problem may look to their parents to select their clothes, diets, schools or colleges, even their friends. Adults with the disorder allow others to make important decisions for them. Sometimes they are so dependent on others that they allow their parents to determine whom they will marry, as in the case of Matthew.

◆

A Case of Dependent Personality Disorder

Matthew, a 34-year-old single accountant who lives with his mother, sought treatment when his relationship with his girlfriend came to an end. His mother had objected to marriage because his girlfriend was of a different religion, and—because "blood is thicker than water"—Matthew acceded to his mother's wishes and ended the relationship. Yet he is angry with himself and at his mother because he feels that she is too possessive to ever grant him permission to get married. He describes his mother as a domineering woman who "wears the pants" in the family and is accustomed to having things her way. Matthew alternates between resenting his mother and thinking that perhaps she knows what's best for him.

Matthew's position at work is several levels below what would be expected of someone of his talent and educational level. Several times he has declined promotions in order to avoid increased responsibilities that would require him to supervise others and make independent decisions. He has maintained close relationships with two friends since early childhood and has lunch with one of them on every working day. On days his friend calls in sick, Matthew feels lost. Matthew has lived his whole life at home, except for one year away at college. He returned home because of homesickness.

—Adapted from Spitzer et al., 1994, pp. 179–180

After marriage, people with dependent personality disorder may rely on their spouses to make decisions such as where they should live, which neighbors they should cultivate, how they should discipline the children, what jobs they should take, how they should budget money, and where they should vacation. Like Matthew, individuals with dependent personality disorder avoid positions of responsibility. They turn down challenges and promotions and work beneath their potential. They tend to be overly sensitive to criticism and preoccupied with fears of rejection and abandonment. They may be devastated by the end of a close relationship or by the prospect of living on their own. Because of fear of rejection, they often subordinate their wants and needs to those of others. They may agree with outlandish statements about themselves and do degrading things to please others.

Before going further, we should note that dependence needs to be examined through the lens of culture. Arranged marriages are the norm in some traditional cultures, so people from those cultures who let their parents decide whom they will marry would not be classified as having dependent personality disorder. Similarly, in strongly patriarchal cultures, women may be expected to defer to their fathers and husbands in making many life decisions, even small everyday decisions.

But we needn't look beyond our own society to consider the role of culture. Evidence shows that dependent personality disorder in our culture is diagnosed more frequently in women than in men (APA, 2000; Bornstein, 1997). The diagnosis is often applied to women who, for fear of abandonment, tolerate husbands who openly cheat on them, abuse them, or gamble away the family's resources. Underlying feelings of inadequacy and helplessness discourage them from taking effective action. In a vicious cycle, their passivity encourages further abuse, leading them to feel yet more inadequate and helpless. Applying the diagnosis to women with this pattern is controversial and may be seen as unfairly "blaming the victim," because women in our society are often socialized to dependent roles. Women typically encounter greater stress than men in contemporary life as well as greater social pressures to be passive, demure, or deferential. Therefore, dependent behaviors in women may reflect cultural influences rather than an underlying personality disorder.

Dependent personality disorder has been linked to other psychological disorders, including major depression, bipolar disorder, and social phobia, and to physical problems, such as hypertension, cancer, and gastrointestinal disorders like ulcers and colitis (Bornstein, 1999b; Loranger, 1996; Reich, 1996). There also appears to be a link between dependent personality and what psychodynamic theorists refer to as "oral" behavior problems, such as smoking, eating disorders, and alcoholism (Bornstein, 1999b). Psychodynamic writers trace dependent behaviors to the utter dependence of the newborn baby and the baby's seeking of nourishment through oral means (suckling). Food may come to symbolize love, and persons with dependent personalities may overeat to ingest love symbolically. People with dependent personalities often attribute their problems to physical rather than emotional causes and seek support and advice from medical experts rather than psychologists or counselors (Greenberg & Bornstein, 1988a, 1988b).

Obsessive–Compulsive Personality Disorder The defining features of **obsessive–compulsive personality disorder** include excessive orderliness, perfectionism, rigidity, difficulty coping with ambiguity, difficulty expressing feelings, and meticulousness in work habits. About 1% of people in community samples are diagnosed with the disorder (APA, 2000). The disorder is about twice as common in men than women. Unlike obsessive–compulsive anxiety disorder, people with obsessive–compulsive personality disorder do not necessarily experience outright obsessions or compulsions. If they do, both diagnoses may be deemed appropriate.

Persons with obsessive–compulsive personality disorder are so preoccupied with the need for perfection that they cannot complete work on time. Their efforts inevitably fall short of their expectations, so they redo their work. Or they ruminate about how to prioritize their work and never seem to start working. They focus on details that others perceive as trivial. As the saying goes, they fail to see the forest for the trees. Their rigidity impairs their social relationships; they insist on doing things their way rather than compromising. Their zeal for work keeps them from participating in, or enjoying, social and leisure activities. They tend to be stingy with money. They find it difficult to make decisions and postpone or avoid them for fear of making the wrong choice. They tend to be inflexible and overly rigid in issues of morality and ethics, to be overly formal in relationships, and to find it difficult to express feelings. It is hard for them to relax and enjoy pleasant activities; they worry about the costs of such diversions. Consider the following case example.

obsessive–compulsive personality disorder A personality disorder characterized by rigid ways of relating to others, perfectionistic tendencies, lack of spontaneity, and excessive attention to detail.

A Case of Obsessive–Compulsive Personality Disorder

Jerry, a 34-year-old systems analyst, was perfectionistic, overly concerned with details, and rigid in his behavior. Jerry was married to Marcia, a graphics artist. He insisted on scheduling their free time hour by hour and became unnerved when they deviated from his agenda. He would circle a parking lot repeatedly in search of just the right parking spot to ensure that another car would not scrape his car. He refused to have the apartment painted for over a year because he couldn't decide on the color. He had arranged all the books in their bookshelf alphabetically and insisted that every book be placed in its proper position.

Jerry never seemed to relax. Even on vacation, he was bothered by thoughts of work that he had left behind and by fears that he might lose his job. He couldn't understand how people could lie on the beach and let all their worries evaporate in the summer air. Something can always go wrong, he figured, so how can people let themselves go?

—From the Author's Files

Problems with the Classification of Personality Disorders

Questions remain about the reliability and validity of the diagnostic categories for personality disorders in the *DSM* system. Here we focus on major concerns that clinicians and researchers have raised about how these patterns of behavior are diagnosed or classified.

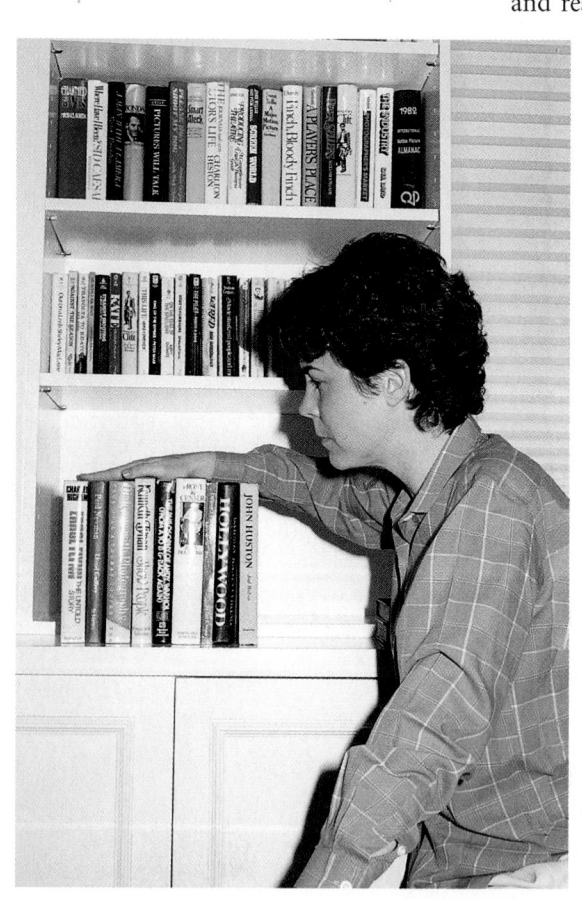

"A place for everything, and everything in its place"? People with obsessive-compulsive personalities may have invented this maxim. Many such people have excessive needs for orderliness in their environment, as suggested in this Laurie Simmons photograph, Red Library #2.

Problems Distinguishing Personality Disorders from Anxiety and Mood Disorders Some reviewers question whether personality disorders can be reliably differentiated from Axis I clinical syndromes such as anxiety or mood disorders (Farmer, 2000). For example, clinicians often have difficulty distinguishing between obsessive–compulsive disorder and obsessive–compulsive personality disorder. Clinical syndromes are believed to be variable over time, whereas personality disorders are held to be generally more enduring patterns of disturbance. Yet features of personality disorders may vary over time with changes in circumstances. On the other hand, some Axis I clinical syndromes (dysthymia, for example) follow a more or less chronic course.

Overlap Among Disorders A high degree of overlap exists among the personality disorders. Although some personality disorders have distinct features, many share common traits, such as problems in romantic relationships (Daley, Burge, & Hammen, 2000). For example, the same person may have traits suggestive of dependent personality disorder (inability to make decisions or initiate activities independently) as well as avoidant personality disorder (extreme social anxiety and heightened sensitivity to criticism).

Co-occurrence (called *comorbidity*) of different personality disorders is also quite common (Grant et al., 2005b). This suggests that the specific types of personality disorders in the *DSM* system may not be sufficiently distinct from one another (Westen & Schedler, 1999). Some personality disorders may not actually be distinct disorders, but rather subtypes or variations of other personality disorders.

Difficulty in Distinguishing Between Normal and Abnormal Behavior Another problem with the diagnosis of personality disorders is that they involve personality traits which, in lesser degrees, describe the behavior of most normal individuals (Warner et al., 2004). Feeling suspicious now and then does not mean you have a paranoid personality disorder. The tendency to exaggerate your own importance does not mean you are narcissistic. You may avoid social interactions for fear of embarrassment or rejection without having an avoidant personality disorder, and you may be especially conscientious in your work without having an obsessive–compulsive personality disorder. Because the defining attributes of these disorders are common personality traits, clinicians should only apply these diagnostic labels when the patterns are so pervasive that they interfere with the individual's functioning or cause significant personal distress. Yet it can be difficult to draw the line between normal behavior and personality disorders. We still lack the evidence we need to determine the particular points at which personality traits become maladaptive to justify a diagnosis of a personality disorder.

Confusing Labels with Explanations It may seem obvious that we should not confuse diagnostic labels with explanations, but in practice the distinction is sometimes clouded. If we confuse labeling with explanation, we may fall into the trap of circular reasoning. What is wrong, for example, with the logic of the following statements?

1. John's behavior is antisocial.
2. Therefore, John has an antisocial personality disorder.
3. John's behavior is antisocial because he has an antisocial personality disorder.

The statements demonstrate circular reasoning because they (a) use behavior to make a diagnosis, and then (b) use the diagnosis as an explanation for the behavior. We may be guilty of circular reasoning in our everyday speech. Consider the following statements: "John never gets his work in on time; therefore, he is lazy. John doesn't get his work in because he's lazy." The label may be acceptable in everyday conversation, but it lacks scientific rigor. For a construct such as *laziness* to have scientific rigor, we need to understand the causes of laziness and the factors that help maintain it. We should not confuse the label we attach to behavior with the cause of the behavior.

Moreover, labeling people with disturbing behavior as having personality disorders overlooks the social and environmental contexts of the behavior. The impact of traumatic life events, which may occur with a greater range or intensity among members of particular gender or cultural groups, is an important underlying factor in maladaptive behavior. However, the conceptual underpinnings of the personality disorders do not consider cultural differences, social inequalities, or power differences between genders or cultural groups. For example, many women diagnosed with personality disorders have a history of childhood physical and sexual abuse. The ways in which people cope with abuse may come to be viewed as flaws in their character rather than as reflections of the dysfunctional societal factors that underlie abusive relationships.

Personality disorders are convenient labels for identifying common patterns of ineffective and self-defeating behavior, but labels do not explain the behaviors they name. Still, the development of an accurate descriptive system is an important step toward scientific explanation. The establishment of reliable diagnostic categories sets the stage for valid research into causation and treatment.

Sexist Biases The construction of certain personality disorders may have sexist underpinnings. The diagnostic criteria seem to label stereotypical feminine behaviors as pathological with greater frequency than stereotypical masculine behaviors. Take the example of histrionic personality, which seems a caricature of the traditional stereotype of the feminine personality: flighty, emotional, shallow, seductive, attention-seeking.

But if the feminine stereotype corresponds to a diagnosable mental disorder, shouldn't we also have a diagnostic category that reflects the masculine stereotype of the "macho male"? We might argue that overly masculinized traits can be associated with significant distress or impairment in social or occupational functioning in certain males. For example, highly masculinized males may get into fights and experience difficulties working for female bosses. Yet there is presently no personality disorder corresponding to the "macho male" stereotype.

Are there sexist biases in the conception of personality disorders? The concept of the histrionic personality disorder seems to be a caricature of the highly stereotyped feminine personality. Why, then, is there not also something akin to a macho male personality disorder, which caricatures the highly stereotyped masculine personality?

Does the diagnosis of dependent personality disorder unfairly stigmatize women who have been socialized into dependent roles by attaching to them a label of a personality disorder? Women may be at greater risk of receiving diagnoses of histrionic or dependent personality disorders simply because clinicians perceive these patterns as common among women or because women are more likely than men to be socialized into these behavior patterns.

Are some personality disorders more likely to be diagnosed in men or in women because of societal expectations rather than underlying pathology? Clinicians tend to show a bias in favor of perceiving women as having histrionic personality disorder and men as having antisocial personality disorder, even when they demonstrate the same symptoms (Garb, 1997). Additional evidence of gender bias is found in a study that examined diagnoses of borderline personality disorder. Researchers presented a hypothetical case example to 311 psychologists, social workers, and psychiatrists (Becker & Lamb, 1994). Half of the sample was presented with a case identified as a female; the other half read the identical case, except that it was identified as male. Clinicians more often diagnosed the case identified as female as having borderline personality disorder.

Is the *DSM* classification of personality disorders gender biased or gender free? Should it be more evenly balanced in its characterizations of disordered personality? What do you think? Consider your own attitudes: Have you ever assumed that women are "just dependent or hysterical" or that men are "just narcissists or antisocial"?

THEORETICAL PERSPECTIVES

In this section we consider theoretical perspectives on the personality disorders. Many theoretical accounts of disturbed personality derive from the psychodynamic model. We thus begin with a review of traditional and modern psychodynamic models.

Psychodynamic Perspectives

Traditional Freudian theory focused on problems arising from the Oedipus complex as the foundation for abnormal behaviors, including personality disorders. Freud believed that children normally resolve the Oedipus complex by forsaking incestuous wishes for the parent of the opposite gender and identifying with the parent of the same gender. As a result, they incorporate the parent's moral principles in the form of a personality structure called the *superego*. Many factors may interfere with appropriate identification and sidetrack the normal developmental process, preventing children from developing moral constraints and the feelings of guilt or remorse that normally follow antisocial behavior. Freud's account of moral development focused mainly on the development of males. He has been criticized for failing to account for the moral development of females.

More recent psychodynamic theories have generally focused on the earlier, pre-Oedipal period of about 18 months to 3 years, during which infants begin to develop identities separate from those of their parents. These theories focus on the development of the sense of self in explaining such disorders as narcissistic and borderline personality disorders.

Hans Kohut One of the principal shapers of modern psychodynamic concepts is Hans Kohut, whose theory is labeled *self psychology* because of its emphasis on processes in the development of a cohesive sense of self. Freud believed that the resolution of the Oedipus complex was central to the development of adult personality. Kohut disagreed, arguing that what matters most is how the self develops—whether the person is able to develop self-esteem, values, and a cohesive and realistic sense of self as opposed to an inflated, narcissistic personality (Anderson, 2003; Goldberg, 2003).

Kohut (1966) believed that people with narcissistic personalities mount a facade of self-importance to cover up deep feelings of inadequacy. The narcissist's self-esteem is like a reservoir that needs to be constantly replenished with a steady stream of praise and attention lest it run dry. A sense of grandiosity helps people with a narcissistic personality mask their underlying feelings of worthlessness. Failures or disappointments threaten to expose these feelings and drive the person into a state of depression, so as a defense against despair, the person attempts to diminish the importance of disappointments or failures.

People with narcissistic personalities may become enraged by others whom they perceive have failed to protect them from disappointment or have declined to shower them with reassurance, praise, and admiration. They may become infuriated by even the slightest criticism, no matter how well intentioned. They may mask feelings of rage and humiliation by adopting a facade of cool indifference. They can make difficult psychotherapy clients because they may become enraged when therapists puncture their inflated self-images to help them develop more realistic self-concepts.

To Kohut, early childhood involves a normal stage of *healthy narcissism*. Infants feel powerful, as though the world revolves around them. Infants also normally perceive their parents as idealized towers of strength and wish to be one with them and to share their power (Edmundson, 2001; Strozier, 2001). Empathic parents reflect their children's inflated perceptions by making them feel that anything is possible and by nourishing their self-esteem (e.g., telling them how terrific and precious they are). Even empathic parents are critical from time to time, however, and puncture their children's grandiose sense of self. Or they fail to measure up to their children's idealized views of them. Gradually, unrealistic expectations dissolve and are replaced by more realistic appraisals of oneself and others. In adolescence, childhood idealization is transformed into realistic admiration for parents, teachers, and friends. In adulthood, these ideas develop into a set of internal ideals, values, and goals.

Lack of parental empathy and support, however, sets the stage for *pathological narcissism*. Children who are not prized by their parents fail to develop a sturdy sense of self-esteem. They develop damaged self-concepts and feel incapable of being loved and admired. Pathological narcissism involves the construction of a grandiose facade of self-perfection that cloaks perceived inadequacies. The facade always remains on the brink of crumbling, however, and must be shored up by a constant flow of reassurance that one is special and unique. This leaves the person vulnerable to painful blows to self-esteem following failure to achieve social or occupational goals.

Kohut's approach to therapy provides clients who have a narcissistic personality with an initial opportunity to express their grandiose self-images and to idealize the therapist. Over time, however, the therapist helps them explore the childhood roots of their narcissism and gently points out imperfections in both client and therapist to encourage clients to form more realistic images of the self and others.

Otto Kernberg Otto Kernberg (1975), a leading psychodynamic theorist, views borderline personality in terms of a failure in early childhood to develop a sense of constancy and unity in one's image of oneself and others. From this perspective, borderline individuals cannot synthesize contradictory (positive and negative) elements of themselves and others into complete, stable wholes. Rather than viewing important people in their lives as sometimes loving and sometimes rejecting, they shift back and forth between pure idealization and utter hatred. This rapid shifting back and forth between viewing others as either "all good" or "all bad" is referred to as *splitting*.

Kernberg tells of a woman in her 30s whose attitude toward him vacillated in such a way. The woman would respond to him in one session as the most wonderful therapist and feel that all her problems were solved. But several sessions later she would turn against him and accuse him of being unfeeling and manipulative, become dissatisfied with treatment, and threaten to drop out (cited in Sass, 1982).

In Kernberg's view, parents, even excellent parents, invariably fail to meet all their children's needs. Infants therefore face the early developmental challenge of reconciling images of the nurturing, comforting "good mother" with those of the withholding, frustrating "bad mother." Failure to reconcile these opposing images into a realistic, unified, and stable parental image may have the effect of psychologically fixating the child in the pre-Oedipal period of psychosexual development. Consequently, as adults, they may continue to have rapidly shifting attitudes toward therapists and others, idealizing them one moment and rejecting them the next.

Separation-individuation. According to the influential psychodynamic theorist Margaret Mahler, young children undergo a process of separation-individuation by which they learn to differentiate their own identities from their mothers. She believed that a failure to successfully master this developmental challenge may lead to the development of a borderline personality.

Margaret Mahler Margaret Mahler, another influential modern psychodynamic theorist, explained borderline personality disorder in terms of childhood separation from the mother figure. Mahler and her colleagues (Mahler & Kaplan, 1977; Mahler, Pine, & Bergman, 1975) believed that during the first year infants develop a symbiotic attachment to their mothers. *Symbiosis,* or interdependence, is a biological term derived from Greek roots meaning "to live together." In psychology, symbiosis is a state of oneness in which the child's identity is fused with the mother's. Normally, children gradually differentiate their own identities or senses of self from their mothers. The process, *separation-individuation,* is the development of a separate psychological and biological identity from the mother (separation) and recognition of personal characteristics that define one's self-identity (individuation). Separation-individuation may be a stormy process. Children may vacillate between seeking greater independence and moving closer to, or "shadowing," the mother, which is seen as a wish for reunion. The mother may disrupt normal separation-individuation by refusing to let go of the child or by too quickly pushing the child toward independence. The tendencies of people with borderline personalities to react to others with ambivalence and to alternate between love and hate is suggestive of earlier ambivalences during the separation-individuation process. Borderline personality disorder may arise from the failure to master this developmental challenge.

Psychodynamic theory provides ways of understanding the development of several types of personality disorders. But a limitation of the theory is that it is based largely on inferences drawn from behavior and retrospective accounts of adults rather than on observations of children. We may also question whether it is valid to compare normal childhood experiences with abnormal behaviors in adulthood. For example, the ambivalences that characterize the adult borderline personality may bear only a superficial relationship, if any, to children's vacillations between closeness and separation during separation-individuation.

Links between abuse in childhood and later development of personality disorders suggest that failure to form close-bonding relationships with parental caretakers in childhood plays a critical role in the development of personality disorders. We will explore the links between abuse and personality disorders later in this chapter.

Learning Perspectives

Learning theorists focus on maladaptive behaviors rather than disorders of personality. They are interested in identifying the learning histories and environmental factors that give rise to maladaptive behaviors associated with diagnoses of personality disorders and the reinforcers that maintain them.

Learning theorists suggest that childhood experiences shape the pattern of maladaptive habits of relating to others that constitute personality disorders. For example, children who are regularly discouraged from speaking their minds or exploring their environments may develop a dependent behavior pattern. Excessive parental discipline may lead to obsessive–compulsive behaviors. Psychologist Theodore Millon (1981) suggests that children whose behavior is rigidly controlled and punished by parents, even for slight transgressions, may develop inflexible, perfectionistic standards. As these children mature, they strive to develop themselves in an area in which they excel, such as schoolwork or athletics, as a way of avoiding parental criticism or punishment. But because of overattention to a single area of development, they do not become well rounded. Thus they squelch expressions of spontaneity and avoid risks. They may also place perfectionistic demands on themselves to avoid punishment or rebuke, or develop other behaviors associated with the obsessive–compulsive personality pattern.

Millon suggests that histrionic personality disorder may be rooted in childhood experiences in which social reinforcers, such as parental attention, are connected to the child's appearance and willingness to perform for others, especially when reinforcers are dispensed inconsistently. Inconsistent attention teaches children not to take approval for granted and to strive for it continually. People with histrionic personalities may also identify with parents who are dramatic, emotional, and attention-seeking.

Extreme sibling rivalry would further heighten motivation to perform for attention from others.

Social-cognitive theories emphasize the role of reinforcement in explaining the origins of antisocial behaviors. In an early influential work, Ullmann and Krasner (1975) proposed that people with antisocial personalities failed to learn to respond to other people as potential reinforcers. Most children learn to treat others as reinforcing agents because others reinforce them with praise for good behavior and punishment for bad. Reinforcement and punishment provide feedback that helps children modify their behavior to maximize the chances of future rewards and minimize the risks of future punishments. As a consequence, children become sensitive to the demands of powerful others, usually parents and teachers, and learn to regulate their behavior accordingly. They thus adapt to social expectations. They learn what to do and what to say, how to dress and how to act to obtain praise and approval (social reinforcement) from others.

People with antisocial personalities, by contrast, may not have become socialized in this way because their early learning experiences lacked consistency and predictability. Perhaps they were sometimes rewarded for doing the "right thing," but just as often not. They may have borne the brunt of harsh physical punishments, delivered at random. As adults, they do not place much value on what other people expect, because as children, they saw no connection between their own behavior and reinforcement. Although Ullmann and Krasner's views may account for some features of antisocial personality disorder, they may not adequately address the development of the "charming" type of antisocial personality; people in this group are skillful at reading the social cues of others and in using them for personal advantage. As psychologists Paul Babiak and David Hare report in their recent book, *Snakes in Suits*, the numbers of psychopathic personalities who attain executive positions in business where they can control others and where they use guile, manipulation, and charm to cause damage to others far exceed the numbers in prisons or in society at large (Babiak & Hare, 2006).

Social-cognitive theorist Albert Bandura has studied the role of observational learning in aggressive behavior, a common component of antisocial behavior. In a classic study, he and his colleagues (e.g., Bandura, Ross, & Ross, 1963) showed that children acquire skills, including aggressive skills, by observing the behavior of others. Exposure to aggression may come from watching violent television programs or observing parents who behave violently. Bandura does not believe children and adults display aggressive behaviors in a mechanical way, however. Rather, people usually do not imitate aggressive behavior unless they are provoked and believe they are more likely to be rewarded than punished for it. Children are most likely to imitate violent role models who get their way with others by acting aggressively. Children may also acquire antisocial behaviors such as cheating, bullying, or lying by direct reinforcement if they find that those behaviors help them avoid blame or manipulate others.

Social-cognitive psychologists have also shown that the ways in which people with personality disorders interpret their social experiences influence their behavior. Evidence shows that antisocial (psychopathic) individuals often have difficulty "reading" emotions in other people's faces (Kosson et al., 2002) and even picking out emotions in people's speech or vocal expressions, especially the emotion of fear (Blair et al., 2002). Antisocial adolescents tend to have hostile cognitive biases—they incorrectly interpret other people's behavior as threatening (Dodge et al., 2002). Often, perhaps because of their family and community experiences, they presume that others intend them ill when they do not. A method of therapy called *problem-solving therapy* helps aggressive, antisocial children and adolescents reconceptualize conflict situations as problems to be solved rather than as threats to be responded to aggressively (Kazdin & Whitley, 2003). Children learn to generate nonviolent solutions to social confrontations and, like scientists, test the most promising ones. In the section on biological perspectives we also see that the antisocial personality's failure to profit from punishment is connected with a cognitive factor: the *meaning* of the aversive stimulus.

What are the origins of antisocial personality disorder? Are youth who develop antisocial personalities largely "unsocialized" because their early learning experiences lack the consistency and predictability that help other children connect their behavior with rewards and punishments? Or are they very "socialized," but socialized to imitate the behavior of other antisocial youth? To what extent does criminal behavior or membership in gangs overlap with antisocial personality disorder?

All in all, learning approaches to personality disorders, like the psychodynamic approaches, have their limitations. They are grounded in theory rather than in observations of family interactions that presage the development of personality disorders. Research is needed to determine whether childhood experiences proposed by psychodynamic and learning theorists actually lead to the development of particular personality disorders as hypothesized.

Family Perspectives

Many theorists have argued that disturbances in family relationships underlie the development of personality disorders. Consistent with psychodynamic formulations, researchers find that people with borderline personality disorder (BPD) remember their parents as having been more controlling and less caring than do reference subjects with other psychological disorders (Zweig-Frank & Paris, 1991). When people with BPD recall their earliest memories, they are more likely than other people to paint significant others as malevolent or evil. They portray their parents and others close to them as likely to injure them or as failing to protect them (Nigg et al., 1992).

A number of researchers link childhood physical or sexual abuse or neglect to the development of personality disorders, including BPD (e.g., Golier et al., 2003; McLean & Gallop, 2003; Trull, 2001). Perhaps the "splitting" observed in people with the disorder is a function of having learned to cope with unpredictable and harsh behavior from parental figures or other caregivers.

Again consistent with psychodynamic theory, family factors such as parental overprotection and authoritarianism (a "do what I said because I said so" style of parenting) are implicated in the development of dependent personality traits (Bornstein, 1992). Extreme fears of abandonment may also be involved, perhaps resulting from a failure to develop secure bonds with parental attachment figures in childhood due to parental neglect, rejection, or death. Subsequently, these individuals develop a chronic fear of abandonment by significant others, leading to the clinginess that typifies dependent personality disorder. Theorists also suggest that obsessive–compulsive personality disorder may emerge within a strongly moralistic and rigid family environment, which does not permit even minor deviations from expected roles or behavior (e.g., Oldham, 1994).

As with BPD, researchers find that childhood abuse, parental neglect, or lack of parental nurturing are important risk factors in the development of antisocial personality disorder (APD) in adulthood (Johnson et al., 2006; Luntz & Widom, 1994). In an early but influential view that straddled the psychodynamic and learning theories, the McCords (McCord & McCord, 1964) focused on the role of parental rejection or neglect in the development of APD. They suggest that children normally learn to associate parental approval with conformity to parental practices and values and disapproval with disobedience. When tempted to transgress, children feel anxious about losing parental love. Anxiety signals the child to inhibit antisocial behavior. Eventually, the child identifies with parents and internalizes these social controls in the form of a conscience. When parents do not show love for their children, this identification does not occur. Children do not fear loss of love, because they have never had it. The anxiety that might have served to restrain antisocial and criminal behavior is absent.

Children who are rejected or neglected by their parents may not develop warm feelings of attachment to others. They may lack the ability to empathize with the feelings and needs of others, developing instead an attitude of indifference. Or perhaps they retain a wish to develop loving relationships but lack the ability to experience genuine feelings.

Although family factors may be implicated in some cases of antisocial personality disorder, many neglected children do not later show antisocial or other abnormal behaviors. We are left to develop other explanations to predict which deprived children will develop antisocial personalities or other abnormal behaviors, and which will not.

Biological Perspectives

Much remains to be learned about the biological underpinnings of personality disorders. Most of the attention in the research community has centered on antisocial personality disorder and the personality traits that underlie the disorder, which is the focus of much of our discussion.

Genetic Factors Research evidence suggests a role for genetic factors in the development of personality disorders (Gabbard, 2005; Ni et al., 2006). For example, we have learned that first-degree biological relatives (parents and siblings) of people with certain personality disorders, especially antisocial, schizotypal, and borderline types, are more likely to be diagnosed with these disorders than are members of the general population (APA, 2000; Battaglia et al., 1995). Genetic factors appear to play a role in the development of certain psychopathic personality traits, such as callousness, impulsivity, and irresponsibility (Larsson, Andershed, & Lichtenstein, 2006).

Studies of familial transmission are limited because family members share common environments as well as genes. Hence researchers have turned to twin and adoption studies to tease out genetic and environmental effects. Evidence from these studies supports a genetic contribution to antisocial behavior (Rhee & Waldman, 2002) and narcissism (Livesley et al., 1993). Bear in mind that these studies drew on twins and adoptees from the general population, not people with diagnosed personality disorders. Therefore, the results may not be generalizable to people with diagnosable disorders. Still, the findings suggest that genetics plays a role in the development of antisocial and narcissistic patterns of behavior that are associated with personality disorders. Yet we also understand that environmental factors play a contributing role in the development of personality disorders (Krueger et al., 2002). For example, people may be more vulnerable to developing personality disorders if they encounter certain environmental influences, such as being reared in a dysfunctional family.

Investigators find that a variant on a particular gene is associated with antisocial behavior in adult men, but only in those who were maltreated in childhood (Caspi et al., 2002). Here again, we see that the development of antisocial personality disorder, like many other abnormal behavior patterns, represents an interaction of genetic factors and life experiences (Gabbard, 2005). A leading expert on the genetic bases of abnormal behavior, psychologist William Iacono of the University of Minnesota, takes a closer look at the question of whether genes determine antisocial behavior in the nearby *Controversies in Abnormal Psychology*.

Lack of Emotional Responsiveness According to a leading theorist, Hervey Cleckley (1976), people with antisocial personalities can maintain their composure in stressful situations that would induce anxiety in most people. Lack of anxiety in response to threatening situations may help explain the failure of punishment to induce antisocial people to relinquish antisocial behavior. For most of us, the fear of getting caught and being punished is sufficient to inhibit antisocial impulses. People with antisocial personalities, however, often fail to inhibit behavior that has led to punishment in the past, perhaps because they experience little if any fear or anticipatory anxiety about being caught and punished.

When people get anxious, their palms tend to sweat. This skin response, called the *galvanic skin response* (GSR), is a sign of activation of the sympathetic branch of the autonomic nervous system (ANS). In an early study, Hare (1965) showed that people with antisocial personalities had lower GSR levels when they were expecting painful stimuli than did normal controls. Apparently, the people with antisocial personalities experienced little anxiety in anticipation of impending pain.

CONTROVERSIES IN ABNORMAL PSYCHOLOGY

Bad Genes, Bad Behavior?

—WILLIAM IACONO

Is antisocial behavior heritable? The simple answer is yes. Results pooled from over 50 twin and adoption studies show that genes account for about 41% of the influence on antisocial behavior (Rhee & Waldman, 2002). Although this reflects a substantial genetic contribution, it's important to recognize that most of the risk potential for antisocial behavior, 59%, reflects environmental effects. Important questions that remain to be addressed involve understanding the nature of the inherited risk (just what is inherited) and how genes and environments interact in the development of antisocial behavior.

Recent work suggests that antisocial personality disorder is part of a heritable spectrum of psychological disorders characterized by *behavioral undercontrol*, which is a pattern of behavior involving tendencies to act impulsively and take risks without considering the potential for adverse consequences. The boundaries of this spectrum can be identified by comparing rates of psychopathology in the offspring of antisocial parents to the offspring of other parents. Disorders that show up disproportionately in families with parental antisociality are likely to be part of this spectrum because they reflect the consequences of the parents' genes and the rearing environment antisocial parents provide for their children. Not surprisingly, by the time they are high school seniors, children of antisocial parents develop conduct disorder and antisocial personality disorder at much higher rates than comparison youth (Herndon & Iacono, 2005). However, they are also at higher risk of developing other disorders within the behavioral undercontrol spectrum, including childhood disruptive disorders (ADHD and oppositional defiant disorder, which are discussed in Chapter 14) and substance use disorders.

To tease apart the effects of genetic and environmental factors in this spectrum of disorders, investigators have turned to twin studies of adolescents (Krueger et al., 2002; Young et al., 2000) and adults (Kendler et al., 2003; McGue et al., 2006). Evidence from these studies suggests that these disorders share common genetic influences, which may help explain why people with one spectrum disorder are likely to have other spectrum disorders as well. For example, we've learned that children with ADHD often have comorbid (co-occurring) conduct disorder and that conduct disorder is a frequent precursor to antisocial personality disorder. We also have learned that antisocial

personality disorder and substance abuse frequently go hand in hand. Research along these lines leads us to recognize that individuals who are prone to develop disorders within this spectrum may inherit a genetic propensity to be behaviorally disinhibited—that is, to have difficulties restraining or inhibiting their impulses. This underlying propensity then increases the potential of developing one or more of these spectrum disorders.

One of the intriguing questions we are trying to answer is why some individuals develop one of the disorders in the spectrum and not others. The same twin studies that point to common genetic links among the disorders also indicate the presence of specific genetic influences and environmental effects unique to each disorder. We suspect that these unique influences determine which of the spectrum disorders, or which combination of disorders, are likely to occur.

These studies point to the nature of the inherited risk for antisociality, but understanding how this risk becomes expressed in behavior requires unraveling the complex gene-environment interplay that fosters the development of antisocial behavior. Studying adopted children who had at least one biological parent who was antisocial helps us better understand the complex interactions of genes and environment. If genes were the only determinant of antisocial behavior, then the family environment in the adoptive family would have no influence on whether the child becomes antisocial. However, adoption research has shown that the nature of the adoptive home has a strong influence on adoptee antisociality, such that children whose biological parent is antisocial are more likely to become antisocial adults if they were raised in dysfunctional or troubled adoptive homes (Cadoret et al., 1997). By analyzing the genes present in an individual's DNA, several molecular genetic studies have shown that child maltreatment at an early age increases the risk for antisocial behavior, but only in the presence of a form of a particular gene, or gene variant, that affects the activity of brain neurotransmitters linked to aggression (Kim-Cohen et al., 2006). This finding may help solve the riddle of why not all abused children become antisocial.

We have also learned that because this gene variant only appears in males, different mechanisms must be at work in females. Twin research has shown that for girls, the timing of puberty may be important. Genetic influences on the development of conduct disorder are strong when the age of first menstruation (menarche) is normal, but they are virtually absent for girls who enter puberty at an earlier stage (Burt et al., 2006). For precocious girls, environmental influences related to their opportunity to form social bonds with older, more deviant youth, coupled with their lack of experience navigating the social expectations of later adolescence may account for their antisociality.

Finally, note that controversy surrounds genetic studies of antisociality in large part because critics equate heritability with determinism, the notion that genetic consequences are inevitable. However, as these findings illustrate, genetic risk, not antisocial behavior per se, is inherited, and the full accounting of antisocial behavior involves understanding the complex interplay of genetic and environmental influences. Genetic studies have become an important tool for highlighting how challenges from the environment influence the development of antisocial behavior.

Critical Thinking

- Is behavioral undercontrol and disinhibition always something to be avoided? Can you think of ways in which acting on the spur of the moment and being comfortable taking risks might be advantageous?
- If someone possesses genetic risk for antisocial personality disorder, does this mean nothing can be done to help them? Can you think of individuals you know who have shown good adjustment despite one of their relatives being antisocial?
- If genes influence antisocial behavior, is it reasonable to hold individuals responsible for their bad deeds? Why or why not?

William Iacono, Ph.D., is a Distinguished McKnight University Professor and Director of the Center for Twin and Family Research at the University of Minnesota. Trained as a clinical psychologist, he conducts longitudinal studies of adolescent twins and adoptees, which are aimed at understanding the development of adult adjustment and mental health.

Hare's findings of a weaker GSR response in people with antisocial personalities has been replicated a number of times in studies showing lower levels of physiological responsiveness in people with psychopathic or antisocial personalities (e.g., Fung et al., 2005; Lorber, 2005). This lack of emotionality may help explain why the threat of punishment seems to have so little effect on deterring their antisocial behavior. It is conceivable that the autonomic nervous system (ANS) of people with antisocial personalities is underresponsive to threatening stimuli.

The Craving-for-Stimulation Model Other investigators have attempted to explain the antisocial personality's lack of emotional response in terms of the levels of stimulation necessary to maintain an optimum level of arousal. Your optimum level of arousal is the degree of arousal at which you feel best and function most efficiently.

People with antisocial or psychopathic personalities appear to have exaggerated cravings for stimulation (Arnett et al., 1997). Perhaps they require a higher-than-normal threshold of stimulation to maintain an optimum state of arousal. In other words, they may need more stimulation than other people to maintain interest and function normally.

A need for higher levels of stimulation may explain why people with antisocial personality traits tend to become bored easily and gravitate to stimulating but potentially dangerous activities, like the use of intoxicants such as drugs or alcohol, motorcycling, skydiving, high-stakes gambling, or sexual adventures. A higher-than-normal threshold for stimulation would not directly cause antisocial or criminal behavior; after all, astronauts, soldiers, police officers, and firefighters must also exhibit this trait to some respect. However, the threat of boredom and inability to tolerate monotony may influence some sensation seekers to drift into crime or reckless behavior.

Brain Abnormalities Brain-imaging techniques link borderline personality disorder and antisocial personality disorder to dysfunctions in parts of the brain involved in regulating emotions and impulsive aggressive behavior, specifically the prefrontal cortex of the frontal lobes and the deeper brain structures comprising the limbic system (Berlin, Rolls, & Iversen, 2006; Kiehl, 2006; Kiehl et al., 2006; Schmahl & Bremner, 2006). The prefrontal cortex is responsible for such functions as controlling impulsive behavior, weighing consequences of our actions, and problem solving (Brown et al., 2006). Brain abnormalities could help account for many features of antisocial personality disorder, including lack of conscience, failure to inhibit impulsive behavior, low arousal states, poor problem-solving efforts, and failure to think about the consequences of one's behavior (Raine et al., 2000). Nevertheless, we do not know how many people with antisocial personality disorder have underlying brain abnormalities.

Sociocultural Perspectives

Social conditions may contribute to the development of personality disorders. Because antisocial personality disorder is reported most frequently among people from lower socioeconomic classes, the kinds of stressors encountered by disadvantaged families may contribute to antisocial behavior patterns. Many inner-city neighborhoods are beset by social problems such as alcohol and drug abuse, teenage pregnancy, and disorganized and disintegrating families. These stressors are associated with an increased likelihood of child abuse and neglect, which may in turn contribute to lower self-esteem and breed feelings of anger and resentment in children. Neglect and abuse may become translated into the lack of empathy and a callous disregard for the welfare of others that are associated with antisocial personalities.

Children reared in poverty are also more likely to be exposed to deviant role models, such as neighborhood drug dealers. Maladjustment in school may lead to alienation

QUESTIONNAIRE
The Sensation-Seeking Scale

Do you crave stimulation or seek sensation? Are you satisfied by reading or in watching television, or must you ride the big wave or bounce your motorbike over desert dunes? Zuckerman (1980) finds four factors related to sensation seeking: (a) pursuit of thrill and adventure, (b) *disinhibition* (that is, tendency to express impulses), (c) pursuit of experience, and (d) susceptibility to boredom. Although some sensation seekers use drugs or have trouble with the law, many are law abiding and limit their sensation seeking to sanctioned activities. Thus sensation seeking should not be interpreted as criminal or antisocial in itself.

Zuckerman developed several sensation-seeking scales that assess the levels of stimulation people seek to feel at their best and function efficiently. A brief one follows. To assess your own sensation-seeking tendencies, pick the choice, A or B, that best depicts you. Then compare your responses to those in the key at the end of the chapter.

1. **a.** I would like a job that requires a lot of traveling.
    b. I would prefer a job in one location.
2. **a.** I am invigorated by a brisk, cold day.
    b. I can't wait to get indoors on a cold day.
3. **a.** I get bored seeing the same old faces.
    b. I like the comfortable familiarity of everyday friends.
4. **a.** I would prefer living in an ideal society in which everyone is safe, secure, and happy.
    b. I would have preferred living in the unsettled days of our history.

5. **a.** I sometimes like to do things that are a little frightening.
    b. A sensible person avoids activities that are dangerous.
6. **a.** I would not like to be hypnotized.
    b. I would like to have the experience of being hypnotized.
7. **a.** The most important goal in life is to live it to the fullest and experience as much as possible.
    b. The most important goal in life is to find peace and happiness.
8. **a.** I would like to try parachute jumping.
    b. I would never want to try jumping out of a plane, with or without a parachute.
9. **a.** I enter cold water gradually, giving myself time to get used to it.
    b. I like to dive or jump right into the ocean or a cold pool.
10. **a.** When I go on a vacation, I prefer the change of camping out.
    b. When I go on a vacation, I prefer the comfort of a good room and bed.
11. **a.** I prefer people who are emotionally expressive even if they are a bit unstable.
    b. I prefer people who are calm and even-tempered.
12. **a.** A good painting should shock or jolt the senses.
    b. A good painting should give one a feeling of peace and security.
13. **a.** People who ride motorcycles must have some kind of unconscious need to hurt themselves.
    b. I would like to drive or ride a motorcycle.

Source: Reprinted with permission of John Wiley & Sons, Inc.

A high need for sensation-seeking? The actor Jason Priestly, whose interests in thrill-seeking extended to motorcycles, racing boats, and bungee jumping, nearly died when the racing car he was driving at 186 miles an hour crashed into a wall of race track. Priestly reported that he had suffered 14 concussions in his life. Looking back at the accident, he admitted to an interviewer that he was never the brightest bulb in the bunch.

and frustration with the larger society, leading to antisocial behavior. Addressing the problem of antisocial personality may thus require attempts at a societal level to redress social injustice and improve social conditions.

Little information is available about the rates of personality disorders in other cultures. One initiative in this direction involved a joint program sponsored by the World Health Organization (WHO) and the U.S. Alcohol, Drug Abuse, and Mental Health Administration (ADAMHA). The goal of the program was to develop and standardize diagnostic instruments that could be used to arrive at psychiatric diagnoses worldwide. One result of this effort was the development of the International Personality Disorder Examination (IPDE), a semistructured interview protocol for diagnosing personality disorders (Loranger et al., 1994). The IPDE was pilot-tested by psychiatrists and clinical psychologists in 11 countries (India, Switzerland, the Netherlands, Great Britain, Luxembourg, Germany, Kenya, Norway, Japan, Austria, and the United States). The interview protocol diagnoses personality disorders reasonably reliably among the different languages and cultures that were sampled. Although more research is needed to determine the rates of particular personality disorders in other countries, investigators found the borderline and avoidant types to be the most frequently diagnosed. Perhaps the characteristics associated with these personality disorders reflect some dimensions of personality disturbance that are common throughout the world.

TYING IT TOGETHER

Throughout the text we've endorsed the value of a multifactorial model of abnormal behavior, the view that psychological disorders result from a complex web of psychological, sociocultural, and biological factors. Our understanding of personality disorders is no exception. A history of childhood abuse, neglectful or punitive parents, and learning experiences that breed fear of social interactions rather than self-confidence may underlie the development of personality disorders. Social-cognitive factors, such as the effects of modeling aggressive behavior and cognitive biases that predispose people to misconstrue other people's behavior as threatening, also influence the development of maladaptive ways of relating to others that become identified with personality disorders. Evidence also suggests a genetic contribution to several types of personality disorders, including antisocial, schizotypal, and borderline types. Other biological factors implicated in antisocial personality disorder include a lack of emotional responsiveness to threatening cues, excessive need for stimulation, and underlying brain abnormalities. Sociocultural factors, such as social stressors associated with poverty and living in a disintegrating, crime-ridden neighborhood, are linked to a greater likelihood of child abuse and neglect, which in turn sets the stage for lingering resentments and lack of empathy for others that typify the antisocial personality.

How are these factors linked together? Typically, we find common themes in the development of specific personality disorders, such as harsh or punitive parenting in the case of antisocial personality. However, we need to allow for different combinations of factors and causal pathways to come into play. For example, some people with antisocial personality disorder were raised in economically deprived conditions and lacked consistent parenting. Others were raised in middle-class families but experienced neglectful or harsh parenting. Clinicians need to evaluate how each person's developmental history may have shaped his or her way of relating to others.

The *Concept Map for Abnormal Psychology* at the end of the chapter lists the *DSM* clusters of personality disorders, the major theoretical perspectives discussed in this chapter, and several key treatment approaches. The concept map also illustrates a potential causal pathway leading to the development of antisocial personality disorder.

TREATMENT OF PERSONALITY DISORDERS

We began the chapter with a quote from the eminent psychologist William James, who suggested that people's personalities seem to be "set in plaster" by a certain age. James's view is applicable to many people with personality disorders, who are typically highly resistant to change.

People with personality disorders usually see their behaviors, even maladaptive, self-defeating behaviors, as natural parts of themselves. Even when unhappy and distressed, they are unlikely to perceive their own behavior as causative. Like Marcella, whom we described as showing features of a histrionic personality disorder, they may condemn others for their problems and believe others, not they, need to change. Thus they usually do not seek help on their own. Or they begrudgingly acquiesce to treatment at the urging of others but drop out or fail to cooperate with the therapist. Even if they go for help, they commonly feel overwhelmed by anxiety or depression and terminate treatment as soon as they find some relief, rather than probe more deeply for the underlying causes of their problems. People with personality disorders also tend to respond poorly to treatment of other problems, like depression, perhaps because of the negative influence of their maladaptive behavioral patterns (Shea, Widiger, & Klein, 1992). Despite these obstacles, evidence supports the effectiveness of both psychodynamic therapy and cognitive-behavioral therapy in treating personality disorders (Leichsenring & Leibing, 2003; Salekin, 2002).

Psychodynamic Approaches

Psychodynamic approaches are often used to help people diagnosed with personality disorders become aware of the roots of their self-defeating behavior patterns and learn more adaptive ways of relating to others. However, people with personality disorders, especially those with borderline and narcissistic personality disorders, often present particular challenges to the therapist. For example, people with borderline personality disorder tend to have turbulent relationships with therapists, sometimes idealizing them, sometimes denouncing them as uncaring.

Promising results have been reported using psychodynamically oriented therapies in treating personality disorders (Bateman & Fonagy, 2001; Clarkin et al., 2007; Svartberg, Stiles, & Seltzer, 2004). These therapies emphasize the client's problem behaviors in relating to others and generally adopt a more active, confrontational style to address the client's defenses than is the case with traditional psychoanalysis.

Behavioral Approaches

Behavior therapists see their task as changing clients' behaviors rather than their personality structures. Many behavioral theorists do not think in terms of clients' "personalities" at all, but rather in terms of acquired maladaptive behaviors that are maintained by reinforcement contingencies. Behavioral therapists therefore focus on attempting to replace maladaptive behaviors with adaptive behaviors through techniques such as extinction, modeling, and reinforcement. If clients are taught behaviors that are likely to be reinforced by other people, the new behaviors may well be maintained.

Despite difficulties in treating borderline personality disorder (BPD), two groups of therapists headed by Aaron Beck (e.g., Beck et al., 2003) and Marsha Linehan (Koerner & Linehan, 2002; Linehan et al., 2006) report promising results using cognitive-behavioral techniques. Beck's approach focuses on helping the individual identify and correct distorted thinking, such as tendencies to see oneself as completely defective, bad, and helpless (Dingfelder, 2004). Linehan's technique, called *dialectical behavior therapy* (DBT), is a form of cognitive-behavioral and supportive therapy techniques specifically designed to treat borderline personality disorder. Behavioral techniques are used to help clients improve their relationships with others, develop problem-solving skills, and learn more adaptive ways of handling confusing feelings (Dingfelder, 2004). Because people with BPD tend to be overly sensitive to even the slightest cues of rejection, therapists provide continuing acceptance and support, even when clients become manipulative or overly demanding. DBT has yielded promising results in treating BPD (e.g., Kröger et al., 2006; Linehan et al., 2006).

Some antisocial adolescents have been placed, often by court order, in residential and foster-care programs that contain numerous behavioral-treatment components. These programs have concrete rules and clear rewards for obeying them. Some residential programs rely on *token economies,* in which prosocial behaviors are rewarded with tokens such as plastic chips that can be exchanged for privileges. Although participants in such programs often show improved behavior, it remains unclear whether such programs reduce the risk that adolescent antisocial behavior will continue into adulthood.

Biological Approaches

Drug therapy does not directly treat personality disorders. Antidepressants or antianxiety drugs are sometimes used to treat associated depression or anxiety in people with personality disorders, especially borderline personality disorder (Rinne et al., 2002; Sansone, Rytwinski, & Gaither, 2003). Antidepressants of the SSRI class (e.g., Prozac) may also help temper anger and rage in people with borderline personality disorder and help them control anger and impulsive and aggressive behaviors, including self-mutilation (Rivas-Vazquez & Blais, 2002). Researchers suspect that impulsive and aggressive behavior may be related to serotonin deficiencies. Prozac and similar drugs increase the availability of serotonin in the synaptic connections in the brain. Atypical antipsychotic drugs have also been used with some success in treating borderline personality disorder (Nickel et al., 2006; Soler et al., 2005). However, drugs alone do not target long-standing patterns of maladaptive behavior that are the defining features of personality disorders.

Much remains to be learned about working with people who have personality disorders. The major challenges involve recruiting people who do not see themselves as being disordered into treatment and prompting them to develop insight into their self-defeating or injurious behaviors. Current efforts to help such people are too often reminiscent of the old couplet:

> He that complies against his will,
> Is of his own opinion still.

—Samuel Butler, Hudibras

IMPULSE CONTROL DISORDERS

People with borderline personalities often have difficulty controlling their impulses. But problems with impulse control are not limited to people with personality disorders. The *DSM* includes a category of mental disorders called **impulse control disorders** that are characterized by difficulties controlling or restraining impulsive behavior. Compulsive gambling (called *pathological gambling* in the *DSM*) is a type of impulse control disorder, as is *kleptomania* (compulsive stealing), *pyromania* (compulsive fire setting), *trichotillomania* (compulsive hair-pulling resulting in noticeable bald patches), and *intermittent explosive disorder* (failure to resist aggressive impulses, leading to serious assault or property destruction). Other impulse control problems, such as compulsive Internet use and compulsive shopping, are presently under consideration for inclusion in the diagnostic manual.

Have you ever blown your budget on a sale item? Have you ever made a bet you could not afford? Have you ever lost and screamed at someone, even though you knew you should be keeping your cool?

Most of us keep our impulses under control most of the time. Although we may sometimes surrender to a tempting desert or occasionally blurt out an obscentity in anger, we generally hold our impulsive behaviors in check. People with impulse control disorders, however, have persistent difficulty resisting harmful impulses, temptations, or drives. They experience a rising level of tension or arousal just prior to the impulsive act, followed by a sense of relief or release after the act is completed. People with impulse control disorders often have other psychological disorders, especially mood disorders, a fact that leads investigators to question whether these disorders should be classified within a broader spectrum of mood disorders. Our focus here is on two major types of impulse control disorders: *pathological gambling* and *kleptomania*.

impulse control disorders A category of psychological disorders characterized by failure to control impulses, temptations, or drives, resulting in harm to oneself or others.

Pathological Gambling

Gambling has probably never been more popular in the United States. Legalized gambling encompasses many forms, including state lotteries, offtrack betting (OTB) parlors, casino nights sponsored by religious and fraternal organizations, and gambling meccas like Atlantic City and Las Vegas. Technological developments, especially the advent of Internet gambling, has mushroomed in recent years, despite attempts by legal authorities to crack down on it.

Most people who gamble are able to maintain self-control and can stop whenever they wish. Others, like the man in the following case example, fall into a pattern of problem or compulsive gambling, which is classified by the *DSM* as a mental disorder called **pathological gambling.**

pathological gambling A type of impulse control disorder characterized by a pattern of habitual gambling and impaired control over the behavior.

◇

Twenty-eight years after his first two-bit bet at the race track, the double life of lies and deception caught up with an insurance executive whose gambling debts had climbed into the hundreds of thousands of dollars. The business he had built went bankrupt. His marriage ended in bitter divorce. Often, he considered killing himself.

(continued)

The former executive does not look like an addict, a liar, a manipulator or some-one who would ignore his two young daughters, but he admits to having been all of these.

"Gambling," he said, dragging hard on a cigarette, "took me from a good man, which I basically am, to a person I didn't know. I was only happy when I was in action and I felt most at home when I was in action. The more I won, the more I gambled. The more I lost, the more I gambled. It was a no-win situation."

—*Gately, 1989, p. 31. Copyright © 1989 by the New York Times Company. Reprinted by permission.*

By the time he sought treatment, he had lost more than $1 million. Many pathological or compulsive gamblers only seek treatment during a financial or emotional crisis, such as a bankrupty or divorce. Pathological gambling can take many forms, from excessive wagering on horse races or in card games and casinos, to extravagant betting on sporting events, and to chancy stock picks. Estimates are that about 1% of the general population suffers from pathological gambling and the rates may be rising as the result of the increasing spread of legalized gambling (Petry et al., 2006). But where should we draw the line between recreational gambling and pathological gambling? A leading researcher, Wendy Slutske of the University of Missouri, takes a closer look at the question in the *Controversies in Abnormal Psychology* feature.

Pathological gamblers often report they had experienced a big win, or a series of winnings, early in their gambling careers. Eventually, however, their losses begin to mount, and they feel driven to bet with increasing desperation to reverse their luck and recoup their losses. Losses sometimes begin with the first bet, and pathological gamblers often become trapped in a negative spiral of betting yet more frequently to recover losses even as their losses—and their debts—multiply. At some point, most pathological gamblers hit rock bottom, a state of despair characterized by loss of control over gambling, financial ruin, suicide attempts, and shattered family relationships. They may attempt to reduce their mounting losses by gambling more frequently, hoping for the one "big score" that will put them "into the black." They may sometimes be bouncing with energy and overconfidence and at other times feel anxious and filled with despair.

Many compulsive gamblers suffer from low self-eseteem and were rejected or abused as children by their parents. Gambling may become a means of boosting their self-esteem by proving that they are winners. Far too often, however, winnings are elusive and losses mount. Losing only strengthens their negative self-image, which can lead to depression and even suicide.

Gambling and other Nonchemical Addictions We can think of pathological gambling as a kind of nonchemical addiction. It shares with chemical dependence (addiction) a loss of control over the behavior, a state of high arousal or pleasurable excitement experienced when the behavior is performed, and withdrawal symptoms, such as headaches, insomnia, and loss of appetite, when the person cuts back or stops the compulsive behavior. Personality characteristics of pathological gamblers and chemical abusers also overlap, with psychological test profiles of both groups showing such traits as self-centeredness, anxiety, low tolerance for frustration, impulsivity, and manipulativeness (Vitaro, Arseneault & Tremblay, 1997). Pathological gamblers and alcohol-dependent patients also show similar kinds of performance deficits on neuropsychological tests that are suggestive of dysfunctions in the frontal lobes of the brain, the part of the brain that constrains impulsive behavior (Goudriaan et al., 2006).

Gambling American style. Gambling is big business in the United States. Although most gamblers can control their gambling behavior, compulsive gamblers are unable to resist impulses to gamble. Many compulsive gamblers seek help only when their losses throw them into financial or emotional crisis.

Investigators also find high rates of comorbidity (co-occurrence) between pathological gambling and substance use disorders (Dannon et al., 2006; Zimmerman, Chelminski, & Young, 2006).

The addiction model may apply more directly to some compulsive gamblers than others. Some forms of pathological gambling may be more closely aligned to mood disorders or obsessive–compulsive disorder than to substance use disorders.

Treatment of Pathological Gambling   Treatment of pathological gambling remains a challenge. Helping professionals face an uphill battle in working with compulsive gamblers who, like people with personality disorders and substance use disorders, make maladaptive choices and show little insight into the causes of their problems. They may resist efforts to help them. Yet some successful treatment efforts are reported, including cognitive-behavioral programs that focus on helping gamblers correct cognitive biases (e.g., beliefs that they can control gambling outcomes that are actually governed by chance, and tendencies to credit themselves for wins and explain away losses) (e.g., Petry et al., 2006). Promising results are also reported from the use of antidepressant drugs and mood stabilizing drugs, which suggests that pathological gambling and mood disorders may share common features (Dannon et al., 2006; Grant, Williams, & Kim, 2006).

Many treatment programs involve peer support programs, like Gamblers Anonymous (GA), which models itself on Alcoholics Anonymous. This program emphasizes personal responsibility for one's behavior and ensures anonymity of group members so as to encourage participation and sharing of experiences. Within a supportive group setting, members gain insight into their self-destructive behaviors. In some cases, hospital-based or residential treatment programs may be used to sequester pathological gamblers, so that they can help break away from their usual destructive routines. Upon release, they are encouraged to continue treatment by participating in GA or similar programs. To ensure anonymity, lay programs like GA do not keep records of participants. Unfortunately, from the information we do have, it appears that abstinence rates among attendees is low (Petry, 2003; Petry et al., 2006).

Some pathological gamblers show improvement on their own, indeed some become free of symptoms, even without receiving any formal treatment. The problem is that we don't know which problem gamblers are likely to improve on their own. A recent analysis of data from two nationally representative samples in the United States showed that about four of ten pathological gamblers were symptom-free during the previous year (Slutske, 2006a,b).

Kleptomania

Kleptomania derives from the Greek *kleptes,* meaning thief, and is characterized by a pattern of compulsive stealing. The stolen objects are typically of little value or use to the person. The person may give them away, return them secretly, discard them, or just keep them hidden at home. In most cases, people with kleptomania can easily afford the items they steal. Even wealthy people have been known to be compulsive shoplifters. The thefts are apparently unmotivated by anger or vengeance. The are usually crimes resulting from a momentary impulse, poorly planned, and sometimes resulting in arrest.

Although shoplifting is common, kleptomania—a recurring pattern of compulsive stealing—is considered rare, although the prevalence of the disorder in the general population remains unclear. We have little scientific evidence on kleptomania to guide our understanding of the disorder. The presence of an irresistible, repetitive pattern in kleptomania suggests common features with obsessive–compulsive disorder (OCD). However, there is an important distinction. People with obsessive–compulsive disorder experience only temporary relief from anxiety when they peform compulsive acts; by contrast, people with kleptomania experience pleasurable excitement or gratification when they engage in compulsive stealing. Another difference is that kleptomania appears to be an end in itself, whereas compulsions in OCD are performed to avoid potential unfortunate events (like repeatedly checking the gas jets to prevent a gas explosion).

kleptomania A type of impulse control disorder characterized by a pattern of compulsive stealing.

T R U T H or F I C T I O N

Kleptomania, or compulsive stealing, is usually motivated by poverty.

✔ **FALSE.** People with kleptomania typically steal items of little value to them.

CONTROVERSIES IN ABNORMAL PSYCHOLOGY

Losing $10 Million: A Case of Pathological Gambling?

—WENDY SLUTSKE

Would you consider it abnormal for a person to lose $10 million gambling? Do you think this behavior would constitute grounds for a diagnosis of pathological (compulsive) gambling? In making judgments about abnormality, we need to take many factors into account. For most all of us, gambling behavior that leads to a loss of a magnitude counted in five or six digits, let alone eight digits, would be associated with significant emotional distress and affect our ability to meet our ordinary responsibilities, such as paying the rent. These factors would weigh heavily in a clinician's judgment that the behavior is abnormal. But what if the person reporting the loss claims to be able to afford it? This was the case recently when former basketball great Charles Barkley said during an *ESPN* interview that he had lost probably $10 million gambling over a period of years. He went on to say that he doesn't consider his gambling to be problem ". . . because I can afford to gamble" (cited in "Barkley Claims Gambling Problem," 2006).

I can't say whether the Barkley case in particular crosses the line into pathological or problem gambling. But for the typical individual of average financial means, there is no question that a sizeable loss, let alone a multimillion dollar loss, would be indicative of a significant gambling problem.

Having studied problems caused by pathological gambling, my belief is that for most people, gambling is a fun and relatively harmless recreational activity. But for a minority of people who gamble, serious legal, financial, interpersonal, and health problems do develop as a consequence of gambling. Drawing the line between recreational gambling and pathological gambling remains a challenge. One difficulty is that we lack any clear metric to determine whether someone is gambling (or losing) too much. First, it is very difficult for people to keep track of and remember how much money they have spent on gambling. Some people even have difficulty understanding what is meant by "money spent on gambling." Second, as the Barkley case illustrates, the same amount of money spent on gambling will have a much different meaning for someone with fewer versus one with more financial resources. One way of resolving the issue is to base our judgment on percentage of total income that is spent on gambling. More importantly, however, we need to carefully examine how gambling behavior and any resulting losses affect a person's mental state and life situation.

In the end, the more fundamental question that we would like to know the answer to is whether gambling has overtaken other important life goals or activities—things such as career, studies, family or friends—as a primary focus in a gambler's life. When this occurs, gambling is no longer a fun or harmless recreational activity. This is when gambling has indeed become a problem.

Critical Thinking

There is a law unique to the state of Missouri, developed in an effort to curb gambling problems, that places a limit on how much an individual can lose at a casino.

- What do you think would be an appropriate limit to set for losses?
- Do you believe that imposing a limit on losses would prevent or reduce gambling problems?
- How would you evaluate whether the program actually reduced gambling problems?

Wendy Slutske received her Ph.D. in clinical psychology from the University of Minnesota and is currently an Associate Professor of Psychology at the University of Missouri–Columbia. She studies the etiology and descriptive psychopathology of addictive disorders (primarily alcoholism and pathological gambling) by conducting large scale community-based epidemiologic surveys of individuals, twin pairs, and the families of twins. Dr. Slutske's recent research shows that pathological gambling may be caused, in part, by genetic risk factors (yet to be identified) that are also associated with the development of alcohol dependence and antisocial personality disorder and that many individuals with the disorder appear to recover on their own, most without any formal treatment or involvement in programs like Gambler's Anonymous.

All in all, some forms of kleptomania may be like OCD, whereas others forms may have more in common with substance use or mood disorders (Grant, 2006). Perhaps the thrill of theft is a way in which some people attempt to fend off feelings of depression. By coming to better understand the subtypes, we many be better equipped to tailor more effective treatment approach. As it stands, the few isolated treatment studies are limited to a few cases.

Traditional psychodynamic formulations viewed kleptomania as a defense against unconsious penis envy in women and castration anxiety in men. The belief is that people with kleptomania are motivated to steal phallic objects (symbols of the penis) as a magical way of protecting themselves against the apparent loss (in females) or threatened loss (in males) of the penis (Fenichel, 1945). Whether this theoretical speculation has merit remains uncertain, as we lack any supportive evidence of these unconscious processes.

There is little formal research on the treatment of kleptomania (Kohn & Antonuccio, 2002; Grant, 2006). In the following case example, we describe a behavioral approach to treating kleptomania:

A Case of Kleptomania

The client was a 56-year-old woman, who has shoplifted everyday of the preceding 14 years. Her compulsive urges to steal fit the clinical criteria that may distinguish kleptomania from other types of shoplifting, although her booty had no apparent meaning to her. Typical loot consisted of a pair of baby shoes, although there was no baby in her family to whom she could give the shoes. The compulsion to steal was so strong that she felt powerless to resist it. She told her therapist that she wished she could be "chained to a wall" (Glover, 1985, p. 213) in order to prevent her from acting out. She expressed anger that it was so easy to steal from a supermarket, in effect blaming the store for her own misconduct.

Her treatment, called covert sensitization, involved the pairing in imagination of an aversive stimulus with the undesired behavior. The therapist directed the woman to imagine feeling nauseous and vomiting while stealing. She was instructed to picture herself in the supermarket, approaching an object she intends to steal, and becoming nauseated and vomiting as she attempts to remove it, which draws the scowling attention of other shoppers. She is then directed to imagine herself replacing the object and consequently feeling relief from the nausea.

In a subsequent session, she imagines the nausea starting as she approached the object, but the nausea disappeared when she turned away rather than removing it. She was also asked to practice the imaginal scenes on her own throughout the week, as homework assignments. She reported a decline in stealing behavior during the treatment program. She reported only one instance of shoplifting between the completion of treatment and a 19-month follow-up evaluation.

—Adapted from Glover, 1985

Was the treatment effective? Perhaps. But then again, uncontrolled case studies cannot ascertain cause-and-effect relationships. For example, we cannot know whether the treatment itself or other factors, such as the client's motivation to change her life, were responsible for the changes in her behavior.

SUMMING UP

Types of Personality Disorders

What are personality disorders? Personality disorders are maladaptive or rigid behavior patterns or personality traits associated with states of personal distress that impair the person's ability to function in social or occupational roles. People with personality disorders do not generally recognize a need to change themselves.

What are the classes of personality disorders within the* DSM *system? The *DSM* classifies personality disorders on Axis II and categorizes them according to the following clusters of characteristics: odd or eccentric behavior; dramatic, emotional, or erratic behavior; or anxious or fearful behavior.

What are the features of personality disorders characterized by odd or eccentric behavior? People with paranoid personality disorder are unduly suspicious and mistrustful of others, to the point that their relationships suffer. But they do not hold the more flagrant paranoid delusions typical of schizophrenia. Schizoid personality disorder describes people who have little if any interest in social relationships, show a restricted range of emotional expression, and appear distant and aloof. People with schizotypal personalities appear odd or eccentric in their thoughts, mannerisms, and behavior, but not to the degree found in schizophrenia.

What are the features of personality disorders characterized by dramatic, emotional, or erratic behavior? Antisocial personality disorder describes people who persistently engage in behavior that violates social norms and the rights of others and who tend to show no remorse for their misdeeds. Borderline personality disorder is defined in terms of instability in self-image, relationships, and mood. People with borderline personality disorder often engage in impulsive acts, which are frequently self-destructive. People with histrionic personality disorder tend to be highly dramatic and emotional in their behavior, whereas people diagnosed with narcissistic personality disorder have an inflated or grandiose sense of self, and like those with histrionic personalities, they demand to be the center of attention.

What are the features of personality disorders characterized by anxious or fearful behavior? Avoidant personality disorder describes people who are so terrified of rejection and criticism that they are generally unwilling to enter relationships without unusually strong reassurances of acceptance. People with dependent personality disorder are overly dependent on others and have extreme difficulty acting independently or making even the smallest decisions on their own. People with obsessive–compulsive personality disorder have various traits such as orderliness, perfectionism, rigidity, and overattention to detail, but are without the true obsessions and compulsions associated with obsessive–compulsive (anxiety) disorder.

What are some problems associated with the classification of personality disorders? Various controversies and problems attend the classification of personality disorders, including overlap among the categories, difficulty in distinguishing between variations in normal behavior and abnormal behavior, confusion of labels with explanations, and possible underlying sexist biases.

Theoretical Perspectives

How do traditional Freudian concepts of disturbed personality development compare with more recent psychodynamic approaches? Earlier Freudian theory focused on unresolved Oedipal conflicts in explaining normal and abnormal personality development. More recent psychodynamic theorists have focused on the pre-Oedipal period in explaining the development of such personality disorders as narcissistic and borderline personality.

How do learning theorists view personality disorders? Learning theorists view personality disorders in terms of maladaptive patterns of behavior rather than personality traits. Learning theorists seek to identify the early learning experiences and present reinforcement patterns that explain the development and maintenance of personality disorders.

What is the role of family relationships in personality disorders? Many theorists argue that disturbed family relationships play formative roles in the development of personality disorders. For example, theorists have connected antisocial personality to parental rejection or neglect and parental modeling of antisocial behavior.

How do antisocial adolescents interpret social cues? Antisocial adolescents are more likely to interpret social cues as provocations or intentions of ill will. This cognitive bias may lead them to be confrontational in their relationships with peers.

What roles might biological factors play in antisocial personality disorder? People with antisocial personalities may lack emotional responsiveness to physically threatening stimuli and have reduced levels of autonomic nervous system (ANS) reactivity. People with antisocial personalities may also require higher levels of stimulation to maintain optimal levels of arousal.

What role do sociocultural factors play in the development of personality disorders? The effects of poverty, urban blight, and drug abuse can lead to family disorganization and disintegration, making it less likely that children will receive the nurturance and support they need to develop more socially adaptive behavior patterns. Sociocultural theorists believe that such factors may underlie the development of personality disorders, especially antisocial personality disorder.

Treatment of Personality Disorders

How do therapists approach the treatment of personality disorders? Therapists from different schools of therapy help people with personality disorders become aware of their self-defeating behavior patterns and learn more adaptive ways of relating to others. Despite difficulties in working therapeutically with people with personality disorders, promising results have emerged from the use of relatively short-term psychodynamic therapy and cognitive-behavioral treatment approaches.

Impulse Control Disorders

What are impulse control disorders? They are psychological disorders characterized by a pattern of repeated failure to resist impulses to perform acts that are harmful to oneself or to others. People affected by these disorders experience a rising level of tension or arousal just before the act, then a sense of relief or release when the act is committed.

What are some types of impulse control disorders? Examples include pathological gambling, kleptomania, pyromania, trichotillomania, and intermittent explosive disorder.

What do we know about the features and treatment of pathological gambling? Pathological gambling can be likened to a type of nonchemical addiction in which people experience a loss of control over the behavior, a state of high arousal or pleasurable excitement when the behavior is performed, and withdrawal symptoms when they stop gambling. People with the disorder frequently have comorbid conditions, especially substance use disorders and mood disorders. Promising treatment approaches have been introduced, including use of psychiatric drugs and cognitive-behavioral therapy. Many compulsive gamblers participate in peer support groups, such as Gamblers Anonymous.

What do we know about the features and treatment of kleptomania? Kleptomania is characterized by a compulsion to steal, usually involving items of little value to the person. Little is known about effective treatments for this disorder.

KEY TERMS

personality disorders *(p. 435)*
ego syntonic *(p. 436)*
ego dystonic *(p. 436)*
paranoid personality disorder *(p. 437)*
schizoid personality disorder *(p. 438)*
schizotypal personality disorder *(p. 438)*
antisocial personality disorder *(p. 440)*

borderline personality disorder (BPD) *(p. 443)*
splitting *(p. 445)*
histrionic personality disorder *(p. 445)*
narcissistic personality disorder *(p. 447)*
avoidant personality disorder *(p. 449)*
dependent personality disorder *(p. 450)*

obsessive–compulsive personality disorder *(p. 451)*
impulse control disorders *(p. 465)*
pathological gambling *(p. 465)*
kleptomania *(p. 467)*

KEY FOR SENSATION-SEEKING SCALE

Because this is an abbreviated version of a questionnaire, no norms are applicable. However, answers that agree with the following key are suggestive of sensation seeking:

1. A
2. A
3. A
4. B
5. A
6. B
7. A
8. A
9. B
10. A
11. A
12. A
13. B

MEDIA TOOLS

A variety of digital and online learning tools are available to enrich your learning experience and help you succeed in the course. These resources include:

- **MyPsychLab,** an online learning system for your course in abnormal psychology that allows you to test your mastery of concepts in the book by using chapter-by-chapter diagnostic tests. Results from the diagnostic tests help you build a customized study plan. To access **MyPsychLab,** visit www.prenhall.com/mypsychlab and follow the instructions on the site.

- **"SPEAKING OUT" PATIENT INTERVIEWS,** a set of video case examples of actual patients you can access on the companion

CD-ROM included with the text. Icons in the margins of the chapter highlight the video case examples included on the CD-ROM.

- **COMPANION WEB SITE,** an online study center that offers computer-scored quizzes you can use to test your knowledge, along with other study tools and links to related sites to enhance your learning of abnormal psychology. To access the companion Web site, visit www.prenhall.com/nevid and use the various tabs and links on the site to access these learning resources.

Personality Disorders

are characterized by

Rigid, inflexible and maladaptive patterns of behavior or ways of relating to others

and are classified within these three major clusters

- Cluster A: Personality disorders characterized by odd or eccentric behaviors (paranoid, schizoid, and schizotypal personality disorders)
- Cluster B: Personality disorders characterized by dramatic, emotional, or erratic behavior (antisocial, borderline, histrionic, and narcissistic personality disorders)
- Cluster C: Personality disorders characterized by anxious or fearful behavior (avoidant, dependent, and obsessive–compulsive personality disorders)

and are conceptualized in terms of

- Psychodynamic perspectives
- Learning perspectives
- Family perspectives
- Sociocultural perspectives
- Biological perspectives
- Multiple factors, as in this conceptual model of antisocial personality disorder:

and may be treated by

- Drug therapy to control troubling symptoms
- Cognitive-behavioral therapy to foster adaptive behavior and effective social and problem-solving skills, as well as correcting faulty thinking
- Psychodynamic therapy to gain insight into possible childhood origins of problem behavior and to develop more effective ways of relating to others

A Multifactorial Model of Antisocial Personality Disorder

Parenting and Modeling Influences

- Exposure to deviant role models
- Harsh and neglectful parenting

Biological Factors

- Possible genetic contribution
- Brain abnormalities involving the prefrontal cortex may play a role in some cases
- Lack of emotional responsiveness to threatening cues

Poor Socialization

- Lack of empathy
- Failure to internalize social rules and mores

Vulnerability Factors

Increased Risk Potential

Cognitive factors

- Difficulty "reading" emotions in other people's faces or vocal expressions
- Incorrectly interpreting other people's behavior as threatening or hostile

Antisocial Personality Disorder

- Callous treatment of others
- Failure to inhibit impulses
- Criminal or aggressive behavior

Abnormal Behavior in Childhood and Adolescence

CHAPTER OUTLINE

NORMAL AND ABNORMAL BEHAVIOR IN CHILDHOOD AND ADOLESCENCE 475–478

Cultural Beliefs About What Is Normal
 and Abnormal
Prevalence of Mental Health Problems
 in Children and Adolescents
Risk Factors for Childhood Disorders

**PERVASIVE DEVELOPMENTAL
DISORDERS 478–485**

Autism

MENTAL RETARDATION 485–489

Causes of Mental Retardation
Intervention

LEARNING DISORDERS 489–492

Types of Learning Disorders
Understanding and Treating Learning
 Disorders

COMMUNICATION DISORDERS 492–493

**ATTENTION-DEFICIT AND DISRUPTIVE
BEHAVIOR DISORDERS 493–499**

Attention-Deficit Hyperactivity Disorder
Conduct Disorder
Oppositional Defiant Disorder

**CHILDHOOD ANXIETY AND
DEPRESSION 499–506**

Separation Anxiety Disorder

Understanding and Treating Childhood
 Anxiety Disorders
Childhood Depression
Understanding and Treating Childhood
 Depression
Suicide in Children and Adolescents

ELIMINATION DISORDERS 506–509

Enuresis
Encopresis

SUMMING UP 509–510

An autistic woman, Donna Williams, reflects on what it is like to be an autistic child. In this excerpt from her memoir *Nobody Nowhere*, she speaks about her need to keep the world out. She was about 3 years old when her parents took her to a doctor out of concern that she appeared malnourished.

"I"

"A World of My Own Creation"

My parents thought I had leukemia and took me for a blood test. The doctor took some blood from my earlobe. I cooperated. I was intrigued by a multicolored cardboard wheel the doctor had given me. I also had hearing tests because, although I mimicked everything, it appeared that I was deaf. My parents would stand behind me and make sudden loud noises without my so much as blinking in response. "The world" simply wasn't getting in. . . . The more I became aware of the world around me, the more I became afraid. Other people were my enemies, and reaching out to me was their weapon, with only a few exceptions—my grandparents, my father, and my Aunty Linda. . . .

Donna also recalled how, for her, people became things and things existed to offer her protection and shield her from a fear of vulnerability:

I collected scraps of colored wool and crocheted bits and would put my fingers through the holes so that I could fall asleep securely. For me, the people I liked were their things, and those things (or things like them) were my protection from the things I didn't like—other people.

The habits I adopted of keeping and manipulating these symbols were my equivalent of magic spells cast against the nasties who could invade me if I lost my cherished objects or had them taken away. My strategies were not the result of insanity or hallucination, but simply harmless imagination made potent by my overwhelming fear of vulnerability. . . .

People were forever saying that I had no friends. In fact my world was full of them. They were far more magical, reliable, predictable, and real than other children, and they came with guarantees. It was a world of my own creation where I didn't need to control myself or the objects, animals, and nature, which were simply being in my presence.

—*Williams, 1992, pp. 5, 6, 9*

PSYCHOLOGICAL DISORDERS OF CHILDHOOD AND ADOLESCENCE OFTEN HAVE A SPECIAL poignancy, perhaps none more than autism. These disorders affect children at ages when they have little capacity to cope. Some of these problems, such as autism and mental retardation, prevent children from fulfilling their developmental potentials. Some psychological problems in childhood and adolescents mirror those found in adults—problems such as mood disorders and anxiety disorders. In some cases, the problems are unique to childhood, such as separation anxiety; in others, such as ADHD, or attention-deficit hyperactivity disorder, the problem manifests itself differently in childhood than in adulthood.

NORMAL AND ABNORMAL BEHAVIOR IN CHILDHOOD AND ADOLESCENCE

To determine what is normal and abnormal among children and adolescents, we consider, in addition to the criteria outlined in Chapter 1, the child's age and cultural background (USDHHS, 1999a). Many problems are first identified when the child enters school. Although these problems may have existed earlier, they may have been tolerated or not seen as "problems" in the home. Sometimes the stress of starting school contributes to their onset. Keep in mind, however, that what is socially acceptable

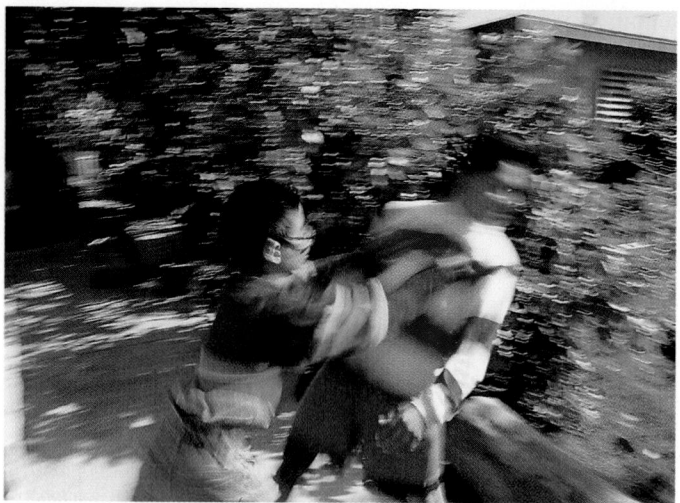

How serious is this problem? Thai parents might judge the behavior shown by these children to be less serious than American parents would. Thai-Buddhist values tolerate broad variations in children's behavior and assume that it will change for the better.

at one age, such as intense fear of strangers at about 9 months, may be socially unacceptable at more advanced ages. Many behavior patterns that would be considered abnormal among adults—such as intense fear of strangers and lack of bladder control—are perfectly normal for children at certain ages.

Cultural Beliefs About What Is Normal and Abnormal

Cultural beliefs help determine whether people view behavior as normal or abnormal. Because children rarely label their own behavior as abnormal, definitions of normality depend largely on how a child's behavior is filtered through the family's cultural lenses. Cultures vary with respect to the types of behaviors they classify as unacceptable as well as the threshold for labeling child behaviors as deviant.

Parents judge the unusualness of children's behavior from their own cultural perspective. For example, groups of American and Thai parents were presented with vignettes depicting two children, one with problems of "overcontrol" (for example, shyness and fears) and one with problems of "undercontrol" (for example, disobedience and fighting). The Thai parents rated *both* sets of problems as less serious and worrisome than did American parents (Weisz et al., 1988). Thai parents also rated the children as more likely to improve over time, even without treatment. These viewpoints are embedded within traditional Thai-Buddhist beliefs and values, which tolerate broad variations in children's behavior and assume that change is inevitable.

Like definitions of abnormality, methods of treatment differ for children. Children may not have the verbal skills to express their feelings through speech or the attention span required to sit through a typical therapy session. Therapy methods must be tailored to the level of the child's cognitive, physical, social, and emotional development. For example, psychodynamic therapists have developed techniques of *play therapy* in which children enact family conflicts symbolically through their play activities, such as by play acting with dolls or puppets. Or they might be given drawing materials and asked to draw pictures, in the belief that their drawings will reflect their underlying feelings.

As with other forms of therapy (see Chapter 4), child therapy needs to be offered in a culturally sensitive framework. Therapists need to tailor their interventions to the cultural backgrounds and social and linguistic needs of children in order to establish effective therapeutic relationships.

Prevalence of Mental Health Problems in Children and Adolescents

Just how common are mental health problems among America's children and adolescents? Unfortunately, quite common.

According to a report from the U.S. Surgeon General, 1 in 10 children suffers from a mental disorder severe enough to impair development ("A Children's Mental Illness 'Crisis,'" 2001). The most commonly diagnosed psychological disorders in children age 6 to 17 are learning disabilities (11.5%) and attention-deficit hyperactivity disorder (8.8%) (Blanchard, Gurka, & Blackman, 2006). A telephone survey based on a national probability sample of American youth ages 12 to 17 found that 7% of the boys and 14% of the girls had suffered from major depression in the 6-month period preceding the survey (Kilpatrick et al., 2003).

Overall, more American children suffer from mental disorders than from diabetes, AIDS, and leukemia combined. Yet 60% to 80% of children with mental health disorders fail to get the treatment they need (Goldberg, 2001). Children who have *internalized* problems, such as anxiety and depression, are at higher risk of going untreated than are children with *externalized* problems (problems involving acting out or aggressive behavior) that are disruptive or annoying to others.

Risk Factors for Childhood Disorders

Many factors contribute to increased risk of developmental disorders, including genetic susceptibility, environmental stressors (such as living in decaying neighborhoods), and family factors (such as inconsistent or harsh discipline, neglect, or physical or sexual abuse). Children with parents who suffer from depression also stand a higher risk of developing psychological disorders, perhaps because it leads to greater family stress (Essex et al., 2006; Weissman et al., 2005, 2006).

Gender is yet another discriminating factor. Boys are at greater risk for developing many childhood disorders, ranging from autism to hyperactivity to elimination disorders. Problems of anxiety and depression also affect boys more often than girls. In adolescence, however, anxiety and mood disorders become more common among girls and remain so throughout adulthood (USDHHS, 1999a).

Physical and sexual abuse and neglect figure prominently in the developmental histories of children, adolescents, and adults with psychological disorders (Gamble et al., 2006; Joiner et al., 2007). (Effects of childhood sexual abuse are discussed in Chapter 11.) Physically abused or neglected children often have difficulty forming healthy peer relationships and healthy attachments to others. They may lack the capacity for empathy or fail to develop a sense of conscience or concern about the welfare of others. They may act out in ways that mirror the cruelty they've experienced in their lives, such as by torturing or killing animals, setting fires, or picking on smaller, more vulnerable children. Other common psychological effects of neglect and abuse include lowered self-esteem, depression, immature behaviors such as bed-wetting or thumb-sucking, suicide attempts and suicidal thinking, poor school performance, behavior problems, and failure to venture beyond the home to explore the outside world (Saywitz et al., 2000; Wolfe et al., 2001). The behavioral and emotional consequences of child abuse often extend into adulthood (Briere & Elliott, 2003).

Child abuse is hardly an isolated problem. Each year more than 1.5 million children in the United States are victims of child abuse or neglect (Gershater-Molkoa, Lutzker, & Sherman, 2002). More than 1,000 children in the United States die each year as the result of abuse or neglect. As horrific as these numbers are, they greatly understate the problem, as most incidents of child maltreatment are never publicly identified. Concerns about physical abuse are understandable, but we should not lose sight of the emotional consequences of verbal abuse, of parents harshly scolding, belittling, and swearing at their children (Yager, 2006b). Yes, "sticks and stones" can break bones, but words can also do emotional harm (Teicher et al., 2006).

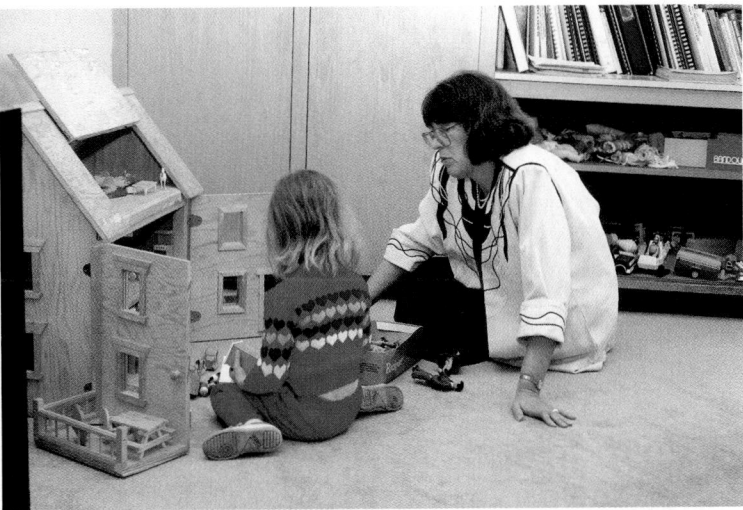

Play therapy. In play therapy, children may enact scenes with dolls or puppets that symbolically represent conflicts occurring within their own families.

TABLE 14.1 Overview of Disorders of Childhood and Adolescence

TYPES OF DISORDERS

	Description	Major Types/Estimated Prevalence Rates, If Known	Features
Pervasive Developmental Disorder	Marked impairment in multiple areas of development	• Autistic Disorder (0.66%)* • Asperger's Disorder	• Autism: Major deficits in relating to others, impaired language and cognitive functioning, and restricted range of activities and interests • Asperger's Disorder: Poor social interactions and stereotyped behavior but without the significant language or cognitive deficits of autism
Mental Retardation	A broad-based delay in the development of cognitive and social functioning	• Deficits vary with level of severity from mild to profound (1%)	• Diagnosed on the basis of low IQ score and poor adaptive functioning
Learning Disorders	Deficiencies in specific learning abilities in the context of at least average intelligence and exposure to learning opportunities	• Mathematics Disorder • Disorder of Written Expression • Reading Disorder (Dyslexia) (4%)	• Mathematics Disorder: Difficulty understanding basic mathematical operations • Disorder of Written Expression: Grossly deficient writing skills • Reading Disorder: Difficulty recognizing words and comprehending written text
Communication Disorders	Difficulties in understanding or using language	• Expressive Language Disorder • Mixed Receptive/Expressive Language Disorder • Phonological Disorder • Stuttering (1%)	• Expressive Language Disorder: Difficulty using spoken language • Mixed Receptive/Expressive Disorder: Difficulty understanding and producing speech • Phonological Disorder: Difficulty articulating the sounds of speech • Stuttering: Difficulty speaking fluently without interruption
Attention-Deficit and Disruptive Behavior Disorders	Patterns of disturbed behavior that are generally disruptive to others and to adaptable social functioning	• Attention-Deficit Hyperactivity Disorder (3%–7%) • Conduct Disorder (12% males; 7% females) • Oppositional Defiant Disorder (6%–15%)	• ADHD: Problems of impulsivity, inattention, and hyperactivity • Conduct Disorder: Antisocial behavior that violates social norms and the rights of others • Oppositional Defiant Disorder: Pattern of noncompliant, negativistic, or oppositional behavior
Anxiety and Mood Disorders	Emotional disorders affecting children and adolescents	• Separation Anxiety Disorder (4%–5%) • Specific Phobia • Social Phobia • Generalized Anxiety Disorder • Major Depression • Bipolar Disorder	• Anxiety and depression often have similar features in children as in adults, but some differences exist • Children may suffer from school phobia as a form of separation anxiety • Depressed children may fail to label their feelings as depression or may show behaviors, such as conduct problems and physical complaints, that mask depression
Elimination Disorders	Persistent problems with controlling urination or defecation that cannot be explained by organic causes	• Enuresis (lack of control over urination) (7% boys; 3% girls) • Encopresis (lack of control over defecation) (1%)	• Enuresis: Nighttime-only enuresis (bed-wetting) is the most common type • Encopresis: Occurs most often during daytime hours

Sources for prevalence rates: APA, 2000; Frick & Silverthorn, 2001; Loeber et al., 2000; Masi et al., 2001; Nock et al., 2006; Shute et al., 2000; Wingert, 2000; Yeargin-Allsopp et al., 2003, CDC, 2007.

*Prevalence rate refers to autism spectrum disorders.

We now turn to consider the specific types of psychological disorders of childhood and adolescence. We will examine the features of these disorders, their causes, and the treatments used to help children who suffer from them. Before we begin, you may wish to review Table 14.1, which provides an overview of disorders of childhood and adolescence.

pervasive developmental disorders (PDDs) A class of developmental disorders characterized by significantly impaired behavior or functioning in multiple areas of development.

PERVASIVE DEVELOPMENTAL DISORDERS

Children with **pervasive developmental disorders (PDDs)** show markedly impaired behavior or functioning in many areas of development. These types of disorders usually become evident in the first few years of life and are often associated with mental retardation. They were originally thought to reflect childhood forms of adult psychoses like schizophrenia because they share such features as social and emotional impairment, oddities of communication, and stereotyped motor behaviors. Mental health professionals today recognize that they are distinct disorders from schizophrenia and other psychoses. Only very rarely in children do we find evidence of the prominent hallucinations or delusions that would justify a diagnosis of schizophrenia.

The major type of PDD, and hence the focus of our discussion, is **autism** (also called *autistic disorder*). But first let us note some other types of pervasive developmental disorders. **Asperger's disorder,** a milder form of pervasive developmental disorder, is characterized by poor social interactions and development of narrow, obsessive or repetitive behavior (Murphy et al., 2002). The narrowing of behavior may take the form of fixations with obscure topics or interests. For example, one Asperger child became obsessed with vacuum cleaners (Osborne, 2002). However, in contrast to autism, Asperger's children are not impaired by significant intellectual or language deficits (APA, 2000).

Other, less-common types of pervasive developmental disorder include **Rett's disorder,** a disorder reported only in females; and **childhood disintegrative disorder,** a rare condition that appears to be more common among males. Many investigators believe that autism and these other PDDs share enough in common that they represent a spectrum or continuum of autism-related disorders called *autism spectrum disorders.* Asperger's disorder falls at the mild end of the spectrum, with autism in the middle, and childhood disintegrative disorder and Rett's disorder at the most severe or lower functioning end. The diagnostic features of autistic disorder are found in Table 14.2. Table 14.3 lists the diagnostic features of other types of pervasive developmental disorders.

autism A pervasive developmental disorder characterized by failure to relate to others, lack of speech, disturbed motor behaviors, intellectual impairment, and demands for sameness in the environment.

Asperger's disorder A pervasive developmental disorder characterized by social deficits and stereotyped behavior but without the significant language or cognitive delays associated with autism.

Rett's disorder A pervasive developmental disorder characterized by a range of physical, behavioral, motor, and cognitive abnormalities that begin after a few months of apparently normal development.

childhood disintegrative disorder A pervasive developmental disorder involving loss of previously acquired skills and abnormal functioning following a period of apparently normal development during the first 2 years of life.

TABLE 14.2
Diagnostic Features of Autistic Disorder

A. Diagnosis requires a combination of features from the following groups. Not all of the features from each group need be present for a diagnosis to be made.

Impaired Social Interactions

1. Impairment in the nonverbal behaviors such as facial expressiveness, posture, gestures, and eye contact that normally regulate social interaction
2. Does not develop age-appropriate peer relationships
3. Failure to express pleasure in the happiness of other people
4. Does not show social or emotional reciprocity (give and take)

Impaired Communication

1. Delay in development of spoken language (nor is there an effort to compensate for this lack through gestures)
2. When speech development is adequate, there is nevertheless lack of ability to initiate or sustain conversation
3. Shows abnormalities in form or content of speech (e.g., stereotyped or repetitive speech, as in echolalia; idiosyncratic use of words; speaking about the self in the second or third person—using "you" or "he" to mean "I")
4. Does not show spontaneous social or imaginative (make-believe) play

Restricted, Repetitive, and Stereotyped Behavior Patterns

1. Shows restricted range of interests
2. Insists on routines (e.g., always uses same route to go from one place to another)
3. Shows stereotyped movements (e.g., hand flicking, head banging, rocking, spinning)
4. Shows preoccupation with parts of objects (e.g., repetitive spinning of wheels of toy car) or unusual attachments to objects (e.g., carrying a piece of string)

B. Onset occurs prior to the age of 3 through display of abnormal functioning in at least one of the following: social behavior, communication, or imaginative play.

Source: Adapted from the *DSM-IV-TR* (APA, 2000).

TABLE 14.3

Diagnostic Features of Other Pervasive Developmental Disorders

Disorder	Diagnostic Features
Asperger's Disorder	• Markedly impaired social interactions (e.g., failure to maintain eye contact or to develop age-appropriate peer relationships, or failure to seek out others to share enjoyable activities or interests) • Development of narrow, repetitive, and stereotyped behaviors, interests, and activities (e.g., twisting hands or fingers; rigidly adhering to fixed routines or rituals that lack any clear purpose; fascination with train schedules) • No clinically significant delay in language or cognitive development or in development of self-help skills or adaptive behaviors apart from social interactions
Rett's Disorder	After apparently normal development during the first few months of life, the following abnormalities develop: • Slowing of head growth • Deteriorating motor skills (loss of purposeful hand skills) • Development of stereotyped hand movements, typically resembling hand-wringing or hand washing • Development of poorly coordinated gait or movement of whole body • Loss of social interest • Severe deficits in language development • Typically associated with profound or severe mental retardation
Childhood Disintegrative Disorder	After apparently normal development for at least the first 2 years of life: • Significant loss of previously acquired skills in such areas as understanding or using language, social or adaptive functioning, bowel or bladder control, play, or motor skills • Abnormal functioning as shown by impaired social interactions or communication, and development of narrow, stereotyped, and repetitive behaviors, interests, or activities

Source: Adapted from the *DSM-IV-TR* (APA, 2000).

Autism

Autism is one of the severest disorders of childhood. It is a chronic, lifelong condition. Children with autism, like Peter, seem utterly alone in the world, despite parental efforts to bridge the gulf that divides them.

A Case of Autism

Peter nursed eagerly, sat and walked at the expected ages. Yet some of his behavior made us vaguely uneasy. He never put anything in his mouth. Not his fingers nor his toys—nothing. . . .

More troubling was the fact that Peter didn't look at us, or smile, and wouldn't play the games that seemed as much a part of babyhood as diapers. He rarely laughed, and when he did, it was at things that didn't seem funny to us. He didn't cuddle, but sat upright in my lap, even when I rocked him. But children differ and we were content to let Peter be himself. We thought it hilarious when my brother, visiting us when Peter was 8 months old, observed that "That kid has no social instincts, whatsoever." Although Peter was a first child, he was not isolated. I frequently put him in his playpen in front of the house, where the schoolchildren stopped to play with him as they passed. He ignored them, too.

It was Kitty, a personality kid, born two years later, whose responsiveness emphasized the degree of Peter's difference. When I went into her room for the late feeding, her little head bobbed up and she greeted me with a smile that reached from her head to her toes. And the realization of that difference chilled me more than the wintry bedroom.

Peter's babbling had not turned into speech by the time he was 3. His play was solitary and repetitious. He tore paper into long thin strips, bushel baskets of it every day. He spun the lids from my canning jars and became upset if we tried to divert him. Only rarely could I catch his eye, and then saw his focus change from me to the reflection in my glasses. . . .

[Peter's] adventures into our suburban neighborhood had been unhappy. He had disregarded the universal rule that sand is to be kept in sandboxes, and the children themselves had punished him. He walked around a sad and solitary figure, always carrying a toy airplane, a toy he never played with. At that time, I had not heard the word that was to dominate our lives, to hover over every conversation, to sit through every meal beside us. That word was autism.

—Adapted from Eberhardy, 1967

The word *autism* derives from the Greek *autos*, meaning "self." The term was first used in 1906 by the Swiss psychiatrist Eugen Bleuler to refer to a peculiar style of thinking among people with schizophrenia. Autistic thinking is the tendency to view oneself as the center of the universe, to believe that external events somehow refer to oneself. In 1943, another psychiatrist, Leo Kanner, applied the diagnosis "early infantile autism" to a group of disturbed children who seemed unable to relate to others, as if they lived in their own private worlds. Unlike children suffering from mental retardation, these children seemed to shut out any input from the outside world, creating a kind of "autistic aloneness" (Kanner, 1943).

Autism. Autism, one of the most severe childhood disorders, is characterized by pervasive deficits in the ability to relate to and communicate with others and by a restricted range of activities and interests. Children with autistic disorder lack the ability to relate to others and seem to live in their own private worlds.

Scientists today face a baffling mystery: What accounts for a nearly tenfold rise in reported cases of autism in recent years? The causes remain unclear, although improved diagnostic practices and greater awareness of the disorder among physicians probably contributes to some of the increase. Many children who in the past may have been incorrectly diagnosed with mental retardation or learning disabilities are now classified as autistic (Shattuck, 2006a, 2006b).

Scientists are also actively investigating whether other factors, such as prenatal or childhood infections or exposure to environmental toxins, may play a role in explaining the increased incidence of the disorder. Presently, no one really knows (Ault, 2004). Suspicion has also focused on possible contamination from a preservative in the widely used *MMR* (measles, mumps, rubella) vaccine. However, scientists have failed to find any association between autism and vaccines (Madsen et al., 2002). Dr. Fred Volkmar, an autism expert at the Yale Child Study Center, says, "hard scientific evidence to support any specific environmental cause has been lacking" (quoted in Goode, 2004b, p. A17).

According to the U.S. Centers for Disease Control and Prevention (CDC), about 1 in 150 children in the United States are affected by *autism spectrum disorders*, which includes autism and related disorders such as Asperger's disorder (CDC, 2007).

Autism is more common in boys than in girls, about four times as common (Baron-Cohen, Knickmeyer, & Belmonte, 2005). The disorder generally becomes evident in toddlers between 18 and 30 months of age, but the average child is not diagnosed until about age 6. Delays in diagnosis can be detrimental, because the earlier children with autism are diagnosed and treated, the better they generally do (Fox, 2000).

Children with autism are often described by their parents as having been "good babies" early in infancy. This generally means they were not demanding. As they develop, however, they begin to reject physical affection, such as cuddling, hugging, and kissing. Their speech development begins to fall behind the norm. Although Eric did quite well through his first 16 months, signs of social detachment often begin during the first year of life, such as failure to look at other people's faces. The clinical features of the disorder appear prior to 3 years of age (APA, 2000).

Autism seems always to have been with Peter. However, in the following case example, the disorder apparently developed between the ages of 12 and 24 months.

◇

The Case of Eric

"People used to say to me they hoped they [would have] a baby just like mine," Sarah said of Eric, 3 years old at the time. As an infant, Eric smiled endearingly, laughed, and hugged. He uttered a dozen words by his first birthday. By 16 months he had memorized the alphabet and could read some signs. "People were very impressed," Sarah said.

Gradually, things changed, but it took months for Sarah to realize that Eric had a problem. At the age of 2, other members of Eric's play group bubbled with conversation. Eric had abandoned words completely. Instead, Eric combined letters and numbers in idiosyncratic ways, such as "B–T–2–4–6–Z–3."

Eric grew increasingly withdrawn. His diet was essentially self-limited to peanut butter and jelly sandwiches. He spent hour after hour arranging letters and numbers on a magnetic board. But the "symptom" that distressed Sarah most was impossible to measure: when she gazed into Eric's eyes, she no longer saw a "sparkle."

—Adapted from Martin, 1989

Features of Autism Perhaps the most poignant feature of autism is the child's utter aloneness (see Table 14.2). Other features include language and communication problems and ritualistic or stereotyped behavior. The child may also be mute, or if some language skills are present, they may be characterized by peculiar usage, as in *echolalia* (parroting back what the child has heard in a high-pitched monotone); pronoun reversals (using "you" or "he" instead of "I"); use of words that have meaning only to those who have intimate knowledge of the child; and tendencies to raise the voice at the end of sentences, as if asking a question. Nonverbal communication may also be impaired or absent. For example, autistic children may avoid eye contact and show an absence of any facial expressions (Dalton et al., 2005). They are also slow to respond to adults who try to grab their attention, if they attend at all. Although they may be unresponsive to others, however, they display strong emotions, especially strong negative emotions, such as anger, sadness, and fear.

A primary feature of autism is repeated purposeless stereotyped movements—interminably twirling, flapping the hands, or rocking back and forth with the arms around the knees. Some children with autism mutilate themselves, even as they cry out in pain. They may bang their heads, slap their faces, bite their hands and shoulders, or pull out their hair. They may also throw sudden tantrums or panics. Another feature of autism is aversion to environmental changes—a feature termed *preservation of sameness*. When familiar objects are moved even slightly from their usual places, children with autism may throw tantrums or cry continually. Like Eric, children with autistic disorder may insist on eating the same food every day.

Children with autism are bound by ritual. The teacher of a 5-year-old girl with autistic disorder learned to greet her every morning by saying, "Good morning, Lily, I am very, very glad to see you" (Diamond, Baldwin, & Diamond, 1963). Although Lily would not respond to the greeting, she would shriek if the teacher omitted even one of the *very*s.

Like Donna Williams, the woman whose childhood experiences opened this chapter, autistic children often view people as a threat. Reflecting back on his childhood, a high-functioning autistic young man speaks about his needs for sameness and for performing repetitive, stereotyped behaviors. For this young man, people were a threat because they were not always the same and were made up of pieces that didn't quite fit together:

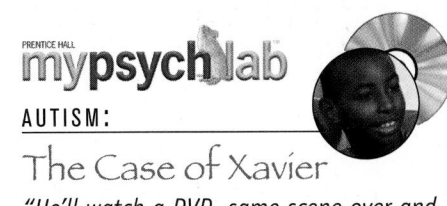

PRENTICE HALL
mypsychlab
AUTISM:
The Case of Xavier
"He'll watch a DVD, same scene over and over and over again."

"I Didn't Know What They Were For"

I loved repetition. Every time I turned on a light I knew what would happen. When I flipped the switch, the light went on. It gave me a wonderful feeling of security because it was exactly the same each time. Sometimes there were two switches on one plate, and I like those even better; I really liked wondering which light would go on from which switch. Even when I knew, it was thrilling to do it over and over. It was always the same.

People bothered me. I didn't know what they were for or what they would do to me. They were not always the same and I had no security with them at all. Even a person who was always nice to me might be different sometimes. Things didn't fit together to me with people. Even when I saw them a lot, they were still in pieces, and I couldn't connect them to anything. . . .

—*From Barron & Barron, 2002, pp. 20–21*

Autistic children appear to have failed to develop a differentiated self-concept, a sense of themselves as distinct individuals. Despite their unusual behavior, they are often quite attractive and have an "intelligent look" about them. However, as measured by scores on standardized tests, their intellectual development tends to lag below the norm. Though some autistic children have normal IQs, most show evidence of mental retardation (Noonan, 2003). Even those without intellectual impairment have difficulty acquiring the ability to symbolize, such as recognizing emotions, engaging in symbolic play, and solving problems conceptually. They also display difficulty in performing tasks that require interaction with other people. The relationship between autism and intelligence is clouded, however, by difficulties in administering standardized IQ tests to these children. Testing requires cooperation, a skill that is dramatically lacking in children with autism. At best, we can only estimate their intellectual ability.

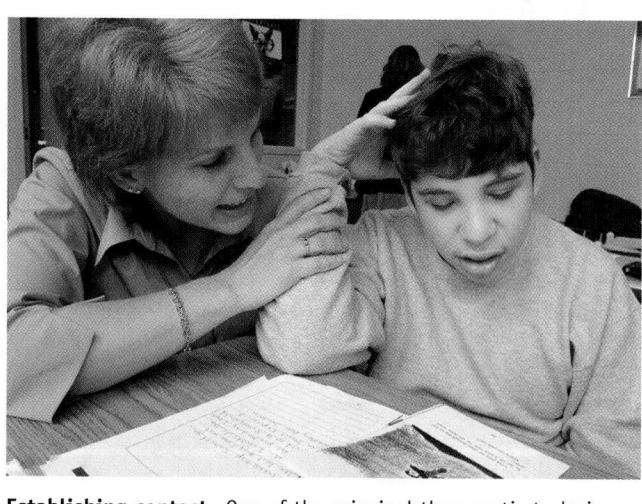

Establishing contact. One of the principal therapeutic tasks in working with children with autism is the establishment of interpersonal contact. Behavioral therapists use reinforcers to increase adaptive social behaviors, such as paying attention to the therapist and playing with other children. Behavioral therapists may also use punishments to suppress self-mutilative behavior.

Theoretical Perspectives An early and now discredited belief held that the autistic child's aloofness was a reaction to parents who were cold and detached—"emotional refrigerators" who lacked the ability to establish warm relationships with their children.

Psychologist O. Ivar Lovaas and his colleagues (1979) offered a cognitive-learning perspective on autism. They suggest that children with autism have perceptual deficits that limit them to processing only one stimulus at a time. As a result, they are slow to learn by means of classical conditioning (association of stimuli). From the learning-theory perspective, children become attached to their primary caregivers through associations with primary reinforcers such as food and hugging. Autistic children, however, attend either to the food or to the cuddling and do not connect it with the parent.

Research on cognitive deficits shows that autistic children do often have difficulties integrating information from various senses (e.g., Toichi et al., 2002). At times they seem unduly sensitive to stimulation. At other times they become so insensitive that an observer might wonder whether they are deaf. Perceptual and cognitive deficits seem to diminish their capacity to make use of information—to comprehend and apply social rules.

But what is the basis of these perceptual and cognitive deficits? Although we don't yet know what causes autism, the many clinical features of the disorder, including mental retardation, language deficits, bizarre motor behavior, even seizures, point to a neurological basis involving brain abnormalities (Grossberg & Seidman, 2006). Mounting evidence from MRI, PET scan, and other brain-imaging studies shows a range of abnormalities in the brains of autistic patients, including malfunctions of neural circuitry and apparent loss of brain tissue (e.g., Friedman et al., 2006; Hardan et al., 2006; Haznedar et al., 2006; Silk et al., 2006). Many scientists today believe that the brain of the autistic child develops abnormally due to a combination of genetic factors and (presently unknown) environmental influences, possibly involving exposure to toxins or viruses (Glasson et al., 2004; Ramoz et al., 2004; Wallis, 2006). Multiple genes may be responsible for determining susceptibility to autism; work is now proceeding to track down suspected genes (e.g., Cantor et al., 2005; Wassink et al., 2007).

Treatment Although there is no cure for autism, we've learned that early, intensive behavioral treatment programs that apply learning principles can significantly improve learning and communication skills and reduce disturbed behaviors (Ben-Itzchak & Zachor, 2006; Matson, 2006; Sherer & Schreibman, 2005; Wallis, 2006). No other treatment approach has produced comparable results. Using operant conditioning methods, therapists and parents engage in the painstaking work, systematically using rewards and mild punishments to increase the child's ability to attend to others, to play with other children, to develop academic skills, and to eliminate self-mutilative behavior.

The most widely used behavioral treatment programs are highly intensive and structured, offering a great deal of individual, one-to-one instruction. In a classic study, psychologist O. Ivar Lovaas of UCLA demonstrated impressive gains in autistic children who received more than 40 hours of one-to-one behavior modification each week for at least 2 years (Lovaas, 1987). Unfortunately, intensive one-to-one treatment is expensive (estimates range from $40k to more than $60k annually), and parents seeking publically supported programs are often put on long waiting lists (Carey, 2004; Gross, 2004). Also, although long-term follow-ups remain to be reported, some children make great progress and others do not (Smith, 1999). Children who are better functioning at the start of treatment typically gain the most.

Biomedical treatments have been limited largely to the use of psychiatric drugs to control disruptive behavior. For example, antipsychotic drugs normally used to treat schizophrenia have been used to help control tantrums, aggression, self-injurious, and stereotyped behavior in autistic children (e.g., McDougle et al., 2005). But drugs do not produce consistent improvement in cognitive and language development.

mypsych lab

AUTISM:

Dr. Kathy Pratt

Autistic traits generally continue into adulthood to one degree or another. Yet some autistic children do go on to earn college degrees and function independently. Others need continuing treatment throughout their lives, even institutionalized care. However, even the highest functioning adults with the disorder manifest deficient social and communication skills and a highly limited range of interests and activities (APA, 2000).

MENTAL RETARDATION

About 1% of the general population is affected by **mental retardation,** a broad-ranging impairment in the development of cognitive and social functioning (APA, 2000). The course of mental retardation is variable. Many children with mental retardation improve over time, especially if they receive support, guidance, and enriched educational opportunities. Those who are reared in impoverished environments may fail to improve or may deteriorate further.

Mental retardation is diagnosed by a combination of three criteria: (a) low scores on formal intelligence tests (an IQ score of approximately 70 or below); (b) impaired functioning in performing life tasks expected of someone of the same age in a given cultural setting; and (c) development of the disorder before the age of 18 (APA, 2000; Kanaya, Scullin, & Ceci, 2003).

The *DSM* classifies mental retardation according to level of severity, as shown in Table 14.4. Most children with mental retardation (about 85%) fall into the mildly retarded range. These children are generally capable of meeting basic academic demands, such as learning to read simple passages. As adults they are generally capable of independent functioning, although they may require some guidance and support. Table 14.5 provides a description of the deficits and abilities associated with various degrees of mental retardation.

Causes of Mental Retardation

The causes of mental retardation include biological factors, psychosocial factors, or a combination of these factors (APA, 2000). Biological causes include chromosomal and genetic disorders, infectious diseases, and maternal alcohol use during pregnancy. Psychosocial causes include exposure to an impoverished home environment marked by the lack of intellectually stimulating activities during childhood.

Down Syndrome and Other Chromosomal Abnormalities The most frequently identified cause of mental retardation is **Down syndrome** (formerly called Down's syndrome), which is characterized by an extra chromosome on the 21st pair of chromosomes, resulting in 47 chromosomes rather than the normal complement of 46 (Arron et al., 2006). Down syndrome occurs in about 1 in 800 births. It usually occurs when the

mental retardation A generalized delay or impairment in the development of intellectual and adaptive abilities.

Down syndrome A condition caused by the presence of an extra chromosome on the 21st pair and characterized by mental retardation and various physical anomalies.

TABLE 14.4
Levels of Mental Retardation

Degree of Severity	Approximate IQ Range	Percentage of People with Mental Retardation within the Range
Mild mental retardation	50–55 to approximately 70	Approximately 85%
Moderate mental retardation	35–40 to 50–55	10
Severe mental retardation	20–25 to 35–40	3–4
Profound mental retardation	Below 20 or 25	1–2

Source: Adapted from the *DSM-IV-TR* (APA, 2000).

TABLE 14.5

Levels of Retardation, Typical Ranges of IQ Scores, and Types of Adaptive Behaviors Shown

Severity/Approximate IQ Score Range	Preschool Age (0–5) Maturation and Development	School Age (6–21) Training and Education	Adult (21 and Over) Social and Vocational Adequacy
Mild/50–70	Often not noticed as retarded by casual observer, but is slower to walk, feed self, and talk than most children.	Can acquire practical skills and useful reading and arithmetic to a 3rd- to 6th-grade level with special education. Can be guided toward social conformity.	Can usually achieve social and vocational skills adequate to self-maintenance; may need occasional guidance and support when under unusual social or economic stress.
Moderate/35–49	Noticeable delays in motor development, especially in speech; responds to training in various self-help activities.	Can learn simple communication, elementary health and safety habits, and simple manual skills; does not progress in functional reading or arithmetic.	Can perform simple tasks under sheltered conditions; participates in simple recreation; travels alone in familiar places; usually incapable of self-maintenance.
Severe/20–34	Marked delay in motor development; little or no communication skill; may respond to training in elementary self-help—e.g., self-feeding.	Usually walks, barring specific disability; has some understanding of speech and some response; can profit from systematic habit training.	Can conform to daily routines and repetitive activities; needs continuing direction and supervision in protective environment.
Profound/Below 20	Gross retardation; minimal capacity for functioning in sensorimotor areas; needs nursing care.	Obvious delays in all areas of development; shows basic emotional responses; may respond to skillful training in use of legs, hands, and jaws; needs close supervision.	May walk, may need nursing care, may have primitive speech; will usually benefit from regular physical activity; incapable of self-maintenance.

Source: From *Essentials of Psychology* (6th ed.) by S. A. Rathus (1996). Copyright © 2001. Reprinted with permission of Brooks/Cole, an imprint of the Wadsworth Group, a division of Thomson Learning. FAX 800-730-2215.

21st pair of chromosomes in either the egg or the sperm fails to divide normally, resulting in an extra chromosome. Chromosomal abnormalities become more likely as parents age, so expectant couples in their mid-30s or older often undergo prenatal genetic tests to detect Down syndrome and other genetic abnormalities. Down syndrome can be traced to a defect in the mother's chromosomes in about 95% of cases, with the remainder attributable to defects in the father's sperm (Antonarakas et al., 1991).

People with Down syndrome are recognizable by distinctive physical features: a round face, broad, flat nose, and small, downward-sloping folds of skin at the inside corners of the eyes, which gives the impression of slanted eyes. A protruding tongue, small, squarish hands and short fingers, a curved fifth finger, and disproportionately small arms and legs in relation to their bodies also characterize children with Down syndrome. Nearly all of these children have mental retardation, and many suffer from physical problems, such as malformations of the heart and respiratory difficulties. Sadly, the average life expectancy of Down syndrome patients is only 49 years (Yang, Rasmussen, & Friedman, 2002). In their later years, people with Down syndrome tend to suffer memory losses and experience childish emotions that represent a form of senility.

Children with Down syndrome suffer various deficits in learning and development. They tend to be uncoordinated and to lack proper muscle tone, which makes it difficult for them to carry out physical tasks and play like other children. Down syndrome children suffer memory deficits, especially for information presented verbally, which makes it difficult for them to learn in school. They also have difficulty following instructions from teachers and expressing their thoughts or needs clearly in speech. Despite their disabilities, most can learn to read, write, and perform simple arithmetic, if they receive appropriate schooling and encouragement.

Although less common than Down syndrome, chromosomal abnormalities on the sex chromosome may also result in mental retardation, such as in Klinefelter's syndrome and Turner's syndrome. *Klinefelter's syndrome*, which only occurs among males, is characterized by the presence of an extra X chromosome, resulting in an XXY chromosomal pattern rather than the normal XY pattern. Estimates of the prevalence of Klinefelter's syndrome range from 1 in 500 to 1 in 1,000 male births (Brody, 1993). These men fail to develop appropriate secondary sex characteristics, resulting in small, underdeveloped testes, low sperm production, enlarged breasts, poor muscular development, and infertility. Mild retardation or learning disabilities are also common. Men with Klinefelter's syndrome often don't discover they have the condition until they undergo tests for infertility.

Turner's syndrome, found only among females, is characterized by the presence of a single X sex chromosome instead of the normal two. Although such girls develop normal external genitals, their ovaries remain poorly developed, producing reduced amounts of estrogen. As women, they tend to be shorter than average and infertile. They also tend to show evidence of mild retardation, especially in skills relating to math and science.

Fragile X Syndrome and Other Genetic Abnormalities Scientists have identified several genetic causes of mental retardation (Burton, 2006; Sharp et al., 2006). The most commonly identified genetic cause is **fragile X syndrome** (Hall, 2006; Huber, 2007). The syndrome is the second most common form of retardation overall, after Down syndrome. The disorder is caused by a defective gene in an area of the X sex chromosome that appears fragile, hence the name. Fragile X syndrome causes mental retardation in 1 out of 1,000 to 1,500 males and (generally less severe) mental handicaps in 1 out of 2,000 to 2,500 females (Rousseau et al., 1991). The effects of fragile X syndrome range from mild learning disabilities to retardation so profound that those affected can hardly speak or function.

Females normally have two X chromosomes, whereas males have only one. For females, having two X chromosomes seems to provide some protection against the disorder if the defective gene turns up on one of the two chromosomes. This may explain why the disorder usually has more profound effects on males than on females. Yet the mutation does not always manifest itself. Many males and females carry the fragile X mutation without showing any clinical signs. Such carriers can still pass the syndrome to their offspring.

A genetic test can detect the genetic defect that causes fragile X syndrome. Although there is no treatment for the syndrome, genetic research focused on identifying the molecular cause of the disorder may lead to effective treatments (Huber et al., 2002).

Phenylketonuria (PKU) is a genetic disorder that occurs in 1 in 10,000 births (Plomin et al., 1994). It is caused by a recessive gene that prevents the child from metabolizing the amino acid phenylalanine, which is found in many foods. Consequently, phenylalanine and its derivative, phenylpyruvic acid, accumulate in the body, causing damage to the central nervous system, resulting in mental retardation. PKU can be detected in newborns by analyzing blood or urine samples. Although there is no cure for PKU, children with the disorder may suffer less damage or develop normally if they are placed on a diet low in phenylalanine soon after birth. These children receive protein supplements that compensate for their nutritional loss.

Today, various prenatal tests can detect chromosomal abnormalities and genetic disorders. In *amniocentesis,* which is usually conducted about 14 to 15 weeks following conception, a sample of amniotic fluid is drawn with a syringe from the amniotic sac that contains the fetus. Cells from the fetus can then be separated from the fluid, allowed to grow in a culture, and examined for abnormalities, including Down syndrome. Blood tests are used to detect carriers of other disorders.

Prenatal Factors Some cases of mental retardation are caused by maternal infections or substance abuse during pregnancy. Rubella (German measles) in the mother, for example, can be passed along to the unborn child, causing brain damage resulting in retardation. It may also play a role in autism. Although the mother may experience mild symptoms or none at all, the effects on the fetus can be tragic. Other maternal infections that may cause retardation in the child include syphilis, cytomegalovirus, and genital herpes.

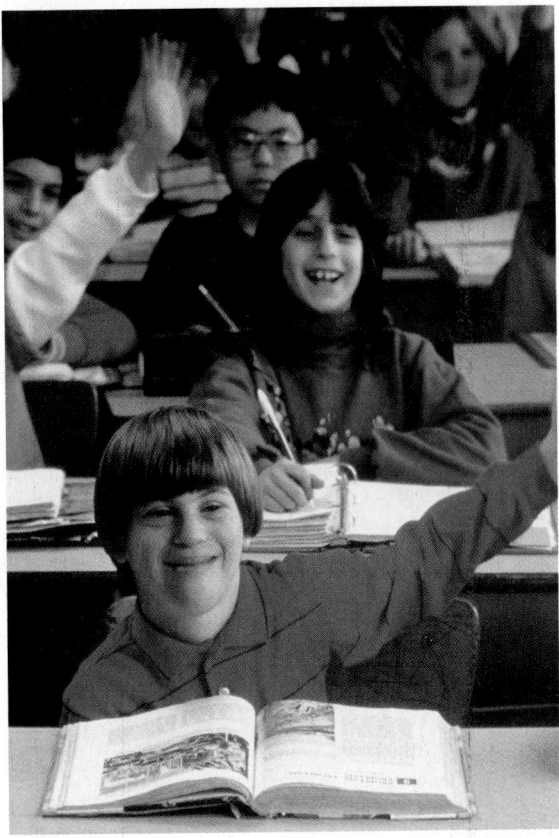

Striving to achieve. Most children with Down syndrome can learn basic academic skills if they are afforded opportunities to learn and are provided with encouragement.

fragile X syndrome An inherited form of mental retardation caused by a mutated gene on the X chromosome.

phenylketonuria (PKU) A genetic disorder that prevents the metabolization of phenylpyruvic acid, leading to mental retardation unless the diet is strictly controlled.

488   Chapter 14

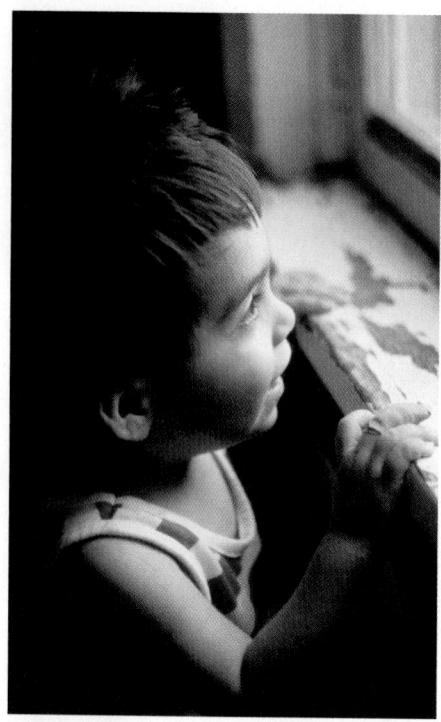

Environmental hazards. Children who are exposed to environmental hazards, such as paint chips containing lead-based paint, may suffer brain damage that can lead to mental retardation.

cultural–familial retardation A mild form of mental retardation that is influenced by impoverishment of the home environment.

Widespread programs that immunize women against rubella before pregnancy and tests for syphilis during pregnancy have reduced the risk of transmission of these infections to children. Most children who contract genital herpes from their mothers do so during delivery by coming into contact with the herpes simplex virus in the birth canal. Therefore, delivery by caesarean section (C-section) can prevent viral transmission during childbirth.

Drugs that the mother ingests during pregnancy may pass through the placenta to the child. Some can cause severe birth deformities and mental retardation. Children whose mothers drink alcohol during pregnancy are often born with *fetal alcohol syndrome* (described in Chapter 9), one of the most prominent causes of mental retardation.

Birth complications, such as oxygen deprivation or head injuries, place children at increased risk for neurological disorders, including mental retardation. Prematurity also places children at risk of retardation and other developmental problems. Brain infections, such as encephalitis and meningitis, or traumas during infancy and early childhood can cause mental retardation and other health problems. Children who ingest toxins, such as paint chips containing lead, may also suffer brain damage that produces mental retardation.

Cultural-Familial Causes   Most cases of mental retardation fall in the mild range of severity and have no apparent biological cause or distinguishing physical feature. Psychosocial factors, such as an impoverished home or social environment that is intellectually unstimulating, or parental neglect or abuse, may contribute to mental retardation. Such cases these are classified as **cultural-familial retardation.**

Children in impoverished families may lack toys, books, or opportunities to interact with adults in intellectually stimulating ways. Consequently, they may not develop appropriate language skills or acquire any motivation to learn. Economic burdens, such as the need to hold multiple jobs, may prevent their parents from spending time reading to them, talking to them at length, and exposing them to creative play or activities. They may spend most of their days glued to the TV set. The parents, most of whom were also reared in poverty, may lack the reading or communication skills to help develop these skills in their children. A vicious cycle of poverty and impoverished intellectual development is repeated from generation to generation.

Children with this form of retardation may respond dramatically when provided with enriched learning experiences, especially at an early age. Social programs, such as Head Start, have helped children at risk of cultural-familial retardation to function within the normal range of ability (e.g., Barnett & Escobar, 1990).

Intervention

The services that children with mental retardation need depend on the level of severity and type of retardation. With appropriate training, children with mild retardation may approach a sixth-grade level of competence. They can acquire vocational skills and support themselves minimally through meaningful work. Many such children can be mainstreamed in regular classes. At the other extreme, children with severe or profound mental retardation may need institutional care or placement in a residential care facility in the community, such as a group home. Placement in an institution is often based on the need to control destructive or aggressive behavior, not because of the severity of the individual's intellectual impairment. Consider the case of a child with moderate retardation.

A Case of Moderate Mental Retardation

The mother pleaded with the emergency room physician to admit her 15-year-old son, claiming that she couldn't take it anymore. Her son, a Down syndrome patient with an IQ of 45, had alternated since the age of 8 between living in institutions and at home. Each visiting day he pleaded with his mother to take him home, and after about a year at each placement, she would bring him home but find herself unable to control his behavior. During temper tantrums, he would break dishes and destroy furniture and had recently become physically assaultive toward his mother, hitting her on the arm and shoulder during a recent scuffle when she attempted to stop him from repeatedly banging a broom on the floor.

—Adapted from Spitzer et al., 1989, pp. 338–340

Educators sometimes disagree about whether children with mental retardation should be mainstreamed in regular classes or placed in special education classes. Although some children with mild retardation achieve better when they are mainstreamed, others do not. They may find these classes overwhelming and withdraw from their schoolmates. There has also been a trend toward deinstitutionalization of people with more severe mental retardation, motivated in large part by public outrage over the appalling conditions that formerly existed in many institutions serving this population. The Developmentally Disabled Assistance and Bill of Rights Act, which Congress passed in 1975, provided that persons with mental retardation have the right to receive appropriate treatment in the least-restrictive treatment setting. Nationwide, the population of institutions for people with mental retardation shrank by nearly two-thirds from the 1970s to the 1990s.

People with mental retardation who are capable of functioning in the community have the right to receive less-restrictive care than is provided in large institutions. Many are capable of living outside the institution and have been placed in supervised group homes. Residents typically share household responsibilities and are encouraged to participate in meaningful daily activities, such as training programs or sheltered workshops. Others live with their families and attend structured day programs. Adults with mild retardation often work in outside jobs and live in their own apartments or share apartments with other persons with mild retardation. Although the large-scale dumping of mental patients in the community from psychiatric institutions resulted in massive social problems and swelled the ranks of America's homeless population, deinstitutionalization of people with mental retardation has largely been a success story that has been achieved with rare dignity (Winerip, 1991).

People with mental retardation (MR) stand a high risk of developing other psychiatric disorders, such as anxiety and depression, as well as behavioral problems (Einfeld et al., 2006; McGillivray & McCabe, 2006). Unfortunately, the emotional life of people with MR has received little attention in the literature (Ross & Oliver, 2003). Many professionals even assumed (wrongly) that people with mental retardation were somehow immune from psychological problems or that they lacked the verbal skills needed to benefit from psychotherapy. However, evidence shows that people with mental retardation can benefit from psychotherapy (Bütz, Bowling, & Bliss, 2000).

People with MR often need psychological help dealing with adjustment to life in the community. Many have difficulty making friends and become socially isolated. Problems with self-esteem are also common, especially because people who have mental retardation are often demeaned and ridiculed. Psychological counseling may be supplemented with behavioral techniques that help people acquire skills in areas such as personal hygiene, work, and social relationships. Structured behavioral approaches can be used to teach persons with more severe retardation such basic hygienic behaviors as toothbrushing, self-dressing, and hair combing. Other behavioral treatment techniques include social skills training, which focuses on increasing the individual's ability to relate effectively to others, and anger management training to help individuals develop effective ways of handling conflicts without acting out.

LEARNING DISORDERS

Nelson Rockefeller was a governor of New York State and a vice president of the United States. He was brilliant and well educated. However, despite the best of tutors, he always had trouble reading. Rockefeller suffered from

Imparting skills. In 1975, Congress enacted legislation that requires public schools to provide children with disabilities with educational programs that meet their individual needs.

dyslexia A learning disorder characterized by impaired reading ability.

learning disorder A deficiency in a specific learning ability in the context of normal intelligence and exposure to learning opportunities.

dyslexia, a condition whose name is derived from the Greek roots *dys-*, meaning "bad," and *lexikon,* meaning "of words." Dyslexia is the most common type of **learning disorder** (also called a *learning disability*), accounting for perhaps 80% of cases. People with dyslexia have trouble reading despite possessing at least average intelligence (Anthony & Francis, 2005). People with learning disorders show poor development in reading, math, or writing skills to a point that it impairs their school performance or daily functioning.

Learning disorders are typically chronic disorders that affect development well into adulthood. Children with learning disorders tend to perform poorly in school. Their teachers and families often view them as failures. It is not surprising that children with learning disorders often have other psychological problems, such as low self-esteem. They are also more likely than their peers to be diagnosed with attention-deficit hyperactivity disorder (Faraone et al., 2000).

Types of Learning Disorders

Types of learning disorders include *mathematics disorder, disorder of written expression,* and *reading disorder.*

Mathematics Disorder *Mathematics disorder* describes children with deficiencies in arithmetic skills. They may have problems understanding basic mathematical terms or operations, such as addition or subtraction; decoding mathematical symbols (+, =, etc.); or learning multiplication tables. The problem may become apparent as early as the first grade (age 6) but is not generally recognized until about the second or third grade.

Disorder of Written Expression *Disorder of written expression* refers to children with grossly deficient writing skills. The deficiency may be characterized by errors in spelling, grammar, or punctuation, or by difficulty in composing sentences and paragraphs. Severe writing difficulties generally become apparent by age 7 (second grade), although milder cases may not be recognized until the age of 10 (fifth grade) or later.

Reading Disorder Reading disorder—*dyslexia*—characterizes children who have poorly developed skills in recognizing words and comprehending written text. Dyslexia is estimated to affect about 4% of school-age children (APA, 2000) and is much more common in boys than in girls (Rutter et al., 2004). Boys with dyslexia are also more likely than girls to show disruptive behavior in class and so are more likely to be referred for evaluation.

Children with dyslexia may read slowly and with great difficulty and may distort, omit, or substitute words when reading aloud. They have trouble decoding letters and letter combinations and translating them into the appropriate sounds (Miller-Medzon, 2000). They may also misperceive letters as upside down (for example, confusing *w* for *m*) or in reversed images (*b* for *d*). Dyslexia is usually apparent by the age of 7, coinciding with the second grade, although it is sometimes recognized in 6-year-olds. Children and adolescents with dyslexia are prone to such problems as depression, low self-worth, and attention-deficit hyperactivity disorder.

Rates of dyslexia vary with respect to native language. Rates of dyslexia are high in English-speaking and French-speaking countries, where the language contains a large number of ways to spell words containing the same meaningful sounds (e.g., the same "o" sound in the words "toe" and "tow"). They are low in Italy, where the language has a smaller ratio of sounds to letter combinations (Paulesu et al., 2001).

Understanding and Treating Learning Disorders

Much of the research on learning disorders focuses on dyslexia, with mounting evidence pointing to underlying abnormalities in the ways the brain of a dyslexic child processes visual and auditory information (Anthony & Francis, 2005; Paulesu et al., 2001). People with dyslexia have difficulty processing the sounds corresponding to particular letters (e.g., seeing an *f* or a *ph* or a *gh* and saying or hearing in our minds

A CLOSER LOOK

The Savant Syndrome

Got a minute? Try the following:

1. Without referring to a calendar, calculate the day of the week that March 15, 2079, will fall on.
2. List the prime numbers between 1 and 1 billion. (Hint: the list starts 1, 2, 3, 5, 7, 11, 13, 17 . . .)
3. Repeat verbatim the newspaper stories you read over coffee this morning.
4. Sing accurately every note played by the first violin in Beethoven's *Ninth Symphony*.

Give up? Don't feel badly about yourself, because very few people can perform such mental feats. Ironically, the people most likely to be able to accomplish these tasks suffer from autism, mental retardation, or both. Clinicians use the label *savant syndrome* to refer to someone with severe mental deficiencies who possesses some remarkable mental abilities. Commonly, these people are called *savants* (the term *savant* is derived from the French *savoir*, meaning "to know"). People with the savant syndrome have shown remarkable though circumscribed mental skills, such as calendar calculating, rare musical talent, even accomplished poetry (Dowker, Hermelin, & Pring, 1996)—all of which stand in contrast to their limited general intellectual abilities. Some people with the syndrome engage in lightning calculations, such as calendar calculating. One young man could tell you in a few seconds the day of the week of any given date—for example, what day of the week October 23, 1996 was (Thioux et al., 2006).

There are also cases of savant persons who were blind but could play back any musical piece, no matter how complex, or repeat long passages of foreign languages without losing a syllable. Others could make exact estimates of elapsed time. One could reportedly repeat verbatim the contents of a newspaper he had just read; another could repeat backward what he had just read (Tradgold, 1914, cited in Treffert, 1988).

The savant syndrome phenomenon occurs more frequently in males by a ratio of about 6 to 1. The special skills of people with the savant syndrome tend to appear out of the blue and may disappear as suddenly.

Many theories have been proposed to explain the savant syndrome, but scientists have yet to reach a consensus. One theory is that people with savant syndrome may inherit two sets of hereditary factors, one for retardation and the other for special memory abilities. Other theorists speculate that the brains of savants are wired with specialized circuitry that allows them to perform concrete and narrowly defined tasks, such as perceiving number relationships (Treffert, 1988). An environment that reinforces savant abilities and provides opportunities for practice and concentration would give further impetus to the development of these unusual abilities. Still the savant syndrome remains a mystery.

Savant syndrome. Leslie Lemke, a blind autistic savant musician, played music he heard verbatim and composed his own music, even though he had no music education. One day when he was about 14, he played flawlessly the entirety of Tchaikovsky's Piano Concerto No. 1 after having heard it once the night before.

an *f* sound). They also have trouble distinguishing speech sounds. In one study, investigators found that the normally dominant speech centers in the left hemisphere of the brain were not as active in dyslexic children as they were in children without reading problems (Breier et al., 2003). These underlying brain deficits may have a genetic basis, as evidence connects genetic factors with a greater risk of dyslexia (Meng et al., 2006; Schumacher et al., 2006).

Recently, scientists speculated that dyslexia may take two general forms, one more genetically influenced and the other more environmentally influenced (Morris, 2003; Shaywitz et al., 2003). The predominant genetic type appears to involve defects in the neural circuitry in the brain that normal readers use to process speech sounds (Shaywitz, Mody, & Shaywitz, 2006). These people learn to compensate for these defects by relying on other brain capabilities, although they continue to read slowly. In the more environmentally influenced type, neural circuity is intact but people rely more on memory than on decoding strategies to understand written words. This second type may be more prevalent in children from disadvantaged educational backgrounds and is associated with more persistent reading disability (Kersting, 2003).

Linking learning disorders to defects in brain circuitry responsible for processing sensory (visual and auditory) information may point toward development of treatment programs that help children adjust to their sensory capabilities. Therapists need to design strategies tailored to each child's particular type of disability and educational needs.

Brain-imaging study of dyslexic adults.
Brain scans taken during a reading task show that stronger activation of the reading systems in the left hemisphere (shown here by areas tinted in yellow) is associated with better reading skills in nondyslexic readers. By contrast, more competent dyslexic readers rely more on the right hemisphere (as shown by blue-tinted areas). More capable dyslexic readers seem to rely on different neural pathways than normal readers. By examining differences in activation of particular areas of the brain, scientists hope to learn more about the neurological underpinnings of dyslexia.

communication disorders A class of psychological disorders characterized by difficulties in understanding or using language.

For example, a child who retains auditory information better than visual information might be taught verbally, by using recordings rather than written materials. Other intervention approaches focus on evaluating children's learning competencies and designing strategies to help them acquire skills needed to perform basic academic tasks, such as arithmetic skills. In addition, language specialists can help dyslexic children grasp the structure and use of words.

COMMUNICATION DISORDERS

Communication disorders are persistent difficulties in understanding or using language. The categories of communication disorders include expressive language disorder, mixed receptive/expressive language disorder, phonological disorder, and stuttering. Each of these disorders interferes with academic or occupational functioning or ability to communicate socially. Table 14.6 lists the *DSM-IV* classification of learning disorders and communication disorders.

Expressive language disorder is a persistent impairment in the use of spoken language, such as slow vocabulary development, errors in tense, difficulties recalling words, and problems producing sentences of appropriate length and complexity for the individual's age. Affected children may also have a phonological (articulation) disorder, compounding their speech problems.

Mixed receptive/expressive language disorder refers to difficulties both understanding and producing speech. There may be difficulty understanding words or sentences. In some cases, children have difficulty understanding certain word types (such as words expressing differences in quantity—*large, big,* or *huge*), spatial terms (such as *near* or *far*), or sentence types (such as sentences that begin with the word *unlike*). Other cases are marked by difficulties understanding simple words or sentences.

Phonological disorder is a persistent difficulty articulating the sounds of speech in the absence of defects in the oral speech mechanism or neurological impairment. Children with the disorder may omit, substitute, or mispronounce certain sounds—especially *ch, f, l, r, sh,* and *th,* which most children articulate properly by the time they reach the early school years. It may sound as if they are uttering "baby talk." Children with more severe cases have problems articulating sounds usually mastered during the preschool years: *b, m, t, d, n,* and *h.* Speech therapy is often helpful, and mild cases often resolve themselves by the age of 8.

Stuttering is a disturbance in the ability to speak fluently with appropriate timing of speech sounds. The lack of normal fluency must be inappropriate for the person's age in order to justify the diagnosis. Stuttering usually begins between 2 and 7 years of age and affects about 1 child in 100 before puberty (APA, 2000). The disorder is characterized by one or more of the following characteristics: (a) repetitions of sounds and syllables; (b) prolongations of certain sounds; (c) interjections of inappropriate sounds; (d) broken words, such as pauses occurring within a spoken word; (e) blocking of

TABLE 14.6		
DSM-IV Classification of Learning Disorders and Communication Disorders		
Learning Disorders	Reading Disorder Mathematics Disorder Disorder of Written Expression	
Communication Disorders	Expressive Language Disorder Mixed Receptive/Expressive Language Disorder Phonological Disorder Stuttering	

Source: Adapted from the *DSM-IV-TR* (APA, 2000).

speech; (f) circumlocutions (substitutions of alternative words to avoid problematic words); (g) displaying an excess of physical tension when emitting words; and (h) repetitions of monosyllabic whole words (for example, "I-I-I-I am glad to meet you") (APA, 2000).

Stuttering occurs in three times as many males as females. The good news is that most children who stutter, upwards of 80%, overcome the problem without any treatment, typically before age 16. What causes stuttering? Although the question is still unresolved, most experts believe that genetic and environmental influences interact in producing stuttering (Shugart et al., 2004; Starkweather, 2002). Brain scans reveal abnormal patterns of neural activity in certain regions of the brain (Ingham, 2003; Neumann et al., 2003). Stuttering also appears to have an emotional component. Recent evidence indicates that children who stutter tend to be more emotionally reactive than nonstutterers—when faced with stressful or challenging situations, they become more upset or excited (Karrass et al., 2006). Social anxiety, or overconcern with how others see them, may also contribute to the problem (Kraaimaat, Vanryckeghem, & Van Dam-Baggen, 2002). Treatment of communication disorders is generally approached with specialized speech therapy or fluency training and with psychological counseling for anxiety or other emotional problems.

ATTENTION-DEFICIT AND DISRUPTIVE BEHAVIOR DISORDERS

Attention-deficit and disruptive behavior disorders are a diverse range of problem behaviors, including *attention-deficit hyperactivity disorder (ADHD), conduct disorder (CD),* and *oppositional defiant disorder (ODD).* These disorders are socially disruptive and usually more upsetting to other people than to the children who are diagnosed with these problems. The rate of comorbidity (co-occurrence) among these disorders is very high.

Attention-Deficit Hyperactivity Disorder

Many parents believe that their children are not attentive toward them—that they run around on whim and do things their own way. Some inattention, especially in early childhood, is normal enough. In **attention-deficit hyperactivity disorder (ADHD),** however, children display impulsivity, inattention, and **hyperactivity** that are inappropriate to their developmental levels (Krain & Castellanos, 2006).

ADHD is divided into three subtypes: (a) a predominantly inattentive type; (b) a predominantly hyperactive or impulsive type; and (c) a combination type characterized by high levels of both inattention and hyperactivity–impulsivity (APA, 2000). The disorder is usually first diagnosed during elementary school, when problems with attention or hyperactivity–impulsivity make it difficult for the child to adjust to school. Although signs of hyperactivity are often observed earlier, many overactive toddlers do not go on to develop the disorder. ADHD affects between 3% and 7% of school-age children, or some two million American youngsters in total (APA, 2000; Bradley & Golden, 2001; Wingert, 2000). ADHD is diagnosed two to nine times more often in boys than girls. Black and Hispanic children are less likely to receive the diagnosis than Euro American children (Schneider & Eisenberg, 2006).

Although inattention appears to be the basic problem, associated problems include inability to sit still for more than a few minutes, bullying, temper tantrums, stubbornness, and failure to respond to punishment (see Table 14.7). Boys with ADHD tend to be judged by their teachers as showing more inattention and hyperactivity in the classroom than are girls with the disorder (Hartung et al., 2002).

Children with ADHD have great difficulty in school. They seem incapable of sitting still. They fidget and squirm in their seats, butt into other children's games, have outbursts of temper, and may

attention-deficit hyperactivity disorder (ADHD) A behavior disorder characterized by excessive motor activity and inability to focus one's attention.

hyperactivity An abnormal behavior pattern characterized by difficulty in maintaining attention and extreme restlessness.

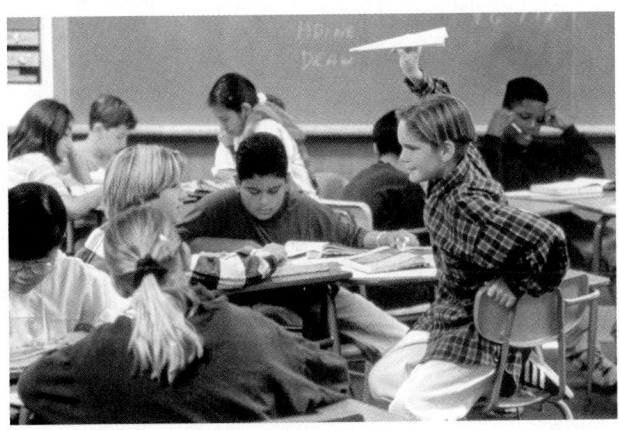

Attention-deficit hyperactivity disorder (ADHD). ADHD is more common in boys than girls and is characterized by attentional difficulties, restlessness, impulsivity, excessive motor behavior (continuous running around or climbing), and temper tantrums.

TABLE 14.7

Diagnostic Features of Attention-Deficit Hyperactivity Disorder (ADHD)

Kind of Problem	Specific Behavior Pattern
Lack of attention	Fails to attend to details or makes careless errors in schoolwork, etc.
	Has difficulty sustaining attention in schoolwork or play
	Doesn't appear to pay attention to what is being said
	Fails to follow through on instructions or to finish work
	Has trouble organizing work and other activities
	Avoids work or activities that require sustained attention
	Loses work tools (e.g., pencils, books, assignments, toys)
	Becomes readily distracted
	Is forgetful in daily activities
Hyperactivity	Fidgets with hands or feet or squirms in his or her seat
	Leaves seat in situations such as the classroom in which remaining seated is required
	Is constantly running around or climbing on things
	Has difficulty playing quietly
Impulsivity	Frequently "calls out" in class
	Fails to wait his/her turn in line, games, etc.

To receive a diagnosis of ADHD, the disorder must begin by the age of 7; must have significantly impaired academic, social, or occupational functioning; and must be characterized by a designated number of clinical features shown in this table occurring over a 6-month period in at least two settings, such as at school, at home, or at work.

Source: Adapted from the *DSM-IV-TR* (APA, 2000).

engage in dangerous behavior, such as running into the street without looking. All in all, they can drive parents and teachers to despair.

Where does "normal" age-appropriate overactivity end and hyperactivity begin? Assessment of the degree of hyperactive behavior is crucial, because many normal children are called "hyper" from time to time. Some critics of the ADHD diagnosis argue that it merely labels children who are difficult to control as mentally disordered or sick. Most children, especially boys, are highly active during the early school years. Proponents of the diagnosis counter that there is a difference in quality between normal overactivity and ADHD. Normally overactive children are usually goal directed and can exert voluntary control over their behavior. But children with ADHD appear hyperactive without reason and seem unable to conform their behavior to the demands of teachers and parents. Put another way: Most children can sit still and concentrate for a while when they want to; children who are hyperactive seemingly cannot.

Although children with ADHD tend to be of average or above-average intelligence, they often underachieve in school. They are frequently disruptive in the classroom and tend to get into fights (especially the boys). They may fail to follow or remember instructions or complete assignments. Compared to children not diagnosed with ADHD, they are more likely to have learning disabilities, to repeat grades, to suffer physical injuries, and to be placed in special education classes. They are also more likely to have mood disorders, anxiety disorders, and problems getting along with family members. Investigators find that ADHD boys tend to lack empathy, or awareness of other people's feelings (Braaten & Rosén, 2000). Not surprisingly, children with ADHD tend to be less well liked by their classmates and more likely to be rejected than other children (Hoza et al., 2005). Teenagers with ADHD are more likely than their peers to use alcohol, tobacco, and illicit drugs (e.g., Molina & Pelham, 2003).

ADHD symptoms tend to decline with age, but the disorder often persists in milder form into adolescence and adulthood (Okie, 2006; Volkmar, 2003). ADHD affects about 4.4% of U.S. adults at some point in their lives (Kessler et al., 2006). Adult forms of ADHD primarily involve problems of inattention and distractabilty rather than hyperactivity.

Theoretical Perspectives Increasing evidence points to an important role for genetics in the development of ADHD. We know that ADHD tends to run in families, which is suggestive of a genetic contribution. But more direct evidence comes from findings of a higher concordance rate for the disorder among monozygotic (MZ) twins than among DZ (dizygotic) twins (Waldman & Gizera, 2006). Researchers recognize that genes do not operate in a vacuum; they believe that environmental factors and the interaction of genes and environment play important roles in ADHD (Bradley & Golden, 2001). For example, ADHD is much more common in children whose mothers smoked during pregnancy than in other children (Milberger et al., 1996). Maternal smoking may cause defects in the brain during prenatal development. Investigators continue to track down other possible environmental factors, such as a high level of family conflict, emotional stress during pregnancy, and poor parenting skills in handling children's misbehavior. Scientists are also seeking to track down the specific genes involved in ADHD (Langley et al., 2004; Wigg et al., 2002).

Rapidly accumulating evidence from brain-imaging studies of children with ADHD shows dysfunctions in parts of the brain, especially the prefrontal cortex, that regulate attention and impulsive behavior (e.g., Fassbender, & Schweitzer, 2006; Krain & Castellanos, 2006; Mackie et al., 2007; Pliszka et al., 2006; Shaw et al., 2006; Smith et al., 2006). The most prominent view among researchers today is that ADHD involves a breakdown in the executive control functions of the brain that normally allow people to focus attention and restrain impulsive behavior (Casey & Durston, 2006; Winstanley, Eagle, & Robbins, 2006).

Treatment It may seem odd that many of the drugs used to help ADHD children calm down and attend better in school are actually stimulants, such as the widely used drug Ritalin and longer-acting stimulants, including Concerta, a one-dose-a-day drug. Concerta quickly became the most commonly prescribed drug for treating ADHD (Bauchner, 2003). Perhaps it's not so odd that these drugs are effective, especially when you consider that stimulant drugs activate the prefrontal cortex, the part of the brain that regulates attentional processes and control over impulsive, acting-out behavior (Faraone, 2003b; Tanaka et al., 2006).

Stimulant drugs not only reduce disruptive, hyperactive behavior but also improve attention spans of ADHD children (Biederman, 2003; Chronis, Jones, & Raggi, 2006). Stimulant drugs are even being used with preschoolers as young as 3 to 5 years of age. Although use of stimulants is not without critics, these drugs can help many children with ADHD calm down and concentrate better on tasks and schoolwork, perhaps for the first times in their lives.

Although stimulant medication can help reduce restlessness and increase attention in school, it remains unclear whether these gains translate into improved academic performance (Stein et al., 2003). We should also note a common problem with stimulant medication, as with other psychiatric drugs, is a high rate of relapse after the person stops taking the medication. Also, the range of effectiveness is limited, as in the following case example.

TRUTH or FICTION

Women who smoke during pregnancy increase the risk of attention-deficit hyperactivity disorder in their offspring.

✓ **TRUE.** Maternal smoking during pregnancy is associated with an increased risk of ADHD in children.

TRUTH or FICTION

Children who are hyperactive are often given depressants to help calm them down.

✓ **FALSE.** Children with ADHD are often given stimulant drugs, such as Ritalin, not depressants. These stimulants have a paradoxical effect of calming them down and increasing their attention spans.

Eddie Hardly Ever Sits Still

Nine-year-old Eddie is a problem in class. His teacher complains that he is so restless and fidgety that the rest of the class cannot concentrate on their work. He hardly ever sits still. He is in constant motion, roaming the classroom, talking to other children while they are working. He has been suspended repeatedly for outrageous behavior, most recently swinging from a fluorescent light fixture and unable to get himself down.

(continued)

His mother reports that Eddie has been a problem since he was a toddler. By the age of 3 he had become unbearably restless and demanding. He has never needed much sleep and always awakened before anyone else in the family, making his way downstairs and wrecking things in the living room and kitchen. Once, at the age of 4, he unlocked the front door and wandered into traffic, but was rescued by a passerby.

Psychological testing shows Eddie to be average in academic ability but to have a "virtually nonexistent" attention span. He shows no interest in television or in games or toys that require concentration. He is unpopular with peers and prefers to ride his bike alone or to play with his dog. He has become disobedient at home and at school and has stolen small amounts of money from his parents and classmates.

Eddie has been treated with methylphenidate (Ritalin), but it was discontinued because it had no effect on his disobedience and stealing. However, it did seem to reduce his restlessness and increase his attention span at school.

—Adapted from Spitzer et al., 1989, pp. 315–317

mypsychlab

ATTENTION-DEFICIT/
HYPERACTIVITY DISORDER
(ADHD):

Dr. Raun Melmed

Then there's the matter of side effects. Although short-term side effects (e.g., loss of appetite or insomnia) usually subside within a few weeks or may be eliminated by lowering the dose, stimulant drugs may lead to other effects, including a slowdown of physical growth (DeNoon, 2006; Wingert, 2000). Fortunately, we have evidence that children taking stimulant medication eventually catch up to their peers in physical stature (e.g., Gorman, 1998).

The first nonstimulant drug approved for use in treating ADHD was Strattera. Strattera works differently than stimulant medication. It is a *selective norepinephrine reuptake inhibitor*, which means that it increases the availability of the neurotransmitter norepinephrine in the brain by interfering with the reuptake of the chemical by transmitting neurons. Although we don't know precisely how the drug works on ADHD, the increased availability of norepinephrine may enhance the brain's ability to regulate impulsive behavior and attention.

Whatever the benefits of ADHD medication may be, drugs cannot teach new skills. So researchers are focusing on whether a combination of stimulant medication and behavioral or cognitive-behavioral techniques can produce greater benefits than either approach alone (e.g., Arnold et al., 2003).

Behavioral interventions also demonstrate therapeutic benefits in treating ADHD (Chronis, Jones, & Raggi, 2006). Behavior modification, involving programs to train parents and teachers to use contingent reinforcement for appropriate behaviors (for example, a teacher praising the child for sitting quietly), may be combined with cognitive modification (for example, training the child to silently talk himself or herself through the steps involved in solving challenging academic problems). Cognitive-behavioral therapists can help train ADHD children to "stop and think" before giving in to angry impulses and acting out aggressively (Miranda & Presentacion, 2000). Although evidence on combining medication and CBT is mixed, some children may do well with therapeutic drugs alone, others with CBT alone, and still others with a combination of both treatments (Abikoff, 2001; Pelham et al., 2005).

Conduct Disorder

conduct disorder A psychological disorder in childhood and adolescence characterized by disruptive, antisocial behavior.

Although it also involves disruptive behavior, **conduct disorder** differs in important ways from ADHD. Whereas children with ADHD seem literally incapable of controlling their behavior, children with conduct disorder purposefully engage in patterns of antisocial behavior that violate social norms and the rights of others. Whereas children with ADHD throw temper tantrums, children diagnosed as conduct disordered are intentionally aggressive and cruel. Like antisocial adults, many conduct-disordered children are callous and apparently do not experience guilt or remorse for their misdeeds. As children, they steal or destroy property; as adolescents they commit rape, armed robbery, even homicide. They may cheat in school—when they bother to attend—and lie to cover their tracks. They frequently engage in substance abuse and sexual activity.

Conduct disorder is a surprisingly common problem, affecting about 12% of males and 7% of females (9.5% overall) (Nock et al., 2006). Conduct disorder is not only more common among boys than girls, but it also takes a somewhat different form. In boys, conduct disorder is more likely to be exhibited in stealing, fighting, vandalism, or disciplinary problems at school, whereas in girls it is more likely to involve lying, truancy, running away, substance use, and prostitution. Children with conduct disorder often present with other disorders or problem behaviors, including ADHD, social withdrawal, and major depression (Decker et al., 2001; Lahey et al., 2003; Lambert et al., 2001). The average (median) age of onset is 11.6 years, although it can develop at younger or older ages (Nock et al., 2006). Conduct disorder is typically a chronic or persistent disorder. Although conduct disorder is closely linked to antisocial behavior, other commonly found traits include callousness (uncaring, mean, cruel) and an unemotional way of relating to others.

Oppositional Defiant Disorder

Conduct disorder (CD) and **oppositional defiant disorder (ODD)** are often combined under the general heading of "conduct problems." Though the disorders may be related, evidence suggests that ODD is a separate diagnostic category, not merely a milder form of CD (Greene et al., 2002; Silverthorn, 2001). ODD is more closely related to nondelinquent (negativistic or oppositional) conduct disturbance, whereas conduct disorder involves more outright delinquent behavior, such as truancy, stealing, lying, and aggression. Yet oppositional defiant disorder, which typically develops earlier than CD, may lead to the development of antisocial behavior and conduct disorder at later ages.

Children with ODD tend to be negativistic or oppositional. They defy authority by arguing with parents and teachers and refusing to follow requests or directives. They may deliberately annoy other people, become easily angered or lose their temper, become touchy or easily annoyed, blame others for their mistakes or misbehavior, feel resentful toward others, or act in spiteful or vindictive ways toward others. The disorder typically begins before age 8 and develops gradually over a period of months or years. It typically starts in the home environment but may extend to other settings, such as school.

ODD is one of the most common diagnoses among children. The disorder is believed to affect between 6% and 12% of school-age children and upwards of 15% of adolescents (Frick & Silverthorn, 2001). ODD is more common overall among boys than girls. However, this overall effect masks a gender shift that occurs with age. Among children age 12 or younger, ODD appears to be more than twice as common among boys. Among adolescents, the rate is higher among girls. By contrast, most studies find conduct disorder to be more common in boys than girls across all age groups.

Theoretical Perspectives on ODD and CD The causal factors in ODD remain obscure. Some theorists believe that oppositionality is an expression of an underlying temperament described as the "difficult-child" type (Rey, 1993). Others believe that unresolved parent–child conflicts or overly strict parental control lie at the root of the disorder. Psychodynamic theorists look at ODD as a sign of fixation at the anal stage of psychosexual development, when conflicts between the parent and child emerge over toilet training. Leftover conflicts may later become expressed in the form of rebelliousness against parental wishes. Learning theorists view oppositional behaviors as arising from parental use of inappropriate reinforcement strategies. In this view, parents may inappropriately reinforce oppositional behavior by giving in when the child refuses to comply with their wishes, which can become a pattern.

Family factors are also implicated in the development of conduct disorder. Some forms of conduct disorder are associated with ineffective parenting styles, such as failure to provide positive reinforcement for appropriate behavior and use of harsh and inconsistent discipline for misbehavior. Family interactions of families of children with CD are often characterized by negative, coercive interactions. Children with CD are

oppositional defiant disorder (ODD)
A psychological disorder in childhood and adolescence characterized by excessive oppositionality or tendencies to refuse requests from parents and others.

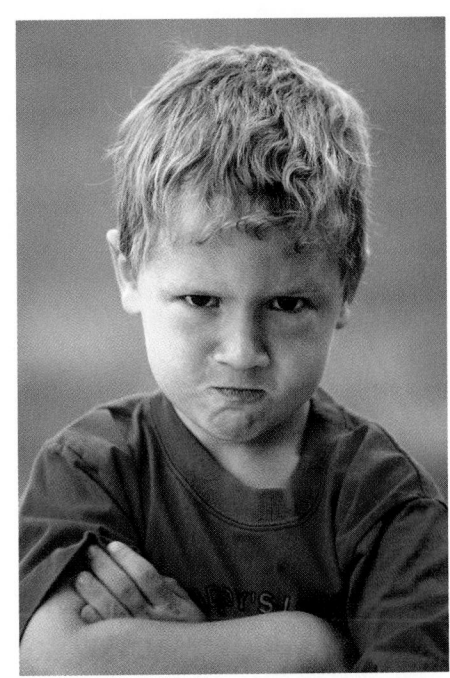

Oppositional defiant disorder (ODD). ODD is characterized by negativistic and oppositional behavior in response to directives from parents, teachers, or other authority figures. Children with ODD may act spitefully or vindictively toward others, but do not typically show the cruelty, aggressivity, and delinquent behavior associated with conduct disorder.

often very demanding and noncompliant with their parents and other family members. Family members often reciprocate by using negative behaviors, such as threatening or yelling at the child or using physical means of coercion. Parental aggression against children with conduct behavior problems commonly includes pushing, grabbing, slapping, spanking, hitting, or kicking. Parents of children with oppositional defiant disorders or severe conduct disorder display high rates of antisocial personality disorder and substance abuse (Frick et al., 1992). It's not too much of a stretch to speculate that parental modeling of antisocial behaviors can lead to antisocial conduct in children.

Conduct disorders often occur in a context of parental distress, such as marital conflict. Coercive parental discipline and poor parental monitoring are also linked to increased risk of conduct disorder (Kilgore et al., 2002). Poor parenting behaviors, such as harsh discipline and lack of monitoring, may foster the lack of empathy for others and the poor control over disruptive behavior we find in conduct disordered children.

Children with disruptive behavior disorders also tend to show biased ways of processing social information. For example, they may wrongly assume that others intend them ill. They are often quick to blame others for the scrapes they get into. They tend to view others as treating them unfairly regardless of the evidence. They may also show other cognitive deficits, such as an inability to generate alternative, nonviolent, responses to social conflicts.

As with many psychological disorders, evidence points to a genetic contribution to conduct disorder (Scourfield et al., 2004; Hudziak, 2001). For example, investigators find more evidence of antisocial behavior in the biological parents of adopted-away children with conduct disorder than in the adoptive parents (Langbehn & Cadoret, 2001). Genetic factors may also be involved in the development of oppositional defiant disorder.

Treatment Parent-training programs are used widely in treating conduct problems (Kazdin, 2003; Silverthorn, 2001). Parents are trained in behavioral techniques to alter the child's aggressive and oppositional behavior in the home and increase the child's adaptive behavior. Treatment generally targets several goals, including helping parents develop more consistent and effective discipline strategies, increasing the use of positive reinforcement for rewarding compliant behavior, and increasing the frequency of positive interactions between the parent and child. Parents must learn not only how to alter disruptive behaviors in their children but also to pay attention to their children and reward them when they act appropriately. Anger control training may also be of value in treating children with anger problems and aggressive behavior (Sukhodolsky et al., 2005).

The following example illustrates the involvement of the parents in the behavioral treatment of a child with oppositional defiant disorder.

A Case of Oppositional Defiant Disorder

Billy was a 7-year-old second grader referred by his parents. The family was relocated frequently because the father was in the Navy. Billy usually behaved when his father was taking care of him, but he was noncompliant with his mother and yelled at her when she gave him instructions. His mother was incurring great stress in the effort to control Billy, especially when her husband was at sea.

Billy had become a problem at home and in school during the first grade. He ignored and violated rules in both settings. Billy failed to carry out his chores and frequently yelled at and hit his younger brother. When he acted up, his parents would restrict him to his room or the yard, take away privileges and toys, and spank him. But all of these measures were used inconsistently. He also played on the railroad tracks near his home, and twice the police brought him home after he had thrown rocks at cars.

A home observation showed that Billy's mother often gave him inappropriate commands. She interacted with him as little as possible and showed no verbal praise, physical closeness, smiles, or positive facial expressions or gestures. She paid attention to him only when he misbehaved. When Billy was noncompliant, she would yell back at him and then try to catch him to force him to comply. Billy would then laugh and run from her.

Billy's parents were informed that the child's behavior was a product of inappropriate cueing techniques (poor directions), a lack of reinforcement for appropriate behavior, and lack of consistent sanctions for misbehavior. They were taught the appropriate use of reinforcement, punishment, and time out. The parents then charted Billy's problem behaviors to gain a clearer idea of what triggered and maintained them. They were shown how to reinforce acceptable behavior and use time out as a contingent punishment for misbehavior. Billy's mother was also taught relaxation training to help desensitize her to Billy's disruptions. Biofeedback was used to enhance the relaxation response.

During a 15-day baseline period, Billy behaved in a noncompliant manner about four times per day. When treatment was begun, Billy showed an immediate drop to about one instance of noncompliance every two days. Follow-up data showed that instances of noncompliance were maintained at a bearable level of about one per day. Fewer behavioral problems in school were also reported, even though they had not been addressed directly.

—Adapted from Kaplan, 1986, pp. 227–230

Children with conduct disorder are sometimes placed in residential treatment programs that establish explicit rules with clear rewards and mild punishments (e.g., withdrawal of privileges). Many children with conduct disorders, especially boys, display aggressive behavior and have problems controlling their anger. Many can benefit from programs designed to help them develop skills to manage conflict without resorting to aggressive behavior (Webster-Stratton et al., 2001).

Cognitive-behavioral therapy (CBT) is also used to teach aggressive children to reconceptualize social provocations as problems to be solved rather than as challenges to answer with violence. These children learn to use calming self-talk to inhibit impulsive behavior and control anger and to find and use nonviolent solutions to social conflicts.

CHILDHOOD ANXIETY AND DEPRESSION

Anxieties and fears are a normal feature of childhood, just as they are a normal feature of adult life. Childhood fears—of the dark or of small animals—are common, and most children outgrow them naturally. Anxiety is abnormal, however, when it is excessive and interferes with normal academic or social functioning or becomes troubling or persistent. Children, like adults, may suffer from different types of diagnosable anxiety disorders, including specific phobias, social phobias, generalized anxiety disorder (GAD), obsessive–compulsive disorder (OCD), and posttraumatic stress disorder (PTSD). Although these disorders may develop at any age, we consider further a type of disorder that typically develops during early childhood: separation anxiety disorder.

Some children show the more general pattern of avoidance of social interactions that characterizes avoidant personality disorder. Although children who are socially avoidant or have social anxiety disorder (also called social phobia) may have warm relationships with family members, they tend to be shy and withdrawn around others. This interferes with their development of social relationships with their peers. Such problems tend to develop after normal fear of strangers fades, at age 2 $\frac{1}{2}$ or later. Their distress at being around other children at school can also affect their academic progress. Having a social anxiety disorder during adolescence or young adulthood also increases the likelihood of later developing a depressive disorder (Stein et al., 2001).

Separation Anxiety Disorder

It is normal for young children to show anxiety when they are separated from their caregivers. Famed attachment researcher Mary Ainsworth (1989) chronicled the development of attachment behaviors and found that separation anxiety normally begins

separation anxiety disorder A childhood disorder characterized by extreme fear of separation from parents or other caretakers.

Social avoidance. Socially avoidant children tend to be excessively shy and withdrawn and have difficulty interacting with other children.

Separation anxiety. In separation anxiety disorder, a child shows persistent anxiety when separated from her or his parents that is inconsistent with her or his developmental level. Such children tend to cling to their parents and resist even brief separations.

during the first year. The sense of security normally provided by bonds of attachment apparently encourages children to explore their environments and become progressively independent of their caregivers.

Separation anxiety disorder is diagnosed when separation anxiety is persistent and excessive or inappropriate for the child's developmental level. That is, 3-year-olds ought to be able to attend preschool without nausea and vomiting brought on by anxiety. Similarly, 6-year-olds ought to be able to attend first grade without persistent dread that something awful will happen to them or their parents. Children with separation anxiety disorder tend to cling to their parents and follow them around the house. They may voice concerns about death and dying and insist that someone stay with them while they are falling asleep. Other features of the disorder include nightmares, stomachaches, nausea and vomiting when separation is anticipated (as on school days), pleading with parents not to leave, or throwing tantrums when parents are about to depart. Children may refuse to attend school for fear that something will happen to their parents while they are away.

Separation anxiety disorder affects an estimated 4% to 5% of children and young adolescents (APA, 2000; Shear et al., 2006). The disorder occurs most often in girls and is often associated with school refusal. It also frequently occurs together with social anxiety (Ferdinand et al., 2006). The disorder may persist into adulthood, leading to an exaggerated concern about the well-being of one's children and spouse and difficulty tolerating any separation from them.

In previous years, separation anxiety disorder was usually referred to as *school phobia*. However, separation anxiety disorder may occur at preschool ages. In young children, refusal to attend school is usually viewed as separation anxiety. In adolescents, however, refusal to attend school is frequently connected with academic and social concerns, so the label of separation anxiety disorder would not apply.

The development of separation anxiety disorder frequently follows a stressful life event, such as illness, the death of a relative or pet, or a change of schools or homes. In the following example, Alison's problems followed the death of her grandmother.

Alison's Fear of Death

Alison's grandmother died when Alison was 7 years old. Her parents decided to permit her request to view her grandmother in the open coffin. Alison took a tentative glance from her father's arms across the room, then asked to be taken out of the room. Her 5-year-old sister took a leisurely close-up look, with no apparent distress.

Alison had been concerned about death for two or three years by this time, but her grandmother's passing brought on a new flurry of questions: "Will I die?," "Does everybody die?," and so on. Her parents tried to reassure her by saying, "Grandma was very, very old, and she also had a heart condition. You are very young and in perfect health. You have many, many years before you have to start thinking about death."

Alison could not be alone in any room in her house. She pulled one of her parents or her sister along with her everywhere she went. She also reported nightmares about her grandmother and, within a couple of days, insisted on sleeping in the same room with her parents. Fortunately, Alison's fears did not extend to school. Her teacher reported that Alison spent some time talking about her grandmother, but her academic performance was apparently unimpaired.

Alison's parents decided to allow Alison time to "get over" the loss. Alison gradually talked less and less about death, and by the time 3 months had passed, she was able to go into any room in her house by herself. She wanted to continue to sleep in her parents' bedroom, however. So her parents "made a deal" with her. They would put off the return to her own bedroom until the school year ended (a month away), if Alison would agree to return to her own bed at that time. As a further incentive, a parent would remain with her until she fell asleep for the first month. Alison overcame the anxiety problem in this fashion with no additional delays.

—From the Author's Files

Understanding and Treating Childhood Anxiety Disorders

Theoretical perspectives on anxiety disorders in children parallel to some degree explanations of anxiety disorders in adults. Psychoanalytic theorists argue that childhood anxieties and fears, like their adult counterparts, symbolize unconscious conflicts. Cognitive theorists focus on the role of cognitive biases. Anxious children tend to show the types of cognitive distortions found in adults with anxiety disorders, including interpreting ambiguous situations as threatening and expecting bad things to happen (Hadwin, Garner, & Perez-Olivas, 2006; Kazdin, 2003). They also tend to engage in negative self-talk (Kendall & Treadwell, 2007). Expecting the worst, combined with having low self-confidence, encourages avoidance of feared activities—with friends, in school, and elsewhere. Negative expectations also heighten feelings of anxiety to the point where they impair performance in the classroom or the athletic field.

Learning theorists suggest that generalized anxiety may arise from fears of rejection or failure that carry across situations. Underlying fears of rejection or feelings of inadequacy generalize to most areas of social interaction and achievement. Genetic factors also appear to contribute to the development of anxiety disorders in children, including separation anxiety and specific phobias (Bolton et al., 2006).

Whatever the causes, overanxious children can benefit from the same cognitive-behavioral techniques for treating anxiety that we discussed in Chapter 6, such as gradual exposure to phobic stimuli and relaxation training. Cognitive techniques can help children test their anxiety-generating thoughts and replace them with adaptive alternative thoughts. CBT has shown good results in treating various types of anxiety disorders in children and adolescents (Kendall et al., 2004; Turner, 2006; Valderhaug et al., 2006, 2007). The drug *fluvoxamine* (brand name Luvox), a selective serotonin-reuptake

Is this child too young to be depressed? Although we tend to think of childhood as the happiest and most carefree time of life, depression is actually quite common among older children and adolescents. Depressed children may report feelings of sadness and lack of interest in previously enjoyable activities. Many, however, do not report or are not aware of feelings of depression, even though they may look depressed to observers. Depression may also be masked by other problems, such as conduct or school-related problems, physical complaints, and overactivity.

T R U T H (or) **F I C T I O N**

Difficulties at school, problem behaviors, and physical complaints may actually be signs of depression in children.

☑ **TRUE.** Children may not label what they are feeling as depression or be able to put into words how they feel. Depression is often masked by conduct problems, academic problems, and physical complaints.

inhibitor, also shows good therapeutic effects in treating children and adolescents with anxiety disorders such as social phobia, separation anxiety disorder, and generalized anxiety disorder (Pine et al., 2001; Walkup et al., 2001).

Childhood Depression

We may think of childhood as the happiest time of life. Most children are protected by their parents and are unencumbered by adult responsibilities. From the perspective of aging adults, their bodies seem made of rubber and free of aches. They have apparently boundless energy. However, children and adolescents can suffer from diagnosable mood disorders, including major depression and bipolar disorder (Birmaher et al., 2006; Masi et al., 2006; Raman et al., 2007). An estimated three million adolescents in the United States suffer from major depression (Wright & Kantrowitz, 2002). Major depression even occurs among preschoolers, although it is rare. During childhood there is no discernible gender difference in the risk of depression, but after age 15, girls are about twice as likely to become depressed as boys.

Like depressed adults, depressed children and adolescents typically have feelings of hopelessness; distorted thinking patterns and tendencies to blame themselves for negative events; and lower self-esteem, self-confidence, and perceptions of competence. They report episodes of sadness and crying, feelings of apathy, as well as insomnia, fatigue, and poor appetite. They may also experience suicidal thoughts or even attempt suicide. Yet depression in children is also associated with some distinctive features, such as refusal to attend school, fears of parents' dying, and clinging to parents. Depression may also be masked by behaviors that appear unrelated. Conduct disorders, academic problems, physical complaints, and even hyperactivity may stem from unrecognized depression. Among adolescents, aggressive and sexual acting out may also be signs of depression.

Depressed children or adolescents may not label what they are feeling as depression. They may not report feeling sad even though they appear sad to others. Part of the problem is cognitive–developmental. Children are not usually capable of recognizing internal feeling states until about the age of 7. They may not be able to identify negative feeling states, such as depression, in themselves. Some children appear bored or irritable rather than sad, at least in the early stages of depression.

Depressed children often lack academic, athletic, and social skills. They may find it hard to concentrate in school and may suffer from impaired memory, making it difficult for them to keep their grades up. They often keep their feelings to themselves, which may prevent their parents from recognizing the problem and seeking help. The child may express negative feelings in the form of anger, sullenness, or impatience, leading to conflicts with parents that in turn can accentuate and prolong depression.

Major depressive episode in childhood or adolescence may last upwards of a year or longer and may occur again later in life. Yet childhood depression rarely occurs by itself. Depressed children often have other significant psychological problems, including anxiety disorders, conduct or oppositional defiant disorders, and among adolescent girls, eating disorders. A sizable percentage of depressed adolescents (between 20% and 40%) later also develop bipolar disorder (USDHHS, 1999a).

Understanding and Treating Childhood Depression

Depression and suicidal behavior in childhood are frequently related to family problems and conflicts. Children exposed to stressful life events affecting the family, such as parental conflict or unemployment, stand an increased risk of depression (Nolen-Hoeksema, Girgus, & Seligman, 1992; Rudolph et al., 2001). Rejection and lack of social support from friends and family members also contribute to depression in adolescents (Nolan, Glynn, & Garber, 2003). Depression in adolescents can be triggered by such stressful life events as conflicts with parents and dissatisfaction with school grades. In girls, disturbed eating behaviors and body dissatisfaction after puberty often predict the development of major depression during adolescence (Stice et al., 2000). Interestingly, the relationship between loss of a parent in childhood and later depression during childhood or adolescence is not consistent; some studies show a connection whereas others do not (Lewinsohn et al., 1994).

As children mature and their cognitive abilities develop, cognitive factors, such as negative thinking styles, appear to play a stronger role in the development of depression (Garber, Keiley, & Martin, 2002). Like their adult counterparts, children and adolescents with depression tend to adopt a cognitive style characterized by negative attitudes toward themselves and the future (Garber, Weiss, & Shanley, 1993). They also tend to adopt a more helpless or pessimistic attributional style than their nondepressed peers (Lewinsohn et al., 1994). This means that they attribute negative events to internal, stable, and global causes and positive events to external, unstable, and specific causes.

Investigators find distorted thinking patterns in depressed children in other cultures. For example, a study of 582 Chinese children in secondary schools in Hong Kong linked feelings of depression to distorted thinking patterns involving tendencies to minimize accomplishments and blow failures and shortcomings out of proportion (Leung & Poon, 2001). European researchers linked several thinking patterns to depression in young people, including blaming onself for things that were not one's fault, ruminating about one's problems (mulling over them again and again in one's mind), and blowing problems out of proportion (Garnefski et al., 2001).

All in all, the distorted cognitions of depressed children include the following:

1. Expecting the worst (pessimism)
2. Catastrophizing the consequences of negative events
3. Assuming personal responsibility for negative outcomes, even when this is unwarranted
4. Minimizing accomplishments and focusing only on negative aspects of events

Although there are links between cognitive factors and depression, we do not know which comes first; that is, whether children become depressed because of a depressive mindset or whether depression leads to distorted, negative thoughts. Quite possibly the relationship is reciprocal, with depression affecting thinking patterns and thinking patterns affecting emotional states. Genetic factors also appear to play a role in explaining depressive symptoms in adolescents (O'Connor et al., 1998).

Adolescent girls tend to show greater levels of depressive symptoms than do adolescent boys, a finding that mirrors the gender gap in depression among adults (Stewart et al., 2004). Girls who adopt a passive, ruminative coping style (e.g., brooding and obsessing about their problems) may be at greatest risk of developing depression.

CBT has been used with some success in treating depressed children and adolescents (e.g., Berman et al., 2000; Braswell & Kendall, 2001). However, the effects of CBT and other forms of psychotherapy for childhood depression appear to be rather modest in size (Weisz, McCarty, & Valeri, 2006). Although individual approaches vary, CBT usually involves social skills training (e.g., learning how to start a conversation or make friends) to increase the likelihood of obtaining social reinforcement. CBT typically also includes training in problem-solving skills and ways of increasing the frequency of rewarding activities and countering depressive styles of thinking. In addition, family therapy may help families resolve underlying conflicts and reorganize their relationships so that members can become more supportive of each other.

Lithium has been used with generally favorable results in children and adolescents with bipolar disorder (USDHHS, 1999a). The SSRI-type antidepressant drugs *fluoxetine* (brand name Prozac), *sertraline* (Zoloft), and *citalopram* (brand name Celexa) show promise in treating childhood and adolescent depression (Harris, 2004; TADS Team, 2004; Wagner et al., 2004). However, concerns that stimulants and antidepressants are being prescribed too widely in treating childhood disorders has prompted a heated debate, as we examine in *Controversies in Abnormal Psychology* feature.

CONTROVERSIES IN ABNORMAL PSYCHOLOGY

Are We Overmedicating Our Kids?

The rising use of psychiatric drugs in recent years to treat ADHD, depression, and other psychological disorders in children has been nothing short of explosive. Some 3.6 million children in the United States were treated with drugs for ADHD in 2005 (the latest year for which data were available) (Harris, 2006). Nearly 2 million children received antidepressants for emotional problems such as depression, panic disorder, and eating disorders. In just the 3-year period between 2002 and 2005, the number of prescriptions written for treating ADHD jumped an incredible 90% (Okie, 2006). Increasing numbers of young people are also receiving other psychiatric drugs commonly used to treat adults, including mood stabilizers (anticonvulsants), antianxiety drugs, sleep medications, and even antipsychotic drugs (Olfson et al., 2006). The use of potent antipsychotic drugs for treating problems in children and teens, such as aggressive behavior and bipolar disorders, increased more than fivefold from 1993 to 2002 (Carey, 2006).

With so many children receiving powerful psychiatric drugs, critics claim that we are too ready to seek a "quick fix" for problem behavior rather than examine contributing factors, such as family conflicts, that may take more effort and time to treat. As one pediatrician put it, "It takes time for parents and teachers to sit down and talk to kids. . . . It takes less time to get a child a pill" (Hancock, 1996, p. 52).

The two sides of the debate are clearly drawn. Critics contend that we are overusing psychiatric drugs, especially Ritalin. They point to the risk of potentially troubling side effects, such as weight loss and sleeplessness from Ritalin, and express concerns that we just don't know how stimulants and other powerful psychiatric drugs affect still-developing brains (Geller, 2006; Lagacea et al., 2006; Stambor, 2006). Critics also contend that alternative treatments, such as cognitive-behavioral therapy, are available to treat many of these problems, but are underused in comparison with the prescription pad.

On the other side of the debate, proponents of drug therapy point to the therapeutic benefits of treating such disorders as ADHD and childhood depression. Stimulant drugs such as Ritalin can help calm down hyperactive children and improve concentration. That said, the scientific jury is still out on the question of the long-term effectiveness of stimulant medication and whether use of such drugs results in significant improvement in academic performance.

What about antidepressants? The earlier generation of tricyclic antidepressants proved ineffective in treating childhood depression. However, as we noted earlier, the newer generation of SSRI-type antidepressants (Prozac and Zoloft, for example) shows promise in treating childhood depression, although lingering doubts remain about whether the therapeutic benefits are clinically meaningful.

Clouding the picture further are warnings issued by the Food and Drug Administration (FDA) about a small increased risk of suicidal symptoms in youths and young adults treated with antidepressant medication (Friedman & Leon, 2007; Hammad et al., 2006; Simon et al., 2006). However, more recent evidence tip the scales in favor of antidepressants, by showing their therapeutic benefits to more than offset the small increased risk of suicidal thoughts and behavior (Bridge et al., 2007). Still, these increased risks place demands on providers and family members to watch for warning signs of suicidal thinking.

Drug therapy advocates express concerns that young people with serious depression will fail to be treated adequately if the FDA warnings discourage physicians from prescribing antidepressant medications (Friedman & Leon, 2007). They contend that failure to treat depression can increase the risk of suicide and that leaving ADHD untreated or undertreated may lead to serious substance abuse and academic problems down the road (Kluger, 2003). Moreover, they point out that the FDA did not advise against antidepressant treatment with children or adolescents, but rather urged more careful monitoring of young patients as well as closer collaboration between practitioners and their patients and families (Pfeffer, 2007).

Should this child be medicated? The use of psychiatric drugs in children has skyrocketed in recent years. Do you know any children who have benefited from psychiatric drugs? What concerns does the use of these drugs pose? What alternatives are available?

Not only are millions of children taking psychiatric drugs, but an estimated 1.6 million are taking two or more drugs, sometimes even three or more, at a time. For example, many kids are taking stimulants for ADHD and antidepressants or mood stabilizers for mood disorders. However, we have only minimal evidence to support the use of taking two psychiatric drugs at the same time and no evidence at all to support the use of three or more drugs (Harris, 2006). As psychiatrist Daniel Safer, a leading authority on the use of psychiatric drugs in children, put it, "No one has been able to show that the benefits of these combinations outweigh the risks in children" (cited in Harris, 2006, p. A28.)

One thing on which both sides seem to agree is that drug therapy alone is not sufficient to treat psychological problems in children and adolescents. The child with academic difficulties, problems at home, and low self-esteem needs more than a pill (or a combination of pills). Any use of therapeutic drugs needs to be supplemented by psychological interventions to help troubled children develop more adaptive behaviors. Perhaps drug therapy should be considered a secondline treatment when nonpharmacological approaches prove ineffective. Sometimes a combination approach works best. A recent study of depressed adolescents showed that whereas treatment with Prozac was superior to cognitive-behavioral therapy alone, the combination of the two was more effective than either treatment alone (Harris, 2004).

Critical Thinking

- Why is the prescription of stimulant drugs and antidepressants in treating childhood disorders controversial?
- In many comparable countries drugs are prescribed much less frequently for childhood disorders than they are in the United States. What does this suggest?

Suicide in Children and Adolescents

Suicide is rare among children and early adolescents but becomes more common in late adolescence and early adulthood (Pelkonen & Marttunen, 2003). Among college students, suicide is the second leading cause of death, after motor vehicle accidents (Rawe & Kingsbury, 2006). Among young people overall in the 15- to 24-year-old age group, suicide is the third most common cause of death, after accidents and homicides (NIMH, 2003b; Winerman, 2004). Approximately 1 person per 10,000 (0.01%) in this age range commits suicide.

Teenage suicide rates rose sharply in the early 1990s but have headed downward in recent years (Goode, 2003c; Gould et al., 2003). Even so, youth suicide remains a major public health problem in the United States and Canada (Koplin & Agathen, 2002; Langlois & Morrison, 2002). Official statistics only account for reported suicides; some apparent accidental deaths, such as those due to falling from a window, may be suicides as well.

Despite the commonly held view that children and adolescents who talk about suicide are only venting their feelings, most young people who kill themselves send out signals beforehand (Bongar, 2002). In fact, those who discuss their plans are the ones most likely to carry them out. Unfortunately, parents tend not to take their children's suicidal talk seriously.

In addition to increasing age, other factors associated with heightened risk of suicide in children and adolescents include the following (e.g., Fergusson & Woodward, 2002; Lewinsohn et al., 2001; NIMH, 2003b; Pelkonen & Marttunen, 2003; USDHHS, 1999a; Wu et al., 2001):

- *Gender.* Girls, like women, are three times more likely than boys to attempt suicide. However, boys, like men, are more likely to succeed, perhaps because boys, like men, are more apt to use lethal means, such as guns.
- *Geography.* Adolescents in less-populated areas are more likely to commit suicide. Adolescents in the rural western regions of the United States have the highest suicide rate.
- *Ethnicity.* The suicide rates for African American, Asian American, and Hispanic American youth are about 30% to 60% lower than that of (non-Hispanic) White youth. Yet, as noted in Chapter 8, the highest suicide rates in the U.S. are among Native American adolescent and young adult males (Meyers, 2007).
- *Depression and hopelessness.* Depression figures as prominently in youth suicide as it does in adult suicide, especially when it is combined with feelings of hopelessness and low self-esteem.
- *Previous suicidal behavior.* One quarter of adolescents who attempt suicide are repeaters. More than 80% of adolescents who take their lives have talked about it before doing so. Suicidal teenagers may carry lethal weapons, talk about death, make suicide plans, or engage in risky or dangerous behavior.
- *Prior sexual abuse.* In an Australian sample, young people with a history of childhood sexual abuse had more than 10 times higher rates of suicide than the national average (Plunkett et al., 2001). Moreover, about one-third of young people who had been abused had attempted suicide, compared to none in a nonabused control group.
- *Family problems.* Family problems contribute to an increased risk of suicide attempts and actual suicides. These problems include family instability and conflict, physical or sexual abuse, loss of a parent due to death or separation, and poor parent–child communication.
- *Stressful life events.* Many suicides among young people are directly preceded by stressful or traumatic events, such as breaking up with a girlfriend or boyfriend, having an unwanted pregnancy, getting arrested, having problems at school, moving to a new school, or having to take an important test.
- *Substance abuse.* Addiction in the adolescent's family, or by the adolescent, is a factor.
- *Social contagion.* Adolescent suicides sometimes occur in clusters, especially when a

TRUTH or FICTION

Suicide is unfortunately quite common among young teens around the time of puberty.

☑ **FALSE.** Actually, suicide is rare among children and young adolescents. But the risks increase with age into late adolescence and early adulthood.

suicide or a group of suicides receives widespread publicity. Adolescents may romanticize suicide as a heroic act of defiance. There are often suicides or attempts among the siblings, friends, parents, or adult relatives of suicidal adolescents. Perhaps the suicide of a family member or schoolmate renders suicide a more "real" option for managing stress or punishing others. Perhaps the other person's suicide gives the adolescent the impression that he or she is "doomed" to commit suicide. Adolescent suicides may occur in bunches in a community, especially when adolescents are subjected to mounting academic pressures, such as competing for admission to college. Note the case of Pam.

◇

Pam, Kim, and Brian

Pam was an exceptionally attractive 17-year-old who was hospitalized after cutting her wrists. "Before we moved to [an upper-middle-class town in suburban New York]," she told the psychologist, "I was the brightest girl in the class. Teachers loved me. If we had had a yearbook, I'd have been the most likely to succeed. Then we moved, and suddenly I was hit with it. Everybody was bright, or tried to be. Suddenly I was just another ordinary student planning to go to college.

"Teachers were good to me, but I was no longer special, and that hurt. Then we all applied to college. Do you know that 90 percent of the kids in the high school go on to college? I mean four-year colleges? And we all knew—or suspected—that the good schools had quotas on kids from here. I mean you can't have 30 kids from our senior class going to Yale or Princeton or Wellesley, can you? You're better off applying from Utah.

"Then Kim got her early-acceptance rejection from Brown. Kim was number-one in the class. Nobody could believe it. Her father'd gone to Brown and Kim had almost 1500 SATs. Kim was out of commission for a few days—I mean she didn't come to school or anything—and then, boom, she was gone. She offed herself, kaput, no more, the end. Then Brian was rejected from Cornell. A few days later, he was gone, too. And I'm like, 'These kids were better than me.' I mean their grades and their SATs were higher than mine, and I was going to apply to Brown and Cornell. I'm like, 'What chance do I have? Why bother?'"

—From the Author's Files

You can see how catastrophizing thoughts play a role in such tragic cases. Consistent with the literature on suicide among adults, young people who attempt suicide do not use active problem-solving strategies in handling stressful situations. They may see no other way out of their perceived failures or stresses. As with adults, one approach to working with suicidal children helps them challenge distorted thinking and generate alternative strategies for handling problems and stressors. Promising prevention programs, including school-based skills training programs, have been developed, but evidence supporting their effectiveness remains to be demonstrated (Gould et al., 2003).

ELIMINATION DISORDERS

Fetuses and newborn children eliminate waste products reflexively. As children develop and undergo toilet training, they develop the ability to inhibit the natural reflexes that govern urination and bowel movements. For some children, however,

TABLE 14.8

Diagnostic Features of Enuresis

The child repeatedly wets bedding or clothes (whether intentional or involuntary).

The child's chronological age is at least 5 (or child is at an equivalent developmental level).

The behavior occurs at least twice a week for 3 months or causes significant impairment in functioning.

The disorder does not have an organic basis.

Source: Adapted from the *DSM-IV-TR* (APA, 2000).

problems with control elimination persist in the form of *enuresis* and *encopresis*, disorders of elimination that are not due to organic causes.

Enuresis

The term *enuresis* derives from the Greek roots *en-*, meaning "in," and *ouron*, meaning "urine." **Enuresis** is failure to control urination after one has reached the "normal" age for attaining such control. Conceptions of what age is normal for achieving control vary among clinicians. *DSM-IV* standards are shown in Table 14.8. Enuresis, like so many other developmental disorders, is more common among boys. Enuresis is estimated to affect 7% of boys and 3% of girls by age 5. Bed-wetting affects upwards of 7 million children age 6 and over in the United States (Lim, 2003). The disorder usually resolves itself by adolescence if not earlier, although in about 1% of cases the problem continues into adulthood (APA, 2000).

As you might suspect, enuresis can be extremely distressing, especially to the older child (Butler, 2004). Wetting may occur during nighttime sleep only, during waking hours only, or during both nighttime sleep and waking hours. Nighttime-only enuresis is the most common type, and accidents occurring during sleep are referred to as *bed-wetting.* Achieving bladder control at night is more difficult than achieving daytime control. When asleep at night, children must learn to wake up when they feel the pressure of a full bladder and then go to the bathroom to relieve themselves. The younger the "trained" child is, the more likely she or he is to wet the bed at night. It is perfectly normal for children who have acquired daytime control over their bladders to have nighttime accidents for a year or more. Bed-wetting usually occurs during the deepest stage of sleep and may reflect immaturity of the nervous system. The diagnosis of enuresis applies in cases of repeated bed-wetting or daytime wetting of clothes by children of at least 5 years of age.

Theoretical Perspectives Psychodynamic explanations of enuresis suggest that it represents the expression of hostility toward children's parents because of harsh toilet training. It may represent regression in response to the birth of a sibling or some other stressor or life change, such as starting school or suffering the death of a parent or relative. Learning theorists point out that enuresis occurs most commonly in children whose parents attempted to train them early. Early failures may have connected anxiety with efforts to control the bladder. Conditioned anxiety, then, induces rather than curbs urination.

Evidence from a Danish study strongly suggests that *primary enuresis*, the most prevalent form of the disorder, which characterizes children who have persistent bed-wetting and have never established urinary control, is genetically transmitted (Eiberg, Berendt, & Mohr, 1995). We don't yet understand the genetic mechanism in enuresis, but one possibility implicates the genes that regulate the rate of development of motor control over eliminatory reflexes by the cerebral cortex. Although genetic factors

enuresis Failure to control urination after one has reached the expectable age for attaining such control.

Urine alarm. The urine alarm method is widely used in the treatment of nighttime enuresis. How does the method illustrate the principles of classical conditioning?

Principles of classical conditioning can be applied to treat bed-wetting in children.

☑ **TRUE.** The use of a urine alarm can help condition the enuretic child to awaken to the pressure of a full bladder. In this paradigm, what is the unconditioned stimulus and what is the conditioned stimulus?

encopresis Lack of control over bowel movements that is not caused by an organic problem in a child who is at least 4 years old.

appear to be involved in the transmission of primary enuresis, it is likely that environmental and behavioral factors also come into play in determining the development and course of the disorder. The other type of enuresis, *secondary enuresis,* is apparently not genetically influenced and characterizes children with occasional bed-wetting who developed the problem after having established urinary control.

Treatment Enuresis usually resolves itself as children mature. Behavioral methods have been shown to be helpful when enuresis endures or causes parents or children great distress, however. Such methods condition children to wake up when their bladders are full. One dependable example is the use of a urine alarm method, a variation on a technique introduced by psychologist O. Hobart Mowrer in the 1930s.

The problem in bed-wetting is that children with enuresis continue to sleep despite bladder tension that awakens most other children (Butler, 2004). As a consequence, they reflexively urinate in bed. Mowrer pioneered the use of the urine alarm, which in its present form involves a moisture-activated alarm that is placed beneath the sleeping child. A sensor sounds the alarm when the child wets the bed, which awakens the child (Lim, 2003). After several repetitions, most children learn to awaken in response to bladder tension—*before* the alarm is sounded. The technique is usually explained through principles of classical conditioning. Tension in children's bladders is paired repeatedly with a stimulus (an alarm) that wakes them up when they wet the bed. The bladder tension (a conditioned stimulus, or CS) elicits the same response (waking up—the conditioned response, or CR) that is elicited by the alarm (the unconditioned stimulus, or US).

Treatment for enuresis, generally involving the urine alarm technique or drug therapy, is often helpful (Fitz et al., 2004). Certain psychiatric drugs can be helpful, such as *fluvoxamine* (brand name Luvox), a SSRI-type antidepressant that works on brain systems that control urination (Horrigan, & Barnhill, 2000; Kano & Arisaka, 2000). However, the urine alarm technique has the highest cure rates and the lowest relapse rates among available treatments (Glazener, Evans, & Peto, 2000; Thiedke, 2003). The higher relapse rates associated with drug treatment underscores the fact that therapeutic drugs by themselves do not teach any new skills or adaptive behaviors that can be retained beyond the active treatment period.

Encopresis

The term *encopresis* derives from the Greek roots *en-* and *kopros,* meaning "feces." **Encopresis** is lack of control over bowel movements that is not caused by an organic problem. The child must have a chronological age of at least 4, or in children with intellectual impairment, a mental age of at least 4 years. About 1% of 5-year-olds have encopresis (APA, 2000). Like enuresis, this condition is most common among boys. Soiling may be voluntary or involuntary and is not caused by an organic problem, except in cases in which constipation is involved. Among the possible predisposing factors are inconsistent or incomplete toilet training and psychosocial stressors, such as the birth of a sibling or beginning school.

Soiling, unlike enuresis, is more likely to happen during the day than at night. It can thus be keenly embarrassing to the child. Classmates often avoid or ridicule soilers. Because feces have a strong odor, teachers may find it hard to act as though nothing has happened. Parents, too, are eventually galled by recurrent soiling and may increase their demands for self-control and employ powerful punishments for failure. As a result, children may hide soiled underwear, distance themselves from classmates, or feign sickness to stay at home. Their levels of anxiety concerning soiling increase. Because anxiety, which involves arousal of the sympathetic branch of the autonomic nervous system, promotes bowel movements, control may become yet more elusive.

Not surprisingly, children who soil have more emotional and behavioral problems than those who do not soil (Joinson et al., 2006).

When soiling is involuntary, it is often associated with constipation, impaction, or retention that results in subsequent overflow. Constipation may be related to psychological factors, such as fears associated with defecating in a particular place or with a more general pattern of negativistic or oppositional behavior. Or constipation may be related to physiological factors, such as complications from an illness or from medication. Much less frequently, encopresis is deliberate or intentional.

Soiling often appears to follow harsh punishment for an accident or two, particularly in children who are already highly stressed or anxious. Harsh punishment may rivet children's attention on soiling. They may then ruminate about soiling, raising their level of anxiety so that self-control is impaired.

Behavior therapy techniques are helpful in treating encopresis (Loening-Baucke, 2002). Treatment generally involves the parents rewarding (by praise and other means) successful attempts at self-control and using mild punishments for continued accidents (for example, gentle reminders to attend more closely to bowel tension and having the child clean her or his own underwear). When encopresis persists, thorough medical and psychological evaluation is recommended to determine possible causes and appropriate treatments.

Before moving on to the next chapter, you may wish to review the *Concept Map for Abnormal Psychology,* which outlines causal factors and treatment approaches discussed in the chapter relating to psychological disorders affecting children and adolescents.

SUMMING UP

Normal and Abnormal Behavior in Childhood and Adolescence

What factors do we need to consider in distinguishing normal and abnormal behavior in childhood and adolescence? In addition to the criteria described in Chapter 1, we need to take into account the child's age and cultural background.

What are the effects of child abuse? The effects of child abuse range from physical injuries, even death, to emotional consequences, such as difficulties forming healthy attachments, low self-esteem, suicidal thinking, depression, and failure to explore the outside world, among other problems. The emotional and behavioral consequences of child abuse and neglect often extend into adulthood.

Pervasive Developmental Disorders

What are pervasive developmental disorders? Pervasive developmental disorders involve marked deficiencies in multiple areas of development. They develop within the first years of life and are often associated with mental retardation. Autistic disorder is the most prominent pervasive developmental disorder.

What are the clinical features of autism? Children with autism shun affectionate behavior, engage in stereotyped behavior, attempt to preserve sameness, and tend to have peculiar speech habits such as echolalia, pronoun reversals, and idiosyncratic speech. The causes of autism remain unknown, but gains in academic and social functioning have been obtained through the use of intensive behavior therapy.

Mental Retardation

What is mental retardation and how is it assessed? Mental retardation involves impaired development of intellectual and adaptive abilities. It is assessed by intelligence tests and measures of functional ability. Most cases fall in the mildly retarded range.

What are the causes of mental retardation? Mental retardation is caused by chromosomal abnormalities, such as Down syndrome; genetic disorders, such as fragile X syndrome and phenylketonuria; prenatal factors, such as maternal diseases and alcohol use; and familial/cultural factors associated with intellectually impoverished home environments.

Learning Disorders

What are learning disorders? Learning disorders (also called learning disabilities) are specific deficits in the development of arithmetic, writing, or reading skills.

What are the causes of learning disorders and approaches to treatment? The causes remain under study but probably involve underlying brain dysfunctions that make it difficult to process or decode visual and auditory information. Intervention focuses mainly on attempts to remediate specific skill deficits.

Communication Disorders

What are communication disorders? These disorders are characterized by impaired understanding or use of language. The specific types of communication disorders include expressive language disorder, mixed receptive/expressive language disorder, phonological disorder, and stuttering.

Attention-Deficit and Disruptive Behavior Disorders

What are attention-deficit and disruptive behavior disorders? This category includes attention-deficit hyperactivity disorder (ADHD), conduct disorder, and oppositional defiant disorder (ODD). ADHD is characterized by impulsivity, inattention, and hyperactivity. Children with conduct disorders intentionally engage in antisocial behavior. Children with ODD show negativistic or oppositional behavior but not outright delinquent or antisocial behavior characteristic of conduct disorder. However, ODD may lead to the development of conduct disorder.

How are these disorders treated? Stimulant medication is generally effective in reducing hyperactivity, but it has not led to general academic gains. Behavior therapy may help ADHD children adapt better to school. Behavior therapy may also be helpful in modifying behaviors of children with conduct disorders and oppositional defiant disorder.

Childhood Anxiety and Depression

What types of anxiety disorders affect children? Anxiety disorders that occur commonly among children and adolescents include specific phobias, social phobia, and generalized anxiety disorder. Children may also show separation anxiety disorder, which involves excessive anxiety at times when they are separated from their parents. Cognitive biases, such as expecting negative outcomes, negative self-talk, and interpreting ambiguous situations as threatening, figure prominently in anxiety disorders in children and adolescents, as they often do among adults.

What are the distinguishing features of depression in childhood and adolescence? Depressed children, especially younger children, may not report or be aware of feeling depressed. Depression may also be masked by seemingly unrelated behaviors, such as conduct disorders. Depressed children also tend to show cognitive biases associated with depression in adulthood, such as adoption of a pessimistic explanatory style and distorted thinking. Although rare, suicide in children does occur and threats should be taken seriously. Risk factors for adolescent suicide include gender, age, geography, race, depression, past suicidal behavior, strained family relationships, stress, substance abuse, and social contagion.

Elimination Disorders

What are elimination disorders? These are problems of impaired control over urination (enuresis) and bowel movements (encopresis) that cannot be accounted for by organic causes. Both disorders are more common in boys.

What is the urine alarm method for treating enuresis? The urine alarm method conditions children with enuresis to respond to bladder tension by awakening before urinating.

KEY TERMS

pervasive developmental disorders (PDDs) *(p. 478)*
autism *(p. 479)*
Asperger's disorder *(p. 479)*
Rett's disorder *(p. 479)*
childhood disintegrative disorder *(p. 479)*
mental retardation *(p. 485)*
Down syndrome *(p. 485)*

fragile X syndrome *(p. 487)*
phenylketonuria (PKU) *(p. 487)*
cultural-familial retardation *(p. 488)*
dyslexia *(p. 490)*
learning disorder *(p. 490)*
communication disorders *(p. 492)*
attention-deficit hyperactivity disorder (ADHD) *(p. 493)*

hyperactivity *(p. 493)*
conduct disorder *(p. 496)*
oppositional defiant disorder (ODD) *(p. 497)*
separation anxiety disorder *(p. 500)*
enuresis *(p. 507)*
encopresis *(p. 508)*

MEDIA TOOLS

A variety of digital and online learning tools are available to enrich your learning experience and help you succeed in the course. These resources include:

- **MYPSYCHLAB,** an online learning system for your course in abnormal psychology that allows you to test your mastery of concepts in the book by using chapter-by-chapter diagnostic tests. Results from the diagnostic tests help you build a customized study plan. To access **MyPsychLab,** visit www. prenhall.com/mypsychlab and follow the instructions on the site.

- **"SPEAKING OUT" PATIENT INTERVIEWS,** a set of video case examples of actual patients you can access on the companion CD-ROM included with the text. Icons in the margins of the chapter highlight the video case examples included on the CD-ROM.

- **COMPANION WEB SITE,** an online study center that offers computer-scored quizzes you can use to test your knowledge, along with other study tools and links to related sites to enhance your learning of abnormal psychology. To access the companion Web site, visit www.prenhall.com/nevid and use the various tabs and links on the site to access these learning resources.

Disorders of Childhood and Adolescence

are characterized by

Disturbed behavior patterns developing in childhood or adolescence

and include

- Pervasive Developmental Disorders
- Mental Retardation
- Learning Disorders
- Communication Disorders
- Attention-Deficit and Disruptive Behavior Disorders
- Anxiety and Mood Disorders
- Elimination Disorders

and may be caused by such factors as

- Biological factors such as genetics, prenatal infections, and brain abnormalities
- Family factors such as childhood abuse and neglect, family conflict, poor parenting behaviors
- Learning factors such as lack of reinforcement for appropriate behavior and conditioned fear (in elimination disorders)
- Psychosocial factors such as stressful life events
- Cognitive factors such as dysfunctional thinking patterns in depressed and anxious children

and may be treated by

- Psychiatric drugs for ADHD and depression
- Behavioral treatment for autistic disorder and elimination disorders
- Cognitive-behavioral therapy to help anxious and depressed children develop more adaptive thinking patterns and coping skills
- Psychoeducational interventions (for mental retardation and learning disorders), residential treatment programs (for conduct disorder), parent training programs (for conduct disorder) and speech therapy (for communication disorders)

Attention-Deficit Hyperactivity Disorder (ADHD)

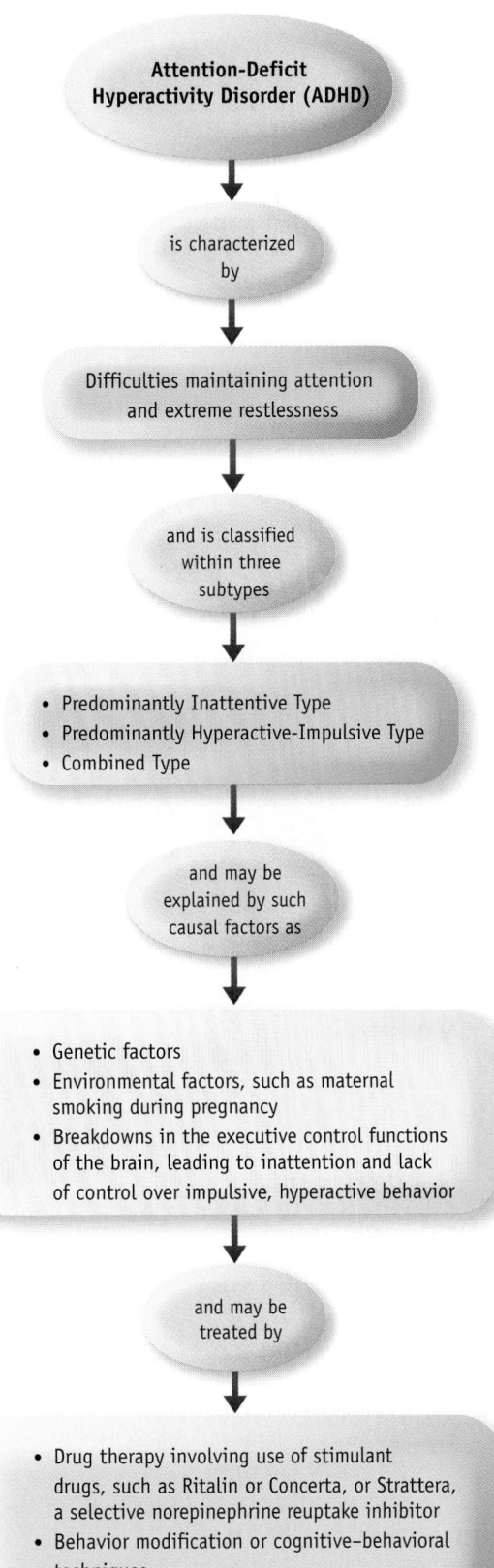

Attention-Deficit Hyperactivity Disorder (ADHD)

is characterized by

Difficulties maintaining attention and extreme restlessness

and is classified within three subtypes

- Predominantly Inattentive Type
- Predominantly Hyperactive-Impulsive Type
- Combined Type

and may be explained by such causal factors as

- Genetic factors
- Environmental factors, such as maternal smoking during pregnancy
- Breakdowns in the executive control functions of the brain, leading to inattention and lack of control over impulsive, hyperactive behavior

and may be treated by

- Drug therapy involving use of stimulant drugs, such as Ritalin or Concerta, or Strattera, a selective norepinephrine reuptake inhibitor
- Behavior modification or cognitive–behavioral techniques
- Combination of drug therapy and behavioral or cognitive-behavioral treatment

Cognitive Disorders and Disorders Related to Aging

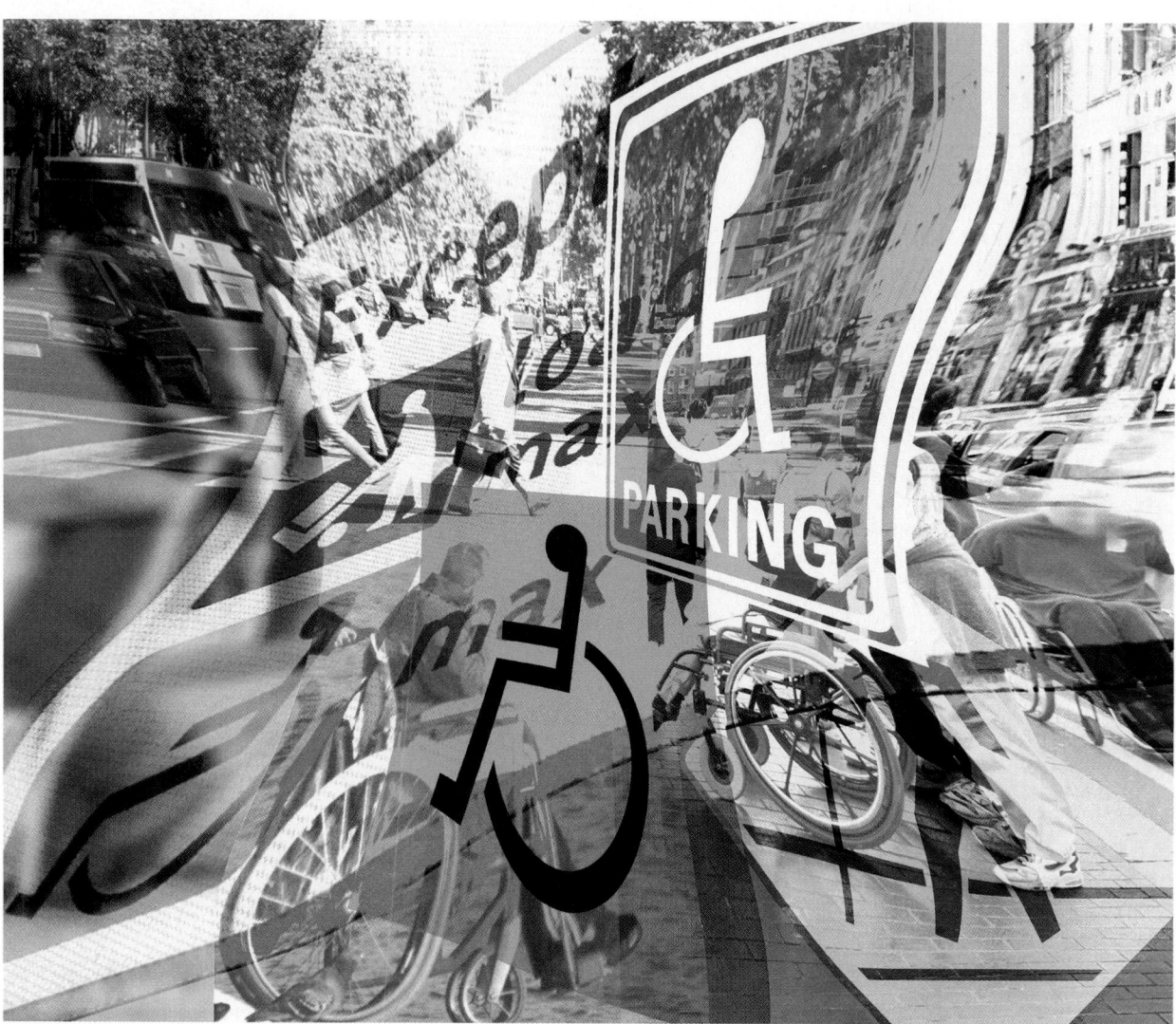

CHAPTER OUTLINE

COGNITIVE DISORDERS 515–522

Dementia
Delirium
Amnestic Disorders

PSYCHOLOGICAL DISORDERS RELATED TO AGING 522–532

Anxiety Disorders and Aging
Depression and Aging

Sleep Problems and Aging
Dementia of the Alzheimer's Type
Vascular Dementia

DEMENTIAS DUE TO GENERAL MEDICAL CONDITIONS 532–537

Dementia Due to Pick's Disease
Dementia Due to Parkinson's Disease
Dementia Due to Huntington's Disease

Dementia Due to HIV Disease
Dementia Due to Creutzfeldt-Jakob Disease
Dementia Due to Head Trauma
Neurosyphilis

SUMMING UP 537–538

"You should pray for a sound mind in a sound body."
—Juvenal, Roman poet, A.D. 55–127

"I"

"Now Is the Last Best Time"

The disease [Alzheimer's disease] works slowly, destroying the mind, stealing life in a tedious, silent dance of death. Slowly the memory is impaired, and then you wander in a world without certainty and names. Yesterdays disappear, except those long ago. Eventually there is a descent into silence and a dependence on caretakers. Hands other than yours feed and bathe you. A cipher takes your place amid the tubes and tragedy. By the end, Alzheimer's leaves its victims silent, quivering in their flesh, awaiting the last rites. Some common illness often takes credit on the death certificate. . . .

I am alone and I can hear water running somewhere in the house. I don't remember going to the bathroom. Who else turned on the water?

Writing sometimes becomes difficult. Words vanish before they reach the page. Most of the time the biggest drawback is my plummeting typing accuracy. So far there are few words the spell checker cannot correct. . . .

I do not want to succumb to this illness, but I am powerless in its clutches. Words come when I sit down to write, but they dance away seductively, and meaning and substance disappear quickly. Of course, this is not new; such things happen many times, but before they were retrievable and now they are not. . . .

There are many days of tears now. Some mornings I wake and my eyes are wet. I cry, choked with emotion I cannot express. I am having trouble reading the writing I do with a pencil or pen. It used to be clear and sharp; now it wobbles and is full of uncertainty. The words come normally but the letters are sometimes not in the proper order. I spend valuable time deciphering the meaning in each letter of the alphabet until the word's meaning becomes clear. Progress is slow and I am losing time. A few months ago I had no trouble writing. I have to be careful to spell correctly but sometimes. . . .

I am aware of the loss of language more than ever before. I am afraid to write because watching the words come out distorted is painful and it reveals the destructive power of the disease over which I have no control.

Now is the last best time.

—From DeBaggio, 2002

HAVING A "SOUND MIND IN A SOUND BODY" IS AN ANCIENT PRESCRIPTION FOR A HEALTHY AND happy life. However, brain diseases and injuries can make us unsound in both body and mind. When damage to the brain results from an injury or stroke, the deterioration in cognitive, social, and occupational functioning can be rapid and severe. In the case of a more gradual but progressive form of deterioration, such as in Alzheimer's disease, the decline of mental functioning is more gradual but leads eventually to a state of virtual helplessness. Sadly, people with Alzheimer's may come to realize that each day is their last best time.

In this chapter, we focus on the class of psychological disorders called *cognitive disorders*. These disorders arise from injuries or diseases that affect the brain.

Some of these diseases, including Alzheimer's disease, primarily affect older adults. Consequently we focus in this chapter on the types of psychological problems that often affect people in late adulthood.

COGNITIVE DISORDERS

Cognitive disorders are disturbances of thinking or memory that represent a marked change from the individual's prior level of functioning (APA, 2000). Cognitive disorders are not psychologically based; they are caused by physical or medical conditions,

cognitive disorders A class of psychological disorders characterized by impairment in cognitive abilities and daily functioning in which biological causation is either known or presumed.

including drug use or withdrawals, which affect the functioning of the brain. In some cases the specific cause of the cognitive disorder can be pinpointed; in others, it cannot. Although these disorders are biologically based, psychological and environmental factors play key roles in determining the impact and range of disabling symptoms as well as the individual's ability to cope with them.

Our ability to perform cognitive functions—to think, reason, and store and recall information—depends on the functioning of the brain. Cognitive disorders arise when the brain is either damaged or impaired in its ability to function due to injury, illness, exposure to toxins, or use or abuse of psychoactive drugs. The more widespread the damage to the brain, the greater and more extensive the impairment in functioning. The extent and location of brain damage largely determine the range and severity of impairment. The location of the damage is also critical because many brain structures or regions perform specialized functions. Damage to the temporal lobe, for example, is associated with defects in memory and attention, whereas damage to the occipital lobe may result in visual–spatial deficits, such as in the famous case of Dr. P., a distinguished musician and teacher who lost the ability to visually recognize objects, including faces.

In *The Man Who Mistook His Wife for a Hat,* the neurologist Oliver Sacks (1985) recounts how Dr. P. failed to recognize the faces of his students at the music school. When a student spoke, however, Dr. P. immediately recognized his or her voice. Not only did the professor fail to discriminate faces visually, but sometimes he perceived faces where none existed. He patted the heads of fire hydrants and parking meters, which he took to be children. He warmly addressed the rounded knobs on furniture. Dr. P. and his colleagues generally dismissed these peculiarities as jokes—after all, Dr. P. was well known for his oddball humor and jests. His music remained as accomplished as ever, and his general health seemed fine, so these misperceptions seemed little to be concerned about.

Not until 3 years later did Dr. P. seek a neurological evaluation. His ophthalmologist had found that although Dr. P.'s eyes were healthy, he had problems interpreting visual stimulation. So he made the referral to Dr. Sacks, a neurologist. When Dr. Sacks engaged Dr. P. in conversation, Dr. P.'s eyes fixated oddly on miscellaneous features of Dr. Sack's face—his nose, then his right ear, then his chin, sensing parts of his face but apparently not connecting them in a meaningful pattern. When Dr. P. sought to put on his shoe after a physical examination, he confused his foot with the shoe. When preparing to leave, Dr. P. looked around for his hat, and then . . .

> [Dr. P.] reached out his hand, and took hold of his wife's head, tried to lift it off, to put it on. He had apparently mistaken his wife for a hat! His wife looked as if she was used to such things. (Sacks, 1985, p. 10)

Dr. P.'s peculiar behavior may seem amusing to some, but his loss of visual perception was tragic. Although Dr. P. could identify abstract forms and shapes—a cube, for example—he no longer recognized the faces of his family, or his own. Some features of particular faces would strike a chord of recognition. For example, he could recognize a picture of Einstein from the distinctive hair and mustache and a picture of his own brother from the square jaw and big teeth. But he was responding to isolated features, not grasping the facial patterns as wholes.

Sacks recounts a final test:

> It was still a cold day, in early spring, and I had thrown my coat and gloves on the sofa.
> "What is this?" I asked, holding up a glove.
> "May I examine it?" he asked, and, taking it from me, he proceeded to examine it as he had examined the geometrical shapes.
> "A continuous surface," he announced at last, "infolded on itself. It appears to have"—he hesitated—"five outpouchings, if this is the word."
> "Yes," I said cautiously. "You have given me a description. Now tell me what it is."

Does this man's singing help him coordinate his actions? In a celebrated case study, Dr. Oliver Sacks discussed the case of "Dr. P.," who was discovered to be suffering from a brain tumor that impaired his ability to interpret visual cues. Yet he could still eat meals and wash and dress himself so long as he could sing to himself.

"A container of some sort?"

"Yes," I said, "and what would it contain?"

"It would contain its contents!" said Dr. P., with a laugh. "There are many possibilities. It could be a change-purse, for example, for coins of five sizes. It could . . ."

I interrupted the blarney flow. "Does it not look familiar? Do you think it might contain, might fit, a part of your body?"

No light of recognition dawned on his face.

No child would have the power to see and speak of "a continuous surface . . . infolded on itself," but any child, any infant, would immediately know a glove as a glove, see it as familiar, as going with a hand. Dr. P. didn't. He saw nothing as familiar. Visually, he was lost in a world of lifeless abstractions. (Sacks, 1985, p. 13)

Later, we might add, Dr. P. accidentally put the glove on his hand, exclaiming, "My God, it's a glove!" (Sacks, 1985, p. 13). His brain immediately seized the pattern of tactile information, although his visual brain centers were powerless to interpret the shape as a whole. Dr. P., that is, showed lack of visual knowledge—a symptom referred to as visual **agnosia,** derived from Greek roots meaning "without knowledge." Still, Dr. P.'s musical abilities and verbal skills remained intact. He was able to function, to dress himself, take a shower, and eat his meals by singing various songs to himself—for example, eating songs and dressing songs—that helped him coordinate his actions. However, if his dressing song was interrupted while he was dressing himself, he would lose his train of thought and be unable to recognize not only the clothes his wife had laid out but also his own body. When the music stopped, so did his ability to make sense of the world. Sacks later learned that Dr. P. had a massive tumor in the area of the brain that processes visual information. Dr. P. was apparently unaware of his deficits, having filled his visually empty world with music in order to function and imbue his life with meaning and purpose.

Dr. P.'s case is unusual in the peculiarity of his symptoms, but it illustrates the universal dependence of psychological functioning on an intact brain. The case also shows how some people adjust—sometimes so gradually that the changes are all but imperceptible—to developing physical or organic problems. Dr. P.'s visual problems might have been relatively more debilitating in a person who was less talented or who had less social support to draw on. The tragic case of Dr. P. illustrates how psychological and environmental factors determine the impact and range of disabling symptoms as well as the individual's ability to cope with them.

People who suffer from cognitive disorders may become completely dependent on others to meet basic needs in feeding, toileting, and grooming. In other cases, although some assistance in meeting the demands of daily living may be required, people are able to function at a level that permits them to live semi-independently. The cognitive deficit that Dr. P. developed, *agnosia,* is often a feature of dementia, a type of cognitive disorder involving a general deterioration of mental functioning. Dementia, along with delirium and amnestic disorders, are three major types of cognitive disorders. Table 15.1 provides an overview of these three major types of cognitive disorders.

agnosia A disturbance of sensory perception, usually affecting visual perception.

Dementia

Dementia is a profound deterioration in mental functioning characterized by severe problems with memory and by one or more of the cognitive deficits listed in Table 15.2 (APA, 2000). There are many causes of dementia, including brain diseases, such as Alzheimer's disease (AD) and Pick's disease, and infections or disorders that affect the functioning of the brain, such as meningitis, HIV infection, and encephalitis. In some cases, the dementia can be halted or reversed, especially when it is caused by certain types of tumors, seizures, metabolic disturbances, and treatable infections, or when it results from depression or substance abuse. But the great majority of dementias, including the most common form, dementia associated with AD, are progressive and irreversible (Kasl-Godley & Gatz, 2000). AD accounts for most cases of dementia in older adults (Wilson & Bennett, 2003).

dementia Profound deterioration of mental functioning, characterized by impaired memory, thinking, judgment, and language use.

TABLE 15.1 Overview of Cognitive Disorders

TYPE OF DISORDER	Specific Disorders	Lifetime Prevalence in Population (approx.)	Description	Associated Features
Delirium	• Delirium due to a general medical condition • Substance intoxication delirium • Substance withdrawal delirium	Unknown	States of extreme mental confusion interfering with concentration and ability to speak coherently	• Difficulty filtering out irrelevant stimuli or shifting attention; excited speech that conveys little meaning • Disorientation as to time and place; frightening hallucinations or other perceptual distortions • Motor behavior may slow to a stupor or fluctuate between states of restlessness and stupor • Mental states may fluctuate between lucid intervals and periods of confusion
Dementia	• Dementia of the Alzheimer's type • Vascular dementia • Dementia due to HIV disease • Dementia due to head trauma • Dementia due to Parkinson's disease • Dementia due to Huntington's disease • Dementia due to Pick's disease • Dementia due to Creutzfeldt-Jakob disease	Alzheimer's disease: 10% over age 65	Profound deterioration of mental functioning, including memory	• Most forms, such as dementia of the Alzheimer's type, are irreversible and progressive • Associated with specific cognitive deficits, such as aphasia, apraxia, agnosia, and disturbance in executive functioning • Types of dementias are grouped by age of onset into senile dementias (beginning after age 65) and presenile dementias (beginning at age 65 or earlier)
Amnestic Disorders	• Amnestic disorder due to a general medical condition • Substance-induced persisting amnestic disorder	Unknown	Profound deficit in memory not associated with delirium or dementia	• May involve anterograde or retrograde amnesia • Person may be disoriented, especially as to place and time

Sources: APA, 2000; Herbert et al., 2003.

---

senile dementias Forms of dementia that begin after age 65.

presenile dementias Forms of dementia that begin at or before age 65.

T R U T H or F I C T I O N

Dementia is a normal part of the aging process.

☑ **FALSE.** Dementia is not a normal part of aging. It is caused by an underlying disease affecting brain functioning.

---

delirium A state of mental confusion, disorientation, and inability to focus attention.

Dementias usually occur in people over the age of 80. Those that begin after age 65 are called late-onset or **senile dementias.** Those that begin at age 65 or earlier are termed early-onset or **presenile dementias**. Although the risk of dementia is greater in later life, dementia is not a consequence of normal aging. It is a sign of a degenerative brain disease, such as Alzheimer's disease.

Delirium

The word *delirium* derives from the Latin roots *de-*, meaning "from," and *lira,* meaning "line" or "furrow." It means straying from the line, or the norm, in perception, cognition, and behavior. **Delirium** is a state of extreme mental confusion in which people have difficulty concentrating and speaking clearly and coherently (see Table 15.3). People suffering from delirium may find it difficult to tune out irrelevant stimuli or to shift their attention to new tasks. They may speak excitedly, but their speech carries little if any meaning. Disorientation as to time (not knowing the current date, day of the week, or time) and place (not knowing where you are) is common. Disorientation to person (the identities of oneself and others) is not. People in a state of delirium may experience terrifying hallucinations, especially visual hallucinations.

Disturbances in perceptions often occur, such as misinterpretations of sensory stimuli (for example, confusing an alarm clock for a fire bell) or illusions (for instance, feeling as if the bed has an electrical charge passing through it). There can be a

TABLE 15.2

Cognitive Deficits in Dementia

Cognitive Deficit	Definition	Description
Aphasia	Impaired ability to comprehend and/or produce speech	There are several types of aphasia. In sensory or receptive aphasia, people have difficulty understanding written or spoken language, but retain the ability to express themselves through speech. In motor aphasia, the ability to express thoughts through speech is impaired, but the person can understand spoken language. A person with a motor aphasia may not be able to summon up the names of familiar objects or may scramble the normal order of words.
Apraxia	Impaired ability to perform purposeful movements despite an absence of any defect in motor functioning	There may be an inability to tie a shoelace or button a shirt, although the person can describe how these activities should be performed and despite the fact that there is nothing wrong with the person's arm or hand. The person may have difficulty pantomiming the use of an object (e.g., combing one's hair).
Agnosia	Inability to recognize objects despite an intact sensory system	Agnosias may be limited to specific sensory channels. A person with a visual agnosia may not be able to identify a fork when shown a picture of the object, although he or she has an intact visual system and may be able to identify the object if allowed to touch it and manipulate it by hand. Auditory agnosia is marked by impairment in the ability to recognize sounds; in tactile agnosia, people are unable to identify objects (such as coins or keys) by holding them or touching them.
Disturbance in Executive Functioning	Deficits in planning, organizing, or sequencing activities or in engaging in abstract thinking	An office manager who formerly handled budgets and scheduling loses the ability to manage the flow of work in the office or adapt to new demands. An English teacher loses the ability to extract meaning from a poem or story.

Source: Adapted from *DSM-IV-TR* (APA, 2000).

dramatic slowing down of movement into a state resembling catatonia. There may be rapid fluctuations between restlessness and stupor. Restlessness is characterized by insomnia, agitated, aimless movements, even bolting out of bed or striking out at nonexistent objects. This may alternate with periods in which victims have to struggle to stay awake.

TABLE 15.3

Features of Delirium

Domain	Level of Severity		
	Mild	**Moderate**	**Severe**
Emotion	Apprehension	Fear	Panic
Cognition and Perception	Confusion, racing thoughts	Disorientation, delusions	Meaningless mumbling, vivid hallucinations
Behavior	Tremors	Muscle spasms	Seizures
Autonomic Activity	Abnormally fast heartbeat (tachycardia)	Perspiration	Fever

Source: Adapted from Freemon (1981), p. 82.

The prevalence of delirium is estimated at about 1% to 2% in the general community, but rises to 14% among people over the age of 85 (Inouye, 2006). Delirium can result from a variety of underlying conditions including head trauma; metabolic disorders, such as hypoglycemia (low blood sugar); fluid or electrolyte imbalances; seizure disorders (epilepsy); deficiencies of the B vitamin thiamine; brain lesions; and various diseases that affect the functioning of the central nervous system, including Parkinson's disease, AD, viral encephalitis (a type of brain infection), liver disease, and kidney disease (APA, 2000; Lichtenberg & Duffy, 2000). Delirium may also occur due to exposure to toxic substances (such as eating certain poisonous mushrooms), as a side effect of using certain medications, or during states of drug or alcohol intoxication. Among young people, delirium is most commonly the result of abrupt withdrawal from psychoactive drugs, especially alcohol. However, among older patients, it is often a sign of life-threatening medical conditions (Inouye, 2006).

People with chronic alcoholism who abruptly stop drinking may experience a form of delirium called *delirium tremens* or DTs. During an acute episode of the DTs, the person may be terrorized by wild and frightening hallucinations, such as "bugs crawling down walls" or on the skin. The DTs can last for a week or more and are best treated in a hospital, where the patient can be carefully monitored and the symptoms treated with mild tranquilizers and environmental support. Although there are many known causes of delirium, in many cases the specific cause cannot be identified.

Whatever the cause, delirium is a generalized disruption of the brain's cortical functioning, possibly owing to imbalances in the levels of brain neurotransmitters (Burns et al., 2004; Inouye, 2006). As a result, the ability to process information is impaired and confusion reigns. The ability to think and speak clearly declines, as does the ability to attend to one's surroundings and interpret stimuli accurately. Delirium may occur abruptly, as in cases resulting from seizures or head injuries, or gradually over hours or days, as in cases involving infections, fever, or metabolic disorders. During the course of delirium, the person's mental state often fluctuates between periods of clarity ("lucid intervals"), which are most common in the morning, and periods of confusion and disorientation. Delirium is generally worse in the dark and following sleepless nights.

Unlike dementia, in which there is a steady deterioration of mental ability, states of delirium often clear up spontaneously when the underlying organic or drug-related cause is resolved. The course of delirium is relatively brief, usually lasting about a week, but rarely longer than a month. However, if the underlying cause persists or leads to further deterioration, delirium may progress to disability, coma, and even death (Inouye, 2006).

Amnestic Disorders

amnestic disorders Disturbances of memory associated with inability to learn new material or recall past events or personal information.

Amnestic disorders (commonly called amnesias) are characterized by a dramatic decline in memory functioning that is not connected with states of delirium or dementia. Unlike the memory disorders of dissociative amnesia and dissociative fugue discussed in Chapter 7, amnestic disorder is amnesia that results from a physical cause.

Amnestic disorders frequently follow a traumatic event, such as a blow to the head, an electric shock, or an operation. A head injury may prevent people from remembering events that occurred shortly before the accident. An automobile accident victim may not remember anything that transpired after getting into the car. A football player who develops amnesia from a blow to the head during the game may not remember anything after leaving the locker room. In some cases, people retain memories for the remote past but lose those for recent events. People with amnesia may be more likely to remember events from their childhood than last evening's dinner, for example. Consider the following case.

Amnestic disorder. An amnestic disorder syndrome can follow a traumatic injury such as a blow to the head. This football player may not be able to recall the events that happened just prior to his being tackled, nor the collision itself.

Who Is She?

A medical student was rushed to the hospital after he was thrown from a motorcycle. His parents were with him in his hospital room when he awakened. As his parents were explaining what had happened to him, the door suddenly flew open and his flustered wife, whom he had married a few weeks earlier, rushed into the room, leaped onto his bed, began to caress him, and expressed her great relief that he was not seriously injured. After several minutes of expressing her love and reassurance, his wife departed and the flustered student looked at his mother and asked, "Who is she?"

—*Adapted from Freemon, 1981, p. 96*

The medical student's long-term memory loss included memories dating not only to the accident but also further back to the time before he was married or had met his wife. Like most victims of posttraumatic amnesia, the medical student recovered his memory fully.

There are two general types of amnesia—**retrograde amnesia** (loss of memory of past events and personal information) and **anterograde amnesia** (inability or difficulty forming or storing new memories). A football player who does not remember anything after leaving the locker room has retrograde amnesia, but some cases are reported in the medical annals of people for whom information literally "goes in one ear and out the other" because they are unable to form new memories. These patients are experiencing anterograde amnesia. Problems with forming new memories may be revealed by an inability to remember the names of, or to recognize, people whom the person met 5 or 10 minutes earlier. Immediate memory, as measured by ability to repeat back a series of numbers, seems to be unimpaired in states of amnesia. The person is unlikely to remember the number series later, however, no matter how often it is rehearsed.

TRUTH or FICTION

After a motorcycle accident, a medical student failed to recognize the woman he had married a few weeks earlier.

☑ **TRUE.** After a motorcycle accident, a medical student failed to recognize his wife of a few weeks, although he remembered his parents.

retrograde amnesia Loss or impairment of ability to recall past events.

anterograde amnesia Loss or impairment of ability to form or store new memories.

In a famous medical case, an epileptic patient, known by the initials HM, developed anterograde amnesia as a complication of surgery performed to control his seizures. After the surgery, he became unable to learn any new information. He is quoted as having said: "Every day is alone by itself, whatever enjoyment I have had, whatever sorrow I have had."

People with an amnestic disorder may experience disorientation, more commonly involving disorientation to place (not knowing where one is at the time) and time (not knowing the day, month, and year) than disorientation as to self (not knowing one's own name). They may not be aware of their memory loss or may attempt to deny or mask their memory deficits even when evidence of their impairment is presented to them. They may attempt to fill the gaps in their memories with imaginary events. Or they may admit they have a memory problem but appear apathetic about it, showing a kind of emotional blandness.

Although people with amnestic disorder may suffer profound memory losses, their general intelligence tends to remain within a normal range. In contrast, in progressive dementias such as AD, memory and intellectual functioning both deteriorate. Early detection and diagnosis of the causes of memory problems are critical because they are often correctible if the underlying cause is treated successfully.

In addition to brain trauma, other causes of amnesia include brain surgery; **hypoxia,** or sudden loss of oxygen to the brain; brain infection or disease; **infarction,** or blockage of the blood vessels supplying the brain; and chronic, heavy use of certain psychoactive substances, most commonly alcohol.

Alcohol-Induced Persisting Amnestic Disorder (Korsakoff's Syndrome) A common cause of amnestic disorder is thiamine deficiency linked to chronic abuse of alcohol. Alcohol abusers tend to take poor care of their nutritional needs and may not follow a diet rich enough in vitamin B_1, or thiamine. Thiamine deficiencies may produce an irreversible form of memory loss called *alcohol-induced persisting amnestic disorder,* commonly known as **Korsakoff's syndrome.** The word *persisting* is used because the memory deficits persist even years after the person stops drinking (APA, 2000). Korsakoff's syndrome is not limited to people with chronic alcoholism, however. It has been reported in other groups who experience thiamine deficiencies during times of deprivation, such as prisoners of war.

People with Korsakoff's syndrome have major gaps in their memory of past experiences (Phaf, Geurts, & Eling, 2000). Their memory deficits are believed to result from the loss of brain tissue due to bleeding in the brain. Despite their memory losses, patients with Korsakoff's syndrome may retain their general level of intelligence. They are often described as being superficially friendly but lacking in insight, unable to discriminate between actual events and wild stories they invent to fill the gaps in their memories. They sometimes become grossly disoriented and confused and require custodial care.

Korsakoff's syndrome often follows an acute attack of **Wernicke's disease,** another brain disorder caused by thiamine deficiency. Wernicke's disease is characterized by confusion and disorientation, **ataxia,** or difficulty maintaining balance while walking, and paralysis of the muscles that control eye movements. These symptoms may pass, but the person is often left with Korsakoff's syndrome and enduring memory impairment. If, however, Wernicke's disease is treated promptly with major doses of vitamin B_1, Korsakoff's syndrome may not develop. Once Korsakoff's syndrome has set in, it is usually permanent, although slight improvement is possible with treatment.

PSYCHOLOGICAL DISORDERS RELATED TO AGING

Many physical changes occur with aging. Changes in calcium metabolism cause the bones to grow brittle and heighten the risk of breaks from falls. The skin grows less elastic, creating wrinkles and folds. The senses become less keen, so older people see and hear less acutely. Older people need more time (called *reaction time*) to respond to stimuli, whether they are driving or taking intelligence tests. For example, older drivers

hypoxia Decreased supply of oxygen to the brain or other organs.

infarction The development of an infarct, or area of dead or dying tissue, resulting from the blocking of blood vessels normally supplying the tissue.

Korsakoff's syndrome A syndrome associated with chronic alcoholism that is characterized by memory loss and disorientation (also called *alcohol-induced persisting amnestic disorder*).

Wernicke's disease A brain disorder, associated with chronic alcoholism, characterized by confusion, disorientation, and difficulty maintaining balance while walking.

ataxia Loss of muscle coordination.

require more time to react to traffic signals and other cars. The immune system functions less effectively with increasing age, so people become more vulnerable to illness.

Cognitive changes occur as well. It is normal for people in later life to experience some decline in memory functioning and general cognitive ability, as measured by tests of intelligence, or IQ tests. The decline is sharpest on timed items, such as the performance subtests of the Wechsler Adult Intelligence Scale (discussed in Chapter 3). Some abilities, such as vocabulary and accumulated store of knowledge, hold up well and may actually improve over time. However, people typically experience some reduction in memory as they age, especially memory for names or recent events. But apart from the occasional social embarrassment resulting from forgetting a person's name, cognitive declines do not significantly interfere in most cases with the person's ability to meet social or occupational responsibilities. Declines in cognitive functioning may also be offset to a certain extent by increased knowledge and life experience.

The important point here is that dementia, or senility, is not the result of normal aging (USDHHS, 1999a). It is a sign of degenerative brain disease. Screening and testing on neurological and neuropsychological tests can help distinguish dementias from normal aging processes. Generally speaking, the decline in intellectual functioning in dementia is more rapid and severe.

Let us now turn to consider relationships between various psychological disorders and aging, beginning with anxiety disorders, the most common mental disorder of older adults.

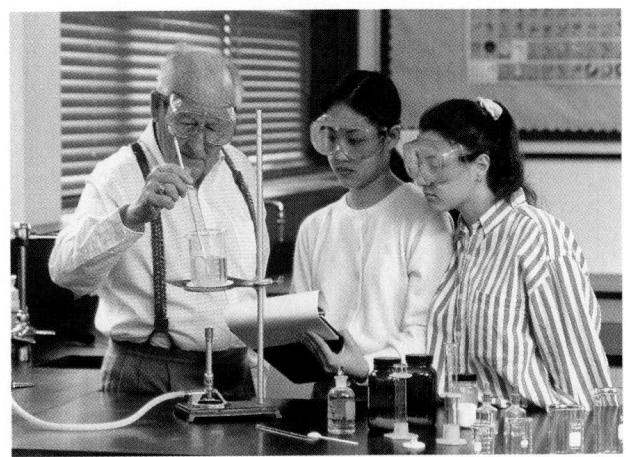

What changes take place as we age? How do they affect our moods? Although some declines in cognitive and physical functioning are connected with aging, older adults who remain active and engage in rewarding activities can be highly satisfied with their lives.

Anxiety Disorders and Aging

Although anxiety disorders may develop at any point in life, they tend to be less prevalent among older adults than their younger counterparts. Still, anxiety disorders are the most commonly occurring psychological disorder among older adults, even more common than depression. Approximately 1 in 10 adults over the age of 55 suffers from a diagnosable anxiety disorder (USDHHS, 1999a). Older women are more likely to be affected than older men, by a ratio of about two to one (Stanley & Beck, 2000). The most frequently occurring anxiety disorders among older adults are generalized anxiety disorder (GAD) and phobic disorders. Panic disorder is rare. Most cases of agoraphobia affecting older adults tend to be of recent origin and may involve the loss of social support systems due to the death of a spouse or close friends. Then again, some older individuals who are frail may have realistic fears of falling on the street and may be misdiagnosed as agoraphobic if they refuse to leave the house alone. Generalized anxiety disorder may arise from the perception that one lacks control over one's life, which may be the case for older people contending with infirmity, loss of friends and loved ones, and lessened economic opportunities. Antianxiety drugs, such as the benzodiazepines (Valium is one), are commonly used to quell anxiety in older adults. Psychological interventions, such as cognitive-behavior therapy, show therapeutic benefits in treating anxiety in older adults and do not carry the risk of drug side effects or potential dependence (Nordhus & Pallesen, 2003; Stanley & Beck, 2000).

Depression and Aging

Although risks of major depression decline with age, many older adults encounter significant periods of depression (Karel & Hinrichsen, 2000). For some older adults, recurring depression is a continuation of a lifelong pattern; in others, it first arises in later life. Between 8% and 20% of older adults experience some symptoms of depression (USDHHS, 1999a), with perhaps about 3% of them suffering from major

Agoraphobia, or a need for support? Some older adults may refuse to venture away from home on their own because of realistic fears of falling in the street. They may be in need of social support, not therapy.

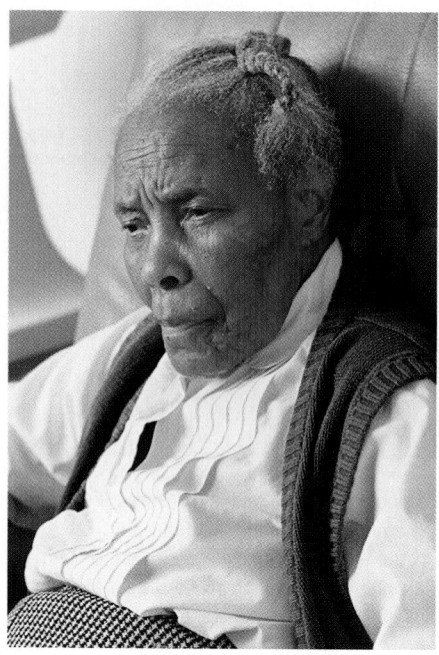

Late-life depression. Many older adults struggle with clinical depression. What factors contribute to depression in late adulthood?

depressive disorder (Rimer, 1999; Steffens et al., 2000). Rates of depression are higher still among residents of nursing homes. Although fewer older adults suffer from major depression than do younger adults, suicide is more frequent among older adults, especially older White males (Bruce et al., 2004; Eddleston, 2006).

Depression in later life is linked to a faster rate of physical decline and a higher death rate (Brenda et al., 1998). Depression may be linked to a higher death rate because of coexisting medical conditions or perhaps because of a lack of compliance with taking necessary medications.

Older people of color often carry an especially heavy stress burden. In one study, a sample of 127 elderly African Americans recruited from senior citizens programs in two large urban centers in the northeastern United States were administered measures of race-related stress, satisfaction with life, and health concerns (Utsey et al., 2002). The investigators found that men reported higher levels of institutional and collective forms of racism than did women. The investigators commented that they weren't surprised by these findings, as African American men have traditionally been subjected to harsher experiences of societal racism and oppression. Going further, the investigators reported that institutional race-related stress was associated with poorer psychological well-being. Many of the elderly men in this sample had experienced institutional racism (i.e., government-sanctioned discrimination in housing, education, employment, health care, and public policy) during their early and middle life. This study contributes to a growing body of literature showing links between race-related stress and mental health functioning of African Americans.

Other investigators have examined the role of acculturative stress in older adults from immigrant groups. A study of Mexican American older adults showed that those who were minimally acculturated to U.S. society had greater rates of depression than either highly acculturated or bicultural individuals (Zamanian et al., 1992).

Depressive disorders occur commonly in people suffering from brain disorders, several of which, such as AD and stroke, disproportionately affect older people. Researchers estimate that depressive disorders occur in as many as half of stroke victims and about a third to a half of people affected by AD or Parkinson's disease (e.g., Chemerinski et al., 2001; Fregn et al., 2006). In the case of Parkinson's disease, depression may result not only from coping with the disease but also from neurobiological changes in the brain caused by the disease.

Social support can help buffer the effects of stress, bereavement, and illness, thereby reducing the risk of depression. Social support is especially important to older people who are challenged because of physical disability. Participation in volunteer or religious organizations may also provide a sense of meaning and purpose as well as a needed social outlet.

Older people may be especially vulnerable to depression because of the stress of coping with life changes—retirement; physical illness or incapacitation; placement in a residential facility or nursing home; the deaths of a spouse, siblings, lifetime friends, and acquaintances; or the need to care for a spouse whose health is declining. Retirement, whether voluntary or forced, may lead to a loss of role identity. Deaths of relatives and friends induce grief and remind older people of their own advanced age as well as reduce the availability of social support. Older adults may feel incapable of forming new friendships or finding new goals in life. The chronic strain of coping with a family member with Alzheimer's disease can lead to depression in the caregiver, even without any prior vulnerability to depression (Mittelman et al., 2004).

Despite the prevalence of depression in older people, physicians often fail to recognize it or to treat it appropriately (Bruce et al., 2002). Health-care providers may be less likely to recognize depression among older people than in middle-aged or young people because they tend to focus on the older patient's physical complaints, and because depression in older people is often masked by physical complaints and sleeping problems.

The good news about geriatric depression is that effective treatment is available, including antidepressant medication, cognitive-behavioral therapy, and interpersonal psychotherapy (Pinquart, Duberstein, & Lyness, 2006; Reynolds et al., 2006; Sammons, 2005; Wei et al., 2005). This evidence of treatment effectiveness should help put to rest the belief that psychotherapy or psychiatric medication is not appropriate for people in late adulthood. Moreover, the memory impairment that can accompany depression often lifts when the underlying depression is resolved.

Sleep Problems and Aging

Sleep problems, especially insomnia, are common among older people. Insomnia in late adulthood is actually more prevalent than depression. Sleep problems reflect age-related changes in sleep physiology, such as sleep apnea and tendencies to wake up earlier in the morning (Martin, Shochat, & Ancoli-Israel, 2000). However, sleep problems may be a feature of other psychological disorders, such as depression, dementia, and anxiety disorders, as well as medical illness. Psychosocial factors, such as loneliness and the related difficulty of sleeping alone after the loss of a spouse, may also be involved. Dysfunctional thoughts, such as excessive concerns about lack of sleep and perceptions of hopelessness and helplessness about controlling sleep, may contribute to insomnia in older people.

Sleep medications are often used in treating late-life insomnia, but long-term use of these drugs can cause dependence and withdrawal symptoms. Fortunately, behavioral approaches, similar to those described in Chapter 10, are effective in treating insomnia in later life and produce as good if not better therapeutic benefits than sleep medications without risks of side effects or drug dependence (Martin, Shochat, & Ancoli-Israel, 2000; Sivertsen et al., 2006). Moreover, older adults are as capable of benefiting from behavioral treatment as younger adults.

Dementia of the Alzheimer's Type

Alzheimer's disease (AD) is a degenerative brain disease that leads to progressive and irreversible dementia, characterized by loss of memory and deterioration of other cognitive functions (Thompson et al., 2003). AD affects about 4.5 million Americans and is the fourth leading cause of death among adults (Grady, 2004). As we noted, AD accounts for more than half of the cases of dementia in the general population.

The risks of AD increase dramatically with advancing age. An estimated 10% of Americans over the age of 65, and about half of those in the 75- to 84-year age range, are believed to suffer from AD (Herbert et al., 2003; Lemonick & Park, 2001). As the U.S. population continues to age, the disease is expected to affect some 13 million Americans by the year 2050 (Shumaker, Legault, & Coker, 2006).

The great majority of cases of AD occur in people over the age of 65, most typically in those in their late 70s and 80s (see Figure 15.1). Women are at higher risk of developing the disease than men, although this may be a consequence of women tending to live longer. Economic costs of AD are estimated at more than $90 billion a year in the United States (Cowan & Kandel, 2001). Yet it is important to again note that although AD is strongly connected with aging, it is a degenerative brain disease and not a consequence of normal aging (Butler, 2001).

The dementia associated with AD takes the form of a progressive deterioration or loss of mental abilities involving memory, language, and problem solving. Occasional memory loss or forgetfulness in middle life (e.g., forgetting where one put one's glasses) is normal and not a sign of the early stages of Alzheimer's disease. People in later life (and some of us not quite that advanced in years) complain of not remembering names as well as they used to or of forgetting names that were once well known to them.

Forgetting where you put your keys is a normal occurrence; forgetting where you live is not. Here, a woman with early-onset Alzheimer's, recounts how her memory began slipping away. She relates an experience that happened to her one day as she was driving home from her husband's office.

Alzheimer's disease (AD) A progressive brain disease characterized by gradual loss of memory and intellectual functioning, personality changes, and eventual loss of ability to care for oneself.

TRUTH or FICTION

People who become occasionally forgetful as they age are probably suffering from the early stages of Alzheimer's disease.

☑ **FALSE.** Occasional memory loss or forgetfulness is a normal consequence of the aging process.

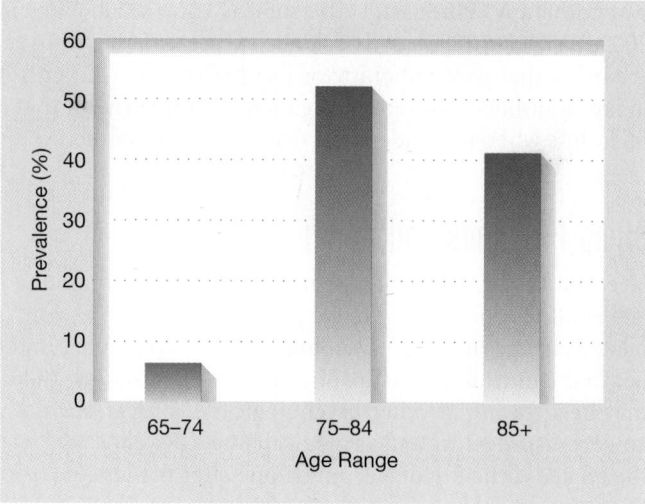

FIGURE 15.1 Prevalence of Alzheimer's disease among older adults.
Among older adults, the risk of Alzheimer's disease is much greater among people over the age of 75 than among those 65 to 74.

Source: Herbert et al., 2003.

"I" Living in the Labyrinth

I was hopelessly lost, and had no idea how to get home. . . . My body was shaking with fear and uncontrollable sobs. What was happening?

A few yards ahead, there was a park ranger building. Trembling, I wiped my eyes, and breathing deeply, tried to calm myself. . . . . The guard smiled and inquired how he could assist me.

"I appear to be lost," I began. . .

"Where do you need to go?" the guard asked politely.

A cold chill enveloped me as I realized I could not remember the name of my street. Tears began to flow down my cheeks. I did not know where I wanted to go. . . .

I felt panic wash over me anew as I searched my memory and found it blank. Suddenly, I remembered bringing my grandchildren to this park. That must mean I lived relatively nearby, surely.

"What is the closest subdivision?" I quavered.

The guard scratched his head thoughtfully.

"The closest Orlando subdivision would be Pine Hills, maybe," he ventured.

"That's right!" I exclaimed gratefully. The name of my subdivision had rung a bell. . . .

I drove carefully in the exact direction he advised and searched each intersection. . . . Finally, . . . I recognized the entrance to the subdivision. . . .

Once home, a wave of relief brought more tears. . . . . I took refuge in the darkened master bedroom, and sat, curled up on my bed, my arms wrapped tightly around myself."

Source: From McGowin, 1993

Suspicions of AD are raised when cognitive impairment is more severe and pervasive, affecting the individual's ability to meet the ordinary responsibilities of daily work and social roles. Over the course of the illness, people with AD may get lost in parking lots or in stores, or even in their own homes. The wife of an AD patient describes how AD affected her husband: "With no cure, Alzheimer's robs the person of who he is. It is painful to see Richard walk around the car several times because he can't find the door" (Morrow, 1998, p. D4). Agitation, wandering behavior, depression, and aggressive behavior are common as the disease progresses (Chen et al., 1999; Slone & Gleason, 1999).

People with AD may become depressed, confused, or even delusional when they sense that their mental ability is slipping away but not understand why. They may experience hallucinations and other psychotic features. Bewilderment and fear may lead to paranoid delusions or beliefs that their loved ones have betrayed them, robbed them,

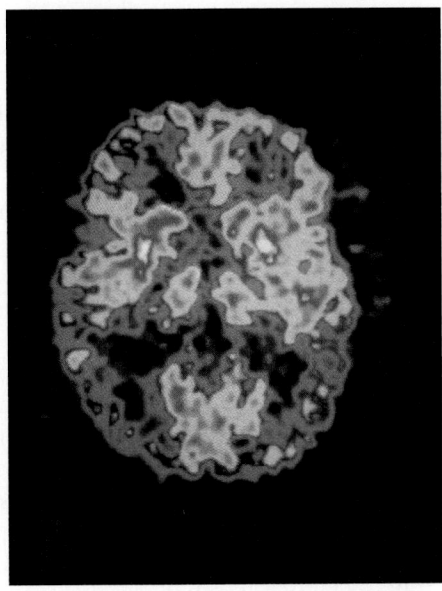

FIGURE 15.2 PET scans of brains from a healthy aged adult (left) and a patient with Alzheimer's disease (right).
The darkly shaded areas in the photo to the right suggest how the neurological changes associated with Alzheimer's disease (as marked by the excess of dark shading) impair brain activity.

Source: Friedland, R. P., Case Western Reserve University, courtesy of *Clinical Neuroimaging.* Copyright © 1988 by John Wiley and Sons, Inc.

or don't care about them. They may forget the names of their loved ones or fail to recognize them. They may even forget their own names.

AD was first described in 1907 by the German physician Alois Alzheimer (1864–1915). During an autopsy of a 56-year-old woman who had suffered from severe dementia, he found two brain abnormalities now regarded as signs of the disease: plaques (portions of degenerative brain tissue) and neurofibrillary tangles (twisted bundles of nerve cells) (Jacobsen et al., 2006; Nunomura et al., 2006) (see Figure 15.2). The darkly shaded areas in the photo to the right in Figure 15.2 show the diminished brain activity associated with AD.

Diagnosis There is no definitive diagnostic test for AD. The diagnosis is generally based on a clinical evaluation and given only when other possible causes of dementia are eliminated. Other medical and psychological conditions may mimic AD, such as severe depression resulting in memory loss and impaired cognitive functioning. Consequently, misdiagnoses may occur, especially in the early stages of the disease. A confirmatory diagnosis of AD can be made only upon inspection of brain tissue by biopsy or autopsy. However, biopsy is rarely performed because of the risk of hemorrhage or infection, and autopsy, of course, occurs too late to help the patient.

Symptoms of Alzheimer's Disease Alzheimer's disease develops gradually but progresses steadily, leading to dementia in about 3 years following onset. Earlier age of onset is associated with poorer cognitive functioning, even when the duration of the illness is taken into account. AD that strikes earlier in life may involve a more severe form of the disease.

The early stages of the disease are marked by limited memory problems and subtle personality changes. People may at first have trouble managing their finances; remembering recent events or basic information such as telephone numbers, area codes, zip codes, and the names of their grandchildren; and performing numerical computations. A business executive who once managed millions of dollars may become unable to perform simple arithmetic. There may be subtle personality changes, such as signs of withdrawal

Alzheimer's disease. Alzheimer's disease (AD) has struck a number of notable people, including former President Ronald Reagan, here shown with his wife, Nancy, at his first public appearance after being diagnosed with AD. Reagan died of the disease in June 2004.

in people who had been outgoing or irritability in people who had been gentle. In these early stages, people with AD generally appear neat and well-groomed and are generally cooperative and socially appropriate.

Some people with AD are not aware of their deficits. Others deny them. At first they may attribute their problems to other causes, such as stress or fatigue. Denial may protect people with AD in the early or mild stages of the disease from recognition that their intellectual abilities are in decline. Or the recognition that one's mental abilities are slipping away may lead to depression.

In moderately severe AD, people require assistance in managing everyday tasks. At this stage, the Alzheimer's patient may be unable to select appropriate clothes or recall their addresses or names of family members. When they drive, they begin making mistakes, such as failing to stop at stop signs or accelerating when they should be braking. They may encounter difficulties in toileting and bathing themselves. They often make mistakes in recognizing themselves in mirrors. They may no longer be able to speak in full sentences. Verbal responses may become limited to a few words.

Movement and coordination functions deteriorate further. People with AD at the moderately severe level may begin walking in shorter, slower steps. They may no longer be able to sign their names, even when assisted by others. They may have difficulty handling a knife and fork. Agitation becomes a prominent feature at this stage, and victims may act out in response to the threat of having to contend with an environment that no longer seems controllable. They may pace or fidget or display aggressive behavior such as yelling, throwing, or hitting. Patients may wander off because of restlessness and be unable to find their way back.

People with advanced AD may start talking to themselves or experience visual hallucinations or paranoid delusions. They may believe someone is attempting to harm them or is stealing their possessions, or that their spouses are unfaithful to them. They may believe their spouses are actually other people.

At the most severe stage, cognitive functions decline to the point where people become essentially helpless. They may lose the ability to speak or control body movement. They become incontinent; are unable to communicate, walk, or even sit up; and require assistance in toileting and feeding. In the end state, seizures, coma, and death result.

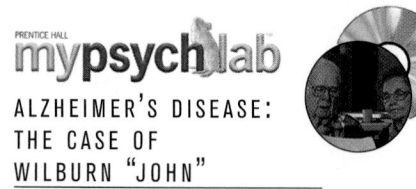

ALZHEIMER'S DISEASE: THE CASE OF WILBURN "JOHN"

"You kinda have hope whenever you have cancer . . . but then, [with] Alzheimer's . . . you die, just a little each day."

Do you know my name? Alzheimer's disease can devastate patients' families. Spouses usually provide the bulk of daily care. This man has been caring for his wife for several years, and he believes that his hugs and kisses sometimes prompt his wife to murmur his name.

The following case illustrates the major features of Alzheimer's disease, such as memory loss, disorientation, and behavior problems.

A Case of Dementia of the Alzheimer's Type

A 65-year-old draftsman began to have problems remembering important details at work; at home he began to have difficulty keeping his financial records up-to-date and remembering to pay bills on time. His intellectual abilities progressively declined, forcing him eventually to retire from his job. Behavioral problems began to appear at home, as he grew increasingly stubborn and even verbally and physically abusive toward others when he felt thwarted.

On neurological examination, he displayed disorientation as to place and time, believing that the consultation room was his place of employment and that the year was "1960 or something," when it was actually 1982. He had difficulty with even simple memory tests, failing to remember any of six objects shown to him 10 minutes earlier, not recalling the names of his parents or siblings, or the name of the president of the United States. His speech was vague and filled with meaningless phrases. He couldn't perform simple arithmetical computations, but he could interpret proverbs correctly.

Shortly following the neurological consultation, the man was placed in a hospital because his family was no longer able to control his increasingly disruptive behavior. In the hospital, his mental abilities continued to decline, while his aggressive behavior was largely controlled by major tranquilizers (antipsychotic drugs). He was diagnosed as suffering from a primary degenerative dementia of the Alzheimer type. He died at age 74, some 8 years following the onset of his symptoms.

—Adapted from Spitzer et al., 1989, pp. 131–132

AD wreaks havoc not only on the affected person but also on the entire family. Families who helplessly watch their loved ones slowly deteriorate have been described as attending a "funeral that never ends" (Aronson, 1988). The symptoms of advanced AD, such as wandering away, aggressiveness, destructiveness, incontinence, screaming, and remaining awake at night, cause high levels of stress imposed on caregivers. Living with a person with advanced AD may seem like living with a stranger, so profound are the changes in personality and behavior. Not surprisingly, caregivers experience more health problems and higher levels of stress hormone than do noncaregivers (Vitaliano, Zhang, & Scanlan, 2003). Typically, the caretaking burden falls disproportionately on the adult daughters in the family, who are often middle-aged women feeling "sandwiched" between their responsibilities to their children and to their affected parents. Here is one woman's story.

"A Daughter's Dilemma"

Mom is 86 years old and is in the third stage of Alzheimer's disease. I first recognized a change in Mom about 10 years ago when she became emotionally volatile. My dilemma is: How much responsibility do I have for Mom's care while maintaining my own family life?

I am a 52-year-old married woman raising three teenage boys. My career is in clinical psychology, and I have a Ph.D. in gerontology. I seem to be the logical one to coordinate her care, because I am her only daughter and have the knowledge of Alzheimer's disease. But I left my parents' home in Brooklyn, New York, long ago and now live in Colorado. How do I manage Mom's care long distance?

In an effort to help, I suggested that Mom spend time in my home in Colorado. . . . I accompanied Mom on the plane trip to Colorado, and that trip brought me into the stark, cold reality that Mom had Alzheimer's. She did not know where she was or where she was going. Upon arrival, she did not recognize my home, although she had visited me numerous times in the past.

She tried sleeping in the bathtub the first night. She said that she was trying to find her bed. She stayed for two months, and during that time she rarely found the bathroom, which was adjacent to her bedroom. . . .

During our first month together, I was feeling good about forgetting myself and serving her. I told her that I loved her and wanted to give her the care that she deserved. But I began to burn out during the second month. I stopped looking forward to the weekends when she was in my constant care. At work, I was helping other caretakers keep a balance in their lives, yet I found myself always putting Mom first. Many of my personal, marital, and family's needs went unmet.

—*Source: Smoller, 1997, pp. 23, 28, 33, 36*

Causal Factors AD is a brain disease of unknown origin. However, we do know that plaques, the steel-wool-like clumps that form in the brains of people with Alzheimer's disease, are composed of a material called *beta amyloid,* which consists of fibrous protein fragments (Goedert & Spillantini, 2006; Jacobsen et al., 2006). Whether or not the accumulation of plaque plays a role in explaining memory loss and other symptoms of AD remains unclear (Lesné et al., 2006; Nunomura et al., 2006). Laboratory experiments on other animals suggest that memory deficits may actually precede the formation of significant deposits of plaque (Jacobsen et al., 2006).

On another front, we have compelling evidence from twin studies and other sources that genetic factors play an important role in AD (Bird, 2005; Gatz et al., 2006; Silverman et al., 2005). Environmental factors also appear to play a role, although scientists haven't yet determined what these factors might be (Gatz et al., 2006). Importantly, investigators need to better understand the relative contributions of genes and environmental influences, as well as their interactions, in how the disease develops (Bird, 2005).

Some forms of AD are linked to genes that regulate production of a protein called *apolipoprotein E* (APOe) (Bartzokis et al., 2006). This protein transports cholesterol through the bloodstream. People with defects in these genes may begin to show signs of brain deterioration even before memory symptoms appear. The brain appears to work harder when performing a memory task, which suggests that it is trying to compensate for underlying abnormalities (Bookheimer et al., 2000). Other genes likely play a role AD, including genes involved in production of beta amyloid (Goedert & Spillantini, 2006; Li, 2000).

Treatment and Prevention Presently available drugs for AD offer at best modest benefits in slowing cognitive decline and boosting cognitive functioning (Grady, 2004; Reisberg et al., 2003). None is a cure (Roberson & Mucke, 2006). One widely used drug, *donepezil* (brand name Aricept), increases levels of the neurotransmitter acetylcholine (ACh). AD patients show reduced levels of ACh, possibly because of the death of brain cells in ACh-producing areas of the brain. Another drug, *memantine* (brand name Axura), blocks the neurotransmitter glutamate, a brain chemical found in abnormally high concentrations in AD patients. High levels of glutamate may damage brain cells. Memantine is the first drug designed to tackle moderate to severe AD (Tariot et al., 2004). Recent evidence also shows donepezil to yield some modest improvements in cognitive functioning and activities of daily living in cases of severe AD (Winblad et al., 2006). However, it remains doubtful whether donepezil can lead to clinically meaningful changes in severe AD (Hogan, 2006). Psychosocial interventions, such as memory training programs, can also help AD patients make optimal use of their remaining abilities (Kasl-Godley & Gatz, 2000).

Hopes for the future lie in the development of an effective vaccine that might prevent this devastating disease. In the meantime, investigators report that lifestyle changes, such as engaging in intellectually challenging tasks and following a regular exercise program, may delay or even prevent the development of dementia in later life (Larson et al., 2006; Verghese et al., 2003).

Plaques linked to Alzheimer's disease. In Alzheimer's disease, nerve tissue in the brain degenerates, forming steel-wool-like clumps or plaques composed of beta-amyloid protein fragments, shown here as blue-stained areas in a section of the cerebral cortex.

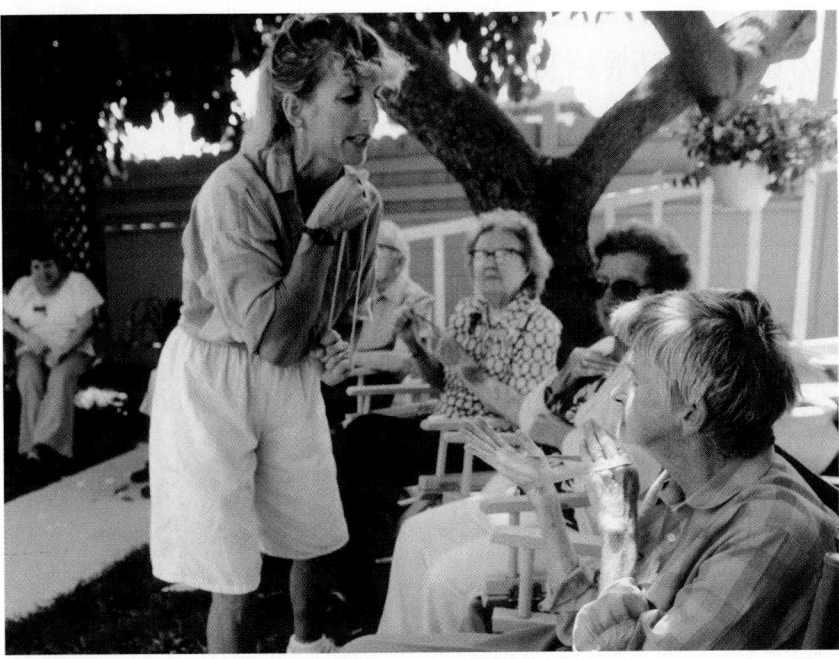

Boosting memory. Memory training programs are not a cure, but they may help Alzheimer's patients make the best use of their remaining abilities.

Vascular Dementia

The brain, like other living tissues, depends on the bloodstream to supply it with oxygen and glucose and to carry away its metabolic wastes. A stroke, also called a **cerebrovascular accident (CVA),** occurs when part of the brain becomes damaged because of a disruption in its blood supply, usually as the result of a blood clot that becomes lodged in an artery that services the brain and obstructs circulation (Adler, 2004). Areas of the brain may be damaged or destroyed, leaving the victim with disabilities in motor, speech, and cognitive functions. Death may also occur.

Vascular dementia (formerly called *multi-infarct dementia*) is a form of dementia that results from repeated strokes (Wright et al, 2006). An *infarct* refers to the death of tissue caused by insufficient blood supply. Vascular dementia, the second most common form of dementia after Alzheimer's disease, most often affects people in later life but at somewhat earlier ages than dementia due to AD (APA, 2000; Wilkinson et al., 2003). The disease affects more men than women and accounts for about one in five cases of dementia. Unlike AD, heredity does not appear to play a major role in vascular dementia (Bergem et al., 1997).

Single strokes may produce gross impairments in specific functions, such as **aphasia,** but single strokes do not typically cause the more generalized cognitive declines that characterize dementia. Vascular dementia generally results from multiple strokes that occur at different times and that have cumulative effects on a wide range of mental abilities.

Features of Vascular Dementia The symptoms of vascular dementia are similar to those of dementia of the Alzheimer's type, including impaired memory and language ability, agitation and emotional instability, and loss of ability to care for one's own basic needs. However, AD is characterized by an insidious onset and a gradual decline of mental functioning, whereas vascular dementia typically occurs abruptly and follows a stepwise course of deterioration involving rapid declines in cognitive functioning that are believed to reflect the effects of additional strokes (e.g., Kasl-Godley & Gatz, 2000). Some cognitive functions in people with vascular dementia

cerebrovascular accident (CVA) A stroke, or brain damage resulting from a rupture or blockage of a blood vessel supplying oxygen to the brain.

vascular dementia Dementia resulting from a number of strokes in the brain.

aphasia Impaired ability to understand or express speech.

QUESTIONNAIRE
Examining Your Attitudes Toward Aging

What are your assumptions about late adulthood? Do you see older people as basically different from the young in their behavior patterns and their outlooks, or just as more mature?

To evaluate the accuracy of your attitudes toward aging, mark each of the following items true or false. Then turn to the answer key at the end of the chapter.

	TRUE	FALSE
1. By age 60 most couples have lost their capacity for satisfying sexual relations.	___	___
2. Older people cannot wait to retire.	___	___
3. With advancing age people become more externally oriented, less concerned with the self.	___	___
4. As individuals age, they become less able to adapt satisfactorily to a changing environment.	___	___
5. General satisfaction with life tends to decrease as people become older.	___	___
6. As people age they tend to become more homogeneous—that is, all old people tend to be alike in many ways.	___	___
7. For the older person, having a stable intimate relationship is no longer highly important.	___	___
8. The aged are susceptible to a wider variety of psychological disorders than young and middle-aged adults.	___	___
9. Most older people are depressed much of the time.	___	___
10. Church attendance increases with age.	___	___
11. The occupational performance of the older worker is typically less effective than that of the younger adult.	___	___
12. Most older people are just not able to learn new skills.	___	___
13. Compared to younger persons, older people tend to think more about the past than the present or the future.	___	___
14. Most people in later life are unable to live independently and reside in nursing homes or similar institutions.	___	___

Source: Adapted from Rathus, S. A., & Nevid, J. S. (1995). *Adjustment and growth: The challenges of life* (6th ed.), p. 440. Reprinted with permission of Brooks/Cole, an imprint of Wadsworth Group, a division of Thomson Learning. FAX 800-730-2215.

remain relatively intact in the early course of the disorder, leading to a pattern of patchy deterioration in which islands of mental competence remain while other abilities suffer gross impairment, depending on the particular areas of the brain that have been damaged by multiple strokes.

DEMENTIAS DUE TO GENERAL MEDICAL CONDITIONS

We have examined relationships between aging and psychological disorders, such as dementia and depression. Next we consider a number of physical disorders that affect psychological functioning in various ways.

Dementia Due to Pick's Disease

Pick's disease causes a progressive dementia that is symptomatically similar to AD. Symptoms include memory loss and social inappropriateness, such as a loss of modesty or the display of flagrant sexual behavior. Diagnosis is confirmed only upon autopsy by the *absence* of the neurofibrillary tangles and plaques that are found in AD and by the presence of other abnormal structures—Pick's bodies—in nerve cells. Pick's disease is believed to account for about 6% to 12% of dementias (Kertesz, 2006). Unlike AD, it becomes evident most often between the ages of 50 and 60, although it can occur at later ages (APA, 2000). The risk declines with advancing age after 70. Men are more likely than women to suffer from Pick's disease. Pick's disease often runs in families and a genetic component is suspected in its development (Hutton, 2001; Kertesz, 2006).

Pick's disease A form of dementia, similar to Alzheimer's disease, but distinguished by specific abnormalities (Pick's bodies) in nerve cells and absence of neurofibrillary tangles and plaques.

Dementia Due to Parkinson's Disease

Parkinson's disease is a slowly progressing neurological disease that affects between half a million and one million people in the United States, including the former heavyweight champion Muhammad Ali and the actor Michael J. Fox (Carroll, 2004; Deuschl et al., 2006). The disease affects men and women about equally and most often strikes between the ages of 50 and 69. Dementia occurs in perhaps 20% to as many as 75% or more of Parkinson's patients over the course of the illness (Aarsland et al., 2003; APA, 2000).

Parkinson's disease A progressive disease of the basal ganglia characterized by muscle tremor and shakiness, rigidity, difficulty walking, poor control of fine motor movements, lack of facial muscle tone, and in some cases, cognitive impairment.

Parkinson's disease is characterized by uncontrollable shaking or tremors, rigidity, disturbances in posture (leaning forward), and lack of control over body movements. People with Parkinson's disease may be able to control their shaking or tremors, but only briefly. Some cannot walk at all. Others walk laboriously, in a crouch. Some execute voluntary body movements with difficulty, have poor control over fine motor movements, such as finger control, and have sluggish reflexes. They may look expressionless, as if they are wearing masks, a symptom that apparently reflects the degeneration of brain tissue that controls facial muscles. It is particularly difficult for patients to engage in sequences of complex movements, such as those required to sign their names. People with Parkinson's disease may be unable to coordinate two movements at the same time, as seen in this description of a Parkinson's patient who had difficulty walking and reaching for his wallet at the same time.

Battling Parkinson's disease. Actor Michael J. Fox has been waging a personal battle against Parkinson's disease and has brought national attention to the need to fund research efforts to develop more effective treatments for this degenerative brain disease.

◆

Motor Impairment in a Case of Parkinson's Disease

A 58-year-old man was walking across the hotel lobby in order to pay his bill. He reached into his inside jacket pocket for his wallet. He stopped walking instantly as he did so and stood immobile in the lobby in front of strangers. He became aware of his suspended locomotion and resumed his stroll to the cashier; however, his hand remained rooted in his inside pocket, as though he were carrying a weapon he might display once he arrived at the cashier.

—*Adapted from Knight, Godfrey, & Shelton, 1988*

Despite the severity of motor disability, cognitive functions seem to remain intact during the early stages of the disease. Dementia is more common in the later stages or among those with more severe forms of the disease (APA, 2000). The form of dementia associated with Parkinson's disease typically involves a slowing down of thinking processes, impaired ability to think abstractly or plan or organize a series of actions, and difficulty retrieving memories. Overall, the cognitive impairments associated with Parkinson's disease tend to be more subtle than those associated with AD. Parkinson's patients often become socially withdrawn and depressed, either because of difficulty coping with the disease or biochemical changes that are part and parcel of the disease (Rao et al., 1992).

Parkinson's disease is characterized by destruction or impairment of dopamine-producing nerve cells in the *substantia nigra* ("black substance"), an area of the brain that helps regulate body movement. The underlying causes of the disease remain unknown, but scientists today suspect an interaction between genetic influences and environmental factors, perhaps involving exposure to certain toxins (Lesage et al., 2006; Mosharov et al., 2006; Ozelius et al., 2006). According to one expert, "Dopamine is like the oil in the engine of a car. . . . If the oil is there, the car runs smoothly. If not, it seizes up" (cited in Carroll, 2004, p. F5).

Whatever the underlying cause, the symptoms of the disease—the uncontrollable tremors, shaking, rigid muscles, and difficulty walking—are tied to deficiencies in the amount of dopamine in the brain. The drug L-dopa, which increases dopamine levels, brought hope to Parkinson's patients when it was introduced in the 1970s. L-dopa is converted in the brain into dopamine.

L-dopa helps control the symptoms of the disease and slows its progress, but it does not cure it (Kaiser et al., 2003; Parkinson Study Group, 2000). About 80% of people with Parkinson's disease show significant improvement in their tremors and motor symptoms following treatment with L-dopa. After a few years, however, L-dopa begins to lose its effectiveness, and the disease continues to progress. Several other drugs are in the experimental stage, offering hope for further advances in treatment. Other sources of hope comes from experimental use of electrical stimulation of deep-brain structures and from genetic studies that may one day lead to an effective gene therapy for the disease (Deuschl et al., 2006; Schüpbach et al., 2006; Smeding et al., 2006).

Dementia Due to Huntington's Disease

Huntington's disease, also known as *Huntington's chorea,* was first recognized by the neurologist George Huntington in 1872. In Huntington's disease, there is progressive deterioration of the basal ganglia, a part of the brain that helps regulate body movement and posture.

The most prominent physical symptoms of the disease are involuntary, jerky movements of the face (grimaces), neck, limbs, and trunk—in contrast to the poverty of movement that typifies Parkinson's disease (Higgins, 2006). These twitches are termed *choreiform,* which derives from the Greek *choreia,* meaning "dance." Unstable moods, alternating with states of apathy, anxiety, and depression, are common in the early stages of the disease. As the disease progresses, paranoia may develop, and people may become suicidally depressed. Difficulties retrieving memories in the early course of the disease may develop later into dementia. Eventually, there is loss of control of bodily functions, leading to death occurring within about 15 years after onset of the disease.

Huntington's disease, which afflicts about 1 in 10,000 people, typically begins in the prime of adulthood, between the ages of 30 and 45. Men and women are equally likely to develop the disease (APA, 2000). One of the victims of the disease was the folksinger Woody Guthrie, who gave us the beloved song "This Land Is Your Land," among many others. He died of Huntington's disease in 1967, after 22 years of battling the malady. Because of the odd, jerky movements associated with the disease, Guthrie, like many other Huntington's victims, was misdiagnosed as suffering from alcoholism. He spent several years in mental hospitals before the correct diagnosis was made.

Huntington's disease is caused by a genetic defect on a single defective gene (Cowan & Kandel, 2001; Nucifora et al., 2001). The defective gene produces a flawed protein that somehow damages the basal ganglia and cerebral cortex (Society for Neuroscience, 2006). The disease is transmitted genetically from either parent to children of either gender. People who have a parent with Huntington's disease stand a 50% chance of inheriting the gene. People who inherit the gene eventually contract the disease. Although there is no cure or effective treatment, scientists are closely examining the defective gene in the attempt to find ways of counteracting its influence. A glimmer of hope for a possible cure appeared in 2006, when scientists reported a breakthrough: They had discovered a cure for Huntington's disease in mice by means of engineering a corrective mutation into the disease gene (Graham et al., 2006). Whether this animal model eventually leads to an effective treatment or even a cure for humans with Huntington's remains to be seen.

Dementia Due to HIV Disease

The human immunodeficiency virus (HIV), which causes AIDS, can invade the central nervous system and cause a cognitive disorder—*dementia due to HIV disease.* The most typical signs of dementia due to HIV disease include forgetfulness and impaired concentration and problem-solving ability (APA, 2000). Dementia is rare in persons with HIV who have not yet developed full-blown AIDS. Common behavioral features of dementia associated with HIV disease are apathy and social withdrawal. As AIDS progresses, the dementia grows more severe, taking the form of delusions, disorientation, further impairments in memory and thinking processes, and perhaps even delir-

---

Huntington's disease An inherited degenerative disease that is characterized by jerking and twisting movements, paranoia, and mental deterioration.

TRUTH or FICTION

A famous folksinger and songwriter was misdiagnosed with alcoholism and spent several years in mental hospitals until the correct diagnosis was made.

☑ **TRUE.** The folksinger and songwriter was Woody Guthrie, whose Huntington's disease went misdiagnosed for years.

ium. In its later stages, the dementia may resemble the profound deficiencies found among people with advanced Alzheimer's disease.

Dementia Due to Creutzfeldt-Jakob Disease

Creutzfeldt-Jakob disease is a rare and fatal brain disease (Cowley, 2001a; Spencer et al., 2002). It is characterized by the formation of small cavities in the brain that resemble the holes in a sponge. Dementia is a common feature of the disease. The disease typically affects people in the 40- to 60-year-old age range, although it may develop in adults at any age (APA, 2000). There are no treatments for the disease, and death usually results within months of onset of symptoms. In about 5% to 15% of cases there is evidence of familial transmission, which suggests that a genetic component contributes to determining susceptibility to the disease. The human form of mad-cow disease, a fatal illness spread by eating infected beef, is a variant of Creutzfeldt-Jakob disease (Cowan & Kandel, 2001; McNeil, 2001).

Dementia Due to Head Trauma

Head trauma resulting from jarring, banging, or cutting brain tissues, usually because of accident or assault, can injure the brain, sometimes severely so (Teasdale & Engberg, 2003). Progressive dementia due to head trauma is more likely to result from multiple head traumas (as in the case of boxers who receive multiple blows to the head during their careers) than from a single blow or head trauma (APA, 2000; Guskiewicz et al., 2003; McCrea et al., 2003). Yet even a single head trauma can have psychological effects, and if severe enough, can lead to physical disability or death. Specific changes in personality following traumatic injury to the brain vary with the site and extent of the injury, among other factors. Damage to the frontal lobe, for example, is associated with a range of emotional changes involving alterations of mood and personality.

Neurosyphilis

General paresis (from the Greek *parienai*, meaning "to relax") is a form of dementia—or "relaxation" of the brain in its most negative connotation—that results from neurosyphilis, a form of later-stage syphilis in which the bacterium that causes the disease directly attacks the brain. General paresis is of historical significance to abnormal psychology. The 19th-century discovery of the connection between this form of dementia and a concrete physical illness, syphilis, strengthened the medical model and held out the promise that organic causes would eventually be found for other abnormal behavior patterns. Syphilis is a sexually transmitted disease caused by the bacterium *Treponema pallidum.*

General paresis is associated with physical symptoms such as tremors, slurred speech, impaired motor coordination, and, eventually, paralysis—all of which are suggestive of relaxed control over the body. Psychological signs include shifts in mood states, blunted emotional responsiveness, and irritability; delusions; changes in personal habits, such as suspension of personal grooming and hygiene; and progressive intellectual deterioration, including impairments of memory, judgment, and comprehension. Some people with general paresis grow euphoric and entertain delusions of grandiosity. Others become lethargic and depressed. Eventually, people with general paresis lapse into a state of apathy and confusion, characterized by the inability to care for themselves or to speak intelligibly. Death results either from renewed infection or the damage caused by the existing infection.

Late-stage syphilis once accounted for upwards of thirty percent of admissions to psychiatric hospitals. However, advances in detection and the development of

TRUTH or FICTION

A form of dementia is linked to mad-cow disease.

☑ **TRUE.** A form of dementia is caused by the human form of mad-cow disease.

general paresis A form of dementia resulting from neurosyphilis.

CONTROVERSIES IN ABNORMAL PSYCHOLOGY

The Danger Lurking Within: Would You Want to Know?

Until recently, children of patients with Huntington's disease had to wait until they developed symptoms themselves—usually in midlife—to know whether they had inherited the disease. Today, a genetic test is available that can detect carriers of the defective gene, those who will eventually develop the disease should they live long enough (Timman et al., 2004). Eventually, perhaps, genetic engineering may provide a means of modifying the defective gene or its effects. Because researchers have not yet developed ways to cure or control Huntington's disease, some potential carriers, such as the folksinger Arlo Gurthie, son of the famed folksinger Woody Guthrie, who died from the disease, preferred not knowing whether they had inherited the gene. Now in his 60s, Arlo seems to have escaped his father's fate.

If you were in Arlo's position, would you want to undergo genetic testing to see if you are a carrier? Would you want to know? Or would you prefer keeping yourself in the dark and living your life as best as you could?

What about Alzheimer's disease? If a reliable test were available to detect early signs of Alzheimer's or predict its development, would you take the test? Although such tests are not yet available, scientists in late 2006 reported finding a possible "fingerprint" of Alzheimer's disease in spinal fluid, comprising a pattern of particular proteins found in Alzheimer's patients ("Spinal Fluid," 2006). Yet scientists caution that more research is needed before a spinal-tap test (or other biomarker) would be available to reliably detect disease in its early stages or predict its development in people presently free of symptoms.

In thinking critically about these questions, you may wish to challenge some common assumptions, such as that knowledge is necessarily better than ignorance. Gaining knowledge is valued when it can be used to help stave off or limit the impact of disease. But what if knowledge carried no health benefits? Might ignorance be better than knowledge?

Deciding upon genetic testing for defective genes is a personal choice. But controversy arises over whether people who may be potential carriers of genetic diseases have an ethical or moral responsibility to determine their genetic risk before deciding whether to bear children. We pose the question to encourage you to examine the issue critically. Do you believe people at genetic risk have an obligation to determine their genetic risk before becoming parents? Going further, should people who discover they are carrying a potentially lethal or disabling gene be morally (or perhaps legally) obliged not to bear children? How might you look at this question differently if you were a fundamentalist Christian, an orthodox Jew, or a practicing Buddhist or Muslim?

Genetics plays an important role in many diseases discussed in this chapter, such as Parkinson's disease and Alzheimer's disease. Genes are also implicated in many physical conditions, such as Tay-Sachs disease, sickle-cell disease, and cystic fibrosis. As we gain more knowledge and the ability to determine whether people carry many different conditions, insurance companies might

Would you want to know? Folksinger Arlo Guthrie decided no. What do you think you would do if you had been in Arlo's place?

require expectant parents to undergo genetic testing. Knowledge about the genetic causes of devastating disease has deep ramifications for society.

Critical Thinking

- Should people be required to be tested for genetic defects?
- Should we be required to reveal our relative risk of developing a wide range of diseases as a condition for obtaining health insurance or for getting a job? What are the effects of requiring such disclosure? Of not requiring it?

antibiotics that cure the infection have sharply reduced the incidence of late-stage syphilis and the development of general paresis. The effectiveness of treatment depends on when antibiotics are introduced and the extent of brain damage. In cases where extensive tissue damage has occurred, antibiotics can stem the infection and prevent further damage, producing some improvement in intellectual performance; however, they cannot restore people to their original levels of functioning.

Before moving ahead, you may wish to review the *Concept Map for Psychology*, which reviews causal factors in cognitive disorders and approaches to treating these disorders.

Heading toward brain damage? Multiple blows to the head may lead to a progressive form of dementia.

SUMMING UP

Cognitive Disorders

What are cognitive disorders? Cognitive disorders are disturbances of thinking or memory that represent a marked decline in intellectual or memory functioning. They are caused by physical or medical conditions or drug use or withdrawal affecting the functioning of the brain.

What is delirium? Delirium is a state of mental confusion characterized by symptoms such as impaired attention, disorientation, disorganized thinking and rambling speech, reduced level of consciousness, and perceptual disturbances. Delirium is most commonly caused by alcohol withdrawal, as in the form of delirium tremens (DTs).

What is dementia? Dementia is a cognitive deterioration or impairment, as evidenced by memory deficits, impaired judgment, personality changes, and disorders of higher cognitive functions such as problem-solving ability and abstract thinking.

Is dementia a normal part of aging? No, dementia is not a normal consequence of aging but a sign of a degenerative brain disorder. There are various causes of dementias, including Alzheimer's disease and Pick's disease, and brain infections or disorders.

What are amnestic disorders? Amnestic disorders are memory deficits caused by organic factors. A common cause of amnestic syndrome is alcohol-induced persisting amnestic disorder, or Korsakoff's syndrome, which results from thiamine deficiency typically associated with a pattern of chronic alcohol abuse.

Psychological Disorders Related to Aging

What types of psychological problems affect people in later life? Generalized anxiety disorder and phobic disorders are the most commonly occurring anxiety disorders among older people. Depression to varying degrees is common among people in later life and may be associated with memory deficits that may lift as the depression clears. Dementia of the Alzheimer's type primarily affects people in later life. It involves irreversible and progressive memory impairment. Certain sleep disorders, such as insomnia and sleep apnea, are also common among older people.

What are Alzheimer's disease and vascular dementia? Alzheimer's disease (AD) is a progressive brain disease characterized by progressive loss of memory and cognitive ability, as well as deterioration in personality functioning and self-care skills. There is no cure or effective treatment for AD. Research into its causes has focused on genetic factors and imbalances in neurotransmitters, especially acetylcholine. Vascular dementia results from multiple strokes (blood clots that block the supply of blood to parts of the brain, damaging or destroying brain tissue).

Dementias Due to General Medical Conditions

What other general medical conditions can lead to dementia?
Various other medical conditions can lead to dementia, including Pick's disease, Parkinson's disease, Huntington's disease, Creutzfeldt-Jakob disease, HIV disease, head trauma, and neurosyphilis.

Scoring Key for Attitudes Toward Aging Scale

1. False. Most healthy couples continue to engage in satisfying sexual activities into their 70s and 80s.
2. False. This is too general a statement. Those who find their work satisfying are less desirous of retiring.
3. False. In late adulthood, we tend to become more concerned with internal matters—our physical functioning and our emotions.
4. False. Adaptability remains reasonably stable throughout adulthood.
5. False. Age itself is not linked to noticeable declines in life satisfaction. Of course, we may respond negatively to disease and losses, such as the death of a spouse.
6. False. Although we can predict some general trends for older adults, we can also do so for younger adults. Older adults, like their younger counterparts, are heterogeneous in personality and behavior patterns.
7. False. Older adults with stable intimate relationships are more satisfied.
8. False. We are susceptible to a wide variety of psychological disorders at all ages.
9. False. Only a minority are depressed.
10. False. Actually, church attendance declines, but not verbally expressed religious beliefs.
11. False. Although reaction time may increase and general learning ability may undergo a slight decline, older adults usually have little or no difficulty at familiar work tasks. In most jobs, experience and motivation are more important than age.
12. False. Learning may just take a bit longer.
13. False. Older adults do not direct a higher proportion of thoughts toward the past than do younger people. Regardless of our age, we may spend more time daydreaming at any age if we have more time on our hands.
14. False. Fewer than 10% of older adults require some form of institutional care.

KEY TERMS

cognitive disorders *(p. 515)*
agnosia *(p. 517)*
dementia *(p. 517)*
senile dementias *(p. 518)*
presenile dementias *(p. 518)*
delirium *(p. 518)*
amnestic disorders *(p. 520)*
retrograde amnesia *(p. 521)*

anterograde amnesia *(p. 521)*
hypoxia *(p. 522)*
infarction *(p. 522)*
Korsakoff's syndrome *(p. 522)*
Wernicke's disease *(p. 522)*
ataxia *(p. 522)*
Alzheimer's disease (AD) *(p. 525)*
cerebrovascular accident (CVA) *(p. 531)*

vascular dementia *(p. 531)*
aphasia *(p. 531)*
Pick's disease *(p. 532)*
Parkinson's disease *(p. 532)*
Huntington's disease *(p. 534)*
general paresis *(p. 535)*

MEDIA TOOLS

A variety of digital and online learning tools are available to enrich your learning experience and help you succeed in the course. These resources include:

- **MYPSYCHLAB,** an online learning system for your course in abnormal psychology that allows you to test your mastery of concepts in the book by using chapter-by-chapter diagnostic tests. Results from the diagnostic tests help you build a customized study plan. To access **MyPsychLab,** visit www. prenhall.com/mypsychlab and follow the instructions on the site.
- **"SPEAKING OUT" PATIENT INTERVIEWS,** a set of video case examples of actual patients you can access on the companion

CD-ROM included with the text. Icons in the margins of the chapter highlight the video case examples included on the CD-ROM.

- **COMPANION WEB SITE,** an online study center that offers computer-scored quizzes you can use to test your knowledge, along with other study tools and links to related sites to enhance your learning of abnormal psychology. To access the companion Web site, visit www.prenhall.com/nevid and use the various tabs and links on the site to access these learning resources.

Cognitive Disorders

which are characterized by

Disturbances of thinking or memory that reflect a significant change from the prior level of functioning

and includes these major types

- Delirium
- Dementia
- Amnestic Disorders

and may be caused by such factors as

- Medical conditions such as head trauma, metabolic disorders, neurosyphillis, multiple strokes, fluid or electrolyte imbalances, epilepsy, vitamin B deficiencies, and brain lesions
- Brain diseases such as Parkinson's disease, Alzheimer's disease, Pick's disease, Huntington's disease, HIV disease, Creutzfeldt-Jakob disease, and brain infections such as meningitis and encephalitis
- Blows to the head, complications from surgery, blockage of blood supply to the brain, and heavy use of certain psychoactive substances

and may be treated by

- Drugs for Alzheimer's disease to bolster cognitive functioning and slow the rate of cognitive decline
- Medical treatment of any underlying condition, such as head trauma

MODEL SPOTLIGHT

Alzheimer's Disease (AD)

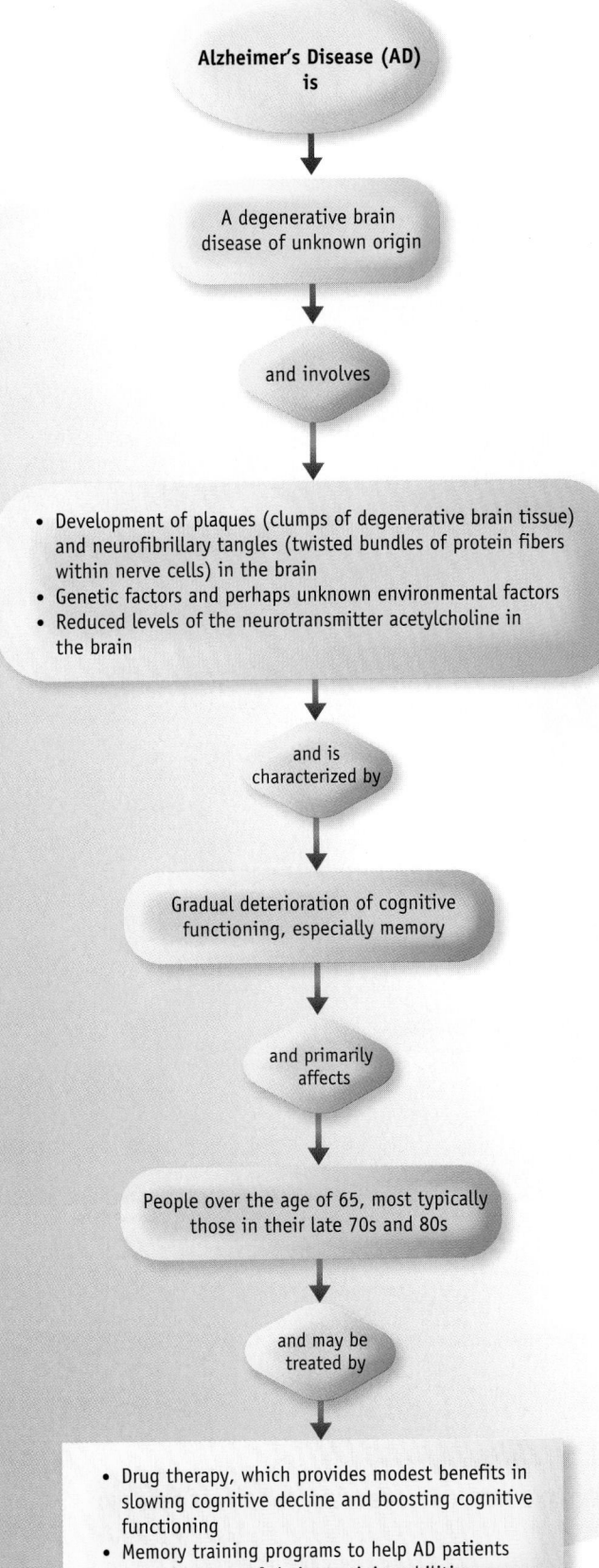

Alzheimer's Disease (AD) is

↓

A degenerative brain disease of unknown origin

↓

and involves

↓

- Development of plaques (clumps of degenerative brain tissue) and neurofibrillary tangles (twisted bundles of protein fibers within nerve cells) in the brain
- Genetic factors and perhaps unknown environmental factors
- Reduced levels of the neurotransmitter acetylcholine in the brain

↓

and is characterized by

↓

Gradual deterioration of cognitive functioning, especially memory

↓

and primarily affects

↓

People over the age of 65, most typically those in their late 70s and 80s

↓

and may be treated by

↓

- Drug therapy, which provides modest benefits in slowing cognitive decline and boosting cognitive functioning
- Memory training programs to help AD patients make best use of their remaining abilities

16

CHAPTER

Abnormal Psychology and the Law

CHAPTER OUTLINE

PSYCHIATRIC COMMITMENT AND PATIENTS' RIGHTS 544–554

Predicting Dangerousness
Patients' Rights

THE INSANITY DEFENSE 555–560

Legal Bases of the Insanity Defense
Determining the Length of Criminal
  Commitment

Perspectives on the Insanity Defense
Competency to Stand Trial

SUMMING UP 560–561

"I"
"Please Look Into Your Heart"

Dear Jodie,

There is a definite possibility that I will be killed in my attempt to get Reagan. It is for this very reason that I am writing you this letter now.

As you well know by now I love you very much. Over the past seven months I've left you dozens of poems, letters and love messages in the faint hope that you could develop an interest in me. . . .

Jodie, I would abandon this idea of getting Reagan in a second if I could only win your heart and live out the rest of my life with you, whether it be in total obscurity or whatever.

I will admit to you that the reason I'm going ahead with this attempt now is because I just cannot wait any longer to impress you. I've got to do something now to make you understand, in no uncertain terms, that I am doing all of this for your sake! By sacrificing my freedom and possibly my life, I hope to change your mind about me. This letter is being written only an hour before I leave for the Hilton Hotel. Jodie, I'm asking you to please look into your heart and at least give me the chance, with this historical deed, to gain your respect and love.

—*John Hinckley's letter to actress Jodie Foster, written on March 31, 1980, shortly before he attempted to assassinate President Ronald Reagan*

Source: Linder, 2004, "The John Hinckley Trial"

GUNSHOTS RANG OUT AS PRESIDENT RONALD REAGAN STEPPED OUT OF THE WASHINGTON Hilton that cold day in March 1981. Secret Service agents formed a human shield around the president; one shoved him into a waiting limousine, which sped to a hospital. Agents seized the gunman, John Hinckley, a 25-year-old drifter. The president had been wounded; James Brady, his press secretary, was hit by a stray bullet that shattered his spine and left him partially paralyzed; and a Secret Service agent was shot.

The letter Hinckley left in his hotel room, parts of which are cited above, revealed his hope that his assassination of the president would impress a young actress, Jodie Foster. Hinckley had never met Foster but had a crush on her.

At Hinckley's trial, there was never any question whether Hinckley had fired the wounding bullets, but the prosecutor was burdened to demonstrate beyond a reasonable doubt that Hinckley had the capacity to control his behavior and appreciate its wrongfulness. The defense presented testimony that portrayed Hinckley as an incompetent schizophrenic who suffered under the delusion that he would achieve a "magic union" with Foster as a result of killing the president. The prosecutor claimed that Hinckley made a conscious and willful choice to kill the president and that, whatever mental disorder Hinckley might have, it did not prevent him from controlling his behavior. The jury sided with the defense and found Hinckley not guilty by reason of insanity (Janofsky, 2003). He was remanded to a federal psychiatric facility, St. Elizabeth's Hospital in Washington, D.C., where he has remained ever since.

Fast-forward 22 years. In 2003, Hinckley, then 48, petitioned the courts to allow him to leave the grounds of the hospital for day trips in the company of his parents (Sokolove, 2003). In December, 2005, a federal judge ruled that Hinckley was permitted home visits to be supervised by his parents for three or four nights at a time. By the time this book reaches your hands, Hinckley may well have been granted a full release.

Hinckley's doctors have argued that his psychiatric condition (a combination of psychosis and depression) was "in full remission." The idea that Hinckley might one

Not guilty by reason of insanity. In 1981, John Hinckley Jr. attempted to assassinate President Ronald Reagan outside a Washington hotel. Hinckley was later found not guilty by reason of insanity. Here we see President Reagan at the moment he was struck by a bullet from the gun fired by Hinckley.

civil commitment The legal process of placing a person in a mental institution, even against his or her will.

criminal commitment The legal process of confining a person found not guilty by reason of insanity in a mental institution.

day be granted full release is an unsettling thought to many people. Should someone who has committed such grievous acts have been found "not guilty" at all, even by "reason of insanity"? Shouldn't he have been imprisoned rather than treated in a mental hospital? How should society treat mentally disturbed individuals who commit crimes? Then again, had Hinckley been convicted of a crime, might he have already been set free or at least paroled?

The Hinckley case provides an example of the interface of society and abnormal behavior. In this chapter we will discuss the insanity defense, its history in U.S. law, and the legal and moral arguments that underlie its use. We will also examine the legal rights of mental patients and the legal responsibility that falls on mental health-care providers to warn third parties of threats made by patients. We will address questions that touch on the general issue of how to balance the rights of the individual with the rights of society. Do people who are obviously mentally disturbed have the right to refuse treatment? Do psychiatric institutions have the right to administer antipsychotic and other drugs to patients against their will? Should mental patients with a history of disruptive or violent behavior be hospitalized indefinitely or permitted to live in supervised residences in the community once their conditions are stabilized? When severely disturbed people break the law, should society respond to them with the criminal justice system or with the mental health system?

We begin with psychiatric commitment, the process by which individuals are involuntarily confined in mental hospitals because they are deemed to be mentally ill and a danger to either themselves or others. As with other issues we consider in this chapter, the practice of psychiatric commitment brings into focus the interface between the rights of individuals and the rights of society.

PSYCHIATRIC COMMITMENT AND PATIENTS' RIGHTS

Legal placement of people in psychiatric institutions against their will is called **civil commitment** (also called *psychiatric commitment*). Through civil commitment, individuals who are judged to be mentally ill and a threat to themselves or others can be involuntarily confined to psychiatric institutions to provide them with treatment and help ensure their own safety and that of others (Failer, 2002; Glenn, 2003).

Civil commitment should be distinguished from *voluntary hospitalization,* in which an individual voluntarily seeks treatment in a psychiatric institution and can, with adequate notice, leave the institution when she or he so desires. Even in such cases, however, when the hospital staff believes that a voluntary patient presents a threat to her or his own welfare or to others, they may petition the court to change the patient's legal status from voluntary to involuntary.

We also need to distinguish civil commitment from **criminal commitment,** in which an individual who is acquitted of a crime by reason of insanity is placed in a psychiatric institution for treatment. In criminal commitment, a defendant's unlawful act is judged by a court of law to result from a mental disorder or defect, and the defendant is committed to a psychiatric hospital where treatment can be provided rather than incarcerated in a prison.

Civil commitment in a psychiatric hospital usually requires that a relative or professional file a petition with the court, which empowers psychiatric examiners to evaluate the person. Finally, a judge hears psychiatric testimony and decides whether or not to commit the individual. In the event of commitment, the law usually requires periodic legal review and recertification of the patient's involuntary status. The legal process is intended to ensure that people are not indefinitely "warehoused" in psychiatric hospitals. Hospital staff must demonstrate the need for continued inpatient treatment.

Legal safeguards protect people's civil rights in commitment proceedings. Defendants have the right to due process and to be assisted by an attorney, for example. But when individuals are deemed to present a clear and imminent threat to themselves or others, the court may order immediate hospitalization until a formal commitment hearing can be held. Such emergency powers are usually limited to a specific period, usually 72 hours (Failer, 2002). If a formal commitment petition is not filed with the court during this time, the individual has a right to be discharged.

Standards for psychiatric commitment have been tightened over the past generation, and the rights of individuals who are subject to commitment proceedings are more strictly protected. In the past, psychiatric abuses were more common. People were often committed without clear evidence that they posed a threat. Not until 1979, in fact, did the U.S. Supreme Court rule, in *Addington* v. *Texas,* that in order for individuals to be hospitalized involuntarily, they must be judged both to be "mentally ill" and to present a clear and present danger to themselves or others. Thus people cannot be committed because of their odd behavior or eccentricity.

Few would argue that contemporary tightening of civil commitment laws protects the rights of the individual. Even so, some critics of the psychiatric system have called for the abolition of psychiatric commitment on the grounds that commitment deprives the individual of liberty in the name of therapy, and that such a loss of liberty cannot be justified in a free society. Perhaps the most vocal and persistent critic of the civil commitment statutes is psychiatrist Thomas Szasz (Szasz, 1970, 2003a, 2003b). Szasz argued that the label of *mental illness* is a societal invention that transforms social deviance into medical illness. In Szasz's view, people should not be deprived of their liberty because their behavior is perceived to be socially deviant or disruptive. Szasz likens involuntary hospitalization to institutional slavery (Szasz, 2003b). According to Szasz, people who violate the law should be prosecuted for criminal behavior, not confined to a psychiatric hospital. Although psychiatric commitment may prevent some individuals from acting violently, it does violence to many people who are innocent of any crime by depriving them of the fundamental right of liberty:

> The mental patient, we say, *may be* dangerous: he may harm himself or someone else. But we, society, *are* dangerous: we rob him of his good name and of his liberty, and subject him to tortures called "treatments."
>
> *(Szasz, 1970, p. 279)*

> It is a fundamental principle of English and American law that only persons charged with and convicted of certain crimes are subject to imprisonment. Persons who respect other people's rights to life, liberty, and property have an inalienable right to their own life, liberty, and property.
>
> *(Szasz, 2003a, p. 228).*

Szasz's strident opposition to institutional psychiatry and his condemnation of psychiatric commitment focused attention on abuses in the mental health system. Many patients who have experienced psychiatric commitment rail against the practice. A recent survey in Germany showed that most patients believed that their court-mandated commitment was not justified and could have been avoided (Langle et al., 2003).

Szasz was effective in persuading many professionals to question the legal, ethical, and moral bases of coercive psychiatric treatment in the forms of involuntary hospitalization and forced medication. Many caring and concerned professionals draw the line at abolishing psychiatric commitment, however. They argue that people may not be acting in their considered best interests when they threaten suicide or harm to others, or when their behavior becomes so disorganized that they cannot meet their basic needs (McMillan, 2003; Sayers, 2003). Most countries, including the United States and Canada, have laws that permit commitment of dangerous, mentally ill people (Appelbaum, 2003). Yet the issue of psychiatric commitment continues to rouse debate. In the feature *Controversies in Abnormal Psychology,* we frame the issue by looking more closely at two celebrated cases, that of the so-called "Wild Man of West 96th Street" and that of a psychiatrically disturbed homeless woman, Joyce Brown.

Predicting Dangerousness

Mental health professionals are often called on to judge whether patients are a danger to themselves or others as part of the legal proceedings to determine whether people should be involuntarily hospitalized or maintained involuntarily in the hospital.

Predicting dangerousness. Should mental health professionals or school administrators have recognized signs of impending violence by Seung-Hui Cho, the man who went on a killing rampage at Virginia Tech in 2007? It is always easier after the fact to piece together fragments of a person's prior behaviors as signs of impending violent behavior. Predicting a violent act before it occurs is a much more difficult task, however, even for professionals.

But how accurate are the judgments of professionals when predicting dangerousness? Do professionals have special skills or clinical wisdom that renders their predictions accurate, or are their predictions no more accurate than those of laypeople?

Unfortunately, psychologists and other mental health professionals who rely on their clinical judgments are not very accurate when it comes to predicting dangerousness of the people they treat. Mental health professionals tend to overpredict dangerousness—that is, to label many individuals as dangerous when they are not. Clinicians tend to err on the side of caution in predicting the potential for dangerous behavior, perhaps because they believe that failure to predict violence may have more serious consequences than overprediction. Overprediction of dangerousness does deprive many people of liberty. According to Szasz and other critics of the practice of psychiatric commitment, the commitment of the many to prevent the violence of the few is a form of preventive detention that violates basic constitutional principles.

The leading professional organizations, the American Psychological Association (1978) and the American Psychiatric Association (1998), have both gone on record as stating that neither psychologists nor psychiatrists, respectively, can reliably predict violent behavior. As a leading authority in the field, John Monahan of the University of Virginia, said, "When it comes to predicting violence, our crystal balls are terribly cloudy" (Rosenthal, 1993, p. A1).

Clinician predictions are generally also less accurate than predictions based on evidence of past violent behavior (Gardner et al., 1996; Odeh, Zeiss, & Huss, 2006). Basically, clinicians do not possess any special knowledge or ability for predicting violence beyond that of the average person. In fact, a layperson supplied with information concerning an individual's past violent behavior may predict the individual's potential for future violence more accurately than the clinician, who bases a prediction solely on a clinical interview (Mossman, 1994). Unfortunately, although past violent behavior is the best predictor of future violence, hospital staff may not be permitted access to

CONTROVERSIES IN ABNORMAL PSYCHOLOGY

What Should We Do About the "Wild Man of West 96th Street"?

We have lost track of the whereabouts of Larry Hogue, but his case continues to resonate with how society deals with the problems of the psychiatric homeless population. We first learned about Hogue—the "wild man of West 96th Street"—in the early 1990s. Hogue was a homeless Vietnam War veteran who inhabited the alleyways and doorways of Manhattan's affluent Upper West Side. He went barefoot in winter, ate from garbage cans, and muttered to himself. A reporter characterized Hogue as conducting a personal war of terror on the neighborhood (Kolker, 2002). He reportedly stalked a teacher and threatened to cook and eat her fawn-colored Akita. He also became violent when he smoked crack and was once arrested for pushing a schoolgirl in front of a school bus (Shapiro, 1992). (Miraculously, she escaped injury.)

Hogue was shuttled in and out of state psychiatric hospitals and prisons more than 40 times. For Hogue, the criminal justice, social services, and mental health systems were nothing but revolving doors. Typically, Hogue would improve during a brief hospital stay and be released, only to return to using crack instead of his psychiatric medication. His behavior would then deteriorate. For many people, Larry Hogue became a national symbol of the many cracks in the system.

Then there was the celebrated case of Joyce Brown, a middle-aged woman who also lived on the streets of New York. At one time she slept above a hot air vent on the sidewalk on the Upper East Side of Manhattan, in the midst of some of the most expensive real estate in the world. Sometimes she was observed defecating in her clothes or on the sidewalk. She hurled insults at strangers and refused to go to a shelter, preferring to live in the streets, despite the obvious dangers of potential attack and the risks of exposure to the elements.

In New York, a program was begun to provide outreach services to homeless people in need of psychological treatment. Teams of specialists, each consisting of a nurse, a social worker, and a psychiatrist, were charged with identifying and monitoring behaviorally disordered homeless people, helping them obtain services, bringing them soup and sandwiches, and taking them to the hospital if they were deemed to represent an immediate threat to themselves or others under the authority provided by state laws governing psychiatric commitment, even if it was against the individual's will.

Brown had been picked up and brought against her will to a city hospital for evaluation, where she was diagnosed with paranoid schizophrenia and judged to be in need of treatment. She resisted treatment and claimed that she had a right to live her life as she saw fit, even if it offended other people. As long as she committed no crime, what right did society have to deprive her of her liberty? Yes, she admitted, she had defecated in the streets. But there were no public restrooms available, and establishments such as restaurants had refused her access.

Brown sued for her release, and while her case meandered through the courts, she remained in the hospital, although her doctors were prevented from medicating her against her will. Because she refused medication, the doctors released her, claiming there was little they could do for her.

It may seem obvious that people such as Hogue and Brown need care and that it is the responsibility of a humane society to provide that care, whether through an outpatient clinic or a locked psychiatric facility. But critics of the mental health system, such as Thomas Szasz, argue that by the very nature of a free society, people should be free to make their own decisions, even when those decisions are not in the best interests of their health or welfare. Others argue that society has a duty to protect such people from themselves, as well as to protect citizens from the dangers they pose to others. Now extend the argument: If society has an obligation to protect individuals such as Joyce Brown from themselves, or to protect citizenry from individuals such as Hogue—does it not have obligations to protect individuals whose behavior is harmful in other ways, such as those who smoke cigarettes, drink alcohol to excess, or become obese? Where would you draw that line?

What should society do about the "Larry Hogue's" and "Joyce Brown's" of our cities and towns? What do you think should be done? The cases of Larry Hogue and Joyce Brown touch on the more general issue of how to balance the rights of the individual with the rights of society. Cases like these prompt us to consider a number of questions about the rights of individuals in society to act in ways that offend others—questions that challenge us to think critically about these issues.

Critical Thinking

- Do people in a free society have the right to live on the streets under unsanitary conditions?
- Do people who are obviously mentally disturbed have the right to refuse treatment?
- Should mental patients with a history of disruptive or violent behavior be hospitalized indefinitely or permitted to live in supervised residences in the community once their conditions are stabilized?
- Do people have a right to be mentally ill and be left alone, so long as they do not break any laws? Or do you agree with psychiatrist E. Fuller Torrey and attorney Mary Zdanowicz (1999) that "... for individuals whose brain is impaired by severe mental illness, defending their right to remain mentally ill is mindless"?
- When severely disturbed people do break the law, should society respond to them with the criminal justice system or with the mental health system?

"The wild man of West 96th Street." Larry Hogue, the so-called "Wild Man of West 96th Street" in New York City, has become a symbol of the cracks in the mental health, criminal justice, and social services systems.

TRUTH or FICTION

Psychologists and other mental health professionals can rely on their clinical judgment to accurately predict dangerous of their patients.

☑ **FALSE.** Psychologists and other mental health professionals who rely on their clinical judgments are not very accurate when it comes to predicting the dangerousness of the people they treat. The best predictor of future violence is a history of past violence.

criminal records or may lack the time or resources to track down these records. The prediction problem has been cited by some as grounds for abandoning dangerousness as a criterion for civil commitment.

Why is predicting dangerousness so difficult? Investigators have identified a number of factors that lead to inaccurate predictions, including the following.

The Post Hoc Problem Recognizing violent tendencies after a violent incident occurs (post hoc) is easier than predicting it beforehand. It is often said that hindsight is 20/20. Like Monday morning quarterbacking, it is easier to piece together fragments of people's prior behaviors as evidence of violent tendencies *after* they have committed acts of violence. Predicting a violent act before the fact is a more difficult task, however.

The Problem in Leaping from the General to the Specific Generalized perceptions of violent tendencies may not predict specific acts of violence. Most people who have "general tendencies" toward violence never act on them. Nor is a diagnosis associated with aggressive or dangerous behavior, such as antisocial personality disorder, a sufficient basis for predicting specific violent acts in individuals.

Problems in Defining Dangerousness One difficulty in predicting dangerousness is the lack of agreement over what types of behavior are violent or dangerous. Most people would agree that crimes such as murder, rape, and assault are acts of violence. There is less agreement, even among authorities, for labeling other acts—for example, driving recklessly, harshly criticizing one's spouse or children, destroying property, selling drugs, shoving into people at a tavern, or stealing cars—as violent or dangerous. Consider, also, the behavior of business owners and corporate executives who produce and market cigarettes despite widespread knowledge of the death and disease these substances cause. Clearly, the determination of which behaviors are regarded as dangerous involves moral and political judgments within a given social context.

Base-Rate Problems The prediction of dangerousness is complicated by the fact that violent acts such as murder, assault, or suicide are infrequent within the general population, even if newspaper headlines sensationalize them regularly. Other rare events—such as earthquakes—are also difficult to predict with any degree of certainty concerning when or where they will strike.

The relative difficulty of making predictions about infrequent or rare events is known as the *base-rate problem.* Consider as an example the problem of suicide prediction. If the suicide rate in a given year has a low base rate of about 1% of a clinical population, the likelihood of accurately predicting that any given person in this population will commit suicide is very small. You would be correct 99% of the time if you predicted that any given individual in this population would *not* commit suicide in a given year. But if you predicted the nonoccurrence of suicide in every case, you would fail to predict the relatively few cases in which suicide does occur, even though virtually all your predictions would likely be correct. Yet predicting the one likely case of suicide among those 100 people is likely to be tricky. When clinicians make predictions, they weigh the relative risks of incorrectly failing to predict the occurrence of a behavior (a *false negative*) against the consequences of incorrectly predicting it (a *false positive*). Clinicians often err on the side of caution by overpredicting dangerousness. From the clinician's perspective, erring on the side of caution might seem like a no-lose situation. Yet many people committed to an institution under such circumstances are denied their liberty when they would not actually have acted violently against themselves or others.

The Unlikelihood of Disclosure of Direct Threats of Violence How likely is it that truly dangerous people will disclose their intentions to a health professional who is evaluating them or to their own therapist? The client in therapy is not likely to inform a therapist

What are the rights of mental patients? Popular books and films, such as *One Flew Over the Cuckoo's Nest* starring Jack Nicholson, have highlighted many of the abuses of mental hospitals. In recent years, a tightening of standards of care and the adoption of legal safeguards have led to better protection of the rights of patients in mental hospitals.

of a clear threat, such as "I'm going to kill _____ next Wednesday morning." Threats are more likely to be vague and nonspecific, as in "I'm so sick of _____; I could kill her," or "I swear he's driving me to murder." In such cases, therapists must infer dangerousness from hostile gestures and veiled threats. Vague, indirect threats of violence are less-reliable indicators of dangerousness than specific, direct threats.

The Difficulty of Predicting Behavior in the Community from Behavior in the Hospital Mental health professionals fall well short of the mark when making long-term predictions of dangerousness (Buchanan, 1999). They are often wrong when predicting whether patients will become dangerous following release from the hospital. One reason is that they often base their predictions on patients' behavior in the hospital. But violent or dangerous behavior may be situation specific. A model patient who is able to adapt to a structured environment like that of a psychiatric hospital may be unable to cope with the pressures of independent community life. We can expect clinicians to be more accurate when they base their predictions on the patient's previous behavior in the community than in the controlled setting of a mental hospital.

Overall, clinician predictions of dangerousness are significantly better than predictions based on chance alone, but they are still often inaccurate (Kaplan, 2000). Although their crystal balls may be cloudy, mental health professionals who work in institutional settings continue to be called on to make predictions—deciding whom to commit and whom to discharge based largely on how they appraise the potential for violence (McNiel et al., 2003). Rather than expecting clinicians to rely on clinical judgment, investigators are developing better decision-based tools, such as structured screening methods, to guide assessment of violence risk (e.g., McNiel et al., 2002, 2003; Swets, Dawes, & Monahan, 2000).

These efforts are helping to improve the ability to predict the likelihood of violent behavior, at least with respect to short-term predictions (e.g., McNiel et al., 2003). Clinicians may be more successful in predicting violence by basing predictions on a composite of factors, including evidence of past violent behavior, than on any single factor. A promising new method is the decision-tree model (Lehmann, 2002). In this branching technique, clinicians ask specific questions based on the patient's previous responses to determine the likelihood of future violence (Monahan et al., 2001).

All told, however, professionals lack valid instruments for assessing the risk of dangerousness (Bauer et al., 2003). Not surprisingly, the accuracy of clinician predictions of violence is generally greater when clinicians agree with one another than when they disagree (McNiel, Lam, & Binder, 2000). Accuracy is also improved when clinicians make short-term predictions of dangerousness, such as predictions of imminent violence (Binder, 1999).

Violence and Mental Disorders The importance of developing tools to predict dangerousness is underscored by evidence of an increased risk of violence among people with severe mental disorders (Fazel & Grann, 2006). However, interpretation of these links needs be tempered by the recognition that people with mental disorders account for a relatively small proportion of violent crimes in society (Applebaum, 2006). Public perceptions of the mentally ill as dangerous is exaggerated by the disproportionate attention given to a few highly publicized cases in the media (Applebaum, 2006).

Research evidence shows that mental illness is at best a weak predictor of violent behavior (Corrigan & Watson, 2005). Only a small minority of people with mental disorders commit violent crimes. Hence, we need to identify factors to help us better appraise the risk of violence. We've learned that particular clusters of symptoms are associated with heightened risk of serious violence, especially active psychotic symptoms such as delusions of persecution (Swanson et al., 2006). Another important factor is substance abuse, as evidence shows a greater potential for violence in patients with serious psychiatric disorders who use alcohol, crack, or other drugs. The risk potential is also greater among patients living in economically distressed neighborhoods (Applebaum, 2006).

The issue of substance abuse was put into perspective in a recent large-scale study of 951 mental patients, which showed that patients who did not abuse drugs were

TABLE 16.1

Mental Health and the Law

Case	Year	Legal Issue
Durham v. *United States*	1954	Insanity defense
Wyatt v. *Stickney*	1972	Minimum standard of care
O'Connor v. *Donaldson*	1975	Patients' rights
Jackson v. *Indiana*	1972	Competency to stand trial
Tarasoff v. *the Regents of the University of California*	1976	Duty to warn
Rogers v. *Okin*	1979	Right to refuse treatment
Youngberg v. *Romeo*	1982	Right to confinement in less-restrictive conditions
Jones v. *United States*	1983	Length of criminal commitment
Medina v. *California*	1992	Burden of proof for determining mental competency
Sell v. *United States*	2003	Forced medication of mentally ill defendants

no more likely than controls to engage in violent behavior (Monahan et al., 2001). However, those patients who abused alcohol or drugs were twice as likely as control subjects with substance abuse problems to engage in violent acts. The likelihood of violence is also heightened among schizophrenia patients who experience command hallucinations—voices commanding them to harm themselves or others (McNiel, Lam, & Binder, 2000). Having noted these increased risks of mental patients acting violently, let us also point out that people with severe psychiatric disorders stand an increased risk of being victims of crimes themselves as compared to people in the general population (Teplin et al., 2005).

As we explore in *A Closer Look,* the problem of predicting dangerousness also arises when therapists need to evaluate the seriousness of threats made by their patients against others. Do therapists have a "duty to warn"—a legal obligation to warn the intended targets of these threats? The "duty to warn" is one of many legal issues arising from society's response to problems of abnormal behavior. In the following sections, we discuss such major legal issues as patients' rights, the insanity defense, and the right of mental patients to refuse treatment. Table 16.1 contains a listing of the landmark court cases that underpin our discussion of these issues.

Patients' Rights

We have considered society's right to hospitalize involuntarily people who are judged to be mentally ill and to pose a threat to themselves or others. But what happens after commitment? Do involuntarily committed patients have the right to receive or demand treatment? Or can society just warehouse them in psychiatric facilities indefinitely without treating them? Consider the opposite side of the coin as well: May people who are involuntarily committed refuse treatment? Such issues—which have been brought into public light by landmark court cases—fall under the umbrella of *patients' rights.* Generally speaking, the history of abuses in the mental health system, as highlighted in such popular books and movies as *One Flew Over the Cuckoo's Nest,* have led to a tightening of standards of care and adoption of legal guarantees to protect patients' rights. The legal status of some issues, such as the right to treatment, remains unsettled, however.

Right to Treatment We might assume that mental health institutions that accept people for treatment would provide them with treatment. Not until the 1972 landmark federal court case of *Wyatt* v. *Stickney,* however, did a federal court establish a minimum standard of care to be provided by hospitals. The case was a class action suit against Stickney, the commissioner of mental health for the State of Alabama, brought on behalf of Ricky Wyatt, a mentally retarded young man, and other patients at a state hospital and school in Tuscaloosa.

The federal district court in Alabama held both that the hospital had failed to provide treatment to Wyatt and others and that living conditions at the hospital were inadequate and dehumanizing. The court described the hospital dormitories as "barn-like structures" that afforded no privacy to the residents. The bathrooms had no partitions between stalls, the patients were outfitted with shoddy clothes, the wards were filthy and crowded, the kitchens were unsanitary, and the food was substandard. In addition, the staff was inadequate in numbers and poorly trained. The case of *Wyatt* v. *Stickney* established certain patient rights, including the right not to be required to perform work that is performed for the sake of maintaining the facility. The court held that mental hospitals must, at a minimum, provide the following:

1. A humane psychological and physical environment,
2. Qualified staff in numbers sufficient to administer adequate treatment, and
3. Individualized treatment plans (*Wyatt* v. *Stickney,* 1972).

The court established that the state was obliged to provide adequate treatment for people who were involuntarily confined to psychiatric hospitals. The court further ruled that to commit people to hospitals for treatment involuntarily, and then not to provide treatment, violated their rights to due process under the law.

A listing of some of the rights granted institutionalized patients under the court's ruling is shown in Table 16.2. Although the ruling of the court was limited to Alabama,

T R U T H or F I C T I O N

Patients in mental hospitals may be required to perform general housekeeping duties in a mental facility.

☑ **FALSE.** The Alabama case of *Wyatt* v. *Stickney* established certain patient rights, including the right not to be required to perform work that is performed for the sake of maintaining the psychiatric hospital.

TABLE 16.2

Partial Listing of the Patient's Bill of Rights Under *Wyatt* v. *Stickney*

1. Patients have rights to privacy and to be treated with dignity.
2. Patients shall be treated under the least restrictive conditions that can be provided to meet the purposes that commitment was intended to serve.
3. Patients shall have rights to visitation and telephone privileges unless special restrictions apply.
4. Patients have the right to refuse excessive or unnecessary medication. In addition, medication may not be used as a form of punishment.
5. Patients shall not be kept in restraints or isolation except in emergency conditions in which their behavior is likely to pose a threat to themselves or others and less-restrictive restraints are not feasible.
6. Patients shall not be subject to experimental research unless their rights to informed consent are protected.
7. Patients have the right to refuse potentially hazardous or unusual treatments, such as lobotomy, electroconvulsive shock, or aversive behavioral treatments.
8. Unless it is dangerous or inappropriate to the treatment program, patients shall have the right to wear their own clothing and keep possessions.
9. Patients have rights to regular exercise and to opportunities to spend time outdoors.
10. Patients have rights to suitable opportunities to interact with the opposite gender.
11. Patients have rights to humane and decent living conditions.
12. No more than six patients shall be housed in a room, and screen or curtains must be provided to afford a sense of privacy.
13. No more than eight patients shall share one toilet facility, with separate stalls provided for privacy.
14. Patients have a right to nutritionally balanced diets.
15. Patients shall not be required to perform work that is performed for the sake of maintenance of the facility.

A CLOSER LOOK

The Duty to Warn

One of the most difficult dilemmas a therapist faces is whether to disclose confidential information that may protect third parties from harm. Part of the difficulty lies in determining whether the client has made a bona fide threat. The other part is that information a client discloses in psychotherapy is generally protected as privileged communication, which carries a right to confidentiality. But this right is not absolute. State courts have determined that a therapist is obligated to breach confidentiality under certain conditions, such as when there is clear and compelling evidence that an individual poses a serious threat to others.

A 1976 court ruling in California in the case of *Tarasoff* v. *the Regents of the University of California* established the legal basis for the therapist's **duty to warn** (Jones, 2003). In 1969, a graduate student at the University of California at Berkeley, Prosenjit Poddar, a native of India, became depressed when his romantic overtures toward a young woman, Tatiana Tarasoff, were rebuffed. Poddar entered psychotherapy with a psychologist at a student health facility and informed the psychologist that he intended to kill Tatiana when she returned from her summer vacation. The psychologist, concerned about Poddar's potential for violence, first consulted with his colleagues and then notified the campus police that Poddar was dangerous, recommending that he be taken to a facility for psychiatric treatment.

The campus police interviewed Poddar. They believed he was rational and released him after he promised to keep away from Tatiana. Poddar then terminated treatment with the psychologist and shortly afterward killed Tatiana. Poddar was found guilty of the lesser sentence of voluntary manslaughter rather than murder, based on testimony of three psychiatrists that he suffered from diminished mental capacity and paranoid schizophrenia. Under California law, his diminished capacity prevented the finding of malice that was necessary for a murder conviction. Following a prison term, Poddar returned to India, where he reportedly made a new life for himself (Schwitzgebel & Schwitzgebel, 1980).

Tatiana's parents, however, sued the university. They claimed that the university health center had failed in its responsibility to warn Tatiana of the threat made against her by Poddar. The California Supreme Court agreed with the parents. They ruled that a therapist who has reason to believe that a client poses a serious threat to another person is obligated to warn the potential victim, not merely to notify police. This ruling imposed on therapists a duty-to-warn obligation when their clients show the potential for violence by making threats against others.

The ruling recognized that the rights of the intended victim outweigh the rights of confidentiality. Under *Tarasoff*, the therapist does not merely have a *right* to breach confidentiality and warn potential victims of danger, but is *obligated* by law to divulge such confidences to the victim.

TRUTH or FICTION

Therapists may not breach confidentiality even if a client makes a death threat against a specific person.

☑ **FALSE.** Therapists are actually obligated under some state laws to breach client confidentiality to warn people when threats of violence are made against them by their clients.

The duty-to-warn provision poses ethical and practical dilemmas for clinicians. Under *Tarasoff*, therapists may feel obliged to protect their personal interests and those of others by breaching confidentiality on the mere suspicion that their clients harbor violent intentions. Because clients' threats are seldom carried out, the *Tarasoff* ruling may deny many clients their rights to confidentiality in order to prevent such rare instances. Although some clinicians may "overreact" to *Tarasoff* and breach confidentiality without sufficient cause, it can be argued that the interests of the few potential victims outweigh the interests of the many who may suffer a loss of confidentiality.

Another problem with applying the *Tarasoff* standard is the lack of any special ability on the therapist's part to predict dangerousness. Nevertheless, the *Tarasoff* ruling obliges therapists to judge whether or not their clients' disclosures indicate an imminent intent to harm others (VandeCreek & Knapp, 2001). In the *Tarasoff* case, the threat was obvious. In most cases, however, threats are not so clear cut. We have no clear criteria for determining whether a therapist "should have known" that a client was dangerous before a violent act

occurs. In the absence of guidelines that specify the criteria therapists should use to fulfill their duty to warn, they must rely on their best clinical judgment.

The ethical issues become even murkier when therapists treat HIV-infected patients who put their sexual partners at risk by concealing their HIV status. Therapists must balance their duty-to-warn obligations with their ethical responsibility to protect patient confidentiality. Presently, we lack a clear set of professional standards that therapists can follow to resolve these dilemmas (Huprich, Fuller, & Schneider, 2003). Psychologists must follow the laws of the states in which they practice regarding the requirements for maintaining confidentiality of their clients' HIV status and become aware of any exceptions that might exist for breaching confidentiality (APA, 2003).

Although the intent of the *Tarasoff* decision was to protect potential victims, it may inadvertently increase the risks of violence when applied to clinical practice, as in the following situations (Weiner, 2003):

1. *Clients may be less willing to confide in their therapists,* making it more difficult for therapists to help them diffuse violent feelings.
2. *Potentially violent people may be less likely to enter therapy,* fearing that disclosures made to a therapist will be revealed.
3. *Therapists may be less likely to probe violent tendencies,* seeking to avoid legal complications. Therapists may avoid asking clients about potential violence or may avoid treating patients who are believed to have violent tendencies.

It remains unclear whether *Tarasoff* has done more good than harm (Herbert, 2002; Weiner, 2003). It is clear, however, that *Tarasoff* has raised concerns for clinicians who are trying to meet their legal responsibilities under *Tarasoff* and their clinical responsibilities to their clients.

A survey of psychiatric residents in San Francisco showed that nearly half had issued Tarasoff-type warnings (Binder & McNiel, 1996). In most cases, the intended victim was already aware of the threat. Most of the therapists told their patients about the warnings. Although issuing a warning produced no clear effects on the therapeutic relationship in most cases, negative effects were reported in some cases.

The *Tarasoff* case was brought in California, and the decision applied only in that state (Weiner, 2003). Other states have different statutes. Some states permit therapists to breach confidentiality to warn third parties of a patient's threats against them, but do not impose an obligation on therapists to do so (Herbert & Young, 2002). Therapists must be aware of local statutes and legal precedents. Therapists must also not lose sight of the primary therapeutic responsibility to their clients when legal issues arise. They must balance the obligation to meet their responsibilities under duty-to-warn provisions with the need to help their clients resolve the feelings of rage and anger that give rise to violent threats.

Tatiana Tarasoff and Prosenjit Poddar. Poddar, Tatiana's killer, was a rejected suitor who had made threats against her to his therapist at a university health center. Poddar was subsequently convicted of voluntary manslaughter in her death. A suit brought by Tatiana's parents against the university led to a landmark court ruling that established an obligation on therapists to warn third parties of threats made against them by their clients.

many other states have revised their mental hospital standards to ensure that involuntarily committed patients are not denied basic rights.

Other court cases have further clarified patients' rights.

O'Connor v. Donaldson

The 1975 case of Kenneth Donaldson is another landmark in patients' rights. Donaldson, a former patient at a state hospital in Florida, sued two hospital doctors on the grounds that he had been involuntarily confined without receiving treatment for 14 years, despite the fact that he posed no serious threat to himself or others. Donaldson had been originally committed on the basis of a petition filed by his father, who had perceived him as delusional. Despite the fact that Donaldson received no treatment during his confinement and was denied grounds privileges and occupational training, his repeated requests for discharge were denied. He was finally released when he threatened to sue the hospital. Once discharged, Donaldson did sue his doctors and was awarded damages of $38,500 from O'Connor, the superintendent of the hospital. The case was eventually argued before the U.S. Supreme Court.

Court testimony established that although the hospital staff had not perceived Donaldson to be dangerous, they had refused to release him. The hospital doctors argued that continued hospitalization had been necessary because they had believed Donaldson was unlikely to adapt successfully to community living. The doctors had prescribed antipsychotic medications, but Donaldson had refused to take them because of his Christian Science beliefs. As a result, he received only custodial care.

The Supreme Court held that "mental illness [alone] cannot justify a State's locking a person up against his will and keeping him indefinitely in simple custodial confinement. There is still no constitutional basis for confining such persons involuntarily if they are dangerous to no one and can live safely in freedom" (*O'Connor* v. *Donaldson*, 1975, p. 2493). The ruling addressed patients who are not considered dangerous. It is not yet clear whether the same constitutional rights would be applied to committed patients who are judged to be dangerous.

In its ruling in *O'Connor* v. *Donaldson,* the Supreme Court did not deal with the larger issue of the rights of patients to receive treatment. The ruling does not directly obligate state institutions to treat involuntarily committed, nondangerous people, because the institutions may elect to release them instead.

The Supreme Court did touch on the larger issue of society's rights to protect itself from individuals who are perceived as offensive. In delivering the opinion of the Court, Justice Potter Stewart wrote,

> May the State fence in the harmless mentally ill solely to save its citizens from exposure to those whose ways are different? One might as well ask if the State, to avoid public uneasiness, could incarcerate all who are physically unattractive or socially eccentric. Mere public intolerance or animosity cannot constitutionally justify the deprivation of a person's physical liberty.

(O'Connor *v.* Donaldson, *1975*)

Youngberg v. Romeo

In a 1982 case, *Youngberg* v. *Romeo,* the U.S. Supreme Court more directly addressed the issue of the patient's right to treatment. Even so, it seemed to retreat somewhat from the patients' rights standards established in *Wyatt* v. *Stickney*. Nicholas Romeo, a 33-year-old man with profound retardation who was unable to talk or care for himself, had been institutionalized in a state hospital and school in Pennsylvania. While in the state facility he had a history of injuring himself through his violent behavior and was often kept in restraints. The case was brought by the patient's mother, who alleged that the hospital was negligent in not preventing his injuries and in routinely using physical restraints for prolonged periods while not providing adequate treatment.

The Supreme Court ruled that involuntarily committed patients, such as Nicholas, have a right to be confined in less-restrictive conditions, such as being freed from physical restraints whenever it is reasonable to do so. The Supreme Court ruling also included

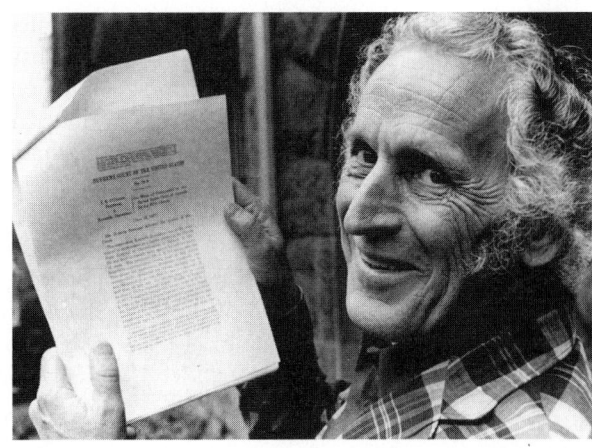

Kenneth Donaldson. Donaldson points to the U.S. Supreme Court decision that ruled that people who are considered mentally ill but not dangerous cannot be confined against their will if they can be maintained safely in the community.

duty to warn The therapist's obligation to warn third parties of threats made against them by clients.

a limited recognition of the committed patient's right to treatment. The Court held that institutionalized patients have a right to minimally adequate training to help them function free of physical restraints, but only to the extent that such training can be provided in reasonable safety. Reasonableness, the Court held, should be determined on the basis of the judgment of qualified professionals. The federal courts should not interfere with the internal operations of the facility, the Court held, because "there's no reason to think judges or juries are better qualified than appropriate professionals in making such decisions" (*Youngberg* v. *Romeo,* 1982, p. 2462). The courts should only second guess the judgments of qualified professionals when such judgments depart from professional standards of practice. But the Supreme Court did not address the broader issues of the rights of committed patients to receive training that might eventually enable them to function independently outside the hospital.

The related issue of whether people with severe psychological disorders who reside in the community have a constitutional right to receive mental health services (and whether states are obliged to provide these services) continues to be argued in the courts at both the state and federal levels.

Right to Refuse Treatment   Consider the following scenario. A person, John Citizen, is involuntarily committed to a mental hospital for treatment. The hospital staff determines that John suffers from a psychotic disorder, paranoid schizophrenia, and should be treated with antipsychotic medication. John, however, decides not to comply with treatment. He claims that the hospital has no right to treat him against his will. The hospital staff seeks a court order to mandate treatment, arguing it makes little sense to commit people involuntarily unless the hospital is empowered to treat them as the staff deems fit.

Does an involuntary patient, such as John, have the right to refuse treatment? If so, does this right conflict with states' rights to commit people to mental institutions to receive treatment? One might also wonder whether people who are judged in need of involuntary hospitalization are competent to make decisions about which treatments are in their best interests.

The rights of committed patients to refuse psychotropic medications was tested in a 1979 case, *Rogers* v. *Okin,* in which a Massachusetts federal district court imposed an injunction on a Boston state hospital prohibiting the forced medication of patients except in emergency situations. The court ruled that committed patients could not be forcibly medicated, except in the case of emergency—for example, when patients' behaviors posed a significant threat to themselves or others. The court recognized that a patient may be unwise to refuse medication, but it held that a patient with or without a mental disorder has the right to exercise bad judgment so long as the effects of the "error" do not impose "a danger of physical harm to himself, fellow patients, or hospital staff" (*Rogers* v. *Okin,* 1979).

Despite the concerns some mental health professionals raised that patients who refused medications would be "rotting with their rights on" (Gutheil, 1980), legal protections ensuring patients' rights to refuse psychiatric treatments do not appear to have had seriously damaging or disruptive effects on mental health services or on the people receiving these services (Kapp, 1994).

Although statutes and regulations vary from state to state, cases in which hospitalized patients refuse medications are often first brought before an independent review panel. If the panel rules against the patient, the case may then be brought before a judge, who makes the final decision about whether the patient is to be forcibly medicated. In practice, only about 10% of patients refuse medication. Furthermore, between 70% and 90% of refusals that reach the review process are eventually overridden. Hospitalized patients in one study who refused medication tended to be more assaultive, were more likely to require seclusion and restraint, and had longer hospitalizations than did compliant patients (Kasper et al., 1997). However, the refusal episodes tended to be brief, about 3 days on the average, and all initial refusers were eventually treated.

Our discussion of legal issues and abnormal behavior now turns to the controversy concerning the insanity defense.

Should he be released? In 2003, some 22 years after he shot President Ronald Reagan, John Hinckley, Jr. was permitted unsupervised daytime visits with his parents. If his psychiatric condition remains "in remission," should Hinckley be released?

THE INSANITY DEFENSE

John Hinckly, a man who was seen by millions of TV viewers attempting to assassinate President Reagan, was found "not guilty by reason of insanity." The verdict led to a public outcry, with many calling for the abolition of the insanity defense. Public opinion polls taken several days after the Hinckley verdict was returned showed the public had little confidence in the psychiatric testimony offered at the trial (Slater & Hans, 1984). One objection focused on the fact that once the defense presented evidence to support a plea of insanity, the federal prosecutor had the responsibility of proving *beyond a reasonable doubt* that the defendant was sane. It can be difficult enough to demonstrate that someone is sane or insane in the present, so imagine the problems that attend proving someone was sane at the time a criminal act was committed.

In the aftermath of the Hinckley verdict, the federal government and many states changed their statutes to shift the burden of proof to the defense to prove insanity (Ogloff, Roberts, & Roesch, 1993). Even the American Psychiatric Association went on record as stating that psychiatric expert witnesses should not be called on to render opinions about whether defendants can control their behavior. In the opinion of the psychiatric association, these are not medical judgments that psychiatrists are trained to provide.

Perceptions of the use of the **insanity defense** tend to stray far from the facts. Despite the common perception that the insanity defense is widely and often successfully used, the facts are that it is used rarely and is usually unsuccessful. In actuality, it is used in far fewer than 1% of felony cases and succeeds in but a fraction of these cases (Martin, 1998). Thus, despite public perceptions, the use of the insanity defense is rare, and the rate of acquittals is rarer still.

The public also overestimates the proportion of defendants acquitted on the basis of insanity who are set free rather than confined to mental health institutions and underestimates the length of hospitalization of those who are confined (Silver et al., 1994). People found not guilty on the basis of insanity are often confined to mental hospitals for longer periods of time than they would have served in prison (Lymburner & Roesch, 1999). The net result is that although changes in the insanity defense, or its abolition, might prevent a few flagrant cases of abuse, they would not afford the public much broader protection.

In the wake of the Hinckley acquittal, a number of states adopted a new type of verdict, the "guilty-but-mentally-ill" (GBMI) verdict (Boudouris, 2000). The GBMI verdict offers juries the option of finding that the defendant is mentally ill but that the mental illness did not cause the defendant to commit the crime. People convicted under a GBMI statute go to prison but receive treatment while incarcerated.

Fourteen states have permitted GMBI verdicts (Melville & Naimark, 2002). However, the verdict has sparked controversy. Although GBMI was intended to reduce the number of NGRI (not guilty by reason of insanity) verdicts, it has failed to do so (Melville & Naimark, 2002). All in all, the GBMI verdict is widely seen as a social experiment that has thus far failed to prove its usefulness (Palmer & Hazelrigg, 2000). Critics argue that the verdict merely stigmatizes defendants who are found guilty as also being mentally ill. Some even call for the abolition of the verdict (Melville & Naimark, 2002).

In a celebrated case, John E. du Pont, an heir to the du Pont family fortune, was found guilty but mentally ill following trial for the 1996 murder of Olympic gold medalist wrestler David Schultz ("Du Pont Heir Found Guilty," 1997). Du Pont was subsequently remanded to a state psychiatric hospital for treatment rather than to prison. At trial, it was reported that du Pont exhibited bizarre behavior and suffered from delusions of being spied on by Nazis and of having his body inhabited by bugs.

Although the public outrage over the Hinckley and other celebrated insanity verdicts led to a reexamination of the insanity defense, society has long held to the doctrine of free will as a basis for determining responsibility for wrongdoing. The doctrine of free will, as applied to criminal responsibility, requires that people can be held guilty of a crime only if they are judged to have been in control of their actions at the time.

T R U T H or F I C T I O N

An attempt to assassinate the president of the United States was seen by millions of television viewers, but the would-be assassin was found not guilty by a court of law.

☑ **TRUE.** A man who was seen by millions of TV viewers attempting to assassinate President Reagan was found "not guilty by reason of insanity" by a court of law.

insanity defense A legal defense in which a defendant in a criminal case pleads not guilty on the basis of insanity.

T R U T H or F I C T I O N

The insanity defense is used in a large number of trials, usually successfully.

☑ **FALSE.** The insanity defense is rarely used in felony cases, and the rate of acquittals based on the defense is even rarer.

Guilty but mentally ill? John du Pont, an heir to the du Pont family fortune, was tried for the 1996 murder of Olympic gold medalist wrestler David Schultz. Du Pont was found guilty but mentally ill, a verdict that remains controversial in part because it is seen by some people as merely a way of stigmatizing defendants who are found guilty as also being mentally ill.

Not only must a court of law determine, beyond a reasonable doubt, that a defendant had committed a crime, but the individual's state of mind must be considered as well in determining guilt. The court must thus rule not only on whether a crime was committed but also on whether an individual is morally responsible and deserving of punishment. The insanity defense is based on the belief that when a criminal act derives from a distorted state of mind, and not from the exercise of free will, the individual should not be punished but rather treated for the underlying mental disorder. The insanity defense has a long legal history.

Legal Bases of the Insanity Defense

Three major modern court rulings bear on the insanity defense. The first was an 1834 case in Ohio that was ruled that people could not be held responsible if they are compelled to commit criminal actions because of impulses they are unable to resist.

The second major legal test of the insanity defense is referred to as the M'Naghten rule, based on a case in England in 1843 of a Scotsman, Daniel M'Naghten, who had intended to assassinate the prime minister of England, Sir Robert Peel. Instead, he killed Peel's secretary, whom he had mistaken for the prime minister. M'Naghten claimed that the voice of God had commanded him to kill Peel. The English court acquitted M'Naghten on the basis of insanity, finding that the defendant had been ". . . labouring under such a defect of reason, from disease of the mind, as not to know the nature and quality of the act he was doing; or, if he did know it, that he did not know he was doing what was wrong." The M'Naghten rule holds that people do not bear criminal responsibility if, by reason of a mental disease or defect, they either have no knowledge of their actions or are unable to tell right from wrong.

The third major case that helped lay the foundation for the modern insanity defense was *Durham* v. *United States* of 1954. This case held that the "accused [person] is not criminally responsible if his unlawful act was the product of mental disease or mental defect" (pp. 874–875). Under the *Durham* rule, juries were expected to decide not only whether the accused suffered from a mental disease or defect but also whether this mental condition was causally connected to the criminal act. The court recognized that criminal intent is a precondition of criminal responsibility:

> The legal and moral traditions of the western world require that those who, of their own free will and with evil intent . . . commit acts which violate the law, shall be criminally responsible for those acts. Our traditions also require that where such acts stem from and are the product of a mental disease or defect . . . moral blame shall not attach, and hence there will not be criminal responsibility.
>
> (Durham v. United States, *214 F2d 862, D.C. circ. 1954*)

The intent of the *Durham* rule was to reject as outmoded the two earlier standards of legal insanity, the irresistible impulse rule and the "right–wrong" principle. The court argued that the "right–wrong test" was outmoded because the concept of "mental disease" is broader than the ability to recognize right from wrong. The legal basis of insanity should thus not be judged on just one feature of a mental disorder, such as deficient reasoning ability. The irresistible impulse test was denied because the court recognized that in certain cases, criminal acts arising from "mental disease or defect" might occur in a cool and calculating manner rather than in the manner of a sudden, irresistible impulse. Defendants may have known they were committing criminal acts, but were not driven to do so by an irresistible impulse (Sokolove, 2003).

The *Durham* rule, however, has proved to be unworkable for several reasons, such as a lack of precise definitions of such terms as *mental disease* or *mental defect* (Maeder, 1985). Courts were confused, for example, about whether a personality disorder (e.g., antisocial personality disorder) constituted a "disease." Also, juries found it difficult to draw conclusions about whether an individual's "mental disease" was causally connected to the criminal act. Without clear or precise definitions of terms, juries came to rely increasingly on expert psychiatric testimony, their verdicts simply endorsing the testimony of expert witnesses (Maeder, 1985).

By 1972, the *Durham* rule was replaced in many jurisdictions by legal guidelines formulated by the American Law Institute (ALI) to define the legal basis of insanity (Van Susteren, 2002). These guidelines, which essentially combine the M'Naghten principle with the irresistible impulse principle, include the following provisions:

1. A person is not responsible for criminal conduct if at the time of such conduct as a result of mental disease or defect he lacks substantial capacity either to appreciate the criminality (wrongfulness) of his conduct or to conform his conduct to the requirements of law.

2. . . . the terms "mental disease or defect" do not include an abnormality manifested only by repeated criminal or otherwise antisocial conduct. (American Law Institute, 1962, p. 66)

The first guideline incorporates aspects of the M'Naghten test (being unable to appreciate right from wrong) and the irresistible impulse test (being unable to conform one's behavior to the requirements of law) of insanity. The second guideline asserts that repeated criminal behavior (such as a pattern of drug dealing) is not sufficient in itself to establish a mental disease or defect that might relieve the individual of criminal responsibility. Although many legal authorities believe the ALI guidelines are an improvement over earlier tests, questions remain as to whether a jury composed of ordinary citizens can be expected to make complex judgments about the defendant's state of mind, even on the basis of expert testimony. Under the ALI guidelines, juries must determine whether defendants lack substantial capacity to be aware of, or capable of, conforming their behavior to the law. By adding the term *substantial capacity* to the legal test, the ALI guidelines broaden the legal basis of the insanity defense, implying that defendants need not be completely incapable of controlling their actions to meet the legal test of not guilty by reason of insanity.

Under our system of justice, juries must struggle with the complex question of determining criminal responsibility, not merely criminal actions. But what of those individuals who successfully plead not guilty by reason of insanity? Should they be committed to a mental institution for a fixed sentence, as they might have been had they been incarcerated in a penal institution? Or should their commitments be of an indeterminate term and their release depend on their mental status? The legal basis for answering such questions was decided in the case of a man named Michael Jones.

Determining the Length of Criminal Commitment

The issue of determinate versus indeterminate commitment was addressed in the case of Michael Jones (*Jones* v. *United States*), who was arrested in 1975 and charged with petty larceny for attempting to steal a jacket from a Washington, D.C., department store. Jones was first committed to a public mental hospital, St. Elizabeth's Hospital (the same hospital where John Hinckley remains committed as of this writing). Jones was diagnosed as suffering from paranoid schizophrenia and was kept hospitalized until he was judged competent to stand trial, about 6 months later. Jones offered a plea of not guilty by reason of insanity, which the court accepted without challenge, remanding him to St. Elizabeth's. Despite the fact that Jones's crime carried a maximum sentence of 1 year in prison, Jones's repeated attempts to obtain release were denied in subsequent court hearings.

The U.S. Supreme Court eventually heard his appeal *7 years* after Jones was hospitalized and reached its decision in 1983. It ruled against Jones's appeal and affirmed the decision of the lower courts that he was to remain in the hospital. The Supreme Court thereby established a principle that individuals who are acquitted by reason of insanity "constitute a special class that should be treated differently" than civilly committed individuals (Morris, 2002). They may be committed for an indefinite period to a mental institution under criteria that require a less-stringent level of proof of dangerousness than is ordinarily applied in cases of civil commitment. Thus people found not guilty by reason of insanity may remain confined to a mental hospital for many years longer than they would have been sentenced to prison had they been found guilty.

Among other things, the Supreme Court ruling in *Jones* v. *United States* provides that the usual and customary sentences that the law provides for particular crimes have no bearing on criminal commitment. In the words of the Court,

> . . . different considerations underlie commitment of an insanity acquittee. As he was not convicted, he may not be punished. His confinement rests on his continuing illness and dangerousness. There simply is no necessary correlation between severity of the offense and length of time necessary for recovery.

(Jones *v.* United States, *103 S.Ct. 3043, 1983*)

The ruling held that a person who is criminally committed may be confined "to a mental institution until such time as he has regained his sanity or is no longer a danger to society" (p. 3053). As in the case of Michael Jones, people who are acquitted on the basis of insanity may remain confined for much longer periods of time than they would have been sentenced to prison. They may also be released earlier than they might have been released from prison, if their "mental condition" improves. However, public outrage over a speedy release, especially for a major crime, might prevent rapid release.

The indeterminateness of criminal commitment raises various questions. Is it reasonable to deny people such as Michael Jones their liberty for an indefinite and possibly lifelong term for a relatively minor crime, such as petty larceny? On the other hand, is justice served by acquitting perpetrators of heinous crimes by reason of insanity and then releasing them early if they are deemed by professionals to be able to rejoin society?

The Supreme Court's ruling in *Jones* v. *United States* seems to imply that we must separate the notion of legal sentencing from that of legal or criminal commitment. Legal sentencing rests on the principle that the punishment should fit the crime: The more serious the crime, the longer the punishment. In criminal commitment, however, persons acquitted of their crimes by reason of insanity are guiltless in the eyes of the law, and their length of confinement is determined by their mental state.

Perspectives on the Insanity Defense

The insanity defense places special burdens on juries. In assessing criminal responsibility, the jury must determine not only that the accused committed a crime but also the defendant's state of mind at the time. In rejecting the *Durham* decision, courts have relieved psychiatrists and other expert witnesses from responsibility for determining whether the defendant's behavior is a product of a "mental disease or defect." But is it reasonable to assume that juries are better able to assess defendants' states of mind than mental health professionals? In particular, how can a jury evaluate the testimony of expert conflicting witnesses? The jury's task is made even more difficult by the mandate to decide whether the defendant was mentally incapacitated *at the time of the crime.* The defendant's courtroom behavior may bear little resemblance to his or her behavior during the crime.

Thomas Szasz and others who deny the existence of mental illness have raised another challenge to the insanity defense. If mental illness does not exist, then the insanity defense becomes groundless. Szasz argues that the insanity defense is ultimately degrading because it strips people of personal responsibility for their behavior. People who break laws are criminals, Szasz argues, and should be prosecuted and sentenced accordingly. Acquittal of defendants by reason of insanity treats them as nonpersons, as unfortunates who are not deemed to possess the basic human qualities of free choice, self-determination, and personal responsibility. We are each responsible for our behavior, Szasz contends, and we should each be held accountable for our misdeeds.

 Szasz argues that the insanity defense has historically been invoked in crimes that were particularly heinous or perpetrated against persons of high social rank. When persons of low social rank commit crimes against persons of higher status, Szasz argues, the insanity defense directs attention away from the social ills that may have motivated the crime. Despite Szasz's contention, however, the insanity defense is invoked in many cases of less-shocking crimes or in cases involving persons from similar social classes.

How, then, are we to evaluate the insanity defense? To abolish it would reverse hundreds of years of legal tradition that recognizes that people are not to be held responsible for their criminal behavior when their ability to control themselves is impaired by a mental disorder or defect.

Consider a hypothetical example. John Citizen commits a crime, say a heinous crime such as murder, while acting on a delusional belief that the victim was intent on assassinating him. The accused claims that voices from his TV set informed him of the identity of the would-be assassin and commanded him to kill the person to save himself and other potential victims. Cases like this are thankfully rare. Few mentally disturbed persons, even few people with psychotic features, commit violent crimes, and even fewer commit murder.

Recently, Morris Hoffman, a state trial judge in Denver, and Stephen Morse, a professor of law and psychiatry at the University of Pennsylvania, had this to say about the moral basis of the insanity defense:

> Punishing the deserving wrongdoers among us—those who intentionally violate the criminal law and are cognitively unimpaired—takes people seriously as moral agents and lies at the heart of what being civilized is all about. But being civilized also means not punishing those whom we deem morally impaired by mental disorder. Convicting and punishing a defendant who genuinely believed that God commanded him to kill is not unscientific, it is immoral and unjust.
>
> —*Hoffman & Morse, 2006*

In reaching a judgment on the insanity plea, we need to consider whether the law should apply special standards in cases such as John Citizen's, or whether one standard of criminal responsibility should apply to all. If we assert the legitimacy of the insanity defense in some cases, we still need a standard of insanity that can be interpreted and applied by juries of ordinary citizens. The furor over the Hinckley verdict suggests that issues concerning the insanity plea remain unsettled and are likely to continue to be so for a long period of time.

Competency to Stand Trial

There is a basic rule of law that those who stand accused of crimes must be able to understand the charges and proceedings brought against them and be able to participate in their own defense. The concept of **competency to stand trial** should not be confused with the insanity defense. A defendant can be held competent to stand trial but still be judged not guilty of a crime by reason of insanity. A clearly delusional person, for example, may understand the court proceedings and be able to confer with defense counsel, but still be acquitted by reason of insanity. On the other hand, a person may be incapable of standing trial at a particular time, but be tried at a later time when competency is restored.

Far more people are confined to mental institutions on the basis of a determination that they lack the mental competence to stand trial than on the basis of the insanity verdict (Roesch et al., 1999). There may be 45 people committed under the mental competency to stand trial criteria for every one committed following a verdict of not guilty by reason of insanity (Steadman, 1979).

People declared incompetent to stand trial are generally confined to a mental institution until they are deemed competent or it is determined that they are unlikely to regain competency. Abuses may occur, however, if the accused are kept incarcerated for indefinite periods awaiting trial. In 1972, the U.S. Supreme Court ruled, in the case of *Jackson* v. *Indiana*, that a person could not be kept in a mental hospital awaiting trial longer than it would take to determine whether treatment was likely to restore competency. Under *Jackson*, psychiatric examiners must determine whether there exists a substantial probability that the defendant would regain competency through treatment within the foreseeable future (Hubbard, Zapf, & Ronan, 2003). If it does not seem the person would ever become competent, even with treatment, the individual must either be released or committed under the procedures for civil commitment.

competency to stand trial The ability of criminal defendants to understand the charges and proceedings brought against them and to participate in their own defense.

TRUTH or FICTION

A defendant may be held competent to stand trial but still be judged not guilty of a crime by reason of insanity.

☑ **TRUE.** Yes, a defendant can be held competent to stand trial but then be found not guilty of a crime by reason of insanity at trial.

However, compliance with the *Jackson* standard has been inconsistent, with some states imposing a minimum length of treatment (e.g., 5 years) before acknowledging that a defendant is deemed permanently incompetent (Morris, 2002).

A 1992 ruling by the U.S. Supreme Court, in the case of *Medina* v. *California*, held that the burden of proof for determining competency to stand trial lies with the defendant, not the state (Greenhouse, 1992). Then, in 2003, the U.S. Supreme Court held in the case of *Sell* v. *United States* that mentally ill defendants could be forcibly medicated to render them competent to stand trial, at least under some limited circumstances (Bassman, 2005). The decision allows a defendant to be involuntarily medicated if it is deemed medically appropriate and would not cause side effects that would compromise the fairness of the trial (Greenhouse, 2003; Heilbrun & Kramer, 2005). The effect of the *Sell* decision may be to bring to trial many defendants whose trials were delayed due to a lack of mental competence.

We opened this book by noting that despite the popular impression that abnormal behavior affects only a few of us, it actually affects every one of us in one way or another. Let us close by suggesting that if we all work together to foster research into the causes, treatment, and prevention of abnormal behavior, perhaps we can meet the multifaceted challenges that abnormal behavior poses to our society at large.

SUMMING UP

Psychiatric Commitment and Patients' Rights

What is the difference between civil commitment and criminal commitment? The legal process by which people are placed in psychiatric institutions against their will is called civil or psychiatric commitment. Civil commitment is intended to provide treatment to people who are deemed to suffer from mental disorders and to pose a threat to themselves or others. Criminal commitment, by comparison, involves the placement of a person in a psychiatric institution for treatment who has been acquitted of a crime by reason of insanity. In voluntary hospitalization, people voluntarily seek treatment in a psychiatric facility and can leave of their own accord unless a court rules otherwise.

How successful are mental health professionals in predicting the dangerousness of patients they evaluate? Although people must be judged dangerous to be placed involuntarily in a psychiatric facility, mental health professionals have not demonstrated any special ability to predict dangerousness. Factors that may account for the failure to predict dangerousness include (a) recognizing violent tendencies post hoc is easier than predicting it; (b) generalized perceptions of violent tendencies may not predict specific acts of violence; (c) lack of agreement in defining violence or dangerousness; (d) base-rate problems; (e) unlikelihood of direct threats of violence; and (f) predictions based on hospital behavior may not generalize to community settings.

What is meant by the duty to warn? Although information disclosed by a client to a therapist generally carries a right to confidentiality, the California *Tarasoff* ruling held that therapists have a duty or obligation to warn third parties of threats made against them by their clients.

What landmark court cases dealt with the rights of patients in psychiatric facilities? In *Wyatt* v. *Stickney*, a court in Alabama imposed a minimum standard of care. In *O'Connor* v. *Donaldson*, the U.S. Supreme Court ruled that nondangerous mentally ill people could not be held in psychiatric facilities against their will if such people could be maintained safely in the community. In *Youngberg* v. *Romeo*, the Supreme Court ruled that involuntarily confined patients have a right to less-restrictive types of treatment and to receive training to help them function. Court rulings, such as that of *Rogers* v. *Okin* in Massachusetts, have established that patients have a right to refuse medication, except in case of emergency.

The Insanity Defense

What are the legal bases of the insanity defense? Three court cases established legal precedents for the insanity defense. In 1834, a court in Ohio applied a principle of irresistible impulse as the basis of an insanity defense. The M'Naghten rule, based on a case in England in 1843, treated the failure to appreciate the wrongfulness of one's action as the basis of legal insanity. The *Durham* rule was based on a case in the United States in 1954 in which it was held that persons did not bear criminal responsibility if their criminal behavior was the product of "mental disease or mental defect." Another set of standards developed by the American Law Institute that combines the M'Naghten and irresistible impulse principles. People who are criminally committed may be hospitalized for an indefinite period of time, with their eventual release dependent on a determination of their mental status.

What is meant by the legal concept of competency to stand trial? People who are accused of crimes but are incapable of understanding the charges against them or assisting in their own defense can be found incompetent to stand trial and remanded to a psychiatric facility. In the case of *Jackson* v. *Indiana*, the U.S. Supreme Court placed restrictions on the length of time a person judged incompetent to stand trial could be held in a psychiatric facility.

KEY TERMS

civil commitment *(p. 544)*
criminal commitment *(p. 544)*

duty to warn *(p. 553)*
insanity defense *(p. 555)*

competency to stand trial *(p. 559)*

MEDIA TOOLS

A variety of digital and online learning tools are available to enrich your learning experience and help you succeed in the course. These resources include:

- **MyPsychLab,** an online learning system for your course in abnormal psychology that allows you to test your mastery of concepts in the book by using chapter-by-chapter diagnostic tests. Results from the diagnostic tests help you build a customized study plan. To access **MyPsychLab,** visit www. prenhall.com/mypsychlab and follow the instructions on the site.

- **"SPEAKING OUT" PATIENT INTERVIEWS,** a set of video case examples of actual patients you can access on the companion CD-ROM included with the text. Icons in the margins of the chapter highlight the video case examples included on the CD-ROM.

- **COMPANION WEB SITE,** an online study center that offers computer-scored quizzes you can use to test your knowledge, along with other study tools and links to related sites to enhance your learning of abnormal psychology. To access the companion Web site, visit www.prenhall.com/nevid and use the various tabs and links on the site to access these learning resources.

A

Abnormal psychology. The branch of psychology that deals with the description, causes, and treatment of abnormal behavior patterns.

Acculturative stress. Pressure to adjust to a host or mainstream culture.

Acute stress disorder (ASD). A traumatic stress reaction occurring during the month following exposure to a traumatic event.

Addiction. Impaired control over the use of a chemical substance, accompanied by physiological dependence.

Adjustment disorder. A maladaptive reaction to an identified stressor, characterized by impaired functioning or emotional distress that exceeds what would normally be expected.

Adoptee studies. Studies that compare the traits and behavior patterns of adopted children to those of their biological parents and their adoptive parents.

Agnosia. A disturbance of sensory perception, usually affecting visual perception.

Agoraphobia. Excessive, irrational fear of open or public places.

Alarm reaction. The first stage of the GAS, characterized by heightened sympathetic activity.

Alcoholism. An alcohol dependence disorder or addiction that results in serious personal, social, occupational, or health problems.

Alzheimer's disease (AD). A progressive brain disease characterized by gradual loss of memory and intellectual functioning, personality changes, and eventual loss of ability to care for oneself.

Amnestic disorders. Disturbances of memory associated with inability to learn new material or recall past events or personal information.

Amphetamine psychosis. A psychotic state induced by ingestion of amphetamines.

Amphetamines. A class of stimulants that activate the central nervous system, producing heightened states of arousal and feelings of pleasure.

Anorexia nervosa. An eating disorder characterized by maintenance of an abnormally low body weight, a distorted body image, intense fears of gaining weight, and in females, amenorrhea.

Anterograde amnesia. Loss or impairment of ability to form or store new memories.

Antianxiety drugs. Drugs that combat anxiety and reduce states of muscle tension.

Antidepressants. Drugs used to treat depression that affect the availability of neurotransmitters in the brain.

Antipsychotic drugs. Drugs used to treat schizophrenia or other psychotic disorders.

Antisocial personality disorder. A personality disorder characterized by antisocial and irresponsible behavior and lack of remorse for misdeeds.

Anxiety. An emotional state characterized by physiological arousal, unpleasant feelings of tension, and a sense of apprehension or foreboding.

Anxiety disorder. A class of psychological disorders characterized by excessive or maladaptive anxiety reactions.

Aphasia. Impaired ability to understand or express speech.

Archetypes. Primitive images or concepts that reside in the collective unconscious.

Asperger's disorder. A pervasive developmental disorder characterized by social deficits and stereotyped behavior but without the significant language or cognitive delays associated with autism.

Ataxia. Loss of muscle coordination.

Attention-deficit hyperactivity disorder (ADHD). A behavior disorder characterized by excessive motor activity and inability to focus one's attention.

Autism. A pervasive developmental disorder characterized by failure to relate to others, lack of speech, disturbed motor behaviors, intellectual impairment, and demands for sameness in the environment.

Autonomic nervous system. The division of the peripheral nervous system that regulates the activities of the glands and involuntary functions.

Avoidant personality disorder. A personality disorder characterized by avoidance of social relationships due to fears of rejection.

Axon. The long, thin part of a neuron along which nerve impulses travel.

B

Barbiturates. Sedative drugs which are depressants with high addictive potential.

Basal ganglia. An assemblage of neurons located between the thalamus and cerebrum, involved in coordinating motor (movement) processes.

Behavior therapy. The therapeutic application of learning-based techniques.

Behavioral assessment. The approach to clinical assessment that focuses on the objective recording and description of problem behavior.

Behaviorism. The school of psychology that defines psychology as the study of observable behavior.

Binge-eating disorder (BED). A disorder characterized by recurrent eating binges without purging; classified as a potential disorder requiring further study.

Biofeedback training (BFT). A method of feeding back to the individual information about bodily functions so that the person can gain some degree of control over these functions.

Biopsychosocial model. An integrative model for explaining abnormal in terms of the interactions of biological, psychological, and sociocultural factors.

Bipolar disorder. A psychological disorder characterized by mood swings between states of extreme elation and depression.

Blind. A state of being unaware of whether one has received an experimental treatment.

Body dysmorphic disorder (BDD). A somatoform disorder characterized by preoccupation with an imagined or exaggerated physical defect of appearance.

Body mass index (BMI). A standard measure of overweight and obesity that takes both body weight and height into account.

Borderline personality disorder (BPD). A personality disorder characterized by abrupt shifts in mood, lack of a coherent sense of self, and unpredictable, impulsive behavior.

Breathing-related sleep disorder. A sleep disorder in which sleep is repeatedly disrupted by difficulty with breathing normally.

Brief psychotic disorder. A psychotic disorder lasting from a day to a month that often follows exposure to a major stressor.

Bulimia nervosa. An eating disorder characterized by recurrent binge eating followed by self-induced purging, accompanied by overconcern with body weight and shape.

C

Cardiovascular disease. A disease or disorder of the cardiovascular system, such as coronary heart disease or hypertension.

Case study. A carefully drawn biography based on clinical interviews, observations, and psychological tests.

Catatonic type. The subtype of schizophrenia characterized by gross disturbances in motor activity, such as catatonic stupor.

Central nervous system. The brain and spinal cord.

Cerebellum. A structure in the hindbrain involved in coordination and balance.

Cerebral cortex. The wrinkled surface area of the cerebrum responsible for processing sensory stimuli and controlling higher mental functions, such as thinking and use of language.

Cerebrovascular accident (CVA). A stroke, or brain damage resulting from a rupture or blockage of a blood vessel supplying oxygen to the brain.

Cerebrum. The large mass of the forebrain, consisting of the two cerebral hemispheres.

Childhood disintegrative disorder. A pervasive developmental disorder involving loss of previously acquired skills and abnormal functioning following a period of apparently normal development during the first 2 years of life.

Circadian rhythm sleep disorder. A sleep disorder characterized by a mismatch between the body's normal sleep–wake cycle and the demands of the environment.

Civil commitment. The legal process of placing a person in a mental institution, even against his or her will.

Classical conditioning. A form of learning in which a response to one stimulus can be made to occur to another stimulus by pairing or associating the two stimuli.

Cocaine. A stimulant derived from the leaves of the coca plant.

Cognitive assessment. Measurement of thoughts, beliefs, and attitudes that may be associated with emotional problems.

Cognitive disorders. A class of psychological disorders characterized by impairment in cognitive abilities and daily functioning in which biological causation is either known or presumed.

Cognitive restructuring. A cognitive therapy method that involves replacing irrational thoughts with rational alternatives.

Cognitive therapy. A form of therapy that helps clients identify and correct faulty cognitions (thoughts, beliefs, and attitudes) believed to underlie their emotional problems and maladaptive behavior.

Cognitive triad of depression. The view that depression derives from adopting negative views of oneself, the environment or world at large, and the future.

Cognitive-behavioral therapy (CBT). A learning-based approach to therapy incorporating cognitive and behavioral techniques.

Cognitive-specificity hypothesis. The belief that different emotional disorders are linked to particular kinds of automatic thoughts.

Communication disorders. A class of psychological disorders characterized by difficulties in understanding or using language.

Competency to stand trial. The ability of criminal defendants to understand the charges and proceedings brought against them and to participate in their own defense.

Compulsion. A repetitive or ritualistic behavior that the person feels compelled to perform.

Conditional positive regard. Valuing other people on the basis of whether their behavior meets one's approval.

Conditioned response. In classical conditioning, a learned response to a previously neutral stimulus.

Conditioned stimulus. A previously neutral stimulus that evokes a conditioned response after repeated pairings with an unconditioned stimulus that had previously evoked that response.

Conduct disorder. A psychological disorder in childhood and adolescence characterized by disruptive, antisocial behavior.

Confidentiality. Protection of the identity of participants by keeping records secure and not disclosing their identities.

Congruence. The fit between one's thoughts, behaviors, and feelings.

Conscious. To Freud, the part of the mind that corresponds to our present awareness.

Construct validity. (a) In testing, the degree to which a test measures the hypothetical construct that it purports to measure; (b) in an experiment, the degree to which treatment effects can be accounted for by the theoretical mechanisms (constructs) represented by the independent variables.

Content validity. The degree to which the content of a test or measure represents the content domain of the construct it purports to measure.

Control group. In an experiment, a group that does not receive the experimental treatment.

Conversion disorder. A somatoform disorder characterized by loss or impairment of physical function in the absence of any apparent organic cause.

Correlation coefficient. A statistical measure of the strength of the relationship between two variables expressed along a continuum that varies between −1.00 and +1.00.

Correlational method. A scientific method of study that examines the relationships between factors or variables expressed in statistical terms.

Countertransference. In psychoanalysis, the transfer of feelings or attitudes that the analyst holds toward other persons in her or his life onto the client.

Couple therapy. A form of therapy that focuses on resolving conflicts in distressed couples.

Crack. The hardened, smokable form of cocaine.

Criminal commitment. The legal process of confining a person found not guilty by reason of insanity in a mental institution.

Criterion validity. The degree to which a test correlates with an independent, external criterion or standard.

Critical thinking. Adoption of a questioning attitude and careful scrutiny of claims and arguments in the light of evidence.

Cultural–familial retardation. A mild form of mental retardation that is influenced by impoverishment of the home environment.

Culture-bound syndromes. Patterns of abnormal behavior found within only one or a few cultures.

Cyclothymic disorder. A mood disorder characterized by a chronic pattern of less-severe mood swings than are found in bipolar disorder.

D

Defense mechanisms. The reality-distorting strategies used by the ego to shield the self from awareness of anxiety-provoking materials.

Deinstitutionalization. The policy of shifting care for patients with severe or chronic mental health problems from inpatient facilities to community-based facilities.

Delirium. A state of mental confusion, disorientation, and inability to focus attention.

Delusional disorder. A type of psychosis characterized by persistent delusions, often of a paranoid nature, that do not have the bizarre quality of the type found in paranoid schizophrenia.

Dementia. Profound deterioration of mental functioning, characterized by impaired memory, thinking, judgment, and language use.

Dementia praecox. The term given by Kraepelin to the disorder now called schizophrenia.

Dendrites. The rootlike structures at the ends of neurons that receive nerve impulses from other neurons.

Dependent personality disorder. A personality disorder characterized by difficulty making independent decisions and overly dependent behavior.

Dependent variables. Outcomes of an experiment believed to be dependent on the effects of an independent variable.

Depersonalization. Feelings of unreality or detachment from one's self or one's body.

Depersonalization disorder. A disorder characterized by persistent or recurrent episodes of depersonalization.

Depressant. A drug that lowers the level of activity of the central nervous system.

Derealization. A sense of unreality about the outside world.

Detoxification. The process of ridding the system of alcohol or other drugs under supervised conditions.

Dhat syndrome. A culture-bound somatoform disorder, found primarily among Asian Indian males, characterized by excessive fears over the loss of seminal fluid.

Diathesis. A vulnerability or predisposition to a particular disorder.

Diathesis–stress model. A model that posits that abnormal behavior problems involve the interaction of a vulnerability or predisposition and stressful life events or experiences.

Disorganized type. The subtype of schizophrenia characterized by disorganized behavior, bizarre delusions, and vivid hallucinations.

Dissociative amnesia. A dissociative disorder in which a person experiences memory loss without any identifiable organic cause.

Dissociative disorder. A disorder characterized by disruption, or dissociation, of identity, memory, or consciousness.

Dissociative fugue. A dissociative disorder in which one suddenly flees from one's life situation, travels to a new location, assumes a new identity, and has amnesia for personal material.

Dissociative identity disorder. A dissociative disorder in which a person has two or more distinct, or alter, personalities.

Dopamine hypothesis. The prediction that schizophrenia involves overactivity of dopamine receptors in the brain.

Double depression. Concurrent major depressive disorder and dysthymic disorder.

Down syndrome. A condition caused by the presence of an extra chromosome on the 21st pair and characterized by mental retardation and various physical anomalies.

Downward drift hypothesis. The theory that explains the linkage between low socioeconomic status and behavior problems by suggesting that problem behaviors lead people to drift downward in social status.

Duty to warn. The therapist's obligation to warn third parties of threats made against them by clients.

Dyslexia. A learning disorder characterized by impaired reading ability.

Dyspareunia. Persistent or recurrent pain experienced during or following sexual intercourse.

Dyssomnias. Sleep disorders involving disturbances in the amount, quality, or timing of sleep.

Dysthymic disorder. A mild but chronic type of depressive disorder.

E

Eating disorder. A psychological disorder characterized by disturbed patterns of eating and maladaptive ways of controlling body weight.

Eclectic therapy. An approach to psychotherapy that incorporates principles or techniques from various systems or theories.

Ego. The psychic structure that corresponds to the concept of the self, governed by the reality principle and characterized by the ability to tolerate frustration.

Ego dystonic. Referring to behaviors or feelings that are perceived to be alien to one's self-identity.

Ego psychology. Modern psychodynamic approach that focuses more on the conscious strivings of the ego than on the hypothesized unconscious functions of the id.

Ego syntonic. Referring to behaviors or feelings that are perceived as natural parts of the self.

Electroconvulsive therapy (ECT). A method of treating severe depression by administering electrical shock to the head.

Emotion-focused coping. A coping style that attempts to minimize emotional responsiveness rather than deal with the stressor directly.

Empathy.   The ability to understand someone's experiences and feelings from that person's point of view.

Encopresis.   Lack of control over bowel movements that is not caused by an organic problem in a child who is at least 4 years old.

Endocrine system.   The system of ductless glands that secrete hormones directly into the bloodstream.

Endophenotypes.   Measurable processes or mechanisms not apparent to the naked eye, which are the means by which an organism's genetic code comes to affect its observable characteristics or phenotypes.

Endorphins.   Natural substances that function as neurotransmitters in the brain and are similar in their effects to morphine.

Enuresis.   Failure to control urination after one has reached the expectable age for attaining such control.

Epidemiological studies.   Research studies that track rates of occurrence of particular disorders among different population groups.

Erotomania.   A delusional disorder characterized by the belief that one is loved by someone of high social status.

Exhaustion stage.   The third stage of the GAS, characterized by lowered resistance, increased parasympathetic activity, and eventual physical deterioration.

Exhibitionism.   A type of paraphilia almost exclusively occurring in males, in which the man experiences persistent and recurrent sexual urges and sexually arousing fantasies involving the exposure of his genitals to a stranger and either has acted upon these urges or feels strongly distressed by them.

Expectancies.   Beliefs about expected outcomes.

Experimental group.   In an experiment, a group that receives the experimental treatment.

Experimental method.   A scientific method that aims to discover cause-and-effect relationships by manipulating independent variables and observing the effects on the dependent variables.

External validity.   The degree to which experimental results can be generalized to other settings and conditions.

Eye movement desensitization and reprocessing (EMDR).   A controversial form of therapy for PTSD that involves eye tracking of a visual target while holding images of the traumatic experience in mind.

F

Factitious disorder.   A disorder characterized by intentional fabrication of psychological or physical symptoms for no apparent gain.

Family therapy.   A form of therapy in which the family, not the individual, is the unit of treatment.

Fear-stimulus hierarchy.   An ordered series of increasingly fearful stimuli.

Female orgasmic disorder.   A type of sexual dysfunction involving persistent difficulty achieving orgasm despite adequate stimulation.

Female sexual arousal disorder.   A type of sexual dysfunction in women involving difficulty becoming sexually aroused or lack of sexual excitement or pleasure during sexual activity.

Fetishism.   A type of paraphilia in which a person uses an inanimate object as a focus of sexual interest and as a source of arousal.

Fight-or-flight reaction.   The inborn tendency to respond to a threat by either fighting or fleeing.

Fixation.   In Freudian theory, a constellation of personality traits associated with a particular stage of psychosexual development, resulting from either too much or too little gratification at the stage.

Flooding.   A behavior therapy technique for overcoming fears by means of exposure to high levels of fear-inducing stimuli.

Fragile X syndrome.   An inherited form of mental retardation caused by a mutated gene on the X chromosome.

Free association.   The method of verbalizing thoughts as they occur without a conscious attempt to edit or censure them.

Frotteurism.   A type of paraphilia involving sexual urges or sexually arousing fantasies involving bumping and rubbing against nonconsenting persons for sexual gratification.

G

Gender identity.   One's psychological sense of being female or being male.

Gender identity disorder (GID).   A type of psychological disorder characterized by conflict between one's anatomic sex and one's gender identity.

General adaptation syndrome (GAS).   The body's three-stage response to states of prolonged or intense stress.

General paresis.   A degenerative brain disease occurring when the bacterium that causes syphilis directly invades brain tissue.

Generalized anxiety disorder (GAD).   A type of anxiety disorder characterized by general feelings of dread and foreboding and heightened states of bodily arousal.

Genotype.   The set of traits specified by an individual's genetic code.

Genuineness.   The ability to recognize and express one's true feelings.

Gradual exposure.   A behavior therapy technique for overcoming fears through direct exposure to increasingly fearful stimuli.

Group therapy.   A form of therapy in which a group of clients meets together with a therapist.

H

Hallucinations.   Perceptions occurring in the absence of external stimuli that become confused with reality.

Hallucinogens.   Substances that cause hallucinations.

Health psychologist.   A psychologist who studies the role of psychological factors in physical illness.

Heroin.   A narcotic derived from morphine that has strong addictive properties.

Heterosexism.   The culturally based belief system that holds that only reproductive sexuality between men and women is psychologically healthy and morally correct.

Histrionic personality disorder.   A personality disorder characterized by excessive need for attention, praise, reassurance, and approval.

Homophobia.   Hatred and fear of lesbians and gay males.

Hormones.   Substances secreted by endocrine glands that regulate body functions and promote growth and development.

Humors.   According to the ancient Hippocratic belief system, the vital bodily fluids (phlegm, black bile, blood, yellow bile).

Huntington's disease.   An inherited degenerative disease that is characterized by jerking and twisting movements, paranoia, and mental deterioration.

Hyperactivity.   An abnormal behavior pattern characterized by difficulty in maintaining attention and extreme restlessness.

Hypersomnia.   A pattern of excessive sleepiness during the day.

Hypoactive sexual desire disorder.   Persistent or recurrent lack of sexual interest or sexual fantasies.

Hypochondriasis.   A somatoform disorder characterized by misinterpretation of physical symptoms as signs of underlying serious disease.

Hypomania.   A relatively mild state of mania.

Hypothalamus.   A structure in the forebrain involved in regulating body temperature, emotion, and motivation.

Hypothesis.   An assumption that is tested through experimentation.

Hypoxia.   Decreased supply of oxygen to the brain or other organs.

Hypoxyphilia.   A paraphilia in which a person seeks sexual gratification by being deprived of oxygen by means of using a noose, plastic bag, chemical, or pressure on the chest.

I

Id.   The unconscious psychic structure, present at birth, that contains primitive instincts and is regulated by the pleasure principle.

Immune system.   The body's system of defense against disease.

Impulse control disorders.   A category of psychological disorders characterized by failure to control impulses, temptations, or drives, resulting in harm to oneself or others.

Incidence.   The number of new cases of a disorder that occurs within a specific period of time.

Independent variables.   Factors that are manipulated in experiments.

Infarction.   The development of an infarct, or area of dead or dying tissue, resulting from the blocking of blood vessels normally supplying the tissue.

Informed consent.   The principle that subjects should receive enough information about an experiment beforehand to decide freely whether to participate.

Insanity defense.   A legal defense in which a defendant in a criminal case pleads not guilty on the basis of insanity.

Insomnia.   Difficulties falling asleep, remaining asleep, or achieving restorative sleep.

Internal validity.   The degree to which manipulation of the independent variables can be causally related to changes in the dependent variables.

Intoxication.   A state of drunkenness.

K

Kleptomania.   A type of impulse control disorder characterized by a pattern of compulsive stealing.

Koro syndrome. A culture-bound somatoform disorder, found primarily in China, in which people fear that their genitals are shrinking.

Korsakoff's syndrome. A syndrome associated with chronic alcoholism that is characterized by memory loss and disorientation (also called *alcohol-induced persisting amnestic disorder*).

L

Learned helplessness. A behavior pattern characterized by passivity and perceptions of lack of control.

Learning disorder. A deficiency in a specific learning ability in the context of normal intelligence and exposure to learning opportunities.

Limbic system. A group of forebrain structures involved in learning, memory, and basic drives.

Longitudinal study. A research study in which subjects are followed over time.

M

Major depressive disorder. A severe mood disorder characterized by major depressive episodes.

Male erectile disorder. A sexual dysfunction in males characterized by difficulty in achieving or maintaining erection during sexual activity.

Male orgasmic disorder. Persistent or recurrent delay in achieving orgasm or inability to achieve orgasm despite a normal level of sexual interest and arousal.

Malingering. Faking illness in order to avoid work or duty.

Managed care systems. Health care delivery systems that impose limits on the number of treatment sessions they will approve for payment and the fees they will allow for reimbursement.

Mania. A state of unusual elation, energy, and activity.

Manic episode. A period of unrealistically heightened euphoria, extreme restlessness, and excessive activity characterized by disorganized behavior and impaired judgment.

Marijuana. A hallucinogenic drug derived from the leaves and stems of the plant *Cannabis sativa*.

Medical model. A biological perspective in which abnormal behavior is viewed as symptomatic of underlying illness.

Medulla. An area of the hindbrain involved in regulation of heartbeat and respiration.

Mental retardation. A generalized delay or impairment in the development of intellectual and adaptive abilities.

Methadone. An artificial narcotic that is used to help people who are addicted to heroin to abstain from it without a withdrawal syndrome.

Modeling. (a) Learning by observing and imitating the behavior of others; (b) in behavior therapy, a technique for helping an individual acquire a new behavior by having a therapist or another person demonstrate the target behavior that is then imitated by the client.

Mood disorders. Psychological disorders characterized by disturbances of mood.

Morphine. A strongly addictive narcotic derived from the opium poppy that relieves pain and induces feelings of well-being.

Münchausen syndrome. A type of factitious disorder characterized by the fabrication of medical symptoms.

N

Naltrexone. A drug that blocks the high from alcohol as well as from opiates.

Narcissistic personality disorder. A personality disorder characterized by adoption of an inflated self-image and demands for attention and admiration.

Narcolepsy. A sleep disorder characterized by sudden, irresistible episodes of sleep.

Narcotics. Drugs that are used medically for pain relief but that have strong addictive potential.

Naturalistic observation. A form of research in which behavior is observed and measured in its natural environment.

Negative reinforcers. Reinforcers that, when removed, increase the frequency of the preceding behavior.

Negative symptoms. Behavioral deficiencies associated with schizophrenia, such as social skills deficits, social withdrawal, flattened affect, poverty of speech and thought, psychomotor retardation, and failure to experience pleasure.

Neurons. Nerve cells.

Neuropsychological assessment. Measurement of behavior or performance that may be indicative of underlying brain damage or defects.

Neurotransmitters. Chemical substances that transmit messages from one neuron to another.

Nightmare disorder. A sleep disorder characterized by recurrent awakenings due to frightening nightmares.

Nonspecific treatment factors. Factors not specific to any one form of psychotherapy, such as therapist attention and support, and creating positive expectancies of change.

O

Obesity. A condition of excess body fat; generally defined by a BMI of 30 or higher.

Object-relations theory. The psychodynamic viewpoint that focuses on the influences of internalized representations of the personalities of parents and other strong attachment figures (called "objects").

Objective tests. Self-report personality tests that can be scored objectively and that are based on a research foundation.

Obsession. A recurring thought or image that the individual cannot control.

Obsessive–compulsive disorder (OCD). A type of anxiety disorder characterized by recurrent obsessions, compulsions, or both.

Obsessive–compulsive personality disorder. A personality disorder characterized by rigid ways of relating to others, perfectionistic tendencies, lack of spontaneity, and excessive attention to detail.

Operant conditioning. A form of learning in which behavior is acquired and strengthened when it is reinforced.

Oppositional defiant disorder (ODD). A psychological disorder in childhood and adolescence characterized by excessive oppositionality or tendencies to refuse requests from parents and others.

P

Pain disorder. A somatoform disorder in which psychological factors are presumed to play a sig-

nificant role in the development, severity, or course of chronic pain.

Panic disorder. A type of anxiety disorder characterized by repeated episodes of intense anxiety or panic.

Paranoid personality disorder. A personality disorder characterized by undue suspiciousness of others' motives, but not to the point of delusion.

Paranoid type. The subtype of schizophrenia characterized by hallucinations and systematized delusions, commonly involving themes of persecution.

Paraphilias. Sexual deviations or types of sexual disorders in which the person experiences recurrent sexual urges and sexually arousing fantasies involving nonhuman objects (such as articles of clothing), inappropriate or nonconsenting partners (for example, children), or situations producing humiliation or pain to oneself or one's partner.

Parasomnias. Sleep disorders involving abnormal behaviors or physiological events that occur during sleep or while falling asleep.

Parasympathetic nervous system. Pertaining to the division of the autonomic nervous system whose activity reduces states of arousal and regulates bodily processes that replenish energy reserves.

Parkinson's disease. A progressive disease of the basal ganglia characterized by muscle tremor and shakiness, rigidity, difficulty walking, poor control of fine motor movements, lack of facial muscle tone, and in some cases, cognitive impairment.

Pathological gambling. A type of impulse control disorder characterized by a pattern of habitual gambling and impaired control over the behavior.

Pedophilia. A type of paraphilia involving sexual attraction to children.

Peripheral nervous system. The somatic and autonomic nervous systems.

Person-centered therapy. The establishment of a warm, accepting therapeutic relationship that frees clients to engage in self-exploration and achieve self-acceptance.

Personality disorders. Excessively rigid behavior patterns, or ways of relating to others, that ultimately become self-defeating.

Pervasive developmental disorders (PDDs). A class of developmental disorders characterized by significantly impaired behavior or functioning in multiple areas of development.

Phenotype. An individual's actual or expressed traits.

Phenylketonuria (PKU). A genetic disorder that prevents the metabolization of phenylpyruvic acid, leading to mental retardation unless the diet is strictly controlled.

Phobia. An excessive, irrational fear.

Physiological assessment. Measurement of physiological responses that may be associated with abnormal behavior.

Physiological dependence. A condition in which the drug user's body comes to depend on a steady supply of the substance.

Pick's disease. A form of dementia, similar to Alzheimer's disease, but distinguished by specific abnormalities (Pick's bodies) in nerve cells and absence of neurofibrillary tangles and plaques.

Placebo. An inert medication or bogus treatment that is intended to control for expectancy effects.

Pleasure principle. The governing principle of the id, involving demands for immediate gratification of needs.

Pons. A structure in the hindbrain involved in respiration and other functions.

Positive psychology. A growing contemporary movement within psychology that focuses on the positive attributes of human behavior.

Positive reinforcers. Reinforcers that, when introduced, increase the frequency of the preceding behavior.

Positive symptoms. Flagrant symptoms of schizophrenia, such as hallucinations, delusions, bizarre behavior, and thought disorder.

Postpartum depression (PPD). Persistent and severe mood changes that occur after childbirth.

Posttraumatic stress disorder (PTSD). A prolonged maladaptive reaction to a traumatic event.

Preconscious. To Freud, the part of the mind whose contents lie outside present awareness but can be brought into awareness by focusing attention.

Premature ejaculation. A type of sexual dysfunction involving a pattern of unwanted rapid ejaculation during sexual activity.

Presenile dementias. Forms of dementia that begin at or before age 65.

Prevalence. The overall number of cases of a disorder in a population within a specific period of time.

Primary insomnia. A sleep disorder characterized by chronic or persistent insomnia not caused by another psychological or physical disorder or by the effects of drugs or medications.

Primary prevention. Efforts designed to prevent problems from arising.

Proband. The case first diagnosed of a given disorder.

Problem-focused coping. A coping style that attempts to confront the stressor directly.

Prodromal phase. In schizophrenia, the period of decline in functioning that precedes the first acute psychotic episode.

Projective tests. Psychological tests that present ambiguous stimuli onto which the examinee is thought to project his or her personality and unconscious motives.

Psychoanalysis. The method of psychotherapy developed by Sigmund Freud.

Psychoanalytic theory. The theoretical model of personality developed by Sigmund Freud; also called psychoanalysis.

Psychodynamic model. The theoretical model of Freud and his followers, in which abnormal behavior is viewed as the product of clashing forces within the personality.

Psychodynamic therapy. Therapy that helps individuals gain insight into, and resolve, unconscious conflicts.

Psychological dependence. Compulsive use of a substance to meet a psychological need.

Psychological disorder. Abnormal behavior pattern that involves a disturbance of psychological functioning or behavior.

Psychological hardiness. A cluster of stress-buffering traits characterized by commitment, challenge, and control.

Psychopharmacology. The field of study that examines the effects of therapeutic or psychiatric drugs.

Psychosis. A severe form of disturbed behavior characterized by impaired ability to interpret reality and difficulty meeting the demands of daily life.

Psychosomatic. Pertaining to a physical disorder in which psychological factors play a causal or contributing role.

Psychotherapy. A structured form of treatment derived from a psychological framework that consists of one or more verbal interactions or treatment sessions between a client and a therapist.

Punishment. Application of aversive or painful stimuli that reduces the frequency of the behavior it follows.

R

Random assignment. A method of assigning research subjects at random to experimental or control groups to balance these groups on the characteristics of people that comprise them.

Random sample. A sample that is drawn in such a way that every member of a population has an equal chance of being included.

Rape. Forced sexual intercourse with a nonconsenting person. Note that the legal definition of rape varies from state to state.

Rational emotive behavior therapy (REBT). A therapeutic approach that focuses on helping clients replace irrational, maladaptive beliefs with alternative, more adaptive beliefs.

Reality principle. The governing principle of the ego, which involves considerations of social acceptability and practicality.

Reality testing. The ability to perceive the world accurately and to distinguish reality from fantasy.

Rebound anxiety. The experiencing of strong anxiety following withdrawal from a tranquilizer.

Receptor site. A part of a dendrite on a receiving neuron that is structured to receive a neurotransmitter.

Reinforcement. A stimulus or event that increases the frequency of the response that it follows.

Reliability. In psychological assessment, the consistency of a measure or diagnostic instrument or system.

Residual phase. In schizophrenia, the phase that follows an acute phase, characterized by a return to the level of functioning of the prodromal phase.

Resistance stage. The second stage of the GAS, involving the body's attempt to withstand prolonged stress and preserve resources.

Reticular activating system. Brain structure involved in processes of attention, sleep, and arousal.

Retrograde amnesia. Loss or impairment of ability to recall past events.

Rett's disorder. A pervasive developmental disorder characterized by a range of physical, behavioral, motor, and cognitive abnormalities that begin after a few months of apparently normal development.

Reversal design. An experimental design that consists of repeated measurement of a subject's behavior through a sequence of alternating baseline and treatment phases.

S

Sadomasochism. Sexual activities between partners involving the attainment of gratification by means of inflicting and receiving pain and humiliation.

Sanism. The negative stereotyping of people who are identified as mentally ill.

Schizoaffective disorder. A type of psychotic disorder in which individuals experience both severe mood disturbance and features associated with schizophrenia.

Schizoid personality disorder. A personality disorder characterized by persistent lack of interest in social relationships, flattened affect, and social withdrawal.

Schizophrenia. A chronic psychotic disorder characterized by disturbed behavior, thinking, emotions, and perceptions.

Schizophreniform disorder. A psychotic disorder lasting less than 6 months in duration, with features that resemble schizophrenia.

Schizotypal personality disorder. A personality disorder characterized by eccentricities of thought and behavior, but without clearly psychotic features.

Scientific method. A systematic method of conducting scientific research in which theories or assumptions are examined in the light of evidence.

Secondary prevention. Efforts to ameliorate existing problems at an early stage.

Selection factor. A type of bias in which differences between experimental and control groups result from differences in the type of participants in the groups, not from the independent variable.

Self-actualization. In humanistic psychology, the tendency to strive to become all that one is capable of being. The motive that drives one to reach one's full potential and express one's unique capabilities.

Self-efficacy expectancies. Beliefs in one's ability to accomplish particular tasks.

Self-monitoring. The process of observing or recording one's own behaviors, thoughts, or emotions.

Semistructured interview. Interview in which the clinician follows a general outline of questions designed to gather essential information but is free to ask them in any order and to branch off in other directions.

Senile dementias. Forms of dementia that begin after age 65.

Separation anxiety disorder. A childhood disorder characterized by extreme fear of separation from parents or other caretakers.

Sexual aversion disorder. A type of sexual dysfunction characterized by aversion to, and avoidance, of genital sexual contact.

Sexual dysfunctions. Persistent or recurrent problems with sexual interest, arousal, or response.

Sexual masochism. A type of paraphilia characterized by sexual urges and sexually arousing fantasies involving receiving humiliation or pain.

Sexual sadism. A type of paraphilia or sexual deviation characterized by recurrent sexual urges and sexually arousing fantasies involving inflicting humiliation or physical pain on sex partners.

Single-case experimental design. A type of case study in which the subject is used as his or her own control.

Sleep disorders. Persistent or recurrent sleep-related problems that cause distress or impaired functioning.

Sleep terror disorder. A sleep disorder characterized by recurrent episodes of sleep terror resulting in abrupt awakenings.

Sleepwalking disorder. A sleep disorder involving repeated episodes of sleepwalking.

Social causation model. The belief that social stressors, such as poverty, account for the greater risk of severe psychological disorders among people of lower socioeconomic status.

Social phobia. Excessive fear of social interactions or situations.

Social-cognitive theory. A learning-based theory that emphasizes observational learning and incorporates roles for cognitive variables in determining behavior.

Somatic nervous system. The division of the peripheral nervous system that relays information from the sense organs to the brain and transmits messages from the brain to the skeletal muscles.

Somatization disorder. A somatoform disorder characterized by repeated multiple complaints that cannot be explained by physical causes.

Somatoform disorders. A disorder characterized by complaints of physical problems or symptoms that cannot be explained by physical causes.

Specific phobia. A phobia that is specific to a particular object or situation.

Splitting. An inability to reconcile the positive and negative aspects of the self and others, resulting in sudden shifts between positive and negative feelings.

Stimulants. Psychoactive substances that increase the activity of the nervous system.

Stress. A demand made on an organism to adapt or adjust.

Stressor. A source of stress.

Structured interview. Interview that follows a preset series of questions in a particular order.

Substance abuse. The continued use of a psychoactive drug despite the knowledge that it is causing a social, occupational, psychological, or physical problem.

Substance dependence. Impaired control over the use of a psychoactive substance; often characterized by physiological dependence.

Substance use disorders. Disorders characterized by maladaptive use of psychoactive substances (e.g., substance dependence).

Substance-induced disorders. Disorders, such as intoxication, that can be induced by using psychoactive substances.

Superego. The psychic structure that incorporates the values of the parents and important others and functions as a moral conscience.

Survey method. A research method in which large samples of people are questioned by means of a survey instrument.

Sympathetic nervous system. Pertaining to the division of the autonomic nervous system whose activity leads to heightened states of arousal.

Synapse. The junction between one neuron and another through which nerve impulses pass.

Systematic desensitization. A behavior therapy technique for overcoming phobias by means of exposure to progressively more fearful stimuli while one remains deeply relaxed.

T

Tardive dyskinesia (TD). A disorder characterized by involuntary movements of the face, mouth, neck, trunk, or extremities and caused by long-term use of antipsychotic medication.

Terminals. The small branching structures at the tips of axons.

Thalamus. A structure in the forebrain involved in relaying sensory information to the cortex and in processes related to sleep and attention.

Theory. A formulation of the relationships underlying observed events.

Thought disorder. A disturbance in thinking characterized by the breakdown of logical associations between thoughts.

Token economy. Behavioral treatment program in which a controlled environment is constructed such that people are reinforced for desired behaviors by receiving tokens that may be exchanged for desired rewards.

Tolerance. Physical habituation to a drug such that with frequent use, higher doses are needed to achieve the same effects.

Transference relationship. In psychoanalysis, the client's transfer or generalization to the analyst of feelings and attitudes the client holds toward important figures in his or her life.

Transvestic fetishism. A type of paraphilia in heterosexual males involving sexual urges and sexually arousing fantasies involving dressing in female clothing. Also termed *transvestism*.

Trephination. A harsh, prehistoric practice of cutting a hole in a person's skull, possibly in an attempt to release demons.

Two-factor model. A theoretical model that accounts for the development of phobic reactions on the basis of classical and operant conditioning.

Type A behavior pattern (TABP). A behavior pattern characterized by a sense of time urgency, competitiveness, and hostility.

U

Unconditional positive regard. Valuing other people as having basic worth regardless of their behavior at a particular time.

Unconditioned response. An unlearned response.

Unconditioned stimulus. A stimulus that elicits an unlearned response.

Unconscious. To Freud, the part of the mind that lies outside the range of ordinary awareness and that contains instinctual urges.

Unstructured interview. Interview in which the clinician adopts his or her own style of questioning rather than following any standard format.

V

Vaginismus. The involuntary spasm of the muscles surrounding the vagina when vaginal penetration is attempted, making sexual intercourse difficult or impossible.

Validity. The degree to which a test or diagnostic system measures the traits or constructs it purports to measure.

Vascular dementia. Dementia resulting from a number of strokes in the brain.

Virtual reality therapy. A form of exposure therapy involving the presentation of phobic stimuli in a virtual reality environment.

Voyeurism. A type of paraphilia involving sexual urges and sexually arousing fantasies focused on acts of watching unsuspecting others who are naked, in the act of undressing, or engaging in sexual activity.

W

Wernicke's disease. A brain disorder, associated with chronic alcoholism, characterized by confusion, disorientation, and difficulty maintaining balance while walking.

Withdrawal syndrome. A characteristic cluster of symptoms following the sudden reduction or cessation of use of a psychoactive substance after physiological dependence has developed.

A

Aarre, T. F., Dahl, A. A., Johansen, J. B., Kjonniksen, I., & Neckelmann, D. (2003). Efficacy of repetitive transcranial magnetic stimulation in depression: A review of the evidence. *Nordic Journal of Psychiatry, 57*, 227–232.

Aarsland, D., Andersen, K., Larsen, J. P., Lolk, A., & Kragh-Sorensen, P. (2003). Prevalence and characteristics of dementia in Parkinson disease: An 8-year prospective study. *Archives of Neurology, 60*, 387–392.

Abbey, A., Zawackia, T., Bucka, O., Clinton, A. M., & McAuslan, P. (2004). Sexual assault and alcohol consumption: What do we know about their relationship and what types of research are still needed? *Aggression and Violent Behavior, 9*, 271–303.

Abikoff, H. (2001). Tailored psychosocial treatments for ADHD: The search for a good fit. *Journal of Clinical Child Psychology, 30* (1), 122–125.

Abkevich, V., Camp, N. J., Hensel, C. H., Neff, C. D., Russell, D. L., Hughes, D. C., et al. (2003). Predisposition locus for major depression at chromosome 2q22–12q23.2. *American Journal of Human Genetics, 73*, 1271–1281.

Abracen, J., & Looman, J. (2004). Issues in the treatment of sexual offenders: Recent developments and directions for future research. *Aggression and Violent Behavior, 9*, 229–246.

Abraham, K. (1948). The first pregenital stage of the libido (1916). In D. Bryan & A. Strachey (Eds.), *Selected papers of Karl Abraham, M. D.* London: The Hogarth Press.

Abramowitz, J. S. (1996). Variants of exposure and response prevention in the treatment of obsessive-compulsive disorder: A meta-analysis. *Behavior Therapy, 27*, 583–600.

Abramowitz, J. S., Foa, E. B., & Franklin, M. E. (2003). Exposure and ritual prevention for obsessive-compulsive disorder: Effects of intensive versus twice-weekly sessions. *Journal of Consulting and Clinical Psychology, 71*, 394–398.

Abramowitz, J. S., Franklin, M. E., Schwartz, S. A., & Furr, J. M. (2003). Symptom presentation and outcome of cognitive-behavioral therapy for obsessive-compulsive disorder. *Journal of Consulting and Clinical Psychology, 71*, 1049–1057.

Abramson, J. L., Williams, S. A., Krumholz, H. M., & Vaccarino, V. (2001). Moderate alcohol consumption and risk of heart failure among older persons. *Journal of the American Medical Association, 285*, 1971–1977.

Achenbach, T. M., & Dumenci, L. (2001). Levent Advances in empirically based assessment: Revised cross-informant syndromes and new *DSM*-oriented scales for the CBCL, YSR, and TRF: Comment on Lengua, Sadowski, Friedrich, and Fisher (2001). *Journal of Consulting and Clinical Psychology, 69*, 699–702.

Achenbach, T. M., & Edelbrock, C. S. (1979). The Child Behavior Profile: I. Boys aged 12–16 and girls aged 6–11 and 12–16. *Journal of Consulting and Clinical Psychology, 47*, 223–233.

Achenbach, T. M., Krukowski, R. A., Dumenci, L., Ivanova, M. Y., & Masha Y. (2005). Assessment of adult psychopathology: meta-analyses and implications of cross-informant correlations. *Psychological Bulletin, 131*, 361–382.

Ackerman, S. J., & Hilsenroth, M. J. (2003). A review of therapist characteristics and techniques positively impacting the therapeutic alliance. *Clinical Psychology Review, 23*, 1–33.

Acklin, M. W., et al. (2000). Interobserver agreement, intraobserver reliability, and the Rorschach comprehensive system. *Journal of Personality Assessment, 74*, 15–47.

Adam, M. B., McGuire, H. J., Walsh, M., Basta, J., & LeCroy, C. (2005). Acculturation as a predictor of the onset of sexual intercourse among Hispanic and white teens. *Archives of Pediatrics & Adolescent Medicine, 159*, 261–265.

Addis, M. E. (2002). Methods for disseminating research products and increasing evidence-based practice: promises, obstacles, and future directions. *Clinical Psychology: Science and Practice, 9*, 367–378.

Addis, M. E., Hatgis, C., Krasnow, A. D., Jacob, K., Bourne, L., & Mansfield, A. (2004). Effectiveness of cognitive–behavioral treatment for panic disorder versus treatment as usual in a managed care setting. *Journal of Consulting and Clinical Psychology, 72*, 625–635.

Addolorato, G., Leggio, L., Abenavoli, L., Gasbarrini, G., and on behalf of the Alcoholism Treatment Study Group (2005). Neurobiochemical and clinical aspects of craving in alcohol addiction: A review. *Addictive Behaviors, 30*, 1209–1224.

Adelson, R. (2006a, January). Cultural factors in alcohol abuse. *Monitor on Psychology, 37*, p. 32.

Adelson, R. (2006b, January). Nationwide survey spotlights U.S. alcohol abuse. *Monitor on Psychology, 37*, pp. 30–32.

Ader, R., Felten, D. L., & Cohen, N. (2001). *Psychoneuroimmunology* (3rd ed.). New York: Academic Press.

Adler, J. (2004, March 8). The war on strokes. *Newsweek*, 42–48.

Agras, W. S., et al. (2000a). A multicenter comparison of cognitive-behavioral therapy and interpersonal psychotherapy for bulimia nervosa. *Archives of General Psychiatry, 57*, 459–466.

Agras, W. S., et al. (2000b). Outcome predictors for the cognitive behavior treatment of bulimia nervosa: Data from a multisite study. *American Journal of Psychiatry, 157*, 1302–1308.

Ahluwalia, J. S., Harris, K. J., Catley, D., Okuyemi, K. S., & Mayo, M. S. (2002). Sustained release bupropion for smoking cessation in African Americans: A randomized controlled trial. *Journal of the American Medical Association, 288*, 468–474.

Ainsworth, M. D. S. (1989). Attachments beyond infancy. *American Psychologist, 44*, 709–716.

Akhtar, A. (1987). Schizoid personality disorder: A synthesis of developmental, dynamic, and descriptive features. *American Journal of Psychotherapy, 41*, 499–517.

Akhtar, S. (1988). Four culture-bound psychiatric syndromes in India. *The International Journal of Social Psychiatry, 34*, 70–74.

Akhtar, S. (2003). Things: Developmental, psychopathological, and technical aspects of inaminate objects. *Canadian Journal of Psychoanalysis, 11*, 1–44.

Akiskal, H. S., & Benazzi, F. (2006). The *DSM-IV* and *ICD-10* categories of recurrent [major] depressive and bipolar II disorders: Evidence that they lie on a dimensional spectrum. *Journal of Affective Disorders, 92*, 45–54.

Alao, A. O., & Dewan, M. J. (2001). Evaluating the tolerability of the newer mood stabilizers. *Journal of Nervous & Mental Disease, 189*, 60–63.

Albarracin, D., Durantini, M. R., & Ear, A. (2006). Empirical and theoretical conclusions of an analysis of outcomes of HIV-prevention interventions. *Current Directions in Psychological Science, 15*, 73–78.

Aldrich, M. S. (1992). Narcolepsy. *Neurology, 42*(7, Suppl. 6), 34–43.

Aleman, A., Kahn, R. S., & Selten, J.-P. (2003). Sex differences in the risk of schizophrenia: Evidence from meta-analysis. *Archives of General Psychiatry, 60*, 565–571.

Allderidge, P. (1979). Hospitals, madhouses and asylums: Cycles in the care of the insane. *British Journal of Psychiatry, 134*, 1476–1478.

Allen, G., & Courchesne, E. (2003). Differential effects of developmental cerebellar abnormality on cognitive and motor functions in the cerebellum: An fMRI study of autism. *American Journal of Psychiatry, 160*, 262–273.

Allen, M. H., Hirschfeld, R. M., Wozniak, P. J., Baker, J. D., & Bowden, C. L. (2006). Linear relationship of valproate serum concentration to response and optimal serum levels for acute mania. *American Journal of Psychiatry, 163*, 272–275.

Allgulander, C., Dahl, A. A., Austin, C., Morris, P. L. P., Sogaard, J. A., Fayyad, R., et al. (2005). Efficacy of sertraline in a 12-week trial for generalized anxiety disorder. *American Journal of Psychiatry, 161*, 1642–1649.

Alloy, L. B., Abramson, L. Y., Urosevic, S., Walshaw, P. D., Nusslock, R., & Neeren, A. M. (2005). The psychosocial context of bipolar disorder: Environmental, cognitive, and developmental risk factors. *Clinical Psychology Review, 25*, 1043–1075.

Alloy, L. B., et al. (2000). The Temple-Wisconsin cognitive vulnerability to depression project: Lifetime history of Axis I psychopathology in individuals at high and low cognitive risk for depression. *Journal of Abnormal Psychology, 109*, 403–418.

Alter, J. (2001, February 12). The war on addiction. *Newsweek*, 36–39.

Altman, L. K. (1994, February 22). Stomach microbe offers clues to cancer as well as ulcers. *The New York Times*, C3.

Altschuler, E. L., Haroun, A., Ho, B., & Weimer, A. (2001). Did Samson have antisocial personality disorder? *Archives of General Psychiatry, 58*, 202.

Alzheimer's vaccine passes key test. (2001, July 23). *CNN Web Posting.* Retrieved July 25, 2001, from http://www.cnn.com/2001/HEALTH/07/23/alzheimers.vaccine/index.html.

American Cancer Society. (2004). *Questions about smoking, tobacco, and health.* Retrieved May 5, 2004, from http://www.cancer.org/docroot/PED/content/PED_10_2x_Questions_About_Smoking_Tobacco_and_Health.asp.

American Law Institute. (1962). Model penal code: Proposed official draft. Philadelphia: Author.

American Psychiatric Association. (1994). *DSM-IV: Diagnostic and statistical manual of mental disorders* (4th ed.). Washington, DC: Author.

American Psychiatric Association. (1998). *Fact sheet: Violence and mental illness.* Washington, DC: Author.

American Psychiatric Association. (2000). *DSM-IV-TR: Diagnostic and statistical manual of mental disorders* (4th ed., text revision). Washington, DC: Author.

American Psychological Association (APA) (1978). Report of the Task Force on the Role of Psychology in the Criminal Justice System. *American Psychologist, 33*, 1099–1113.

American Psychological Association (APA) (2002). Ethical principles of psychologists and code of conduct. *American Psychologist, 57*, 1060–1073.

American Psychological Association (2003). A guide for including information on HIV/AIDS in graduate courses in psychology. *APA Online.* Retrieved January 14, 2004 from http://www.apa.org/pi/aids/toc.html.

Amering, M., & Katschnig, H. (1990). Panic attacks and panic disorder in cross-cultural perspective. *Psychiatric Annals, 20*, 511–516.

Ames, M. A., & Houston, D. A. (1990). Legal, social, and biological definitions of pedophilia. *Archives of Sexual Behavior, 19*, 333–342.

Amminger, G. P., Pape, S., Rock, D., Roberts, S. A., Ott, S. L., Squires-Wheeler, E., et al. (1999). Relationship between childhood behavioral disturbance and later schizophrenia in the New York High-Risk Project. *American Journal of Psychiatry, 156*, 525–530.

Ancoli-Israel, S., Klauber, M. R., Butters, N., Parker, L., & Kripke, D. F. (1991). Dementia in institutionalized elderly: Relation to sleep apnea. *Journal of the American Geriatrics Society, 39*, 258–263.

Anderluh, M. B., Tchanturia, K., Rabe-Hesketh, S., & Treasure, J. (2003). Childhood obsessive–compulsive personality traits in adult women with eating disorders: Defining a broader eating disorder phenotype. *American Journal of Psychiatry, 160*, 242–247.

Andersen, B. L. (1992). Psychological interventions for cancer patients to enhance the quality of life. *Journal of Consulting and Clinical Psychology, 60*, 552–568.

Andersen, B. L. (2002). Biobehavioral outcomes following psychological interventions for cancer patients. *Journal of Consulting and Clinical Psychology, 70*, 590–610.

Andersen, B. L., Golden-Kreutz, D. M., & DiLillo, V. (2001). Cancer. In A. Baum, T. A. Revenson, & J. E. Singer (Eds.), *Handbook of health psychology* (pp. 709–726). Mahwah, NJ: Lawrence Erlbaum Associates.

Anderson, D. Q., & Maloney, K. C. (2001). The efficacy of cognitive–behavioral therapy on the core symptoms of bulimia nervosa. *Clinical Psychology Review, 21*, 971–988.

Anderson, E. M., & Lambert, M. J. (1995). Short-term dynamic ally oriented psychotherapy: A review and meta-analysis. *Clinical Psychology Review, 15*, 503–514.

Anderson, E. M., & Lambert, M. J. (2001). A survival analysis of clinically significant change in outpatient psychotherapy. *Journal of Clinical Psychology, 57*, 875–888.

Anderson, J. W. (2003). "Mr. Psychoanalysis" breaks with Freud. *Contemporary Psychology: APA Review of Books, 48*, 855–857.

Anderson, L. P. (1991). Acculturative stress: A theory of relevance to Black Americans. *Clinical Psychology Review, 11*, 685–702.

Anderson, R. A., & Rees, C. S. (2006). Group versus individual cognitive-behavioural treatment for obsessive-compulsive disorder: A controlled trial. *Behaviour Research and Therapy, 45*, 123–137.

Anderson, S. W., & Booker, M. B., Jr. (2006). Cognitive behavioral therapy versus psychosurgery for refractory obsessive-compulsive disorder. *Journal of Neuropsychiatry & Clinical Neurosciences, 18*, 129.

Andersson, G., Carlbring, P., Holmström, A., Sparthan, E., Furmark, T., et al. (2006). Internet-based self-help with therapist feedback and in vivo group exposure for social phobia: A randomized controlled trial. *Journal of Consulting and Clinical Psychology, 74*, 677–686.

Andreasen, A. (2003). From molecule to mind: Genetics, genomics, and psychiatry. *American Journal of Psychiatry, 160*, 613. [Editorial]

Andrews, B., Brewin, C. R., Rose, S., & Kirk, M. (2000). Predicting PTSD symptoms in victims of violent crime: The role of shame, anger, and childhood abuse. *Journal of Abnormal Psychology, 109*, 69–73.

Andrews, E. L. (1997, September 9). In Germany, humble herb is a rival to Prozac. *The New York Times*, pp. C1, C7.

Angier, N. (1991, August 4). Kids who can't sit still. *The New York Times*, Section 4A, pp. 30–33.

Angier, N. (1999). *Woman: An intimate geography.* Boston: Houghton Mifflin.

Angier, N. (2000a, July 21). Study finds region of brain may be key problem solver. *The New York Times*, pp. C1, C4.

Angier, N. (2000b, November 7). Who is fat? It depends on culture. *The New York Times*, pp. F1–F2.

Angier, N. (2003, February 25). Not just genes: Moving beyond nature vs. nurture. *The New York Times*, pp. F1, F10.

Angold, A., & Costello, E. J. (1993). Depressive comorbidity in children and adolescents: Empirical, theoretical, and methodological issues. *American Journal of Psychiatry, 150*, 1779–1791.

Angold, A., & Costello, J. (1996). Toward establishing an empirical basis for the diagnosis of oppositional defiant disorder. *Journal of the American Academy of Child and Adolescent Psychiatry, 35*, 1205–1212.

Anonymous. (1985, June 13). Schizophrenia—A mother's agony over her son's pain. *Chicago Tribune*, Section 5, pp. 1–3.

Another worry for aging baby boomers—pot and their hearts. (2000, March 3). *CNN Web Posting.* Retrieved March 13, 2000, from www.canoe.ca/Health0003/03_pot.html.

Ansell, B. J. (2001, January 9). Fearing one fate, women ignore a killer. *The New York Times*, p. F8.

Anthony, J. C., & Helzer, J. E. (1991). Syndromes of drug abuse and dependence. In L. N. Robins & D. A. Regier (Eds.), *Psychiatric disorders in America: The epidemiologic catchment area study* (pp. 116–154). New York: The Free Press.

Anthony, J. C., Warner, L. A., & Kessler, R. C. (1994). Comparative epidemiology of dependence on tobacco, alcohol, controlled substances, and inhalants: Basic findings from the National Comorbidity Survey. *Experimental and Clinical Psychopharmacology, 2*, 244–268.

Anthony, J. L., & Francis, D. J. (2005). Development of phonological awareness. *Current Directions in Psychological Science, 14*, 255–259.

Anthony, W. A., & Liberman, R. P. (1986). The practice of psychiatric rehabilitation: Historical, conceptual, and research base. *Schizophrenia Bulletin, 12*, 542–559.

Antidepressants may be tied to modest suicide risk in children. (2006, March 7). *PsycPort.com.* Retrieved March 16, 2006, from http://www.psycport.com/showArticle.cfm?xmlFile=nytsyn%5F2006%5F03%5F07%5Fmedic%5F3445%2D0007%2Dpat%5Fnytimes%2Exml&provider=New%20York%20Times%20Syndicate.

Anton, R. F., Moak, D. H., Latham, P., K., Waid, L. R., Malcolm, R. J., Dias, J. K., et al. (2001). Posttreatment results of combining naltrexone with cognitive-behavior therapy for the treatment of alcoholism. *Journal of Clinical Psychopharmacology, 21*, 72–77.

Anton, R. F., O'Malley, S. S., Ciraulo, D. A., Cisler, R. A., Couper, D., Donovan, D. M. et al. (2006). Combined pharmacotherapies and behavioral interventions for alcohol dependence. The COMBINE Study: A randomized controlled trial. *Journal of the American Medical Association, 295*, 2003–2017.

Antonarakas, S. E., et al. (1991). Prenatal origin of the extra chromosome trisomy 21 as indicated by analysis of DNA polymorphisms. *The New England Journal of Medicine, 324*, 872–876.

Antoni, M. H., Levine, J., Tischer, P., Green, C., & Millon, T. (1986). Refining personality assessments by combining MCMI high-point profiles and MMPI codes: IV. MMPI 89/98. *Journal of Personality Assessment, 50*, 65–72.

Antony, M. M., Ledley, D. R., Liss, A., & Swinson, R. P. (2006). Responses to symptom induction exercises in panic disorder. *Behaviour Research and Therapy, 44*, 85–98.

Anxiety: Most common mental health problem. (2000, February 2). *CNN Web Posting.* Retrieved February 4, 2000, from www.cnn.com/2000/HEALTH/02/02/mental.health.wmd/.

APA Task Force on Evidence-Based Practice. (2006). Evidence-based practice in psychology. *American Psychologist, 61*, 271–285.

Apopolinario, J. C., et al. (2003). A randomized, double-blind, placebo-controlled study of sibutramine in the treatment of binge-eating disorder. *Archives of General Psychiatry, 60*, 1109–1116.

Appelbaum, P. S. (2003). Dangerous persons, moral panic, and the uses of psychiatry. *Psychiatric Services, 54*, 441–442.

Arango, C., Kirkpatrick, B., & Buchanan, R. W. (2000). Neurological signs and the heterogeneity of schizophrenia. *American Journal of Psychiatry, 157*, 566–572.

Arbisi, P. A., Ben-Porath, Y., S., & McNulty, J. A. (2002). A comparison of MMPI-2 validity in African American and Caucasian psychiatric inpatients. *Psychological Assessment, 14*, 3–15.

Arena, K., & Frieden, T. (2003, December 17). Judge grants Hinckley unsupervised visits with his parents. Retrieved December 17, 2003, from http://www.cnn.com/2003/LAW/12/17/hinckley.decision/index.html.

Arieti, S. (1974). *Interpretation of schizophrenia* (2nd ed.). New York: Basic Books.

Armfield, J. M. (2006). Cognitive vulnerability: A model of the etiology of fear. *Clinical Psychology Review, 26*, 746–768.

Arnett, P. A. (1997). Autonomic responsivity in psychopaths: A critical review and theoretical proposal. *Clinical Psychology Review, 17*, 903–936.

Arnett, P. A., Smith, S. S., & Newman, J. P. (1997). Approach and avoidance motivation in psychopathic criminal offenders during passive avoidance. *Journal of Personality and Social Psychology, 72*, 1413–1428.

Arnold, L. E., Elliott, M., Sachs, L., Bird, H., Kraemer, H. C., Wells, K. C., et al. (2003). Effects of ethnicity on treatment attendance, stimulant response/dose, and 14-month outcome in ADHD. *Journal of Consulting and Clinical Psychology, 71*, 713–727.

Arnold, P. D., Sicard, T., Burroughs, E., Richter, M. A., & Kennedy, J. L. (2006). Glutamate transporter gene slc1a1 associated with obsessive-compulsive disorder. *Archives of General Psychiatry, 63*, 769–776.

Arnow, B., Kenardy, J., & Agras, W. S. (1992). Binge eating among the obese: A descriptive study. *Journal of Behavioral Medicine, 15*, 155–170.

Arnulf, I., Merino-Andreu, M., Perrier, A., Birolleau, S., Similowski, T., Derenne, J.-P., et al. (2002). Obstructive sleep apnea and venous thromboembolism. *Journal of the American Medical Association, 287*.

Aronson, M. K. (1988). Patients and families: Impact and long-term-management implications. In M. K. Aronson (Ed.), *Understanding Alzheimer's disease* (pp. 74–78). New York: Charles Scribners Sons.

Arron, J. R., Winslow, M. M., Polleri, A., Chang, C., Wu, H., Gao, X., et al. (2006). NFAT dysregulation by increased dosage of DSCR1 and DYRK1A on chromosome 21. *Nature, 441*, 595–600.

Arseneault, L., et al. (2002). Cannabis use in adolescence and risk for adult psychosis: Longitudinal prospective study. *British Medical Journal, 325*, 1212–1213.

Artaloytia, J. F., Arango, C., Lahti, A., Sanz, J., Pascual, A., Cubero, P., et al. (2006). Negative signs and symptoms secondary to antipsychotics: A double-blind, randomized trial of a single dose of placebo, haloperidol, and risperidone in healthy volunteers. *American Journal of Psychiatry, 163*, 488–493.

Asaad, G., & Shapiro, B. (1986). Hallucinations: Theoretical and clinical overview. *American Journal of Psychiatry, 143*, 1088–1097.

Asarnow, R. F., et al. (1991). Span of apprehension in schizophrenia. In J. Zubin, S. Steinhauer, & J. Gruzelier (Eds.), *Handbook of schizophrenia: Vol. 5. Neuropsychology, psychophysiology, and information-processing* (pp. 353–370). Amsterdam: Elsevier Science.

Ashton, A. K., Ahrens, K., Gupta, S., & Masand, P. S. (2000). Antidepressant-induced sexual dysfunction and ginkgo biloba. *American Journal of Psychiatry, 157*, 836–837.

Ashton, C. H. (2001). Pharmacology and effects of cannabis: A brief review. *British Journal of Psychiatry, 178*, 101–106.

Attention disorder linked with drug abuse. (2003, August 18). Retrieved September 12, 2003, from http://www.cnn.com/2003/HEALTH/parenting/08/18/adhd.study.reut/index.html.

Audrain-McGovern, J., Lerman, C., Wileyto, E. P., Rodriguez, D., & Shields, P. G. (2004). Interacting effects of genetic predisposition and depression on adolescent smoking progression. *American Journal of Psychiatry, 161*, 1224–1230.

Augusto, A., et al. (1996). Post-natal depression in an urban area of Portugal: Comparison of childbearing women and matched controls. *Psychological Medicine, 26*, 135–141.

Ault, A. (2004, February 10). Federal panel hears testimony on vaccinations and autism. *The New York Times,* p. A20.

Auranen, M., Vanhala, R., Varilo, T., Ayers, K., Kempas, E. A., Ylisaukko-oja, T., et al. (2002). Genomewide screen for autism-spectrum disorders: evidence for a major susceptibility locus on chromosome 3q25–27. *American Journal of Human Genetics, 71*, 777–790.

Autism rate about 1 in 150, higher than previous estimates. (2007, February 8). Retrieved February 9, 2007, from http://www.cnn.com/2007/HEALTH/conditions/02/08/autism.prevalence.ap/index.html.

Avery, D. H., Holtzheimerii, P. E., Fawaz, W., Russo, J., et al. (2006). A controlled study of repetitive transcranial magnetic stimulation in medication-resistant major depression. *Biological Psychiatry, 59*, 187–194.

Ayoub, C. C., Alexander, R., Beck, D., et al., & the APSAC Taskforce on Münchausen by Proxy, Definitions Working Group. (2002). Position paper: Definitional issues in Münchausen by proxy. *Child Maltreatment, 7*, 105–112.

Azrin, N. H., & Peterson, A. L. (1989). Reduction of an eye tick by controlled blinking. *Behavior Therapy, 20*, 467–473.

B

Babiak, P., & Hare, R. D. (2006). Snakes in suits: When psychopaths go to work . New York: HarperBusiness.

Babulas, V., Factor-Litvak, P., Goetz, R., Schaefer, C. A., & Brown, A. S. (2006). Prenatal exposure to maternal genital and reproductive infections and adult schizophrenia. *American Journal of Psychiatry, 163*, 927–929.

Bachmann, G., Bancroft, J., Braunstein, G., Burger, H., Davis, S., Dennerstein, L., Goldstein, I., et al. (2002). Female androgen insufficiency: The Princeton consensus statement on definition, classification, and assessment. *Fertility and Sterility, 77*, 660–665.

Bäckman, L., & Forsell, Y. (1994). Episodic memory functioning in a community-based sample of old adults with major depression: Utilization of cognitive support. *Journal of Abnormal Psychology, 103*, 361–370.

Baer, L., Rauch, S. L., Ballantine, H. T., Jr., Martuza, R., Cosgrove, R., Cassem, E., et al. (1995). Cingulotomy for intractable obsessive-compulsive disorder: Prospective long-term follow-up of 18 patients. *Archives of General Psychiatry, 52*, 384–392.

Baer, R. A. (2003). Mindfulness training as a clinical intervention: A conceptual and empirical review. *Clinical Psychology: Science and Practice, 10*, 125–143.

Bagary, M. S., Symms, M. R., Barker, G. J., Mutsatsa, S. H., Joyce, E. M., & Ron, M. A. (2003). Gray and white matter brain abnormalities in first-episode schizophrenia inferred from magnetization transfer imaging. *Archives of General Psychiatry, 60*, 779–788.

Bagby, R. M., Nicholson, R., & Buis, T. (1998). Effectiveness of the MMPI-2 validity indicators. *Journal of Personality Assessment, 70*, 405–415.

Bagge, C., Nickell, A., Stepp, S., Durrett, C., Jackson, K., & Trull, T. J. (2004). Borderline persoanlity disorder features predict negative outcomes 2 years later. *Journal of Abnormal Psychology, 113*, 279–288.

Bagley, C., & D'Augelli, A. R. (2000). Suicidal behaviour in gay, lesbian, and bisexual youth. *British Medical Journal, 320*, 1617–1618.

Bailar, J. C., III. (2001). The powerful placebo and the wizard of Oz. *New England Journal of Medicine, 344*, 1630–1632.

Bailey, D. S. (2003a, November). The "Sylvia Plath" effect. *Monitor on Psychology, 34*, 42–43.

Bailey, D. S. (2003b, October). *Monitor on Psychology, 34*, p. 20.

Bailey, J. M. (1999). Homosexuality and mental illness. *Archives of General Psychiatry, 56*, 883–884.

Bailey, J. M. (2003a). Personal communication.

Bailey, J. M. (2003b). *The man who would be queen: The science of gender-bending and transsexualism.* Washington, DC: Joseph Henry Press.

Bain, J. (2002, April 30). New treatments may help control sleep apnea. *New York Times Online.* Retrieved May 3, 2002, from http://www.nytimes.com/2002/04/30/health/30APNE.html.

Baity, M. R., & Hilsenroth, M. J. (2002). Rorschach aggressive content (AgC) variable: A study of criterion validity. *Journal of Personality Assessment, 78*, 275–287.

Bakalard, N. (2006, April 18). Research ties lack of sleep to risk for hypertension. *The New York Times,* p. F7.

Baker, R. C., & Kirschenbaum, D. S. (1993). Self-monitoring may be necessary for successful weight control. *Behavior Therapy, 24*, 377–394.

Baldessarini, R. J., & Tondo, L. (2000). Does lithium treatment still work? Evidence of stable responses over three decades. *Archives of General Psychiatry, 57*, 187–190.

Baldessarini, R. J., & Tondo, M. D. (2003). Suicide risk and treatments for patients with bipolar disorder. *Journal of the American Medical Association, 290*, 1517–1519.

Baldessarini, R. J., Tohen, M., & Tondo, L. (2000). Maintenance treatment in bipolar disorder. *Archives of General Psychiatry, 57*, 490–492.

Baldeweg, T., et al. (1997). Neurophysiological changes associa ted with psychiatric symptoms in HIV-infected individuals without AIDS. *Biological Psychiatry, 41*, 474–487.

Ballie, R. (2002, January). Kay Redfield Jamison receives $500,000 "genius award." *Monitor on Psychology.* Retrieved March, 15, 2003, from http://www.apa.org/monitor/jan02/redfield.html.

Baltimore, D. (2000, June 25). 50,000 genes, and we know them all (almost). *The New York Times,* Section 4, p. 17.

Bancroft, J., Carnes, L. Janssen, E., Goodrich, D., & Long, J. S. (2005a). Erectile and ejaculatory problems in gay and heterosexual men. *Archives of Sexual Behavior, 34*, 285–297.

Bancroft, J., et al. (2005b). The relevance of the dual control model to male sexual dysfunction: The Kinsey Institute/BASRT collaborative project. *Sexual & Relationship Therapy, 20*, 13–30.

Bancroft, J., Loftus, J., & Long, J. S. (2003). Distress about sex: A national survey of women in heterosexual relationships. *Archives of Sexual Behavior, 32*, 193–208.

Bandura, A. (1982). Self-efficacy mechanism in human agency. *American Psychologist, 37*, 122–147.

Bandura, A. (1986). *Social foundations of thought and action: A social-cognitive theory.* Englewood Cliffs, NJ: Prentice Hall.

Bandura, A. (2001). Social cognitive theory: An agentic perspective. *Annual Review of Psychology, 52*, 1–26.

Bandura, A. (2004). Swimming against the mainstream: The early years from chilly tributary to transformative mainstream. *Behaviour Research and Therapy, 42*, 613–630.

Bandura, A., Barr-Taylor, C., Williams, S. L., Mefford, I. N., & Barchas, J. D. (1985). Catecholamine secretion as a function of perceived coping self-efficacy. *Journal of Consulting and Clinical Psychology, 53*, 406–414.

Bandura, A., Jeffery, R. W., & Wright, C. L. (1974). Efficacy of participant modeling as a function of response induction aids. *Journal of Abnormal Psychology, 83*, 56–64.

Bandura, A., Ross, S. A., & Ross, D. (1963). Imitation of film-mediated aggressive models. *Journal of Abnormal and Social Psychology, 66*, 3–11.

Barbaree, H. E., & Marshall, W. L. (1991). The role of male sexual arousal in rape: Six models. *Journal of Consulting and Clinical Psychology, 59*, 621–631.

Barber, J., Connolly, M. B., Crits-Christoph, P., Gladis, L., & Siqueland, L. (2000). Alliance predicts patients' outcome beyond in-treatment change in symptoms. *Journal of Consulting and Clinical Psychology, 68*, 1027–1032.

Barber, M. E., et al. (1998). Aborted suicide attempts: A new classification of suicidal behavior. *American Journal of Psychiatry, 155*, 385–389.

Barch, D. M. (2003). Cognition in schizophrenia: Does working memory work? *Current Directions in Psychological Science, 12*, 146–150.

Barch, D. M., & Csernansky, J. G. (2007). Abnormal parietal cortex activation during working memory in schizophrenia: Verbal phonological coding disturbances versus domain-general executive dysfunction. *American Journal of Psychiatry, 164*, 1090–1098.

Barch, D. M., Carter, C. S., Braver, T. S., Sabb, F. W., MacDonald, A. III, Noll, D. C., et al. (2001). Selective deficits in prefrontal cortex function in medication-naive patients with schizophrenia. *Archives of General Psychiatry, 58*, 280–288.

Barclay, L., & Vega, C. (2006, July 7). Varenicline may be more effective than bupropion for smoking cessation *Medscape Medical News.* Retrieved August 17, 2006, from http://www.medscape.com/viewarticle/540203.

Bardone-Cone, A. M., Author, L. Y., Abramson, K. D., Vohs, T. F. Heatherton, T. F., & Joiner, T. E., Jr. (2006). Predicting bulimic symptoms: An interactive model of self-efficacy, perfectionism, and perceived weight status. *Behaviour Research and Therapy, 44*, 27–42.

Bardwell, W. A., Moore, P., Ancoli-Israel, S., & Dimsdale, J. E. (2003). Fatigue in obstructive sleep apnea: Driven by depressive symptoms instead of apnea severity? *American Journal of Psychiatry, 160*, 350–355.

Barefoot, J. C., Mortensen, E. L., Helms, M. J., Avlund, K., & Schroll, M. (2001). A longitudinal study of gender differences in depressive symptoms from age 50 to 80. *Psychology and Aging, 16*, 342–345.

Barkham, M., Rees, A., Stiles, W. B., Shapiro, D. A., Hardy, G. E., & Reynolds, S. (1996). Dose-effect relations in limited psychotherapy for depression. *Journal of Consulting and Clinical Psychology, 64*, 927–935.

Barkley claims gambling problem has cost him $10M (2006, May 5). *ESPN.com News Service*. Retrieved December 6, 2006, from http://sports.espn.go.com/nba/news/story?id=2432043.

Barkley, R. A. (2001). Executive function and ADHD: A reply. *Journal of the American Academy of Child & Adolescent Psychiatry, 40*, 501–502.

Barlow, D. H., Esler, J. L., & Vitali, A. E. (1998). Psychosocial treatments for panic disorders, phobias, and generalized anxiety disorder. In P. E. Nathan & J. M. Gorman (Eds.), *A guide to treatments that work* (pp. 288–318). New York: Oxford University Press.

Barlow, D. H., Gorman, J. M., Shear, M. K., & Woods, S. W. (2000). Cognitive-behavioral therapy, imipramine, or their combination for panic disorder: A Randomized controlled trial. *Journal of the American Medical Association, 283*, 2529–2536.

Barnett, W. S., & Escobar, C. M. (1990). Economic costs and benefits of early intervention. In S. J. Meisels & J. P. Shonkoff (Eds.), *Handbook of early childhood intervention* (pp. 560–582). New York: Cambridge University Press.

Baron-Cohen, S., Knickmeyer, R. C., & Belmonte, M. K. (2005). Sex differences in the brain: implications for explaining autism. *Science, 310*, 819–823.

Barrera, M., Jr., & Sandler, I. N. (2006). Prevention: A report of progress and momentum into the future. *Clinical Psychology: Science and Practice, 13*, 221–226.

Barrett, P. M., et al. (2001). Cognitive-behavioral treatment of anxiety disorders in children: Long-term (6-year) follow-up. *Journal of Consulting and Clinical Psychology, 69*, 135–141.

Barron, J., & Barron, S. (2002). *There's a boy in here.* Arlington, TX: Future Horizons.

Barrowclough, C., Tarrier, N., Humphreys, L., Ward, J., Gregg, L., & Andrews, B. (2003). Self-esteem in schizophrenia: relationships between self-evaluation, family attitudes, and symptomatology. *Journal of Abnormal Psychology, 112*, 92–99.

Barry, C. T., et al. (2000). The importance of callous–unemotional traits for extending the concept of psychopathy to children. *Journal of Abnormal Psychology, 109*, 335–340.

Barry, D. T., & Grilo, C. M. (2002). Cultural, psychological, and demographic correlates of willingness to use psychological services among East Asian immigrants. *Journal of Nervous & Mental Disease, 190*, 32–39.

Barsky, A. J., & Ahern, D. K. (2004). Cognitive behavior therapy for hypochondriasis: A randomized controlled trial. *Journal of the American Medical Association, 291*, 1464–1470.

Barsky, A. J., Ahern, D. K., Bailey, E. D., Saintfort, R., Liu, E. B., & Peekna, H. M. (2001). Hypochondriacal patients' appraisal of health and physical risks. *American Journal of Psychiatry, 158*, 783–787.

Barsky, A. J., Fama, J. M., Bailey, E. D., & Ahern, D. K. (1998). A prospective 4- to 5-year study of *DSM-III-R* hypochondriasis. *Archives of General Psychiatry, 55*, 737–744.

Barsky, A. J., Orav, E. J., & Bates, D. W. (2005) Somatization increases medical utilization and costs independent of psychiatric and medical comorbidity. *Archives of General Psychiatry, 62*, 903–910.

Barsky, A. J., Wool, C., Barnett, M. C., & Cleary, P. D. (1994). Histories of childhood trauma in adult hypochondriacal patients. *American Journal of Psychiatry, 151*, 397–401.

Barsky, A. J., Wyshak, G., & Klerman, G. L. (1992). Psychiatric comorbidity in *DSM-III-R* hypochondriasis. *Archives of General Psychiatry, 49*, 101–108.

Bartholow, B. D., & Heinz, A. (2006). Alcohol and aggression without consumption alcohol cues, aggressive thoughts, and hostile perception bias. *Psychological Science, 17*, 30–37.

Bartzokis, G., Lu, P. H., Geschwind, D. H., Edwards, N., Mintz, J., & Cummings, J. L. (2006). Apolipoprotein E genotype and age-related myelin breakdown in healthy individuals: Implications for cognitive decline and dementia. *Archives of General Psychiatry, 63*, 63–72.

Basch, M. F. (1980). *Doing psychotherapy.* New York: Basic Books.

Basile, K. C. (2002). Attitudes toward wife rape: Effects of social background and victim status. *Violence & Victims, 17*(3), 341–354.

Bassman, R. (2005). Mental Illness and the freedom to refuse treatment: Privilege or right. *Professional Psychology: Research and Practice, 36*, 488–497.

Bastien, C. H., Morin, C. M., Ouellet, M.-C., Blais, F. C., & Bouchard, S. (2004). Cognitive-behavioral therapy for insomnia: Comparison of individual therapy, group therapy, and telephone consultations. *Journal of Consulting and Clinical Psychology, 72*, 653–659.

Bateman, A. B., & Fonagy, P. (2001). Treatment of borderline personality disorder with psychoanalytically oriented partial hospitalization: An 18-month follow-up. *American Journal of Psychiatry, 158*, 36–42.

Bateson, G. D., Jackson, D., Haley, J., & Weakland, J. (1956). Toward a theory of schizophrenia. *Behavioral Science, 1*, 251–264.

Battaglia, M., Bernardeschi, L., Franchini, L., Bellodi, L., & Smeraldi, E. (1995). A family study of schizotypal disorder. *Schizophrenia Bulletin, 21*, 33–45.

Bauchner, H. (2003, December 23). Response to medication differs for adhd subtypes. *Journal Watch Psychiatry*. Retrieved December 24, 2003, from http://psychiatry.jwatch.org/cgi/content/full/2003/1223/10?q=etoc.

Bauer, A. Rosca, P., Khawalled, R., Gruzniewski, A., & Grinshpoon, A. (2003). Dangerousness and risk assessment: The state of the art. *Israeli Journal of Psychiatry and Related Sciences, 40*, 182–190.

Bauer, M. S., & Mitchner, L. (2004). What is a "mood stabilizer"? An evidence-based response. *American Journal of Psychiatry, 161*, 3–18.

Baumeister, R. F., Catanese, K. R., & Vohs, K. D. (2001). Is there a gender difference in strength of sex drive? Theoretical views, conceptual distinctions, and a review of relevant evidence. *Personality & Social Psychology Review, 5*, 242–273.

Baumeister, R. F., Catanese, K. R., & Wallace, H. M. (2002). Conquest by force: A narcissistic reactance theory of rape and sexual coercion. *Review of General Psychology, 6*, 92–135.

Baxter, L. R., Jr. (2003). Basal ganglia systems in ritualistic social displays: Reptiles and humans; function and illness. *Physiology and Behavior, 79*, 451–460.

Bayer, B. A., Bubel, D., Jacobs, S. R., Knolls, M. L., Harwell, V. D., et al. (2002). Posttraumatic stress in women with breast cancer and their daughters. *American Journal of Family Therapy, 30*, 323–338.

Bazell, R. (2000, August 29). Cause of narcolepsy pinpointed. *MSNBC Web Posting*. Retrieved August 29, 2000, from http://www.msnbc.com/news/452884.asp.

Bazell, R., The Associated Press, & Reuters (2002, August 7). Hunger hormone may fight obesity: Natural chemical shown to make people feel full in buffet experiment. *MSNBC Web Posting*. Retrieved August 9, 2002, from http://www.msnbc.com/news/791118.asp.

Beals, J., Novins, D. K., Whitesell, N. R., Spicer, P., Mitchell, C. M., & Manson, S. M. (2005). Prevalence of mental disorders and utilization of mental health services in two American Indian reservation populations: mental health disparities in a national context. *American Journal of Psychiatry, 162*, 1723–1732.

Bean, J. L. (2002). Expressions of female sexuality. *Journal of Sex & Marital Therapy, 28* (Suppl 1), 29–38.

Beardslee, W. R., & Goldman. S. (2003, September 22). Living beyond sadness. *Newsweek*, p. 70.

Beauvais, F. (1998). American Indians and alcohol. *Alcohol Health and Research World, 22*, 253–259.

Bechdolf, A., Knost, B., Kuntermann, C., Schiller, S., Klosterkotter, J., Hambrecht, M., et al. (2004). A randomized comparison of group cognitive-behavioural therapy and group psychoeducation in patients with schizophrenia. *Acta Psychiatrica Scandinavica, 110*, 21–28.

Bechtoldt, H., Norcross, J. C., Wyckoff, L. A., Pokrywa, M. L., Campbell, L. F., et al. (2001, Winter). Theoretical orientations and employment settings of clinical and counseling psychologists: A comparative study. *Clinical Psychologist, 54*, 3–6.

Beck, A. T. (1976). *Cognitive therapy and the emotional disorders.* New York: International Universities Press.

Beck, A. T., & Clark, D. A. (1997). An information processing model of anxiety: Automatic and strategic processes. *Behaviour Research and Therapy, 35*, 49–58.

Beck, A. T., & Young, J. E. (1985). Depression. In D. H. Barlow (Ed.), *Clinical handbook of psychological disorders* (pp. 206–244). New York: Guilford Press.

Beck, A. T., Brown, G., Steer, R. A., Eidelson, J. I., & Riskind, J. H. (1987). Differentiating anxiety and depression: A test of the cognitive content-specificity hypothesis. *Journal of Abnormal Psychology, 96*, 179–183.

Beck, A. T., et al. (1990). Relationship between hopelessness and ultimate suicide: A replication with psychiatric outpatients. *American Journal of Psychiatry, 147*, 190–195.

Beck, A. T., Freeman, A., Davis, D. D., & Associates. (2003). *Cognitive therapy of personality disorders* (2nd ed.). New York: Guilford.

Beck, A. T., Rush, A. J., Shaw, B. F., & Emery, G. (1979). *Cognitive therapy of depression.* New York: Guilford Press.

Becker, D., & Lamb, S. (1994). Sex bias in the diagnosis of borderline personality disorder and posttraumatic stress disorder. *Professional Psychology: Research and Practice, 25*, 55–61.

Bedwell, J. S., Kamath, V., & Baksh, E. (2006). Comparison of three computer-administered cognitive tasks as putative endophenotypes of schizophrenia. *Schizophrenia Research, 88*, 36–46.

Begley, S. (1995, November 20). Lights of madness. *Newsweek*, pp. 76–77.

Begley, S. (2001, June 11). How it all starts inside your brain. *Newsweek*, pp. 40–42.

Behrman, A. (2002). *Electroboy: A memoir of mania.* New York: Random House.

Being fat at 40 cuts years off life. (2003, January 6). *CNN Web Posting*. Retrieved January 8, 2003, from http://www.cnn.com/2003n/HEALTH/diet.fitness/01/06/obesity.mortality/index.html.

Beitman, B. D., Goldfried, M. R., & Norcross, J. C. (1989). The movement toward integrating the psychotherapies: An overview. *American Journal of Psychiatry, 146*, 138–147.

Bejerot, S. (2003). Psychosurgery for obsessive-compulsive disorder—concerns remain. *Acta Psychiatrica Scandinavica, 107*, 241–243.

Belkin, L. (2005, May 22). Can you catch obsessive-compulsive disorder? *The New York Times Online*. Retrieved May 22, 2005, from http://www.nytimes.com/2005/05/22/magazine/22OCD. html?

Bell, A. P., & Weinberg, M. S. (1978). *Homosexualities: A study of diversity among men and women.* New York: Simon & Schuster.

Bell, M., Bryson, G., & Wexler, B. E. (2003). Cognitive remediation of working memory deficits: durability of training effects in severely impaired and less severely impaired schizophrenia. *Acta Psychiatrica Scandinavica, 108*, 101–109.

Bellack, A. S., & Mueser, K. T. (1990). Schizophrenia. In A. S. Bellack, M. Hersen, & A. E. Kazdin (Eds.), *International handbook of behavior modification and therapy* (2nd ed., pp. 353–370). New York: Plenum Press.

Bellack, A. S., & Mueser, K. T. (1993). Psychosocial treatment for schizophrenia. *Schizophrenia Bulletin, 19*, 317–336.

Bellack, A. S., Schooler, N. R., Marder, S. R., Kane, J. M., Brown, C. H., & Yang, Y. (2004). Do clozapine and risperidone affect social competence and problem solving? *American Journal of Psychiatry, 161*, 364–367.

Belluck, P. (2003, February 9). Methadone, once the way out, suddenly grows as a killer drug. *The New York Times*, pp. A1, A30.

Benazon, N. R. (2000). Predicting negative spousal attitudes toward depressed persons: A test of Coyne's interpersonal model. *Journal of Abnormal Psychology, 109*, 500–554.

Bender, L. (1938). A visual motor gestalt test and its clinical use. *Research Monograph of the American Orthopsychiatric Association, 3, XI*, 176.

Ben-Itzchak, E., & Zachor, D. A. (2006). The effects of intellectual functioning and autism severity on outcome of early behavioral intervention for children with autism. *Research in Developmental Disabilities*, in press.

Benjamin, L., & Wonderlich, S. A. (1994). Social perceptions and borderline personality disorder: The relation to mood disorders. *Journal of Abnormal Psychology, 103*, 610–624.

Bennett, D. (1985). Rogers: More intuition in therapy. *APA Monitor, 16*, p. 3.

Bennett, D., Sharpe, M., Freeman, C., & Carson, A. (2004). Anorexia nervosa among female secondary school students in Ghana. *British Journal of Psychiatry, 185*, 312–317.

Benowitz, N. L. (2002). Smoking cessation trials targeted to racial and economic minority groups. *New England Journal of Medicine, 344*, 1351–1357.

Benson, H. (1975). *The relaxation response.* New York: Morrow.

Benson, H., Manzetta, B. R., & Rosner, B. (1973). Decreased systolic blood pressure in hypertensive subjects who practiced meditation. *Journal of Clinical Investigation, 52*, 8.

Bentall, R. P. (1990). The illusion of reality: A review and integration of psychological research on hallucinations. *Psychological Bulletin, 107*, 82–95.

Bentall, R. P., Haddock, G., & Slade, P. (1994). Cognitive behavior therapy for persistent auditory hallucinations: From theory to therapy. *Behavior Therapy, 25*, 51–66.

Ben-Ya'acov, Y., & Amir, M. (2004). Posttraumatic symptoms and suicide risk. *Personality and Individual Differences, 36*, 1257–1264.

Berenbaum, H., & Fujita, F. (1994). Schizophrenia and personality: Exploring the boundaries and connections between vulnerability and outcome. *Journal of Abnormal Psychology, 103*, 148–158.

Berenbaum, H., & Oltmanns, T. F. (1990). Emotional experience and expression in schizophrenia and depression. *Journal of Abnormal Psychology, 101*, 37–44.

Bergem, A. L. M., et al. (1997). Heredity in late-onset Alzheimer's disease and vascular dementia. *Archives of General Psychiatry, 54*, 264–270.

Bergner, R. M. (1997). What is psychopathology? And so what? *Clinical Psychology: Science and Practice, 4*, 235–248.

Berlin, H. A., Rolls, E. T., & Iversen, S. D. (2005). Borderline personality disorder, impulsivity, and the orbitofrontal cortex. *American Journal of Psychiatry, 162*, 2360–2373.

Berlin, I. N. (1987). Effects of changing Native American cultures on child development. *Journal of Community Psychology, 15*, 299–306.

Berman, J. R., Berman, L. A., Lin, H., Flaherty, E., Lahey, N., Goldstein, I., & Cantey-Kiser, J. (2001). Effect of sildenafil on subjective and physiologic parameters of the female sexual response in women with sexual arousal disorder. *Journal of Sex & Marital Therapy, 27* (5), 411–420.

Berman, J. R., Berman, L. A., Toler, S. M., Gill, J., Haughie, S., & Sildenafil Study Group. (2003). Safety and efficacy of sildenafil citrate for the treatment of female sexual arousal disorder: A double-blind, placebo controlled study. *Journal of Urology, 170*, 2333–2338.

Berman, L. A. (2000). Cited in "Women, too, may benefit from Viagra" (2000, May 1). *CNN Web Posting.* Retrieved February 23, 2004, from http://www.cnn.com/2000/HEALTH/women/05/01/women.sex.function/.

Berman, S. L., et al. (2000). Predictors of outcome in exposure-based cognitive and behavioral treatments for phobic and anxiety disorders in children. *Behavior Therapy, 31,* 713–731.

Bernstein, D. P., et al. (1996). Childhood antecedents of adolescent personality disorders. *American Journal of Psychiatry, 153,* 907–913.

Bernstein, E. M., & Putnam, F. W. (1986). Development, reliability, and validity of a dissociation scale. *The Journal of Nervous and Mental Disease, 174,* 727–735.

Bernstein, R. L., & Gaw, A. C. (1990). Koro: Proposed classification for *DSM-IV. American Journal of Psychiatry, 147,* 1670–1674.

Berton, O., & Nestler, E. J. (2006). New approaches to antidepressant drug discovery: Beyond monoamines. *Nature Reviews, 7,* 137–151.

Bertram, L., Blacker, D., Mullin, K., Keeney, D., Jones, J., Basu, S., Yhu, S., et al. (2000). Evidence for genetic linkage of Alzheimer's disease to chromosome 10q. *Science, 290,* 2302–2303.

Beutler, L. E., Harwood, T. M., & Caldwell, R. (2001). Cognitive-behavioral therapy and psychotherapy integration. In K. S. Dobson (Ed.), *Handbook of cognitive-behavioral therapies* (2nd ed., pp. 138–170). New York: Guilford Press.

Bick, P. A., & Kinsbourne, M. (1987). Auditory hallucinations and subvocal speech in schizophrenic patients. *American Journal of Psychiatry, 144,* 222–225.

Bickel, W. K., et al. (1997). Effects of adding behavioral treatment to opioid detoxification with buprenorphine. *Journal of Consulting and Clinical Psychology, 65,* 803–810.

Biederman, J. (2003, August). *Current concepts on the pharmacotherapy of ADHD.* Paper presented at the meeting of the American Psychological Association, Toronto, CA.

Biederman, J., Faraone, S., Milberger, S., Guite, J., Mick, E., Chen, L., & Mennin, D. (1996b). A prospective 4-year follow-up study of attention-deficit hyperactivity and related disorders. *Archives of General Psychiatry, 53,* 437–446.

Biederman, J., Faraone, S., Milberger, S., Jetton, J. G., Chen, L., Mick, E. et al. (1996a). Is childhood oppositional defiant disorder a precursor to adolescent conduct disorder? Findings from a four-year follow-up study of children with ADHD. *Journal of the American Academy of Child and Adolescent Psychiatry, 35,* 1193–1204.

Biever, J. L., Castaño, M. T., de las Fuentes, C., González, C., Servín-López, S., Sprowls, C., et al. (2002). The role of language in training psychologists to work with Hispanic clients. *Professional Psychology: Research and Practice, 33,* 330–336.

Bigler, E. D., & Ehrenfurth, J. W. (1981). The continued inappropriate singular use of the Bender Visual Motor Gestalt Test. *Professional Psychology, 12,* 562–569.

Binder, R. L. (1999). Are the mentally ill dangerous? *Journal of the American Academy of Psychiatry and the Law, 27,* 189–201.

Binder, R. L., & McNiel, D. E. (1996). Application of the Tarasoff ruling and its effect on the victim and the therapeutic relationship. *Psychiatric Services, 47,* 1212–1215.

Binik, Y. M. (2005). Should dyspareunia be retained as a sexual dysfunction in *DSM-V?* A painful classification decision. *Archives of Sexual Behavior, 34,* 11–21.

Biran, M. (1988). Cognitive and exposure treatment for agoraphobia: Re-examination of the outcome research. *Journal of Cognitive Psychotherapy: An International Quarterly, 2,* 165–178.

Birchwood, M., Cochrane, R., Macmillan, F., Copestake, S., Kucharska, J., & Carriss, M. (1992). The influence of ethnicity and family structure on relapse in first-episode schizophrenia: A comparison of Asian, Afro-Caribbean, and White patients. *British Journal of Psychiatry, 161,* 783–790.

Bird, T. D. (2005). Genetic factors in Alzheimer's disease. *New England Journal of Medicine, 352,* 862–864.

Birmaher, B., Axelson, D., Strober, M., Gill, M. K., Valeri, S., Chiappetta, L. et al. (2006). Clinical course of children and adolescents with bipolar spectrum disorders. *Archives of General Psychiatry, 63,* 175–183.

Birnbaum, M. H., Martin, H., & Thomann, K. (1996). Visual function in multiple personality disorder. *Journal of the American Optometric Association, 67,* 327–334.

Bjerklie, D. (2005, January 17). Can sunny thoughts halt cancer? *Time Magazine,* p. A14.

Blackman, S. J. (1996). Has drug culture become an inevitable part of youth culture? A critical assessment of drug education. *Educational Review, 48,* 131–142.

Blackmore, E. R., et al. (2006). Obstetric variables associated with bipolar affective puerperal psychosis. *British Journal of Psychiatry, 188,* 32–36.

Blair, R. J. R., Mitchell, D. G. V., Richell, R., Kelly, S., Leonard, A., Newman, C., et al. (2002). Turning a deaf ear to fear: Impaired recognition of vocal affect in psychopathic individuals. *Journal of Abnormal Psychology, 111,* 682–686.

Blais, M. A., et al. (2001). Predicting *DSM-IV* cluster B personality disorder criteria from MMPI-2 and Rorschach data: A test of incremental validity. *Journal of Personality Assessment, 76,* 150–168.

Blais, M. A., Holdwick, D. J., Jr. McLean, R. Y., Otto, M. W., Pollack, M. H., & Hilsenroth, M. J. (2003). Exploring the psychometric properties and construct validity of the MCMI-III anxiety and avoidant personality scales. *Journal of Personality Assessment, 81,* 237–241.

Blakeslee, S. (1997a, June 27). Brain studies tie marijuana to other drugs. *The New York Times,* p. A16.

Blanchard, E. B., & Diamond, S. (1996). Psychological treatment of benign headache disorders. *Professional Psychology, 27,* 541–547.

Blanchard, E. B., & Hickling, E. J. (2004). *After the crash: Psychological assessment and treatment of survivors of motor vehicle accidents* (2nd ed.). Washington, DC: American Psychological Association.

Blanchard, E. B., Appelbaum, K. A., Radnitz, C. L. & Morrill, B., et al. (1990). A controlled evaluation of thermal biofeedback and thermal feedback combined with cognitive therapy in the treatment of vascular headache. *Journal of Consulting and Clinical Psychology, 58,* 216–224.

Blanchard, E. B., Hickling, E. J., Devi neni, T., Veazey, C. H., & Galovski, T. E. (2003). A controlled evaluation of cognitive–behavioral therapy for posttraumatic stress in motor vehicle accident survivors. *Behavior Research and Therapy, 41,* 79–96.

Blanchard, L. T., Gurka, M. J., & Blackman, J. A. (2006). Emotional, developmental, and behavioral health of American children and their families: A report from the 2003 National Survey of Children's Health. *Pediatrics, 117,* 1202–1212.

Blanchard, R., & Hucker, S. J. (1991). Age, transvestism, bondage, and concurrent paraphilic activities in 117 fatal cases of autoerotic asphyxia. *British Journal of Psychiatry, 159,* 371–377.

Blanker, M. H., Bosch, J. L., Groeneveld, E. P., Bohnen, A. M., Prins, A., Thomas, J., et al. (2001). Erectile and ejaculatory dysfunction in a community-based sample of men 50 to 78 years old: Prevalence, concern, and relation to sexual activity. *Urology, 57,* 763–768.

Blankstein, K. R., & Segal, Z. V. (2001). Cognitive assessment: Issues and methods. In K. S. Dobson (Ed.), *Handbook of cognitive-behavioral therapies* (2nd ed., pp. 40–85). New York: Guilford Press.

Blatt, S. J., et al. (1998). When and how perfectionism impedes the brief treatment of depression: Further analyses of the National Institute of Mental Health Treatment of Depression Collaborative Research Program. *Journal of Consulting and Clinical Psychology, 66,* 423–428.

Bleiberg, K. L., & Markowitz, J. C. (2005). A pilot study of interpersonal psychotherapy for posttraumatic stress disorder. *American Journal of Psychiatry, 162,* 181–183.

Bliss, E. L., & Jeppsen, E. A. (1985). Prevalence of multiple personality among inpatients and outpatients. *American Journal of Psychiatry, 142,* 250–251.

Blonigen, D. M., Hicks, B. M., Krueger, R. F., Christopher, J., & Iacono, W. (2006). Continuity and change in psychopathic traits as measured via normal-range personality: A longitudinal-biometric study. *Journal of Abnormal Psychology, 115,* 85–95.

Bloom, J. D., & Rogers, J. L. (1987). The legal basis for forensic psychiatry: Statutorily mandated psychiatric diagnosis. *American Journal of Psychiatry, 144,* 847–853.

Blowers, L. C., Loxton, N. J., Grady-Flesser, M., Occhipinti, S., & Dawe, S. (2003). The relationship between sociocultural pressure to be thin and body dissatisfaction in preadolescent girls. *Eating Behaviors, 4,* 229–244.

Blumberg, H. P., Kaufman, J., Martin, A., Whiteman, R., Zhang, J. H., Gore, J. C., et al. (2003). Amygdala and hippocampal volumes in adolescents and adults with bipolar disorder. *Archives of General Psychiatry, 60,* 1201–1208.

Blumenthal, J. A., Sherwood, A., Babyak, M. A., Watkins, L. L., Waugh, R., Georgiades, A., et al. (2005). Effects of exercise and stress management training on markers of cardiovascular risk in patients with ischemic heart disease: A randomized controlled trial. *Journal of the American Medical Association, 293,* 1626–1634.

Bocking, C. L. H., Schene, A. H., Spinhoven, P., Koeter, M. W. J., Wouters, L. F., Huyser, J., et al. (2005). Preventing relapse/recurrence in recurrent depression with cognitive therapy: A randomized controlled trial. *Journal of Consulting and Clinical Psychology, 73,* 647–657.

Bockting, W. O., & Fung, L. C. T. (2006). Genital reconstruction and gender identity disorders. In Sarwer, D. B., et al. (Eds.), *Psychological aspects of reconstructive and cosmetic plastic surgery: Clinical, empirical, and ethical perspectives* (pp. 207–229). Lippincott Williams & Wilkins Publishers.

Boles, S. M., & Miottoa, K. (2003). Substance abuse and violence: A review of the literature. *Aggression and Violent Behavior, 8,* 155–174.

Bolton, D., Eley, T. C., O'Connor, T. G., Perrin, S., Rabe-Hesketh, S., Rijsdijk, F., et al. (2006). Prevalence and genetic and environmental influences on anxiety disorders in 6-year-old twins. *Psychological Medicine, 36,* 335–344.

Bolton, J., Cox., F., Clara, I., & Sareen, J., (2006). Use of alcohol and drugs to self-medicate anxiety disorders in a nationally representative sample. *Journal of Nervous & Mental Disease, 194,* 818–825.

Bolton, P. (2001). Cross-cultural validity and reliability testing of a standard psychiatric assessment instrument without a gold standard. *Journal of Nervous & Mental Disease, 189,* 238–242.

Bolton, P., Bolton, P., Neugebauer, R., Verdeli, H., Clougherty, K. F., Wickramaratne, P., Speelman, L., et al. (2003). Group interpersonal psychotherapy for depression in rural Uganda: A randomized controlled trial. *Journal of the American Medical Association, 289,* 3117–3124.

Bonanno, G. A., Galea, S., Bucciarelli, A., & Vlahov, D. (2006). Psychological resilience after disaster: New York City in the aftermath of the September 11th terrorist attack. *Psychological Science, 17,* 181–186.

Bondareff, W., Alpert, M., Friedhoff, A. J., Richter, E. M., Clary, C. M., & Batzar, E. (2000). Comparison of sertraline and nortriptyline in the treatment of major depressive disorder in late life. *American Journal of Psychiatry, 157,* 745–750.

Bongar, B. (2002). *The suicidal patient: Clinical and legal standards of care* (2nd ed.). Washington, DC: American Psychological Association.

Bonifati, V., Rizzu, P., van Baren, M. J., Schaap, O., Breedveld, G. J., Krieger, E. et al. (2003). Mutations in the DJ-1 Gene associated with autosomal recessive early-onset Parkinsonism. *Science, 299,* 256–258.

Bonné, J. (2001, February 6). Meth's deadly buzz. *MSNBC.com Special Report.* Retrieved February 8, 2001, from http://www.msnbc.com/news/510835.asp?bt=nm&btu=http://www.msnbc.com/tools/newstools/d/news_menu. asp&cp1=1.

Bookheimer, S. Y., Strojwas, M. H., Cohen, M. S., Saunders, A. M., Pericak-Vance, M. A., Mazziotta, J. C., et al. (2000). Patterns of brain activation in people at risk for Alzheimer's disease. *The New England Journal of Medicine, 343,* 450–456.

Boren, T., Faulk, P., Roth, K. A., Larson, G., & Normark, S. (1993). Attachment of *Helicobacter pylori* to human gastric epithelium mediated by blood group antigens. *Science, 262,* 1892–1895.

Borjesson, M., & Dahlof, B. (2005). Physical activity has a key role in hypertension therapy. *Lakartidningen, 102,* 123–124, 126, 128–129.

Borkovec, T. D., Newman, M. G., Pincus, A. L., & Lytle, R. (2002). A component analysis of cognitive-behavioral therapy for generalized anxiety disorder and role of interpersonal problems. *Journal of Consulting and Clinical Psychology, 70,* 288–298.

Bornstein, R. F. (1992). The dependent personality: Developmental, social, and clinical perspectives. *Psychological Bulletin, 112,* 3–23.

Bornstein, R. F. (1993). *The dependent personality.* New York: The Guilford Press.

Bornstein, R. F. (1997). Dependent personality disorder in the *DSM-IV* and beyond. *Clinical Psychology: Science and Practice, 4,* 175–187.

Bornstein, R. F. (1999). Dependent and histrionic personality disorders. In T. Millon, et al. (Eds.), *Oxford textbook of psychopathology. Oxford textbooks in clinical psychology, Vol. 4* (pp. 535–554). New York: Oxford University Press.

Boskind-White, M., & White, W. C. (1983). *Bulimarexia: The binge–purge cycle.* New York: W. W. Norton.

Bostwick, J. M., & Pankratz, V. S. (2000). Affective disorders and suicide risk: A reexamination. *American Journal of Psychiatry, 157,* 1925–1932.

Botelho, R. J., & Richmond, R. (1996). Secondary prevention of excessive alcohol use: Assessing the prospects of implementation. *Family Practice, 13,* 182–193.

Bouchard, C., Rhéaume, J., & Ladouceur, R. (1999). Responsibility and perfectionism in OCD: An experimental study. *Behaviour Research & Therapy, 37,* 239–248.

Bouchard, S., et al. (1996). Cognitive restructuring in the treatment of psychotic symptoms in schizophrenia: A critical analysis. *Behavior Therapy, 27,* 257–277.

Boudouris, J. (2000). The insanity defense in Polk County, Iowa. *American Journal of Forensic Psychology, 18,* 41–79.

Bouwer, C., & Stein, D. J. (1997). Association of panic disorder with a history of traumatic suffocation. *American Journal of Psychiatry, 154,* 1566–1570.

Bowden, C. L., Calabrese, J. R., McElroy, S. L., Gyulai, L., Wassef, A., Petty, F., et al. (2000). A randomized, placebo-controlled 12-month trial of divalproex and lithium in treatment of outpatients with bipolar I disorder. *Archives of General Psychiatry, 57,* 481–489.

Bowden, C. L., Calabrese, J. R., Sachs, G., Yatham, L. N., Asghar, S. A., Hompland, M., et al. (2003). A placebo-controlled 18-month trial of lamotrigine and lithium maintenance treatment in recently manic or hypomanic patients with bipolar I disorder. *Archives of General Psychiatry, 60,* 392–400.

Bowers, T. G., & Clum, G. A. (1988). Relative contribution of specific and nonspecific treatment effects: Meta-analysis of placebo-controlled behavior therapy research. *Psychological Bulletin, 103,* 315–323.

Bowlby, J. (1988). *A secure base.* New York: Basic Books.

Boyd-Franklin, N. (1989). *Black families in therapy: A multisystems approach.* New York: Guilford Press.

Boyle, M. H., Offord, D. R., Racine, Y. A., Szatmari, P., Fleming, J. E., & Links, P. S. (1992). Predicting substance use in late adolescence: Results from the Ontario Child Health Study Follow-up. *American Journal of Psychiatry, 149,* 761–767.

Boyles, S. (2002, July 10). Are antidepressants effective? *WebMD Web Posting.* Retrieved July 12, 2002, from http://my.webmd.com/condition_center_content/mhl/article/1663.53542.

Braaten, E. B., & Rosén, L. E. (2000). Self-regulation of affect in attention deficit–hyperactivity disorder (ADHD) and non-ADHD boys: Differences in empathic responding. *Journal of Consulting and Clinical Psychology, 68,* 313–321.

Braddock, D. (1992). Community mental health and mental retardation services in the United States: A comparative study of resource allocation. *American Journal of Psychiatry, 149,* 175–183.

Bradford, J. M. W. (2001). The neurobiology, neuropharmacology, and pharmacological treatment of the paraphilias and compulsive sexual behaviour. *Canadian Journal of Psychiatry, 46*(1) 26–34.

Bradley, J. D. D., & Golden, C. J. (2001). Biological contributions to the presentation and understanding of attention-deficit/hyperactivity disorder: A review. *Clinical Psychology Review, 21,* 907–929.

Bradley, R., Greene, J., Russ, E., Dutra, L., & Westen, D. (2005). A multidimensional meta-analysis of psychotherapy for PTSD. *American Journal of Psychiatry, 162,* 214–227.

Bradley, R. G., & Follingstad, D. R. (2001). Utilizing disclosure in the treatment of the sequelae of childhood sexual abuse. A theoretical and empirical review. *Clinical Psychology Review, 21,* 1–32.

Brady, K., Pearlstein, T., Asnis, G. M., Baker, D., Rothbaum, B., Sikes, C. R., & Farfel, G. M. (2000). Efficacy and safety of sertraline treatment of posttraumatic stress disorder: A randomized controlled trial. *Journal of the American Medical Association, 283,* 1837–1844.

Braff, D. L. (1993). Information processing and attention dysfunction in schizophrenia. *Schizophrenia Bulletin, 19,* 233–259.

Braff, D., Schork, N. J., & Gottesman, I. I. (2007). Endophenotyping schizophrenia. *American Journal of Psychiatry, 164,* 705–707.

Braham, L. G., Trower, P., & Birchwood, M. (2004). Acting on command hallucinations and dangerous behavior: A critique of the major findings in the last decade. *Clinical Psychology Review, 24,* 513–528.

Bramon, E., & Sham, P. C. (2001). The common genetic liability between schizophrenia and bipolar disorder: A review. *Current Psychiatry Reports, 3,* 332–337.

Brandes, J. L. (2006). The influence of estrogen on migraine: A systematic review. *Journal of the American Medical Association, 295,* 190–198.

Brannigan, G. G., & Decker, S. L. (2006). The Bender-Gestalt II. *American Journal of Orthopsychiatry, 76,* 10–12.

Branson, R., Potoczna, N., Kral, J. G., Lentes, K-U., Hoehe, M. R., et al. (2003). Binge eating as a major phenotype of melanocortin 4 receptor gene mutations. *New England Journal of Medicine, 348,* 1096–1103.

Braswell, L., & Kendall, P. C. (2001). Cognitive-behavioral therapy with youth. In K. S. Dobson (Ed.), *Handbook of cognitive-behavioral therapies* (2nd ed., pp. 246–294). New York: The Guilford Press.

Braun, B. G. (Ed.). (1986). *Treatment of multiple personality disorder.* Washington, DC: American Psychiatric Press.

Braun, S. (2001, Spring). Seeking insight by prescription. *Cerebrum,* 10–21.

Breaux, C., Matsuoka, J. K., & Ryujin, D. H. (1995, August). *National utilization of mental health services by Asian/Pacific Islanders.* Paper presented at the meeting of the American Psychological Association, New York, NY.

Breier, J. I., Simos, P. G., Fletcher, J. M., Castillo, E. M., Zhang, W., & Papanicolaou, A. C. (2003). Abnormal activation of temporoparietal language areas during phonetic analysis in children with dyslexia. *Neuropsychology, 17,* 610–621.

Breitner, J. C. S., & Zandi, P. P. (2001). Do nonsteroidal antiinflammatory drugs reduce the risk of Alzheimer's disease? *New England Journal of Medicine, 345,* 1567–1568.

Bremmer, J. D., Southwick, S. M., Darnell, A., & Charney, D. S. (1996). Chronic PTSD in Vietnam combat veterans: Course of illness and substance abuse. *American Journal of Psychiatry, 153,* 369–375.

Bremner, J. D., Vythilingam, M., Ng, C. K., Vermetten, E., Nazeer, A., Oren, D. A., et al. (2003). Regional brain metabolic correlates of methylparatyrosine–induced depressive symptoms implications for the neural circuitry of depression. *Journal of the American Medical Association, 289,* 3125–3134.

Brenda, W. J. H., et al. (1998). Depressive symptoms and physical decline in community-dwelling older persons. *Journal of the American Medical Association, 279,* 1720–1726.

Brent, D. A., Oquendo, M., Birmaher, B., Greenhill, L., Kolko, D., Stanley, B. et al. (2002). Familial pathways to early-onset suicide att empt: Risk for suicidal behavior in offspring of mood-disordered suicide attempters. *Archives of General Psychiatry, 59,* 801–807.

Breslau, J., Aguilar-Gaxiola, S., Kendler, K. S., Su, M., Williams, D., & Kessler, R. C. (2006). Specifying race-ethnic differences in risk for psychiatric disorder in a USA national sample. *Psychological Medicine, 36,* 57–68.

Breslau, J., Kendler, K. S., Su, M., Gaxiola-Aguilar, S., & Kessler, R.C. (2005). Lifetime risk and persistence of psychiatric disorders across ethnic groups in the United States. *Psychological Medicine, 35,* 317–327.

Breslau, N., Johnson, E. O., Hiripi, E., & Kessler, R. (2001). Nicotine dependence in the United States: Prevalence, trends, and smoking persistence. *Archives of General Psychiatry, 58,* 810–816.

Breslau, N., Peterson, E. L., Schultz, L. R., Chilcoat, H. D., & Andreski, P. (1998). Major depression and stages of smoking: A longitudinal investigation. *Archives of General Psychiatry, 55,* 161–166.

Breslau, N., Roth, T., Rosenthal, L., & Andreski, P. (1996). Sleep disturbance and psychiatric disorders: A longitudinal epidemiological study of young adults. *Biological Psychiatry, 39,* 411–418.

Breslow, N. (1989). Sources of confusion in the study and treatment of sadomasochism. *Journal of Social Behavior and Personality, 4,* 263–274.

Brewin, C. R., Andrews, B., & Valentine, J. D. (2000). Meta-analysis of risk factors for posttraumatic stress disorder in trauma-exposed adults. *Journal of Consulting and Clinical Psychology, 68,* 748–766.

Bricker, J. B., Peterson, A. V., Jr., Andersen, M. R., Rajana, K. B., Leroux, B. G., & Sarasona, I. G. (2006). Childhood friends who smoke: Do they influence adolescents to make smoking transitions? *Addictive Behaviors, 31,* 889–900.

Bridge, J. A., Iyengar, S., Salary, C. B., Barbe, R. P., Birmaher, B., Pincus, H. A., et al. (2007). Clinical response and risk for reported suicidal ideation and suicide attempts in pediatric antidepressant treatment: A meta-analysis of randomized controlled trials. *Journal of the American Medical Association, 297,* 1683–1696.

Briere, J., & Elliott, D. M. (2003). Prevalence and psychological sequelae of self-reported childhood physical and sexual abuse in a general population sample of men and women. *Child Abuse & Neglect, 27,* 1205–1222.

Brody, J. E. (1990, June 7). A search to bar retardation in a new generation. *The New York Times,* p. B9.

Brody, J. E. (1993, December 15). Living with a common genetic abnormality. *The New York Times,* p. C17.

Brody, J. E. (1996, November 20). Controlling anger is good medicine for the heart. *The New York Times,* p. C15.

Brody, J. E. (1997, March 26). Race and weight. *The New York Times,* p. C8.

Brody, J. E. (2000, May 16). Cybersex give s birth to a psychological disorder. *The New York Times,* pp. F7, F11.

Brody, J. E. (2002, December 24). Adolescent angst or a deeper disorder? Tips for spotting serious symptoms. *The New York Times,* p. F5.

Brody, J. E. (2006, April 18). A slight change in habits could lull you to sleep. *The New York Times,* p. F7.

Broussard, B. A., Johnson, A., Himes, J. H., Story, M., Fichtner, R., Hauck, F., et al. (1991). Prevalence of obesity in American Indians and Alaska Natives. *American Journal of Clinical Nutrition, 53* (6 Suppl.), 1535S–1542S.

Brown, A. S., Begg, M. D., Gravenstein, S., Schaefer, C. A., Wyatt, R. J., Bresnahan, M., et al. (2004). Serologic evidence of prenatal influenza in the etiology of schizophrenia *Archives of General Psychiatry, 61,* 774–780.

Brown, D. R., Ahmed, F., Gary, L. E., & Milburn, N. G. (1995). Major depression in a community sample of African Americans. *American Journal of Psychiatry,* 373–378.

Brown, G. K., Beck, A. T., Steer, R. A., & Grisham, J. R. (2000). Risk factors for suicide in psychiatric outpatients: A 20-year prospective study. *Journal of Consulting and Clinical Psychology, 68,* 371–377.

Brown, G. R., & Haaser, R. C. (2005). Sexual disorders. In Levenson, J. L. (Ed.). *The American psychiatric publishing textbook of psychosomatic medicine.* (pp. 359–386). Washington, DC: American Psychiatric Publishing, Inc.

Brown, K. W., & Ryan, R. M. (2003). The benefits of being present: Mindfulness and its role in psychological well-being. *Journal of Personality and Social Psychology, 84,* 822–848.

Brown, L. S. (1992). A feminist critique of the personality disorders. In L. Brown & M. Balou (Eds.), *Personality and psychopathology: Feminist reappraisals* (pp. 206–228). New York: Guilford Press.

Brown, L. S. (1997, November). Recovered memories of abuse: Research and clinical update. *Clinician's Research Digest, Supplemental Bulletin, 17,* 1–2.

Brown, M. J., et al. (2006). Hypertension and ethnic group. *British Medical Journal, 332,* 833–836.

Brown, M. Z., Comtois, K. A., & Linehan, M. M. (2002). Reasons for suicide attempts and nonsuicidal self-injury in women with borderline personality disorder. *Journal of Abnormal Psychology, 111,* 198–202.

Brown, R. J., Schrag, A., & Trimble, M. R. (2005). Dissociation, childhood interpersonal trauma, and family functioning in patients with somatization disorder. *American Journal of Psychiatry, 162,* 899–905.

Brown, S. L., & Forth, A. E. (1997). Psychopathy and sexual assault: Static risk factors, emotional precursors, and rapist subtypes. *Journal of Consulting and Clinical Psychology, 65,* 848–857.

Brown, T. A., Di Nardo, P. A., Lehman, C. L., & Campbell, L. A. (2001). Reliability of *DSM-IV* anxiety and mood disorders: Implications for the classification of emotional disorders. *Journal of Abnormal Psychology, 110,* 49–58.

Bruce, M. L., McAvay, G. J., Raue, P. J., Brown, E. L., Meyers, B. S., Keohane, D. J., et al. (2002). Major depression in elderly home health care patients. *American Journal of Psychiatry, 159,* 1367–1374.

Bruce, M. L., Ten Have, T. R., Reynolds, C. F., III, Katz, I. I., Schulberg, H. C., Mulsant, B. H., Brown, G. K., et al. (2004). Reducing suicidal ideation and depressive symptoms in depressed older primary care patients: A randomized controlled trial. *Journal of the American Medical Association, 291,* 1081–1091.

Bruce, T. J., & Alahi, P. (2006, Winter/Spring), Pharmacotherapy for schizophrenia: Will CATIE open doors? *The Clinical Psychologist, 59,* 12–13.

Bruce, T. J. & Sanderson, W. C. (2004). "Evidence-based psychosocial practices: The past, present, and future," in C. Stout & R. Hayes (Eds.), *Evidence-based practice: Methods, models and tolls for mental health professionals.* New York: John Wiley and Sons, pp. 220–243.

Bruch, H. (1973). *Eating disorders: Obesity, anorexia and the person within.* New York: Basic Books.

Bruch, M. A. (1997). Positive thoughts or cognitive balance as a moderator of the negative life events—dysphoria relationship: A reexamination. *Cognitive Therapy and Research, 21,* 25–38.

Brun, A. (1996). Frontal lobe degeneration of non-Alzheimer type. *Acta Neurologica Scandinavica Supplementum, 168,* 28–30.

Bryant, R. A. (2001). Posttraumatic stress disorder and traumatic brain injury: Can they co-exist? *Clinical Psychology Review, 21,* 931–948.

Bryant, R. A., Moulds, M. L., Guthrie, R. M., Dang, S. T., & Nixon, R. D. V. (2003). Imaginal exposure alone and imaginal exposure with cognitive restructuring in treatment of posttraumatic stress disorder. *Journal of Consulting and Clinical Psychology, 71,* 706–712.

Buchanan, A. (1999). Risk and dangerousness. *Psychological Medicine, 29,* 465–473.

Buchanan, R. W., & Carpenter, W. T., Jr. (1997). The neuroanatomies of schizophrenia. *Schizophrenia Bulletin, 23,* 367–372.

Buchanan, T., (2002). Online assessment: Desirable or dangerous? *Professional Psychology: Research and Practice, 33,* No. 2, 148–154.

Buchert, R., Thomasius, R., Wilke, F., Petersen, K., Nebeling, B., Obrocki, J., et al. (2004). A voxel-based pet investigation of the long-term effects of "ecstasy" consumption on brain serotonin transporters. *American Journal of Psychiatry, 161,* 1181–1189.

Buddie, A. M., & Testa, M. (2005). Rates and predictors of sexual aggression among students and nonstudents. *Journal of Interpersonal Violence, 20,* 713–724.

Budney, A. J., Hughes, J. R., Moore, B. A., & Vandrey, R. (2004). Review of the validity and significance of cannabis withdrawal syndrome. *American Journal of Psychiatry, 161,* 1967–1977.

Buhlmann, U., McNally, R. J., Wilhelm, S., & Florin, I. (2002). Selective processing of emotional information in body dysmorphic disorder. *Journal of Anxiety Disorders, 16,* 289–298.

Bulik, C. M., Sullivan, P. F., Tozzi, F., Furberg, H., Lichtenstein, P. & Pedersen, N. L. (2006). Prevalence, heritability, and prospective risk factors for anorexia nervosa. *Archives of General Psychiatry, 63,* 305–312.

Bulmash, E. L., Moller, H. J., Kayumov, L., Shen, J., Wang, X., & Shapiro, C. M. (2006). Psychomotor disturbance in depression: Assessment using a driving simulator paradigm. *Journal of Affective Disorders, 93,* 213–218.

Bunde, J., & Suls, J. (2006). A quantitative analysis of the relationship between the Cook-Medley Hostility Scale and traditional coronary artery disease risk factors. *Health Psychology, 25,* 493–500.

Bunney, W. E., Bunney, B. G., Vawter, M. P., Tomita, H., Li, J., Evans, S. J., et al. (2003). Microarray technology: A review of new strategies to discover candidate vulnerability genes in psychiatric disorders. *American Journal of Psychiatry, 160,* 657–666.

Burgess, A. W., & Morgenbesser, L. I. (2005). Sexual violence and seniors. *Brief Treatment and Crisis Intervention, 5,* 193–202.

Buriel, R., Calzada, S., & Vazquez, R. (1982). The relationship of traditional Mexican American culture to adjustment and delinquency among three generations of Mexican American male adolescents. *Hispanic Journal of Behavioral Sciences, 4,* 41–55.

Burns, A., Gallagley, A., Byrne, J. (2004). Delirium. *Journal of Neurology, Neurosurgery, and Psychiatry with Practical Neurology. 75,* 362–367.

Burns, D. D. (1980). *Feeling good: The new mood therapy.* New York: Morris.

Burns, D. D., & Beck, A. T. (1978). Modification of mood disorders. In J. P. Foreyt & D. P. Rathjen (Eds.), *Cognitive behavior therapy: Research and application* (pp. 109–134). New York: Plenum Press.

Burns, D. D., & Nolen-Hoeksema, S. (1992). Therapeutic empathy and recovery from depression in cognitive-behavioral therapy: A structural equation model. *Journal of Consulting and Clinical Psychology, 60,* 441–449.

Burros, M. (1994, July 17). Despite awareness of risks, more in U.S. are getting fat. *The New York Times,* pp. A1, A8.

Burt, S. A., McGue, M., DeMarte, J. A., Krueger, R. F., & Iacono, W. G. (2006). Timing of menarche and the origins of conduct disorder. *Archives of General Psychiatry, 63,* 890–896.

Burton, K. W. (2006, August 17). Missing genes tied to mental retardation. ScienceNOW Daily News. Retrieved August 19, 2006, from http://sciencenow.sciencemag.org/cgi/content/full/2006/817/1.

Burton, N., & Lane, R. C. (2001). The relational treatment of dissociative identity disorder. *Clinical Psychology Review, 21,* 301–320.

Bushman, B. J., Bonacci, A. M., van Dijk, M., & Baumeister, R. F. (2003). Narcissism, sexual refusal, and aggression: Testing a narcissistic reactance model of sexual coercion. *Journal of Personality and Social Psychology, 84,* 1027–1040.

Busseri, M. A., & Tyler, J. D. (2003). Interchangeability of the Working Alliance Inventory and Working Alliance Inventory, Short Form. *Psychological Assessment, 15,* 193–197.

Bustillo, J. R., Lauriello, J., Horan, W., & Keith, S. (2001). The psychosocial treatment of schizophrenia: An update. *American Journal of Psychiatry, 158,* 163–175.

Butcher, J., Derksen, J., Sloore, H., & Sirigatti, S. (2003). Objective personality assessment of people in diverse cultures: European adaptations of the MMPI-2. *Behaviour Research and Therapy, 41,* 819–840.

Butler, A. C., & Beck, A. T. (1995, Summer). Cognitive therapy for depression. *The Clinical Psychologist, 48,* 3–5.

Butler, A. C., Chapman, J. E., Forman, E .M. & Beck, A. T. (2006). The empirical status of cognitive-behavioral therapy: A review of meta-analyses. *Clinical Psychology Review, 26,* 17–33.

Butler, G. (1989). Issues in the application of cognitive and behavioral strategies to the treatment of social phobia. *Clinical Psychology Review, 9,* 91–106.

Butler, L. D., et al. (1996). Hypnotizability and traumatic experience: A diathesis–stress model of dissociative symptomatology. *American Journal of Psychiatry, 153*(Suppl.), 42–63.

Butler, R. J. (2004). Childhood nocturnal enuresis: Developing a conceptual framework. *Clinical Psychology Review, 24,* 909–931.

Butler, R. N. (2001, Fall/Winter). The myth of old age. *Newsweek Special Issue,* p. 33.

Bütz, M. R., Bowlling, J. B., & Bliss, C. A. (2000). Psychotherapy with the mentally retarded: A review of the literature and the implications. *Professional Psychology: Research and Practice, 31,* 42–47.

Byers, E. S., & Grenier, G. (2003). Premature or rapid ejaculation: Heterosexual couples' perceptions of men's ejaculatory behavior. *Archives of Sexual Behavior, 32*(3), 261–270.

Byne, W., Buchsbaum, M. S., Kemether, E. Hazlett, E. A., Shinwari, A., Mitropoulou, V., et al. (2001). Magnetic resonance imaging of the thalamic mediodorsal nucleus and pulvinar in schizophrenia and schizotypal personality disorder. *Archives of General Psychiatry, 58,* 133–140.

C

Cable, N., & Sacker, A. (2006). The role of adolescent social disinhibition expectancies in moderating the relationship between psychological distress and alcohol use and misuse. *Addictive Behaviors,* in press.

Cable, N., & Sacker, A. (2007). The role of adolescent social disinhibition expectancies in moderating the relationship between psychological distress and alcohol use and misuse. *Addictive Behaviors, 32,* 282–295.

Caddy, G. R., Addington, H. J. Jr., & Perkins, D. (1978). Individualized behavior therapy for alcoholics. A third year independent double-blind follow-up., *Behavioral Research & Therapy, 16,* 345–362.

Cadoret, R. J., Leve, L. D., & Devor, E. (1997). Genetics of aggressive and violent behavior. Psychiatric Clinics of North America, *20,* 301–322.

Caetano, R. (1987). Acculturation and drinking patterns among U.S. Hispanics. *British Journal of Addiction, 82,* 789–799.

Cafri, G., Yamamiya, Y., Brannick, M., & Thompson, J. K. (2005). The influence of sociocultural factors on body image: a meta-analysis. *Clinical Psychology: Science and Practice, 12,* 421–433.

Cahn, W., Pol, H. E. H., Lems, E. B. T., van Haren, N. E. M., Schnack, H. G., van der Linden, J. A., et al. (2002). Brain volume changes in first-episode schizophrenia: a 1-year follow-up study. *Archives of General Psychiatry, 59,* 1002–1010.

Cale, E. M., & Lilienfeld, S. O. (2002). Sex differences in psychopathy and antisocial personality disorder. A review and integration. *Clinical Psychology Review, 22,* 1179–1207.

Calhoon, S. K. (1996). Confirmatory factor analysis of the Dysfunctional Attitude Scale in a student sample. *Cognitive Therapy and Research, 20,* 81–91.

Calhoun, P. S., et al. (2000). Drug use and validity of substance use self-reports in veterans seeking help for posttraumatic stress disorder. *Journal of Consulting and Clinical Psychology, 68,* 923–927.

Callicott, J. H., Mattay, V. S., Verchinski, B. A., Marenco, S., Egan, M. F., & Weinberger, D. R. (2003). Complexity of prefrontal cortical dysfunction in schizophrenia: More than up or down. *American Journal of Psychiatry, 160,* 2209–2215.

Cameron, N. (1963). *Personality development and psychopathology: A dynamic approach.* Boston: Houghton Mifflin.

Campbell, R. (2006). Rape survivors' experiences with the legal and medical systems: Do rape victim advocates make a difference? *Violence Against Women, 12,* 30–45.

Campbell, R., & Wasco, S. M. (2005). Understanding rape and sexual assault: 20 years of progress and future directions. *Journal of Interpersonal Violence, 20,* 127–131.

Campbell, T. (2000). First person account: Falling on the pavement. *Schizophrenia Bulletin, 26,* 507–509.

Campbell, W. K., Foster, C. A., & Finkel, E. J. (2002). Does self-love lead to love for others? A story of narcissistic game playing. *Journal of Personality and Social Psychology, 83,* 340–354.

Cannon, T. D., Glahn, D. C., Kim, J., Van Erp, T. G. M., Karlsgodt, K., Cohen, M. S. et al. (2005). Dorsolateral prefrontal cortex activity during maintenance and manipulation of information in working memory in patients with schizophrenia. *Archives of General Psychiatry, 62,* 1071–1080.

Cantor, R. M., Kono, N., Duvall, J. A., Alvarez-Retuerto, A., Stone, J. L., Alarcon, M., et al. (2005). Replication of autism linkage: fine-mapping peak at 17q21. American Journal of Human Genetics, *76,* 1050–1056.

Capps, L., et al. (1993). Parental perception of emotional expressiveness in children with autism. *Journal of Consulting and Clinical Psychology, 61,* 475–484.

Cardemil, E. V., & Battle, C. L. (2003). Guess who's coming to therapy? Getting comfortable with conversations about race and ethnicity in psychotherapy. *Professional Psychology: Research and Practice, 34,* 278–286.

Carey, B. (2004, December 27). Autism therapies still a mystery, but parents take a leap of faith. *The New York Times,* pp. A1–A15.

Carey, B. (2006a, December 6). Study finds medication raises suicide risks in young adults. *The New York Times,* p. A25.

Carey, B. (2006b, June 6). Use of antipsychotics by the young rose five-fold. *The New York Times,* p. A18.

Carey, G., & DiLalla, D. L. (1994). Personality and psychopathology: Genetic perspectives. *Journal of Abnormal Psychology, 103,* 32–43.

Carey, M. P., Carey, K. B., Maisto, S. A., Gordon, C. M., Schroder, K. E. E., & Vanable, P. A. (2004). Reducing HIV-risk behavior among adults receiving outpatient psychiatric treatment: Results from a randomized controlled trial. *Journal of Consulting and Clinical Psychology, 72,* 252–268.

Carey, M. P., Wincze, J. P., & Meisler, A. W. (1998). Sexual dysfunction: Male erectile disorder. In D. H. Barlow (Ed.), *Clinical handbook for psychological disorders* (pp. 442–480). New York: Guilford Press.

Carini, M. A., & Nevid, J. S. (1992). Social appropriateness and impaired perspective in schizophrenia. *Journal of Clinical Psychology, 48,* 170–177.

Carlbring, P., Bohman, S., Brunt, S., Buhrman, M., Westling, B. E., Ekselius, L., et al. (2006). Remote treatment of panic disorder: a randomized trial of Internet-based cognitive behavior therapy supplemented with telephone calls. *American Journal of Psychiatry, 163,* 2119–2125.

Carmichael, M. (2002, December 2). Ginkgo on your mind? *Newsweek,* p. 59.

Carmichael, M. (2003, May 5). The fat factor. *Newsweek,* p. 69.

Carney, R. M., Freedland, K. E., & Jaffe, A. S. (2001). Depression as a risk factor for coronary heart disease mortality. *Archives of General Psychiatry, 58.*

Carpenter, S. (2000, September). Psychologists tackle neuroimaging at APA-sponsored Advanced Training Institute. *Monitor on Psychology,* pp. 42–43.

Carpenter, S. (2001, May). Stimulants boost achievement in ADHD teens. *Monitor on Psychology,* pp. 26–27.

Carroll, L. (2003, November 4). Fetal brains suffer badly from effects of alcohol. *New York Times Online.* Retrieved November 4, 2003, from http://www.nytimes.com/2003/11/04/health/04FETA.html?th.

Carroll, L. (2004, February 10). Parkinson's research focuses on links to genes and toxins. *The New York Times,* p. F5.

Carroll, R. T. (2002). *Occam's razor.* From the "Skeptic's Dictionary" by Robert T. Carroll. Retrieved January 12, 2004, from http://skepdic.com/occam.html.

Carter, M. M., Hollon, S. D., Carson, R., & Shelton, R. C. (1995). Effects of a safe person on induced distress following a biological challenge in panic disorder with agoraphobia. *Journal of Abnormal Psychology, 104,* 156–163.

Carver, C. S., & Gaines, J. G. (1987). Optimism, pessimism, and postpartum depression. *Cognitive Therapy & Research, 11,* 449–462.

Carver, C. S., Smith, R. G., Antoni, M., Petronis, V. M., Weiss, S., & Derhagopian, R. P. (2005). Optimistic personality and psychosocial well-being during treatment predict psychosocial well-being among long-term survivors of breast cancer. *Health Psychology, 24,* 508–516.

Casey, B. J., & Durston, S. (2006). From behavior to cognition to the brain and back: What have we learned from functional imaging studies of attention deficit hyperactivity disorder? *American Journal of Psychiatry, 163,* 957–960.

Casey, L. M., Oei, T. P. S., & Newcombe, P. A. (2004). An integrated cognitive model of panic disorder: The role of positive and negative cognitions. *Clinical Psychology Review 24,* 529–555.

Casey, P., Maracy, M, Kelly, B. D., Lehtinend, V., Ayuso-Mateose, J.-L., Dalgard, O. S., & Dowrick, C. (2006). Can adjustment disorder and depressive episode be distinguished? Results from ODIN. *Journal of Affective Disorders, 92,* 291–297.

Caspi, A., McClay, J., Moffitt, T. E., Mill, J., Martin, J., Craig, I. W., et al. (2002). Role of genotype in the cycle of violence in maltreated children. *Science, 297,* 851–854.

Caspi, A., Sugden, K., Moffitt, T. E., Taylor, A., Craig, I. W., Harrington, H. L., McClay, J., et al. (2003). Influence of life stress on depression: Moderation by a polymorphism in the 5-HTT Gene. *Science, 301,* 386–389.

Castellanos, F. X., Giedd, J. N., Berquin, P. C., Walter, J. M., Sharp, W., Tran, T., et al. (2001). Quantitative brain magnetic resonance imaging in girls with attention-deficit/hyperactivity disorder. *Archives of General Psychiatry, 58,* 289–295.

Castellanos, F. X., Sharp, W. S., Gottesman, R. F., Greenstein, D. K., Giedd, J. N., & Rapoport, J. L. (2003). Anatomic brain abnormalities in monozygotic twins discordant for attention deficit hyperactivity disorder. *American Journal of Psychiatry, 160,* 1693–1696.

Catz, S. L., & Kelly, J. A. (2001). Living with HIV disease. In A. Baum, T. A. Revenson, & J. E. Singer (Eds.), *Handbook of health psychology* (pp. 841–850). Mahwah, NJ: Erlbaum.

Cavell, T. A. (2001). Updating our approach to parent training. I: The case against targeting noncompliance. *Clinical Psychology: Science & Practice, 8*(3), 299–318.

CDC finds gaping racial disparities in health. (2005, January 13). Retrieved February 3, 2006, from http://www.msnbc.msn.com/id/6823541/.

Celio, A. A., Winzelberg, A. J., Wilfley, D. E., Eppste in-Herald, D., Springer, E. A., Dev, P., et al. (2000). Reducing risk factors for eating disorders: Comparison of an Internet- and a classroom-delivered psychoeducational program. *Journal of Consulting and Clinical Psychology, 68,* 650–657.

Center for Mental Health Services (CMHS). (1994). *Mental health statistics.* Office of Consumer, Family and Public Information, Center for Mental Health Services, U.S. Department of Health and Human Services. Rockville, MD: Author.

Center for Mental Health Services (2001, May). *National Strategy for Suicide Prevention: Goals and objectives for action: Summary. A joint effort of SAMHS, CDC, NIH, and HRSA.* Washington, DC: Author.

Centers for Disease Control (CDC) (2000). Tobacco use among middle and high school students—United States, 1999. *Morbidity and Mortality Weekly Report, 49,* 49–53.

Centers for Disease Control (CDC) (2001a, October 12). Cigarette smoking among adults—United States, 1999. *Morbidity and Mortality Weekly Report, 50* (40). Retrieved November 15, 2001, from http://www.cdc.gov/tobacco/research_data/adults_prev/mm5040.htm.

Centers for Disease Control (CDC) (2001b). *Suicide in the United States.* National Center for Injury Prevention and Control, Centers for Disease Control. Atlanta: Author.

Centers for Disease Control (CDC). (2007, February). FAQs–Prevalence of ASDs. Retrieved September 18, 2007 from http://www.cdc.gov/ncbddd/autism/faq_prevalence.htm.

Centers for Disease Control and Prevention (CDC) (2004a). Asthma prevalence and control characteristics by race/ethnicity—United States, 2002. *Morbidity and Mortality Weekly Report, 53,* 145–148.

Centers for Disease Control and Prevention (CDC) (2004b). Morbidity and Mortality Weekly Report, *Journal of the American Medical Association, 291,* 1317–1318.

Centers for Disease Control and Prevention (CDC) (2005). Cigarette smoking among adults—United States, 2004. (2005, November 11). *Morbidity and Mortality Weekly Report, 54.*

Centers for Disease Control and Prevention (CDC) (2006, January 30). National Center for Injury Prevention and Control. *WISQARS Injury Mortality Reports, 1999–2003.* Retrieved December 14, 2006, from http://webappa.cdc.gov/sasweb/ncipc/mortrate10_sy.html.

Cepeda-Benito, A., Reynoso, J. T., & Erath, S. (2004). Meta-analysis of the efficacy of nicotine replacement. *Journal of Consulting and Clinical Psychology, 72,* 712–722.

Chadda, R. K., & Ahuja, N. (1990). Dhat syndrome: A sex neurosis of the Indian subcontinent. *British Journal of Psychiatry, 156,* 577–579.

Chakrabarti, S., & Fombonne, E. (2001). Pervasive developmental disorders in preschool children. *Journal of the American Medical Association, 285,* 3093–3099.

Chamberlin, J. (2001, July/August). Putting a face on child mental illness. *Monitor on Psychology,* pp. 28–29.

Chambless, D. L., & Ollendick, T. H. (2001). Empirically supported psychological interventions: Controversies and evidence. *Annual Review of Psychology, 52,* 685–716.

Chan, D. W. (1991). The Beck Depression Inventory: What difference does the Chinese version make? *Psychological Assessment, 3,* 616–622.

Chang, D. F. (2002). Understanding the rates and distribution of mental disorders. In K. S. Kurasaki, S. Okazaki, & S. Sue (Eds.), *Asian American mental health: Assessment, theories, and methods.* (pp. 9–28). New York: Kluwer Academic/Plenum Publishers.

Chang, S. C. (1984). Review of I. Yamashita "Taijin-kyofu." *Transcultural Psychiatric Research Review, 21,* 283–288.

Chang, T., & Yeh, & C. J. (2003). Using online groups to provide support to Asian American men: Racial, cultural, gender, and treatment issues. *Professional Psychology: Research and Practice, 34,* 634–643.

Charney, D. S., Nemeroff, C. B., Lewis, L., Laden, S. K., Gorman, J. M., Laska, E. M. (2002). National depressive and manic-depressive association consensus statement on the use of placebo in clinical trials of mood disorders. *Archives of General Psychiatry, 59,* 262–270.

Chassin, L., Pitts, S. C., & Prost, J. (2002). Binge drinking trajectories from adolescence to emerging adulthood in a high-risk sample: Predictors and substance abuse outcomes. *Journal of Consulting and Clinical Psychology, 70,* 67–78.

574 References

Chassin, L., Presson, C. C., Sherman, S. J., & Kim, K. (2003). Historical changes in cigarette smoking and smoking-related beliefs after 2 decades in a Midwestern community. *Health Psychology, 22*, 347–353.

Chavira, D. A., Grilo, C., Carlos, M., Shea, M. T., Yen, S., Gunderson, J. G., et al. (2003). Ethnicity and four personality disorders. *Comprehensive Psychiatry, 44*, 483–491.

Check, E. (2003). Battle of the mind. *Nature, 422*, 370–372.

Chemerinski, E., et al. (2001). The specificity of depressive symptoms in patients with Alzheimer's disease. *American Journal of Psychiatry, 158*, 68–72.

Chen, E., Bloomberg, G. R., Fisher, E. B., Jr., & Strunk, R. C. (2003). Predictors of repeat hospitalizations in children with asthma: The role of psychosocial and socioenvironmental factors. *Health Psychology, 22*, 12–18.

Chen, H., Zhang, S. M., Hernan, M. A., Schwarzchild, M. A., Willett, W. C., Colditz, G. A., et al. (2003). Nonsteroidal anti-inflammatory drugs and the risk of Parkinson disease. *Archives of Neurology, 60*, 1059–1064.

Chen, J., Rathore, S. S., Radford, M. J., Wang, Y., Krumholz, H. M., et al. (2001). Racial differences in the use of cardiac catheterization after acute myocardial infarction. *The New England Journal of Medicine, 344*, 1443–1449.

Chen, P., Ganguli, M., Mulsant, B. H., & DeKosky, S. T. (1999). The temporal relationship between depressive symptoms and dementia: A community-based prospective study. *Archives of General Psychiatry, 56*, 261–266.

Cheung, F. M. (1991). The use of mental health services by ethnic minorities. In H. F. Myers, et al. (Eds.), *Ethnic minority perspectives on clinical training and services in psychology* (pp. 23–31). Washington, DC: American Psychological Association.

Cheung, F. M., Song, W., & Butcher, J. N. (1991). An infrequency scale for the Chinese MMPI. *Psychological Assessment, 3*, 648–653.

Cheung, F. M., & Ho, R. M. (1997). Standardization of the Chinese MMPI-A in Hong Kong: A preliminary study. *Psychological Assessment, 9*, 499–502.

Cheung, F. M., Kwong, J. Y. Y., & Zhang, J. (2003). Clinical validation of the Chinese Personality Assessment Inventory. *Psychological Assessment, 15*, 89–100.

Children's mental illness "crisis," A: Report: 1 in 10 children suffers enough to impair development. (2001, January 3). *Associated Press Web Posting.* Retrieved January 5, 2001, from http://www.msnbc.com/news/510934.asp.

Ching, J. W. J., McDermott, J. F., Fukunaga, C. & Yanagida, E. (1995). Perceptions of family values and roles among Japanese Americans: Clinical considerations. *American Journal of Orthopsychiatry, 65*, 216–224.

Chipperfield, B., & Vogel-Sprott, M. (1988). Family history of problem drinking among young male social drinkers: Modeling effects on alcohol consumption. *Journal of Abnormal Psychology, 97*, 423–428.

Chobanian, A. V., Bakris, G. L., Black, H. R., Cushman, W. C., Green, L. A., Izzo, J. L. Jr., Jones, D. W. et al. (2003). The seventh report of the Joint National Committee on Prevention, Detection, Evaluation, and Treatment of High Blood Pressure: The JNC 7 report. *Journal of the American Medical Association, 289*, 2560–2572.

Chorpita, B. F., Yim, L. M., Donkervoet, J. C., Arensdorf, A., Amundsen, M. J., McGee, C., Serrano, A., et al. (2002). Toward large-scale implementation of empirically supported treatments for children: A review and observations by the Hawaii Empirical Basis to Services Task Force. *Clinical Psychology: Science and Practice, 9*, 165–190.

Chovil, I. (2000). First person account: I and I, dancing fool, challenge you the world to a duel. *Schizophrenia Bulletin, 26 (3)*, 745–747.

Chowdhury, A. N. (1996). The definition and classification of Koro. *Culture, Medicine and Psychiatry, 20*, 41–65.

Choy, Y., Fyer, A. J., & Lipsitz, J. D. (2006). Treatment of specific phobia in adults. *Clinical Psychology Review*, in press.

Christensen, A., Atkins, D. C., Berns, S., Wheeler, J., Baucom, D. H., & Simpson, L. E. (2004). Traditional versus integrative behavioral couple therapy for significantly and chronically distressed married couples. *Journal of Consulting and Clinical Psychology, 72*, 176–191.

Christensen, H., Griffiths, K. M., & Jorm, A. F. (2004). Delivering interventions for depression by using the Internet: Randomised controlled trial. *British Medical Journal, 328*, 265.

Chronis, A. M., Jones, H. A., & Raggi, V. L. (2006). Evidence-based psychosocial treatments for children and adolescents with attention-deficit/hyperactivity disorder. *Clinical Psychology Review*, in press.

Chu, J. A., Frey, L. M., Ganzel, B. L., & Matthews, J. A. (1999). Memoreis of childhood abuse: Dissociation, amnesia, and corroboration. *American Journal of Psychiatry, 156*, 749–755.

Chung, T., & Maisto, S. A. (2006). Relapse to alcohol and other drug use in treated adolescents: Review and reconsideration of relapse as a change point in clinical course. *Clinical Psychology Review, 26*, 149–161.

Ciechanowski, P., Wagner, E., Schmaling, K., Schwartz, S., Williams, B., Diehr, P., et al. (2004). Community-integrated home-based depression treatment in older adults: A randomized controlled trial. *Journal of the American Medical Association, 291*, 1569–1577.

Cipriani, A., Pretty, H., Hawton, K., & Geddes, J. R. (2005). Lithium in the prevention of suicidal behavior and all-cause mortality in patients with mood disorders: A systematic review of randomized trials. *American Journal of Psychiatry, 162*, 1805–1819.

Clark, D. A., (2004). *Cognitive-behavioral therapy for OCD.* New York: Guilford.

Clark, D. A., Cook, A., & Snow, D. (1998). Depressive symptom differences in hospitalized, medically ill, depressed psychiatric inpatients and nonmedical controls. *Journal of Abnormal Psychology, 107*, 38–48.

Clark, D. M. (1986). A cognitive approach to panic. *Behaviour Research and Therapy, 24*, 461–470.

Clark, D. M., Ehlers, A., McManus, F., Hackmann, A., Fennell, M., Campbell, H., et al. (2003). Cognitive therapy versus fluoxetine in generalized social phobia: a randomized placebo-controlled trial. *Journal of Consulting and Clinical Psychology, 71*, 1058–1067.

Clark, D. M., Salkovskis, P. M., Ost, L. G., Breitholtz, E., Koehler, K. A., Westling, B. E., et al. (1997). Misinterpretation of body sensations in panic disorder. *Journal of Consulting and Clinical Psychology, 65*, 203–213.

Clark, H. W. (2003). Office-based practice and opioid-use disorders. *New England Journal of Medicine, 349*, 928–930.

Clark, R. (2006). Perceived racism and vascular reactivity in Black college women: moderating effects of seeking social support. *Health Psychology, 25*, 20–25.

Clark, S. E., & Loftus, E. F. (1996). The construction of space alien abduction memories. *Psychological Inquiry, 7*, 140–143.

Clarkin, J. F., Levy, K. N., Lenzenweger, M. F., & Kernberg, O. F. (2007). Evaluating three treatments for borderline personality disorder: A multiwave study. *American Journal of Psychiatry, 164*, 922–928.

Clay, R. A. (2001a, January). Bringing psychology to cardiac care. *Monitor on Psychology*, pp. 46–49.

Clay, R. A. (2001b, January). To the heart of the matter. *Monitor on Psychology*, pp. 42–45.

Cleckley, H. (1976). *The mask of sanity* (5th ed.). St. Louis: Mosby.

Cleghorn, J. M., Franco, S., Szechtman, B., Kaplan, R. D., Szechtman, H., Brown, G. M., et al. (1992). Toward a brain map of auditory hallucinations. *American Journal of Psychiatry, 149*, 1062–1069.

Clemetson, L. (2003, January 21). Hispanics now largest minority, census shows. *The New York Times*, pp. A1, A17.

Cloitre, M. (2004). Aristotle revisited: The case of recovered memories. *Clinical Psychology: Science and Practice, 11*, 42–46.

CNS Spectrums, 7, 585–587.

Cocaine use tied to loss of pleasure sense. (2003, January 7). *The New York Times*, p. F10.

Cochran, S. D., Sullivan, J. G., & Mays, V. M. (2003). prevalence of mental disorders, psychological distress, and mental health services use among lesbian, gay, and bisexual adults in the United States. *Journal of Consulting and Clinical Psychology, 71, No. 1*, 53–61.

Cochran, S. V., & Rabinowitz, F. E. (2003). Gender-sensitive recommendations for assessment and treatment of depression in men. *Professional Psychology: Research and Practice, 34*, 132–140.

Cockell, S. J., Hewitt, P. L., Seal, B., Sherry, S., Goldner, E. M., Flett, G. L., et al. (2002). Trait and self-presentational dimensions of perfectionism among women with anorexia nervosa. *Cognitive Therapy and Research, 26*, 745–758.

Cognitive impairment linked to early death in HIV-infected patients (1996, March 29). *Reuters News Service.*

Cohen, A. C., Gold, D. P., Shulman, K. I., Wortley, J. T., McDonald, G., & Wargon, M. (1993). Factors determining the decision to institutionalize dementing individuals: A prospective study. *The Gerontologist, 22*, 714–720.

Cohen, D. (1986). Psychopathological perspectives: Differential diagnosis of Alzheimer's disease and related disorders. In L. W. Poon (Ed.), *Handbook for clinical memory assessment of older adults* (pp. 81–88). Washington, DC: American Psychological Association.

Cohen, F. L., Ferrans, C. E., & Eshler, B. (1992). Reported accidents in narcolepsy. *Loss, Grief and Care, 5*, 71–80.

Cohen, H., Kaplan, Z., Kotler, M., Kouperman, I., Moisa, R., & Grisaru, N. (2004). Repetitive transcranial magnetic stimulation of the right dorsolateral prefrontal cortex in posttraumatic stress disorder: A double-blind, placebo-controlled study. *American Journal of Psychiatry, 161*, 515–524.

Cohen, J. A., & Mannarino, A. P. (1997). A treatment study for sexually abused preschool children: Outcome during a one-year follow-up. *Journal of the American Academy of Child and Adolescent Psychiatry, 36*, 1228–1235.

Cohen, S., Doyle, W., J., Turner, R., Alper, C. M., & Skoner, D. P. (2003). Sociability and susceptibility to the common cold. *Psychological Science, 14*, 389–395.

Cohen, S., Frank, E., Doyle, W. J., Skoner, D. P., Rabin, B. S., & Gwaltney, J. M., Jr. (1998). Types of stressors that increase susceptibility to the common cold in healthy adults. *Health Psychology, 17*, 214–223.

Cohen, S., Tyrrell, D. A. J., & Smith, A. P. (1991). Psychological stress and susceptibility to the common cold. *The New England Journal of Medicine, 325*, 606–612.

Cohen-Kettenis, P. T. (2001). Gender identity disorder in *DSM? Journal of American Academy of Child & Adolescent Psychiatry, 40*, 391.

Cohen-Kettenis, P. T., & van Goozen, S. H. M. (1997). Sex reassignment of adolescent transsexuals: A follow-up study. *Journal of the American Academy of Child and Adolescent Psychiatry, 36*, 263–271.

Colas, E. (1988). *Just checking.* New York: Simon & Schuster.

Coldwell, C. M., & Bender, W. S. (2007). The effectiveness of assertive community treatment for homeless populations with severe mental illness: A meta-analysis. *American Journal of Psychiatry, 164*, 393–399.

Cole, D. A., et al. (1998). A longitudinal look at the relation between depression and anxiety in children and adolescents. *Journal of Consulting and Clinical Psychology, 66*, 451–460.

Cole, S. W., Naliboff, B. D., Kemen y, M. E., Griswold, M. P., Fahey, J. I., & Zack, J. A. (2002). Impaired response to HAART in HIV-infected individuals with high autonomic nervous system activity. *Proceedings of the National Academy of Science, 98*, 12695–12700.

Coleman, D., & Baker, F. M. (1994). Misdiagnosis of schizophrenia in older, Black veterans. *Journal of Nervous and Mental Disease, 182*, 527–528.

Collaer, M. L., & Hill, E. M. (2006). Large sex difference in adolescents on a timed line judgment task: Attentional contributors and task relationship to mathematics. *Perception, 35*, 561–572.

College binge drinking worries (1999, August 27). *Associated Press, NewsReal, Inc.*

Collins, B. N., & Brandon, T. H. (2002). Effects of extinction context and retrieval cues on alcohol cue reactivity among nonalcoholic drinkers. *Journal of Consulting and Clinical Psychology, 70*, 390–397.

Collins, P. H. (1990). *Black feminist thought: Knowledge, consciousness, and the politics of empowerment.* Boston: Unwin Hyman.

Comas-Diaz, L. (2006). The present and future of clinical psychology in private practice, *Clinical Psychology: Science and Practice, 13*, 273–277.

Comas-Diaz, L., & Griffith, E. (1988). Introduction: On culture and psychotherapeutic care. In L. Comas-Diaz & E. Griffith (Eds.), *Clinical guidelines in cross-cultural mental health.* New York: Wiley.

Comer, S. D., Sullivan, M. A., Yu, E., Rothenberg, J. L., Kleber, H. D., Kampman, K., et al. (2006). Injectable, sustained-release naltrexone for the treatment of opioid dependence: A randomized, placebo-controlled trial. *Archives of General Psychiatry, 63*, 210–218.

Compton, W. M., Grant, B. F., Colliver, J. D., Glantz, M. D., & Stinson, F. S. (2005). Prevalence of marijuana use disorders in the United States: 1991–1992 and 2001–2002. *Journal of the American Medical Association, 291*, 2114–2121.

Conklin, C. Z., & Westen, D. (2005). Borderline personality disorder in clinical practice. *American Journal of Psychiatry, 162*, 867–875.

Conley, R. R., & Buchanan, R. W. (1997). Evaluation of treatment-resistant schizophrenia. *Schizophrenia Bulletin, 23*, 663–674.

Constantino, M. J., Arnow, B. A., Blasey, C., & Agras, W. S. (2005). The association between patient characteristics and the therapeutic alliance in cognitive-behavioral and interpersonal therapy for bulimia nervosa. *Journal of Consulting and Clinical Psychology, 73*, 203–211.

Conway, K. P., Compton, W., Stinson, F. S., & Grant, B. F. (2006). Lifetime comorbidity of *DSM-IV* mood and anxiety disorders and specific drug use disorders: results from the National Epidemiologic Survey on Alcohol and Related Conditions. *Journal of Clinical Psychiatry, 67*, 247–257.

Cooke, D. J., & Michie, C. (1997). An item response theory analysis of the Hare Psychopathy Checklist—Revised. *Psychological Assessment, 9*, 3–14.

Coons, P. M. (1986). Treatment progress in 20 patients with multiple personality disorder. *Journal of Nervous and Mental Disease, 174*, 715–721.

Cooper, A., Delmonico, D. L., & Burg, R. (2000). Cybersex users, abusers, and compulsives: New findings and implications. *Sexual Addiction & Compulsivity, 7(1–2)*, 5–29.

Cooper, A., Scherer, C. R., Boies, S. C., & Gordon, B. L. (1999). Sexuality on the Internet: From sexual exploration to pathological expression. *Professional Psychology: Research & Practice, 30 (2)*, 154–164.

Cooper, P. J., Murray, L., Wilson, A., & Romaniuk, H. (2003). Controlled trial of the short- and long-term effect of psychological treatment of postpartum depression: 1. Impact on maternal mood. *British Journal of Psychiatry, 182*, 412–419.

Cooper, P. J., Tomlinson, M., Swartz, L., Woolgar, M., Murray, L., & Molteno, C. (1999). Post-partum depression and the mother-infant relationship in a South African peri-urban settlement. *British Journal of Psychiatry, 175*, 554–558.

Corbett, J., Saccone, N. L., Foroud, T., Goate, A., Edenberg, H., Nurnberger, J., et al. (2005). Sex adjusted and age adjusted genome screen for nested alcohol dependence diagnoses. *Psychiatric Genetics, 15*, 25–30.

Corbitt, E. M., & Widiger, T. A. (1995). Sex differences among the personality disorders: An exploration of the data. *Clinical Psychology: Science and Practice, 2*, 225–238.

Corcoran, D. (2002, December 3). What's normal? A look at Asperger Syndrome. *The New York Times*, p. F6.

Cordova, M. J., Andrykowski, M. A., Kenady, D. E., McGrath, P. C., Sloan, D. A, & Redd, W. H. (1995). Frequency and correlates of posttraumatic-stress-disorderlike symptoms after treatment for breast cancer. *Journal of Consulting and Clinical Psychology, 63,* 981–986.

Corina, D. P., Richards, T. L., Serafini, S., Richards, A. L., Steury, K., Abbott, R. D., Echeland, D. R., et al. (2001). fMRI auditory language differences between dyslexic and able reading children. *Neuroreport: For Rapid Communication of Neuroscience Research, 12*(6), 1195–1201.

Coronado, S. F., & Peake, T. H. (1992). Culturally sensitive therapy: Sensitive principles. *Journal of College Student Psychotherapy, 7,* 63–72.

Cororve, M. B., & Gleaves, D. H. (2001). Body dysmorphic disorder: A review of conceptualizations, assessment, and treatment strategies. *Clinical Psychology Review, 21,* 949–970.

Correll, C. U., Leucht, S., & Kane, J. M. (2004). Lower risk for tardive dyskinesia associated with second-generation antipsychotics: A systematic review of 1 year studies. *American Journal of Psychiatry, 161,* 414–425.

Corrigan, P. W., & Watson, A. C. (2005). Findings from the National Comorbidity Survey on the frequency of violent behavior in individuals with psychiatric disorders. *Psychiatry Research, 136,* 153–162.

Cortina, L. M., & Kubiak, S. S. P. (2006). Gender and posttraumatic stress: sexual violence as an explanation for women's increased risk. *Journal of Abnormal Psychology, 115,* 753–759.

Coryell, W., Endicott, J., & Keller, M. (1992). Rapidly cycling affective disorder: Demographics, diagnosis, family history, and course. *Archives of General Psychiatry, 49,* 126–131.

Coryell, W., Pine, D., Fyer, A., & Klein, D. (2006). Anxiety responses to CO_2 inhalation in subjects at high-risk for panic disorder. *Journal of Affective Disorders, 92,* 63–70.

Coryell, W., Solomon, D., Turvey, C., Keller, M., Leon, A. C., Endicott, J., et al. (2003). The long-term course of rapid-cycling bipolar disorder. *Archives of General Psychiatry, 60,* 914–920.

Costa, P. T., Jr., & McCrae, R. R. (1985). Hypochondriasis, neuroticism, and aging: When are somatic complaints unfounded? *American Psychologist, 40,* 19–28.

Costello, E. J., Compton, S. N., Keele, G., & Angold, A. (2003). Relationships between poverty and psychopathology: A natural experiment. *Journal of the American Medical Association, 290,* 2023–2029.

Costin, C. (1997). *Your dieting daughter: Is she dying for attention?* New York: Brunner/Mazel.

Courchesne, E., Carper, R., & Akshoomoff, N. (2003). Evidence of brain overgrowth in the first year of life in autism. *Journal of the American Medical Association, 290,* 337–344.

Coursey, R. D., Alford, J., & Safarjan, B. (1997). Significant advances in understanding and treating serious mental illness. *Professional Psychology: Research and Practice, 28,* 205–216.

Couzin, J. (2006, April 13). Gene variant may boost obesity risk. *ScienceNOW Daily News.* Retrieved May 26, 2006, from http://sciencenow.sciencemag.org/cgi/content/full/2006/413/1

Cowan, W. M., & Kandel, E. R. (2001). Prospects for neurology and psychiatry. *Journal of the American Medical Association, 285,* 594–600.

Cowley, G. (2001a, March 12). Cannibals to cows: The path of a deadly disease. *Newsweek,* pp. 53–61.

Cowley, G. (2001b, February 12). New ways to stay clean. *Newsweek,* pp. 45–47.

Cowley, G. (2003, September 8). Girls, boys, and autism. *Newsweek,* pp. 42–46.

Cox, B. J., MacPherson, P. S., & Enns, M. W. (2004). Psychiatric correlates of childhood shyness in a nationally representative sample. *Behavior Research and Therapy, 43,* 1019–1027.

Coyle, J. P. (2006). Treating difficult couples: Helping clients with coexisting mental and relationship disorders. *Family Relations: Interdisciplinary Journal of Applied Family Studies, 55*(1), 146–147.

Coyle, J. T. (2001). Drug treatment of anxiety disorders in children. *The New England Journal of Medicine, 344,* 1326–1327.

Coyne, J. C. (1976). Toward an interactional description of depression. *Psychiatry, 39,* 14–27.

Craighead, W. E., Craighead, L. W., & Ilardi, S. S. (1998). Psychosocial treatments for major depressive disorder. In P. E. Nathan & J. M. Gorman (Eds.), *A guide to treatments that work* (pp. 226–239). New York: Oxford University Press.

Cramer, P. (2000). Defense mechanisms in psychology today: Further processes for adaptation. *American Psychologist, 55,* 637–646.

Craske, M. G., Brown, T. A., & Barlow, D. H. (1991). Behavioral treatment of panic disorder: A two-year follow-up. *Behavior Therapy, 22,* 289–304.

Cravchik, A., & Goldman, D. (2000). Neurochemical individuality: Genetic diversity among human dopamine and serotonin receptors and transporters. *Archives of General Psychiatry, 57,* 1105–1114.

Crerand, C. E., Phillips, K. A., Menard, W., & Fay, C. (2005). Nonpsychiatric medical treatment of Phbody dysmorphic disorder. *Psychosomatics, 46,* 549–555.

Crits-Christoph, P. (1992). The efficacy of brief dynamic psychotherapy: A meta-analysis. *American Journal of Psychiatry, 149,* 151–158.

Crits-Christoph, P., Wilson, G. T., & Hollon, S. D. (2005). Empirically supported psychotherapies: Comment on Westen, Novotny, and Thompson-Brenner (2004). *Psychological Bulletin, 131,* 412–417.

Cross-National Collaborative Group. (1992). The changing rate of major depression: Cross-national comparisons. *Journal of the American Medical Association, 268,* 3098–3105.

Cryan, J. F., O'Leary, O. F., Jin, S. H., Friedland, J. C., Ouyang, M., Hirsch, B. R., et al. (2004). Norepinephrine-deficient mice lack responses to anti-depressant drugs, including selective serotonin reuptake inhibitors. *Proceedings of the National Academy of Science, 101,* 8186–8191.

Csernansky, J. G., Schindler, M. K., Splinter, N. R., Wang, L., Gado, M., Selemon, L. D., et al. (2004). Abnormalities of thalamic volume and shape in schizophrenia. *American Journal of Psychiatry, 161,* 896–902.

Cui, X-J., & Vaillant, G. E. (1997). Does depression generate negative life events? *Journal of Nervous and Mental Disease, 185,* 145–150.

Cuijpers, P., & Smit, F. (2005). Preventing the incidence of new cases of mental disorders: A meta-analytic review. *Journal of Nervous & Mental Disease, 193,* 119–125.

Cunningham, J. A., & Breslin, F. C. (2004). Only one in three people with alcohol abuse or dependence ever seek treatment. *Addictive Behaviors, 29,* 221–223.

Curb, J. D., & Marcus, E. B. (1991). Body fat and obesity in Japanese-Americans. *American Journal of Clinical Nutrition, 53,* 1552S–1555S.

Curbing the obesity epidemic. (2006). *The Lancet, 367.* Retrieved May 20, 2006, from http://www.thelancet.com/journals/lancet/article/PIIS0140673606686649/fulltext.

Curry, S., Marlatt, G. A., & Gordon, J. R. (1987). Abstinence violation effect: Validation of an attributional construct with smoking cessation. *Journal of Consulting and Clinical Psychology, 55,* 145–149.

Curtin, J. J., Patrick, C. J., Lang, A. R, Cacioppo, J. T., & Birbaumer, N. (2001). Alcohol affects emotion through cognition. *Psychological Science, 12,* 527–531.

Curtner-Smith, M. E. (2000). Mechanisms by which family processes contribute to school-age boy's bullying. *Child Study Journal, 30*(3), 169–186.

Cuthbert, B. N. (2005). Dimensional models of psychopathology: Research agenda and clinical utility. *Journal of Abnormal Psychology, 114,* 565–569.

Cutrona, C. E., Russell, D. W., Hessling, R. M., Brown, P. A., & Murry, V. (2000). Direct and moderating effects of community context on the psychological well-being of African American women. *Journal of Personality and Social Psychology, 79,* 1088–1101.

Cutrona, C. E., Wallace, G., & Wesner, K. A. (2006). Neighborhood characteristics and depression: An examination of stress processes. *Current Directions in Psychological Science, 15,* 188–192.

Cutting, L. P., & Docherty, N. M. (2000). Schizophrenia outpatients' perceptions of their parents: Is expressed emotion a factor? *Journal of Abnormal Psychology, 109,* 266–272.

Cyranowski, J. M., Frank, E., Young, E., & Shear, M. K. (2000). Adolescent onset of the gender difference in lifetime rates of major depression: A theoretical model. *Archives of General Psychiatry, 57,* 21–27.

D

Dadds, M. R., Sanders, M. R., Morrison, M., & Rebgetz, M. (1992). Childhood depression and conduct disorder: II. An analysis of family interaction patterns in the home. *Journal of Abnormal Psychology, 101,* 505–513.

Dahl, R. E. (1992). The pharmacologic treatment of sleep disorders. *Psychiatric Clinics of North America, 15,* 161–178.

Daley, S. E., Burge, D., & Hammen, C. (2000). Borderline personality disorder symptoms as predictors of 4-year romantic relationship dysfunction in young women: Addressing issues of specificity. *Journal of Abnormal Psychology, 109,* 451–460.

Daley, S. E., Hammen, C., Burge, D., Davila, J., Paley, B., Lindberg, N., et al. (1997). Predictors of the generation of episodic stress: A longitudinal study of late adolescent women. *Journal of Abnormal Psychology, 106,* 251–259.

Dalton, K. M., Nacewicz, B. M., Johnstone, T., Schaefer, H. S., Gernsbacher, M. A., Goldsmith, H. H., et al. (2005). Gaze fixation and the neural circuitry of face processing in autism. *Nature Neuroscience, 8,* 519–526.

Daly, R. C., Danaceau, M.A., Rubinow, D. R., & Schmidt, P. J. (2003). Concordant restoration of ovarian function and mood in perimenopausal depression. *American Journal of Psychiatry, 160,* 1842–1846.

Damasio, A. R. (1997). Towards a neuropathology of emotion and mood. *Nature, 386,* 769–770.

Damasio, R. (2000). A neural basis for sociopathy. *Archives of General Psychiatry, 57,* 128–129.

Dana, R. H. (Ed.) (2000). Handbook of cross-cultural and multicultural personality assessment. Mahwah, NJ: Lawrence Erlbaum Associates.

Dannon, P. N., Lowengrub, K., Aizer, A., & Kotler, M. (2006). Pathological gambling: Comorbid psychiatric diagnoses in patients and their families. *Israel Journal of Psychiatry and Related Sciences, 43,* 88–92.

Dao., T. K., & Prevatt, F. (2006). A psychometric evaluation of the Rorschach Comprehensive System's Perceptual Thinking Index. *Journal of Personality Assessment, 86,* 180–189.

Dar, R., Stronguin, F., & Etter, J.-F. (2005). Assigned versus perceived placebo effects in nicotine replacement therapy for smoking reduction in Swiss smokers. *Journal of Consulting and Clinical Psychology, 73,* 350–353.

David, D., & Szentagotaia, A. (2006). Cognitions in cognitive-behavioral psychotherapies; toward an integrative model. *Clinical Psychology Review, 26,* 284–298.

Davidson, J. R. T., Rothbaum, B. O., van der Kolk, B. A., Sikes, C. R., & Farfel, G. M. (2001). Multicenter, double-blind comparison of sertraline and placebo in the treatment of posttraumatic stress disorder. *Archives of General Psychiatry, 58,* 485–492.

Davidson, P. R., & Parker, K. C. H. (2001). Eye movement desensitization and reprocessing (EMDR): A meta-analysis. *Journal of Consulting and Clinical Psychology, 69,* 305–316.

Davidson, R. J. (2000). Affective style, psychopathology, and resilience: Brain mechanisms and plasticity. *American Psychologist, 55,* 1196–1214.

Davidson, R. J., Pizzagalli, D., Nitschke, J. B., & Putnam, K. (2002). Depression: Perspectives from affective neuroscience. *Annual Review of Psychology, 53,* 545–574.

Davis, J. L. (2002, November 4). Depression: Genetic or environmental? Genetics plus temperament affect mood disorders. *WebMD Medical News.* Retrieved November 9, 2002, from http://my.webmd.com/content/article/53/61257.htm?z=1663_00000_2409_f1_05.

Davis, J. M., Chen, N, & Glick, I. D. (2003). A meta-analysis of the efficacy of second-generation antipsychotics. *Archives of General Psychiatry, 60,* 553–564.

Davis, M., Myers, K. M., Ressler, K. J., & Rothbaum, B. O. (2006). Facilitation of extinction of conditioned fear by D-cycloserine: Implications for psychotherapy. *Current Directions in Psychological Science, 14,* 214–219.

Davis, S. R., Davison, S. L., Donath, S., & Bell, R. J. (2005). Circulating androgen levels and self-reported sexual function in women. *Journal of the American Medical Association, 294,* 91–96.

Davis, T. L., & Liddell, D. L. (2002). Getting inside the house: The effectiveness of a rape prevention program for college fraternity men. *Journal of College Student Development, 43* (1), 35–50.

Daw, J. (2001, April). Survey uncovers communication breakdown in the treatment of depression. *Monitor on Psychology,* p. 69.

Dawe, S., Rees, V. W., Mattick, R., Sitharthan, T., & Heather, N. (2002). Efficacy of moderation-oriented cue exposure for problem drinkers: A randomized controlled trial. *Journal of Consulting and Clinical Psychology, 70,* 1045–1050.

De Gucht, V., & Maes, S. (2006). Explaining medically unexplained symptoms: Toward a multidimensional, theory-based approach to somatization. *Journal of Psychosomatic Research, 60,* 349–352.

De La Cancela, V., & Guzman, L. P. (1991). Latino mental health service needs: Implications for training psychologists. In H. F. Myers et al. (Eds.), *Ethnic minority perspectives on clinical training and services in psychology* (pp. 59–64). Washington, DC: American Psychological Association.

de Moor, C., Sterner, J., Hall, M., Warneke, C., Gilani, Z. Amato, R. et al. (2003). A pilot study of the effects of expressive writing on psychological and behavioral adjustment in patients enrolled in a Phase II trial of vaccine therapy for metastatic renal cell carcinoma. *Health Psychology, 21,* 615–619.

De Silva, P. (1993). Post-traumatic stress disorder: Cross-cultural aspects. *International Review of Psychiatry, 5,* 217–229.

de Waal, M. W. M., Arnold, I. A., Eekhof, J. A., & van Hemert, A. M. (2004). Somatoform disorders in general practice: Prevalence, functional impairment and comorbidity with anxiety and depressive disorders. *British Journal of Psychiatry, 184,* 470–476.

DeAngelis, T. (2002, June). How do mind-body interventions affect breast cancer? *Monitor on Psychology, 33,* pp. 51–53.

DeBaggio, T. (2002). *Losing my mind. An intimate look at life with Alzheimer's.* New York: The Free Press.

Decker, S. L., McIntosh, D. E., Kelly, A. M., Nicholls, S. K., & Dean, R. S. (2001). Comorbidity among individuals classified with attention disorders. *International Journal of Neuroscience, 110*(1–2), 43–54.

Deegear, J., & Lawson, D. M. (2003). The utility of empirically supported treatments. *Professional Psychology: Research and Practice, 34,* 271–277.

Deffenbacher, J. L., et al. (2000). An application of Beck's cognitive therapy to general anger reduction. *Cognitive Therapy & Research, 24,* 689–697.

Dekker, J. (1993). Inhibited male orgasm. In W. O'Donohue & J. H. Geer (Eds.), *Handbook of sexual dysfunctions: Assessment and treatment* (pp. 279–301). Boston: Allyn & Bacon.

Del Boca, F. K., Darkes, J., Greenbaum, P. E., & Goldman, M. S. (2004). Up close and personal: Temporal variability in the drinking of individual college students during their first year. *Journal of Consulting and Clinical Psychology, 72,* 155–164.

Delahanty, D. L., & Baum, A. (2001). Stress and breast cancer. In A. Baum, T. A. Revenson, & J. E. Singer (Eds.), *Handbook of health psychology* (pp. 747–756). Mahwah, NJ: Erlbaum.

Della Sala, S. (Ed.). (1999). *Mind myths: Exploring popular assumptions about the mind and brain.* New York: Wiley.

Dement, W. C. (1992). The proper use of sleeping pills in the primary care setting. *Journal of Clinical Psychiatry, 53* (12, Suppl.), 50–56.

Denizet-Lewis, B. (2006, June 25). An anti-addiction pill? *The New York Times Magazine*, pp. 48–53.

Denneby, J. A., Appleby, L., Thomas, C. S., Faragher, E. B., et al. (1996). Case-control study of suicide by discharged psychiatry patients. *British Medical Journal, 312*, 1580.

Dennis, C. (2004, January 29). Brain development: The most important sexual organ. *Nature, 427*, 390–392.

Denollet, J., et al. (1996). Personality as independent predictor of long-term mortality in patients with coronary heart disease. *Lancet, 347*, 417–421.

DeNoon, D. (2006, May 1). Do ADHD drugs stunt kids' growth? *WebMD Medical News*. Retrieved May 12, 2006, from http://www.webmd.com/content/article/121/114370Reviewed.

Depression Guideline Panel. (1993b). *Depression in primary care: Vol. 2. Treatment of major depression.* Clinical Practice Guideline No. 5. Rockville, MD: U.S. Department of Health and Human Services, Public Health Service, Agency for Health Care Policy and Research (AHCPR Pub. No. 93–0551).

Derby, C. A. (2000, October 2). Cited in, "Study finds exercise reduces the risk of impotence." *CNN.com*. Retrieved November 12, 2002, from http://www.cnn.com/2000/HEALTH/men/10/02/fitness. impotence.ap/.

DeRosse, P., Funke, B., Burdick, K. E., Lencz, T., Ekholm, J. M., Kane, J. M., et al. (2006). Dysbindin genotype and negative symptoms in schizophrenia. *American Journal of Psychiatry, 163*, 532–534.

DeRubeis, R. J., & Crits-Christoph, P. (1998). Empirically supported individual and group psychological treatments for adult mental disorders. *Journal of Consulting and Clinical Psychology, 66*, 37–52.

DeRubeis, R. J., Gelfand, L. A., Tang, T. Z., & Simons, A. D. (1999). Medications versus cognitive behavior therapy for severely depressed outpatients: Meta-analysis of four randomized comparisons. *American Journal of Psychiatry, 156*, 1007–1013.

DeRubeis, R. J., Hollon, S. D., Amsterdam, J. D., Shelton, R. C., Young, P. R., Salomon, R. M., et al. (2005). Cognitive therapy vs medications in the treatment of moderate to severe depression. *Archives of General Psychiatry, 62*, 409–416.

DeRubeis, R. J., Shelton, R. C., Amsterdam, J. D., Salomon, R. M., O'Reardon, J. P., Lovett, M. L., et al. (2005). Prevention of relapse following cognitive therapy vs. medications in moderate to severe depression. *Archives of General Psychiatry, 62*, 417–422.

DeRubeis, R. J., Tang, T. Z., & Beck, A. T. (2001). Cognitive therapy. In K. S. Dobson (Ed.), *Handbook of cognitive-behavioral therapies* (2nd ed., pp. 349–392). New York: Guilford Press.

Dettmer, K., Saunders, B., & Strang, J. (2001). Take home naloxone and the prevention of deaths from opiate overdose: Two pilot schemes. *British Medical Journal, 322*, 895–896.

Deuschl, G., Schade-Brittinger, C., Krack, P., Volkmann, J., Schäfer, H., Bötzel, K., et al. (2006). A randomized trial of deep-brain stimulation for Parkinson's disease. *New England Journal of Medicine, 355*, 896–908.

Devan, G. S. (1987). Koro and schizophrenia in Singapore. *British Journal of Psychiatry, 150*, 106–107.

Devilly, G. J. (2002). Eye movement desensitization and reprocessing: A chronology of its development and scientific standing. *Scientific Review of Mental Health Practice, 1*, 113–138.

Devlin, M. J., Yanovski, S. Z., & Wilson, G. T. (2000). Obesity: What mental health professionals need to know. *American Journal of Psychiatry, 157*, 854–866.

Di Castelnuovo, A., Costanzo, S., Bagnardi, V., Donati, M. B., Iacoviello, L., & de Gaetano, G. (2006). Alcohol dosing and total mortality in men and women: An updated meta-analysis of 34 prospective studies. *Archives of Internal Medicine, 166*, 2437–2445.

Diamond, S., Baldwin, R., & Diamond, R. (1963). *Inhibition and choice.* New York: Harper & Row.

Dick, D. M., Rose, R. J., Viken, R. J., Kaprio, J., & Koskenvuo, M. (2001). Exploring gene-environment interactions: Socioregional moderation of alcohol use. *Journal of Abnormal Psychology, 110*, 625–632.

Dickel, D. E., Veenstra-VanderWeele, J., Cox, N. J., Wu, A., Fischer, D. J., Van Etten-Lee, M., Himle, J. A., et al. (2006). Association testing of the positional and functional candidate gene SLC1A1/EAAC1 in early-onset obsessive-compulsive disorder. *Archives of General Psychiatry, 63*, 778–785.

Dickens, B. M., Doob, A. N., Warwick, O. H., & Winegard, W. C. (1982). *Report of the Committee of Enquiry into Allegations Concerning Drs. Linda and Mark Sobell.* Toronto: Addiction Research Foundation.

Dickerson, F. B., Tenhula, W. N., & Green-Paden, L. D. (2005). The token economy for schizophrenia: review of the literature and recommendations for future research. *Schizophrenia Research, 75*, 405–416.

Dickey, C. C., McCarley, R. W., Xua, M. L., Seidman, L. J., Voglmaiera, M. M., Niznikiewicz, M. A., Connor, E., et al. (2007). fMRI abnormalities of the hippocampus and cavum septi pellucidi in females with schizotypal personality disorder. *Schizophrenia Research, 89*, 49–58.

Dickey, C. C., McCarley, R. W., Xua, M. L., Seidman, L. J., Voglmaier, M. M., Niznikiewicza, M. A., et al. (2006). MRI abnormalities of the hippocampus and cavum septi pellucidi in females with schizotypal personality disorder. *Schizophrenia Research*, in press.

DiClemente, R. J., Wingood, G. M., Harrington, K. F., Lang, D. L., Davies, S. L., Hook, E. W. III. (2004). Efficacy of an HIV prevention intervention for African American adolescent girls: A randomized controlled trial. *Journal of the American Medical Association, 292*, 171–179.

Dimidjian, S., Hollon, S. D., Dobson, K. S., Schmaling, K. B., Kohlenberg, R. J., Addis, M. E., et al. (2006). Randomized trial of behavioral activation, cognitive therapy, and antidepressant medication in the acute treatment of adults with major depression. *Journal of Consulting and Clinical Psychology, 74*, 658–670.

Dingfelder, S. F. (2004, March). Treatment for the "untreatable." *Monitor on Psychology, 35*, pp. 46–49.

Dingfelder, S. F. (2006, November). The hunt for endophenotypes. *Monitor on Psychology, 37*, pp. 20–21.

Dishion, T. J., & Owen, L. D. (2002). A longitudinal analysis of friendships and substance use: Bidirectional influence from adolescence to adulthood. *Developmental Psychology, 38*, 480–491.

Dittman, M. (2003, February). Psychology's first prescribers. *Monitor on Psychology*, pp. 36–37.

Dixit, A. R., & Crum, R. M. (2000). Prospective study of depression and the risk of heavy alcohol use in women. *American Journal of Psychiatry, 157*, 801–807.

Dixon, L., Adams, C., & Lucksted, A. (2000). Update on family psychoeducation for schizophrenia. *Schizophrenia Bulletin, 26 (1)*, 5–20.

Dixon, L., Weiden, P., Torres, M., & Lehman, A. (1997). Assertive community treatment and medication compliance in the homeless mentally ill. *American Journal of Psychiatry, 154*, 1302–1304.

Dobson, K. S., & Dozois, D. J. A. (2001). Historical and philosophical bases of the cognitive-behavioral therapies. In K. S. Dobson (Ed.), *Handbook of cognitive-behavioral therapies* (2nd ed., pp. 3–40). New York: Guilford Press.

Docherty, N. M., Cohen, A. S., Nienow, T. M., Dinzeo, T. J., & Dangelmaier, R. E. (2003). Stability of formal thought disorder and referential communication disturbances in schizophrenia. *Journal of Abnormal Psychology, 112*, 469–475.

Docherty, N. M., Gordinier, S. W., Hall, M. J., & Dombrowski, M. E. (2004). Referential communication disturbances in the speech of nonschizophrenic siblings of schizophrenia patients. *Journal of Abnormal Psychology, 113*, 399–405.

Dodge, K. A., Laird, R., Lochman, J. E., & Zelli, A. (2002). Multidimensional latent-construct analysis of children's social information processing patterns. *Psychological Assessment, 14*, 60–73.

Dodge, K. A., Lochman, J. E., Harnish, J. D., Bates, J. E., & Pettit, G. S. (1997). Reactive and proactive aggression in school children and psychiatrically impaired chronically assaultive youth. *Journal of Abnormal Psychology, 106*, 37–51.

Dohrenwend, B. P. (2006). Inventorying stressful life events as risk factors for psychopathology: toward resolution of the problem of intracategory variability. *Psychological Bulletin, 132*, 477–495

Dohrenwend, B. P., Turner, J. B., Turse, N. A., Adams, B. G., Koenen, K. C., & Marshall, R. (2006). The psychological risks of Vietnam for U.S. veterans: A revisit with new data and methods. *Science, 313*, 979–982.

Donker, F. J. S. (2000). Cardiac rehabilitation: A review of current developments. *Clinical Psychology Review, 20*, 923–943.

Dooren, J. C. (2004, September 14). FDA panel says antidepressants increase children suicide risk. *Wall Street Journal Online*. Retrieved September 15, 2004, from http://online.wsj.com/search.

Dorahy, M. J. (2001). Dissociative identity disorder and memory dysfunction: The current state of experimental research and its future directions. *Clinical Psychology Review, 21*, 771–795.

Dougall, A. L., & Baum, A. (2001). Stress, health, and illness. In A. Baum, T. A. Revenson, & J. E. Singer (Eds.), *Handbook of health psychology* (pp. 339–348). Mahwah, NJ: Erlbaum.

Dougherty, D. M., Mathias, C. W., Marsh, D. M., Moeller, F. G., and Swann, A. C. (2004). Suicidal behaviors and drug abuse: Impulsivity and its assessment. *Drug & Alcohol Dependence, 76*, S93–S105.

Dowker, A., Hermelin, B., & Pring, L. (1996). A savant poet. *Psychological Medicine, 26*, 913–924.

Draguns, J. G., & Tanaka-Matsumi, J. (2003). Assessment of psychopathology across and within cultures: Issues and findings *Behaviour Research and Therapy, 41*, 755–776.

Drake, R. E., Wallach, M. A., Teague, G. B., Freeman, D. H., Paskus, T. S., & Clark, T. A. (1991). Housing instability and homelessness among rural schizophrenic patients. *American Journal of Psychiatry, 148*, 211–215.

Drakenberg, K., et al. (2006). μ opioid receptor A118G polymorphism in association with striatal opioid neuropeptide gene expression in heroin abusers. *Proceedings of the National Academy of Sciences, 103*, 7883–7888.

Drewnowski, A. (1997). Taste preferences and food intake. *Annual Review of Nutrition, 17*, 237–253.

Drews, C. D., Yeargin-Allsopp, M., Decoufle, P., & Murphy, C. C. (1995). Variation in the influence of selected sociodemographic risk factors for mental retardation. *American Journal of Public Health, 85*, 329–334.

Drieling, T., van Calker, D., & Hecht, H. (2006). Stress, personality and depressive symptoms in a 6.5 year follow-up of subjects at familial risk for affective disorders and controls. *Journal of Affective Disorders, 91*, 195–203.

Druss, B. G., Miller, C. L., Rosenheck, R. A., Shih, S. C., & Bost, J. E. (2002). Mental health care quality under managed care in the United States: A view from the Health Employer Data and Information Set (HEDIS). *American Journal of Psychiatry, 159*, 567–572.

Druss, B. G., Rosenheck, R. A., & Sledge, W. H. (2000). Health and disability costs of depressive illness in a major U.S. corporation. *American Journal of Psychiatry, 157*, 1274–1278.

Dryden, W., & Ellis, A. (2001). Rational emotive behavior therapy. In K. S. Dobson (Ed.), *Handbook of cognitive-behavioral therapies* (2nd ed., pp. 295–348). New York: Guilford Press.

Du Pont heir found guilty of murder but mentally ill. (1997, February 26). *The New York Times*, p. A10.

Dubovsky, S. (2000, September). Lithium: The oldest specific psychotropic medication. *Journal Watch for Psychiatry*, pp. 73, 76.

Dubovsky, S. (2004, March). Neuroanatomimc responses to psychotherapy for depression. *Journal Watch Psychiatry, 10 (3)*, p. 24.

Dubovsky, S. (2006a). A new drug for the information-processing defect in schizophrenia. *Journal Watch Psychiatry*. Retrieved July 25, 2006, from http://psychiatry.jwatch.org/cgi/content/full/2006/724/2.

Dubovsky, S. (2006b). An update on the neurobiology of addiction. *Journal Watch Psychiatry*. Retrieved February 23, 2006, from http://psychiatry.jwatch.org/cgi/content/full/2006/222/7?q=etoc.

Dubovsky, S. (2006c, March 8). rTMS for Refractory Depression? *Journal Watch Psychiatry*. Retrieved August 14, 2006, from http://psychiatry.jwatch.org/cgi/content/full/2006/308/1.

Duckworth, G., & McBride, H. (1996). Suicide in old age: A tragedy of neglect. *Canadian Journal of Psychiatry, 41*, 217–222.

Duenweld, M. (2003, June 18). More Americans seeking help for depression. *The New York Times*, pp. A1, A22.

Duffy, A., Alda, M., Kutcher, S., Fusee, C., & Grof, P. (1998). Psychiatric symptoms and syndromes among adolescent children of parents with lithium-responsive or lithium-nonresponsive bipolar disorder. *American Journal of Psychiatry, 155*, 431–433.

Duffy, F. H. (1994). The role of quantified electroencephalography in psychological research. In G. Dawson & K. W. Fischer (Eds.), *Human behavior and the developing brain* (pp. 93–132). New York: Guilford Press.

Dugas, M. J. (2002). Generalized anxiety disorder. In M. Hersen (Ed.), *Clinical behavior therapy: Adults and children* (pp. 125–143). New York: Wiley.

Dugas, M. L., Ladouceur, R., Léger, E., Freeston, M. H., Langlis, F., Provencher, M. D., et al. (2003). Group cognitive-behavioral therapy for generalized anxiety disorder: Treatment outcome and long-term follow-up. *Journal of Consulting and Clinical Psychology, 71*, 821–825.

Dugger, C. W. (1992, September 3). Threat only when on crack, homeless man foils system. *The New York Times*, pp. A1, B4.

Dugger, C. W. (1994, July 15). Larry Hogue is arrested in Westchester. *The New York Times*, pp. B1, B2.

Dulit, R. A., Fyer, M. R., Leon, A. C., Brodsky, B. S., & Frances, A. J. (1994). Clinical correlates of self-mutilation in borderline personality disorder. *American Journal of Psychiatry, 151*, 1305–1311.

Dumais, A., Lesage, A. D., Alda, M., Rouleau, G., Dumont, M., Chawky, N., et al. (2005). Risk factors for suicide completion in major depression: A case-control study of impulsive and aggressive behaviors in men. *American Journal of Psychiatry, 162*, 2116–2124.

Duman, R. S., Heninger, G. R., & Nestler, E. J. (1997). A molecular and cellular theory of depression. *Archives of General Psychiatry, 54*, 597–606.

Duncan, J., Seitz, R. J., Kolodny, J., Bor, D., Herzog, H., Ahmed, A., et al. (2000). A neural basis for general intelligence. *Science, 289*, 457–460.

Durham, P. L. (2004). CGRP-receptor antagonists—a fresh approach to migraine therapy? *New England Journal of Medicine, 350*, 1073–1075.

Duran, B., Oetzel, J., Lucero, J., Jiang, Y., Novins, D. K., Manson, S., et al. (2005). Obstacles for rural American Indians seeking alcohol, drug, or mental health treatment. *Journal of Consulting and Clinical Psychology, 73*, 819–829.

Durantini, M. R., Albarracin, D., Mitchell, A. L., Earl, A. N., & Gillette, J. C. (2006). Conceptualizing the influence of social agents of behavior change: a meta-analysis of the effectiveness of HIV-prevention interventionists for different groups. *Psychological Bulletin, 132*, 212–248.

Durham v. United States, 214 F. 2d 862 (DC Circ 1954).

Durkheim, E. (1958). *Suicide* (J. A. Spaulding & G. Simpson, Trans.). New York: Free Press. (Original work published 1897.)

Dwyer, M. (1988). Exhibitionism/voyeurism. *Journal of Social Work and Human Sexuality, 7*, 101–112.

Dykens, E. M., & Hodapp, R. M. (1997). Treatment issues in genetic mental retardation syndromes. *Professional Psychology: Research and Practice, 28*, 263–270.

Dyslexia: The interaction of culture and biology. (2001, March 15). *CNN Web Posting*. Retrieved March 16, 2001, from http://www.cnn.com/2001/fyi/teachers.ednews/03/15/dyslexia.reading.ap.

E

Earnst, K. S., & Kring, A. M. (1997). Construct validity of negative symptoms: An empirical and conceptual review. *Clinical Psychology Review, 17*, 167–189.

Eaton, W. W., Dryman, A., & Weissman, M. M. (1991). Panic and phobia. In L. N. Robins & D. A. Regier (Eds.), *Psychiatric disorders in America: The Epidemiologic Catchment Area Study* (pp. 155–179). New York: Free Press.

Eaton, W. W., Kessler, R. C., Wittchen, H. U., & Magee, W. J. (1994). Panic and panic disorder in the United States. *American Journal of Psychiatry, 151,* 413–420.

Eberhardy, F. (1967). The view from "the couch." *Journal of Child Psychological Psychiatry, 8,* 257–263.

Ebigbo, P. O. (1993). Situation analysis of child abuse and neglect in Nigeria. *Journal of Psychology in Africa, 1,* 159–178.

Ebmeier, K. P., Donaghey, C., & Steele, J. D. (2006). Recent developments and current controversies in depression. *The Lancet, 367,* 153–167.

Eddleston, M. (2006). Physical vulnerability and fatal self-harm in the elderly. *British Journal of Psychiatry, 189,* 278–279.

Edelson, E. (1998, March 9). Migraines come into focus. *Newsday,* p. C7.

Edenberg, H. J., Strother, W. N., McClintick, J. N., Tian, H., Stephens, M., Jerome, R. E., et al. (2005). Gene Expression in the hippocampus of inbred alcohol-preferring and -nonpreferring rats. *Genes, Brain & Behavior, 4,* 20–30.

Edinger, J. D., Wohlgemuth, W. K., Radtke, R. A., Marsh, G. R., & Quillian, R. E. (2001). Cognitive behavioral therapy for treatment of chronic primary insomnia: A randomized controlled trial. *Journal of the American Medical Association, 285,* 1856–1864.

Edman, J. L., & Johnson, R. C. (1999). Filipino American and Caucasian American beliefs about the causes and treatment of mental problems. *Cultural Diversity and Ethnic Minority Psychology, 5,* 380–386.

Edmundson, M. (2001, June 3). I'm O.K, and then some. *The New York Times Book Review,* 33.

Edwards, J., Jackson, H. R., & Pattison, P. E. (2002). Emotion recognition via facial expression and affective prosody in schizophrenia: A methodological review. *Clinical Psychology Review, 22,* 789–832.

Edwards, V. J., Holden, G. W., Felitti, V. J., & Anda, R. F. (2003). Relationship between multiple forms of childhood maltreatment and adult mental health in community respondents: Results from the Adverse Childhood Experiences Study. *American Journal of Psychiatry, 160,* 1453–1460.

Egan, B. M. (2006). Sleep and hypertension: Burning the candle at both ends really is hazardous to your health. *Hypertension, 47,* 816–817.

Egan, J. (1991). Oppositional defiant disorder. In J. M. Wiener (Ed.), *Textbook of child and adolescent psychiatry.* Washington, DC: American Psychiatric Press.

Ehlers, A. (1995). A 1-year prospective study of panic attacks: Clinical course and factors associated with maintenance. *Journal of Abnormal Psychology, 104,* 164–172.

Ehlers, A., Clark, D. M., Hackmann, A., McManus, F., Fennell, M., Herbert, C., & Mayou, R. (2003). A randomized controlled trial of cognitive therapy, a self-help booklet, and repeated assessments as early interventions for posttraumatic stress disorder. *Archives of General Psychiatry, 60,* 1024–1032.

Ehlers, A., Mayou, R. A., & Bryant, B. (1998). Psychological predictors of chronic posttraumatic stress disorder after motor vehicle accidents. *Journal of Abnormal Psychology, 107,* 508–519.

Eiberg, H., Berendt, I., & Mohr, J. (1995). Assignment of dominant inherited nocturnal euresis (ENUR1) to chromosome 13q. *Nature Genetics, 10,* 354–356.

Eichstedt, J. A., & Arnold, S. L. (2001). Childhood-onset obsessive-compulsive disorder. A tic-related subtype of OCD? *Clinical Psychology Review, 21,* 137–157.

Einfeld, S. L., Piccinin, A. M., Mackinnon, A., Hofer, S. M., Taffe, J., Gray, K. M. et al. (2006). Psychopathology in young people with intellectual disability. *Journal of the American Medical Association, 296,* 1981–1989.

Eisenbruch, M. (1992). Toward a culturally sensitive *DSM:* Cultural bereavement in Cambodian refugees and the traditional healer as taxonomist. *Journal of Nervous and Mental Disease, 180,* 8–10.

Eisler, I., Dare, C., Hodes, M., Russell, G., Dodge, E., & Le Grange, D. (1997). Family and individual therapy in anorexia nervosa: A 5-year follow-up. *Archives of General Psychiatry, 54,* 1025–1030.

Eisner, D. A. (2000). *The death of psychotherapy: From Freud to alien abduction.* Westport, CT: Praeger.

El Nasser, H. (2003, June 19). 39 million make Hispanics largest minority group. *USA Today,* pp. 1, 3.

Elkin, I., Shea, M. T., Watkins, J. T., Imber, S. D., Sotsky, S. M., Collins, J. F., et al. (1989). National Institute of Mental Health treatment of depression collaborative research program: General effectiveness of treatments. *Archives of General Psychiatry, 46,* 971–982.

Ellason, J. W., & Ross, C. A. (1997). Two-year follow-up of inpatients with dissociative identity disorder. *American Journal of Psychiatry, 154,* 832–839.

Ellenbogen, J. M., Hulbert, J. C., Stickgold, R., Dinges, D. F., & Thompson-Schill, S. L. (2006). Interfering with theories of sleep and memory: sleep, declarative memory, and associative interference. *Current Biology, 16,* 1290–1294.

Ellickson, P. L., Hays, R. D., & Bell, R. M. (1992). St epping through the drug use sequence: Longitudinal scalogram analysis of initiation and regular use. *Journal of Abnormal Psychology, 101,* 441–451.

Elliott, A. J., Uldall, K. K., Bergam, K., Russo, J., Claypoole, K., & Roy-Byrne, P. P. (1998). Randomized, placebo-controlled trial of paroxetine versus imipramine in depressed HIV-positive outpatients. *American Journal of Psychiatry, 155,* 367–372.

Ellis, A. (1977b). The basic clinical theory of rational-emotive therapy. In A. Ellis & R. Grieger (Eds.), *Handbook of rational-emotive therapy.* (pp. 3–34) New York: Springer.

Ellis, A. (1993). Reflections on rational-emotive therapy. *Journal of Consulting and Clinical Psychology, 61,* 199–201.

Ellis, A. (1997). Using rational emotive behavior therapy techniques to cope with disability. *Professional Psychology: Research and Practice, 28,* 17–22.

Ellis, A. (2001). *Overcoming destructive beliefs, feelings, and behaviors: New directions for rational emotive behavior therapy.* Amherst, NY: Prometheus Books.

Ellis, A., & Dryden, W. (1987). *The practice of rational emotional therapy.* New York: Springer.

Ellis, B. J., Jackson, J. J., & Boyce, W. T. (2006). The stress response systems: universality and adaptive individual differences. *Developmental Review, 26,* 175–212.

Ellis, L., & Bonin, S. L. (2003). Genetics and occupation-related preferences. Evidence from adoptive and non-adoptive families. *Personality and Individual Differences, 35,* 929–937.

Epping-Jordan, J. E., Compas, B. E., & Howell, D. C. (1994). Predictors of cancer progression in young adult men and women: Avoidance, intrusive thoughts, and psychological symptoms. *Health Psychology, 13,* 539–547.

Epstein, D. H., Hawkins, W. E., Covia, L., Umbrichtc, A., & Preston, K. L. (2003). Cognitive–behavioral therapy plus contingency management for cocaine use: Findings during treatment and across 12-month followup. *Psychology of Addictive Behaviors, 17,* 73–82.

Epstein, H. (2003, October 12). Enough to make you sick? *The New York Times Magazine,* pp. 75–81, *98,* 102–108.

Erlenmeyer-Kimling, L., et al. (1997). The New York high-risk project: Prevalence and comorbidity of Axis I disorders in offspring of schizophrenic parents at 25-year follow-up. *Archives of General Psychiatry, 54,* 1096–1102.

Ernst, T., Chang, L., Leonido-Yee, M., & Speck, O. (2000). Evidence for long-term neurotoxicity associated with methamphetamine abuse: A 1HMRS study. *Neurology, 54,* 1344–1349.

Ertekin-Taner, N., Graff-Radford, N., Younkin, L. H., Eckman, C., Baker, M., Adamson, J., et al. (2000). Linkage of plasma A42 to a quantitative locus on chromosome 10 in late-onset Alzheimer's disease pedigrees. *Science, 290,* 2303–2304.

Escobar, J. I. (1998). Immigration and mental health: Why are immigrants better off? *Archives of General Psychiatry, 55,* 781–782.

Esparza, J., Fox, C., Harper, I. T., Bennett, P. H., Schulz, L. O., Valencia, M. E., et al. (2000). Daily energy expenditure in Mexican and USA Pima Indians: Low physical activity as a possible cause of obesity. *International Journal of Obesity and Related Metabolic Disorders, 24,* 55–59.

Espie, C. A. (2002). Insomnia. *Annual Review of Psychology, 53,* 215–243.

Espie, C. A., Inglis, S. J., & Harvey, L. (2001). Predicting clinically significant response to cognitive behavior therapy for chronic insomnia in general medical practice: Analyses of outcome data at 12 months posttreatment. *Journal of Consulting and Clinical Psychology, 69,* 58–66.

Espie, C. A., Inglis, S. J., Tessier, S., & Harvey, L. (2001). The clinical effectiveness of cognitive behaviour therapy for chronic insomnia: Implementation and evaluation of a sleep clinic in general medical practice. *Behaviour Research and Therapy, 39,* 45–60.

Essex, M. J., Kraemer, H. C., Armstrong, J. M., Boyce, W. T., Goldsmith, H. H., Klein, M. H. et al. (2006). Exploring risk factors for the emergence of children's mental health problems. *Archives of General Psychiatry, 63,* 1246–1256.

Essock, S. M., et al. (2000). Cost-effectiveness of clozapine compared with conventional antipsychotic medication for patients in state hospitals. *Archives of General Psychiatry, 57,* 987–994.

Esterling, B. A., L'Abate, L., Murray, E. J., & Pennebaker, J. W. (1999). Empirical foundations for writing in prevention and psychotherapy: Mental and physical health outcomes. *Clinical Psychology Review, 19,* 79–96.

Etminan, M., Gill, S., & Samii, A. (2003). Effect of non-steroidal anti-inflammatory drugs on risk of Alzheimer's disease: Systematic review and meta-analysis of observational studies. *British Medical Journal, 327,* 128–131.

Evans, S. W., Pelham, W. E., Smith, B. H., Bukstein, O., Gnagy, E. M., Greiner, A. R., et al. (2001). Dose-response effects of methylphenidate on ecologically valid measures of academic performance and classroom behavior in adolescents with ADHD. *Experimental and Clinical Psychopharmacology, 9,* 163–175.

Ewing, R., Schmid, T., Killingsworth, R., Zlot, A., & Raudenbush, S. (2003). Relationship between urban sprawl and physical activity, obesity and morbidity. *American Journal of Health Promotion, 18* (1), 47–57.

Exner, J. E. (1991). *The Rorschach: A comprehensive system: Vol. 2. Interpretation.* New York: Wiley.

Exner, J. E. (1993). *The Rorschach: A comprehensive system: Vol. 1. Basic foundations* (3rd ed.). New York: Wiley.

Exner, J. E., Jr. (2002). Early development of the Rorschach test. *Academy of Clinical Psychology Bulletin, 8,* 9–24.

F

Fabian, J. L. (1991). "Koro: Proposed classification for *DSM-IV*": Comment. *American Journal of Psychiatry, 148,* 1766.

Fabrega, H., Jr. (1990). Hispanic mental health research: A case for cultural psychiatry. *Journal of Behavioral Sciences, 12,* 339–365.

Fabrega, H., Jr. (1992). Diagnosis interminable: Toward a culturally sensitive *DSM-IV. Journal of Nervous and Mental Disease, 180,* 5–7.

Fackelmann, K. (2003, August 19). Alzheimer's cases expected to rise at a more rapid rate. *USA Today,* p. 7D.

Failer, J. L. (2002). *Who qualifies for rights? Homelessness, mental illness, and civil commitment.* Ithaca, NY: Cornell University Press.

Fairburn, C. G., & Wilson, G. T. (Eds.). (1993). *Binge eating: Nature, assessment, and treatment.* New York: Guilford Press.

Fairburn, C. G., Stice, E., Cooper, Z., Doll, H. A., Norman, P. A., & O'Connor, E. E. (2003). Understanding persistence in bulimia nervosa: A 5-year naturalistic study. *Journal of Consulting and Clinical Psychology, 71,* 103–109.

Fairburn, C. G., Welch, S. L., Doll, H. A., Davies, B. A., & O'Connor, M. E. (1997). Risk factors for bulimia nervosa: A community-based case-control study. *Archives of General Psychiatry, 54,* 509–517.

Fallon, B. A., et al. (1993). Fluoxetine for hypochondriacal patients without major depression. *Journal of Clinical Psychopharmacology, 13,* 438–441.

Fals-Stewart, W. (2003). The occurrence of partner physical aggression on days of alcohol consumption: A longitudinal diary study. *Journal of Consulting and Clinical Psychology, 71,* 41–52.

Fanous, A. H., van den Oord, E. J., Riley, B. P., Aggen, S. H., Neale, M. C., O'Neill, A., et al. (2005). Relationship between a high-risk haplotype in the dtnbp1 (dysbindin) gene and clinical features of schizophrenia. *American Journal of Psychiatry, 162,* 1824–1832.

Faraone, S. V. (2003a, August). *ADHD: Facts and fiction.* Paper presented at the meeting of the American Psychological Association, Toronto, CA.

Faraone, S. V. (2003b, August). *The persistence of attention-deficit/hyperactivity disorder through adolescence and adulthood.* Paper presented at the meeting of the American Psychological Association, Toronto, CA.

Faraone, S. V., Biederman, J., Feighner, J. A., & Monuteaux, M. C. (2000). Assessing symptoms of attention deficit hyperactivity disorder in children and adults: Which is more valid? *Journal of Consulting and Clinical Psychology, 68,* 830–842.

Faraone, S. V., Biederman, J., Mick, E., Williamson, S., Wilens, T., Spencer, T., et al. (2000). Family study of girls with attention deficit hyperactivity disorder. *American Journal of Psychiatry, 157*(7), 1077–1083.

Faraone, S. V., Biederman, J., Spencer, T., Mick, E., Murray, K., Petty, C, et al. (2006). Diagnosing adult attention deficit hyperactivity disorder: Are late onset and subthreshold diagnoses valid? *American Journal of Psychiatry 163,* 1720–1729.

Faraone, S. V., Doyle, A. E., Mick, E., & Biederman, J. (2001). Meta-analysis of the association between the 7-repeat allele of the dopamine d4 receptor gene and attention deficit hyperactivity disorder. *American Journal of Psychiatry, 158,* 1052–1057.

Faraone, S. V., et al. (1993). Intellectual performance and school failure in children with attention deficit hyperactivity disorders and their siblings. *Journal of Abnormal Psychology, 102,* 616–623.

Farber, B. A., Brink, D. C., & Raskin, P. M. (1996). *The psychotherapy of Carl Rogers: Cases and commentary* (pp. 74–75). New York: The Guilford Press.

Farmer, R. F. (2000). Issues in the assessment and conceptualization of personality disorders. *Clinical Psychology Review, 20,* 823–851.

Farooqi, I. S., Keogh, J. M., Yeo, G. S. H., Lank, E. J., Cheetham, T., et al. (2003). Clinical spectrum of obesity and mutations in the melanocortin 4 receptor gene. *New England Journal of Medicine, 348,* 1085–1095.

Farr, C. B. (1994). Benjamin Rush and American psychiatry. *American Journal of Psychiatry, 151*(Suppl.), 65–73.

Farrell, A. D., & White, K. S. (1998). Peer influences and drug use among urban adolescents: Family structure and parent/adolescent relationship as protective factors. *Journal of Consulting and Clinical Psychology, 66,* 248–258.

Farrell, A. D., Camplair, P. S., & McCullough, L. (1987). Identification of target complaints by computer interview: Evaluation of the Computerized Assessment System for Psychotherapy Evaluation and Research. *Journal of Consulting and Clinical Psychology, 55,* 691–700.

Fassbender, C., & Schweitzer, J. B. (2006). Is there evidence for neural compensation in attention deficit hyperactivity disorder? A review of the functional neuroimaging literature. *Clinical Psychology Review, 26,* 445–465.

Fava, M., Bless, E., Otto, M. W., Pava, J. A., & Rosenbaum, J. F. (1994). Dysfunctional attitudes in major depression: Changes with pharmacotherapy. *Journal of Nervous and Mental Disease, 182,* 45–49.

FDA approves nicotine lozenge (2002, November 1). Retrieved November 1, 2002, from http://www.cnn.com/2002/HEALTH/11/01/tobacco.lozenge.ap/index.html.

Feldman, L. B., & Rivas-Vazquez, R. A. (2003). Assessment and treatment of social anxiety disorder *Professional Psychology: Research and Practice, 34,* 396–405.

Feldman, M. D. (2003). Foreword to *"Sickened, the memoir of a Munchausen by proxy childhood"* (pp. v–ix). New York: Bantam.

Feng, Y., Niu, T., Xing, H., Xu, X., Chen, C., Peng, S., et al. (2004). A common haplotype of the nicotine acetylcholine receptor alpha 4 subunit gene is associated with vulnerability to nicotine addiction in men. *American Journal of Human Genetics, 75,* 112–121.

Fensterheim, H., & Kantor, J. S. (1980). Behavioral approach to sexual disorders. In B. Wolman & J. Money (Eds.), *Handbook of human sexuality.* Englewood Cliffs, NJ: Prentice Hall.

Ferdinand, R. F., Bongersa, I. L., van der Ende, J., van Gastela, W., Tick, N., Utens, E. et al. (2006). Distinctions between separation anxiety and social anxiety in children and adolescents. *Behaviour Research and Therapy, 44,* 1523–1535.

Ferguson-Peters, M. (1985). Racial socialization of young black children. In H. & J. L. McAdoo (Eds.), *Black children* (pp. 159–173). Beverly Hills, CA: Sage Publications.

Fergusson, D. M., & Woodward, L. J. (2002). Mental health, educational, and social role outcomes of adolescents with depression. *Archives of General Psychiatry, 59,* 225–231.

Fergusson, D. M., Horwood, L. J., & Meautrais, A. L. (1999). Is sexual orientation related to mental health problems and suicidality in young people? *Archives of General Psychiatry, 56,* 876–880.

Ferketich, A. K., Schwartzbaum, J. A., Frid, D. J., & Moeschberger, M. L. (2000). Depression as an antecedent to heart disease among women and men in the NHANES I Study. *Archives of Internal Medicine, 160,* 1261–1268.

Ferrans, C. E., Cohen, F. L., & Smith, K. M. (1992). The quality of life of persons with narcolepsy. *Loss, Grief and Care, 5,* 23–32.

Ferri, M., Amato, L., & Davoli, M. (2006). Alcoholics Anonymous and other 12-step programmes for alcohol dependence. *The Cochrane Database of Systematic Reviews,* No. 3. Retrieved September 23, 2006, from http://dx.doi.org/10.1002/14651858.CD005032.pub2.

Fertuck, E. A., Lenzenweger, M. F., Clarkin, J. F., Hoermann, S., & Stanley, B. (2006). Executive neurocognition, memory systems, and borderline personality disorder. *Clinical Psychology Review, 26,* 346–375.

Fewer teens using drugs. (2004). Retrieved March 3, 2004, from http://www.cnn.com/2004/HEALTH/parenting/02/25/teen.drug/index.html.

Field, A. P. (2006). Is conditioning a useful framework for understanding the development and treatment of phobias? *Clinical Psychology Review, 26,* 857–875.

Fiellin, D. A., O'Connor, P. G., Chawarski, M., Pakes, J. P. Pantalon, M. V., & Schottenfeld, R. S. (2001). Methadone maintenance in primary care: A randomized controlled trial. *Journal of the American Medical Association, 286,* 1724–1731.

Fieve, R. R. (1975). *Moodswings: The third revolution in psychiatry.* New York: Morrow.

Fiez, J. A. (2001). Bridging the gap between neuroimaging and neuropsychology: Using working memory as a case-study. *Journal of Clinical & Experimental Neuropsychology, 23,* 19–31.

Finkelhor, D., Hotaling, G., Lewis, I. A., & Smith, C. (1990). Sexual abuse in a national survey of adult men and women: Prevalence, characteristics, and risk factors. *Child Abuse and Neglect, 14,* 19–28.

Finney, J. W., & Monahan, S. C. (1996). The cost-effectiveness of treatment for alcoholism: A second approximation. *Journal of Studies on Alcohol, 57,* 229–243.

Firestone, R. W., Firestone, L. A., & Catlett, J. (2006). *Sex and love in intimate relationships.* Washington, DC: American Psychological Association.

First, M. (2006). Beyond clinical utility: Broadening the *DSM-V* research appendix to include alternative diagnostic constructs. *American Journal of Psychiatry, 163,* 1679–1681.

First, M. B. (2005). Clinical utility: A prerequisite for the adoption of a dimensional approach in *DSM. Journal of Abnormal Psychology, 114,* 560–564.

Fishbain, D. A. (1991). "Koro: Proposed classification for *DSM-IV*": Comment. *American Journal of Psychiatry, 148,* 1765–1766.

Fisher, B. S., Daigle, L. E., Cullen, F. T., & Turner, M. G. (2003). Reporting sexual victimization to the police and others: Results from a national-level study of college women. *Criminal Justice & Behavior, 30*(1), 6–38.

Fisher, J. D., Fisher, W. A., Bryan, A. D., & Misovich, S. J. (2002). Information-motivation-behavioral skills model-based HIV risk behavior change intervention for inner-city high school youth. *Health Psychology, 21,* 177–186.

Fisher, P. L., & Wells, A. (2005). How effective are cognitive and behavioral treatments for obsessive–compulsive disorder? A clinical significance analysis. *Behaviour Research and Therapy, 43,* 1543–1558.

Fisher, W. A., Rosen, R. C., Mollen, M., Brock, G., Karlin G, Pommerville, P. et al. (2005). Improving the sexual quality of life of couples affected by erectile dysfunction: A double-blind, randomized, placebo-controlled trial of vardenafil. *Journal of Sexual Medicine, 2*(5), 699–708.

Fitzgerald, P. B., Benitez, J., de Castella, A., Daskalakis, J., Brown, T. L., & Kulkarni, J. (2005). A randomized, controlled trial of sequential bilateral repetitive transcranial magnetic stimulation for treatment-resistant depression. *American Journal of Psychiatry, 163,* 88–94.

Fitzgerald, P. B., Brown, T. L., Marston, N. A. U., Daskalakis, J., de Castella, A., & Kulkarni, J. (2003). Transcranial magnetic stimulation in the treatment of depression: A double-blind, placebo-controlled trial. *Archives of General Psychiatry, 60,* 1002–1008.

Flegal, K. M., Graubard, B. I., Williamson, D. F., & Gail, M. H. (2005). Excess deaths associated with underweight, overweight, and obesity. *Journal of the American Medical Association, 293,* 1861–1867.

Foa, E. B. (1996). The efficacy of behavioral therapy with obsessive-compulsives. *The Clinical Psychologist, 49,* 19–21.

Foa, E. B., & Kozak, M. J. (1995). *DSM-IV* field trial: Obsessive-compulsive disorder. *American Journal of Psychiatry, 152,* 90–96.

Foa, E. B., & Rothbaum, B. O. (1998). *Treating the trauma of rape: Cognitive-behavioral therapy for PTSD.* New York: Guilford Press.

Foderaro, L. W. (1994, November 8). "Clubhouse" helps mentally ill find the way back. *The New York Times,* p. B1.

Folsom, D. P., Hawthorne, W., Lindamer, L., Gilmer, T., Bailey, A., Golshan, S., Garcia, P., et al. (2005). Prevalence and risk factors for homelessness and utilization of mental health services among 10,340 patients with serious mental illness in a large public mental health system. *American Journal of Psychiatry, 162,* 370–376.

Fombonne, E. (2003a). The prevalence of autism. *Journal of the American Medical Association, 287,* 87–89.

Fombonne, E. (2003b). Epidemiological surveys of autism and other pervasive developmental disorders: An update. *Journal of Autism and Developmental Disorders, 33,* 365–382.

Fontaine, K. R., Redden, D. T., Wang, C., Westfall, A. O., & Allison, D. B. (2003). Years of life lost due to obesity. *Journal of the American Medical Association, 289,* 187–193.

Food and Drug Administration (FDA) (2004, March). Antidepressant use in children, adolescents, and adults. *FDA/Center for Drug Evaluation and Research Online Posting.* Retrieved April 23, 2004, from http://www.fda.gov/cder/drug/antidepressants/default.htm.

Foote, B., et al. (2005). Prevalence of dissociative disorders in psychiatric outpatients. *American Journal of Psychiatry, 163,* 623–629.

Ford, J. M., Mathalon, D. H., Kalba, S., Whitfield, S., Faustman, W. O., & Roth, W. T. (2001). Cortical responsiveness during inner speech in schizophrenia: An event-related potential study. *American Journal of Psychiatry, 158,* 1914–1916.

Forman, D. N., et al. (2000). Postpartum depression: Identification of women at risk. *British Journal of Obstetrics and Gynaecology, 107,* 1210–1217.

Foster, S. E., Vaughan, R. D., Foster, W. H., & Califano, Jr., J. A. (2003). Alcohol consumption and expenditures for underage drinking and adult excessive drinking. *Journal of the American Medical Association, 289,* 989–995.

Fouquereau, E., Fernandez, A., Mullet, E., & Sorum, P. C. (2003). Stress and the urge to drink. *Addictive Behaviors, 28,* 669–685.

Fowles, D. C. (1993). Electrodermal activity and antisocial behavior: Empirical findings and theoretical issues. In J. C. Roy, et al. (Eds.), *Psychological theories of drinking and alcoholism* (pp. 181–226). New York: Guilford Press.

Fox, M. (2000, August 21). Autism checks urged for all babies. *Reuters Limited, MSNBC Web Posting.* Retrieved August 23, 2000, from http://www.msnbc.com/news/449244.asp.

Foxhall, K. (2001, March). Study finds marital stress can triple women's risk of recurrent coronary event. *Monitor on Psychology, 32,* p. 14.

Frackiewicz, E. J., Sramek, J. J., Herrera, J. M., & Cutler, N. R. (1999). Review of neuroleptic dosage in different ethnic groups. In J. M. Herrera, et al. (Eds.), *Cross cultural psychiatry* (pp. 107–130). Chichester, England: Wiley.

Fraga, M. F., Ballestar, E., Paz, M. F., Ropero, S., Setien, F., Ballestar, M. L., et al. (2005). Epigenetic differences arise during the lifetime of monozygotic twins. *Proceedings of the National Academy of Sciences, 102,* 10604–10609.

Frangou, S., Lewis, M., & McCrone, P. (2006). Efficacy of ethyl-eicosapentaenoic acid in bipolar depression: Randomised double-blind placebo-controlled study. *British Journal of Psychiatry, 188,* 46–50.

Frank, E., & Kupfer, D. J. (2000). Peeking through the door to the 21st century. *Archives of General Psychiatry, 57,* 83–85.

Frank, E., & Kupfer, D. J. (2003). Progress in the therapy of mood disorders: Scientific support. *American Journal of Psychiatry, 160,* 1207–1208.

Frank, E., Kupfer, D. J., Thase, M. E., Mallinger, A. G., Swartz, H. A., Fagiolini, A. M. (2005). Two-year outcomes for interpersonal and social rhythm therapy in individuals with bipolar I disorder. *Archives of General Psychiatry, 62,* 996–1004.

Frankle, W. G., Perlis, R. H., Deckersbach, T., Grandin, L. D., Gray, S. M., Sachs, et al. (2002). Bipolar depression: Relationship between episode length and antidepressant treatment. *Psychological Medicine, 32,* 1417–1423.

Franklin, M. E., Abramowitz, J. S., Bux Jr., D. A., Zoellner, L. A., & Feeny, N. C. (2002). Cognitive–behavioral therapy with and without medication in the treatment of obsessive–compulsive disorder. *Professional Psychology: Research and Practice, 33,* 162–168.

Franklin, M. E., Rynn, M., March, J. S., & Foa, E. B. (2002). Obsessive-compulsive disorder. In M. Hersen (Ed.), *Clinical behavior therapy: Adults and children.* (pp. 276–303). New York: John Wiley & Sons, Inc.

Franko, D. L., &. Keel, P. K. (2006). Suicidality in eating disorders: Occurrence, correlates, and clinical implications. *Clinical Psychology Review, 26,* 769–782.

Fraser, J. S. (1996). All that glitters is not always gold: Medical offset effects and managed behavioral health care. *Professional Psychology: Research & Practice, 27,* 335–344.

Frasure-Smith, N., & Lespérance, F. (2005). Depression and coronary heart disease: complex synergism of mind, body, and environment. *Current Directions in Psychological Science, 14,* 39–43.

Frattaroli, J. (2006). Experimental disclosure and its moderators: A meta-analysis. *Psychological Bulletin, 132,* 823–865.

Frauenglass, S., et al. (1997). Family support decreases influence of deviant peers on Hispanic adolescent's substance use. *Journal of Clinical Child Psychology, 26,* 15–23.

Fredrickson, B. L., Tugade, M. M., Waugh, C. E., & Larkin, G. R. (2003). What good are positive emotions in crises? A prospective study of resilience and emotions following the terrorist attacks on the United States on September 11th, 2001. *Journal of Personality and Social Psychology, 84,* 365–376.

Freedman, R. (2003). Schizophrenia. *New England Journal of Medicine, 349,* 1738–1749.

Freedman, R. (2005). The choice of antipsychotic drugs for schizophrenia. *New England Journal of Medicine, 355,* 1286–1288.

Freedman, R., et al. (1987). Neurobiological studies of sensory gating in schizophrenia. *Schizophrenia Bulletin, 13,* 669–678.

Freemon, F. R. (1981). *Organic mental disease.* Jamaica, NY: Spectrum.

Fregni, F., Ono, C. R. Santos, C. M., Bermpohl, F., Buchpiguel, C., Barbosa, E. R., et al. (2006). Effects of antidepressant treatment with rTMS and fluoxetine on brain perfusion in PD. *Neurology, 66,* 1629–1637.

Freiberg, P. (1995, June). Psychologists examine attacks on homosexuals. *APA Monitor, 26*(6), 30–31.

Freud, S. (1957). Mourning and melancholia. (1917). In J. Rickman (Ed.), *A general selection from the works of Sigmund Freud.* Garden City, NY: Doubleday.

Freud, S. (1964). New introductory lectures. In *Standard edition of the complete psychological works of Sigmund Freud* (Vol. 22). London: Hogarth. (Original work published in 1933) (pp. 3–182).

Fricchione, G. (2004). Generalized anxiety disorder. *New England Journal of Medicine, 351,* 675–682.

Frick, P. J., & Silverthorn, P. (2001). Psychopathology in children and adolescents. In H. E. Adams (Ed.), *Comprehensive handbook of psychopathology* (3rd ed., 879–919). New York: Plenum Press.

Frick, P. J., Lahey, B. B., Loeber, R., Stouthamer-Loeber, M., Christ, M. A., & Hanson, K. (1992). Familial risk factors to oppositional defiant disorder and conduct disorder: Parental psychopathology and maternal parenting. *Journal of Consulting and Clinical Psychology, 60,* 49–55.

Friedman, M., & Ulmer, D. (1984). *Treating Type A behavior and your heart.* New York: Fawcett Crest.

Friedman, M., et al. (1986). Alteration of type A behavior and its effect on cardiac recurrences in postmyocardial infarction patients: Summary results of the recurrent coronary prevention project. *American Heart Journal, 112,* 653–665.

Friedman, M. A., Friedman, M. A., Leventhal, H. E., Horne, R., Keitner, G. I., & Miller, I. W. (2004). Combined psychotherapy and pharmacotherapy for the treatment of major depressive disorder. *Clinical Psychology: Science and Practice, 11,* 47–68.

Friedman, R. A. (2002, December 31). Born to be happy, through a twist of human hard wire. *The New York Times,* p. F5.

Friedman, R. A. (2005). The changing face of teenage drug abuse—the trend toward prescription drugs. *New England Journal of Medicine, 354,* 1448–1450.

Friedman, R. A., & Leon, A. C. (2007). Expanding the black box—depression, antidepressants, and the risk of suicide. *New England Journal of Medicine, 356,* 2343–2346.

Friedman, S. D., Shaw, D. W. W., Artru, A. A., Dawson, G., Petropoulos, H., & Dager, S. R. (2006). Gray and white matter brain chemistry in young children with autism. *Archives of General Psychiatry, 63,* 786–794.

Fritz, G., Rockney, R., and Work Group on Quality Issues (2004). Summary of the practice parameter for the assessment and treatment of children and adolescents with enuresis. *Journal of the American Academy of Child and Adolescent Psychiatry, 43,* 123–125.

Frueh, B. C., et al. (1996). Trauma management therapy: A preliminary evaluation of a multicomponent behavioral treatment for chronic combat-related PTSD. *Behaviour Research and Therapy, 34,* 533–543.

Fuchs, C. S., Stampfer, M. J., Colditz, G. A., Giovannucci, E. L., Manson, J. E., Kawachi, I., et al. (1995). Alcohol consumption and mortality among women. *The New England Journal of Medicine, 332,* 1245–1250.

Fuchs, M. (2001, June 9). For Alzheimer's patients, some solace, if not hope. *The New York Times,* pp. B1, B6.

Fuertes, J. N., & Brobst, K. (2002). Clients' ratings of counselor multicultural competency. *Cultural Diversity and Ethnic Minority Psychology, 8,* 214–223.

Fuller, R. L., Luck, S. J., McMahon, R. P., & Gold, J. M. (2005). Working memory consolidation is abnormally slow in schizophrenia. *Journal of Abnormal Psychology, 114,* 279–290.

Fung, M. T., Raine, A., Loeber, R., Lynam, D. R., Steinhauer, S. R., Venables, P. H. et al. (2005). Reduced electrodermal activity in psychopathy-prone adolescents. *Journal of Abnormal Psychology, 114,* 187–196.

Furlong, M., & Oei, T. P. S. (2002). Changes to automatic thoughts and dysfuntional attitudes in group: CBT for depression. *Behavioural and Cognitive Psychotherapy, 30,* 351–360.

Furukawa, T. A., McGuire, H., & Barbui, C. (2002). Meta-analysis of effects and side effects of low dosage tricyclic antidepressants in depression: Systematic review. *British Medical Journal, 325,* 991–995.

G

Gabb, J., Sonderegger, L., Scherrer, S., & Ehlert, U. (2006). Psychoneuroendocrine effects of cognitive-behavioral stress management in a naturalistic setting—a randomized controlled trial. *Psychoneuroendocrinology, 31,* 428–438.

Gabbard, G. O. (2005). Mind, brain, and personality disorders. *American Journal of Psychiatry, 162,* 648–655.

Gabbard, G. O., et al. (1997). The economic impact of psychotherapy: A review. *American Journal of Psychiatry, 154,* 147–155.

Gable, S. L., & Haidt, J. (2005). What (and why) is positive psychology? *Review of General Psychology, 9,* 103–110.

Galea, S., Nandi, A., & Vlahov, D. (2005). The epidemiology of post-traumatic stress disorder after disasters. *Epidemiologic Reviews, 27,* 78–91.

Galea, S., Vlahov, D., Resnick, H., Kilpatrick, D., Bucuvalas, M. J., & Morgan, M. D. (2002) An investigation of the psychological effects of the September 11, 2001, attacks on New York City: Developing and implementing research in the acute postdisaster period. *CNS Spectrums, 7,* 585–587.

Gall, R., Isaac, L., & Kryger, M. (1993). Quality of life in mild obstructive sleep apnea. *Sleep, 16*(Suppl.), S59–S61.

Gallant, J. E. (2000). Strategies for long-term success in the treatment of HIV infection. *Journal of the American Medical Association, 283,* 1329–1334.

Gamble, S. A., Talbot, N. L., Duberstein, P. R., Conner, K. R., Franus, N., Beckman, A., et al. (2006). Childhood sexual abuse and depressive symptom severity: the role of neuroticism. *Journal of Nervous & Mental Disease, 194,* 382–385.

Ganellen, R. J. (1996). Comparing the diagnostic efficiency of the MMPI, MCMIII, and Rorschach: A review. *Journal of Personality Assessment, 67,* 219–243.

Gangwisch, J. E.,. Heymsfield, S. B., Boden-Albala, B., Buijs, R. M., Kreier, F., Pickering, T. G., et al. (2006). Short sleep duration as a risk factor for hypertension: Analyses of the first National Health and Nutrition Examination Survey. *Hypertension, 47,* 1–2.

Gara, M. A., Woolfolk, R. L., Cohen, B. D., Goldston, R. B., Allen, L. A., & Novalany, J. (1993). Perceptions of self and other in major depression. *Journal of Abnormal Psychology, 102,* 93–100.

Garb, H. N. (1997). Race bias, social class bias, and gender bias in clinical judgment. *Clinical Psychology: Science and Practice, 4,* 99–120.

Garb, H. N. (2000). Computers will become increasingly important for psychological assessment: Not that there's anything wrong with that! *Psychological Assessment, 12,* 31–39.

Garb, H. N. (2003a). Incremental validity and the assessment of psychopathology in adults. *Psychological Assessment, 15,* 508–520.

Garb, H. N. (2003b, Winter). Letter to the editor. *The Clinical Psychologist, 56,* p. 5.

Garb, H. N., Wood, J. M., Lilienfeld, S. O., & Nezworski, M. T. (2002). Effective use of projective techniques in clinical practice: Let the data help with selection and interpretation. *Professional Psychology: Research and Practice, 33,* 454–463.

Garb, H. N., Wood, J. M., Lilienfeld, S. O., & Nezworski, M. T. (2005). Roots of the Rorschach controversy. *Clinical Psychology Review, 25,* 97–118.

Garber, J., Keiley, M. K., & Martin, N. C. (2002). Developmental trajectories of adolescents' depressive symptoms: Predictors of change. *Journal of Consulting & Clinical Psychology, 70,* 79–95.

Garber, J., Weiss, B., & Shanley, N. (1993). Cognitions, depressive symptoms, and development in adolescents. *Journal of Abnormal Psychology, 102,* 47–57.

Garbutt, J. C., Kranzler, H. R., O'Malley, S. S., Gastfriend, D. R., Pettinati, H. M., Silverman, B. L., et al. (2005a). Efficacy and tolerability of long-acting injectable naltrexone for alcohol dependence: A randomized controlled trial. *Journal of the American Medical Association, 293,* 1617–1625.

Garbutt, J. C., Kranzler, H. R., O'Malley, S. S., Gastfriend, D. R., Silverman, B. L., Loewy, J. W., et al. (2005b). Naltrexone treatment for alcohol dependency—Reply. *Journal of the American Medical Association, 294,* 900.

Garbutt, J. C., West, S. L., Carey, T. S., Lohr, K. N., & Crews, F. T. (1999). Pharmacological treatment of alcohol dependence. *Journal of the American Medical Association, 281,* 1318–1325.

Garcia-Lopez, L.-J., Olivares, J., Beidel, D., Albano, A.-M., Turner, S., & Rosa, A. I. (2006). Efficacy of three treatment protocols for adolescents with social anxiety disorder: A 5-year follow-up assessment. *Journal of Anxiety Disorders, 20,* 175–191.

Gardner, W., Lidz, C. W., Mulvey, E. P., & Shaw, E. C. (1996). Clinical versus actuarial predictions of violence in patients with mental illnesses. *Journal of Consulting and Clinical Psychology, 64,* 602–609.

Garfield, S. L. (1994). Eclecticism and integration in psychotherapy: Developments and issues. *Clinical Psychology: Science and Practice, 1,* 123–137.

Garlick, D. (2003). Integrating brain science research with intelligence research. *Current Directions in Psychological Science, 12,* 185–189.

Garnefski, N., Kraaij, V., & Spinhoven, P. (2001). De relatie tussen cognitieve copingstrategieen en symptomen van depressie, angst en suiecidaliteit. *Gedrag & Gezondheid: Tijdschrift voor Psychologie & Gezondheid, 29,* 148–158.

Garner, D. M. (1993). Binge eating in anorexia nervosa. In C. G. Fairburn & G. T. Wilson (Eds.), *Binge eating: Nature, assessment, and treatment* (pp. 50–76). New York: Guilford.

Gaser, C., Nenadic, I., Buchsbaum, B. R., Hazlett, E. A., & Buchsbaum, M.S. (2004). Ventricular enlargement in schizophrenia related to volume reduction of the thalamus, striatum, and superior temporal cortex. *American Journal of Psychiatry, 161,* 154–156.

Gatchel, R. J. (2001). Biofeedback and self-regulation of physiological activity: A major adjunctive treatment modality in health psychology. In A. Baum, T. A. Revenson, & J. E. Singer (Eds.), *Handbook of health psychology* (pp. 95–104). Mahwah, NJ: Erlbaum.

Gatz, M., Reynolds, C. A., Fratiglioni, L., Johansson, B., Mortimer, J. A., Berg, S., et al. (2006). Role of genes and environments for explaining Alzheimer Disease. *Archives of General Psychiatry, 63,* 168–174.

Gauthier, J. G., Ivers, H., & Carrier, S. (1996). Nonpharmacological approaches in the management of recurrent headache disorders and their comparison and combination with pharmacotherapy. *Clinical Psychology Review, 16,* 543–571.

Gavin, N. I., Gaynes, B. N., Lohr, K. N., Meltzer-Brody, S., Gartlehner, G., & Swinson, T. (2005). Perinatal depression: A systematic review of prevalence and incidence. *Obstetrics & Gynecology, 106,* 1071–1083.

Gawin, F. H. (1991). Cocaine addiction: Psychology and neurophysiology. *Science, 251,* 1581.

Gebhard, P. H., Gagnon, J. H., Pomeroy, W. B., & Christenson, C. V. (1965). *Sex offenders: An analysis of types.* New York: Harper & Row.

Geddes, J. R., Burgess, S., Hawton, K., Jamison, K., & Goodwin, G. M. (2004). Long-term lithium therapy for bipolar disorder: Systematic review and meta-analysis of randomized controlled trials. *American Journal of Psychiatry, 161,* 217–222.

Geddes, J., Freemantle, N., Harrison, P., & Bebbington, P. (2000). Atypical antipsychotics in the treatment of schizophrenia: Systematic overview and meta-regression analysis. *British Medical Journal, 321,* 1371–1376.

Geer, J., Heiman, J., & Leitenberg, H. (1984). *Human sexuality.* Englewood Cliffs, NJ: Prentice Hall.

Geipert, N. (2007, January). Don't be mad: More research links hostility to coronary risk. *Monitor on Psychology, 38,* pp. 50–51.

Gelernter, J., Page, G. P., Stein, M. B., & Woods, S. W. (2004). Genome-wide linkage scan for loci predisposing to social phobia: Evidence for a chromosome 16 risk locus. *American Journal of Psychiatry, 161,* 59–66.

Geller, B. (2006, October 16). Early use of methylphenidate: The jury on neuronal effects is still out. *Journal Watch Psychiatry.* Retrieved October 16, 2006, from http://psychiatry.jwatch.org/cgi/content/full/2006/1016/2.

Geller, B., & DelBello, M. P. (Eds.). (2003). *Bipolar disorder in childhood and early adolescence.* New York: Guilford.

Geller, B., Craney, J. L., Bolhofner, K., Nickelsburg, M. J., Williams, M., & Zimerman, B. (2002). Two-year prospective follow-up of children with a prepubertal and early adolescent bipolar disorder phenotype. *American Journal of Psychiatry, 159,* 927–933.

Geller, B., Tillman, R., Craney, J. L., & Bolhofner, K. (2005). Four-year prospective outcome and natural history of mania in children with a prepubertal and early adolescent bipolar disorder phenotype. *Archives of General Psychiatry, 61,* 459–467.

Gelman, D. (1994, April 18). The mystery of suicide. *Newsweek,* pp. 44–49.

George, M. S., Anton, R. F., Bloomer, C., Teneback, C., Drobes, D. J., Lorberbaum, J. P., et al. (2001). Activ ion of prefrontal cortex and anterior thalamus in alcoholic subjects on exposure to alcohol-specific cues. *Archives of General Psychiatry, 58,* 345–352.

George, M. S., Nahas, Z., Molloy, M., Speer, A. M., Oliver, N. C., Li, X. B., et al. (2000). A control led trial of daily left prefrontal cortex TMS for treating depression. *Biological Psychiatry, 48,* 382–389.

Gerevich, J., Treuer, T., Danics, Z., & Herr, J. (2005). Diagnostic and psychodynamic aspects of sexual addiction appearing as a non-paraphiliac form of compulsive sexual behaviour. *Journal of Substance Use, 10,* 253–259.

Gershater-Molkoa, R. M., Lutzker, J. R., & Sherman, J. A. (2002). Intervention in child neglect: An applied behavioral perspective. *Aggression and Violent Behavior, 7,* 103–124.

Gershon, A. A., Dannon, P. N., & Grunhaus, L. (2003). Transcranial magnetic stimulation in the treatment of depression. *American Journal of Psychiatry, 160,* 835–845.

Gershon, E. S., & Rieder, R. O. (1992). Major disorders of mind and brain. *Scientific American, 267*(3), 126–133.

Gershuny, B. S., & Thayer, J. F. (1999). Relations among psychological trauma, dissociative phenomena, and trauma-related distress: A review and integration. *Clinical Psychology Review, 19,* 631–657.

Ghaderi, A. (2006). Does individualization matter? A randomized trial of standardized (focused) versus individualized (broad) cognitive behavior therapy for bulimia nervosa. *Behaviour Research and Therapy, 44,* 273–288.

Ghaemi, S. N., Rosenquist, K. J., Ko, J. Y., Baldassano, C. F., Kontos, N. J., &. Baldessarini, R. J. (2004). Antidepressant treatment in bipolar versus unipolar depression. *American Journal of Psychiatry, 161,* 163–165.

Ghizzani, A. (2003). Aging and male sexuality. *Archives of Sexual Behavior, 32* (3), 294–295.

Gidron, Y., & Davidson, K. (1996). Development and preliminary testing of a brief intervention for modifying CHD-predictive hostility components. *Journal of Behavioral Medicine, 19,* 203–220.

Gidron, Y., Davidson, K., & Bata, I. (1999). The short-term effects of a hostility-reduction intervention on male coronary heart disease patients. *Health Psychology, 18,* 416–420.

Giembycz, M. A., & O'Connor, B. J. (2000). *Asthma: Epidemiology, anti-inflammatory therapy and future trends.* Boston: Birkhauser.

Gil, K. M., Williams, D. A., Keefe, F. J., & Beckham, J. C. (1990). The relationship of negative thoughts to pain and psychological distress. *Behavior Therapy, 21,* 349–362.

Gilbert, S. (1997, June 25). Social ties reduce risk of a cold. *The New York Times,* p. C11.

Gilbert, S. (2004, March 16). New clues to women veiled in black. *The New York Times, Science Times,* pp. F1, F7.

Gilbert, S. C. (2003). Eating disorders in women of color. *Clinical Psychology: Science and Practice, 10,* 444–455.

Gill, A. R. (2001). Interventions for autism. In reply. *Journal of the American Medical Association, 286,* 670–671. [Letter]

Gist, R., & Devilly, G. J. (2002). Post-trauma debriefing: The road too frequently travelled. *Lancet, 360,* 741–742.

Gitlin, M. (2003). Sexual dysfunction with psychotropic drugs. *Expert Opinion on Pharmacotherapy, 4,* 2259–2269.

Gittelman-Klein, R., & Mannuzza, S. (1990). Hyperactive boys almost grown up. *Archives of General Psychiatry, 45,* 1131–1134.

Glantz, K., et al. (1996). Virtual reality (VR) for psychotherapy: From the physical to the social environment. *Psychotherapy, 33,* 464–473.

Glaser, R., Kiecolt-Glaser, J. K., Speicher, C. E., & Holliday, J. E. (1985). Stress, loneliness, and changes in herpes virus latency. *Journal of Behavioral Medicine, 8,* 249–260.

Glaser, R., Rice, J., Sheridan, J., Fertel, R., Stout, J., Speicher, C., Pinsky, D., et al. (1987). Stress-related immune suppression: Health implications. *Brain, Behavior, and Immunity, 1,* 7–20.

Glass, R. M. (2001). Panic disorder—It's real and it's treatable. *Journal of the American Medical Association, 283,* 2573–2574. [Editorial]

Glasson, E. J., Bower, C., Petterson, B., de Klerk, N., Chaney, G., & Hallmayer, J. F. (2004). Perinatal factors and the development of autism: A population study. *Archives of General Psychiatry, 61,* 618–627.

Glazener, C. M., Evans, J. H., & Peto, R. E. (2000). Tricyclic and related drugs for nocturnal enuresis in children. *Cochrane Database Systems Review, 3,* CD002117.

Gleaves, D. H. (1996). The sociocognitive model of dissociative identity disorder: A reexamination of the evidence. *Psychological Bulletin, 120,* 42–59.

Gleaves, D. H., Smith, S. M., Butler, L. D., & Spiegel, D. (2004). False and recovered memories in the laboratory and clinic: A review of experimental and clinical evidence. *Clinical Psychology: Science and Practice, 11,* 3–28.

Glenn, D. (2003, January 27). Liberty, sanity, equality. *The Chronicle of Higher Education,* Retrieved November 14, 2003, from http://www.alternet.org/story.html?StoryID=15034.

Glidden, L. M. (2002). *International review of research in mental retardation* (Vols. 24 & 25). San Francisco: Academic Press.

Glover, J. H. (1985). A case of kleptomania treated by covert sensitization. *British Journal of Clinical Psychology, 24,* 213–214.

Glueckauf, R. L., Pickett, T. C., Ketterson, T. U., Loomis, J. S., & Rozensky, R. H. (2003). Preparation for the delivery of telehealth services: A self-study framework for expansion of practice. *Professional Psychology: Research and Practice, 34,* 159–163.

Glynn, S., & Mueser, K. T. (1986). Social learning for chronic mental inpatients. *Schizophrenia Bulletin, 12,* 648–668.

Glynn, S., & Mueser, K. T. (1992). Social learning. In R. P. Liberman (Ed.), *Handbook of psychiatric rehabilitation* (pp. 127–152). New York: Macmillan.

Goddard, A. W., Mason, G. F., Almai, A., Rothman, D. L., Behar, K. L., et al. (2001). Reductions in occipital cortex GABA levels in panic disorder detected with 1h-magnetic spectroscopy. *Archives of General Psychiatry, 58,* 556–561.

Godtfredsen, N. S., Prescott, E., & Osler, M. S. (2005). Effect of smoking reduction on lung cancer risk. *Journal of the American Medical Association, 294,* 1505–1510.

Goedert, M., & Spillantini, M. G. (2006, November 3). A century of Alzheimer's disease. *Science, 314,* 777–781.

Goenjian, A. K., Molina, L., Steinberg, A. M., Fairbanks, L. A., Alvarez, M. L., Goenjian, H. A., et al. (2001). Posttraumatic stress and depressive reactions among Nicaraguan adolescents after Hurricane Mitch. *American Journal of Psychiatry, 158,* 788–794.

Goetz, K. L., & Price, T. R. P. (1994). The case of koro: Treatment response and implications for diagnostic classification. *Journal of Nervous and Mental Disease, 182,* 590–591.

Goff, D. C., & Summs, C. A. (1993). Has multiple personality disorder remained consistent over time? A comparison of past and recent cases. *Journal of Nervous and Mental Disease, 181,* 595–600.

Goisman, R. M., et al. (1994). Panic, agoraphobia, and panic disorder with agoraphobia: Data from a multicenter anxiety disorders study. *Journal of Nervous and Mental Disease, 182,* 72–79.

Goldapple, K., Segal, Z., Garson, C., Lau, M., Bieling, P., Kennedy, S., et al. (2004). Modulation of cortical-limbic pathways in major depression: treatment-specific effects of cognitive behavior therapy. *Archives of General Psychiatry, 61,* 34–41.

Goldberg, A. (2003). Heinz Kohut, 1913–1981. *American Journal of Psychiatry, 160,* 670.

Goldberg, C. (2001, July 9). Children trapped by mental illness. *The New York Times,* pp. A1, A11.

Goldberg, I. J., et al. (2001). Wine and your heart: A science advisory for healthcare professionals from the Nutrition Committee, Council on Epidemiology and Prevention, and Council on Cardiovascular Nursing of the American Heart Association. *Circulation, 103,* 472–475.

Goldberg, J. H., Halpern-Felsher, B. L., & Millstein, S. G. (2002). Beyond invulnerability: The importance of benefits in adolescents' decision to drink alcohol. *Health Psychology, 21,* 477–484.

Goldberg, T. E., Egan, M. F., Gscheidle, T., Coppola, R., Weickert, T., Kolachana, B. S., et al. (2003). Executive subprocesses in working memory. *Archives of General Psychiatry, 60,* 889–896.

Golden, O. (2000). The federal response to child abuse and neglect. *American Psychologist, 55,* 1050–1053.

Goldfarb, L. A., Dynens, E. M., & Gerrard, M. (1985). The Goldfarb fear of fat scale. *Journal of Personality Assessment, 49,* 329–332.

Goldstat, R., Briganti, E., Tran, J., Wolfe, R., & Davis, S. R. (2003). Transdermal testosterone therapy improves well-being, mood, and sexual function in premenopausal women. *Menopause, 10,* 390–398.

Goldstein, A. J., de Beurs, E. E., Chambless, D. L., & Wilson, K. A. (2000). EMDR for panic disorder with agoraphobia: Comparison with waiting list and credible attention-placebo control conditions. *Journal of Consulting and Clinical Psychology, 68,* 947–956.

Goldstein, I., et al. (1998). Oral sildenafil in the treatment of erectile dysfunction. *The New England Journal of Medicine, 338,* 1397–1404.

Goldstein, I., Meston, C., Davis, S., & Traish, A. (Eds.). (2006). *Female sexual dysfunction.* New York: Parthenon.

Goldstein, R. L. (1986). Erotomania. *American Journal of Psychiatry, 143,* 802.

Goleman, D. (1988, November 1). Narcissism looming larger as root of personality woes. *The New York Times,* pp. C1, C16.

Goleman, D. (1992, December 8). A rising cost of modernity: Depression. *The New York Times,* pp. C1, C13.

Goleman, D. (1993, December 7). Stress and isolation tied to a reduced life span. *The New York Times,* p. C5.

Goleman, D. (1994a, January 11). Childhood depression may herald adult ills. *The New York Times,* pp. C1, C10.

Goleman, D. (1994b, April 26). Mental decline in aging need not be inevitable. *The New York Times,* pp. C1, C10.

Goleman, D. (1995, October 4). Eating disorder rates surprise the experts. *The New York Times,* C11.

Goleman, D. (1995a, July 13). A genetic clue to bedwetting is located. *The New York Times,* p. A8.

Goleman, D. (1995b, June 21). "Virtual reality" conquers fear of heights. *The New York Times,* p. C11.

Golier, J. A., Yehuda, R., Bierer, L. M., Mitropoulou, V., New, A. S., Schmeidler, J., et al. (2003). The relationship of borderline personality disorder to posttraumatic stress disorder and traumatic events. *American Journal of Psychiatry, 160,* 2018–2024.

Gone, J. (2004). Mental health services for Native Americans in the 21st century United States. *Professional Psychology: Research and Practice, 35,* 10–18.

Gonzales, D., Rennard, S. I., Nides, M., Oncken, C., Azoulay, S., Billing, C. B., et al. (2006). Varenicline, an $\alpha_4\beta_2$ nicotinic acetylcholine receptor partial agonist, vs sustained-release bupropion and placebo for smoking cessation: A randomized controlled trial. *Journal of the American Medical Association, 296,* 47–55.

González, B., Huerta-Sánchez, E., Ortiz-Nieves, A., Vázquez-Alvarez, T., & Kribs-Zaleta, C. (2003). Am I too fat? Bulimia as an epidemic. *Journal of Mathematical Psychology, 47,* 515–526.

Goode, E. (2001, February 20). Samson diagnosis: Antisocial personality disorder, with muscles. *The New York Times,* p. F7.

Goode, E. (2003a, April 15). To curb cravings, and maybe more. *The New York Times,* p. F5.

Goode, E. (2003b, May 6). Experts see mind's voices in new light. *The New York Times Online.* Retrieved July 18, 2003, from http://notes.utk.edu/bio/greenberg.nsf/0/611983b95a021f7985256d1f003e1949?OpenDocument.

Goode, E. (2003c, October 14). Study links prescriptions to decrease in suicides. *The New York Times,* p. F5.

Goode, E. (2003d, December 11) British warning on antidepressant use for youth. *The New York Times,* pp. A1, A6.

Goode, E. (2004a). Lifting the veils of autism, one by one by one. *The New York Times,* pp. F1, F4.

Goode, E. (2004b, January 26). Autism cases up; cause is unclear. *The New York Times,* pp. A1, A17.

Goodstein, L., & Connelly, M. (1998, April 30). Teen-age poll finds a turn to the traditional. *The New York Times,* p. A20.

Goodwin, P. J., Leszcz, M., Ennis, M., Koopmans, J., Vincent, L., Guther, H., et al. (2001). The effect of group psychosocial support on survival in metastatic breast cancer. *New England Journal of Medicine, 345,* 1719–1726.

Gooren, L. J. G., & Kruijver, P. M. (2002). Androgens and male behavior. *Molecular and Cellular Endocrinology, 198,* 31–40.

Gordis, E. (1995). The National Institute on Alcohol Abuse and Alcoholism. *Alcohol Health & Research World, 19,* 5–11.

Gordis, E. (1999, May 5). *What we know: Conceptual advances in alcohol research.* National Institute on Alcohol Abuse and Alcoholism (NIAAA). Retrieved July 13, 2000, from http://www.niaaa.nih.gov/about/conceptual.htm.

Gordon, C. M., & Carey, M. P. (1996). Alcohol's effects on requisites for sexual risk reduction in men: An initial experimental investigation. *Health Psychology, 15,* 56–60.

Gormally, J., Sipps, G., Raphael, R., Edwin, D., & Varvil-Weld, D. (1981). The relationship between maladaptive cognitions and social anxiety. *Journal of Consulting and Clinical Psychology, 49,* 300–301.

Gorman, C. (1998, November 30). How does it work? *Time,* p. 92.

Gorman, C. (2003, October 20). How to eat smarter. *Time,* pp. 48–59.

Gorman, J. M., Kent, J., Martinez, J., Browne, S., Coplan, J., & Papp, L. A. (2001). Physiological changes during carbon dioxide inhalation in patients with panic disorder, major depression, and premenstrual dysphoric disorder: Evidence for a central fear mechanism. *Archives of General Psychiatry, 58,* 125–131.

Gorman, J. M., Kent, J. M., Sullivan, G. M., & Coplan, J. D. (2000). Neuroanatomical hypothesis of panic disorder, revised. *American Journal of Psychiatry, 57,* 493–505.

Gorwood, P., Leboyer, M., Jay, M., Payan, C., & Feingold, J. (1995). Gender and age at onset in schizophrenia: Impact of family history. *American Journal of Psychiatry, 152,* 208–212.

Gosselin, C., & Wilson, G. (1980). *Sexual variations.* New York: Simon & Schuster.

Gottesman, I. I. (1991). *Schizophrenia genetics: The origins of madness.* New York: Freeman.

Gottesman, I. I., & Gould, T. D. (2003). The endophenotype concept in psychiatry: Etymology and strategic intentions. *American Journal of Psychiatry, 160,* 636–645.

Gottesman, I. I., McGuffin, P., & Farmer, A. E. (1987). Clinical genetics as clues to the "real" genetics of schizophrenia. *Schizophrenia Bulletin, 13,* 23–47.

Gottesman, I. J. (2001). Psychopathology through a life span-genetic prism. *American Psychologist, 56,* 867–878.

Goudriaan, A. E., Oosterlaan, J., de Beurs, E., & van den Brink, W. (2006). Neurocognitive functions in pathological gambling: a comparison with alcohol dependence, Tourette syndrome and normal controls. *Addiction, 101,* 534–547.

Gould, M. S., Greenberg, T., Velting, D. M., & Shaffer, D. (2003). Youth suicide risk and preventive interventions: A review of the past 10 years. *Journal of the American Academy of Child and Adolescent Psychiatry; 42,* 386–405.

Gould, M. S., Greenberg, T., Velting, D. M., & Shaffer, D. (2003). Youth suicide risk and preventive interventions: A review of the past 10 years. *Evidence Based Mental Health, 6,* 121.

Gould, R. A., et al. (1997). Cognitive-behavioral and pharmacological treatment for social phobia: A meta-analysis. *Clinical Psychology: Science and Practice, 4,* 291–306.

Gould, R., Miller, B. L., Goldberg, M. A., & Benson, D. F. (1986). The validity of hysterical signs and symptoms. *The Journal of Nervous and Mental Disease, 174,* 593–597.

Gouzoulis-Mayfrank, E., et al. (2000). Impaired cognitive performance in drug free users of recreational ecstasy (MDMA). *Journal of Neurology, Neurosurgery, & Psychiatry, 68,* 719–725.

Grady, D. (1997, January 21). Brain-tied gene defect may explain why schizophrenics hear voices. *The New York Times,* pp. C1, C3.

Grady, D. (2002, November 26). Why we eat (and eat and eat). *The New York Times,* pp. F1, F4.

Grady, D. (2003, April 15). Quest for weight-loss drug takes an unusual turn. *The New York Times,* p. F5

Grady, D. (2004, April 7). Minimal benefit is seen in drugs for Alzheimer's. *The New York Times,* pp. A1, A16.

Graham, J. R. (2000). *MMPI-2: Assessing personality and psychopathology.* New York: Oxford University Press.

Graham, R. K., Deng, Y., Slow, E. J., Haigh, B., Bissada, N., Lu, G., Pearson, J., et al. (2006). Cleavage at the Caspase-6 site is required for neuronal dysfunction and degeneration due to mutant huntingtin. *Cell, 125,* 1179–1191.

Grange, D., Telch, C. F., & Tibbs, J. (1998). Eating attitudes and behaviors in 1,435 South African caucasian and non-caucasian college students. *American Journal of Psychiatry, 155,* 250–254.

Granholm, E., McQuaid, J. R., McClure, F. S., Auslander, L. A., Perivoliotis, D., Pedrelli, P., et al. (2005). A randomized, controlled trial of cognitive behavioral social skills training for middle-aged and older outpatients with chronic schizophrenia. *American Journal of Psychiatry, 162,* 520–529.

Grant, B. F. (1997). Prevalence and correlates of alcohol use and *DSM-IV* alcohol dependence in the United States: Results of the National Longitudinal Alcohol Epidemiologic Survey. *Journal of Studies on Alcohol, 58,* 464–473.

Grant, B. F., et al. (1994). Prevalence of *DSM-IV* alcohol abuse and dependence: United States, 1992. *Alcohol Health & Research World, 18,* 243–248.

Grant, B. F., Harford, T. C., Muthen, B. O., Yi, H. Y., Hasin, D. S., & Stinson, F. S. (2006a). *DSM-IV* alcohol dependence and abuse: Further evidence of validity in the general population. *Drug and Alcohol Dependence,* in press.

Grant, B. F., Hasin, D. S., Blanco, C., Stinson, F. S., Chou, S. P., Goldstein, R. B., et al. (2006c). The epidemiology of social anxiety disorder in the United States: results from the National Epidemiologic Survey on Alcohol and Related Conditions. *Journal of Clinical Psychiatry, 66,* 1351–1361.

Grant, B. F., Hasin, D. S., Stinson, F. S., Dawson, D. A., Goldstein, R. B., Smith, S., et al. (2006b). The epidemiology of *DSM-IV* panic disorder and agoraphobia in the United States: Results from the National Epidemiologic Survey on Alcohol and Related Conditions. *Journal of Clinical Psychiatry, 67,* 363–374.

Grant, B. F., Hasin, D. S., Stinson, F. S., Dawson, D. A., Ruan, W. J., Goldstein, R. B., et al. (2005a). Prevalence, correlates, co-morbidity, and comparative disability of *DSM-IV* generalized anxiety disorder in the USA: results from the National Epidemiologic Survey on Alcohol and Related Conditions. *Psychological Medicine, 35,* 1747–1759.

Grant, B. F., Stinson, F. S., Dawson, D. A., Chou, P., Ruan, W. J., & Pickering, R. P. (2004). Co-occurrence of 12-month alcohol and drug use disorders and personality disorders in the United States: Results from the national epidemiologic survey on alcohol and related conditions. *Archives of General Psychiatry, 61,* 361–368.

Grant, B. F., Stinson, F. S., Dawson, D. A., Chou, S. P., & Ruan, W. J. (2005b). Co-occurrence of *DSM-IV* personality disorders in the United States: results from the National Epidemiologic Survey on Alcohol and Related Conditions. *Comprehensive Psychiatry, 46,* 1–5.

Grant, J. E. (2006). Understanding and treating kleptomania: new models and new treatments. *Israel Journal of Psychiatry and Related Sciences, 43,* 81–87.

Grant, J. E., Williams, K. A., & Kim, S. W. (2006). Update on pathological gambling. *Currrent Psychiatry Reports, 8,* 53–58.

Gratz, K. L., Rosenthal, M. Z., Tull, M. T., Lejuez, C. W., & Gunderson, J. G. (2006). an experimental investigation of emotion dysregulation in borderline personality disorder. *Journal of Abnormal Psychology, 115,* 850–855.

Gray, M. J., & Acierno, R. (2002) Posttraumatic stress disorder. In M. Hersen (Ed.), *Clinical behavior therapy: Adults and children.* (pp. 106–124). New York: John Wiley & Sons, Inc.

Gray, N. S., Brown, A. S., MacCulloch, M. J., Malcolm, J., Smith, J., & Snowden, R. J. (2005). An implicit test of the associations between children and sex in pedophiles. *Journal of Abnormal Psychology, 114,* 304–308.

Gray-Little, B., & Hafdahl, A. R. (2000). Factors influencing racial comparisons of self-esteem: A quantitative review. *Psychological Bulletin, 126,* 26–54.

Greenberg, R. P., & Bornstein, R. F. (1988a). The dependent personality: I. Risk for physical disorders. *Journal of Personality Disorders, 2,* 126–135.

Greenberg, R. P., & Bornstein, R. F. (1988b). The dependent personality: II. Risk for psychological disorders. *Journal of Personality Disorders, 2,* 136–143.

Greenberg, R. P., et al. (1994). A meta-analysis of fluoxetine outcome in the treatment of depression. *Journal of Nervous and Mental Disease, 182,* 547–551.

Greenberger, E., Chen, C., & Tally, S. R. (2000). Family, peer, and individual correlates of depressive symptomatology among U.S. and Chinese adolescents. *Journal of Consulting and Clinical Psychology, 68,* 209–219.

Greene, B. A. (1985). Considerations in the treatment of Black patients by White therapists. *Psychotherapy, 22,* 389–393.

Greene, B. A. (1986). When the therapist is White and the patient is Black: Considerations for psychotherapy in the feminist heterosexual and lesbian communities. *Women & Therapy, 5,* 41–65.

Greene, B. A. (1990). Sturdy bridges: The role of African American mothers in the socialization of African American children. *Women & Therapy, 10,* 205–225.

Greene, B. A. (1992a). Black feminist psychotherapy. In E. Wright (Ed.), *Psychoanalysis and feminism: A critical dictionary* (pp. 34–35). Oxford, UK: Basil Blackwell.

Greene, B. A. (1992b). Still here: A perspective on psychotherapy with African American women. In J. Chrisler & D. Howard (Eds.), *New directions in feminist psychology* (pp. 13–25). New York: Springer.

Greene, B. A. (1993a). African American women. In L. Comas-Diaz & B. Greene (Eds.), *Women of color and mental health* (pp. 13–25). New York: Guilford Press.

Greene, B. A. (1993b, Spring). Psychotherapy with African American women: The integration of feminist and psychodynamic approaches. *Journal of Training and Practice in Professional Psychology, 7,* 49–66.

Greene, R. L., Robin, R. W., Albaugh, B., Caldwell, A., & Goldman, D. (2003). Use of the MMPI-2 in American Indians: II. Empirical correlates. *Psychological Assessment, 5,* 360–369.

Greene, R. W., & Ablon, J. S. (2001). What does the MTA study tell us about effective psychosocial treatment for ADHD? *Journal of Clinical Child Psychology, 30* (1), 114–121.

Greene, R. W., Biederman, J., Zerwas, S., Monuteaux, M. C., Goring, J. G., & Faraone, S. V., (2002). Psychiatric comorbidity, family dysfunction, and social impairment in referred youth with oppositional defiant disorder. *American Journal of Psychiatry, 159,* 1214–1224.

Greenfield, S. A. (1997). *The human brain: A guided tour.* HarperCollins: New York.

Greengrass, M. (2002, September). Psychological aspects of asthma: 10 years of research. *Monitor on Psychology,* p 13.

Greenhill, L. L. (1998). Childhood attention deficit hyperactivity disorder: Pharmacological treatments. In P. E. Nathan & J. M. Gorman (Eds.), *A guide to treatments that work* (pp. 42–64). New York: Oxford University Press.

Greenhouse, L. (1992, June 23). Defendants must prove incompetency. *The New York Times,* p. A17.

Greenhouse, L. (2003, July 1). In a momentous term, justices remake the law, and the court. *The New York Times,* pp. A1, A18, A19.

Greenspan, R. (2003, September 25). Porn pages reach 260 million. *ClickZ Network Web Posting.* Retrieved April 23, 2004, from http://www.clickz.com/stats/big_picture/traffic_patterns/article.php/3083001.

Greenwood, A. (2006, April 25). Natural killer cells power immune system response to cancer. *NCI Cancer Bulletin, 3* (17). Retrieved April 28, 2006, from http://www.cancer.gov/ncicancerbulletin/NCI_Cancer_Bulletin_042506/page4.

Gregg, E. W., Cheng, Y. J., Cadwell, B. L., Imperatore, G., Williams, D. E., Flegal, K. M., et al. (2005). Secular trends in cardiovascular disease risk factors according to body mass index in U.S. adults. *Journal of the American Medical Association, 293,* 1868–1874.

Gregory, J. (2003). *Sickened, the memoir of a Münchausen by proxy childhood.* New York: Bantam.

Griffith, J. (1983). Relationship between acculturation and psychological impairment in adult Mexican-Americans. *Hispanic Journal of Behavioral Sciences, 5,* 431–459.

Grilo, C. M., & Masheb, R. M. (2005). A randomized controlled comparison of guided self-help cognitive behavioral therapy and behavioral weight loss for binge eating disorder. *Behaviour Research and Therapy, 43,* 1509–1525.

Grissom, R. J. (1996). The magical number .7 + 2.2: Meta-meta-analysis of the probability of superior outcome in comparisons involving therapy, placebo, and control. *Journal of Consulting and Clinical Psychology, 64,* 973–982.

Grob, G. N. (1983). *Mental illness and American society, 1875–1940.* Princeton, NJ: Princeton University Press.

Grob, G. N. (1994). *The mad among us: A history of the care of America's mentally ill.* New York: Free Press.

Grob, G. N. (2001). Mental health policy in 20th-Century America. In R. W. Manderscheid & M. J. Henderson (Eds.), *Mental health, United States, 2000.* Washington, D. C.: U.S. Government Printing Office.

Grof, P., & Alda, M. (2000). Discrepancies in the efficacy of lithium. *Archives of General Psychiatry, 57,* 191.

Gross, B. (2006). The pleasure of pain. *Forensic Examiner, 15,* 57–61.

Gross, J. (2004, January 30). As autism cases rise, parent run frenzied race to get help. *The New York Times,* pp. A1, B7.

Grossberg, S., & Seidman, D. (2006). Neural dynamics of autistic behaviors: cognitive, emotional, and timing substrates. *Psychological Review, 113,* 483–525.

Grossman, L. (2003, January 20). Can Freud get his job back? *Time,* pp. 48–51.

Groth, A. N., & Birnbaum, H. J. (1979). *Men who rape: The psychology of the offender.* New York: Plenum Press.

Grothe, K. B., Dutton, G. R., Jones, G. N., Bodenlos, J., Ancona, M., & Brantley, P. J. (2005). Validation of the Beck Depression Inventory-II in a low-income African American sample of medical outpatients. *Psychological Assessment, 17,* 110–114.

Grunder, G., Carlsson, A., & Wong, D. F. (2002). Mechanism of new antipsychotic medications: Occupancy is not just antagonism. *Archives of General Psychiatry, 60,* 974–977.

Guarnaccia, P. J., & Rodriguez, O. (1996). Concepts of culture and their role in the development of culturally competent mental health services. *Hispanic Journal of Behavioral Sciences, 18,* 419–443.

Guertin, T. L. (1999). Eating behavior of bulimics, self-identified binge eaters, and non-eating disordered individuals: What differentiates these populations? *Clinical Psychology Review, 19,* 1–24.

Gullette, E. C. D., et al. (1997). Effects of mental stress on myocardial ischemia during daily life. *Journal of the American Medical Association, 277,* 1521–1526.

Gunderson, E. W., Vosburg, S. K., & Hart, C. L. (2002). Does marijuana use cause long-term cognitive deficits? *Journal of the American Medical Association, 287,* 2652. [Letter]

Gunderson, J. G. (1996). The borderline patient's intolerance of aloneness: Insecure attachments and therapist availability. *American Journal of Psychiatry, 153,* 752–758.

Gunderson, J. G. (2001). *Borderline personality disorder: A clinical guide.* Washington DC: American Psychiatric Press.

Gupta, S. (2003, January 20). If everyone were on Prozac. *Time,* p. 49.

Gur, R. E., Cowell, P. E., Latshaw, A., Turetsky, B. I., Grossman, R. I., Arnold, S. E., et al. (2002). Reduced dorsal and orbital prefrontal gray matter volumes in schizophrenia. *Archives of General Psychiatry, 57,* 761–768.

Gur, R. E., Nimgaonkar, V. L., Almasy, L., Calkins, M. E., Ragland, J. D., Pogue-Geile, M. Fl., et al. (2007). Neurocognitive endophenotypes in a multiplex multigenerational family study of schizophrenia. *American Journal of Psychiatry, 164,* 813–817.

Gur, R. E., Turetsky, B. I., Cowell, P. E., Finkelman, C., Maany, V., Grossman, R. I., et al. (2000). Temporolimbic volume reductions in schizophrenia. *Archives of General Psychiatry, 57,* 769–775.

Guralnik, O., Schmeidler, J., & Simeon, D. (2000). Feeling unreal: Cognitive processes in depersonalization. *American Journal of Psychiatry, 157,* 103–109.

Guskiewicz, K. M., McCrea, M., Marshall, S. W., Cantu, R. C., Randolph, C., Barr, W., et al. (2003). Cumulative effects associated with recurrent concussion in collegiate football players: The NCAA concussion study. *Journal of the American Medical Association, 290,* 2549–2555.

Gutheil, T. G. (1980). In search of true freedom: Drug refusal, involuntary medication, and "rotting with your rights on." *American Journal of Psychiatry, 137,* 327–328.

Guthrie, P. C., & Mobley, B. D. (1994). A comparison of the differential diagnostic efficiency of three personality disorder inventories. *Journal of Clinical Psychology, 50,* 656–665.

Guydish, J., Werdegar, D., Sorensen, J. L., Clark, W., & Acampora, A. (1998). Drug abuse day treatment: A randomized clinical trial comparing day and residential treatment programs. *Journal of Consulting and Clinical Psychology, 66,* 280–289.

Guze, S. B. (1993). Genetics of Briquet's syndrome and somatization disorder: A review of family, adoption, and twin studies. *Annals of Clinical Psychiatry, 5,* 225–230.

H

Haaga, D. A. F. (1995). Metatraits and cognitive assessment: Application to attributional style and depressive symptoms. *Cognitive Therapy and Research, 19,* 121–142.

Haaga, D. A. F. (2004). A healthy dose of criticism for randomized trials: Comment on Westen, Novotny, and Thompson-Brenner (2004). *Psychological Bulletin, 130,* 674–676.

Haake, P., Schedlowski, M., Exton, M. S., Giepen, C., Hartmann, U., et al. (2003). Acute neuroendocrine response to sexual stimulation in sexual offenders. *Canadian Journal of Psychiatry, 48* (4), 265–271.

Habib, M. (2000). The neurological basis of developmental dyslexia: An overview and working hypothesis. *Brain, 123*(12), 2373–2399.

Hadwin, J. A., Garner, M., & Perez-Olivas, G. (2006). The development of information processing biases in childhood anxiety: A review and exploration of its origins in parenting. *Clinical Psychology Review, 26,* 876–894.

Häfner, H., an der Heiden, W., Behrens, S., Gattaz, W. F., Hambrecht, M., Loffler, W., et al. (1998). Causes and consequences of the gender difference in age at onset of schizophrenia. *Schizophrenia Bulletin, 24,* 99–113.

Hagen, S., & Carouba, M. (2002). *Women at Ground Zero: Stories of Courage and Compassion* Indianapolis, IN: Alpha Books.

Hajjar, I., & Kotchen, T. A. (2003). Trends in prevalence, awareness, treatment, and control of hypertension in the United States, 1988–2000. *Journal of the American Medical Association, 290,* 199–206.

Hall, G. N. (2003). Cultual competence in clinical psychology research. *Clinical Psychologist, 56,* 11–16.

Hall, J. G. (2006, November 1). Grandfathers of Fragile X boys need evaluation. *Journal Watch Pediatrics and Adolescent Medicine.* Retrieved November 2, 2006, from http://pediatrics.jwatch.org/cgi/content/full/2006/1101/4.

Hall, M.-H., Rijsdijk, F., Picchioni, M., Schulze, K., Ettinger, U., Toulopoulou, T., et al. (2007). Substantial shared genetic influences on schizophrenia and event-related potentials. *American Journal of Psychiatry, 164,* 804–812.

Halmi, K., Agras, W. S., Mitchell, J., Wilson, G. T., Crow, S., Bryson, S. W., et al. (2002). Relapse predictors of patients with bulimia nervosa who achieved abstinence through cognitive-behavioral therapy. *American Journal of Psychiatry, 59,* 1105–1109.

Halmi, K. A., et al. (2000). Perfectionism in anorexia nervosa: Variation by clinical subtype, obsessionality, and pathological eating behavior. *American Journal of Psychiatry, 157,* 1799–1805.

Ham, L. S., & Hope, D. A. (2003). College students and problematic drinking: A review of the literature. *Clinical Psychology Review, 23,* 719–759.

Hamel, M., Shafer, T. W., & Erdberg, P. (2003). A study of nonpatient preadolescent Rorschach protocols. *Journal of Personality Assessment, 75,* 280–294.

Hamilton, K. E., & Dobson, K. S. (2002). Cognitive therapy of depression: Pretreatment patient predictors of outcome. *Clinical Psychology Review, 22,* 875–893.

Hamilton, S. P., Slager, S. L., De Leon, A. B., Heiman, G. A., Klein, D. F., Hodge, S. E., et al. (2004). Evidence for genetic linkage between a polymorphism in the adenosine 2A receptor and panic disorder. *Neuropsychopharmacology, 29,* 558–565.

Hammad, T. A., Laughren, T., & Racoosin, J. (2006). Suicidality in pediatric patients treated with antidepressant drugs. *Archives of General Psychiatry, 63,* 332–339.

Hammen, C., & Compas, B. E. (1994). Unmasking unmasked depression in children and adolescents: The problem of comorbidity. *Clinical Psychology Review, 14,* 585–603.

Hammen, C., & de Mayo, R. (1982). Cognitive correlates of teacher stress and depressive symptoms: Implications for attributional models of depression. *Journal of Abnormal Psychology, 91,* 96–101.

Hammen, C., & Gitlin, M. (1997). Stress reactivity in bipolar patients and its relation to prior history of disorder. *American Journal of Psychiatry, 154,* 856–857.

Hammen, C., Henry, R., & Daley, S. E. (2000). Depression and sensitization to stressors among young women as a function of childhood adversity. *Journal of Consulting and Clinical Psychology, 68,* 782–787.

Hammer, S. M., Saag, M. S., Schechter, M., Montaner, J. S., Schooley, R. T., et al. (2006). Treatment for adult HIV infection: 2006 recommendations of the International AIDS Society–USA Panel. *Journal of the American Medical Association, 295,* 190–198.

Hampton, T. (2006). Alcoholism genes. *Journal of the American Medical Association, 295,* 190–198.

Hancock, L. (1996, March 18). Mother's little helper. *Newsweek,* pp. 51–56.

Hankin, B. L., Abramson, L. Y., Moffitt, T. E., Silva, P. A., McGee, R., & Angell, K. E. (1998). Development of depression from preadolescence to young adulthood: Emerging gender differences in a 10-year longitudinal study. *Journal of Abnormal Psychology, 107,* 128–140.

Hanna, F. J. (2003). Confronting the controversy. *Contemporary Psychology: APA Review of Books, 48,* 835–836.

Hansen, N. B., Lambert, M. J., & Forman, E. M. (2002). The psychotherapy dose-response effect and its implication for treatment delivery services. *Clinical Psychology: Science and Practice, 9,* 329–343.

Hansen, N. D., Randazzo, K. V., Schwartz, A., Marshall, M., Kalis, D., Frazier, E., et al. (2006). Do we practice what we preach? An exploratory survey of multicultural psychotherapy competencies. *Professional Psychology: Research and Practice, 37,* 66–74.

Hardan, A. Y., Muddasani, S., Vemulapalli, M., Keshavan, M. S., & Minshew, N. J. (2006). An MRI study of increased cortical thickness in autism. *American Journal of Psychiatry, 163,* 1290–1292.

Hare, R. D. (1965). Temporal gradient of fear arousal in psychopaths. *Journal of Abnormal Psychology, 70,* 442–445.

Hariri, A. R., Mattay, V. S., Tessitore, A., Kolachana, B., Fera, F., Goldman, D. (2002). Serotonin transporter genetic variation and the response of the human amygdala. *Science, 19,* 400–403.

Harmer, C. J., Bhagwagar, Z., Perrett, D. I., Vollm, B. A., Cowen, P. J., et al. (2003). Acute SSRI administration affects the processing of social cues in healthy volunteers. *Neuropsychopharmacology, 28,* 148–152.

Harpur, T. J., & Hare, R. D. (1994). Assessment of psychopathy as a function of age. *Journal of Abnormal Psychology, 103,* 604–609.

Harris, A. E., & Curtin, L. (2002). Parental perceptions, early maladaptive schemas, and depressive symptoms in young adults. *Cognitive Therapy and Research, 26,* 405–416.

Harris, A. H. S., Cronkite, R., & Moos, R. (2006). Physical activity, exercise coping, and depression in a 10-year cohort study of depressed patients. *Journal of Affective Disorders, 93,* 79–85.

Harris, G. (2004a, June 2). Antidepressants seen as effective for adolescents. *The New York Times,* pp. A1, A16.

Harris, G. (2004b, September 16). Doctors say they will cut antidepressant use. *The New York Times,* p. A18.

Harris, G. (2006, November 23). Proof is scant on psychiatric drug mix for young. *The New York Times*, pp. A1, A28.

Harrop, C., & Trower, P. (2001). Why does schizophrenia develop at late adolescence? *Clinical Psychology Review, 21*, 241–266.

Hartung, C. M., & Widiger, T. A. (1998). Gender differences in the diagnosis of mental disorders: Conclusions and controversies of the *DSM-IV*. *Psychological Bulletin, 123*, 260–278.

Hartung, C. M., Willcutt, E. G., Lahey, B. B., Pelham, W. E., Loney, J., et al. (2002). Sex differences in young children who meet criteria for attention deficit hyperactivity disorder. *Journal of Clinical Child and Adolescent Psychology, 31*, 453–464.

Harvey, A. G., & Bryant, R. A. (2002). Two-year prospective evaluation of the relationship between acute stress disorder and posttraumatic stress disorder following mild traumatic brain injury. *American Journal of Psychiatry, 157*, 629–631.

Harvey, P. D., et al. (1997). Age-related differences in formal thought disorder in chronically hospitalized schizophrenic patients: A cross-sectional study. *American Journal of Psychiatry, 154*, 205–210.

Hasin, D., Hatzenbuehler, M. L., Keyes, K., & Ogburn, E. (2006). Substance use disorders: Diagnostic and Statistical Manual of Mental Disorders, fourth edition (*DSM-IV*) and International Classification of Diseases, tenth edition (ICD-10). *Addiction, 101 Suppl. 1*, 59–75.

Hasin, D. S., Goodwin, R. D., Stinson, F. S., & Grant, B. F. (2005). Epidemiology of major depressive disorder: Results from the National Epidemiologic Survey on Alcoholism and Related Conditions. *Archives of General Psychiatry, 62*, 1097–1106.

Hatzichristou, D. G., Cuzin, B., Martin-Morales, A., Buvat, J., Porst, H., Laferriere, N., et al. (2005). Vardenafil improves satisfaction rates, depressive symptomatology, and self-confidence in a broad population of men with erectile dysfunction. *Journal of Sexual Medicine, 2*, 109–116.

Haughton, E., & Ayllon, T. (1965). Production and elimination of symptomatic behavior. In L. P. Ullmann & L. Krasner (Eds.), *Case studies in behavior modification.* (pp. 94–98) New York: Holt, Rinehart and Winston.

Havermans, R. C., &. Jansen, A. T. M. (2003). Increasing the efficacy of cue exposure treatment in preventing relapse of addictive behavior. *Addictive Behaviors, 28*, 989–994.

Hawkins, E. H., Cummins, L. H., & Marlatt, G. A. (2004). Preventing substance abuse in American Indian and Alaska Native Youth: Promising strategies for healthier communities. *Psychological Bulletin, 130*, 304–323.

Hawton, K., & Catalan, J. (1990). Sex therapy for vaginismus: Characteristics of couples and treatment outcomes. *Sexual and Marital Therapy, 5*, 39–48.

Hayes, B. (2001). *Sleep demons: An insomniac's memoir.* New York: Washington Square Press.

Hayes, S. C., & Wilson, K. G. (2003). Mindfulness: Method and process. *Clinical Psychology: Science and Practice, 10*, 161–165.

Haynes, P. L. (2005). The role of behavioral sleep medicine in the assessment and treatment of sleep disordered breathing. *Clinical Psychology Review, 25*, 673–705.

Hazlett, E. A., Buchsbaum, M. S., Kemether, E., Bloom, R., Platholi, J., et al. (2004). Abnormal glucose metabolism in the mediodorsal nucleus of the thalamus in schizophrenia. *American Journal of Psychiatry, 161*, 305–314.

Haznedar, M. M., Buchsbaum, M. S., Hazlett, E. A., LiCalzi, E. M., Cartwright, C., & Hollander, E. (2006). Volumetric analysis and three-dimensional glucose metabolic mapping of the striatum and thalamus in patients with autism spectrum disorders. *American Journal of Psychiatry, 163*, 1252–1263.

Haznedar, M. M., Buchsbaum, M. S., Wei, T. C., Hof, P. R., Cartwright, C., Bienstock, C. A., et al. (2000). Limbic circuitry in patients with autism spectrum disorders studied with positron emission tomography and magnetic resonance imaging. *American Journal of Psychiatry, 157*, 1994–2001.

Headache coping strategies depend on the cause. (2000, August 14). CNN Web Posting. Retrieved August 20, 2000, from http://www.cnn.com/2000/HEALTH/08/14/headache.redux/index.html.

Heckman, T. G., Anderson, E. S., Sikkema, K. J., Kochman, A., Kalichman, S. C., & Anderson, T. (2004). Emotional distress in nonmetropolitan persons living with HIV disease enrolled in a telephone-delivered, coping improvement group intervention. *Health Psychology, 23*, 94–100.

Hedley, A. A., Ogden, C. L., Johnson, C. L., Carroll, M. D., Curtin, L. R., & Flegal, K. M. (2004). Prevalence of overweight and obesity among US children, adolescents, and adults, 1999–2002. *Journal of the American Medical Association, 291*, 2847–2850.

Heidrich, S. M., Forsthoff, C. A., & Ward, S. E. (1994). Psychological adjustment in adults with cancer: The self as mediator. *Health Psychology, 13*, 346–353.

Heilbrun, K., & Kramer, G. M. (2005). Involuntary medication, trial competence, and clinical dilemmas: Implications of Sell v. United States for psychological practice. *Professional Psychology: Research and Practice, 36*, 459–466.

Heimberg, R. G., Turk, C. L., & Mennin, D. S. (Eds.). (2004). *Generalized anxiety disorder.* New York: Guilford.

Heinrichs, M., Wagner, D., Schoch, W., Soravia, L. M., Hellhammer, D. H., & Ehlert, U. (2005). Predicting posttraumatic stress symptoms from pretraumatic risk factors: A 2-year prospective follow-up study in firefighters. *American Journal of Psychiatry, 162*, 2276–2286.

Helgeson, V. S. (2005). Recent advances in psychosocial oncology. *Journal of Consulting and Clinical Psychology, 73*, 268–271.

Hellmich, N. (2003, April 24). Being overweight linked to dying of cancer. *USA Today*, p. 1A.

Hellstrom, W. J. G., Nehra, A., Shabsigh, R., & Sharlip, I. D. (2006). Premature ejaculation: the most common male sexual dysfunction. *Journal of Sexual Medicine, 3* (Suppl. 1), 1–3.

Helmuth, L. (2001). Commentary: Dyslexia: Same brains, different languages. *Science, 291*, 2064.

Hendin, H., Maltsberger, J. T., Lipschitz, A., Pollinger H., & Kyle, J. (2001). Recognizing and responding to a suicide crisis. *Suicide & Life-Threatening Behavior, 31* (2), 115–128.

Henkin, W. A. (1985). Toward counseling the Japanese in America: A cross-cultural primer. *Journal of Counseling and Development, 63*, 500–503.

Henriques, G., Wenzel, A., Brown, G. K., & Beck, A. T. (2005). Suicide attempters' reaction to survival as a risk factor for eventual suicide. *American Journal of Psychiatry, 162*, 2180–2182.

Henry, M., Pascual-Leone, A., & Cole, J. (2003). Electromagnetic stimulation shows promise for treatment-resistant depression. *HealthPlace.com Depression Community.* Retrieved November 14, 2003, from http://www.healthyplace.com/communities/depression/treatment/tms/index.asp.

Herbert, A., Gerry, N. P., McQueen, M. B., Heid, I. M., Pfeufer, A., Illig, T., et al. (2006). A common genetic variant is associated with adult and childhood obesity. *Science, 312*, 279–283.

Herbert, J. D., et al. (2000). Science and pseudoscience in the development of eye movement desensitization and reprocessing. *Clinical Psychology Review, 20*, 945–972.

Herbert, L. E., Scherr, P. A., Bienias, J. L., Bennett, D. A., & Evans, D. A. (2003). Alzheimer's disease in the U.S. population: Prevalence estimates using the 2000 census. *Archives of Neurology, 60*, 1119–1122.

Herbert, M. R., Harris, G. J., Adrien, K. T., Ziegler, D. A., Makris, N., Kennedy, D. N., et al. (2002). Abnormal asymmetry in language association cortex in autism. *Annals of Neurology, 52*, 588–596.

Herbert, P. B. (2002). The duty to warn: A reconsideration and critique. *The Journal of the American Academy of Psychiatry and the Law, 30*, 417–424.

Herbert, P. B., & Young, K. A. (2002). *Tarasoff* at twenty-five. *The Journal of the American Academy of Psychiatry and the Law, 30*, 275–281.

Herek, G. M. (1996). Heterosexism and homophobia. In R. P. Cabaj & T. S. Stein (Eds.), *Textbook of homosexuality and mental health* (pp. 101–113). Washington, DC: American Psychiatric Association Press.

Heres, S., Davis, J., Maino, K., Jetzinger, E., Kissling, W., & Leucht, S. (2006). Why olanzapine beats risperidone, risperidone beats quetiapine, and quetiapine beats olanzapine: An exploratory analysis of head-to-head comparison studies of second-generation antipsychotics. *American Journal of Psychiatry, 163*, 185–194.

Herkov, M. J., Gynther, M. D., Thomas, S., & Myers, W. C. (1996). MMPI differences among adolescent inpatients, rapists, sodomists, and sexual abusers. *Journal of Personality Assessment, 66*, 81–90.

Hernandez, R. (2000, August 2). In new drug battle, use of ecstasy among young soars. *The New York Times*, p. A21.

Herndon, R. W., & Iacono, W. G. (2005). Psychiatric disorder in the children of antisocial parents. *Psychological Medicine, 35*, 1815–1824.

Herrera, V. M., & McCloskey, L. A. (2003). Sexual abuse, family violence, and female delinquency: Findings from a longitudinal study. *Violence & Victims, 18*, 319–334.

Hertz, M. R. (1986). Rorschach bound: A 50-year memoir. *Journal of Personality Assessment, 50*, 396–416.

Herwig, U., Lampe, Y., Juengling, F. D., Wunderlich, A., Walter, H., Spitzer, M., et al. (2003). Add-on rTMS for treatment of depression: A pilot study using stereotaxic coil-navigation according to PET data. *Journal of Psychiatric Research, 37*, 267–275.

Herzog, W., Schellberg, D., & Deter, H. C. (1997). First recovery in anorexia nervosa patients in the long-term course: A discrete-time survival analysis. *Journal of Consulting and Clinical Psychology, 65*, 169–177.

Heston, L. L., White, J. A., & Mastri, A. R. (1987). Pick's disease: Clinical genetics and natural history. *Archives of General Psychiatry, 44*, 409–411.

Hettema, J. M., Annas, P., Neale, M. C., Kendler, K. S., & Fredrikson, M. (2003). A twin stud y of the genetics of fear conditioning. *Archives of General Psychiatry, 60*, 702–708.

Hettema, J. M., Neale, M. C., & Kendler, K. S. (2001). A review and meta-analysis of the genetic epidemiology of anxiety disorders. *American Journal of Psychiatry, 158*, 1568–1578.

Heun, R., Papassotiropoulos, A., Jessen, F., Maier, W., & Breitner, J. C. (2001). A family study of Alzheimer disease and early- and late-onset depression in elderly patients. *Archives of General Psychiatry, 58*, 190–196.

Hicks, T. V., Leitenberg, H., Barlow, D. H., Gorman, J. M., Shear, M. K., & Woods, S. W. (2005). Physical, mental, and social catastrophic cogni-

tions as prognostic factors in cognitive-behavioral and pharmacological treatments for panic disorder. *Journal of Consulting and Clinical Psychology, 73*, 506–514.

Higgins, D. S., Jr. (2006). Huntington's disease. *Current Treatment Options in Neurology, 8*, 236–244.

Higgins, S. T. (2006). Extending contingency management to the treatment of methamphetamine use disorders. *American Journal of Psychiatry, 163*, 1870–1872.

Higgins, S. T., Heil, S. H., & Lussier, J. P. (2004). Clinical implications of reinforcement as a determinant of substance use disorders *Annual Review of Psychology, 55*, 431–461.

Hilchey, T. (1994, November 11). High anxiety raises risk of heart failure in men, study finds. *The New York Times*, p. A17.

Hill, K. G., et al. (2000). Early adult outcomes of adolescent binge drinking: Person- and variable-centered analyses of binge drinking trajectories. *Alcohol: Clinical Experimental Research, 24*, 892–901.

Hingson, R. W., Heeren, T., Jamanka, A., & Howland, J. (2000). Age of drinking onset and unintentional injury involvement after drinking. *Journal of the American Medical Association, 284*, 1527–1533.

Hinton, D. E., Pich, B., Safren, S. A., Pollack, M. H., & McNally, R. J. (2006). Anxiety sensitivity among Cambodian refugees with panic disorder: A factor analytic investigation. *Journal of Anxiety Disorders, 20*, 281–295.

Hirsch, S. R., & Leff, J. P. (1975). *Abnormalities in parents of schizophrenics.* Oxford, U.K.: Oxford University Press.

Hirvonen, J., van Erp, T. G. M., Huttunen, J., Aalto, S., Någren, K., et al. (2006). Brain dopamine D_1 receptors in twins discordant for schizophrenia. *American Journal of Psychiatry, 163*, 1747–1753.

Hitti, M. (2006, March 6). Eating disorders may run in families. *WebMD Medical News.* Retrieved March 19, 2006, from http://psychologytoday.webmd.com/content/article/119/113378?src=rss_psychtoday.

Ho, B.-C., Milev, P., O'Leary, D. S., Librant, A., Andreasen, N. C., & Wassink, T. H. (2006). Cognitive and magnetic resonance imaging brain morphometric correlates of brain-derived neurotrophic factor val66met gene polymorphism in patients with schizophrenia and healthy volunteers. *Archives of General Psychiatry, 63*, 731–740.

Hochhausen, N. M., Lorenz, A. R., & Newman, J. P. (2002). Specifying the impulsivity of female inmates with borderline personality disorder. *Journal of Abnormal Psychology, 111*, 495–501.

Hoffman, M. B., & Morse, S. J. (2006, July 30). The insanity defense goes back on trial. *The New York Times Online.* Retrieved November 10, 2006, from http://www.nytimes.com/2006/07/30/opinion/30hoffman.html?ex=1311912000&en=4687219d882295b3&ei=5088&partner=rssnyt&emc=rss.

Hoffman, R. E., Rapaport, J., Mazure, C. M., & Quinlan, D. M. (1999). Selective speech perception alterations in schizophrenic patients reporting hallucinated "voices." *American Journal of Psychiatry, 156*, 393–399.

Hoffman, S. G. (2000a). Self-focused attention before and after treatment of social phobia. *Behavior Research and Therapy, 38*, 717–725.

Hoffman, S. G. (2000b). Treatment of social phobia: Potential mediators and moderators. *Clinical Psychology: Science and Practice, 7*(1), 3–16.

Hoffman, S. G., Newman, M. G., Ehlers, A., & Roth, W. T. (1995). Psychophysiological differences between subgroups of social phobia. *Journal of Abnormal Psychology, 104*, 224–231.

Hoffman, W., & Prior, M. (1982). Neuropsychological dimensions of autism in children: A test of the hemispheric dysfunction hypothesis. *Journal of Clinical Neuropsychology, 4*, 27–42.

Hofmann, S. G., Meuret, A. E., Smits, J. A. J., Simon, N. M., Pollack, M. H., Eisenmenger, K., et al. (2006). Augmentation of exposure therapy with d-cycloserine for social anxiety disorder. *Archives of General Psychiatry, 63*, 298–304.

Hofmann, S. G., Moscovitch, D. A., Kim, H. J., & Taylor, A. N. (2004). Changes in self-perception during treatment of social phobia. *Journal of Consulting and Clinical Psychology, 72*, 588–596.

Hogan, B. E., Linden, W., & Najarian, B. (2002). Social support interventions. Do they work? *Clinical Psychology Review, 22*, 381–440.

Hogan, D. B. (2006). Donepezil for severe Alzheimer's disease. *Lancet, 367*, 1031–1032.

Hogarty, G. E., et al. (1997). Three-year trials of personal therapy among schizophrenic patients living with or independent of family, II: Effects on adjustment of patients. *American Journal of Psychiatry, 154*, 1514–1524.

Hogarty, G. E., Flesher, S., Ulrich, R., Carter, M., Greenwald, D., Pogue-Geile, M., et al. (2004). Cognitive enhancement therapy for schizophrenia: Effects of a 2-year randomized trial on cognition and behavior. *Archives of General Psychiatry, 61*, 866–876.

Hogarty, G. E., Schroeder, N. R., Ulrich, R., Mussare, N., Peregino, F., & Herron, E. (1979). Fluphenazine and social therapy in the aftercare of schizophrenic patients. *Archives of General Psychiatry, 36*, 1283–1294.

Holahan, C. J., Moos, R. H., Holahan, C. K., Brennan, P. L., & Schutte, K. K. (2005). Stress generation, avoidance coping, and depressive symptoms: A 10-year model. *Journal of Consulting and Clinical Psychology, 73*, 658–666.

Holcomb, D. R., Savage, M. P., Seehafer, R., & Waalkes, D. M. (2002). A mixed-gender date rape prevention intervention targeting freshman college athletes. *College Student Journal, 36* (2), 165–179.

Holder-Perkins, V., & Wise, T. N. (2002). Somatization disorder. In K. A. Phillips (Ed), *Somatoform and factitious disorders. Review of psychiatry, Vol. 20* (pp. 1–26). Washington, DC: American Psychiatric Association.

Holland, A. J., Sicotte, N., & Treasure, J. (1988). Anorexia nervosa: Evidence of a genetic basis. *Journal of Psychosomatic Research, 32*, 561–571.

Hollingshead, A. B., & Redlich, F. C. (1958). *Social class and mental illness: A community study*. New York: Wiley.

Hollon, S. D., & Kendall, P. C. (1980). Cognitive self-statements in depression: Development of an automatic thoughts questionnaire. *Cognitive Therapy and Research, 4*, 383–395.

Hollon, S. D., DeRubeis, R. J., Shelton, R. C., Amsterdam, J. D., Salomon, R. M., & O'Reardon, J. P., et al. (2005). Prevention of relapse following cognitive therapy vs medications in moderate to severe depression. *Archives of General Psychiatry, 62*, 417–422

Hollon, S. D., Stewart, M. O., & Strunk, D. (2006). Enduring effects for cognitive behavior therapy in the treatment of depression and anxiety. *Annual Review of Psychology, 57*, 285–315.

Holloway, J. D. (2003, December). Snapshot from the therapy room. *Monitor on Psychology*, p. 31.

Holloway, J. D. (2004a). New Mexico closing in on RxP implementation. *Monitor on Psychology, 35*, 13.

Holloway, J. D. (2004b, June). Gaining prescriptive knowledge. *Monitor on Psychology*, pp. 22–24.

Holloway, L. (1998, February 12). A mental patient skips care and West Siders worry again. *The New York Times*, p. B5.

Holroyd, K. A. (2002). Assessment and psychological management of recurrent headache disorders. *Journal of Consulting and Clinical Psychology, 70*, 656–677.

Holroyd, K. A., et al. (2001). Management of chronic tension-type headache with tricyclic antidepressant medication, stress management therapy, and their combination: A randomized controlled trial. *Journal of the American Medical Association, 285*, 2208–2215.

Holt, C. S., Heimberg, R. G., & Hope, D. A. (1992). Avoidant personality disorder and the generalized subtype of social phobia. *Journal of Abnormal Psychology, 101*, 318–325.

Holzman, P. S. (1987). Recent studies of psychophysiology in schizophrenia. *Schizophrenia Bulletin, 13*, 49–75.

Holzman, P. S., Levy, D. L., Matthysse, S. W., & Abel, L. A. (1997). Smooth pursuit eye tracking in twins: A critical commentary. *Archives of General Psychiatry, 54*, 429–431.

Hong, L., E., Summerfelt, A., Wonodi, I., Adami, H., Buchanan, R. W., & Thaker, G. K. (2007). Independent domains of inhibitory gating in schizophrenia and the effect of stimulus interval. *American Journal of Psychiatry, 164*, 61–65.

Honig, A., et al. (1998). A uditory hallucinations: A comparison between patients and nonpatients. *Journal of Nervous and Mental Disease, 186*, 646–651.

Hook, J. N., & Valentiner, D. P. (2002). Are specific and generalized social phobias qualitatively distinct? *Clinical Psychology: Science and Practice, 9*, 379–395.

Hooley, J. M., & Hiller, J. B. (2000). Personality and expressed emotion. *Journal of Abnormal Psychology, 109*, 40–44.

Horne, L. R., Van Vactor, J. C., & Emerson, S. (1991). Disturbed body image in patients with eating disorders. *American Journal of Psychiatry, 148*, 211–215.

Horrigan, J. P., & Barnhill, J. L. J. (2000). "Fluvoxamine and enuresis:" Comment. *Journal of the American Academy of Child & Adolescent Psychiatry, 39*, 1465–1466.

Houry, D. (2004). Suicidal patients in the emergency department: Who is at greatest risk? *Annals of Emergency Medicine, 43*, 731–732.

Houston, T. K., Cooper, L. A., & Ford, D. E. (2002). Internet support groups for depression: A 1-year prospective cohort study. *American Journal of Psychiatry, 159*, 2062–2068.

Howard, B. V., Manson, J. E., Stefanick, M. L., Beresford, S. A., Frank, G., Jones, B., et al. (2006). Low-fat dietary pattern and weight change over 7 years: The Women's Health Initiative Dietary Modification Trial. *Journal of the American Medical Association, 295*, 39–49.

Howard, C. E., & Porzelius, L. K. (1999). The role of dieting in binge eating disorder: Etiology and treatment implications. *Clinical Psychology Review, 19*, 25–44.

Howard, K. I., Kopta, S. M., Krause, M. S., & Orlinksy, D. E. (1986). The dose-effect relationship in psychotherapy. *American Psychologist, 41*, 159–164.

Howland, R. H., & Thase, M. E. (1993). A comprehensive review of cyclothymic disorder. *Journal of Nervous and Mental Disease, 18*, 485–493.

Hoza, B., Mrug, S., Gerdes, A. C., Hinshaw, S. P., Bukowski, W. M., Gold, J. A., et al. (2005). What aspects of peer relationships are impaired in children with attention-deficit/hyperactivity disorder? *Journal of Consulting and Clinical Psychology, 73*, 411–423.

Hrobjartsson, A., & Gotzsche, P. C. (2001). Is the placebo powerless? An analysis of clinical trials comparing placebo with no treatment. *The New England Journal of Medicine, 344*, 1594–1602.

Hu, F. B., & Willett, W. C. (2002). Optimal diets for prevention of coronary heart disease. *Journal of the American Medical Association, 288*, 2569–2578.

Hu, M.-C., Davies, M., &. Kandel, D. B. (2006). Epidemiology and correlates of daily smoking and nicotine dependence among young adults in the United States. *American Journal of Public Health, 96*, 299–308.

Huang, L. H. (1994). An integrative approach to clinical assessment and intervention with Asian-American adolescents. *Journal of Clinical Child Psychology, 23*, 21–31.

Huang, W., & Cuvo, A. J. (1997). Social skills training for adults with mental retardation in job-related settings. *Behavior Modification, 21*, 3–44.

Hubbard, K. L., Zapf, P. A., & Ronan, K. A. (2003). Competency restoration: An examination of the differences between defendants predicted restorable and not restorable to competency. *Law and Human Behavior, 27*, 127–139.

Huber, K. (2007). Fragile X Syndrome: Molecular mechanisms of cognitive dysfunction. *American Journal of Psychiatry, 164*, 556.

Huber, K. M., Gallagher, S. M., Warren, S. T., & Bear, M. F. (2002). Altered synaptic plasticity in a mouse model of fragile X mental retardation. *Proceedings of the National Academy of Sciences of the United States of America, 99*, 7746–7750.

Hublin, C., et al. (1997). Prevalence and genetics of sleepwalking: A population-based twin study. *Neurology, 48*, 177–181.

Hudson, J. I., Lalonde, J. K., Berry, J. M., Pindyck, L. J., Bulik, C. M., Crow, S. J., et al. (2006). Binge-eating disorder as a distinct familial phenotype in obese individuals. *Archives of General Psychiatry, 63*, 313–319.

Hudson, J. I., Mangweth, B., Pope, H. G. Jr., De Col, C., Hausmann, A., Gutweniger, S., et al. (2003). Family study of affective spectrum disorder. *Archives of General Psychiatry, 60*, 170–177.

Hudziak, J. J. (2001). Latent class analysis of ADHD and comorbid symptoms in a population sample of adolescent female twins. *Journal of Child Psychology & Psychiatry & Allied Disciplines, 42*, 933–942.

Huffman, J. C., & Stern, T. A. (2003). The diagnosis and treatment of Munchausen's. *General Hospital Psychiatry, 25*, 358–363.

Hufford, M. R. (2001). Alcohol and suicidal behavior. *Clinical Psychology Review, 21*, 797–811.

Hugdahl, K., Rund, B. R., Lund, A., Asbjørnsen, A., Egeland, J., Ersland, L., et al. (2004). Brain activation measured with fmri during a mental arithmetic task in schizophrenia and major depression. *American Journal of Psychiatry, 161*, 286–293.

Hugh-Jones, S., Gough, B., & Littlewood, A. (2005). Sexual exhibitionism as sexuality and individuality: A critique of psycho-medical discourse from the perspectives of women who exhibit. *Sexualities, 8*, 259–281.

Hummelen, B., Wilberg, T., Pedersen, G. F., & Karterud, S. (2006). An investigation of the validity of the Diagnostic and Statistical Manual of Mental Disorders, Fourth Edition avoidant personality disorder construct as a prototype category and the psychometric properties of the diagnostic criteria. *Comprehensive Psychiatry, 47*, 376–383.

Humphrey, L. L. (1986). Family dynamics in bulimia. In S. C. Feinstein, et al. (Eds.), *Adolescent psychiatry* (pp. 315–332). Chicago: University of Chicago Press.

Hunsley, J., & Bailey, J. M. (2001). Whither the Rorschach? An analysis of the evidence *Psychological Assessment, 13*, 472–485.

Hunter, E. C. M., Phillips, M. L., Chalder, T., Sierra, M., & David, A. S. (2003). Depersonalisation disorder: A cognitive–behavioural conceptualization. *Behaviour Research and Therapy, 41*, 1451–1467.

Hunter, M. D., Eickhoff, S. B., Miller, T. W. R., Farrow, F. D., Wilkinson, I. D., & Woodruff, P.W. R. (2006). Neural activity in speech-sensitive auditory cortex during silence. *Proceedings of the National Academy of Sciences, 103*, 189–194.

Huntjens, R. J. C., Peters, M. L., Postma, A., Woertman, L., Effting, M., & van der Hart, O. (2005). Transfer of newly acquired stimulus valence between identities in dissociative identity disorder (DID). *Behaviour Research and Therapy, 43*, 243–255.

Huprich, S. K., Fuller, K. M., & Schneider, R. B. (2003). Divergent ethical perspectives on the duty-to-warn principle with HIV patients. *Ethics Behavior, 13*, 263–278.

Hurlburt, G., & Gade, E. (1984). Personality differences between Native American and Caucasian women alcoholics: Implications for alcoholism counseling. *White Cloud Journal, 3*, 35–39.

Hussong, A. M., et al. (2001). Specifying the relations between affect and heavy alcohol use among young adults. *Journal of Abnormal Psychology, 110*, 449–461.

Hutton, M. (2001). Missense and splice site mutations in tau associated with FTDP-17: Multiple pathogenic mechanisms. *Neurology, 56*(Suppl. 4), S21–S25.

Huxley, N. A., Rendall, M., & Sederer, L. (2000). Psychosocial treatments in schizophrenia: A review of the past 20 years. *Journal of Nervous & Mental Disease, 188*, 187–201.

Hwang, W.-C. (2006). The psychotherapy adaptation and modification framework: Application to Asian Americans. *American Psychologist, 61*, 702–715.

I

Ickovics, J. R., et al. (2001). Mortality, CD4 cell count decline, and depressive symptoms among HIV-seropositive women: Longitudinal analysis from the HIV Epidemiology Research Study. *Journal of the American Medical Association, 285*, 1466–1474.

Ilardi, S. S., & Craighead, W. E. (1994). The role of nonspecific factors in cognitive-behavior therapy for depression. *Clinical Psychology: Science and Practice, 1*, 138–156.

in 't Veld, B. A., Ruitenberg, A., Hofman, A., Launer, L. J., van Duijn, C. M., et al. (2001). Nonsteroidal antiinflammatory drugs and the risk of Alzheimer's disease. *New England Journal of Medicine, 345*, 1515–1521.

Ingham, R. J. (2003). Brain imaging and stuttering: Some reflections on current and future developments. *Journal of Fluency Disorders, 28*, 411–420.

Ingram, R. E. (1991). Tilting at windmills: A response to Pyszczynski, Greenberg, Hamilton, and Nix. *Psychological Bulletin, 110*, 544–550.

Ingram, R. E., & Siegle, G. J. (2001). Cognition and clinical science: From revolution to evolution. In K. S. Dobson (Ed.), *Handbook of cognitive-behavioral therapies* (2nd ed., pp. 111–137). New York: Guilford Press.

Inouye, S. K. (2006). Delirium in older persons. *New England Journal of Medicine, 354*, 1157–1165.

Insanity: A defense of last resort. (1992, February 3). *Newsweek*, p. 49.

Institute of Medicine. (1990). *Broadening the base of treatment for alcohol problems*. Washington, DC: National Academy Press.

International Human Genome Sequencing Consortium (2001). Initial sequencing and analysis of the human genome. *Nature 409*, 860–921.

Ioannidis, J. P. A., & Karassa, P. (2001). Comparison of evidence of treatment effects in randomized and nonrandomized studies. *Journal of the American Medical Association, 286*, 821–830.

Irle, E., Exner, C., Thielen, K., Weniger, G., & Ruether, E. (1998). Obsessive-compulsive disorder and ventromedial frontal lesions: Clinical and neuropsychological findings. *American Journal of Psychiatry, 155*, 255–263.

Ironson, G., Wynings, C., Schneiderman, N., Baum, A., Rodriguez, M., Greenwood, D., et al. (1997). Posttraumatic stress symptoms, intrusive thoughts, loss, and immune function after hurricane Andrew. *Psychosomatic Medicine, 59*, 128–141.

Irwin, M. L., Yasui, Y., Ulrich, C. M., Bowen, D., Rudolph, R. E., Schwartz, R. S., et al. (2002). Effect of exercise on total and intra-abdominal body fat in postmenopausal women: A randomized controlled trial. *Journal of the American Medical Association, 289*, 323–330.

Irwin, M. R., Cole, J. C., & Nicassio, P. M. (2006). Comparative meta-analysis of behavioral interventions for insomnia and their efficacy in middle-aged adults and in older adults 55+ years of age. *Health Psychology, 25*, 3–14.

Isacsson, G. (2000). Suicide prevention—A medical breakthrough? *Acta Psychiatrica Scandinavica, 102*, 113–117.

Iversen, L. L. (2000). *The science of marijuana*. New York: Oxford University Press.

Iwamasa, G. Y, Soroccco, K. H., & Koonce, D. A. (2002). Ethnicity and clinical psychology: A content analysis of the literature. *Clinical Psychology Review, 22*, 931–944.

Iwata, N., Tsubuki, S., Takaki Y., Shirotani, K., Lu, B., Gerard, N. P., et al. (2001). Metabolic regulation of brain abeta by neprilysin. *Science, 292*, 1550–1552.

J

Jablensky, A., Sartorius, N., Ernberg, G., & Anker, M. (1992). Schizophrenia: Manifestations, incidence and course in different cultures: A World Health Organization ten-country study (Monograph Suppl.). *Psychological Medicine, 20* (Monograph Suppl.), 1–97.

Jablensky, A. V., Morgan, V., Zubrick, S. R., Bower, C., & Yellachich, L.-A. (2005). Pregnancy, delivery, and neonatal complications in a population cohort of women with schizophrenia and major affective disorders. *American Journal of Psychiatry, 162*, 79–91.

Jackson, J., Calhoun, K. S., Amick, A. E., Maddever, H. M., & Habifm V. L. (1990). Young adult women who report childhood intrafamilial sexual abuse: Subsequent adjustment. *Archives of Sexual Behavior, 19*, 211–221.

Jacobi, C., Hayward, C., de Zwaan, M., Kraemer, H. C., & Agras, W. S. (2004). Coming to terms with risk factors for eating disorders: Application of risk terminology and suggestions for a general taxonomy. *Psychological Bulletin, 130*, 19–65.

Jacobs, B. L. (2004). Depression: The brain finally gets into the act. *Current Directions in Psychological Science, 13*, 103–106.

Jacobs, M. K., Christensen, A., Snibbe, J. R., Dolezal-Wood, S., Huber, A., & Polterok, A. (2001). A comparison of computer-based versus traditional individual psychotherapy. *Professional Psychology: Research and Practice, 32*, 92–96.

Jacobs, W., Newman, G. H., & Burns, J. C. (2001). The Homeless Assessment Program: A service-training model for providing disability evaluations for homeless, mentally ill individuals. *Professional Psychology: Research and Practice, 32,* 319–323.

Jacobsen, J. S., Wu, C.-C., Redwine, J. M., Comery, T. A., Arias, R., Bowlby, M., Martone, R., et al. (2006). Early-onset behavioral and synaptic deficits in a mouse model of Alzheimer's disease. *Proceedings of the National Academy of Sciences, 103,* 5161–5166.

Jacobson, N. S., Dobson, K. S., Truax, P. A., Addis, M. E., Koerner, K., Gollan, J. K., et al. (1996). A component analysis of cognitive-behavioral treatment for depression. *Journal of Consulting and Clinical Psychology, 64,* 295–304.

Jaffe, A. B., & Levine, J. (2003). Efficacy and effectiveness of first- and second-generation antipsychotics in schizophrenia. *Clinical Psychiatry, 64, Suppl 17,* 3–6.

James, S., & Prilleltensky, I. (2002). Cultural diversity and mental health: Towards integrative practice. *Clinical Psychology Review, 22,* 1133–1154.

Jamison, K. R. (1993). *Touched with fire.* New York: Free Press.

Jamison, K. R. (1995). *An unquiet mind.* New York: Knopf.

Janeck, A. S., Calamari, J. E., Riemann, B. C., & Heffelfinger, S. K. (2003). Too much thinking about thinking? Metacognitive differences in obsessive-compulsive disorder. *Journal of Anxiety Disorders, 17,* 181–195.

Janofsky, J. S., Dunn, M. H., Roskes, E. J., Briskin, J. K., & Rudolph, M. S. (1996). Insanity defense pleas in Baltimore City: An analysis of outcome. *American Journal of Psychiatry, 153,* 1464–1468.

Janofsky, M. (2003, December 18). Man who shot Reagan allowed to visit parents unsupervised. *The New York Times,* pp. A1, A38.

Janssen, E. & Bancroft, J. (2006). The dual-control Model: The role of sexual inhibition & excitation in sexual arousal and behavior. In E. Janssen (Ed.), *The psychophysiology of sex.* Bloomington, IN: Indiana University Press, in press.

Januzzi, J., & DeSanctis, R. (1999). Looking to the brain to save the heart. *Cerebrum, 1,* 31–43.

Jarrett, R. B., Kraft, D., Doyle, J., Foster, B. M., Eaves, G. G., & Silver, P. C. (2001). Preventing recurrent depression using cognitive therapy with and without a continuation phase: A randomized clinical trial. *Archives of General Psychiatry, 58,* 381–388.

Jarrett, R. B., Schaffer, M., McIntire, D., Witt-Browder, A., Kraft, D., & Risser, R. C. (1999). Treatment of atypical depression with cognitive therapy or phenelzine. *Archives of General Psychiatry, 56,* 431–437.

Jason Priestley: Q & A. (2003, November 1). *Newsweek,* p. 73.

Javier, R. A. (1993). Cited in Rathus, S.A. (1993). *Psychology* (5th ed.). Fort Worth, TX: Harcourt Brace Jovanovich.

Jaycox, L. H., Reivich, K. J., Gillham, J., & Seligman, M. E. P. (1994). Prevention of depressive symptoms in school children. *Behaviour Research and Therapy, 32,* 801–816.

Jefferson, D. J. (2005, August 8). America's most dangerous drug. *Newsweek,* p. 41–48.

Jeffery, R. W. (1991). Population perspectives on the prevention and treatment of obesity in minority populations. *American Journal of Clinical Nutrition, 53* (6 Suppl.), 1621A–1624S.

Jemmott, J. B., et al. (1983, June 25). Academic stress, power motivation, and decrease in secretion rate of salivary secretory immunoglobin A. *Lancet,* 1400–1402.

Jenkins, C. D. (1988). Epidemiology of cardiovascular diseases. *Journal of Consulting and Clinical Psychology, 56,* 324–332.

Jenkins, J. H. (1988). Ethnopsychiatric interpretations of schizophrenic illness: The problem of nervios within Mexican-American families. *Culture, Medicine, and Psychiatry, 12,* 301–329.

Jenkins, J. H., & Karno, M. (1992). The meaning of expressed emotion: Theoretical issues raised by cross-cultural research. *American Journal of Psychiatry, 149,* 9–21.

Jensen, P. S., Martin, D., & Cantwell, D. P. (1997). Comorbidity in ADHD: Implications for research practice, and DSM-V. *Journal of the American Academy of Child and Adolescent Psychiatry, 36,* 1065–1079.

Jerome, L. W., et al. (2000). The coming of age in telecommunications in psychological research and practice. *American Psychologist, 55,* 407–421.

Jeste, D. V., & Caligiui, M. P. (1993). Tardive dyskinesia. *Schizophrenia Bulletin, 19,* 303–315.

Jeste, D. V., Lindamer, L. A., Evans, J., & Lacro, J. P. (1996). Relationship of ethnicity and gender to schizophrenia and pharmacology of neuroleptics. *Psychopharmacology Bulletin, 32,* 243–251.

Jeste, D. V., Wragg, R. E., Salmon, D. P., Harris, M. J., & Thal, L. J. (1992). Cognitive deficits of patients with Alzheimer's disease with and without delusions. *American Journal of Psychiatry, 149,* 184–188.

Jiang, H., & Chess, L. (2006). Regulation of immune responses by T Cells. *New England Journal of Medicine, 354,* 1166–1176.

Joe, S., Baser, E., Breeden, G., Neighbors, H. W., & Jackson, J. S. (2006). Prevalence and risk factors for lifetime suicide attempts Among Blacks in the United States. *Journal of the American Medical Association, 296,* 2112–2123.

Johns, A. (2001). Psychiatric effects of cannabis. *British Journal of Psychiatry, 178,* 116–122.

Johnson, B. A., Roache, J. D., Javors, M. A., DiClemente, C. C., Cloninger, C. R., Prihoda, T. J., et al. (2000). Ondansetron for reduction of drinking among biologically predisposed alcoholic patients: A randomized controlled trial. *Journal of the American Medical Association, 284,* 963–971.

Johnson, D. B., Oyama, N., LeMarchand, L., & Wilkens, L. (2004). Native Hawaiians mortality, morbidity, and lifestyle: comparing data from 1982, 1990, and 2000. *Pacific Health Dialog, 11,* 120–130.

Johnson, J. G., Cohen, P., Chen, H., Kasen, S., & Brook, J. S. (2006). Parenting behaviors associated with risk for offspring personality disorder during adulthood. *Archives of General Psychiatry, 63,* 579–587.

Johnson, R. E., Chutuape, M. A., Strain, E. C., Walsh, S. L., Stitzer, M. L., & Bigelow, G. E. (2000). A comparison of levomethadyl acetate, buprenorphine, and methadone for opioid dependence. *The New England Journal of Medicine, 343,* 1290–1297.

Johnson, R. J., & McFarland, B. H. (1996). Lithium use and discontinuation in a health maintenance organization. *American Journal of Psychiatry, 153,* 993–1000.

Johnson, S., Winett, C. A., Meyer, B., Greenhouse, W. J., & Miller, I. (1999). Social support and the course of bipolar disorder. *Journal of Abnormal Psychology, 108,* 558–566.

Johnson, S. L. (2005). Life events in bipolar disorder: Towards more specific models. *Clinical Psychology Review, 25,* 1008–1027.

Johnson, S. L., & Leahy, R. L. (2003) (Eds). *Psychological treatment of bipolar disorder.* New York: Guilford.

Johnson, T. J. (2002). College students' self-reported reasons for why drinking games end. *Addictive Behaviors, 27,* 145–153.

Johnson, W. G., Tsoh, J. Y., & Varnado, P. J. (1996). Eating disorders: Efficacy of pharmacological and psychological interventions. *Clinical Psychology Review, 16,* 457–478.

Johnston, L. D., O'Malley, P. M., Bachman, J. G., & Schulenberg, J. E. (2004). *Monitoring the Future National Survey Results on Drug Use, 1975(2003. Volume II: College Students and Adults Ages 1945* (NIH Publication No. 04-5508). Bethesda, MD: National Institute on Drug Abuse.

Johnston, T. D., & Edwards, L. (2002). Genes, interactions, and the development of behavior. *Psychological Review, 109,* 26–34.

Joiner, T. E., Conwell, Y., Fitzpatrick, K. K., Witte, T. K., Schmidt, N. B., Berlim, M.T., et al. (2005). Four studies on how past and current suicidality relate even when "everything but the kitchen sink" is covaried. *Journal of Abnormal Psychology, 114,* 291–303.

Joiner, T. E., Jr., Sachs-Ericsson, N. J., Wingate, L. R., Brown, J. S., Anestis, M. D., & Selby, E. A. (2007). Childhood physical and sexual abuse and lifetime number of suicide attempts: A persistent and theoretically important relationship. *Behaviour Research and Therapy, 45,* 539–547.

Joinson, C., Heron, J., Butler, U., von Gontard, A., & the Avon Longitudinal Study of Parents and Children Study Team. (2006). Psychological differences between children with and without soiling problems. *Pediatrics, 117,* 1575–1584.

Jones v. United States, 103 S. Ct. 3043 (1983).

Jones, B. E., & Hill, M. J. (2002). *Mental health issues in lesbian, gay, bisexual, and transgender communities: Review of Psychiatry, Volume 21.* Washington, DC: American Psychiatric Publishing.

Jones, C. (2003). Tightropes and tragedies: 25 years of Tarasoff. *Medicine, Science, and the Law, 43,* 13–22.

Jones, E. (1953). *The life and work of Sigmund Freud.* New York: Basic Books.

Jones, M. P. (2006). The role of psychosocial factors in peptic ulcer disease: Beyond Helicobacter pylori and NSAIDs. *Journal of Psychosomatic Research, 60,* 407–412.

Jones, P. B., et al. (1998). Schizophrenia as a long-term outcome of pregnancy, delivery, and perinatal complications: A 28-year follow-up of the 1966 North Finland general population birth cohort. *American Journal of Psychiatry, 155,* 355–364.

Jones, S. R., & Fernyhough, C. (2007). Neural correlates of inner speech and auditory verbal hallucinations: A critical review and theoretical integration. *Clinical Psychology Review, 27,* 140–154.

Jorenby, D. E., Hays, J. T., Rigotti, N. A., Azoulay, S., Watsky, E. J., Williams, K. E., Billing, C. B., et al. (2006). Efficacy of varenicline, an $\alpha_4\beta_2$ nicotinic acetylcholine receptor partial agonist, vs placebo or sustained-release bupropion for smoking cessation: A randomized controlled trial. *Journal of the American Medical Association, 296,* 56–63.

Jouriles, E. N., et al. (1997). Psychometric properties of family members' reports of parental physical aggression toward clinic-referred children. *Journal of Consulting and Clinical Psychology, 65,* 309–318.

Judd, L. J. (1997). The clinical course of unipolar major depressive disorders. *Archives of General Psychiatry, 54,* 989–991.

Judd, L. L., Akiskal, H. S., Schettler, P. J., Coryell, W., Endicott, J., Maser, J. D., et al. (2003b). A prospective investigation of the natural history of the long-term weekly symptomatic status of bipolar II disorder. *Archives of General Psychiatry, 60,* 261–269.

Judd, L. L., Akiskal, H. S., Schettler, P. J., Coryell, W., Maser, J., Rice, J. A., et al. (2003a). The comparative clinical phenotype and long term longitudinal episode course of bipolar I and II. *Journal of Affective Disorders, 73,* 19–32.

Judd, L. L., Akiskal, H. S., Zeller, P. J., Paulus, M., Leon, A. C., Maser, J. D., et al. (2000a). Psychosocial disability during the long-term course of unipolar major depressive disorder. *Archives of General Psychiatry, 57,* 375–380.

Judd, L. L., Paulus, M. J., Schettler, P. J., Akiskal, H. S., Endicott, J., Leon, A. C., et al. (2000b). Does incomplete recovery from first lifetime major depressive episode herald a chronic course of illness? *American Journal of Psychiatry, 157,* 1509–1511.

Just, N., & Alloy, L. B. (1997). The response styles theory of depression: Tests and an extension of the theory. *Journal of Abnormal Psychology, 106,* 221–229.

Just, N., Abramson, L. Y., & Alloy, L. B. (2001). Remitted depression studies as tests of the cognitive vulnerability hypotheses of depression onset. A critique and conceptual analysis. *Clinical Psychology Review, 21,* 63–83.

K

Kabat-Zinn, J. (2003). Mindfulness-based interventions in context: Past, present, and future. *Clinical Psychology: Science and Practice, 10,* 144–156.

Kaczmarek, P., LeVine, E., & Segal, A. F. (2006). Section 6. Civil and criminal trial matters. In Kaczmarek, P., LeVine, E., & Segal, A. F. *Law & mental health professionals: New Mexico* (pp. 269–296). Washington, DC: American Psychological Association.

Kafka, M. P. (2003). Sex offending and sexual appetite: The clinical and theoretical relevance of hypersexual desire. *International Journal of Offender Therapy & Comparative Criminology, 47*(4) 439–451.

Kahn, M. W. (1982). Cultural clash and psychopathology in three aboriginal cultures. *Academic Psychology Bulletin, 4,* 553–561.

Kaiser, R., Hofer, A., Grapengiesser, A., Gasser, T., Kupsch, A., Roots, I., & Brockmoller, J. (2003). L-Dopa-induced adverse effects in PD and dopamine transporter gene polymorphism. *Neurology, 60,* 1750–1755.

Kakiuchi, C., et al. (2003). Impaired feedback regulation of XBP1 as a genetic risk factor for bipolar disorder. *Nature Genetics, 35,* 171–175.

Kalb, C. (2001a). Can this pill stop you from hitting the bottle? *Newsweek,* pp. 46–48.

Kalb, C. (2001b, January 22). Seeing a virtual shrink. *Newsweek,* pp. 34–37.

Kalb, C. (2002, December 2). How to lift the mind. *Newsweek,* pp. 67–70.

Kalichman, S. C. (2000). HIV transmission risk behaviors of men and women living with HIV-AIDS: Prevalence, predictors, and emerging clinical intervention. *Clinical Psychology: Science and Practice, 7,* 32–47.

Kamphuis, J. H., Emmelkamp, P. M. G., & Krijn, M. U. (2002). Specific phobia. In M. Hersen (Ed.), *Clinical behavior therapy: Adults and children* (pp. 75–89). New York: Wiley.

Kanai, T., Takeuchi, H., Furukawa, T. A., Yoshimura, R., Imaizumi, T., & Kitamura, T. (2003). Time to recurrence after recovery from major depressive episodes and its predictors. *Psychological Medicine, 33,* 839–845.

Kanaya, T., Scullin, M. H., & Ceci, S. J. (2003). The Flynn Effect and U.S. policies: The impact of rising IQ scores on American society via mental retardation diagnoses. *American Psychologist, 58,* 778–790.

Kandel D. B. (Ed.) (2002). *Stages and pathways of drug involvement: Examining the gateway hypothesis.* Cambridge, England: Cambridge University Press.

Kandel, D. B. (2003). Does marijuana use cause the use of other drugs? *Journal of the American Medical Association, 289,* 482–483.

Kane, J. M. (1996). Drug therapy: Schizophrenia. *The New England Journal of Medicine, 334,* 34–41.

Kane, J. M., & Marder, S. R. (1993). Psychopharmalogic treatment of schizophrenia. *Schizophrenia Bulletin, 19,* 287–302.

Kangas, M., Henry, J. L., & Bryant, R. A. (2005). The relationship between acute stress disorder and posttraumatic stress disorder following cancer. *Journal of Consulting and Clinical Psychology, 73,* 360–364.

Kanner, A. D., Coyne, J. C., Schaefer, C., & Lazarus, R. S. (1981). Comparison of two modes of stress measurement: Daily hassles and uplifts versus major life events. *Journal of Behavioral Medicine, 4,* 1–39.

Kanner, L. (1943). Autistic disturbances of affective content. *Nervous Child, 2,* 217–240.

Kano, K., & Arisaka, O. (2000). Fluvoxamine and enuresis. *Journal of the American Academy of Child & Adolescent Psychiatry, 39,* 1464–1465.

Kantor, M. (1998). *Homophobia: Description, development and dynamics of gay bashing.* Westport, CT: Praeger.

Kaplan, H. S. (1986). *Sexual aversion, sexual phobias, and panic disorder.* New York: Brunner/Mazel.

Kaplan, R. M. (2000). Two pathways to prevention. *American Psychologist, 55,* 382–396.

Kapp, M. B. (1994). Treatment and refusal rights in mental health: Therapeutic justice and clinical accommodation. *American Journal of Orthopsychiatry, 64,* 223–234.

Kaptchuk, R., Eisenberg, D., & Komaroff, A. (2002, December 2). Pondering the placebo effect. *Newsweek,* pp. 71–73.

Kapur, S., & Remington, G. (2000). Atypical antipsychotics: Patients value the lower incidence of extrapyramidal side effects. *British Medical Journal, 321,* 1360–1361.

Karel, J. J., & Hinrichsen, G. (2000). Treatment of depression in late life: Psychotherapeutic interventions. *Clinical Psychology Review, 20,* 707–729.

Karlsson, R. (2005). Ethnic matching between therapist and patient in psychotherapy: An overview of findings, together with methodological and conceptual issues. *Cultural Diversity and Ethnic Minority Psychology, 11,* 113–129.

Karno, M., et al. (1987). Expressed emotions and schizophrenic outcome among Mexican-American families. *Journal of Nervous and Mental Disease, 175,* 143–151.

Karp, B. I., Garvey, M., Jacobsen, L. K., Frazier, J. A., Hamburger, S. D., Bedwell, J. S., et al. (2001). Abnormal neurologic maturation in adolescents with early-onset schizophrenia. *American Journal of Psychiatry, 158,* 118–122.

Karrass, J., Walden, T. A., Conturea, E. G., Graham, C. G., Arnold, H. S., Hartfield, K. N., et al. (2006). Relation of emotional reactivity and regulation to childhood stuttering. *Journal of Communication Disorders, 39,* 402–423.

Karver, M. S., Handelsman, J. B., Fields, S., & Bickman, L. (2006). Meta-analysis of therapeutic relationship variables in youth and family therapy: The evidence for different relationship variables in the child and adolescent treatment outcome literature. *Clinical Psychology Review, 26,* 50–65.

Kasari, D., et al. (1993). Affective development and communication in children with autism. In A. P. Kaiser & D. B. Gray (Eds.), *Enhancing children's communication: Research foundation for intervention* (pp. 201–222). New York: Brookes.

Kasen, S., Cohen, P., Skodol, A. E., Johnson, J. G., Smailes, E., & Brook, J. S. (2001). Childhood depression and adult personality disorder: Alternative pathways of continuity. *Archives of General Psychiatry, 58,* 231–236.

Kasl-Godley, J., & Gatz, M. (2000). Psychosocial interventions for individuals with dementia: An integration of theory, therapy, and a clinical understanding of dementia. *Clinical Psychology Review, 20,* 755–782.

Kaslow, N. J., Thompson, M. P., Okun, A., Price, A., Young, S., Bender, M., et al. (2002). Risk and protective factors for suicidal behavior in abused African American women. *Journal of Consulting and Clinical Psychology, 70,* 311–319.

Kasper, J. A., Hoge, S. K., Feucht-Haviar, T., Cortina, J., & Cohen, B. (1997). Prospective study of patients' refusal of antipsychotic medication under a physician discretion review procedure. *American Journal of Psychiatry, 154,* 483–489.

Kasper, M. E., Rogers, R., & Adams, P. A. (1996). Dangerousness and command hallucinations: An investigation of psychotic inpatients. *Bulletin of the American Academy of Psychiatry and the Law, 24,* 219–224.

Kates, W. R., Burnette, C. P., Eliez, S., Strunge, L. A., Kaplan, D., Landa, R., et al. (2004). Neuroanatomic variation in monozygotic twin pairs discordant for the narrow phenotype for autism. *American Journal of Psychiatry, 161,* 539–546.

Katon, W., Russo, J., Sherbourne, C., Russo, J., Sherbourne, C., Stein, M. B., et al. (2006). Incremental cost-effectiveness of a collaborative care intervention for panic disorder. *Psychological Medicine, 36,* 353–363.

Katon, W. J. (2006). Panic disorder. *New England Journal of Medicine, 354,* 2360–2367.

Katz, J. N. (1995). *The invention of heterosexuality.* New York: Dutton.

Kauer, J. A. (2003). Addictive drugs and stress trigger a common change at VTA synapses. *Neuron, 37,* 549–550.

Kaufman, N. K., Rohde, P., Seeley, J. R., Clarke, G. N., & Stice, E. (2005). Potential mediators of cognitive-behavioral therapy for adolescents with comorbid major depression and conduct disorder. *Journal of Consulting and Clinical Psychology, 73,* 38–46.

Kawachi, I., Colditz, G. A., Ascherio, A., Rimm, E. B., Giovannucci, E., Stampfer, M. J., & Willett, W. C. (1994). Prospective study of phobic anxiety and risk of coronary heart disease in men. *Circulation, 89,* 1992–1997.

Kay, A. B. (2006). Natural Killer T Cells and asthma. *New England Journal of Medicine, 354,* 1186–1188.

Kay, S. R. (1990). Significance of the positive-negative distinction in schizophrenia. *Schizophrenia Bulletin, 16,* 635–652.

Kaysen, S. (1994). *Girl, interrupted.* New York: Random House.

Kazdin, A. E. (1992). *Research design in clinical psychology* (2nd ed.). Boston: Allyn & Bacon.

Kazdin, A. E. (2003). Psychotherapy for children and adolescents. *Annual Review of Psychology, 54,* 253–276.

Kazdin, A. E., & Whitley, M. K. (2003). Treatment of parental stress to enhance therapeutic change among children referred for aggressive and antisocial behavior. *Journal of Consulting and Clinical Psychology, 71,* 504–515.

Keating, G. M., McClellan, K., & Jarvis, B. (2001). Methylphenidate (OROS(R) formulation). *CNS Drugs, 15* (6), 495–500.

Keel, P. K., Mitchell, J. E., Miller, K. B., Davis, T. L., & Crow, S. J. (1999). Long-term outcome of bulimia nervosa. *Archives of General Psychiatry, 56,* 63–69.

Keesey R. E., & Powley, T. L. (1986). The regulation of body weight. *Annual Review of Psychology, 37,* 109–133.

Kellner, C. H., Fink, M., Knapp, R., Petrides, G., Husain, M., Rummans, T., et al. (2005). Relief of expressed suicidal intent by ECT: A Consortium for Research in ECT Study. *American Journal of Psychiatry, 162,* 977–982.

Kellner, C. H., Knapp, R. G., Petrides, G., Rummans, T. A., Husain, M. M., Rasmussen, K., et al. (2006). Continuation electroconvulsive therapy vs pharmacotherapy for relapse prevention in major depression. *Archives of General Psychiatry, 63,* 1337–1344.

Kelly, B. D., Kennedy, N., & Shanley, D. (2000). Delusion and desire: erotomania revisited. *Acta Psychiatrica Scandinavica, 102,* 74–75.

Kelly, J. A., & Kalichman, S. C. (2002). Behavioral research in HIV/AIDS primary and secondary prevention: Recent advances and future directions. *Journal of Consulting and Clinical Psychology, 70,* 626–639.

Kelly, S. J., Macaruso, P., & Sokol, S. M. (1997). Mental calculation in an autistic savant: A case study. *Journal of Clinical and Experimental Neuropsychology, 19,* 172–184.

Kelner, K., & Helmuth, L. (2003). Obesity—What is to be done? *Science, 299,* 845.

Kemeny, M. E. (2003). The psychobiology of stress. *Current Directions in Psychological Science, 12,* 124–129.

Kenardy, J. A., Dow, M. G. T., Johnston, D. W., Newman, M. G., Thomson, A., & Taylor, C. B. (2003). A comparison of delivery methods of cognitive–behavioral therapy for panic disorder: An international multicenter trial. *Journal of Consulting and Clinical Psychology, 71,* 1068–1075.

Kendall, P. C., & Treadwell, K. R. H. (2007). The role of self-statements as a mediator in treatment for youth with anxiety disorders. *Journal of Consulting and Clinical Psychology, 75,* 380–389.

Kendall, P. C., Safford, S., Flannery-Schroeder, E., & Webb, A. (2004). Child anxiety treatment: Outcomes in adolescence and impact on substance use and depression at 7.4-year follow-up. *Journal of Consulting and Clinica l Psychology, 72,* 276–287.

Kendell, R., & Jablensky, A. (2003). Distinguishing between the validity and utility of psychiatric diagnoses. *American Journal of Psychiatry, 160,* 4–12.

Kendler, K. S. (1994). Twin studies of psychiatric illness: Current status and future directions. *Archives of General Psychiatry, 50,* 905–918.

Kendler, K. S. (2001). A psychiatric dialogue on the mind-body problem. *American Journal of Psychiatry, 158,* 989–1000.

Kendler, K. S. (2005). "A gene for . . .": The nature of gene action in psychiatric disorders. *American Journal of Psychiatry, 162,* 1243–1252.

Kendler, K. S., & Diehl, S. R. (1993). The genetics of schizophrenia: A current, genetic-epidemiologic perspective. *Schizophrenia Bulletin, 19,* 261–295.

Kendler, K. S., & Gardner, C. O. (1998). Boundaries of major depression: An evaluation of *DSM-IV* criteria. *American Journal of Psychiatry, 155,* 172–177.

Kendler, K. S., & Prescott, C. A. (1999). A population-based twin study of lifetime major depression in men and women. *Archives of General Psychiatr y, 56,* 39–44.

Kendler, K. S., & Walsh, D. (1995). Schizotypal personality disorder in parents and the risk for schizophrenia in siblings. *Schizophrenia Bulletin, 21,* 47–52.

Kendler, K. S., Bulik, C. M., Silberg, J., Hettema, J. M., Myers, J., & Prescott, C. A. (2000). Childhood sexual abuse and adult psychiatric and substa nce use disorders in women: An epidemiological and co-twin control analysis. *Archives of General Psychiatry, 57* (10), 953–959.

Kendler, K. S., et al. (1991). The genetic epidemiology of bulimia nervosa. *American Journal of Psychiatry, 148,* 1627–1637.

Kendler, K. S., et al. (1992a). The genetic epidemiology of phobias in women: The interrelationship of agoraphobia, social phobia, situational phobia, and simple phobia. *Archives of General Psychiatry, 49,* 273–281.

Kendler, K. S., et al. (1993). The lifetime history of major depression in women: Reliability of diagnosis and heritability. *Archives of General Psychiatry, 50,* 863–870.

Kendler, K. S., et al. (1997). Resemblance of psychotic symptoms and syndromes in affected sibling pairs from the Irish study of high-density schizophrenia families: Evidence for possible etiologic heterogeneity. *American Journal of Psychiatry, 154,* 191–198.

Kendler, K. S., et al. (2001). The genetic epidemiology of irrational fears and phobias in men. *Archives of General Psychiatry, 58,* 257–265.

Kendler, K. S., Gardner, C. O., & Prescott, C. A. (2002). Toward a comprehensive developmental model for major depression in women. *American Journal of Psychiatry, 159,* 1133–1145.

Kendler, K. S., Gruenberg, A. M., & Tsuang, M.T. (1985). Psychiatric illness in first-degree relatives of schizophrenic and surgical control patients, a family study using *DSM-III* criteria. *Archives of General Psychiatry, 42,* 770–779.

Kendler, K. S., Hettema, J. M., Butera, F., Gardner, C. O., & Prescott, C. A. (2003). Life event dimensions of loss, humiliation, entrapment, and danger in the predict- ion of onsets of major depression and generalized anxiety. *Archives of General Psychiatry, 60,* 789–796.

Kendler, K. S., Jacobson, K. C., Prescott, C. A., & Neale, M. C. (2003). Specificity of genetic and environmental risk factors for use and abuse/dependence of cannabis, cocaine, hallucinogens, sedatives, stimu-

lants, and opiates in male twins. *American Journal of Psychiatry, 160,* 687–695.

Kendler, K. S., Kuhn, J., & Prescott, C. A. (2004). The interrelationship of neuroticism, sex, and stressful life events in the prediction of episodes of major depression. *American Journal of Psychiatry, 161,* 631–636.

Kendler, K. S., Thornton, L. M., & Gardner, C. O. (2000). Stressful life events and previous episodes in the etiology of major depression in women: An evaluation of the "kindling" hypothesis. *American Journal of Psychiatry, 157,* 1243–1251.

Kendler, K. S., Thornton, L. M., & Pedersen, N. L. (2000). Tobacco consumption in Swedish twins reared apart and reared together. *Archives of General Psychiatry, 57,* 886–892.

Kennedy, N., Abbott, R., & Paykel, E. S. (2003). Remission and recurrence of depression in the maintenance era: Long-term outcome in a Cambridge cohort. *Psychological Medicine, 33,* 827–838.

Kennedy, N., McDonough, M., Kelly, B., & Berrios, G. E. (2002). Erotomania revisited: Clinical course and treatment. *Comprehensive Psychiatry, 43,* 1–6.

Kent, A., & Waller, G. (2000). Childhood emotional abuse and eating psychopathology. *Clinical Psychology Review, 20,* 887–903.

Kent, J. M., Papp, L. A., Martinez, J. M., Browne, S. T., Coplan, J. D., Klein, D. F., et al. (2001). Specificity of panic response to CO_2 inhalation in panic disorder: A comparison with major depression and premenstrual dysphoric disorder. *American Journal of Psychiatry, 158,* 58–67.

Kernberg, O. F. (1975). *Borderline conditions and pathological narcissism.* New York: Jason Aronson.

Kersting, K. (2003, November). Study shows two types of reading disability. *Monitor on Psychology.* Retrieved February 3, 2004, from http://www.apa.org/monitor/nov03/study.html.

Kessler, R. C., Adler, L., Barkley, R., Biederman, J., Conners, C. K., et al. (2006). The prevalence and correlates of adult ADHD in the United States: Results from the National Comorbidity Survey Replication. *American Journal of Psychiatry, 163,* 716–723.

Kessler, R. C., Berglund, P., Demler, O., Jin, R., Koretz, D., Merikangas, K. R., et al. (2003). The epidemiology of major depressive disorder: Results from the National Comorbidity Survey Replication (NCS-R). *Journal of the American Medical Association, 289,* 3095–3105.

Kessler, R. C., Berglund, P.A., Demler, O., Jin, R., & Walters, E. E. (2005a). Lifetime prevalence and age-of-onset distributions of *DSM-IV* disorders in the National Comorbidity Survey Replication (NCS-R). *Archives of General Psychiatry, 62,* 593–602.

Kessler, R. C., Borges, G., & Walters, E. E. (1999). Prevalence of and risk factors for lifetime suicide attempts in the National Comorbidity Survey. *Archives of General Psychiatry, 56,* 617–626.

Kessler, R. C., Chiu, W. T., Demler, O., & Walters, E. E. (2005b). Prevalence, severity, and comorbidity of 12-month *DSM-IV* disorders in the National Comorbidity Survey Replication. *Archives of General Psychiatry, 62,* 617–627.

Kessler, R. C., Crum, R. M., Warner, L. A., Nelson, C. B., Schulenberg, J., & Anthony, J. C. (1997). Lifetime co-occurrence of *DSM-III-R* alcohol abuse and dependence with other psychiatric disorders in the National Comorbidity Survey. *Archives of General Psychiatry, 54,* 313–321.

Kessler, R. C., Demler O., Frank, R. G., Olfson, M., Pincus, H. A., Walters, E. E., et al. (2005c). Prevalence and treatment of mental disorders, 1990 to 2003. *New England Journal of Medicine, 352,* 2515–2523.

Kessler, R. C., Downey, G., Milavsky, J. R., & Stipp, H. (1990). Clustering of teenage suicides after television news stories about suicides: A reconsideration. *American Journal of Psychiatry, 145,* 1379–1383.

Kessler, R. C., McGonagle, K. A., Swartz, M., Blazer, D. G., & Nelson, C. B. (1993). Sex and depression in the National Comorbidity Survey I: Lifetime prevalence, chronicity, and recurrence. *Journal of Affective Disorders, 29,* 85–96.

Kessler, R. C., McGonagle, K. A., Zhao, S., Nelson, C. B., Hughes, M., Eshleman, S., et al. (1994). Lifetime and 12-month prevalence of *DSM-III-R* psychiatric disorders in the United States: Results from the National Comorbidity Survey. *Archives of General Psychiatry, 51,* 8–19.

Kessler, R. C., Sonnega, A., Bromet, E., Hughes, M., & Nelson, C. B. (1995). Posttraumatic stress disorder in the National Comorbidity Survey. *Archives of General Psychiatry, 52,* 1048–1060.

Kety, S., Wender, P. H., Jacobsen, B., Ingraham, L. J., Jansson, L., Faber, B., et al. (1994). Mental illness in the biological and adoptive relatives of schizophrenic adoptees: Replication of the Copenhagen study in the rest of Denmark. *Archives of General Psychiatry, 51,* 442–455.

Kety, S. S. (1980). The syndrome of schizophrenia: Unresolved questions and opportunities for research. *British Journal of Psychiatry, 136,* 421–436.

Kety, S. S., Rosenthal, D., Wender, P. H., Schulsinger, F., & Jacobsen, B. (1975). Mental illness in the biological and adoptive families of adoptive individuals who have become schizophrenic: A preliminary report based on psychiatric interviews. In R. R. Fieve, D. Rosenthal, & H. Brill (Eds.), *Genetic research in psychiatry* (pp. 147–165). Baltimore: The Johns Hopkins University Press.

Kety, S. S., Rosenthal, D., Wender, P. H., Schulsinger, F., & Jacobsen, B. (1978). The biological and adoptive families of adopted individuals who become schizophrenic. In C. Wynne, R. L. Cromwell, & S. Mathysse (Eds.), *The nature of schizophrenia* (pp. 25–37). New York: Wiley.

Keyes, D. (1982). *The minds of Billy Milligan.* New York: Bantam Books.

Kiecolt-Glaser, J. K., et al. (1987). Marital quality, marital disruption, and immune function. *Psychosomatic Medicine, 49,* 13–34.

Kiecolt-Glaser, J. K., Kennedy, S., Malkoff, S., Fisher, L., Speicher, C. E., & Glaser, R. (1988). Marital discord and immunity in males. *Psychosomatic Medicine, 50,* 213–229.

Kiecolt-Glaser, J. K., Marucha, P. T., Malarkey, W. B., Mercado, A. M., & Glaser, R. (1995). Slowing of wound healing by psychological stress. *Lancet, 346,* 1194–1196.

Kiecolt-Glaser, J. K., McGuire, L., Robles, T. F., & Glaser, R. (2002a). Emotions, morbidity, and mortality: New perspectives from psychoneuroimmunology. *Annual Review of Psychology, 53,* 83–107.

Kiecolt-Glaser, J. K., McGuire, L., Robles, T. F., & Glaser, R. (2002b). Psychoneuroimmunology and psychosomatic medicine: Back to the future. *Psychosomatic Medicine, 64,* 15–28.

Kiecolt-Glaser, J. K., Preacher, K. J., MacCallum, R. C., Atkinson, C., Malarkey, W. B., & Glaser, R. (2003). Chronic stress and age-related increases in the proinflammatory cytokine IL-6. *Proceedings of the National Academy of Sciences, 100,* 9090–9095.

Kiecolt-Glaser, J. K., Speicher, C. E., Holliday, J. E., & Glaser, R. (1984). Stress and the transformation of lymphocytes in Epstein-Barr virus. *Journal of Behavioral Medicine, 7,* 1–12.

Kiefer, F., Jahn, H., Tarnaske, T., Helwig, H., Briken, P., Holzbach, R., et al. (2003). Comparing and combining naltrexone and acamprosate in relapse prevention of alcoholism: A double-blind, placebo-controlled study. *Archives of General Psychiatry, 60,* 92–99.

Kiehl, K. A., et al. (2006). A cognitive neuroscience perspective on psychopathy: Evidence for paralimbic system dysfunction. *Psychiatry Research, 142,* 107–128.

Kiely, D. K., Bergmann, M. A., Jones, R. N., Murphy, K. M., Orav, E. J., & Marcantonio, E. R. (2004). Characteristics associated with delirium persistence among newly admitted post-acute facility patients. *The Journals of Gerontology Series A: Biological Sciences and Medical Sciences, 59,* 344–349.

Kieseppä, T., Partonen, T., Haukka, J., Kaprio, J., & Lönnqvist, J. (2004). High concordance of Bipolar I disorder in a nationwide sample of twins. *American Journal of Psychiatry, 161,* 1814–1821.

Kiesler, C. A., & Sibulkin, A. E. (1987). *Mental hospitalization: Myths and facts about a national crisis.* Newbury Park, CA: Sage.

Kiesler, D. J. (1999). *Beyond the disease model of mental disorders.* Westport, CT: Praeger Publishers.

Kihlstrom, J. F. (2004). An unbalanced balancing act: Blocked, recovered, and false memories in the laboratory and clinic. *Clinical Psychology: Science and Practice, 11,* 34–39.

Kilgore, K., Snyder, J., & Lentz, C. (2002). The contribution of parental discipline, parental monitoring, and school risk to early-onset conduct problems in African American boys and girls. *Developmental Psychology, 36* (6), 835–845.

Kilpatrick, D. G., et al. (2000). Risk factors for adolescent substance abuse and dependence: Data from a national sample. *Journal of Consulting and Clinical Psychology, 68,* 19–30.

Kilpatrick, D. G., Ruggiero, K. J., Acierno, R., Saunders, B. E., Resnick, H. S., & Best, C. L. (2003). Violence and risk of PTSD, major depression, substance abuse/dependence, and comorbidity: Results from the National Survey of Adolescents. *Journal of Consulting & Clinical Psychology, 71,* 692–700.

Kilts, C. D., et al. (2001). Neural activity related to drug craving in cocaine addiction. *Archives of General Psychiatry, 58,* 334–341.

Kilts, C. D., Gross, R. E., Ely, T. D., & Drexler, K. P. G. (2004). The neural correlates of cue-induced craving in cocaine-dependent women. *American Journal of Psychiatry, 161,* 233–241.

Kim-Cohen, J., Caspi, A., Taylor, A., Williams, B., Newcombe, R., Craig, I. W., et al. (2006). MAOA, maltreatment, and gene-environment interaction predicting children's mental health: New evidence and a meta-analysis. *Molecular Psychiatry, 11,* 903–913.

Kinetz, E. (2006, September 26). Is hysteria real? Brain images say yes. *The New York Times,* pp. F1, F4.

King, S., & Dixon, M. J. (1995). Expressed emotion, family dynamics, and symptom severity in a predictive model of social adjustment for schizophrenic young adults. *Schizophrenia Research, 14,* 121–132.

King, S., & Dixon, M. J. (1999). Expressed emotion and relapse in young schizophrenia outpatients. *Schizophrenia Bulletin, 25,* 377–386.

Kingsberg, S. A. (2002). The impact of aging on sexual function in women and their partners. *Archives of Sexual Behavior, 31* (5), 431–437.

Kinney, D. K., Holzman, P. S., Jacobsen, B., Jansson, L., Faber, B., Hildebrand, W., Kasell, E., et al. (1997). Thought disorder in schizophrenic and control adoptees and their relatives. *Archives of General Psychiatry, 54,* 475–479.

Kirisci, L., Vanyukov, M., & Tarter, R. (2005). Detection of youth at high risk for substance use disorders: A longitudinal study. *Psychology of Addictive Behaviors, 19,* 243–252.

Kirmayer, L. J., Robbins, J. M., & Paris, J. (1994). Somatoform disorders: Personality and the social matrix of somatic distress. *Journal of Abnormal Psychology, 103,* 125–136.

Kirsch, I. (2004). Conditioning, expectancy, and the placebo effect: Comment on Stewart-Williams and Podd (2004). *Psychological Bulletin, 130,* 341–343.

Kirsch, I., Moore, T. J., Scoboria, A., & Nicholls, S. S. (2002). The emperor's new drugs: An analysis of antidepressant medication data submitted to the U.S. Food and Drug Administration. *Prevention & Treatment, 5,* Posted July 15, 2002. Retrieved July 16, 2003, from http://journals.apa.org/prevention/volume5/pre0050023a.html.

Klassen, D., & O'Connor, W. A. (1988). Predicting violence in schizophrenic and non-schizophrenic patients: A prospective study. *Journal of Community Psychology, 16,* 217–227.

Klein, D. F. (1994). "Klein's suffocation theory of panic": Reply. *Archives of General Psychiatry, 51,* 506.

Klein, D. N., Lewinsohn, P. M., Seeley, J. R., & Rohde, P. (2001). A family study of major depressive disorder in a community sample of adolescents. *Archives of General Psychiatry, 58,* 13–20.

Klein, D. N., Schwartz, J. E., Santiago, J. J., Vivian, D., Vocisano, C., Castonguay, L. G., et al. (2003). Therapeutic alliance in depression treatment: Controlling for prior change and patient characteristics. *Journal of Consulting and Clinical Psychology, 71,* 997–1006.

Kleinman, A. (1987). Anthropology and psychiatry: The role of culture in cross-cultural research on illness. *British Journal of Psychiatry, 151,* 447–454.

Kleinplatz, P. J. (2003). What's new in sex therapy? From stagnation to fragmentation. *Sexual & Relationship Therapy, 18* (1), 95–106.

Klerman, G. L. (1984). Ideology & science in the individual psychotherapy of schizophrenia. *Schizophrenia Bulletin, 10,* 608–612.

Klerman, G. L., Weissman, M. M., Rounsaville, B. J., & Chevron, E. S. (1984). *Interpersonal psychotherapy of depression.* New York: Basic Books.

Klesges, R. C., Johnson, K. C., & Somes, G. (2006). Varenicline for smoking cessation: definite promise, but no panacea. *Journal of the American Medical Association, 296,* 94–95.

Klonoff, E. A., & Landrine, H. (1997). *Preventing misdiagnosis of women: A guide to physical disorders that have psychiatric symptoms.* Thousand Oaks, CA: Sage.

Kluft, R. P. (1988). The dissociative disorders. In J. Talbott, R. Hales, & S. Yudofsky (Eds.), *Textbook of psychiatry.* Washington, DC: American Psychiatric Press.

Kluger, J. (2001, June 18). How to manage teen drinking (the smart way). *Time,* pp. 42–44.

Kluger, J. (2003, October 26). Medicating young minds. *Time Magazine Online.* Retrieved October 27, 2003, from http://www.time.com/time/magazine/article/0,9171, 1101031103-526331,00.html.

Knight, R. G., Godfrey, H. P. D., & Shelton, E. J. (1988). The psychological deficits associated with Parkinson's disease. *Clinical Psychology Review, 8,* 391–410.

Knoll, J. L., IV, Garver, D. L., Ramberg, J. E., Kingsbury, S. J., Croissant, D., & McDermott, B. (1998). Heterogeneity of the psychoses: Is there a neurodegenerative psychosis? *Schizophrenia Bulletin, 24,* 365–379.

Knudsen, D. D. (1991). Child sexual coercion. In E. Grauerholz & M. A. Koralewski (Eds.), *Sexual coercion: A sourcebook on its nature, causes, and prevention* (pp. 17–28). Lexington, MA: Lexington Books.

Kobak, K. A., Greist, J. H., Jefferson, J. W., & Katzelnick, D. J. (1996). Computer-administered clinical rating scales: A review. *Psychopharmacology, 127,* 291–301.

Kobak, K. A., Taylor, L. H., Dottl, S. L., Greist, J. H., Jefferson, J. W., Burroughs, D., et al. (1997). A computer-administered telephone interview to identify mental disorders. *Journal of the American Medical Association, 278,* 905–910.

Kobasa, S. C. (1979). Stressful life events, personality, and health: An inquiry into hardiness. *Journal of Personality and Social Psychology, 37,* 1–11.

Kobasa, S. C., Maddi, S. R., & Kahn, S. (1982). Hardiness and health: A prospective study. *Journal of Personality and Social Psychology, 42,* 168–177.

Koenen, K. C., Stellman, J. M., & Stellman, S. D. (2003). Risk factors for course of posttraumatic stress disorder among Vietnam veterans: A 14-year follow-up of American Legionnaires. *Journal of Consulting and Clinical Psychology, 71,* 980–986.

Koenigsberg, H. W., Harvey, P. D., Mitropoulou, V., Schmeidler, J., New, A. S., Goodman, M., et al. (2002). Characterizing affective instability in borderline personality disorder. *American Journal of Psychiatry, 159,* 789–796.

Koerner, K., & Linehan, M. M. (2002). Dialectical behavior therapy for borderline personality disorder. In S. G. Hofmann & M. Tompson (Eds.), *Treating chronic and severe mental disorders: A handbook of empirically supported interventions* (pp. 317–342). New York: Guilford Press.

Kohler, C. G., Turner, T. H., Bilker, W. B., Brensinger, C. M., Siegel, S. J., et al. (2003). Facial emotion recognition in schizophrenia: intensity effects and error pattern. *American Journal of Psychiatry, 160,* 1768–1774.

Kohn, C. S., & Antonuccio, D. O. (2002). Treatment of kleptomania using cognitive and behavioral strategies. *Clinical Case Studies, 1,* 25–38.

Kolata, G. (2000a, October 18). Days off are not allowed, experts argue. *The New York Times,* pp. A1, A20.

Kolata, G. (2000b, October 17). How the body knows when to gain or lose. *The New York Times,* pp. F1, F8.

Kolbert, E. (1994, January 21). Demons replace dolls and bicycles in world of children of the quake. *The New York Times,* p. A19.

Kolker, R. (2002, January 14). *Quality-of-life control. New York Magazine Online.* Retrieved November 14, 2003, from http://www.newyorkmetro.com/nymetro/news/politics/newyork/features/5581/.

Kolko, D. J., & Rickard-Figueroa, J. L. (1985). Effects of video games on the adverse corollaries of chemotherapy in pediatric oncology patients: A single-case analysis. *Journal of Consulting and Clinical Psychology, 53,* 223–228.

Konradi, C., Eaton, M., MacDonald, M. L., Walsh, J., Benes, F. M., & Heckers, S. (2004). Molecular evidence for mitochondrial dysfunction in bipolar disorder. *Archives of General Psychiatry, 61,* 300–308.

Koocher, G. P., & Keith-Spiegel, P. (2007). *Ethics in psychology* (3rd ed.). New York: Oxford University Press.

Kopell, B., H., Machado, A. G., & Rezai, A.R. (2005). Not your father's lobotomy: Psychiatric surgery revisited. *Clinical Neurosurgery, 52,* 315–330.

Kopelowicz, A., Liberman, R. P., & Zarate, R. (2006). *Schizophrenia Research, 32*(1 Suppl), S12–S23.

Koplin, B., & Agathen, J. (2002). Suicidality in children and adolescents: A review. *Current Opinions in Pediatrics, 14,* 713–717.

Kordower, J. H., Emborg, M. E., Bloch, J., Ma, S. Y., Chu, Y., Leventhal, L., McBride, J., & Chen, E. Y. (2000). Neurodegeneration prevented by lentiviral vector delivery of GDNF in primate models of Parkinson's disease. *Science, 290,* 767–773.

Koss, M. P. (1988). Stranger and acquaintance rape: Are there differences in the victim's experience? *Psychology of Women Quarterly, 12,* 1–24.

Koss, M. P., & Kilpatrick, D. G. (2001). Rape and sexual assault. In E. Gerrity, et al. (Eds.), *The mental health consequences of torture. Plenum series on stress and coping* (pp. 177–193). Dordrecht, Netherlands: Kluwer Academic Publishers.

Koss, M. P., Bailey, J. A., Yuan, N. P., Herrera, V. M., & Lichter, E. L. (2003). Depression and PTSD in survivors of male violence: Research and training initiatives to facilitate recovery. *Psychology of Women Quarterly, 27* (2), 130–142.

Koss, M. P., Figueredo, A. J., & Prince, R. J. (2002). Cognitive mediation of rape's mental, physical and social health impact: Tests of four models in cross-sectional data. *Journal of Consulting & Clinical Psychology, 70* (4), 926–941.

Koss, M. P., Gidycz, C. A., & Wisniewski, N. (1987). The scope of rape: Incidence and prevalence of sexual aggression and victimization in a national sample of higher education s tudents. *Journal of Consulting and Clinical Psychology, 55,* 162–170.

Kosson, D. S., Lorenz, A. R., & Newman, J. P. (2006). Effects of comorbid psychopathy on criminal offending and emotion processing in male offenders with antisocial personality disorder. *Journal of Abnormal Psychology, 115,* 798–780.

Kosson, D. S., Suchy, Y., Mayer, A. R., & Libby, J. (2002). Facial affect recognition in criminal psychopaths. *Emotion, 4,* 398–411.

Kotler, M. (1997). Excess dopamine D4 receptor (D4DR) exon III seven repeat allele in opioid-dependent subjects. *Molecular Psychiatry, 2,* 251–254.

Kouyoumdjian, H., Zamboanga, B. L., & Hansen, D. J. (2003). Barriers to community mental health services for Latinos: Treatment considerations. *Clinical Psychology: Science and Practice, 10,* 394–422.

Kovacs, M. (1996). Presentation and course of major depressive disorder during childhood and later years of the life span. *Journal of the American Academy of Children and Adolescent Psychiatry, 35,* 705–715.

Kraaimaat, F. W., Vanryckeghem, M., & Van Dam-Baggen, R. (2002). Stuttering and social anxiety. *Journal of Fluency Disorders, 27,* 319–330.

Krack, P., Batir, A., Van Blercom, N., Chabardes, S., Fraix, V., Ardouin, C., et al. (2003). Five-year follow-up of bilateral stimulation of the subthalamic nucleus in advanced Parkinson's disease. *New England Journal of Medicine, 349,* 1925–1934.

Kraepelin, E. (1909–1913). *Psychiatrie* (8th ed.). Leipzig: J. A. Barth.

Krahe, B., Waizenhofer, E., & Moller, I. (2003). Women's sexual aggression against men: Prevalence and predictors. *Sex Roles, 49,* 219–232.

Krain, A. L., & Castellanos, F. X. (2006). Brain development and ADHD. *Clinical Psychology Review, 26,* 433–444.

Krakauer, S. Y. (2001). *Treating dissociati ve identity disorder: The power of the collective heart.* Philadelphia: Brunner-Routledge.

Kramer, M. S., et al. (1998, September 11). Distinct mechanism for antidepressant activity by blockade of central substance P receptors. *Science,* pp. 1640–1645.

Krantz, D. S., Contrada, R. J., Hills, D. R., & Friedler, E. (1988). Environmental stress and biobehavioral antecedents of coronary heart disease. *Journal of Consulting and Clinical Psychology, 56,* 333–341.

Krantz, M. J., & Mehler, P. S. (2004). Treating opioid dependence: Growing implications for primary care. *Archives of Internal Medicine, 164,* 277–288.

Kranzler, H. R. (2000). Medications for alcohol dependence: New vistas. *Journal of the American Medical Association, 284,* 1016–1017. [Editorial]

Kranzler, H. R. (2006). Evidence-based treatments for alcohol dependence: New Results and New Questions. *Journal of the American Medical Association, 295*, 2075–2076.

Krehbiel, K. (2000, October). Diagnosis and treatment of bipolar disorder. *Monitor on Psychology*, p. 22.

Kremer, T. G., & Gesten, E. L. (2003). Managed mental health care: The client's perspective. *Professional Psychology: Research & Practice, 34*, 187–196.

Kring, A. M., & Neale, J. M. (1996). Do schizophrenic patients show a disjunctive relationship among expressive, experiential, and psychophysiological components of emotion? *Journal of Abnormal Psychology, 105*, 249–257.

Kristof, N. D. (2002, December 5). Love and race. *The New York Times Online*. Retrieved July 23, 2003, from http://www.racematters.org/loveandrace.htm.

Kröger, C., Schweiger, U., Sipos, V., Arnold, R., Kahl, K. G., Schunert, T., et al. (2006). Effectiveness of dialectical behaviour therapy for borderline personality disorder in an inpatient setting. *Behaviour Research and Therapy, 44*, 1211–1217.

Kromkamp, M, Uylings, H. B., Smidt, M. P., Hellemons, A. J., Burbach, J. P., & Kahn, R. S. (2003). Decreased thalamic expression of the home-obox gene DLX1 in psychosis. *Archives of General Psychiatry, 60*, 869–874.

Krueger, R. B., & Kaplan, M. S. (2002). Behavioral and psychopharmacological treatment of the paraphilic and hypersexual disorders. *Journal of Psychiatric Practice, 8*(1), 21–32.

Krueger, R. F., & Markon, K. E. (2006). Understanding psychopathology: Melding behavior genetics, personality, and quantitative psychology to develop an empirically based model. *Current Directions in Psychological Science, 15*, 113–117.

Krueger, R. F., Hicks, B. M., Patrick, C. J., Carlson, S. R., Iacono, W. G., & McGue, M. (2002). Etiologic connections among substance dependence, antisocial behavior, and personality: Modeling the externalizing spectrum. *Journal of Abnormal Psychology, 111,* 411–424.

Krug, E., Kresnow, M., Peddicord, J. P., Dahlberg, L. L., Powell, K. E., Crosby, A. E., & Annest, J. L. (1998). Suicide after natural disasters. *The New England Journal of Medicine, 338*, 373–378.

Kryger, M. H., Roth, T., & Dement, W. C. (Eds.). (2000). *Principles and practice of sleep medicine* (3rd ed.). Philadelphia: W. B. Saunders.

Kubany, E. S., Hill, E. E., Owens, J. A., Iannce-Spencer, C., McCaig, M. A., et al. (2004). Cognitive trauma therapy for battered women with PTSD (CTT-BW). *Journal of Consulting and Clinical Psychology, 72*, 3–18.

Kubiszyn, T. W., et al. (2000). Empirical support for psychological assessment in clinical health care settings. *Professional Psychology: Research and Practice, 31*, 119–130.

Kuhn, C. M., & Wilson, W. A. (2001, Spring). Our dangerous love affair with ecstasy. *Cerebrum*, pp. 22–33.

Kuno, E., & Rothbard, A. B. (2002). Racial disparities in antipsychotic prescription patterns for patients with schizophrenia. *American Journal of Psychiatry, 159*, 567–572.

Kuperberg, G. R., Broome, M. R., McGuire, P., K., David, A. S., Eddy, M., Ozawa, F., et al. (2003). Regionally localized thinning of the cerebral cortex in schizophrenia. *Archives of General Psychiatry, 60*, 878–888.

Kupfer, D. J. (1999). Research in affective disorders comes of age. *American Journal of Psychiatry, 156*, 165–167. [Editorial]

Kupfer, D. J. (2005a). Dimensional models for research and diagnosis: A current dilemma. *Journal of Abnormal Psychology, 114*, 557–559.

Kupfer, D. J. (2005b). The increasing medical burden in bipolar disorder. *Journal of the American Medical Association, 293*, 2528–2530.

Kupfer, D. J., & Reynolds, C. F. (1997). Current concepts: Management of insomnia. *The New England Journal of Medicine, 336*, 341–346.

Kurth, T., Gaziano, J. M., Berger, K., Kase, C. S., Rexrode, K. M., Cook, N. R., et al. (2002). Body mass index and the risk of stroke in men. *Archives of Internal Medicine, 162*, 2557–2562.

Kwon, H., Menon, V., Eliez, S, Warsofsky, I. S., White, C. D., Dyer-Friedman, J. J., et al. (2001). Functional neuroanatomy of visuospatial working memory in Fragile X syndrome: Relation to behavioral and molecular measures. *American Journal of Psychiatry, 158*, 1040–1051.

Kwon, S., & Oei, T. P. S. (1994). The roles of two levels of cognitions in the development, maintenance, and treatment of depression. *Clinical Psychology Review, 14*, 331–358.

Kymalainen, J. A., Weisman, A. G., Rosales, G. A., & Armesto, J. C. (2006). Ethnicity, expressed emotion, and communication deviance in family members of patients with schizophrenia. *Journal of Nervous and Mental Disease, 194*, 391–396.

L

La Roche, M. J., & Maxie, A. (2003). Ten considerations in addressing cultural differences in psychotherapy. *Professional Psychology: Research and Practice, 34*, 180–186.

Ladouceur, R., Dugas, M. J., Freeston, M. H., Leger, E., Gagnon, F., & Thibodeau, N. (2000). Efficacy of a cognitive–behavioral treatment for generalized anxiety disorder: Evaluation in a controlled clinical trial. *Journal of Consulting and Clinical Psychology, 68*, 957–964.

Lagacea, D. C., Yee, J. K., Bolaños, C. A., &. Eisch, A. J. (2006). Juvenile administration of methylphenidate attenuates adult hippocampal neurogenesis. *Biological Psychiatry*, in press.

Lahey, B. B., et al. (1995). Four-year longitudinal study of conduct disorder in boys: Patterns and predictors of persistence. *Journal of Abnormal Psychology, 104*, 83–93.

Lahey, B. B., Loeber, R., Burke, J. D, & Applegate, B. (2005). Predicting future antisocial personality disorder in males from a clinical assessment in childhood. *Journal of Consulting and Clinical Psychology, 73*, 389–399.

Lahey, B. B., Loeber, R., Burke, J., Rathouz, P. J., & McBurnett, K. (2003). Waxing and waning in concert: Dynamic comorbidity of conduct disorder with other disruptive and emotional problems over 7 years among clinic-referred boys. *Journal of Abnormal Psychology, 111*, 556–567.

Lam, D. H., Watkins, E. R., Hayward, P., Bright, J., Wright, K., Kerr, N., et al. (2000). Cognitive therapy for bipolar illness: A pilot study of relapse prevention. *Cognitive Therapy & Research, 24*, 503–520.

Lam, D. H., Watkins, E. R., Hayward, P., Bright, J., Wright, K., Kerr, N., et al. (2003). A randomized controlled study of cognitive therapy for relapse prevention for bipolar affective disorder: Outcome of the first year. *Archives of General Psychiatry, 60*, 145–152.

Lam, R. W., Levitt, A. J., Levitan, R. D., Enns, M. W., Morehouse, R., Michalak, E. E., et al. (2006). The Can-SAD Study: A randomized controlled trial of the effectiveness of light therapy and fluoxetine in patients with winter seasonal affective disorder. *American Journal of Psychiatry, 163*, 805–811.

Lamb, H. R. (2001). A century and a half of psychiatric rehabilitation in the United States. In H. R. Lamb & L. E. Weinberger (Eds.), *Deinstitutionalization: Promise and problems. New directions for mental health services* (pp. 99–110). San Francisco: Jossey-Bass/Pfeiffer.

Lamb, H. R., & Weinberger L. (Eds). (2001). *Deinstitutionalization: Promise and problems. New directions for mental health services.* San Francisco: Jossey-Bass/Pfeiffer.

Lamberg, L. (2000). Sleep disorders, often unrecognized, complicate many physical illnesses. *Journal of the American Medical Association, 284*, 2173–2175.

Lamberg, L. (2003). Advances in eating disorders offer food for thought. *Journal of the American Medical Association, 290*, 1437–1442.

Lamberg, L. (2006). Rx for obesity: Eat less, exercise more, and—maybe—get more sleep. *Journal of the American Medical Association, 295*, 2341–2344.

Lambert, E. W., Wahler, R. G., Andrade, A. R., & Bickman, L. (2001). Looking for the disorder in conduct disorder. *Journal of Abnormal Psychology, 110*, 110–123.

Lambert, G., Johansson, M., Agren, H., & Friberg, P. (2000). Reduced brain norepinephrine and dopamine release in treatment-refractory depressive illness: Evidence in support of the catecholamine hypothesis of mood disorders. *Archives of General Psychiatry, 57*, 787–793.

Lambert, G., Reid, C., Kaye, D., Jennings, G., & Esler, M. (2003). Increased suicide rate in the middle-aged and its association with hours of sunlight. *American Journal of Psychiatry, 160*, 793–795.

Lambert, M. C., Weisz, J. R, Knight, F., Desrosiers, M. F., Overly, K., & Thesiger, C. (1992). Jamaican and American adult perspectives on child psychopathology: Further exploration of the threshold model. *Journal of Consulting and Clinical Psychology, 60*, 146–149.

Lambert, N. M., Hartsough, C. S., Sassone, D., & Sandoval, J. (1987). Persistence of hyperactivity symptoms from childhood to adolescence and associated outcomes. *American Journal of Orthopsychiatry, 57*, 22–32.

Landerman, L. R., Burns, B. J., Swartz, M. S., Wagner, H. R., & George, K. K. (1994). The relationship between insurance coverage and psychiatric disorder in predicting use of mental health services. *American Journal of Psychiatry, 151*, 1785–1790.

Landolt, H. P., Roth, C., Dijk, D. J., & Borbely, A. A. (1996). Late-afternoon ethanol intake affects nocturnal sleep and the sleep EEG in middle-aged men. *Journal of Clinical Psychopharmacolog y, 16*, 428–436.

Lane, E. (1994, December 6). Losing weight isn't enough. *New York Newsday*, p. A6.

Langbehn, D. R., & Cadoret, R. J. (2001). The adult antisocial syndrome with and without antecedent conduct disorder: Comparisons from an adoption study. *Comprehensive Psychiatry, 42* (4), 272–282.

Lange, A., Rietdijk, D., Hudcovicova, M., van de Ven, J.-P., Schrieken, B., &. Emmelkamp, P. M. G. (2003). Interapy: A controlled randomized trial of the standardized treatment of posttraumatic stress through the Internet. *Journal of Consulting and Clinical Psychology, 71*, 901–909.

Langenbucher, J. W., & Chung, T. (1995). Onset and staging of *DSM-IV* alcohol dependence using mean age and survival-hazard methods. *Journal of Abnormal Psychology, 104*, 346–354.

Langenbucher, J. W., Martin, C. S., Labouvie, E., Sanjuan, P. M., Bavly, L., & Pollock, N. K. (2000). Toward the DSM-V: The withdrawal-gate model versus the *DSM-IV* in the diagnosis of alcohol abuse and dependence. *Journal of Consulting and Clinical Psychology, 68*, 799–809.

Langle, G., Renner, G., Gunthner, A., Stuhlinger, M., Eschweiler, G., U'Ren, R., et al. (2003). Psychiatric commitment: patients' perspectives. *Med Law, 22*, 39–53.

Langlois, S., & Morrison, P. (2002) Suicide deaths and suicide at tempts. *Health Reports, 13*(2), 9–22.

Langly, K., Marshall, L., van den Bree, M., Thomas, H., Owen, M., O'Donovan, M., et al. (2004). Association of the Dopamine D4 Receptor Gene 7-repeat allele with neuropsychological test performance of children with ADHD. *American Journal of Psychiatry, 161*, 133–138.

Långström, N., & Zucker, K. J. (2005). Transvestic fetishism in the general population: Prevalence and correlates. *Journal of Sex & Marital Therapy, 31*, 87–95.

Lara, M. E., Leader, J., & Klein, D. N. (1997). The association between social support and course of depression: Is it confounded with personality? *Journal of Abnormal Psychology, 106*, 478–482.

Largo-Marsh, L., & Spates, C. R. (2002). The effects of writing therapy in comparison to EMDR on traumatic stress: The relationship between hypnotizability and client expectancy to outcome. *Professional Psychology: Research and Practice, 33*, 581–586.

Larson, E. B., Wang, M.S., Bowen, J. D., McCormick, W. C., Teri, L., Crane, P., et al. (2006). Exercise is associated with reduced risk for incident dementia among persons 65 years of age and older. *Annals of Internal Medicine, 144*, 73–81.

Larsson, H., Andershed, H., & Lichtenstein, P. A. (2006). A genetic factor explains most of the variation in the psychopathic personality. *Journal of Abnormal Psychology, 115*, 221–230.

Lauerman, C. (2000, November 7). *Psychological counseling is now just a computer click away.* Retrieved November 21, 2000, from http://www.psycport.com/news/2000/11/07/Knigt/3822-0076-MEDE-.

Laumann, E. O., Gagnon, J. H., Michael, R. T., & Michaels, S. (1994). *The social organization of sexuality: Sexual practices in the United States.* Chicago: University of Chicago Press.

Laumann, E. O., Paik, A., & Rosen, R. C. (1999). Sexual dysfunction in the United States: Prevalence and predictors. *Journal of the American Medical Association, 281*, 537–544.

Launer, L. J. (2003). Nonsteroidal anti-inflammatory drugs and Alzheimer disease: What's next? *Journal of the American Medical Association, 289*, 2865.

Lawrence, A. A. (2005). Sexuality before and after male-to-female sex reassignment surgery. *Archives of Sexual Behavior, 34*(2), 147–166.

Lawrence, J., Mayers, D. L., Hullsiek, K. H., Collins, G., Abrams, D. I., Reisler, R. B., et al. (2003). Structured treatment interruption in patients with multidrug-resistant human immunodeficiency virus. *New England Journal of Medicine, 349*, 837–846.

Laws, D. R., & Marshall, W. L. (2003). A brief history of behavioral and cognitive behavioral approaches to sexual offenders: Part 1. Early developments. *Sexual Abuse: Journal of Research & Treatment, 15* (2), 75–92.

Lawson, W. B. (1986). Racial and ethnic factors in psychiatric research. *Hospital and Community Psychiatry, 37*, 50–54.

Lawson, W. B. (1996). Clinical issues in the pharmacotherapy of African-Americans. *Psychopharmacology Bulletin, 32*, 275–281.

Lawson, W. B., Helper, N., Holladay, J., & Cuffel, B. (1994). Race as a factor in inpatient and outpatient admissions and diagnosis. *Hospital and Community Psychiatry, 45*, 72–74.

Lazarus, A. A. (1992). Multimodal therapy: Technical eclecticism with minimal integration. In J. C. Norcross & M. R. Goldfried (Eds.), *Handbook of psychotherapy integration* (pp. 231–263). New York: Basic Books.

Lazarus, R. S., & Folkman, S. (1984). *Stress, appraisal, and coping.* New York: Springer.

Leary, W. E. (1996, December 18). Responses of alcoholics to therapies seem similar. *The New York Times*, p. A17.

Leber, P. (2000). Placebo controls: No news is good news. *Archives of General Psychiatry, 57*, 319–320.

Lechner, S. C., Antonia, M. H., Lydstona, D., LaPerrierea, A., Ishiia, M., Devieuxa, J., et al. (2003). Cognitive– behavioral interventions improve quality of life in women with AIDS. *Journal of Psychosomatic Research, 54*, 253–261.

Leckman, J. F., & Kim, Y. S. (2006). A primary candidate gene for obsessive-compulsive disorder. *Archives of General Psychiatry, 63*, 717–720.

Lecrubier, Y., Clerc, G., Didi, R., & Kieser, M. (2002). Efficacy of St. John's Wort extract vs 5570 in major depression: A double-blind, placebo-controlled trial. *American Journal of Psychiatry, 159*, 1361–1366.

Lee, C. C., & Richardson, B. L. (1991). *Multicultural issues in counseling: New approaches to diversity.* Alexandria, VA: AACD.

Lee, D. T. S., et al. (2001). A psychiatric epidemiological study of postpartum Chinese women. *American Journal of Psychiatry, 158*, 220–226.

Lee, J. K P., Jackson, H. J., Pattison, P., & Ward, T. (2002). Developmental risk factors for sexual offending. *Child Abuse & Neglect, 26*, 73–92.

Lee, J., & Park, S. (2005). Working memory impairments in schizophrenia: a meta-analysis. *Journal of Abnormal Psychology, 114*, 599–611.

Lee, T. M. C., et al. (1998). Seasonal affective disorder. *Clinical Psychology: Science and Practice, 5*, 275–290.

Leekam, S. R., & López, B. (2000). Attention and joint attention in preschool children with autism. *Developmental Psychology, 36*, 261–273.

Lefley, H. P. (1990). Culture and chronic mental illness. *Hospital and Community Psychiatry, 41*, 277–286.

Lehmann, C. (2002, June). Computer program helps identify violent patients. *Psychiatric News, 87(12)*, p. 4.

Lehrer, M., et al. (1994). Relaxation and music therapies for asthma among patients prestabilized on asthma medication. *Journal of Behavioral Medicine, 17*, 1–24.

Lehrer, P. M., Feldman, J., Giardino, N., Song, H.-S., & Schmaling, K. (2002). Psychological aspects of asthma. *Journal of Consulting and Clinical Psychology, 70*, 691–711.

Lehrer, P. M., Sargunaraj, D., & Hochron, S. (1992). Psychological approaches to the treatment of asthma. *Journal of Consulting and Clinical Psychology, 60*, 639–643.

Leibenluft, E. (1996). Women with bipolar illness: Clinical and research issues. *American Journal of Psychiatry, 153*, 163–173.

Leiblum, S. R., & Rosen, R. C. (Ed.). (2000). *Principles and practice of sex therapy* (3rd ed.). New York: Guilford Press.

Leiblum, S. R., Koochaki, P. E., Rodenberg, C. A., Barton, I. P., & Rosen, R. C. (2006). Hypoactive sexual desire disorder in postmenopausal women: US results from the Women's International Study of Health and Sexuality (WISHeS). *Menopause, 13*, 46–56.

Leibson, C. L., et al. (2001). Use and costs of medical care for children and adolescents with and without attention- deficit/hyperactivity disorder. *Journal of the American Medical Association, 285*, 60–66.

Leichsenring, F. (2001). Comparative effects of short-term psychodynamic psychotherapy and cognitive–behavioral therapy in depression: A meta-analytic approach. *Clinical Psychology Review, 21*, 401–419.

Leichsenring, F., & Leibing, E. (2003). The effectiveness of psychodynamic therapy and cognitive behavior therapy in the treatment of personality disorders: A meta-analysis. *American Journal of Psychiatry, 160*, 1223–1232.

Lemonde, S., Turecki, G., Bakish, D., Du, L., Hrdina, P. D., Bown, C. D., Sequeira, A., et al. (2003). Impaired repression at a 5-hydroxytryptamine 1A receptor gene polymorphism associated with major depression and suicide. *Journal of Neuroscience, 23*, 8788–8799.

Lemonick, M. D. (2003a, January 20). Your mind your body. *Time*, p. 35

Lemonick, M. D. (2003b, January 20). The power of mood. *Time*, pp. 36–41

Lemonick, M. D., & Park, A. (2001, May 14). Alzheimer's: The nun study. *Time*, pp . 54–64.

Leocani, L., et al. (2001). Abnormal pattern of cortical activation associated with voluntary movement in obsessive-compulsive disorder: An EEG study. *American Journal of Psychiatry, 158*, 140–142.

Leon, A. C. (2000). Placebo protects subjects from nonresponse: A paradox of power. *Archives of General Psychiatry, 57*, 329–330.

Leon, A. C., Solomon, D. A., Mueller, T. L., Endicott, J., Rice, J. P., Maser, J. D., et al. (2003). A 20-year longitudinal observational study of somatic antidepressant treatment effectiveness. *American Journal of Psychiatry, 160*, 727–733.

Leonard, S., Gault, J., Hopkins, J., Logel, J., Vianzon, R., Short, M., Drebing, C., et al. (2002). Association of promoter variants in the 7 nicotinic acetylcholine receptor subun it gene with an inhibitory deficit found in schizophrenia. *Archives of General Psychiatry, 59*, 1085–1096.

Lépine, J.-P., Caillard, V., Bisserbe, J.-C., Troy, S., Hotton, J.-M., & Boyer, P. (2004). A randomized, placebo-controlled trial of sertraline for prophylactic treatment of highly recurrent major depressive disorder. *American Journal of Psychiatry, 161*, 836–842.

Lesage, S., Durr, A., Tazir, M., Lohmann, E., Leutenegger, A.-L., Janin, S., Pollak, P., Brice, A., the French Parkinson's Disease Genetics Study Group, (2006). LRRK2 G2019S as a cause of Parkinson's disease in North African Arabs. *New England Journal of Medicine, 354*, 422–423.

Lesch, K. P., et al. (1996). Association of anxiety-related traits with a polymorphism in the serotonin transporter gene regulatory region. *Science, 274*, 1527–1531.

Leserman, J., Petitto, J. M., Golden, R. N., Gaynes, B. N., Gu, H., Perkins, D. O., et al. (2000). Impact of stressful life events, depression, social support, coping, and cortisol on progression to AIDS. *American Journal of Psychiatry, 157*, 1221–1228.

Lesné, S., Koh, M. T., Kotilinek, L., Kayed, R., Glabe, C. G. Yang, A., et al. (2006). A specific amyloid-bold beta protein assembly in the brain impairs memory. *Nature 440*, 352–357.

Lespérance F. Frasure-Smith, N., Koszycki, D., Laliberte, M. A., van Zyl, L. T., Baker, B., Swenson, J. R., et al. (2007). Effects of citalopram and interpersonal psychotherapy on depression in patients with coronary artery disease: The Canadian Cardiac Randomized Evaluation of Antidepressant and Psychotherapy Efficacy (CREATE) trial. *Journal of the American Medical Association, 297*, 367–379.

Lesser, I. (1992, December). *Ethnic differences in response to psychotropic drugs.* Paper presented at a symposium, Anxiety Disorders in African Americans, presented by the State University of New York Health Science Center at Brooklyn, Brooklyn, NY.

Leucht, S., Barnes, T. R., Kissling, W., Engel, R. R., Correll, C., & Kane, J. M. (2003). Relapse prevention in schizophrenia with new-generation antipsychotics: A systematic review and exploratory meta-analysis of randomized, controlled trials. *American Journal of Psychiatry, 160*, 1209–1222.

Leung, P. W. L., & Poon, M. W. L. (2001). Dysfunctional schemas and cognitive distortions in psychopathology: A test of the specificity hypothesis.

Journal of Child Psychology & Psychiatry & Allied Disciplines, 42 (6), 755–765.

Levenson, J. L., & Bemis, C (1991). The role of psychological factors in cancer onset and progression. *Psychosomatics, 32*, 124–132.

Levenstein, S., Ackerman, S., Kiecolt-Glaser, J. K., & Dubois, A. (1999). Stress and peptic ulcer disease. *Journal of the American Medical Association, 281*, 10–11.

Levine, A. (2000, December 22). Tomorrow's education, made to measure. *The New York Times*, p. A33.

Levine, E. S., & Schmelkin, L. P. (2006). The move to prescribe: A change in paradigm? *Professional Psychology: Research and Practice, 37*, 205–209.

Levitan, R. D., Kaplan, A. S., Joffe, R. T., Levitt, A. J., & Brown, G. M. (1997). Hormonal and subjective responses to intravenous metachlorophenylpiperazine in bulimia nervosa. *Archives of General Psychiatry, 54*, 521–527.

Levitan, R. D., Rector, N. A., & Bagby, R. M. (1998). Negative attributional style in season al and nonseasonal depression. *American Journal of Psychiatry, 155*, 428–430.

Lewin, T. (2001, April 15). Ask not for whom the clock ticks. *The New York Times Week in Review*, p. 4.

Lewinsohn, P. M. (1974). A behavioral approach to depression. In R. J. Friedman & M. M. Katz (Eds.), *The psychology of depression: Contemporary theory and research.* Washington, DC: Winston-Wiley.

Lewinsohn, P. M., & Clarke, G. N. (1999). Psychosocial treatments for adolescent depression. *Clinical Psychology Review, 19*, 329–342.

Lewinsohn, P. M., & Libet, J. M. (1972). Pleasant events, activity schedules and depression. *Journal of Abnormal Psychology, 79*, 291–295.

Lewinsohn, P. M., Clarke, G. N., Rhode, P., Hops, H., & Seely, J. (1996). A course in coping: A cognitive–behavioral approach to the treatment of adolescent depression. In D. Hibbs & P. S. Jensen (Eds.), *Psychosocial treatments for child and adolescent disorders: Empirically based strategies for clinical practice* (pp. 109–135). Washington, DC: American Psychological Association.

Lewinsohn, P. M., Duncan, E. M., Stanton, A. K., & Hautzinger, M. (1986). Age at first onset for nonpolar depression. *Journal of Abnormal Psychology, 95*, 378–383.

Lewinsohn, P. M., et al. (1994). Adolescent psychopathology: II. Psychosocial risk factors for depression. *Journal of Abnormal Psychology, 103*, 302–315.

Lewinsohn, P. M., Joiner, T. E., & Rohde, P. (2001). Evaluation of cognitive diathesis–stress models in predicting major depressive disorder in adolescents. *Journal of Abnormal Psychology, 110*, 203–215.

Lewinsohn, P. M., Rohde, P., & Seeley, J. R. (1994). Psychosocial risk factors for future adolescent suicide attempts. *Journal of Consulting and Clinical Psychology, 62*, 297–305.

Lewinsohn, P. M., Rohde, P., & Seeley, J. R. (1996). Adolescent suicidal ideation and attempts: Prevalence, risk factors, and clinical implications. *Clinical Psychology: Science and Practice, 3*, 25–46.

Lewinsohn, P. M., Rohde, P., Seeley, J. R., & Baldwin, C. L. (2001). Gender differences in suicide attempts from adolescence to young adulthood. *Journal of American Academy of Child & Adolescent Psychiatry, 40*, 427–434.

Lewis, D. O., et al. (1997). Objective documentation of child abuse and dissociation in 12 murderers with dissociative identity disorder. *American Journal of Psychiatry, 154*, 1703–1710.

Lewis, S. W., Barnes, T. R., Davies, L., Murray, R. M., Dunn, G., Hayhurst, K. P., et al. (2006). Randomized controlled trial of effect of prescription of clozapine vs other second-generation antipsychotic drugs in resistant schizophrenia. *Schizophrenia Bulletin, 32*, 715–723.

Lewis-Hall, F. (1992, December). *Overview of DSM-III-R: Focus on panic disorder and obsessive-compulsive disorder.* Paper presented at a symposium, Anxiety Disorders in African Americans, presented by the State University of New York Health Science Center at Brooklyn, Brooklyn, NY.

Lewy, A. J., Lefler, B. J., Emens, J. S., & Bauer, V. K. (2006). The circadian basis of winter depression. *Proceedings of the National Academy of Sciences, 103*, 7414–7419.

Lex, B. W. (1987). Review of alcohol problems in ethnic minority groups. *Journal of Consulting and Clinical Psychology, 55*, 293–300.

Ley, R. (1997). The Ondine curse, false suffocation alarms, trait-state suffocation fear, and dyspnea-suffocation fear in panic attacks. *Archives of General Psychiatry, 54*, 677.

Leyton, M., Boileau, I., Benkelfat, C., Diksic, M., Baker, G., & Dagher, A. (2002). Amphetamine-induced increases in extracellular dopamine, drug wanting, and novelty seeking: A PET/[11C]raclopride study in healthy men. *Neuropsychopharmacology, 27*, 1027–1035.

Li, G., Baker, S. P., Smialek, J. E., & Soderstrom, C. A. (2001). Use of alcohol as a ri sk factor for bicycling injury. *Journal of the American Medical Association, 284*, 893–896.

Li, Y. M., Xu, M., Lai, M. T., Huang, Q., Castro, J. L., DiMuzio-Mower, J., et al. (2000). Photoactivated-secretase inhibitors directed to the active site covalently label presenilin, 1. *Nature, 405*, 689–693.

Liberman, R. P. (1994). Treatment and rehabilitation of the seriously mentally ill in China: Impressions of a society in transition. *American Journal of Orthopsychiatry, 64*, 68–77.

Lichstein, K. L., Durrence, H. H., Bayen, U. J., & Riedel, B. W. (2001). Primary versus secondary insomnia in older adults: Subjective sleep and daytime functioning. *Psychology and Aging, 16*, 264–271.

Lichstein, K. L., Wilson, N. M., & Johnson, C. T. (2000). Psychological treatment of secondary insomnia. *Psychology and Aging, 15*, 232–240.

Lichtenberg, P. A., & Duffy, M. (2000). Psychological assessment and psychotherapy in long-term care. *Clinical Psychology: Science and Practice*, 317–328.

Lieber, C. S. (1990, January 14). Cited in "Barroom biology: How alcohol goes to a woman's head." *The New York Times*, p. E24.

Lieberman, J. A. (2006). Comparative effectiveness of antipsychotic drugs: A Commentary on: Cost Utility of the Latest Antipsychotic Drugs in Schizophrenia Study (CUtLASS 1) and Clinical Antipsychotic Trials of Intervention Effectiveness (CATIE). *Archives of General Psychiatry, 63*, 1069–1072.

Lieberman, J. A., Stroup, T. S., McEvoy, J. P., Swartz, M. S., Rosenheck, R. A., Perkins, D. O., et al. (2005). Effectiveness of antipsychotic drugs in patients with chronic schizophrenia. *New England Journal of Medicine, 353*, 1209–1233.

Liebowitz, M. R., Gelenberg, A. J., & Munjack, D. (2005). Venlafaxine extended release vs placebo and paroxetine in social anxiety disorder. *Archives of General Psychiatry, 62*, 190–198.

Liebowitz, M. R., Heimberg, R. G., Fresco, D. M., Travers, J., & Stein, M. B. (2000). Social phobia or social anxiety disorder: What's in a name? *Archives of General Psychiatry, 57*, 191–192.

Liebowitz, M. R., Stein, M. B., Tancer, M., Carpenter, D., Oakes, R., & Pitts, C. D. (2002). A randomized, double-blind, fixed-dose comparison of paroxetine and placebo in treatment of generalized social anxiety disorder. *Journal of Clinical Psychiatry, 63*, 66–74.

Lifetime risk and persistence of psychiatric disorders across ethnic groups in the United States. *Psychological Medicine, 35*, 317–327.

Lightsey, O. W., Jr. (1994a). Positive automatic cognitions as moderators of the negative life event-dysphoria relationship. *Cognitive Therapy and Research, 18*, 353–365.

Lightsey, O. W., Jr. (1994b). "Thinking positive" as a stress buffer: The role of positive automatic cognitions in depression and happiness. *Journal of Counseling Psychology, 41*, 325–334.

Lilenfeld, L. R. R., Wonderlich, S., Riso, L. P., Crosby, R., & Mitchell, J. (2006). Eating disorders and personality: A methodological and empirical review. *Clinical Psychology Review, 26*, 299–320.

Lilienfeld, S. O. (1997). The relation of anxiety sensitivity to higher and lower order personality dimensions: Implications for the etiology of panic attacks. *Journal of Abnormal Psychology, 106*, 539–544.

Lilienfeld, S. O. (2007). Psychological treatments that cause harm. *Perspectives on Psychological Science, 2*, 53–70.

Lilienfeld, S. O., & Andrews, B. P. (1996). Identifying noncriminal psychopaths. *Journal of Personality Assessment, 66*, 488–524.

Lilienfeld, S. O., & Marino, L. (1995). Mental disorder as a Roschian concept: A critique of Wakefield's "harmful dysfunction" analysis. *Journal of Abnormal Psychology, 104*, 411–420.

Lilienfeld, S. O., Fowler, K. A, & Lohr, J. M. (2003). And the band played on: Science, pseudoscience, and the Rorschach Inkblot Method. *The Clinical Psychologist, 56*(1), 6–7.

Lilienfeld, S. O., Lynn, S. J., & Lohr, J. M. (Ed.). (2003). *Science and pseudoscience in clinical psychology.* New York: Guilford.

Lilienfeld, S. O., Wood, J. M., & Garb, H. N. (2000). The scientific status of projective techniques. *Psychological Science in the Public Interest, 1*, 27–66.

Lim, S. (2003, September 2). Beating the bed-wetting blues. *MSNBC Online.* Retrieved September 3, 2003, from http://www.msnbc.com/news/954846.asp.

Lin, K., et al. (1991). Ethnicity and family involvement in the treatment of schizophrenic patients. *Journal of Nervous & Mental Disease, 179*, 631–633.

Lin, T. Y., et al. (1978). Ethnicity and patterns of help-seeking. *Culture, Medicine, and Psychiatry, 2*, 3–14.

Linde, K., Streng, A., Jurgens, S., Hoppe, A., Brinkhaus, B., Witt, C., Wagenpfeil S., et al. (2005). Acupuncture for patients with migraine: A randomized controlled trial. *Journal of the American Medical Association, 293*, 2118–2125.

Linder, D. (2004). *The John Hinckley Trial (Hinkley's Communications with Jodie Foster).* Retrieved April 24, 2004, from http://www.law.umkc.edu/faculty/projects/ftrials/hinckley/hinckleytrial.html.

Lindsey, K. P., & Paul, G. L. (1989). Involuntary commitments to public mental institutions: Issues involving the overrepresentation of blacks and assessment of relevant functioning. *Psychological Bulletin, 106*, 171–183.

Linehan, M. M. (1993). *Cognitive-behavioral treatment of borderline personality disorder.* New York: Guilford Press.

Linehan, M. M., Camper, P., Chiles, J. A., Strosahl, K., & Shearin, E. (1987). Interpersonal problem solving and parasuicide. *Cognitive Therapy and Research, 11*, 1–12.

Linehan, M. M., Comtois, K. A., Murray, A. M., Brown, M. Z., Gallop, R. J., Heard, H. L., et al. (2006). Two-year randomized controlled trial and follow-up of dialectical behavior therapy vs. therapy by experts for suicidal behaviors and borderline personality disorder. *Archives of General Psychiatry, 63,* 757–766.

Liotti, G., et al. (2000). Predictive factors for borderline personality disorder. *Acta Psychiatrica Scandinavica, 102,* 282–289.

Lipsey, M. W., & Wilson, D. B. (1993). The efficacy of psychology, educational, and behavioral treatment: Confirmation from meta-analysis. *American Psychologist, 48,* 1181–1209.

Lipsey, M. W., & Wilson, D. B. (1995). Reply to comments on Lispey and Wilson (1993). *American Psychologist, 50,* 113–115.

Lipton, R. B., et al. (1998). Efficacy and safety of acetaminophen, aspirin, and caffeine in alleviating migraine headache pain. *Archives of Neurology, 55,* 210–217.

Lipton, R. B., Stewart, W. F., Stone, A. M., Láinez, M. J., & Sawyer, J. P. (2000). Stratified care vs step care strategies for migraine: The disability in strategies of Care (DISC) Study: A randomized trial. *Journal of the American Medical Association, 284,* 2599–2605.

Little, S. J., Holte, S., Routy, J. P., Daar, E. S., Markowitz, M., Collier, A. C., et al. (2002). Antiretroviral-drug resistance among patients recently infected with HIV. *New England Journal of Medicine, 347,* 385–394.

Litz, B. T., Gray, M. J., Bryant, R. A., & Adler, A. B. (2002). Early intervention for trauma: Current status and future directions. *Clinical Psychology: Science and Practice, 9,* 112–134.

Litz, B. T., Williams, L., Wang, J., Bryant, R., & Engel, C. A. (2005). Therapist-assisted Internet self-help program for traumatic stress. *Professional Psychology: Research & Practice, 35,* 628–634.

Liu, I.-C., Blacker, D. L., Xu, R., Fitzmaurice, G., Lyons, M. J., & Tsuang, M. T. (2004). Genetic and environmental contributions to the development of alcohol dependence in male twins. *Archives of General Psychiatry, 61,* 897–903.

Livesley, W. J., et al. (1993). Genetic and environmental contributions to dimensions of personality disorder. *American Journal of Psychiatry, 150,* 1826–1831.

Livesley, W. J., Schroeder, M. L., Jackson, D. N., & Jang, K. L. (1994). Categorical distinctions in the study of personality disorder: Implications for classification. *Journal of Abnormal Psychology, 103,* 6–17.

Lobel, M., DeVincent, C. J., Kaminer, A., & Meyer, B. A. (2000). The impact of prenatal maternal stress and optimistic disposition on birth outcomes in medically high-risk women. *Health Psychology, 19,* 544–553.

Lochman, J. E. (1992). Cognitive-behavioral intervention with aggressive boys: Three-year follow-up and preventive effects. *Journal of Consulting and Clinical Psychology, 60,* 426–432.

Lochman, J. E., & Dodge, K. A. (1994). Social-cognitive processes of severely violent, moderately aggressive, and nonaggressive boys. *Journal of Consulting and Clinical Psychology, 62,* 366–374.

Loeb, K. L., Wilson, G. T., Labouvie, E., Pratt, E. M., Hayaki, J., Walsh, B., et al. (2005). Therapeutic alliance and treatment adherence in two interventions for bulimia nervosa: A study of process and outcome. *Journal of Consulting and Clinical Psychology, 73,* 1097–1107.

Loeber, R., Burke, J. D., Lahey, B. B., Winters, A., & Zera, M. (2000). Oppositional defiant and conduct disorder: A review of the past 10 years. *Journal of the American Academy of Child and Adolescent Psychiatry, 39,* 1468–1484.

Loening-Baucke, V. (2002). Encopresis. *Current Opinions in Pediatrics, 14,* 570–575.

Loewenstein, R. J. (1991). Psychogenic amnesia and psychogenic fugue: A comprehensive review. *Annual Review of Psychiatry, 10,* 223–247.

Loftus, E. F. (1993). The reality of repressed memories. *American Psychologist, 48,* 518–537.

Loftus, E. F. (1996). The myth of repressed memory and the realities of science. *Clinical Psychology: Science and Practice, 3,* 356–365.

Loftus, E. F. (1997). Creating childhood memories. *Applied Cognitive Psychology, 11,* S75–S86.

Logan, T. K., Walker, R., Jordan, C. E., & Leukefeld, C. G. (2006). Justice system options and responses. In Logan, T. K., Walker, R., Jordan, C. E., & Leukefeld, C. G. (Eds.), *Women and victimization: Contributing factors, interventions, and implications* (pp. 161–194). Washington, DC: American Psychological Association.

Logsdon-Conradsen, S. (2002). Using mindfulness meditation to promote holistic health in individuals with HIV/AIDS. *Cognitive and Behavioral Practice, 9,* 67–71.

Lohman, J. J. H. M. (2001). Treatment strategies for migraine headache. *Journal of the American Medical Association, 285,* 1014.

Lohr, B. A., Adams, H. E., & Davis, J. M. (1997). Sexual arousal to erotic and aggressive stimuli in sexually coercive and noncoercive men. *Journal of Consulting and Clinical Psychology, 106,* 230–242.

Looper, K. J., & Kirmayer, L. J. (2002). Behavioral medicine approaches to somatoform disorders. *Journal of Consulting and Clinical Psychology, 70,* 810–827.

Lopes, C. L., Vergara, A., Agani, F., & Gotway, C. A. (2000). Mental health, social functioning, and attitudes of Kosovar Albanians following the war in Kosovo. *Journal of the American Medical Association, 284,* 569–577.

Lopez, S. R., Nelson, H. K., Polo, A. J., Jenkins, J. H., Karno, M., Vaughn, C., et al. (2004). Ethnicity, expressed emotion, attributions, and course of schizophrenia: Family warmth matters. *Journal of Abnormal Psychology, 113,* 428–439.

López, S. R. (2002). Teaching culturally informed psychological assessment: Conceptual issues and demonstrations. *Journal of Personality Assessment, 79,* 226–234.

López-Larson, M. P., DelBello, M. P., Zimmerman, M. E., Schwiers, M. L., & Strakowski, S. M. (2002). Regional prefrontal gray and white matter abnormalities in bipolar disorder. *Biological Psychiatry, 52,* 93–100.

López-Muñoza, F., Vieta, E., Rubio, G., García-Garcia, P., & Alamo, C. (2006). Bipolar disorder as an emerging pathology in the scientific literature: A bibliometric approach. *Journal of Affective Disorders, 92,* 161–170.

LoPiccolo, J., & Stock, W. E. (1986). Treatment of sexual dysfunction. *Journal of Consulting and Clinical Psychology, 54,* 158–167.

Loranger, A. W. (1996). Dependant personality disorder: Age, sex, and Axis I comorbidity. *Journal of Nervous and Mental Disease, 184,* 17–21.

Loranger, A. W., Sartorius, N., Andreoli, A., Berger, P., Buchheim, P., Channabasavanna, S. M., et al. (1994). The international personality disorder examination: The World Health Organization/Alcohol, Drug, Abuse and Mental Health Administration International Pilot Study of Personality Disorders. *Archives of General Psychiatry, 51,* 215–224.

Lorber, M. F. (2004). Psychophysiology of aggression, psychopathy, and conduct problems: A meta-analysis. *Psychological Bulletin, 130,* 531–552.

Loring, D. W., & Larrabee, G. J. (2006). Sensitivity of the Halstead and Wechsler Test Batteries to brain damage: Evidence from Reitan's original validation sample. *Clinical Neuropsychology, 20,* 221.

Lothane, Z. (2006). Freud's legacy—is it still with us? *Psychoanalytic Psychology, 23,* 285–301.

Lovaas, O. I. (1987). Behavioral treatment and normal educational and intellectual functioning in young autistic children. *Journal of Consulting and Clinical Psychology, 55,* 3–9.

Lovaas, O. I., Koegel, R. L., & Schreibman, L. (1979). Stimulus overselectivity in autism: A review of the research. *Psychological Bulletin, 86,* 1236–1254.

Low, C. A., Stanton, A. L., & Danoff-Burg, S. (2006). Expressive disclosure and benefit finding among breast cancer patients: Mechanisms for positive health effects. *Health Psychology, 25,* 181–189.

Lowe, M. R., Gleaves, D. H., Murphy-Eberenz, K. P. (1998). On the relation of dieting and bingeing in bulimia nervosa. *Journal of Abnormal Psychology, 107,* 263–271.

Lowenstein, L. F. (2002). Recent research into dealing with the problem of malingering. *Medico Legal Journal, 70,* 38–49.

Lubell, S. (2004, February 19). On the therapist's couch, a jolt of virtual reality. *The New York Times,* p. G5.

Luborsky, I., et al. (1996). Factors in outcomes of short-term dynamic psychotherapy for chronic vs. non-chronic major depression. *Journal of Psychotherapy: Practice and Research, 5,* 152–159.

Luborsky, L., et al. (1988). *Who will benefit from psychotherapy? Predicting therapeutic outcomes.* New York: Basic Books.

Luntz, B. K., & Widom, C. S. (1994). Antisocial personality disorder in abused and neglected children grown up. *American Journal of Psychiatry, 151,* 670–674.

Luoma, J. B., Martin, C. E., & Pearson, J. L. (2002). Contact with mental health and primary care providers before suicide: A review of the evidence. *American Journal of Psychiatry, 159,* 909–916.

Lupski, J. R. (2007). Structural variation in the human genome. *New England Journal of Medicine, 356,* 1169–1171.

Lutgendorf, S. K., Antoni, M. H., Ironson, G., Klimas, N., Kumar, M., Starr, K., et al. (1997). Cognitive-behavioral stress management decreases dysphoric mood and herpes simplex virus-type 2 antibody titer in symptomatic HIV-seropositive gay men. *Journal of Consulting and Clinical Psychology, 65,* 31–43.

Lyketsos C. G., Sheppard, J. M., Steele, C. D., Kopunek, S., Steinberg, M., Baker, A. S., et al. (2000). Randomized, placebo-controlled, double-blind clinical trial of sertraline in the treatment of depression complicating Alzheimer's disease: Initial results from the Depression in Alzheimer's Disease Study. *American Journal of Psychiatry, 157,* 1686–1689.

Lymburner, J. A., & Roech, R. (1999). The insanity defense: Five years of research (1993–1997). *International Journal of Law and Psychiatry, 22,* 213–240.

Lynch, F. L., Hornbrook, M., Clarke, G. N., Perrin, N., Polen, M. R., O'Connor, E., et al. (2005) Cost-effectiveness of an intervention to prevent depression in at-risk teens. *Archives of General Psychiatry, 62,* 1241–1248.

Lyubomirsky, S., Sheldon, K. M., & Schkade, D. (2005). Pursuing happiness: The architecture of sustainable change. *Review of General Psychology, 9,* 111–131.

M

Ma, S. H., & Teasdale, J. D. (2004). Mindfulness-based cognitive therapy for depression: Replication and exploration of differential relapse prevention effects. *Journal of Consulting and Clinical Psychology, 72,* 31–40.

Machan, D. (2000, December). Forget the champagne. *Forbes,* pp. 118–120.

Mackie, S., Shaw, P., Lenroot, R., Pierson, R., Greenstein, D. K., Nugent III, T. F., Sharp, W. S., et al. (2007). Cerebellar development and clinical outcome in attention deficit hyperactivity disorder. *American Journal of Psychiatry, 164,* 647–655.

MacPhillamy, D. J., & Lewinsohn, P. M. (1974). Depression as a function of levels of desired and obtained pleasure. *Journal of Abnormal Psychology, 83,* 651–657.

Maddi, S. R., & Kobasa, S. C. (1984). *The hardy executive: Health under stress.* Homewood, IL: Dow Jones-Irwin.

Madsen, K. M., Hviid, A., Vestergaard, M., Schendel, D., Wohlfahrt, J., Thorsen, P., et al. (2002). A population-based study of measles, mumps, and rubella vaccination and autism. *New England Journal of Medicine, 347,* 1477–1482.

Madsen, K. M., Lauritsen, M. B., Pedersen, C. B., Thorsen, P., Plesner, A-M., Andersen, P. H., & Mortensen, P. B. (2003). Thimerosal and the occurrence of autism: negative ecological evidence from Danish population-based data. *Pediatrics, 112,* 604–606.

Maeder, T. (1985). *Crime and madness: The origins and evolution of the insanity defense.* New York: Harper & Row.

Maher, W. B., & Maher, B. A. (1985). Psychopathology: I. From ancient times to the eighteenth century. In G. A. Kimble & K. Schlesinger (Eds), *Topics in the history of psychology* (Vol. 2, pp. 251–294). Hillsdale, NJ: Erlbaum.

Maheu, M. M., & Gordon, B. L. (2000). Counseling and therapy on the Internet. *Professional Psychology: Research and Practice, 31,* 484–489.

Mahler, M., & Kaplan, L. (1977). Developmental aspects in the assessment of narcissistic and so-called borderline personalities. In P. Hartocollis (Ed.), *Borderline personality disorders: The concept, the syndrome, the patient* (pp. 71–85). New York: International Universities Press.

Mahler, M. S., Pine, F., & Bergman, A. (1975). The borderline syndrome: The role of the mother in the genesis and psychic structure of the borderline personality. *International Journal of Psychoanalysis, 56,* 163–177.

Maier, S. F., & Seligman, M. E. P. (1976). Learned helplessness: Theory and evidence. *Journal of Experimental Psychology (General), 105,* 3–46.

Maier, S. F., Watkins, L. R., & Fleshner, M. (1994). Psychoneuroimmunology: The interface between behavior, brain, and immunity. *American Psychologist, 49,* 1004–1017.

Maj, M., Starace, F., & Pirozzi, R. (1991). A family study of *DSM-III-R* schizoaffective disorder, depressive type, compared with schizophrenia and psychotic and nonpsychotic major depression. *American Journal of Psychiatry, 148,* 612–616.

Malamuth, N. M., Huppin, M., & Paul, B. (2005). Sexual coercion. In Buss, D. M. (Ed.). *The handbook of evolutionary psychology* (pp. 394–418). Hoboken, NJ: Wiley.

Malaspina, D., Harlap, S., Fennig, S., H eiman, D., Nahon, D., Feldman, D., & Susser, E. S. (2001). Advancing paternal age and the risk of schizophrenia. *Archives of General Psychiatry, 58,* 361–367.

Maldonado, J. R., Butler, L. D., & Spiegel, D. (1998). Treatments for dissociative disorders. In P. E. Nathan & J. M. Gorman (Eds.), *A guide to treatments that work* (pp. 423–446). New York: Oxford University Press.

Male eating disorders on rise, experts say (2004, May 12). *CNN Web Posting.* Retrieved May 26, 2004, from http://www.cnn.com/2004/HEALTH/diet.fitness/05/12/male.eating.disorder.ap/index.html.

Maletzky, B. M. (1980). Self-referred vs. court-referred sexually deviant patients: Success with assisted covert sensitization. *Behavior Therapy, 11,* 306–314.

Maletzky, B. M., & Steinhauser, C. (2002). A 25-year follow-up of cognitive/behavioral therapy with 7,275 sexual offenders. *Behavior Modification, 26* (2), 123–147.

Malinauskas, B. M., Raedeke, T. D., Aeby, V. G., Smith, J. L., & Dallas, M. B. (2006). Dieting practices, weight perceptions, and body composition: A comparison of normal weight, overweight, and obese college females. *Nutrition Journal, 5,* 11.

Malone, K. M., Oquendo, M. A., Haas, G. L., Ellis, S. P., Li, S., & Mann, J. J. (2000). Protective factors against suicidal acts in major depression: Reasons for living. *American Journal of Psychiatry, 157,* 1084–1088.

Malone, K. M., Waternaux, C., Haas, G. L., Cooper, T. B., Li, S., & Mann, J. J. (2003). Cigarette smoking, suicidal behavior, and serotonin function in major psychiatric disorders. *American Journal of Psychiatry, 160,* 773–779.

Mann, J. J. (2005). The medical management of depression. *New England Journal of Medicine, 353,* 1819–1834.

Mann, J. J., Apter, A., Bertolote, J., Beautrais, A., Currier, D., Haas, A., et al. (2005). Suicide prevention strategies: A systematic review. *Jouyrnal of the American Medical Association, 294,* 2064–2074.

Mann, J. J., et al. (1996). Postmortem studies of suicide victims. In S. J. Watson (Ed.), *Biology of schizophrenia and affective disease* (pp. 179–221). Washington, DC: American Psychiatric Press.

Mansell, W., Colom, F., & Scott, J. (2005). The nature and treatment of depression in bipolar disorder: A review and implications for future psychological investigation. *Clinical Psychology Review, 25,* 1076–1100.

Manson, J. E., & Bassuk, S. S. (2003). Obesity in the United States: A fresh look at its high toll. *Journal of the American Medical Association, 289,* 229–230.

Manson, J. E., Skerrett, P. J., Greenland, P., & VanItallie, T. B. (2004). The escalating pandemics of obesity and sedentary lifestyle a call to action for clinicians. *Archives of Internal Medicine, 164,* 249–258.

Marcus, D. K., & Nardone, M. E. (1992). Depression and interpersonal rejection. *Clinical Psychology Review, 12,* 433–449.

Marijuana leads to hard drugs. (2002, January 21). *MSNBC Web Posting.* Retrieved January 22; 2002, from http://www.msnbc.com/news/862289.asp.

Marion, I. J. (2005, December). The neurobiology of cocaine addiction. *Science Practice Perspectives, National Institute on Drug Abuse, 3*(1), 25–31.

Maris, R. W. (2002). Suicide. *Lancet, 360,* 1892.

Mark, D. H. (1998). Editor's Note. *Journal of the American Medical Association, 279,* 151.

Markel, H. (2002, October 27). For addicts, relief may be an office visit away. *The New York Times Week in Review,* p. 14.

Markovitz, J. H., et al. (1993). Psychological predictors of hypertension in the Framingham Study: Is there tension in hypertension? *Journal of the American Medical Association, 270,* 2439–2443.

Marks, M., & De Silva, P. (1994). The "match/mismatch" mode of fear: Empirical status and clinical implications. *Behaviour Research and Therapy, 32,* 759–770.

Marlatt, G. A. (1978). Craving for alcohol, loss of control, and relapse: A cognitive-behavioral analysis. In P. E. Nathan, G. A. Marlatt, & T. Loberg (Eds.), *Alcoholism: New directions in behavioral research and treatment* (pp. 271–314). New York: Plenum Press.

Marlatt, G. A. (1983). The controlled drinking controversy: A commentary. *American Psychologist,* 38, 1097–1110.

Marlatt, G. A., & Gordon, J. R. (1985). *Relapse prevention: Maintenance strategies in the treatment of addictive behaviors.* New York: Guilford Press.

Marlatt, G. A., Baer, J. S., Kivlahan, D. R., Dimeff, L. A., Larimer, M. E., Quigley, L. A., et al. (1998). Screening and brief intervention for high-risk college student drinkers: Results from a 2-year follow-up assessment. *Journal of Consulting and Clinical Psychology, 66,* 604–615.

Marlatt, G. A., Demming, B., & Reid, J. B. (1973). Loss of control drinking in alcoholics: An experimental analogue. *Journal of Abnormal Psychology, 81,* 233–241.

Marlatt, G. A., Somers, J. M., & Tapert, S. F. (1993). Harm reduction: Application to alcohol abuse problems. *NIDA Research Monographs, 137,* 147–166.

Marneros, A. (2003). The schizoaffective phenomenon: The state of the art. *Acta Psychiatrica Scandinavica,* Suppl, 418, 29–33.

Marsh, D. T., & Johnson, D. L. (1997). The family experience of mental illness: Implications for intervention. *Professional Psychology: Research & Practice, 28,* 229–237.

Marshal, M. P. (2003). For better or for worse? The effects of alcohol use on marital functioning. *Clinical Psychology Review, 23,* 959–997.

Mart, E. G. (2003). Munchausen's syndrome by proxy reconsidered. *Child Maltreatment: Journal of the American Professional Society of the Abuse of Children, 8,* 72–73.

Martin, D. (1989, January 25). Autism: Illness that can steal a child's sparkle. *The New York Times,* p. B1.

Martin, D. J., Garske, J. P., & Davis, M. K. (2000). Relation of the therapeutic alliance with outcome and other variables: A meta-analytic review. *Journal of Consulting and Clinical Psychology, 68,* 438–450.

Martin, E. K., Taft, C. T., & Resick, P. A. (2007). A review of marital rape. *Aggression and Violent Behavior,* in press.

Martin, J., Shochat, T., & Ancoli-Israel, S. (2000). Assessment and treatment of sleep disturbances in older adults. *Clinical Psychology Review, 20,* 783–805.

Martin, J. L., Barbanoj, M. J., Schlaepfer, T. E., Thompson, E., Perez, V., & Kulisevsky, J. (2003). Repetitive transcranial magnetic stimulation for the treatment of depression. Systematic review and meta-analysis. *British Journal of Psychiatry, 182,* 480–491.

Martin, J. P. (1998, February 27). The insanity defense: A closer look. *The Washington Post.* Retrieved November 16, 2006, from http://www.washingtonpost.com/wp-srv/local/longterm/aron/qa227.htm.

Martin, P. R., & Seneviratne, H. M. (1997). Effects of food deprivation and a stressor on head pain. *Health Psychology, 16,* 310–318.

Marx, E. M., Williams, J. M. G., & Claridge, G. C. (1992). Depression and social problem solving. *Journal of Abnormal Psychology, 101,* 78–86.

Masi, G., et al. (2006). The clinical phenotypes of juvenile bipolar disorder: Toward a validation of the episodic-chronic-distinction. *Biological Psychiatry, 59,* 603–610.

Masi, G., Mucci, M., & Millepiedi, S. (2001). Separation anxiety disorder in children and adolescents: Epidemiology, diagnosis, and management. *CNS Drugs, 15* (2), 93–104.

Mason, M. (1994, September). Why ulcers run in families. *Health,* pp. 44, 48.

Masters, W. H., & Johnson, V. E. (1970). *Human sexual inadequacy.* Boston: Little, Brown.

Mataix-Cols, D., Wooderson, S., Lawrence, N., Brammer, M. J., Speckens, A., & Phillips, M. L. (2004). Distinct neural correlates of washing, checking, and hoarding symptom dimensions in obsessive-compulsive disorder. *American Journal of Psychiatry, 61,* 564–576.

Mathalno, D. H., et al. (2001). Progressive brain volume changes and the clinical course of schizophrenia in men: A longitudinal magnetic resonance imaging study. *Archives of General Psychiatry, 58,* 148–157.

Mathews, K. A. (2005). Psychological perspective on the development of coronary heart disease. *American Psychologist, 60,* 783–706.

Mathews, M., Mathews, M., & Mathews, J. (2004). Efficacy of sertraline in the treatment of children and adolescents with major depressive disorder. *Journal of the American Medical Association, 291,* 40.

Mathias, R. (2000). Cocaine, marijuana, and heroin abuse up, methamphetamine abuse down. *NIDA Notes, 15* (3), 4–5.

Matson, J. L. (2006). Current status of differential diagnosis for children with autism spectrum disorders. *Research in Developmental Disabilities, 27,* in press.

Mattson, M. P. (2003). Neurobiology: Ballads of a protein quartet. *Nature, 422,* 385–387.

Maxwell, C. D., Robinson, A. L., & Post, L. A. (2003). The nature and predictors of sexual victimization and offending among adolescents. *Journal of Youth & Adolescence, 32* (6) 465–477.

May, R. (2005). How do we know what works? *Journal of College Student Psychotherapy, 19,* 69–73.

Mayo-Smith, M. F. (1997). Pharmacological management of alcohol withdrawal. A meta-analysis and evidence-based practice guideline. American Society of Addiction Medicine Working Group on Pharmacological Management of Alcohol Withdrawal. *Journal of the American Medical Association, 278,* 144–151.

Mayou, R., Kirmayer, L. J., Simon, G., Kroenke, K., & Sharpe, M. (2005). Somatoform disorders: Time for a new approach in *DSM-V. American Journal of Psychiatry, 162,* 847–855.

Mays, V. M. (1985). The Black American and psychotherapy: The dilemma. *Psychotherapy, 22,* 379–388.

Mazure, C. M. (1998). Life stressors as risk factors in depression. *Clinical Psychology: Science and Practice, 5,* 291–313.

McCabe, M. P. (2005). The role of performance anxiety in the development and maintenance of sexual dysfunction in men and women. *International Journal of Stress Management, 12,* 379–388.

McCarthy, B. W., Ginsberg, R. L., & Fucito, L. M. (2006). Resilient sexual desire in heterosexual couples. *Family Journal: Counseling and Therapy for Couples and Families, 14,* 59–64.

McCarty, D., et al. (1991). Alcoholism, drug abuse, and the homeless. *American Psychologist, 46,* 1139–1148.

McCaul, M. E., & Furst, J. (1994). Alcoholism treatment in the United States. *Alcohol Health & Research World, 18,* 253–260.

McClure, E. B., Kubisyn, T., & Kaslow, N. J. (2002). Advances in the diagnosis and treatment of childhood mood disorders. *Professional Psychology: Research and Practice, 33,* 125–134.

McClure, M. M., Romero, M. J., Bowie, C. R., Reichenberg, A., Harvey, P. D., & Siever, L. J. (2007). Visual-spatial learning and memory in schizotypal personality disorder: Continued evidence for the importance of working memory in the schizophrenia. *Archives of Clinical Neuropsychology.*

McCord, W., & McCord, J. (1964). *The psychopath: An essay on the criminal mind.* New York: D. Van Nostrand.

McCracken, J. T., McGough, J., Shah, B., Cronin, P., Hong, D., Aman, M. G., et al. (2002). Risperidone in children with autism and serious behavioral problems. *New England Journal of Medicine, 347,* 314–321.

McCrady, B. S. (1993). Alcoholism. In D. H. Barlow (Ed.), *Clinical handbook of psychological disorders* (2nd ed., pp. 362–393). New York: Guilford Press.

McCrady, B. S. (1994). Alcoholics Anonymous and behavior therapy: Can habits be treated as diseases? Can diseases be treated as habits? *Journal of Consulting and Clinical Psychology, 62,* 1159–1166.

McCrady, B. S., & Langenbucher, J. W. (1996). Alcohol treatment and health care system reform. *Archives of General Psychiatry, 53,* 737–746.

McCrae R. R., Costa, P. T., Jr. Martin, T. A., Oryol, V. E., Rukavishnikov, A. A., Senin, I. G., et al. (2004). Consensual validation of personality traits across cultures. *Journal of Research in Personality, 38,* 17–20.

McCrea, M., Guskiewicz, K. M., Marshall, S. W., Barr, W., Randolph, C., Cantu, R. C., et al. (2003). Acute effects and recovery time following concussion in collegiate football players: The NCAA Concussion Study. *Journal of the American Medical Association, 290,* 2556–2563.

McCrone, P., Knapp, M., Proudfoot J., Ryden, C., Cavanagh, K., Shapiro, D. A., et al. (2004). Cost-effectiveness of computerised cognitive-behavioural therapy for anxiety and depression in primary care: Randomised controlled trial. *British Journal of Psychiatry, 185,* 55–62.

McDermott, J. F. (2001). Emily Dickinson revisited: A study of periodicity in her work. *American Journal of Psychiatry, 158,* 686–690.

McDermut, W., Miller, I. W., & Brown, R. A. (2001). The efficacy of group psychotherapy for depression: A meta-analysis and review of the empirical research. *Clinical Psychology: Science and Practice, 8,* 98–116.

McDonagh, A., Friedman, M., McHugo, G., Ford, J., Sengupta, A., Mueser, K., et al. (2005). Randomized trial of cognitive-behavioral therapy for chronic posttraumatic stress disorder in adult female survivors of childhood sexual abuse. *Journal of Consulting and Clinical Psychology, 73,* 515–524.

McDougle, C. J., Scahill, L., Aman, M. G., McCracken, J. T., Tierney, E., Davies, M., et al. (2005). Risperidone for the core symptom domains of autism. *American Journal of Psychiatry, 162,* 1142–1148.

McElroy, S. L., Casuto, L. S., Nelson, E. B., Lake, K. A., Soutullo, C. A., Keck, P. E., Jr., & Hudson, J. I. (2000). Placebo-controlled trial of sertraline in the treatment of binge eating disorder. *American Journal of Psychiatry, 157,* 1004–1006.

McElroy, S. L., Hudson, J. I., Malhotra, S., Welge, J. A., Nelson, E. B, & Keck, P. E. Jr. (2003). Citalopram in the treatment of binge-eating disorder: A placebo-controlled trial. *Journal of Clinical Psychiatry, 64,* 807–813.

McGillivray, J. A., & McCabe, M. P. (2006). Early detection of depression and associated risk factors in adults with mild/moderate intellectual disability. *Research in Developmental Disabilities,* in press.

McGinn, L. K., & Sanderson, W. C. (2001). What allows cognitive behavioral therapy to be brief: Overview, efficacy, and crucial factors facilitating brief treatment. *Clinical Psychology: Science and Practice, 8,* 23–37.

McGirra, A., Tousignant, M., Routhier, D., Pouliot, L., Chawky, N., Margolese, H. C., et al. (2006). Risk factors for completed suicide in schizophrenia and other chronic psychotic disorders: A case–control study. *Schizophrenia Research,* in press.

McGlashan, T. H., & Fenton, W. S. (1992). The positive-negative distinction in schizophrenia: Review of natural history validators. *Archives of General Psychiatry, 49,* 63–72.

McGlashan, T. H., & Hoffman, R. E. (2000). Schizophrenia as a disorder of developmentally reduced synaptic connectivity. *Archives of General Psychiatry, 57,* 637–648.

McGlashan, T. H., Zipursky, R. B., Perkins, D., Addington, J., Miller, T., Woods, S. W., et al. (2006). Randomized, double-blind trial of olanzapine versus placebo in patients prodromally symptomatic for psychosis. *American Journal of Psychiatry, 163,* 790–799.

McGlinchey, J. B., Zimmerman, M., Young, D., & Chelminski, I. (2006). Diagnosing Major Depressive Disorder VIII: Are some symptoms better than others? *Journal of Nervous & Mental Disease, 194,* 785–790.

McGovern, P. G., Pankow, J. S., Shahar, E., Doliszny, K. M., Folsom, A. R., Blackburn, H., et al. (1996). Recent trends in acute coronary heart disease. *The New England Journal of Medicine, 334,* 884–190.

McGowan, S., Lawrence, A. D., Sales, T., Quested, D., & Grasby, P. (2004). Presynaptic Dopaminergic dysfunction in schizophrenia: A positron emission tomographic [18f]fluorodopa study. *Archives of General Psychiatry, 61,* 134–142.

McGrath, E., Keita, G. P., Strickland, B. R., & Russo, N. F. (1990). *Women and depression: Risk factors and treatment issues.* Washington DC: American Psychological Association.

McGrath, P. J., Stewart, J. W., Janal, M. N., Petkova, E., Quitkin, F. M., & Klein, D. F. (2000). A placebo-controlled study of fluoxetine versus imipramine in the acute treatment of atypical depression. *American Journal of Psychiatry, 157,* 344–350.

McGrath, R. E, Pogge, D. L., & Stokes, J. M. (2002). Incremental validity of selected MMPI—A content scales in an inpatient setting . *Psychological Assessment, 14,* 401–409.

McGrath, R. E., Wiggins, J. G., Sammons, M. T., Levant, R. F., Brown, A., & Stock, W. (2004). Professional issues in pharmacotherapy for psychologists. *Professional Psychology: Research and Practice, 35,* 158–163.

McGue, M. (1993). From proteins to cognitions: The behavioral genetics of alcoholism. In R. Plomin & G. E. McClearn (Eds.), *Nature, nurture & psychology* (pp. 245–268). Washington, DC: American Psychological Association.

McGue, M., Iacono, W. G., & Krueger, R. (2006). The association of early adolescent problem behavior and adult psychopathology: a multivariate behavioral genetic perspective. *Behavior Genetics, 36,* 591–602.

McGue, M., Slutske, W., & Iaono, W. G. (1999). Personality and substance use disorders: II. Alcoholism versus drug use disorders. *Journal of Consulting and Clinical Psychology, 67,* 394–404.

McGuffin, P., Rijsdijk, F., Andrew, M., Sham, P., Katz, R., & Cardno, A. (2003). The heritability of bipolar affective disorder and the genetic relationship to unipolar depression. *Archives of General Psychiatry, 60,* 497–502.

McGuire, P. K., Shah, G. M. S., & Murray, R. M. (1993). Increased blood flow in Broca's area during auditory hallucinations in schizophrenia. *The Lancet, 342,* 703–706.

McKee, B. (2003, September 4). As suburbs grow, so do waistlines. *The New York Times,* pp. F1, F13.

McKellar, J., Stewart, E., & Humphreys, K. (2003). Alcoholics Anonymous involvement and positive alcohol- related outcomes: Cause, consequence, or just a correlate? A prospective 2-year study of 2,319 alcohol-dependent men. *Journal of Consulting and Clinical Psychology, 71,* 302–308.

McKenna, M. C., Zevon, M. A., Corn, B., & Rounds, J. (1999). Psychosocial factors and the development of breast cancer: A meta-analysis. *Health Psychology, 18,* 520–531.

McLean, L. M., & Gallop, R. (2003). Implications of childhood sexual abuse for adult borderline personality disorder and complex posttraumatic stress disorder. *American Journal of Psychiatry, 160,* 369–371.

McLean, P. D., et al. (2001). Cognitive versus behavior therapy in the group treatment of obsessive-compulsive disorder. *Journal of Consulting and Clinical Psychology, 69,* 205–214.

McLeod, B. D., & Weisz, J. R. (2004). Using dissertations to examine potential bias in child and adolescent clinical trials. *Journal of Consulting and Clinical Psychology, 72,* 235–251.

McMillan, J. R. (2003). Dangerousness, mental disorder, and responsibility. *Journal of Medical Ethics, 29,* 232–235.

McMurtrie, B. (1994, July 19). Overweight fatten ranks. *New York Newsday,* p. A26.

McNally, R. (1987). Preparedness and phobias: A review. *Psychological Bulletin, 101,* 283–303.

McNally, R. J., & Eke, M. (1996). Anxiety sensitivity, suffocation fear, and breath-holding duration as predictors of response to carbon dioxide challenge. *Journal of Abnormal Psychology, 105,* 146–149.

McNally, R. J., Bryant, R. A., & Ehlers, A. (2003). Does early psychological intervention promote recovery from posttraumatic stress? *Psychological Science in the Public Interest, 4(2),* 45–79.

McNally, R. J., Cassiday, K. L., & Calamari, J. E. (1990). Taijin-kyofu-sho in a Black American woman: Behavioral treatment of a "culture-bound" anxiety disorder. *Journal of Anxiety Disorders, 4,* 83–87.

McNally, R. J., et al. (1995). Clinical versus nonclinical panic: A test of suffocation false alarm theory. *Behaviour Research & Therapy, 33,* 127–131.

McNeil, D. E., Borum, R., Douglas, K. S., Hart, S. D., Lyon, D., Sullivan, L. E., & Hemphill, J. F. (2002). Risk assessment. In J. P. Ogloff (Ed.), *Taking psychology and law into the 21st century: Reviewing the discipline—A bridge to the future* (pp. 147–170). New York: Plenum.

McNeil, D. G., Jr. (2001, February 4). Epidemic errors. *The New York Times Week in Review,* pp. 1, 5.

McNiel, D. E., Gregory, A. L., Lam, J. N., Binder, R. L., Sullivan, G. R. (2003). Utility of decision support tools for assessing acute risk of violence *Journal of Consulting and Clinical Psychology, 71,* 945–953.

McNiel, D. E., Lam, J. N., & Binder, R. L. (2000). Relevance of interrater agreement to violence risk assessment. *Journal of Consulting and Clinical Psychology, 68,* 6, 1111–1115.

McNulty, J. L., Graham, J. R., Ben-Porath, Y. S., & Stein, L. A. R. (1997). Comparative validity of MMPI-2 scores of African American and Caucasian mental health center clients. *Psychological Assessment, 9,* 464–470.

McQuiston, J. T. (1997, February 5). New mother on Long Island suffering from depression is found, apparently a suicide. *The New York Times,* p. B5.

Meacham, J. (2000, September 18). The new face of race. *Newsweek,* pp. 38–41.

Mead, M. (1935). *Sex and temperament in three primitive societies.* New York: Morrow.

Medalia, A., Aluma, M., Tryon, W., & Merriam, A. E. (1998). Effectiveness of attention training in schizophrenia. *Schizophrenia Bulletin, 24,* 147–152.

Mednick, S. A., & Schulsinger, F. (1968). Some premorbid characteristics related to breakdown in children with schizophrenic mothers. In D. Rosenthal & S. S. Kety (Eds.), *The transmission of schizophrenia* (pp. 267–291). New York: Pergamon Press.

Mednick, S. A., Parnas, J., & Schulsinger, F. (1987). The Copenhagen High-Risk project, 1962–86. *Schizophrenia Bulletin, 13,* 485–495.

Meehl, P. E. (1962). Schizotaxia, schizotypy, schizophrenia. *American Psychologist, 17,* 827–838.

Meehl, P. E. (1972). A critical afterword. In I. I. Gottesman & J. Shields (Eds.), *Schizophrenia and genetics: A twin study vantage point* (pp. 367–415). New York: Academic Press.

Mehrabian, A., & Weinstein, L. (1985). Temperament characteristics of suicide attempters. *Journal of Consulting and Clinical Psychology, 53,* 544–546.

Meichenbaum, D. (1993). Changing conceptions of cognitive behavior modification: Retrospect and prospect. *Journal of Consulting and Clinical Psychology, 61,* 202–204.

Meichenbaum, D., & Deffenbacher, J. L. (1988). Stress inoculation training. *The Counseling Psychologist, 16* (1), 69–90.

Meier, B. F., Robinson, M. D., Gaither, G. A., & Heinert, N. J. (2006). A secret attraction or defensive loathing? Homophobia, defense, and implicit cognition. *Journal of Research in Personality, 40,* 377–394.

Melani, D. (2001, January 17). Emotions can pull trigger on heart attack. *Evansville Courier & Press, Scripps Howard News Service.* Retrieved January 19, 2001, from http://www.psycport.com/news/2001/01/17/eng-courierpress_features/eng-courierpress_features_134435_74_9803814571351.html.

Melchert, T. P. (1996). Childhood memory and a history of different forms of abuse. *Professional Psychology: Research and Practice, 27,* 438–446.

Mellor, C. S. (1970). First rank symptoms of schizophrenia. *British Journal of Psychiatry, 177,* 15–23.

Melville, J. D., & Naimark, D. (2002). Punishing the insane: The verdict of guilty but mentally ill. *Journal of the American Academy of Psychiatry and the Law, 30,* 553–55.

Mendelsohn, M. E., & Karas, R. H. (2005). Molecular and cellular basis of cardiovascular gender differences. *Science, 308,* 583–1587.

Mendez, J. L. (2005). Conceptualizing sociocultural factors within clinical and research contexts. *Clinical Psychology: Science and Practice, 12,* 434–437.

Meng, H., Smith, S. D., Hager, K., Held, M., Liu, J., Olson, R K., et al. (2006). DCDC2 is associated with reading disability and modulates neuronal development in the brain. *Proceedings of the National Academy of Sciences, 102,* 17053–17058.

Merckelbach, H., Arntz, A., & de Jong, P. (1991). Conditioning experiences in spider phobics. *Behaviour Research and Therapy, 29,* 301–304.

Merckelbach, H., et al. (1996). The etiology of specific phobias: A review. *Clinical Psychology Review, 16,* 337–361.

Merikangas, K. R., & Risch, N. (2003). Will the genomics revolution revolutionize psychiatry? *American Journal of Psychiatry, 160,* 625–635.

Merrill, K. A., Tolbert, V. E., & Wade, W. A. (2003). Effectiveness of cognitive therapy for depression in a community mental health center: A benchmarking study. *Journal of Consulting and Clinical Psychology, 71,* 404–409.

Messari, S., & Hallam, R. (2003). CBT for psychosis: a qualitative analysis of clients' experiences. *British Journal of Clinical Psychology, 42,* 171–188.

Messer, S. B. (2001a). Empirically supported treatments: What's a nonbehaviorist to do? In B. D. Slife & R. N. Williams (Eds.), *Critical issues in psychotherapy: Translating new ideas into practice* (pp. 3–19). Thousand Oaks, CA: Sage.

Messer, S. B. (2001b). What makes brief psychodynamic therapy time efficient? *Clinical Psychology: Science and Practice, 8,* 5–22.

Messias, E., Kirkpatrick, B., Bromet, E., Ross, D., Buchanan, R. W., & Carpenter, W. T. (2005). Summer birth and deficit schizophrenia: A pooled analysis from 6 countries. *Archives of General Psychiatry, 61,* 970–985.

Messinis, L., Kyprianidou, A., Malefaki, S., & Papathanasopoulos, P. (2006). Neuropsychological deficits in long-term frequent cannabis users. *Neurology, 66,* 737–739.

Meston, C. M., & Frohlich, P. F. (2000). The neurobiology of sexual function. *Archives of General Psychiatry, 57,* 1012–1030.

Meston, C. M., & Heiman, J. R. (2000). Sexual abuse and sexual function: An examination of sexually relevant cognitive processes. *Journal of Consulting and Clinical Psychology, 68* (3), 399–406.

Meyer, B., Pilkonis, P. A., Krupnick, J. L., Egan, M. K., Simmens, S. J., & Sotsky, S. M. (2002). Treatment expectancies, patient alliance, and outcome: Further analyses from the National Institute of Mental Health treatment of depression collaborative research program. *Journal of Consulting and Clinical Psychology, 70,* 1051–1055.

Meyer, G. J. (1997). Assessing reliability: Critical corrections for a critical examination of the Rorschach comprehensive system. *Psychological Assessment, 9,* 480–489.

Meyer, G. J. (2000). Incremental validity of the Rorschach Prognostic Rating Scale over the MMPI Ego Strength Scale and IQ. *Journal of Personality Assessment, 74,* 365–370.

Meyer, G. J. (2001). To the final special section in the special series on the utility of the Rorschach for clinical assessment. *Psychological Assessment, 13,* 419–422.

Meyer, G. J., & Archer, R. P. (2001). The hard science of Rorschach research: What do we know and where do we go? *Psychological Assessment, 13,* 486–502.

Meyer, G. J., et al. (2001). Psychological testing and psychological assessment: A review of evidence and issues. *American Psychologist, 56,* 128–165.

Meyer, G. J., Hilsenroth, M. J., Baxter, D., Exner, J. E., Jr., et al. (2002). An examination of interrater relaibity for scoring the Rorschach comprehensive system in eight data sets. *Journal of Personality Assessment, 78,* 219–274.

Meyer, I. H. (2003). Prejudice, social stress, and mental health in lesbian, gay, and bisexual populations: Conceptual issues and research evidence. *Psychological Bulletin, 129,* 674–697.

Meyer, J. H., McMain, S., Kennedy, S. H., Korman, L., Brown, G. M., DaSilva, J. N., et al. (2003). Dysfunctional attitudes and 5-HT2 receptors during depression and self-harm. *American Journal of Psychiatry, 160,* 90–99.

Meyers, L. (2005). Psychologists back increased parity, prescriptive authority and professional access. *Monitor on Psychology, 36,* 42–43.

Michaud, E. (2000, October). Women's secret terror. *Prevention,* pp. 118–127.

Michelson, D., Bancroft, J., Targum, S., Kim, Y., & Tepner, R. (2000). Female sexual dysfunction associated with antidepressant administration: A randomized, placebo-controlled study of pharmacologic intervention. *American Journal of Psychiatry, 157,* 239–243.

Mignot, E., & Thorsby, E. (2001). Narcolepsy and the HLA System. *The New England Journal of Medicine, 344,* 692.

Miklowitz, D. J. (1994). Family risk indicators in schizophrenia. *Schizophrenia Bulletin, 20,* 137–149.

Miklowitz, D. J., & Alloy, L. B. (1999). Psychosocial factors in the course and treatment of bipolar disorder: Introduction to the special section. *Journal of Abnormal Psychology, 108,* 555–557.

Miklowitz, D. J., George, E. L., Richards, J. A., Simoneau, T. L., & Suddath, R. L. (2003). A randomized study of family-focused psychoeducation and pharmacotherapy in the outpatient management of bipolar disorder. *Archives of General Psychiatry, 60,* 904–912.

Milad, R. R., & Quirk, G. J. (2002). Neurons in medial prefrontal cortex signal memory for fear extinction. *Nature 420,* 70–74.

Milberger, S., et al. (1996). Is maternal smoking during pregnancy a risk factor for attention deficit hyperactivity disorder in children? *American Journal of Psychiatry, 153,* 1138–1142.

Miller, A. L., Wyman, S. E., Huppert, J. D., Glassman, S. L., & Rathus, J. H. (2000). Analysis of behavioral skills utilized by suicidal adolescents receiving dialectical behavior therapy. *Cognitive & Behavioral Practice, 7(2),* 183–187.

Miller, E. (1987). Hysteria: Its nature and explanation. *British Journal of Clinical Psychology, 26,* 163–173.

Miller, G. E., & Cohen, S. (2001). Psychological interventions and the immune system: A meta-analytic review and critique. *Health Psychology, 20,* 47–63.

Miller, L. K. (1999). The savant syndrome: Intellectual impairment and exceptional skills. *Psychological Bulletin, 125,* 31–46.

Miller, M. (2000, August 10). He just said no to the drug war. *The New York Times Magazine,* pp. 32–35.

Miller, M., Azrael, D., & Hemenway, D. (2004). The epidemiology of case fatality rates for suicide in the northeast. *Annals of Emergency Medicine, 43,* 723–730.

Miller, S. D., & Triggiano, P. (1991). The psychophysiological investigation of multiple personality disorder: Review and update. *American Journal of Clinical Hypnosis, 35,* 47–61.

Miller, S. D., Blackburn, R., Scholes, G., White, G. L., & Mamalis, N. (1991). Optical differences in multiple personality disorder: A second look. *Journal of Nervous & Mental Disease, 179,* 132–135.

Miller, T. Q., Turner, C. W., Tindale, R. S., Posavac, E. J., & Dugoni, B. L. (1991). Reasons for the trend toward null findings in research on Type A Behavior. *Psychological Bulletin, 110,* 469–485.

Miller, W. R., & Brown, S. A., (1997). Why psychologists should treat alcohol and drug problems. *American Psychologist, 52,* 1269–1279.

Miller, W. R., & Hester, R. K. (1986). Inpatient alcoholism treatment: Who benefits? *American Psychologist, 41,* 794–805.

Miller-Medzon, K. (2000, August 20). Early dyslexia detection leads to normal learning. *Boston Herald,* pp. 1, 11.

Millon, T. (1981). *Disorders of personality DSM-III: Axis II.* New York: Wiley.

Millon, T. (1982). *Millon Clinical Multiaxial Inventory manual* (3rd ed.). Minneapolis: National Computer Systems.

Millon, T. (2003). It's time to rework the blueprints: Building a science for clinical psychology. *American Psychologist, 58,* 949–961.

Milrod, B., Leon, A. C., Busch, F., Rudden, M., Schwalberg, M., Clarkin, J., Aronson, A., et al. (2007). A randomized controlled clinical trial of psychoanalytic psychotherapy for panic disorder. *American Journal of Psychiatry, 164,* 265–272.

Minarik, M. L., & Ahrens, A. H. (1996). Relations of eating and symptoms of depression and anxiety to the dimensions of perfectionism among undergraduate women. *Cognitive Research & Therapy, 20,* 155–169.

Mineka, S. (1991, August). Paper presented at the annual meeting of the American Psychological Association, San Francisco. (Cited in Turkington, C. [1991]. Evolutionary memories may have phobia role. *APA Monitor, 22*(11), 14.

Minerd, J., & Jasmer, R. (2006, April). *Forty winks or more to make a healthier America.* Retrieved April 7, 2006, from http://www.medpagetoday.com/PrimaryCare/SleepDisorders/tb/3009.

Minuchin, S., Rosman, B. L., & Baker, L. (1978). *Psychosomatic families: Anorexia nervosa in context.* Cambridge, MA: Harvard University Press.

Miranda, A., & Presentacion, M. J. (2000). Efectos de un tratamiento cognitivo-conductual en ninos contrastorno por deficit de atencion con hiperactividad, agresivos y no agresivos. *Infancia y Aprendizaje, 92,* 51–70.

Miranda, J., Green, B. L., Krupnick, J. L., Chung, J., Siddique, J., Belin, T., et al. (2006). One-year outcomes of a randomized clinical trial treating depression in low-income minority women. *Journal of Consulting and Clinical Psychology, 74,* 99–111.

Mitchell, C. M., Beals, J., & The Pathways of Choice Team. (2006). The development of alcohol use and outcome expectancies among American Indian young adults: A growth mixture model. *Addictive Behaviors, 31,* 1–14.

Mitka, M. (2000). Psychiatrists help survivors in the Balkans. *Journal of the American Medical Association, 283,* 1277–1278.

Mitka, M. (2003, November 19). FDA alert on antidepressants for youth. *Journal of the American Medical Association, 290,* 2354–2355.

Mitte, K. (2005). Meta-analysis of cognitive-behavioral treatments for generalized anxiety disorder: A comparison with pharmacotherapy. *Psychological Bulletin, 131,* 785–795.

Mittelman, M. S., Roth, D. L., Coon, D. W., & Haley, W. E. (2004). Sustained benefit of supportive intervention for depressive symptoms in caregivers of patients with Alzheimer's disease. *American Journal of Psychiatry, 161,* 850–856.

Mixed progress on cancer front. (2003, September 3). *MSNBC Web Posting.* Retrieved September 4, 2003, from http://www.msnbc.com/news/960534.asp.

Modestin, J. (1992). Multiple personality disorder in Switzerland. *American Journal of Psychiatry, 149,* 88–92.

Moffitt, T. E., Caspi, A., & Rutter, M. (2006). Measured gene-environment interactions in psychopathology concepts, research strategies, and implications for research, intervention, and public understanding of genetics. *Perspectives on Psychological Science, 1,* 5–27.

Mohr, D. C., Hart, S. L., Julian, L., Catledge, C., Honos-Webb, L., Vella, L., et al. (2005). Telephone-administered psychotherapy for depression. *Archives of General Psychiatry, 62,* 1007–1014.

Mokdad, A. H., Ford, E. S., Bowman, B. A., Dietz, W. H., Vinicor, F., Bales, V. S., et al. (2003). Prevalence of obesity, diabetes, and obesity-related health risk factors, 2001. *Journal of the American Medical Association, 289,* 76–79.

Mokdad, A. H., Marks, J. S., Stroup, D. F., & Gerberding, J. L. (2004). Actual causes of death in the United States, 2000. *Journal of the American Medical Association, 291,* 1238, 1241.

Mokuau, N. (1990). The impoverishment of native Hawaiians and the social work challenge. *Health and Social Work, 15,* 235–242.

Moldin, S. O. (1994). Indicators of liability to schizophrenia: Perspectives from genetic epidemiology. *Schizophrenia Bulletin, 20,* 169–184.

Molina, B. S. G., & Pelham, W. E. (2003). Childhood predictors of adolescent substance use in a longitudinal study of children with ADHD. *Journal of Abnormal Psychology, 112,* 497–507.

Mollica R. F., Henderson, D. C., & Tor, S. (2002). Psychiatric effects of traumatic brain injury events in Cambodian survivors of mass violence. *British Journal of Psychiatry, 181,* 339–347.

Monahan, J. (1981). *A clinical prediction of violent behavior.* DHHS Publication, Adm. 81–921. Rockville, MD: National Institutes of Mental Health.

Monahan, J., Steadman, H. J., Silver, E., Appelbaum, P. S., Robbins, P. C., Mulvey, E. P., Roth, L. H., et al. (2001). *Rethinking risk assessment: The MacArthur Study of Mental Disorder and Violence.* New York: Oxford University Press.

Moncher, M. S., Holden, G. W., & Trimble, J. E. (1990). Substance abuse among Native-American youth. *Journal of Consulting and Clinical Psychology, 58,* 408–415.

Money, J. (2000). Reflections of a gender biographer. *Men & Masculinities, 3,* 209–216.

Monroe, S. M., Harkness, K., Simons, A. D., & Thase, M. E. (2001). Life stress and the symptoms of major depression. *Journal of Nervous & Mental Disease, 189,* 168–175.

Monson, C. M., Langhinrichsen-Rohling, J., & Binderup, T. (2000). Does "no" really mean "no" after you say "yes"? Attributions about date and marital rape. *Journal of Interpersonal Violence, 15,* 1156–1174.

Monson, C. M., Schnurr, P. P., Resick, P. A., Friedman, M. J., Young-Xu, Y., & Stevens, S. (2006). Cognitive processing therapy for veterans with military-related posttraumatic stress disorder. *Journal of Consulting and Clinical Psychology, 74,* 898–907.

Montemurro, B., Bloom, C., & Madell, K. (2003). Ladies night out: A typology of women patrons of a male strip club. *Deviant Behavior, 24* 333–352.

Monti, P. M., et al. (1987). Reactivity of alcoholics and nonalcoholics to drinking cues. *Journal of Abnormal Psychology, 96,* 122–126.

Mooney, M., White, T., & Hatsukami, D. (2004). The blind spot in the nicotine replacement therapy literature: Assessment of the double-blind in clinical trials. *Addictive Behaviors, 29,* 673–684.

Moore, D. R. & Heiman, J. R. (2006). Women's sexuality in context: Relationship factors and female sexual functioning. In I. Goldstein, C. Meston, S. Davis, & A. Traish (Eds.), *Female sexual dysfunction.* New York: Parthenon.

Moos, R. H., & Moos, B. S. (2004). Long-term influence of duration and frequency of participation in alcoholics anonymous on individuals with alcohol use disorders. *Journal of Consulting and Clinical Psychology, 72,* 81–90.

Moos, R. H., & Moos, B. S. (2005). Paths of entry into alcoholics anonymous: consequences for participation and remission. *Alcoholism: Clinical and Experimental Research, 29,* 1858–1868.

Moos, R. H., Cronkite, R. C., & Moos, B. S. (1998). Family and extrafamily resources and the 10-year course of treated depression. *Journal of Abnormal Psychology, 107,* 450–460.

Moos, R. H., McCoy, L., & Moos, B. S. (2000). Global Assessment of Functioning (GAF) ratings: Determinants and roles as predictors of one-year treatment outcomes. *Journal of Clinical Psychology, 56,* 449–461.

Mor, N., & Winquist, J. (2002). Self-focused attention and negative affect: A meta-analysis. *Psychological Bulletin, 128,* 638–662.

Moran, P., Walsh, E., Tyrer, P., Burns, T., Creed, F., & Fahy, T. (2003). Does comorbid personality disorder increase the risk of suicidal behaviour in psychosis? *Acta Psychiatrica Scandinavica, 107,* 441–448.

Morgan, D. L., & Morgan, R. K. (2001). Single-participant research design: Bringing science to managed care. *American Psychologist, 56,* 119–127.

Morgan, K. (1996). Mental health factors in late-life insomnia. *Reviews in Clinical Gerontology, 6,* 75–83.

Morgenstern, J., Bux, D. A., Labouvie, E., Morgan, T., Blanchard, K. A., & Muench, F., et al. (2002). Examining mechanisms of action in 12-step treatment: The role of 12-step cognitions. *Journal of Studies on Alcohol, 63,* 665–672.

Morimoto, K., Miyatake, R., Nakamura, M., Watanabe, T., Hirao, T., & Suwaki, H. (2002). Delusional disorder: Molecular genetic evidence for dopamine psychosis. *Neuropsychopharmacology, 26,* 794–801.

Morin, C. M. (2000). The nature of insomnia and the need to refine our diagnostic criteria. *Psychosomatic Medicine, 62,* 483–485.

Morin, C. M., & Ware, J. C. (1996). Sleep and psychopathology. *Applied and Preventive Psychology, 5,* 211–224.

Morin, C. M., & Wooten, V. (1996). Psychological and pharmacological approaches to treating insomnia: Critical issues in assessing their separate and combined effects. *Clinical Psychology Review, 16,* 521–542.

Morin, C. M., Stone, J., Trinkle, D., Mercer, J., & Remsberg, S. (1993). Dysfunctional beliefs and attitudes about sleep among older adults with and without insomnia complaints. *Psychology and Aging, 8,* 463–467.

Morris, B. R. (2003, July 8). Two types of brain problems are found to cause dyslexia. *The New York Times,* p. F5.

Morris, E. P., Stewart, S. H., & Ham, L. S. (2005). The relationship between social anxiety disorder and alcohol use disorders: A critical review. *Clinical Psychology Review, 25,* 734–760.

Morris, G. H. (2002). Commentary: Punishing the unpunishable—the abuse of psychiatry to confine those we love to hate. *Journal of the American Academy of Psychiatry and the Law, 30,* 556–562.

Morris, M. C., Evans, D. A., Bienias, J. L., Tangney, C. C., & Wilson, R. S. (2002). Vitamin E and cognitive decline in older persons. *Archives of Neurology, 59,* 1125–1132.

Morrison, J. (1989). Childhood sexual histories of women with somatization disorder. *American Journal of Psychiatry, 146,* 239–241.

Morrison, M. F., Petitto, J. M., Have, T. T., Gettes, B. S., Chiappini, M. S., Weber, A. L., et al. (2002). Depressive and anxiety disorders in women with HIV infection. *American Journal of Psychiatry, 159,* 860–862.

Morrison, T., Waller, G., & Lawson, R. A. (2006). Attributional style in the eating disorders. *Journal of Nervous & Mental Disease, 194,* 303–305.

Morrow, D. J. (1998, March 5). Stumble on the road to market. *The New York Times,* p. D1.

Mörtberg, E., Karlsson, A., Fyring, C., & Sundin, O. (2006). Intensive cognitive-behavioral group treatment (CBGT) of social phobia: A randomized controlled study. *Journal of Anxiety Disorders, 20,* 646–660.

Mortensen, P. B., Pedersen, C. B., Westergaard, T., Wohlfahrt, J., Ewald, H., Mors, O., et al. (1999). Effects of family history and place and season of birth on the risk of schizophrenia. *New England Journal of Medicine, 340,* 603–608.

Mosharov, E. V., Staal, R. G. W., Bové, J., Prou, D., Hananiya, A., Markov, D., et al. (2006). α-synuclein overexpression increases cytosolic catecholamine concentration. *The Journal of Neuroscience, 26,* 9304–9311.

Mossman, D. (1994). Assessing predictions of violence: Being accurate about accuracy. *Journal of Consulting and Clinical Psychology, 62,* 783–792.

Moulds, M. L., & Nixon, R. D. (2006). In vivo flooding for anxiety disorders: Proposing its utility in the treatment posttraumatic stress disorder. *Journal of Anxiety Disorder, 20,* 498–509.

Mowrer, O. H. (1948). Learning theory and the neurotic paradox. *American Journal of Orthopsychiatry, 18,* 571–610.

MTF Survey finds overall decline in teen substance abuse. (2006). *NIDA Notes, 20*(10), 19.

Mueller, T. I., Leon, A. C., Keller, M. B., Solomon, D. A., Endicott, J., Coryell, W., et al. (1999). Recurrence after recovery from major depressive disorder during 15 years of observational follow-up. *The American Journal of Psychiatry, 156,* 1000–1006.

Mueser, K. T., & Liberman, R. P. (1995). Behavior therapy in practice. In B. Bongar & L. E. Beutler (Eds.), *Comprehensive textbook of psychotherapy: Theory and practice* (pp. 84–110). New York: Oxford.

Mueser, K. T., Sengupta, A., Schooler, N. R., Bellack, A. S., Xie, H., Glick, I. D., & Keith, S. J., et al. (2001). Family treatment and medication dosage reduction in schizophrenia: Effects on patient social functioning, family attitudes, and burden. *Journal of Consulting and Clinical Psychology, 69,* 3–12.

Mukamal, K. J., Conigrave, K. M., Mittleman, M. A., Camargo, C. A., Jr., Stampfer, M. J., Willett, W. C., et al. (2003). Roles of drinking pattern and type of alcohol consumed in coronary heart disease in men. *New England Journal of Medicine, 348,* 109–118.

Mullen, A. (2000). Risperidone and tardive dyskinesia: A case of blepharospasm. *Australian and New Zealand Journal of Psychiatry, 34,* 879–880.

Müller, R. A., Kleinhans, N., Kemmotsu, N., Pierce, K., & Courchesne, E. (2003). Abnormal variability and distribution of functional maps in autism: an fMRI study of visuomotor learning. *American Journal of Psychiatry, 160,* 1847–1862.

Munarriz, R., Talakoub, L., Flaherty, E., Gioia, M., Hoag, L., Kim, N. N., et al. (2002). Androgen replacement therapy with dehydroepiandrosterone for androgen insufficiency and female sexual dysfunction: Androgen and questionnaire results. *Journal of Sex & Marital Therapy, 28* (Suppl. 1), 165–173.

Muñoz, R. F., & Mendelson, T. (2005). Toward evidence-based interventions for diverse populations: The San Francisco General Hospital prevention and treatment manuals. *Journal of Consulting and Clinical Psychology, 73,* 790–799.

Muñoz, R. F., Mrazek, P. J., & Haggerty, R. J. (1996). Institute of Medicine Report on Prevention of Mental Disorders: Summary and commentary. *American Psychologist, 51,* 1116–1121.

Munsey, C. (2006, October). Drug may accelerate phobia therapy. *Monitor on Psychology, 37,* p. 22.

Muraven, M. (2005). Self-focused attention and the self-regulation of attention: Implications for personality and pathology. *Journal of Social and Clinical Psychology, 24,* 382–400.

Murphy, C. M., Winters, J., O'Farrell, T. J., Fals-Stewart, W., & Murphy, M. (2005). Alcohol consumption and intimate partner violence by alcoholic men: Comparing violent and nonviolent conflicts. *Psychology of Addictive Behaviors, 19,* 35–42.

Murphy, D. G. M., Critchley, H. D., Schmitz, N., McAlonan, G., van Amelsvoort, T., Robertson, D., et al. (2002). A proton magnetic resonance spectroscopy study of brain. *Archives of General Psychiatry, 59,* 885–891.

Murray, B. (2000a). From brain scan to lesson plan. *Monitor on Psychology, 31,* pp. 22–28.

Murray, B. (2000b, July/August). Psychology seeks to replicate groundbreaking research on the success of drug/psychotherapy treatment. *Monitor on Psychology,* p. 13.

Murray, B. (2003, October). A brief history of RxP. *Monitor on Psychology, 34,* 66–67.

Murray, H. A. (1943). *Thematic Apperception Test: Pictures and manual.* Cambridge, MA: Harvard University Press.

Murray, J. B. (1993). Relationship of childhood sexual abuse to borderline personality disorder, posttraumatic stress disorder, and multiple personality disorder. *Journal of Psychology, 127,* 657–676.

Murray, L., Cooper, P. J., Wilson, A., & Romaniuk, H. (2003). Controlled trial of the short- and long-term effect of psychological treatment of post-partum depression: 2. Impact on the mother-child relationship and child outcome. *British Journal of Psychiatry, 182,* 420–427.

Murstein, B. I., & Mathes, S. (1996). Projection on projective techniques & pathology: The problem that is not being addressed. *Journal of Personality Assessment, 66,* 337–349.

Murtagh, D. R. R., & Greenwood, K. M. (1995). Identifying effective psychological treatments for insomnia: A meta-analysis. *Journal of Consulting and Clinical Psychology, 63,* 79–89.

Mutler, A. (2000, August 3). One-fourth of Kosovo's population suffering mental anguish in the aftermath of war. *Associated Press Web Listing.* Copyrighted by Associated Press. Retrieved August 3, 2000, from http://psycport.com/news/2000/08/03/wstm-/2537-2706-Kosovo-StillatWar.html.

Myin-Germeys, I., Delespaul, P. A. E. G., & deVries, M. W. (2000). Schizophrenia patients are more emotionally active than is assumed based on their behavior. *Schizophrenia Bulletin, 26,* 847–853.

N

Nabel, E. G. (2003). Cardiovascular disease. *New England Journal of Medicine, 349,* 60–72.

Nagayama Hall, G. C. (2005). Introduction to the special section on multicultural and community psychology: Clinical psychology in context. *Journal of Consulting and Clinical Psychology, 73,* 787–789.

Naglieri, J. A., Drasgow, F., Schmit, M., Handler, L., Prifitera, A., Margolis, A., et al. (2004). Psychological testing on the Internet: New problems, old issues. *American Psychologist, 59,* 150–162.

Nagourney, E. (2001a, April 10). Geography of dyslexia is explored. *The New York Times,* p. F7.

Nagourney, E. (2001b, April 24). A good night's sleep, without the pills. *The New York Times,* p. F8.

Naimi, T. S., Brewer, R. D., Mokdad, A., Denny, C., Serdula, M. K., & Marks, J. S. (2003). Binge drinking among US adults. *Journal of the American Medical Association, 289,* 70–75.

Najman, J. M., Dunne, M. P., Purdie, D. M., Boyle, F. M., & Coxeter, P. D. (2005). Sexual abuse in childhood and sexual dysfunction in adulthood: An Australian population-based study. *Archives of Sexual Behavior, 34,* 517–526.

Nakamura, K., Kitanishi, K., Miyake, Y., Hashimoto, K., & Kubota, M. (2002). The neurotic versus delusional subtype of taijin-kyofu-sho: their DSM diagnoses. *Psychiatry and Clinical Neurosciences, 56,* 595–601.

Narrow, W. E., Rae, D. S., Robins, L. N., & Regier, D. A. (2002). Revised prevalence estimates of mental disorders in the United States: Using a clinical significance criterion to reconcile 2 surveys' estimates. *Archives of General Psychiatry, 59,* 115–123.

Näslund, J., et al. (2000). Correlation between elevated levels of amyloid-peptide in the brain and cognitive decline. *Journal of the American Medical Association, 283,* 1571–1577.

Nasrallah, H. A., Ketter, T. A., & Kalali, A. H. (2006). Carbamazepine and valproate for the treatment of bipolar disorder: a review of the literature. *Journal of Affective Disorders, 95,* 69–78.

Natenshon, A. (2000–2002). Parental influence takes precedence over Barbie and the media. *Empowered Parents Website.* Retrieved November 19, 2003, from http://www.empoweredparents.com/1prevention/prevention_09.htm.

Nathan, P. E., Stuart, S. P., & Dolan, S. L. (2000). Research on psychotherapy efficacy and effectiveness: Between Scylla and Charybdis? *Psychological Bulletin, 126,* 964–981.

National Crime Victimization Survey. (2006). *U.S. Bureau of Justice Statistics.* Washington, DC: U.S. Department of Justice.

National Institute of Mental Health (NIMH). (2000). *Depression Research at the National Institute of Mental Health.* (2000). NIH Publication No. 004501. Retrieved from http://www.nimh.nih.gov/publicat/depresfact.cfm.

National Institute of Mental Health (NIMH). (2001). *Bipolar disorder.* Retrieved December 14, 2006, from http://www.nimh.nih.gov/publicat/bipolar.cfm.

National Institute of Mental Health (NIMH). (2003a, July 17). Gene more than doubles risk of depression following life stresses. *NIMH Press Office.* Retrieved July 19, 2003, from http://www.nih.gov/news/pr/jul2003/nimh-17.htm.

National Institute of Mental Health (NIMH). (2003b, December 23). *Suicide facts.* Retrieved February 12, 2004, from http://www.nimh.nih.gov/research/suifact.cfm.

National Institutes of Diabetes and Digestive and Kidney Diseases (NIDDK). (2001, Summer). New obesity gene discovered. *WIN Notes,* p. 2.

National Institutes of Health (NIH). (2003). *HIV/AIDS, severe mental illness and homelessness.* Retrieved March 24, 2004, from http://grants.nih.gov/grants/guide/pa-files/PA-04-024.html.

National Institutes of Health, National Heart, Lung, and Blood Institute. (1998). *Clinical guidelines on the identification, evaluation, and treatment of overweight and obesity in adults:* Bethesda, MD: Author.

National Institutes of Health, Office of Research on Women's Health, Office of the Director. (1999). *Women of color health data book: Adolescents to seniors.* NIH Publication 99–4247. Bethesda, MD: Author.

National Strategy for Suicide Prevention. (2001, May). *Goals and Objectives for Action: Summary.* A joint effort of SAMHSA, CDC, NIH, and HRSA. The Center for Mental Health Services. Rockville, MD: Author.

Naughton, K. (2004, February 2). *The soft sell.* Newsweek, pp. 46–47.

Navarro, M. (2004, January 17). Blacks and Latinos try to find balance in touchy new math. *The New York Times,* pp. A1, B2.

Ndetei, D. M., & Singh, A. (1983). Hallucinations in Kenyan schizophrenic patients. *Acta Psychiatrica Scandinavica, 67,* 144–147.

Ndetei, D. M., & Vadher, A. (1984). A comparative crosscultural study of the frequencies of hallucination in schizophrenia. *Acta Psychiatrica Scandinavica, 70,* 545–549.

Neal, A. M., & Turner, S. M. (1991). Anxiety disorders research with African Americans: Current status. *Psychological Bulletin, 109,* 400–410.

Needles, D. J., & Abramson, L. Y. (1990). Positive life events, attributional style, and hopefulness: Testing a model of recovery from depression. *Journal of Abnormal Psychology, 99,* 156–165.

Negy, C., & Snyder, D. K. (1997). Ethnicity and acculturation: Assessing Mexican American couples' relationships using the marital satisfaction inventory—revised. *Psychological Assessment, 9,* 414–421.

Negy, C., & Snyder, D. K. (2004). A research note on male chauvinism and MexicanAmericans. *Psychology and Education, 41,* 22–27.

Negy, C., & Woods, D. J. (1992a). Mexican Americans' performance on the Psychological Screening Inventory as a function of acculturation. *Journal of Clinical Psychology, 48,* 315–319.

Negy, C., & Woods, D. J. (1992b). A note on the relationship between acculturation and socioeconomic status. *Hispanic Journal of Behavioral Sciences, 14,* 248–251.

Negy, C., & Woods, D. J. (1993). Mexican- and Anglo-American differences on the Psychological Screening Inventory. *Journal of Personality Assessment, 60,* 543–555.

Negy, C., Snyder, & Diaz-Loving, R. (2004). A cross-national comparison of Mexican and Mexican American couples using the Marital Satisfaction Inventory-revised. *Assessment, 11,* 49–56.

Neighbors, H. (1992, December). *The help seeking behavior of black Americans: A summary of the National Survey of Black Americans.* Paper presented at a symposium, Anxiety Disorders in African Americans, presented by the State University of New York Health Science Center at Brooklyn, Brooklyn, NY.

Nelson, C. B., Heath, A. C., & Kessler, R. C. (1998). Temporal progression of alcohol dependence symptoms in the U.S. household population: Results from the National Comorbidity Survey. *Journal of Consulting and Clinical Psychology, 66,* 474–483.

Nelson, J. C. (2006). The STAR*D Study: A four-course meal that leaves us wanting more. *American Journal of Psychiatry, 163,* 1864–1866.

Nemets, H., Nemets, B., Apter, A., Bracha, Z., & Belmaker, R. H. (2006). Omega-3 treatment of childhood depression: A controlled, double-blind pilot study. *American Journal of Psychiatry, 163,* 1098–1100.

Nemiah, J. C. (1978). Psychoneurotic disorders. In A. M. Nicholi (Ed.), *Harvard guide to modern psychiatry.* Cambridge, MA: Harvard University Press.

Nestadt, G., et al. (2000). A family study of obsessive-compulsive disorder. *Archives of General Psychiatry, 57,* 358–363.

Nestler, E. J. (2005, December). Research review: The neurobiology of cocaine addiction. *Science and Practice Perspectives.* Retrieved January 4, 2007, from http://www.drugabuse.gov/PDF/Perspectives/vol3no1/Neurobiology.pdfR.

Nestler, E. J. (2005). Is there a common molecular pathway for addiction? *Nature Neuroscience, 8,* 1445–1449.

Nettle, D. (2001). *Strong imagination: Madness, creativity, and human nature.* New York: Oxford University Press.

Neugebauer, R. (1979). Medieval and early modern theories of mental illness. *Archives of General Psychiatry, 36,* 477–484.

Neumann, K., Euler, H. A., von Gudenberg, A. W., Giraud, A. L., Lanfermann, H., Gall, V., et al. (2003). The nature and treatment of stuttering as revealed by fMRI A within- and between-group comparison. *Journal of Fluency Disorders, 28,* 381–409.

Nevid, J. S., & Javier, R. A. (1997). Preliminary investigation of a culturally-specific smoking cessation intervention for Hispanic smokers. *American Journal of Health Promotion, 11,* 198–207.

Nevid, J. S., & Rathus, S. A. (2005). Psychology and the challenges of life: Adjustment in the new millennium (9th ed.). New York: Wiley.

Nevid, J. S., Javier, R. A., & Moulton, J. (1996). Factors predicting participant attrition in a community-based culturally-specific smoking cessation program for Hispanic smokers. *Health Psychology, 15,* 226–229.

Nevid, J. S., Rathus, S. A., & Rubenstein, H. R. (1998). *Health in the new millennium.* New York: Worth.

Neville, H. A., et al. (1996). The impact of multicultural training on white racial identity attitudes and therapy competencies. *Professional Psychology: Research & Practice, 27,* 83–89.

New studies help patients with treatment-resistant bipolar disorder. (2006, February 1). *American Psychiatric Association, News Release.* Retrieved June 30, 2006, from http://www.psych.org/news_room/press_releases/06_07_%20STEP_BD.pdf.

New use of brain scan may yield delays in Alzheimer's symptoms. (2000, May 15). *CNN Web Posting.* Retrieved May 16, 2000, from http://www.cnn.com/2000/HEALTH/aging/05/15/alzheimers.diagnosis/.

Newcomer, J. W. (2005). Second-generation (atypical) antipsychotics and metabolic effects: A comprehensive literature review. *CNS Drugs, 19* (Suppl 1), 1–93.

Nezu, A. M. (1994). In troduction to special section: Mental retardation and mental illness. *Journal of Consulting and Clinical Psychology, 62,* 4–5.

Ni, X., Chan, K., Bulgin, N., Sicard, T., Bismil, R., McMain, S., et al. (2006). Association between serotonin transporter gene and borderline personality disorder. *Journal of Psychiatric Research, 40,* 448–453.

NIAAA report links drinking and early death. (1990, October). *The Addiction Letter, 6,* p. 5.

Niaura, R., Todaro, J. F., Stroud, L., Spiro III, A., Ward, K. D., & Weiss, S. (2002). Hostility, the metabolic syndrome, and incident coronary heart disease. *Health Psychology, 21,* 588–593.

Nicholson, R. A., et al. (1997). Utility of MMPI-2 indicators of response distortion: Receiver operating characteristic analysis. *Psychological Assessment, 9,* 471–479.

Nickel, M. K., Muehlbacher, M., Nickel, C., Kettler, C. C., Gil, F. P., Bachler, E., et al. (2006). Aripiprazole in the treatment of patients with borderline personality disorder: A double-blind, placebo-controlled study. *American Journal of Psychiatry, 163,* 833–838.

Nickerson, K. J., Helms, J. E., & Terrell, F. (1994). Cultural mistrust, opinions about mental illness, and Black students' attitudes toward seeking psychological help from White counselors. *Journal of Counseling Psychology, 41,* 378–385.

Nicolosi, A., Laumann, E. O., Glasser, D. B., Brock, G., King, R., & Gingell, C. (2006). Sexual activity, sexual disorders and associated help-seeking behavior among mature adults in five anglophone countries from the Global Survey of Sexual Attitudes and Behaviors (GSSAB). *Journal of Sex & Marital Therapy, 32,* 331–342

Nierenberg, A. A., et al. (2000). Timing of onset of antidepressant response with fluoxetine treatment. *American Journal of Psychiatry, 157,* 1429–1435.

Nierenberg, A. A., Ostacher, M. J., Calabrese, J. R., Ketter, T. A., Marangell, L. B., Miklowitz, D. J., et al. (2006). Treatment-resistant bipolar depression: A step-BD equipoise randomized effectiveness trial of antidepressant augmentation with lamotrigine, inositol, or risperidone. *American Journal of Psychiatry, 163,* 210–216.

Nigg, J. T. (2001). Is ADHD a disinhibitory disorder? *Psychological Bulletin, 127*(5), 571–598.

Nigg, J. T., & Casey, B.J. (2005). An integrative theory of attention-deficit/hyperactivity disorder based on the cognitive and affective neurosciences. *Developmental Psychopathology, 17,* 785–806.

Nigg, J. T., & Goldsmith, H. H. (1994). Genetics of personality disorders: Perspectives from personality and psychopathology research. *Psychological Bulletin, 115,* 346–380.

Nigg, J. T., et al. (1992). Malevolent object representations in borderline personality disorder and major depression. *Journal of Abnormal Psychology, 101,* 61–67.

NIH (National Institutes of Health). (2002). Mimicking brain's "all clear" quells fear in rats, *NIH News Release,* Posted November 6, 2002.

Nishith, P., Mechanic, M. B., & Resick, P. A. (2000). Prior interpersonal trauma: The contribution to current PTSD symptoms in female rape victims. *Journal of Abnormal Psychology, 109,* 20–25.

Nix, G., Watson, C., Pyszczynski, T., & Greenberg, J. (1995). Reducing depressive affect through external focus of attention. *Journal of Social and Clinical Psychology, 14,* 36–52.

Noaghiul, S., & Hibbeln, J. R. (2003). Cross-national comparisons of seafood consumption and rates of bipolar disorders. *American Journal of Psychiatry, 160,* 2222–2227.

Nock, M. K. (2002). A multiple-baseline evaluation of the treatment of food phobia in a young boy. *Journal of Behavior Therapy and Experimental Psychiatry, 33,* 217–225.

Nock, M. K., Kazdin, A. E., Hiripi, E., & Kessler, R. C. (2006). Prevalence, subtypes, and correlates of *DSM-IV* conduct disorder in the National Comorbidity Survey Replication. *Psychological Medicine, 36,* 699–710.

Nolan, S. A., Glynn, C., & Garber, J. (2003). Prospective relations between rejection and depression in young adolescents, *Journal of Personality and Social Psychology, 85,* 745–755.

Nolen-Hoeksema, S. (1991). Responses to depression and their effects on the duration of depressive episodes. *Journal of Abnormal Psychology, 100,* 569–582.

Nolen-Hoeksema, S. (2000). The role of rumination in depressive disorders and mixed anxiety/depressive symptoms. *Journal of Abnormal Psychology, 109,* 504–511.

Nolen-Hoeksema, S., & Girgus, J. S. (1994). The emergence of gender differences in depression during adolescence. *Psychological Bulletin, 115,* 424–443.

Nolen-Hoeksema, S., Girgus, J. S., & Seligman, M. E. P. (1992). Predictors and consequences of childhood depressive symptoms: A 5-year longitudinal study. *Journal of Abnormal Psychology, 101,* 405–422.

Nolen-Hoeksema, S., Morrow, J., & Fredrickson, B. L. (1993). Response styles and the duration of episodes of depressed mood. *Journal of Abnormal Psychology, 102,* 20–28.

Noonan, D. (2000, September 25). Why drugs cost so much. *Newsweek,* pp. 22–30.

Noonan, D. (2003, September 8). "Allowed to be odd." *Newsweek,* p. 50.

Norcross, J. C., Beutler, L. E., & Levant, R. F. (Eds.). (2005). *Evidence-based practices in mental health: Debate and dialogue on the fundamental questions.* Washington, DC: American Psychological Association.

Norcross, J. C., Koocher, G. P., & Garofalo, A. (2006). Discredited psychological treatments and tests: A Delphi poll. *Professional Psychology: Research & Practice, 37,* 515–522.

Nordhus, I. H., & Pallesen, S. (2003). Psychological treatment of late-life anxiety: An empirical review. *Journal of Consulting and Clinical Psychology, 71,* 643–651.

Norris, F. N., Murphy, A. D., Baker, C. K., Perilla, J. L., Rodriguez, F. G, & Rodriguez, J. de J. (2003). Epidemiology of trauma and posttraumatic stress disorder in Mexico. *Journal of Abnormal Psychology, 112,* 646–656.

North, C. S., & Pfefferbaum, B. (2002). Research on the mental health effects of terrorism. *Journal of the American Medical Association, 288,* 633–636.

Nowell, P. D., et al. (1998). Effective treatments for selected sleep disorders. In P. E. Nathan & J. M. Gorman (Eds.), *A guide to treatments that work* (pp. 531–543). New York: Oxford University Press.

Noyes, R., et al. (1993). The validity of *DSM-III-R* hypochondriasis. *Archives of General Psychiatry, 50,* 961–970.

Nucifora, F. C., Jr., Sasaki, M., Peters, M. F., Huang, H., Cooper, J. K., Yamada, M., et al. (2001). Interference by Huntington and atrophin-1 with cbp-mediated transcription leading to cellular toxicity. *Science, 291,* 2423–2428.

Nunes, E. V., & Levin, F. R. (2004). Treatment of depression in patients with alcohol or other drug dependence: A meta-analysis. *Journal of the American Medical Association, 291,* 1887–1896.

Nunomura, A., Castellani, R. J., Lee, H., Moreira, P. I., Zhu, X., Perry, G., et al. (2006). Neuropathology in Alzheimer's Disease: Awaking from a hundred-year-old dream. *Science of Aging Knowledge Environment, 2006,* e10.

Nurnberger, J. I., et al. (2001). Evidence for a locus on chromosome 1 that influences vulnerability to alcoholism and affective disorder. *American Journal of Psychiatry, 158,* 718–724.

Nussbaum, R. L., & Ellis, C. E. (2003). Alzheimer's disease and Parkinson's disease. *New England Journal of Medicine, 348,* 1356–64.

Nutrition, obesity and perception. (2001, January 9). *CNN Web Posting.* Retrieved January 11, 2001, from http://www.cnn.com/2001/HEALTH/children/01/09/overweight.kids/index.html.

O

O'Brien, C. P., & McKay, J. (1998). Psychopharmacological treatments of substance use disorders. In P. E. Nathan & J. M. Gorman (Eds.), *A guide* to treatments that work (pp. 127–155). New York: Oxford University Press.

O'Brien, C. P., Volkow, N., & Li, T.-K. (2006). What's in a word? Addiction versus dependence in DSM-V. American Journal of Psychiatry, 163, 764–765.

O'Brien, K. M., & Vincent, N. K. (2003). Psychiatric comorbidity in anorexia and bulimia nervosa: Nature, prevalence, and causal relationships. Clinical Psychology Review, 23, 57–74.

O'Connor v. Donaldson, 95 S. Ct. 2486 (1975).

O'Connor, A. (2004, March 16). In sex, brain studies show, "la difference" still holds. The New York Times, Science Times, p. F5.

O'Connor, E. (2001a, January). Law sanctions new treatment for heroin addiction—and recommends psychological counseling. Monitor on Psychology, p. 18.

O'Connor, E. (2001b, February). Researchers pinpoint potential cause of autism. Monitor on Psychology, p. 13.

O'Connor, P. G. (2000). Treating opioid dependence—new data and new opportunities. The New England Journal of Medicine, 343, 1332–1334. [Editorial]

O'Connor, T. G., McGuire, S., Reiss, D., Hetherington, E. M., & Plomin, R. (1998). Co-occurrence of depressive symptoms and antisocial behavior in adolescence: A common genetic liability. Journal of Abnormal Psychology, 107, 27–37.

O'Donnell, J. (2003, April 24). Traffic deaths rise to 12-year high. USA Today, p. 1D.

O'Donohue, W., McKay, J. S., & Schewe, P. A. (1999). Rape: The roles of outcome expectancies and hypermasculinity. Sexual Abuse Journal of Research and Treatment, 8, 133–141.

O'Farrell, T. J., et al. (1996). Cost-benefit and cost-effectiveness analyses of behavioral marital therapy as an addition to outpatient alcoholism treatment. Journal of Substance Abuse, 8, 145–166.

O'Hara, M. W. (2003, November). Clinician's Research Digest, Supplemental Bulletin 29. 1–2.

O'Hara, M. W., Stuart, S., Gorman, L. L., & Wenzel, A. (2000). Efficacy of interpersonal psychotherapy for postpartum depression. Archives of General Psychiatry, 57, 1039–1045.

O'Leary, A. (1990). Stress, emotion, and human immune functions. Psychological Bulletin, 108, 382–383.

O'Leary, D. S., Andreasen, N. C., Hurtig, R. R., Kesler, M. L., Rogers, M., Arndt, S., et al. (1996). Auditory attentional deficits in patients with schizophrenia: A positron emission tomography study. Archives of General Psychiatry, 53, 633–641.

Odeh, M. S., Zeiss, R. A., & Huss, M. T. (2006). Cues they use: Clinicians' endorsement of risk cues in predictions of dangerousness. Behavioral Sciences & the Law, 24, 147–156.

Oei, T. P. S., & Shuttlewood, G. J. (1996). Specified and nonspecific factors in psychotherapy: A case of cognitive therapy for depression. Clinical Psychology Review, 16, 83–103.

Oei, T. P. S., Bullbeck, K., & Campbell, J. M. (2006). Cognitive change process during group cognitive behaviour therapy for depression. Journal of Affective Disorders, 92, 231–241.

Ogdie, M. N., Fisher, S. E., Yang, M. Ishii, J., Francks, C., Loo, S. K., et al. (2004). Attention deficit hyperactivity disorder: Fine mapping supports linkage to 5p13, 6q12, 16p13, and 17p11. American Journal of Human Genetics, 75, 661–668.

Ogloff, J. R. P., Roberts, C. F., & Roesch, R. (1993). The insanity defense: Legal standards and clinical assessment. Applied & Preventive Psychology, 2, 163–178.

Öhman, A., & Mineka, S. (2001). Fears, phobias, and preparedness: Toward an evolved module of fear and fear learning. Psychological Review, 108, 483–522.

Okie, S. (2006). ADHD in adults. New England Journal of Medicine, 354, 2637–2641.

Okubo, Y., et al. (1997). Decreased prefrontal dopamine D1 receptors in schizophrenia revealed by PET. Nature, 385, 634–636.

Olatunjia, B. O., Sawchuk, C. N., Deacon, B. J., Tolin, D. F., Lilienfeld, S. O., Williams, N. L., et al. (2005). The Anxiety Sensitivity Profile revisited: Factor structure and psychometric properties in two nonclinical samples. Journal of Anxiety Disorders, 19, 603–625.

Oldham, J. M. (1994). Personality disorders: Current perspectives. Journal of the American Medical Association, 272, 213–220.

Oldham, J. M. (2006). Borderline personality disorder and suicidality. American Journal of Psychiatry, 163, 20–26.

Olesen, J. (1994). Understanding the biologic basis of migraine. New England Journal of Medicine, 331, 1713–1714.

Olff, M., Langeland, W., Draijer, N., & Gersons B. P. R. (2007). Gender differences in posttraumatic stress disorder. Psychological Bulletin, 133, 183–204.

Olfson, M., Blanco, C., Liu, L., Moreno, C., & Laje, G. (2006). National trends in the outpatient treatment of children and adolescents with antipsychotic drugs. Archives of General Psychiatry, 63, 679–685.

Olfson, M., Gameroff, M. J., Marcus, S. C., Greenberg T., & Shaffer, D. (2005). Emergency treatment of young people following deliberate self-harm. Archives of General Psychiatry, 62, 1122–1128.

Olfson, M., Guardino, M., Struening, E., Schneier, F. R., Hellman, F., & Klein, D. F. (2000). Barriers to the treatment of social anxiety. American Journal of Psychiatry, 157, 542–548.

Olfson, M., Marcus, S., Sackeim, H. A., Thompson, J., & Pincus, H. A. (1998). Use of ECT for the inpatient treatment of recurrent major depression. American Journal of Psychiatry, 155, 22–29.

Olfson, M., Uttaro, T., Carson, W. H., & Tafesse, E. (2005). Male sexual dysfunction and quality of life in schizophrenia. Journal of Clinical Psychiatry, 66, 331–338.

Olincy, A., Harris, J.G., Johnson, L.L., Pender, V., Kongs, S., Allensworth, D., et al. (2006). Proof-of-concept trial of an alpha 7 nicotinic agonist in schizophrenia. Archives of General Psychiatry, 63, 630–638.

Olivardia, R., Pope, H. G. Jr., Borowiecki III, J. J., & Cohane, G. H. (2004). Biceps and body image: The relationship between muscularity and self-esteem, depression, and eating disorder symptoms. Psychology of Men & Masculinity, 5, 2, 112–120.

Olson, E. (2001, October 7). Countries lag in treating mental illness, W. H. O. says. The New York Times, p. A24.

Olson, L. (2000). Combating Parkinson's disease—Step three. Science, 290, 721–724.

Olson, S. E. (1997). Becoming one: A story of triumph over multiple personality disorder. Pasadena, CA: Trilogy Books.

Onitsuka, T., Niznikiewicz, M. A., Spencer, K. M., Frumin, M., Kuroki, N., Lucia, L.C., et al. (2006). Functional and structural deficits in brain regions subserving face perception in schizophrenia. American Journal of Psychiatry, 163, 455–462.

Onstad, S., Skre, I., Torgensen, S., & Kringlen, E. (1991). Twin concordance for DSM-III-R schizophrenia. Acta Psychiatrica Scandinavica, 83, 395–401.

Oquendo, M.A., Friend, J. M., Halberstam, B., Brodsky, B. S., Burke, A. K., Grunebaum, M. F., Malone, K. M., & Mann, J. J. (2003). Association of comorbid posttraumatic stress disorder and major depression with greater risk for suicidal behavior. American Journal of Psychiatry, 160, 580–582.

Ormel, J., Oldehinkel, A. J., & Brilman, E. I. (2001). The interplay and etiological continuity of neuroticism, difficulties, and life events in the etiology of major and subsyndromal, first and recurrent depressive episodes in later life. American Journal of Psychiatry, 158, 885–891.

Ortega, A. N., Rosenheck, R., Alegria, M., & Desai, R. A. (2000). Acculturation and the lifetime risk of psychiatric and substance use disorders among Hispanics. Journal of Nervous & Mental Disease, 188, 728–735.

Orth-Gomér, K., Wamala, S. P., Horsten, M., Schenck-Gustafsson, K., Schneiderman, N., & Mittleman, M. A. (2000). Marital stress worsens prognosis in women with coronary heart disease: The Stockholm Female Coronary Risk Study. Journal of the American Medical Association, 284, 3008–3014.

Osborn, I. (1998). The hidden epidemic of obsessive-compulsive disorder. New York: Random House.

Osborne, L. (2001, May 6). Regional disturbances. The New York Times, p. A17.

Osborne, L. (2002). American normal: The hidden world of Asperger Syndrome. Katlenburg-Lindau, Germany: Copernicus Books.

Osman, S. L. (2003). Predicting men's rape perceptions based on the belief that "No" really means "Yes." Journal of Applied Social Psychology, 33(4), 683–692.

Öst, L. (1987). Age of onset in different phobias. Journal of Abnormal Psychology, 96, 223–229.

Öst, L. (1992). Blood and injection phobia: Background and cognitive, physiological, and behavioral variables. Journal of Abnormal Psychology, 101, 68–74.

Öst, L-G., Svensson, L., Hellström, K., & Lindwall, R. (2001). One-session treatment of specific phobias in youths: A randomized clinical trial. Journal of Consulting and Clinical Psychology, 69, 814–824.

Ostir, G. V., Berges, I. M., Markides, K. S., & Ottenbacher, K. J. (2006) Hypertension in older adults and the role of positive emotions. Psychosomatic Medicine, 68, 727–733.

Ostler, K., Thompson, C., Kinmonth, A. L., Peveler, R. C., Stevens, L., & Stevens, A. (2001). Influence of socio-economic deprivation on the prevalence and outcome of depression in primary care. British Medical Journal, 178, 12–17.

Otto, M. W. (2001, February). A pilot study of CBT for bipolar disorders. Journal Watch Psychiatry, 7, 9.

Otto, M. W. (2006, September 1). Three types of treatment for depression: a comparison. Journal Watch Psychiatry. Retrieved September 4, 2006, from http://psychiatry.jwatch.org/cgi/content/full/2006/901/2.

Otto, M. W., Pollack, M. H., & Maki, K. M. (2000). Empirically supported treatments for panic disorder: Costs, benefits, and stepped care. Journal of Consulting and Clinical Psychology, 68, 556–563.

Ouellette, S. C., & DiPlacido, J. (2001). Personality's role in the protection and enhancements of health: Where the research has been, where it is stuck, how it might move. In A. Baum, T. A. Revenson, & J. E. Singer (Eds.), Handbook of health psychology (pp. 3–318). Mahwah, NJ: Lawrence Erlbaum Associates.

Ouimette, P. C., Finney, J. W., & Moos, R. H. (1997). Twelve-step and cognitive-behavioral treatment for substance abuse: A comparison of treatment

effectiveness. Journal of Consulting and Clinical Psychology, 65, 230–240.

Overholser, J. C. (2000). Cognitive-behavioral treatment of panic disorder. Psychotherapy: Theory, Research, Practice, Training, 37, 247–256.

Overmier, J. B. L., & Seligman, M. E. P. (1967). Effect of inescapable shock upon subsequent escape and avoidance learning. Journal of Comparative and Physiological Psychology, 63, 28–33.

Ozelius, L. J., Senthil, G., Saunders-Pullman, R., Ohmann, E., Deligtisch, A., Tagliati, M., et al. (2006). LRRK2 G2019S as a Cause of Parkinson's disease in Ashkenazi Jews. New England Journal of Medicine, 354, 424–425.

Ozer, E. J., & Weiss, D. S. (2004). Who develops posttraumatic stress disorder? Current Directions in Psychological Science, 13, 169–172.

Ozer, E. J., Best, S. R., Lipsey, T. L., & Weiss, D. S. (2003). Predictors of posttraumatic stress disorder and symptoms in adults: A meta-analysis. Psychological Bulletin, 129, 52–73.

P

Palinkas, L. A., Wingard, D. L., & Barrett-Connor, E. (1990). The biocultural context of social networks and depression among the elderly. Social Science and Medicine, 4, 441–447.

Pallesen, S., Hilde, I. N., Havik, O. E., & Nielsen, G. H. (2001). Clinical assessment and treatment of insomnia. Professional Psychology: Research and Practice, 32, 115–124.

Pallesen, S., Molde, H., Arnestad, H. M., Skutle, A., Menzoni, R. & Holsten, F. (2006). Pharmacological treatment of pathological gambling. Tidsskr Nor Laegeforen, 126, 2408.

Palmer, C. A., & Hazelrigg, M. (2000). The guilty but mentally ill verdict: A review and conceptual analysis of intent and impact. Journal of the American Academy of Psychiatry and the Law, 28, 47–54.

Palmiter, D. Jr., & Renjilian, D. (2003). Clinical Web pages: Do they meet expectations? Professional Psychology: Research and Practice, 34, 164–169.

Panagiotakos, D. B., Pitsavos, C., Chrysohoou, C., Kavouras, S., Stefanadis, C., & ATTICA Study. (2005). The associations between leisure-time physical activity and inflammatory and coagulation markers related to cardiovascular disease: The ATTICA Study. Preventive Medicine, 40, 432–437.

Panek, R. (2002, November 24). Hmm, what did you mean by all that, Dr. Freud? The New York Times, Section AR, p. 36.

Pankratz, N., Nichols, W. C., Uniacke, S. K., Halter, C., Rudolph, A., Shults, C., et al. (2002). Genome screen to identify susceptibility genes for Parkinson disease in a sample without Parkinson mutations. American Journal of Human Genetics, 71, 124–135.

Park, C. L. (2004). Positive and negative consequences of alcohol consumption in college students. Addictive Behaviors, 29, 311–321.

Parker, G., Gibson, N. A., Brotchie, H., Heruc, G., Rees, A.-M., & Hadzi-Pavlovic, D. (2006). Omega-3 fatty acids and mood disorders. American Journal of Psychiatry, 163, 969–978.

Parker, G., Gladstone, G., & Chee, K. T. (2001). Depression in the planet's largest ethnic group: The Chinese. American Journal of Psychiatry, 158, 857–864.

Parkinson Study Group. (2000). Pramipexole vs. levodopa as initial treatment for Parkinson disease: A randomized controlled trial. Journal of the American Medical Association, 284, 1931–1938.

Parloff, R. (2003, February 3). Is fat the next tobacco? Fortune, pp. 51–54.

Parnas, J., et al. (1993). Lifetime DSM-III-R diagnostic outcomes in the offspring of schizophrenic mothers: Results from the Copenhagen High-Risk Study. Archives of General Psychiatry, 50, 707–714.

Parsey, R.V., Ramin, S., Hastings, M. A., Quendon, X., H., Goldman, D., Huang, Y.-Y., Simpson, N., et al. (2006). Lower serotonin transporter binding potential in the human brain during major depressive episodes. American Journal of Psychiatry, 163, 52–58.

Pato, M. T., Pato, C. N., & Pauls, D. L. (2002). Recent findings in the genetics of OCD. Clinical Psychiatry, 63, (Suppl. 6):30–33.

Pato, M. T., Schindler, K. M., & Pato, C. N (2001). The genetics of obsessive-compulsive disorder. Currrent Psychiatry Reports, 3, 163–168.

Patrick, C. J., Cuthbert, B. N., & Lang, P. J. (1994). Emotion in the criminal psychopath: Fear image processing. Journal of Abnormal Psychology, 103, 523–534.

Patrick, D. L., et al. (2005). Premature ejaculation: An observational study of men and their partners. Journal of Sexual Medicine, 2, 358–367.

Patton, G. C., Coffey, C., Carlin, J. B., Degenhardt, L., Lynskey, M., Hall, W., et al. (2002). Cannabis use and mental health in young people: Cohort study. British Medical Journal, 325, 1195–1198.

Paul, G. L., & Lentz, R. J. (1977). Psychosocial treatment of chronic mental patients: Milieu versus social-learning programs. Cambridge, MA: Harvard University Press.

Paul-Labrador, M., Polk, D., Dwyer, J. H., Velasquez, I., Nidich, S., Rainforth, M., et al. (2006). Effects of a randomized controlled trial of transcendental meditation on components of the metabolic syndrome in subjects with coronary heart disease. Archives of Internal Medicine, 166, 1218–1224.

Paulesu, E., Demonet, J. F., Fazio, F., McCrory, E., Chanoine, V., Brunswick, N., et al. (2001). Dyslexia: Cultural diversity and biological unity. *Science, 291,* 2165–2167.

Paulesu, E., Frith, C. D., & Frackowisk, R. S. J. (1993). The neural correlates of the verbal component of working memory. *Nature, 362,* 342–344.

Pauli, P., Dengler, W., Wiedemann, G., Montoya, P., Flor, H., Birbaumer, N., et al. (1997). Behavioral and neurophysiological evidence for altered processing of anxiety-related words in panic disorder. *Journal of Abnormal Psychology, 106,* 213–220.

Pear, R. (2000, March 20). White House seeks to curb pills used to calm young. *The New York Times online.*

Pearson, C. A., & Gleaves, D. H. (2006). The multiple dimensions of perfectionism and their relation with eating disorder features. *Personality and Individual Differences, 41,* 225–235.

Peirce, T. R., Bray, N. J., Williams, N. M., Norton, N., Moskvina, V., Preece, B., et al. (2005). Convergent evidence for 2',3'-cyclic nucleotide 3'-phosphodiesterase as a possible susceptibility gene for schizophrenia. *Archives of General Psychiatry, 63,* 18–24.

Pelham, W. E., Burrows-MacLean, L., Gnagy, E.M., Fabiano, G., A., Coles, E. K., Tresco, K. E., et al. (2005). Transdermal methylphenidate, behavioral, and combined treatment for children with ADHD. *Experimental and Clinical Psychopharmacology, 13,* 111–126.

Pelham, W. E., Hoza, B., Pillow, D. R., Gna gy, E. M., Kipp, H. L., Greiner, A. R., et al. (2002). Effects of Methylphenidate and expectancy on children with ADHD: Behavior, academic performance, and attributions in a summer treatment program and regular classroom settings. *Journal of Consulting and Clinical Psychology, 70,* 320–335.

Pelkonen, M., & Marttunen, M. (2003). Child and adolescent suicide: Epidemiology, risk factors, and approaches to prevention. *Paediatric Drugs, 5,* 243–65.

Peltzer, K., & Machleidt, W. (1992). A traditional (African) approach towards the therapy of schizophrenia and its comparison with Western models. *Therapeutic Communities International Journal for Therapeutic and Supportive Organizations, 13,* 229–242.

Penadés, R., Catalán. R., Salamero, M., Boget, T., Puig, O., Guarch, J., et al. (2006). Cognitive Remediation therapy for outpatients with chronic schizophrenia: A controlled and randomized study. *Schizophrenia Research, 87,* 323–331.

Pengilly, J. W., & Dowd, E. T. (2000). Hardiness and social support as moderators of stress. *Journal of Clinical Psychology, 56,* 813–820.

Penn, D. L. (1998, June). Assessment and treatment of social dysfunction in schizophrenia. *Clinician's Research Digest, Supplemental Bulletin 18,* 1–2.

Penn, D. L., & Mueser, K. T. (1996). Research update on the psychosocial treatment of schizophrenia. *American Journal of Psychiatry, 153,* 607–617.

Penn, D. L., Combs, D. R., Ritchie, M., Francis, J., Cassisi, J., Morris, S., et al. (2000). Emotion recognition in schizophrenia: Further investigation of generalized versus specific deficit models. *Journal of Abnormal Psychology, 109,* 555–558.

Penn, D. L., Waldheter, E. J., Perkins, D. O., Mueser, K. T., & Lieberman, J. A. (2005). Psychosocial treatment for first-episode psychosis: A research update. *American Journal of Psychiatry, 162,* 2220.

Penninx, B. W., Guralnik, J. M., Bandeen-Roche, K., Kasper, J. D., Simonsick, E. M., Ferrucci, L., et al. (2001). The protective effect of emotional vitality on adverse health outcomes in disabled older women. *Journal of the American Geriatrics Society, 48,* 1359–1366.

Peplau, L. A. (2003). Human sexuality: How do men and women differ? *Current Directions in Psychological Science, 12,* 37–40.

Peppard, P. E., Szklo-Coxe, M., Hla, K. M., & Young, T. (2006). Longitudinal association of sleep-related breathing disorder and depression. *Archives of Internal Medicine, 166,* 1709–1715.

Peppard, P. E., Young, T., Palta, M., & Skatrud, J. (2000). Prospective study of the association between sleep-disordered breathing and hypertension. *The New England Journal of Medicine, 342,* 1378–1384.

Perälä, J., Suvisaari, J., Saarni, S. I., Kuoppasalmi, K., Isometsä, E., Pirkola, S., Partonen, T., et al. (2007). Lifetime Prevalence of psychotic and bipolar I disorders in a general population. *Archives of General Psychiatry, 64,* 19–28.

Perlin, M. L. (1994). Law and the delivery of mental health services in the community. *American Journal of Orthopsychiatry, 64,* 194–208.

Perry, J. C., & Bond M. (2000). Empirical studies of psychotherapy for personality disorders. In J. G. Gunderson & G. O. Gabbard, *Psychotherapy for personality disorders* (pp. 1–31). Washington, DC: American Psychiatric Press.

Perry, W. (2003). Let's call the whole thing off: A response to Dawes (2001). *Psychological Assessment, 15,* 582–585.

Persaud, R. (2000). Recurrent depression and stressful life events: In reply. *Archives of General Psychiatry, 57,* 617. [Letter]

Peterson, A. V., Jr., Lerouxa, B. G., Bricker, J., Kealeya, K. A., Marek, P. M., Sarason, I. G., et al. (2006). Nine-year prediction of adolescent smoking by number of smoking parents. *Addictive Behaviors, 31,* 788–801.

Peterson, E. D., Shaw, L. K., DeLong, E. R., Pryor, D. B., Califf, R. M., & Mark, D. B. (1997). Racial variation in the use of coronary-revascular-

ization procedures—Are the differences real? Do they matter? *The New England Journal of Medicine, 336,* 480–486.

Petrie, K. J., Booth, R. J., & Pennebaker, J. W. (1998). The immunological effects of thought suppression. *Journal of Personality and Social Psychology, 75,* 1264–1272.

Petry, N. M. (2003). Patterns and correlates of Gamblers Anonymous attendance in pathological gamblers seeking professional treatment. *Addictive Behavior, 27,* 1–14.

Petry, N. M., & Martin, B. (2002). Low-cost contingency management for treating cocaine- and opioid-abusing methadone patients. *Journal of Consulting and Clinical Psychology, 70,* 398–405.

Petry, N. M., Alessi, S. M., Marx, J., Austin, M., & Tardif, M. (2005). Vouchers versus prizes: Contingency management treatment of substance abusers in community settings. *Journal of Consulting and Clinical Psychology, 73,* 1005–1014.

Petry, N. M., Ammerman, Y., Bohl, J., Doersch, A., Gay, H., Kadden, R., et al. (2006). Cognitive-behavioral therapy for pathological gamblers. *Journal of Consulting and Clinical Psychology, 74,* 555–567.

Petticrew, M., Bell, R. & Hunter, D. (2002). Influence of psychological coping on survival and recurrence in people with cancer: Systematic review. *British Medical Journal, 325,* 1066–1069.

Pettingale, K. W. (1985). Towards a psychobiological model of cancer: Biological considerations. Special issue: Cancer and the mind. *Social Science and Medicine, 20,* 779–787.

Peyron, C., Faraco, J., Rogers, W., Ripley, B., Overeem, S., & Charnay, Y. (2000). A mutation in a case of early onset narcolepsy and a generalized absence of hypocretin peptides in human nacroleptic brains. *Nature Medicine, 6,* 991–997.

Pfammatter, M., Junghan, U. M., & Brenner, H. D. (2006). Efficacy of psychological therapy in schizophrenia: Conclusions from meta-analyses. *Schizophrenia Research, 32*(1 Suppl), S64-S80.

Pfeffer, C. R. (2007). The FDA pediatric advisories and changes in diagnosis and treatment of pediatric depression. *American Journal of Psychiatry, 164,* 843–846.

Phaf, R. H., Geurts, H., & Eling, P. A. T. M. (2000). Word frequency and word stem completion in Korsakoff patients. *Journal of Clinical & Experimental Neuropsychology, 22,* 817–829.

Philaretou, A. G. (2006). Female exotic dancers: Intrapersonal and interpersonal perspectives. *Sexual Addiction & Compulsivity, 13,* 41–52.

Philaretou, A. G., Mahfouz, A. Y., & Allen, K. R. (2005). Use of Internet pornography and men's well-being. *International Journal of Men's Health, 4,* 149–169.

Phillips, K. A., & Menard, W. (2006). Suicidality in body dysmorphic disorder: A prospective study. *American Journal of Psychiatry, 163,* 1280–1282.

Phillips, K. A., Albertini, R. S., & Rasmussen, S. A. (2002). A randomized placebo-controlled trial of fluoxetine in body dysmorphic disorder. *Archives of General Psychiatry, 59,* 381–388.

Phillips, K. A., Pagano, M. E., Menard, W., &. Stout, R. L. (2006). A 12-month follow-up study of the course of body dysmorphic disorder. *American Journal of Psychiatry, 163,* 907–912.

Phinney, J. (1989). Stages of ethnic identity in minority group adolescents. *Journal of Early Adolescence, 9,* 34–49.

Phinney, J., & Alipuria, L. (1990). Ethnic identity in older adolescents from four ethnic groups. *Journal of Adolescence, 13,* 171–183.

Phinney, J., Lochner, B., & Murphy, R. (1990). Ethnic identity development and psychological adjustment in adolescence. In A. Stiffman & L. Davis (Eds.), *Ethnic issues in adolescent mental health* (pp. 53–72). Newbury Park, CA: Sage.

Pianta, R. C., & Egeland, B. (1994). Relation between depressive symptoms and stressful life events in a sample of disadvantaged mothers. *Journal of Consulting and Clinical Psychology, 62,* 1229–1234.

Piasecki, T. M., Jorenby, D. E., Smith, S. S., Fiore, M. C., & Baker, T. B. (2003). Smoking withdrawal dynamics: I. Abstinence distress in lapsers and abstainers. *Journal of Consulting and Clinical Psychology, 112,* 3–13.

Pickering, T. G., (2003). Lifestyle modification and blood pressure control: Is the glass half full or half empty? *Journal of the American Medical Association, 289,* 2131–2132.

Pierce, R. C., & Kumaresan, V. (2006). The mesolimbic dopamine system: The final common pathway for the reinforcing effect of drugs of abuse? *Neuroscience & Biobehavioral Reviews, 30,* 215–238.

Pihl, R. O., Peterson, J., & Finn, P. (1990). Inherited predispostion to alcoholism: Characteristics of sons of male alcoholics. *Journal of Abnormal Psychology, 99,* 291–301.

Pike, K. M., & Rodin, J. (1991). Mothers, daughters, and disordered eating. *Journal of Abnormal Psychology, 101,* 198–204.

Pilling, S., Bebbington, P., Kuipers, E., Garety, P., Geddes, J., Orbach, G., et al. (2002) Psychological treatments in schizophrenia: I. Meta-analysis of family intervention and cognitive behaviour therapy. *Psychological Medicine, 32,* 763–782.

Pinderhughes, E. (1989). *Understanding race, ethnicity and power: Keys to efficacy in clinical practice.* New York: Free Press.

Pine, D. S., and the Research Unit on Pediatric Psychopharmacology Anxiety Study Group (2001). Fluvoxamine for the treatment of anxiety

disorders in children and adolescents. *New England Journal of Medicine, 344*(17), 1279–1285.

Pinel, J. P. J., Assanand, S., & Lehman, D. R. (2000). Hunger, eating, and ill health. *American Psychologist, 55,* 1105–1116.

Pi-Sunyer, X. (2003). A clinical view of the obesity problem. *Science, 299,* 859–860.

Pitman, R. K. (2006). Combat effects on mental health: The more things change, the more they remain the same. *Archives of General Psychiatry, 63,* 127–128.

Pitschel-Walz, G., Leucht, S., Bauml, J., Kissling, W., & Engel, R. R. (2001). The effect of family interventions on relapse and rehospitalization in schizophrenia—a meta-analysis. *Schizophrenia Bulletin, 27*(1), 73–92.

Pliszka, S. R., Glahn, D. C., Semrud-Clikeman, M., Franklin, C., Perez, R. III, Xiong, J., et al. (2006). Neuroimaging of inhibitory control areas in children with attention deficit hyperactivity disorder who were treatment naive or in long-term treatment. *American Journal of Psychiatry, 163,* 1052–1060.

Plomin, R. (2001). Genetic factors contributing to learning and language delays and disabilities. *Child & Adolescent Psychiatric Clinics of North America, 10*(2), 259–277.

Plomin, R. (2003, April). 65 years of DNA. *APS Observer, 16*(4), 7–8.

Plomin, R., & Crabbe, J. C. (2001). DNA. *Psychological Bulletin, 126,* 806–828.

Plomin, R., & McGuffin, P. (2003). Psychopathology in the postgenomic era. *Annual Review of Psychology, 54,* 205–228.

Plomin, R., DeFries, J. C., Craig, I. W., & McGuffin, P. (Eds.). (2003). *Behavioral genetics in the postgenomic era.* Washington, DC: APA Books.

Plomin, R., Owen, M. J., & McGuffin, P. (1994). The genetic basis of complex human behaviors. *Science, 264,* 1733–1739.

Plunkett, A., O'Toole, B., Swanston, H., Oates, R. K., Shrimpton, S., & Parkinson, P. (2001). Suicide risk following child sexual abuse. *Ambulatory Pediatrics, 5,* 262–266.

Polcin, D. L. (1992). Issues in the treatment of dual diagnosis clients who have chronic mental illness. *Professional Psychology: Research and Practice, 23,* 30–37.

Pole, N., Best, S. R., Metzler, T., & Marmar, C. R. (2005). Why are Hispanics at greater risk for PTSD? *Cultural Diversity and Ethnic Minority Psychology, 11,* 144–161

Poling, J., Oliveto, A., Petry, N., Sofuoglu, M., Gonsai, K., Gonzalez, G., et al. (2006). Six-month trial of bupropion with contingency management for cocaine dependence in a methadone-maintained population. *Archives of General Psychiatry, 63,* 219–228.

Polivy, J., & Herman, C. P. (2002). Causes of eating disorders. *Annual Review of Psychology, 53,* 187–213.

Pollack, A. (2004a, January 13). Putting a price on a good night's sleep. *The New York Times,* pp. CF1, F8.

Pollack, A. (2004b, January 13). Sleep experts debate root of insomnia: Body, mind or a little of each. *The New York Times,* p. F8.

Pollan, M. (2003, October 12). The (Agri)cultural contradictions of obesity. *The New York Times Magazine,* pp. 41, 48.

Pollock, V. E. (1992). Meta-analysis of subjective sensitivity to alcohol in sons of alcoholics. *American Journal of Psychiatry, 149,* 1534–1538.

Pope, H. G., Jr. (2002). Cannabis, cognition, and residual confounding. *Journal of the American Medical Association, 287,* 1172–1174.

Pope, H. G., Jr., & Yurgelun-Todd, D. (1996). The residual cognitive effects of heavy marijuana use in college students. *Journal of the American Medical Association, 275,* 521–527.

Pope, H. G., Oliva, P. S., Hudson, J. I., Bodkin, J. A., & Gruber, A. J. (1999). Attitudes towards *DSM-IV* dissociative disorders diagnoses among board-certified American psychiatrists. *American Journal of Psychiatry, 156,* 321–323.

Posener, J. A., Wang, L., Price, J. L., Gado, M. H., Province, M. A., Miller, M. I., et al. (2003). High-dimensional mapping of the hippocampus in depression. *American Journal of Psychiatry, 160,* 83–89.

Potash, J. B., Zandi, P. P., Willour, V. L., Lan, T.-H., Huo, Y., Avramopoulos, D., et al. (2003). Suggestive linkage to chromosomal regions 13q31 and 22q12 in families with psychotic bipolar disorder. *American Journal of Psychiatry, 160,* 680–686.

Potter, J. D. (1997). Hazards and benefits of alcohol. *The New England Journal of Medicine, 337,* 1763–1764.

Poulakis, Z., & Wertheim, E. H. (1993). Relationships among dysfunctional cognitions, depressive symptoms, and bulimic tendencies. *Cognitive Therapy and Research, 17,* 549–559.

Powchik, P., et al. (1998). Postmortem studies in schizophrenia. *Schizophrenia Bulletin, 24,* 325–341.

Power, K., McGoldrick, T., Brown, K., Buchanan, R., Sharp, D., Swanson, V., & Karatzias, A. (2002). A controlled comparison of eye movement desensitization and reprocessing versus exposure plus cognitive restructuring versus wait list in the treatment of post-traumatic stress disorder. *Clinical Psychology and Psychotherapy, 9,* 299–318.

PracticeNet (2003, Summer). Survey results—clinical practice patterns. *American Psychological Association Online.* Retrieved December 11, 2003, from www.apapracticenet.net/results/Summer2003/13.asp.

Pressman, S. D., & Cohen, S. (2005). Does positive affect influence health? *Psychological Bulletin, 131,* 925–971.

Preuss, U. W., Schuckit, M. A., Smith, T. L., Danko, G. P., Bucholz, K. K., Hesselbrock, M. N., et al. (2003). Predictors and correlates of suicide attempts over 5 years in 1,237 alcohol-dependent men and women. *American Journal of Psychiatry, 160,* 56–63.

Price, D. (2004a). Efficacy of sertraline in the treatment of children and adolescents with major depressive disorder. *Journal of the American Medical Association, 291,* 40–41.

Price, D. (2004b). To the editor. *Journal of the American Medical Association, 291,* 40–41. [Letter]

Prigatano, G. P. (1992). Personality disturbances associated with traumatic brain injury. *Journal of Consulting and Clinical Psychology, 60,* 360–368.

Prigerson, H. G., Maciejewski, P. K., & Rosenheck, R. A. (2001). Combat trauma: Trauma with highest risk of delayed onset and unresolved posttraumatic stress disorder symptoms, unemployment, and abuse among men. *Journal of Nervous & Mental Disease, 189,* 99–108.

Prisciandaro, J. J., & Roberts, J. E. A (2005). Taxometric investigation of unipolar depression in the National Comorbidity Survey. *Journal of Abnormal Psychology, 114,* 718–728.

Project MATCH Research Group. (1997). Matching alcoholism treatments to client heterogeneity: Project MATCH posttreatment drinking outcomes. *Journal of Studies on Alcohol, 58,* 7–29.

Proudfoot, J., Ryden, C., Everitt, B., Shapiro, D. A., Goldberg, D., Mann, A., et al. (2004). Clinical efficacy of computerised cognitive-behavioural therapy for anxiety and depression in primary care: Randomised controlled trial. *British Journal of Psychiatry, 185,* 46–54.

Prudic, J., et al. (1996). Resistance to antidepressant medications and short-term clinical response to ETC. *American Journal of Psychiatry, 153,* 985–992.

Prudic, J., et al. (2004). Effectiveness of electroconvulsive therapy in community settings. *Biological Psychiatry, 55,* 301–312.

Prudic, J., Olfson, M., Marcus, S. C., Fuller, R. B., & Sackeim, H. A. (2004). Effectiveness of electroconvulsive therapy in community settings. *Biological Psychiatry, 55,* 301–312.

Pumariega, A. J. (1986). Acculturation and eating attitudes in adolescent girls: A comparative correlational study. *Journal of the American Academy of Child Psychiatry, 25,* 276–279.

Purdum, T. S. (2001, March 30). Non-Hispanic whites a minority, California census figures show. *The New York Times,* pp. A1, A18.

Purisch, A. D. (2001). Misconceptions about the Luria-Nebraska Neuropsychological Battery. *NeuroRehabilitation, 16,* 275–280.

Putnam, F. W., & Carlson, E. B. (1994). "Screening for multiple personality disorder with the Dissociative Experiences Scale": A reply. *American Journal of Psychiatry, 151,* 1249–1250.

Putnam, F. W., Guroff, J. J., Silberman, E. K., Barban, L., & Post, R. M. (1986). The clinical phenomenology of multiple personality disorder: Review of 100 recent cases. *Journal of Clinical Psychiatry, 47,* 285–293.

Pyszczynski, T., & Greenberg, J. (1987). Self-regulatory perseveration and the depressive self-focusing style: A self-awareness theory of reactive depression. *Psychological Bulletin, 102,* 122–138.

Q

Qin, P., Agerbo, E., & Mortensen, P. B. (2003). Suicide risk in relation to socioeconomic, demographic, psychiatric, and familial factors: A national register–based study of all suicides in Denmark, 1981–1997. *American Journal of Psychiatry, 160,* 765–77 2.

Quesnel, C., Savard, J., Simard, S., Ivers, H., & Morin, C. M. (2003). Efficacy of cognitive–behavioral therapy for insomnia in women treated for nonmetastatic breast cancer. *Journal of Consulting and Clinical Psychology, 71,* 189–200.

Quiet Storm. (2004). *I have dissociative identity disorder.* Retrieved March 23, from http://homepage.smc.edu/hart_christian/lectures/14/QStorm.pdf.

R

Rabasca, L. (2000, March). Listening instead of preaching. *Monitor on Psychology, 31,* pp. 50–51.

Rabkin, J. G., Wagner, G. J., & Rabkin R. (2000). A double-blind, placebo-controlled trial of testosterone therapy for HIV-positive men with hypogonadal symptoms. *Archives of General Psychiatry, 57,* 141–147.

Rachman, S. J. (2000). Joseph Wolpe (1915–1997). *American Psychologist, 55,* 431.

Rachman, S. J., & Bichard, S. (1988). The overprediction of fear. *Clinical Psychology Review, 8,* 303–312.

Radel, M., Vallejo, R. L., Iwata, N., Aragon, R., Long, J. C., Virkkunen, M., et al. (2005). Haplotype based localization of an alcohol dependence gene in the 5q34 γ Aminobutyric Acid Type A Gene Cluster. *Archives of General Psychiatry, 62,* 47–55.

Ragland, J. D., et al. (1999). Neuropsychological laterality indices of schizophrenia: Interactions with gender. *Schizophrenia Bulletin, 25,* 79–89.

Ragland, J. D., et al. (2001). Effect of schizophrenia on frontotemporal activity during word encoding and recognition: A PET cerebral blood flow study. *American Journal of* Psychiatry, *158,* 1114–1125.

Ragland, J. D., Gur, R. C., Valdez, J., Turetsky, B. I., Elliott, M., Kohler, C., et al. (2004). Event-related fMRI of frontotemporal activity during word encoding and recognition in schizophrenia. *American Journal of Psychiatry, 161,* 1004–1015.

Räikkönen. K., et al. (1999). Effects of hostility on ambulatory blood pressure and mood during daily living in healthy adults. *Health Psychology, 18,* 44–53.

Raine, A., et al. (2000). Reduced prefrontal gray matter volume and reduced autonomic activity in antisocial personality disorder. *Archives of General Psychiatry, 57,* 119–127.

Rakic, Z., Starcevic, V., Starcevic, V. P., & Marinkovic, J. (1997). Testosterone treatment in men with erectile disorder and low levels of total testosterone in serum. *Archives of Sexual Behavior, 26,* 495–504.

Ralph, D., & McNicholas, T. (2000). UK management guidelines for erectile dysfunction. *British Medical Journal, 321,* 499–503.

Raman, R. P. B., Sheshadri, Y. C., Reddy, J., Girimaji, S. C, Srinath, S., & Raghunandan, V.N.G.P. Is bipolar II disorder misdiagnosed as major depressive disorder in children? *Journal of Affective Disorders, 98,* 263–266.

Ramoz, N., Reichert, J. G., Smith, C. J., Silverman, J. M., Bespalova, I. N., Davis, K. L., et al. (2004). Linkage and association of the mitochondrial aspartate/glutamate carrier SLC25A12 gene with autism. *American Journal of Psychiatry, 161,* 662–669.

Rao, K., DiClemente, R. J., & Ponton, L. E. (1992). Child sexual abuse of Asians compared with other populations. *Journal of the American Academy of Child and Adolescent Psychiatry, 31,* 880–886.

Rao, S. M., Huber, S. J., & Bornstein, R. A. (1992). Emotional changes with multiple sclerosis and Parkinson's disease. *Journal of Consulting and Clinical Psychology, 60,* 369–378.

Rapee, R. M. (1987). The psychological treatment of panic attacks: Theoretical conceptualization and review of evidence. *Clinical Psychology Review, 7,* 427–438.

Rapee, R. M. (1991). Generalized anxiety disorder: A review of clinical features and theoretical concepts. *Clinical Psychology Review, 11,* 419–440.

Raphael, A., J, Golden, C., & Cassidy-Feltgen, S. (2002). The Bender-Gestalt Test (BGT) in forensic assessment. *Journal of Forensic Psychology Practice, 2,* 93–106.

Rapin, I. (1997). Autism. *The New England Journal of Medicine, 337,* 97–104.

Rashotte, C. A., MacPhee, K., & Torgesen, J. K. (2001). The effectiveness of a group reading instruction program with poor readers in multiple grades. *Learning Disability Quarterly, 24*(2), 119–134.

Raskind, W. H. (2001). Current understanding of the genetic basis of reading and spelling disability. *Learning Disability Quarterly, 24*(3), 141–157.

Rasmussen, K. M., Negy, C., Carlson, R., & Burns, J. M. (1997). Suicide ideation and acculturation among low socioeconomic status Mexican American adolescents. *Journal of Early Adolescence, 17,* 390–407.

Rathus, S. A., & Nevid, J. S. (1977). *Behavior therapy.* Garden City, NY: Doubleday.

Rathus, S. A., Nevid, J. S., & Fichner-Rathus, L. (2005). *Human sexuality in a world of diversity* (6th ed.). Boston: Allyn & Bacon.

Ratti, L. A., Humphrey, L. L., & Lyons, J. S. (1996). Structural analysis of families with a polydrug-dependent, bulimic, or normal adolescent daughter. *Journal of Consulting & Clinical Psychology, 64,* 1255–1262.

Ratti, M. T., Bo, P., Giardini, A., & Soragna, D. (2002). Chronic alcoholism and the frontal lobe: Which executive functions are impaired? *Acta Neurology Psychiatrica Scandinavica, 105,* 276–281.

Rauch, S. L., & Jenike, M. A. (1998). Pharmacological treatment of obsessive compulsive disorder. In P. E. Nathan & J. M. Gorman (Eds.), *A guide to treatments that work* (pp. 358–376). New York: Oxford University Press.

Rauschenberger, S. L., & Lynn, S. J. (1995). Fantasy proneness, *DSM-III-R* Axis I psychopathology, and dissociation. *Journal of Abnormal Psychology, 104,* 373–380.

Rawe, J., & Kingsbury, K. (2006, May 22). When colleges go on suicide watch. *Time,* pp. 62–63.

Rawson, R. A., Washton, A., Domier, C. P., & Reiber, C. (2002). Drugs and sexual effects: Role of drug type and gender. *Journal of Substance Abuse Treatment, 22,* 103–108.

Read, J., et al. (2001). Assessing suicidality in adults: Integrati ng childhood trauma as a major risk factor. *Professional Psychology: Research and Practice, 32,* 367–372.

Ready, T. (2000, June 7). Meditation apparently good for the heart as well as the mind. *CNN Web Posting.* Retrieved June 8, 2000, from http://www.cnn.com/2000/HEALTH/06/07/minding. heart.wmd/.

Redd, W. H. (1995). Behavioral research in cancer as a model for health psychology. *Health Psychology, 14,* 99–100.

Redd, W. H., & Jacobsen, P. (2001). Behavioral intervention in comprehensive cancer care. In A. Baum, T. A. Revenson, & J. E. Singer (Eds.), *Handbook of health psychology* (pp. 757–776). Mahwah, NJ: Erlbaum.

Reed, G. M., McLaughlin, C. J., & Milholland, K. (2000). Ten interdisciplinary principles for professional practice in telehealth: Implications for psychology. *Professional Psychology: Research and Practice, 31,* 170–178.

Regehr, C., Hill, J., & Glancy, G. D. (2000). Individual predictors of traumatic reactions in firefighters. *Journal of Nervous & Mental Disease, 188,* 333–339.

Reich, J. (1996). The morbidity of *DSM-III-R* dependent personality disorder. *Journal of Nervous & Mental Disease, 184,* 22–26.

Reichman, M. E. (1994). Alcohol and breast cancer. *Alcohol Health and Research World, 18,* 182–183.

Reifler, B. V. (2006). Play it again, Sam—depression is recurring. *New England Journal of Medicine, 354,* 1189–1190.

Reinisch, J. M. (1990). *The Kinsey Institute new report on sex: What you must know to be sexually literate.* New York: St. Martin's Press.

Reisberg B., Doody, R., Stoffler, A., Schmitt, F., Ferris, S., Mobius, H. J., & Memantine Study Group. (2003). Memantine in moderate-to-severe Alzheimer's disease. *New England Journal of Medicine, 348,* 1333–1341.

Reisberg, B., et al. (1986). Assessment of presenting symptoms. In L. W. Poon (Ed.), *Handbook for clinical memory assessment of older adults* (pp. 108–128). Washington, DC: American Psychological Association.

Reisner, A. D. (1994). Multiple personality disorder diagnosis: A house of cards? *American Journal of Psychiatry, 151,* 629.

Reiss, D. (2005). The interplay between genotypes and family relationships: Reframing concepts of development and prevention. *Current Directions in Psychological Science, 14,* 139–143.

Reitan, R. M., & Wolfson, D. (2000). The neuropsychological similarities of mild and more severe head injury. *Archives of Clinical Neuropsychology, 15,* 433–442.

Remington, G. (2006). Schizophrenia, antipsychotics, and the metabolic syndrome: is there a silver lining? *American Journal of Psychiatry, 163,* 1132–1134

Reneman, L., Lavalaye, J., Schmand, B., de Wolff, F. A., van den Brink, W., den Heeten, G. J., et al. (2001). Cortical serotonin transporter density and verbal memory in individuals who stopped using 3,4-methylenedioxymethamphetamine (MDMA or "Ecstasy"): Preliminary findings. *Archives of General Psychiatry, 58,* 901–906.

Renfrey, G. S. (1992). Cognitive-behavior therapy and the Native American client. *Behavior Therapy, 23,* 321–340.

Researchers gain insight into Huntington's. (2001, March 22). *CNN Web Posting.* Retrieved March 24, 2001, from http://www.cnn.com/2001/HEALTH/conditions/03/22/huntingtons.gene/index.html.

Resick, P. A. (2003). Post hoc reasoning in possible cases of child sexual abuse: Just say no. *Clinical Psychology: Science & Practice, 10* (3), 349–351.

Resick, P. A., Nishith, P., Weaver, T. L., Astin, M. C., & Feuer, C. A. (2002). A comparison of cognitive-processing therapy with prolonged exposure and a waiting condition for the treatment of chronic posttraumatic stress disorder in female rape victims. *Journal of Consulting and Clinical Psychology, 70,* 867–879.

Rey, J. M. (1993). Oppositional defiant disorder. *American Journal of Psychiatry, 150,* 1769–1778.

Rey, J. M., & Tennant, C. C. (2002). Cannabis and mental health: More evidence establishes clear link between use of cannabis and psychiatric illness, *British Medical Journal, 325,* 1183–1184.

Reyna, V. F., & Farley, F. (2006). Risk and rationality in adolescent decision making implications for theory, practice, and public policy. *Psychological Science in the Public Interest, 7,* 2–44.

Reynolds, C. F., Dew, M. A., Pollock, B. J., Mulsant, B. H., Frank, E., Miller, M. D., et al. (2006). Maintenance treatment of major depression in old age. *New England Journal of Medicine, 354,* 1130–1138.

Reynolds, C. F., III, et al. (1996). Treatment outcome in recurrent major depression: A post hoc comparison of elderly ("Young Old") and midlife patients. *American Journal of Psychiatry, 153,* 1288–1292.

Reynolds, K., Lewis, L. B., Nolen, J. D. L., Kinney, G. L., Sathya, B., He, J., et al. (2003). Alcohol consumption and risk of stroke. *Journal of the American Medical Association, 289,* 579–588.

Rhee, S. H., & Waldman, I. D. (2002). Genetic and environmental influences on antisocial behavior: A meta-analysis of twin and adoption studies. *Psychological Bulletin, 128,* 490–529.

Rhee, S. H., Hewitt, J. K., Young, S. E., Corley, R. P., Crowley, T. J., & Stallings, M. C. (2003). Genetic and environmental influences on substance initiation, use, and problem use in adolescents. *Archives of General Psychiatry, 60,* 1256–1264.

Ribisl, K. M., et al. (2000). English language use as a risk factor for smoking initiation among Hispanic and Asian American Adolescents: Evidence for mediation by tobacco-related beliefs and social norms. *Health Psychology, 19,* 403–410.

Ricaurte, G. A., Yuan, J., Hatzidimitriou, G., Cord, B. J., & McCann, U. D. (2002). Severe dopaminergic neurotoxicity in primates after a common recreational dose regimen of MDMA ("ecstasy"). *Science, 297,* 2260–2263.

Ricciardelli, L. A., & McCabe, M. P. (2001). Children's body image concerns and eating disturbance: A review of the literature. *Clinical Psychology Review, 21,* 325–344.

Ricciardelli, L. A., & McCabe, M. P. (2004). A biopsychosocial model of disordered eating and the pursuit of muscularity in adolescent boys. *Psychological Bulletin, 130,* 179–205.

Rice, N., & O'Donohue, W. (2002). Cultural sensitivity: A critical examination. *New Ideas in Psychology, 20,* 35–48.

Richard, D. C. S., & Bobicz, K. (2003, January). Computers and behavioral assessment: 6 years later. *The Behavior Therapist,* pp. 219–223.

Richards, J. C., Edgar, L. V., & Gibbon, P. (1996). Cardiac acuity in panic disorder. *Cognitive Therapy and Research, 20,* 361–376.

Richardson, M. A., Bevans, M. L., Read, L. L., Chao, H. M., Clelland, J. D., et al. (2003). Efficacy of the branched-chain amino acids in the treatment of tardive dyskinesia in men. *American Journal of Psychiatry, 160,* 1117–1124.

Riddle, M. A., Reeve E A., Yaryura-Tobias, J. A, Yang, H. M., Claghorn, J. L., Gaffney, G., et al. (2001). Fluvoxamine for children and adolescents with obsessive-compulsive disorder: A randomized controlled, multicenter trial. *Journal of the American Academy of Child and Adolescent Psychiatry, 40,* 222–229.

Ridley, C. R. (1984). Clinical treatment of the nondisclosing Black client: A therapeutic paradox. *American Psychologist, 39,* 1234–1244.

Ridley, M. (2003). *Nature via nurture genes, experience, and what makes us human.* New York: HarperCollins.

Riedel, B. R. W., & Lichstein, K. L. (2001). Strategies for evaluating adherence to sleep restriction treatment for insomnia. *Behaviour Research and Therapy, 39,* 201–212.

Riether, A. M., & Stoudemire, A. (1988). Psychogenic fugue states: A review. *Southern Medical Journal, 81,* 568–571.

Riley, V. (1981). Psychoneuroendocrine influences on immunocompetence and neoplasia. *Science, 212,* 1100–1109.

Rimer, S. (1999, September 5). Gaps seen in treating depression in elderly. *The New York Times,* pp. 1, 18.

Rimm, E. (2000, May). *Lifestyle may play role in potential for impotence.* Paper presented to the annual meeting of the American Urological Association, Atlanta, GA.

Rinne, T., van den Brink, W., Wouters, L., & van Dyck, R. (2002). SSRI treatment of borderline personality disorder: A randomized, placebo-controlled clinical trial for female patients with borderline personality disorder. *American Journal of Psychiatry, 159,* 2048–2054.

Riso, L. P., duToit, P. L., Blandino, J. A., Penna, S., Dacey, S., Duin, J. S., et al. (2003). Cognitive aspects of chronic depression. *Journal of Abnormal Psychology, 112,* 72–80.

Ritter, C., et al. (2000). Stress, psychosocial resources, and depressive symptomatology during pregnancy in low-income, inner-city women. *Health Psychology, 19,* 576–585.

Ritterband, L. M., Cox, D. J., Walker, L. S., Kovatchev, B., McKnight, L., Patel, K., et al. (2003). An Internet intervention as adjunctive therapy for pediatric encopresis. *Journal of Consulting and Clinical Psychology, 71,* 910–917.

Rivas-Vazquez, R. A., & Blais, M. A. (2002). Pharmacologic treatment of personality disorder. *Professional Psychology: Research and Practice, 33,* 104–107.

Rivas-Vazquez, R. A., Johnson, S. L., Rey, G. J., Blais, M. A., & Rivas-Vazquez, A. (2002). Current treatments for bipolar disorder: A review and update for psychologists. *Professional Psychology: Research and Practice, 33,* 212–223.

Robb, A. S., Silber, T. J., Orrell-Valente, J. K., Valadez-Meltzer, A., Ellis, N., & Dadson, M. J. (2002). Supplemental nocturnal nasogastric refeeding for better short-term outcome in hospitalized adolescent girls with anorexia nervosa. *American Journal of Psychiatry, 159,* 1347–1353.

Roberson, E. D., & Mucke, L. (2006, November 3). 100 years and counting: Prospects for defeating Alzheimer's Disease. *Science, 314,* 781–784.

Robin, R. W., Greene, R. L., Albaugh, B., Caldwell, A., & Goldman, D. (2003). Use of the MMPI-2 in American Indians: I. Comparability of the MMPI2 between two tribes and with the MMPI-2 normative group. *Psychological Assessment, 15,* 351–359.

Robins, L. N., Locke, B. Z., & Reiger, D. A. (1991). An overview of psychiatric disorders in America. In L. N. Robins & D. A. Regier (Eds.), *Psychiatric disorders in America: The Epidemiologic Catchment Area Study* (pp. 328–366). New York: Free Press.

Robins, L. N., Tipp, J., & Przybeck, T. (1991). Antisocial personality. In L. N. Robins & D. A. Regier (Eds.), *Psychiatric disorders in America: The Epidemiologic Catchment Area Study* (pp. 258–290). New York: Free Press.

Robinson, N. M., Zigler, E., & Gallagher, J. J. (2001). Two tails of the normal curve: Similarities and differences in the study of mental retardation and giftedness. *American Psychologist, 55,* 1413–1424.

Robinson, T., et al. (1996). Ethnicity and body dissatisfaction: Are Hispanic and Asian girls at increased risk of eating disorders. *Journal of Adolescent Health, 19,* 384–393.

Rocha, B. A., Scearce-Levie, K., Lucasm J. J., Hiroi, N., Castanon, N., Crabbe, J. C., et al. (1998). Increased vulnerability to cocaine in mice lacking the serotonin-1 B receptor. *Nature, 393,* 175. [Letter]

Rock, C. L., & Curran-Celentano, J. (1996). Nutritional management of eating disorders. *The Psychiatric Clinics of North America, 19,* 701–713.

Rodin, J., Bartoshuk, L., Peterson, C., & Schank, D. (1990). Bulimia and taste: Possible interactions. *Journal of Abnormal Psychology, 99,* 32–39.

Rodríguez de Fonseca, F., Carrera, M. R., Navarro, M., Koob, G. F., & Weiss, R. (1997). Activation of corticotropin- releasing factor in the limbic system during cannabinoid withdrawal. *Science, 276,* 2050–2054.

Roelofs, K., Keijsers, G. P. J., Hoogduin, K. A. L., Näring, G. W. B., & Moene, F. C. (2002). Childhood abuse in patients with conversion disorder. *American Journal of Psychiatry, 159,* 1908–1913.

Roemer, L., & Orsillo, S. M. (2003). Mindfulness: A promising intervention strategy in need of further study. *Clinical Psychology: Science and Practice, 10,* 172–178.

Roesch, R., Zapf, P. A., Golding, S. L., & Skeem, J. L. (1999). Defining and assessing competence to stand trial. In A. K. Hess, I. B. Weiner, et al. (Eds.), *The handbook of forensic psychology* (2nd ed., pp. 327–349). New York: Wiley.

Roesler, A., & Witztum, E. (2000). Pharmacotherapy of paraphilias in the next millennium. *Behavioral Sciences & the Law, 18*(1), 43–56.

Rogan, A. (1986, Fall). Recovery from alcoholism: Issues for black and Native American alcoholics. *Alcohol Health and Research World, 10,* 42–44.

Rogers v. Okin, 478 F. Supp. 1242 (D.Mass. 1979).

Rogers, C. R. (1951). *Client-centered therapy.* Boston: Houghton Mifflin.

Rogers, R., Gillis, J. R., Turner, R. E., & Frise-Smith, T. (1990). The clinical presentation of command hallucinations in a forensic population. *American Journal of Psychiatry, 147,* 1304–1307.

Rogler, L. H., Cortes, D. E., & Malgady, R. G. (1991). Acculturation and mental health status among Hispanics: Convergence and new directions for research. *American Psychologist, 46,* 584–597.

Rohan, K. J., Sigmon, S. T., & Dorhofer, D. M. (2003). Cognitive-behavioral factors in seasonal affective disorder. *Journal of Consulting and Clinical Psychology, 71,* 22–30.

Rohde, P., Lewinsohn, P. M., & Seeley, J. R. (1991). Comorbidity of unipolar depression: II. Comorbidity with other mental disorders in adolescents and adults. *Journal of Abnormal Psychology, 101,* 214–222.

Rojas-Vilches, A. P., & Negy, C. (under review). Latinos' attitudes toward seeking therapy: An intergenerational study between college students and their parents.

Roll, J. M., Petry, N. M., Stitzer, M. L., Brecht, M. L., Peirce, J. M., McCann, M. J., Blaine, J., MacDonald, M., et al. (2006). Contingency management for the treatment of methamphetamine use disorders. *American Journal of Psychiatry, 163,* 1993–1999.

Rose, J. (1996). Anger management: A group treatment program for people with mental retardation. *Journal of Developmental and Physical Disabilities, 8,* 133–149.

Rosen, J. C. (1996). Body dysmorphic disorder: Assessment and treatment. In J. K. Thompson (Ed.), *Body image, eating disorders, and obesity* (pp. 149–170). Washington, DC: American Psychological Association.

Rosen, R. C., & Laumann, E. O. (2003). The prevalence of sexual problems in women: How valid are comparisons across studies? Commentary on Bancroft, Loftus, and Long's (2003) "Distress about sex: A national survey of women in heterosexual relationships." *Archives of Sexual Behavior, 32*(3), 209–211.

Rosen, R. C., & Leiblum, S. R. (1995). Treatment of sexual disorders in the 1990s: An integrated approach. *Journal of Consulting and Clinical Psychology, 63,* 877–890.

Rosen, R. C., Fisher, W. A., Eardley, I., Niederberger, C., Nadel, A., & Sand, M. (2004). Men's Attitudes to Life Events and Sexuality (MALES) Study. *Current Medical Research Opinion, 20,* 607–617.

Rosenberg, D. A. (2003). Münchausen syndrome by proxy: Medical diagnostic criteria. *Child Abuse and Neglect, 27,* 421–430.

Rosenberg, H., & Davis, L. A. (1994). Acceptance of moderate drinking by alcohol treatment services in the United States. *Journal of Studies on Alcohol, 55,* 167–172.

Rosenfarb, I. S., Bellack, A. S., & Aziz, N. (2006). Family interactions and the course of schizophrenia in African American and white patients. *Journal of Abnormal Psychology. 115,* 112–120.

Rosenheck, R. (2000). Cost-effectiveness of services for mentally ill homeless people: The application of research to policy and practice. *American Journal of Psychiatry, 157,* 1563–1570.

Rosenheck, R. A., Leslie, D. L., Sindelar, J., Miller, E. A., Lin, H., Stroup, T. S., et al. (2006). Cost-Effectiveness of second-generation antipsychotics and perphenazine in a randomized trial of treatment for chronic schizophrenia. *American Journal of Psychiatry, 163,* 2080–2089

Rosenheck, R., Kasprow, W., Frisman, L., & Liu-Mares, W. (2003). Cost-effectiveness of supported housing for homeless persons with mental illness. *Archives of General Psychiatry, 60,* 940–951.

Rosenheck, R., Leslie, D., Keefe, R., McEvoy, J., Swartz, M., Perkins, D., et al. (2006). Barriers to employment for people with schizophrenia. *American Journal of Psychiatry, 163,* 411–417.

Rosenheck, R., Perlick, D., Bingham, S., & Collins, J. (2004). In reply. *Journal of the American Medical Association, 291,* 1065–1066.

Rosenheck, R., Perlick, D., Bingham, S., Liu-Mares, W., Collins, J., Warren, S., et al. (2003). Effectiveness and cost of olanzapine and haloperidol in the treatment of schizophrenia: A randomized controlled trial. *Journal of the American Medical Association, 26,* 2693–2702.

Rosenthal, D., et al. (1968). Schizophrenics' offspring reared in adoptive homes. In D. Rosenthal & S. S. Kety (Eds.), *The transmission of schizophrenia.* Oxford: Pergamon Press.

Rosenthal, D., et al. (1975). Parent-child relationships and psychopathological disorder in the child. *Archives of General Psychiatry, 32,* 466–476.

Rosenthal, E. (1993, April 9). Who will turn violent? Hospitals have to guess. *The New York Times;* pp. A1, C12.

Ross, C. A., Anderson, G., Fleisher, W. P., & Norton, G. R. (1991). The frequency of multiple personality disorder among psychiatric inpatients. *American Journal of Psychiatry, 148,* 1717–1720.

Ross, C. A., Miller, S. D., Reagor, P., Bjornson, L., Fraser, G. A., & Anderson, G. (1990). Structured interview data on 102 cases of multiple personality disorder from four centers. *American Journal of Psychiatry, 147,* 596–601.

Ross, C. A., Norton, G. R., & Wozney, K. (1989). Multiple personality disorder: An analysis of 236 cases. *Canadian Journal of Psychiatry, 34,* 413–418.

Ross, D. E. (2000). The deficit syndrome and eye tracking disorder may reflect a distinct subtype within the syndrome of schizophrenia. *Schizophrenia Bulletin, 26,* 855–866.

Ross, E., & Oliver, C. (2003). The assessment of mood in adults who have severe or profound mental retardation. *Clinical Psychology Review, 23,* 225–245.

Ross, R., Dagnone, D., Jones, P. J., Smith, H., Paddags, A., & Hudson, R. (2000). Reduction in obesity and related comorbid conditions after diet-induced weight loss or exercise-induced weight loss in men: A randomized, controlled trial. *Annals of Internal Medicine, 133,* 92–103.

Roth, R. M., Flashman, L. A., Saykin, A. J., McAllister, T. W., & Vidaver, R. (2004). Apathy in schizophrenia: Reduced frontal lobe volume and neuropsychological deficits. *American Journal of Psychiatry, 161,* 157–159.

Roth, T., Soubrane, C., Titeux, L. & Walsh, J. K., on behalf of the Zoladult Study Group (2006). Efficacy and safety of zolpidem-MR: A double-blind, placebo-controlled study in adults with primary insomnia. *Sleep Medicine, 7,* 397–406.

Rothbaum, B. O., Hodges, L., Anderson, P. L., Price, L., & Smith, S. (2002). Twelve-month follow-up of virtual reality and standard exposure therapies for the fear of flying. *Journal of Consulting and Clinical Psychology, 70,* 428–432.

Rotter, J. B. (1966). Generalized expectancies for internal vs. external control of reinforcement. *Psychological Monographs, 1,* 210–609.

Rounsaville, B. J., & Kosten, T. R. (2000). Treatment for opioid dependence: Quality and access. *Journal of the American Medical Association, 283,* 1337–1339. [Editorial]

Rousseau, F., et al. (1991). Direct diagnosis by DNA analysis of the fragile X syndrome of mental retardation. *New England Journal of Medicine, 325,* 1673–1681.

Roy, A. (2003). Characteristics of HIV patients who attempt suicide. *Acta Psychiatrica Scandinavica 107,* 41–44.

Roy, E. (2000). Relation of family history of suicide to suicide attempts in alcoholics. *American Journal of Psychiatry, 157,* 2050–2051.

Roy-Byrne, P. (2006a, February 8). Omega-3 Fatty acids in bipolar depression: Are you what you eat? *Journal Watch Psychiatry.* Retrieved January 14, 2007, from http://psychiatry.jwatch.org/cgi/content/full/2006/208/1.

Roy-Byrne, P. (2006b, September 11). Debriefing after trauma: The final word? *Journal Watch Psychiatry.* Retrieved January 7, 2007, from http://psychiatry.jwatch.org/cgi/content/full/2006/911/1.

Roy-Byrne, P. P., Craske, M. G., Stein, M. B., Sullivan, G., Bystritsky, A., Katon, W., et al. (2005). A randomized effectiveness trial of cognitive-behavioral therapy and medication for primary care panic disorder. *Archives of General Psychiatry, 62,* 290–298.

Rozee, P. D., & Koss, M. P. (2001). Rape: A century of resistance. *Psychology of Women Quarterly, 25*(4), 295–311.

Rozin, P., Bauer, R., & Catanese, D. (2003). Food and life, pleasure and worry, among American college students: gender differences and regional similarities. *Journal of Personality and Social Psychology, 85,* 132–141.

Rubin, L. J. (1996). Childhood sexual abuse: False accusations of "false memory"? *Professional Psychology: Research and Practice, 27,* 447–451.

Rubinstein, S., & Caballero, B. (2000). Is Miss America an undernourished role model? *Journal of the American Medical Association, 283,* 1569.

Rudolph, K. D., Kurlakowsky, K. D., & Conley, C. S. (2001). Developmental and social-contextual origins of depressive control-related beliefs and behavior. *Cognitive Therapy & Research, 25*(4), 447–475.

Rugino, T., & Copley, T. C. (2001). Effects of modafinil in children with attention-deficit/hyperactivity disorder: An open-label study. *Journal of American Academy of Child & Adolescent Psychiatry, 40,* 230–235.

Ruscio, A. M., Borkovec, T. D., & Ruscio, J. (2001). A taxometric investigation of the latent structure of worry. *Journal of Abnormal Psychology, 110,* 413–422.

Rush, A. J., & Weissenburger, J. E. (1994). Do thinking patterns predict depressive symptoms? *Cognitive Therapy and Research, 10,* 225–236.

Rush, A. J., Kraemer, H. C., Sackeim, H. A., Fava, M., Trivedi, M. H., Frank. E., et al. (2006a). Report by the ACNP Task Force on response and remission in major depressive disorder. *Neuropsychopharmacology, 31,* 1841–1853.

Rush, A. J., Trivedi, M. H., Wisniewski, S. R., Stewart, J. W., Nierenberg, A. A., Thase, M. E., et al. (2006b). Bupropion-SR, sertraline, or venlafaxine-XR after failure of SSRIs for depression. *New England Journal of Medicine, 354,* 1231–1242.

Rutledge, T., & Hogan, B. E. (2002). A quantitative review of prospective evidence linking psychological factors with hypertension development. *Psychosomatic Medicine, 64,* 758–766.

Rutter, M. (2003). Poverty and child mental health: Natural experiments and social causation. *Journal of the American Medical Association, 290,* 2063–2064.

Rutter, M., Caspi, A., Fergusson, D., Horwood, L. J., Goodman, R., Maughan, B., et al. (2004). Sex differences in developmental reading disability: New findings from 4 epidemiological studies. *Journal of the American Medical Association, 291,* 2007–2012.

Ryan, R. (2002). Samson was heroic, exhausted, depressed, and in love, but he does not have antisocial personality disorder. *Archives of General Psychiatry, 59,* 564–565.

Rybarczyk, B., Lopez, M., Benson, R., Alsten, C., & Stepanski, E. (2002). Efficacy of two behavioral treatment programs for comorbid geriatric insomnia. *Psychology and Aging, 17,* 288–298.

Rybarczyk, B., Stepanski, E., Fogg, L., Lopez, M., Barry, P., & Davis, A. A. (2005). A placebo-controlled test of cognitive-behavioral therapy for comorbid insomnia in older adults. *Journal of Consulting and Clinical Psychology, 73,* 1164–1174.

Rychtarik, R. G., et al. (2000). Treatment settings for persons with alcoholism: Evidence for matching clients to inpatient versus outpatient care. *Journal of Consulting and Clinical Psychology, 68,* 277–289.

Ryder, A. G., Alden, L. E., & Paulhus, D. L. (2000). Is acculturation unidimensional or bidimensional? A head-to-head comparison in the prediction of personality, self-identity, and adjustment. *Journal of Personality and Social Psychology, 79*(1), 49–65.

Ryffa, C. D., Lovea, G. D., Urry, H. L., Muller, D., Rosenkranz, M. A., Friedman, E. M., et al. (2006). Psychological well-being and ill-being: Do they have distinct or mirrored biological correlates. *Psychotherapy and Psychosomatics, 75,* 85–95.

S

Sachdev, P., & Hay, P. (1996). Site and size of lesion and psychosurgical outcome in obsessive-compulsive disorder: A magnetic resonance imaging study. *Biological Psychiatry, 39,* 739–742.

Sack, W. H., Clarke, G. N., & Seeley, J. (1996). Multiple forms of stress in Cambodian adolescent refugees. *Child Development, 67,* 107–116.

Sackeim, H. A., Haskett, R. F., Mulsant, B. H., Thase, M. E., Mann, J. J., Pettinati, H. M., et al. (2001). Continuation pharmacotherapy in the prevention of relapse following electroconvulsive therapy. *Journal of the American Medical Association, 285,* 1299–1307.

Sackeim, H. A., et al. (1994). Effects of stimulus intensity and electrode placement on the efficacy and cognitive effects of electroconvulsive therapy. *New England Journal of Medicine, 328,* 839–846.

Sackeim, H. A., Prudic, J., & Devanand, D. P. (1990). Treatment of medication-resistant depression with electroconvulsive therapy. In A. Tasman, et al. (Eds.), *Review of psychiatry* (Vol. 9). Washington, DC: American Psychiatric Press.

Sacks, O. (1985). *The man who mistook his wife for a hat and other clinical tales.* New York: Summit.

Sadeh, A. (2005). Cognitive-behavioral treatment for childhood sleep disorders. *Clinical Psychology Review, 25,* 612–628.

Sadler, A. G., Booth, B. M., Nielson, D., & Doebbeling, B. N. (2000). Health-related consequences of physical and sexual violence: Women in the military. *Obstetrics & Gynecology, 96*(3), 473–480.

Safran, J. D., & Messer, S. B. (1997). Psychotherapy integration: A postmodern critique. *Clinical Psychology: Science and Practice, 4,* 140–152.

Saigal, C. S. (2004). Obesity and erectile dysfunction: Common problems, common solution? *Journal of the American Medical Association, 291,* 3011–3012.

Salekin, R. T. (2002). Psychopathy and therapeutic pessimism: Clinical lore or clinical reality? *Clinical Psychology Review, 22,* 79–112.

Salekin, R. T., Ziegler, T. A., Larrea, M. A., Anthony, V. L., et al. (2003). Predicting dangerousness with two million Adolescent Clinical Inventory psychopathy scales: The important of egocentric and callous traits. *Journal of Personality Assessment, 80,* 154–163.

Salgado de Snyder, V. N. (1987). Factors associated with acculturative stress and depressive symptomatology among married Mexican immigrant women. *Psychology of Women Quarterly, 11,* 475–488.

Salgado de Snyder, V. N., Cervantes, R. C., & Padilla, A. M. (1990). Gender and ethnic differences in psychosocial stress and generalized distress among Hispanics. *Sex Roles, 22,* 441–453.

Salkovskis, P. M., & Clark, D. M. (1993). Panic disorder and hypochondriasis. Special issue: Panic, cognitions and sensations. *Advances in Behaviour Research and Therapy, 15,* 23–48.

Salkovskis, P. M., Thorpe, S. J., Wahl, K., Wroe, A. L., & Forrester, E. (2003). Neutralizing increases discomfort associated with obsessional thoughts: An experimental study with obsessional patients. *Journal of Abnormal Psychology, 112,* 709–715.

Sammons, M. T. (2005a). Late-life depression: Detection, risk reduction, and somatic intervention: Commentary on Delano-Wood and Abeles. *Clinical Psychology: Science and Practice, 12,* 218–221.

Sammons, M. T. (2005b). Pharmacotherapy for delusional disorder and associated conditions. *Professional Psychology: Research and Practice, 36,* 476–479.

Sammons, M. T., & Brown, A. B. (1997). The Department of Defense psychopharmacology demonstration project: An evolving program for postdoctoral education in psychology. *Professional Psychology: Research and Practice, 28,* 107–112.

Samuels, Y., Wang, Z., Bardelli, A., Silliman, N., Ptak, J., Szabo, S., et al. (2004). High frequency of mutations of the PIK3CA gene in human cancers. *Science, 23,* 554.

Sanders Thompson, V. L., Bazile, A., & Akbar, M. (2004). African Americans' perceptions of psychotherapy and psychotherapists. *Professional Psychology: Research and Practice, 35,* 19–26.

Sanders, B., & Green, J. A. (1995). The factor structure of the Dissociative Experiences Scale in college students. *Dissociation Progress in the Dissociative Disorders, 7,* 23–27.

Sanders, L. (2006, June 18). Heartache. *The New York Times,* pp. 27–28.

Sanderson, W. C., & Rego, S. A. (2000). Empirically supported treatment for panic disorder: Research, theory, and application of cognitive behavioral therapy. *Journal of Cognitive Psychotherapy, 14,* 219–244.

Sanislow, C. A., Grilo, C. M., & McGlashan, T. H. (2000). Factor analysis of the *DSM-III-R* borderline personality disorder criteria in psychiatric inpatients. *American Journal of Psychiatry, 157,* 1629–1633.

Sansone, R. A., Rytwinski, D., & Gaither, G. A. (2003). Borderline personality and psychotropic medication prescription in an outpatient psychiatry clinic. *Comprehensive Psychiatry, 44,* 454–458.

Sapolsky, R. M. (2000, April 10). It's not "all in the genes." *Newsweek, 68,* pp. 43–44.

Sapolsky, R. M. (2003). Gene therapy for psychiatric disorders. *American Journal of Psychiatry, 160,* 208–220.

Sar, V., Yargic, L. I., & Tutkun, H. (1996). Structured interview data on 35 cases of dissociative identity disorder in Turkey. *American Journal of Psychiatry, 153,* 1329–1333.

Sass, L. (1982, August 22). The borderline personality. *The New York Times Magazine,* pp. 12–15, 66–67.

Satcher, D. (2000). Mental health: A report of the Surgeon General—Executive summary. *Professional Psychology: Research and Practice, 31,* 5–13.

Sato, T. (1997). Seasonal affective disorder and phototherapy: A critical review. *Professional Psychology: Research and Practice, 28,* 164–169.

Sawa, A., & Snyder, S. H. (2002). Schizophrenia: Diverse approaches to a complex disease. *Science, 296,* 692–695.

Sayers, G. M. (2003). Psychiatry and the control of dangerousness: A comment. *Journal of Medical Ethics, 29,* 235–236.

Saywitz, K. J., Mannarino, A. P., Berliner, L., & Cohen, J. A. (2000). Treatment for sexually abused children and adolescents. *American Psychologist, 55,* 1040–1049.

Schaffer, S. J. (2000, November/December). New NY Tarasoff/confidentiality ruling. *NYSPA Notebook,* p. 5.

Schatzberg, A. F. (2002). Brain imaging in affective disorders: More questions about causes versus effects. *American Journal of Psychiatry, 159,* 1807–1808.

Scheel, K. R. (2000). The empirical basis of dialectical behavior therapy: Summary, critique, and implications. *Clinical Psychology: Science and Practice, 7,* 68–86.

Scheier, L. M., Botvin, G. J., & Baker, E. (1997). Risk and protective factors as predictors of adolescent alcohol involvement and transitions in alcohol use: A prospective analysis. *Journal of Studies on Alcohol, 58,* 652–767.

Scheier, M. F., & Carver, C. S. (1985). Optimism, coping, and health: Assessment and implications of generalized outcome expectancies. *Health Psychology, 4,* 219–247.

Scheier, M. F., & Carver, C. S. (1992). Effects of optimism on psychological and physical well-being: Theoretical overview and empirical update. Special issue: Cognitive perspectives in health psychology. *Cognitive Therapy and Research, 16,* 201–228.

Scheier, M. F., Matthews, K. A., Owens, J. F., Schulz, R., Bridges, M. W., Magovern, G. J., et al. (1999). Optimism and rehospitalization after coronary artery bypass graft surgery. *Archives of Internal Medicine, 159,* 829–935.

Schiess, M. (2003). Nonsteroidal anti-inflammatory drugs protect against Parkinson neurodegeneration: Can an NSAID a day keep Parkinson disease away? *Archives of Neurology, 60,* 1043–1044.

Schiller, L., & Bennett, A. (1994). *The quiet room: A journey out of the torment of madness.* New York: Warner Books, Inc.

Schizophrenia Update—Part I (1995, June). *The Harvard Mental Health Letter, 11,* 1–4.

Schlenger, W. E., Caddell, J. M., Ebert, L., Jordan, B. K., Rourke, K. M., Wilson, D., et al. (2002). Psychological reactions to terrorist attacks: Findings from the National Study of Americans' Reactions to September 11. *Journal of the American Medical Association, 288,* 581–588.

Schmahl, C., & Bremner, J. D. (2006). Neuroimaging in borderline personality disorder. *Journal of Psychiatric Research, 40,* 419–427.

Schmidt, N. B., & Mallott, M. (2006). Evaluating anxiety sensitivity and other fundamental sensitivities predicting anxiety symptoms and fearful responding to a biological challenge. *Behaviour Research and Therapy, 44,* 1681–1688.

Schmidt, N. B., Lerew, D. R., & Jackson, R. J. (1997). The role of anxiety sensitivity in the pathogenesis of panic: Prospective evaluation of spontaneous panic attacks during acute stress. *Journal of Abnormal Psychology, 106,* 355–364.

Schmidt, N. B., Trakowski, J. H., & Staab, J. P. (1997). Extinction of panicogenic effects of a 35% CO_2 challenge in patients with panic disorder. *Journal of Abnormal Psychology, 106,* 630–638.

Schmidt, N. B., Woolaway-Bickel, K., Trakowski, J., Santiago, H., Storey, J., Koselka, M., et al. (2000). Dismantling cognitive-behavioral treatment for panic disorder: Questioning the utility of breathing retraining. *Journal of Consulting and Clinical Psychology, 68,* 417–424.

Schmitt, E. (2001a, April 1). U.S. now more diverse, ethnically and racially. *The New York Times,* p. A20.

Schmitt, E. (2001b, March 13). For 7 million people in census, one race category isn't enough. *The New York Times,* pp. A1, A14.

Schneck, C. D., Miklowitz, D. J., Calabrese, J. R., Allen, M. H., Thomas, M. R., Wisniewski, S. R., et al. (2004). Phenomenology of rapid-cycling bipolar disorder: data from the first 500 participants in the systematic treatment enhancement program. *American Journal of Psychiatry, 161,* 1902–1908.

Schneider, F., Gur, R. G., Koch, K., Backes, V., Amunts, K., Shah, N. J., et al. (2006). Impairment in the specificity of emotion processing in schizophrenia. *American Journal of Psychiatry, 163,* 442–447.

Schneider, H., & Eisenberg, D. (2006). Who receives a diagnosis of attention-deficit/hyperactivity disorder in the United States elementary school population? *Pediatrics, 117,* e601–e609.

Schneider, J. P. (2003). The impact of compulsive cybersex behaviours on the family. *Sexual and Relationship Therapy, 18,* 329–354.

Schneider, J. P. (2004). Editorial: Sexual addiction & compulsivity: Twenty years of the field, ten years of the journal. *Sexual Addiction & Compulsivity, 11,* 3–5.

Schneider, J. P. (2005). Addiction is addiction. *Sexual Addiction & Compulsivity, 12,* 75–77.

Schneider, L. S. (2004). Estrogen and dementia: Insights from the Women's Health Initiative Memory Study. *Journal of the American Medical Association, 291,* 3005–3007.

Schneider, L. S., Nelson, J. C., Clary, C. M., Newhouse, P., Krishnan, K. R. R., Shiovitz, T., et al. (2003). An 8-week multicenter, parallel-group, double-blind, placebo. *American Journal of Psychiatry, 160,* 1277–1285.

Schneiderman, N., Antoni, M. H., Saab, P. G., & Ironson, G. (2001). Health psychology: Psychosocial and biobehavioral aspects of chronic disease management. *Annual Review of Psychology, 52,* 555–580.

Schneier, F. R. (2006). Social anxiety disorder. *New England Journal of Medicine, 355,* 1029–1036.

Schneier, F. R., Wexler, K. B., & Liebowitz, M. R. (1997). Social phobia and stuttering. *American Journal of Psychiatry, 154,* 131.

Schniering, C. A., & Rapee, R. M. (2004). The relationship between automatic thoughts and negative emotions in children and adolescents: A test of the cognitive content-specificity hypothesis. *Journal of Abnormal Psychology, 113,* 464–470.

Schnurr, P. P., Ford, J. D., & Friedman, M. J. (2000). Predictors and outcomes of posttraumatic stress disorder in World War II veterans exposed to mustard gas. *Journal of Consulting and Clinical Psychology, 68,* 258–268.

Schoenman, T. J. (1984). The mentally ill witch in text books of abnormal psychology: Current status and implications of a fallacy. *Professional Psychiatry, 15,* 299–314.

Schonwald, A. D., & Rappaport, L. (2003, September 22). New options for ADHD. *Newsweek,* p. 77.

Schooler, N., Rabinowitz, J., Davidson, M., Emsley, R., Harvey, P. D., et al. (2005). Risperidone and haloperidol in first-episode psychosis: A Long-Term Randomized Trial. *American Journal of Psychiatry, 162,* 947–953.

Schopp, L. H., Johnstone, B., & Reid-Arndt, S. (2005). Telehealth brain injury training for rural behavioral health generalists: Supporting and enhancing rural service delivery networks. *Professional Psychology: Research and Practice, 36,* 158–163.

Schreier, H., & Ricci, L. R. (2002). Follow-up of a case of Münchausen by proxy syndrome. *Journal of the American Academy of Child and Adolescent Psychiatry, 41,* 1395–1396.

Schteingart, J. S., et al. (1995). Homeless and child functioning in the context of risk and protective factors moderating child outcomes. *Journal of Clinical Child Psychology, 24,* 320–331.

Schuckit, M. A. (1987). Biological vulnerability to alcoholism. *Journal of Consulting and Clinical Psychology, 55,* 301–309.

Schuckit, M. A. (1996). Recent developments in the pharmacotherapy of alcohol dependence. *Journal of Consulting and Clinical Psychology, 64,* 669–676.

Schulze, T. G., Ohlraun, S., Czerski, P. M., Schumacher, J., Kassem, L., Deschner, M., et al. (2005). Genotype-phenotype studies in bipolar disorder showing association between the DAOA/G30 locus and persecutory delusions: A first step toward a molecular genetic classification of psychiatric phenotypes. *American Journal of Psychiatry, 162,* 2101–2108.

Schumacher, J., Anthoni, H., Dahdouh, F., Konig, I. R., Hillmer, A. M., Kluck, N., et al. (2006). Strong genetic evidence of DCDC2 as a susceptibility gene for dyslexia. *American Journal of Human Genetics, 78,* 52–62.

Schüpbach, M., Gargiulo, M., Welter, M. L., Mallet, L., Béhar, C., Houeto, J. L., Maltête, D., et al. (2006). Neurosurgery in Parkinson disease: A distressed mind in a repaired body? *Neurology, 66,* 1811–1816.

Schwartz, B. S., Stewart, W. F., Simon, D., & Lipton, R. B. (1998). Epidemiology of tension-type headache. *Journal of the American Medical Association, 279,* 381–383.

Schwartz, C. E., Wright, C. I., Shin, L. M., Kagan, J., & Rauch, S. L. (2003). Inhibited and uninhibited infants "grown up": Adult amygdalar response to novelty. *Science, 300,* 1952 –1953.

Schwartz, J. M. (1998). Neuroanatomical aspects of cognitive-behavior therapy response in obsessive– compulsive disorder. *British Journal of Psychiatry, 35,* 38–44.

Schwartz, R. P., Highfield, D. A., Jaffe, J. H., Brady, J. V., Butler, C. B., Rouse, C. A., et al. (2006). A randomized controlled trial of interim methadone maintenance. *Archives of General Psychiatry, 63,* 102–109.

Schwitzgebel, R. L., & Schwitzgebel, R. K. (1980). *Law and psychological practice.* New York: Wiley.

Scientists discover migraine gene (2003, January 21). Retrieved February 2, 2003, from http://www.msnbc.com/news/862298.asp.

Scientists learn why stress can kill (2003, June 30). Retrieved July 1, 2003 from http://www.msnbc.com/news/933118.asp?cp1=1.

Scogin, F., & McElreath, L. K. (1994). Efficacy of psychosocial treatments for geriatric depression: A quantitative review. *Journal of Consulting and Clinical Psychology, 62,* 69–74.

Scourfield, J., Van den Bree, M., Martin, N., & McGuffin, P. (2004). Conduct problems in children and adolescents: A twin study. *Archives of General Psychiatry, 61,* 489–496.

Scroppo, J. C., Drob, S. L., Weinberger, J. L., & Eagle, P. (1998). Identifying dissociative identity disorder: A self-report and projective study. *Journal of Abnormal Psychology, 107,* 272–284.

Sears, M. R., Greene, J. M., Willan, A. R., Wiecek, E. M., Taylor, D. R., Flannery, E. M., et al. (2003). A longitudinal, population-based, cohort study of childhood asthma followed to adulthood. *New England Journal of Medicine, 349,* 1414–1422.

Sears, R. R., Maccoby, E. E., & Levin, H. (1957). *Patterns of child rearing.* New York: Harper & Row.

See, L. (1999, November). My face doesn't match my race. *Self,* pp. 60–61.

Seeman, M. V. (1997). Psychopathology in women and men: Focus on female hormones. *American Journal of Psychiatry, 154,* 1641–1647.

Sees, K. L., et al. (2000). Methadone maintenance vs. 180-day psychosocially enriched detoxification for treatment of opioid dependence. *Journal of the American Medical Association, 283,* 1303–1310.

Segal, J. H. (1989). Erotomania revisited: From Kraepelin to *DSM-III-R. American Journal of Psychiatry, 146,* 1261–1266.

Segal, S. P., Bola, J. R., & Watson, M. A. (1996). Race, quality of care, and antipsychotic prescribing practices in psychiatric emergency services. *Psychiatric Services, 47,* 282–286.

Segerstrom, S. C., & Miller, G. E. (2004). Psychological stress and the human immune system: A meta-analytic study of 30 years of inquiry. *Psychological Bulletin, 130,* 601–630.

Segraves, R. T., & Althof, S. (1998). Psychotherapy and pharmacotherapy of sexual dysfunctions. In P. E. Nathan & J. M. Gorman (Eds.), *A guide to treatments that work* (pp. 447–471). New York: Oxford University Press.

Segrin, C., & Abramson, L. Y. (1994). Negative reactions to depressive behaviors: A communication theories analysis. *Journal of Abnormal Psychology, 103,* 655–668.

Segrin, C., & Dillard, J. P. (1992). The international theory of depression: A meta-analysis of the research literature. *Journal of Social and Clinical Psychology, 11,* 43–70.

Selemon, L. D., Kleinman, J. E., Herman, M. M., & Goldman-Rakic, P. S. (2002). Smaller frontal gray matter volume in postmortem schizophrenic brains. *American Journal of Psychiatry, 159,* 1983–1991.

Seligman, L., & Hardenburg, S. A. (2000). Assessment and treatment of paraphilias. *Journal of Counseling & Development, 78*(1), 107–113.

Seligman, M. E. P. (1973). Fall into helplessness. *Psychology Today, 7,* 43–48.

Seligman, M. E. P. (1975). *Helplessness: On depression, development, and death.* San Francisco: Freeman.

Seligman, M. E. P. (1991). *Learned optimism.* New York: Knopf.

Seligman, M. E. P. (1998, August). *Prevention of depression and positive psychology.* Paper presented at the meeting of the American Psychological Association, San Francisco.

Seligman, M. E. P., & Maier, S. F. (1967). Failure to escape traumatic shock. *Journal of Experimental Psychology, 74,* 1–9.

Seligman, M. E. P., Castellon, C., Cacciola, J., Schulman, P., Luborsky, L., Ollove, M., et al. (1988). Explanatory style change during cognitive therapy for unipolar depression. *Journal of Abnormal Psychology, 97,* 13–18.

Seligman, M. E. P., Steen, T. A., Park, N., & Peterson, C. (2005). Positive psychology progress: Empirical validation of interventions. *American Psychologist, 60,* 410–421.

Sellbom, M., Graham, J. R., & Schenk, P. W. (2006). Incremental validity of the MMPI–2 Restructured Clinical (RC) Scales in a private practice sample. *Journal of Personality Assessment, 86,* 196–205.

Selvin, B. W. (1993, June 1). Transsexuals are coming to terms with themselves and society. *New York Newsday,* pp. 55, 58, 59.

Selye, H. (1976). *The stress of life* (Rev. ed.) New York: McGraw-Hill.

Semrud-Clikeman, M., et al. (2000). Using MRI to examine brain-behavior relationships in males with attention deficit disorder with hyperactivity. *Journal of the American Academy of Child & Adolescent Psychiatry, 39,* 477–484.

Sensky, T., et al. (2000). A randomized controlled trial of cognitive-behavioral therapy for persistent symptoms in schizophrenia resistant to medication. *Archives of General Psychiatry, 57,* 165–172.

Seppa, N. (1997, June). Children's TV remains steeped in violence. *APA Monitor, 28*(6), 36.

Serrano-Blanco, A., Gabarron, E., Garcia-Bayo, I., Soler-Vila, M., Caramés, E., Peñarrubia-Maria, M.T., et al. (2006). Effectiveness and cost-effectiveness of antidepressant treatment in primary health care: A six-month randomised study comparing fluoxetine to imipramine. *Journal of Affective Disorders, 91,* 153–163.

Shabsigh, R., Perelman, M. A., Lockhart, D. C., Lue, T. F., & Broderick, G. A. (2005). Health issues of men: Prevalence and correlates of erectile dysfunction. *Journal of Urology, 174,* 662–766.

Shadish, W. R., Lurigio, A. J., & Lewis, D. A. (1989). After deinstitutionalization: The present and future of mental health long-term care policy. *Journal of Social Issues, 45,* 1–15.

Shadish, W. R., Matt, G. E., Navarro, A. M., & Phillips, G. (2000). The effects of psychological therapies under clinically representative conditions: A meta-analysis. *Psychological Bulletin, 126,* 512–529.

Shaffer, C. E., Jr., Waters, W. F., & Adams, S. G., Jr. (1994). Dangerousness: Assessing the risk of violent behavior. *Journal of Consulting and Clinical Psychology, 62,* 1064–1068.

Shafran, R., & Mansell, W. (2001). Perfectionism and psychopathology: A review of research and treatment. *Clinical Psychology Review, 21,* 879–906.

Shahar, E., Whitney, C. W., Redline, S., et al. (2002). Sleep-disordered breathing and cardiovascular disease: Cross-sectional results of the Sleep Heart Health Study. *American Journal of Respiratory Critical Care Medicine, 163,* 19–25.

Shalev, A. Y., & Freedman, S. (2005). PTSD following terrorist attacks. *American Journal of Psychiatry, 162,* 1188–1191.

Shao, Y., Cuccaro, M. L., Hauser, E. R., Raiford, K. L., Menold, M. M., Wolpert, C. M., et al. (2003). Fine mapping of autistic disorder to chromosome 15q11-q13 by use of phenotypic subtypes. *American Journal of Hum an Genetics, 72,* 539–548.

Shapiro, D. A., Rees, A., Barkham, M., Hardy, G., Reynolds, S., & Startup, M. (1995). Effects of treatment duration and severity of depression on the maintenance of gains after cognitive-behavioral and psychodynamic interpersonal psychotherapy. *Journal of Consulting and Clinical Psychology, 63,* 378–387.

Shapiro, E. (1992, August 22). Fear returns to sidewalks of West 96th Street. *The New York Times,* pp. B3–B4.

Shapiro, F. (1995). *Eye movement desensitization and reprocessing: Basic principles, protocols, and procedures.* New York: Guilford Press.

Shapiro, F. (2001). *Eye movement desensitization and reprocessing: Basic principles, protocols, and procedures.* (2nd ed.). New York: Guilford Press.

Sharkansky, E. J., King, D. W., King, L. A., & Wolfe, J. (2000). Coping with Gulf War combat stress: Mediating and moderating effects. *Journal of Abnormal Psychology, 109,* 188–197.

Sharp, A. J., Hansen, S., Selzer, R. R., Cheng, Z., Regan, R., Hurst, J. A., et al. (2006, August 15). Discovery of previously unidentified genomic disorders from the duplication architecture of the human genome. *Nature Genetics.* Retrieved August 15, 2006, from DOI 10.1038/ng1862.

Sharp, T. A. (2006). New molecule to brighten the mood. *Science, 311,* 45–46.

Sharp, T. J., & Harvey, A. G. (2001). Chronic pain and posttraumatic stress disorder: Mutual maintenance? *Clinical Psychology Review, 21,* 857–877.

Sharpe, M., & Williams, A. C. de-C. (2002). Treating patients with somatoform pain disorder and hypochondriasis. Turk, D. C., & Gatchel, R. J. (Eds.), *Psychological approaches to pain management: A practitioner's handbook* (2nd ed.), (pp. 515–533). New York: Guilford Press.

Shattuck, P. T. (2006a). The contribution of diagnostic substitution to the growing administrative prevalence of autism in US special education. *Pediatrics, 117,* 1028–1037.

Shattuck, P. T. (2006b). Diagnostic substitution and changing autism prevalence. *Pediatrics, 117,* 1438–1439.

Shaw, H., Ramirez, L., Trost, A., Randall, P., & Stice, E. (2004). Body image and eating disturbances across ethnic groups: More similarities than differences. *Psychology of Addictive Behaviors, 18,* 12–18.

Shaw, P., Lerch, J., Greenstein, D., Sharp, W., Clasen, L., Evans, A., Giedd, J., et al. (2006). Longitudinal mapping of cortical thickness and clinical outcome in children and adolescents with attention-deficit/hyperactivity disorder. *Archives of General Psychiatry, 63,* 540–549.

Shaw, R., Cohen, F., Doyle, B., & Palesky, J. (1985). The impact of denial and repressive style on information gain and rehabilitation outcomes in myocardial infarction patients. *Psychosomatic Medicine, 47,* 262–273.

Shaywitz, S. E., Mody, M., & Shaywitz, B. A. (2006). Neural mechanisms in dyslexia. *Current Directions in Psychological Science, 15,* 278–281.

Shaywitz, S. E., Shaywitz, B. A., Fulbright, R. K., Skudlarski, P., Mencl, W. E., et al. (2003). Neural systems for compensation and persistence: Young adult outcome of childhood reading disability. *Biological Psychiatry, 54,* 25–33.

Shea, M. T., Widiger, T. A., & Klein, M. H. (1992). Comorbidity of personality disorders and depression: Implications for treatment. *Journal of Consulting and Clinical Psychology, 60,* 857–868.

Shear, K., Jin, R., Ruscio, A. M., Walters, E. E., & Kessler, R. C. (2006). Prevalence and correlates of estimated *DSM-IV* child and adult separation anxiety disorder in the National Comorbidity Survey Replication. *American Journal of Psychiatry 163,* 1074–1083.

Sheehan, D. V., & Mao, C. G. (2003). Paroxetine treatment of generalized anxiety disorder. *Psychopharmacology Bulletin, 37,* (Suppl. 1): 64–75.

Sheitman, B. B., et al. (1998). Pharmacological treatments of schizophrenia. In P. E. Nathan & J. M. Gorman (Eds.), *A guide to treatments that work* (pp. 167–189). New York: Oxford University Press.

Shelton, R. C., et al. (2001). Effectiveness of St. John's Wort in major depression: A randomized controlled trial. *Journal of the American Medical Association, 285,* 1978–1986.

Sher, L. (2005). Suicide and alcoholism. *Nordic Journal of Psychiatry, 59,* 152.

Sherbourne, C. D., Hays, R D., Fleishman, J. A., Vitiello, B., Magruder, K. M., Bing, E. G., et al. (2000). Impact of psychiatric conditions on health-related quality of life in persons with HIV infection. *American Journal of Psychiatry, 157,* 248–254.

Sherbourne, C. D., Hays, R. D., & Wells, K. B. (1995). Personal and psychosocial risk factors for physical and mental health outcomes and course of depression among depressed patients. *Journal of Consulting and Clinical Psychology, 63,* 345–355.

Sherer, M.R., & Schreibman, L. (2005). Individual behavioral profiles and predictors of treatment effectiveness for children with autism. *Journal of Consulting and Clinical Psychology, 73,* 525–538.

Sheridan, M. S. (2003). The deceit continues: An updated literature review of Münchausen syndrome by proxy. *Child Abuse and Neglect, 27,* 431–451.

Sherman, D. K., McGue, M. K., & Iacono, W. G. (1997). Twin concordance for attention deficit hyperactivity disorder: A comparison of teachers' and mothers' reports. *American Journal of Psychiatry, 154,* 532–535.

Sherwood, N. E., et al. (2000). The perceived function of eating for bulimic, subclinical bulimic, and non-eating disordered women. *Behavior Therapy, 31,* 777–793.

Sheung-Tak, C. (1996). A critical review of Chinese koro. *Culture, Medicine and Psychiatry, 20,* 67–82.

Shields, A. E., Lerman, C., & Sullivan, P. (2005). The use of race variables in genetic studies of complex traits and the goal of reducing health disparities: A transdisciplinary perspective. *American Psychologist, 60,* 77–103.

Shiffman, S., Dresler, C. M., Hajek, P., Gilburt, S. J. A., Targett, D. A., & Strahs, K. R. (2002). Efficacy of a nicotine lozenge for smoking cessation. *Archives of Internal Medicine, 162,* 1267–1276.

Shifren, J., & Ferrari, N. A. (2004, May 10). A better sex life. *Newsweek,* pp. 86–87.

Shneidman, E. (2005). Prediction of suicide revisited: a brief methodological note. *Suicide & Life-Threatening Behavior, 35,* 1–2.

Shneidman, E. S. (1985). *Definition of suicide.* New York: Wiley.

Shnek, Z. M., et al. (2005). Psychological factors and depressive symptoms in ischemic heart disease. *Health Psychology, 141–145.*

Shonk, S. M., & Cicchetti, D. (2001). Maltreatment, competency deficits, and risk for academic and behavioral maladjustment. *Developmental Psychology, 37,* 3–17.

Shugart, Y. Y., Mundorff, J., Kilshaw, J., Doheny, K., Doan, B., Wanyee, J., et al. (2004). Results of a genome-wide linkage scan for stuttering. *American Journal of Medical Genetics, 124A*, 133–135.

Shukla, P. R., & Singh, R. H. (2000). Supportive psychotherapy in Dhat syndrome patients. *Journal of Personality & Clinical Studies, 16*, 49–52.

Shultz, S. K., Scherman, A., & Marshall, L. J. (2000). Evaluation of a university-based date rape prevention program: Effect on attitudes and behavior related to rape. *Journal of College Student Development, 41*(2), 193–201.

Shumaker, S. A., Legault, C., & Coker, L. H. (2006). Behavior-based interventions to enhance cognitive functioning and independence in older adults. *Journal of the American Medical Association, 296*, 2852–2854.

Shute, N., Locy, T., & Pasternak, D. (2000, March 6). The perils of pills. *U.S. News & World Report*, pp. 44–50.

Siegel, J. (2001, January 18). St. John's Wort: Nature's antidepressant? *HealthGate Web Posting. NBCI.com*. Retrieved January 28, 2001, from http://healthgate.nbci.com/getcontent.asp?siteid=nbci&docid=/healthy/alternative/2000/johnwort/index.

Siegel, J. M. (2004). Hypocretin (orexin): Role in normal behavior and neuropathology. *Annual Review of Psychology, 55*, 125–148.

Siegel, L. J. (1992). *Criminology* (4th ed.). St. Paul, MN: West.

Sierra, M., Gomez, J., Molina, J. J., Luque, R., Munoz, J. F., & David, A. S. (2006). Depersonalization in psychiatric patients: A transcultural study. *Journal of Nervous & Mental Disease, 194*, 356–361.

Siever, L. J., & Davis, K. L. (2004). The pathophysiology of schizophrenia disorders: perspectives from the spectrum. *American Journal of Psychiatry, 161*, 398–413.

Sijbrandij, M., Olff, M., Reitsma, J. B., Carlier, I. V., & Gersons, B. P. (2006). Emotional or educational debriefing after psychological trauma: Randomised controlled trial. *British Journal of Psychiatry, 189*, 150–155.

Silber, M. H. (2005). Chronic insomnia. *New England Journal of Medicine, 353*, 803–810.

Silberstein, R. B., Farrow, M. M., Levy, F., Pipingas, A., Hay, D. A., & Jarman, C. (1998). Functional brain electrical activity mapping in boys with attention-deficit/hyper activity disorder. *Archives of General Psychiatry, 55*, 1105–1112.

Silberstein, S. D., Massiou, H., Le Jeunne, C., Johnson-Pratt, L., McCarroll, K. A., & Lines, C. R. (2000). Rizatriptan in the treatment of menstrual migraine. *Obstetrics & Gynecology, 96*, 237–242.

Silva, R. R., Alpert, M., Munoz, D. M., Singh, S., Matzner, F., & Dummit, S. (2000). Stress and vulnerability to posttraumatic stress disorder in children and adolescents. *American Journal of Psychiatry, 157*, 1229–1235.

Silver, E., Cirincione, C., & Steadman, H. J. (1994). Demythologizing inaccurate perceptions of the insanity defense. *Law and Human Behavior, 18*, 63–70.

Silver, H., Feldman, P., Bilker, W., & Gur, R. C. (2003). Working memory deficit as a core neuropsychological dysfunction in schizophrenia. *American Journal of Psychiatry, 160*, 1809–1816.

Silver, S. M., Rogers, S., Knipe, J., & Colelli, G. (2005). EMDR therapy following the 9/11 terrorist attacks: A community-based intervention project in New York City. *International Journal of Stress Management, 12*, 29–42.

Silverman, J. M., Ciresi, G., Smith, C. J., Marin, D. B., & Schnaider-Beeri, M. (2005). Variability of familial risk of Alzheimer disease across the late life span. *Archives of General Psychiatry, 62*, 565–573.

Silverthorn, P. (2001). Oppositional defiant disorder. In H. Orvaschel, et al. (Eds.), *Handbook of conceptualization and treatment of child psychopathology* (pp. 41–56). Amsterdam, Netherlands: Pergamon/Elsevier Science.

Simeon, D., Greenberg, J., Knutelska, M., Schmeidler, J., & Hollander, E. (2003). Peritraumatic reactions associated with the World Trade Center disaster. *American Journal of Psychiatry, 160*, 1702–1705.

Simeon, D., Gross, S., Guralnik, O., Stein, D. J., Schmeidler, J. & Hollander, E. (1997). Feeling unreal: 30 Cases of *DSM-III-R* depersonalization disorder. *American Journal of Psychiatry, 154*, 1107–1113.

Simeon, D., Guralnik, O., Hazlett, E. A., Spiegel-Cohen, J., Hollander, E., & Buchsbaum, M. S. (2000). Feeling unreal: A PET study of depersonalization disorder. *American Journal of Psychiatry, 157*, 1782–1788.

Simeon, D., Guralnik, O., Schmeidler, J., &, Knutelska, M. (2004). Fluoxetine therapy in depersonalisation disorder: Randomised controlled trial. *British Journal of Psychiatry, 185*, 31–36.

Simeon, D., Guralnik, O., Schmeidler, J., Sirof, B., & Knutelska, M. (2001). The role of childhood interpersonal trauma in depersonalization disorder. *American Journal of Psychiatry, 158*, 1027–1033.

Simon, G. E. (1998). Management of somatoform and factitious disorders. In P. E. Nathan & J. M. Gorman (Eds.), *A guide to treatments that work* (pp. 408–422). New York: Oxford University Press.

Simon, G. E., Fleck, M., Lucas, R., & Bushnell, D. M. (2004). Prevalence and predictors of depression treatment in an international primary care study. *American Journal of Psychiatry, 161*, 1626–1634.

Simon, G. E., Savarino, J., Operskalski, B., & Wang, P. S. (2006). Suicide risk during antidepressant treatment. *American Journal of Psychiatry, 163*, 41–47.

Simonsen, G., Blazina, C., & Watkins, C. E., Jr. (2000). Gender role conflict and psychological well-being among gay men. *Journal of Counseling Psychology, 47*(1), 85–89.

Simons-Morton, B., Haynie, D. L., Crump, A. D., Eitel, S. P., & Saylor, K. E. (2001). Peer and parent influences on smoking and drinking among early adolescents. *Health Education & Behavior, 28*, 95–107.

Simonton, D. K., & Baumeister, R. F. (2005). Positive psychology at the summit. *Review of General Psychology, 9*, 99–102.

Simpson, D. D., Joe, G. W., Fletcher, B. W., Hubbard, R. L., & Anglin, M. D. (1999). A national evaluation of treatment outcomes for cocaine dependence. *Archives of General Psychiatry, 57*, 507–514.

Sin, D. D., Man, J., Sharpe, H., Gan, W. Q., & Man, S. F. P. (2004). Pharmacological management to reduce exacerbations in adults with asthma: A systematic review and meta-analysis. *Journal of the American Medical Association, 292*, 367–376.

Singh, G. (1985). Dhat syndrome revisited. *Indian Journal of Psychiatry, 27*, 119–122.

Sink, M. (2004, November 9). Drinking deaths draw attention to old campus problem. *The New York Times*, p. A16.

Sivertsen, B., Omvik, S., Pallesen, S., Bjorvatn, B., Havik, O. E., Kvale, G., et al. (2006). Cognitive behavioral therapy vs zopiclone for treatment of chronic primary insomnia in older adults: A randomized controlled trial. *Journal of the American Medical Association, 295*, 2851–2858.

Six-year outcome of cognitive behavior therapy for prevention of recurrent depression. *American Journal of Psychiatry, 161*, 1872–1876.

Skaar, K. L., et al. (1997). Smoking cessation 1: An overview of research. *Behavioral Medicine, 23*, 5–13.

Skegg, K., Nada-Raja, S., Dickson, N., Paul, C., & Williams, S. (2003). Sexual orientation and self-harm in men and women. *American Journal of Psychiatry, 160*, 541–546.

Skinner, B. F. (1938). *The behavior of organisms: An experimental analysis.* New York: Appleton.

Skoog, G., & Skoog, I. (1999). A 40-year follow-up of patients with obsessive–compulsive disorder. *Archives of General Psychiatry, 56*, 121–127.

Skoog, I. (2000). Detection of preclinical Alzheimer's disease. *The New England Journal of Medicine, 343*, 502–503.

Slater, D., & Hans, V. P. (1984). Public opinion on forensic psychiatry following the Hinckley verdict. *American Journal of Psychiatry, 141*, 675–679.

Sloan, D. M., & Marx, B. P. (2004). A closer examination of the structured written disclosure procedure. *Journal of Consulting and Clinical Psychology, 72*, 165–175.

Sloan, D. M., Marx, B. P., & Epstein, E. M. (2005). Further examination of the exposure model underlying the efficacy of written emotional disclosure. *Journal of Consulting and Clinical Psychology, 73*, 549–554.

Slone, D. G., & Gleason, C. E. (1999). Behavior management planning for problem behaviors in dementia: A practical model. *Professional Psychology: Research and Practice, 30*, 27–36.

Slutske, W. S. (2006a). Natural recovery and treatment-seeking in pathological gambling: results of two U.S. national surveys. *American Journal of Psychiatry, 163*, 297–302.

Slutske, W. S. (2006b). On the limits of cross-sectional retrospective data for characterizing the course of pathological gambling and its relation with comorbid psychopathology: A Reply to Afifi, Cox, and Sareen. *American Journal of Psychiatry, 163*, 1297–1298. [Letter]

Slutske, W. S., Heath, A. C., Madden, P. A. F., Bucholz, K. K., Statham, D. J., & Martin, N. G. (2002). Personality and the genetic risk for alcohol dependence. *Journal of Abnormal Psychology, 111*, 124–133.

Small, J. G., et al. (1997). Quetiapine in patients with schizophrenia: A high- and low-dose double-blind comparison with placebo. *Archives of General Psychiatry, 54*, 549–557.

Smeding, H. M., Speelman, J. D., Koning-Haanstra, M., Schuurman, P. R., Nijssen, P., van Laar, T., et al. (2006). Neuropsychological effects of bilateral STN stimulation in Parkinson disease: A controlled study. *Neurology, 66*, 1830–1836.

Smith, A. B., Taylor, E., Brammer, M., Toone, B., & Rubia, K. (2006). Task-specific hypoactivation in prefrontal and temporoparietal brain regions during motor inhibition and task switching in medication-naive children and adolescents with attention deficit hyperactivity disorder. *American Journal of Psychiatry 163*, 1044–1051.

Smith, D. (2001, October). Sleep psychologists in demand. *Monitor on Psychology*, pp. 36–38.

Smith, D. (2003, March). Hostility associated with immune function. *Monitor on Psychology*, p. 47.

Smith, D. (2003, April). Women and sex: What is "dysfunctional?" *Monitor on Psychology, 34*, pp. 54–56.

Smith, G. R. (1994). The course of somatization and its effects on utilization of health care resources. *Psychosomatics, 35*, 263–267.

Smith, G. T. (2005). On construct validity: Issues of method and measurement. *Psychological Assessment, 17*, 396–408.

Smith, J. E., & Krejci, J. (1991). Minorities join the majority: Eating disturbances among Hispanic and Native American youth. *International Journal of Eating Disorders, 10*, 179–186.

Smith, M. L., & Glass, G. V. (1977). Meta-analysis of psychotherapy outcome studies. *American Psychologist, 32*, 752–760.

Smith, M. L., Glass, G. V., & Miller, T. I. (1980). *The benefits of psychotherapy.* Baltimore: Johns Hopkins University Press.

Smith, R. E., Smoll, F. L., & Ptacek, J. T. (1990). Conjunctive moderator variables in vulnerability and reliency research: Life stress, social support and coping skills, and adolescent sport injuries. *Journal of Personality and Social Psychology, 58*, 360–370.

Smith, S. C. (1983). *The great mental calculators.* New York: Columbia University Press.

Smith, T. (1999). Outcome of early intervention for children with autism. *Clinical Psychology: Science and Practice, 6*, 33–49.

Smith, T. K. (2003, February). We've got to stop eating like this. *Fortune*, pp. 58–70.

Smith, T. W., & Ruiz, J. M. (2002). Psychosocial influences on the development and course of coronary heart disease: Current status and implications for research and practice. *Journal of Consulting and Clinical Psychology, 70*, 548–568.

Smith, T. W., Snyder, C. R., & Perkins, S. C. (1983). The self-serving function of hypochondriacal complaints: Physical symptoms as self-handicapping strategies. *Journal of Personality and Social Psychology, 44*, 787–797.

Smith, Y. L. S., et al. (2001). Adolescents with gender identity disorder who were accepted or rejected for sex reassignment surgery: A prospective follow-up study. *Journal of American Academy of Child & Adolescent Psychiatry, 40*, 472–481.

Smith, Y. L. S., Van Goozen, S. H. M., Kuiper, A. J., & Cohen-Kettenis, P. T. (2005). Sex reassignment: Outcomes and predictors of treatment for adolescent and adult transsexuals. *Psychological Medicine, 35*, 89–99.

Smoller, E. S. (1997). *I can't remember: Family stories of Alzheimer's disease.* Philadelphia: Temple University Press.

Smyth, J. M., & Pennebaker, J. W. (2001). What are the health effects of disclosure? In A. Baum, T. A. Revenson, & J. E. Singer (Eds.), *Handbook of health psychology* (pp. 339–348). Mahwah, NJ: Erlbaum.

Smyth, J. M., et al. (1999). Effects of writing about stressful experiences on symptom reduction in patients with asthma or rheumatoid arthritis. *Journal of the American Medical Association, 281*, 1304–1309.

Snell, M. E. (1997). Teaching children and young adults with mental retardation in school programs: Current research. *Behaviour Change, 14*, 73–105.

Snitz, B. E., MacDonald, A. III, Cohen, J. D., Cho, R. Y., Becker, T., & Carter, C. S. (2005). Lateral and medial hypofrontality in first-episode schizophrenia: functional activity in a medication-naive state and effects of short-term atypical antipsychotic treatment. *American Journal of Psychiatry, 162*, 2322–2329.

Snyder, S. H. (2002). Forty years of neurotransmitters: A personal account. *Archives of General Psychiatry, 59*, 983–994.

Sobell, M. B., & Sobell, L. C. (1973a). Alcoholics treated by individualized behavior therapy: One-year treatment outcome, *Behaviour Research and Therapy, 11*, 599–618.

Sobell, M. B., & Sobell, L. C. (1973b). Individualized behavior therapy for alcoholics, *Behavior Therapy, 4*, 49–72.

Sobell, M. B., & Sobell, L. C. (1976). Second-year treatment outcome of alcoholics treated by individualized behavior therapy: Results, *Behaviour Research and Therapy, 14*, 195–215.

Sobell, M. B., & Sobell, L. C. (1984). The aftermath of heresy: A response to Pendery et al.'s (1982) critique of "Individualized behavior therapy for alcoholics," *Behaviour Research and Therapy, 22*, 413–440.

Sobell, M. B., & Sobell, L. C. (1995). Controlled drinking after 25 years: How important was the great debate? *Addiction, 90*, 1149–1153.

Society for Neuroscience (2006, March). *Huntington's disease.* Retrieved April 17, 2006, from http://web.sfn.org/content/Publications/BrainBriefings/huntingtons_disease.html.

Society for Neuroscience. (2005a). *Alcoholism.* Retrieved March 29, 2006, from http://web.sfn.org/content/Publications/BrainResearch.

Society for Neuroscience. (2005b). *Bipolar disorder: Making a difference today.* Retrieved March 29, 2006, from http://web.sfn.org/content/Publications/BrainResearch SuccessStories/BRSS_Dyslexia.pdf.

Sokolove, M. (2003, November 16). Should John Hinckley go free? *The New York Times Magazine*, pp. 54–57.

Soler, J., Pascual, J. C., Campins, J., Barrachina, J., Puigdemont, D., Avarez, E., et al. (2005). Double-blind, placebo-controlled study of dialectical behavior therapy plus olanzapine for borderline personality disorder. *American Journal of Psychiatry, 162*, 1221–1224.

Solomon, D. A., et al. (1997). Recovery from major depression: A 10-year prospective follow-up across multiple episodes. *Archives of General Psychiatry, 54*, 1001–1006.

Solomon, D. A., et al. (2000). Multiple recurrences of major depressive disorder. *American Journal of Psychiatry, 157*, 229–233.

Solowij, N., Stephens, R. S., Roffman, R. A., Babor, T., Kadden, R., Miller, M., et al. (2002). Cognitive functioning of long-term heavy cannabis users seeking treatment. *Journal of the American Medical Association, 287*, 1123–1131.

Sørensen, H. J., Mortensen, E. L., Reinisch, J. M., & Mednick, S. A. (2003). Do hypertension and diuretic treatment in pregnancy increase the risk of schizophrenia in offspring? *American Journal of Psychiatry, 160*, 464–468.

Southwick, S. M., et al. (1997). Noradrenergic and serotonergic function in posttraumatic stress disorder. *Archives of General Psychiatry, 54,* 749–758.

Spanos, N. P. (1978). Witchcraft in histories of psychiatry: A critical analysis and an alternative conceptualization. *Psychological Bulletin, 85,* 417–439.

Spanos, N. P. (1994). Multiple identity enactments and multiple personality disorder: A sociocognitive perspective. *Psychological Bulletin, 116,* 143–165.

Spanos, N. P., Weekes, J. R., & Bertrand, L. D. (1985). Multiple personality: A social psychological perspective. *Journal of Abnormal Psychology, 94,* 362–376.

Spataro, J., Mullen, P. E., Burgess, P. M., Wells, D. L., & Moss, S. A. (2004). Impact of child sexual abuse on mental health: Prospective study in males and females. *British Journal of Psychiatry, 184,* 416–421.

Spechler, S. J., Fischbach, L., & Feldman, M. (2000). Clinical aspects of genetic variability in Helicobacter pylori. *Journal of the American Medical Association, 283,* 1264–1266.

Spencer, D. J. (1983). Psychiatric dilemmas in Australian aborigines. *International Journal of Social Psychiatry, 29* (3), 208–214.

Spencer, M. D., Knight, R. S., & Will, R. G. (2002). First hundred cases of variant Creutzfeldt-Jakob disease: Retrospective case note review of early psychiatric and neurological features. *British Medical Journal, 324,* 1479–1482.

Spiegel, D. (2006). Recognizing traumatic dissociation. *American Journal of Psychiatry, 163,* 566–568.

Spiegel, D. A., & Bruce, T. J. (1997). Benzodiazepines and exposure-based cognitive behavior therapies for panic disorder: Conclusions from combined treatment trials. *American Journal of Psychiatry, 154,* 773–781.

Spielmans, G. I. (2004). To the editor. *Journal of the American Medical Association, 291,* 41. [Letter]

Spinal fluid may be key to detecting Alzheimer's (2006, December 12). Retrieved December 12, 2006, from http://www.msnbc.msn.com/id/16160428/.

Spitzer, R. L. (2005). Peer commentaries on Binik: A more radical proposal: Dyspareunia is not a mental disorder. *Archives of Sexual Behavior, 34,* 48.

Spitzer, R. L., et al. (1992). Binge eating disorder: A multisite field trial of the diagnostic criteria. *International Journal of Eating Disorders, 11,* 191–203.

Spitzer, R. L., et al. (1994). *DSM-IV case book* (4th ed.). Washington, DC: American Psychiatric Press.

Spitzer, R. L., Gibbon, M., Skodol, A. E., Williams, J. B. W., & First, M. B. (1989). *DSM-III-R casebook.* Washington, DC: American Psychiatric Press.

Springen, K. (2004, May 10). Women, cigarettes and death. *Newsweek,* p. 69.

Squier, L. H., & Domhoff, G. W. (1998). The presentation of dreaming and dreams in introductory psychology textbooks: A critical examination with suggestions for textbook authors and course instructors. *Dreaming, 8,* 149–168.

St. John's wort doesn't help with major depression. (2001, June). *Tufts University Health & Nutrition Letter,* p. 2.

Staddon, J. E., R., & Cerutti, D. T. (2003). Operant conditioning. *Annual Review of Psychology, 4,* 115–144.

Stader, S. R., & Hokanson, J. E. (1998). Psychosocial antecedents of depressive symptoms: An evaluation using daily experiences methodology. *Journal of Abnormal Psychology, 107,* 17–26.

Stafford, R. S., & Radley, D. C. (2003). National trends in antiobesity medication use. *Archives of Internal Medicine, 163,* 1046–1050.

Stahl, S. M. (2001). Sex and psychopharmacology: Is natural estrogen a psychotropic drug in women? *Archives of General Psychiatry, 58,* 537–538. [Letter]

Stambor, (2006, October). Psychologist calls for more research on adolescents' brains. *Monitor on Psychology, 37,* p. 16.

Stamm, B. H., & Perednia, D. A. (2000). Evaluating psychosocial aspects of telemedicine and telehealth systems. *Professional Psychology: Research and Practice, 31,* 184–189.

Stangier, U., Heidenreicha, T., Peitza, M., Lauterbach, W., & Clark, D. M. (2003). Cognitive therapy for social phobia: Individual versus group treatment. *Behaviour Research and Therapy, 41,* 991–1007.

Stanley, M. A., & Beck, J. G. (2000). Anxiety disorders. *Clinical Psychology Review, 20,* 731–754.

Stanley, M. A., & Turner, S. M. (1995). Current status of pharmacological and behavioral treatment of obsessive-compulsive disorder. *Behavior Therapy, 26,* 163–186.

Starkstein, S. E., Jorge, R., Mizrahi, R., & Robinson, R. G. (2005). The construct of minor and major depression in Alzheimer's Disease. *American Journal of Psychiatry, 162,* 2086–2093.

Starkweather, C. W. (2002). The epigenesis of stuttering. *Journal of Fluency Disorders, 27,* 269–287.

Steadman, H. J. (1979). *Beating a rap: Defendants found incompetent to stand trial.* Chicago: University of Chicago Press.

Steadman, H. J., et al. (1993). *Before and after Hinckley: Evaluating insanity defense reform.* New York: Guilford Press.

Steffens, D. C., Skoog, I., Norton, M. C., Hart, A. D., Tschanz, J. T., Plassman, B. L., et al. (2000). Prevalence of depression and its treatment in an elderly population: The Cache County Study. *Archives of General Psychiatry, 57,* 601–607.

Stein, A. L., Trana, G. Q., Lund, L. M., Haji, U., Dashevsky, B. A., & Baker, D. G. (2005). Correlates for posttraumatic stress disorder in Gulf War veterans: A retrospective study of main and moderating effects. *Journal of Anxiety Disorders, 19,* 861–876.

Stein, D., Asherov, J., Lublinksy, E., Sobol-Havia, D., et al. (2002). Sociodemographic factors associated with attempted suicide in two Israeli cities between 1990 and 1998. *Journal of Nervous & Mental Disease, 190,* 115–118.

Stein, D., Brom, D., Elizur, A., & Witztum, E. (1998). The association between attitudes toward suicide and suicidal ideation in adolescents. *Acta Psychiatrica Scandinavia, 97,* 195–201.

Stein, M. A., Sarampote, C. S., Waldman, I. D., Robb, A. S., Conlon, C., Pearl, P. L., et al. (2003). A dose-response study of OROS methylphenidate in children with attention-deficit/hyperactivity disorder. *Pediatrics, 112,* 404–413.

Stein, M. B., & Kean, Y. M. (2000). Disability and quality of life in social phobia: Epidemiologic findings. *American Journal of Psychiatry, 157,* 1606–1613.

Stein, M. B., Fuetsch, M., Muller, N., Hofler, M., Lieb, R., & Wittchen, H. U. (2001). Social anxiety disorder and the risk of depression: A prospective community study of adolescents and young adults. *Archives of General Psychiatry, 58,* 251–256.

Stein, M. B., Goldin, P. R., Sareen, J., Zorrilla, L. T. E., & Brown, G. G. (2002). Increased amygdala activation to angry and contemptuous faces in generalized social phobia. *Archives of General Psychiatry, 59,* 1027–1034.

Stein, M. B., Torgrud, L. J., & Walker, J. R. (2000). Social phobia symptoms, subtypes, and severity: Findings from a community survey. *Archives of General Psychiatry, 57,* 1046–1052.

Stein, M. B., Walker, J. R., & Forde, D. R. (1996). Public-speaking fears in a community sample: Prevalence, impact on functioning, and diagnostic classification. *Archives of General Psychiatry, 53,* 169–174.

Steinberg, M. (1991). The spectrum of depersonalization: Assessment and treatment. *Annual Review of Psychiatry, 10,* 223–247.

Steinbrook, R. (2006). The potential of human papillomavirus vaccines. *New England Journal of Medicine, 354,* 1109–1112.

Steinhausen, H.-C. (2002). The outcome of anorexia nervosa in the 20th century. *American Journal of Psychiatry, 159,* 1284–1293.

Stemberger, R. R., et al. (1995). Social phobia: An analysis of possible developmental factors. *Journal of Abnormal Psychology, 194,* 526–531.

Stenson, J. (2001, August 26). Burden of mental illness in America falls on minorities. *MSNBC Web Posting.* Retrieved August 26, 2001, from http://www.msnbc.com/news/619545.asp.

Stephenson, J. (2004). Global AIDS epidemic worsens. *Journal of the American Medical Association, 291,* 31–32.

Steptoe, A., Wardle, J., & Marmot, M. (2005). Positive affect and health-related neuroendocrine, cardiovascular, and inflammatory processes. *Proceedings of the National Academy of Sciences, 102,* 6508–6512.

Stern, E., & Silbersweig, D. A. (2001). Advances in functional neuroimaging methodology for the study of brain system underlying human neuropsychological function and dysfunction. *Journal of Clinical & Experimental Neuropsychology, 23,* 3–18.

Stevens, J. E. (1995, January 30). Virtual therapy. *The Boston Globe,* pp. 25, 29.

Stevens, J. R. (1997). Anatomy of schizophrenia revisited. *Schizophrenia Bulletin, 23,* 373–383.

Stevens, S. E., Hynan, M. T., & Allen, M. (2000). A meta-analysis of common factor and specific treatment effects across the outcome domains of the phase model of psychotherapy. *Clinical Psychology: Science and Practice, 7,* 273–290.

Stevenson, J., Meares, R., & Comerford, A. (2003). Diminished impulsivity in older patients with borderline personality disorder. *American Journal of Psychiatry, 160,* 165–166.

Stewart, M. W., et al. (1994). Differential relationships between stress and disease activity for immunologically distinct subgroups of people with rheumatoid arthritis. *Journal of Abnormal Psychology, 1103,* 251–258.

Stewart, S. M., Kennard, B. D., Lee, P. W. H., Hughes, C. W., Mayes, T. L., Emslie, G. J., et al. (2004). A cross-cultural investigation of cognitions and depressive symptoms in adolescents. *Journal of Abnormal Psychology, 113,* 248–257.

Stewart, W. F., Ricci, J. A., Chee, E., Hahn, S. R., & Morganstein, D. (2003). Cost of lost productive work time among US workers with depression. *Journal of the American Medical Association, 289,* 3135–3141.

Stice, E. (1994). Review of the evidence for a sociocultural model of bulimia nervosa and an exploration of the mechanisms of action. *Clinical Psychology Review, 14,* 633–661.

Stice, E. (2001). A prospective test of the dual-pathway model of bulimic pathology: Mediating effects of dieting and negative affect. *Journal of Abnormal Psychology, 110,* 124–135.

Stice, E., Burton, E. M., & Shaw, H. (2004). Prospective relations between bulimic pathology, depression, and substance abuse: Unpacking comorbidity in adolescent girls. *Journal of Consulting and Clinical Psychology, 72,* 62–71.

Stice, E., Hayward, C., Cameron, R. P., Killen, J. D., & Taylor, C. B. (2000). Body-image and eating disturbances predict onset of depression among female adolescents: A longitudinal study. *Journal of Abnormal Psychology, 109,* 438–444.

Stinson, F. S., Grant, B. F., Dawson, D. A., Ruan, W. J., Huang, B., & Saha, T. (2005). Comorbidity between DSM-IV alcohol and specific drug use disorders in the United States: Results from the National Epidemiologic Survey on Alcohol and Related Conditions. *Drug and Alcohol Dependence, 80,* 105–116.

Stipp, D. (2003, February). The quest for the antifat pill. *Fortune,* pp. 66–67.

Stokstad, E. (2001). New hints into the biological basis of autism. *Science, 294,* pp. 34–37.

Stolberg, S. G. (1998, March 13). New cancer cases decreasing in U.S. as deaths do, too. *The New York Times,* pp. A1, A14.

Stolberg, S. G. (2001, May 10). Blacks found on short end of heart attack procedure. *The New York Times,* p. A20.

Stolberg, S. G. (2002, November 17). Preschool meds. *The New York Times Magazine,* pp. 58–61.

Stoller, R. J. (1969). Parental influences in male transsexualism. In R. Green & J. Money (Eds.), *Transsexualism and sex reassignment.* Baltimore: Johns Hopkins University Press.

Stone J., Smyth R., Carson, A., Lewis, S., Prescott, R., Warlow, C., & Sharpe, M. (2006). La belle indifférence in conversion symptoms and hysteria: Systematic review. *British Journal of Psychiatry, 188,* 204–209.

Stone, A. (1976). The *Tarasoff* decisions: Suing psychotherapists to safeguard society. *Harvard Law Review, 90,* 358–378.

Stone, A. A., et al. (2000). Structured writing about stressful events: Exploring potential psychological mediators of positive health effects. *Health Psychology, 19,* 619–624.

Stone, A. A., Neale, J. M., Cox, D. S., & Napoli, A., et al. (1994). Daily events are associated with a secretory immune response to an oral antigen in men. *Health Psychology, 13,* 440–446.

Stone, J., Smyth, R., Carson, A., Lewis, S., Prescott, R., Warlow, C., & Sharpe, M. (2005). Systematic review of misdiagnosis of conversion symptoms and "hysteria." *British Medical Journal, 331,* 989.

Stone, M. H. (1980). *The borderline syndromes: Constitution, personality, and adaptation.* New York: McGraw-Hill.

Stoney, C. M. (2003). Gender and cardiovascular disease: a psychobiological and integrative approach. *Current Directions in Psychological Science, 12,* 129–133.

Stotland, N. L. (2000, July 26). Sertraline: An effective treatment for binge-eating disorder? *Journal Watch Women's Health,* pp. 1, 4.

Stotland, N. L. (2004, September 8). Somatoform psychiatric disorders, physical symptoms. Journal Watch Psychiatry. Retrieved June 16, 2006, from http://psychiatry.jwatch.org/cgi/content/full/2004/908/11.

Stotland, N. L. (2006, June). Postpartum psychosis: Risk factors. *Journal Watch for Psychiatry, 12,* p. 51.

Stout, D. (2000, September 1). Use of illegal drugs is down among young, survey finds. *The New York Times,* p. A18.

Stover, E. S., et al. (1996). Perspectives from the National Institute of Mental Health: Preventing or living with AIDS. *Annals of Behavioral Medicine, 18,* 58–60.

Strakowski, S. M., DelBello, M. P., Zimmerman, M. E., Getz, G. E., Mills, N. P., Ret, J., et al. (2002). Ventricular and periventricular structural volumes in first-versus multiple-episode bipolar disorder. *American Journal of Psychiatry, 159,* 1841–1847.

Strasser, A. A., Kaufmann, V., Jepson, C., Perkins, K. A., Pickworth, W. B., & Wileyto, E. P. (2005). Effects of different nicotine replacement therapies on postcessation psychological responses. *Addictive Behaviors, 30,* 9–17.

Straub, R. E., Jiang, Y., MacLean, C. J., Ma, Y., Webb, B. T., Myakishev, M. V., et al. (2002). Genetic variation in the 6p22.3 gene DTNBP1, the human ortholog of the mouse dysbindin gene, is associated with schizophrenia. *American Journal of Human Genetics, 71,* 337–348.

Strauss, J. L., Hayes, A. M., Johnson, S. L., Newman, C. F., Browne, G. K., Barber, J. P. et al. (2006). Early alliance, alliance ruptures, and symptom change in a nonrandomized trial of cognitive therapy for avoidant and obsessive–compulsive personality disorders. *Journal of Consulting and Clinical Psychology, 74,* 337–345.

Stricker, G. (2003). Is this the right book at the wrong time? *Contemporary Psychology, 48,* 726–728.

Stricker, G., & Gold, J. R. (1999). The Rorschach: Toward a nomothetically based, idiographically applicable configurational model. *Psychological Assessment, 11,* 240–250.

Stricker, G., & Gold, J. R. (2001, January). An introduction to psychotherapy integration. *NYS Psychologist, 13,* 7–12.

Striegel-Moore, R. H., Dohm, F. A., Kraemer, H. C., Taylor, C. B., Daniels, S. D., Crawford, P. B., et al. (2003). Eating disorders in white and black women. *American Journal of Psychiatry, 160*, 1326–1331.

Strike, P. C., Magid, K., Whitehead, D. L., Brydon, L., Bhattacharyya, M. R., & Steptoe, A. (2006) Pathophysiological processes underlying emotional triggering of acute cardiac events. *Proceedings of the National Academy of Sciences*. Retrieved March 16, 2006, from http://www.pnas.org/cgi/content/abstract/103/11/4322.

Strober, M., Freeman, R., Lampert, C., Diamond, J., & Kaye, W. (2000). Controlled family study of anorexia nervosa and bulimia nervosa: Evidence of shared liability and transmission of partial syndromes. *American Journal of Psychiatry, 157*, 393–401.

Stroebe, M., Stroebe, W., & Abakoumkin, G. (2005). The broken heart: Suicidal ideation in bereavement. *American Journal of Psychiatry, 162*, 2178–2180.

Strollo, P. J., & Rogers, R. M. (1996). Obstructive sleep apnea. *The New England Journal of Medicine, 334*, 99–104.

Ström, L., Pettersson, R., & Andersson, G. (2004). Internet-based treatment for insomnia: A controlled evaluation. *Journal of Consulting and Clinical Psychology, 72*, 113–120.

Strote, J., Lee, J. E., & Wechsler, H. (2002). Increasing MDMA use among college students: Results of a national survey. *Journal of the American Academy of Child & Adolescent Psychiatry, 41*, 1215.

Strozier, C. B. (2001). *Heinz Kohut: The making of a psychoanalyst*. New York: Farrar, Straus & Giroux.

Stuart, G. L., Treat, T. A., & Wade, W. A., (2000). Effectiveness of an empirically based treatment for panic disorder delivered in a service clinic setting: 1-year follow-up. *Journal of Consulting and Clinical Psychology, 68*, 506–512.

Stuart, R. B. (2004). Twelve practical suggestions for achieving multicultural competence. *Professional Psychology: Research and Practice, 35*, 3–9.

Stuart, S., O'Hara, M. W., & Gorman, L. L. (2003). The prevention and treatment of postpartum depression. *Archives of Women's Mental Health, 6* (Suppl. 2), S57–S69.

Study finds psychotherapy can treat those with disease fears. (2004, March 23). *CNN Web Posting.* Retrieved March 23, 2004, from http://www.cnn.com/2004/HEALTH/03/23/hypochondria.treatment.ap/index.html.

Study links binge eating to mutation in a gene. (2003, March 20). *The New York Times*, p. A27.

Stunkard, A. J., & Sørensen, T. I. A. (1993). Obesity and socioeconomic status—A complex relation. *New England Journal of Medicine, 329*, 1036–1037.

Stutts, J. T., Hickey, S. E., & Kasdan, M. L. (2003) Malingering by proxy: A form of pediatric condition falsification. *Journal of Developmental and Behavioral Pediatrics, 24*, 276–278.

Styron, W. (1990). *Darkness visible*. New York: Random House.

Substance Abuse and Mental Health Services Administration (SAMHSA). (2006, updated August 29). *2004 National Survey on Drug Use & Health: Detailed tables*. Retrieved November 18, 2006, from http://www.drugabusestatistics.samhsa.gov/NSDUH/2k4nsduh/2k4tabs/Sect1peTabs1to66.htm#tab1.1b.

Sue, S. (2003). In defense of cultural competency in psychotherapy and treatment. *American Psychologist, 58*, 964–970.

Suinn, R. M. (2001). The terrible twos—Anger and anxiety: Hazardous to your health. *American Psychologist, 56*, 27–36.

Sukhodolsky, D. G., Golub, A., Stone, E. C., & Orban, L. (2005). Dismantling anger control training for children: A randomized pilot study of social problem-solving versus social skills training components. *Behavior Therapy, 36*, 15–23.

Sullivan, H. S. (1962). *Schizophrenia as a human process*. New York: Norton.

Sullivan, M. D. (2000). DSM-IV pain disorder: A case against the diagnosis. *International Review of Psychiatry, 12*, 91–98.

Sullivan, P. F., Neale, M. C., & Kendler, K. S. (2000). Genetic epidemiology of major depression: Review and meta-analysis. *American Journal of Psychiatry, 157*, 1552–1562.

Sulloway, F. J. (1983). *Freud: Biologist of the mind*. New York: Basic Books.

Suls, J., Wan, C. K., & Blanchard, E. B. (1994). A multilevel data-analytic approach for evaluation of relationships between daily life stressors and symptomatology: Patients with irritable bowel syndrome. *Health Psychology, 13*, 103–113.

Sun, P., & Swindle, R. (2005). Are men with erectile dysfunction more likely to have hypertension than men without erectile dysfunction? A naturalistic national cohort study. *Journal of Urology, 174*, 244–248.

Sun, P., Cameron, A., Seftel, A., Shabsigh, R, Niederberger, C., & Guay, A. (2006). Erectile dysfunction—an observable marker of diabetes mellitus? A large national epidemiological study. *Journal of Urology, 176*, 1081–1085.

Sutker, P. B., Davis, J, M., Uddo, M., & Ditta, S. R. (1995). War zone stress, personal resources, and PTSD in Persian Gulf War returnees. *Journal of Abnormal Psychology, 104*, 444–452.

Svartberg, M., Stiles, T. C., & Seltzer, M. H. (2004). Randomized, controlled trial of the effectiveness of short-term dynamic psychotherapy and cognitive therapy for Cluster C personality disorders. *American Journal of Psychiatry, 161*, 810–817.

Svikis, D. S., Velez, M. L., & Pickens, R. W. (1994). Genetic aspects of alcohol use and alcoholism in women. *Alcohol Health & Research World, 18*, 192–196.

Swanson, H. L., Mink, J., & Bocian, K. M. (1999). Cognitive processing deficits in poor readers with symptoms of reading disabilities and ADHD: More alike than different? *Journal of Educational Psychology, 91* (2), 321–333.

Swanson, J. W., Swartz, M. S., Van Dorn, R. A., Elbogen, E. B., Wagner, R., Rosenheck, R. A., et al. (2006). A national study of violent behavior in persons with schizophrenia. *Archives of General Psychiatry, 63*, 490–499.

Swartz, M., et al. (1991). Somatization disorder. In L. N. Robins & D. A. Regier (Eds.), *Psychiatric disorders in America: The Epidemiologic Catchment Area Study* (pp. 220–257). New York: Free Press.

Swartz, M. S., Perkins, D. O., Stroup, T. S., Davis, S. M., Capuano, G., Rosenheck, R. A., et al. (2007). Effects of antipsychotic medications on psychosocial functioning in patients with chronic schizophrenia: Findings from the NIMH CATIE Study. *American Journal of Psychiatry, 164*, 428–436.

Sweeney, J. A., Clementz, B. A., Haas, G. L., Escobar, M. D., Drake, K., & Frances, A. J. (1994). Eye tracking dysfunction in schizophrenia: Characterization of component eye movement abnormalities, diagnostic specificity, and the role of attention. *Journal of Abnormal Psychology, 103*, 222–230.

Swendsen, J. D., & Mazure, C. M. (2000). Life stress as a risk factor for postpartum depression: Current research and methodological issues. *Clinical Psychology: Science and Practice, 7*, 17–31.

Swets, J. A., Dawes, R. M., & Monahan, J. (2000). Psychological science can improve diagnostic decisions. *Psychological Science in the Public Interest, 1*, 1–26.

Szasz, T. (2003a). Psychiatry and the control of dangerousness: On the apotropaic function of the term "mental illness." *Journal of Medical Ethics, 29*, 227–230.

Szasz, T. (2003b). Response to: Comments on psychiatry and the control of dangerousness: On the apotropaic function of the term "mental illness." *Journal of Medical Ethics, 29*, 237.

Szasz, T. S. (1961). *The myth of mental illness*. New York: Harper & Row.

Szasz, T. S. (1970). *Ideology and insanity: Essays on the psychiatric dehumanization of man*. New York: Doubleday Anchor.

Szasz, T. S. (2000). Second commentary on "Aristotle's function argument." *Philosophy, Psychiatry, & Psychology, 7*(1), 3–16.

Szatmari, P., Bryson, S. E., Streiner, D. L., Wilson, F., Archer, L., & Ryerse, C. (2000). Two-year outcome of preschool children with autism or Asperger's syndrome. *American Journal of Psychiatry, 157*, 1980–1987.

Szeszko, P. R., Ardekani, B. A., Ashtari, M., Malhotra, A. K., Robinson, D. G., Bilder, R. M., & Lim, K. O. (2005). White matter abnormalities in obsessive-compulsive disorder: A diffusion tensor imaging study. *Archives of General Psychiatry, 62*, 782–790.

T

Takahashi, C. (2001, April 8). Selling to Gen Y: A far cry from Betty Crocker. *The New York Times Week in Review*, p. 3.

Tamm, L., Menon, V., & Reiss, A. L. (2006). Parietal attentional system aberrations during target detection in adolescents with attention deficit hyperactivity disorder: Event-related fMRI evidence. *American Journal of Psychiatry, 163*, 1033–1043.

Tanaka, K., Shintani, N., Hashimoto, H., Kawagishi, N., Ago, Y., Matsuda, T., et al. (2006). Calming an "ADHD" Mouse. *The Journal of Neuroscience, 26*, 5091–5097.

Tanasescu, M., Leitzmann, M. F., Rimm, E. B., Willett, W. C., Stampfer, M. J., & Hu, F. B. (2002). Exercise type and intensity in relation to coronary heart disease in men. *Journal of the American Medical Association, 288*, 1994–2000.

Tang, C. S., Critelli, J. W., & Porter, J. F. (1995). Sexual aggression and victimization in dating relationships among Chinese college students. *Archives of Sexual Behavior, 24*, 47–53.

Tapert, S. F., Brown, G. G., Baratta, M. V., & Brown, S. A. (2004). fMRI BOLD response to alcohol stimuli in alcohol dependent young women. *Addictive Behavior, 29*, 33–50.

Tardiff, K., Marzuk, P. M., Leon, A. C., Portera, L., & Weiner, C. (1997). Violence by patients admitted to a private psychiatric hospital. *American Journal of Psychiatry, 154*, 88–93.

Tariot, P. N., Farlow, M. R., Grossberg, G. T., Graham, S. M., McDonald, S., Gergel, I., et al. (2004). Memantine treatment in patients with moderate to severe Alzheimer disease already receiving donepezil: A randomized controlled trial. *Journal of the American Medical Association, 291*, 317–324.

Tarrier, N., & Wykes, T. (2004). Is there evidence that cognitive behaviour therapy is an effective treatment for schizophrenia? A cautious or cautionary tale? *Behaviour Research and Therapy, 42*, 1377–1401.

Tarrier, N., Kinney, C., McCarthy, E., Humphreys, L., Wittkowski, A., & Morris, J. (2000). Two-year follow-up of cognitive-behavioral therapy and supportive counseling in the treatment of persistent symptoms in chronic schizophrenia. *Journal of Consulting and Clinical Psychology, 68*, 917–922.

Tate, D. F., Wing, R. R., & Winett, R. A. (2001). Internet technology to deliver a behavioral weight loss program. *Journal of the American Medical Association, 285*, 1172–1177.

Taylor, C. B., & Luce, K. H. (2003). Computer- and Internet-based psychotherapy interventions. *Current Directions in Psychological Science, 12*, 18–22.

Taylor, K. L., Lamdan, R. M., Siegel, J. E., Shelby, R., Moran-Klimi, K., & Hrywna, M. (2003). Psychological adjustment among African American breast cancer patients: One-year follow-up results of a randomized psychoeducational group intervention. *Health Psychology, 22*, 316–323.

Taylor, M. A., & Fink, M. (2003). Catatonia in psychiatric classification: A home of its own. *American Journal of Psychiatry, 160*, 1233–1241.

Taylor, M. J., Freemantle, N., Geddes, J. R., & Bhagwagar, Z. (2006). Early onset of selective serotonin reuptake inhibitor antidepressant action: Systematic review and meta-analysis. *Archives of General Psychiatry, 63*, 1217–1223.

Taylor, M. J., Rudkin, L., & Hawton, K. (2005). Strategies for managing antidepressant-induced sexual dysfunction: Systematic review of randomised controlled trials. *Journal of Affective Disorders, 88*, 241–254.

Taylor, S. (1995). Assessment of obsessions and compulsions: Reliability, validity, and sensitivity to treatment effects. *Clinical Psychology Review, 15*, 261–296.

Taylor, S., & Rachman, S. J. (1994). Klein's suffocation theory of panic. *Archives of General Psychiatry, 51*, 505–506.

Taylor, S., Fedoroff, I. C., Koch, W. J., Thordarson, D. S., Fecteau, G., & Nicki, R. M. (2001). Posttraumatic stress disorder arising after road traffic collisions: Patterns of response to cognitive–behavior therapy. *Journal of Consulting and Clinical Psychology, 69*, 541–551.

Taylor, S., Thordarson, D. S., Maxfield, L., Fedoroff, I. C., Lovell, K., & Ogrodniczuk J. (2003). Comparative efficacy, speed, and adverse effects of three PTSD treatments: Exposure therapy, EMDR, and relaxation training. *Journal of Consulting and Clinical Psychology, 71*, 330–338.

Taylor, V., & Rupp, L. J. (2004). Chicks with dicks, men in dresses: What it means to be a drag queen. *Journal of Homosexuality, 46*, 113–133.

Teasdale, T. W., & Engberg, A. W. (2003). Cognitive dysfunction in young men following head injury in childhood and adolescence: A population study. *Journal of Neurology and Neurosurgical Psychiatry, 74*, 933–936.

Tecott, L. H. (2003). The genes and brains of mice and men. *American Journal of Psychiatry, 160*, 646–656.

Teens see little risk in ecstasy. (2003, February 11). *CNN Web Posting.* Retrieved February 15, 2003, from http://www.cnn.com/2003/HEALTH/parenting/02/11/drug.survey/index.html.

Teicher, M. H., Samson, J. A., Polcari, A., & McGreenery, C. E. (2006). Sticks, stones, and hurtful words: Relative effects of various forms of childhood maltreatment. *American Journal of Psychiatry, 163*, 993–1000.

Tein, J. Y., Sandler, I. N., MacKinnon, D. P., & Wolchik, S. A. (2004). How did it work? Who did it work for? Mediation in the context of a moderated prevention effect for children of divorce. *Journal of Consulting and Clinical Psychology, 72*, 617–624.

Teplin, L. A., McClelland, G. M., Abram, K. M., & Weiner, D. A. (2005). Crime victimization in adults with severe mental illness: Comparison with the National Crime Victimization Survey. *Archives of General Psychiatry, 62*, 911–921.

ter Kuile, M. M., van Lankveld, J. J. D. M., de Groot, E., Melles, R., Neffs, J., & and Zandbergen, M. (2006). Cognitive-behavioral therapy for women with lifelong vaginismus: Process and prognostic factors. *Behaviour Research and Therapy, 45*, 359–373.

Teri, L., & Wagner, A. (1992). Alzheimer's disease and depression. *Journal of Consulting and Clinical Psychology, 60*, 379–391.

Terman, J. S., et al. (2001). Circadian time of morning light administration and therapeutic response in winter depression. *Archives of General Psychiatry, 58*, 69–75.

Teunisse, R. J., Cruysberg, J. R., Hoefnagels, W. H., Verbeek, A. L., & Zitman, F. G., (1996). Visual hallucinations in psychologically normal people: Charles Bonnnet's syndrome. *Lancet, 347*, 794–797.

Thakker, J., & Ward, T. (1998). Culture and classification: The cross-cultural application of the DSM-IV. *Clinical Psychology Review, 18*, 501–529.

Thannickal, T. C., et al. (2000). Reduced number of hypocretin neurons in human narcolepsy. *Neuron, 17*, 469–474.

Thase, M. E. (2006). A tale of two paradigms. *Clinical Psychology: Science and Practice, 13*, 94–98.

Thase, M. E., et al. (1997). Treatment of major depression with psychotherapy or psychotherapy-pharmacotherapy combinations. *Archives of General Psychiatry, 54*, 1009–1015.

The Center on Alcohol Marketing and Youth. (2005). *Underage drinking in the United States: A Status Report, 2004*. Retrieved February 12, 2006, from http://camy.org/research/underage2004/report.pdf.

The McKnight Investigators. (2003). Risk factors for the onset of eating disorders in adolescent girls: Results of the McKnight Longitudinal Risk Factor Study. *American Journal of Psychiatry, 160,* 248–254.

The Pediatric OCD Treatment Study (POTS) Team (2004). Cognitive-behavior therapy, sertraline, and their combination for children and adolescents with obsessive-compulsive disorder. *Journal of the American Medical Association, 292,* 1969–1976.

Theorell, T. (1992). Critical life changes. A review of research. *Psychotherapy and Psychomatics, 57,* 108–117.

Therapy and hypochondriacs often make poor mix, study says. (2004, March 25). *The New York Times,* p. A19.

Thibodeau, R., Jorgensen, R. S., & Kim, S. (2006). Depression, anxiety, and resting frontal EEG asymmetry: A meta-analytic review. *Journal of Abnormal Psychology, 115,* 715–729.

Thiedke, C. C. (2003). Nocturnal enuresis. *American Family Physician, 67,* 1509–1510.

Thioux, M., Stark, D. E., Klaiman, C., & Schultz, R. (2006). The day of the week when you were born in 700 ms: Calendar computation in an autistic savant. *Journal of Experimental Psychology: Human Perception and Performance, 32,* 1155–1168.

Thoits, P. A. (1983). Dimensions of life events as influences upon the genesis of psychological distress and associated conditions: An evaluation and synthesis of the literature. In H. B. Kaplan (Ed.), *Psychosocial stress: Trends in theory and research.* (pp. 33–103). New York: Academic Press.

Thompson, P. M., Hayashi, K. M., de Zubicaray, G., Janke, A. L., Rose, S. E., Semple, J., et al. (2003). Dynamics of gray matter loss in Alzheimer's Disease. *Journal of Neuroscience, 23,* 994.

Thompson, P. M., Hayashi, K. M., Simon, S. L., Geaga, J. A., Hong, M. S., Sui, Y., et al. (2005). Structural abnormalities in the brains of human subjects who use methamphetamine. *Journal of Neuroscience, 30,* 6028–6036.

Thompson, P. M., Vidal, C., Gledd, J. N., Gochman, P., Blumenthal, J., Nicolson, R., et al. (2001). Mapping adolescent brain change reveals dynamic wave of accelerated gray matter loss in very early-onset schizophrenia. *Proceedings of the National Academy of Science, 98,* 11650–11655.

Thompson, T. (1995). *The beast: A journey through depression.* New York: Putnam.

Thompson-Brenner, H., Glass, S., & Westen, D. (2003). A multidimensional meta-analysis of psychotherapy for bulimia nervosa. *Clinical Psychology: Science and Practice, 10,* 269–287.

Three million teens think suicide. (2002, July 15). *MSNBC Web Posting.* Retrieved July 15 from http://www.msnbc.com/news/780187.asp.

Tienari, P., Wynne, L. C., Läksy, K., Moring, J., Nieminen, P., Sorri, A., et al. (2003). Genetic boundaries of the schizophrenia spectrum: Evidence from the Finnish adoptive family study of schizophrenia. *American Journal of Psychiatry, 160,* 1587–1594.

Tienari, P., Wynne, L.C., Sorri, A., Lahti, I., Laksy, K., Moring, J., et al. (2004). Genotype-environment interaction in schizophrenia spectrum disorder. *British Journal of Psychiatry, 184,* 216–222.

Tiffany, S. T., Cox, L. S., & Elash, C. A. (2000). Effects of transdermal nicotine patches on abstinence-induced and cue-elicited craving in cigarette smokers. *Journal of Consulting and Clinical Psychology, 68,* 233–240.

Tiihonen, J., et al. (1992). Modified activity of the human auditory cortex during auditory hallucinations. *American Journal of Psychiatry, 149,* 255–257.

Tillfors, M., Furmark, T., Ekselius, L., & Fredrikson, M. (2001). Social phobia and avoidant personality disorder as related to parental history of social anxiety: A general population study. *Behaviour Research and Therapy, 39,* 289–298.

Time capsule. (2000, November). *Monitor on Psychology,* p. 10.

Timman, R., Roos, R., Maat-Kievit, A., & Tibben, A. (2004). Adverse effects of predictive testing for Huntington Disease underestimated: Long-term effects 7–10 years after the test. *Health Psychology, 23,* 189–197.

Timpson, J., et al. (1988). Depression in a Native Canadian in Northwestern Ontario: Sadness, grief or spiritual illness? *Canada's Mental Health, 36*(2–3), 5–8.

Tishler, P. V., Larkin, E. K., Schluchter, M. D., & Redline, S. (2003). Incidence of sleep-disordered breathing in an urban adult population: The relative importance of risk factors in the development of sleep-disordered breathing. *Journal of the American Medical Association, 289,* 2230–2237.

Tobacco Information and Prevention Source (TIPS). (2005, December). *Adult Cigarette Smoking in the United States: Current Estimates, Fact sheet,* December 2005, available at http://www.cdc.gov/TOBACCO/factsheets/AdultCigaretteSmoking_FactSheet.htm.

Tobin, D. L., Johnson, C. L., & Dennis, A. B. (1992). Divergent forms of purging behavior in bulimia nervosa patients. *International Journal of Eating Disorders, 11,* 17–24.

Tohen, M., Baker, R. W., Altshuler, L. L., Zarate, C. A., Suppes, T., Ketter, T. A., et al. (2002). Olanzapine versus divalproex in the treatment of acute mania. *American Journal of Psychiatry, 159,* 1011–1017.

Tohen, M., Jacobs, T. G., Grundy, S. L., McElroy, S. L., Banov, M. C., Janicak, P. G., et al. (2000). Efficacy of olanzapine in acute bipolar mania: A double-blind, placebo-controlled study. *Archives of General Psychiatry, 57,* 841–849.

Tohen, M., Ketter, T. A., Zarate, C. A., Suppes, T., Frye, M., Altshuler, L., et al. (2003). Olanzapine versus divalproex sodium for the treatment of acute mania and maintenance of remission: A 47-week study. *American Journal of Psychiatry, 160,* 1263–1271.

Tohen, M., Zarate, C. A., Hennen, J., Khalsa, H.-M. K., Strakowski, S. M., Gebre-Medhin, P., et al. (2003). The McLean-Harvard First-Episode Mania Study: Prediction of recovery and first recurrence. *American Journal of Psychiatry, 160,* 2099–2107.

Toichi, M., Kamio, Y., Okada, T., Sakihama, M., Youngstrom, E. A., Findling, R. F., & Yamamoto, K. (2002). A lack of self-consciousness in autism. *American Journal of Psychiatry, 159,* 1422–1424.

Tolin, D. F., & Foa, E. B. (2006). Sex differences in trauma and posttraumatic stress disorder: A quantitative review of 25 years of research. *Psychological Bulletin, 132,* 959–992.

Tolomiczenko, G. S., Sota, T., & Goering, P. N. (2000). Personality assessment of homeless adults as a tool for service planning. *Journal of Personality Disorders, 14,* 152–161.

Tomlinson, K. L, Tate, S. R., Anderson, K. G., McCarthy, D. M., & Brown, S. A. (2006). An examination of self-medication and rebound effects: Psychiatric symptomatology before and after alcohol or drug relapse. *Addictive Behaviors, 31,* 461–474.

Tonstad, S., Tønnesen, P., Hajek, P., Williams, K. E., Billing, C. B., Reeves, K. R., for the Varenicline Phase 3 Study Group (2006). Effect of maintenance therapy with varenicline on smoking cessation: A randomized controlled trial. *Journal of the American Medical Association, 296,* 64–71.

Toomey, R., et al. (2003). A twin study of the neuropsychological consequences of stimulant abuse. *Archives of General Psychiatry, 60,* 303–310.

Toomey, R., Lyons, M. J., Eisen, S. A., Xian, H., Chantarujikapong, S., Seidman, L. J., et al. (2003). A twin study of the neuropsychological consequences of stimulant abuse. *Archives of General Psychiatry, 60,* 303–310.

Torgersen, S. (1986). Genetic factors in moderately severe and mild affective disorder. *Archives of General Psychiatry, 43,* 222–226.

Torgersen, S., Kringlen, E., & Cramer, V. (2001). The prevalence of personality disorders in a community sample. *Archives of General Psychiatry, 58,* 590–596.

Torgesen, J. K., et al. (2001). Intensive remedial instruction for children with severe reading disabilities: Immediate and long-term outcomes from two instructional approaches. *Journal of Learning Disabilities, 34*(1), 33–58.

Torrey, E. F., & Zdanowicz, M. (1999, May 28). A right to mental illness? *PsychLaws.Org.* Retrieved November 14, 2003, from http://www.psychlaws.org/GeneralResources/article14.htm.

Tough, P. (2001, July 29). The alchemy of OxyContin. *The New York Times Magazine,* pp. 32–37, 52, 62–63.

Tower, R. B., & Kasl, S. V. (1996). Depressive symptoms across older spouses: Longitudinal influences. *Psychology and Aging, 11,* 683–697.

Tradgold, A. F. (1914). *Mental deficiency.* New York: Wainwood.

Trask, P. C., & Sigmon, S. T. (1997). Munchausen syndrome: A review and new conceptualization. *Clinical Psychology: Science and Practice, 4,* 346–358.

Traven, N. D., Kuller, L. H., Ives, D. G., Rutan, G. H., & Perper, J. A. (1995). Coronary heart disease mortality and sudden death: Trends and patterns in 35- to 44-year-old white males, 1970–1990. *American Journal of Epidemiology, 142,* 45–52.

Treatment for Adolescents with Depression Study (TADS) Team. (2004). Fluoxetine, cognitive-behavioral therapy, and their combination for adolescents with depression treatment for adolescents with depression study (TADS) randomized controlled trial. *Journal of the American Medical Association, 292,* 807–820.

Treatment of alcoholism—Part II. (1996, September). *The Harvard Mental Health Letter, 13,* 1–5.

Treffert, D. A. (1988). The idiot savant: A review of the syndrome. *American Journal of Psychiatry, 145,* 563–572.

Tremblay, R. E., et al. (1992). Early disruptive behavior, poor school achievement, delinquent behavior, and delinquent personality: Longitudinal analyses. *Journal of Consulting and Clinical Psychology, 60,* 64–72.

Treynor, W., Gonzalez, R., & Nolen-Hoeksema, S. (2003). Rumination reconsidered: A psychometric analysis. *Cognitive Therapy & Research, 27,* 247–259.

Trimble, J. E. (1991). The mental health service and training needs of American Indians. In H. F. Myers, et al. (Eds.), *Ethnic minority perspectives on clinical training and services in psychology* (pp. 43–48). Washington, DC: American Psychological Association.

Trinh, N.-H., Hoblyn, J., Mohanty, S., & Yaffe, K. (2003). Efficacy of cholinesterase inhibitors in the treatment of neuropsychiatric symptoms and functional impairment in Alzheimer Disease: A meta-analysis. *Journal of the American Medical Association, 289,* 210–216.

Trivedi, M. H., Fava, M., Fava, M., Thase, M. E., Quitkin, F., Warden, D., Ritz, L., et al. (2006). Medication augmentation after the failure of SSRIs for depression. *New England Journal of Medicine, 354,* 1243–1252.

Trivedi, M. H., Rush, A. J., Wisniewski, S. R., Nierenberg, A. A., Warden, D., Ritz, L., et al. (2006). Evaluation of outcomes with citalopram for depression using measurement-based care in STAR*D: Implications for clinical practice. *American Journal of Psychiatry, 163,* 28–40.

Trull, T. J. (2001). Structural relations between borderline personality disorder features and putative etiological correlates. *Journal of Abnormal Psychology, 110,* 471–481.

Trunzo, J. J., & Pinto, B. M. (2003). Social support as a mediator of optimism and distress in breast cancer survivors. *Journal of Consulting and Clinical Psychology, 71,* 805–811.

Trzepacz, P., & van der Mast, R. (2002). The neuropathophysiology of delirium. In: J. Lindesay, K. Rockwood, & A. Macdonald, (Eds.), *Delirium in old age* (pp. 51–90). Oxford: University Press.

Tsang, H. W.-H. (2001). Applying social skills training the context of vocational rehabilitation for people with schizophrenia. *Journal of Nervous & Mental Disease, 189,* 90–98.

Tsao, J. C. I., Lewin, M. R., & Craske, M. G. (2002). Effects of cognitive–behavior therapy for panic disorder on comorbid conditions: Replication and extension. *Behavior Therapy, 33,* 493–509.

Tseng, W., Mo, K. M., Li, L. S., Chen, G. Q., Ou, L. W., & Zheng, H. B. (1992). Koro epidemics in Guangdong, China: A questionnaire survey. *Journal of Nervous & Mental Disease, 180,* 117–123.

Tuiten, A., Van Honk, J., Koppeschaar, H., Bernaards, C., Thijssen, J., & Verbaten, R. (2000). Time course of effects of testosterone administration on sexual arousal in women. *Archives of General Psychiatry, 57,* 149–153.

Turkington, D., Grant, J. B. F., Rao, N., Sanjay, K., Linsley, K. R., & Young, A. H. (2002). A randomized controlled trial of fluvoxamine in prostatodynia, a male somatoform pain disorder. *Journal of Clinical Psychiatry, 63,* 778–781.

Turkington, D., Kingdon, D., &. Weiden, P. J. (2006). Cognitive behavior therapy for schizophrenia. *American Journal of Psychiatry, 163,* 365–373.

Turner, C. M. (2006). Cognitive–behavioural theory and therapy for obsessive–compulsive disorder in children and adolescents: Current status and future directions. *Clinical Psychology Review, 26,* 912–938.

Turner, J., & Reid, S. (2002). Munchausen's syndrome. *Lancet, 359,* 346–349.

Turner, R. M. (2000). Understanding dialectical behavior therapy. *Clinical Psychology: Science and Practice, 7,* 95–98.

Turner, S. M., & Beidel, D. C. (1989). Social phobia: Clinical syndrome, diagnosis, and comorbidity. *Clinical Psychology Review, 9,* 3–18.

Turner, S. M., Beidel, D. C., & Jacob, R. G. (1994). Social phobia: A comparison of behavior therapy and atenolol. *Journal of Consulting and Clinical Psychology, 62,* 350–358.

Turner, S. M., Beidel, D. C., & Townsley, R. M. (1992). Social phobia: A comparison of specific and generalized subtypes and avoidant personality disorder. *Journal of Abnormal Psychology, 101,* 326–331.

Turner, S. M., McCann, B. S., Beidel, D. C., & Mezzich, J. E. (1986). DSM-III classification of the anxiety disorders: A psychometric study. *Journal of Abnormal Psychology, 95,* 168–172.

Turovksy, J., & Barlow, D. H. (1995, Summer). Albany Panic Control Treatment (PCT) for panic disorder and agoraphobia. *The Clinical Psychologist, 48*(3), 5–6.

Tuschen-Caffier, B., Pook, M., & Frank, M. (2001). Evaluation of manual-based cognitive-behavioral therapy for bulimia nervosa in a service setting. *Behaviour Research and Therapy, 39,* 299–308.

Twenge, J. M., & Nolen-Hoeksema, S. (2002). Age, gender, race, socioeconomic status, and birth cohort differences on the Children's Depression Inventory: A meta-analysis. *Journal of Abnormal Psychology, 111,* 578–588.

U

U.N. AIDS deaths, infections at new highs (2003, November 25). *CNN Web Posting.* Retrieved January 14, 2004, from http://www.cnn.com/2003/HEALTH/conditions/11/25/aids.reut/.

U.S. Department of Health and Human Services (USDHHS). (1986). *NIDA capsules: Heroin.* No. 11. Rockville, MD: U.S. Department of Health and Human Services, Public Health Service, Alcohol, Drug Abuse, and Mental Health Administration, National Institute on Drug Abuse.

U.S. Department of Health and Human Services (USDHHS). (1991). *Vital statistics of the United States 1988.* (Vol. 2. Part A. Mortality). Washington, DC: U.S. Government Printing Office. (DHHS Pub. No. PHS 91–1101).

U.S. Department of Health and Human Services (USDHHS) (1992). *NIDA capsules: LSD (lysergic acid diethylamide)* No. 39. Rockville, MD: U.S. Department of Health and Human Services, Public Health Service, Alcohol, Drug Abuse, and Mental Health Administration, National Institute on Drug Abuse, National Institute on Drug Abuse.

U.S. Department of Health and Human Services (USDHHS) (1993). *National household survey on drug abuse: Highlights 1991.* (DHHS Publication No. (SMA) 93–1979). Washington, DC: U.S. Government Printing Office.

U.S. Department of Health and Human Services (USDHHS) (1999a). *Mental Health: A Report of the Surgeon General.* Rockville, MD: U.S.

Department of Health and Human Services, Substance Abuse and Mental Health Services Administration, Center for Mental Health Services, National Institutes of Health, National Institute of Mental Health.

U.S. Department of Health and Human Services (USDHHS) (1999b). *Mental health: A report of the Surgeon General—Executive summary.* Rockville, MD: U.S. Department of Health and Human Services, Substance Abuse and Mental Health Services Administration, Center for Mental Health Services, National Institutes of Health, National Institute of Mental Health.

U.S. Department of Health and Human Services (USDHHS) (2001). *Mental health: Culture, race, and ethnicity: A supplement to mental health: A report of the Surgeon General—Executive summary.* Rockville, MD: U.S. Department of Health and Human Services, Substance Abuse and Mental Health Services Administration, Center for Mental Health Services, National Institutes of Health, National Institute of Mental Health.

U.S. Department of Justice. (2003). National Crime Victimization Survey. Washington, DC: U.S. Department of Justice.

Uhl, G. R., & Grow, R. W. (2004). The burden of complex genetics in brain disorders. *Archives of General Psychiatry, 61,* 223–229.

UK ECT Review Group. (2003). Efficacy and safety of electroconvulsive therapy in depressive disorders: A systematic review and meta-analysis. *Lancet, 361,* 799–808.

Ullmann, L. P., & Krasner, L. (1975). *A psychological approach to abnormal behavior* (2nd ed.). Englewood Cliffs, NJ: Prentice Hall.

Unger, J. B., Cruz, T. B., & Rohrbach, L. A. (2000). English language use as a risk factor for smoking initiation among Hispanic and Asian American adolescents: Evidence for mediation by tobacco-related beliefs and social norms. *Health Psychology, 19,* 403–410.

Utsey, S. O., Chae, M. H., Brown, C. F., & Kelly, D. (2002). Effect of ethnic group membership on ethnic identity, race-related stress, and quality of life. *Cultural Diversity and Ethnic Minority Psychology, 8,* 366–377.

Utsey, S. O., Payne, Y. A., Jackson, E. S., & Jones, M. A. (2002). Race-related stress, quality of life indicators, and life satisfaction among elderly African Americans. *Cultural Diversity and Ethnic Minority Psychology, 8,* 224–233.

V

Valderhaug, R., Larsson, B., Götestam, K., G., & Piacentini, J. (2007). An open clinical trial of cognitive-behaviour therapy in children and adolescents with obsessive–compulsive disorder administered in regular out-patient clinics *Behaviour Research and Therapy, 45,* 577–589.

Valentiner, D. P., Mounts, N. S., & Deacon, B. J. (2004). Panic attacks, depression and anxiety symptoms, and substance use behaviors during late adolescence. *Journal of Anxiety Disorders, 18,* 573–585.

Vallea, M. F., Huebner, E. S., & Suldo, S. M. (2006). An analysis of hope as a psychological strength. *Journal of School Psychology, 44,* 393–406.

Van Ameringen, M. A., et al. (2001). Sertraline treatment of generalized social phobia: A 20-week, double-blind, placebo-controlled study. *American Journal of Psychiatry, 158,* 275–281.

Van Balkom, A. J. L. M., Bakker, A., Spinhoven, P., Blaauw, B. M., Smeenk, S., & Ruesink, B. (1997). A meta-analysis of the treatment of panic disorder with or without agoraphobia: A comparison of psychopharmacological, cognitive-behavioral, and combination treatments. *Journal of Nervous & Mental Disease, 185,* 510–516.

van der Stelt, O., Frye, J., Lieberman, J. A., & Belger, A. (2004). Impaired P3 generation reflects high-level and progressive neurocognitive dysfunction in schizophrenia. *Archives of General Psychiatry, 61,* 237–248.

Van Eerdewegh, P., Little, R. D., Dupuis, J., Del Mastro, R. G., Falls, K., Simon, J., et al. (2002). Association of the ADAM33 gene with asthma and bronchial hyperresponsiveness. *Nature, 418,* 426–430.

van Emmerik, A. A. P., Kamphuis, J. H., Hulsbosch, A. M., & Emmelkamp, P. M. (2002). Single session debriefing after psychological trauma: A meta-analysis. *Lancet, 360,* 766–771.

van Goozen, S. H. M., Slabbekoorn, D., Gooren, L. J. G., Sanders, G., & Cohen-Kettenis, P. T. (2002). Organizing and activating effects of sex hormones in homosexual transsexuals. *Behavioral Neuroscience, 116,* 982–988.

Van Humbeeck, G., Van Audenhove, Ch., De Hert, M., Pieters, G., & Storms, G. (2002). Expressed emotion: A review of assessment instruments *Clinical Psychology Review, 22,* 321–341.

van Lankveld, J. J. D. M., ter Kuile, M. M., de Groot, H. E., Melles, R., Neffs, J., Zandbergen, M. (2006). Cognitive-behavioral therapy for women with lifelong vaginismus: A randomized waiting-list controlled trial of efficacy. *Journal of Consulting and Clinical Psychology, 74,* 168–178.

Van Ommeren, M., de Jong, J. T., Sharma, B., Komproe, I., Thapa, S. B., & Cardena, E. (2001). Psychiatric disorders among tortured Bhutanese refugees in Nepal. *Archives of General Psychiatry, 58,* 475–482.

Van Susteren, N. (2002). The insanity defense, continued. *The Journal of the American Academy of Psychiatry and the Law, 30,* 474–475. [Editorial]

Van Wie, V. E., & Gross, A. M. (2001). The role of woman's explanations for refusal on men's ability to discriminate unwanted sexual behavior in a date rape scenario. *Journal of Family Violence, 16,* 331–344.

VandeCreek, L., & Knapp, S. (2001). *Tarasoff and beyond: Legal and clinical considerations in the treatment of life-endangering patients.* Sarasota, FL: Professional Resource Press.

VandenBos, G. R., & Williams, S. (2000). The Internet versus the telephone: What is telehealth, anyway? *Professional Psychology: Research and Practice, 31,* 490–492.

Vanderkam, L. (2003). *Barbie and fat as a feminist issue.* Retrieved November 19, 2003, from http://www.shethinks.org/articles/an00208.cfm.

Vastag, B. (2004a). National autism summit charts a path through a scientific, clinical wilderness. *Journal of the American Medical Association, 291,* 31–32.

Vastag, B. (2004b). Obesity is now on everyone's plate. *Journal of the American Medical Association, 291,* 1186–1188.

Vazire, S. (2006). Informant reports: A cheap, fast, and easy method for personality assessment. *Journal of Research in Personality, 40,* 472–481.

Vega, W. A., et al. (1998). Lifetime prevalence of DSM-III-R psychiatric disorders among urban and rural Mexican Americans in California. *Archives of General Psychiatry, 55,* 771–778.

Velting, O. N., Setzer, N. J., & Albano, A. M. (2004). Update on and advances in assessment and cognitive–behavioral treatment of anxiety disorders in children and adolescents. *Professional Psychology: Research and Practice, 35,* 42–54.

Verghese, A. (2004, February 22). Hope and clarity: Is optimism a cure? *The New York Times Magazine,* pp. 11–12.

Verghese, J., Lipton, R. B., Katz, M. J., Hall, C. B., Derby, C. A., Kuslansky, G., et al. (2003). Leisure activities and the risk of dementia in the elderly. *New England Journal of Medicine, 348,* 2508–2516.

Verhovek, S. H. (2000). What is the matter with Mary Jane? *The New York Times Week in Review,* p. 3.

Vermeer, S. E., Prins, N. D., den Heijer, T., Hofman, A., Koudstaal, P. J., & Breteler, M. M. B. (2003). Silent brain infarcts and the risk of dementia and cognitive decline. *New England Journal of Medicine, 348,* 1215–1222.

Vermetten E., et al. (2006). Hippocampal and amygdalar volumes in dissociative identity disorder. *American Journal of Psychiatry, 163,* 630–636.

Vickers, K., & McNallly, R. J. (2005). Respiratory symptoms and panic in the National Comorbidity Survey: A test of Klein's suffocation false alarm theory. *Behaviour Research and Therapy, 43,* 1011–1018.

Vidal, C. N., Rapoport, J. L., Hayashi, K. M., Geaga, J. A., Sui, Y., McLemore, L. E., et al. (2006). Dynamically spreading frontal and cingulate deficits mapped in adolescents with schizophrenia. *Archives of General Psychiatry, 63,* 25–34.

Viglione, D. J. (1999). A review of recent research addressing the utility of the Rorschach. *Psychological Assessment, 11,* 251–265.

Vik, P. W., Carrello, P., Tate, S. R., & Field, C. (2000). Progression of consequences among heavy-drinking college students. *Psychology of Addictive Behaviors, 14,* 91–101.

Viken, R. J., Treat, T. A., Nosofsky, R. M., McFall, R. M., & Palmeri, T. J. (2002). Modeling individual differences in perceptual and attentional processes related to bulimic symptoms. *Journal of Abnormal Psychology, 111,* 598–609.

Villarosa, L. (2002, December 3). To prevent sexual abuse, abusers step forward. *The New York Times,* p. F5.

Vincent, J. B., Masellis, M., Lawrence, J., Choi, V., Gurling, H. M., Parikh, S. V., et al. (1999). Genetic association analysis of serotonin system genes in bipolar affective disorder. *American Journal of Psychiatry, 156,* 136–138.

Visser, S., & Bouman, T. K. (2001). The treatment of hypochondriasis: Exposure plus response prevention vs. cognitive therapy. *Behaviour Research and Therapy, 39,* 423–442.

Vitaliano, P. P., Zhang, J., & Scanlan, J. M. (2003). Is caregiving hazardous to one's physical health? A meta-analysis. *Psychological Bulletin, 129,* 946–972.

Vitaro, F., Arseneault, L., & Tremblay, R.E. (1997). Dispositional predictors of problem gambling in adolescent males. *American Journal of Psychiatry, 154,* 1769–1770

Voelker, R. (2000). Recessive Alzheimer gene? *Journal of the American Medical Association, 284,* 1777.

Volkmar, F. R. (2003). Changing perspectives on ADHD. *American Journal of Psychiatry, 160,* 1025–1007.

Volkmar, F., Chawarska, K., & Klin, A. (2005). Autism in infancy and early childhood. *Annual Review of Psychology, 56,* 315–336.

Volkow, N. D. (2006). Map of human genome opens new opportunities for drug abuse research. *NIDA Notes, 20* (4), 3.

Volkow, N. D., Chang, L., Wang, G. J., Fowler, J. S., Leonido-Yee, M., Franceschi, D., et al. (2001). Association of dopamine transporter reduction with psychomotor impairment in methamphetamine abusers. *American Journal of Psychiatry, 158,* 377–382.

Volkow, N. D., Wang, G. J., Fischman, M. W., Foltin, R. W., Fowler, J. S., Abumrad, N. N., et al. (1997). Relationship between subjective effects of cocaine and dopamine transporter occupancy. *Nature, 386,* 827–830.

Vollset, S. E., Tverdal, A., & Gjessing, H. K. (2006). Smoking and deaths between 40 and 70 years of age in women and men. *Annals of Internal Medicine, 144,* 381–389.

W

Wadden, T. A., Berkowitz, R. I., Womble, L. G., Sarwer, D. B., Phelan, S., Cato, R. K., et al. (2005). Randomized trial of lifestyle modification and pharmacotherapy for obesity. *New England Journal of Medicine, 353,* 2111–2120.

Wadden, T A., Brownell, K. D., & Foster, G. D. (2002). Obesity: Responding to the global epidemic. *Journal of Consulting and Clinical Psychology, 70,* 510–525.

Wade, N. (2000, May 9). Scientists decode Down syndrome chromosome. *The New York Times,* pp. C1, C3.

Wade, N. (2003a, April 15). Once again, scientists say human genome is complete. *The New York Times,* p. F1.

Wade, N. (2003b, June 3). Gene sweepstakes ends, but winner may well be wrong. *The New York Times,* pp. F1, F2.

Wade, T. D., Bulik, C. M., Neale, M., & Kendler, K. S. (2000). Anorexia nervosa and major depression: Shared genetic and environmental risk factors. *American Journal of Psychiatry, 157,* 469–471.

Wadsworth, M. E., & Achenbach, T. M. (2005). Explaining the link between low socioeconomic status and psychopathology: Testing two mechanisms of the social causation hypothesis. *Journal of Consulting and Clinical Psychology, 73,* 1146–1153.

Wagner, K. D., Ambrosini, P., Rynn, M., Wohlberg, C., Yang, R., Greenbaum, M. S., et al. (2003). Efficacy of sertraline in the treatment of children and adolescents with major depressive disorder: Two randomized controlled trials. *Journal of the American Medical Association, 290,* 1033–1041.

Wagner, K. D., Robb, A. S., Findling, R. L., Jin, J., Gutierrez, M. M., & Heydorn, W. E. (2004). A randomized, placebo-controlled trial of citalopram for the treatment of major depression in children and adolescents. *American Journal of Psychiatry, 161,* 1079–1083.

Wagner, K. D., Wohlberg, C. J., & Yang, R. (2004). Efficacy of sertraline in the treatment of children and adolescents with major depressive disorder—reply. *Journal of the American Medical Association, 291,* 42.

Wahlbeck, K., Forsen, T., Osmond, C., Barker, D. J., & Eriksson, J. G. (2001). Association of schizophrenia with low maternal body mass index, small size at birth, and thinness during childhood. *Archives of General Psychiatry, 58,* 48–52.

Wahlberg, K. E., et al. (2001). Long-term stability of communication deviance. *Journal of Abnormal Psychology, 110,* 443–448.

Wainwright, N. W. J., & Surtees, P. G. (2002). Childhood adversity, gender and depression over the life-course. *Journal of Affective Disorders, 72,* 33–44.

Waismann, R., Fenwick, P. B. C., Wilson, G. D., Hewett, T. D., & Lumsden, J. (2003). EEG responses to visual erotic stimuli in men with normal and paraphilic interests. *Archives of Sexual Behavior, 32*(2), 135–144.

Wakefield, H., & Underwager, R. (1996). Commentary on Kenneth Pope's review. *Clinical Psychology: Science and Practice, 3,* 366–371.

Wakefield, J. C. (1992a). The concept of mental disorder: On the boundary between biological facts and social values. *American Psychologist, 47,* 373–388.

Wakefield, J. C. (1992b). Disorder as harmful dysfunction: A conceptual critique of DSM-III-R's definition of mental disorder. *Psychological Review, 99,* 232–247.

Wakefield, J. C. (1997). Normal inability versus pathological disability: Why Ossorio's definition of mental disorder is not sufficient. *Clinical Psychology: Science and Practice, 4,* 249–258.

Wakefield, J. C. (2001). Evolutionary history versus current causal role in the definition of disorder: Reply to McNally. *Behaviour Research and Therapy, 39,* 347–366.

Wakeling, A. (1996). Epidemiology of anorexia nervosa. *Psychiatry Research, 62,* 3–9.

Waldinger, M. D., Zwinderman, A. H., & Olivier, B. (2001). Antidepressants and ejaculation: A double-blind, randomized, placebo-controlled, fixed-dose study with paroxetine, sertraline and nefazodone. *Journal of Clinical Psychopharmacology, 21*(3), 293–297.

Waldman, I. D., & Gizera, I. R. (2006). The genetics of attention deficit hyperactivity disorder. *Clinical Psychology Review, 26,* 396–432.

Walker, E. F., & Diforio, D. (1997). Schizophrenia: A neural diathesis-stress model. *Psychological Review, 104,* 667–685.

Walker, E., Kestler, L., Bollini, A., & Hochman, K. M. (2004). Schizophrenia: Etiology and course. *Annual Review of Psychology, 55,* 401–430.

Walker, L. E. (1988). The battered woman syndrome. In G. T. Hotaling, D. Finkelhor, J. T. Kirkpatrick, & M. A. Straus (Eds.), *Family abuse and its consequences: New directions in research* (pp. 139–148). Newbury Park, CA: Sage.

Walker, R. (2004, February 8). Cialis. *The New York Times Magazine,* p. 26.

Walkup, J. T., et al. (2001). Fluvoxamine for the treatment of anxiety disorders in children and adolescents. The Research Unit on Pediatric

Psychopharmacology Anxiety Study Group. *The New England Journal of Medicine, 344,* 1279–1285.

Wall, T. L., Carr, L. G., & Ehlers, C. L. (2003). Protective association of genetic variation in alcohol dehydrogenase with alcohol dependence in Native American Mission Indians. *American Journal of Psychiatry, 160,* 41–46.

Waller, N. G., & Ross, C. A. (1997). The prevalence of biometric structure of pathological dissociation in the general population: Taxometric and behavior genetic findings. *Journal of Abnormal Psychology, 106,* 499–510.

Wallis, C. (2006, May 15). A tale of two schools. *Time,* pp. 49–51.

Walsh, B. T., Agras, W. W., Devlin, M. J., Fairburn, C. G., Wilson, G. T., Kahn, C., et al. (2000). Fluoxetine for bulimia nervosa following poor response to psychotherapy. *American Journal of Psychiatry, 157,* 1332–1334.

Walsh, B. T., Fairburn, C. G., Mickley, D., Sysko, R., & Parides, M. K. (2004). Treatment of bulimia nervosa in a primary care setting. *American Journal of Psychiatry, 161,* 556–561.

Walsh, B. T., Kaplan, A. S., Attia, E., Olmsted, M., Parides, M., Carter, J. C., et al. (2006). Fluoxetine after weight restoration in anorexia nervosa: A randomized controlled trial. *Journal of the American Medical Association, 295,* 2605–2612.

Walsh, B. T., Wilson, G. T., Loeb, K. L., Devlin, M. J., Pike, K. M., Roose, S. P., et al. (1997). Medication and psychotherapy in the treatment of bulimia nervosa. *American Journal of Psychiatry, 154,* 523–531.

Walsh, R., & Shapiro, S. L. (2006). The meeting of meditative disciplines and Western psychology: A mutually enriching dialogue. *American Psychologist, 61,* 227–239.

Walsh, T., Casadei, S., Coats, K. H., Swisher, E., Stray, S. M., & Higgins, J. (2006). Spectrum of mutations in BRCA1, BRCA2, CHEK2, and TP53 in families at high risk of breast cancer. *Journal of the American Medical Association, 295,* 1379–1388.

Walters, S. T., Wright, J. A., & Shegog, R. (2006). A review of computer and Internet-based interventions for smoking behavior. *Addictive Behaviors, 31,* 264–277.

Wampold, B. E. (2001). *The great psychotherapy debate: Models, methods, and findings.* Mahwah, NJ: Erlbaum.

Wampold, B. E., et al. (1997b). The flat earth as a metaphor for the evidence for uniform efficacy of bonafide psychotherapies: Reply to Crits-Christoph (1997) and Howard, et al. (1997). *Psychological Bulletin, 122,* 226–230.

Wang, C., Cunningham, G., Dobs, A., Iranmanesh,A., Matsumoto, A. M., Snyder, P. J., et al. (2004). Long-term testosterone gel (AndroGel) treatment maintains beneficial effects on sexual function and mood, lean and fat mass, and bone mineral density in hypogonadal men. *Journal of Clinical Endocrinology and Metabolism, 89,* 2085–2098.

Wang, P. S., Lane, M., Olfson, M., Pincus, H. A., Wells, K. B., & Kessler, R. C. (2005). RC Twelve-month use of mental health services in the United States: Results from the National Comorbidity Survey Replication. *Archives of General Psychiatry, 62,* 590–592.

Wang, X., Gao, L., Shinfuku, N., Zhang, H., Zhao, C., & Shen, Y. (2000). Longitudinal study of earthquake-related PTSD in a randomly selected community sample in North China. *American Journal of Psychiatry, 157,* 1260–1266.

Warheit, G. J., Vega, W. A., Auth, J., & Meinhardt, K. (1985). Psychiatric symptoms and dysfunctions among Anglos and Mexican Americans: An epidemiological study. In J. R. Greenley (Ed.), *Research in community and mental health* (pp. 3–32). London: JAI Press.

Warner, J. (2002, October 18). Fish oil eases depression. Retrieved October 20, 2002, from http://my.webmd.com/condition_center_content/mhl/article/1663.54436?z=2950_00000_0000_f1_06.

Warner, L. A., Kessler, R. C., Hughes, M., Anthony, J. C., & Nelson, C. B. (1995). Prevalence and correlates of drug use and dependence in the United States. *Archives of General Psychiatry, 52,* 219–229.

Warner, M. B., Morey, L. C., Finch, J. F., Gunderson, J. G., Skodol, A. E., Sanislow, C. A., et al. (2004). The longitudinal relationship of personality traits and disorders. *Journal of Abnormal Psychology, 113,* 217–227.

Wartik, N. (2000, June 25). Depression comes out of hiding. *The New York Times,* pp. MH1, MH4.

Wassertheil-Smoller, S., Shumaker, S., Ockene, J., Talavera, G. A., Greenland, P., Cochrane, B., et al. (2004). Depression and cardiovascular sequelae in postmenopausal women: The Women's Health initiative (WHI). *Archives of Internal Medicine, 164,* 289–298.

Wassink, T. H., Hazlett, H. C., Epping, E. A., Arndt, S., Dager, S. R., Schellenberg, G. D., et al. (2007). Cerebral cortical gray matter overgrowth and functional variation of the serotonin transporter gene in autism. *Archives of General Psychiatry, 64,* 709–717.

Waterworth, D. M., Bassett, A. S., & Brzustowicz, L. M. (2002). Recent advances in the genetics of schizophrenia. *Cellular and Molecular Life Sciences, 59,* 331–348.

Watson, D., & Clark, L. A. (2006). Clinical diagnosis at the crossroads. *Clinical Psychology: Science and Practice, 13,* 210–215.

Watts, C., & Zimmerman, C. (2002). Violence against women: Global scope and magnitude. *Lancet, 359* (9313), 1232–1237.

Weaver, T. L., & Clum, G. A. (1995). Psychological distress associated with interpersonal violence: A meta-analysis. *Clinical Psychology Review, 15,* 115–140.

Webster-Stratton, C., Reid, J., & Hammond, M. (2001). Social skills and problem-solving training for children with early-onset conduct problems: Who benefits? *Journal of Child Psychology & Psychiatry & Allied Disciplines, 42* (7), 943–952.

Wechsler, D. (1975). Intelligence defined and undefined: A relativistic appraisal. *American Psychologist, 30,* 135–139.

Weed, W. S. (2003, December 14). Questions for Raymond Damadian: Scanscam? *The New York Times Online.* Retrieved January 8, 2004, from www.nytimes.com/2003/12/14/magazine/14QUESTIONS.html.

Weems, C. F., Berman, S. L., Silverman, W. K., & Saavedra, L. M. (2001). Cognitive errors in youth with anxiety disorders: The linkages between negative cognitive errors and anxious symptoms. *Cognitive Therapy & Research, 25,* 559–575.

Weems, C. F., Hayward, C., Killen, J., & Taylor, C. B. (2002). A longitudinal investigation of anxiety sensitivity in adolescence. *Journal of Abnormal Psychology, 111,* 471–477.

Weems, C. F., Pina, A. A., Costa, N. M., Watts, S. E., Taylor, L. K., & Cannon, M. F. (2007). Predisaster trait anxiety and negative affect predict posttraumatic stress in youths after Hurricane Katrina. *Journal of Consulting and Clinical Psychology, 75,* 154–159.

Wei, W., Sambamoorthi, U., Olfson, M., Walkup, J. T., & Crystal, S. (2005). Use of psychotherapy for depression in older adults. *American Journal of Psychiatry, 162,* 711–717.

Weich, S., Churchill, R., & Lewis, G. (2003). Dysfunctional attitudes and the common mental disorders in primary. *Journal of Affective Disorders, 75,* 269–278.

Weinberg, G. (1972). *Society and the healthy homosexual.* New York: St. Martin's Press.

Weine, S. M., Razzano, L., Brkic, N., Ramic, A., Miller, K., Smajkic, A., et al. (2000). Profiling the trauma related symptoms of Bosnian refugees who have not sought mental health services. *Journal of Nervous & Mental Disease, 188,* 416–421.

Weiner, I. B. (2001). Advancing the science of psychological assessment: The Rorschach Inkblot Method as exemplar. *Psychological Assessment, 13,* 423–432.

Weiner, I. B., Spielberger, C. D., & Abeles, N. (2002). Scientific psychology and the Rorschach Inkblot Method. *The Clinical Psychologist, 55,* 7–12.

Weiner, I. B., Spielberger, C. D., & Abeles, N. (2003). Once more around the park: Correcting misinformation about Rorschach assessment. *The Clinical Psychologist, 56,* 8–9.

Weiner, J. R. (2003). *Tarasoff* warnings resulting in criminal charges: Two case reports. *The Journal of the American Academy of Psychiatry and the Law, 31,* 239–241.

Weiner, R. D. (2000). Retrograde amnesia with electroconvulsive therapy characteristics and implications. *Archives of General Psychiatry, 57,* 591–592.

Weisberg, R. B., Brown, T. A., Wincze, J. P., & Barlow, D. H. (2001). Causal attributions and male sexual arousal: The impact of attributions for a bogus erectile difficulty on sexual arousal, cognitions, and affect. *Journal of Abnormal Psychology, 110,* 324–334.

Weisman, A., et al. (1993). An attributional analysis of expressed emotion in Mexican-American families with schizophrenia. *Journal of Abnormal Psychology, 102,* 601–606.

Weisman, A. G., et al. (1998). Expressed emotion, attributions, and schizophrenia symptom dimensions. *Journal of Abnormal Psychology, 107,* 355–359.

Weisman, A. G., et al. (2000). Controllability perceptions and reactions to symptoms of schizophrenia: A within-family comparison of relatives with high and low expressed emotion. *Journal of Abnormal Psychology, 109,* 167–171.

Weisman, A. G., Rosales, G. A., Kymalainen, J. A., & Armesto, J. C. (2006). Ethnicity, expressed emotion, and schizophrenia patients' perceptions of their family members' criticism. *Journal of Nervous and Mental Disease, 194,* 644–649.

Weiss, R. D., & Mirin, S. M. (1987). *Cocaine.* Washington, DC: American Psychiatric Press.

Weissman, A. N., & Beck, A. T. (1978, November). *Development and validation of the Dysfunctional Attitudes Scale: A preliminary investigation.* Paper presented at the meeting of the American Educational Research Association, Toronto, Canada.

Weissman, M. M. (1999). Depressed adolescents grown up. *Journal of the American Medical Association, 281,* 1707–1713.

Weissman, M. M., & Markowtiz, J. C. (1994). Interpersonal psychotherapy: Current status. *Archives of General Psychiatry, 51,* 599–606.

Weissman, M. M., et al. (1991). Affective disorders. In L. N. Robins & D. A. Regier (Eds.), *Psychiatric disorders in America: The Epidemiologic Catchment Area Study* (pp. 53–80). New York: Free Press.

Weissman, M. M., Pilowsky, D. J., Wickramaratne, P. J., Talati, A., Wisniewski, S. R., Fava, C. W., et al. (2006). Remissions in maternal depression and child psychopathology: A STAR*D-child report. *Journal of the American Medical Association, 295,* 1389–1398.

Weissman, M. M., Wickramaratne, P., Nomura, Y., Warner, V., Verdeli, H., Pilowsky, D. J., et al. (2005). Families at high and low risk for depression: A 3-generation study. *Archives of General Psychiatry, 62,* 29–36.

Weisstaub, N. V., et al. (2006). Cortical 5-HT2A receptor signaling modulates anxiety-like behaviors in mice. *Science, 313,* 536–540.

Weisz, J. R., Jensen-Doss, A., & Hawley, K., M. (2006). Evidence-based youth psychotherapies versus usual clinical care: A meta-analysis of direct comparisons. *American Psychologist, 61,* 671–689.

Weisz, J. R., McCarty, C. A., & Valeri, S. M. (2006). Effects of psychotherapy for depression in children and adolescents: A meta-analysis. *Psychological Bulletin, 132,* 132–149.

Weisz, J. R., Pilkonis, P. A., Woody, S. R., & Follette, W. C. (2000). Stressing the (other) three Rs in the search for empirically supported treatments: Review procedures, research quality, relevance to practice and the public interest. *Clinical Psychology: Science and Practice, 7,* 243–258.

Weisz, J. R., Suwanlert, S., Chaiyasit, W., Weiss, B., Walter, B. R., & Anderson, W. W. (1988). Thai and American perspectives on over-and undercontrolled child behavior problems: Exploring the threshold model among parents, teachers, and psychologists. *Journal of Consulting and Clinical Psychology, 56,* 601–609.

Weisz, J. R., Weersing, V. R., & Henggeler, S. W. (2005). Jousting with straw men: Comment on Westen, Novotny, and Thompson-Brenner (2004). *Psychological Bulletin, 131,* 418–426.

Welch, M. R., & Kartub, P. (1978). Socio-cultural correlates of incidence of impotence: A cross-cultural study. *Journal of Sex Research, 14,* 218–230.

Welkowitz, L. A., Papp, L., Martinez, J., Browne, S., & Gorman, J. M. (1999). Instructional set and physiological response to CO_2 inhalation. *American Journal of Psychiatry, 156,* 745–748.

Wells, K. B., & Miranda, J. (2006). Promise of interventions and services research: Can it transform practice? *Clinical Psychology: Science and Practice, 13,* 99–104.

Wells, K. B., Sherbourne, C., Schoenbaum, M., Duan, N., Meredith, L., Unutzer, J., et al. (2000). Impact of disseminating quality improvement programs for depression in managed primary care: A randomized controlled trial. *Journal of the American Medical Association, 283,* 212–220.

Welsh, R. S. (2003). Prescription privileges: Pro or con. *Clinical Psychology: Science and Practice, 10,* 371–372. [Letter]

Weltzin, T. E., Cameron, J., Berga, S., & Kaye, W. H. (1994). Prediction of reproductive status in women with bulimia nervosa by past high weight. *American Journal of Psychiatry, 151,* 136–138.

Wender, P. H., Rosenthal, D., Kety, S. S., Schulsinger, F., & Welner, J. (1974). Cross-fostering: A research strategy for clarifying the role of genetic and experiential factors in the etiology of schizophrenia. *Archives of General Psychiatry, 30,* 121–128.

Wenzel, A., Finstroma, N., Jordan, J., & Brendle, J. R. (2005). Memory and interpretation of visual representations of threat in socially anxious and nonanxious individuals. *Behaviour Research and Therapy, 43,* 1029–1044.

Westen, D., & Bradley, R. (2005). Empirically supported complexity rethinking evidence-based practice in psychotherapy. *Current Directions in Psychological Science, 14,* 266–271.

Westen, D., & Gabbard, G. O. (2002). Developments in cognitive neuroscience: 1. Conflict, compromise, and connectionism. *Journal of the American Psychoanalytic Association, 50,* 53–98.

Westen, D., & Shedler, J. (1999). Revising and assessing axis II, Part II: Toward an empirically based and clinically useful classification of personality disorders. *The American Journal of Psychiatry, 156,* 273–285.

Westen, D., Novotny, C. M., & Thompson-Brenner, H. (2004). The empirical status of empirically supported psychotherapies: assumptions, findings, and reporting in controlled clinical trials. *Psychological Bulletin, 130,* 631–663.

Westen, D., Novotny, C. M., & Thompson-Brenner, H. (2005). EBP≠EST: Reply to Crits-Christoph et al. (2005) and Weisz et al. (2005). *Psychological Bulletin, 131,* 427–433.

Wetzler, S., & Marlowe, D. B. (1993). The diagnosis and assessment of depression, mania, and psychosis by self-report. *Journal of Personality Assessment, 60,* 1–31.

Wexler, B. E., Gottschalk, C. H., Fulbright, R. K., Prohovnik, I., Lacadie, C. M., Rounsaville, B. J., et al. (2001). Functional magnetic resonance imaging of cocaine craving. *American Journal of Psychiatry, 158,* 86–95.

Whalen, C. K., Jamner, L. D., Henker, B., & Delfino, R. J. (2001). Smoking and moods in adolescents with depressive and aggressive dispositions: Evidence from surveys and electronic diaries. *Health Psychology, 20,* 99–111.

What causes migraine headaches? (2001) *Nidus Information Services, Inc.* Retrieved January 5, 2004, from http://www.ucdmc.ucdavis.edu/ucdhs/health/a-z/97 migraine/doc97causes.html.

Whiffen, V. E., & Gotlib, I. H. (1993). Comparison of postpartum and nonpostpartum depression: Clinical presentation, psychiatric history, and psychosocial functioning. *Journal of Consulting and Clinical Psychology, 61,* 485–493.

White, K. S., Brown, T. W., Somers, T. J., & Barlow, D. H. (2006). Avoidance behavior in panic disorder: The moderating influence of perceived control. *Behaviour Research and Therapy, 44,* 147–157.

Whittal, M. L., Thordarson, D. S., & McLean, P. (2005). Treatment of obsessive–compulsive disorder: Cognitive behavior therapy vs. exposure and response prevention. *Behaviour Research and Therapy, 43,* 1559–1576.

WHO World Mental Health Survey Consortium. (2004). Prevalence, severity, and unmet need for treatment of mental disorders in the World Health Organization World Mental Health Surveys. *Journal of the American Medical Association, 291,* 2581–2590.

Whooley, M. A., Kiefe, C. I., Chesney, M. A., Markovitz, -J. H., Matthews, K., Hulley, S. B., et al. (2002). Depressive symptoms, unemployment, and loss of income. The CARDIA Study. *Archives of Internal Medicine, 162,* 2614–2620.

Wichman, T., & Delong, M. R. (2006). Deep brain stimulation for neurologic and neuropsychiatric disorders. *Neuron, 52,* 197–204.

Wickenhaver, J. (1992, September 8). After the "Wild Man": Can an insane system be cured? *Manhattan Spirit,* pp. 13, 28.

Wickizer, T. M., Lessler, D., & Travis, K. M. (1996). Controlling inpatient psychiatric utilization through managed care. *American Journal of Psychiatry, 153,* 339–345.

Widiger, T. A. (1991). *DSM-IV* reviews of the personality disorders: Introduction to special series. *Journal of Personality Disorder, 5,* 122–134.

Widiger, T. A. (1992). Generalized social phobia versus avoidant personality disorder: A commentary on three studies. *Journal of Abnormal Psychology, 101,* 340–343.

Widiger, T. A., & Clark, L. A. (2000). Toward *DSM-V* and the classification of psychopathology. *Psychological Bulletin, 126,* 946–963.

Widiger, T. A., & Costa, P. T., Jr. (1994). Personality and personality disorders. *Journal of Abnormal Psychology, 103,* 78–91.

Widiger, T. A., & Simonsen, E. (2005). Alternative dimensional models of personality disorder: Finding a common ground. *Journal of Personality Disorders, 19,* 110–130.

Wiers, R. W., & Kummeling, R. H. C. (2004). An experimental test of an alcohol expectancy challenge in mixed gender groups of young heavy drinkers. *Addictive Behaviors, 29,* 215–220.

Wiersma, D., et al. (2001). Cognitive behaviour therapy with coping training for persistent auditory hallucinations in schizophrenia: A naturalistic follow-up study of the durability of effects. *Acta Psychiatrica Scandinavica, 103,* 393–399.

Wigg, K., Zai, G., Schachar, R., Tannock, R., Roberts, W., Malone, M., Kennedy, J. L., et al. (2002). Attention deficit hyperactivity disorder and the gene for dopamine beta-hydroxylase. *American Journal of Psychiatry, 159,* 1046–1048.

Wilbur, C. B. (1986). Psychoanalysis and multiple personality disorder. In B. G. Braun (Ed.), *Treatment of multiple personality disorder.* Washington, DC: American Psychiatric Press.

Wilcox, M. A., Faraone, S. V., Su, J., Van Eerdewegh, P., & Tsuang, M. T. (2002). Genome scan of three quantitative traits in schizophrenia pedigrees. *Biological Psychiatry, 52,* 847–854.

Wilens, T. E., Biederman, J., Wozniak, J., Gunawardene, S., Wong, J., & Monuteaux, M. (2003). Can adults with attention-deficit/hyperactivity disorder be distinguished from those with comorbid bipolar disorder? Findings from a sample of clinically referred adults. *Biological Psychiatry, 54,* 8.

Wilkie, F. L., et al. (1998). Mild cognitive impairment and risk of mortality in HIV-1 infection. *Journal of Neuropsychiatry and Clinical Neuroscience, 10,* 125–132.

Wilkinson, D., et al. (2003). Donepezil in vascular dementia: A randomized, placebo-controlled study. *Neurology, 61,* 479–486.

Wilkinson-Ryan, T., & Westen, D. (2000). Identity disturbance in borderline personality disorders: An empirical investigation. *American Journal of Psychiatry, 157,* 528–541.

Willer, M. G., Thuras, P., & Crow, S. J. (2005). Implications of the changing use of hospitalization to treat anorexia nervosa. *American Journal of Psychiatry, 162,* 2374–2376.

Williams, A.-L., Katz, D., Alia, A., Girard, C., Goodman, J., & Goodman, J., (2006). Do essential fatty acids have a role in the treatment of depression? *Journal of Affective Disorders, 93,* 117–123.

Williams, D. (1992). *Nobody nowhere: The extraordinary autobiography of an autistic.* New York: Times Books.

Williams, J., Hadjistavropoulos, T., & Sharpe, D. (2006). A meta-analysis of psychological and pharmacological treatments for body dysmorphic disorder. *Behaviour Research and Therapy, 44,* 99–111.

Williams, J. B., et al. (1992). The Structured Clinical Interview for *DSM-III*—(SCID). II: Multisite test-retest reliability. *Archives of General Psychiatry, 49,* 630–636.

Williams, J. E., Paton, C. C., Siegler, I. C., Eigenbrodt, M. L., Nieto, F. J., & Tyroler, H. A. (2000). Anger proneness predicts coronary heart disease risk: Prospective analysis from the Atherosclerosis Risk in Communities (ARIC) Study. *Circulation, 101,* 2034–2039.

Williams, N. M., Preece, A., Morris, D. W., Spurlock, G., Bray, N. J., Stephens, D. M., Norton, N., et al. (2004). Identification in 2 independent samples of a novel schizophrenia risk haplotype of the Dystrobrevin

Binding Protein Gene (DTNBP1). *Archives of General Psychiatry, 61,* 336–344.

Williams, P. G., Wiebe, D. J., & Smith, T. W. (1992). Coping processes as mediators of the relationship between hardiness and health. *Journal of Behavioral Medicine, 15,* 237–255.

Williams, R. B., Marchuk, D. A., Gadde, K. M., Barefoot, J. C., Grichnik, K., Helms, M. J., et al. (2003) Serotonin-related gene polymorphisms and central nervous system serotonin function. *Neuropsychopharmacology, 28,* 533–541.

Willis, D. J. (2003, Fall). The case for prescription privileges. *The Clinical Psychologist, 56,* 1–4.

Wills, T. A., & Filer Fegan, M. (2001). Social networks and social support. In A. Baum, T. A. Revenson, & J. E. Singer (Eds.), *Handbook of health psychology* (pp. 3–18). Makwah, NJ: Lawrence Erlbaum Associates.

Wilson, G. T. (1991). Chemical aversion conditioning in the treatment of alcoholism: Further comments: *Behaviour Research & Therapy, 29,* 415–419.

Wilson, G. T. (1994). Behavioral treatment of childhood obesity: Theoretical and practical implications. *Health Psychology, 13,* 371–372.

Wilson, G. T. (1997). Behavior therapy at century close. *Behavior Therapy, 28,* 449–457.

Wilson, G. T., & Fairburn, C. G. (1998). Treatment for eating disorders. In P. E. Nathan & J. M. Gorman (Eds.), *A guide to treatments that work* (pp. 501–530). New York: Oxford University Press.

Wilson, G. T., Fairburn, C. C., Agras, W. S., Walsh, B. T., Kraemer, H. (2002). Cognitive behavioral therapy for bulimia nervosa: Time course and mechanisms of change. *Journal of Consulting and Clinical Psychology, 70,* 267–274.

Wilson, K. A., & Hayward, C. (2006). Unique contributions of anxiety sensitivity to avoidance: A prospective study in adolescents. *Behaviour Research and Therapy, 44,* 601–609.

Wilson, R. S., & Bennett, D. A. (2003). Cognitive activity and risk of Alzheimer's disease. *Current Directions in Psychological Science, 12,* 87–90.

Wilson, R. S., Barnes, L. L., Mendes de Leon, C. F., Aggarwal, N. T., Schneider, J. S., Bach, J., et al. (2002). Depressive symptoms, cognitive decline, and risk of AD in older persons. *Neurology, 59,* 364–370.

Wilson, S. A., Becker, L. A., & Tinker, R. H. (1997). Fifteen-month follow-up of eye movement desensitization and reprocessing (EMDR) treatment for posttraumatic stress disorder and psychological trauma. *Journal of Consulting and Clinical Psychology, 65,* 1047–1056.

Winblad, B., Kilander, L., Eriksson, S., Minthon, L., Batsman, S., Wetterholm, A. L., et al (2006). Donepezil in patients with severe Alzheimer's disease: double-blind, parallel-group, placebo-controlled study. *Lancet, 367,* 1057–1065.

Winefield, H. R., & Harvey, E. J. (1994). Needs of family caregivers in chronic schizophrenia. *Schizophrenia Bulletin, 20,* 557–566.

Winerip, M. (1991, December 18). Soldier in battle for the retarded. *The New York Times,* pp. B1, B6.

Winerip, M. (1998, January 4). Binge nights. *The New York Times,* Education Section 4A, pp. 28–31, 42.

Winerip, M. (1999, May 23). Bedlam on the streets. *The New York Times,* pp. 42–49.

Winerman, L. (2004, May). Panel stresses youth suicide prevention. *Monitor on Psychology, 35,* p. 18.

Winerman, L. (2005, July/August). A virtual cure. *Monitor on Psychology, 36,* pp. 87–89.

Wing, R. R., & Polley, B. A. (2001). Obesity. In A. Baum, T. A. Revenson, & J. E. Singer (Eds.), *Handbook of health psychology* (pp. 263–279). Mahwah, NJ: Erlbaum.

Wingert, P. (2000, December 4). No more "afternoon nasties." *Newsweek,* p. 59.

Winstanley, C. A., Eagle, D. M., & Robbins, T. W. (2006). Behavioral models of impulsivity in relation to ADHD: Translation between clinical and preclinical studies. *Clinical Psychology Review, 26,* 379–395.

Winston, A., Laikin, M., Pollack, J., Samstag, L. W., McCullough, L., & Muran, J. C. (1994). Short-term psychotherapy of personality disorders. *American Journal of Psychiatry, 51,* 190–194.

Winston, A., Pollack, J., McCullough, L., Flegenheimer, W., Kestenbaum, R., & Trujillo, M. (1991). Brief psychotherapy of personality disorders. *Journal of Nervous & Mental Disease, 179,* 188–193.

Winterer, G., Coppola, R., Goldberg, T. E., Egan, M. F., Jones, D. W., et al. (2004). Prefrontal broadband noise, working memory, and genetic risk for schizophrenia. *American Journal of Psychiatry, 161,* 490–500.

Winterer, G., Musso, F., Beckmann, C., Mattay, V., Egan, M. F., Jones, D. W., et al. (2006). Instability of prefrontal signal processing in schizophrenia. *American Journal of Psychiatry, 163,* 1960–1968.

Wintersteen, M. B., Mensinger, J. L., & Diamond, G. S. (2005). Do gender and racial differences between patient and therapist affect therapeutic alliance and treatment retention in adolescents? *Professional Psychology: Research and Practice, 36,* 400–408.

Wisner, K. L., Parry, B. L., & Piontek, C. M. (2002). Postpartum depression. *New England Journal of Medicine, 347,* 194–199.

Witkiewicz, K., & Marlatt, G. A. (2004). Relapse prevention for alcohol and drug problems: That was Zen, this is Tao. *American Psychologist, 59,* 224–235.

Wittstein, I. S., Thiemann, D. R., Lima, J. A. C., Baughman, K. L., Schulman, S. P., Gerstenblith, G., et al. (2006). Neurohumoral features of myocardial stunning due to sudden emotional stress. *New England Journal of Medicine, 352,* 539–548.

Woerner, M. G., Robinson, D. G., Alvir, J. M., Sheitman, B. B., Lieberman, J. A., & Kane, J. M. (2003). *American Journal of Psychiatry, 160,* 1514–1516.

Wolfe, D. A., et al. (2001). Child maltreatment: Risk of adjustment problems and dating violence in adolescence. *Journal of American Academy of Child & Adolescent Psychiatry, 40,* 282–289.

Wolpe, J. (1958). *Psychotherapy by reciprocal inhibition.* Stanford, CA: Stanford University Press.

Wolpe, J., & Lazarus, A. A. (1966). *Behavior therapy techniques.* New York: Pergamon Press.

Wonderlich, S. A., Brewerton, T. D., Jocic, Z., Dansky, B. S., & Abbott, D. W. (1997). Relationship of childhood sexual abuse and eating disorders. *Journal of the American Academy of Child and Adolescent Psychiatry, 36,* 1107–1115.

Wong, E. C., Kim, B. S. K., Zane, N. W. S., Kim, I. J., & Huang, J. S. (2003). Examining culturally based variables associated with ethnicity: Influences on credibility perceptions of empirically supported interventions. *Cultural Diversity and Ethnic Minority Psychology, 9,* 88–96.

Wong, J. L., & Whitaker, D. J. (1993). Depressive mood states and their cognitive and personality correlates in college students: They improve over time. *Journal of Clinical Psychology, 49,* 615–621.

Wong, M. M., Klingle, R. S., & Price, R. K. (2004). Alcohol, tobacco, and other drug use among Asian American and Pacific Islander Adolescents in California and Hawaii. *Addictive Behaviors, 29,* 127–141.

Wood, J. M., Bootzin, R. R., Rosenhan, D., Nolen-Hoeksema, S., & Jourden, R. (1992). Effects of 1989 San Francisco earthquake on frequency and content of nightmares. *Journal of Abnormal Psychology, 101,* 219–234.

Wood, M. D., Vinson, D. C., & Sher, K. J. (2001). Alcohol use and misuse. In A. Baum, T. A. Revenson, & J. E. Singer (Eds.), *Handbook of health psychology* (pp. 280–320). Mahwah, NJ: Erlbaum.

Woods, C. M., Vevea, J. L., Chambless, D. L., & Bayen, U. J. (2002). Are compulsive checkers impaired in memory? A meta-analytic review. *Clinical Psychology: Science and Practice, 9,* 353–366.

Woods, S. C., Schwartz, M. W., Baskin, D. G., & Seeley, R. J. (2000). Food intake and the regulation of body weight. *Annual Review of Psychology, 51,* 255–277.

Woodward, A. M., Dwinell, A. D., & Arons, B. S. (1992). Barriers to mental health care for Hispanic Americans: A literature review and discussion. *Journal of Mental Health Administration, 19,* 224–236.

Woodworth, M., & Porter, S. (2002). In cold blood: Characteristics of criminal homicides as a function of psychopathy. *Journal of Abnormal Psychology, 111,* 436–445.

Wootton, J. M., et al. (1997). Ineffective parenting and childhood conduct problems: The moderating role of callous-unemotional traits. *Journal of Consulting and Clinical Psychology, 65,* 301–308.

Wright, J. H., Wright, A. S., Albano, A. M., Basco, M. R., Goldsmith, J., Raffield, T., et al. (2006). Computer-assisted cognitive therapy for depression: maintaining efficacy while reducing therapist time/*American Journal of Psychiatry, 162,* 1158–1164.

Wright, P., & Kantrowitz, B. (2002, October 7). Young and depressed. *Newsweek,* pp. 53–60.

Writing Group of the PREMIER Collaborative Research Group. (2003). Effects of comprehensive lifestyle modification on blood pressure control: Main results of the PREMIER Clinical Trial. *Journal of the American Medical Association, 289,* 2083–2093.

Wu, P., Hoven, C. W., Cohen, P., Liu, X., Moore, R. E., Tiet, Q., et al. (2001). Factors associated with use of mental health services for depression by children and adolescents. *Psychiatric Services, 52* (2), 189–195.

Wyatt v. Stickney, 334 F. Supp. 1341 (1972).

X

Xu, K., Lichtermann, D., Lipsky, R. H., Franke, P., Liu, X., Hu, Y., et al. (2004). Association of specific haplotypes of D2 dopamine receptor gene with vulnerability to heroin dependence in 2 distinct populations. *Archives of General Psychiatry, 61,* 597–606.

Y

Yager, J. (2003, December 23). Is there something fishy about bipolar disorder? *Journal Watch Psychiatry.* Retrieved December 24, 2003, from http://psychiatry.jwatch.org/cgi/content/full/2003/1223/5?q=etoc.

Yager, J. (2005, May 18). Which psychotherapy for acute anorexia nervosa? *Journal Watch Psychiatry.* Retrieved April 7, 2006, from http://psychiatry.jwatch.org/cgi/content/full/2005/518/1.

Yager, J. (2006a, October 16). Which patients with major depression will relapse despite maintenance fluoxetine? *Journal Watch Psychiatry.*

Retrieved October 16, 2006, from http://psychiatry.jwatch.org/cgi/content/full/2006/1016/4.

Yager, J. (2006b, July 11). How destructive is parental verbal abuse? *Journal Watch Psychiatry.* Retrieved July 11, 2006, from http://psychiatry.jwatch.org/cgi/content/citation/2006/711/4.

Yancey, K. B. (2000, August 18). Treatment virtually cures fear of flying. *USA Today Online.* Retrieved November 23, 2003, from http://www.usatoday.com/life/cyber/tech/review/crh424.htm.

Yang, L. H., Phillips, M. R., Licht, D. M., & Hooley, J. M. (2004). Causal attributions about schizophrenia in families in China: Expressed emotion and patient relapse. *Journal of Abnormal Psychology, 113,* 592–602.

Yang, Q., Rasmussen, S. A., & Friedman, J. M. (2002). Mortality associated with Down's syndrome in the USA from 1983 to 1997: A population-based study. *The Lancet, 359,* 1019–1025.

Yates, W. R. (2000). Testosterone in psychiatry: Risks and benefits. *Journal of the American Medical Association, 57,* 155–156.

Yatham, L. M., Liddle, P. F., Shiah, I. S., Scarrow, G., Lam, R. W., Adam, M. J., Zis, A. P., et al. (2000). Brain serotonin2 receptors in major depression: A positron emission tomography study. *Archives of General Psychiatry, 57,* 850–858.

Yeap, S., Kelly, S. P., Sehatpour, P., Magno, E., Javitt, D. C., Garavan, H., et al. (2006). Visual sensory deficits as endophenotypes for schizophrenia: High-density electrical mapping in clinically unaffected first-degree relatives. *Archives of General Psychiatry, 63,* 1180–1188.

Yeargin-Allsopp, M., Rice, C., Karapurkan, T., Doernberg, N., Boyle, C., & Murphy, C. (2003). Prevalence of autism in a US metropolitan area. *Journal of the American Medical Association, 289,* 49–55.

Yeh, C. J. (2003). Age, acculturation, cultural adjustment, and mental health symptoms of Chinese, Korean, and Japanese immigrant youths. *Cultural Diversity and Ethnic Minority Psychology, 9,* 34–48.

Yeni, P. G., Hammer, S. M., Carpenter, C. C., Cooper, D. A., Fischl, M. A., Gatell, J. M., et al. (2002). Antiretroviral treatment for adult HIV infection in 2002: Updated Recommendations of the International AIDS Society-USA Panel. *Journal of the American Medical Association, 288,* 222–235.

Yeung, A., Howarth, S., Chan, R., Sonaw alla, S., Nierenberg, A. A., & Fava, M. (2002). Use of the Chinese version of the Beck Depression Inventory for screening depression in primary care. *Journal of Nervous & Mental Disease, 190,* 94–99.

Yeung, P. P., & Greenwald, S. (1992). Jewish Americans and mental health: Results of the NIMH Epidemiologic Catchment Area Study. *Social Psychiatry and Psychiatric Epidemiology, 27,* 292–297.

Yoder, V. C., Virden, T. B. III, & Amin, K. (2005). Internet pornography and loneliness: An association? *Sexual Addiction & Compulsivity, 12,* 19–44.

Young, E. A., McFatter, R., & Clopton, J. R. (2001). Family functioning, peer influence, and media influence as predictors of bulimic behavior. *Eating Behaviors, 2,* 323–337.

Young, M. A., Fogg, L. F., Scheftner, W. A., & Fawcett, J. A. (1994). Interactions of risk factors in predicting suicide. *American Journal of Psychiatry, 51,* 434–435.

Young, S. E., Stallings, M. C., Corley, R. P., Krauter, K. S., & Hewitt, J. K. (2000). Genetic and environmental influences on behavioral disinhibition. *American Journal of Medical Genetics, 96,* 684–695.

Young, T. J., & French, L. A. (1996). Suicide and homicide rates among U.S. Indian health service areas: The income inequality hypothesis. *Social Behavior and Personality, 24,* 365–366.

Young, T. K., & Sevenhuyser, G. (1989). Obesity in northern Canadian Indians: Patterns, determinants, and consequences. *American Journal of Clinical Nutrition, 49,* 786–793.

Youngberg v. Romeo, 102 S. Ct. 2452, 2463 (1982).

Yu, C. E., Dawson, G., Munson, J., D'Souza, I., Osterling, J., Estes, A., et al. (2002). Presence of large deletions in kindreds with autism. *American Journal of Human Genetics, 71,* 100–115.

Z

Zamanian, K., et al. (1992). Acculturation and depression in Mexican-American elderly. *Gerontologist, 11,* 109–121.

Zammit, S., Allebeck, P., Adreasson, S., Lundberg, I., & Lewis, G. (2002). Self reported cannabis use as a risk factor for schizophrenia in Swedish conscripts of 1969: Historical cohort study. *British Medical Journal, 325,* 1199.

Zanardi, R., Franchini, L., Gasperini, M., Perez, J., & Smeraldi, E. (1996). Double-blind controlled trial of sertraline versus paroxetine in the treatment of delusional depression. *American Journal of Psychiatry, 153,* 1631–1633.

Zanarini, M. C., Frankenburg, F. R., Hennen, J., & Silk, K. R. (2003). The longitudinal course of borderline psychopathology: 6-year prospective follow-up of the phenomenology of borderline personality disorder. *American Journal of Psychiatry, 160,* 274–283.

Zane, N., & Sue, S. (1991). Culturally responsive mental health services for Asian Americans: Treatment and training issues. In H. F. Myers, et al. (Eds.), *Ethnic minority perspectives on clinical training and services in psychology* (pp. 49–58). Washington, DC: American Psychological Association.

Zangen, A., Solinas, M., Ikemoto, S., Goldberg, S. R., & Wise, R. A. (2006). Two brain sites for cannabinoid reward. *The Journal of Neuroscience, 26,* 4901–4907.

Zernike, K., & Petersen, M. (2001, August 19). Schools' backing of behavior drugs comes under fire. *The New York Times Online.*

Zhang, C. H., Hernan, M. A., Schwarzschild, M. A., Willett, W. C., Colditz, G. A., Speizer, F. E., et al. (2003). Nonsteroidal anti-inflammatory drugs and the risk of Parkinson disease. *Archives of Neurology, 60,* 1059–1064.

Zhou, Z., Roy, A., Lipsky, R., Kuchipudi, K., Zhu, G., Taubman, J., et al. (2005). Haplotype-based linkage of tryptophan hydroxylase 2 to suicide attempt, major depression, and cerebrospinal fluid 5-hydroxyindoleacetic acid in 4 populations. *Archives of General Psychiatry, 62,* 1109–1118.

Zickler, P. (2000). Brain imaging studies show long-term damage from methamphetamine abuse. *NIDA Notes, 15*(3), 11, 13.

Zickler, P. (2004, April). Smoking decreases key enzyme throughout body research findings. National Institute on Drug Abuse. *NIDA Notes, 19.* Retrieved May 10, 2004, from http://www.drugabuse.gov/NIDA_notes/NNvol19N1/Smoking.html.

Zickler, P. (2006, October). Marijuana smoking is associated with a spectrum of respiratory disorders. *NIDA Notes, 21*(1), pp. 12–13.

Zimand, E., Anderson, P., Gershon, G., Graap, K., Hodges, L., & Rothbaum, B. (2003). Virtual reality therapy: Innovative treatment for anxiety disorders. *Primary Psychiatry, 9,* 51–54.

Zimmerman, M., Chelminski, I., & Young, D. (2006). Prevalence and diagnostic correlates of *DSM-IV* pathological gambling in psychiatric outpatients. *Journal of Gambling Studies, 22,* 255–262.

Zimmerman, M., McGlinchey, J. B., Young, D., & Chelminski, I. (2006). Diagnosing major depressive disorder III: Can some symptoms be eliminated from the diagnostic criteria? *Journal of Nervous & Mental Disease, 194,* 313–317.

Zinbarg, R. E., Brown, T. A., Barlow, D. H., & Rapee, R. M. (2001). Anxiety sensitivity, panic, and depressed mood: A reanalysis teasing apart the contributions of the two levels in the hierarchical structure of the Anxiety Sensitivity Index. *Journal of Abnormal Psychology, 110,* 372–377.

Zito, J. M., Safer, D. J., dosReis, S., Gardner, J. F., Boles, M., & Lynch, F. (2000). Trends in the prescribing of psychotropic medications to preschoolers. *Journal of the American Medical Association, 283,* 1025–1030.

Zlotnick, C., Bruce, S. E., Shea, M. T., & Keller, M. B. (2001). Delayed posttraumatic stress disorder (PTSD) and predictors of first onset of PTSD in patients with anxiety disorders. *Journal of Nervous & Mental Disease, 189,* 404–406.

Zoellner, L. A., Foa, E. B., Brigidi, B. D., & Przeworski, A. (2000). Are trauma victims susceptible to "false memories"? *Journal of Abnormal Psychology, 109,* 517–524.

Zola, S. M. (1999). Memory, amnesia, and the issue of recovered memory: Neurobiological aspects. *Clinical Psychology Review, 19,* 915–932.

Zorumski, C. F., & Isenberg, K. E. (1991). Insights into the structure and function of GABA-benzodiazepine receptors: Ion channels and psychiatry. *American Journal of Psychiatry, 148,* 162–172.

Zubenko, G. S., Mulsant, B. H., Sweet, R. A., Pasternak, R. E., & Tu, X. M. (1997). Mortality of elderly patients with psychiatric disorders. *American Journal of Psychiatry, 154,* 1360–1368.

Zubin, J., & Spring, B. (1977). Vulnerability—New view of schizophrenia. *Journal of Abnormal Psychology, 86,* 103–126.

Zucker, K. J. (2005a). Gender identity disorder in children and adolescents. *Annual Review of Clinical Psychology, 1,* 467–492.

Zucker, K. J. (2005b). Gender identity disorder in girls. In D. J. Bell, S. L. Foster, & E. J. Mash (Eds.), *Handbook of behavioral and emotional problems in girls: Issues in clinical child psychology* (pp. 285–319). Kluwer Academic/Plenum Publishers.

Zuckerman, M. (1980). Sensation seeking. In H. London & J. Exner (Eds.), *Dimensions of personality.* New York: Wiley.

Zuroff, D. C., & Blatt, S. (2006). The therapeutic relationship in the brief treatment of depression: Contributions to clinical improvement and enhanced adaptive capacities. *Journal of Consulting and Clinical Psychology, 74,* 130–140.

Zvolensky, M. J., & Eifert, G. H. (2001). A review of psychological factors/processes affecting anxious responding during voluntary hyperventilation and inhalations of carbon dioxide-enriched air. *Clinical Psychology Review, 21,* 375–400.

Zvolensky, M. J., Arrindell, W. A., Taylor, S., Bouvard, M., Cox, B. J., Stewart, S. H., et al. (2003). Cross-cultural assessment and abnormal psychology. *Behaviour Research and Therapy, 41,* 841–859.

Zvolensky, M. J., McNeil, D. W., Porter, C. A., & Stewart, S. H. (2001). Assessment of anxiety sensitivity in young American Indians and Alaska Natives. *Behaviour Research and Therapy, 39,* 477–493.

Zweig-Frank, H., & Paris, J. (1991). Parents' emotional neglect and overprotection according to the recollections of patients with borderline personality disorder. *American Journal of Psychiatry, 148,* 648–651.

Zwillich, C. W. (2000). Is untreated sleep apnea a contributing factor for chronic hypertension? *Journal of the American Medical Association, 283,* 1880–1881. [Editorial]

PHOTO CREDITS

Chapter 1   page 2: Tomek Sikora; page 6: David Stluka/Getty Images, Inc.; page 7 (top): Kathleen Finlay; page 7 (bottom): Pierre Perrin; page 9: Arne hodalic; page 11: Image #283253. Photo by: Bierwert. American Museum of Natural History Library; page 12 (top): The Granger Collection; page 12 (bottom): The Granger Collection; page 13: The Granger Collection; page 14: Corbis/Bettmann; page 16: © Bettmann/CORBIS; page 17 (left): The Granger Collection; page 17 (right): The Granger Collection; page 18: © Thinkstock/CORBIS All Rights Reserved; page 23: Richard Hutchings/PhotoEdit Inc.; page 25: Corbis RF; page 28: Rachel Epstein/PhotoEdit Inc.; page 33: Gerry Koocher.

Chapter 2   page 36: Erwin Redl; page 44: Gabriel M. Covian/Getty Images, Inc.; page 47: David DeLossy/Photodisc/Getty Images, Inc.; page 48 (top): David Muir/Masterfile Corporation; page 48 (bottom): Altrendo Images/Getty Images, Inc.; page 49: LucasFilm/20th Century Fox/Picture Desk, Inc./Kobal Collection; page 50 (left): Corbis/Bettmann; page 50 (center): Scott Camazine/Corbis/Bettmann; page 50 (right): PhotoEdit Inc.; page 52: Nina Leen/Getty Images/Time Life Pictures; page 53: The Granger Collection; page 56 (top): Nancy Sheehan/Photolibrary.com; page 56 (bottom): AP Wide World Photos; page 57 (left): Corbis/Rogers Ressmeyer/Corbis/Bettmann; page 57 (right): Ann Kaplan/Corbis/Corbis/Bettmann; page 58: © Ellen B. Senisi/Ellen B. Senisi; page 59: Albert Ellis Institute; page 60: Aaron T. Beck, M.D.; page 64: Frank Siteman/Jupiter Images-FoodPix-Creatas-Brand X-Banana Stock-PictureQuest.

Chapter 3   page 68: Diana Ong/SuperStock, Inc.; page 75 (top): Jeff Greenberg/PhotoEdit Inc.; page 75 (bottom): Charles Gupton/Getty Images Inc.-Stone Allstock; page 78: Thomas A. Widiger; page 79: The Image Works/The Image Works; page 80: Spencer Grant/PhotoEdit Inc.; page 82: IT Stock Free/Jupiter Images; page 89: Pearson Education/PH College; page 90: Reprinted by permission of the publishers from Henry A. Murray, THEMATIC APPERCEPTION TEST, Cambridge, Mass.: Harvard University Press, © 1943 by the President and Fellows of Harvard College, © 1971 by Henry A. Murray; page 94: David Young Wolff/PhotoEdit Inc.; page 96: Richard T. Nowitz/Corbis/Bettmann; page 97: Scott Camazine/Photo Researchers, Inc.; page 98 (top): Brookhaven National Laboratory; page 98 (bottom): Visuals Unlimited; page 99 (left): Alexander Tsiaras/Science Source/Photo Researchers, Inc.; page 99 (right): Magnetic Resonance Imaging of the Brain in Schizophrenia, pg. 35–44, 1990; 47: 35/Archive of General Psychiatry/American Medical Association.

Chapter 4   page 102: Rob Colvin/Stock Illustration Source/Getty Images, Inc.; page 104: ©Columbia/Everett Collection; page 107: Zigy Kaluzny/Getty Images Inc.-Stone Allstock; page 108: Kactus Foto/SuperStock, Inc.; page 109: Grantpix/Photo Researchers, Inc.; page 112: Drawing by Mike Ewers. Reprinted by permission; page 118 (top): Jim Pickerell/The Stock Connection; page 118 (bottom): David Young Wolff/PhotoEdit Inc.; page 119: © Teri Stratford. All rights reserved; page 122: Dr. William C. Sanderson; page 123: From the Wall Street Journal—permission, Cartoon Features Syndicate; page 124: Nancy Sheehan/PhotoEdit Inc.; page 128: Will McIntyre/Photo Researchers, Inc.; page 131: © Stephane Klein/CORBIS All Rights Reserved; page 133: Michael Newman/PhotoEdit Inc.; page 136: Robert Ginn/PhotoEdit Inc.

Chapter 5   page 140: Esbin-Anderson/The Image Works; page 142: Phyllis Picardi/Stock Boston; page 145: Biology Media/Science Source/Photo Researchers, Inc.; page 146: Richard Radstone/Getty Images, Inc.; page 148: IN THE BLEACHERS ©2006 Steve Moore. Reprinted with permission of UNIVERSAL PRESS SYNDICATE. All rights reserved; page 149 (left): Esbin/Anderson/Omni-Photo Communications, Inc.; page 149 (right): David Young Wolff/PhotoEdit Inc.; page 152: Lawrence Migdale/Stock Boston; page 153: Charles Negy, Ph.D.; page 155: Photos.com; page 156: Mark Adams/Getty Images, Inc.-Taxi; page 158: Joel Gordon Photography/Design Conceptions; page 160: Getty Images, Inc.; page 161: Michael Banks/Getty Images Inc.-Stone Allstock; page 166: Alon Reininger/Woodfin Camp & Associates.

Chapter 6   page 170: Sandy Skoglund/Sandy Skoglund; page 172: Walter Smith/Corbis/Bettmann; page 174: Martin Barraud/Stone/Getty Images; page 180 (left): Geri Engberg/Geri Engberg Photography; page 180 (top right): SuperStock, Inc.; page 180 (bottom right): David E. Dempster/Pearson Education/PH College; page 184: Corbis/Stephanie Maze/Corbis/Bettmann; page 186: M.H. Sharp/Photo Researchers, Inc.; page 187: © Robert Michael/CORBIS All Rights Reserved; page 190: Laima E. Druskis/Pearson Education/PH College; page 192: Bob Mahoney/The Image Works; page 196: Getty Images Inc.-Stone Allstock; page 197: Sony Pictures/Photofest; page 201 (left): Charles Piatiau/Corbis/Bettmann; page 201 (right): © Matt Rainey/Star Ledger/CORBIS All Rights Reserved; page 203: Dave Schwarz/St. Cloud Times/AP Wide World Photos.

Chapter 7   page 210: Jean Metzinger (1883–1956), "Woman, frontal and profile". 1917. Musee National d'Art Moderne. Centre National d'Art et de Culture. Georges Pompidou. Reunion des Musees Nationaux/Art Resource, NY. ©2009 Artist Rights Society (ARS), NY; page 214 (left): Film Still Archive/The Museum of Modern Art/Film Stills Archive; page 214 (center): Film Still Archive/The Museum of Modern Art/Film Stills Archive; page 214 (right): Film Still Archive/The Museum of Modern Art/Film Stills Archive; page 218: Susan Greenwood/Getty Images, Inc.-Liaison; page 220: Siner Jeff/Corbis/Sygma; page 221: © Mika/Zefa/CORBIS All Rights Reserved; page 224: Michael Newman/PhotoEdit Inc.; page 229: Matthew Borkoski/Stock Boston; page 223: Bald Headed Pictures/Taxi/Getty Images; page 234: BSIP/Phototake NYC; page 237: Peter Turnley/Corbis/Bettmann; page 238: Stock Montage/Hulton Archive/Getty Images.

Chapter 8   page 246: Images.com/CORBIS Images.com; page 248: Sean Gallup/Getty Images, Inc.; page 250: Joel Gordon Photography/Design Conceptions; page 254: Laurent/Laeticia/Photo Researchers, Inc.; page 255: Bill Aron/PhotoEdit Inc.; page 256: AP Wide World Photos; page 257: Loomis Dean/Time Life Pictures/Getty Images/Time Life Pictures; page 260: Tom & Dee Ann McCarthy/Corbis/Bettmann; page 261: Marvi Lacar/Getty Images, Inc.; page 262: © Nice One Productions/CORBIS All Rights Reserved; page 264: SuperStock, Inc.; page 267: Noel Hendrickson/Getty Images, Inc.; page 270: Michal Heron/Michal Heron Photography; page 278: John Ulan/Canadian Press/Phototake NYC; page 281: Doug Dreyer/AP Wide World Photos; page 282: Gemeente Museum, The Hague, Netherlands/SuperStock, Inc.; page 284: Mary Kate Denny/PhotoEdit Inc.

Chapter 9   page 290: © Kevin Belford/Images.com/CORBIS All Rights Reserved; page 292 (left): Walter Bibikow/Getty Images Inc.-Image Bank; page 292 (right): Lawrence Migdale/Pix; page 299 (top): Ken Fisher/Getty Images Inc.-Stone Allstock; page 299 (bottom right): © Tribune Media Services, Inc. All Rights Reserved. Reprinted with permission; page 300 (left): D. Wells/The Image Works; page 300 (right): © Redlink/CORBIS All Rights Reserved; page 301: © Image Source/CORBIS All Rights Reserved; page 304: Don Farrall/Getty Images, Inc.- Photodisc; page 305: AP Wide World Photos; page 313: Catherine Ursillo/Photo Researchers, Inc.; page 316: Tom & DeeAnn McCarthy/Corbis/Stock Market; page 317: Joel Gordon Photography/Design Conceptions; page 319: Ted. S. Warren/AP Wide World Photos; page 323 (top): Linda & Mark Sobell; page 323 (bottom): Linda & Mark Sobell.

Chapter 10   page 330: ©Images.Com/Corbis; page 334: Tony Freeman/PhotoEdit Inc.; page 338: REUTERS/L'Equipe Agence/ HO/Landov LLC; page 339 (left): Jill Greenberg Studio, Inc.; page 344: Tom Raymond/Getty Images Inc.-Stone Allstock; page 346: Alex Wong/Getty Images, Inc.-Liaison; page 339 (right): WENN/Landov LLC; page 348: Russell D. Curtis/Photo Researchers, Inc.; page 350: Pictor/ImageState/International Stock Photography Ltd.; page 353: Ogust/The Image Works.

Chapter 11   page 358: Eric Fischel, "The Bed, The Chair, The Sitter." 78" x 93". Oil on Linen. 1999–2000. Courtesy: Mary Boone Gallery, New York; page 360: Dr. Jayne Thomas, Deceased/Peg Greene; page 362 (top): PhotoDisc/Getty Images; page 362 (bottom): George Holton/Photo Researchers, Inc.; page 364: Corbis/Sygma; page 369: Roy Morsch/Corbis/Stock Market; page 372: Ira Wyman/Corbis/Sygma; page 375: Bob Daemmrich/The Image Works; page 377: Randy Matusow/Randy Matusow; page 383: Fredrik D. Bodin; page 384: Michael Newman/PhotoEdit Inc.; page 388: Dazzo/Masterfile Corporation.

Chapter 12   page 396: Elia Alba Doll heads (multiplicities) copyright 2001. Courtesy of the artist and Henrique Faria Fine Art; page 398: Getty Images, Inc.; page 403: Sikora, Tomek/Getty Images Inc.-Image Bank; page 404: © Paul Almasy/CORBIS All Rights Reserved; page 408: Bob Benyas Photography; page 410: Grunnitus Studio/Photo Researchers, Inc.; page 411: Frieman Photography/Photo Researchers, Inc.; page 412: Corbis/Bettmann; page 414: Monte S. Buchsbaum, M.D., Mount Sinai School of Medicine, New York, N.Y.; page 415 (top right): Courtesy of Thompson, et al., in PNAS; page 415 (bottom left): Nancy C. Andreasen, M.D./University of Iowa Hospitals & Clinics; page 415 (bottom right): Nancy C. Andreasen, M.D./University of Iowa Hospitals & Clinics; page 416: Monte S. Buchsbaum, M.D., Mount Sinai School of Medicine, New York, N.Y.; page 417: David Lees/Corbis/Bettmann; page 421: Amy Etra/PhotoEdit Inc.; page 426: Patrick Molnar/Getty Images Inc.-Stone Allstock.

Chapter 13   page 434: Barbara Kruger, "Power Pleasure Desire Disgust." Installation: November 1997. Courtesy: Mary Boone Gallery, New York; page 438: Savino/The Image Works; page 440: AP Wide World Photos; page 441: © Bettmann/CORBIS All Rights Reserved; page 444: Dr. P. Marazzi/Photo Researchers, Inc.; page 445: Douglas Kirkland/Corbis/Bettmann; page 446: Greg Ceo/Image Bank/Getty Images; page 450: Penny Tweedie/Getty Images Inc.-Stone Allstock; page 452: Laima E. Druskis/Pearson Education/PH College; page 453: Bob Daemmrich/Stock Boston; page 456: Bob Daemmrich/Stock Boston; page 457: Richard Renaldi/Richard Renaldi; page 460: William G. Iacono; page 462: L. G. Patterson/AP Wide World Photos; page 466: Lexxox McLendon/AP Wide World Photos; page 468: Wendy S. Slutske, Ph.D.

Chapter 14   page 474: SuperStock, Inc.; page 476: Tony Freeman/PhotoEdit Inc.; page 477: M. Siluk/The Image Works; page 481: Erika Stone/Erika Stone; page 484: Robin Nelson/PhotoEdit Inc.; page 487: Richard Hutchings/Photo Researchers, Inc.; page 488: Tony Freeman/PhotoEdit Inc.; page 489: Paul Conklin/PhotoEdit Inc.; page 491: AP Wide World Photos; page 492: Dr. Judith Rumsey/National Institute of Mental Health; page 493: David Young Wolff/PhotoEdit Inc.; page 497: Pascal Quittemelle/Stock Boston; page 500 (top): Image 100/Corbis, Inc.; page 500 (bottom): David Young Wolff/PhotoEdit Inc.; page 502: Jean Claude LeJeune/Stock Boston; page 504: Michael Newman/PhotoEdit Inc.; page 508: Palco Labs, Inc.

Chapter 15   page 514: Wire Design/Photodisc/Getty Images; page 516: Frank Siteman/Stock Boston; page 521: Jeff Persons/Stock Boston; page 523 (top): David Young Wolff/PhotoEdit Inc.; page 523 (bottom): ARTHUR TILLEY/Getty Images, Inc.-Taxi; page 524: Michael Newman/PhotoEdit Inc.; page 527 (left): Robert P. Friedland, MD, Case Western Reserve University; page 527 (right): Robert P. Friedland, MD, Case Western Reserve University; page 527 (bottom): AP/Wide World Photos; page 528: AP Wide World Photos; page 530: Spike Walker/Getty Images Inc.-Stone Allstock; page 531: Karen Kasmauski/Woodfin Camp & Associates; page 533: Getty Images, Inc.; page 536: Catherine Bauknight/Corbis/Bettmann; page 537: AP Wide World Photos.

Chapter 16   page 542: Shannon Stapleton/REUTERS/Landov LLC; page 544: AP Wide World Photos; page 546: NewsCom; page 547: AP/Wide World Photos; page 548: Republic Pictures/Stringer/Getty Images, Inc.; page 552 (left): AP Wide World Photos; page 552 (right): AP Wide World Photos; page 553: AP Wide World Photos; page 554: Brendan Smialowski/Stringer/Reuters NewsMedia/Corbis/Bettmann; page 556: AP Wide World Photos.

Aalto, S., 414, 420
Aarre, T. F., 278
Aarsland, D., 532
Abakoumkin, G., 280
Abbey, A., 302
Abeles, N., 552
Abenavoli, L., 311
Abgott, R., 252
Abikoff, H., 496
Abracen, J., 385
Abram, K. M., 550
Abramowitz, J. S., 197, 198
Abramson, K. D., 338
Abramson, L. Y., 65, 262, 264, 270, 277
Achenbach, T. M., 94, 95
Acierno, R., 202, 204, 476
Ackerman, S. J., 120
Acklin, M. W., 88
Adam, M. B., 151
Adami, H., 414
Adams, B. G., 203
Adams, C., 419
Adams, H. E., 391
Adams et al., 343
Addington, H. J. Jr., 323
Addington, J., 423
Addis, M. E., 179, 271
Addolorato, G., 311
Adelson, R., 294, 298
Adler, L., 4, 5, 495
Aeby, V. G., 337
Agathen, J., 505
Aggen, S. H., 413
Ago, Y., 495
Agras, W. S., 120, 338, 340, 341, 342
Aguilar-Gaxiola, S., 205
Ahern, D. K., 232, 240
Ahmed, F., 134
Ahrens, A. H., 263
Ahuja, N., 236
Ainsworth, M. D. S., 499
Aizer, A., 467
Akhtar, S., 236, 237, 438
Akiskal, H. S., 77, 252, 256
Alahi, P., 423
Alamo, C., 276
Alarcon, M., 484
Albano, A.-M., 193, 531
Albaugh, B., 100
Albertini, R. S., 240
Alcoholism Treatment Study Group, 311
Alden, L. E., 152
Aldrich, M. S., 349
Alegria, M., 151, 152
Aleman, A., 400
Alessi, S. M., 322
Alford, J., 415
Alia, A., 269
Alipuria, L., 155
Allen, K. R., 384
Allen, M. H., 257
Allgulander, C., 200
Alloy, L. B., 65, 253, 268, 270, 277
Almai, A., 176
Almasy, L., 411
Alper, C. M., 146
Alpert, M., 202
Alter, J., 303
Althof, S., 375
Alvarez-Retuerto, A., 484
Alvir, J. M., 428
Aman, M. G., 484
Amato, L., 320
Amato, R., 146
American Heart Association, 164
American Law Institute, 557
American Psychiatric Association (APA), 70, 71, 72, 73, 74, 76, 142, 143,

174, 181, 194, 195, 199, 203, 213, 215, 216, 219, 220, 221, 222, 228, 231, 232, 235, 249, 250, 252, 254, 256, 257, 258, 291, 293, 294, 303, 305, 306, 308, 309, 311, 332, 333, 335, 347, 348, 349, 351, 352, 359, 361, 366, 376, 400, 401, 409, 412, 426, 429, 437, 438, 439, 440, 441, 442, 443, 444, 446, 447, 449, 451, 459, 478, 479, 480, 482, 485, 490, 492, 493, 494, 500, 507, 508, 515, 517, 519, 520, 522, 531, 532, 533, 534, 535, 546
American Psychological Association (APA), 21, 148, 215, 216, 436, 450, 518, 546, 552
Ames, M. A., 381
Amin, K., 384
Ammerman, Y., 466, 467
Amminger, G. P., 421
Amsterdam, J. D., 116, 273
Amunts, K., 398
Ancoli-Israel, S., 349, 525
Ancona, M., 100
Anda, R. F., 381, 382
Andersen, K., 532
Andershed, H., 459, 530
Anderson, E. M., 120
Anderson, E. S., 166
Anderson, G., 217
Anderson, J. W., 454
Anderson, L. P., 156
Anderson, P., 192
Anderson, P. L., 192
Anderson, R. A., 198
Anderson, S. W., 128
Anderson, T., 166
Anderson, W. W., 476
Andersson, G., 119
Andrade, A. R., 497
Andreasen, A., 268
Andreasen, A. C., 45
Andreasen, N. C., 411, 413
Andreoli, A., 462
Andrew, M., 268, 269
Andrews, B., 202, 418
Andrykowski, M. A., 203
Anestis, M. D., 477
Angier, N., 337
Angold, A., 63
Anipova, A. V., 65
Anker, M., 10, 400
Annas, P., 261
Annest, J. L., 281
Anthoni, H., 491
Anthony, J. C., 298
Anthony, J. L., 178, 490
Anton, R. F., 314
Antonarakas, S. E., 486
Antoni, M., 155
Antoni, M. H., 166
Antonia, M. H., 166
Antonuccio, D. O., 469
APA Presidential Task Force on Evidence-Based Practice, 120
Apopolinario, J. C., 342
Appelbaum, K. A., 160
Appelbaum, P. S., 545, 549, 550
Applegate, B., 441
Aragon, R., 312
Arango, C., 422
Arbisi, P. A., 100
Ardekani, B. A., 196
Arias, R., 527, 530
Arieti, S., 409, 424
Arisaka, O., 508
Armesto, J. C., 418, 419
Armfield, J. M., 187

Armstrong, J. M., 477
Arndt, S., 484
Arnett, P. A., 461
Arnold, H. S., 493
Arnold, I. A., 239
Arnold, L. E., 496
Arnold, P. D., 196
Arnold, R., 464
Arnold, S. E., 397
Arnold, S. L., 196
Arnow, B. A., 120
Arntz, A., 185
Arnulf, I., 350
Aronson, A., 179
Aronson, M. K., 529
Arrindell, W. A., 176
Arseneault, L., 466
Artaloytia, J. F., 422
Artru, A. A., 304, 484
Asaad, G., 406
Asbjørnsen, A., 415
Asghar, S. A., 276
Ashtari, M., 196
Assanand, S., 344
Atkinson, C., 146
Attia, E., 165, 341
ATTICA Study, 161
Audrain-McGovern, J., 311
Augusto, A., 254
Ault, A., 482
Auslander, L. A., 425
Austin, C., 200
Austin, M., 322
Auth, J., 152
Author, L. Y., 338
"Autism Rate" (2007), 482
Avarez, E., 464
Avery, D. H., 278
Avlund, K., 252
Avon Longitudinal Study of Parents and Children Study Team, 509
Axelson, D., 502
Ayllon, T., 411
Ayuso-Mateose, J.-L., 143
Aziz, N., 419
Azoulay, S., 317
Azrael, D., 280
Azrin, N. H., 30

Babiak, P., 457
Babor, T., 310
Babulas, V., 414
Babyak, M. A., 161
Bachler, E., 464
Bachman, J. G., 298
Backes, V., 398
Baer, J. S., 133
Baer, R. A., 158
Bagary, M. S., 414
Bagge, C., 444, 445
Bagley, C., 18
Bagnardi, V., 302
Bailar, J. C., 25
Bailey, A., 136
Bailey, D. S., 257, 361, 363, 378, 384
Bailey, E. D., 232, 233
Bailey, J. A., 388
Bailey, J. M., 18, 89, 385
Baity, M. R., 89
Baker, B., 125
Baker, C. K., 202
Baker, D. G., 154
Baker, F. M., 135
Baker, L., 339
Baker, R. C., 94
Baker, S. P., 301
Baker, T. B., 324
Bakish, D., 282
Bakris, G. L., 161
Baksh, E., 420, 439

Balddessarini, R. J., 256
Baldwin, R., 483
Baldwin, S. A., 120
Bales, V. S., 343
Ballestar, E., 45
Ballestar, M. L., 45
Ballie, R., 256
Baltimore, D., 44
Bancroft, J., 274, 366, 367, 375
Bandeen-Roche, K., 162
Bandura, A., 55, 111, 145, 154, 457
Barbanoj, M. J., 278
Barbe, R. P., 504
Barbosa, E. R., 524
Barch, D. M., 400, 415, 416
Barclay, L., 317
Bardelli, A., 165
Bardone-Cone, A. M., 338
Bardwell, W. A., 349
Barefoot, J. C., 252
Barker, G. J., 414
Barkham, M., 120
"Barkley Claims Gambling Problem" (2006), 468
Barkley, R., 4, 5, 495
Barlow, D. H., 174, 177, 179, 369
Barnes, T. R., 422
Barnett, M. C., 233
Barnett, W. S., 488
Barnhill, J. L. J., 508
Barr-Taylor, C., 155
Barr, W., 535
Barrachina, J., 464
Barrera, M. Jr., 133
Barron, J., 483
Barron, S., 483
Barrowclough, C., 418
Barry, D. T., 135
Barry, P., 354
Barsky, A. J., 232, 235, 239, 240
Bartholow, B. D., 297
Bartzokis, G., 530
Basch, M. F., 110
Basco, M. R., 531
Baser, E., 279, 280
Basile, K. C., 390
Baskin, D. G., 197, 344
Bassman, R., 560
Bassuk, S. S., 344
Basta, J., 151
Bastien, C. H., 353
Bata, I., 162
Bateman, A. B., 463
Bates, D. W., 235
Batsman, S., 530
Battaglia, M., 459
Battle, C. L., 123
Bauchner, H., 495
Bauer, A., 549
Bauer, R., 336
Bauer, V. K., 252
Baughman, K. L., 162
Baum, A., 165
Baum et al., 269
Baumeister, R. F., 156, 390
Baxter, L. R., Jr., 197
Bayer, B. A., 203
Bazell, R., 344, 349
Beals, J., 62, 82, 300, 315
Bean, J. L., 366, 368
Bear, M. F., 487
Beauvais, F., 300
Bebbington, P., 276, 426
Bechdolf, A., 425
Bechtoldt, H., 117
Beck, A. T., 59, 95, 96, 114, 116, 120, 263, 265, 281, 464
Beck, J. G., 523
Becker, D., 454

Becker, T., 415
Beckham, J. C., 155
Beckman, A., 477
Bedwell, J. S., 415, 420, 439
Begg, M. D., 414
Begley, S., 219, 303
Béhar, C., 534
Behar, K. L., 176
Behrman, A., 257
Beidel, D., 193
Beidel, D. C., 182
Beitman, B. D., 117
Bejerot, S., 128
Belger, A., 405
Belin, T., 273
Belkin, L., 195
Bell, A. P., 18
Bell, M., 416
Bell, R. J., 193
Bellack, A. S., 419, 423, 426
Bellodi, L., 459
Belluck, P., 318
Ben-Itzchak, E., 484
Ben-Porath, Y., 100
Benazon, N. R., 262
Benazzi, F., 77
Bender, M., 284
Bender, W. S., 137
Bennett, A., 397, 423
Bennett, D., 112, 337
Bennett, D. A., 517, 518, 525
Benson, H., 157
Bentall, R. P., 406, 407
Berendt, I., 507
Beresford, S. A., 344
Berg, S., 530
Bergem, A. L. M., 531
Berger, P., 462
Berglund, P. A., 4, 5, 248, 251
Bergman, A., 456
Berkowitz, R. I., 346
Berlim, M., 281
Berlin, H. A., 461
Berliner, L., 381, 477
Berman, J. R., 375
Berman, L. A., 375
Berman, S. L., 503
Bermpohl, F., 524
Bernardeschi, L., 459
Bernstein, E. M., 223
Bernstein, R. L., 236
Berrios, G. E., 427
Berry, J. M., 332, 342
Berton, O., 268, 273
Bespalova, I. N., 484
Best, C. L., 476
Best, S. R., 202
Beutler, L. E., 32, 117
Bevans, M. L., 422
Bhagwagar, Z., 40, 268
Bhattacharyya, M. R., 162
Bichard, S., 187
Bickman, L., 120, 497
Biedermann, J., 4, 5, 76, 495, 497
Bienias, J. L., 518, 525
Bierer, L. M., 458
Biever, J. L., 135
Bilder, R. M., 196
Bilker, W. B., 397
Billing, C. B., 317
Binder, R. L., 549, 550, 552
Binderup, T., 390
Binik, Y. M., 367, 368
Biran, M., 116
Birbaumer, N., 176
Birchwood, M., 406
Bird, H., 496
Bird, T. D., 530
Birmaher, B., 282, 502, 504
Birnbaum, H. J., 390

Birnbaum, M. H., 214
Birolleau, S., 350
Bismil, R., 459
Bissada, N., 86, 534
Bisserbe, J.-C., 274
Bjerklie, D., 155
Bjorvatn, B., 354, 525
Black, H. R., 161
Blackburn, R., 214
Blacker, D. L., 311
Blackman, J. A., 476
Blackmore, E. R., 254
Blaine, J., 322
Blair, R. J. R., 457
Blais, F. C., 353
Blais, M. A., 87, 89, 464
Blanchard, E. B., 160, 202
Blanchard, K. A., 320
Blanchard, L. T., 476
Blanco, C., 182, 183, 205, 281, 504
Blandino, J. A., 265, 268
Blankstein, K. R., 95–96
Blasey, C., 120
Blatt, S. J., 263
Blazer, D. G., 252
Blazina, C., 18
Bleiberg, K. L., 270
Bless, E., 266
Bliss, C. A., 489
Blonigen, D. M., 441
Bloom, C., 380
Bloom, R., 416
Bloomberg, G. R., 164
Bloomer, C., 314
Blowers, L. C., 336
Blumenthal, J., 415
Blumenthal, J. A., 161
Boag, S., 46
Bockting, C. L. H., 116, 275
Bockting, W. O., 363
Bodenlos, J., 100
Bodkin, J. A., 215
Boget, T., 425
Bohl, J., 466, 467
Bohman, S., 119
Bolaños, C. A., 504
Boles, S. M., 301
Bollini, A., 281, 400, 414, 415, 425
Bolton, D., 501
Bolton, P., 99, 270
Bonacci, A. M., 390
Bonanno, G. A., 202
Bongar, B., 505
Bongersa, I. L., 500
Booker, M. B. Jr., 128
Bookheimer, S. Y., 530
Booth, B. M., 388
Bootzin, R. R., 351
Borges, G., 278
Borjesson, M., 161
Borkovec, T. D., 198, 200
Bornstein, R. A., 533
Bornstein, R. F., 451, 458
Borowiecki, J. J. III, 336
Borum, R., 549
Boskind-White, M., 335
Bost, J. E., 123
Botelho, R. J., 133
Bötzel, K., 532, 534
Bouchard, C., 197
Bouchard, S., 353
Boudouris, J., 555
Bouman, T. K., 240
Bourne, L., 179
Bouvard, M., 176
Bové, J., 533
Bowden, C. L., 276
Bowen, D., 346
Bower, C., 64, 484
Bowie, C. R., 415

Bowlby, M., 527, 530
Bowlling, J. B., 489
Bowman, B. A., 343
Bown, C. D., 282
Boyce, W. T., 147, 477
Boyd-Franklin, N., 124
Boyer, P., 274
Boyle, F. M., 366, 368
Boyles, S., 274
Braaten, E. B., 494
Bradford, J. M. W., 386
Bradley, J. D. D., 493, 495
Bradley, R., 204
Brady, J. V., 318
Braff, D., 411, 420
Braff, D. L., 404
Braham, L. G., 406
Brammer, M., 495
Brammer, M. J., 196
Bramon, E., 428
Brandes, J. L., 160
Brandon, T. H., 314
Brannick, M., 336
Brannigan, G. G., 90
Branson, R., 342
Brantley, P. J., 100
Braswel, L., 503
Braswell, L., 111
Braun, B. G., 214
Braun, S., 305
Bray, N. J., 413
Breaux, Matsuoka, & Ryujin (1995), 134
Brecht, M. L., 322
Breeden, G., 279, 280
Breier, J. I., 491
Breitholtz, E., 176
Bremner, J. D., 40, 445, 461
Brenda, W. J. H., 524
Brendle, J. R., 187
Brennan, P. L., 154
Brenner, H. D., 407, 425, 426
Brensinger, C. M., 397
Brent, D. A., 282
Breslau, J., 61, 205, 295
Breslin, F. C., 325
Breslow, N., 383
Bresnahan, M., 414
Brewer, R. D., 301
Brewin, C. R., 202
Briand, 423
Brice, A., 533
Bricker, J., 315
Bridge, J. A., 504
Briere, J., 477
Briganti, E., 375
Bright, J., 277
Brigidi, B. D., 219
Brink, D. C., 112
Brinkhaus, B., 159
Brobst, K., 123
Brock, G., 365
Brockmoller, J., 533
Broderick, G. A., 370
Brodsky, B. S., 269
Brody, J. E., 254, 353–354, 384, 487
Bromet, E., 173, 400
Brook, J. S., 445, 458
Brotchie, H., 269
Brown, A. S., 381, 414
Brown, C. F., 524
Brown, C. H., 423
Brown, D. R., 134
Brown, E. L., 524
Brown, G., 265
Brown, G. G., 186
Brown, G. K., 279, 281
Brown, G. M., 40, 340
Brown, G. R., 372, 375
Brown, J. S., 477
Brown, K., 205

Brown, L. S., 219
Bowlling, J. B., 489
Brown, M. J., 156, 461
Brown, M. Z., 445, 464
Brown, P. A., 156
Brown, R. J., 235
Brown, S. A., 324
Brown, T. A., 369
Brown, T. L., 278
Brown, T. W., 174
Browne, S., 176
Brownell, K. D., 344
Browning, 381
Bruce, M. L., 279, 281, 524
Bruce, T. J., 122, 423
Bruch, H., 339
Brunswick, N., 490
Brunt, S., 119
Bryant, R., 119
Bryant, R. A., 200, 203, 204
Brydon, L., 162
Bryson, G., 416
Bubel, D., 203
Bucciarelli, A., 202
Buchanan, A, 549
Buchanan, R., 205
Buchanan, R. W., 400, 414
Buchert, R., 311
Buchheim, P., 462
Buchpiguel, C., 524
Buchsbaum, B. R., 416
Buchsbaum, M. S., 224, 416, 484
Bucka, O., 302
Bucuvalas, M. J., 147
Buddie, A. M., 297
Budney, A. J., 310
Buhlmann, U., 239
Buhrman, M., 119
Bukowski, W. M., 494
Bulgin, N., 459
Bulik, C. M., 332, 340, 342
Bullbeck, K., 266
Bulmash, E. L., 251
Bunde, J., 161
Bunney, B. G., 44
Bunney, W. E., 44
Burdick, K. E., 413
Burg, R., 384
Burge, D., 452
Burgess, A. W., 389
Burgess, S., 276
Buriel, R., 151
Burke, A. K., 269
Burke, J., 497
Burke, J. D., 441, 478
Burns, A., 520
Burns, B. J., 123
Burns, D. D., 114, 263
Burns, J. C., 136, 137
Burns, T., 281
Burroughs, D., 82
Burroughs, E., 196
Burrows-MacLean, L., 496
Burt, 391
Burt, S. A., 460
Burton, E. M., 340
Burton, K. W., 487
Burton, M., 425
Burton, N., 224, 225, 226
Busch, F., 179
Bushman, B. J., 390
Bushnell, D. M., 251
Busseri, M. A., 120
Bustillo, J. R., 424
Butcher, J., 99
Butcher, J. N., 100
Butera, F., 259, 460
Butler, A. C., 116, 120
Butler, C. B., 318
Butler, L. D., 217, 219, 220, 224, 227
Butler, R. J., 507, 508
Butler, R. N., 525

Butler, U., 509
Bütz, M. R., 489
Bux, D. A., 320
Bux Jr., D. A., 197, 198
Byers, E. S., 367
Byrne, J., 520
Bystritsky, A., 179

Caballero, B., 336, 337
Cable, N., 315
Cacciola, J., 268
Caddell, J. M., 147
Caddy, G. R., 323
Cadoret, R. J., 460, 498
Cadwell, B. L., 343
Caetano, R., 151
Cafri, G., 336
Caillard, V., 274
Calabrese, J. R., 257, 276
Calamari, J. E., 197
Caldwell, A., 100
Caldwell, R., 117
Cale, E. M., 440
Calker, D. van, 31
Calkins, M. E., 411
Callicott, J. H., 415
Calzada, S., 151
Camargo, C. A. Jr., 302
Cameron, A., 371
Cameron, N., 218
Campbell, H., 193
Campbell, J. M., 266
Campbell, L. F., 117
Campbell, R., 389
Campbell, T., 4
Campbell, W. K., 448
Campins, J., 464
Cannon, M. F., 202
Cannon, T. D., 415
Cantey-Kiser, J., 375
Cantor, R. M., 484
Cantu, R. C., 535
Capuano, G., 423
Caramés, E., 274
Cardemil, E. V., 123
Cardno, A., 268, 269
Carey, B., 166, 484, 504
Carini, M. A., 407
Carlbring, P., 119
Carlier, I. V., 204
Carlos, M., 439, 444
Carlson, S. R., 459, 460
Carlsson, A., 414
Carnes, L., 366, 367, 375
Carney, R. M., 162
Carpenter, D., 200
Carpenter, W. T., 400
Carrier, S., 160
Carroll, L., 302, 532, 533
Carroll, M. D., 344
Carroll, R. T., 205
Carson, A., 232, 337
Carson, R., 177
Carter, C. S., 415
Carter, J. C., 165, 341
Carter, M., 425
Carter, M. M., 177
Cartwright, C., 484
Carver, C. S., 155, 157
Casey, B. J., 495
Casey, L. M., 176
Casey, P., 143
Caspi, A., 268, 459, 460, 490
Cassisi, J., 407
Castaño, M. T., 135
Castellani, R. J., 527, 530
Castellanos, F. X., 493, 495
Castellon, C., 268
Castillo, E. M., 491
Castonguay, L. G., 120, 254

Castro, J. L., 530
Catalán, R., 425
Catanese, D., 336
Catanese, K. R., 390
Catlett, J., 366
Cato, R. K., 346
"CDC Finds Gaping Racial Disparities in Health" (2005), 156
Ceci, S. J., 485
Celio, A. A., 342
Center on Alcohol Marketing and Youth, 298
Centers for Disease Control (CDC), 163, 165, 306, 307
Cepeda-Benito, A., 318
Cervantes, R. C., 61, 152
Chadda, R. K., 236
Chae, M. H., 524
Chaiyasit, W., 476
Chalder, T., 221
Chambless, D. L., 120, 205
Chan, D. W., 99
Chan, K., 459
Chaney, G., 484
Chang, D. F., 62
Chang, T., 119
Channabasavanna, S. M., 462
Chanoine, V., 490
Chantarujikapong, S., 305
Chao, H. M., 422
Chapman, J. E., 116, 120
Chassin, L., 301, 315
Chavira, D. A., 439, 444
Chawky, N., 281
Chee, E., 251
Chee, K. T., 10
Cheetham, T., 342, 344
Chelminski, I., 467
Chemerinski, E., 524
Chen, C., 311
Chen, E., 164
Chen, G. Q., 236
Chen, H., 445, 458
Chen, J., 162
Chen, P., 526
Cheng, Y. J., 343
Cheng, Z., 487
Chesney, M. A., 260
Chess, L., 145
Cheung, F. M., 99, 100, 134, 135
Chevron, E. S., 270
Chiappetta, L., 502
Chiappini, M. S., 166
"Children's Mental Illness 'Crisis', A" (2001), 476
Cho, R. Y., 415
Chobanian, A. V., 161
Chou, S. P., 182, 183, 199, 205, 452
Chovil, I., 399, 400
Chowdhury, 236
Choy, Y., 190, 193
Christ, M. A., 498
Christopher, J., 441
Chronis, A. M., 495, 496
Chrysohoou, C., 161
Chu, J. A., 219
Chung, J., 273
Chung, T., 323
Cipriani, A., 276
Cirincione, C., 555
Claghorn, J. L., 198
Claridge, G. C., 260
Clark, D. A., 198, 265
Clark, D. M., 176, 177, 193, 239
Clark, R., 156
Clark, T. A., 136
Clarke, G. N., 96, 133
Clarkin, J., 179
Clarkin, J. F., 444, 445, 463
Clasen, L., 495

Clay, R. A., 161
Cleary, P. D., 233
Cleckley, H., 441, 459
Clelland, J. D., 422
Clerc, G., 275
Clinton, A. M., 302
Cloitre, M., 219
Clopton, J. R., 336
Clougherty, K. F., 270
Clum, G. A., 226
Cochran, S. D., 18
Cochran, S. V., 253
Cohane, G. H., 336
Cohen, A. S., 400
Cohen, B., 554
Cohen, F., 154
Cohen, F. L., 349
Cohen, H., 278
Cohen, J. A., 156, 381, 477
Cohen, J. D., 415
Cohen-Kettenis, P. T., 362, 363, 364
Cohen-Kettensi, P. T., 361
Cohen, M. S., 415, 530
Cohen, P., 445, 458, 505
Cohen, S., 146, 161
Coker, L. H., 525
Colas, E., 195
Coldwell, C. M., 137
Cole, 391
Cole, J., 278
Cole, J. C., 354
Colelli, G., 205
Coleman, D., 135
Coles, E. K., 496
Collins, B. N., 314
Collins, P. H., 124
Colliver, J. D., 294, 295
Comas-Diaz, L., 119
Combs, D. R., 407
Comer, S. D., 318
Comerford, A., 445
Comery, T. A., 527, 530
Compas, B. E., 154
Compton et al., 309
Compton, S. N., 63, 251
Compton, W., 173, 181, 182, 199, 248, 254, 255, 294
Compton, W. M., 294, 295
Comtois, K. A., 445, 464
Conigrave, K. M., 302
Conklin, C. Z., 444
Conley, C. S., 502
Conlon, C., 495
Connelly, 344
Conner, K. R., 477
Conners, C. K., 4, 5, 495
Connor, E., 439
Constantino, M. J., 120
Contrada, R. J., 162
Conturea, E. G., 493
Conway, K. P., 173, 181, 182, 199, 248, 251, 254, 255, 294
Conwell, Y., 281
Cook, A., 265
Coon, D. W., 524
Coons, P. M., 227
Cooper, A., 384
Cooper, J. K., 534
Cooper, L. A., 119
Cooper, P. J., 254
Cooper, T. B., 282
Cooper, Z., 342
Coplan, J., 176
Coppola, R., 405, 415, 416
Corbett, J., 312
Cord, B. J., 305
Cordova, M. J., 203
Corley, R. P., 460
Coronado, S. F., 125
Cororve, M. B., 234, 239, 240

Corrigan, P. W., 549
Cortina, J., 554
Cortina, L. M., 202
Coryell, W., 176, 185, 256, 257
Costa, N. M., 202
Costanzo, S., 302
Costello, E. J., 63
Costin, C., 331
Coursey, R. D., 415
Couzin, J., 344
Cowan, W. M., 281, 398, 414, 525, 534, 535
Cowell, P. E., 397
Cowen, P. J., 40
Cowley, G., 317
Cox, B. J., 176
Cox, D. S., 146
Cox, MacPherson, & Enns, 182
Cox, N. J., 196
Coxeter, P. D., 366, 368
Coyle, J. P., 372
Coyne, J. C., 262
Craig, I. W., 268, 459, 460
Cramer, V., 435
Craske, M. G., 179
Crawford, P. B., 337
Creed & Barsky, 239
Creed, F., 281
Crerand, C. E., 233
Critchley, H. D., 479
Crits-Christoph, P., 121
Croghan et al., 317
Cronkite, R., 262
Crosby, A. E., 281
Crosby, R., 338
Crow, 410
Crow, S. J., 332, 341, 342
Crum, R. M., 312
Cruysberg, J. R., 406
Cruz, T. B., 151
Crystal, S, 525
Csernansky, J. G., 415, 416
Cubero, P., 422
Cuffel, B., 135
Cuijpers, P., 133
Cuijpers, van Straten, & Warmerdam, 271
Cullen, F. T., 389
Cummings, J. L., 530
Cummins, L. H., 300
Cunningham, G., 372
Cunningham, J. A., 325
Curb, J. D., 345
"Curbing the Obesity Epidemic" (2006), 344
Curtin, L., 65
Curtin, L. R., 344
Cushman, W. C., 161
Cuthbert, B. N., 77, 442
Cutler, N. R., 136
Cutrona, C. E., 156, 259
Cyranowski, J. M., 253
Czerski, P. M., 258, 269

Dacey, S., 265, 268
Dager, S. R., 304, 484
Dahdouh, F., 491
Dahl, A. A., 200, 278
Dahl, R. E., 351
Dahlberg, L. L., 281
Dahlof, B., 161
Daigle, L. E., 389
Daley, S. E., 260, 452
Dalgard, O. S., 143
Dallas, M. B., 337
Dalton, K. M., 483
Dana, R. H., 10
Dang, S. T., 204
Dangelmaier, R. E., 400
Danics, Z., 384
Daniels, S. D., 337

Dannon, P. N., 278, 467
Danoff-Burg, S., 146
Dao., T. K., 89
Dar, R., 25
Darkes, J., 298
Dashevsky, B. A., 154
DaSilva, J. N., 40
Daskalakis, J., 278
D'Augelli, A. R., 18
Dauvilliers, Arnulf, & Mignot, 349
David, A. S., 221, 222
David, D., 116
Davidson, K., 162
Davidson, M., 422
Davidson, R. J., 185, 269
Davies, B. A., 339, 340
Davies, L., 422
Davies, M., 316, 484
Davies, S. L., 133
Davis, 370
Davis, A. A., 354
Davis, D. D., 464
Davis, J., 422
Davis, J. M., 203, 391
Davis, K. L., 439, 484
Davis, S., 366, 368, 440
Davis, S. M., 423
Davis, S. R., 193, 375
Davis, T. L., 342, 391
Davison, S. L., 193
Davoli, M., 320
Daw, J., 82
Dawe, S., 314, 336
Dawes, R. M., 549
Dawson, D. A., 173, 174, 175, 199, 294, 452
Dawson, G., 304, 484
de Beurs, E., 466
de Beurs, E. E., 205
de Castella, A., 278
De Col, C., 342
de Gaetano, G., 302
de Groot, E., 375
de Groot, H. E., 375
De Gucht, V., 227, 239
De Hert, M., 418
de Jong, P., 185
de Klerk, N., 484
De La Cancela, V., 125, 134
de las Fuentes, C., 135
De Leon, A. B., 185
de Moor, C., 146
De Silva, P., 187
de Waal, M. W. M., 239
de Wolff, F. A., 305
De Zubicaray, G., 525
de Zwaan, M., 338, 340
Deacon, B. J., 176
Dean, R. S., 497
DeBaggio, T., 515, 517
Decker, S. L., 90, 497
Deegear, J., 120
Deffenbacher, J. L., 162
Dekker, J., 367
DeKosky, S. T., 526
Del Boca, F. K., 298
Del Mastro, R. G., 163
Delahanty, D. L., 165
Delespaul, P. A. E. G., 407
Deligtisch, A., 533
Della Salla, S., 32
Delmonico, D. L., 384
Delong, M. R., 128
DeMarte, J. A., 460
Dement, W. C., 352
Demler, O., 4, 5, 104, 248, 251
Demonet, J. F., 490
den Heeten, G. J., 305
Deng, Y., 86, 534
Dengler, W., 176

Denizet-Lewis, B., 310
Dennis, C., 364
Denny, C., 301
DeNoon, D., 496
Depression Guideline Panel, 125, 276
Derby, C. A., 371, 530
Derenne, J.-P., 350
Derhagopian, R. P., 155
Derksen, J., 99
DeRosse, P., 413
DeRubeis, R. J., 96, 114, 116, 273
Desai, R. A., 151, 152
DeSanctis, R., 161
Deschner, M., 258, 269
Deuschl, G., 532, 534
Dev, P., 342
Devan, G. S., 236
Devieuxa, J., 166
Devilly, G. J., 205
Devlin, M. J., 342
Devor, E., 460
deVries, M. W., 407
Dew, M. A., 525
Di Castelnuovo, A., 302
Diamond, R., 483
Diamond, S., 483
Diaz-Loving, R., 153
Dick, D. M., 312
Dickel, D. E., 196
Dickens, B. M., 323
Dickerson, F. B., 424
Dickey, C. C., 439
DiClemente, R. J., 133
Didi, R., 275
Diehl, S. R., 412
Dietz, 344
Dietz, W. H., 343
Diforio, D., 421
Dimeff, L. A., 133
Dimidjian, S., 271
Dimsdale, J. E., 349
DiMuzio-Mower, J., 530
Dingfelder, S. F., 420, 464
Dinzeo, T. J., 400
DiPlacido, J., 155
Dishion, T. J., 316
Ditta, S. R., 203
Dixit, A. R., 312
Dixon, L., 419
Dixon, M. J., 418
Doan, B., 493
Dobs, A., 372
Dobson, K. S., 116, 271, 273
Docherty, N. M., 400, 418
Dodge, K. A., 457
Doebbeling, B. N., 388
Doersch, A., 466, 467
Doheny, K., 493
Dohm, F. A., 337
Dohrenwend, B. P., 149, 203
Doll et al., 306
Doll, H. A., 339, 340, 342
Dombrowski, M. E., 418
Domier, C. P., 371
Donaghey, C., 128, 275
Donath, S., 193
Donati, M. B., 302
Doob, A. N., 323
Doody, R., 530
Dorahy, M. J., 215, 223
Dorhofer, D. M., 253
Dottl, S. L., 82
Dougall, A. L., 165
Dougherty, D. M., 297
Douglas, K. S., 549
Dow, M. G. T., 179
Dowd, E. T., 155
Dowker, A., 491
Downey, G., 282
Dowrick, C., 143

Doyle, B., 154
Doyle, W. J., 146
Dozois, D. J. A., 116
Draguns, J. G., 10
Draijer, N., 202
Drake, R. E., 136
Drakenberg, K., 311
Dresler, C. M., 318
Drewnowski, A., 335
Drieling, T., 31, 259
Drob, S. L., 226
Drobes, D. J., 314
Druss, B. G., 123, 251
Dryden, W., 113
Du, L., 282
"Du Pont Heir Found Guilty" (1997), 555
Duan, N., 251
Duberstein, P. R., 477
Dubovsky, S., 276, 278, 310, 405
Duenweld, M., 251
Duffy, F. H., 99
Duffy, M., 520
Dugas, M. J., 198
Dugas, M. L., 200
Duin, J. S., 265, 268
Duke & Hochman, 283
Dumenci, L., 94, 95
Dummit, S., 202
Dunn, G., 422
Dunn, H., 425
Dunne, M. P., 366, 368
Dupuis, J., 163
Duran, B., 125
Durantini, M. R., 133, 166
Durham, P. L., 159
Durham v. United States (1954), 556
Durr, A., 533
Durrett, C., 444, 445
Durston, S., 495
duToit, P. L., 265, 268
Dutra, L., 204
Dutton, G. R., 100
Duvall, J. A., 484
Dwyer, J. H., 157
Dykens, E. M., 341

Eagle, D. M., 495
Eagle, P., 226
Ear, A., 133, 166
Eardley, I., 370, 371
Earl, A. N., 133
Earnst, K. S., 410, 414
Eberhardy, F., 481
Ebert, L., 147
Ebmeier, K. P., 128, 275
Eddleston, M., 524
Eddy, Hennessey, & Thompson-Brenner, 337
Edenberg, H., 312
Edenberg, H. J., 312
Edgar, L. V., 176
Edmundson, M., 455
Edwards, N., 530
Edwards, V. J., 381, 382
Edwin, D., 188
Eekhof, J. A., 239
Effting, M., 215
Egan, M. F., 405, 415, 416
Egeland, J., 415
Ehlers, A., 193
Ehlert, U., 145, 203
Eiberg, H., 507
Eichstedt, J. A., 196
Eickhoff, S. B., 406
Eidelson, J. L., 265
Einfeld, S. L., 489
Eisch, A. J., 504
Eisen, S. A., 305
Eisenberg, D., 493
Eisenmenger, K., 190

Eisner, D. A., 32
Ekholm, J. M., 413
Ekselius, L., 119
Elbogen, E. B., 549
Eley, T.C., 501
Eling, P. A. T. M., 522
Ellason, J. W., 227
Elliott, D. M., 477
Elliott, M., 415, 416, 496
Ellis, A., 58, 59, 113, 368
Ellis, B. J., 147
Ellis, S. P., 284
Ely, T. D., 314
Emens, J. S., 252
Emery, G., 59, 95, 114, 263
Emmelkamp, P. M. G., 187, 190, 192
Emsley, R., 422
Endicott, J., 252, 256, 257
Engberg, A. W., 535
Engel, C. A., 119
Enns, M. W., 253
Epping, E. A., 484
Epping-Jordan, J. E., 154
Eppste in-Herald, D., 342
Epstein, E. M., 146
Epstein, H., 145
Erath, S., 318
Erdberg, P., 89
Eriksson, S., 530
Erlenmeyer-Kimling, L., 421
Ernberg, C., 10
Ernberg, G., 400
Ersland, L., 415
Eschweiler, G., 545
Escobar, C. M., 488
Escobar, J. I., 152
Eshleman, S., 440
Esposito et al., 370
Essex, M. J., 477
Etter, J.-F., 25
Ettinger, U., 405, 411, 420
Euler, H. A., 493
Evans, A., 495
Evans, D. A., 518, 525
Evans, J. H., 508
Evans, S. J., 44
Ewing, R., 345
Exner, J., 462
Exner, J. E., Jr., 88
Exton, M. S., 385

Faber, B., 412
Fabian, J. L., 236
Fabiano, G. A., 496
Fabrega, H., Jr., 100
Factor-Litvak, P., 414
Fagiolini, A. M., 277
Fahy, T., 281
Failer, J. L., 544, 545
Fairburn, C. G., 332, 339, 340, 341, 342
Falls, K., 163
Fals-Stewart, W., 302
Fama, J. M., 233
Fanous, A. H., 413
Faraone, S. V., 76, 490, 495, 497
Farber, B. A., 112
Farlow, M. R., 530
Farmer, R. F., 452
Farooqi, I. S., 342, 344
Farr, C. B., 13
Farrell, A. D., 316
Farrow, F. D., 406
Farrow, M. M., 160
Fassbender, C., 495
Faustman, W. O., 407
Fava, M., 125, 266, 274
Fawaz, W., 278
Fay, C., 233
Fayyad, R., 200
Fazel & Grann, 549

Fazio, F., 490
Fecteau, G., 205
Fedoroff, I. C., 205
Feeny, N. C., 197, 198
Feighner, J. A., 76
Feingold, J., 402
Feldman, J., 163, 164
Feldman, L. B., 193
Feldman, M. D., 230
Felitti, V. J., 381, 382
Feng, Y., 311
Fenichel (1945), 469
Fennell, M., 193
Fenwick, P. B. C., 385
Fera, F., 185
Ferdinand, R. F., 500
Ferguson-Peters, M., 124
Fergusson, D., 490
Fergusson, D. M., 505
Fernandez, A., 318
Fernyhough, C., 406, 407
Ferrans, C. E., 349
Ferri, M., 320
Ferris, S., 530
Ferrucci, L., 162
Fertuck, E. A., 444, 445
Feucht-Haviar, T., 554
"Fewer Teens" (2004), 305
Fichner-Rathus, L., 360, 384
Fields, S., 120
Fiellin et al., 318
Figueredo, A. J., 388
Filer Fegan, M., 156
Finch, J. F., 452
Findling, R. F., 484
Findling, R. L., 503
Fink, M., 275, 409
Finkel, E. J., 448
Finney, J. W., 322
Finstroma, N., 187
Fiore, M. C., 324
Firestone, L. A., 366
Firestone, R. W., 366
First, M., 77
First, M. B., 16, 252
Fischer, D. J., 196
Fishbain, D. A., 236
Fisher, B. S., 389
Fisher, E. B., Jr., 164
Fisher, P. L., 198
Fisher, W. A., 370, 371
Fitz et al., 508
Fitzgerald, P. B., 278
Fitzmaurice, G., 311
Fitzpatrick, K. K., 281
Flaherty, E., 372, 375
Flannery, E. M., 164
Flannery-Schroeder, E., 501
Flashman, L. A., 410
Fleck, M., 251
Flegal, K. M., 343, 344
Fleisher, W. P., 217
Flesher, S., 425
Fletcher, J. M., 491
Flor, H., 176
Florin, I., 239
Foa, E. B., 198, 202, 219
Fogg, L., 354
Folkman, S., 154
Folsom, D. P., 136
Fombonne, E., 482
Fonagy, P., 463
Fontaine, K. R., 343
Foote, B., 224, 226
Ford, D. E., 119
Ford, E. S., 343
Ford, J., 204
Ford, J. D., 203
Ford, J. M., 407
Forman, D. N., 254

Forman, E. M., 116, 120
Foroud, T., 312
Forrester, E., 195
Foster, C. A., 448
Fouquereau, E., 318
Fowler, K. A., 89
Fox, M., 482
Foxhall, K., 162
Frackiewicz, E. J., 136
Fraga, M. F., 45
Franchini, L., 459
Francis, D. J., 490
Francis, J., 407
Frangou, S., 269
Frank, E., 125, 253, 256, 274, 277, 525
Frank et al., 270
Frank, G., 344
Frank, R. G., 104
Franke, P., 311
Frankenburg, F. R., 444
Franklin, C., 495
Franklin, M. E., 197, 198
Franko, D. L., 281, 334, 336
Franus, N., 477
Fraser, J. S., 123
Frasure-Smith, N., 125, 161
Fratiglioni, L., 530
Frattaroli, J., 146
Frauenglass, S., 316
Frazier, E., 123
Frazier, J. A., 415
Fredrickson, B. L., 147, 253
Fredrikson, M., 261
Freedland, K. E., 162
Freedman, R., 400, 404
Freedman, S., 202
Freeman, A., 464
Freeman, C., 337
Freeman, D. H., 136
Freemantle, N., 268
Freemon, F. R., 519, 521
Freeston, M. H., 200
Fregni, F., 524
Freiberg, P., 364
French Parkinson's Disease Genetics Study Group, 533
Freud, S., 45
Frey, L. M., 219
Fricchione, G., 198
Frick, P. J., 478, 497, 498
Friedland, R. P., 526
Friedler, E., 162
Friedman, E. M., 141
Friedman, J. M., 486
Friedman, M., 204
Friedman, M. A., 273, 275
Friedman, M. J., 203, 204
Friedman, R. A., 254, 423, 504
Friedman, S. D., 304, 484
Friend, J. M., 269
Fromm-Reichmann, F., 416
Frumin, M., 414
Frye, J., 405
Fucito, L. M., 366, 372
Fuertes, J. N., 123
Fuetsch, M., 499
Fulbright, R. K., 491
Fuller, K. M., 552
Fuller, R. B., 275
Fung, L. C. T., 363
Fung, M. T., 461
Funke, B., 413
Furberg, H., 340
Furmark, T., 119
Furukawa, T. A., 252
Fyer, A., 176, 185
Fyer, A. J., 190, 193
Fyring, C., 193

Gabarron, E., 274

Gabb, J., 145
Gabbard, G. O., 123, 459
Gable, S. L, 156
Gade, E., 319
Gado, M., 416
Gaffney, G., 198
Gagnon, J. H., 365
Gail, M. H., 343
Gaither, G. A., 364, 464
Galea, S., 147, 202
Gall, V., 493
Gallagher, S. M., 487
Gallagley, A., 520
Gallop, R., 458
Gallop, R. J., 464
Gamble, S. A., 477
Gameroff, M. J., 371
Gan, W. Q., 164
Ganellen, R. J., 86
Ganguli, M., 526
Ganzel, B. L., 219
Garb, H. N., 82, 86, 88, 89, 135, 454
Garber, J., 502, 503
Garbutt, J. C., 318
García-Bayo, I., 274
Garcia-García, P., 276
Garcia-Lopez, L.-J., 193
Garcia, P., 136
Garety, P., 426
Garfield, S. L., 117
Gargiulo, M., 534
Garnefski, N., 503
Garner, M., 501
Garofalo, A., 32
Gartlehner, G., 254
Garvey, M., 415
Gary, L. E., 134
Gasbarrini, A., 311
Gaser, C., 416
Gasser, T., 533
Gastfriend, D. R., 318
Gatchel, R. J., 157, 160
Gately, 466
Gatz, M., 517, 530, 531
Gauthier, J. G., 160
Gavin, N. L., 254
Gaw, A. C., 236
Gaxiola-Aguilar, S., 61, 295
Gay, H., 466, 467
Gaynes, B. N., 166, 254
Geaga, J. A., 370, 414
Gebre-Medhin, P., 256
Geddes, J., 426
Geddes, J. R., 268, 276
Geer, J., 377
Geipert, N., 161
Gelenberg, A. J., 193
Gelernter, J., 185
Geller, B., 504
Gelman, D., 284
George, E. L., 277
George, K. K., 123
George, M. S., 314
Georgiades, A., 161
Gerberding, J. L., 278
Gerdes, A. C., 494
Gerevich, J., 384
Gergel, I., 530
Gernsbacher, M.A., 483
Gerrard, M., 341
Gerry, N. P., 344
Gershater-Molkoa, R. M., 477
Gershon, A. A., 278
Gershon, E. S., 415
Gershon, G., 192
Gershuny, B. S., 221
Gersons, B. P., 204
Gersons, B. P. R., 202

Gerstenblith, G., 162
Geschwind, D. H., 530
Gesten, E. L., 86
Gettes, B. S., 166
Geurts, H., 522
Ghaderi, A., 341
Ghizzani, A., 366, 367
Giardino, N., 163, 164
Gibbon, M., 16, 252
Gibbon, P., 176
Gibson, N. A., 269
Gidron, Y., 162
Giedd, J., 495
Giembycz, M. A., 163
Giepen, C., 385
Gil, F. P., 464
Gil, K. M., 155
Gilani, Z., 146
Gilbert, S., 253
Gilbert, S. C., 337
Gilburt, S. J. A., 318
Gill, J., 375
Gill, M. K., 502
Gillette, J. C., 133
Gillham, J., 133
Gilmer, T., 136
Gingell, C., 365
Ginsberg, R. L., 366, 372
Gioia, M., 372, 375
Girard, C., 269
Giraud, A. L., 493
Girgus, J. S., 502
Girimaji, S. C., 502
Gizera, I. R., 495
Gjessing, H. K., 306
Glabe, C. G., 530
Gladstone, G., 10
Glahn, D. C., 415, 495
Glancy, G. D., 202
Glantz, M. D., 294, 295
Glaser, R., 144, 145, 146, 161
Glass, R. M., 172, 176, 179, 275
Glass, S., 342
Glasser, D. B., 365
Glasson, E. J., 484
Glazener, C. M., 508
Gleason, C. E., 526
Gleaves, D. H., 217, 219, 234, 239, 240, 338
Gledd, J. N., 415
Glenn, D., 544
Glick, I. D., 426
Glover, J. H., 469
Glynn, C., 502
Gnagy, E. M., 496
Goate, A., 312
Gochman, P., 415
Goddard, A. W., 176
Godfrey, H. P. D., 533
Godtfredsen, N. S., 165
Goedert, M., 530
Goetz, K. L., 236
Goetz, R., 414
Goff, D. C., 215
Gold, J. A., 494
Goldberg, A., 454
Goldberg, C., 476
Goldberg, I. J., 302
Goldberg, S. R., 311
Goldberg, T. E., 405, 415, 416
Golden, C. J., 493, 495
Golden, R. N., 166
Goldfarb, L. A., 341
Goldfried, M. R., 117
Goldin, P. R., 186
Golding, S. L., 559
Goldman, D., 100, 185, 269
Goldman, M. S., 298
Goldman-Rakic, P. S., 415
Goldsmith, H. H., 477, 483

Goldsmith, J., 531
Goldstat, R., 375
Goldstein, A. J., 205
Goldstein, I., 366, 368, 375, 440
Goldstein, R. B., 173, 174, 175, 182, 183, 205
Goldstein, R. L., 427
Goleman, D., 192, 447
Golier, J. A., 458
Golshan, S., 136
Golub, A., 498
Gomez, J., 221, 222
Gonsai, K., 322
Gonzales, D., 317
González, B., 332
González, C., 135
Gonzalez, G., 322
Gonzalez, R., 253
Goode, E., 405, 482, 505
Goodman, J., 269
Goodman, M., 444
Goodman, R., 490
Goodrich, D., 366, 367, 375
Goodwin, R. D., 252
Gooren, L. J. G., 363, 364
Gordinier, S. W., 418
Gordis, E., 312
Gordon, J. R., 324
Goring, J. G., 497
Gormally, J., 188
Gorman, C., 343, 496
Gorman, J. M., 176, 177, 179
Gorwood, P., 402
Gosselin, C., 378
Götestam, K. G., 501
Gotlib et al., 267
Gotlib, I. H., 254
Gottesman & Hanson, 411
Gottesman, I. I., 411, 412, 413, 420, 421
Gotzsche, P. C., 25
Goudriaan, A. E., 466
Gough, B., 378
Gould, M. S., 505, 506
Gould, T. D., 420
Graap, K., 192
Grady, D., 344, 404, 525, 530
Grady-Flesser, M., 336
Graham, C. G., 493
Graham, R. K., 86, 534
Graham, S. M., 530
Granholm, E., 425
Grant, B. F., 75, 173, 174, 175, 181, 182, 183, 199, 205, 248, 251, 252, 254, 255, 294, 295, 298, 452
Grant et al., 173, 174, 183
Grant, J. B. F., 240
Grant, J. E., 467, 468, 469
Grapengiesser, A., 533
Grasby, P., 414
Gratz, K. L., 444
Graubard, B. I., 343
Gravenstein, S., 414
Gray, K. M., 489
Gray-Little, B., 156
Gray, M. J., 202, 204
Gray, N. S., 381
Green, B. L., 273
Green, L. A., 161
Green-Paden, L. D., 424
Greenbaum, P. E., 298
Greenberg, J., 261
Greenberg, R. P., 451
Greenberg, T., 371, 505, 506
Greene, B. A., 124
Greene, J., 204
Greene, J. M., 164
Greene, R. L., 100
Greene, R. W., 497
Greengrass, M., 163

Greenhill, L., 282
Greenhouse, L., 560
Greenhouse, W. J., 270
Greenland, P., 346
Greenstein, D., 495
Greenstein, D. K., 495
Greenwald, D., 425
Greenwood, A., 145
Gregg, E. W., 343
Gregg, L., 418
Gregory, A. L., 549
Greist, J. H., 82
Grenier, G, 367
Grilo, C., 439, 444
Grilo, C. M., 135, 342, 443
Grinshpoon, A., 549
Grisaru, N., 278
Grob, G. N., 14, 15
Gross, B., 383
Gross, J., 484
Gross, R. E., 314
Grossberg, G. T., 530
Grossberg, S., 484
Grossman, L., 108
Grossman, R. I., 397
Groth, A. N., 390
Grothe, K. B., 100
Gruber, A. J., 215
Gruenberg, A. M., 429
Grunder, G., 414
Grunebaum, M. F., 269
Grunhaus, L., 278
Gruzniewski, A., 549
Gscheidle, T., 416
Gu, H., 166
Guarch, J., 425
Guarnaccia, P. J., 125
Guay, A., 371
Guertin, T. L., 335
Gunderson, E. W., 443
Gunderson, J. G., 439, 444, 452
Gunthner, A., 545
Gupta, S., 40
Gur, R. C., 415, 416
Gur, R. E., 397, 411
Gur, R. G., 398
Guralnik, J. M., 162
Guralnik, O., 221, 224, 227
Gurka, M. J., 476
Gurling et al., 413
Gurling et al., 203
Harwood, T. M., 117
Hashimoto, H., 495
Hasin, D., 75
Hasin, D. S., 75, 173, 174, 175, 182, 183, 205, 252, 300
Hasin et al, 298
Hastings, M. A., 269
Hatgis, C., 179
Hatsukami, D., 25
Hatzenbuehler, M. L., 75
Hatzidimitriou, G., 305
Haughie, S., 375
Haughton, E., 411
Haukka, J., 269
Hausmann, A., 342
Have, T. T., 166
Havermans, R. C., 314
Hadzi-Pavlovic, D., 269
Havik, O. E., 347, 354, 525
Hawkins, E. H., 300
Hawthorne, W., 136
Hawton, K., 276, 371
Hay, D. A., 160
Hayaki, J., 120
Hayashi, K. M., 370, 414, 525
Hayes, B., 352
Hayhurst, K. P., 422
Haynes, P. L., 349, 353
Hays, J. T., 317
Hays, R. D., 260
Hayward, C., 177, 338, 340

Hayward, P., 277
Hazelrigg, M., 555
Hazlett, E. A., 224, 416, 484
Hazlett, H. C., 484
Hallmayer, J. F., 484
Haznedar, M. M., 484
He, J., 302
Heard, H. L., 464
Heather, N., 314
Heatherton, T. F., 338
Hecht, H., 31, 259
Heckman, T. G., 166
Hedley, A. A., 344
Heffelfinger, S. K., 197
Heid, I. M., 344
Heidenreicha, T., 193
Heil, S. H., 314, 322
Heilbrun, K., 560
Heiman, G. A., 185
Heiman, J., 377
Heiman, J. R., 368, 369
Heimberg, R. G., 116, 200
Heinert, N. J., 364
Heinrichs, M., 202
Heinz, A., 297
Held, M., 491
Helgeson, V. S., 165
Hellhammer, D. H., 203
Hellmich, N., 344
Helms, M. J., 252
Helper, N., 135
Hemenway, D., 280
Hemphill, J. F., 549
Hennen, J., 256, 444
Henriques, G., 211
Henry, J. L, 200
Henry, M., 278
Henry, R., 260
Herbert, A., 344
Herbert, J. D., 205
Herbert, L. E., 518, 525
Herbert, P. B., 552
Herek, G. M., 364
Heres, S., 422
Herman, C. P., 336
Herman, M. M., 415
Hermelin, B., 491
Hernandez, R., 305
Herndon, R. W., 460
Heron, J., 509
Herr, J., 384
Herrera, J. M., 136
Herrera, V. M., 381, 388
Heruc, G., 269
Herwig, U., 278
Hessling, R. M., 156
Hester, R. K., 322
Hetherington, E. M., 503
Hettema, J. M., 176, 259, 261, 460
Hewett, T. D., 385
Hewitt, J. K., 460
Heydorn, W. E., 503
Hibbeln, J. R., 269
Hickey, S. E., 230
Hickling, E. J., 202
Hicks, B. M., 441, 459, 460
Hicks, T. V., 177
Higgins, D. S., Jr., 534
Higgins, S. T., 314, 322
Highfield, D. A., 318
Hilde, I. N., 347
Hildebrand, W., 412
Hill, J., 202
Hill, M. J., 361
Hiller, J. B., 418
Hillmer, A. M., 491
Hills, D. R., 162
Hilsenroth, M. J., 87, 89, 120
Himle, J. A., 196
Hinrichsen, G., 523
Hinshaw, S. P., 494

Hinton, D. E., 176
Hirao, T., 428
Hiripi, E., 478, 497
Hirsch, S. R., 416
Hirvonen, J., 414, 420
Hitti, M., 340
Hla, K. M., 350
Ho, B.-C., 411, 413
Ho, R. M., 100
Hoag, L., 372, 375
Hochman, K. M., 281, 400, 414, 425
Hodge, S. E., 185
Hodges, L., 192
Hoefnagels, W. H., 406
Hoehe, M. R., 342
Hoermann, S., 444, 445
Hofer, A., 533
Hofer, S. M., 489
Hoffman, M. B., 559
Hofler, M., 499
Hofmann, S. G., 187, 190
Hogan, B. E., 161
Hogan, D. B., 530
Hogarty, G. E., 424, 425
Hoge, S. K., 554
Holahan, C. J., 154
Holahan, C. K., 154
Holden, G. W., 381, 382
Holder-Perkins, V., 235, 239
Holdwick, D. J. Jr., 87
Holladay, J., 135
Holland, A. J., 340
Hollander, E., 224, 484
Holliday, J. E., 146
Hollingshead, A. B., 63
Hollon, S. D., 95, 116, 121, 177, 271, 273, 275
Holloway, J. D., 110
Holmans et al., 268
Holmström, A., 119
Holroyd, K. A., 159, 160
Holtzheimeriii, P. E., 278
Holzman, P. S., 412
Hompland, M., 276
Hong, L. E., 414
Hong, M. S., 370
Honig, A., 406
Hook, E. W. III, 133
Hooley, J. M., 418
Hoppe, D. A., 298, 301
Hoppe, A., 159
Horan, W., 424
Hornbrook, M., 133
Horne, R., 273, 275
Horrigan, J. P., 508
Horsten, M., 161, 162
Horwood, L. J., 490
Hotchkiss, 448
Hotton, J.-M., 274
Houeto, J. L., 534
Houry, D., 280
Houston, D. A., 381
Houston, T. K., 119
Hoven, C. W., 505
Howard, B. V., 344
Howard, C. E., 342
Howell, D. C., 154
Hoza, B., 494
Hrdina, P. D., 282
Hrobjartsson, A., 25
Hrywna, M., 165, 205
Hu, F. B., 160
Hu, M.-C., 316
Hu, Y., 311
Huang, B., 294
Huang, H., 534
Huang, L. H., 152
Huang, Q., 530
Huang, Y.-Y., 269
Hubbard, K. L., 559

Huber, K., 487
Huber, K. M., 487
Huber, S. J., 533
Hublin, C., 352
Hudson, J. I., 215, 332, 342
Hudziak, J. J., 498
Huebner, E. S., 156
Huerta-Sánchez, E., 332
Huffman, J. C., 229
Hugdahl, K., 415
Hugh-Jones, S., 378
Hughes, J. R., 310
Hughes, M., 173, 440
Hulley, S. B., 260
Hummelen, B., 75
Humphrey, L. L., 302, 340
Humphreys, K., 320
Humphreys, L., 418
Hunsley, J., 89
Hunter, E. C. M., 221
Hunter, M. D., 406
Huntjens, R. J., 215
Huppin, M., 391
Huprich, S. K., 552
Hurlburt, G., 319
Hurst, J. A., 487
Husain, M., 275
Huss, M. T., 546
Hutton, M., 532
Huttunen, J., 414, 420
Huyser, J., 116
Hviid, A., 482
Hwang, W.-C., 124, 125
Hyman & Pavlik, 161

Iacono, W., 441
Iacono, W. G., 459, 460
Iacoviello, L., 302
Iaono, W. G., 312
Ikemoto, S., 311
Illig, T., 344
Imaizumi, T., 252
Imperatore, G., 343
Ingham, R. J., 493
Ingram, R. E., 197, 261
Inouye, S. K., 520
International Human Genome, 44
Iranmanesh, A., 372
Ironson, G., 166
Irwin, M. L., 346
Irwin, M. R., 354
Ishiia, M., 166
Isometsä, E., 400
Ivanova, M. Y, 94
Ivers, H., 160
Iversen, S. D., 461
Iwata, N., 312
Iyengar, S., 504
Izzo, J. L. Jr., 161

Jablensky, A., 10, 400
Jablensky, A. V., 64
Jackson, E. S., 156
Jackson, H. J., 385
Jackson, J. J., 147
Jackson, J. S., 279, 280
Jackson, K., 444, 445
Jacob et al., 312
Jacob, K., 179
Jacobi, C., 338, 340
Jacobs, B. L., 268
Jacobs, S. R., 203
Jacobs, W., 136, 137
Jacobsen, B., 412
Jacobsen, J. S., 527, 530
Jacobsen, L. K., 415
Jacobsen, P., 165
Jaffe, A. B., 428
Jaffe, A. S., 162
Jaffe, J. H., 318

Jamison, K. R., 256, 277
Janeck, A. S., 197
Janin, S., 533
Janke, A. L., 525
Janofsky, M., 543
Jansen, A. T. M, 314
Janssen, E., 366, 367, 375
Jansson, L., 412
Januzzi, J., 161
Jarman, F. C., 160
Jasmer, R., 350
Javier, R. A., 319, 371
Jay, M., 402
Jaycox, L. H., 133
Jee, 343
Jefferson, J. W., 82
Jeffery, R. W., 111
Jemal et al., 164
Jemmott, J. B., 146
Jenike, M. A., 198
Jenkins, J. H., 419
Jepson, C., 317, 318
Jerome, R. E., 312
Jetzinger, E., 422
Jiang, H., 145
Jiang, Y., 125, 176
Jin, J., 503
Jin, R., 4, 5, 248, 251, 500
Joe, S., 279, 280
Joffe, R. T., 340
Johansen, J. B., 278
Johansson, B., 530
Johns, A., 310
Johnson, C. L., 344
Johnson, D. B., 62
Johnson, J. G., 445, 458
Johnson, K. C., 317
Johnson, S., 270
Johnson, S. L., 260, 277
Johnson, V. E., 372
Johnston, D. W., 179
Johnston L. D., 298
Johnstone, T., 483
Joiner, Brown, & Wingate, 282
Joiner, T. E., 64, 266, 281, 477, 505
Joiner, T. E. Jr., 338
Joinson, C., 509
Jokela et al., 268
Jokela et al., 268
Jones, B., 344
Jones, B. E., 361
Jones, C., 552
Jones, D. W., 161, 405, 415
Jones, E., 17
Jones, G. N., 100
Jones, H. A., 495, 496
Jones, M. A., 156
Jones, M. P., 141, 159
Jones, P. B., 421
Jones, S. R., 406, 407
Jones v. United States (1983), 557, 558
Jordan, B. K., 147
Jordan, C. E., 389
Jordan, J., 187
Jorenby, D. E., 317, 324
Jorge, R., 280
Jourden, R., 351
Joyce, E. M., 414
Judd, L. J., 252
Judd, L. L., 256
Juengling, F. D., 278
Junghan, U. M., 407, 425, 426
Jurgens, S., 159
Just, N., 65, 253

Kabat-Zinn, J., 158
Kaczmarek, P., 388
Kadden, R., 310, 466, 467
Kafka, M. P., 385
Kahl, K. G., 464
Kahn, C., 342

Kahn, M. W., 125, 300
Kahn, R. S., 400
Kahn, S., 155
Kaiser, R., 533
Kalali, A. H., 276
Kalb, C., 269, 275
Kalba, S., 407
Kalichman, S. C., 166
Kalis, D., 123
Kamath, V., 420, 439
Kamio, Y., 484
Kamphuis, J. H., 187, 190, 192
Kampman, K., 318
Kanai, T., 252
Kanaya, T., 485
Kandel, D. B., 310, 316
Kandel, E. R., 281, 398, 414, 525, 534, 535
Kane, J. M., 413, 422, 423, 428
Kangas, M., 200
Kanner, L., 481
Kano, K., 508
Kantor, M., 364
Kantrowitz, B, 502
Kaplan, A. S., 165, 340, 341
Kaplan, H. S., 499
Kaplan, L., 456
Kaplan, M. S., 386
Kaplan, Z., 278
Kapp, M. B., 554
Kaprio, J., 269, 312
Karas, R. H., 161
Karatzias, A., 205
Karel, J. J., 523
Karlsgodt, K., 415
Karlsson, A., 193
Karlsson, R., 123
Karno, M., 419
Karp, B. I., 415
Karrass, J., 493
Karterud, S., 75
Kartub, P., 372
Karver, M. S., 120
Kasdan, M. L., 230
Kasell, E., 412
Kasen, S., 445, 458
Kasl-Godley, J., 517, 530, 531
Kaslow, N. J., 284
Kasper, J. A., 554
Kasper, J. D., 162
Kassem, L., 258, 269
Katon, W., 179
Katon, W. J., 175, 176, 177, 178
Katz, D., 269
Katz, I. I., 279, 281, 524
Katz, J. N., 364
Katz, M. J., 530
Katz, R., 268, 269
Kaufman, N. K., 96
Kaufmann, V., 317, 318
Kavouras, S., 161
Kawagishi, N., 495
Kay, A. B., 145
Kayed, R., 530
Kaysen, S. 1994, 103
Kayumov, L., 251
Kazdin, A. E., 93, 457, 478, 497, 498, 501
Kealeya, K. A., 315
Keck, P.E. Jr., 342
Keefe, F. J., 155
Keel, P. K., 281, 334, 336, 342
Keele, G., 63
Keesey R. E., 344
Keiley, M. K., 503
Keita, G. P., 253
Keith, S., 424
Keith, S. J., 426
Keith-Spiegel, P., 32
Keitner, G. I., 273, 275

Keller et al., 254
Keller, M., 257
Kellner, C. H., 274, 275
Kelly, A. M., 497
Kelly, B., 427
Kelly, B. D., 143, 427
Kelly, D., 524
Kelly, S., 457
Kemeny, M. E., 145
Kemether, E., 416
Kenady, D. E., 203
Kenardy, J. A., 179
Kendall, P. C., 95, 111, 501, 503
Kendell & Jablensky, 75
Kendler, 43, 44, 45
Kendler, K. S., 31, 61, 176, 184, 185, 205, 259, 261, 268, 295, 340, 412, 413, 429, 460
Kennard et al., 266
Kennedy, J. L., 196, 495
Kennedy, N., 252, 427
Kennedy, S. H., 40
Kent, A., 340
Kent, J., 176
Keogh, J. M., 342, 344
Keohane, D. J., 524
Kernberg, O. F., 455, 463
Kerr, N., 277
Kersting, K., 491
Kertesz, 532
Keshavan, M. S., 484
Kessler, R. C., 4, 5, 61, 104, 173, 205, 248, 251, 278, 282, 295, 298, 440, 478, 495, 497, 500
Kestler, L., 281, 400, 414, 415, 425
Ketter, T. A., 276
Kettler, C. C., 464
Kety, S. S., 412
Keyes, K., 75
Khalsa, H.-M. K., 256
Khawalled, R., 549
Kiecolt-Glaser, J. K., 144, 145, 146, 161
Kiefe, C. I., 260
Kiehl, K. A., 440, 461
Kieseppä, T., 269
Kieser, M., 275
Kihlstrom, J. F., 219
Kilander, L., 530
Kilgore, K., 498
Killen, J., 177
Killingsworth, R., 345
Kilpatrick, D., 147
Kilpatrick, D. G., 295, 389, 476
Kilshaw, J., 493
Kilts, C. D., 314
Kim-Cohen, J., 460
Kim, H. J., 187
Kim, J., 415
Kim, K., 315
Kim, N. N., 372, 375
Kim, S. W., 467
Kim, Y., 274
Kim, Y. S., 196
Kinetz, E., 237
King, D. W., 202
King, L. A., 202
King, R., 365
King, S., 418
Kingdon, D., 425
Kingsbury, K., 279, 505
Kinmonth, A. L., 277
Kinney, D. K., 412
Kinney, G. L., 302
Kirisci, L., 315
Kirkpatrick, B., 400
Kirmayer, L. J., 224, 239, 240
Kirsch, I., 274
Kirschenbaum, D. S., 94
Kissling, W., 422
Kitamura, T., 252

Kivlahan, D. R., 133
Kjonniksen, I., 278
Klaiman, C., 491
Kleber, H. D., 318
Klein, D., 176, 185
Klein, D. F., 185
Klein, D. N., 120, 254, 255, 268
Klein, Keller, et al., 254
Klein, M. H., 463, 477
Kleinman, A., 9, 10
Kleinman, J. E., 415
Klerman, G. L., 233, 239, 270
Klesges, R. C., 317
Klimas, N., 166
Klingle, R. S., 298
Klonoff, E. A., 235
Klosterkotter, J., 425
Kluck, N., 491
Kluft, R. P., 226
Kluger, J., 316, 504
Knapp, R., 275
Knapp, R. G., 274
Knapp, S., 552
Knight, A., 425
Knight, R. G., 533
Knipe, J., 205
Knolls, M. L., 203
Knost, B., 425
Knutelska, M., 227
Kobak, K. A., 82
Kobasa, S. C., 155
Koch, K., 398
Koch, W. J., 205
Kochman, A., 166
Koegel, R. L., 484
Koehler, K. A., 176
Koenen, K. C., 202, 203
Koenigsberg, H. W., 444
Koerner, K., 464
Koeter, M. W. J., 116
Koh, M. T., 530
Kohlenberg, R. J., 271
Kohler, C., 415, 416
Kohler, C. G., 397
Kohn, C. S., 469
Kohut, H., 454
Kolachana, B., 185
Kolachana, B. S., 416
Kolbert, E., 351
Kolker, R., 546
Konig, I. R., 491
Koning-Haanstra, M., 534
Kono, N., 484
Koocher, G. P., 32
Koocher, P., 32
Kopell, B. H., 128
Kopelowicz, A., 418, 425
Koplin, B., 505
Koretz, D., 4, 5
Korman, L., 40
Koskenvuo, M., 312
Koss, M. P., 388, 389
Kosson, D. S., 441, 457
Koszycki, D., 125
Kotilinek, L., 530
Kotler, M., 278, 467
Kotov, R., 65
Kouperman, I., 278
Kouyoumdjian, H., 134
Kraaij, V., 503
Kraaimaat, F. W., 493
Krack, P., 532, 534
Kraemer, H. C., 125, 274, 337, 338, 340, 477, 496
Kragh-Sorensen, P., 532
Krahe, B., 390
Krain, A. L., 493, 495
Krakauer, S. Y., 225
Kral, J. G., 342
Kramer, G. M., 560

Krantz, D. S., 162
Krantz, M. J., 303, 304, 318
Kranzler, H. R., 297, 318, 325
Krasner, L., 457
Krasnow, A. D., 179
Krauter, K. S., 460
Krejci, J., 337
Kremer, T. G., 86, 123
Kresnow, M., 281
Kreutz, M., 425
Kribs-Zaleta, C., 332
Krijn, M. U., 187, 190, 192
Kring, A. M., 410, 414
Kringlen, E., 412, 435
Kroenke, K., 239
Kröger, C., 464
Krueger, R., 460
Krueger, R. B., 386
Krueger, R. F., 77, 441, 459, 460
Krug, E., 281
Kruijver, P. M., 364
Krukowski, R. A., 94
Krumholz, H. M., 162
Krupnick, J. L., 273
Kryger, M. H., 352
Kubiak, S. S. P., 202
Kubisyzn, T. W., 86, 87, 89
Kuchipudi, K., 282
Kuhn, J., 31, 259
Kuiper, A. J., 362
Kuipers, E., 426
Kulisevsky, J., 278
Kulkarni, J., 278
Kumar, M., 166
Kumaresan, V., 310
Kuno, E., 424
Kuntermann, C., 425
Kuoppasalmi, K., 400
Kupfer, D. J., 77, 256, 277, 353
Kupsch, A., 533
Kurlakowsky, K. D., 502
Kuroki, N., 414
Kuslansky, G., 530
Kvale, G., 354, 525
Kwon, S., 266
Kwong, J. Y. Y., 99
Kymalainen, J. A., 418, 419
Kyprianidou, A., 310

Labouvie, E., 120, 320
Ladouceur, R., 197, 200
Lagacea, D. C., 504
Lahey, B. B., 441, 478, 493, 497, 498
Lahey, N., 375
Lahti, A., 422
Lai, M. T., 530
Laird, R., 457
Laje, G., 281, 504
Läksy, K., 419
Laliberte, M. A., 125
Lalonde, J. K., 332, 342
Lalumière et al., 391
Lam, D. H., 253, 277
Lam, J. N., 549, 550
Lamb, S., 454
Lamberg, L., 279, 337, 340, 343, 344
Lambert, E. W., 497
Lambert, M. J., 120
Lamberti et al., 423
Lamdan, R. M., 165, 205
Lampe, Y., 278
Landerman, L. R., 123
Landrine, H., 235
Lane, R. C., 224, 225, 226
Lanfermann, H., 493
Lang, D. L., 133
Lang, P. J., 442
Langbehn, D. R., 498
Langeland, W., 202
Langhinrichsen-Rohling, J., 390

Langle, G., 545
Langlis, F., 200
Langlois, S., 505
Langly, K., 495
Långström, N., 378
Lank, E. J., 342, 344
LaPerrierea, A., 166
Larimer, M. E., 133
Larkin, E. K., 349
Larkin, G. R., 147
Larrabee, G. J., 90
Larsen, J. P., 532
Larsson, B., 501
Larsson, H., 459, 530
Latshaw, A., 397
Laughren, T., 504
Laumann, E. O., 365
Lauriello, J., 424
Lauterbach, W., 193
Lavalaye, J., 305
Lawrence, A. A., 362
Lawrence, A. D., 414
Lawrence, N., 196
Laws, D. R., 385
Lawson, D. M., 120
Lawson, R. A., 338
Lawson, W. B., 135
Lazarus, A. A., 158
Lazarus, R. S., 154
Leahy, R. L., 277
Lear, 230
Leber, P., 25
Leboyer, M., 402
Lechner, S. C., 166
Leckman, J. F., 196
LeCroy, C., 151
Lecrubier, Y., 275
Lee, D. T. S., 254
Lee, H., 527, 530
Lee, J., 415
Lee, J. E., 305
Lee, J. K. P., 385
Leff, J. P., 416
Lefler, B. J., 252
Lefley, H. P., 125
Legault, C., 525
Léger, E., 200
Leggio, L., 311
Lehman, D. R., 344
Lehmann, C., 549
Lehrer, P. M., 163, 164
Lehtinend, V., 143
Leibing, E., 463
Leiblum, S. R., 366, 367, 373, 374
Leichsenring, F., 463
Leitenberg, H., 177, 377
Lejuez, C. W., 444
LeMarchand, L., 62
Lemonde, S., 282
Lemonick, M. D., 278, 294, 525
Lencz, T., 413
Lenroot, R., 495
Lentes, K-U., 342
Lentz, C., 498
Lenzenweger, M. F., 444, 445, 463
Leocani, L., 196
Leon, A. C., 179, 252, 257, 504
Leonard, A., 457
Lépine, J.-P., 274
Lerch, J., 495
Lerman, C., 156, 311
Lerouxa, B. G., 315
Lesage, S., 533
Leserman, J., 166
Leslie, D. L., 398, 422
Lesné, S., 530
Lespérance, F., 125, 161
Leucht, S., 422
Leukefeld, C. G., 389
Leung, P. W. L., 503

Leutenegger, A.-L., 533
Levant, R. F., 32
Leve, L. D., 460
Leventhal, H. E., 273, 275
Levin, F. R., 324
LeVine, E., 388
Levine, E. S., 19
Levine, J., 428
Levinson et al., 268
Levitan, R. D., 253, 340
Levitt, A. J., 253, 340
Levy, F., 160
Levy, K. N., 463
Lewin, M. R., 179
Lewinsohn, P. M., 64, 262, 266, 268, 503, 505
Lewis, D. O., 226
Lewis-Hall, F., 134
Lewis, L. B., 302
Lewis, M., 269
Lewis, S., 232
Lewis, S. W., 422
Lewy, A. J., 252
Li, G., 301
Li, J., 44
Li, L. S., 236
Li, S., 282, 284
Li, T.-K., 294
Li, Y. M., 530
Libby, J., 457
Liberman, R. P., 418, 424, 425
Librant, A., 411, 413
LiCalzi, E. M., 484
Licht, D. M., 418
Lichtenberg, P. A., 520
Lichtenstein, P., 340
Lichtenstein, P. A., 459, 530
Lichter, E. L., 388
Lichtermann, D., 311
Liddell, D. L., 391
Lidz, C. W., 546
Lieb, R., 499
Lieber, C. S., 298
Lieberman, J. A., 405, 422, 425, 428
Liebowitz, M. R., 193, 200
Lilenfeld, L. R. R., 338
Lilienfeld, S. O., 32, 88, 89, 116, 176, 440
Lim, K. O., 196
Lim, S., 507, 508
Lima, J. A. C., 162
Lin, H., 375, 398, 422
Lin, K., 424
Lindamer, L., 136
Lindblad, Lindberg, & Hjern, 341
Linde, K., 159
Linder, D., 543
Lindsey, K. P., 135
Linehan, M. M., 445, 464
Linsley, K. R., 240
Liotti, G., 445
Lipsey, T. L., 202
Lipsitz, J. D., 190, 193
Lipsky, R. H., 311
Lipton, R. B., 530
Little, R. D., 163
Littlewood, A., 378
Litz, B. T., 119
Liu, E. B., 232
Liu, I.-C., 311
Liu, J., 491
Liu, L., 281, 504
Liu, X., 311, 505
Livesley, W. J., 459
Lochman, J. E., 457
Locke, B. Z., 441, 442
Lockhart, D. C., 370
Loeb, K. L., 120
Loeber, R., 441, 461, 478, 497, 498
Loening-Baucke, V., 509

Loewenstein, R. J., 226
Loewy, J. W., 318
Loftus, E. F., 219
Logan, T. K., 389
Logsdon-Conradsen, S., 158
Lohmann, E., 533
Lohr, B. A., 391
Lohr, J. M., 32, 89
Lohr, K. N., 254
Lolk, A., 532
London, H., 462
Loney, J., 493
Long, J. C., 312
Long, J. S., 366, 367, 375
Lönnqvist, J., 269
Looman, J., 385
Looper, K. J., 240
Lopez, M., 354
López-Muñoza, F., 276
Lopez, S. R., 419
Loranger, A. W., 451, 462
Lorber, M. F., 461
Lorberbaum, J. P., 314
Lorenz, A. R., 441
Loring, D. W., 90
Lothane, Z., 45, 51
Lovaas, O. I., 484
Lovea, G. D., 141
Low, C. A., 146
Lowengrub, K., 467
Loxton, N. J., 336
Lu, G., 86, 534
Lu, P. H., 530
Lubell, S., 192
Luborsky, L., 268
Lucas, R., 251
Lucero, J., 125
Lucia, L.C., 414
Lucksted, A., 419
Luczak, Glatt, & Wall, 298, 325
Lue, T. F., 370
Lumsden, J., 385
Lund, A., 415
Lund, L. M., 154
Luntz, B. K., 458
Luoma, J. B., 284
Lupski, J. R., 27
Luque, R., 221
Lussier, J. P., 314, 322
Lutgendorf, S. K., 166
Lutzker, J. R., 477
Lydstona, D., 166
Lymburner, J. A., 555
Lynam, D. R., 461
Lynch, F. L., 133
Lynn, S. J., 32, 224
Lyon, D., 549
Lyons, J. S., 302, 340
Lyons, M. J., 305, 311
Lytle, R., 200
Lyubomirsky, S., 156

Ma, S. H., 158
Ma, Y., 176
Maat-Kievit, A., 536
MacCallum, R. C., 146
MacCulloch, M. J., 381
MacDonald, A. III, 415
MacDonald, M., 322
Machado, A. G., 128
Machleidt, W., 424
Maciejewski, P. K., 202
Mackie, S., 495
Mackinnon, A., 489
MacLean, C. J., 176
Maddi, S. R., 155
Madell, K., 380
Madsen, K. M., 482
Maeder, T., 556
Maes, S., 227, 239

Magid, K., 162
Maher, B. A., 10
Maher, W. B., 10
Mahfouz, A. Y., 384
Mahler, M., 456
Mahler, M. S., 456
Maier, S. F., 266
Maino, K., 422
Maisto, S. A., 323
Maj, M., 429
Maki, K. M., 179
Malamuth, N. M., 391
Malcolm, J., 381
Maldonado, J. R., 217, 219, 220, 227
"Male Eating Disorders" (2004), 339
Malefaki, S., 310
Maletzky, B. M., 386
Malhotra, A. K., 196
Malhotra, S., 342
Malinauskas, B. M., 337
Mallet, L., 534
Mallinger, A. G., 277
Mallott, M., 176
Malone, K. M., 269, 282, 284
Malone, M., 495
Maltête, D., 534
Mamalis, N., 214
Man, J., 164
Man, S. F. P., 164
Mangweth, B., 342
Mann, J. J., 268, 269, 273, 274, 282, 284
Mannarino, A. P., 156, 381, 477
Mansell, W., 197
Mansfield, A., 179
Manson, J. E., 344, 346
Manson, S., 125
Manson, S. M., 62, 82
Manzetta, B. R., 157
Maracy, M., 143
Marangell, L. L., 276
March, J. S., 198
Marcus, S. C., 275, 371
Marder, S. R., 422, 423
Marek, P. M., 315
Marenco, S., 415
Margolese, H. C., 281
Marion, I. J., 318
Markel, H., 318
Markon, K. E., 77
Markov, D., 533
Markovitz, J. H., 260
Markowitz, J. C., 270, 271
Marks, J. S., 278, 301
Marks, M., 187
Marlatt, G. A., 133, 300, 315, 322, 323, 324
Marmot, M., 161
Marneros, A., 428
Marsh, D. M., 297
Marshal, M. P., 297, 302
Marshall, L., 495
Marshall, M., 123
Marshall, R., 203
Marshall, S. W., 535
Marshall, W. L., 385
Marston, N. A. U., 278
Mart, E. G., 230
Martin, B., 322
Martin, C. E., 284
Martin, D., 482
Martin, E. K., 390
Martin, H., 214
Martin, J., 459, 525
Martin, J. L., 278
Martin, J. P., 555
Martin, N., 498
Martin, N. C., 503
Martinez, J., 176

Martone, R., 527, 530
Marttunen, M., 505
Marx, B. P., 146
Marx, E. M., 260
Marx, J., 322
Maser, J. D., 256
Masha, Y., 94
Masheb, R. M., 342
Masi, G., 502
Mason & Kreger (1998), 445
Mason, G. F., 176
Masters, W. H., 372
Mataix-Cols, D., 196
Mathalon, D. H., 407
Mathews, K. A., 161
Mathias, C. W., 297
Matson, J. L., 484
Matsuda, T., 495
Matsumoto, A. M., 372
Mattay, V. S., 185, 415
Matthews, J. A., 219
Matthews, K., 260
Mattick, R., 314
Matzner, F., 202
Maughan, B., 490
Maxwell, C. D., 391
Mayer, A. R., 457
Mayou, R., 239
Mays, V. M., 18, 124
Mazrek, P. J., 132
Mazure, C. M., 254
Mazziotta, J. C., 530
McAllister, T. W., 410
McAlonan, G., 479
McAuslan, P., 302
McAvay, G. J., 524
McBurnett, K., 497
McCabe, M. P., 336, 339, 367, 489
McCann, M. J., 322
McCann, U. D., 305
McCarley, R. W., 439
McCarthy, B. W., 366, 372
McCarty, C. A., 503
McClay, J., 268, 459
McClelland, G. M., 550
McClintick, J. N., 312
McCloskey, L. A., 381
McClure, F. S., 425
McClure, M. M., 415
McCord, J., 458
McCord, W., 458
McCracken, J. T., 484
McCrady, B. S., 312
McCrea, M., 535
McCrone et al., 119
McCrone, P., 269
McCrory, E., 490
McCurry et al., 353
McDermott, J. F., 257
McDermut, Miller, & Brown, 120
McDonagh, A., 204
McDonald, S., 530
McDonough, M., 427
McDougle, C. J., 484
McElroy, S. L., 342
McFall, R. M., 336
McFatter, R., 336
McGillivray, J. A., 489
McGinn & Sanderson, 116
McGirra, A., 281
McGlashan, T. H., 423, 443
McGlinchey et al., 75
McGoldrick, T., 205
McGonagle, K. A., 252, 440
McGorry, P. D., 77
McGowan, S., 414
McGowin, 526
McGrath, E., 253
McGrath, P. C., 203
McGrath, Pogge, & Stokes, 86

McGrath et al., 274
McGreenery, C. E., 477
McGue, M., 312, 459, 460
McGuffin, P., 268, 269, 412, 487, 498
McGuire, J. K., 151
McGuire, L., 144, 145, 161
McGuire, S., 503
McHugo, G., 204
McIntosh, D. E., 497
McIntosh et al., 342
McKay, J. S., 373
McKee, B., 345
McKellar, J., 320
McKnight Investigators, The, 336
McLean, L. M., 458
McLean, P., 198
McLean, R. Y., 87
McLemore, L. E., 414
McLeod & Weisz, 120
McMain, S., 40, 459
McManus, F., 193
McMillan, J. R., 545
McNally, 203
McNally, R. J., 176, 239
McNally et al., 73
McNeil, D. W., 177
McNicholas, T., 371
McNiel, D. E., 535, 549, 550, 552
McNulty, J. L., 100
McQuaid, J. R., 425
McQueen, M. B., 344
Mead, M., 7
Meares, R., 445
Mechanic, M. B., 202
Mednick, S. A., 23, 415, 421
Meehl, P. E., 420
Mefford, I. N., 155
Mehler, P. S., 303, 304, 318
Mehrabian, A., 281
Meichenbaum, 58
Meier, B. F., 364
Meinhardt, K., 152
Melani, D., 161
Melchert, T. P., 219
Melles, R., 375
Mellor, C. S., 403
Meltz-Brody, S., 254
Melville, J. D., 555
Memantine Study Group, 530
Menard, W., 233, 234
Mencl, W. E., 491
Mendelsohn, M. E., 161
Mendez, J. L., 336
Meng, H., 491
Mennin, D. S., 116, 200
Mental Health Services, 279
Menza, 274
Merckelbach, H., 181, 184, 185
Meredith, L., 251
Merikangas, K. R., 4, 5, 44
Merino-Andreu, M., 350
Merrill, K. A., 273
Messari, S., 407
Messer, 109, 120
Messias, E., 400
Messinis, L., 310
Meston, C., 366, 368, 440
Meuret, A. E., 190
Meyer & Archer, 89
Meyer, B., 270
Meyer et al., 82, 89
Meyer, G. J., 89
Meyer, I. H., 18
Meyer, J. H., 40
Meyers, B. S., 524
Meyers, L., 280, 505
Michael, R. T., 365
Michaels, S., 365
Michalak, E. E., 253
Michelson, D., 274

Mickley, D., 340, 341
Mignot, E., 349
Miklowitz, D. J., 257, 276, 277
Milad, R. R., 186
Milavsky, J. R., 282
Milburn, N. G., 134
Milev, P., 411, 413
Mill, J., 459
Miller & Blackwell, 162
Miller, C. L., 123
Miller, E., 238, 239
Miller, E. A., 398, 422
Miller, G. E., 145, 146
Miller, I., 270
Miller, I. W., 273, 275
Miller, K. B., 342
Miller, M., 280, 310
Miller, M. D., 525
Miller-Medzon, K., 490
Miller, S. D., 214
Miller, T., 423
Miller, T. W. R., 406
Miller, W. R., 322, 324
Millon, 86
Millon, T., 456
Milrod, B., 179
Minarik, M. L., 263
Mineka, S., 185
Minerd, J., 350
Minshew, N. J., 484
Minthon, L., 530
Mintz, J., 530
Minuchin, S., 339
Miottoa, K., 301
Miranda, A., 496
Miranda, J., 273
Mirin, S. M., 291, 296, 314
Mitchell, A. L., 133
Mitchell, C., 62
Mitchell, C. M., 300, 315
Mitchell, D. G. V., 457
Mitchell, J., 338
Mitchell, J. E., 342
Mitka, M., 343
Mitropoulou, V., 444, 458
Mitte, K., 200
Mittelman, M. S., 524
Mittle, K., 200
Mittleman, M. A., 161, 162, 302
Miyatake, R., 428
Mizrahi, R., 280
Mo, K. M., 236
Mobius, H. J., 530
Modestin, J., 216
Mody, M., 491
Moeller, F. G., 297
Moffitt, T. E., 268, 459
Mohr et al., 119
Mohr, J., 507
Moisa, R., 278
Mokdad, A., 301
Mokdad, A. H., 278, 343
Moldin, S. O., 412
Molina, B. S. G., 494
Molina, J. J., 221
Moller, H. J., 251
Moller, I., 390
Monahan, J., 549, 550
Monahan, S. C., 322
Money, J., 385
Monroe et al., 259
Monroe, S. M., 31
Monson, C. M., 204, 390
Montaner, J. S. G., 165
Montemurro, B., 380
Monti, P. M., 314
Montoya, P., 176
Monuteaux, M. C., 76, 497
Mooney, M., 25
Moore, B. A., 310

Moore, D. R., 368, 369
Moore, P., 349
Moore, R. E., 505
Moore, T. J., 274
Moos, B. S., 320, 324
Moos, McCoy, & Moos, 75
Moos, R., 262
Moos, R. H., 154, 320, 324
Mor, N., 261
Moran-Klimi, K., 165, 205
Moran, P., 281
Morehouse, R., 253
Moreira, P. I., 527, 530
Moreno, C., 281, 504
Morey, L. C., 452
Morgan, D. L., 29
Morgan, M. D., 147
Morgan, R. K., 29
Morgan, T., 320
Morgan, V., 64
Morganstein, D., 251
Morgenbesser, L. I., 389
Morgenstern, J., 320
Morimoto, K., 428
Morin, C. M., 353
Morrill, B., 160
Morris, B. R., 491
Morris, E. P., 324
Morris, G. H., 557, 560
Morris, P. L. P., 200
Morris, S., 407
Morrison, A. P., 425
Morrison, M. F., 166
Morrison, P., 505
Morrison, T., 338
Morrow, D. J., 526
Morrow, J., 253
Morse, S. J., 559
Mörtberg, E., 193
Mortensen, E. L., 252, 415
Mortimer, J. A., 530
Moscovitch, D. A., 187
Mosharov, E. V., 533
Moskvina, V., 413
Mossman, D., 546
Moulds, M. L., 191, 204
Moulton, J., 319
Mrug, S., 494
MTF Survey, 304
Mucke, L., 530
Muddasani, S., 484
Muehlbacher, M., 464
Muench, F., 320
Mueser, K., 204
Mueser, K. T., 425, 426
Mukamal, K. J., 302
Muller, D., 141
Muller, N., 499
Mullet, E., 318
Mulsant, B. H., 279, 281, 524, 525, 526
Mulvey, E. P., 546
Mulvey, E. P., 546
Munarriz, R., 372, 375
Mundorff, J., 493
Munjack, D., 193
Muñoz, & Mendelson, 123
Munoz, D. M., 202
Munoz, J. F., 221, 222
Muñoz, Mrazek, & Haggerty, 132
Munsey, C., 193
Muraven, M., 261
Murphy, A. D., 202
Murphy, D. G. M., 479
Murray, A. M., 464
Murray, I., 254
Murray, R. M., 422
Murry, V., 156
Murstein & Mathes, 89
Muthen, B. O., 75, 173, 174

Mutsatsa, S. H., 414
Myakishev, M. V., 176
Myin-Germeys, I., 407

Nabel, E. G., 160, 161
Nacewicz, B. M., 483
Nadel, A., 370, 371
Naglieri et al., 82
Nagourney, E., 347
Någren, K., 414, 420
Naimark, D., 555
Naimi, T. S., 301
Najman, J. M., 366, 368
Nakamura et al., 73
Nakamura, M., 428
Nandi, A., 202
Napoli, A., 146
Nasrallah, H. A., 276
National Institute of Mental Health (NIMH), 44, 249, 253, 259, 268, 270, 278, 505
National Institutes of Health (NIH), 136, 186
National Strategy for Suicide Prevention, 278
Naughton, K., 375
Nazeer, A., 40
NCI, 343
Ndetei, D. M., 400
Neale, J. M., 146
Neale, M. C., 176, 261, 413
Nebeling, B., 311
Neckelmann, D., 278
Needles, D. J., 264
Neeren, A. M., 270, 277
Neffs, J., 375
Negy, C., 152, 153
Neighbors et al., 134
Neighbors, H. W., 279, 280
Nelson, 125
Nelson, C. B., 173, 252, 440
Nelson, E. B., 342
Nelson, H. K., 419
Nemiah, J. C., 215
Nenadic, I., 416
Nestler, E. J., 268, 273, 310
Nettle, D., 257
Neugebauer, R., 13, 270
Neumann, K., 493
Nevid, J. S., 41, 47, 65, 83, 105, 107, 148, 248, 283, 319, 360, 384, 391, 532
New, A. S., 444, 458
New York City Voices, 324, 435
Newcombe, P. A., 176
Newcombe, R., 460
Newcomer, J. W., 423
Newman, C., 457
Newman, G. H., 136, 137
Newman, J. P., 441, 461
Newman, M. G., 179, 200
Newsweek, 298
Nezworski, M. T., 88, 89
Ng, C. K., 40
Ni, X., 459
Nicassio, P. M., 354
Nicholls, S. K., 497
Nicholls, S. S., 274
Nickel, C., 464
Nickel, M. K., 464
Nickell, A., 444, 445
Nickerson, Helms, & Terrell, 124
Nicki, R. M., 205
Nicolosi, A., 365
Nicolson, R., 415
Nides, M., 317
Nidich, S., 157
Niederberger, C., 370, 371
Nielsen, G. H., 347
Nielson, D., 388

Nieminen, P., 419
Nienow, T. M., 400
Nierenberg, A. A., 276
Nigg, J. T., 458
Nijssen, P., 534
Nirngaonkar, V. L., 411
Nishith, P., 202
Nitschke, J. B., 269
Niu, T., 311
Nixon, R. D., 191
Nixon, R. D. V., 204
Niznikiewicz, M. A., 414, 439
Noaghiul, S., 269
Nock, M. K., 478, 497
Nolan, S. A., 502
Nolen-Hoeksema, S, 253, 351, 502
Nolen, J. D. L., 302
Nomura, Y., 477
Noonan, D., 483
Norcross, J. C., 117
Nordhus, I. H., 523
Norman, P. A., 342
Normandi & Rorak, 338
Norris, F. N., 202
Norton & Price, 116
Norton, G. R., 217
Norton, M. C., 524
Norton, N., 413
Nosofsky, R. M., 336
Novins, D. K., 62, 125
Noyes, R., 233
Nucifora, F. C., Jr., 534
Nunes, E. V., 324
Nunomura, A., 527, 530
Nurnberger, J., 312
Nusslock, R., 270, 277
"Nutrition, Obesity and Perception" (2001), 338

Oakes, R., 200
Oates, R. K., 505
O'Brien, C. P., 294
O'Brien, K. M., 340
Obrocki, J., 311
Occhipinti, S., 336
O'Connor, 302
O'Connor, A., 375
O'Connor, B. J., 163
O'Connor, E., 133, 318
O'Connor, E. E., 342
O'Connor, M. E., 339, 340
O'Connor, P. E., 318
O'Connor, T. G., 501, 503
O'Connor v. Donaldson, 553
Odeh, M. S., 546
O'Donnell, J., 297
O'Donohue, W., 373
O'Donovan, M., 495
Oei, T. P. S., 176, 266
Oetzel, J., 125
O'Farrell, Fals-Stewart, & Murphy, 297
O'Farrell, T. J., 322
Ogburn, E., 75
Ogden, C. L., 344
Ogide et al., 495
Ogloff, J. R. P., 555
O'Hara, M. W., 253
Ohlraun, S., 258, 269
Öhman, A., 185
Ohmann, E., 533
Okada, T., 484
Okie, S., 495, 504
Okun, A., 284
Olatunjia, B. O., 176
Oldham, J. M., 445, 458
O'Leary, D. S., 411, 413
Olff, M., 202, 204
Olfson, M., 104, 275, 281, 371, 504, 525
Oliva, P. S., 215

Olivardia, R., 336
Olivares, J., 193
Oliver, C., 489
Oliveto, A., 322
Olivier, B., 375
Ollendick, T. H., 120
Ollove, M., 268
Olmsted, M., 165, 341
Olsen et al., 161
Olson, E., 251, 400
Olson, R. K., 491
O'Malley, P. M., 298
O'Malley, S. S., 318
Omvik, S., 354, 525
Oncken, C., 317
O'Neill, A., 413
Onitsuka, T., 414
Ono, C. R., 524
Onstad, S., 412
Oosterlaan, J., 466
Operskalski, B., 504
Oquendo, M., 282
Oquendo, M. A., 269, 284
Oquendo, X. H., 269
Orav, E. J., 235
Orbach, G., 426
Orban, L., 498
O'Reardon, J. P., 116
Oren, D. A., 40
Orsillo, S. M., 158
Ortega, A. N., 151, 152
Orth-Gomér, K., 161, 162
Ortiz-Nieves, A., 332
Orton, H., 82
Osborn, I., 194
Osborne, L., 479
Osler, M. S., 165
Osman, S. L., 391
Öst et al., 94
Ost, L. G., 176
Ostacher, M. J., 276
Ostler, K., 277
O'Toole, B., 505
Ott, S. L., 421
Otto, M. W., 87, 179, 262, 266
Ou, L. W., 236
Ouellet, M.-C., 353
Ouellette, S. C., 155
Overmier, J. B. L., 266
Owen, L. D., 316
Owen, M., 495
Owen, M. J., 412, 487
Oyama, N., 62
Ozelius, L. J., 533
Ozer, E. J., 173, 202, 203

Padilla, A. M., 61, 152
Page, G. P., 185
Paik, A., 365
Palesky, J., 154
Pallesen, S., 347, 354, 523, 525
Palmer, C. A., 555
Palmeri, T. J., 336
Panagiotakos, D. B., 161
Panek, 51
Papanicolaou, A. C., 491
Papathanasopoulos, P., 310
Pape, A., 421
Papp, L. A., 176
Parides, M., 165, 341
Parides, M. K., 340
Paris, J., 224, 458
Park, A., 525
Park, C. L., 315
Park, N., 156
Park, S., 415
Parker, G., 269
Parkinson, P., 505
Parkinson Study Group, 533
Parloff, R., 345

Parnas, J., 23, 421
Parsey, R. V., 269
Partonen, T., 269, 400
Pascual, A., 422
Pascual, J. C., 464
Pascual-Leone, A., 278
Paskus, T. S., 136
Pato, C. N., 196
Pato, M. T., 196
Patrick, C. J., 442, 459, 460
Pattison, P., 385
Paul, B., 391
Paul, G. L., 135
Paul-Labrador, M., 157
Paulesu, E., 490
Paulhus, D. L., 152
Pauli, P., 176
Pauls, D. L., 196
Paulus, M. J., 252
Pava, J. A., 266
Payan, C., 402
Paykel, E. S., 252
Payne, Y. A., 156
Paz, M. F., 45
Peake, T. H., 125
Pearl, P. L., 495
Pearson, C. A., 338
Pearson, J., 86, 534
Pearson, J. L., 284
Peddicord, J. P., 281
Pedersen, G. F., 75
Pedersen, N. L., 340
Pedrelli, P., 425
Peekna, H. M., 232
Peirce, J. M., 322
Peirce, T. R., 413
Peitza, M., 193
Pelham, W. E., 493, 494, 496
Pelkonen, M., 505
Peltzer, K., 424
Penadés, R., 425
Peng, S., 311
Pengilly, J. W., 155
Penn, D. L., 407, 425
Penna, S., 265, 268
Pennebaker, J. W., 146
Penninx, B. W., 162
Peppard, P. E., 350
Perälä, J., 400
Perelman, M. A., 370
Perez-Olivas, G., 501
Perez, R. III, 495
Perez, V., 278
Pericak-Vance, M. A., 530
Perilla, J. L., 202
Perivoliotis, D., 425
Perkins, D., 323, 423
Perkins, D. O., 166, 423, 425
Perkins, K. A., 317, 318
Perkins, S. C., 239
Perlin, 77
Perrett, D. I., 40
Perrier, A., 350
Perrin, N., 133
Perrin, S., 501
Perry, G., 527, 530
Peters, M. F., 534
Peters, M. L., 215
Petersen, K., 311
Peterson, A. L., 30
Peterson, A. V. Jr., 315
Peterson, C., 156
Petitto, J. M., 166
Peto, R. E., 508
Petrides, G., 274, 275
Petronis, V. M., 155
Petropoulos, H., 304, 484
Petry, N., 322
Petry, N. M., 322, 466, 467

Petterson, B., 484
Peveler, R. C., 277
Pew Research Center, 147
Pfammatter, M., 407, 425, 426
Pfeffer, C. R., 504
Pfeufer, A., 344
Phaf, R. H., 522
Phelan, S., 346
Philaretou, A. G., 378, 384
Phillips et al., 44
Phillips, K. A., 233, 234, 240
Phillips, M. L., 196, 221
Phillips, M. R., 418
Phinney, J., 152
Pi-Sunyer, X., 343
Piacentini, J., 501
Piasecki, T. M., 324
Picchioni, M., 405, 411, 420
Piccinin, A. M., 489
Pich, B., 176
Pickens, R. W., 312
Pickering, T. G., 161
Pickworth, W. B., 317, 318
Pierson, R., 495
Pieters, G., 418
Pike, K. M., 340
Pilling, S., 426
Pilowsky, D. J., 477
Pina, A. A., 202
Pincus, A. L., 200
Pincus, H. A., 104, 504
Pinderhughes, 1989, 124
Pindyck, L. J., 332, 342
Pine, D., 176, 185
Pine, D. S., 502
Pine, F., 456
Pinel, J. P. J., 344
Pinquart, Duberstein, & Lyness, 525
Pinto, B. M., 155
Pipingas, A., 160
Pirkola, S., 400
Pirozzi, R., 429
Pitman, R. K., 202
Pitsavos, C., 161
Pitts, C. D., 200
Pitts, S. C., 301
Pizzagalli, D., 269
Plant & Plant, 384
Plassman, B. L., 524
Platholi, J., 416
Pliszka, S. R., 495
Plomin, 44
Plomin & McGuffin, 44
Plomin et al., 43, 44
Plomin, R., 412, 487, 503
Plunkett, A., 505
Pogue-Geile, M., 425
Pogue-Geile, M. Fl., 411
Pokrywa, M. L., 117
Polcari, A., 477
Polen, M. R., 133
Poling, J., 322
Polivy, J., 336
Polk, D., 157
Pollack, A., 348, 352, 353, 354
Pollack, M. H., 87, 176, 179, 190
Pollak, P., 533
Pollan, M., 343
Polley, B. A., 344, 346
Pollock, B. J., 525
Polo, A. J., 419
Poon, M. W. L., 503
Pope, H. G., 215
Pope, H. G. Jr., 336, 342
Porter, C. A., 177
Porter, S., 443
Porzelius, L. K., 342
Post, L. A., 391
Postma, A., 215
Potoczna, N., 342

Pouliot, L., 281
Powell, K. E., 281
Power, K., 205
Powley, T. L., 344
PracticeNet, 110
Pratt, E., M., 120
Preacher, K. J., 146
Preece, B., 413
Prescott, C. A., 259, 261, 268, 460
Prescott, E., 165
Prescott, R., 232
Presentacion, M. J., 496
Pressman, S. D., 161
Presson, C. C., 315
Pretty, H., 276
Prevatt, F., 89
Price, A., 284
Price et al., 377
Price, L., 192
Price, R. K., 298
Price, T. R. P., 236
Prigerson, H. G., 202
Prince, R. J., 388
Pring, L., 491
Prisciandaro & Roberts, 77
Project MATCH Research Group, 324
Prost, J., 301
Prou, D., 533
Provencher, M. D., 200
Prudic, J., 275
Przeworski, A., 219
Psychological Corporation, 84
Ptak, J., 165
Puig, O., 425
Puigdemont, D., 464
Pumariega, A. J., 151
Purdie, D. M., 366, 368
Putnam, F. W., 223
Putnam, K., 269
Pyszczynski, T., 261

Quello, Brady, & Sonne, 324
Quested, D., 414
Quigley, L. A., 133
Quinn, S., 49
Quirk, G. J., 186

Rabasca, 62, 125
Rabe-Hesketh, S., 501
Rabinowitz, F. E., 253
Rabinowitz, J., 422
Rachman, S. J., 187, 189
Racoosin, J., 504
Radel, M., 312
Radford, M. J., 162
Radnitz, C. L., 160
Raeburn, 269
Raedeke, T. D., 337
Raffield, T., 531
Raggi, V. L., 495, 496
Raghunandan, V. N. G. P., 502
Ragland, J. D., 402, 411, 415, 416
Ragland, J. D., 415, 416
Raine, A., 461
Rainforth, M., 157
Ralph, D., 371
Raman, R. P. B., 502
Ramin, S., 269
Ramirez, L., 337
Ramoz, N., 484
Randall, P., 337
Randazzo, K. V., 123
Randolph, C., 535
Rao, N., 240
Rao, S. M., 533
Rapee, R. M., 266
Raphael, Golden, & Cassidy-Feltgen, 90
Raphael, R., 188
Rapoport, J. L., 414

Raskin, P. M., 112
Rasmussen, K., 274
Rasmussen, S. A., 240, 486
Rathore, S. S., 162
Rathouz, P. J., 497
Rathus, S. A., 148, 360, 384, 391, 486, 532
Ratti, L. A., 302, 340
Rauch, S. L., 198
Raudenbush, S., 345
Raue, P. J., 524
Rauschenberger, S. L., 224
Rawe, J., 279, 505
Rawson, R. A., 371
Rayner, R., 54
Read, L. L., 422
Redd, W. H., 165, 203
Redden, D. T., 343
Reddy, J., 502
Redlich, F. C., 63
Redline, S., 349, 350
Redwine, J. M., 527, 530
Rees, A., 120
Rees, A.-M., 269
Rees, C. S., 198
Rees, Fowler & Maas, 371
Rees, V. W., 314
Reeve E. A., 198
Reeves, K. R, 317
Regan, R., 487
Regehr, C., 202
Reiber, C., 371
Reich, J., 451
Reichenberg, A., 415
Reichert, J. G., 484
Reid, J., 499
Reifler, B. V., 275
Reiger, D. A., 441, 442
Reinisch, J. M., 383, 415
Reisberg B., 530
Reisner, A. D., 216
Reiss, D., 411, 419, 503
Reitan & Wolfson, 90
Reitsma, J. B., 204
Reivich, K. J., 133
Remington, G., 423
Reneman, L., 305
Renfrey, 125
Rennard, S. I., 317
Renner, G., 545
Renton, J. C, 425
Research Unit on Pediatric
    Psychopharmacology Anxiety Study
    Group, 502
Resick, P. A., 202, 204, 381, 390
Resnick, H., 147
Resnick, H. S., 476
Rey, J. M., 497
Reynolds, C. A., 530
Reynolds, C. F., 353, 525
Reynolds, C. F. III, 279, 281, 524
Reynolds, K., 302
Reynolds, S., 120
Reynoso, J. T., 318
Rezai, A. R., 128
Rhéaume, J., 197
Rhee, S. H., 459, 460
Ribisl, K. M., 151
Ricaurte, G. A., 305
Ricci, J. A., 251
Ricci, L. R., 230
Ricciardelli, L. A., 336, 339
Rice, J. A., 256
Richard & Bobicz, 82
Richards, J. A., 277
Richards, J. C., 176
Richardson, M. A., 422
Richell, R., 457
Richmond, R., 133
Richter, M. A., 196

Riddle, M. A., 198
Ridley, 124
Rieder, R. O., 415
Rief & Sharpe, 227, 228, 240
Riemann, B. C., 197
Riether, A. M., 226
Rigotti, N. A., 317
Rijsdijk, F., 268, 269, 405, 411, 420, 501
Riley, B. P., 413
Rimer, S., 524
Rimm, E., 371
Rinne, T., 464
Risch, 44
Riskind, J. H., 265
Riso, L. P., 265, 268, 338
Ritchie, M., 407
Ritter, C., 254
Ritz, L., 274
Rivas-Vazquez, R. A., 193, 464
Robb, A. S., 495, 503
Robbins, J. M., 224
Robbins, P. C., 549, 550
Robbins, T. W., 495
Roberson, E. D., 530
Roberts, C. F., 555
Roberts, S. A., 421
Roberts, W., 495
Robertson, D., 479
Robin et al., 100
Robin, R. W., 100
Robins, L. N., 441, 442
Robinson, A. L., 391
Robinson, D. G., 196, 428
Robinson, M. D., 364
Robinson, R. G., 280
Robinson, T., 337
Robles, T. F., 144, 145, 161
Rock, D., 421
Rodin, J., 340
Rodriguez, D., 311
Rodriguez, F. G, 202
Rodriguez, J. de J., 202
Rodriguez, O., 125
Roech, R., 555
Roemer, L., 158
Roesch, R., 555, 559
Roesler, A., 386
Roffman, R. A., 310
Rogan, A., 319
Rogers, C., 111
Rogers, C. R., 112
Rogers, S., 205
Rogers v. Okin, 554
Rohan et al., 253
Rohan, K. J., 253
Rohde, P., 64, 96, 266, 268, 505
Rohrbach, L. A., 151
Rojas-Vilches, A. P., 153
Roll, J. M., 322
Rolls, E. T., 461
Romaniuk, H., 254
Romero, M. J., 415
Ron, M. A., 414
Ronan, K. A., 559
Roos, R., 536
Roots, I., 533
Ropero, S., 45
Rosa, A. I., 193
Rosales, G. A., 418, 419
Rosca, P., 549
Rose, R. J., 312
Rose, S. E., 525
Rosén, L. E., 494
Rosen, R. C., 365, 366, 367, 370, 371, 373, 374
Rosenbaum, J. F., 266
Rosenberg, D. A., 230
Rosenfarb, I. S., 419
Rosenhan, D., 351

Rosenheck, 137
Rosenheck, Kasprow et al., 137
Rosenheck, R., 151, 152
Rosenheck, R. A., 123, 202, 251, 398, 422, 423, 549
Rosenkranz, M. A., 141
Rosenthal, D., 412
Rosenthal, E., 546
Rosenthal, M. Z., 444
Rosman, B. L., 339
Rosner, B., 157
Ross, C. A., 217, 227
Ross, D., 400, 457
Ross, D. E., 404
Ross, E., 489
Ross, S. A., 457
Roth, D. L., 524
Roth, L. H., 549, 550
Roth, R. M., 410
Roth, T., 352
Roth, W. T., 407
Rothard, A. B., 424
Rothbaum, B., 192
Rothbaum, B. O., 192
Rothenberg, J. L., 318
Rothman, D. L., 176
Rotter, J. B., 155
Rougeta & Aubry, 277
Rounsaville, B. J., 270
Rourke, K. M., 147
Rouse, C. A, 318
Rousseau, F., 487
Routhier, D., 281
Roy, A., 282
Roy-Byrne, P., 269
Roy-Byrne, P. P., 179
Royes, R., 233
Rozee, P. D., 389
Rozin, P., 336
Ruan, W. J., 199, 294, 452
Rubia, K, 495
Rubin, L. J., 219
Rubinstein, S., 336, 337
Rubio, G., 276
Rudden, M., 179
Rudkin, L., 158
Rudolph, K. D., 502
Rudolph, R. E., 346
Ruggiero, K. J., 476
Rummans, T., 275
Rummans, T. A., 274
Rund, B. R., 415
Rupp, L. J., 378
Ruscio, A. M., 198, 500
Ruscio, J., 198
Rush, A. J., 59, 95, 114, 125, 263, 266, 274
Russ, E., 204
Russell, D. W., 156
Russo, J., 278
Russo, N. F., 253
Rutledge, T., 161
Rutter, 63
Rutter, M., 490
Rybarczyk, B., 354
Ryder, A. G., 152
Ryffa, C. D., 141
Rynn, M., 198
Rytwinski, D., 464

Saag, M. S., 165
Saarni, S. I., 400
Saccone, N. L., 312
Sachs-Ericsson, N. J., 477
Sachs, G, 276
Sachs, L., 496
Sackeim et al., 128, 275
Sackeim, H. A., 125
Sacker, A., 315
Sackheim, H. A., 274, 275

Sacks, O., 516, 517
Sadeh, A., 354
Sadler, A. G., 388
Safarjan, B., 415
Safford, S., 501
Safran & Messer, 117
Safren, S. A., 176
Saha, T., 294
Saigal, C. S., 370, 372
Saintfort, R., 232
Sakihama, M., 484
Salamero, M., 425
Salary, C. B., 504
Salekin et al., 87
Salekin, R. T., 463
Sales, T., 414
Salgado de Snyder, V. N., 61, 152
Salkovskis, P. M., 176, 195, 239
Salomon, R. M., 116, 273
Sambamoorthi, U., 525
Sammons, M. T., 428, 525
Samson, J. A., 477
Samuels et al., 165
Samuels, Y., 165
Sand, M., 370, 371
Sanders, G., 363, 364
Sanders, L., 162
Sanders Thompson et al., 134, 135
Sanderson, W. C., 122
Sandler, I. N., 133
Sanislow, C. A., 443, 452
Sanjay, K., 240
Sansone, R. A., 464
Santiago, J. J., 120, 254, 255
Santos, C. M., 524
Sanz, J., 422
Sapolsky, 44
Sar, V., 226
Sarampote, C. S., 495
Sarason, I. G., 315
Sareen, J., 186
Sartorius, N., 10, 400, 462
Sarwer, D. B., 346
Sasaki, M., 534
Sass, L., 455
Satcher, 5
Sathya, B., 302
Saunders, A. M., 530
Saunders, B. E., 476
Saunders-Pullman, R., 533
Savarino, J., 504
Savin, D., 82
Sawchuk, C. N., 176
Saxena et al., 198
Sayers, G. M., 545
Saykin, A. J., 410
Saywitz, K. J., 381, 477
Scahill, L., 484
Scanlan, J. M., 529
Schachar, R., 495
Schade-Brittinger, C., 532, 534
Schaefer, C. A., 414
Schaefer, H. S., 483
Schäfer, H., 532, 534
Schatzberg, A. F., 269
Schechter, M., 165
Schedlowski, M., 385
Scheier, M. F., 157
Schellenberg, G. D., 484
Schenck-Gustafsson, K., 161, 162
Schendel, D., 482
Schene, A. H., 116
Scherk, Pajonk & Leucht, 276
Scherr, P. A., 518, 525
Schettler, P. J., 252
Schettler, P. J., 256
Schewe, P. A., 373
Schiller, L., 397, 423
Schiller, S., 425
Schindler, M. K., 416

Schkade, D., 156
Schlaepfer, T. E., 278
Schlenger, W. E., 147
Schluchter, M. D ., 349
Schmahl, C., 445, 461
Schmaling, K., 163, 164
Schmaling, K. B., 271
Schmand, B., 305
Schmeidler, J., 221, 227, 444, 458
Schmelkin, L. P., 19
Schmid, T., 345
Schmidt et al., 341
Schmidt, N. B., 65, 176, 177, 281
Schmitt, 61
Schmitt, F., 530
Schmitz, N., 479
Schneck, C. D., 257
Schneider, F., 397
Schneider, H., 493
Schneider, J. P., 384
Schneider, R. B., 552
Schneiderman, N., 161, 162
Schneier, F. R., 193
Schniering, C. A., 266
Schnurr, P. P., 203, 204
Schoch, W., 203
Schoenbaum, M., 251
Schoenman, T. J., 12
Scholes, G., 214
Schooler, N., 422
Schooler, N. R., 423, 426
Schooley, R. T., 165
Schopp, Johnstone, & Reid-Arndt, 119
Schork, N. J., 411, 420
Schrag, A., 235
Schreibman, L., 484
Schreier, H., 230
Schroll, M., 252
Schteingart et al., 1995, 136
Schulberg, H. C., 279, 281, 524
Schulenberg, J. E., 298
Schulman, P., 268
Schulman, S. P., 162
Schulsinger, F., 23, 412, 421
Schultz, R., 491
Schulze, K., 405, 411, 420
Schulze, T. G., 258, 269
Schumacher, J., 258, 269, 491
Schunert, T., 464
Schüpbach, M., 534
Schutte, K. K., 154
Schuurman, P. R., 534
Schwalberg, M., 179
Schwartz, 253
Schwartz, A., 123
Schwartz, J. E., 120, 254, 255
Schwartz, M. W., 197, 344
Schwartz, R. P., 318
Schwartz, R. S., 346
Schweiger, U., 464
Schweitzer, J. B., 495
Schwitzgebel, R. K., 552
Schwitzgebel, R. L., 552
"Scientists discover migraine gene" 160, 160
Scoboria, A., 274
Scourfield, J., 498
Scroppo, J. C., 226
Scullin, M. H., 485
Sears, M. R., 164
Seeley, J. R., 96, 268
Seeley, R. J., 197, 344
Seftel, A., 371
Segal, A. F., 388
Segal, Bola, & Watson, 1996, 136
Segal, Z. V., 95–96
Segerstrom, S. C., 145
Segraves, R. T., 375
Segrin, C., 262
Seidman, D., 484

Seidman, L. J., 305, 439
Selby, E. A., 477
Selemon, L. D., 415, 416
Seligman, Abramson, Seligman, &
    Teasdale, 267
Seligman, L., 376
Seligman, M., 133
Seligman, M. E. P., 133, 156, 266, 267,
    268, 502
Selten, J.-P., 400
Seltzer, M. H., 463
Selvin, B. W., 361
Selye, H., 147
Selzer, R. R., 487
Semple, J., 525
Semrud-Clikeman, M., 495
Sengupta, A., 204, 426
Senthil, G., 533
Sequeira, A., 282
Serdula, M. K., 301
Serrano-Blanco, A., 274
Servín-López, S., 135
Setien, F., 45
Shabsigh, R., 370, 371
Shadish, W. R., 120
Shafer, T. W., 89
Shaffer, D., 371, 505, 506
Shafran, R., 197
Shah, N. J., 398
Shahar, E., 350
Shalev, A. Y., 202
Sham, P., 268, 269
Sham, P. C., 428
Shanley, D., 427
Shanley, N., 503
Shapiro, B., 406
Shapiro, C. M., 251
Shapiro, D. A., 120
Shapiro, E., 547
Shapiro, F., 205
Shapiro, S. L., 157
Sharkansky, E. J., 202
Sharp, A. J., 487
Sharp, D., 205
Sharp, T. A., 269
Sharp, W., 495
Sharp, W. S., 495
Sharpe, D., 240
Sharpe, H., 164
Sharpe, M., 232, 235, 239, 337
Shattuck, P. T., 482
Shaw, B. F., 59, 95, 114
Shaw, D. W. W., 304, 484
Shaw, E. C., 546
Shaw, H., 337, 340
Shaw, P., 495
Shaw, R., 154
Shaywitz, B. A., 491
Shaywitz, S. E., 491
Shea, M. T., 439, 444, 463
Shear, K., 179, 500
Shear, M. K., 177
Shedler, J., 452
Sheitman, B. B., 428
Shelby, R., 165, 205
Sheldon, K. M., 156
Shelton, E. J., 533
Shelton, R. C., 116, 177, 273, 275
Shen, J., 251
Sher, K. J., 312, 315
Sher, L., 297
Sherbourne, C., 251
Sherbourne, C. D., 260
Sherer, M. R., 484
Sherman, J. A., 477
Sherman, S. J., 315
Sherwood, A., 161
Sherwood, N. E., 340
Sheshadri, Y. C., 502
Sheung-Tak, C., 236

Shields, A. E., 156
Shields, P. G., 311
Shiffman, S., 318
Shih, S. C., 123
Shintani, N., 495
Shneidman, E., 297
Shneidman, E. S., 282, 285
Shnek, Z. M., 155
Shochat, T., 525
Shore, J. H., 82
Shrimpton, S., 505
Shugart, Y. Y., 493
Shukla, P. R., 372
Shumaker, S. A., 525
Sicard, T., 196, 459
Sicotte, N., 340
Siddique, J., 273
Siegel, J. E., 165
Siegel, S. J., 397
Siegle, G. J., 197
Sierra, M., 221, 222
Siever, L. J., 415, 439
Sigmon, S. T., 230, 253
Sijbrandij, M., 204
Sikkema, K. J., 166
Silber, M. H., 347, 353
Silberstein et al., 99
Silberstein, R. B., 160
Sildenafil Study Group, 375
Silk, K. R., 444, 484
Silliman, N., 165
Silva, R. R., 202
Silver, E., 549, 550, 555
Silver, S. M., 205
Silverman, B. L., 318
Silverman, J. M., 484
Silverthorn, P., 478, 497, 498
Simeon, D., 221, 224, 227
Similowski, T., 350
Simon, G., 239, 251
Simon, G. E., 504
Simon, J., 163
Simon, N. M., 190
Simon, S. L., 370
Simoneau, T. L., 277
Simons, A. D., 31
Simonsen, G., 18
Simonsick, E. M., 162
Simonton, D. K., 156
Simos, P. G., 491
Simpson, N., 269
Sin, D. D., 164
Sindelar, J., 398, 422
Singh, A., 400
Singh, G., 237
Singh, R. H., 372
Singh, S., 201
Sink, M., 301
Sipos, V., 464
Sipps, G., 188
Sirigatti, S., 99
Sitharthan, T., 314
Sivertsen, B., 354, 525
Skeem, J. L., 559
Skerrett, P. J., 346
Skinner, B. F., 54
Skodol, A. E., 16, 252, 452
Skoner, D. P., 146
Skoog, G., 195
Skoog, I., 195, 524
Skre, I., 412
Skudlarski, P., 491
Slabbekoorn, D., 363, 364
Slade, P., 407
Slager, S. L., 185
Slater, D., 555
Sledge, W. H., 251
Sloan, D. A, 203
Sloan, D. M., 146
Slone, D. G., 526

Sloore, H., 99
Slow, E. J., 86, 534
Slutske, W., 312
Slutske, W. S., 298, 467
Smeding, H. M., 534
Smeraldi, E., 459
Smialek, J. E., 301
Smit, F., 133
Smith, 80
Smith & Perlis, 347, 354
Smith, A. B., 495
Smith, C. J., 484
Smith, D., 345
Smith, J., 381
Smith, J. E., 337
Smith, J. L., 337
Smith, K. M., 349
Smith, M. L. and Glass, 120
Smith, M. L. and Glass & Miller, 120
Smith, R. G., 155
Smith, S., 173, 174, 175, 192
Smith, S. D, 491
Smith, S. M., 219
Smith, S. S., 324, 461
Smith, T., 484
Smith, T. W., 239
Smith, Y. L. S., 362
Smits, J. A. J., 190
Smoller, E. S., 530
Smyth, J. M., 146
Smyth, R., 232
Snitz, B. E., 415
Snow, D., 265
Snowden, R. J., 381
Snyder, 125
Snyder, C. R., 239
Snyder, D. K., 152, 153
Snyder, J., 498
Snyder, P. J., 372
Snyder, S. H., 40
Sobell, L. C., 322, 323
Sobell, M. B., 322, 323
Society for Neuroscience, 269, 297, 310,
    534
Soderstrom, C. A., 301
Sofuoglu, M., 322
Sogaard, J. A., 200
Sokolove, M., 543, 556
Soler, J., 464
Soler-Vila, M., 274
Solinas, M., 311
Solomon, D., 257
Solomon, D. A., 146, 252
Solowij, N., 310
Somers, J. M., 322
Somers, T. J., 174
Somes, G., 317
Sonderegger, L., 145
Song, H.-S., 163, 164
Song, W., 100
Sonnega, A., 173
Soravia, L. M., 203
Sørensen, H. J., 415
Sorri, A., 419
Sorum, P. C., 318
Soubrane, C., 352
Spanos, N. P., 12, 13, 216
Spark, 370
Sparthan, E., 119
Speckens, A., 196
Speelman, J. D., 534
Speelman, L., 270
Speicher, C. E., 146
Spencer, D. J., 10
Spencer, K. M., 414
Spicer, P., 62
Spiegel-Cohen, J., 224
Spiegel, D., 217, 219, 220, 224, 227
Spielberger, C. D., 552
Spillantini, M. G., 530

"Spinal fluid ...", 536
Spinhoven, P., 116, 503
Spitzer, M., 278
Spitzer, R. L., 16, 220, 222, 233, 252,
    255, 259, 367, 370, 380, 409, 428,
    437, 438, 443, 450, 489, 496, 529
Splinter, N. R., 416
Spring, B., 420
Springen, K., 307
Springer, E. A., 342
Sprowls, C., 135
Squier & Domhoff, 108
Squires-Wheeler, E., 421
Sramek, J. J., 136
Staab, J. P., 177
Staal, R. G. W., 533
Staddon & Cerutti, 54
Stallings, M. C., 460
Stambor, 504
Stampfer, M. J., 302
Stangier, U., 193
Stanley, B., 282, 444, 445
Stanley, M. A., 523
Stanton, A. L., 146
Starace, F., 429
Stark, D. E., 491
Starkman, 147
Starkstein, S. E., 280
Starkweather, C. W., 493
Starr, K., 166
Steadman, H. J., 549, 550, 555, 559
Steele et al., 269
Steele, J. D., 128, 275
Steen, T. A., 156
Steer, R. A., 265
Stefanadis, C., 161
Stefanick, M. L., 344
Steffens, D. C., 524
Stein, A. L., 154
Stein et al., 154
Stein, M. A., 495
Stein, M. B., 179, 182, 185, 186, 200,
    499
Steinhauer, S. R., 461
Steinhausen, H.-C., 342
Steinhauser, C., 386
Stellman, J. M., 202
Stellman, S. D., 202
Stenson, 133, 134
Stepanski, E., 354
Stephens, M., 312
Stephens, R. S., 310
Stepp, S., 444, 445
Steptoe, A., 161, 162
Stern, T. A., 229
Sterner, J., 146
Stevens, A., 277
Stevens, J. E., 193
Stevens, L., 277
Stevens, S., 204
Stevenson, J., 445
Stewart, E., 320
Stewart et al., 196
Stewart, M. O., 116, 273, 275
Stewart, M. W., 503
Stewart, S. H., 176, 177, 324
Stewart, W. F., 251
Stice, E., 96, 336, 337, 340, 342
Stice et al., 133
Stiles, T. C., 463
Stiles, W. B., 120
Stinson, F. S., 75, 173, 174, 175, 181,
    182, 183, 199, 205, 248, 251, 252,
    254, 255, 294, 452
Stitzer, M. L., 322
Stoffler, A., 530
Stolberg, S. G., 162
Stoller, R. J., 363
Stone, A. A., 146
Stone, E. C., 498

Stone, J., 232
Stone, J. L., 484
Stone, M. H., 445
Storms, G., 418
Stotland, N. L., 227, 254, 342
Stoudemire, A., 226
Stouthamer-Loeber, M., 498
Strahs, K. R., 318
Strasser, A. A., 317, 318
Straub, R. E., 176
Strauss et al., 120
Streng, A., 159
Stricker & Gold, 89, 117
Strickland, B. R., 253
Striegel-Moore, R. H., 337
Strike, P. C., 162
Strober, M., 502
Stroebe, M., 280
Stroebe, W., 280
Strojwas, M. H., 530
Stronguin, F., 25
Strote, J., 305
Strother, W. N., 312
Stroup, D. F., 278
Stroup, T. S., 398, 422, 423
Strozier, C. B, 455
Strunk, D., 116, 273, 275
Strunk, R. C., 164
Stuart, 123
Stuart, G. L., 179
Stuhlinger, M., 545
Stutts, J. T., 230
Su, M., 61, 205, 295
Substance Abuse and Mental Health
    Services Administration (SAMHSA),
    305, 306, 309
Suchy, Y., 457
Suddath, R. L., 277
Sugden, K., 268
Sui, Y., 370, 414
Suinn, R. M., 161
Sukhodolsky, D. G., 498
Suldo, S. M., 156
Sullivan, G., 179
Sullivan, G. R., 549
Sullivan, H. S., 411
Sullivan, J. G., 18
Sullivan, L. E., 549
Sullivan, M. A., 318
Sullivan, M. D., 235
Sullivan, P., 156
Sullivan, P. F., 340, 413
Sulloway, F. J., 17
Suls, J., 161
Summerfelt, A., 414
Summs, C. A., 215
Sun, P., 370, 371
Sundin, O., 193
Surtees, P. G., 260
Sutker, P. B., 203
Suvisaari, J., 400
Suwaki, H., 428
Suwanlert, S., 476
Svartberg, M., 463
Svikis, D. S., 312
Swann, A. C., 297
Swanson, J. W., 549
Swanson, V., 205
Swanston, H., 505
Swartz, H. A., 277
Swartz, M., 235, 252
Swartz, M. S., 123, 423, 549
Swendsen, J. D., 254
Swenson, J. R., 125
Swets, J. A., 549
Swindle, R., 370
Swinson, T., 254
Symms, M. R., 414
Sysko, R., 340, 341

Szabo, S., 165
Szasz, T., 60, 545
Szasz, T. S., 545
Szentagotaia, A., 116
Szeszko, P. R., 196
Szklo-Coxe, M., 350

TADS Team, 503
Taffe, J., 489
Taft, C. T., 390
Tagliati, M., 533
Takahashi, 61
Takeuchi, H., 252
Talakoub, L., 372, 375
Talbot, N. L., 477
Tanaka, K., 495
Tanaka-Matsumi, J., 10
Tancer, M., 200
Tang et al., 275
Tang, T. Z., 96, 114
Tannock, R., 495
Tapert, S. F., 322
Tardif, M., 322
Targett, D. A., 318
Targum, S., 274
Tariot, P. N., 530
Tarrier, N., 418, 425
Tarter, R., 315
Taubman, J., 282
Taylor & Luce, 82, 119
Taylor, A., 268, 460
Taylor, A. N., 187
Taylor, C. B., 177, 179, 337
Taylor, D. R., 164
Taylor, E., 495
Taylor, K. L., 165, 205
Taylor, L. H., 82
Taylor, L. K., 202
Taylor, M. A., 409
Taylor, M. J., 268, 371
Taylor et al., 2006, 133
Taylor, S., 176, 195, 205
Taylor, V., 378
Tazir, M., 533
Teague, G. B., 136
Teasdale, J. D., 158
Teasdale, T. W., 535
Tecott, 44
Teicher, M. H., 477
Tein et al., 133
Ten Have, T. R., 279, 281, 524
Teneback, C., 314
Tenhula, W. N., 424
Teo et al., 306
Teplin, L. A., 550
Tepner, R., 274
ter Kuile, M. M., 375
Tessitore, A., 185
Testa, M., 297
Teunisse, R. J., 406
Thaker, G. K., 414
Thakker, J., 10
Thase, 121
Thase, M. E., 31, 277
Thayer, J. F., 221
Thiedke, C. C., 508
Thiemann, D. R., 162
Thioux, M., 491
Thomann, K., 214
Thomas, H., 495
Thomas, J., 360, 363
Thomas, M. R., 257
Thomasius, R., 311
Thompson-Brenner, H., 342
Thompson, C., 277
Thompson, E., 278
Thompson et al., 305
Thompson, J. K., 336
Thompson, M. P., 284
Thompson, P. M., 370, 415, 525

Thompson, T., 250
Thomson, A., 179
Thordarson, D. S., 198, 205
Thorpe, S. J., 195
Thorsby, E, 349
Thorsen, P., 482
Thuras, P., 341
Tian, H., 312
Tibben, A., 536
Tick, N., 500
Tienari, P., 419
Tierney, E., 484
Tiet, Q., 505
Tiggemann, Martins, & Kirkbride, 339
Tiihonen, J., 407
"Time Capsule" (2000), 88
Timpson et al., 62
Tishler, P. V., 349
Titeux, L., 352
Tobacco Information and Prevention Source (TIPS), 306
Tohen, M., 256
Toichi, M., 484
Tolbert, V. E., 273
Toler, S. M., 375
Tolin, D. F., 176, 202
Tolomiczenko, Sota, & Goering, 137
Tomita, H., 44
Tondo, L., 256
Tønnesen, P., 317
Tonstad, S., 317
Toomey, R., 305
Toone, B., 495
Torgensen, S., 412
Torgersen, S., 435
Torgrud, L. J., 182
Torrey, F., 547
Toulopoulou, T., 405, 411, 420
Tousignant, M., 281
Tozzi, F., 340
Tradgold, A. F., 491
Traish, A., 366, 440
Trakowski, J. H., 177
Tran, J., 375
Trana, H. Q., 154
Trask, P. C., 230
Treadwell, K. R. H., 501
Treasure, J., 340
Treat, T. A., 179, 336
Treffert, D. A., 491
Tremblay, R. E., 466
Tresco, K. E, 496
Treuer, T., 384
Treynor, W., 253
Triggiano, P., 214
Trimble, J. E., 9
Trimble, M. R., 235
Trivedi, M. H., 125, 274
Trost, A., 337
Trower, P., 398, 406
Troy, S., 274
Trull, T. J., 444, 445, 458
Trunzo, J. J., 155
Tsao, J. C. I., 179
Tschanz, J. T., 524
Tseng, W., 236
Tsuang, M. T., 311, 429
Tugade, M. M., 147
Tull, M. T., 444
Turecki, G., 282
Turetsky, B. I., 397, 415, 416
Turk, C. L., 116, 200
Turkington, D., 240, 425
Turner, C. M., 501
Turner, J. B., 203
Turner, M. G., 389
Turner, R., 146
Turner, S., 193
Turner, S. M., 182
Turner, T. H., 397

Turse, N. A., 203
Turvey, C., 257
Tutkun, H., 226
Tverdal, A., 306
Tyler, J. D., 120
Tyrer, P., 281

Uddo, M., 203
UK ECT Review Group, 128, 275
Ullmann, L. P., 457
Ulrich, C. M., 346
Ulrich, R., 425
Underwager, R., 219
Unger, J. B., 151
Unutzer, J., 251
U'Ren, R., 545
Urosevic, S., 270, 277
Urry, H. L., 141
U.S. Department of Health and Human Services (USDHHS), 5, 7, 9, 14, 50, 62, 63, 104, 122, 123, 124, 133, 134, 135, 136, 173, 174, 181, 185, 189, 195, 203, 248, 252, 254, 256, 259, 260, 269, 275, 400, 410, 423, 475, 477, 502, 503, 505, 523
U.S. Department of Justice, 389
Utens, E., 500
Utsey, S. O., 156, 524

Vadher, A., 400
Valderhaug, R., 501
Valdez, J., 415, 416
Valentine, J. D., 202
Valeri, S., 502
Valeri, S. M., 503
Vallea, M. F., 156
Vallejo, R. L., 312
van Amelsvoort, T., 479
Van Audenhove, Ch., 418
van Calker, D., 259
Van Dam-Baggen, R, 493
Van den Bree, M., 495, 498
van den Brink, W., 305, 464, 466
van den Oord, E. J., 413
van der Ende, J., 500
van der Hart, O., 215
van der Stelt, O., 405
van Dijk, M., 390
Van Dorn, R. A., 549
van Dyck, R., 464
Van Eerdewegh, P., 163
van Erp, T. G. M., 414
Van Erp, T. G. M., 415
van Erp, T. G. M., 420
Van Etten-Lee, M., 196
van Gastela, W., 500
Van Goozen, S. H. M., 362
van Goozen, S. H. M., 363, 364
van Hemert, A. M., 239
Van Humbeeck, G., 418
van Laar, T., 534
van Lankveld, J. J. D. M., 375
Van Straten, A., 133
Van Susteren, L., 557
Van Zyl, L. T., 125
VandeCreek, L., 552
Vanderkam, I. D., 339
Vandrey, R., 310
VanItallie, T. B., 346
Vanryckeghem, M., 493
Vanyukov, M., 315
Varenicline Phase 3 Study Group, 317
Varvil-Weld, D., 188
Vastag, B., 344
Vaughn, C., 419
Vawter, M. P., 44
Vázquez-Alvarez, T., 332
Vazquez, R., 151
Veenstra-VanderWeele, J., 196
Vega, C., 317

Vega, W. A., 152
Velasquez, I., 157
Velez, M. L., 312
Velting, D. M., 505, 506
Vemulapalli, M., 484
Venables, P. H., 461
Verbeek, A. L., 406
Verchinski, B. A., 415
Verdeli, H., 477
Verghese, J., 530
Vermetten, E., 40
Vermetten E., 224
Vestergaard, M., 482
Vickers, K., 176
Vidal, C., 415
Vidal, C. N., 414
Vidaver, R., 410
Vieta, E., 276
Viken, R. J., 312, 336
Villarosa, L., 381
Vincent, N. K., 340
Vinicor, F., 343
Vinson, D. C., 312, 315
Virden, T. B. III, 384
Virkkunen, M., 312
Visser, S., 240
Vitaliano, P. P., 529
Vitaro, F., 466
Vivian, D., 120, 254, 255
Vlahov, D., 147, 202
Vocisano, C., 120, 254, 255
Voglmaiera, M. M., 439
Vohs, T. F., 338
Volkmann, J., 532
Volkmar, F. R., 495
Volkow et al., 310
Volkow, N., 294
Volkow, N. D., 27
Vollm, B. A., 40
Vollset, S. E., 306
von Gontard, A., 509
von Gudenberg, A. W., 493
Vosburg, S. K., 443
Vythilingam, M., 40

Wadden, T. A., 344, 346
Wade, 44
Wade, W. A., 179, 273
Wadsworth & Achenbach, 63
Wagenpfeil S., 159
Wagner, D., 203
Wagner, H. R., 123
Wagner, K. D., 503
Wagner, R., 549
Wahl, K., 195
Wahlbeck, K., 415
Wahlberg, K. E., 417
Wahler, R. G., 497
Wainwright, N. W. J., 260
Waismann, R., 385
Waizenhofer, E., 390
Wakefield, H., 219
Wakeling, A., 336, 337
Walden, T. A., 493
Waldheter, E. J., 425
Waldinger, M. D., 375
Waldman, I. D., 459, 460, 495
Walker, E., 281, 400, 414, 415, 425
Walker, E. F., 421
Walker, J. R., 182
Walker, R., 375, 389
Walkup, J. T., 502, 525
Wallace, G., 259
Wallace, H. M., 390
Wallach, M. A., 136
Waller, G., 338, 340
Wallis, C., 484
Walsh, B., 120
Walsh, B. T., 165, 340, 341, 342
Walsh, E., 281

Walsh, J. K., 352
Walsh, M., 151
Walsh, R., 157
Walshaw, P. D., 270, 277
Walter, B. R., 476
Walter, H., 278
Walters, E. E., 104, 248, 251, 278, 500
Wamala, S. P., 161, 162
Wampold, 120
Wang, C., 343, 372
Wang et al., 104
Wang, J., 119
Wang, L., 416
Wang, P. S., 504
Wang, X., 251
Wang, Y., 162
Wang, Z., 165
Wanyee, J., 493
Ward, J., 418
Ward, T., 10, 385
Warden, D., 274
Wardle, J., 161
Warheit, G. J., 152
Warlow, C., 232
Warneke, C., 146
Warner, L. A., 298
Warner, M. B., 452
Warner, V., 477
Warren, S. T., 487
Wartik, N., 253
Warwick, O. H., 323
Wasco, S. M., 389
Washton, A., 371
Wassink, T. H., 411, 413, 484
Watanabe, T., 428
Waternaux, C., 282
Waterworth et al., 44
Watkins, C. E. Jr., 18
Watkins, E. R., 277
Watkins, L. L., 161
Watsky, E. J., 317
Watson & Clark, 75
Watson, A. C., 549
Watson, J. B., 54
Watts, C., 389
Watts, S. E., 202
Waugh, C. E., 147
Waugh, R., 161
Weaver, T. L., 226
Webb, A., 501
Webb, B. T., 176
Weber, A. L., 166
Webster-Stratton, C., 499
Wechsler, D., 82
Wechsler, H., 305
Weed, 98
Weems, C. F., 177, 202
Wei, W., 525
Weich, Churchill, & Lewis, 96
Weickert, T., 416
Weiden, P. J., 425
Weinberg, G., 363
Weinberg, M.S., 18
Weinberger, D. R., 415
Weinberger, J. L., 226
Weiner, D. A., 550
Weiner, I. B., 552
Weiner, Spielberger, & Abeles, 89
Weinstein, L., 281
Weisberg, R. B., 369
Weisman, A., 419
Weisman, A. G., 418, 419
Weiss, B., 476, 503
Weiss, D. S., 173, 202, 203
Weiss, R. D., 291, 296, 314
Weiss, S., 155
Weissenburger, J. E., 266
Weissman, 270
Weissman, M. M., 260, 270, 271, 477
Weisstaub, N. V., 176

Weisz, J. R., 476, 503
Weisz, Weersing, & Henggeler, 121
Welch, M. R., 372
Welch, S. L., 339, 340
Welge, J. A., 342
Wells & Miranda, 120
Wells, A., 198
Wells, K. B., 251, 260
Wells, K. C., 496
Welner, J., 412
Welter, M. L., 534
Wender, P. H., 412
Wenzel, A., 187, 281
Wesner, K. A., 259
Westen, D., 204, 342, 444, 452
Westen, Novotny, & Thompson-Brenner, 121
Westfall, A. O., 343
Westling, B. E., 119, 176
Westra, Dozois, & Marcus, 120
Wetterholm, A. L., 530
Wexler, B. E., 416
Wexler et al., 98–99
Whalen et al., 94
Whiffen, V. E., 254
White, A., 324
White, G. L., 214
White, K. S., 174, 316
White, T., 25
White, W. C., 335
Whitehead, D. L., 162
Whitesell, N. R., 62
Whitfield, S., 407
Whitley, M. K., 457
Whitney, C. W., 350
Whittal, M. L., 198
Whitten, 303
Whooley, M. A., 260
Wichmann, T., 128
Wickramaratne, P., 270, 477
Widiger & Clark, 75
Widiger & Simonsen, 75
Widiger, T. A., 446, 450, 463
Widom, C. S., 458
Wiecek, E. M., 164
Wiedemann, G., 176
Wigg, K., 495
Wilberg, T., 75
Wilbur, C. B., 225
Wileyto, E. P., 311, 317, 318
Wilfley, D. E., 342

Wilhelm, S., 239
Wilke, F., 311
Wilkens, L., 62
Wilkinson, D., 531
Wilkinson, I. D., 406
Willan, A. R., 164
Willcutt, E. G., 493
Willer, M. G., 341
Willett, W. C., 160, 302
Williams, A. C. de-C., 235
Williams, A.-L., 269
Williams, B., 460
Williams, D., 205, 475
Williams, D. A., 155
Williams, D. E., 343
Williams, J., 240
Williams, J. B., 81
Williams, J. B. W., 16, 252
Williams, J. M. G., 260
Williams, K. A., 467
Williams, K. E., 317
Williams, L., 119
Williams, N. L., 176
Williams, N. M., 413
Williams, S., 425
Williams, S. L., 155
Williamson, D. F., 343
Wills, T. A., 156
Wilson, A., 254
Wilson, D., 147
Wilson, G., 378
Wilson, G. D., 385
Wilson, G. T., 120, 121, 332, 341, 342
Wilson, Grilo, & Vitousek, 341, 342
Wilson, K. A., 177, 205
Wilson, R. S., 517
Winblad, B., 530
Wincze, J. P., 369
Winegard, W. C., 323
Winerip, 136
Winerip, M., 301, 489
Winerman, L., 191, 505
Winett, C. A., 270
Wing, R. R., 344, 346
Wingate, L. R., 477
Wingert, P., 493, 496
Wingood, G. M., 133
Winquist, J., 261
Winstanley, C. A., 495
Winterer, G., 405, 415
Winters, A., 478

Wintersteen, Mensinger, & Diamond, 123
Winzelberg, A. J., 342
Wise, R. A., 311
Wise, T. N., 235, 239
Wisniewski, S. R., 257, 274
Witkiewicz, K., 323
Witt, C., 159
Wittchen, H. U., 499
Witte, T. K., 281
Wittstein, I. S., 162
Witztum, E., 386
Woerner, M. G., 428
Woertman, L., 215
Wohlberg, C. J., 415
Wohlfahrt, J., 482
Wolfe, D. A., 477
Wolfe, J., 202
Wolfe, R., 375
Wolpe, J., 158
Womble, L. G., 346
Wonderlich, S., 338
Wong, D. F., 414
Wong, M. M., 298
Wonodi, I., 414
Wood, J. M., 88, 89, 351
Wood, M. D., 312, 315
Wooderson, S., 196
Woodruff, P.W. R., 406
Woods, D. J., 153
Woods, S. C., 197, 344
Woods, S. W., 177, 179, 185, 423
Woodward, Dwinell, & Arons, 134
Woodward, L. J., 505
Woodworth, M., 443
Wool, C., 233
World Health Organization (WHO), 5
Wouters, L., 464
Wouters, L. F., 116
Wright, A. S., 531
Wright, C. L., 111
Wright et al., 119
Wright, J. H., 531
Wright, K., 277
Wright, P., 502
Wroe, A. L., 195
Wu, A., 196
Wu, C.-C., 527, 530
Wu, P., 354, 505
Wunderlich, A., 278
Wyatt, R. J., 414
Wyatt v. Stickney, 551

Wyckoff, L. A., 117
Wykes, T., 425
Wynne, L. C., 419
Wyshak, G., 233, 239

Xian, H., 305
Xie, H., 426
Xing, H., 311
Xiong, J., 495
Xu, K., 311
Xu, M., 530
Xu, R., 311
Xu, X., 311
Xua, M. L., 439

Yager, J., 269, 274, 341, 477
Yamada, M., 534
Yamamiya, Y., 336
Yamamoto, K., 484
Yan, 343
Yancey, K. B., 192
Yang, A., 530
Yang, H. M., 198
Yang, L. H., 418
Yang, Q., 486
Yang, R., 415
Yang, Y., 423
Yargic, L. I., 226
Yaryura-Tobias, J. A., 198
Yasui, Y., 346
Yatham, L. N., 276
Yee, J. K., 504
Yeh, C. J., 119, 152
Yehuda, R., 458
Yellachich, L.-A., 64
Yen, S., 439, 444
Yeo, G. S. H., 342, 344
Yeung et al., 99
Yi, H. Y., 75, 173, 174
Yoder, V. C., 384
Yoshimura, R., 252
Young, A. H., 240
Young, D., 467
Young, E., 253
Young, E. A., 336
Young, J. E., 263
Young, K. A., 552
Young, P. R., 116, 273
Young, S., 284
Young, S. E., 460
Young, T., 350

Young-Xu, Y., 204
Youngberg v. Romeo, 554
Youngstrom, E. A., 484
Yu, E., 318
Yuan, J., 305
Yuan, N. P., 388

Zachor, D. A., 484
Zai, G., 495
Zamanian, K., 151, 524
Zamboanga, B. L., 134
Zanarini, M. C., 444
Zandbergen, M., 375
Zane & Sue, 124
Zangen, A., 311
Zapf, P. A., 559
Zarate, C. A., 256
Zarate, R., 418, 425
Zawackia, T., 302
Zdanowicz, M., 547
Zeiss, R. A., 546
Zelli, A., 457
Zera, M., 478
Zerwas, S., 497
Zhang, J., 99, 529
Zhang, W., 491
Zhao, S., 440
Zheng, H. B., 236
Zhou, Z., 282
Zhu, G., 282
Zhu, X., 527, 530
Zickler, P., 306, 310
Zimand, E., 192
Zimmerman, C., 389
Zimmerman, M., 467
Zimmerman et al., 75, 76
Zipursky, R. B., 423
Zitman, F. G., 406
Zlot, A., 345
Zoellner, L. A., 197, 198, 219
Zola, S. M., 219
Zorrilla, L. T. E., 186
Zubin, J., 420
Zubrick, S. R., 64
Zucker, K. J., 361, 378
Zuckerman, M., 461
Zuroff, & Blatt, 120
Zvolensky, M. J., 65, 176, 177
Zweig-Frank, H., 458
Zwinderman, A. H., 375

A-B-A-B (reversal) design, diagram of, 30
Aberrant forms of thought, 403
Abnormal behavior:
    assessment of, 68–101
    and asylums, 13
    biological perspective, 15–16, 38–43, 65
        evaluating, 43–45
    biopsychosocial perspective, 19, 63–66, 65
    classification of, 68–101
    contemporary perspectives on, 15–19, 36–67
    cultural bases of, 9–10
    and defense mechanisms, 46–47
    defined, 6–10, 18
    definitions, 8
    demonological model of, 10–11
    DSM and models of, 70–77
    historical perspectives on, 10–19
    humanistic concepts of, 56–58
    medical model, 5, 15–16
    and moral therapy, 14
    psychological perspective, 16–17, 65
    sociocultural perspective, 19, 60–63, 65
    and structural or functional abnormalities of
        brain, 42–43
    symptomatic nature of, 52
    and witchcraft, 12–13
Abnormal psychology:
    dangerousness, predicting, 545–550
    defined, 4, 19
    and the law, 542–561
        case study, 543–544
    psychiatric commitment, 544–554
    research methods in, 19–33
    thinking critically about, 31
Abnormality:
    criteria for determining, 6–9
    psychodynamic views on, 50–51
Absolutist thinking, 59
Abstinence syndrome, 293
Abstraction, selective, 264, 272
Abuse, See also Subtraction
    pedophilia, 380–381
    rape, 387–391
    recovered memories of, 217, 219
    sexual, 381–382, 387–391
Acculturation:
    among Hispanic Americans, 151–152, 153
    among Mexican Americans, 151, 152
    defined, 150
Acculturative stress, 150–152
Acetylcholine (ACh), 40
Acquaintance rape, 389
Acquired dysfunctions, 365
Acquired immunodeficiency syndrome (AIDS),
        165–167
    adjustment of people with, 165
    prevention, 167
    support groups, 166
Acute stress disorder (ASD), 200–204
    defined, 200
    features of, 203
    theoretical perspectives, 204
    treatment approaches, 204
Addiction, 294–295
    cybersex, 384
    dependence vs., 296, See also Substance
        abuse
Addington v. Texas, 545
Adipose tissue, 344
Adjustment disorders, 142–143
    as mental disorder, 143
    subtypes of, 143
Adjustment problems, and anxiety, 172
Adler, Alfred, 49, 51
Adoptee studies, 28–29, 311, 412
Adrenal cortex, 144
Adrenal medulla, 145
Adrenaline (epinephrine), 175
Adrenocorticotrophic hormone (ACTH), 144
African Americans, See also Ethnic differences

and alcohol use and abuse, 299–300
and cardiovascular disease (CVD), 162
and eating disorders, 337
and mental health care, 133–134
and psychotherapy, 124
and schizophrenia, 135, 419
and social anxiety disorder, 205
and somatoform disorders, 236
and stress, 156
and substance abuse, 295
Age:
    and alcoholism/alcohol dependence, 298
    and depression, 226
    and suicide, 279
Aggression, 58
Aging:
    and Alzheimer's disease, 16, 40, 44, 217, 226,
        280
    and anxiety disorders, 523
    cognitive changes, 523
    delirium and, 293, 406
    and depression, 523–525
    examining your attitudes toward (questionnaire),
        532
    and Parkinson's disease, 406, 520, 524,
        532–534, 536
    and Pick's disease, 517, 532
    psychological disorders related to, 522–532
    reaction time, 522–523
    and sleep problems, 525
    and vascular dementia, 531, 537
Agnosia, 517–519
Agoraphobia, 116, 174, 179, 183
    defined, 183
AIDS, See Acquired immunodeficiency syndrome
        (AIDS)
Al-Anon, 320
Alarm reaction, 147
    stress-related changes in the body associated
        with, 148
Alaska Natives:
    anxiety sensitivity, 177
    suicide rate, 133
Alateen, 320
Alcohol, 62, 291, 297
    binge drinking, 301
    case study, 313
    delirium tremens, 293
    drinking among college students, 298
    ethnicity and alcohol use and abuse, 299–300
    fetal alcohol syndrome (FAS), 302
    moderate drinking, health benefit of, 302–303
    operant conditioning, 313
    and peer pressure, 316
    and physical health, 302
    psychological effects of, 300–302
    and rape, 391
    as self-medication, 313
    and sexual arousal/excitement, 302
    and tension reduction, 313
Alcohol, Drug Abuse, and Mental Health
        Administration (ADAMHA), 462
Alcohol-induced persisting amnestic disorder, 302
Alcoholic hepatitis, 302
Alcoholics Anonymous (AA), 297, 319–320, 325
Alcoholism/alcohol dependence, 297
    culturally sensitive treatment of, 319
    and domestic abuse, 297
    example of, 324
    genetic factors, 311
    Korsakoff 's syndrome, 236
    risk factors for, 298–299
    role of heredity in, 311–312
    withdrawal from, 293–294
All-or-nothing thinking, 263
Alprazolam (Xanax), 126, 176, 177, 200, 291,
        371
Alter personalities, 214–215
Alzheimer, Alois, 527

Alzheimer's disease (AD), 16, 40, 43, 44, 217,
        226, 280, 517–518, 525–531
    case study, 515, 526, 529–530
    causal factors, 530
    defined, 525
    dementia associated with, 525
    diagnosis, 527
    genetic factors, 536
    plaques linked to, 530
    prevalence of, 526
    prevention, 530
    risks of, 525
    symptoms of, 527–529
    treatment, 530
American Indians:
    anxiety sensitivity, 177
    suicide rate, 133
American Law Institute, 557, 560
American Psychiatric Association, 10, 18, 69, 71,
        75, 78, 174, 275, 359, 546, 555
American Psychological Association (APA), 106
Amitriptyline (Elavil), 127, 273
Amnesia, See also Dissociative amnesia
    anterograde, 521
    continuous, 218
    defined, 217
    generalized, 218
    localized, 218
    retrograde, 521
    selective, 218
    systematized, 218
Amnestic disorders, 520–521
    defined, 520
Amniocentesis, 487
Amobarbital, 303
Amok, 76
Amphetamine psychosis, 305
Amphetamines, 291, 293, 305
Amygdala, 185–186
Anal stage, 47–48
Analgesia, 303
Analogue measures, 94
Analytical psychology, 49
Ancient Greece, abnormal behavior in, 11
Angel dust, See Phencyclidine (PCP)
Anger, 161
    and depression, 260
Animal phobia, 179
Anomie, 282
Anorexia nervosa, 331, 331–334, See also Eating
        disorders
    binge-eating/purging type, 334
    case study, 333
    causes of, 336–341
        biological factors, 340–341
        family factors, 340
        psychosocial factors, 337–340
        sociocultural factors, 336–337
    defined, 332
    diagnostic features of, 333
    medical complications of, 334
    onset of, 333
    restrictive type, 334
    subtypes, 334
Anterograde amnesia, 521
Antianxiety drugs, 126–127, 129, 130, 294,
        352–353
    rebound anxiety, 127
    side effects of, 126
    and sleep problems, 353
Antibodies, 145
Anticonvulsant drugs, 276, 286, 504
Antidepressant drugs, 127–128, 129, 130
    and depressive disorders, 268–270, 273–275
    and dissociative disorders, 227
    and HIV/AIDS, 166
    and obsessive-compulsive disorder (OCD), 198
    and personality disorders, 464
Antidepressants, 317
Antigens, 145

Antimanic drugs, 129
Antipsychotic drugs, 127, 129, 130
    atypical, 276, 422
    and delusional disorders, 428
Antisocial behavior, heritability of, 460
Antisocial personality disorder, 436, 440–443,
        457
    and alcoholism/alcohol dependence, 298
    antisocial behavior, heritability of, 460
    case study, 442–443
    craving-for-stimulation model, 461
    and criminality, 441
    defined, 440
    diagnostic features of, 442
    lifetime prevalence of, 440
    profile of the antisocial personality, 441
    sociocultural factors, 441
Anxiety, 7, 79–80, 171
    adjustment disorder with, 143
    among Westerners, 9
    automatic thoughts associated with, 265
    behavioral features, 172
    in children, 499–507
    cognitive features, 172
    free floating, 196, 207
    physical features, 171
Anxiety disorders, 5, 170–209
    acute stress disorder (ASD), 200–204
    and aging, 523
    classification as neuroses, 172
    concept map, 208
    defined, 171
    ethnic differences in, 204–205
    generalized anxiety disorder (GAD), 198–200
    obsessive-compulsive disorder (OCD),
        194–198
    overview of, 171–172, 173
    panic disorder, 172–179
    phobic disorders, 179–193
    posttraumatic stress disorder (PTSD), 200–204
Anxiety sensitivity (AS), 177
Aphasia, 518–519, 531
Apnea, 349, 353
Apolipoprotein E (APOe), 530
Archetypes, 49
Are You Depressed? (questionnaire), 254
Are You Hooked? (questionnaire), 298
Arousal:
    female sexual arousal disorder, 365–366
    sexual, 365, 366–367
Arousal disorders, 373
Arteriosclerosis, 160
Asian Americans:
    and alcohol use and abuse, 299
    anxiety sensitivity, 177
    care sought for mental illness, 133
    and eating disorders, 337
    and mental heal care, 134
    psychological disorders, 62
    and psychotherapy, 124–125
    and social anxiety disorder, 205
Asperger's disorder, 479, 482
Asperger's disorder, 479
    diagnostic features of, 480
Assessment:
    behavioral, 91–95
    clinical interview, 80–81
    cognitive, 95–96
    computerized assessment protocol, 81–82
    methods of, 80–99
    neurological, 89–91
    neuropsychological, 89–91
    physiological, 96–99
    psychological tests, 82–89
    reliability in, 77–79
    sociocultural and ethnic factors in, 99–100
    standards of, 77–80
    validity in, 79–80
Asthma, 163–164
    bronchodilators, 164

and stress, 163–164
    theoretical perspectives, 163–164
    treatment, 164
    triggers, 163
Asylums, 13
Ataque de nervios ("attack of nerves"), 76, 205
Ataxia, 522, 538
Atherosclerosis, 160
Attention-deficit and disruptive behavior disorders:
    behavioral interventions, 496
    oppositional defiant disorder (ODD), 493,
        497–499
Attention-deficit hyperactivity disorder (ADHD):
    concept map, 512–513
    defined, 493
    diagnostic features of, 494
    medication, 495–496
    stimulant drugs, 495
    symptoms, 495
    theoretical perspectives, 495
    treatment, 495–497
Attention-placebo studies, 25
Attentional deficiencies, 403–404
Attentional deficit hyperactivity disorder (ADHD),
    403–404
Attributional style, 267–268
Atypical antipsychotics, 276, 422
Auditory hallucinations, 405, 406
Australian aborigines, fears of sorcery among, 10
Autism, 44, 417, 475, 477, 478–482, 480, 482
    autistic thinking, 481
    biomedical therapies, 484
    case study, 480–481, 482, 483
    features, 482–483
    gender differences, 482
    preservation of sameness, 483
    primary feature of, 483, 483–484
    relationship between intelligence and, 483
    savant syndrome, 491
    theoretical perspectives, 484
    treatment, 484–485
Autism spectrum disorders, 479, 480
Autistic disorder, 479
Automatic Thoughts Questionnaire (ATQ), 95–96
    items defining factors, 97
Autonomic, use of term, 43
Autonomic nervous system (ANS), 43, 145, 459
Aversive conditioning, 111, 322
Avoidant personality disorder, 436, 449–450
    case study, 449
    defined, 449
    overlap between social phobia and, 450
Axons, 38

Bandura, Albert, 55
Barbie dolls, and eating disorders, 339
Barbiturates, 293, 303
Basal ganglia, 42, 197
Base-rate problems, 548
Basic anxiety, 49
Basic hostility, 49
BEAM (brain electrical activity mapping), 99
Beautiful Mind, A (film), 398
Beck, Aaron, 58, 59–60, 95, 113, 115
Beck Depression Inventory (BDI), Chinese version of,
    99–100
Beck's cognitive therapy, 115
Bed-wetting, 477, 478, 507–508
Bedlam, 13
Behavior coding systems, 92–93
Behavior modification, 55
Behavior patterns, 40
Behavior therapy, 55, 110–111, 115
    dialectical behavior therapy (DBT), 464
    encopresis, 478, 508–509
        defined, 508
    rational-emotive, 113–115
    techniques, 55–56
    treatment, 110–111
Behavior undercontrol, 460

Behavioral activation, 271
Behavioral Approach Task (BAT), 94
Behavioral approaches, 320–321
Behavioral assessment, 91–95
    analogue measures, 94
    behavioral rating scales, 95
    defined, 91
    self-monitoring, 93–94
Behavioral diary/log, 93–94
Behavioral dimension, 441
Behavioral interview, 92
Behavioral observation, 92
Behavioral rating scales, 95
Behaviorism, 52
Belle indifférence, la (phenomenon), 232
Bender Visual Motor Gestalt Test, 90–91
Benzodiazepines, 176, 200, 297, 352
Bereavement, 9, 70, 72, 200, 250, 260, 524
Beta amyloid, 530
Bicultural theory, 151
Binet Alfred, 82–83
Binge drinking, 301
Binge-eating disorder (BED), 331–332, 342–346
    defined, 342
    obesity, causes of, 343–346
    treatment, cognitive-behavioral therapy (CBT), 342
Biofeedback training (BFT), 160
Biological perspectives:
    abnormal behavior, 15–16, 38–43, 65
        evaluating, 43–45, 65–66
    anorexia nervosa, 340–341
    bulimia nervosa, 340–341
    depressive disorders, 268–269
    panic disorder, 176
    paraphilias, 385
    personality disorders, 459
    schizophrenia, 411–412
    sexual dysfunctions, 370–371
    substance abuse, 310–312
        genetic factors, 311–312
        neurotransmitters, 310–311
    suicide, 282
Biomedical therapies, 126–130
    drugs, 126–128
    electroconvulsive therapy (ECT), 128
    evaluation of, 130
    paraphilias, 386
    psychosurgery, 130
Biopsychosocial perspective, of abnormal behavior,
    19, 63–66, 65
Bipolar disorder, 8, 15, 248, 256–258
    bipolar I disorder, 256
    bipolar II disorder, 256
    case study, 256
    causal factors in, 269–270
    gender differences, 257
    lifetime prevalence rates, 256–257
    manic episodes/manic depression, 257–258
    treatment, 276–277
        lithium, 276–277
        mood stabilizers, 276–277
        psychological approaches, 277
    types of, 256
"Black box," 96
Blacking out, 76
Blaming the victim, 451
Blind, use of term, 24
Blocking, 403, 410
Blood phobia, 179
Blunted affect, 407
Body dissatisfaction, 338
Body dysmorphic disorder (BDD), 228, 233–234,
    240
    case study, 234
    defined, 233
    treatment, 240
Body mass index (BMI), 336
Borderline personality disorder (BPD), 436, 443–445
    case study, 444–445
    defined, 443

impulsive behavior, 445
    Kernberg on, 455
    Mahler on, 456
    self-mutilation, 445
    splitting, 445
Brain:
    abnormalities, 268–269, 414–416, 461
    geography of, 42
Brain electrical activity mapping (BEAM), 99
Brain-imaging and recording technique:
    brain electrical activity mapping (BEAM), 99
    computed tomography (CT), 96–97
    computerized axial tomography (CAT scan), 97
    functional magnetic resonance imaging (fMRI),
        98–99
    magnetic resonance imaging (MRI), 98
    positron emission tomography (PET scan), 97–98
Brain waves, 96–97
Breathing-related sleep disorder, 347, 349–350
Breathing retraining, 178
    and panic disorder, 178
Breuer, Joseph, 17
Brief psychotic disorder, 426
Briquet's syndrome, 235
"Broken-heart syndrome," 162
Bronchodilators, 164
Brown, Joyce, 547
Building rapport, 80
Bulimia nervosa, 37, 270, 331–333. *See also* Eating
    disorders
    and binge eating, 335
    case study, 334–335
    causes of, 336–341
        biological factors, 340–341
        family factors, 340
        psychosocial factors, 337–340
        sociocultural factors, 336–337
    defined, 332
    diagnostic features of, 335
    example of, 331
    medical complications of, 336
    self-induced vomiting, 335
Buprenorphine, 318
Bupropion (Zyban), 317

Cancer, 164–165
    death rates, 165
    and erectile disorder, 371
    metastasize, use of term, 164
    and stress, 165
Cannon, Walter, 147–148
Carbamazepine, 276
Cardiovascular disease (CVD), 160–163
    "broken-heart syndrome," 162
    defined, 161
    and ethnicity, 162–163
    and negative emotions, 161–162
    prevention, 161
Case studies, 29–30
    types of, 29
Castration anxiety, 383
CAT scan, 97
Cataplexy, 349
Catastrophizing, 264
Catatonic type of schizophrenia, 409–410
Catharsis, 17
Central nervous system (CNS), 40, 41–42
    and antianxiety drugs, 126
Cerebellum, 41
Cerebral cortex, 42, 43, 196
Cerebral hemispheres, 43
Cerebrum, 42
Cerletti, Ugo, 128
Charcot, Jean-Martin, 16–17
Checking rituals, 197
Child abuse:
    and child/adolescent suicide, 505
    and childhood disorders, 477
    prevalence of, 477
Child Behavior Checklist (CBCL), 95

Childhood/adolescence:
    attentional deficit hyperactivity disorder (ADHD),
        concept map, 512–513
    externalized problems, 476
    internalized problems, 476
    normal/abnormal behavior in, 475–478
        case study, 475
    prevalence of mental health problems in,
        476–477
    suicide in, 505
        case study, 506
Childhood anxiety and depression, 499–507
    childhood anxiety disorders:
        learning perspectives, 501
        understanding and treating, 501–502
        separation anxiety disorder, 499–501
            case study, 501
Childhood depression:
    gender differences, 503
    understanding and treating, 502–503
Childhood disintegrative disorder, diagnostic features
    of, 480
Childhood disorders:
    anxiety disorders, 478
    attention-deficit and disruptive behavior disorders:
        attention-deficit hyperactivity disorder (ADHD),
            493–496
        conduct disorder (CD), 493, 496–497
        oppositional defiant disorder (ODD), 493,
            497–499
    attentional deficit hyperactivity disorder (ADHD),
        478
    childhood anxiety and depression, 499–507
    communication disorders, 478, 492–493
        DSM-IV classification of, 492
        expressive language disorder, 492
        mixed receptive/expressive language disorder,
            492
        phonological disorder, 492
        stuttering, 492–493
    elimination disorders, 478
    gender differences, 477
    learning disorders, 478, 489–492
        disorder of written expression, 490
        DSM-IV classification of, 492
        dyslexia, 490–492
        mathematics disorder, 490
        reading disorder, 490
        types of, 490
        understanding and treating, 490–491
    mental retardation, 478, 485–489
        amniocentesis, 487
        and birth complications, 488
        causes of, 485–487
        chromosomal abnormalities, 485–486
        Down syndrome, 485–486
        fetal alcohol syndrome (FAS), 488
        fragile X syndrome, 487
        intervention, 488–489
        Klinefelter's syndrome, 486–487
        levels of, 485
        phenylketonuria (PKU), 487
        prenatal factors, 487–488
        Turner's syndrome, 487
    mood disorders, 478
    overmedication of children, 504
    overview, 478
    pervasive developmental disorder, 478–485
    risk factors for, 477–478
Childhood sexual abuse, 226
    effects on children, 381–382
    pedophilia, 380–381
    recovered memories of, 217
China, postpartum depression among women in, 254
Chlordiazepoxide (Librium), 297
Chlorpromazine (Thorazine), 127, 422
Choleric, use of term, 11
Choreiform, 534
Chovil, Ian, 398–399
Chromosomal abnormalities, 485–486

Chromosomes, 27
Chronic insomnia, 331
Chronicity, of psychological disorders, 61–62
Circadian rhythm sleep disorder, 347, 350
Cirrhosis of the liver, 299, 302
Civil commitment, 544, 548, 559–560
Clanging, 403
Classical conditioning, 52
  role of, 53
  schematic diagram of the process of, 53
Classical psychoanalysis, 115
Claustrophobia, 8, 179
Cleaning rituals, 195
Client-centered therapy, 57, 111–112, 115
Clinial social workers, 105
Clinical interviews, 80–81
  types of, 81
Clinical psychologists, 105
Clitoris, 367
Clomipramine (Anafranil), 177, 198
Clozapine (Clozaril), 127, 422–423
Cocaine, 291, 293, 305–306, 310
  and depression, 306
  effect on brain, 311
  effects of, 306
Cocaine Anonymous, 319
Cognitions, defined, 95
Cognitive assessment, 95–96
Cognitive-behavioral therapy (CBT), 60, 115, 116, 193
  binge-eating disorder (bed), 342
  and childhood depression, 503
  eating disorders, 341–342
  generalized anxiety disorder (GAD), 200
  and oppositional defiant disorder (ODD), 499
  panic disorder, 193
  paraphilias, 385–386
  phobic disorders, 193
  somatoform disorders, 240
Cognitive disorders:
  amnestic disorders, 518
  delirium, 518
    delirium tremens (DTs), 520
    features of, 519
    prevalence of, 520
  dementia, 518
    cognitive deficits in, 519
  overview of, 518
  presenile dementias, 518
  senile dementias, 518
Cognitive disorders, 516–522
  defined, 515–516
  dementia, 517–518
    due to Creutzfeldt-Jakob disease, 535
    due to head trauma, 535
    due to HIV disease, 534–535
    due to Huntington's disease, 534
    due to Pick's disease, 532–534
    general paresis, 535–536
    neurosyphilis, 535–536
  vascular dementia, 531–532
    defined, 531
    features of, 531–532
    symptoms, 531
Cognitive distortions, 58, 114, 263
  and rational responses, 272
Cognitive models, 58–59
  evaluating, 59–60
Cognitive restructuring, 193
Cognitive therapy, 113–115
  and Beck, 114–115
  and depression, 271–273
  rational emotive behavior therapy (REBT), 113
Cognitive–behavioral therapy (CBT):
  and schizophrenia, 425
  and sleep disorders, 354
"Cold-blooded" killers, 443
Collective unconscious, 49
College Life Stress Inventory, 149
Command hallucinations, 406

Common cold, and stress, 146
Communication deviance (CD), 417–418
Communication disorders, 478, 492–493
  DSM-IV classification of, 492
  expressive language disorder, 492
  mixed receptive/expressive language disorder, 492
  phonological disorder, 492
  stuttering, 492–493
Community mental health centers (CMHCs), 15, 131–133
  spectrum of prevention, 132–133
Community mental health movement, 15
Comorbidity, 8, 324, 436, 452
Competency to stand trial, 559–560
Compulsion to utter, 108
Compulsions, 194, See also Obsessive–compulsive personality disorder
Computed tomography (CT) scan, 97
Computerized axial tomography (CAT scan), 97
Computerized interviews, 81–82
Concerta, 495
Concordance rate, 28, 411–412
Conditional positive regard, 56
Conditioned response (CR), 53
Conditioned stimulus (CS), 53
Conditioning, and phobia, 185
Conduct disorder (CD):
  defined, 496
  genetic factors, 498
  and parental distress, 498
  prevalence of, 497
  theoretical perspectives, 497–498
  treatment, 498–499
Confidentiality, 22
Confounds, 26
Congruence, 112
Conscious/consciousness, 45
Construct validity, 25, 26, 79–80
  of a test of anxiety, 80
Content scales, 85
Content validity, 79
Contingency management (CM) programs, 322
Continuous amnesia, 218
Control groups, 24
Controlled drinking, 322–323
Controlling behavior, defined, 20
Conversion, 231
Conversion disorder, 228, 231–232
  cognitive theory, 239
  conceptual models, 241
  defined, 231
  diagnostic features of, 231
  learning theory, 238–239
  psychodynamic theory, 238
  symptoms, 231–232
  theoretical perspectives, 237–238
Coping, styles of, 154
Coping responses, development of, 178
Coping-skills training, and cancer, 165
Coprophilia, 383
Copycat suicides, 282
Coronary heart disease (CHD), 160–161
Correlation coefficient, 22
Correlational method, 22–23
Cortical steroids, 144, 149
Corticosteroids, 144
Counseling psychologists, 105
Counselors, 105
Countertransference, 108–109
Couple therapy, 118–119
Covert sensitization, 386
Craving-for-stimulation model, 461
Cravings:
  case study, 314
  conditioning model of, 314–315
Creative self, 49
Creutzfeldt-Jakob disease, dementia due to, 535
Criminal commitment, 544
  determining the length of, 557–558
Criterion validity, 79

Critical thinking, defined, 32
Cross-fostering study, 412–413
Crystal meth (ice), 305
Cullen, William, 172
Cultural barriers, to mental health care, 134–135
Cultural differences, in alcohol consumption, 316
Cultural mistrust, and mental health care, 134
Cultural sensitivity, 124
Cultural–familial retardation, 488
Culturally sensitive treatment approach, alcoholism/alcohol dependence, 319
Culture-bound dissociative syndromes, 223
Culture-bound syndromes, 73–74
  from other cultures, 76
Cybersex addiction, 384
Cyclothymia, defined, 258
Cyclothymic disorder, 258–259
  boundaries between bipolar disorder and, 259
  case study, 259
  defined, 258
  hypomanic episodes, 258
Cyclothymic disorder/cyclothymia, 248

"Daily Record of Dysfunctional Thoughts," 95
Dalmane (flurazepam), 126
Dangerousness:
  and abnormality, 8
  base-rate problems, 548
  clinician predictions of, 549
  duty to warn, 552
  O'Connor v. Donaldson, 553
  post hoc problem, 548
  predicting, 545–550
  problems in defining, 548
  unlikelihood of disclosure of direct threats of violence, 548–549
  violence, and mental disorders, 549–550
  Youngberg v. Romeo, 553–554
Darvon, 303
Data rape, 387, 390
Day hospitals, 131
Defense mechanisms, 46–47
Deinstitutionalization, 131
  evaluation of, 136–137
  new services, 137
  and the psychiatric homeless population, 136–137
Deliriant, 309
Delirium, defined, 293
Delirium tremens (DTs), 293, 406
Delta-9-tetrahydrocannabinol (THC), 309
Delusion, 7
Delusional disorders, 426–428, 429
  and antipsychotic medication, 428
  case study, 427–428
  types of, 429
Delusions, 75
  of being controlled, 402
Dementia, 217, 517–518, 532–537
  of the Alzheimer's type, 525–531
  cognitive deficits in, 519
  due to Creutzfeldt-Jakob disease, 535
  due to head trauma, 535
  due to HIV disease, 534–535
  due to Huntington's disease, 534
  due to Pick's disease, 532–534
  general paresis, 535–536
  neurosyphilis, 535–536
  senile, 518
Dementia praecox, 15–16
Demerol, 303
Demonological model, of abnormal behavior, 10–11
Dendrites, 48
Denial, as defense mechanism, 47
Denial of illness, forms of, 154
Dental phobia, 179
Dependence, 62
Dependent personality disorder, 436, 450–451
  case study, 450
  defined, 450

  links to other psychological disorders, 451
Dependent variables, 23–24
  examples of, 24
Depersonalization, defined, 221
Depersonalization disorder, 213, 221–222, 224
  case study, 222
  cultural influences, 222
  diagnostic features of, 222
  example of, 221
Depressant drugs, 41, 296–304
  alcohol, 297
  barbiturates, 303
  defined, 296
  and erectile disorder, 371
  heroin, 304
  morphine, 304
  opoids, 303–304
Depressants:
  alcohol, 297
  barbiturates, 303
  heroin, 304
  morphine, 304
  opoids, 303–304
Depressed mood, adjustment disorder with, 143
Depression, 9, 10, 40, 62, 247, See also Major depressive disorder (MDD); Suicide
  and aging, 523–525
  and anger, 260
  and anxiety, 172
  Are You Depressed? (questionnaire), 254
  automatic thoughts associated with, 265
  case study, 265
  and child/adolescent suicide, 505
  in children, 499–507
  clinical practice guidelines for, 276
  and cocaine use, 306
  and cognitions, research evidence on, 266
  cognitive triad of, 263
  common features of, 249
  economic costs of, 251
  and omega-3 fatty acids, 269
  and perfectionism, 263
  postpartum, 253–254
  research evidence, 261
  and stress, 259–260
  treatment:
    antidepressants, 273–275
    behavioral approaches, 271
    case study, 271
    cognitive therapy, 271–273
    electroconvulsive therapy (ECT), 275
    magnetic stimulation therapy, 278
    psychodynamic approaches, 270–271
    St. John's Wort, 275
  in women, 253
Depressive disorders, 248
  biochemical factors and brain abnormalities, 268–269
  biological factors, 268–269
  cognitive theorists, 263–266
  genetic factors, 268
  humanistic theories, 261
  learned helplessness (attributional) theory, 266–268
  learning theories, 261–262
    interactional theory, 262
    reinforcement, role of, 262
  psychodynamic theories, 260–261
  stress and depression, 259–260
Derealization, 221
Descartes, Rene, 141
Descriptions, 19–20
Desipramine (Norpramin), 273
Detoxification, 317
Developmentally Disabled Assistance and Bill of Rights Act (1975), 489
Dhat syndrome, 76, 236–237, 372
Diabetes mellitus, 162, 251, 301, 343, 371, 476, 620
  and sexual dysfunctions, 370–371

Diagnostic and Statistical Manual of Mental Disorders (DSM), 18, 70, 78, 172
  advantages/disadvantages of, 75–76
  as bible of psychiatry, 78
  criticisms leveled against, 76–77
  evaluating, 75–76
  features of, 71–73
Dialectical behavior therapy (DBT), 464
Diathesis, defined, 64
Diathesis-stress model, 64–65, 182, 260, 277, 420, 433
  and dissociative disorders, 224, 226
  research evidence supporting, 421
Diazepam (Valium), 126, 130, 176, 200, 291, 297, 361
Direct observation, 92, 92–93
Discredited treatments, 32
Disorganized type of schizophrenia, 408–409
Displacement, as defense mechanism, 47
Disqualifying the positive, 264
Dissociation, 203
Dissociative amnesia, 213, 217–219, 224
  compared to malingering, 219
  defined, 217
  recovered memories, 219
  types of memory problems associated with, 218
Dissociative disorders, 211–212, 224
  brain dysfunction, 224
  concept map, 244
  culture-bound dissociative syndromes, 223
  defined, 212
  depersonalization disorder, 221–222
  diathesis-stress model, 224, 226
  dissociative amnesia, 217–219
  dissociative fugue, 219–220
  dissociative identity disorder, 212–217
  psychodynamic views, 223
  social-cognitive theory, 224
  theoretical perspectives, 223–224
  treatment, 224–227
Dissociative experiences, 203
Dissociative Experiences Scale (questionnaire), 223
Dissociative fugue, 213, 219–220, 224
  compared to malingering, 220
  defined, 219
  incidence of, 220
Dissociative identity disorder (DID), 211, 212–217
  controversies, 215–217
  example of, 225
  features of, 215
  and suicide, 217
Disturbance of conduct, adjustment disorder with, 143
Disturbances of volition, 408
Disulfiram (Antabuse), 317
Divalproex (Depakote), 276
Dix, Dorothea, 14
Dizygotic (DZ) twins, 28
  and alcoholism, 312
  concordance rates found among, 410–411
  and depressive disorders, 268–269
  and eating disorders, 340–341
  and schizophrenia, 412–414
Donepezil (Aricept), 530
Dopamine, 40
Dopamine hypothesis, 414
Double-blind placebo design, 25
Double depression, 255
Down syndrome, 485–486
Downward drift hypothesis, 63
Doxepin (Sinequan), 127, 273
Dream analysis, 108
Dreser, Heinrich, 304
Drug-induced hallucinations, 406
Drug therapy, 126–128, 353
  antianxiety drugs, 126–127
  antidepressant drugs, 127–128
  antipsychotic drugs, 127
  lithium, 128
du Pont, John E., 555

Dualism, 141
Duke, Patty, 282–283
Durham v. United States, 550, 556–557
Durkheim, Emile, 282
Duty to warn, 552
Dysfunctional Attitudes Scale (DAS), 96
Dyslexia, 490–492
Dyspareunia, 365, 367, 375
Dyssomnias, 346, 347–350
Dysthymia, 248
Dysthymic disorder, 248, 254–255, 270
  case study, 255
  defined, 254
  demographics, 254
  lifetime prevalence rates, 255

Eating disorders, 330–357, *See also* Eating disorders
  anorexia nervosa, 331–334
    case study, 333
    defined, 332
    diagnostic features of, 333
    medical complications of, 334
    onset of, 333
    subtypes, 334
  binge-eating disorder, 331–332
  and body dissatisfaction, 338
  bulimia nervosa, 331–333
    and binge eating, 335
    case study, 334–335
    defined, 332
    diagnostic features of, 335
    medical complications of, 336
    self-induced vomiting, 335
  defined, 332
  in developing countries, 337
  Fear of Fat Scale (questionnaire), 341
  genetic factors, 340–341
  overview of, 333
  and perfectionism, 338
  rates of, 337
  treatment, 341–342
    antidepressants, 341
    cognitive-behavioral therapy (CBT), 341–342
    drug therapy, 342
    interpersonal psychotherapy (IPT), 341
    psychodynamic therapy, 341
  as weight phobia, 338
Eclectic therapy, 117
Economic and accessibility barriers, to mental health care, 135
Ecstasy (MDMA), 305
Ego, 46, 51
Ego analysts, 110
Ego boundaries, 407
Ego dystonic, 436
Ego identity, 50
Ego psychology, 49
Ego syntonic, 436
Elavil (amitriptyline), 127, 273
Electra complex, 48
Electroconvulsive therapy (ECT), 105, 128, 130
  and depression, 275
Electrodermal response, 96
Electroencephalograph (EEG), 96
Electromyograph (EMG), 96
Electromyographic (EMG) biofeedback, 160
Elimination disorders, 478, 506–509
  encopresis, 508–509
    behavior therapy, 508
    defined, 508
  enuresis, 507–508
    defined, 507
    diagnostic features of, 507, 508
    primary, 507
    treatment, 509
Ellis, Albert, 58–59, 113, 115, 188, 264, 369
Emotion-focused coping, 154
Emotional reasoning, 264
Emotional responsiveness, lack of, 459–461
Empathy, 112

Emphysema, and erectile disorder, 371
Empirically supported treatments (ESTs), 120–121, 122
  examples of, 121
Encopresis, 478, 508–509
  behavior therapy, 508
  defined, 508
Endocrine system, 38
  defined, 144
  glands of, 144
  and stress, 144–145
Endophenotypes, 420
Endorphins, 311
  defined, 304
Enuresis, 507–508
  defined, 507
  diagnostic features of, 507
  primary, 507
  treatment, 509
Epidemiological studies, 26–27
Epinephrine (adrenaline), 175
Erectile dysfunction, 370–371
  case study, 373–374
Erikson, Erik, 49–50, 109, 115
Erogenous zones, 47
Erotomania (love delusion/erotomanic type), 427
  delusional disorders, 429
Ethics in research, 21–22
Ethnic differences, and alcohol use and abuse, 299–300
Ethnic identity, and stress, 156
Ethnic stereotyping, and mental health system, 135–136
Ethnicity:
  and cardiovascular disease (CVD), 162–163
  and child/adolescent suicide, 505
  and hypertension, 164
  and mental health, 60–63
Ethyl alcohol (ethanol), 297
European Americans:
  and alcohol use and abuse, 299
  and cardiovascular disease (CVD), 162
  and eating disorders, 337
  and social anxiety disorder, 205
  and substance abuse, 295
Event-related potentials (ERPs), 405
Evidence-based practices (EBPs), 32, 120, 121–122, 122
Examining Your Attitudes Toward Aging (questionnaire), 532
Exhaustion stage, 149
Exhibitionism, 376–378
  case study, 377–378
Exorcists, in medieval times, and abnormal behavior, 11–12
Expectancy effects, 107
Experimental group, 24
Experimental method, 23–24
  controlling for subject expectancies, 24–25
  experimental and control groups, 24–25
  experimental validity, 25–26
Exposure therapy, 190
Exposure with response prevention (ERP), 198, 240
Expressive language disorder, 492
External validity, 25–26, 26
Externalized problems, 476
Extinction, 185
Eye movement desensitization and reprocessing (EMDR), 204, 205

Factitious disorders, 229
Falling out/blacking out, 76
False negatives, 79, 548
False positives, 79, 548
Family history, and alcoholism/alcohol dependence, 298
Family intervention programs, schizophrenia, 425–426
Family problems, and child/adolescent suicide, 505
Family therapy, 118

FAS, *See* Fetal alcohol syndrome (FAS)
Fat cells, 344
Faulty perceptions/interpretations of reality, and abnormality, 7
Fear of Fat Scale (questionnaire), 341
Fear-stimulus hierarchy, 110, 189
Fears, acquisition of, through classical conditioning, 53
Female orgasmic disorder, 365, 367
Female sexual arousal disorder, 365, 366
Fetal alcohol syndrome (FAS), 302, 488
Fetishism, 378
Fight-or-flight reaction, 147–148
Five-factor model for the classification of personality disorders, 78
Fixation, 48–49
  defined, 49
Flashbacks, 308–309
Flat affect, 407
Flooding, 189, 191
Fluoxetine (Prozac), 127, 198, 240, 273–274, 375, 503
Fluphenazine (Prolixin), 127, 422
Flurazepam (Dalmane), 126
Fluvoxamine (Luvox), 240, 508
Forebrain, 41, 42
Formal intelligence tests, 82
Fortune teller error, 264
Fragile X syndrome, 487
Free association, 107–108
Freud, Sigmund, 16–17, 115
  and goal of psychoanalysis, 107
  psychoanalysis, 51
  and psychodynamic theory, 45
  on suicide, 281
  theoretical model, 17
Fromm-Reichmann, Frieda, 424
Frontal lobes, 43, 196–197
Frotteurism, 380
Fugue, *See* Dissociative fugue
Functional analysis of problem behavior, 92
Functional magnetic resonance imaging (fMRI), 98–99

GAD, *See* Generalized anxiety disorder (GAD)
Galen, 11, 37
Galvani, Luigi, 96
Galvanic skin response (GSR), 96, 459
Gamblers Anonymous (GA), 467
Gamma-aminobutyric acid (GABA), 176
Gang rape, 390
Gender differences:
  alcoholism/alcohol dependence, 298
  autism, 482
  and child/adolescent suicide, 505
  childhood depression, 503
  childhood disorders, 477
Gender identity, defined, 360
Gender identity disorder (GID), 359, 360–364
Gender/sexuality, 358–395
  heterosexism, 364
  homophobia, 364
  rape, 387–391
  sexual dysfunctions, 365–375
General adaptation syndrome (GAS), 147–149
General paresis, 16, 535–536
Generalized amnesia, 218
Generalized anxiety disorder (GAD), 198–200
  cognitive-behavioral therapy (CBT), 200
  defined, 198
  interference with daily living, 198–199
  sample diagnostic criteria for, 71
  theoretical perspectives, 199–200
  treatment, 200–201
Generalized dysfunctions, 365
Genes, 27, 43–45
Genetic factors:
  depressive disorders, 268
  eating disorders, 340–341
Genetic predisposition, 28
Genetics, 27, 38

Genital stage, 48
Genotype, 27
Genuineness, 112
Geography, and child/adolescent suicide, 505
Ghost sickness, 76
Girl, Interrupted (Kaysen), 103–104
Global Assessment of Functioning (GAF) Scale, 74
Glutamate, 196
Going Through Changes (questionnaire), 150
Gradual exposure, 110–111, 189, 190
Grandeur, delusions of, 402
Grandiose type, delusional disorders, 429
Griesinger, Wilhelm, 15
Group therapy, 118
Guthrie, Arlo, 536
Guthrie, Woody, 534

H. pylori, 159
Halcion (triazolam), 126
Halfway houses, 131
Hallucinations, 7
    auditory, 405, 406, *See also* "Hearing voices"
    and cognitive–behavioral therapy (CBT), 407
    command, 406
    drug-induced, 406
    hypnagogic, 349
    olfactory, 405
    psychotics, causes of, 406
    tactile, 405
    visual, 405
Hallucinogens (psychedelics), 294, 308–310
    defined, 308
    LSD (lysergic acid diethylamide), 308–309
    marijuana (*cannabis*), 308, 309–310
    mescaline, 308
    phencyclidine (PCP), 308, 309
    psilocybin, 308
Haloperidol (Haldol), 422
Halstead-Reitan Neuropsychological Battery, 90–91
    Category Test, 90–91
    Rhythm Test, 91
    Tactual Performance Test, 91
"Hardening of the arteries," *See* Arteriosclerosis, 160
Hartmann, Heinz, 49, 110, 115
Hashish (hash), 309
Head Start, 488
Head trauma, dementia due to, 535
Headaches, 159–160
    migraines, 160
    and stress, 159–160
    theoretical perspectives, 159–160
    treatment, 160
Health maintenance organizations (HMOs), 122–123
Health psychologists, 141
Healthy narcissism, 455
"Hearing voices," 6–7, 75, 405
    among Native Americans, 9
Helping professionals:
    finding, 106–107
    types of, 104–105
Heroin, 291, 304, 310
    and erectile disorder, 371
Heterosexism, 364
Hinckly, John, 555, 557
Hippocrates, 11, 37, 69–70, 237
Hispanic Americans:
    acculturation among, 152, 153
    acculturaton among, 151
    alcohol use and abuse, 299
    anxiety sensitivity, 177
    and eating disorders, 337
    and health insurance, 133
    and mental heal care, 134
    and psychotherapy, 125
    and schizophrenia, 135, 419
    and social anxiety disorder, 205
    and substance abuse, 295
Histrionic personality disorder, 436, 445–446
    case study, 446
    defined, 445

HIV/AIDS, 165–167
    adjustment of people with, 165
    and antidepressants, 166
    deaths from, compared to suicide rate, 278
    dementia due to, 534–535
    psychological Interventions to reduce risky
        behaviors, 166–167
Homelessness, psychiatric, and deeinstitutionalism,
    136–136
Homophobia, 364
Homosexuality, 18, 48
Hopelessness, and child/adolescent suicide, 505
Hormonal changes, and headaches, 160
Hormones, 144
Horney, Karen, 49–50
Hospitalization, roles for, 131
Hostility, 161
Human immunodeficiency virus (HIV), 165
Humanistic models, 56–58
    evaluating, 57–58
Humanistic therapy, 111–113, 115
Humors, 11
Huntington's disease, 536
    dementia due to, 534
Hyperactivity, defined, 493
Hypersexual desire, 385
Hypersomnia, 347, 348
Hypertension, and ethnicity, 164
Hyperventilation, 175
Hypnagogic hallucinations, 349
Hypoactive sexual desire disorder, 365, 366
Hypochondriasis, 228, 232–233
    case study, 233
    defined, 232, 235
    diagnostic features of, 232
Hypomania, 249
Hypothalamus, 42
Hypothesis, 19, 21
    defined, 21
Hypoxyphilia, 382
Hysteria, 16, 45
Hysteria/hysterical neurosis, *See* Conversion disorder
Hysterical personality, *See* Histrionic personality
    disorder

Id, 46
Identical (MZ) twins, 28
Illness, and stress, 144–156
Imipramine (Tofranil), 127, 177
Immune system:
    defined, 145
    and stress, 145–146
Impulse control disorders, 465–469
    intermittent explosive disorder, 465
    kleptomania, 435, 465, 467–469
    pathological (compulsive) gambling, 435,
        465–467
    pyromania, 465
    trichotillomania, 465
Incidence, 27
Independent variables, 23–24
    examples of, 24
Index case, 28
"Indian sicknesses," 9
Indicated preventive interventions, 132–133
Individual psychology 49, 49
Information-processing models, 58–59
Informed consent, 21–22
Injection phobia, 179
Inner speech (silent self-talk), and hallucinations, 406
Input, 58
Insanity defense, 555–560
    competency to stand trial, 559–560
    defined, 555
    "guilty-but-mentally-ill" (GBMI) verdict, 555
    legal bases, 556–557
    perspectives on, 558–559
Insomnia, 347, 347–348
    chronic, 331
    primary, 347–348

rebound, 352
Instincts, 45
Institutional barriers, to mental health care, 134
Institutional review boards (IRBs), 21
Integrative eclectics, 117
Intelligence quotient (IQ), 83
Intelligence tests, 82–83
Interactional theory, and depressive disorders, 262
Interleukin-6, 146
Intermittent explosive disorder, 465
Internal consistency, 79
Internal validity, 25–26
internalized problems, 476
International Personality Disorder Examination (IPDE),
    462
International Statistical Classification of Diseases and
    Related Health Problems (ICD), 70
Internet therapy, 119
Interpersonal psychotherapy (IPT), 270–271
    case study, 271
Interrater reliability, 79
Intoxication, 292
Introjection, 260

Jackson v. *Indiana*, 550, 559–560
Jamison, Kay Redfield, 256
Jealous type, delusional disorders, 429
Jones v. *United States*, 550, 557–558
Jumping to conclusions, 264
Jung, Carl, 49, 51

Kaysen, Susanna, 103–104
Kidney disease, and erectile disorder, 371
Kinship studies, 27–29
Klein, Melanie, 110, 115
Kleptomania, 435, 467–469
    case study, 469
Klinefelter's syndrome, 486–487
Klismaphilia, 383
Kohut, Hans, 454–455
Koro, 76
Koro syndrome, 236
Korsakoff 's syndrome, 302, 522
Kraepelin, Emil, 15, 70

L-dopa, 20
La belle indifférence (phenomenon), 232
La Bicêtre (Paris), 13–14
Labeling/mislabeling, 264
Labels, confusing with explanations, 453
Lamotrigine (Lamictal), 276
Language barriers, to mental health care, 135
Late-stage syphilis, and admissions to psychiatric
    hospitals, 535–536
Latency stage, 48
Latent content, 108
Latinos, *See* Hispanic Americans
Learned helplessness (attributional) theory, 266–268
    defined, 266
    global factors, 267
    internal factors, 267
    negative attributional style, 268
    stable factors, 267
Learning disabilities, *See* Learning disorders
Learning disorders, 478, 489–492
    disorder of written expression, 490
    DSM-IV classification of, 492
    dyslexia, 490–492
    mathematics disorder, 490
    reading disorder, 490
    types of, 490
    understanding and treating, 490–491
Learning models, evaluating, 55–56
Learning perspectives, 184–185, 312–315, 411,
    456–458
    childhood anxiety disorders, 501
    personality disorders, 456–458
    phobic disorders, 184–185
    schizophrenia, 411
    substance abuse, 312–315

Leukocytes, 145
Level of functioning, assessment of, 75
Life changes, and stress, 149–150
Life events, 149
Life Orientation Test (questionnaire), 157
Lifetime dysfunctions, 365
Limbic system, 42
Lithium, 128, 276–277, 503
Lithium carbonate, 276
"Little Albert," 54
Localized amnesia, 218
Loftus, Elizabeth, 227
Longitudinal study, 23
"Loose" neurotransmitters, 40
LSD (lysergic acid diethylamide), 294, 308–309
Luvox (fluoxamine), 240, 508

Magical thinking, 439
Magnetic resonance imaging (MRI), 98
Magnification, 59
    and minimization, 264
Mahler, Margaret, 50, 110, 115, 456
Major depressive disorder (MDD), 248, 249–254,
    See also Depression
    case study, 250, 252
    postpartum depression (PDD), 253–254
    risk factors, 252
    seasonal affective (mood) disorder (SAD),
        252–253
Major depressive episode:
    diagnostic features of, 250
    resolution of, 252
Maladaptive/self-defeating behavior, and abnormality,
    7–8
Male erectile disorder, 365, 366
Male orgasmic disorder, 365, 367, 371
Male rape, 390
Malingering:
    compared to dissociative amnesia, 219
    compared to dissociative fugue, 220
    compared to somatoform disorders, 229
Malleus Maleficarum (The Witches' Hammer), 12
Man Who Mistook His Wife for a Hat, The (Sacks),
    516
Managed care systems, 122–123
Mania, 249
    use of term, 11
Manic-depressive psychosis, *See* Bipolar disorder
Manic episodes/manic depression, 257–258
Manifest content, 108
Manipulation, 58
Mantras, 157
Marijuana (*cannabis*), 294, 308, 309–310
Marital rape, 390
Marker, 404
Maslow, Abraham, 57
Mathematics disorder, 490
MDD, *See* Major depressive disorder (MDD)
Medical Inquiries and Observations Upon the Diseases
    of the Mind (Rush), 14
Medical model, 5, 15–16, 38
    origins of, 11
    terminological offspring, 16
Medieval times, abnormal behavior in, 11–12
Medina v. *California*, 550, 560
Meditation, 157–158
Medroxyprogesterone acetate (MPA) (Depo-Provera),
    386
Medulla, 41
Melancholia, 11
Melting pot theory, 151
Memantine (Axura), 530
Memory, 58
Memory lymphocytes, 145
Memory training programs, and Alzheimer's disease
    (AD), 531
Mental defect, 556–557
Mental disease, 556–557
Mental disorders:
    diagnosis of, 69–70

DSM classification of, 70
use of term, 4–5
in DSM, 71
Mental filter, 264
Mental health, 10
duty to warn, 552
and ethnicity, 60–63
in Freudian model, 50
and the law, 550
patient's rights, 550–554
Mental health services, ethnic group differences in use
of, 133–135
Mental hospital, 131
Mental illness, 5, 38, 545
Mental institutions, deterioration of, in late 19th
century, 14–15
Mental retardation:
causes of, 485–487
chromosomal abnormalities, 485–486
Down syndrome, 485–486
fetal alcohol syndrome (FAS), 488
fragile X syndrome, 487
intervention, 488–489
Klinefelter's syndrome, 486–487
levels of, 485
phenylketonuria (PKU), 487
prenatal factors, 487–488
Turner's syndrome, 487
Mescaline, 308
Mesmer, Franz Friedrich, 278
Mesmerism, 278
Meta-analysis, 119–120
Metabolic rate, genetic differences in, 344
Methadone, defined, 318
Methadone maintenance programs, 318
Methamphetamine (meth) abuse, 305
Methods of, 102–139
Mexican Americans:
acculturation among, 151, 152
and schizophrenia, 419
Midbrain, 41
Migraine headaches, 160
Millon Clinical Multiaxial Inventory (MCMI), 86–87
Mind, structure of, 45
Mind reading, 264
Mindfulness meditation, 157–158
Minnesota Multiphasic Personality Inventory (MMPI-2),
84–86
clinical scales of, 86
Mischel, Walter, 55
Mislabeling, 264
Mixed anxiety and depressed mood, adjustment
disorder with, 143
Mixed disturbance, adjustment disorder with, 143
Mixed receptive/expressive language disorder, 492
Mixed type, delusional disorders, 429
M'Naghten rule, 556
Modeling, 55, 111
Models, 9
Moniz, António Egas, 130
Monoamine oxidase (MAO) inhibitors, 127, 273–274
potential side effects, 274
Monosodium glutamate (MSG), 160
Monozygotic (MZ) twins, 29
and alcoholism, 312
concordance rates found among, 410–411
and depressive disorders, 268–269
and eating disorders, 340–341
and schizophrenia, 412–414
Mood disorders, 5, See also Suicide
bipolar disorders, 248
defined, 247
depressive disorders, 248
overview, 248
treatment, 270–278
depression, 270–273
types of, 248–259
Mood stabilizers, 276–277
Mood thermometer, 249
Moods, 247

Moral therapy, 14
Morphine, 291, 304
and erectile disorder, 371
Motor cortex, 43
Mowrer, O. Hobart, 184
Multi-infarct dementia, See Vascular dementia
Multiaxial classification system of the DSM-IV-TR, 71,
71–3
clinical syndromes, 71–73
example of a diagnosis in, 74
general medical conditions, 72
global assessment of functioning, 72–73
personality disorders/mental retardation, 72–73
psychosocial and environmental problems, 72–73
Multicultural issues in psychotherapy, 123–125
African Americans, 124
Asian Americans, 124–125
Hispanic Americans, 125
Native Americans, 125
Multigenic determinism, 44
Multiple personality, See Dissociative identity disorder
Münchausen, Baron Karl von, 229
Münchausen syndrome by proxy, 229–230, 240
Münchausenism, 229
Mundugumor (tribe of cannibals), 7
Musterbation, 264
Myth of Mental Illness, The (Szasz), 417

Naltrexone, 318–319
Narcissism:
healthy, 455
pathological, 455
Narcissistic personality disorder, 436, 446–449
case study, 448–449
defined, 446–447
self-defeating narcissism, features of normal self-
interest compared with, 447
Narcolepsy, 348–349
Narcotics, 303–304
and erectile disorder, 371
Narcotics Anonymous, 319
Nasal sprays, for nicotine addiction, 317
Nash, John, 398
Natenshon, Abigail, 339
National Comorbidity Survey Replication (NCS-R),
205
Native Americans:
and eating disorders, 337
and psychotherapy, 125
suicides among adolescents, 62
treatment for alcoholism, 319
Naturalistic observation, 22
"Nature-nurture" (gene vs. environment) debate,
43–45
Necrophilia, 383
Negative correlations, 22
Negative reinforcement, 55, 184–185
Negative reinforcers, 54
Neglected children, and childhood disorders, 477
Negy, Charles, 152
Neologisms, 403
Nervous system, 38–42
organization of, 41
parts of, 40–43
Neuroleptics, 127, 414
Neurologist, 89
Neurons, 43, 48
anatomy of, 38
Neuropsychological assessment, 89–91, 90
Bender Visual Motor Gestalt Test, 90–91
Neuropsychologist, 89–90
Neurosis, 172, 212
Neurosyphilis, 535–536
Neurotransmitters, 38, 268–269
functions and relationships with abnormal, 39
loose, 40
Nicorette, 317
Nicotine, 293, 306–308
Nicotine replacement therapy, 317–318
Nightmare disorder, 347, 350–351

Nondirective therapy, 111
Nonprofessional support groups, 319–320
Nonspecific treatment factors, 107
Norepinephrine (noradrenaline), 40, 145, 175, 268
Normal/abnormal behavior:
in childhood/adolescence, case study, 475
cultural beliefs about, 476
Normality, psychodynamic views on, 50–51

Obesity, 343–346
defined, 344
fat cells, 344
genetic factors, 344
lifestyle factors, 345
metabolic factors, 344
as national epidemic, 344
psychological factors, 345
socioeconomic factors, 345–346
Object-relations approaches, to psychodynamic
therapy, 110
Object-relations theory, 50
Objective tests, 83–84, 83–87
evaluation of, 87
Millon Clinical Multiaxial Inventory (MCMI), 86–87
Minnesota Multiphasic Personality Inventory (MMPI-
2), 84–86
clinical scales of, 86
Observational learning, 56, 185, 315
Observations, 92–93
Observer drift, 93
Obsession, 194
Obsessive-compulsive disorder (OCD), 194–198
antidepressant drugs, 198
compulsion, 194
compulsive checkers, and memory impairment,
197
exposure with response prevention (ERP), 198
obsession, 194
obsessive thoughts and compulsive behaviors,
examples of, 194
psychological models of, 197
theoretical perspectives, 195–197
treatment approaches, 198
Obsessive–compulsive personality disorder, 436,
451–452
case study, 452
defined, 451
Obstructive sleep apnea, 349
Occam's razor, 205
Occipital lobe, 43
OCD, See Obsessive-compulsive disorder (OCD)
O'Connor v. Donaldson, 550, 553
ODD, See Oppositional defiant disorder (ODD)
Oedipus complex, 48
Olanzapine, 400
Olfactory hallucinations, 405
Omega-3 fatty acids, and depression, 269
One Flew Over the Cuckoo's Nest (film), 548, 550
Online therapy, 119
Operant conditioning, 52
role of, 54–55
Operant responses, 54
Opium, 303
Opioids, 293, 303–304
withdrawal syndrome, 304
Oppositional defiant disorder (ODD):
case study, 498–499
theoretical perspectives, 497–498
treatment, 498–499
Optimism, 155–156
Oral-dependent personality, 315
Oral (first year of life) stage, 47
conflict in, 48
Oral fixations, 48
Orgasm disorders, 365, 367, 374–375
Orgone energy accumulator, 32
Outpatient mental health services, use of, by ethnic
minorities, 134–135
Overgeneralization, 59, 263
Overmedication, of children, 504

OxyContin, 303

Pacific Islanders:
care sought for mental illness, 133
and mental heal care, 134
Pain disorder, 228, 234–235
defined, 234
medical pain vs. psychiatric pain, 235
Panic, 7
Panic attacks, 172–173
coping with, 179
cues, 177
diagnostic features of, 174
recurrent, 174
Panic disorder, 171, 172–179
and antidepressants, 177
biological factors, 176
breathing retraining, 178
cognitive-behavioral approach, 177–178
cognitive-biological model of, 209
cognitive factors, 176–177
coping responses, development of, 178
defined, 172
diagnosis of, 174
drug therapy, 177
exposure, 178
hyperventilation, 175
prevalence of, by gender, 175
self-monitoring, 178
theoretical perspectives, 175–177
treatment approaches, 177–178
Panic disorder with agoraphobia (PDA), 183
Pappinheim, Bertha (Anna O.), 17, 29
Paranoid personality disorder, 428, 436, 437–438
case study, 437
Paranoid type of schizophrenia, 409–410
Paraphilias, 376–387
biological perspectives, 385
coprophilia, 383
defined, 376
exhibitionism, 376–378
fetishism, 378
frotteurism, 380
klismaphilia, 383
necrophilia, 383
overview of, 387
partialism, 383
pedophilia, 380–381
psychological perspectives, 383–385
sexual abuse, effects of, on children, 381–382
sexual masochism, 382
sexual sadism, 382–383
telephone scatologia, 383
theoretical perspectives, 383–385
tranvestic fetishism, 378–379
treatment, 385–386
antiandrogen drugs, 386
biomedical therapies, 386
cognitive-behavioral therapy (CBT), 385–386
covert sensitization, 386
psychoanalysis, 385
social skills training, 386
types of, 376–383
urophilia, 383
voyeurism, 379–380
zoophilia, 383
Parasomnias, 346–347, 350–352
nightmare disorder, 350–351
sleep terror disorder, 351
sleepwalking disorder, 351–352
Parasympathetic division, autonomic nervous system,
43
Parent-training programs, and conduct problems, 498
Parietal lobe, 43
Parkinson's disease, 406, 520, 524, 532–534, 536
and aging, 406, 520, 524, 532–534, 536
defined, 532, 533
genetic factors, 536
Paroxetine (Paxil), 177, 193, 198, 200, 375
Partialism, 383

Pathological (compulsive) gambling, 435, 465–467
  case study, 465–466, 468
  Gamblers Anonymous (GA), 467
  personality characteristics of pathological gamblers, 466–467
  treatment, 467
Pathological mourning, 260
Pathological narcissism, 455
Patient's rights, 550–554
  right to refuse treatment, 554
  right to treatment, 551
  Rogers v. Okin, 554
  Wyatt v. Stickney, 551
Pavlov, Ivan, 52–53
Paxil, See Paroxetine (Paxil)
Pedophilia, 380–381
Peel, Robert, 556
Pentobarbital, 303
Peptic ulcers, 159
Perceptual disturbances, 405–408
  case study, 405
  emotional disturbances, 407–408
  hallucinations, 405–407
Perfectionism:
  and depression, 263
  and eating disorders, 338
Performance anxiety, 366, 368–369
  example of, 369
Peripheral nervous system, 40–41, 43
Persecution:
  ideas of, 7
  delusions of, 402
Persecutory type, delusional disorders, 429
Perseveration, 403
Person-centered therapy, 57, 111–112
Personal distress, and abnormality, 7
Personal therapy, 424
Personality, structure of, 46
Personality dimension, 441
Personality disorders, 434–473
  antisocial personality disorder, 436, 440–443
  avoidant personality disorder, 436, 449–450
  biological perspectives, 459
  borderline personality disorder, 436, 443–445
  brain abnormalities, 461
  case study, 435
  clusters A/B/C (DSM), 436
  concept map, 473
  craving-for-stimulation model, 461
  defined, 435
  dependent personality disorder, 436, 450–451
  ego dystonic, 436
  ego syntonic, 436
  emotional responsiveness, lack of, 459–461
  family perspectives, 458–459
  genetic factors, 459
  histrionic personality disorder, 436, 445–446
  learning perspectives, 456–458
  narcissistic personality disorder, 436, 446–449
  obsessive–compulsive personality disorder, 436, 451–452
  overview of, 436
  paranoid personality disorder, 436, 437–438
  problems with the classification of, 452–454
  psychodynamic perspectives, 454–456
  schizoid personality disorder, 436, 438
  schizotypal personality disorder, 436, 438–440
  sociocultural perspectives, 461–463
  theoretical perspectives, 454–463
  treatment, 463–465
    behavioral approaches, 464
    biological approaches, 464–465
    psychodynamic approaches, 463–464
  types of, 435–454
Personalization, 264
Pervasive developmental disorder (PDDs), 478–485
  autism, 480
    autistic thinking, 481
    biomedical therapies, 484
    case study, 480–481, 482, 483

gender differences, 482
  preservation of sameness, 483
  primary feature of, 483
  relationship between intelligence and, 483
  theoretical perspectives, 484
  treatment, 484–485
autism spectrum disorders, 480
autistic disorder, 479
  diagnostic features of, 479
Phallic stage, 48
Phencyclidine (PCP), 308–309
Phenelzine (Nardil), 127, 273
Phenobarbital, 303
Phenothiazines, 15, 127, 414
Phenotype, 27–28, 420
Phenylketonuria (PKU), 487
Phlegmatic, use of term, 11
Phobias, 184
  acquisition of, through classical conditioning, 53
  defined, 179
  multifactorial model of, 188
Phobic disorders, 179–193
  biological perspectives, 185–186
  cognitive perspectives, 186–187
  learning perspectives, 184–185
  overprediction of danger, 187
  oversensitivity to threatening cues, 187
  psychodynamic perspectives, 184
  self-defeating thoughts and irrational beliefs, 187
  social phobias, 181–182
  specific phobias, 180–181
  theoretical perspectives, 184–88
  treatment, 189–193
    cognitive-behavioral therapy (CBT), 193
    drug therapy, 193
    learning-based approaches, 189–191
    virtual reality therapy (VRT), 191–193
  types of, 180–183
Phonological disorder, 492
Phototherapy, 253
Phrenitis, 11
Phrenology, 79, 80
Physical disorders, psychological factors in, 156–167
Physically abused children, and childhood disorders, 477
Physiological assessment, 96–99
  brain-imaging and recording technique, 96–97
Physiological dependence, 294–295
Pick's disease, 517, 532
  dementia due to, 532–534
Pinel, Philippe, 13–14
Pitts, Geraldine, 56
Placebo, 24
Placebo-control groups, 25
Placebo effects, 107
Play therapy, 476
Pleasure principle, 46
Polysomnographic (PSG) recording, 346
Pons, 41
Portuguese, postpartum depression among women in, 254
Positive correlations, 22
Positive psychology, 156
Positive reinforcers, 54
Positron emission tomography (PET scan), 97–98
Post-partum psychosis, 254
Postpartum depression (PDD), 253–254
Postsynaptic (receiving) neuron, 40
Posttraumatic stress disorder (PTSD), 62, 146–147, 200–204, 224, 270
  defined, 200
  factors predictive of, 202
  features of, 203–204
  theoretical perspectives, 204
  treatment approaches, 204
Poverty of speech, 403
Practice (EBP) movement, 32
Preconscious, 45
Prediction, 20, 23
Predictive validity, 75, 79

Prefrontal cortex, 43, 269, 415–416
Prefrontal lobotomy, 130
Premature ejaculation, 365, 367
Premorbid functioning, 410
Prepared conditioning, 186
Prevalence, 27
Prevention, 134
  spectrum of, 132
Primary insomnia, 347–348
Primary narcissism, 410–411
Primary prevention, 132
Proband, 28
Problem-focused coping, 154
Problem-solving therapy, 457
Prodromal phase, 399
Progressive relaxation, 158
Projection, 184
  as defense mechanism, 47
Projective tests, 83–84, 87–89
  evaluation of, 88–89
  Rorschach Inkblot Test, 87–88
  Thematic Apperception Test (TAT), 87–88
Prolixin (fluphenazine), 127, 422
Prozac (fluoxetine), 40, 127, 193, 198, 227, 240, 273–274, 340, 375, 464, 503
Psilocybin, 308
Psychedelics, See Hallucinogens (psychedelics)
Psychiatric commitment, 544–554
Psychiatric drugs, 40
  and dissociative disorders, 227
  and phobic disorders, 193
Psychiatric homelessness, and deeinstitutionalism, 136–136
Psychiatric nurses, 105
Psychiatric social workers, 105
Psychiatrists, 105
Psychiatry, bible of, 78
Psychoactive substances, 308
Psychoanalysis, 46, 51
  classical, 115
Psychoanalysts, 105, 106
  and paraphilias, 385
Psychoanalytic theory, 45
Psychodynamic approaches, 320
Psychodynamic model, 17, 107
Psychodynamic perspectives, 454–456
Psychodynamic theory:
  basis of, 45
  evaluating, 51–52
Psychodynamic therapy, 107–110
  defined, 107
  dream analysis, 108
  free association, 107–108
  modern approaches, 109–110
  object-relations approaches to, 110
  practice of, 110
  transference, 108–109
Psychogenic amnesia, See Dissociative amnesia
Psychogenic fugue, See Dissociative fugue
Psychological dependence, 295
Psychological disorder, use of term, 4–5
Psychological disorders, 4
  diagnosis of, 69–70
  lifetime and past-year prevalences of, 5
Psychological factors in physical disorders, 156–167
  acquired immunodeficiency syndrome (AIDS), 165–167
  asthma, 163–164
  cancer, 164–165
  cardiovascular disease (CVD), 160–163
  headaches, 159–160
Psychological hardiness, 155
Psychological perspective, of abnormal behavior, 16–17, 45–52, 65
Psychological stressors, 145
Psychological tests, 82–89
  intelligence tests, 82–83
  objective tests, 83–87
  projective tests, 87–89
Psychoneuroimmunology, 144

Psychopath, 440
Psychopharmacology, 126
Psychoquackery, 31, 32–33
Psychoses, 172
Psychosexual development, stages of, 47–48
Psychosis, 51
  brief psychotic disorder, 426
  delusional disorder, 426–428
  schizoaffective disorder, 428–429
  schizophrenia, 396–433
  schizophreniform disorder, 426
Psychosocial and environmental problems, 73
Psychosocial rehabilitation, schizophrenia, 425
Psychosomatic disorders, 159
Psychosurgery, 130
Psychotechnology, 119
Psychotherapists, 104
Psychotherapy, 104–107
  abnormal behavior/problem solving/personal growth, 106
  behavior/thoughts/ feelings, 106
  evaluating methods of, 119–23
  multicultural issues in, 123–125
  psychological principles, 105
  systematic interaction, 105
  types of, 115
Psychotic disorder of an unspecified type, 426
Psychotic disorders, and anxiety, 172
Psychotic hallucinations, causes of, 406
Psychotropic drugs, 129
PTSD, See Posttraumatic stress disorder (PTSD)
Punishment, 55
Pussin, Jean-Baptiste, 13
Pyromania, 465

Racial stereotyping, and mental health system, 135–136
Random assignments, 24, 27
Random samples, 26, 27
Random sampling, 27
Rape, 387–391
  acquaintance, 389
  and alcohol, 391
  Cultural Myths That Create a Climate That Supports Rape (questionnaire), 391
  date, 387, 390
  defined, 388
  examples of, 387–388, 390
  gang, 390
  male, 390
  marital, 390
  motives, 390–391
  stranger, 389
  theoretical perspectives, 390–391
  trauma of, 388
  types of, 389–390
Rapid eye movement (REM) sleep, 349
Rapists, and cognitive distortion, 58
Rapport, building, 80
Rational-emotive behavior therapy, 113
Rational emotive behavior therapy (REBT), 113, 115
Rational Recovery, 319–320
Rational restructuring, 354
Rationalization, as defense mechanism, 47
Raves, 305
Rayner, Rosalie, 54
Reaction formation, as defense mechanism, 47
Reaction time, 522–523
Reactivity, 93
Reality principle, 46
Reality testing, 88, 114
Rebound anxiety, 127
Rebound insomnia, 352
Receptor site, 40
Reciprocal interaction, 262
Reference, delusions of, 402
Reflection, 111, 112
Reform Movement and moral therapy, 13–14
Refractory period, 385
Regression, as defense mechanism, 47

Reinforcement, 54
and depression, 262
Relapse-prevention training, 322–324
substance abuse, 322–324
Reliability, 75, 77–79
of direct observation, 93
REM sleep, 349
Renaissance, 12, 13
Repression, 46, 51
as defense mechanism, 47
Residential approaches, 320
Resistance, 108
Response prevention, 198
Reticular activating system (RAS), 41
Retrieval, 58
Retrograde amnesia, 521
Rett's disorder, diagnostic features of, 480
Reuptake, 40, 311
Reversal design, 29–30
Rewards, 54
Right to refuse treatment, 554
Ritalin, 291, 495
Rockefeller, Nelson, 489–490
Rogers, Carl, 56–57, 115
Rogers v. Okin, 554
Rorschach, Hermann, 88
Rorschach Inkblot Test, 87–88
Rothbaum, Barbara, 192
Rotter, Julian B., 55
Rush, 303
Rush, Benjamin, 14

Sacks, Oliver, 516–517
Sadomasochism (S&M), 382–383
Samples, 26
and populations, 27
Sanguine, use of term, 11
Savant syndrome, 491
Schizoaffective disorder, 428–429
Schizoid personality disorder, 436, 438
case study, 438
defined, 438
Schizophrenia, 8–9, 15, 40, 51, 58, 130, 172, 396–433, 399
aberrant forms of thought, 403
abnormal event-related potentials, 405
attentional deficiencies, 403–404
biochemical factors, 414
biological perspectives, 411–412
brain abnormalities, 414–416
case study, 398, 399, 400, 402
communication deviance (CD), 417–418
course of development, 398–399
defined, 397–398
diagnostic features of, 401–405
disturbances of volition, 408
disturbed thought and speech, 402–403
ego boundaries, 407
expressed emotion (EE), 418–419
eye movement dysfunction (eye tracking dysfunction), 404–405
family factors, 419
family intervention programs, 425–426
family theories, 416–419
gender differences, 400
genetic factors, 411–414
learning perspectives, 411
negative symptoms, 402
overview of, 401
perceptual disturbances, 405–408
case study, 405
emotional disturbances, 407–408
hallucinations, 405–407
positive symptoms, 402
prevalence, 400
prodromal phase, 399
psychodynamic perspectives, 410–411
psychosocial rehabilitation, 425
rates of, 10
residual phase, 400

sensory overload, 404
stupor, 408
subtypes of, 408–410
catatonic type, 409–410
disorganized type, 408–409
paranoid type, 409–410
Type I vs. Type II schizophrenia, 410
theoretical perspectives, 410–421
thought broadcasting, 403
thought insertion, 403
thought withdrawal, 403
treatment, 422–426
biological approaches, 422–423
cognitive–behavioral therapy (CBT), 425
learning-based therapies, 424
psychodynamic therapy, 424
social skills training (SST) programs, 425
sociocultural perspectives, 423–424
viral infections, 414
Schizophreniform disorder, 426
Schizophrenogenic mother, 416
Schizotypal personality disorder, 436, 438–440
case study, 439
Schultz, David, 555
Scientific method, 21
Seasonal affective (mood) disorder (SAD), 252–253
phototherapy, 253
Secobarbital, 303
Secondary prevention, 132–133
Sedatives, 293, 303
Selection factor, 24
Selective abstraction, 59, 264, 272
Selective amnesia, 218
Selective norepinephrine reuptake inhibitor, 496
Selective preventive interventions, 132
Selective reinforcement of behavior, 424
Selective serotonin-reuptake inhibitors (SSRIs), 127, 273–274
Self-actualization, 56, 57–58
Self-concept, 56
Self-control strategies, 321
Self-control techniques, 111
Self-defeating narcissism, features of normal self-interest compared with, 447
Self-efficacy expectancies, 154–155
Self-efficacy expectations, 315
Self-esteem, and sexual dysfunctions, 368–369
Self-focusing model, 261
Self-induced vomiting, 335
Self-monitoring, 93–94, 178
disadvantages of, 94
Self-mutilatio, 445
Self psychology, 454
Sell v. United States, 550, 560
Selye, Hans, 147
Semistructured interview, 81
Senile dementias, 518
Sensate focus exercises, 373
Sensation-Seeking Scale (questionnaire), 462
Sensitivity, 79
Sensitization, 310
Sensory area, parietal lobe, 43
Separation anxiety disorder, 499–501
case study, 501
defined, 500
Separation-individuation, 456
September 11, 2001 terrorist attacks, 146–147
Serotonin, 40, 200, 268, 273, 282
Sertraline (Zoloft), 127, 177, 193, 200, 204, 273, 375, 503
Sexist biases,
and the construction of personality disorders, 453–454
Sexual abuse:
and child/adolescent suicide, 505
effects of, on children, 381–382
Sexual arousal disorders, 365, 366–367
Sexual aversion disorder, 365, 366
Sexual desire disorders, 365, 366
treatment, 372

Sexual dysfunctions, 365–375
acquired dysfunctions, 365
biological perspectives, 370–371
biological treatments of, 375–376
and cardiovascular problems, 370–371
case study, 370
defined, 365
and diabetes mellitus, 370–371
dyspareunia, 365, 367, 375
generalized dysfunctions, 365
lifetime dysfunctions, 365
marianismo stereotype, 371–372
orgasm disorders, 365, 367, 374–375
overview of, 365
psychological perspectives, 368
and relationship problems, 369
and self-esteem, 368–369
sexual arousal disorders, 365, 366–367
sexual desire disorders, 365, 366
sexual pain disorders, 365, 367
situational dysfunctions, 365
sociocultural perspectives, 371–372
testosterone treatments, 375
theoretical perspectives, 367–372
treatment, 372–376
arousal disorders, 373
sexual desire disorders, 372
types of, 366–367
vaginismus, 365, 367, 375
Sexual fulfillment, 369
Sexual masochism, 382
Sexual pain disorders, 365, 367
Sexual sadism, 382–383
Sexual skills/competencies, learning, 369
Sexually transmitted diseases (STDs), prevention, 167
Shock therapy, See Electroconvulsive therapy (ECT)
"Should" statements, 264
Simon, Theodore, 82–83
Single-blind placebo-control study, 25
Single-case experimental designs, 29–30
Single-participant research designs, 29
Situational dysfunctions, 365
Skinner, B. F., 52, 54, 55, 96
Sleep, defined, 346
Sleep apnea, 349, 353
obstructive, 349
Sleep disorders, 330, 346–354
and antianxiety drugs, 353
biological approaches, 352–353
breathing-related sleep disorder, 347, 349–350
chronic insomnia, 331
circadian rhythm sleep disorder, 347, 350
and cognitive–behavioral therapy (CBT), 354
defined, 346
drug therapy, 353
dyssomnias, 346, 347–350
hypersomnia, 347, 348
insomnia, 347, 347–348
narcolepsy, 348–349
nightmare disorder, 347, 350–351
overview of, 347
parasomnias, 346–347, 350–352
psychological approaches, 353–354
rational restructuring, 354
sleep-inducing drugs, 352
sleep terror disorder, 347, 351
sleepwalking disorder, 347, 351–352
stimulus control, 353–354
treatment, 352–354
Sleep disorders centers, 346
Sleep-inducing drugs, 352
Sleep medications, 525
Sleep paralysis, 349
Sleep problems, and aging, 525
Sleep terror disorder, 347, 351
Sleep terrors, defined, 351
Sleepwalking disorder, 347, 351–352
Snakes in Suits (Babiak/Hare), 457
Social anxiety disorder, 181–182
Social avoidance, 500

Social causation model, 63
Social-cognitive theory, 55–56, 56
Social contagion, 282
and child/adolescent suicide, 505–506
Social deviance, and abnormality, 7
Social environmental stress, 162
Social phobias, 179, 181–182
agoraphobia, 183
and daily functioning, 182
defined, 181
Social skills training, 111, 322, 424
Social support, and stress, 156
Sociocultural factors, psychological disorders, 6
Sociocultural perspective:
of abnormal behavior, 19, 60–63, 65
evaluating, 63
Sociodemographic factors, and alcoholism/alcohol dependence, 299
Sociopath, 440
Sodium lactate, 176
Somatic hallucinations, 405
Somatic nervous system, 43
Somatic type, delusional disorders, 429
Somatization disorder, 228, 235–236
Somatoform disorders, 211, 227–241, 240
body dysmorphic disorder (BDD), 228, 233–234, 240
cognitive-behavioral therapy (CBT), 240
compared to malingering, 229
conversion disorder, 228, 231–232
diagnostic features of, 231
defined, 227, 227–228, 235
Dhat syndrome, 236–237
factitious disorders, 229
hypochondriasis, 228, 232–233
Koro syndrome, 236
Münchausen syndrome by proxy, 229–230, 240
overview of, 228
pain disorder, 228, 234–235
somatization disorder, 228, 235–236
theoretical perspectives, 237–239
treatment, 240–241
South Africa, postpartum depression among women in, 254
Southeast Asians, and mental health care, 134
Specific phobias, 180–181
gender differences in, 181
onset of, 181
Specificity, 79
Split personality, See Dissociative identity disorder
Splitting, 445
St. John's Wort, and depression, 275
St. Mary's of Bethlehem Hospital, 13
Standardized interviews, 81
State hospitals, exodus from, 15
Stimulants, 129, 305–310
amphetamines, 305
cocaine, 305–306
ecstasy (MDMA), 305
nicotine, 306–308
Stimulus control, 353–354
Stop-start or stop-and-go technique,, 374–375
Storage, 58
Stranger rape, 389
Stress:
acculturative, 150–152
and asthma, 163–164
and cancer, 165
and child/adolescent suicide, 505
and the common cold, 146
defined, 141–142
and depression, 259–260
and the endocrine system, 144–145
and ethnic identity, 156
general adaptation syndrome (GAS), 147–149
and headaches, 159–160
and illness, 144–156
and the immune system, 145–146
and life changes, 149–150
optimism, 155–156

Stress *(cont.)*
  psychological factors moderating, 153–156
  psychological hardiness, 155
  psychological methods for lowering bodily arousal, 157–158
  self-efficacy expectancies, 154–155
  social environmental, 162
  social support, 156
  and suicide, 278
  terrorism-related trauma, 146–147
Stress hormones, 145, 175
Stressor, 142
Structured Clinical Interview for the DSM (SCID), 81
Stupor, 408
Stuttering, 492–493
Styron, William, 248
Sublimation, as defense mechanism, 47
Substance abuse, 290–329
  addiction, 294–295
  biological perspectives, 310–312
    genetic factors, 311–312
    neurotransmitters, 310–311
  and child/adolescent suicide, 505
  cognitive perspectives, 315
  conditioning model of cravings, 314–315
  controlled drinking, 322–323
  and dependence, 292–294
  depressants, 296–297, 296–304
    alcohol, 297
    barbiturates, 303
    heroin, 304
    morphine, 304
    opoids, 303–304
  hallucinogens (psychedelics), 294, 308–310
    defined, 308
    LSD (lysergic acid diethylamide), 308–309
    marijuana (*cannabis*), 308, 309–310
    mescaline, 308
    phencyclidine (PCP), 308, 309
    psilocybin, 308
  incidence of, 294
  intoxication, 292
  learning perspectives, 312–315
  negative reinforcement and withdrawal, 314
  observational learning, 315
  oral-dependent personality, 315
  pathways to drug dependence, 295–296
  psychodynamic perspectives, 315
  racial and ethnic differences, 295
  relapse-prevention training, 322–324
  as self-medication, 313
  sociocultural perspectives, 316
  stimulants, 305–310
    amphetamines, 305
    cocaine, 305–306
    ecstasy (MDMA), 305
    nicotine, 306–308
  treatment, 316–325
    antidepressants, 317
    aversive conditioning, 322
    behavioral approaches, 320–321

contingency management (CM) programs, 322
  detoxification, 317
  disulfiram (Antabuse), 317
  methadone maintenance programs, 318
  naltrexone, 318–319
  nicotine replacement therapy, 317–318
  nonprofessional support groups, 319–320
  psychodynamic approaches, 320
  residential approaches, 320
  self-control strategies, 321
  social skills training, 322
  withdrawal syndromes, substances leading to, 293–294
Substance dependence:
  defined, 292–293
  diagnostic features of, 293
  incidence of, 294
  lifetime prevalence of, 294
  and physiological dependence, 294
  tolerance, 293
  treatment, 316–325
Substance-induced disorders, defined, 291–292
Substance-related disorders, classification of, 291–296
Substance use disorders, 5
  defined, 292
Substantia nigra ("black substance"), 533
substantial capacity, 557
Suffocation false alarm theory, 176
Suicide, 278–285
  anomie, 282
  biological factors, 282
  in childhood/adolescence, 505
  copycat, 282
  demographics, 279–280
  ethnic/racial differences, 280
  Freud on, 281
  gender differences, 280
  motivation, 282–283
  myths about, 283
  in older adults, 280
  parental, 282
  predicting, 284
  preventing, 285
  risk of, 281
  and stress, 278
  suicide hotlines, 284
  theoretical perspectives, 281–283
  U.S. Surgeon General's report on, 279
Sullivan, Harry Stack, 109, 115, 411, 424
Superego, 46
Survey method, 26
Sympathetic division, autonomic nervous system, 43
Synapse, 38
  transmission of neural impulses across, 39
Syphilis, 16, 535
Systematic desensitization, 110, 189–190
Systematized amnesia, 218
Szasz, Thomas, 60

Tactile hallucinations, 405

Taijin-kyofu-sho (TKS), 73–74
Tarasoff v. the Regents of the University of California, 550, 552
Tardive dyskinesia (TD), 127, 422
Tay-Sachs disease, 536
Technical eclectics, 117
Teenage suicide rates, 504
Telephone scatologia, 383
Temporal lobe, 43
Terminals, 38
Terrorism-related trauma, 146–147
Test-retest reliability, 79
Testosterone treatments, 375
Thalmus, 42
Thematic Apperception Test (TAT), 87–88, 90
Theory, defined, 20
Therapeutic alliance, 120
Therapeutic relationship, 107
Therapists, 104
Thermal BFT, 160
Thioridazine (Mellaril), 127, 422
Thomas, Jay, 360
Thought broadcasting, 403
Thought diary, 95
Thought disorder, 403
Thought insertion, 403
Thought withdrawal, 403
Three Faces of Eve, The (film), 213, 215
Tobacco, 291
Token economy, 111, 424, 464
Tolerance, 126, 293
Tranquilizers, and erectile disorder, 371
Transcendental meditation (TM), 157
Transcranial magnetic stimulation (TMS), 278
Transdermal (skin) patches, for nicotine addiction, 317
Transference, 108–109
Transference neurosis, 108
Transference relationship, 108
Tranvestic fetishism, 378–379
  case study, 379
Trauma-related stress, warning signs of, 148
Treatment interventions, 132
Trephination, 10–11
Triazolam (Halcion), 126
Trichotillomania, 465
Tricyclic antidepressants (TCAs), 127, 273–274
  potential side effects, 274
Trifluoperazine (Stelazine), 422
Triggers, asthma, 163
Tuke, William, 14
Turner's syndrome, 487
Twin studies, 28–29
Two-factor model, 184
Type A behavior pattern (TABP), 161
Type I vs. Type II schizophrenia, 410

Unconditional positive regard, 56, 58, 112
Unconditioned response (UR), 53
Unconditioned stimulus (US), 53
Unconscious, 45
Universal preventive interventions, 132

Unstructured interview, 81
Unusualness, and abnormality, 6–7
Urophilia, 383
U.S. Surgeon General, report on the nation's mental health, 5–6

Vagina, 367
Vaginismus, 365, 367, 375
Validity, 75, 79–80
Valium (diazepam), 126, 130, 176, 200, 291, 297, 371
Varenicline, 317
Variables, 22
Vascular dementia, 531–532
  defined, 531
  features of, 531–532
  symptoms, 531
Viagra, 375–376
Vicodin, 303–304
Violence:
  and mental disorders, 549–550
  unlikelihood of disclosure of direct threats of, 548–549
Virtual reality therapy (VRT), 191–193
Visual hallucinations, 405
Voluntary hospitalization, 544
Voyeurism, 379–380

Water-float test, 12
Watson, John B., 52, 54, 55
Waxy flexibility, 409
Wechsler Adult Intelligence Scale (WAIS-III), 83–84, 523
Wernicke's disease, 522
Weyer Johann, 13
When Your Child Has an Eating Disorder (Natenshon), 339
White Americans, and cardiovascular disease (CVD), 162
"White man's sicknesses," 9
Widiger Thomas, 78
"Wild Man of West 96th Street," 545, 547
Witch-hunting, 12
Witchcraft, 12–13
Withdrawal syndromes, substances leading to, 293–294
Working alliance, 120
Worry circuit, 196
Worth, conditions of, 56
Wyatt v. Stickney, 550, 551

Xanax (alprazolam), 126, 176, 177, 200, 291, 371

Youngberg v. Romeo, 550, 553–554

Zar, 76, 223
Zoloft, 40
Zolpidem (Ambien), 352
Zoophilia, 383
Zygotes, 28

DSM-IV-TR CLASSIFICATION (American Psychiatric Association 2000)

AXIS I

Clinical Syndromes

DISORDERS USUALLY FIRST DIAGNOSED IN INFANCY, CHILDHOOD, OR ADOLESCENCE

- **Learning Disorders**
  Reading Disorder
  Mathematics Disorder
  Disorder of Written Expression
  Learning Disorder Not Otherwise Specified

- **Motor Skills Disorder**
  Developmental Coordination Disorder

- **Communication Disorders**
  Expressive Language Disorder
  Mixed Receptive/Expressive Language Disorder
  Phonological Disorder
  Stuttering
  Communication Disorder Not Otherwise Specified

- **Pervasive Developmental Disorders**
  Autistic Disorder
  Rett's Disorder
  Childhood Disintegrative Disorder
  Asperger's Disorder
  Pervasive Developmental Disorder Not Otherwise Specified

- **Attention-Deficit and Disruptive Behavior Disorders**
  Attention-Deficit/Hyperactivity Disorder
  Predominantly Inattentive Type
  Predominantly Hyperactive-Impulsive Type
  Combined Type
  Oppositional Defiant Disorder
  Conduct Disorder
  Attention-Deficit/Hyperactivity Disorder Not Otherwise Specified
  Disruptive Behavior Disorder Not Otherwise Specified

- **Feeding and Eating Disorders of Infancy or Early Childhood**
  Pica
  Rumination Disorder
  Feeding Disorder of Infancy or Early Childhood Not Otherwise Specified

- **Tic Disorders**
  Tourette's Disorder
  Chronic Motor or Vocal Tic Disorder
  Transient Tic Disorder
  Tic Disorder Not Otherwise Specified

- **Elimination Disorders**
  Encopresis
  Enuresis

- **Other Disorders of Infancy, Childhood, or Adolescence**
  Separation Anxiety Disorder
  Selective Mutism
  Reactive Attachment Disorder of Infancy or Early Childhood
  Stereotypic Movement Disorder
  Disorder of Infancy, Childhood, or Adolescence Not Otherwise Specified

DELIRIUM, DEMENTIA, AND AMNESTIC AND OTHER COGNITIVE DISORDERS

- **Delirium**
  Delirium Due to a General Medical Condition
  Substance Intoxication Delirium
  Substance Withdrawal Delirium
  Delirium Due to Multiple Etiologies
  Delirium Not Otherwise Specified

- **Dementia**
  Dementia of the Alzheimer's Type
  Vascular Dementia
  Dementias Due to Other General Medical Conditions
  Dementia Due to HIV Disease
  Dementia Due to Head Trauma
  Dementia Due to Parkinson's Disease
  Dementia Due to Huntington's Disease
  Dementia Due to Pick's Disease
  Dementia Due to Creutzfeldt-Jakob Disease
  Substance-Induced Persisting Dementia
  Dementia Due to Multiple Etiologies
  Dementia Not Otherwise Specified

- **Amnestic Disorders**
  Amnestic Disorder Due to a General Medical Condition
  Substance-Induced Persisting Amnestic Disorder
  Amnestic Disorder Not Otherwise Specified

SUBSTANCE-RELATED DISORDERS

- **Alcohol Use Disorders**
  Alcohol Dependence
  Alcohol Abuse

- **Alcohol-Induced Disorders**
  Alcohol Intoxication
  Alcohol Withdrawal
  Alcohol Intoxication Delirium
  Alcohol Withdrawal Delirium
  Alcohol-Induced Persisting Dementia
  Alcohol-Induced Persisting Amnestic Disorder
  Alcohol-Induced Psychotic Disorder
  Alcohol-Induced Mood Disorder
  Alcohol-Induced Anxiety Disorder
  Alcohol-Induced Sexual Dysfunction
  Alcohol-Induced Sleep Disorder
  Alcohol-Related Disorder Not Otherwise Specified

- **Amphetamine Use Disorders**

- **Amphetamine-Induced Disorders**

- **Caffeine-Induced Disorders**

- **Cannabis Use Disorders**

- **Cannabis-Induced Disorders**

- **Cocaine Use Disorders**

- **Cocaine-Induced Disorders**

- **Hallucinogen Use Disorders**

- **Hallucinogen-Induced Disorders**

- **Inhalant Use Disorders**

- **Inhalant-Induced Disorders**

- **Nicotine Use Disorder**

- **Nicotine-Induced Disorder**

- **Opioid Use Disorders**

- **Opioid-Induced Disorders**

- **Phencyclidine Use Disorders**

- **Phencyclidine-Induced Disorders**

- **Sedative, Hypnotic, or Anxiolytic Use Disorders**

- **Sedative, Hypnotic, or Anxiolytic-Induced Disorders**

- **Polysubstance-Related Disorder**

- **Other (or Unknown) Substance Use Disorders**

- **Other (or Unknown) Substance-Induced Disorders**

SCHIZOPHRENIA AND OTHER PSYCHOTIC DISORDERS

- **Schizophrenia**
  Paranoid Type
  Disorganized Type
  Catatonic Type
  Undifferentiated Type
  Residual Type

- **Schizophreniform Disorder**

- **Schizoaffective Disorder**

- **Delusional Disorder**

- **Brief Psychotic Disorder**

- **Shared Psychotic Disorder (Folie à Deux)**

- **Psychotic Disorder Due to a General Medical Condition**

- **Substance-Induced Psychotic Disorder**

- **Psychotic Disorder Not Otherwise Specified**

MOOD DISORDERS

- **Depressive Disorders**
  Major Depressive Disorder
  Dysthymic Disorder
  Depressive Disorder Not Otherwise Specified

- **Bipolar Disorders**
  Bipolar I Disorder
  Single Manic Episode
  Most Recent Episode Hypomanic
  Most Recent Episode Manic
  Most Recent Episode Mixed
  Most Recent Episode Depressed
  Most Recent Episode Unspecified
  Bipolar II Disorder
  Cyclothymic Disorder
  Bipolar Disorder Not Otherwise Specified

- **Other Mood Disorders**
  Mood Disorder Due to a General Medical Condition
  Substance-Induced Mood Disorder
  Mood Disorder Not Otherwise Specified